La Cuisine

The Complete Book
of French Cooking

La Cuisine

The Complete Book of French Cooking

Valérie-Anne Létoile
Monique Maine
Madeleine Peter

English-language editor: Jill Norman
Wine section: Pamela Vandyke Price

GUILD PUBLISHING
LONDON

This edition published 1986
Book Club Associates by arrangement with Orbis Publishing

Original French edition © Edition No 1 1982
English translation and design © Orbis Publishing Limited, London 1985
First published in Great Britain by Orbis Publishing Limited,
London 1985

Printed in Italy by G. Canale & C. SpA
ISBN 0-85613-719-7

Contents

Symbols

The symbols will enable you to see at a glance how easy a recipe is, and the preparation and cooking times

easy

more difficult

for experienced cooks

preparation time

cooking time

When using the recipes in this book, remember the following points:

All quantities are for six people, unless otherwise stated.

Use only one set of measurements for the recipes, since American, imperial and metric measurements are not exact equivalents.

In the text of the recipes, American quantities and ingredients are listed first, with the British equivalents in square brackets.

CHAPTER 1

Equipment

From a sharp knife to a microwave oven, a well-planned range of high quality kitchen equipment will help you prepare and serve nourishing, delicious and attractive food as easily and quickly as possible.

Equipment

Traditional utensils

The design of many small kitchen tools (wooden spoons, skewers and sieves for example) has remained unchanged for generations, and the efficiency with which they perform their tasks is unlikely to be improved on by even the most technically advanced appliances.

Apple corer

A small, inexpensive metal cylinder that could save you a great deal of time if you often prepare whole fruit for baking, poaching or preserving.

Basting spoon

A large, often stainless steel, spoon for pouring cooking juices or fats over meat during roasting. A bulb baster, which looks like a huge syringe with a rubber bulb at one end, is a particularly useful tool for this purpose.

Bowls

Keep several different sizes to cope with varying quantities of ingredients to be mixed or stored. If you handle many liquid mixtures, a bowl with a pouring lip is useful, while one made of copper is worthwhile if your cooking involves beating a great many egg whites. The slight acidity of copper strengthens the walls of the air bubbles, making a more stable foam of greater volume.

Can opener

The traditional lever-action can opener is difficult and clumsy to manipulate and leaves a dangerous jagged metal edge. It has now largely been superseded by the simple, rotary-action butterfly model that is cheap to buy and easy to use, particularly if you choose a sturdy, well-made one with moulded plastic handles. The most convenient of all the manual can openers is a wall-mounted version, but this type is slightly more expensive than its hand-held counterpart.

Cherry pitter [stoner]

Also used for olives, this small metal tool is probably a worthwhile purchase only if you use a great many of these fruits in cooking.

Colander

A plastic or metal colander is the most efficient means of draining water away from vegetables and fruit. A metal version will last longer and withstand constant dousing with boiling water.

Cutters

Choose good quality cutters with a sharp edge for your pastry and cookies [biscuits] — metal will hold a sharp edge better than plastic. Traditionally, plain cutters are for savory items and fluted models for sweet ones.

Cutting [chopping] boards

Ideally, you should have several sizes — a small one for herbs and garlic, and a couple of larger ones for meat, vegetables etc. Try to keep separate boards (or at least separate *sides* of one board) for sweet foods and those with a strong flavor like onions. Rinse your boards after every use with hot water and a little detergent.

Foil

Invaluable for both cooking and freezing, foil is one of the most indispensable modern cooking aids. Choose a special heavy-duty variety for the freezer to ensure that your food will not dry out.

The main uses of foil in cooking are to conduct heat (when used to wrap dishes such as fish) and to protect food from burning (when placed on top of cakes or pastry).

Grater

A circular or slightly conical metal model with several different-sized shredding surfaces is the most practical choice since you can use it to grate everything from lemon rind to potatoes and carrots. A very small version with tiny holes is made for nutmeg.

Knives

Kitchen knives come in many different shapes and sizes, weights and materials, and it is very important that the ones you choose are suitable for their purpose, as well as easy and safe to use.

A good knife must have a sharp blade. Carbon steel is highly regarded because of its hard finish and sharp cutting edge, but it does blunt quickly. It also stains and rusts, so it needs a lot of care or it will discolor and give food a metallic flavor. After use, rub with a soft cloth or damp cork dipped in scouring powder, then rinse in warm water. Dry immediately and keep in a dry place. If you are not going to use the knife for a while, smear the blade with a little olive oil.

The alternative blade material is stainless steel, which has a less sharp cutting edge but keeps sharp longer and never rusts. Edges can be flat ground (the sides of the blade are smooth), or hollow ground (the length of the blade has a marked bevel giving it a thinner cutting edge that stays sharper longer).

Knives with serrated edges saw gently through soft foods such as tomatoes. Serrated edges are also found on bread knives and carving knives, though some have scalloped edges on which the gaps between the teeth are wider and more curved. Granton-edged knives have two edges, one straight and one with curved or square indentations. They should be stored in a guard for safety.

Always use a wooden cutting [chopping] board (laminated or marble surfaces will blunt blades) and scrub it frequently to prevent bacteria gathering. Straight-edged knives can be sharpened on a knife steel or a dampened carborun-dum stone. Hold knife, with the blade pointing away from you, at a 45° angle to the steel, and with a light stroking movement, draw the knife towards you from base to tip, first on one side, then the other. The movement is the same if you use a carborundum stone. Sharpen serrated, scalloped or granton blades with a small, crossed steel, drawing the blade through where it crosses. Home sharpening will eventually wear down the teeth of serrated knives, so it is advisable to have them professionally reground and sharpened. Store sharp knives separately from other kitchen utensils for safety's sake; a knife rack, magnetized bar or wooden case is best. When buying a knife make sure that: the blade is well riveted into the handle, not just glued on; it is well-balanced with a comfortable handle; and that it is the right length. A good knife will last for years and prove to be a sound investment if you choose it wisely.

Vegetable knives need to be straight-edged with a blade of about 4 inches [10 cm] in length for chopping small vegetables (onions, carrots) and paring and scraping. Longer blades — 10-12 in [25-30 cm] — are best for chopping heftier vegetables such as cabbage. They can also be used for chopping raw meat. Swivel-bladed or rigid peelers are useful for paring fruit and coring apples, as well as peeling vegetables. Knives with small, thin blades, a fine serrated edge and a pointed tip are essential for slicing soft or juicy fruits like tomatoes and oranges. They can also be used for segmenting grapefruit, though a more flexible curved knife is available for this. For chopping fresh herbs, garlic and onions finely, a hachoir (a 'rocking' chopper with a curved blade and a handle at each end), is particularly useful.

Meat knives come in a variety of shapes. A meat cleaver makes quick work of bones and the flat side can also be used for batting out flesh. A boning knife is very sharp to cut through tough sinews. It is long and curved and should be held like a dagger. A carving knife should also be very sharp to cut cleanly without tearing the meat. The blades need to be about 1 inch [2.5 cm] wide with a straight or scallop edge. An electric carving knife is the most efficient while double-edged knives such as the granton will cut through dense blocks of frozen food.

Poultry shears are used for jointing raw or roasted poultry — heavier ones are more likely to cut through bones. Sharp kitchen scissors with serrated edges make a lot of preparation easier (derinding bacon, snipping chives or parsley).

Fish filleting knives have a flexible straight-edged blade with a pointed end and should be between 6 and 10 in [15-25 cm] long. The 10 in [25 cm] size can also be used for carving whole cooked fish such as salmon, since the flexibility of the blade makes it easier to carve large, wafer-thin slices, giving your carving a professional look.

Bread knives should be long-bladed and serrated or scalloped. A scalloped carving knife can be used for bread too.

Palette knives have a long flexible blade with a rounded end and are used for lifting cakes and biscuits and for spreading icings and creams on cakes.

Ladles

You will find it useful to have two ladles: a large one to use in jam-making and for soups and stews, and a small one for sauces and gravies.

Mandoline

Plastic, wooden or metal in construction, mandolines are made in either a simple, one-blade version or with a more complicated design that has two or three adjustable blades. This inexpensive implement makes it possible to slice foods thinner and more quickly than you could manage by hand.

Measuring spoons

These have different capacities from those of ordinary teaspoons and tablespoons meant for use on the table, so you will need a set to ensure that your recipes can be followed precisely.

Mixing spoon

Wooden spoons are better for cooking than metal ones since they do not conduct heat and can be held comfortably. They are available in several sizes, and some have a pointed bowl that allows you to scrape every bit of food from saucepans and straight-sided bowls.

Use a metal spoon for folding a delicate mixture or for dealing with strongly-flavored foods whose taste might be picked up and passed on by wood.

Pastry board

If your ordinary working surface is made from laminate, you can roll pastry directly on it, but if you normally work at a wooden table, you will need a special board for this purpose. Marble is the ideal material, but anything smooth and hard will do.

Pastry brush

A small bristle or nylon brush that is useful for greasing the inside of baking dishes, pans and tins, as well as for brushing milk, butter or beaten egg on to pastry to give a decorative glazed effect.

Pepper mill

The taste of freshly-ground pepper is incomparable and bears little resemblance to that of the grayish ready-ground variety. Try not to over-fill your mill, or you could damage the mechanism.

Piping bag

Although purpose-made cloth or nylon piping bags with different nozzles are widely available, you can improvise one easily using wax [greaseproof] paper. Some cooks prefer the rigid icing tube made of metal or plastic, which is easier to hold and handle, but which makes it more difficult to control the mixture being piped.

Rolling pin

Made from either hardwood or china, the best designs are long and without handles, since this type rolls pastry most evenly. Some ceramic ones can be filled with iced water to keep your pastry cold, and therefore increase its chances of success.

Scales

Used in Europe (in place of the North American cup system) to measure ingredients, scales are useful in every kitchen to weigh foods in bulk. Never overload your scales or store anything heavy in the pan, since this may damage them.

Sieves and strainers

Designed to separate liquids from solids and small particles from large, these are available in plastic or metal. Ideally, you should have a medium-sized, round version in metal (since plastic will not withstand strong heat) for sifting and blending dry ingredients and for draining large items; a wire conical strainer for use with a narrow-necked jug or bottle; a large round metal one for rice or pasta, and a fine nylon 'hair' sieve for soft fruit.

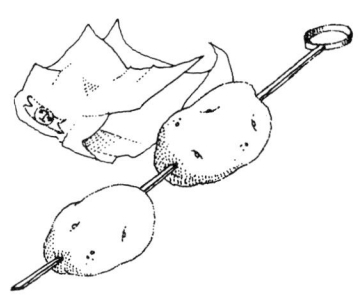

Skewers

Made of stainless steel or wood, skewers have a number of uses in the kitchen: conducting heat to the center of foods (like potatoes and kebabs), trussing poultry and game, fastening food (barding fat for example) into place and testing cakes etc for doneness. Metal skewers conduct heat much more efficiently than wooden ones, but they cannot be used in a microwave oven.

Slotted spoon/skimmer

This implement is used for lifting and draining small foods as well as for skimming fat from the surface of cooked dishes. Do not use a metal spoon for foods containing vinegar since the metal will react with the acid and give an unpleasant flavor.

Spatulas

Keep several handy: a plastic one to scrape bowls and pans and wooden ones in various sizes for lifting and stirring.

String

A ball of medium-weight string or twine is extremely handy in the kitchen for trussing poultry and meat and for tying up bunches of herbs and vegetables.

Thermometers

There are two commonly used types: a meat thermometer, which has a spike that is inserted into the meat, and a sugar thermometer, which is immersed in liquid. To avoid damage, do not subject your cooking thermometers to dramatic changes of temperature.

Pans and molds

The quality of the pans and molds you use will affect your baking, so if your budget is limited, choose a small number

Trussing needle

A long needle with a large eye, and usually made of stainless steel, this implement is used to tie up poultry and game before roasting. These are available straight or curved and in several sizes.

Vegetable mill

Handy for making bread crumbs or purées, or for shredding, grating or slicing vegetables, this gadget is available in plastic and metal. A plastic one may be slightly cheaper, but it will not last as long as the metal version.

Whisks

The two best-known models are the balloon whisk and the coil-rim whisk. Both of these are more efficient for incorporating air into mixtures and for blending ingredients than the costlier and more clumsy rotary whisk.

Wire racks

An essential piece of equipment for cooling cakes, cookies [biscuits] and pastries, a wire rack is also useful as a raised stand on which you can ice cakes.

of good quality items rather than a large range of cheap ones. You should have two layer cake pans [sandwich tins], two deeper round ones (6½ in / 16 cm and 8 in / 20 cm), some muffin [bun] tins, a jelly roll pan [a swiss roll tin], a pie pan or plate and a set of small patty tins. You might also like to have pans or molds for babas, brioches, charlottes, madeleines and savarins.

Electrical appliances

The modern cook has at his or her disposal a range of electrical equipment that has taken most of the tedium and hard physical work out of food preparation.

Traditionally these machines have been limited to a single well-defined function or, at best, to one or two closely-related functions. The last ten years, however, have seen the introduction and rapid spread of the 'food processor', a generic term for a variety of sophisticated multi-function machines. Some of these functions (slicing vegetables, for example) have not previously been generally available to the home cook.

When considering whether to buy an electrical aid for the kitchen you should make an effort to relate the price of the machine to the frequency with which you are likely to use it. This is not always as easy as it might seem, since the very act of acquiring a labor-saving device tends to widen the range of activites that you can undertake.

There are many factors to be taken into consideration:

1. What are the specific functions and characteristics of each of the available makes? Read the descriptive literature that normally accompanies each machine and try to decide which is most likely to meet your present and future needs.

2. What is the capacity of the bowl or container part of the machine? Generally speaking, the larger the machine, the higher the price, and it may be too large for your requirements. On the other hand nothing is more frustrating than a machine with an inadequate capacity.

3. How easy is it to assemble and use the machine and to clean it after use? Before committing yourself have a look at the accompanying instructions to see how clear and helpful they are.

4. How much valuable kitchen space will it take up? Make sure you have room to stand the machine permanently where it can be used with ease.

5. How noisy is the machine? This may be an important factor if it is going to be in very frequent use. Ask your dealer for a demonstration.

6. How *safe* is the machine to use and clean. This is particularly relevant if there are young children in the house.

If you want to extend your range of operations in the kitchen one of the multi-function food processors would be a good investment, although the initial outlay might seem high. Go to a dealer who is capable of offering you expert advice before you make a final choice.

Should you decide to purchase sophisticated electrical appliances for the kitchen, you may need some practice before their full potential is realized. This applies particularly to food processors, which are all too often under-employed.

Grinder [mincer]

Used for grinding [mincing] meat and vegetables and for mixing them together. Much quicker than using a knife when reducing foods to very small pieces.

Blender

Also known as a liquidiser. A very useful device that has been on the market for many years. It incorporates a deep receptacle, at the base of which are small rotating blades that quickly reduce foods to a pulp. It is used in the preparation of soups, sauces, etc. A smaller variation on the same theme is the electric coffee mill (some blenders also have a special attachment for this purpose).

Beater or mixer

The terms are used interchangeably to refer to two different kinds of appliance, which perform very similar functions, i.e. beating or mixing liquids, cake mixtures, dough, etc. They are particularly useful for the rapid and easy beating of egg-whites when making meringue. One type of machine is held in the hand and brought to the mixing bowl, while the other kind is fixed and incorporates a bowl that can be removed.

Food processors

Food processors cope efficiently with a whole range of food preparation tasks and complete them in seconds. They consist of a powerful motor base and a removable work bowl that has a lid complete with feed tube or hopper, plus a variety of changeable blades and discs that slip on to a central spindle inside the work bowl. Food processors have attachments that can chop, slice, purée, blend, mix, grate and mill raw or cooked foods and they make short work of very hard foods such as nuts.

CHAPTER 2

The Value of Food

Wise buying forms the basis of a balanced diet and therefore continuing good health. The table opposite sets out the composition of many basic foods giving details of their energy value, calories and kilojoules, and their nutritional value, carbohydrates and vitamins. Although progress in farming techniques, preserving methods and transport has made it possible for shops to stock many of these items all the year round, most fresh produce is at its tastiest and most nutritious during its natural season and, of course, costs less when it is bought in season.

Nutrition is a very important subject, and specialized books on it will give much more information than is possible to provide here.

Food values

The energy requirement of an adult is between 2,000 calories [10,500 kJ] and 4,000 calories [17,000 kJ] depending on sex and level of energy expended. It is obvious that while a rapidly growing adolescent will need almost 4,500 calories per day, a sedentary woman can manage quite well on 2,000.

While calories represent energy, vitamins provide our bodies with the necessary building elements, so it is extremely important that we consume enough of the appropriate vitamins for our needs. (There is no point in consuming huge quantities, since any excess will be eliminated automatically.)

1 calorie = 4.18 kJ

Under the metric system of measurements, the energy value of foods is calculated in JOULES.

1 kilojoule = 1,000 joules

1 calorie (or kilocalorie) is equivalent to 4.18 kilojoules.

Vitamins for each food are listed in order of the amount contained.

Food values (for 4 oz / 100 g)

Product	cal	kJ	carb	vit
Dairy produce				
Skim milk	34	143	5	—
Whole milk	64	269	5	—
Skim milk plain yogurt	30	126	4	—
Whole milk plain yogurt	45	190	5	—
Camembert cheese	328	1378	2	B_2
Gruyère cheese	400	1680	1	A
Fats				
Butter	770	3234	—	A,D,E
Margarine	770	3234	—	—
Oil	900	3800	—	—
Eggs (each)	151	639	—	A,B
Vegetables				
Asparagus	20	85	3	C,A
Beet [beetroot]	36	153	7	C,A
Carrot	28	119	1	A,C
Cauliflower	33	138	4	C,A,B
Celery	28	119	5	C
Potato chips [crisps]	545	2259	48	—
Cucumber	10	42	1	C,B
Endive [chicory]	20	84	5	A,C
Green beans	32	136	5	C,A
Kidney beans	360	1512	59.6	B
Leek	28	119	5	C
Lentils	340	1428	54.7	B
Lettuce	12	51	1	C,A,E
Mushrooms	35	130	1	B
Peas	60	255	10	C
Potato	84	357	19	C
Radishes	20	84	5	C
Spinach	20	84	4	A,C
Tomato	16	68	3	C,A
Fruit				
Apple	40	170	12	C
Apricot	44	187	10	A
Avocado	200	840	5	A,C
Banana	92	391	22	B_1,A
Cherries	42	179	10	C
Grapefruit	30	126	7	C,B_1
Grapes	66	281	16	C
Lemon	30	125	6	C
Mandarin orange	34	142	8	C
Melon	30	125	7	C
Orange	42	179	10	C,B_1
Peach	35	145	8	A,C
Pear	41	179	10	C
Pineapple	50	210	12	C
Plum	42	179	10	A,C
Strawberries	30	125	6	C
Dried fruit (figs, dates)	300	1250	70	B_1
Nuts (almonds, peanuts)	630	2640	15	—
Starchy foods				
Flour	350	1460	75	—
Pasta	346	1468	24	—
Rice	350	1460	77	B
Bread				
Rusks	360	1512	60	—
White bread	260	1092	55	—
Wholewheat bread	240	1008	50	B,E
Sweet foods				
Cookies [biscuits]	430	1800	80	—
Chocolate	500	2100	58	—
Honey	322	1369	80	B_2
Jam	246	1046	61	—
Sugar	400	1700	100	—
Meat				
Beef	200	840	—	B
Ham	280	1184	—	B
Lamb	220	924	—	B
Pork	325	1374	—	B
Veal	150	630	—	B
Fish and seafood				
Oily fish (eel, salmon, tuna)	170	714	—	—
Non-oily fish (whiting, hake, sole, trout)	100	420	—	—
Lobster	82	344	—	—
Mussels and clams	57	242	2	C
Oysters	49	208	4	B_1,C
Scallops	90	380	—	—
Shrimp [prawns]	120	600	—	B_1,C
Poultry and game				
Chicken	170	714	—	B_1
Duck	341	1442	—	B
Pheasant	205	860	—	—
Rabbit	174	737	—	B
Turkey	143	606	—	—

CHAPTER 3

Preserving

The main ways of preserving food in the home are freezing, sterilizing with heat (canning or bottling), boiling with sugar, immersing in vinegar, oil or alcohol, salting, and drying, and these methods will be outlined in this chapter.

At the end of the chapter, you will find a summary table containing the following information:
1. A list of basic foods.
2. Hints on preparation.
3. Instructions for freezing and canning [bottling], the two simplest methods of preserving food at home.
4. Alternative preserving methods where appropriate, using sugar, vinegar, salt, oil or alcohol.

Freezing

Freezing lowers the temperature of food very quickly to below 0°F / −18°C, thus preventing deterioration without damage to the food's cell walls by the ice crystals that form between 32° and 23°F / 0° and −5°C. Some foods — whole raw tomatoes for example — are not suitable for freezing since their water content is so high that this cell wall damage is inevitable and their texture is completely destroyed.

Deep freezing

During deep-freezing, special industrial equipment freezes the food completely through more rapidly, and brings it to a much lower temperature (−40°F / −40°C) than would be possible with a home freezer. The food is cleaned and all the waste removed, then it is frozen while it is still absolutely fresh, so it comes to you wholesome and easy-to-use. Supermarkets now offer hundreds of different products prepared this way to save you hours of preparation and cooking time: vegetables ready-cleaned, shelled or peeled, sliced, blanched and sometimes even pre-cooked; meats boned and filleted, and poultry and fish cut up and trimmed.

You can save even more time by taking advantage of the many ready-cooked dishes available, which need only thawing or warming through before serving — a particularly speedy process if you have a microwave oven.

Open freezing

Also known as flash freezing this is a method of freezing food uncovered on trays to (1) keep individual pieces separate so they do not freeze in a solid mass and (2) keep delicate, decorative and soft-textured foods intact. Line trays/baking trays with foil or wax [greaseproof] paper, then spread food (fruit, vegetables, rosettes of whipped cream, etc) on top so they aren't touching. Freeze until solid, then remove from tray and pack in bags. Vegetables and fruits can be open frozen at home to produce 'free-flow' packs as sold commercially. Simply shake out the exact amount required. Cakes with decorations of cream or icing are best packed in a rigid container after open freezing. Always remove them from the container before thawing or the elaborate design could be spoilt.

Guidelines for home freezing

1. In order for frozen food to retain its flavor and goodness, it must be completely fresh. Prepare and freeze produce as soon as you get it home (or, better still, as soon as you pick it) and choose your meat from a reliable supermarket or butcher shop whose reputation for freshness and quality can be trusted.
2. Set the temperature of your freezer to its lowest point 6 hours before putting in the food to be frozen.
3. Remember that although freezing prevents the bacteria that cause decay from growing and multiplying, any that are already present when food is frozen will be re-activated when it is thawed, so be sure to do your preparation, cooking and packaging under the most hygienic conditions possible.
4. Once it has been completely frozen (this will take 24 hours) food can be stored at 0°F / −18°C, but you should never let it reach a temperature higher than this.
5. Never re-freeze food that has already been thawed.
6. As you can see from our diagram, commercially frozen food is maintained at extremely low temperatures throughout every stage of packing, shipping and selling. For this cold chain to remain unbroken, you must put frozen food in your freezer no later than one hour after purchase, otherwise it will have begun to thaw and should not be re-frozen.
7. In the event of an electrical failure or a power cut, do not open your freezer. If notice of a cut is given, set your equipment to the maximum cold position; in principle the food should stay frozen for 12 hours without electricity. If the equipment breaks down suddenly, phone the number given in your after-sales emergency service contract immediately.
8. Try not to open your freezer more than once or twice a day.
9. Take advantage of fresh foods in season to get the best quality and the lowest prices.

The cold chain

Factory −58°F / −50°C
Warehouse −22°F / −30°C
Transport −18°F / −28°C
Retailer −0°F / −18°C
Consumer −0°F / −18°C

Freezer accessories

Whether you choose pliable freezer bags or wrappings or rigid containers, freezer packaging materials must first of all be airtight, since extremely cold air will dry out any food with which it comes into contact. (Extreme damaged caused by this process of dehydration is called freezer burn.) Containers must also be strong and good quality to withstand the temperatures involved. Make sure too that storage boxes and jars are designed to stack neatly so that no space is wasted and each item can be identified at a glance.

Flexible packaging

● heavy-duty foil, sometimes called 'freezer foil' is excellent for packaging raw or cooked meat, cheese, butter and bread, and for covering prepared dishes. Waterproof, opaque, pliable and non-flammable, it is invaluable for freezing and for cooking.
● polyethylene [polythene] bags, with or without gussets, are light, flexible and waterproof.
● plastic cling wrap is useful for separating stacked items so they can be removed individually.

Rigid packaging

● plastic boxes with tight-fitting lids contain up to 2 quarts [2 l / 3½ pints] and are ideal for storing fragile fruit and vegetables (raspberries and mushrooms for example), cooked dishes, ice cream, sauces etc. You can get by with far fewer boxes if you line each one with a freezer bag before pouring in the food to be frozen. After 24 hours at −11°F / −24°C the bag will have assumed the shape of the box and can then be removed and stacked, freeing the box for other uses. This process is called preforming.
● foil containers, which sometimes have cardboard lids, are perfect for cooked dishes, pastry cases and cakes. These will go directly into the oven, but the cardboard must be removed first.

- toughened glass jars designed for canning [bottling] will also withstand freezing temperatures. Do not fill them more than three-quarters full since the contents will expand during freezing and could shatter the glass. Make sure lids are closed tightly to keep out the cold, dry air.
- containers made of special material developed for use in microwave ovens are also suitable for freezer use.

Important

Do not fill *any* container more than three-quarters full since food increases in volume considerably when it freezes.

Sealing

Expel as much air as possible from the flexipacks [freezer bags], then twist the top of the bag down as far as the contents, fold the twisted part in two and bind it with a piece of special freezer adhesive tape or a coated wire fastener.

Alternatively, seal the bags with an electrical heat-sealer, which welds the plastic by melting it. This appliance would probably be worthwhile only if you do a great deal of home freezing.

Labeling

Look out for special adhesive labels, ties and marking pens designed for freezer use. You might find it useful to color-code the labels on different types of food — blue for meat, green for vegetables, red for cooked dishes etc. Label every container you put in the freezer with its contents, weight, number of items, condition (raw, cooked, blanched etc) and the latest date for use. You will find precise explanations for each group of products to be frozen, from page 44 onwards in the main preserving table. Hints about how to pack are given at the same time.

To prepare food efficiently for the freezer, you will also need:
- a cutting board
- a set of sharp, good quality kitchen knives
- a swivel-bladed vegetable peeler
- kitchen scales and/or sets of spoon and cup measures
- a large saucepan or stewpan and a basket for blanching vegetables
- one or two strainers
- a fruit pitter [stoner] (useful but not essential)

Thawing

In order that your food reaches the table in the best possible condition, it must be thawed at the correct temperature.

Thawing in the refrigerator

Delicate foods such as poultry, game, raw meat and shellfish, cheese and soft fruits must be thawed gently.

Place them, still in their freezer packaging, in the refrigerator at about 41°F / 5°C, and leave them for 24 hours.

Thawing at room temperature

Foods such as bread, rolls, plain cakes and pastries will thaw at room temperature without any ill-effect.

Thawing in the oven

If you want to eat them warm, the above items can be placed straight into the oven at 350°F / 180°C / Gas Mark 4, as can ready-cooked pastry-based dishes like quiches, pizzas, tarts etc.

All cooked dishes must be brought to boiling point to make them absolutely safe to eat. Commercially frozen items will be marked with instructions for heating.

Thawing during cooking

In water: cook frozen, blanched vegetables by plunging them straight into boiling water.

On the top of the stove: frozen fish fillets or slices, filled crêpes, breaded seafood, ground [minced] beef, croquettes etc should be fried with a little fat.

In a stew, use frozen pieces of meat as you would fresh, adding herbs and liquid according to the recipe you have chosen.

Deep frying: frozen potatoes, fritters etc can be placed directly into the hot fat.

Oven cooking: thaw frozen meat before putting it into the oven, or increase its cooking time considerably. Poultry must always be thawed completely before cooking.

Broiling [grilling]: as long as your element can be set to a high enough temperature, frozen hamburgers and other ground [minced] meat dishes will cook successfully.

Microwave ovens: as well as being excellent for cooking and heating many types of food, a microwave is also useful for defrosting and/or cooking food directly from the freezer. For example:
- 1 cup [250 g / 8 oz] of butter will thaw in 1 minute instead of the 30 minutes it would require at room temperature.
- a 2 lb / 1 kg chicken takes 12 minutes instead of 24 hours at room temperature.
- a roast of beef weighing 1½ lb / 750 g takes 15 minutes instead of 12 hours at room temperature.

Important: anyone who has been fitted with a pacemaker should not use a microwave oven.

Cook's tips

Some foods are unsuitable for freezing:

Vegetables: those containing a large proportion of water, such as salad greens (lettuce, batavia, endive, chicory, lamb's lettuce, cress), celery, cucumber, scallions [spring onions], whole tomatoes, chives, etc., can be frozen but they will not thaw satisfactorily for use in salads. You can still use them in soups and stews however.

Fruit: bananas and avocados do not freeze well unless they have been puréed and mixed with a little lemon juice.

Dairy produce: do not freeze hard-cooked eggs. Fresh eggs can be frozen, but they must be removed from their shells and put in suitable containers. Yogurt and cream cheese freeze well only if they are incorporated in a mixture. Only cream with a very high butterfat content should be frozen.

Baked goods: buttercream icing freezes well, but frosting, meringue icing and royal icing will crumble on thawing.

Miscellaneous: mayonnaise, hollandaise sauce and its derivatives, and gelatin-set desserts do not freeze satisfactorily.

CAUTION

Artificial flavorings: these should be added just before serving since they can be seriously affected by the freezing process.

Spices and salt: use only in moderation when preparing food for freezing, then taste and re-season when food is thawed.

Preserving

Heat-sterilizing (canning or bottling) is accomplished by boiling suitable fruit for varying lengths of time in order to kill the bacteria that cause decay, then sealing it in sterilized containers to protect it from the bacteria in the air. Preserving in this way is still common in France and many families put by fruit throughout the year.

Equipment

To can or bottle a wide range of fruit efficiently, you will need:
● a heavy-bottomed boiler or regular hot-water canner [bottling pan] with a tight fitting lid.
● a rack or trivet for the bottom of the pan to keep the jars away from direct heat, which could cause them to crack.
● toughened glass preserving jars with lids and rubber rings to ensure a perfect seal. It is very important that these rings be changed each time the jars are used since the old rubber will have stretched out of shape so it no longer forms a tight seal.

General recommendations

1. Boil the empty jars upside-down in a large saucepan half full of water for about 15 minutes or 5 minutes in a pressure cooker. Remove the jars with tongs, then, without wiping, drain them upside-down on a perfectly clean cloth. Turn upright.

2. Dip the rubber rings in boiling water, and place them on the necks of the jars.
3. Following the instructions given in your recipe and those in the chart on pages 52 and 53, pack the prepared fruit into the jars. Tap them several times on a folded cloth to settle the contents, then add more fruit until it reaches a level of ¾ in / 2 cm from the rim.
   Cover the fruit with sugar syrup or brine, leaving a space of ½ in / 1 cm under the lid to allow room for the steam to expand without bursting the jar. With a clean cloth, carefully wipe the top of the jar.
4. Seal the filled jars, following the manufacturer's directions. Arrange them in the pan on the rack, making sure they do not touch each other or the sides of the pan.
5. Fill the hot-water canner [bottling pan] with enough hot water to cover the jars by at least 1 in / 2.5 cm, then bring it to a boil. You should not start timing the process until the water has boiled.
6. When the process is completed, carefully remove the jars using tongs and place them on a wooden board or several layers of cloth or newspaper to cool. Complete the seals according to the manufacturer's instructions.
7. Leave the jars upright and undisturbed for 12 hours, then test the seals in the way recommended for the type of jar and lid you have used.
8. Label the jars with their contents and the date and store them in a cool, dark place.
9. Consult the table on pages 52 and 53 for information regarding the shelf-life of canned [bottled] fruits.
   All these operations must be carried out with the utmost care to avoid the very serious danger of food poisoning.
   Preserving food in this way is a very specialized operation, and in this volume we can give only a brief outline of the equipment and techniques involved. For detailed information, you should consult a book devoted to the subject.

Preserving in sugar

Anyone, even a complete beginner, can make delicious preserves from either garden fruit or the more exotic imported varieties. Some vegetables (such as pumpkin) are also suitable, and even flowers can be used to make unusual delicacies like rose-petal jam.

There are four main ways of preserving with sugar: a *jam* is made by cooking fresh fruit whole or in large pieces in a sugar syrup. In a *conserve* the fruit is layered or mixed with sugar, left to macerate, then cooked in the resulting thick syrup, without the addition of any water. In a *jelly*, only the juice of the fruit is cooked with the sugar, while to make a *compote*, the fruit is cooked very lightly in syrup made with only a little sugar.

You will find detailed instructions for all these methods in the following pages, along with a comprehensive table setting out the proportion of sugar, water and fruit required.

Fruit

Your produce should be of the very best quality — ripe, undamaged and free of insects.
1. Wash the fruit thoroughly by putting it into a colander under cold running water. To prevent strawberries, cherries, red and black currants and raspberries from absorbing water, do not top and tail the fruit first or let it stand in water.
2. When the fruit is clean, leave it to drain or pat dry. Then, where necessary, remove the stalks and stones.

Equipment

In order to preserve fruit using sugar, you will need the following items:
To prepare the fruit
● a paring knife
● a fruit pitter [stoner] (useful but not essential)
● earthenware or pyrex bowls
● a colander
● a lemon squeezer
● nutcracker
● sets of cup and spoon measures and/or kitchen scales
● if you are making jelly, you will need a jelly bag for straining the fruit, or a nylon strainer and a wooden spoon or pestle. This process will be easier if you use a blender or food processor to purée the fruit first.

To prepare the syrup
● a sugar thermometer

To cook the fruit
● an aluminum, stainless steel or enamel preserving pan. The traditional design of the preserving pan is ideal for making jam since its wide shape gives the contents a large surface area for evaporation. Copper pans, in spite of their aesthetic appeal, have the serious disadvantage of destroying much of the vitamin C in the fruit. If you do not have a preserving pan, any large pan with a thick base will do.
● a wooden spoon or spatula
● a stainless steel skimming ladle for removing froth

To bottle and seal the preserves
● heat resistant jars or pots that are completely free of chips
● a stainless steel ladle
● paraffin wax, cellophane discs and elastic bands for sealing jelly; lids for other types of preserving jars
● labels

Preparing the syrup

Of the wide range of sugars available, granulated is the most suitable for preserving, since it is quick-dissolving, cheap and easy to measure.

The quality of your preserve will depend on the boiling of the sugar, so follow each recipe carefully to ensure the syrup is brought to the correct stage before the fruit is added.

WARNING:
Once it has come to a boil, your syrup will develop from one stage to the next very quickly, so keep a close check on it with a sugar thermometer dipped into the simmering liquid. If you do not have a sugar thermometer, dip a stainless steel skimmer into the pan, remove a little syrup and let it cool. You can then test it with your thumb and index finger as shown in the illustrations.

Making jams, jellies and preserves

Whichever recipe you choose, it will turn out more successfully if you follow these simple rules:
1. Select only fruit that is just ripe, or even a little underripe, since its pectin level will be at its highest.
2. Be sure all your equipment is absolutely clean.
3. Make your preserve in a heavy-based pan that has a capacity at least twice that of the fruit and sugar to be processed, so the mixture can be brought to a rolling boil without risk of overflowing.
4. Cook the preserve over intense heat so it will reach its setting point as quickly as possible, since long exposure to high temperatures will impair its flavor.
5. Sterilize your jars carefully before filling them with jam.
6. Do not allow the jam to cool in the pan — pour it into jars as soon as it is set.
7. Seal the jars tightly and store them in a dry, dark, cool place.

Common problems and how to deal with them

If your jam becomes moldy, spoon off the mold and cover the jam with a thin layer of paraffin wax. Store it in a dry place and use it as soon as possible.
If your jam becomes frothy, it has begun to ferment and will develop an unpleasant, pungent smell. This means it has not been boiled for long enough, so you should boil it again until it reaches the large thread stage (see page 31).
If your jam crystallizes after several weeks, this indicates a lack of acid in the fruit during boiling. Boil the jam again, adding the juice of a lemon.
If your jam is runny, it does not contain enough pectin, so you must boil it again, adding some commercial pectin to ensure a good set.

Sugar boiling stages

Sugar thermometer ▶
A sugar thermometer should register up to 400°F / 200°C and has the various boiling stages marked. Check its accuracy frequently by bringing it to a boil in water (212°F / 100°C). Always warm it in very hot water before sliding it into the center of the boiling mixture. Hold it firmly and don't let it touch the pan base or you'll get a reading of the metal's heat, not what is being cooked. Bend down so your eye is level with the rim of the pan. When the required temperature is reached, remove pan from heat, then take out thermometer and place it back in jug to cool.

220°F / 105°C

▲
Jam setting point
Remove pan from heat and drop a little jam from a spoon on to a chilled saucer. A skin should form on the surface in less than 5 minutes and should wrinkle when pushed gently with a finger. If it doesn't, cook the jam more.

Large thread, pearl
Boil the syrup for a little longer, then test again as for the thread stage. This time, the thread formed should be shorter and thicker and will snap rather than stretch when pulled. If a little of the syrup is dropped into cold water from a spoon, it should form small, pearl-like balls in the water. The syrup is ready to be used for adding fruits and boiling them until crystallized. ▶

Thread
Don't continue to stir once the sugar has dissolved in the water. Always have a bowl of cold water to hand when testing the various stages of sugar boiling. For thread stage, use a spoon to lift a little syrup out of the pan and pour it slowly into the bowl — it will thicken before it reaches the water. Alternatively, dip fingers in cold water, quickly into the syrup on the back of the spoon, then back into cold water. The sugar should pull into a soft thread as the fingers are separated. At this stage, it's ready to be made into butter cream.

225°F / 108°C

◀

230°F / 110°C

Soft ball
Drop a little syrup into the cold water, leave for 1 minute; when rolled between finger and thumb it should form a soft malleable ball. Use for fondant, fudge, fudge icings, frostings and cooked almond paste. ▶

240°F / 116°C

250°F / 121°C   **Hard ball**
Test once again as for the soft ball stage. This time, the ball that is formed should be harder, firmer and cannot be squashed by the fingers. This is the stage at which it is used for Italian meringue and the softer caramels.

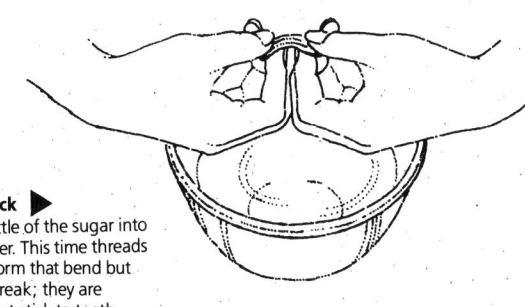

◀

260°F / 125°C

Soft crack ▶
Pour a little of the sugar into cold water. This time threads should form that bend but do not break; they are brittle, but stick to teeth. Use for hard caramels, marshmallow, nougat.

300°F / 149°C

◀ **Hard crack**
Tested again in the cold water, the sugar forms brittle threads that crack like glass and do not stick to the teeth. Use for making hard candy [boiled sweets], barley sugar, spun sugar and glazed fruits.

345°F / 174°C

Caramel ▶
As the sugar continues to boil, it turns a golden brown, then darkens rapidly. Watch it carefully as it quickly burns. Use it for crème caramel, oranges in caramel, some cake toppings.

Jam

Jam is made by cooking whole or quartered fruit in a sugar syrup. For 2 lb / 1 kg fruit, add 3 - 4 cups [750 g - 1 kg / 1½ - 2 lb] of sugar and 1 cup [250 ml / 8 fl oz] of water.

1. Wash the fruit.
2. Prepare the fruit by removing the stalks or pits [stones], peeling, or taking off the bunch.
3. Put the measured sugar and water into a pan.
4. Bring to a boil over a medium heat, stirring to dissolve the sugar. As soon as the syrup becomes clear and transparent, let it boil to the soft ball stage (240°F / 116°C).
5. Add the fruit to the sugar syrup and stir to mix. Return to a boil over a low heat, skimming off the froth or scum that forms on the surface.
6. When the mixture returns to a boil, boil for about 20 minutes or until jell [setting] point is reached. To test, pour a few drops of jam onto a cold plate and cool; if they solidify, the jam is ready. A sugar thermometer will register 220°F / 104°C.
7. Pour the jam into hot sterilized jars, leaving ½ in / 1 cm headroom.
8. For long storage, process in a boiling-water bath for 10 minutes.

Storage time: at least 1 year in a cool, dry place.

Compote

Compote is a mixture of lightly cooked, lightly sugared fruit and syrup. It may be in the form of a purée (stewed apples) or whole or quartered fruit in a syrup (stewed pears, peaches, etc). Expect to use 1½ - 1¾ cups [350 - 400 g / 12 - 14 oz] of sugar per 2 lb / 1 kg of fruit.

1. Wash the fruit.
2. Peel and remove stalks or pits [stones]. Cut the fruit into pieces.
3. Prepare a syrup with 1 quart [1l / 1¾ pints] water and 2 cups [500 g / 1 lb] sugar. Bring to a boil over a low heat, stirring to dissolve the sugar.
4. Add the prepared fruit, completely covering it with syrup.
5. Simmer until the fruit is tender.
6. You may add the juice of ½ lemon to the syrup to sharpen the taste and retain the color of the fruit.
7. Ladle into hot sterilized canning [preserving] jars, leaving ½ in / 1 cm headroom. For long storage, process in a boiling-water bath for 10 minutes.

Storage time: 3 months in a cool, dry place.

Jelly

Jelly is obtained by boiling fruit juices with sugar. To guarantee success, choose fruit which is rich in pectin (an organic vegetable substance which ensures that the jelly sets after boiling) — red currants, apples, raspberries, black currants, blackberries and quinces. Fruit such as cherries and peaches have very little natural pectin, so it needs to be added either as commercially prepared pectin or a pectin stock made from pectin-rich fruit. Select fruits when they have just reached the point of maturity, because they contain more pectin. Add 3 - 4 cups [750 g - 1 kg / 1½ - 2 lb] sugar per 1 quart [1l / 1¾ pints] of juice.

1. Wash the fruit.
2. Extract the juice by puréeing the fruit in a blender or food processor then straining through a nylon strainer. For a clearer jelly, strain through cheesecloth or muslin.
3. Measure the juice and judge the amount of sugar required accordingly.
4. Pour the juice and sugar into a saucepan. Bring to a boil over a low heat, stirring to dissolve the sugar. Skim off any scum or froth that forms on the surface.
5. Boil until jell [setting] point is reached (220°F / 104°C on a sugar thermometer). To test without a thermometer, take a sample of cooled syrup between your thumb and index finger and spread the fingers about ½ in / 1 cm apart: a wide thread should form which will not break.
6. Skim again and pour into hot sterilized jars, leaving ½ in / 1 cm headroom. Seal immediately with paraffin wax or the jar lids.

Storage time: 1 year.

Conserve

To make a conserve, whole fruit, or fruit cut into pieces, is boiled in the sugar in which it has macerated, until the syrup thickens. Conserves need not be as sweet as jam. For 2 lb / 1 kg fruit, add about 2½ - 4 cups [626 g - 1 kg / 1¼ - 2 lb] sugar.

1. Wash the fruit.
2. Prepare the fruit by trimming, removing pits [stones], peeling or taking off the bunch.
3. Place alternate layers of fruit and sugar in an earthenware bowl.
4. Leave to macerate for 12 - 36 hours (12 hours for plums; 24 hours for cherries, strawberries, raspberries, blackberries; 36 hours for oranges, mandarins, lemons, etc). For orange, grapefruit or other citrus conserve, soak the fruit first in cold water (2 - 3 tablespoons of water per 2 lb / 1 kg of fruit for 2 hours).
5. After macerating, bring to a boil, stirring frequently. Skim off scum or froth that forms on the surface. Boil over a low heat for 15 - 20 minutes, according to the type of fruit, until jell [setting] point is reached (220°F / 104°C on a sugar thermometer). To test without a thermometer, see the recipe for jam opposite.
6. Skim the conserve, then pour it into hot sterilized canning [jam] jars leaving ½ in / 1 cm headroom. For long storage, process in a boiling-water bath for 10 minutes.

Storage time: 1 year.

Jams

Fruit	What to make?	Possible mixtures	PROPORTIONS: Fruit	Sugar	Water	Cooking time	Uses
Apples	**Jam**	½ apples and ½ quinces	2 lb / 1 kg	4 cups [1 kg / 2 lb]	2 cups [500 ml / 16 fl oz]	1 hour	Desserts
	Jelly		1 quart [1 l / 1¾ pints] juice	4 cups [1 kg / 2 lb]		30–50 min	Cakes, crêpes
Apricots	**Conserve (semi-crushed fruit)**	Flavor with a few kernels from the pits [stones]	2 lb / 1 kg	4 cups [1 kg / 2 lb]		30 min	On bread and butter
	Jam (whole fruit)	1 vanilla bean [pod]	2 lb / 1 kg	4 cups [1 kg / 2 lb]	1 cup [250 ml / 8 fl oz]	20 min	Cakes, crêpes, sweets
Cherries	**Jam**	Sets in a jelly with ⅓ red currant juice	2 lb / 1 kg	4 cups [1 kg / 2 lb]	⅔ cup [150 ml / ¼ pint]	20 min	Cakes, sweets
Greengages	**Conserve**		2 lb / 1 kg	3 cups [750 g / 1 ½ lb]		20 min	Sauces
Mirabelle plums	**Jam**	½ apricots and ½ mirabelle plums	1 quart [1 l / 1¾ pints] juice	4 cups [1 kg / 2 lb]		20 min	Bread and butter, desserts
Oranges	**Conserve or marmalade**	Other citrus fruits or apples in varying proportions	2 lb / 1 kg	4 cups [1 kg / 2 lb]	1¼ cups [300 ml / ½ pint]	1½ hours	Cakes, tarts, bread and butter
	Jelly		1 quart [1 l / 1¾ pints] juice	4 cups [1 kg / 2 lb]		1 hour	Crêpes, ices, sorbets
Peaches	**Jam**	⅓ raspberries or ¼ lb / 125 g wild strawberries	2 lb / 1 kg	4 cups [1 kg / 2 lb]	⅔ cup [150 ml / ¼ pint]	20–25 min	Cakes, tarts
Pears	**Jam or conserve**	¹⁄₁₀ dried apricots and ¹⁄₁₀ crystallized fruits or 1 vanilla bean [pod]	2 lb / 1 kg	3 cups [750 g / 1 ½ lb]	⅔ cup [150 ml / ¼ pint]	20 min	Desserts
Quinces	**Jam**	½ apples and ½ quinces	2 lb / 1 kg	4 cups [1 kg / 2 lb]	2 cups [500 ml / 16 fl oz]	1 hour	Desserts
	Jelly		1 quart [1 l / 1¾ pints] juice	4 cups [1 kg / 2 lb]		30–50 min	Bread and butter, cakes
Raspberries	**Conserve or jam**	⅔ raspberries and ⅓ peaches	2 lb / 1 kg	4 cups [1 kg / 2 lb]		10 min	Cakes, tarts, sauces
	Jelly	⅔ red currants and ⅓ raspberries	1 quart [1 l / 1¾ pints] juice	4 cups [1 kg / 2 lb]		1 hour	Bread and butter, cakes
Red currants and black currants	**Jelly**	⅓ raspberries or ½ black currants	1 quart [1 l / 1¾ pints] juice	4 cups [1 kg / 2 lb]		3 min after boiling starts	Tart glazing, cakes, yogurt
Rhubarb	**Jam or conserve**	¼ raspberries or strawberries 1 vanilla pod [bean]	2 lb / 1 kg	4 cups [1 kg / 2 lb]		15 min	Tarts, bread and butter
Strawberries	**Conserve**	½ strawberries and ½ raspberries or jam of 4 fruits	2 lb / 1 kg	4 cups [1 kg / 2 lb]		25 min	Bread and butter
	Jam	in equal %: cherries, strawberries, raspberries, red currants	2 lb / 1 kg	4 cups [1 kg / 2 lb]	⅔ cup [150 ml / ¼ pint]		Cakes, sweets, bread and butter

Vegetables

Vegetable	What to make?	Possible mixtures	PROPORTIONS: Vegetable	Sugar	Water	Cooking time	Uses
Pumpkins	**Conserve**	4½ lb / 2 kg pumpkins and 1 orange or 1 lemon or 1 grapefruit	4 lb / 2 kg	6 cups [1.5 kg / 3 lb]		2 hours	Bread and butter, tarts
	Jam	1 lemon cut into slices	4 lb / 2 kg	8 cups [2 kg / 4 lb]		40 min	Bread and butter, tarts
Tomatoes (green)	**Conserve**	2 lemons in slices, 1 vanilla bean [pod], 5 tbsp rum	4 lb / 2 kg	6 cups [1.5 kg / 3 lb]		30 min	Bread and butter, tarts

Flowers

Flower	What to make?	Possible mixtures	PROPORTIONS: Flower petals	Sugar	Water	Cooking time	Uses
Provins roses	**Jam**	1 lemon	1 lb / 500 g	8 cups [2 kg / 4 lb]	2 cups [500 ml / 16 fl oz]	20 min	Bread and butter
Wild violets (March/April)	**Jam**	Juice of 3 lemons	2 lb / 1 kg	6 cups [1.5 kg / 3 lb]		20 min	Bread and butter

Preserving in vinegar, salt and oil

Savory preserves made using vinegar, salt and oil are particularly easy to prepare.

Vinegar
contains a high proportion of acetic acid that penetrates the food and inhibits the growth of micro-organisms. Any type of vinegar (malt, distilled, wine or cider) is suitable for preserving as long as its acid content is at least 6% to prevent fermentation.

Salt
acts by drawing out moisture from the food, making it uninhabitable for micro-organisms. Coarse sea salt gives the best result and can be used dry, in layers with the food, or in solution as a brine.

Oil
is used much less frequently as a preserving medium than either salt or vinegar since it is affected by exposure to light and air, and this instability makes it difficult to judge accurately the shelf life of foods prepared this way.

Guidelines

As with all preserving methods, the foods you choose should be fresh and free of blemishes and insects. Make sure too that they are at their peak of maturity without being over-ripe. Wash each piece carefully and wipe immediately so that no water is absorbed.

Unlike canning or bottling, preserving foods in this way does not require special jars, but the containers you choose must have tightly fitting lids or seals. Do not use metal lids for preserving in vinegar unless they are lined with plastic since vinegar will corrode the metal, causing it to taint and discolor the food. Glass stoppers should fit perfectly or be supplemented by a rubber ring to make an airtight seal. If you want to use a cork stopper, make sure it is exactly the right size for its container, boil it for several minutes, then cover it with plastic wrap.

Keep your preserves in a cool, dry place away from the light and leave them to mature for at least two months. Try to use them up fairly quickly after that to enjoy them at their best, and do not store them for longer than six months. Once you have opened a container, make sure to keep the food covered.

Vinaigre à l'estragon
Tarragon Vinegar

American	Ingredients	Metric/Imperial
00:05		00:00
1 (¼ lb)	Bunch of fresh tarragon	1 (125 g / 4 oz)
1 quart	White wine vinegar	1 l / 1¾ pints

1. Wash the tarragon and shake dry. Put it in the bottle of vinegar.
2. Leave to steep for 2 months before using.

Salt and vinegar are the main preservatives for this selection of vegetables

Citrons confits au sel
Preserved Lemons

American	Ingredients	Metric/Imperial
00:10		00:00
8	Medium-sized lemons	8
6 tbsp	Salt	75 g / 3 oz
2 tbsp	Coriander seeds	2 tbsp
	Virgin olive oil	

1. Quarter the lemons, not cutting them all the way through.
2. Sprinkle the salt into the cuts in the lemons and close them back up. Place in 2 sterilized 1 quart [1l / 2 pint jars]. Leave for 10 days.
3. Carefully wipe the lemons. Clean the jars with boiling water and dry them, then replace the lemons. Add 1 tablespoon coriander seeds to each jar and cover the lemons with olive oil. Seal tightly and leave in a cool, dark place for 2 months.
4. Use as a condiment for chicken, rabbit, beef, etc.

Huile aromatisée
Herb Oil

American	Ingredients	Metric/Imperial
00:05		00:00
1	Bunch of fresh herbs (basil fennel, savory, etc)	1
1 quart	Oil of your choice	1 l / 1¾ pints

1. Put the bunch of herbs into the bottle of oil.
2. Cover and keep in a cool, dark place for 1 month before using.

Concombres au vinaigre

Pickled Cucumbers

🔪	00:15		00:00 🍲
	plus salting		

American	Ingredients	Metric/Imperial
2 lb	Large firm cucumbers	1 kg / 2 lb
⅔ cup	Sea or kosher salt	250 g / 8 oz
1 quart	White vinegar	1 l / 1¾ pints

1. Cut the cucumbers into slices about ¾ in / 2 cm thick. Place in an earthenware jar, sprinkling each layer with salt. Leave for 24 hours, occasionally draining off the water that will exude from the cucumbers.
2. Rinse the cucumber slices. Put them into hot sterilized canning [preserving] jars, filling them three-quarters full.
3. Bring the vinegar to a boil and pour it over the cucumbers, completely covering them, but leaving ½ in / 1 cm headroom. For long storage, process in a boiling-water bath.
4. Wait 1 month before serving.

Echalotes au vinaigre

Pickled Shallots

🔪	00:15		00:05 🍲

American	Ingredients	Metric/Imperial
2 lb	Shallots	1 kg / 2 lb
1 tbsp	Black peppercorns	1 tbsp
1 quart	White vinegar	1 l / 1¾ pints

1. Peel the shallots and place in hot sterilized canning [preserving] jars with the peppercorns.
2. Bring the vinegar to a boil and boil for 5 minutes.
3. Pour the vinegar into the jars, covering the shallots, leaving ½ in / 1 cm headroom. For long storage, process in a boiling-water bath.
4. Leave to steep for 2 months before serving.

Oignons au vinaigre

Pickled Onions

🔪	00:20		00:04 to 00:10 🍲

American	Ingredients	Metric/Imperial
1½ quarts	Water	1.5 l / 2½ pints
2 tbsp	Salt	2 tbsp
2 lb	Small white onions or large mild red onions	1 kg / 2 lb
2 tbsp	Black peppercorns	2 tbsp
1 quart	Boiling flavored white wine vinegar (see pages 36 and 38)	1 l / 1¾ pints

1. Put the water and salt in a saucepan and bring to a boil. Peel the onions and drop into the boiling water. Boil for about 4 minutes for small onions and 10 minutes for large onions.
2. Drain the onions and put them into canning [preserving] jars. Add the peppercorns.
3. Cover with the boiling vinegar. leaving ½ in / 1 cm headroom. For long storage, process for about 10 minutes in a boiling-water bath.
4. Leave for 2 months before eating.

Use flavored oils and vinegar and spiced salt for salad dressings

Cornichons au vinaigre

Pickled Gherkins

	01:00	00:00
	plus marinating	

American	Ingredients	Metric/Imperial
4 lb	Gherkins	2 kg / 4 lb
2 lb (3 cups)	Sea or kosher salt	1 kg / 2 lb
¾ lb	Cocktail [pickling] onions	350 g / 12 oz
2	Hot red peppers [chillies]	2
1	Bunch of fresh tarragon	1
1 tbsp	Black peppercorns	1 tbsp
2 quarts	Boiling white vinegar	2 l / 3½ pints

1. Choose gherkins of equal size. Trim off the stems and scrub the gherkins. Rinse and drain. Thoroughly dry one at a time in a cloth, rubbing them to remove prickles.
2. Place the gherkins in an earthenware pot or bowl, sprinkling each layer with salt. Keep in a cool place for 8 hours.
3. Drain the gherkins, rinse in acidulated water and wipe dry. Arrange them in 2 sterilized 1 quart canning jars [1 l / 2 pint preserving jars]. Add the onions, hot peppers, tarragon and peppercorns. Cover with the boiling vinegar, leaving ½ in / 1 cm headroom.
4. For long storage, process in a boiling-water bath for 20 minutes.
5. Store in a cool, dark place for about 10 days before eating.

Cook's tip: do not remove the gherkins with your fingers or with an iron utensil, but use a stainless steel fork or a special pair of wooden tongs.

Vinaigre à l'echalote

Shallot Vinegar

	00:15	00:00

American	Ingredients	Metric/Imperial
8	Shallots	8
1 quart	White wine vinegar	1 l / 1¾ pints

1. Peel the shallots and quarter them.
2. Place the shallots in the vinegar. Leave to steep for 2 months before using.

Ketchup maison

Tomato Ketchup

	00:20	00:20

American	Ingredients	Metric/Imperial
6 oz	Onions	175 g / 6 oz
2 lb	Tomatoes	1 kg / 2 lb
7 tbsp	Light brown sugar	7 tbsp
⅔ cup	Wine vinegar	150 ml / ¼ pint
	Salt and pepper	
	Paprika	
	Cayenne pepper	
1 tbsp	Mustard powder	1 tbsp
1 tbsp	Ground ginger	1 tbsp
1 tsp	Quatre-épices (see below)	1 tsp
1 tsp	Grated nutmeg	1 tsp

1. Peel and chop the onions. Peel the tomatoes (first plunging them in boiling water for 10 seconds).
2. Place the tomatoes and onions in a saucepan. Sprinkle with the sugar and add the vinegar. Mix thoroughly. Add 1 teaspoon salt, a pinch each of pepper, paprika and cayenne pepper, the mustard, ginger, quatre-épices and nutmeg.
3. Cook over a low heat for 30 minutes, stirring frequently with a wooden spoon.
4. Leave to cool, then purée in a blender or food processor until smooth.
5. Put into sterilized canning [preserving] jars or bottles and seal tightly. The ketchup can be eaten immediately. For longer storage, process in a boiling-water bath. Once the bottle has been opened, keep it in the refrigerator.

Cook's tip: quatre-épices is a ground spice mixture of black pepper, nutmeg, cloves and ginger. Apple pie spice or mixed spice may be substituted.

Champignons à l'huile

Mushrooms in Oil

	00:45	00:30

American	Ingredients	Metric/Imperial
2 lb	Mushrooms (cultivated or wild)	1 kg / 2 lb
2 tbsp	Salt	2 tbsp
2 cups	Water	500 ml / 16 fl oz
2 cups	Vinegar	500 ml / 16 fl oz
1 quart	Olive oil	1 l / 1¾ pints

1. Clean the mushrooms. Dice or cut into quarters.
2. Place the mushrooms in a frying pan and sprinkle with the salt. Cook over a moderate heat until they exude their liquid. Discard the liquid.
3. Cover the the mushrooms with the water and vinegar and bring to a boil. Remove from the heat and leave to drain for 30 minutes.
4. Place in sterilized jars and cover with olive oil. Seal tightly and store in a dry place.

Sel épicé

Spiced Salt

	00:05	00:00

American	Ingredients	Metric/Imperial
2	Dried thyme sprigs	2
1	Bay leaf	1
3	Cloves	3
6 tbsp	Salt	6 tbsp
2 tbsp	Pepper	2 tbsp

1. Crush the thyme, bay leaf and cloves in a mortar with a pestle.
2. Put the salt into a mixing bowl and add the pepper, thyme, bay leaf and cloves. Mix well together.
3. Pour into a jar and seal tightly. Leave for at least 2 months before using.
4. Use the salt to spice sauces, soups and stocks, salads and meat, particularly game.

Olives noires á l'huile

Ripe [Black] Olives in Oil

	00:10		00:00

American	Ingredients	Metric/Imperial
2 lb	Very fresh ripe [black] olives	1 kg / 2 lb
1 cup	Sea or kosher salt	350 g / 12 oz
6	Cloves	6
2 tsp	Black peppercorns	2 tsp
2	Fresh thyme sprigs	2
2	Bay leaves	2
	Virgin olive oil	

1. Wipe the olives. Prick them down to the pit [stone] in 2 places using a sterilized needle. Place the olives in an earthenware pot and cover with the salt. Leave for 10 days, stirring occasionally and draining off the water produced.
2. Rinse the olives and leave to dry, then put them in 2 sterilized jars. Add 3 cloves, 1 teaspoon peppercorns, a sprig of thyme and a bay leaf to each jar. Cover the olives with olive oil.
3. Seal tightly and leave for 2 months before eating.

Basilic à l'huile

Basil Oil

	00:15		00:00

American	Ingredients	Metric/Imperial
2 lb	Fresh basil	1 kg / 2 lb
¼ cup	Salt	4 tbsp
1½ quarts	Virgin olive oil	1.5 l / 2½ pints

1. Rinse the basil and shake dry. Remove the leaves from the stems.
2. Arrange the basil leaves in 1 cup [300 ml / ½ pint] jars in layers about ½ in / 1 cm thick, sprinkling each layer with salt. Cover with olive oil and seal tightly.
3. Leave to soak in a cool dark place for at least 1 month.
4. Use the oil for seasoning soups, salads and meat, and for sprinkling over fresh cream cheeses.

Fromages de chèvre à l'huile

Goat's Milk Cheese in Oil

	00:10		00:00

American	Ingredients	Metric/Imperial
	Small fresh goat's milk cheeses (crottin de Chavignol)	
	Fresh thyme sprigs	
	Fresh rosemary sprigs	
	Bay leaf	
	Virgin olive oil	

1. Place the fresh cheeses in a wide-mouthed jar together with thyme, rosemary and bay leaf. Cover with olive oil and seal the jar tightly.
2. Leave to stand for 1 month.
3. The oil in which the goat's milk cheese has been soaked can be used for making vinaigrette dressings, mayonnaise, etc.

Olive vertes au sel

Salted Green Olives

	00:25		00:00

American	Ingredients	Metric/Imperial
2 lb	Fresh green olives	1 kg / 2 lb
2 quarts	Water	2 l / 3½ pints
1½ lb (2 cups)	Sea or kosher salt	750 g / 1½ lb
3	Fresh fennel sprigs	3
4	Fresh thyme sprigs	4
2	Bay leaves	2

1. Wipe the olives. Prick them down to the pit [stone] with a sterilized needle. Place the olives in an earthenware jar and cover them with cold water. Leave for 12 days, changing the water frequently.
2. Drain the olives. Return them to the jar.
3. Put the water in a saucepan and bring to a boil. Add the fennel sprigs, thyme sprigs and bay leaves. Pour the mixture over the olives and leave to soak for 10 days.
4. Remove the olives with a slotted spoon and place in sterilized jars. Cover them with a fresh brine, prepared as previously and cooled. Seal tightly. Allow to marinate for 2 months before eating.

Goat's milk cheese in oil

Preserving in alcohol

Many fruits — cherries, apricots, plums, grapes and strawberries for example — keep very well in brandy, or in any other alcohol as long as it is not of an unusually high proof. Cognac, Armagnac, whiskey, rum and gin will all make delicious preserves. Like vinegar and salt, alcohol is an antiseptic that penetrates the food and destroys any micro-organisms.

To preserve fruit in this way, you must first soak it in sugar or a sugar syrup since alcohol on its own will harden and shrivel the food. When this is done, add the alcohol to the fruit in the proportion of 1 quart [1 l / 1¾ pints] to 2 lb / 1 kg.

Equipment

To enjoy your preserves at their best, put them in wide-necked jars so you will be able to remove the fruit easily, without damaging it.

If you use a cork stopper, make it more supple by soaking it in water for 12 hours, then drying it for 2-3 weeks before using it to seal the jar.

Cook's tip: Once a corked jar has been opened, line the cork with one thickness of cheesecloth or muslin to prevent air from reaching the alcohol and causing evaporation.

Poires à l'eau-de-vie

Pears in Brandy

	00:30 plus maturing	00:25
American	**Ingredients**	**Metric/Imperial**
2 lb	Small, firm, ripe pears	1 kg / 2 lb
2	Lemons	2
2½ cups	Sugar	625 g / 1¼ lb
1 cup	Water	250 ml / 8 fl oz
1 quart	Eau-de-vie or brandy	1 l / 1¾ pints

1. Peel the pears, leaving their stalks on. Cut them in quarters, trying to cut the stalk equally. Remove the core and seeds. Sprinkle with the juice of 1 lemon to prevent discoloration.

2. Put the sugar, the juice of the remaining lemon and the water in a large heavy saucepan. Cook until syrupy — when the bubbles become very small. If using a sugar thermometer, it should register 212°F/ 100°C.

3. Place the pear quarters in the hot syrup and boil for about 15 minutes over a medium heat until the pears become translucent.

4. Remove the pears with a slotted spoon and arrange in sterilized jars.

5. Boil the syrup until the soft ball stage is reached (240°F / 115°C on a sugar thermometer). Leave the syrup to cool, then pour it over the pears in the jars.

6. Cover the pears with brandy and seal the jars tightly. Leave to mature for 2 months before eating.

Oranges preserved in alcohol

Liqueur d'orange
Orange Liqueur

	00:10 plus maturing		00:05

American	Ingredients	Metric/Imperial
1	Large orange	1
1 cup	Sugar	250 g / 8 oz
1 cup	Water	250 ml / 8 fl oz
1 quart	Fruit eau-de-vie or brandy	1 l / 1¾ pints

1. Scrub the orange carefully, rinse and dry.
2. Put the sugar and water in a heavy saucepan and bring to a boil, stirring to dissolve the sugar. Boil until syrupy, and the bubbles are very small (212°F / 100°C on a sugar thermometer). Leave to cool.
3. Pour the cold syrup into a sterilized large jar and add the brandy. Hang the orange from the cork on a piece of string which you have inserted into the fruit. The orange should be suspended about ½ in / 1 cm above the liquid.
4. Seal the jar and leave in a dry place for 2 months.
5. Throw away the orange which will have darkened and become hard.

Framboises à l'eau-de-vie
Raspberries in Brandy

	00:05 plus maturing		00:10

American	Ingredients	Metric/Imperial
2 lb	Raspberries	1 kg / 2 lb
1½ cups	Sugar	350 g / 12 oz
1 cup	Water	250 ml / 8 oz fl oz
1 quart	Eau-de-vie or brandy	1 l / 1¾ pints

1. Choose only perfectly sound raspberries. You do not have to wash them. However, if they appear dirty, put them in a colander and rinse them quickly under running water. Place in a sterilized jar.
2. Put the sugar and water in a heavy saucepan and bring to a boil, stirring to dissolve the sugar. Boil until syrupy, and the bubbles become very small (212°F / 100°C on a sugar thermometer).
3. Cover the raspberries with the brandy and add the syrup. Seal the jars tightly. Leave for 2 months before eating.

Raisins à l'eau-de-vie
Grapes in Brandy

	00:15 plus maturing		00:15

American	Ingredients	Metric/Imperial
4½ lb	White grapes	2 kg / 4½ lb
⅔ cup	Sugar	150 g / 5 oz
1 cup	Water	250 ml / 8 fl oz
1½ quarts	Eau-de-vie or brandy	1.5 l / 2½ pints

1. Rinse the grapes and drain. Remove them from the stems. Set aside half of the grapes, choosing the most perfect. Put the remaining grapes in a blender or food processor and purée, then strain the purée to extract the juice.

2. Dissolve the sugar in the water in a heavy saucepan. Add the grape juice and boil until syrupy, and small bubbles form on the surface (212°F / 100°C on a sugar thermometer). Leave the syrup to cool.
3. Place the reserved grapes in sterilized jars. Pour the cold syrup over them and add the brandy so that the liquid comes 1 in / 2.5 cm above the level of the fruit. Seal tightly and leave to mature for 2 months before eating.

Pruneaux à l'eau-de-vie
Prunes in Brandy

	00:05 plus maturing		00:00

American	Ingredients	Metric/Imperial
2 lb	Prunes	1 kg / 2 lb
1 quart	Brandy (preferably armagnac)	1 l / 1¾ pints

1. Rinse the prunes and place in a sterilized jar with the brandy. Seal tightly.
2. Leave to mature for 3 months in a dark dry place before eating.

Raspberries in brandy

Cerises à l'eau-de-vie
Cherries in Brandy

	00:15		00:00
	plus maturing		

American	Ingredients	Metric/Imperial
2 lb	Fresh cherries	1 kg / 2 lb
1 tbsp	Coriander seeds	1 tbsp
2	Cinnamon sticks	2
1 cup	Sugar	250 g / 8 oz
1 quart	Fruit eau-de-vie or brandy	1 l / 1¾ pints

1. Rinse the cherries and drain. Trim the stems to ½ in/ 1 cm.
2. Place the cherries in sterilized jars with the coriander, cinnamon and sugar. Seal the jars and leave for 2 days.
3. Add the brandy, seal again and shake the jars gently to mix.
4. Leave to mature in a cool, dark place for 2 months, turning the jar every week.

Storage time: 1 year

Mirabelles à l'eau-de-vie
Plums in Brandy

	00:15		00:05
	plus maturing		

American	Ingredients	Metric/Imperial
2 lb	Plums (preferably mirabelles)	1 kg / 2 lb
1 quart	Eau-de-vie or brandy	1 l / 1¾ pints
1 cup	Sugar	250 g / 8 oz
1 cup	Water	250 ml / 8 fl oz

1. Rinse the plums and drain. Remove the stalks.
2. Place the plums in a sterilized jar and cover with brandy. Seal the jar and leave to mature for 1 month.

3. At the end of 1 month, prepare a sugar syrup by putting the sugar in a heavy saucepan with the water. Bring to a boil, stirring to dissolve the sugar. Boil until syrupy – when the bubbles become very small (212°F / 100°C on a sugar thermometer). Leave the syrup to cool.
4. Pour the cold syrup into the jar of plums and seal tightly. Leave to mature for a further month before eating.

Abricots à l'eau-de-vie
Apricots in Brandy

	00:30		00:35
	plus maturing		

American	Ingredients	Metric/Imperial
2 lb	Apricots	1 kg / 2 lb
2½ cups	Sugar	625 g / 1¼ lb
1 cup	Water	250 ml / 8 fl oz
1 quart	Fruit eau-de-vie or brandy	1 l / 1¾ pints

1. Rinse and dry the apricots. Prick down to the pit [stone] in 2 places with a sterilized needle.
2. Put the sugar in a saucepan with the water and bring to a boil, stirring to dissolve the sugar. Boil to the short thread stage (215°F / 105°C on a sugar thermometer).
3. Put the apricots in the syrup, bring back to a boil and cook for 5 minutes. Remove from the heat and leave to cool for 12 hours.
4. Take out the apricots using a slotted spoon and place in sterilized jars.
5. Boil the syrup again until the long thread stage is reached (225°F / 110°C on a sugar thermometer). Leave the syrup to cool.
6. Cover the apricots with the brandy and pour in the cooled syrup. Seal the jars tightly and shake gently to mix. Allow to mature for 2 months before eating.

A selection of equipment needed for preserving

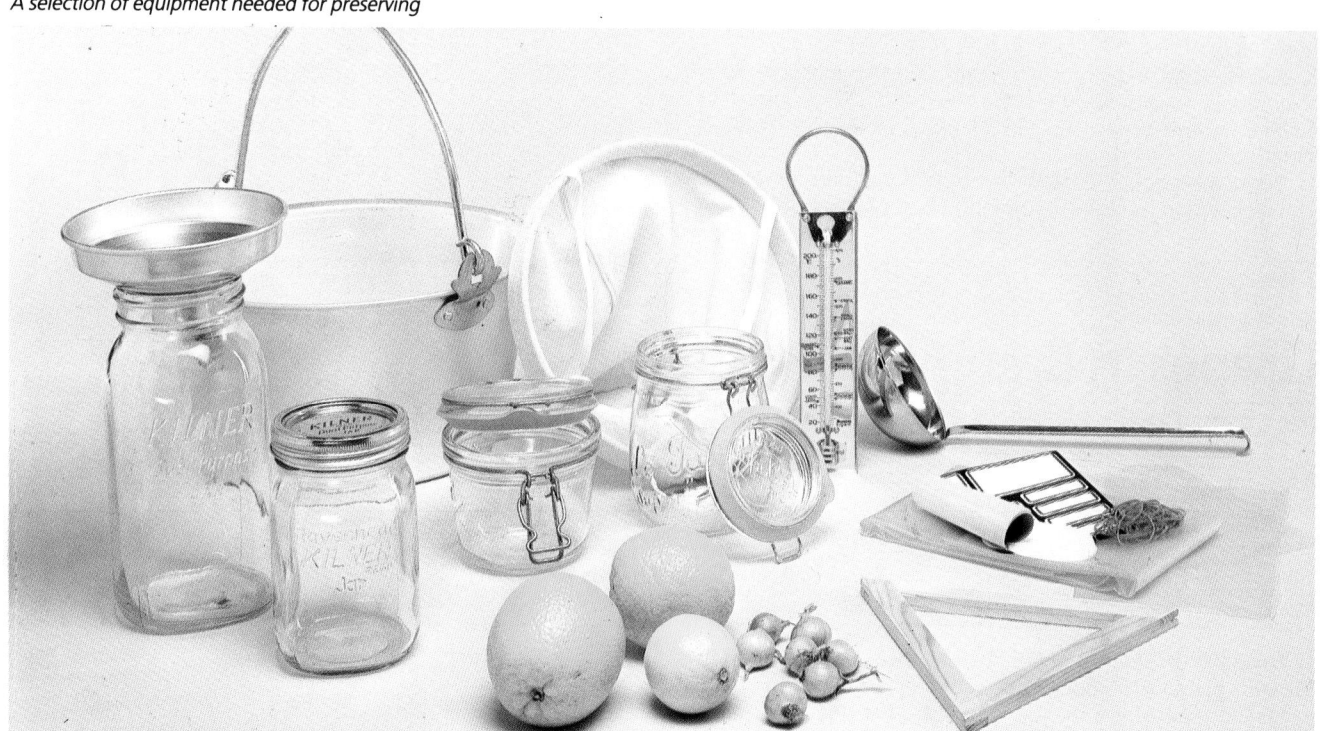

Preserving by drying

The moisture or water content of food provides a suitable environment in which bacteria can multiply, and fermentation and decay can take place. The removal of this water by drying food in the open air, in the sun or in commercial drying cabinets arrests the chemical reactions which cause decay and deterioration.

Drying can be carried out at home and is especially suitable for preserving herbs, mushrooms, beans, apricots etc, but home drying is never perfect and most foods retain a little of their moisture. Beans and lentils however, will dry perfectly if they are picked at the right time (when the stalks have withered in the case of beans).

Drying methods

Sun drying is a cheap and convenient method provided you live in an area where many consecutive days of sunshine (with temperatures of about 90°F / 32°C) can be guaranteed, and where humidity and pollution levels are low. In towns especially it may be difficult to achieve these ideal conditions.

Another method, which is particularly suitable for drying small amounts of food at one time, is to use an electric oven set at the lowest possible temperature. By alternating the heating, evaporation and cooling periods you can achieve the same result as you would had the food been exposed to the sun.

Whichever method you choose, make sure that air can circulate freely on all sides of the food. If it is to be dried on trays, these should be made of stainless steel, nylon or plastic screening, with a durable frame. Aluminum and galvanized metals are not suitable.

Storage

Keep your dried foods in airtight jars to prevent them from absorbing moisture from the air.

To avoid mold and attack by parasites, use an old trick and put a few garlic cloves in with dried vegetables. Store them in a very dry place away from the light.

Use

Dried vegetables must be soaked in cold water for at least 12 hours. Drain and cover them with fresh water before cooking.

Lentils and split peas do not always require soaking. Simply bring them slowly to a boil in a pan of cold water, skimming off any scum that may rise (see also individual recipes).

Garlic

1. Pick the garlic in July or August, leaving a 4-6 in / 10-15 cm length of stalk attached to each bulb.
2. Hang in a dry, well-ventilated place or in the sun for about 10 days.
3. Form into strings by braiding [plaiting] the stalks and hang in a dry place.

Almonds

1. Pick your almonds in June or July. Remove the inner shells (the green outer shells should fall away by themselves), and spread the almonds on a tray. Place them in a dark, ventilated place away from dust and leave to dry for 2 weeks.
2. Put the almonds in an airtight jar and store them in a very dry place.

Herbs

(Basil, tarragon, parsley, celery leaves, mint, rosemary, savory, wild thyme, thyme)
1. Sort the fresh herbs very carefully, keeping only those of the best quality. Wash them in running water and dry with a clean cloth. Tie them in small bunches with raffia or twine.
2. Hang in a dry, well-ventilated place until the leaves crumble easily.
3. Cut the dried herbs with scissors before placing them in jars labeled according to type.

You can dry herbs quickly in a microwave oven (and leaves or flowers for tea: mint, lime, verbena, camomile etc) with a result that is as pleasing to the eye as to the palate. Working with small quantities at a time, spread the leaves or flowers (removing all stalks) on a sheet of paper towel and switch the oven to the defrosting position for less than 1 minute.

Sweet or hot peppers

1. Wash the fresh peppers and dry with a clean cloth.
2. String them together with raffia or twine and hang them in the sun for 2 weeks.
3. Store in airtight jars.

Apricots

(see table on page 52)

Mushrooms

(see table on page 45)

Beans

(see table on page 45)

Apples

1. Peel and core the apples. Cut into rings ½ in / 1 cm thick.
2. Place on the shelf of an electric oven at 150°F / 66°C, (or its lowest setting) with the door open, for 12 hours.
3. Leave for 24 hours in the open air. Put back into the cool oven with the door open, and dry for about 12 hours. Again leave for 24 hours in the open air.
4. Put back in the cool oven with the door open, and dry for 12 hours more. Thread the slices of apple on strings of raffia. Hang in a dry, well-ventilated place for 2-3 days.
5. Store in airtight jars.

Raisins

1. Select 8 bunches of very sweet grapes (currant type), discarding any that are damaged. Wash in fresh water and remove grapes from the stems.
2. Put the grapes into a strainer. Place the strainer with the grapes in a large saucepan full of boiling water for 30 seconds. Lift out, leave to drain and dry.
3. Put the grapes on a tray into an electric oven heated to 150°F / 66°C (or its lowest setting) and dry for 12 hours, with the door open.
4. Leave in a dry, well-ventilated place for 4 hours.
5. Repeat the drying in the oven and open air at least twice until the grapes have dried completely.
6. Store in airtight jars in a very dry place.

Preserving Vegetables

Vegetable	Preparation	Freezing	Other forms of preserving
Beans in shells	1. Shell the beans. 2. Blanch for 5 minutes in unsalted boiling water so as not to harden them. 3. Rinse under cold water.	1. Put in bags. Seal tight and label. 2. **To use:** do not thaw. Boil for 1 hour in water without soaking. Add salt after 20 minutes cooking to avoid hardening.	Drying: 1. Pull up the plants and hang in a dry, airy place. 2. As soon as the shells begin to open, place the beans in a large plastic bag and shake vigorously to separate the shells from the beans. 3. Sort and keep only the soundest beans, putting them into a canvas or paper bag. **To use:** soak for 12 hours. Do not use the soaking water for cooking. Will keep 1 year.
Brussels sprouts	1. Cut off the stalks and remove damaged leaves. 2. Place in acidulated water. 3. Blanch in boiling salted water for 2 minutes, rinse in cold water and drain.	1. Put in plastic bags or boxes. 2. Seal tight and label. **To use:** do not thaw. Cook in boiling water. Will keep 8–10 months.	
Carrots	1. Scrub and peel. 2. Blanch in boiling salted water for 3 minutes if sliced and 5 minutes if left whole. 3. Drain and rinse in cold water.	1. Put in boxes or bags. 2. Seal tight and label. **To use:** do not thaw. Cook for 15 minutes in boiling salted water or 1 hour in a stew. Will keep 12 months.	In the cellar: raw as soon as they are picked. 1. Cut off the stalks, leaving ½ in / 1 cm. 2. Place the carrots in heaps and cover with dry sand. Will keep 4–6 months.
Cauliflower	1. Remove the florets and leave ¾ in / 2 cm of stalk. Wash in acidulated water. 2. Blanch for 2–3 minutes in boiling salted acidulated water. Dry in a thick cloth.	Place in bags and label. **To use:** without thawing, cook in boiling water for 15 minutes. Will keep 6 months.	In vinegar: 1. Place in jars, adding small white onions. 2. Cover with vinegar that has been boiled for 5 minutes and cooled. 3. Seal and leave to marinate for 2 weeks before using as a relish.
Eggplant [Aubergines]	1. Peel and dice or cut into ¾ in / 2 cm slices. 2. Brown for 6 minutes in 6 tbsp [75 g / 3 oz] butter or 3 tbsp oil over a low heat.	1. Pack in bags or boxes. 2. Seal tight and label. **To use:** do not thaw for a slowly stewed dish. Thaw for 12 hours in the refrigerator for a dish cooked *au gratin* or fritters. Will keep 5 months.	
Globe artichokes	1. Break off the artichoke stalks by hand. 2. Remove the hard outside leaves and cut the other leaves level with the heart. Put them into water containing vinegar or lemon as you go along to avoid blackening. 3. Blanch for 10 minutes in salted acidulated water. 4. Free the hearts from their leaves, discard the chokes and rinse in cold water. 5. Leave to cool.	1. Place the very cold hearts in freezer bags and then in plastic containers. 2. Seal tight and label. **To use:** do not thaw. Put directly into boiling water and cook for 12–15 minutes (in a stew: 25 minutes). Will keep 6–9 months.	In oil: (small artichokes) 1. Wash the artichokes and cook whole for 20 minutes in boiling salted water. 2. Drain them and remove the leaves and choke, keeping only the hearts. 3. Place in jars together with black peppercorns, coriander seeds and bay leaves. 4. Cover with oil. Seal the jars. Leave to marinate for 1 month before eating. Will last indefinitely.
Green beans	1. Remove strings and wash. 2. Blanch in boiling salted water for 3 minutes. 3. Rinse for 2 minutes under cold running water.	1. Pack in plastic bags. 2. Seal tight and label. **To use:** without thawing, cook uncovered, in boiling water for 15–20 minutes depending on size.	

Preserving Vegetables

Vegetable	Preparation	Freezing	Other forms of preserving
Mushrooms (*Boletus, cèpes, chanterelles, cultivated mushrooms*)	1. Sort the mushrooms, keeping only those which are fresh and perfectly sound. 2. Trim stems. 3. Clean in fresh water and drain. 4. Wipe with a clean cloth.	Raw mushrooms are not suitable for freezing because they contain too much water and blacken easily.	Drying: 1. Thread the mushrooms on strings, piercing the stem under the head. 2. Hang for 10–15 days in the dry air, in the sun if possible. 3. Put into cool oven, with the door open, and dry for 2 hours, turning occasionally. 4. Place in jars. **To use:** put them dry into a sauce that is simmered or soak first for 1–3 hours.
Peas	1. Shell the peas and sort out the soundest. 2. Blanch for 5 minutes in boiling salted water (1 tbsp salt to 1 quart [1 l / 1¾ pints] water). 3. Rinse under cold water and drain.	Place in plastic sachets. Seal tight and label. **To use:** without thawing, cook in boiling water for 15 minutes. Will keep 10 months.	
Potatoes (*croquettes*)	Make croquettes according to the recipe chosen.	Freeze raw or cooked, spread out on a tray, until hard. Then put into plastic bags. **To use:** if the potatoes are raw, do not thaw but cook gently in butter in a frying pan for about 15 minutes. If they are cooked, warm up in the frying pan for 3-5 minutes.	
Spinach	1. Wash carefully and remove stalks. 2. Blanch in boiling salted water for 3 minutes. 3. Drain and dry.	Place whole leaves or chopped spinach in plastic bags. Seal tight and label. **To use:** do not thaw. Cook in boiling water for 10–15 minutes. Will keep 12 months.	

Preserving raw meat

Meat	Preparation	Freezing
Steaks, fillets, chops, scaloppine [escalopes], tenderloin	Remove sinews and fat. **Cook's tip:** do not freeze ground [minced] meat, otherwise you run the risk of serious food poisoning.	1. Pack separately in foil. 2. Freeze for 6 hours. 3. Gather together in freezer bags, label and return to freezer. **To use:** thaw for 12 hours in refrigerator. Will keep 10 months.
Roasts	Remove excess fat and cut into pieces no heavier than 4 lb / 2 kg.	1. Wrap in foil. 2. Freeze for 24 hours. 3. Place in freezer bags, label and return to freezer. **To use:** thaw for 12 hours in refrigerator. Will keep 10 months.
Legs of mutton or lamb **Ribs of beef**	Remove fat and sinews.	1. To prevent perforations, wrap bones in foil to form protective buffers. 2. Wrap in foil and freeze for 12 hours. 3. Place in freezer bags, label and return to freezer. **To use:** thaw for 12 hours in refrigerator. Will keep 10 months.
Meat for stewing or braising	Cut into pieces.	1. Make up portions according to your requirements and proceed as for steaks. **To use:** thaw for 12 hours in refrigerator. Will keep 10 months.
Charcuterie: dried and smoked sausages, [black or white pudding], crépinettes, faggots, etc.	1. Blanch for 1 minute in boiling water. 2. Drain and dry carefully.	Place in aluminum trays or wrap in foil separately. Label and freeze. **To use:** thaw for 12 hours in refrigerator. Will keep 6 months.
Variety meats [offal]	Except for brains, they do not freeze very well. Eat as soon as you have bought them.	

Fish, meat, vegetables and crustaceans can be frozen and retain their quality

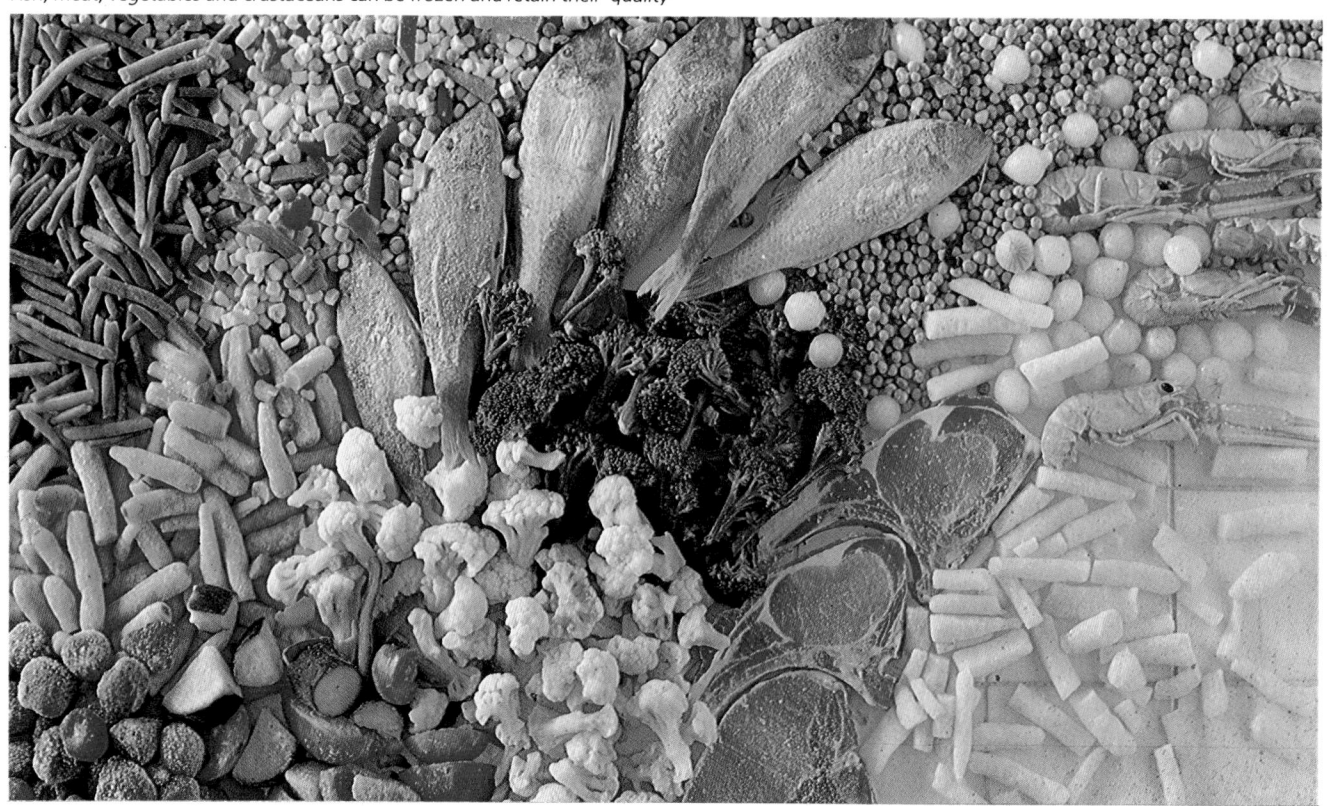

Preserving poultry and game

Meat	Preparation	Freezing	To use
Poultry and game birds	1. Pluck and clean the bird. Cut off the neck and feet. 2. Leave whole or cut up.	1. Whole (place a foil plug inside): wrap in foil. Place in freezer bag. Expel the air. Seal and label. 2. In pieces: wrap each piece in foil and place the individual packages in one bag. Will keep: duck, pheasant: 6–12 months depending on its fat. turkey: 6–8 months. goose: 3–5 months. game fowl: 10 months. chicken: 10 months.	1. Before cooking, with the meat still in the package, thaw in the refrigerator 24 hours for whole birds or 12 hours for pieces. 2. Cook without delay to avoid deterioration.
Game animals (venison, wild boar)	Prepare pieces with a view to future use (roast, chops, braising meats, etc).	1. Wrap in foil. 2. Place in individual bags and seal, expelling the air. Label. Will keep 7 months.	1. For braising pieces: thaw in a marinade for 24 hours in refrigerator (you will not be able to use the marinade liquid to make a sauce). 2. For roasting pieces: with the meat still in its packing, thaw in refrigerator for 24 hours.
Rabbits and hares	1. Skin and clean the animal. 2. Cut off the head and feet. 3. Cut into pieces or leave whole. 4. Leave raw or prepare in cooked dishes without too much flavoring.	1. Whole: wrap in foil and place in a freezer bag. Seal, expelling the air. Label. 2. In pieces: wrap each piece in foil. Place in freezer bags and seal, expelling the air. Label. 3. Cooked: place in plastic containers. Cover and label. Will keep: rabbit: 10 months hare: 6 months	1. Raw: remove from package and thaw in refrigerator for 24 hours or in a marinade. 2. Cooked: do not thaw but cook in the oven or in a casserole.

Meat will thaw more readily if it has been well prepared

Preserving fish

Fish	Preparation	Freezing	To use
Whole fish (with or without scales) anchovies, cod, coley, dabs, grey mullet, herring, mackerel, pike, pike-perch, salmon, sardines, sea bream, shad, snapper, trout, whitebait, whiting	1. Leave the head or cut it off as you please. 2. Clean the fish (see method on page 248). 3. Fill the inside of large fish with crumpled foil.	1. Place the fish on a tray in the freezer at lowest setting for 12 hours. 2. Turn it and replace in middle of freezer for 12 hours. 3. Wrap it in foil. Place it in a double plastic bag and seal tight, expelling the air. Label and return to freezer. Will keep 6 months.	Do not thaw. Cook in a court-bouillon or butter or oil, increasing cooking time by half.
Fish steaks or slices: Bass, burbot, cod, carp, conger eel, eel, gurnet, haddock, hake, lamprey, pike-perch, trout, tuna, turbot	1. Scale the fish, clean and wash. 2. Cut into slices or steaks.	1. Wrap completely flat in foil and place in the freezer set to its lowest point. Freeze for 7 hours. 2. Take out of the freezer and place in plastic wrap in meal portions. Seal tight and label. Return to freezer. Will keep: Lean fish: 6 months Fat fish: 4 months	Do not thaw, but cook according to the recipe chosen.
Fish fillets: Brill, burbot, char, dabs, flounder, grouper, John Dory, monkfish, perch, red mullet, sea bream, sole, turbot	**Prepare fillets:** 1. Having skinned the fish (see method on page 249), make a slit along the center bone from head to tail. Slide the knife under each fillet and separate. 2. Do not soak fillets either in salted or acidulated water, because they might absorb it.	1. Wrap each fillet in foil then place in the freezer on its lowest setting. Freeze for 6 hours. 2. Place in a plastic bag and seal tight, expelling the air. Label and return to freezer. Will keep: Lean fish: 6 months Fat fish: 4 months	For a sauced dish, do not thaw. Cook according to the recipe chosen. For a fried dish, thaw, and before cooking, drain and dip each side in flour.

Freeze fish as quickly as possible after catching. If fish is given to you and you are not sure how fresh it is, eat it as soon as possible.

Preserving shellfish and sea food

Shellfish and sea food	Preparation	Freezing
Clams, cockles, mussels	1. Rinse shellfish. 2. Place in a frying pan without fat and heat, stirring continuously. 3. As soon as the shells open, remove the flesh. 4. Leave to cool in a bowl of salted water (1 tsp salt to each 1 quart [1l / 1¾ pints] water).	1. Put the drained flesh in plastic containers, filling them only to the ¾ mark. 2. Cover with cooled boiled salted water (1 tsp salt to each 1 quart [1l / 1¾ pints] water). Seal the containers and label. Will keep 4 months. To use: without thawing, cook according to the recipe chosen.
Crab	1. Prepare a highly spiced court-bouillon (see recipe page 115). 2. Plunge crabs into the boiling court-bouillon and cook for 8 minutes. 3. Leave to cool. Remove claws, legs, stomach and organs, and shell. Keep only the meat from the body and claws.	1. Wrap the meat, without the shell, in foil, close tightly and freeze. 2. Place in plastic bags and seal, expelling the air. Label and return to the freezer. Will keep 6 months. To use: without thawing, place in boiling court-bouillon to complete cooking.
Scallops	1. Open shells and remove the white flesh (muscle) and coral (if available), using a small pointed knife. 2. Rinse with water and dry.	1. Cover with foil. 2. Freeze before packing. Then place in plastic bags in meal-portions. Seal and label. Will keep 4 months. **To use:** without thawing, cook according to the recipe chosen.
Shrimp [prawns]	1. Boil shelled shrimp for 30 seconds, or unshelled shrimp for 2 minutes in a large quantity of salted water (⅔ cup [150 g / 5 oz] salt to each 1 quart [1l / 1¾ pints] water). 2. Drain and dry on a clean cloth.	1. Place in portions in small containers. 2. Seal and label. **To use:** In shell: without thawing, put shrimp into boiling salted water (2 tsp salt to each 1 quart [1l / 1¾ pints] water), and boil for a few minutes. Shelled: without thawing, cook according to the menu chosen. In salads: thaw in the container in the refrigerator for 12 hours. Will keep 6 months.

Do not confuse keeping on ice with freezing. Crustaceans must be frozen as soon as they are killed, at −13°F / −24°C.

Freezing bread, pastries, creams, ices and sorbets

	Freezing	To use
Bread (all bread provided it is very fresh)	1. Wrap in special foil. 2. Place in freezer bags and label. Will keep 3 months.	Take out of the bag and place in a preheated 280°F / 140°C / Gas Mark 2 oven, in the wrapping, for 15 minutes. Or leave to thaw at room temperature.
Pie [short crust] pastry	1. Cut the pastry into usable portions. 2. Wrap the separate portions in foil. Label. Will keep 2 months.	Leave to thaw for 12 hours, in the wrapping, in the refrigerator, or for 3 hours at room temperature.
Choux pastry	1. Shape the pastry into walnut-size balls. 2. Wrap in foil and label. Will keep 2 months.	Thaw for 24 hours in the refrigerator, in the wrapping.
Puff or flaky pastry	1. Cut the pastry into usable portions. Wrap separately in foil and label. Will keep 2 months.	Thaw for 12 hours in the refrigerator, in the wrapping, for 3 hours at room temperature.
Pizzas	1. Cover the cooked pizzas with foil. 2. Freeze at −13°F / −24°C for 2 hours, then wrap in a freezer bag and return to the freezer. Will keep 2 months.	Reheat in a preheated 425°F / 220°C / Gas Mark 7 oven for 15 minutes.
Creams Custard Sauce	1. Pour the custard sauce into a plastic container. 2. Seal tight and label. Will keep 2 months.	Thaw for 12 hours in the refrigerator.
Confectioners' custard	1. Pour into waxed cardboard cups. 2. Seal tight and label. Will keep 1 month.	Thaw for 12 hours in the refrigerator.
Sponge cake	1. Wrap when cold in foil and then place in the freezer. Will keep 6 months.	Thaw for 12 hours in the refrigerator.
Fruit cake	1. Put the batter into a buttered cake pan, made of special freezer foil. 2. Bake for 45 minutes in a preheated 400°F / 200°C / Gas Mark 6 oven. Cool and freeze. Will keep 3 months.	Heat for 20 minutes in a preheated 400°F / 200°C / Gas Mark 6 oven, in the pan.
Crêpes	1. Leave the crêpes to cool after cooking. 2. Wrap them individually in foil. 3. Put in a freezer bag. Seal tight and label. Will keep 6 months.	1. Steam for a few moments over a pan of boiling water. 2. Heat in a buttered frying pan over a very low heat.
Croissants	1. Leave to cool after cooking (about 20 minutes). 2. Wrap individually in foil and label. Will keep 3 months.	Do not thaw. Heat in a preheated 350°F / 180°C / Gas Mark 4 oven for 15 minutes, in the wrapping.
Chocolate marquise	1. Pour the preparation into a charlotte mold or ribbed mold. 2. Place in a freezer bag. Label and freeze. Will keep 3 months.	To thaw, place in the refrigerator, in the wrapping and leave for 8 hours. To remove from mold, dip briefly in warm water.
Ices and sorbets	1. Place in an aluminium or plastic mold with a lid. 2. Seal tight and label. Place in a freezer bag and seal. Will keep 2 months.	Soften in the refrigerator for at least 30 minutes before serving.

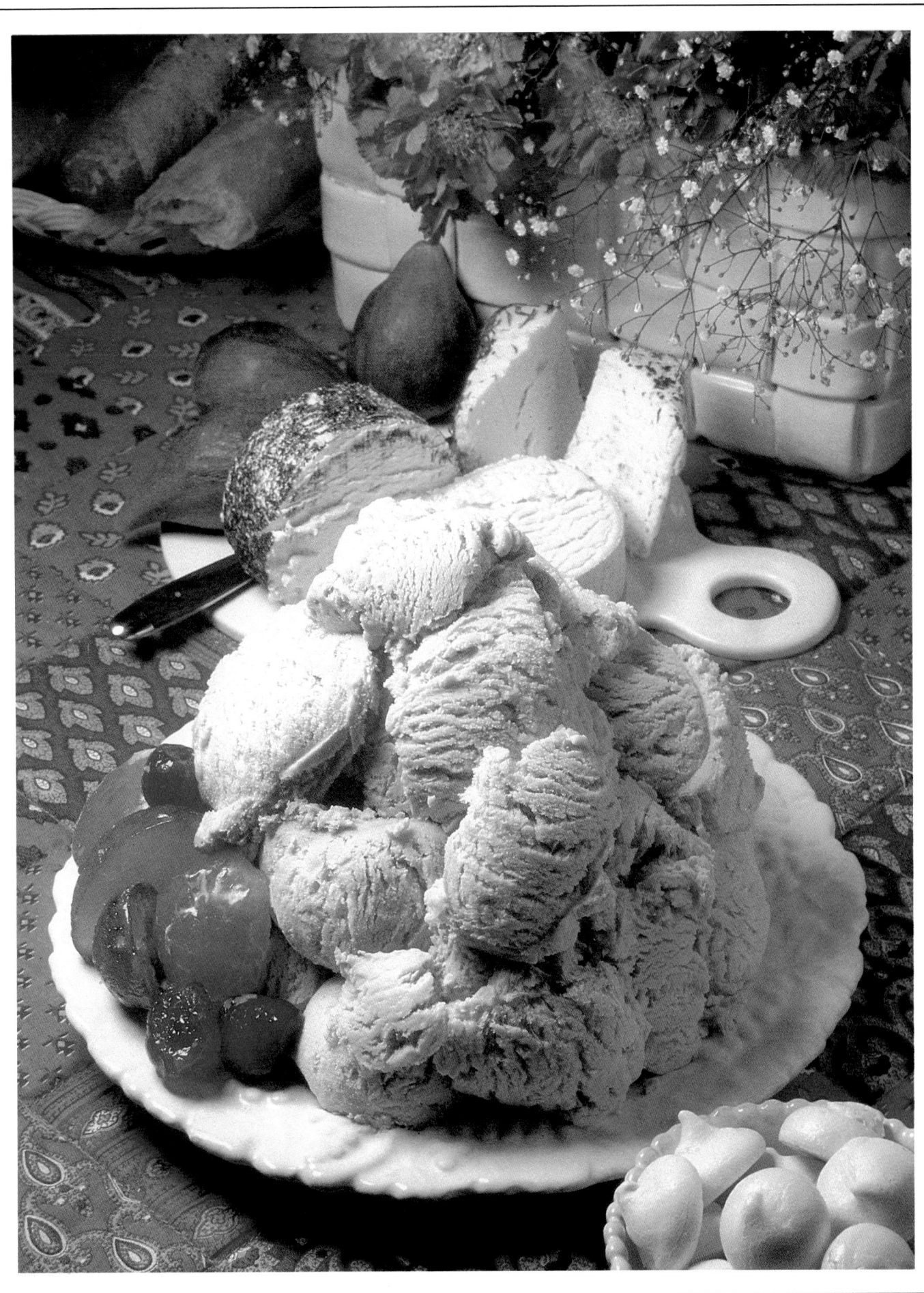

Preserving fruit

Fruit	Preparation	Freezing	Canning [bottling]	Other ways of preserving
Apples and pears	1. Peel and remove the core and seeds.	In slices: 1. Cut into slices ½ in / 1 cm thick. Sprinkle with lemon juice (1 lemon per 2 lb / 1 kg fruit). 2. Roll in sugar (1 cup [250 g / 8 oz] per 2 lb / 1 kg fruit). In compote: 1. Boil for 20 minutes together with 1 cup [250 g / 8 oz] sugar per 2 lb / 1 kg fruit. Place in plastic containers and seal tight. **To use:** thaw in the refrigerator for 8 hours. Will keep 8 months.	Natural: 1. Cut in half. Place in jars, sprinkling with sugar (2 cups [500 g / 1 lb] per 2 lb / 1 kg fruit). Leave to stand for 3 hours in a cool place. 2. Seal and process. In syrup: 1. As you peel them, sprinkle with lemon juice to prevent them turning brown. 2. Plunge for 30 seconds in boiling water and drain. 3. Place in jars to the ⅔ mark. Cover with a syrup made from 1 cup [250 ml / 8 fl oz] water boiled with 1 cup [250 g / 8 oz] sugar and a vanilla pod [bean]. 4. Seal and process. **To use:** as they are. Will keep 1 year.	In sugar: Pear jam. Pear conserve. In alcohol: Pears in brandy. Apple conserve. Apple jelly.
Apricots	1. Wash and cut in half. 2. Remove pits [stones].	1. Place in plastic containers 2. Seal and label. **To use:** do not thaw for cooked dishes. Thaw in the refrigerator to eat cold. Will keep 6–8 months.	1. Put the halved fruit into a jar. 2. Sprinkle with 1 tbsp sugar, or cover with a sugar syrup made from 2 cups [500 g / 1 lb] sugar dissolved in 1 quart [1 l / 1¾ pints] water and boiled for 1 minute. **To use:** as they are with the juice. Will keep 12 months.	In sugar: Apricot jam. Apricot conserve. In alcohol: Apricots in brandy. Drying: 1. Choose apricots which are very ripe but in good condition. 2. Place them whole in a very low electric oven and dry for 6 hours. 3. Leave to cool. Cut in half and remove pits [stones]. 4. Return to the cool oven and dry for a further 6 hours. Leave to cool. 5. Place in the cool oven again for 6 hours. Store in sealed jars. Will keep 8 months.
Blackcurrants	1. Wash and dry on a clean cloth. 2. Destalk with a fork.	1. Place in plastic containers, alternating the layers with sugar (½ cup [100 g / 4 oz] for 2 lb / 1 kg fruit). 2. Seal and label. **To use:** do not thaw for cooked dishes. Thaw to eat cold. Will keep 8 months.	Not suitable for blackcurrants because they break down in the heat.	In sugar: Blackcurrant jam.
Cherries	1. Wash and dry. Remove stalks. 2. Leave the fruit whole with their pits [stones].	1. Place in plastic containers. 2. Cover with a cold syrup made from 1 cup [250 g / 8 oz] sugar dissolved in 1 quart [1 l / 1¾ pints] water. 3. Seal and label. **To use:** do not thaw for cooked dishes. Thaw to eat cold.	Natural: 1. Place in jars sprinkling with sugar (1 cup [250 g / 8 oz] per 1¼ lb / 750 g fruit.) 2. Leave to stand for 3 hours and seal. In syrup: 1. Cover with a cold syrup made from 2 cups [500 g / 1 lb] sugar per 1 quart [1 l / 1¾ pints] water. 2. Seal and process. **To use:** as they are in their juice. Will keep 1 year.	In sugar: Cherry jam. In alcohol: Cherries in brandy.

Preserving fruit

Fruit	Preparation	Freezing	Canning [bottling]	Other ways of preserving
Peaches	1. Plunge for 30 seconds in boiling water. Peel. 2. Cut in half and remove pit [stones].	1. Place in plastic containers. 2. Cover with a cold syrup prepared from 1 cup [250 g / 8 oz] sugar dissolved in 1 quart [1 l / 1¾ pints] water and boiled for 2 minutes. 3. Seal and label. **To use:** thaw in the refrigerator for 8 hours. Will keep 8 months.	Natural or in syrup: 1. Place the halved peaches in jars (with the cavity downwards). Natural: Sprinkle with 1 tbsp sugar per quart [1 l / 2 pint] jar. In syrup: 1. Cover with a syrup made from 3 cups [750 g / 1½ lb] sugar dissolved in 1 quart [1 l / 1¾ pints] water. 2. Seal and process. **To use:** as they are. Will keep 12 months.	In sugar: Peach jam.
Plums	1. Wash and dry. 2. According to your preference, leave the fruit whole with their pits [stones] or cut in half and pit.	1. Place in plastic containers. 2. Seal and label. **To use:** do not thaw for cooked dishes. Thaw for fruit salad. Will keep 8–10 months.	Place in jars: Natural: add 1 tbsp sugar and the juice of 1 lemon per 1 quart [1 l / 2 pint] jar. Seal. In syrup: 1. Cover with a syrup made from 2 cups [500 g / 1 lb] sugar and 1 quart [1 l / 1¾ pints] water and some lemon juice. 2. Seal and process. **To use:** as they are in the juice.	In sugar: Plum jam. Plum marmalade. In alcohol: Plums in brandy. Prunes in brandy.
Raspberries	1. Remove stalks. 2. Wipe without washing.	1. Place in plastic containers. 2. Sprinkle with sugar (1 cup [250 g / 8 oz] per 2 lb / 1 kg fruit). 3. Sprinkle with the juice of a lemon. Seal tightly. **To use:** do not thaw for hot dishes. Thaw to eat cold. Will keep 10 months.	Place in jars: Natural: add sugar (1 cup [250 g / 8 oz] per 2 lb / 1 kg fruit). Leave to stand for 3 hours in a cool place. Seal and process. **To use:** as they are. Will keep 10 months.	In sugar: Raspberry jam. In alcohol: Raspberries in brandy.
Red currants	1. Wash and dry on a clean cloth. 2. Destalk with a fork.	1. Place in plastic containers. 2. Sprinkle with sugar (⅔ cup [150 g / 5 oz] sugar per 2 lb / 1 kg fruit). 3. Sprinkle with the juice of 1 lemon. Seal tightly. **To use:** do not thaw for hot dishes. Thaw to eat cold. Will keep 8 months.	Place in jars: Natural: add sugar (1½ cups [350 g / 12 oz] per 2 lb / 1 kg fruit). Cover and process. **To use:** as they are, in the syrup. Will keep 1 year.	In sugar: Red currant jam, conserve and jelly.
Strawberries	1. Wash and dry on a clean cloth. 2. Remove stalks.	1. Place in plastic containers. 2. Sprinkle with sugar (½ cup [100 g / 4 oz] per 2 lb / 1 kg fruit). 3. Sprinkle with lemon juice. Seal tightly. **To use:** do not thaw for hot dishes. Thaw to eat cold. Will keep 10 months.	Place in jars: Natural: add 1 tbsp sugar per jar. Seal and process.	In sugar: Strawberry jam. Strawberry conserve.
Tomatoes	Pulp: Peel the tomatoes (first plunging them in boiling water for 10 seconds), remove stalks and quarter. Juice: Peel (as above) and purée in a blender or food processor. Strain to remove seeds.	Whole tomatoes do not stand up very well to freezing. Pulp: Fill a plastic container to the ¾ mark. Cover and label. **To use:** without thawing, heat according to chosen recipe. Juice: Fill containers to the ¾ mark. Seal and label. **To use:** thaw and serve cold. Will keep 6 months.	1. Place the peeled tomatoes (whole or in pieces) in jars. 2. Cover with salted water (2 tsp salt to 1 quart [1 l / 1¾ pints] water). 3. Seal and process. **To use:** drain and use according to the recipe chosen. Will keep 8–10 months.	In oil: (whole tomatoes) 1. Heat some salted water (3 tbsp salt to 1 quart [1 l / 1¾ pints] water). As soon as it boils, leave to cool. 2. Wipe the tomatoes. Place in jars. Cover with the cold salted water up to 1½ in / 3 cm of the rim. Fill up to the top with olive oil. 3. Seal and keep cool. **To use:** in salads. Will keep 6 months.

CHAPTER 4

Wine

By Pamela Vandyke Price

Choosing and serving wine

Wines from France

The country that has established the standards, made the news, and given centuries of enjoyment in terms of wine is France. Most regions of France make wine — and many make spirits as well. There are sweet, dry, medium-sweet, medium-dry wines, red, white and rosé; there are fully sparkling, semi-sparkling and very slightly sparkling wines — white, rosé and even red. Today there are hundreds of French wines offering excellent value and much enjoyment that would have been unknown, except in their home regions, as recently as thirty years ago. There are the world-famous names and the world-famous producers, the millionaire estate owners and the peasant proprietors, the businessmen who have taken up wine growing and making because they love it — and who have contributed to the improvement of quality in many regions where previously the wines were only adequate for the locals and holidaymakers.

No single chapter can deal adequately with French wines, about which so much has been written. But the following guidelines should enable you to select from the many wines available — according to where you live and what you can afford — those that will interest you and surprise and delight even the wine-wise people you entertain.

French wine labels

Usually, the finer the wine, the more detailed the information given — according to law and controls — on the main label of the bottle. A merchant or wine shipper may add to this on the back label, often suggesting appropriate foods and how to serve the wine.

The following systems apply to many wines — but, as the subject is complex, you should consult a specialist book if you want to know about them in detail.

Appellation d'origine contrôlée or A.O.C., or A.C.
This is the top category. Wines bearing an A.O.C. must have been grown and made in a specified region, from specific vines, in a particular way. Although an A.O.C. wine should be a good one, there is no law or set of rules that can guarantee quality.

Vin délimité de qualité supérieur or V.D.Q.S.
The same type of controls apply as for A.O.C. wines, but they are a little less demanding.

Vin de pays
This is also subject to controls. The wines are representative of particular regions. They are often excellent value.

Vin de table
The least expensive, and subject to the fewest controls. A vin de table may also be a vin de pays.

Vintages

The majority of all the wines of the world are non-vintage. This means that you can enjoy them as soon as you buy them. If you

PRODUCE OF FRANCE

DOMAINE DU RINGUET ◄ 1

◄ 2

BEAUJOLAIS-VILLAGES

3 ► APPELLATION BEAUJOLAIS-VILLAGES CONTRÔLÉE

MIS EN BOUTEILLE AU DOMAINE ◄ 5

7 ► Georges FAVROT - Propriétaire - LE PERREON (Rhône)

Distribué par JACQUES DÉPAGNEUX, Villefranche (Rhône) ◄ 6

75 cl ◄ 4

IMP. BOUGENHEIM - LYON

1 Name of property where wine was grown

2 Type of wine

3 Designation of quality limited specifically to the area known as Beaujolais-Villages

4 Content by volume

5 Bottled on the estate

6 Name of the distributor of the wine

7 Name of the owner of the estate

keep them indefinitely, they may lose some of their enjoyable quality. An old wine isn't by any means always better than a young one.

Makers of non-vintage wines are able to improve them by using a proportion of the wine of other vintages. Suppose one year there's lots of wine but it lacks something, then it can be helped enormously by the addition of wine from another vintage that can 'lift' the whole.

A vintage date goes onto a bottle for one of two reasons. With wines that are at their best when young, fresh, zippy and crisp, the date enables you to see that the wine really is still young and enjoyable and not old and tired. When you buy Muscadet, some of the Provence wines, many of the vins de pays, it's their youthful charm you want. With certain wines, both white and red, in the top quality categories the vintage date will indicate whether the wine has yet reached its peak, or prime — after which it may decline, just like a person getting old. This can apply to the great white and red wines of Bordeaux, Burgundy, and to certain Rhône wines. But don't forget — these days wines are usually made so that they grow to their peak of maturity rather sooner than they did fifty years ago, when fifty years was almost no time to wait for the great clarets and Burgundies of certain vintages to 'grow up' and be ready to drink. Today, most wines 'come round' in a shorter time. So — get advice about when to drink them.

Always bear in mind that, from year to year, the wines made in the various regions of France will be different from those of the previous year — the climate isn't as unvarying from year to year as it is in, for example, many of the New World vineyards. And in any one year a great vintage in Bordeaux may not coincide with equal quality in Burgundy and so on. Some years are described as 'light', some, even in these days when wine

Château Lafite-Rothschild, one of the largest vineyards in the Médoc

can be made with far more know-how, may be very poor. Get to know something about vintages before merely trying to buy 'a vintage wine', and ask the advice of a good source of supply. Even in poor vintages some quite good wine may be made — and, alas, even in certain great vintages some rather dull wine may also be made. Consult the specialists when you're buying wines in these top categories.

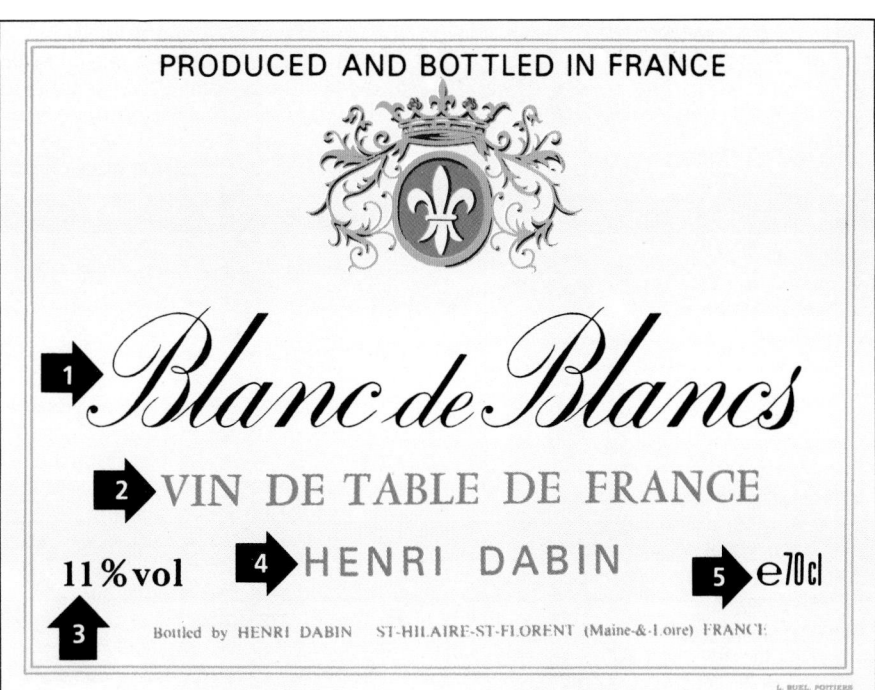

1 Type of wine. Blanc de blancs means 'white of whites', which must by law be a white wine made from white grapes

2 'French table wine'. This basic designation of quality simply means that the wine is from France, not from a particular region and not subject to the strict rules of Appellation Contrôlée or V.D.Q.S.

3 Alcohol by volume

4 Name of wine shipper. The name of the producer of the wine is not shown

5 Content by volume

Alternatives to French wines

Suppose you can't obtain a particular French wine recommended to go with a particular recipe? Don't worry. The French themselves can't often rush out to buy what wine writers suggest. Indeed, most export markets may be able to choose from a far wider range of wines than the average wine buyer in France.

Choose what's likely to be nearest in flavor, style and 'importance' to a French wine and do try to match quality with quality — don't select a cheap wine, however good, to partner a recipe involving expensive ingredients and intended for some special occasion. The suggestions here should give any intelligent wine merchant some notion as to what you want — if, for example, you ask for a dry white wine, he won't hand you something full and red. But mention the type of food and specify the price range in which you're interested.

Go by the grape variety. In many New World vineyards today wines bear the names of the grapes that make them — or are predominant. Thus, if you are looking for the same style of wine as a white Burgundy, you can probably find something made from the Chardonnay grape, which makes all the finest white Burgundies. Red Burgundy is made from the Pinot Noir and this, too, may be available elsewhere. Don't think of such wines as being the same, but they will have a family resemblance. Here are some other family resemblances:

White wines:

Sauvignon — for the dry white wines of Bordeaux, Sancerre, Pouilly Blanc Fumé.
Riesling d'Alsace — Rheinriesling or Johannisberger Riesling, or White Riesling.
Chenin Blanc — the wines of the middle Loire. Don't forget that some, such as Vouvray, can be slightly sweet or even definitely sweet. For this sweeter style of wine you should look for a label that states the wine is late picked.
Chardonnay — white Burgundy and Coteaux Champenoise (the still wine of Champagne).

Red wines:

Pinot Noir — red Burgundy
Syrah/Shiraz — used, often with other grapes, for many red Rhônes, especially those in the north of the region.
Grenache — another red Rhône grape, often predominant in Châteauneuf-du-Pape and found in many wines in the south of France.
Cabernet Sauvignon — this is the backbone of red Bordeaux but in Bordeaux wines it is always used in conjunction with other grapes and there are very few instances of the Cabernet Sauvignon (not to be confused with the Cabernet Franc, another Bordeaux grape, but used alone in many red Loire wines) being used on its own. So a wine labeled 'Cabernet' may bear only a very slight resemblance to a red Bordeaux.
Gamay — the Beaujolais grape. It is often found elsewhere, although authorities do not agree as to whether the grape called 'Gamay beaujolais' in the U.S. is the same as that of the Beaujolais region.
Merlot — another of the grapes used for red Bordeaux, sometimes found making wines on its own.

These are only a few of the many grapes making the huge range of French wines, so if the wine label does not provide additional information, you should try to consult a book — there are many excellent paperbacks on wine.

Long dry summers ripen the grapes for the vintage

Wines from the English-speaking world

Here are some very general indications about the wines of other parts of the world where English is the main language and which you may be able to buy locally. Remember that, everywhere, the finest wines are likely to be both expensive and in short supply, so they may not find their way into shops and, indeed, are unlikely to feature on export lists. This applies — at the time of writing — to the wines of Canada and some of the African states (in addition to the Republic of South Africa), also to the wines of Washington, Oregon and Idaho in the U.S. But in the world of wine this sort of situation can change within a year or two, so don't ever hesitate, if you see a wine that's unfamiliar, to try it. You may get a pleasant surprise.

England: Plenty of good wines are made in England today. In style they tend to resemble some of the German white wines. They can be delicious, interesting apéritifs and partners to fish and light dishes.

California: One single winery may make a complete range of wines — something that astonishes the French! There are some very fine wines — which are also very expensive and in short supply. To a European palate, the medium and cheap white wines can seem very different from French versions, even when the same grape is used, and it's worth noting that in some instances the alcohol content of both whites and reds can be higher than it might be in Europe — so don't quaff regardless! Regulations permit a wine to be labeled with the name of a particular grape — referred to here as a 'varietal' — if there is 75 per cent of that grape in it. Producers proud of their finer wines will usually state on the label if the wine is, say, 100 per cent Chardonnay. The wines of the smaller wineries, which attract praise and comment throughout the world, are often highly distinguished. At the other end of the scale, the popular 'jug' wines from the large establishments can provide agreeable multi-purpose drinks. With few exceptions, vintages do not usually vary as much as they do in France — the climate is more constant.

The wines of other regions of the U.S., as well as those from the most famous areas of California, are all worth study and exploration.

South Africa: Wines have been made at the Cape since the latter part of the seventeenth century and the tradition of wine making and wine appreciation is strong. All types of wine are made. The whites — many made from the Chenin Blanc or Steen as it may be called there — are light and fragrant, particularly in the late-picked wines. The reds, especially those from the individual estates, make use of many classic French grapes too, one estate even making a 'Bordeaux mix' now. Standards are high and controls detailed and effective.

Australia: This huge continent produces enormous quantities of varied wines, ranging from the general branded wines to those with their own unique properties, many of them using classic French grapes. One huge firm may own vineyards in different states and regions, so don't suppose that the single name will indicate the overall style of any particular wine — only the style of the establishment. At one time the Australian reds were thought to be heavy and somewhat coarse, but this is certainly not true today: some very full-bodied wines are made, but also many elegant ones, red and white.

New Zealand: Wine that has won competitions in Paris and London has been made here for nearly two centuries. Emphasis is on the whites and many of these make use of certain German grapes. The reds tend as yet to be somewhat light.

Wines from Europe and South America

As well as French wines, the basic wines of Europe — Germany, Italy, Spain, Portugal, the countries of the central and south-east of the continent — are fully documented. Each of these countries produces wines of individuality and variety, some even being made using grapes of French origin. The only possible guideline that may be useful is that, very often, the cooler countries and regions traditionally produce the finer and more fragrant white wines, the warmer areas make the full, fruity reds.

Don't forget that both Argentina and Chile are important sources of wine today. Many of their exports are in the inexpensive and medium price ranges, and most are very good value. They often bear the names of classic French grapes.

The basic wine glass, plain and colorless, allows you to see the color of the wine

Storing wine

Wine should be stored with the bottles lying down, so that the cork, in contact with the wine, remains swollen, thereby preventing any air from getting in. Spirits should be stored with the bottles upright.

If possible, keep wine in a cool, darkish place, away from vibration. Wines can stand moderate warmth (though ideally not for long) but do not benefit from sharp rises and falls of temperature — so don't keep bottles where they can get very hot or very cold. If you keep them anywhere centrally heated, try to use them up within a few months. And if you're lucky enough to have a real cellar, don't let it get too dry — damp is beneficial to the long, slow maturing of wine.

Serving wine

Wine is more enjoyable if it is served correctly and even the simplest meal can look elegant when glasses are the right size (even chain store cheap ones) and shape (even costly crystal), with the wine itself at the temperature at which it tastes best. Once you get to know something about wine you can be adventurous, but if in doubt, play the entertaining game in accordance with the established rules.

Decanting

The purpose of decanting is twofold: to pour the wine off any deposit in the bottle, so that the wine is clear and bright and — something which is often forgotten — to give a slight 'airing' to the wine, so that it can give off its fragrance and expand its flavor. If you can't decant a wine, then draw the cork on it in advance anyway. Even white wines should have their corks drawn 10-15 minutes ahead of drinking time, so as to get rid of the 'bottle stink' — the air that's been trapped in the bottle.

Wine cradles

The cradle should only be used when you draw a bottle from the wine bin, where it has been lying on its side, so that any deposit is not disturbed. The cork is then carefully drawn and the wine poured into decanter or carafe from this recumbent position in the cradle. But the wine cradle has no place at all on a dining-table where it takes up far more space than a bottle standing upright.

Corkscrews

The purpose of a corkscrew is to pull the cork gradually and steadily — so don't buy the type that merely bores a hole in the cork and, because of its sharp edges and pointed end, breaks the cork anyway. Select a rounded screw, with the sort of spiral that you can look up — like a spiral staircase. Some of the patent devices for pulling corks do facilitate the process, but make sure that you use them correctly. Never use the type that pumps gas into a wine on any sparkling or semi-sparkling wine because it may cause the bottle to explode.

The butterfly-armed corkscrew is generally reliable but with the wooden type you cannot see where the screw is going. The middle one lifts the cork out as part of a continuous, easy, screw action

Serve Champagne in a flûte (left), wines in a Paris goblet or tulip, and fortified wines in a sherry copita (right)

Opening sparkling wines

Never open any sparkling wine without holding a cloth round the bottle; never let go of the cork once the wire muzzle is removed; never point the bottle at anyone or at anything breakable — and, once you really begin to move the cork, *turn the bottle, not the cork*. Hold on to the cork all the time so that it doesn't fly, but comes out with a discreet 'pop' and the wine isn't spilt and wasted but goes into a nearby glass. Remember that, if you've had a bottle of sparkling wine in a shopping basket or in the car, there will be more fizz — so be extra careful.

How much to allow

Be generous. People drink more copiously at some times than at others and they will feel inclined to drink more if you serve very spicy or salty dishes. Work out in advance how much you are likely to need — and don't forget that you should count in the drinks you serve before and after any meal. In general, half a bottle per head, 3-4 glasses (not filled by more than two-thirds), is a minimum and, for a long, special dinner, allow a bottle each. Some people will only drink a little, others are used to taking more. It's far better to pour a cheap wine freely than anxiously eye a more expensive bottle that's going down rather faster than you anticipated.

There is no need to serve more than one wine throughout a meal, but if you do serve one with the first course and another with the main dish, you'll find that people tend to drink more of the second wine. If you offer a sweet wine at the end of the meal a single helping is usually sufficient.

Don't forget that some people truly cannot drink red wine, and do remember that, these days, many like a table water.

Glasses

It's not absolutely necessary to have different glasses for different wines (although you can if you wish). There are some 'regional' glasses in different parts of France, but the basic wine glass is plain, colorless, uncut and unengraved — so that you can see the color of the wine. It's on a stem, to enable you to hold it without warming up a cool white wine and to swing the wine around in the glass so as to release the agreeable smell — the bouquet. Its bowl is either bulbous or tulip-shaped, to contain and direct the bouquet to the drinker's nose. This is why, ideally, the rim of the bowl is slightly smaller than the widest part.

The two most widely available glass shapes are the Paris goblet (like an onion with its top sliced off) and the tulip, which can be elongated or of medium height. These can be used for every type of wine — still, sparkling, white, red, pink and also for port, sherry and madeira, vermouth and, if you wish, cocktails.

The smallest size suitable for civilized wine drinking is around 5½ fluid ounces — about the bulk of a woman's (small) closed hand. If you wish to have different sizes, then keep the 5½ oz glasses for sherry, port, vermouth, but use a larger size — 6½ oz or even 8 oz — for all other wines.

Remember: no glass should ever be filled by more than a half to two-thirds. This is so that you can twirl the wine around and release the bouquet without spilling the drink — you've paid for the bouquet, just as you've paid for the color, so you may as well get your money's worth.

Sparkling wines can be served in the tall triangular glasses, with a point at the base where the bowl joins the stem. But don't ever use the flat, shallow 'saucer' type — this flattens the wine. You've paid for the bubbles, too.

Temperature

All varieties of white wine should be served cool – and this includes sherry, white port, vermouth and anything sparkling – all apéritifs, in fact. But 'cool' doesn't mean iced: over-chilling a wine takes away much of its aroma. Don't simply sling ice into wine either, unless you want a watered-down drink. And never put a bottle in the freezer. Even if you don't forget it and find an alcoholized ice lolly some days later, the shock of the experience won't help the wine at all. (If you're in that much of a hurry, put the glasses in the ordinary part of the refrigerator – they will help along the chilling process when the wine is poured in.)

Most white wines can be cooled for an hour in the middle of a domestic refrigerator. Or – and much quicker – you can put the bottle into a bucket of ice and water (not ice alone, which only cools patches of the bottles) so that the level of the ice and water is up to the level of the wine. This will take 12-15 minutes for most dry wines.

Sweet wines can be cooled to a very slightly lower temperature.

On a stuffy day, whether it's actually summer or winter, or if your home has central heating kept to a high level, you may find it pleasant to give the wines a little more cooling time.

Certain red wines can be very pleasant if cool. Young Beaujolais, many of the young red Loire wines and wines such as the Gamay de l'Ardèche or the inexpensive South of France reds all have their fruitiness enhanced by being lightly chilled.

All rosé wine should be served cool, like white wines.

All sparkling and pétillant wines should also be served cool.

Red wines are usually at their best when served at room temperature – but never warm them up. If you do have a deep, cold cellar and suddenly bring up a bottle to the dining-room for immediate service, then, on a really cold night, you'll be forgiven if you put the bottle in a bucket of just lukewarm (not hot) water after drawing the cork. But otherwise, draw the cork an hour or more before you plan to drink the wine and let it gradually take on the temperature of the room. Never put wine in front of the fire or over a stove – it may acquire a horrible 'scorched' flavor, and heat from below may set up currents in the bottle which can churn up any deposit lying in the bottom.

You can always gently warm a wine by cupping your hand around the bowl of the glass. But, if you heat it in any way, you can never cool it down again to the right temperature. Asking for a wine to be warmed marks you as someone who doesn't know anything about it. The same applies to brandy – even if somebody suggests warming the glass, you should know better; warm it only with your hand.

Wines with – and without – food

Wine between meals: It's chic these days to drink wine casually, between meals. Something white or pink, dry to medium-dry, is usually suitable and, of course, anything sparkling. There are literally hundreds of wines of this type to choose from. You can enjoy the lighter red wines in this way too, although something to nibble is often wise to partner them – they are not necessarily 'stronger' but some people just find red wine more agreeable with a cracker, piece of cheese, potato chips or nuts.

Of the many appropriate French white wines I would mention any of the Sauvignons, less expensive white Burgundies and Bourgogne Aligoté, Alsace Riesling, Sylvaner, Muscat, and the Chenin Blanc wines from the centre of the Loire, Touraine Blanc, any Vouvray, still or sparkling, that isn't definitely sweet, Montlouis, white Saumur (and sparkling Saumur) – and the innumerable pleasant V.D.Q.S. and vins de pays now widely available.

From the rosé wines you might choose rosé d'Anjou, Sancerre rosé, the rosé de Marsannay in the Côte de Nuits and the pink wines of Provence, also those of Bandol, plus those from both ends of the Pyrenees – Béarn on the west, Corbières on the east – and the numerous rosés from Corsica.

Champagne, white and pink, and the many champagne method wines, such as those of Saumur, also the Crémants d'Alsace, Blanquette de Limoux, Clairette de Die and Seyssel, and the 'cuve close' wines, of which Veuve du Vernay is only one, are also possibilities.

Order of wines

This is very simple – but program in your apéritifs too:
Dry before sweet
Young before old
Cheap before costly
White before red – except for sweet white dessert wines at the end of the meal.

One wine can easily go right through from apéritifs to the end of the meal – but if you opt for this, then it may be wise to select something white and fairly full-bodied, such as a white Burgundy, an estate white Graves, a Riesling d'Alsace or Gewurztraminer. Bear in mind that some people cannot easily take red wine in quantity. You can certainly serve Champagne or a sparkling wine all through a meal, but remember that the combination of fizz and food is not to everyone's taste.

For a buffet or informal party, one wine will certainly do – although it may be more enjoyable to have a choice, perhaps something red to go with the cheese, if any. Don't think of vin rosé as the all-purpose 'when in doubt' choice – some pink wines can be drunk with salad dishes, mixtures of meat, fish and poultry and general casual fare, but very often they are too delicate in flavor. If you want to have a pink wine with this sort of food, opt for something from the Rhône or south of France.

Apéritifs

All these wines could be served before a meal. Remember that if you serve a medium dry wine before a meal, such as a medium sherry or perhaps a Bordeaux Sauvignon, then a really bone dry wine such as a Muscadet coming immediately afterwards, with the first course, will taste bitter. Either start with the drier wine or don't serve one with the first course.

The French vermouths are very varied – the pale, fragrant Chambéry is traditionally drunk, lightly chilled, by itself. There's a strawberry version too. Marseilles vermouths tend to be slightly more aromatic. You can serve them straight or with soda, plus a twist of lemon if you like.

First courses

Sometimes these are a bit piquant – anything with a lot of vinegar, a curry flavored dish, or smoked or salt fish with a strong sauce or mustard can swamp a light-bodied wine. Either have a truly 'ordinary' toughish white – Bourgogne Aligoté, Muscadet of ordinary quality, Minervois, a cheapish white Rhône – or skip the wine.

Hors d'oeuvres don't really need an accompanying wine but, if you wish, serve something in the carafe category – inexpensive, light and either white or rosé. Any salad recipe with a vinegar dressing risks conflicting with the wine because of the sharpness of the vinegar, but if you go easy with this, then an ordinary wine will not be overcome. Soup is another course that doesn't really need a wine. If you've put some sherry or madeira in the soup, then a small glass of this alongside is possible, but not essential.

Pâtés are so varied that much depends on the main ingredient and whether the pâté has any accompanying sauce. Follow the suggestions for fish, poultry and meat – but as many pâtés tend to be somewhat rich and fatty, a crisp wine is

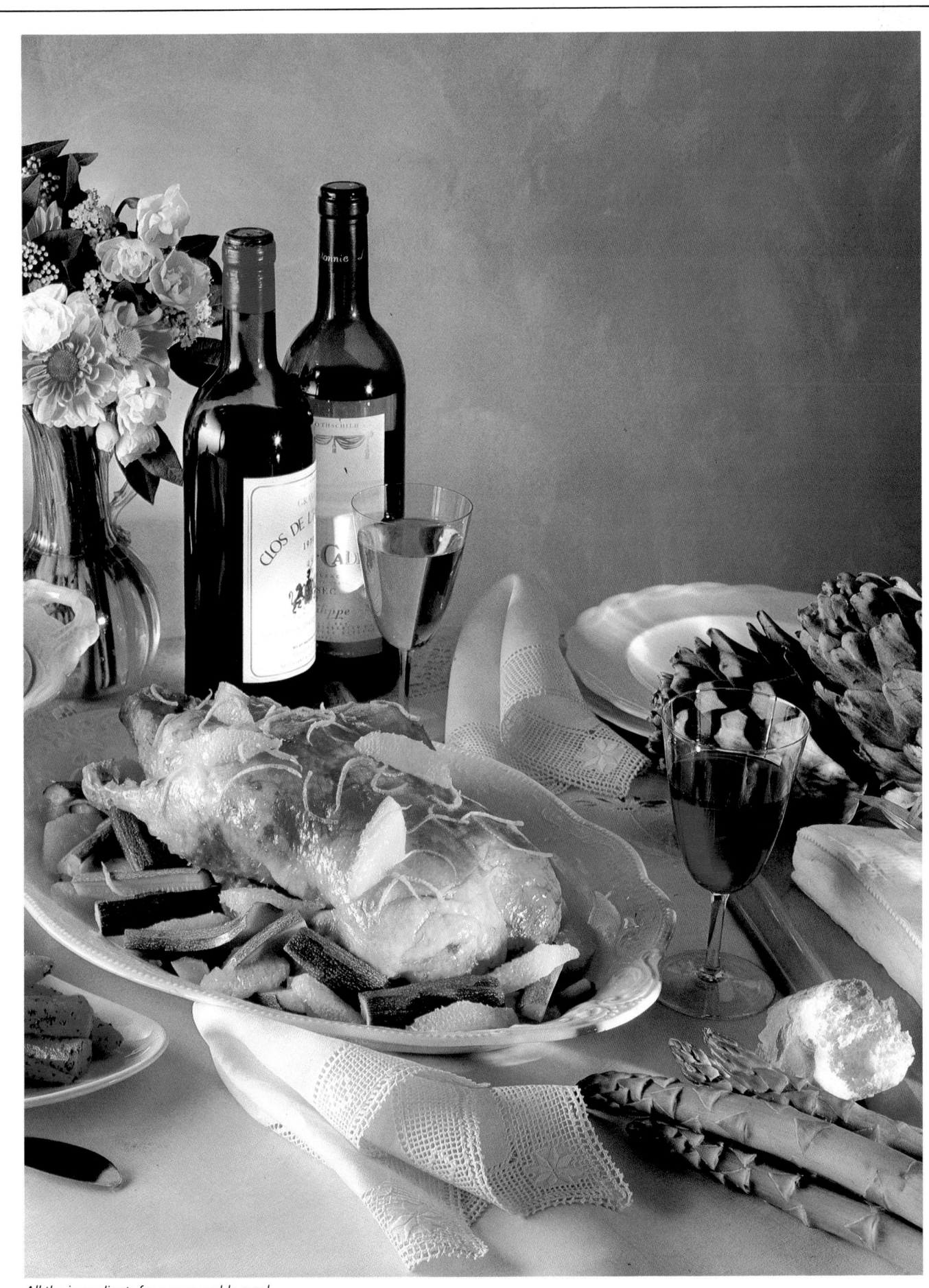

All the ingredients for a memorable meal

probably a good idea. The very rich pâtés, such as pâté de foie gras or anything with truffles, do deserve a fine wine and this would usually be white in France — a very good Riesling d'Alsace would be traditional in the region. The Dordogne whites are possible with many liver pâtés.

Fish pâtés, quenelles de brochet and fish terrines are usually well partnered by a dry, lightish white wine, so don't be afraid of selecting a modest drink to start with.

Eggs   can be a bit of a problem; choose something assertive, white or red, nothing delicate. Asparagus (with hollandaise), fonds d'artichauts and anything with mayonnaise in any form do not need a wine that is too fine. This is where the V.D.Q.S. and vins de pays wines, white or rosé, are so useful.

Main courses

Fish

White wine is served with fish, the choice of wine depending on the sauce — if any. Shellfish and all crustaceans are traditionally partnered by dry white wine; the white butter sauce served with many river fish needn't be an enemy to the wine. Loup, and any of the Mediterranean fish grilled over fennel, need something aromatic and robust as well — a white Côtes du Rhône, white Châteauneuf-du-Pape, white Hermitage, or the many southern whites. Chablis is traditional with oysters — but Muscadet is less costly.

The fine white Burgundies, such as the Meursaults, Puligny-Montrachets, Aloxe-Cortons and the whites from the Côte de Beaune are in general superb with most fine sea or river fish, but don't forget the southern Burgundies — Mâcon, Montagny, Rully, the Chalonais wines, even if you can't manage the grossly inflated price of Pouilly-Fuissé, there's Pouilly-Vinzelles. From the Loire, there are the white Sancerres and Pouilly-Fumé, from Alsace virtually all the white wines with trout and sandre (pike-perch); these last will also be good with char and salmon trout and the finer dishes based on sole, flounder or plaice.

In the Gironde, they drink white dry Bordeaux with the local shellfish. In general, though, it depends on the dish, the sauce (grilled lobster is obviously not the same as lobster mayonnaise or à l'américaine, or flambé au whiskey) or whatever wine can be found and afforded.

Meat and poultry

The notion of white wine with white meat is somewhat silly. Turkey, guinea-fowl, many chicken dishes, veal and pork, are not particularly white by the time the sauces, gravies, stuffings are added. Lovers of red Bordeaux would say there is a wine to go with every single meat, poultry and even all but the most gamy of game, whereas partisans of red Burgundy will advocate the opposite...and lovers of the Rhône reds will state that the finer wines possess a delicacy as well as a power that makes them admirable choices.

In very general terms, claret (red Bordeaux) is traditionally associated with lamb and many grills, including steak, variety meats (offal in the U.K.) and game such as grouse, woodcock, partridge and pheasant, as well as the usual forms of poultry. But beef doesn't have to be partnered by red Burgundy, venison doesn't insist on red Rhône as an accompaniment and casseroles of hare, rabbit, pigeon can be served with red wines according to the seasoning and the wine that may have been included in the dish.

The same applies to dishes of pork and ham: what about the sauce, any added flavorings, any vegetables that may have a pronounced flavor? Is there any fruit in the recipe — or lots of tomatoes, peppers, garlic, herbs, all or any of which can affect a very delicate wine, but go well with a full-bodied one. What about duck with orange sauce? In Alsace they'd drink something white, full and fruity; in Burgundy or the Rhône the choice might be white or red, in the Dordogne or near the Spanish frontier they might opt for the reds of Cahors, or the

Roussillon-Languedoc reds. In the Loire the suggestion would probably include the crisp fruity Cabernet Franc reds from Saumur-Champigny or, as anyone might say, when in doubt, a Beaujolais — of the various categories of quality up to the commune and even the estate wines. The Bordelais would certainly have something red — but whether a full St. Émilion, refined Pomerol, subtle red Graves or complex Médoc is something that would get wine lovers arguing for a long time.

Cheese

This would come after the main course at a French meal when the main wine can be finished. All wine, white as well as red, is extra good with cheese, because the acidity in the wine (which should be there, even in sweetish wines) complements the alkalinity of the cheese admirably. But don't serve a very strong matured cheese or one of the hard cheeses such as cantal or comté with a somewhat elegant red wine. It may be too much for the drink.

Blue cheeses, including roquefort, bleu de bresse and stilton, may, unless in their creamier prime, be too ammoniac for a fine red wine. The gorgeous creamy French cheeses — look for the indication of fat content (matière grasse) on the label — are very good or, if you can't get a brie or camembert as you think it should be, opt for matured edam (for Bordeaux), or a fresh cream cheese, or, for Loire wines, a fresh goat cheese. The small fresh cream cheeses, such as demi-sel or, if it's the real thing, gruyère, will probably be good with most wine.

The sweet course

This can be tricky — anything enriched with liqueurs is really good by itself or with another liqueur alongside. Chocolate is death to a palate attuned to wine — serve a spirit. But the sweet wines of France are not only the great ones of Sauternes and Barsac, so superb that maybe they deserve to be sipped by themselves at the end of the meal, with a dish of fresh fruit (not oranges or pineapple, which are too acid) as the dessert which they complement beautifully.

There are also the lesser-known wines of Cérons, Loupiac, Sainte Croix du Mont, Monbazillac; in the Loire the slightly crisper wines of the Coteaux du Layon, Bonnezeaux, Quart de Chaume; the richer though not always very sweet wines of the Alsace vendanges tardives (late harvest); the rare sweet, but never cloying, Champagnes; and, in the south, the vins doux naturels, of which Muscat de Beaumes de Venise is the best known. Vouvray makes sweet wines too — but you must find those of the great makers to get anything more than a wine that is pleasantly gentle on the palate.

The huge range of the spirits of France, whisked into whipped cream, flamed into the sauce for crêpes, gently dripped over ices, endowing an otherwise routine sauce — or drink — with the 'something special' quality, should be known. But remember, in the kitchen, there are the brandies and the rums for flaming and 'de-greasing', for using as a means both to concentrate the essences of a sauce or gravy and, if poured into a pâté or preserve, as something to keep it from deteriorating. Then there are the spirits that flavor — orange is possibly the most useful and the drop of something orange (Cointreau is the world's best-known orange spirit) is equivalent to the transforming squeeze of lemon in a recipe. But the other fruits, notably kirsch (cherries), can each contribute and merit experiment. Even a miniature of a liqueur can be valuable: a tiny bottle of, say, crème de menthe (peppermint), abricotine (apricot), cassis (blackcurrant) can transform even a shop-bought vanilla ice cream if dribbled over it before serving.

Basic guidelines

When in doubt as to 'what with what', bear in mind that a wine will seem pleasantest if it *either* goes with a dish *or* provides a contrast. So — if you're having a rich, somewhat unctuous recipe, then serve either a crisp, dryish wine, to cut the richness, or else something very full and fruity, to blend in with the flavors of the food.

Don't serve a cheap little wine, which may be a perfectly good drink, with an especially fine dish — the food will overwhelm the wine. If in any doubt, buy a fine wine, because this will help even the modest family-style menu to taste extra-good, whereas a really expensive recipe will gain nothing by having small-scale cheap wine served with it.

If you're following a regional recipe, try to use a wine from the same region, though this isn't always possible. If you can't, don't worry — coq au vin, traditional in Burgundy, won't be spoiled if you put in it and serve with it a red Bordeaux.

Keeping wine once the bottle is opened

All but the very finest and oldest wines — and even some of those — can be corked up and kept in a coolish place, for enjoyment at the next meal — or for the next day. If you've only got the equivalent of a glassful remaining, however, then exposure to the air in the bottle may cause it to deteriorate:

either decant it into a smaller bottle and cork it up or, if it isn't too special, use it for cooking. Wine is perfectly all right for most culinary purposes even after it's ceased to be a very enjoyable drink.

Cooking with wine

There are two main ways of using wine in the kitchen. One is to add it to gravies and sauces shortly before serving, when brisk cooking is involved. For this you should use a wine of at least fair quality. If something is to be simmered or cooked for a long time in wine, however, or if the wine is put into something such as pâté or stuffing, prior to cooking, then a wine of ordinary quality will do. All the alcohol will be given off during the cooking, but if you simply add the wine to a recipe and don't cook it the alcohol remains. Don't, though, use the very cheapest wine for cooking something intended for a special occasion — ideally, use the same wine you'll be drinking. With anything to be cooked for a long time, such as a casserole, this doesn't matter too much but, with a sauce to be enriched with wine and cooked only for a short while, the better the wine the better the end result.

CHAPTER 5

French Cheeses

There are so many varieties and types of French cheese – mellow or dry, bland, delicate or full-bodied, round or square, cow's milk, ewe's milk or goat's milk – that even the most dedicated enthusiast might have trouble recognizing some of them. It is beyond the scope of this chapter to offer detailed information about the more than four hundred local and regional varieties available in France; we can deal here with only a few of the best-known cheeses, but we will teach you how to distinguish their taste, recognize their shape and make a balanced and appropriate selection for your cheeseboard.

The cheeses you serve should compliment the rest of your menu. After game accompanied by a full-bodied wine, for example, serve highly-seasoned varieties with a tang of the soil such as époisses, livarot or any of the blue French cheeses. To follow meat cooked in sauce and washed down with a light wine, choose a good camembert, a brie, a ripe goat's milk cheese or a boursault. A hearty, rustic meal must be backed up by similar cheese – a chèvre fermier, a maroilles or a cantal.

To serve a selection of cheeses, arrange all those that crumble easily (like goat's milk and blue cheese) in the middle of a large platter, and hard cheese (such as gruyère) and those that are difficult to cut around the edge.

Categories of cheese

There are three general categories of cheese:
- **fresh cheeses** are unripened or only slightly ripened and therefore usually whitish in color. They are often acidic and sometimes creamy, and do not normally have a rind. Cottage and curd cheese, petit suisses and cream cheeses are all fresh cheeses.
- **pressed cheeses** have a mild flavor and are either uncooked, with a ripening period of 2-18 months, like cantal, or cooked and ripened for up to 4 years, like gruyère.
- **soft cheeses** are fermented cheeses that are neither cooked nor pressed and can be distinguished by their soft texture. There are several types of soft cheese: velvety crust varieties such as camembert and brie, washed-rind cheeses like pont-l'évêque, blue cheeses, goat's milk cheeses and processed cheeses.

Fresh cheeses

The fat content of any fresh cheese varies with the proportion of cream to milk used in its manufacture.

Fresh factory cheeses are made in both salted and unsalted varieties:

Unsalted fresh cheeses
These include:
- plain white curd cheese, mechanically treated to produce a uniform smooth texture.
- white cheese with a maximum fat content of 40%, sold in draining-molds.
- diet cheeses, sold in small boat-shaped baskets with a fat content of between 0 and 45%.
- cylindrical cream cheeses weighing 1-2 oz / 30-60 g, with a fat content of at least 40%.
- fontainebleau — a mixture of fresh cheese and whipped *crème fraîche*.

Salted fresh cheeses
These include:
- demi-sel (45% fat content)
- gournay, made in the Bray region (Haute-Normandie)
- carré-frais (60% fat content)

There are also many brands of fresh spiced cheeses, enriched and flavored with herbs, garlic, green pepper corns, paprika, etc. These cheeses generally have a slightly sharp tang, and because of their higher fat content are usually firmer in texture (Boursin, for example).

Alongside these fresh factory-made cheeses, there are some that are produced on a regional or local basis, whose taste is creamy and sharp: the caillebottes and jonchées of Poitou,

Roquefort

cremets of the Loire region, brousses of the South, brocciù of Corsica, triple cream boursault with its furry crust and brillat-savarin.

All these fresh cheeses must be stored and displayed for sale at 40°F / 4°C. Their labels should indicate the fat content, any water content above 82% and the expiry date beyond which they may not be sold.

French cheeses obtainable all year round

Bleu de Bresse, boursault, brillat-savarin, cancoillotte, carré de l'Est, emmental, fontainebleau, mimolette, nantais, port-salut, pyrénées, roquefort*, rouy, saint-marcellin, saint-paulin.

Appellation d'origine

Certain cheeses (indicated in the text by an asterisk) have the privilege of an *appellation d'origine*. Under a law passed in 1966, these cheeses are protected from fraudulent imitation.

The *appellation* is based on three main criteria:
1. Adherence to the traditional method of production.
2. Restriction to a limited geographical area, having certain natural features (vegetation, relief, geology) suitable for the production of the milk, and the making and maturing of the cheese.
3. Exercise of quality control over composition (fat and water content), taste and packaging.

Cheeses and labels

French cheese labels carry basic information about the cheese, and it is useful to be able to interpret them.

1. Fat and water content
If the label states 50% ES (Dry element) and 40% MG (fat), this means that for ¼ lb / 100 g cheese, there is 2 oz / 50 g dry matter (that is to say anything which is not water) and ¾ oz / 20 g fat, or 40% of the total weight without water. Fat content relates only to the overall weight without water.
Fat content:
Under 20% = skim-milk cheese (compulsory reference)
40%-45%   = cream cheese
60%   = double-cream cheese
75%   = triple-cream cheese

2. Milk
When milk other than cow's milk is used, this must be made clear, so the label will state *fromage de brebis* (ewe's milk cheese) or *fromage de chèvre* (goat's milk cheese). The words *fromage mi-chèvre* refer to cheese made from at least 50% goat's milk.

3. Farm cheese
The words *fromage fermier* apply only to cheeses made at the farm where the milk is produced.

4. Whole cheeses
All information must appear on the crust or on a hard label.

Pressed cheeses

These are firm-textured cheeses containing less water and more mineral salts than fresh cheeses.
There are two categories:
● uncooked with a dry rind: cantal
● cooked: gruyère; emmental; comté.

Uncooked cheeses

Many well-known French cheeses come into this category.

Cantal*
Cantal cheese has been eaten for almost 2,000 years. Made from cow's milk, it must be smooth, supple and elastic to the touch, and pale yellow in color, with very small holes.

Like a drum in appearance this cheese weighs about 66 lb / 30 kg. It is approximately 16 in / 40 cm in diameter and 14 in / 35 cm in height, with a grayish rind and a nutty, rather spicy taste.

This type of uncooked cheese is marketed under three names:
● cantal or fourme de Cantal*, which is factory-produced and can be made only in the *département* of Cantal.
● salers de haute montagne*, made in summer in the mountainous Salers region.
● languiole*, made from whole unpasteurized cow's milk in a few villages in the mountains of Aveyron, Lozère and Cantal at an altitude of over 2,600 ft / 800 m.

* Appellation d'origine (see page 69)

Saint Nectaire*
Saint Nectaire is one of the oldest cheeses of the Puy-de-Dôme. It is made with milk from the salers cow, and comes in the form of a flat disk 8 in / 20 cm in diameter and 1½ in / 4 cm thick, with a weight of approximately 2 lb / 1 kg. Its crust is gray on a golden yellow background, its texture is rich and smooth and it gives off a delicate scent of its native soil. Its cousins are murol, savaron and vachard, and the last of these can be distinguished from the others by a pronounced earthy flavor and a strong moldy smell.

Saint-Paulin
Saint-Paulin was originally produced in Cistercian abbeys, but this pasteurized cow's-milk cheese is now in widespread production throughout France. It comes in thick disks 8 in / 20 cm in diameter and 2 in / 5 cm thick, weighing approximately 4 lb / 2 kg. The natural crust is orangey and sometimes covered with wax. It is a mild cheese with a soft, smooth texture.

Tomes (or Tommes)
These cow's, goat's or ewe's milk-based cheeses are made in the Alps. They have a strong highly-seasoned taste and are pale yellow and supple. Their gray crusts, which are of varying thickness, show yellow, gray or red mold. The best known varieties are the tome de Savoie and tome de Saint-Marcellin. Tomes may also be flavored with garlic or have their natural crust coated with marc (the skins and pips left in the bottom of wine vats). This last type should not be confused with fondu aux raisins (an emmental-based processed cheese).

Port-Salut
This cheese, which was made at the beginning of the 19th century by the Trappist monks of the Port-du-Salut Abbey at Entrammes in the *département* of Mayenne, has become a commercial brand which, together with bonbel, beaumont and saint-nectaire, makes up the large family of saint-paulin, which in the main are mild cheeses. It is made from pasteurized milk and is a creamy yellow, soft, pressed cheese with a 45-50% fat content. Manufactured in the form of a thick disk, its crust is thin and orangey. In cooking, it is used to make toasted cheese sandwiches, croque-monsieur and various canapés.

Morbier
Morbier, which originates from the Ain and Jura, is recognizable by its horizontal black stripe, because traditionally it was made from cow's milk from two milkings. The curds of the first were protected by a layer of ash before the addition of the second. It comes in a thick disk weighing 12–16 lb / 6–8 kg. Its taste is rather spicy, but is not too strong.

Pyrénées
Creamy in texture, perforated with small holes and characterized by a black shining crust, this very mild cheese is made from cow's milk and has a flavor reminiscent of saint-paulin. It comes in large cylindrical loaves weighing about 8-12 lb / 4-6 kg.

A related cheese, the *brebis des Pyrénées* is made from ewe's milk, as its name implies, but it is stronger and has an orange-gray rind.

Saint Nectaire

Cooked cheeses

Created by milk-producing associations since the end of the Middle Ages, these cheeses are very large and can weigh anything up to 285 lb / 130 kg.

It takes 12 - 15 quarts [12 - 15 l / 10 - 14 quarts] of cow's milk per 2 lb / 1 kg of cheese. The texture of cooked cheeses is fairly firm.

Gruyère

This term designates both the name of a cheese and three varieties of cheese: beaufort, comté and emmental.

Gruyère itself originated in Switzerland, at Gruyères in the canton of Fribourg, and little of it is made in France. Made from cow's milk that is often unpasteurized, it should not have any holes in it, contrary to a widely held view. If it *does* have holes however, they should not be bigger than a pea. Its rind ranges in color from brown to grayish-yellow. Its taste is variable; it may be slightly fruity or very fruity and is sometimes even salty.

The cheeses weigh 65 - 85 lb / 30 - 40 kg and may be as much as 24 - 26 in / 60 - 65 cm in diameter and 5 in / 11 cm thick. It is in cooking that gruyère comes into its own. Easy to use, it enriches purées, béchamel sauces, and creams and it is also used in the preparation of numerous dishes such as soufflés, croquettes, fondue, etc . . .

Beaufort*

Produced in Savoy, Beaufort is made from whole, unpasteurized alpine cow's milk. Its taste is very fruity, and its texture supple, silky and dense. Instead of holes, it has tiny oblique cracks. The cheeses, with their very distinctive concave bottom, can weigh 85 - 130 lb / 40 - 60 kg.

Comté*

Made from unpasteurized cow's milk, this cheese was originally produced in Franche-Comté. It comes in the shape of a millstone weighing about 85 lb / 40 kg. It is firm in texture, fruity in flavor and pale yellow/ivory in color, with holes the size of a pea or a hazelnut and a few cracks. Its crust is rough and grained. It must carry the label of the Franche-Comté Gruyère Association.

Emmental

This cheese, which originated in Switzerland and is made from cow's milk, is also made in Savoy and in Franche-Comté. Compared with gruyère, its holes are quite big, about the size of a walnut. It is the biggest French gruyère: cheeses weigh 130 - 240 lb / 60 - 110 kg. It has a light ivory-yellow texture, and its mild subtle flavor has a touch of fresh walnut about it. Its rind is golden yellow to light brown, solid and dry.

Swiss emmenthal always has an 'h' in its name.

* *Appellation d'origine* (see page 69)

A selection of French cheeses

Soft cheeses

Soft cheeses represent over 35% of the market. They are widely made commercially and are subject to strict regulations to avoid abuse. Since the passing of a law in 1953, these fermented cheeses must have a soft texture which is neither cooked nor pressed. Blue cheeses also belong to this family.

Velvety crust

Camembert
Camembert is the most popular of all velvety crust cheeses. It was invented in 1790 by Marie Harel who had settled in the village of Camembert and had the idea of making a brie in a livarot cheese tub. Since then, this Normandy cheese has spread around the world, and is even made in the United States and West Germany. The label VCN, meaning Genuine Normandy Camembert, is awarded to cheeses that have a fat content of at least 45% and are made from cow's milk from the Pays d'Auge region. (Two quarts [2 l / 3½ pints] of milk are required for an 8 oz / 250 g camembert.) Practically all camemberts are now factory-made, but those produced on a small scale must bear the words *moulé à la main* (hand-made) or *moulé à la louche* (made by ladle).

The taste of a camembert will depend on the degree of fermentation: it may be slightly fruity or very strong.

How to choose a good camembert

Choosing a camembert that is just ready to eat is notoriously difficult.

First of all, look at it closely; if its crust is a velvety white with small red or brown spots, this is a sign that it is ripening, or in other words that it is beginning to ferment.

A perfectly ripe cheese should have a slightly moldy aroma, with no smell of ammonia.

The texture of the camembert should be supple and yielding. This can be checked by feeling the cheese, working from the edge towards the center. Contrary to popular opinion, it should not be runny (nor should any soft cheese), since such a texture would indicate that it has not been dried properly while being made. Instead, check that the inside of the cheese has swelled slightly 2-3 hours after the first cut into it has been made. Experts maintain that a camembert is at its optimum condition for eating when a thin, chalky white layer remains in the middle.

Brie
Brought by Talleyrand from Brie for the Congress of Vienna, and voted 'sacred king of cheeses' there, this cheese was originally produced on a small scale, but it is now mass-produced. It is mellow and mild, slightly salty, with a nutty flavor. The 'rounds', 6-16 in / 15-40 cm in diameter and 1½-2 in / 4-5 cm thick, are usually displayed and served on woven rye-grass mats.

Apart from the *brie laitier,* the mass-produced version, which is made in other countries as well as France, there are 3 types:
- **brie de Meaux*:** is the best-known of the bries, having a white crust and a subtly earthy flavor. It comes in large flat disks 14 in / 35 cm in diameter 1 in / 2.5 cm thick.

- **brie de Coulommiers,** which is similar to the brie de Meaux, but smaller, is the mildest and smoothest of the bries. It is with this brie that Marie Leszczyńska, the wife of Louis XV and Queen of France, prepared the famous bouchées à la reine, or chicken vol-au-vent. Not much of it is sold today. Coulommiers is a cheese of the same type, but it is smaller than the brie of the same name.
- **brie de Melun*** (diameter 10 in / 24 cm) has a crust that is often light brown in color and slightly oily. It is thick, its texture is granular and it has a fruity taste.

Chaource*
Made in the small dairies of Champagne, in the region of Chaource, this cheese is sold in the form of a cylinder 5 in / 12 cm in diameter, 2½ in / 6 cm thick, and weighs approximately 1¼ lb / 600 g. Its crust is covered with a fine white down and the inside is supple with a slight mushroom odor. It is rather a mild cheese with a light fruity flavor.

Neufchâtel*
This comes from the Bray region (Seine-Maritime) and weighs 4 - 8 oz / 100 - 200 g depending on its shape: square, rectangular, cylindrical, oblong or heart-shaped. It has a smooth mellow texture and its savory taste is quite spicy and salty when mature.

Worthy of mention among other soft cheeses with a velvety crust are feuille de Dreux and carré de l'Est, and among the mild, creamy specialty cheeses made from pasteurized milk, the caprice des dieux, monsieur, bouille and suprême.

* *Appellation d'origine* (see page 69)

A delicious brie

Washed crust

These can be distinguished from the velvety crust varieties by their damp appearance, their orange-brown color and their very strong taste.

Munster* gérômé

This cheese comes from Alsace and can be recognized by its glossy smooth bright orange-yellow crust. Its odor is very strong and it has a powerful flavor that is often enhanced with caraway seeds.

Its weight can range from 4 oz / 125 g to 3 lb / 1.5 kg.

Époisses

Made at Époisses (Côte-d'Or) and the surrounding area, this cheese is shaped like a cylinder 4 in / 10 cm in diameter, 2 in / 5 cm thick, and it weighs approximately 14 oz / 400 g.

It has a soft texture and its orangey crust is washed in water containing Burgundy marc, giving it a distinctive spicy taste.

Livarot*

This is made in the Livarot region (Calvados) and is probably one of the oldest of Normandy cheeses. Livarot was traditionally bound in strips of reed but these strips are now made of cardboard. Its orange-pink crust is very smooth and it has a strong smell and a spicy flavor. It is a cylindrical cheese with a diameter of about 4 in / 10 cm, weighing approximately 1 lb / 500 g.

Pont-l'évêque*

Pont l'évêque is rated as one of the richest soft cheeses in France. This very old cheese is now mass-produced, but comes from the Auge region (Calvados), like livarot. It is a square cheese which is extremely smooth and spicy. Its special flavor is said to be due to *monilia candida,* a fungus involved in the fermentation process.

Maroilles*

This cheese originated 1,000 years ago in the Benedictine Abbey of Maroilles, in the heart of Thiérache (Aisne) and it is widely recognized as a soft-textured cheese with a strong flavor and a golden yellow or red ocher color. It varies in weight from 1½ lb / 800 g to 8 oz / 250 g.

Reblochon*

This cheese, a speciality of the Haute-Savoie, was originally made from the particularly rich milk coming from the end of a milking. In former times the cowherds would keep this 'rebloche' milk back illicitly, without the farmer's knowledge, and use it to make the cheese. Nowadays this very mild and creamy cheese is made with any milk that has a high fat content. Reblochon comes in a disk 5 in / 13 cm in diameter and 1 in / 2.5 cm thick, weighing approximately 1 lb / 500 g. Its washed crust is pinkish-white and the cheese itself is soft, creamy and saffron yellow in color. It is allied to the vacherin and colombière cheeses.

Three other spicy cheeses with washed crusts are also worth a mention: langres, a cheese from Champagne shaped like a small drum with a depression in the top; the square saint-rémy from eastern France and the round or heart-shaped rollot from Picardy. The last-named has a strong, earthy flavor.

* Appellation d'origine (see page 69)

Varieties of blue cheeses

Goat's milk cheeses

In France there are at least a hundred varieties of goat's milk cheeses of all shapes – round, pyramidal, heart-shaped and cylindrical, and only cheeses made entirely from goat's milk can be so named. These cheeses have a perfectly regular shape, a fine crust (bluish if charcoal has been used, otherwise pale yellow or pink), a smooth white inside and a fat content of at least 45%. The flavor is nutty or piquant and sometimes very strong.

Noteworthy are:
● **Bougon,** a piquant Poitou cheese made in the form of a flat disk weighing approximately ½ lb / 250 g.
● **Chabichou,** also from Poitou, is a small truncated cone weighing approximately ¼ lb / 100 g.
● **Cabecou de Rocamadour,** from Aquitaine, looks like a coin and weighs approximately 1 oz / 30 g. It may be very nutty.
● **Banon,** a small cheese wrapped in a chestnut leaf, is relatively mild but with a pronounced goaty flavor. It is made in Provence.
● **Crottin de Chavignol*,** weighing 2½ oz / 70 g and made from untreated milk, is slightly nutty.
● **Mâconnais** is also known as *'bouton de culotte'* (trouser buttons) and weighs 2 oz / 50 g. It has a rather mild taste.
● **Saint-Maure,** made in Touraine, is sold in the shape of a log 8 in / 20 cm long, with a piece of straw through it.
● **Valençay,** a mild soft cheese in the shape of a truncated pyramid, is made in Berry. Its crust is sprinkled with wood ash.
● **Selles-sur-cher*,** in the shape of a flattened cone, weighs approximately 5 oz / 150 g.
● **Pouligny-Saint-Pierre*,** which looks like a slightly truncated pyramid, is quite spicy.
● **The other Rhone valley cheeses:** pelardon, rogeret, picodon, etc are very piquant and nutty.
● **The blue cheeses of Savoy,** which weigh anything up to 16 lb / 8 kg, are very piquant.
● **Corsican cheeses:** brindamour, sarteno, venaco, are renowned for their piquant flavor.

Goat's milk cheeses may be eaten fresh, mature, medium-dry or very dry, according to taste. Dry varieties (especially the *crottins* and other *boutons de culotte*) can be preserved in olive oil (see page 39). The fresh varieties should be left in their original wrapping and stored in the vegetable drawer of the refrigerator.

Blue cheeses

Blue cheeses can be made with milk from cows, ewes and goats. They derive their name from their distinctive greenish-blue veining, produced by the action of *penicillium glaucum*, a fungus that is found on moldy rye bread.

Roquefort*
This is undoubtedly the most famous of the French blue cheeses. It was the first cheese to be granted the legal protection of an *appellation d'origine,* defining the area in which it may be produced, the quality of the grazing, and the animals from which the milk is taken.
    The cheese is produced from pure, whole ewe's milk from various regions and is made in the chalk caves of Roquefort (Aveyron), using traditional local methods. After being sprinkled with different varieties of *penicillium*, the curds are poured into round tubs and then salted. The cheese is pierced to admit air and assist the growth of the *penicillium* mold and is then ripened and matured for three months in the cave-cellars of Combalou. The drum-shaped cheeses, weighing 5 lb / 2½ kg, are wrapped in metal foil and labelled. Even mass-produced, roquefort is a remarkable cheese; the taste imparted to it by the ewe's milk from which it is made is quite distinctive.
    Roquefort must not be stored at a temperature above 55°F / 13°C nor too severely chilled. Neither should it be kept under a cheese-cover.
    A good roquefort should be clear white in color, with a regular veining. To be at its best it should not be crumbly, but soft, with a thick buttery texture.

Bleu d'Auvergne*
This cheese from the Auvergne is made from cow's milk in the *départements* of Puy-de-Dôme and Cantal. It is in the form of a wide cylinder approximately 6 in / 15 cm in diameter and weighing 12 oz / 350 g to 6 lb / 3 kg. It must carry the words *syndicat du veritable bleu d'Auvergne* (Bleu d'Auvergne Association). Its taste is quite piquant, almost rough.

Bleu de Bresse
Mass-produced in the Ain *département*, this is a small blue-veined cheese, wrapped in silver foil and weighing ¼ - 1 lb / 125 - 500 g. It has a mild, piquant, smooth flavor.

Bleu des Causses*
This is a sort of roquefort but made from cow's milk and therefore milder. It is made in Aveyron and in a few villages in the *départements* of Gard and Hérault.

Bleu du Haut-Jura*
Known also as bleu de Gex* or septmoncel, it is made, as its name indicates, in the Jura and in the Gex region. It looks like a small millstone weighing 12 - 20 lb / 6 - 9 kg. Its dry crust is reddish yellow, and the veining is deep blue. A highly flavored cheese, it may be farm-produced or made in cooperative dairies.

Fourme d'Ambert
This cheese, which has an unpasteurized milk base, is produced in the Forez region (Auvergne) and comes in the shape of a tall cylinder 9 in / 22 cm high, with a diameter of 4 in / 11 cm. Its dried crust is covered with white and red mold, and it has a very pronounced, somewhat bitter taste. To serve, cut it into slices, then cut each slice into quarters.

Storing cheeses

In the absence of a larder or cellar, the refrigerator is the best place for protecting cheeses from dehydrating and keeping them at a constant temperature.

Soft cheeses with a washed crust (munster or pont-l'évêque) or a velvety crust (camembert or brie). These ripen rapidly. They must be kept in the original packing, placed in the vegetable drawer of the refrigerator, and eaten within 24 hours. (Take them out 1 hour before the meal.)

Pressed cheeses (cantal, tome, etc)
These should be wrapped in wax paper, greaseproof paper or foil, placed in a plastic container and kept in the vegetable drawer of the refrigerator.
    Pre-packed cheeses should be kept in the refrigerator in their vacuum-sealed packs. Once opened, they should be wrapped in foil and returned to the refrigerator.

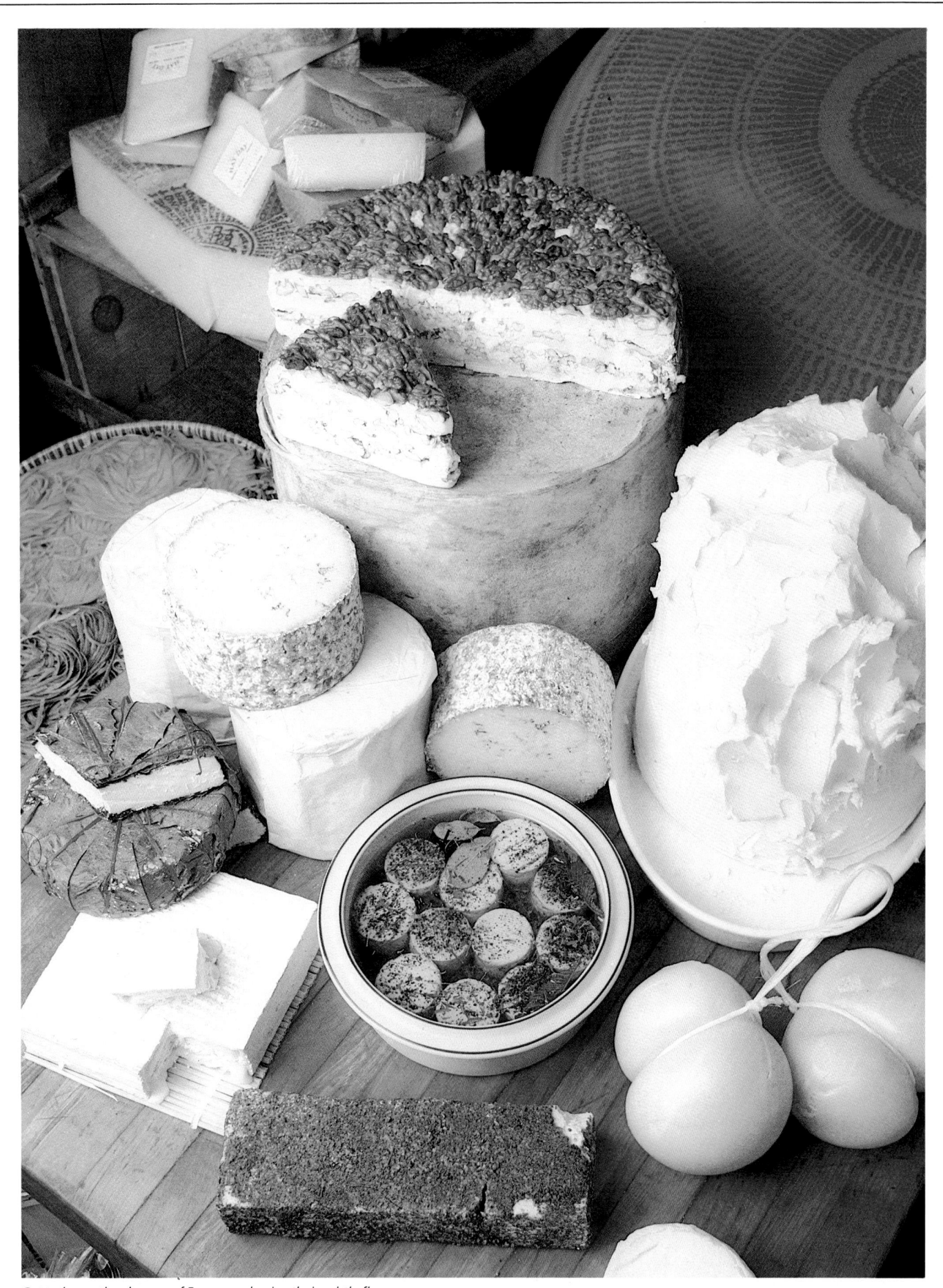

Get to know the cheeses of France and enjoy their subtle flavors

Cheeses in season

	DEC.	NOV.	OCT.	SEPT.	AUG.	JUL.	JUN.	MAY.	APR.	MAR.	FEB.	JAN.
Appenzel	●	●	●			●	●	●	●	●	●	●
Beaufort*	●	●	●	●	●	●	●	●				●
Bleu d'Auvergne*							●	●	●			
Bleu des Causses*							●	●	●			
Bleu du Haut-Jura*	●	●	●	●	●	●	●	●	●	●	●	●
Blue cheeses (various)	●	●	●	●	●	●	●	●	●	●	●	●
Boulette d'Avenses	●	●	●	●	●	●	●	●	●	●	●	●
Bouton de Culotte						●	●	●	●			
Brie* (Meaux and Melun)	●	●	●			●	●	●	●	●	●	
Brocciù	●	●	●	●							●	●
Brousses	●	●	●	●	●							●
Camembert						●	●	●	●	●	●	
Cantal*							●	●	●			
Cendrés					●	●	●	●	●	●		
Chabichou					●	●	●	●	●	●	●	
Chaource*					●	●	●	●	●	●	●	
Comté*	●	●	●					●	●	●	●	●
Crottin de Chavignol*		●	●	●	●	●	●	●	●			
Époisses	●	●	●			●	●	●	●	●	●	●
Fourme d'Ambert or de Montbrison*					●	●	●	●	●	●	●	●
Gaperon								●	●	●		
Gruyère				●	●	●	●	●	●	●		
Laguiole*	●	●										
Langres					●	●	●	●	●	●	●	
Livarot*	●	●	●				●	●	●	●		
Mâconnais						●	●	●	●	●		
Maroilles*	●	●	●		●	●	●	●	●	●	●	
Morbier		●	●	●	●							
Munster géromé					●	●	●	●	●	●		
Murol						●	●	●	●	●		
Neufchâtel*		●	●	●	●	●	●	●	●			
Niolo					●	●	●	●	●	●		
Pavé d'Auge	●	●	●			●	●	●	●	●	●	●
Pélardon					●	●	●	●	●	●	●	
Pont-l'évêque*	●	●	●				●	●	●	●		
Reblochon*					●	●	●	●	●	●		
Sainte-Maure		●	●	●	●	●	●	●	●	●		
Saint Nectaire*					●	●	●	●	●	●	●	
Salers*				●	●	●	●	●	●	●		
Selles-sur-cher*		●	●	●	●	●	●	●	●	●		
Tomes						●	●	●	●	●	●	
Vacherin	●								●	●	●	
Valençay		●	●	●	●	●	●	●	●	●	●	

The following are available all the year round:
Bleu de Bresse, Boursault, Brillat-Savarin, Concoillotte, Carré de l'Est, Emmental, Fontainebleu, Momolette, Nantais, Port-Salut, Pyrénées (cow's milk), Roquefort, Rouy, Saint-Marcellin, Saint-Paulin.

Fromage blanc frais

Fresh White Cheese

⬜ 00:30   00:20 🍲

American	Ingredients	Metric/Imperial
1 quart	Cow's or goat's milk	1 l / 1¾ pints
2	Drops of rennet	2
¼ cup	Water	4 tbsp
	Salt (optional)	

1. If the milk is not pasteurized, boil it for 10 minutes. Otherwise, simply bring the milk to a boil. Pour into a bowl.
2. Dissolve the rennet in the water and mix with the milk. If you want slightly salted cheese, add salt to taste. Leave to stand in a warm place (110°F / 43°C) for 12 hours.
3. Pour into a colander lined with cheesecloth or muslin. Knot the corners of the cheesecloth or muslin and hang in a cool place over a container for 12 hours to drain completely.
4. Refrigerate the cheese, and eat within 4 days.

Yaourt

Yogurt

⬜ 00:30   00:10 🍲

American	Ingredients	Metric/Imperial
1 quart	Cow's milk	1 l / 1¾ pints
1 package	Yogurt culture or	1 packet
1 tbsp	Plain yogurt	1 tbsp

1. Scald the milk and cool to lukewarm (110°F / 43°C).
2. Mix the yogurt culture or prepared plain yogurt with the milk. Pour into 1 or more clean, warm containers. Cover and keep at 110°F / 43°C for 8 - 12 hours. Alternatively, use a commercial yogurt maker.
3. Refrigerate the finished yogurt, which will keep 8 - 10 days in the refrigerator.

Fromage blanc frais aux herbs

Fresh White Cheese with Herbs

⬜ 00:10   00:00 🍲

American	Ingredients	Metric/Imperial
1 quantity	Fresh white cheese	1 quantity
2 tbsp	Chopped mixed fresh chives, parsley and basil	2 tbsp
	Salt and pepper	

1. Put the cheese into a bowl and beat until smooth.
2. Add the herbs, salt and pepper to taste and mix well.
3. Spoon into a serving dish and chill for several hours.

With leftovers . . .
Remove mold and rind. Crush soft cheeses with a fork; grate hard cheeses and mix them in a bowl, adding the same volume of crème fraîche (see page 122). Add pepper, chopped fresh herbs a pinch of grated nutmeg and a teaspoon of Cognac. Blend thoroughly, chill and serve before the dessert.

Using cheeses for cooking

	Appenzel	Bagnes	Beaufort	Comté	Emmental	Gruyère	Parmesan	Raclette
Béchamel sauce				●	●	●		
Cheese pastry					●	●	●	
Fondue			●	●	●	●		
Gratins				●	●	●	●	
Onion soup				●	●			
Raclette	●	●						●

French cheeses

1 – Mimolette
2 – Boulette d'Avesnes
3 – Rollot
4 – Maroilles
5 – Small camembert
6 – Coeur de Bray
7 – Bondon
8 – Camembert
9 – Brie de Meaux
10 – Carré de l'est
11 – Half-camembert
12 – Pont l'Évêque
13 – Livarot
14 – Spicy fresh cheese
15 – Brie de Coulommiers
16 – Processed cheese with walnuts
17 – Small Munster Géromé
18 – Munster Géromé
19 – Triple cream with velvety crust
20 – Processed cheese in portions
21 – Époisses
22 – Fresh cheese
23 – Valençay
24 – Sainte-Maure
25 – Crottin de Chavignol
26 – Pyramide du Poitou
27 – Saint-Paulin
28 – Saint-Paulin in portions
29 – Curé nantais
30 – Small Saint-Paulin
31 – Selles-sur-Cher
32 – Small bleu de Bresse
33 – Bleu de Bresse
34 – Chaource
35 – Gruyère de Comté
36 – Emmental
37 – Beaufort
38 – Cantal
39 – Saint-Nectaire
40 – Bleu d'Auvergne
41 – Fourme d'Ambert
42 – Saint-Marcellin
43 – Rigottes
44 – Tomme de Savoie
45 – Reblochon
46 – Processed cheese with grapes
47 – Bleu des causses
48 – Roquefort
49 – Roquefort in portions
50 – Pyrenean cheese (ewe's milk)
51 – Pyrenean cheese (cow's milk)
52 – Banon de Provence
53 – Poivre d'Ane
54 – Niolo

CHAPTER 6

Buffets

If entertaining friends is no longer synonymous with long meals and sophisticated, carefully thought-out menus, the buffet is an ideal and agreeable solution to your problem, enabling you to serve a variety of food and drink to more guests than could be accommodated at a dinner party.

In this chapter, we have kept to what is the traditional buffet spread, that is to say, anything that can be eaten with the fingers without plates or at least without the need for set places at table. Recipes for canapés, sandwiches, pastries, cocktail snacks and drinks are grouped together according to the type of buffet and the number of guests.

Organizing your buffet

The table: a rectangular table is the most convenient, long and not too wide, so as to give easy access to everybody. A standard dining room table is ideal for a buffet. If you haven't one large enough, trestle tables are adequate. Use a table felt or underlay to protect the surface against spills.

Easy-to-wash tablecloth: choose one that will cope with the inevitable spilt wine and food, and is large enough to come well over the table edges. Have a good supply of paper napkins.

Serving dishes: you should have enough to contain all the items on the menu. For canapés and cocktail snacks, pastries, pizzas etc. choose flat trays for preference, because food can be very easily arranged on them.

Plates: for a buffet with sweet and savory items, allow a minimum of 2 plates per guest.

Glasses: make sure that you have more than enough, to allow for those guests who always want a clean glass for each drink.

Carafes and pitchers are needed for wine, cocktails and fruit juices. However, if it is an informal party, you can just as easily serve wines from the bottle.

Ice buckets: to keep sparkling wines, and vodka cool.

Ice cubes: some refrigerators dispense a large quantity of ice cubes automatically. If yours is a less sophisticated model, make cubes in the ice trays several days in advance, and store them in plastic bags in the freezer compartment. A squirt of carbonated water in the bags helps keep the cubes separate. Reckon on a minimum of 4 cubes per person.

Knives and forks: unless it is all 'finger food' provide knives. Even if not necessary, some people can't do without them!

Trays: useful for clearing up.
Don't forget napkins! Paper ones are ideal, and they can be white or colored, to match or contrast with other decorations.

Coffee cups: you cannot possibly have enough coffee cups to go around all the guests. You can either use paper cups (matching the table cloth and napkins) or hire dishes from a specialist firm or caterer. Glasses and flatware [cutlery] could also be hired if the party is a large one.

A few practical hints
All the buffet recipes given here can quite easily be made the day before.

Prepare as much as possible in advance so that on the day of the party, all you have to do is to add a seasoning, a sauce or possibly reheat food in the oven.

To prevent canapés from drying out, prepare them as late as possible (but still the day before), cover them with a slightly damp cloth, and put them in a cool place, preferably not the refrigerator, where they will dry out especially if left uncovered.

Lay the table in the morning for an evening party, and you will save at least an hour!

In case you have unexpected guests, or the party goes on until dawn, make sure you have food in reserve: pâtés in cans, jars of olives, fruit in syrup, cold cuts, frozen food, cheese.

Working out quantities
These depend on the type of buffet.

If it is a cocktail party, it is usual to reckon on 12 to 15 savory or sweet helpings per person (canapés, quiches, pastries, prunes with bacon for example). If it is a lunch (stand-up meal), you should allow the same quantities as for a sit-down meal. With a great variety of dishes, each guest will find something to his taste.

For drinks, reckon on:
1 bottle of champagne for 4 people
1 bottle of whiskey for 10 people
1 quart [1 l / 1¾ pints] of fruit juice for 4 people
1 bottle of wine for 3 people
1 quart [1 l / 1¾ pints] of mineral water for 3 people
1 quart [1 l / 1¾ pints] of carbonated water for 4 people.

Vary your buffet according to the season

A simple, informal buffet

This buffet for 20 people is a simple answer for people who do not have large rooms where they can hold parties, nor a large kitchen. You can put the meal together yourself in a few hours with very little equipment. It doesn't require any particular skill or special planning.

Cheeses

Offer a minimum of 9 cheeses grouped together on the buffet table in categories, from the mildest to the strongest (see chapter on cheeses). Set them out on the bare table on baskets, or on trays or platters covered with napkins or leaves. Put out two knives: one for the mild flavors and the other for the strong.

Cover the cheeses with a damp cloth to prevent them from drying out, and remove it just before your guests arrive.

You can also offer cheeses cut into cubes. For this, choose varieties of different colors: the pale ones contrasting with the more highly colored ones. Don't forget small cubes of processed cheese in their foil.

Cold meats

Choose a variety of sausages and meats, some of which can be very thinly sliced, and allow about 5 slices per person. Some of the meats can be rolled up and fastened with toothpicks. Serve pâtés or terrines on large plates.

Raw vegetables

Crisp, raw vegetables are refreshing, and are a perfect accompaniment to the cheese board. Choose a head of fresh celery, cleaned, its strings removed, and cut into sections; 10 carrots peeled and cut into 4 lengthwise; a bunch of cleaned radishes or two horseradishes peeled and cut into thin rings; a very fresh, very white cauliflower washed and divided into tiny florets; 3 fennel bulbs cut into thin strips; 2 peeled cucumbers with seeds removed, cut into long sticks.

Sauces

Set out on the buffet table a mayonnaise, a walnut and roquefort sauce, and a basil sauce for the raw vegetables (see chapter on sauces). Put several plates of butter on the table.

Bread

Provide whole wheat loaf, a farmhouse loaf, and crusty baguettes or rolls.

Choosing the wine

Whether you have wine in carafes or bottles, it is best to keep to one variety. Depending on your taste, and that of your guests, offer either a cool young red wine (e.g. Beaujolais), or a Bordeaux, a Burgundy, a Côte-du-Rhône or a Corbières. Do not forget to provide carafes of cool, but not ice cold water.

Quickly prepared sandwiches and canapés

Pain surprise rond
Round Sandwich Surprise

	00:20		00:00
	Makes about:		

American	Ingredients	Metric/Imperial
1	Round loaf of day-old rye bread	1
1 cup	Butter	250 g / 8 oz
½ lb	Roquefort cheese	250 g / 8 oz
1 cup	Green walnuts	125 g / 4 oz

1. Cut off the top crust so the loaf is very flat. Set aside. Cut vertically all around the inside of the crust with a small pointed knife, without cutting through the base. Cut horizontally, at the base this time, keeping the blade of the knife flush with the crust, to separate the cylinder of bread completely from the crust.
2. Carefully remove the cylinder of bread. Cut it horizontally into an equal number of slices about ¼ in / 5 mm thick.
3. Put the butter, roquefort and green walnuts in a food processor or blender and blend until smooth.
4. Spread the mixture generously over half the slices of bread. Cover each slice with a plain slice to make sandwiches, pressing gently to bind them together. Place these sandwiches one on top of the other.
5. Cut down through the stack of sandwiches into 8-10 wedges. Put the reshaped cylinder back in the crust. Cover with the top crust and keep the bread in a cool place until serving.

Pain surprise long
Long Sandwich Surprise

	00:20		00:00
	Makes about 40		

American	Ingredients	Metric/Imperial
1	Day-old rectangular loaf of bread	1
1 cup	Butter, at room temperature	250 g / 8 oz
5	Thin slices of cooked ham	5
14 oz	Gruyère cheese, sliced	400 g / 14 oz

1. Lay the bread on a long side. Cut off the top crust about ½ in / 1 cm thick. Set aside. Cut vertically all around the inside of the crust down to the base (without cutting through it). Cut horizontally, at the base, keeping the blade of the knife flush with the crust. Carefully remove the rectangle of bread.
2. Cut the bread lengthwise into slices about ¼ in / 5 mm thick. Spread them with butter.
3. Cut the ham and gruyère slices to the same size as the slices of bread.

4. Put the ham on one-quarter of the bread slices and the gruyère on another quarter. Cover with the remainder of the slices, buttered side down. Place these sandwiches one on top of the other.
5. Cut small sandwiches of a length equal to the height of the bread, or about 3 in / 7.5 cm. Arrange them inside the crust as you go along. Replace the top crust and keep in a cool place until serving.

Cook's tip: this sandwich surprise can be made using other ingredients such as cooked tongue, smoked ham, salami, etc.

Canapés fromage-radis
Cheese-Radish Canapés

	00:10		00:00
	Makes 12		

American	Ingredients	Metric/Imperial
6	Slices of bread	6
½ lb	Gouda or edam cheese	250 g / 8 oz
1	Bunch of radishes	1
¼ cup	Butter, at room temperature	50 g / 2 oz
1 tsp	Strong prepared mustard	1 tsp
1	Bunch of watercress	1

1. Cut the slices of bread in half. Cut the cheese into thin slices and cut them to the size of the slices of bread. Slice the radishes.
2. Mix the butter with the mustard and spread over the slices of bread.
3. Place a slice of cheese on each slice of bread. Arrange a few radish slices and watercress leaves in the center of each canapé. Keep in a cool place until serving.

Canapés beurre-camembert-oignons au vinaigre
Camembert and Pickled Onion Canapés

	00:20		00:00
	Makes 12		

American	Ingredients	Metric/Imperial
½	Mild-ripe camembert cheese	½
5 tbsp	Butter, at room temperature	65 g / 2½ oz
6	Square slices of rye bread	6
20	Pickled onions	20
	Chopped fresh chives	

1. Remove the crust from the camembert and add the creamy part to the butter. Mix together thoroughly until smooth.
2. Spread the slices of bread with the cheese butter and cut them in half diagonally to obtain triangles.
3. Slice the onions and push into rings. Arrange the onion rings on the canapés and sprinkle with chopped chives. Keep in a cool place until serving.

Salad buffet for twenty

Mixed salads are decorative and fresh and have the advantage of not being fattening. As a basis for a buffet we suggest four mixed salads, for which we give the recipes: Tuna and anchovy rice salad (page 168), lebanese salad (page 175), salami salad (page 182) and swiss salad (page 86).

Multiply the quantities indicated according to the number of guests. We suggest different sorts of canapés. Allow about 100 pieces for a buffet for 20 people.

Pyramide de crudités

Raw Vegetable Pyramid

A raw vegetable pyramid with a roquefort or horseradish sauce will always be welcome in a salad buffet. (In this case, prepare only 2 sorts of salad.)

	01:00 Serves 20	00:00
American	**Ingredients**	**Metric/Imperial**
1	Bunch of celery	1
2	Cucumbers	2
2 lb	Small carrots	1 kg / 2 lb
2	Fennel bulbs	2
2	Sweet red peppers	2
2	Lemons	2
6	Small globe artichokes	6
2	Large onions	2
1	Cauliflower	1
3	Avocados	3
1½ lb	Mushrooms	750 g / 1½ lb
1	Bunch of fresh parsley	1
1	Bunch of fresh chervil	1
1	Head of lettuce	1
1	Head of batavian (curly) endive	1
1	Head of red lettuce or radicchio	1
1	Bunch of radishes	1
2 lb	Tomatoes, preferably plum-type	1 kg / 2 lb

1. Separate the celery into stalks. Trim the bases but retain the leaves. Peel and quarter the cucumbers. Remove the seeds and cut the flesh into sticks. Peel the carrots. Trim the bases from the fennel bulbs and cut into thin slices. Cut the red peppers in half, remove the seeds and cut the flesh into fine strips.
2. Squeeze the juice from the lemons. Quarter the artichokes and sprinkle with some of the lemon juice. Peel and slice the onions and push into rings. Separate the cauliflower into small florets.
3. Cut the avocados in half, remove the seeds and cut each half in half lengthwise. Sprinkle with lemon juice. Trim the mushrooms, but leave them whole. Finely chop the parsley and chervil. Put the herbs into small serving dishes.

4. Rinse and drain the lettuce, batavian endive and red lettuce. Discard any damaged outside leaves.
5. Arrange all the vegetables attractively on a serving dish in a pyramid-shape, mixing the colors and placing the largest vegetables on the bottom. Surround the pyramid with the dishes of chopped herbs, and roquefort or horseradish sauce (see pages 120 and 122).

Cook's tip: you can make up a pyramid using plates of decreasing sizes.

Canapés fromage blanc-raifort-concombre

Cream Cheese, Horseradish and Cucumber Canapés

	00:15	00:00
American	**Ingredients**	**Metric/Imperial**
¼ cup	Grated horseradish	50 g / 2 oz
½ lb	Drained white or cream cheese	250 g / 8 oz
	Salt and pepper	
6	Slices of rye bread	6
6	Slices of cucumber	6
24	Radishes	24

1. Mix together the horseradish, cheese and a little salt and pepper. Spread thinly on the slices of bread. Cut each slice in half.
2. Cut the slices of cucumber in half. Place on the cream cheese.
3. Cut the radishes into flowers and use to garnish the canapés. Keep in a cool place until serving.

Salade suisse

Swiss Salad

	00:15 plus cooling Serves 4	00:30
American	**Ingredients**	**Metric/Imperial**
4	Potatoes	4
	Salt and pepper	
4	Hard-boiled eggs	4
1	Lettuce heart	1
½ lb	Cooked ham	250 g / 8 oz
5 oz	Gruyère cheese	150 g / 5 oz
1	Large bunch of fresh chives	1
⅔ cup	Crème fraîche (see page 122)	150 ml / ¼ pint
1	Lemon	1
1 tsp	Prepared mustard	1 tsp

1. Scrub the potatoes and place in a saucepan of salted water. Bring to a boil and simmer for 30 minutes.
2. Meanwhile, quarter the eggs. Rinse and drain the lettuce leaves. Cut into thin strips with a very sharp knife. Cut the ham and gruyère into small cubes. Chop the chives.
3. Drain the potatoes. When they are cool enough to handle, peel them. Allow to cool, then dice and place in a salad bowl.

4. Put the crème fraîche, juice of the lemon, mustard and salt and pepper to taste in a mixing bowl and mix well.

5. Add the gruyère and ham cubes to the salad bowl. Spoon over the crème sauce, garnish with the egg quarters and sprinkle with the chopped chives. Keep in a cool place until serving.

Canapés jambon-oeufs durs

Ham and Egg Canapés

	00:20		00:00
	Makes 12		

American	Ingredients	Metric/Imperial
1 cup	Shelled hazelnuts	125 g / 4 oz
¼ cup	Butter, at room temperature	50 g / 2 oz
12	Square salted cocktail crackers [biscuits]	12
3	Slices of cooked ham	3
3	Hard-cooked eggs	3
12	Slices of cucumber	12
	Chopped fresh parsley	

1. Coarsely chop the hazelnuts. Add half of the chopped nuts to the butter and mix well. Spread this nut butter over the crackers.

2. Cut the slices of ham into 12 pieces the same size as the crackers. Save the trimmings.

3. Cut each egg into 8 slices.

4. Put a piece of ham on each canapé, top with 2 egg slices and place a slice of cucumber in the center of each.

5. Cut the ham into small pieces. Scatter over the egg slices and sprinkle with the remaining chopped nuts and parsley. Keep in a cool place until serving.

Canapés ronds-beurre d'anchois-sauce tartare

Anchovy Canapés with Tartare Sauce

	00:20		00:00
	Makes 24		

American	Ingredients	Metric/Imperial
½ cup	Anchovy butter (see page 112)	125 g / 4 oz
24	Round slices of bread	24
	Chopped fresh parsley	
6	Hard-cooked eggs	6
½ cup	Tartare sauce (see page 119)	8 tbsp
24	Canned anchovy fillets in oil	24
24	Olives stuffed with pimiento	24

1. Spread a generous layer of anchovy butter over the slices of bread and sprinkle with chopped parsley.

2. Cut the eggs into 24 slices. Arrange them on the canapés and top each with a small teaspoon of tartare sauce. Wrap an anchovy around each stuffed olive and place them in the center of the egg rings.

3. Arrange the canapés on a serving tray and keep in a cool place until serving.

Canapés au salami

Salami Canapés

	00:10		00:00
	Makes 20		

American	Ingredients	Metric/Imperial
10	Square slices of bread	10
6 tbsp	Butter, at room temperature	75 g / 3 oz
10	Slices of salami	10
2	Gherkins	2

1. Using a round fluted pastry cutter the same diameter as the slices of salami, cut a round from each slice of bread. Butter the bread rounds using 2 tablespoons [25 g / 1 oz] of the butter.

2. Remove the skin from the salami. Place 1 slice on each round of buttered bread. Cut the canapés in half. Arrange the canapés on a serving tray.

3. Put the remainder of the butter into a pastry bag fitted with a fluted nozzle and pipe decoratively onto the canapés.

4. Slice the gherkins and place a slice on each canapé. Keep in a cool place until serving.

An attractively presented buffet

Buffets for Special Occasions

The variety and selection of dishes and attractive and careful presentation are the golden rules which you should follow. The recipes here are to serve 50 people or more.

Pruneaux au bacon

Prunes with Bacon

▱ 00:20
Makes 30

00:10

American	Ingredients	Metric/Imperial
30	Tenderized prunes	30
30	Thin bacon slices	30

1. Preheat the oven to 425°F / 220°C / Gas Mark 7.
2. Cut open each prune lengthwise and remove the pit [stone].
3. Wrap each prune in a slice of bacon and secure with a wooden toothpick. Arrange the prunes on a baking sheet.
4. Place in the oven and bake for about 10 minutes or until the bacon is lightly browned. Serve piping hot.

Cook's tip: do not use dried prunes which would have to be soaked.

Pizzas

Individual Pizzas

▱ 00:30
Makes 20–30

00:20 to 00:30

American	Ingredients	Metric/Imperial
1 lb	Tomatoes	500 g / 1 lb
1	Onion	1
2 tbsp	Olive oil	2 tbsp
1	Bouquet garni	1
	Salt and pepper	
	Dried mixed Italian herbs	
	Pastry (see next recipe)	
1	Small can anchovy fillets in oil, drained	1
½ cup	Black olives	50 g / 2 oz

1. Preheat the oven to 400°F / 200°C / Gas Mark 6.
2. Peel the tomatoes (first plunging them into boiling water for 10 seconds). Remove the seeds and chop the tomatoes.
3. Peel the onion and cut into thin slices. Heat the oil in a heavy saucepan, add the onion and cook until softened.
4. Add the tomatoes, bouquet garni, and salt, pepper and herbs to taste. Leave to cook until thickened.
5. Roll out the pastry to about ⅛ in / 3 mm thick and cut out 20-30 small rounds. Use to line buttered tartlet pans. Prick the bottoms with a fork and chill for 15 minutes.
6. Fill the pastry case with the tomato sauce and bake for about 15 minutes.
7. Garnish the tops with a cross of anchovy fillets, cut into strips, and small pieces of olive. Allow to cool.
8. Remove the pizzas from the pans and reheat them when ready to serve.

Petites quiches lorraines

Small Egg and Bacon Quiches

▱ 00:30
plus chilling
Makes 20–30

00:15

American	Ingredients	Metric/Imperial
	Pastry:	
2 cups	Flour	250 g / 8 oz
½ cup	Butter	125 g / 4 oz
1 tsp	Salt	1 tsp
1	Egg yolk	1
	Water	
	Filling:	
1¼ cups	Milk	300 ml / ½ pint
1¼ cups	Crème fraîche (see page 122)	300 ml / ½ pint
2	Eggs	2
1	Egg yolk	1
	Salt	
	Cayenne pepper	
	Grated nutmeg	
¼ lb	Smoked bacon	125 g / 4 oz
1 cup	Grated gruyère cheese	125 g / 4 oz

1. Prepare the pastry: put the flour into a bowl and make a well in the middle. Add the butter, salt, egg yolk and 5 tablespoons water. Mix to a dough, adding more water as necessary. Chill for 20-30 minutes.
2. Mix together the milk, crème fraîche, whole eggs, egg yolk and a pinch each of salt, cayenne pepper and nutmeg. Strain the mixture and set aside.
3. Cut the bacon into small cubes and cook in a frying pan until browned. Drain on paper towels.
4. Roll out the pastry to about ⅛ in / 3 mm thick and cut out 20-30 small rounds. Use to line buttered tartlet pans. Prick the bottoms with a fork and chill for 15 minutes.
5. Preheat the oven to 400°F / 200°C / Gas Mark 6.
6. Fill each pastry case with bacon and grated gruyère and pour in the egg mixture. Bake for 12-15 minutes. As soon as they are out of the oven, remove the quiches from their pans. Reheat them just before serving.

Canapés avocat-moutarde-citron-paprika

Avocado Canapés

▱ 00:30
Makes 20

00:00

American	Ingredients	Metric/Imperial
20	Slices of bread, about ¼ in / 5 mm thick	20
2	Very ripe avocados	2
1 tbsp	Prepared mustard	1 tbsp
1	Lemon	1
	Salt	
	Paprika	

1. Using an oval cutter about 3 in / 7.5 cm long, cut an oval from each slice of bread.
2. Cut the avocado in half. Remove the stones and carefully scoop out the pulp with a spoon. Put the pulp, mustard, juice

of the lemon and salt to taste in a blender or food processor and blend until smooth.

3. Spread the avocado mixture over each canapé, piling it up.

4. Sprinkle the canapés lightly with paprika. Keep in a cool place until serving.

Canapés tomate-oeuf dur-olive

Egg, Tomato and Olive Canapés

⧖ 00:15 Makes 20		00:00 🍲
American	**Ingredients**	**Metric/Imperial**
10	Thin slices of bread	10
2 tbsp	Butter, at room temperature	25 g / 1 oz
4	Hard-cooked eggs	4
5	Firm, medium-sized tomatoes	5
5	Green olives, pitted	5
½	Canned pimiento	½

1. Using a round, fluted cutter the same diameter as the tomatoes, cut 20 rounds from the bread slices. Butter the rounds.

2. Cut the eggs into 20 slices.

3. Cut the tomatoes into 20 equal slices, and place one slice on each canapé. Place a slice of egg on each slice of tomato.

4. Cut the olives into 20 thin slices and place in the middle of the egg yolk.

5. Garnish with small cubes of pimiento. Keep in a cool place until serving.

Canapés beurre-gruyère-saucisson à l'ail

Gruyère and Garlic Sausage Canapés

⧖ 00:30 Makes 20		00:00 🍲
American	**Ingredients**	**Metric/Imperial**
10	Slices of bread, about ¼ in / 5 mm thick	10
½ cup	Butter, at room temperature	125 g / 4 oz
1 cup	Grated gruyère cheese	125 g / 4 oz
	Salt	
	Cayenne pepper	
10	Slices of garlic sausage, 2½ in / 6 cm in diameter	10
10	Slices of gruyère cheese	10

1. Using a 2½ - 3 in / 6 - 7.5 cm round fluted cutter, cut out 2 rounds from each slice of bread.

2. Mix the butter with the grated cheese. Add salt and cayenne pepper to taste. Spread the mixture over the bread rounds, piling it up.

3. Carefully remove the skin from the slices of garlic sausage. Cut each slice in half. Using the cutter, cut rounds out of the slices of gruyère. Cut the rounds in half.

4. Cover each canapé with a ½ round of gruyère and a ½ slice of sausage. Keep in a cool place until serving.

Canapés au caviar

Caviar Canapés

⧖ 00:15 Makes 20		00:00 🍲
American	**Ingredients**	**Metric/Imperial**
5	Slices of bread, about ¼ in / 5 mm thick	5
2 tbsp	Butter, at room temperature	25 g / 1 oz
½ oz	Caviar	15 g / ½ oz
1	Lemon (optional)	1

1. Using a small fluted cutter, cut 4 rounds from each slice of bread. Butter the rounds.

2. Carefully place a teaspoon of caviar on each canapé. If liked, place a slice of lemon on each canapé. Keep in the refrigerator until ready to serve.

Caviar – a gourmet delicacy

Barquettes au saumon fumé
Smoked Salmon Boats

	00:15		00:00
	plus making pastry boats Makes 12		

American	Ingredients	Metric/Imperial
½	Lemon	½
3	Thin slices of smoked salmon	3
1 (3 oz)	Can of salmon	1 (75 g / 3 oz)
¼ cup	Thick crème fraîche (see page 122)	4 tbsp
2 tbsp	Butter	25 g / 1 oz
	Salt and pepper	
12	Baked pastry boats (see page 89)	12

1. Squeeze the juice from the ½ lemon. Cut the slices of smoked salmon to the same length as the pastry boats and reserve the trimmings.
2. Put the drained canned salmon in a blender or food processor, along with the smoked salmon trimmings, crème fraîche, butter and lemon juice. Season to taste with salt and pepper and blend until smooth.
3. Fill each pastry boat with the salmon mixture and garnish each with a piece of smoked salmon. Serve chilled.

Chipolatas cocktail
Cocktail Sausages

	00:05		00:10

American	Ingredients	Metric/Imperial
1½ lb	Small link sausages [chipolatas]	750 g / 1½ lb
2 tbsp	Butter	25 g / 1 oz

1. Prick the sausages to prevent them from bursting.
2. Heat the butter in a frying pan until it froths. Add the sausages and fry them until brown on all sides.
3. Drain the sausages. Arrange them on a dish and spear each with a toothpick. Serve hot.

Canapés asperges
Asparagus Canapés

	00:20		00:00
	Makes 20		

American	Ingredients	Metric/Imperial
5	Cans of asparagus tips	5
10	Slices of bread, ½ in / 1 cm thick	10
1 cup	Mayonnaise (see page 119)	250 ml / 8 fl oz
1	Can of pimientos	1

1. Drain the asparagus.
2. Remove the crusts from the bread. Cut each slice in half to form 2 rectangles and trim the 4 corners with a sharp knife.
3. Spread each rectangle of bread with mayonnaise. Arrange 4, 5 or 6 asparagus tips, according to their size, on each canapé.
4. Drain the pimiento and cut it into thin strips. Arrange them attractively on the canapés. Keep in a cool place until serving.

Barquettes basquaises
Pastry Boats

	00:20	00:12 to 00:15	
	plus making pastry Makes 12		

American	Ingredients	Metric/Imperial
1 quantity	Basic short pastry (see page 457)	1 quantity
	Scrambled egg with tomatoes and peppers (see page 223)	

1. Preheat the oven to 400°F / 200°C / Gas Mark 6.
2. Roll out the pastry about ⅛ in / 3 mm thick. Cut out oval shapes using a pastry cutter, and use to line 12 small boat-shaped molds. Prick the bottoms with a fork. Line the bottom of each with a piece of foil.
3. Bake the boats 'blind' for 10 minutes, then remove the foil and bake for a further 2 minutes. Allow to cool.
4. Unmold the pastry boats and fill with the scrambled egg mixture. Keep in a cool place until serving.

Bouchées au roquefort
Roquefort Puffs
(see page 190)

Cook's tip: complete your buffet by placing on your table two large pieces of meat, such as a whole baked ham and a cold chicken in aspic (see page 314).

Balance your buffet with two salads: périgord salad (see page 180) and swiss salad (see page 86) are good choices since they will add a touch of color and freshness to your table.

For dessert, offer a chocolate cake and a sorbet presented in small cups.

Suggested drinks to go with this party buffet are sparkling wine, fresh fruit juice and mineral water.

A dramatic presentation of buffet food

Drinks for buffets

Your choice of drinks will vary with the kind of buffet you choose. For simple buffets, the most suitable drink is carafes of wine that will go as well with cooked meats as with cheese or salads.

For more formal buffets, there are several options. The most luxurious, and the most expensive, is to serve a single wine – a vintage or fine wine perhaps, or a champagne.

For simpler buffets provide a punch or sangria in a large bowl, from which everyone can help themselves with a ladle. If you are entertaining only a few guests, making cocktails is fun. There is an almost infinite variety of cocktails, but the following pages give a selection of some which are very easy to make, and which require little specialized equipment. A few non-alcoholic cocktails are included, for those who may not wish to drink wine or spirits.

Always serve cocktails cool, as soon as they are made, and do not allow the ice to dilute them, otherwise your cocktails will lose all their flavor and charm.

The amateur barman's equipment
A lemon squeezer
A strainer for fruit juice
A wide variety of bowls; glasses of all sizes
and assorted spoons
A can opener and bottle opener
A mixing goblet
A mixing spoon
Multicolored straws
A stainless steel shaker, or any plastic container
which can be tightly sealed.

A few standard ingredients
Celery salt, salt, cayenne pepper and black peppercorns in a mill, cinnamon, grated nutmeg, worcestershire sauce, tabasco, gherkins, fruit in syrup, confectioners' [icing] sugar, or sugar syrup, and a variety of fruit juices and syrups.

A few base spirits
Angostura, cointreau, cognac, curaçao, gin, pastis, white rum, vermouth (white, red and dry), vodka and whiskey.

Vin chaud
Mulled Wine

	00:10 To serve 6	00:10

American	Ingredients	Metric/Imperial
1 bottle	Red wine	1 bottle
½ tsp	Ground cinnamon	½ tsp
½ tsp	Ground ginger	½ tsp
2	Small oranges studded with cloves	2
3 tbsp	Honey	3 tbsp
¼ cup	Cognac	4 tbsp
½ cup	Water	125 ml / 4 fl oz

1. Heat the wine together with the cinnamon and ginger until the surface of the wine turns white.
2. Add the oranges. Continue to cook until the wine turns white once again. Remove from the heat, and pour into a serving bowl. Add the honey, cognac and boiling water. Serve piping hot.

Laits battus
Milk Shake

	00:05 For 1 large glass	00:00

American	Ingredients	Metric/Imperial
1 cup	Very cold milk	250 ml / 8 fl oz
2 tbsp	Strawberry syrup or peppermint syrup or orange syrup or instant chocolate	2 tbsp

1. Pour the milk and chosen flavoring into a blender. Mix and pour into a large glass.
2. To make a richer drink, add a scoop of vanilla ice cream and blend with the milk and flavoring.

Punch
Rum Punch

	00:15 To serve 10	00:00

American	Ingredients	Metric/Imperial
1	Lemon	1
2 cups	Fresh orange juice	500 ml / ¾ pint
2 cups	Fresh pineapple juice	500 ml / ¾ pint
1 tsp	Ground cinnamon	1 tsp
2 cups	Sugar syrup	500 ml / ¾ pint
3 cups	White rum	750 ml / 1¼ pints

1. Squeeze the lemon and strain the juice.
2. Pour all the juices, cinnamon, syrup and white rum into the punch bowl. Mix and place the punch bowl in the refrigerator. Serve ice cold.

Rum punch

Vegetable Juice

	00:10		00:00
	To serve 4		

American	Ingredients	Metric/Imperial
2	Large carrots	2
2	Tomatoes	2
1	Small leek	1
½	Lemon	½
3	Celery stalks	3
1	Small shallot	1
	Ice cold water	
	A few fresh basil leaves or basil powder	
	Salt and pepper	

1. Peel the carrots and cut into four. Wash the tomatoes and cut into quarters. Wash and peel the leek and cut into four. Squeeze the half lemon. Clean and wash the celery. Cut into pieces. Peel the shallot. Place all the vegetables in a blender goblet and switch on for 3 minutes. Add enough water to the juice to give the cocktail a good consistency. Add the basil, salt and pepper and mix for a few seconds.
2. Pour the mixture into a carafe or pitcher and keep in a cool place until you are ready to serve it.

Vin aux pêches
Wine with Peaches

	00:10		00:05
	the day before		

American	Ingredients	Metric/Imperial
2	Lemons	2
⅔ cup	Water	150 ml / ¼ pint
1	Cinnamon stick	1
1½ bottles	Red wine	1½ bottles
1 cup	Confectioners' [icing] sugar	125 g / 5 oz
3	White or yellow peaches	3

1. Slice the lemons thinly. Boil for 5 minutes in water together with 1 stick cinnamon. Leave to cool. Pass through a conical strainer to extract the juice, pressing with a wooden spoon.
2. Mix the lemon juice with the red wine. Add the sugar and the peaches skinned, pitted [stoned] and cut into pieces. Leave to soak for 24 hours. Serve cool.

Thé glacé aux fruits
Iced Tea with Fruit

	00:15		00:10
	(01:30 before serving) To serve 6		Macerating time 01:00

American	Ingredients	Metric/Imperial
½ can	Pineapple slices	½ can
2	Lemons	2
3	Oranges	3
1	Grapefruit	1
¾ cup	Superfine [caster] sugar	150 g / 6 oz
3 tbsp	Tea (Earl Grey)	3 tbsp

1. Cut the pineapple slices into four and put them together with their syrup into a bowl.
2. Wash 1 lemon and 1 orange and grate the peel of half of each of the two fruits. Add the peel to the pineapple pieces. Squeeze the lemon and pour the juice into the bowl.
3. Peel the oranges, grapefruit and lemons. Cut into thin slices and cut the grapefruit slices into four. Add to the pineapple. Sprinkle with sugar and stir. Leave to stand in a very cold place for at least 1 hour.
4. Make the tea with 1 quart [1 l / 1¾ pints] boiling water and leave to infuse for 5 minutes. Strain and pour over the fruit and place the mixture in the refrigerator. When about to serve, add ice cubes and a few sprigs of mint to the bowl.

Banane flip
Banana Flip

	00:05		00:00
	To serve 4		

American	Ingredients	Metric/Imperial
2	Bananas	2
4	Egg yolks	4
2 tbsp	Confectioners' [icing] sugar	2 tbsp
1 cup	Milk	250 ml / 8 fl oz
	Ground cinnamon	

1. Peel the bananas and cut into pieces. Place in a blender goblet with the other ingredients.
2. Blend and serve in tall glasses.

Iced tea with fruit

Cocktail d'agrumes à la girofle

Citrus Cocktail with Cloves

	00:05 To serve 4		00:00

American	Ingredients	Metric/Imperial
2	Grapefruit	2
4	Oranges	4
1	Lime	1
1	Lemon	1
	Confectioners' [icing] sugar	
2	Cloves	2

1. Squeeze the fruit and pour the juice into a pitcher. Add sugar to taste.
2. Grind the cloves to a fine powder. Add to the juice, together with 5 cubes of crushed ice.

Champagne cobbler

Champagne Cobbler

	00:03 For 1 large glass		00:00

American	Ingredients	Metric/Imperial
2	Cherries	2
2	Pineapple pieces	2
2	Peach slices	2
3 measures	Maraschino	3 measures
3 measures	Orange liqueur	3 measures
3 measures	Orange curaçao	3 measures
	Champagne	

1. Fill the glass half full with finely crushed ice. Put in the cherries, the pieces of pineapple and the slices of peach. Add the maraschino, orange liqueur and curaçao.
2. Stir several times with a mixing spoon and top up with champagne.

Sauternes Cup

	00:05 To serve 10		01:00 Macerating time

American	Ingredients	Metric/Imperial
2	Nectarines	2
4	Apricots	4
6	Strawberries	6
6	Raspberries	6
1	Orange	1
1 thin strip	Cucumber peel	1 thin strip
3 tbsp	Liqueur brandy	3 tbsp
3 tbsp	Orange liqueur	3 tbsp
3 bottles	Sauternes	3 bottles
1⅓ cups	Carbonated mineral water	300 ml / ½ pint

1. Into a large glass jar put the nectarines and apricots, pitted [stoned] and cut into 4, the strawberries and raspberries with their hulls removed, the orange cut into slices and the thin strip of cucumber peel.

2. Pour the liqueur brandy and orange liqueur over the fruit. Cover with foil. Chill in the refrigerator for 1 hour.
3. When you are about to serve, add a dozen ice cubes, the sauternes and the cool mineral water. Stir and serve quickly.

Champagne cobbler

Sangria

Sangria

	00:25 Macerating time: 24:00 to 48:00 hours To serve 15		00:05

American	Ingredients	Metric/Imperial
5 bottles	Red wine (good quality ordinary red wine)	5 bottles
3	Lemons	3
5	Oranges	5
5	Firm peaches	5
12	Apricots (in season)	12
4	Apples	4
4 tsp	Ground cinnamon	4 tsp
1¾ cups	Confectioners' [icing] sugar	200 g / 7 oz
3 cups	Grand Marnier or cognac	750 ml / 1¼ pints
1 quart	Carbonated lemonade	1 l / 1½ pints

1. Pour the wine into a large jar or container.
2. Peel the lemons and oranges, cut into slices ½ in / 1 cm thick and place in the jar.
3. Pit [stone] the peaches and apricots, cut into 4 and put into the jar. Peel the apples, cut into 6 and add to the rest of the fruit.
4. Sprinkle the fruit with the cinnamon and sugar. Add the Grand Marnier or cognac and leave to macerate at room temperature for at least 24 hours.
5. Add the lemonade just before serving and serve very cool with ice cubes.

Menus

Every country has its own particular style of entertaining and these menus, chosen from *La Cuisine*, reflect the flavor of typical French cooking.

Scallops with white butter sauce
Chicken with spring vegetables
Cheese
Rum babas

1. Make the babas the day or the morning before the meal.
2. 1¼ hours before the meal prepare the chicken and put to cook.
3. 40 minutes before the meal clean and cook the scallops and make the white butter sauce.

Leek pie
Chicken with tarragon
Buttered rice
Cheese
Upside-down chocolate custard

1. Make the dessert the day before and keep in the refrigerator until needed.
2. 2 hours before the meal prepare the leek pie.
3. 1 hour before the meal cook the chicken.
4. 30 minutes before the meal put the leek pie to cook, then cook the rice and put it into the oven to finish cooking when the leek pie is served.

Mussels in wine and cream
Pot roast veal, sauté potatoes
Chicory [endive] with garlic-flavoured croûtons
Cheese
Long pineapple tart

1. Make the tart several hours in advance.
2. 1¼ hours before the meal put the veal to cook, then prepare the salad and salad dressing, but do not dress the salad until the last moment. Prepare the sauté potatoes.
3. 30 minutes before the meal make the mussels in wine and cream.

Cheese puffs
Monkfish in tomato sauce
Green salad
Lemon tart

1. Make the lemon tart the day before.
2. 1¼ hours before the meal prepare the salad and its dressing, but do not mix until serving.
3. 1 hour before the meal make the cheese puffs and pipe onto a baking tray.
4. 40 minutes before the meal cook the fish.
5. 10 minutes before the meal bake the cheese puffs.

Languedoc crab salad
Country style lamb
Cheese
Frozen lemon soufflé

1. The day before, prepare the frozen lemon soufflé and place in the refrigerator freezing compartment.
2. 4 hours before the meal, prepare the crab salad and chill in the refrigerator.
3. 2 hours before, prepare everything necessary for the country style lamb, but do not put the meat in the oven until your guests arrive.

Pork and eggplant [aubergine] stew see page 393

Cream of watercress soup
Fried strips of sole
Roast loin of pork with apple compote
Cheese
Profiteroles

1. Make the choux paste for the profiteroles several hours ahead.
2. 2½ hours ahead make the soup, but do not garnish it.
3. 1½ hours before the meal put the pork in the oven and prepare the apples.
4. 1¼ hours before the meal make the hot pepper and potato mayonnaise and cut up the sole.
5. 40 minutes before the meal make the chocolate sauce for the profiteroles and keep warm.
6. 20 minutes before the meal heat the oil for frying, make croûtons and heat the soup gently.
7. 10 minutes before the meal prepare the strips of sole for frying, fry them and keep warm whilst the soup is served. Garnish the soup before bringing it to the table.

Tomato soup
Leg of lamb with potatoes and onions
Cheese
Orange mousse

1. Prepare the mousse and the soup several hours in advance, or the day before.
2. 2½ hours before the meal cook the potatoes.
3. 45 minutes before the meal put in the lamb.
4. 20 minutes before the meal heat the soup gently.

Iced melon with port wine
Veal chops baked in foil
Green salad
Cheese
Ice cream Plombières

1. Make the ice cream 2 or 3 days ahead and keep in the freezer.
2. Prepare the salad and its dressing 1¼ hours before the meal, but do not dress the salad until ready to serve.
3. 1 hour before the meal prepare the veal chops.
4. 40 minutes before the meal prepare the melon and put it to chill.
5. 15 minutes before the meal put the veal chops in the oven.

Lebanese salad
Provençal beef olives with buttered noodles and spinach
Green apple sorbet

1. Make the sorbet 2 or 3 days in advance and keep in the freezer.
2. 2½ hours ahead prepare the beef olives and cook them.
3. 1 hour ahead make the salad and dressing, but keep them separate.
4. 30 minutes before the meal prepare and cook the noodles and spinach.

Chilled leek and potato soup
Marne fish stew
Beef fillet in a pastry case
Radicchio salad and cheese
Chocolate charlotte

1. The day before the meal, make the chocolate charlotte and chilled leek and potato soup. Keep in the refrigerator.
2. 4 hours before, prepare the beef fillet in pastry case. Switch off the oven 30 minutes before cooking has finished and do not switch on again until after serving the fish.
3. 3 hours before, clean the radicchio and prepare the dressing. Do not mix into the salad until ready to serve. Serve the salad with the cheese.
4. 2½ hours before, prepare the fish stew. Keep the fish hot in a bowl standing over a pan of hot water, until the sauce has been reduced, over a low heat. Do not incorporate the butter until the very last moment, when you put the fish into the sauce.

Apricot tart (see page 474)

CHAPTER 7

Basic Cooking Techniques

What is the difference between frying and sautéing? Why can't a chicken be cooked in the same way as a joint? For those who think of cooking as mysterious or bafflingly scientific, this chapter offers a basic outline of the most commonly used cooking methods and explains the special techniques required for success. Remember though that this, like every other worthwhile skill, requires practice, so be prepared for one or two failures at first.

Types of cooking

All foods are cooked in one of two ways — by concentration or expansion.

Concentration involves exposing foodstuffs (meat, poultry, vegetables) to dry heat or immersing them in hot liquid or fat. In this way, the nutritional values are sealed inside by a dry surface crust or a casing formed by the cooking process.

Expansion involves cooking foodstuffs and flavorings slowly in a liquid to effect an exchange between the two.

The term mixed cooking is applied to preparations in which both cooking by concentration and cooking by expansion are used, such as in a recipe for a stew or casserole where meat is browned first to seal in the juices before it is added to the liquid.

Roasting, spit-roasting and barbecuing

Roasting is cooking with butter, oil or other fat, by direct heat on a spit or in the oven, where the intensity of the heat source can be varied depending on the nature and quantity of the food.

Joints of meat that have been cooked on a spit are often much tastier than those cooked in the oven, since the sudden sealing with heat of certain rich meats and game helps to concentrate their flavor.

Some meats need a longer cooking time and a more moderate temperature, so follow the instructions given in the recipes. Be sure to baste the flesh frequently to guarantee an attractive browned appearance.

In the case of oven cooking, certain meats (red meats, game) must be sealed in a very hot oven (at least 525°F / 274°C / Gas Mark 8) and others (white meat and certain game or poultry), after being lightly sealed, are cooked in a moderate oven (see instructions in the recipes).

Making gravy with the juices from the joint
For the juice from the joint to retain all its flavor, it must be mixed with either water (mutton, lamb, poultry, game birds), or (in the case of beef, pork and certain poultry), brown stock or with a stock of the same nature as the joint.

1. Remove from the oven or spit the tray or pan in which the meat has been cooked.

2. Place it over a low heat to color the residue on the bottom slightly. Watch carefully, since any burned material will make the sauce taste bitter. Check the seasoning.

3. Add the appropriate liquid (½ a wine glass per person) and heat, stirring and scraping with a wooden spatula in order to dissolve the residue on the bottom, then reduce by one third.

4. If necessary, strain the resulting gravy and keep it hot before serving.

After making gravy from mutton or lamb juices, you could add a few crushed cloves of garlic or season with Provençal herbs and leave to cook for approximately one minute more. You will then have a savory sauce to pour over meat or vegetables.

Spit-roasting times

For large pieces of meat and poultry, the times are the same as for the oven:

Beef	: 15 minutes per pound (or 10 minutes for rare meat)
Mutton	: 12 to 15 minutes per pound
Lamb	: 15 to 20 minutes per pound
Chicken	: 20 minutes per pound
Pork	: 30 minutes per pound

How to choose your broiler [grill], rotisserie and barbecue equipment

A rotisserie and broiler are used in the kitchen, a barbecue in the open air. The rotisserie (or rotisserie-oven) is suitable for cooking large pieces of meat and poultry and is used also for brochettes (kebabs) and small pieces of meat and fish.

A simpler device, the electric contact broiler with one or two non-stick aluminum plates is more manageable and takes up less room in the kitchen, but it can only be used for cooking small pieces of meat (steak, pork chops, lamb chops, veal fillets, etc.).

A vertical broiler combines the advantages of the rotisserie and the broiler, but it can be used only for small or medium sized pieces of meat, and for brochettes (kebabs).

In the open air, a barbecue can be used both as a broiler and a rotisserie. Its construction is a simple one: a charcoal container covered with a grille, although it is becoming more and more common for it to be fitted with a roasting jack.

Foods for roasting or baking

Meat	What to choose	Cooking time	Weight per serving
Beef	Aitchbone, rib, rib eye, rolled boneless rump, sirloin (tip), tenderloin or fillet, topside	Will vary, depending on taste: per 1 lb / 500 g: 8 min for very rare plus extra 8 min, 15 min for rare plus extra 15 min, 20 min for medium plus extra 20 min, 25 min for well done plus extra 25 min (quick roasting at 425°F / 220°C / Gas Mark 7)	5 - 8 oz / 150 - 250 g
Veal	Breast, fillet, leg, loin, rib (rack or best end), boneless shoulder	25 - 30 min per 1 lb / 500 g plus extra 25 - 30 min, ½ lb / 250 g (quick roasting at 425°F / 220°C / Gas Mark 7)	½ lb / 250 g
Lamb	Breast, crown roast, leg, loin, rib (rack or best end of neck), saddle, shoulder	Will vary, depending on taste: per 1 lb / 500 g: 15 min for rare plus extra 15 min, 25 - 30 min for medium to well done plus extra 25 - 30 min (slow roasting at 350°F / 180°C / Gas Mark 4)	½ lb / 250 g
Pork	Back ribs, blade, crown, hand, knuckle, leg, loin, shoulder, spareribs or fresh belly, tenderloin or fillet	30 - 35 min per 1 lb / 500 g plus extra 30 -35 min (at 375°F / 190°C / Gas Mark 5)	5 oz / 150 g
Pork, cured	Gammon, ham, prime collar bacon, smoked pork	35 min per 1 lb / 500 g (after boiling as necessary and boiling time included in total cooking time)	½ lb / 250 g
Poultry	Chicken, duck, goose, rabbit, turkey	See individual recipes	
Game	All game birds and animals	See individual recipes	
Fish and shellfish	Large whole fish	See individual recipes	

Broiling [grilling]

Broiling is the cooking of meat (red and white), poultry, sausages, brochettes (kebabs), fish or vegetables over a naked heat source and in the open, rather than in an enclosed space such as an oven. Under the action of the heat, a dry crust is formed which seals flavor and nutrients into the food. Its success depends on the temperature used for each food (see table on cooking times) and on close observation and common sense.

Red meats
The cooking time will vary according to taste – as a general rule, large pieces of red meat must be sealed quickly. Once this has been done, lower the cooking temperature so the heat can diffuse inside the meat. When the juices bead on the surface of the raw part, turn the meat over carefully to complete cooking.

White meats and poultry
You must not seal white meats in the same way as red meats – they require less fierce cooking in a moderate heat. Poultry and veal should never be served underdone, so remember that they are not cooked until their juices run clear.

Sausages and brochettes (kebabs)
Chitterlings, sausages, chipolatas, black pudding and white pudding do not require any special cooking. They should be covered in fat before being placed on the broiler, and their cooking time will depend on size and type.

If they are not coated with oil before cooking, brochettes (kebabs) tend to dry out and lose all their taste. There are no strict rules for making brochettes – everything that can be broiled can also be cut into small pieces and threaded on to a skewer. Use your imagination to combine complementary or contrasted flavors, but make sure that all the foods have the same cooking time, or some will be burnt while others remain raw.

A few practical tips for broiling

1. Pre-heat the broiler beforehand.
2. Broiling should be done at the last moment, since the cooked food tastes better if eaten immediately.
3. Oil the broiler using a brush or a piece of rag soaked in oil.
4. Oil foods before putting them on the broiler and again while they are cooking to prevent them from drying out.
5. Do not prick food with a fork during cooking, either to move it or turn it over. Use a steel spatula instead or the juices and the flavor will escape.
6. Do not salt raw meats – use salt after cooking only, since it draws out juices and prevents proper sealing.
7. To serve, present the side which was cooked first, and coat it with clarified butter to make it shinier and more appetizing.
8. For best results, the bars on the broiler and plates must always be kept clean. Never use water for this job, but scrape them instead with a metal brush while they are still hot to remove burnt-on foods. Wipe with a dry cloth.
9. After cleaning, give the broiler a light coating of oil.

Foods for broiling [grilling]

Food	What to choose	Cooking time	Weight per serving
Beef	All prime steaks, cubes for kebabs, ground [minced] beef patties	Will vary, depending on taste	5 - 8 oz / 150 - 250 g
Veal	Steaks or cutlets [escalopes], chops	3 - 8 min per side, depending on thickness	5 oz / 150 g
Lamb	Chops, steaks, cubes for kebabs, ground [minced] lamb patties	3 - 7 min per side, depending on thickness	5 - 8 oz / 150 - 250 g (2 - 3 chops)
Pork	Chops, cutlets [escalopes], cubes for kebabs, ground [minced] pork patties, sausages	12 - 16 min	5 oz / 150 g
Pork, cured	Ham slices [gammon steaks], smoked pork chops, bacon	3 - 10 min per side, depending on thickness	5 - 8 oz / 150 - 250 g
Poultry and game	Chicken and duck pieces, small game birds, venison steaks	See individual recipes	
Fish and shellfish	Steaks, fillets, small whole fish	See individual recipes	
Vegetables	Tomatoes, peppers, eggplant [aubergines], mushrooms, zucchini [courgettes], etc.	See individual recipes	
Dairy foods	Goat's milk cheeses	3 - 4 min	1 or 2

Broiling [grilling] and frying times for red meats (pieces about 1 inch / 2.5 cm thick)

Cooking	Cooking methods	Characteristics of the meat
Extra rare (very quick cooking)	1 to 2 min per side Seal each side of the meat for a very short time (which will vary according to the shape, volume and nature)	Soft, will offer no resistance to touch
Rare (quick cooking)	2 to 4 min per side Turn the meat as soon as blood begins to bead on the surface of the raw part	Contracts to the touch
Medium (rather slow cooking)	3 to 5 min per side Seal the meat vigorously on one side until blood beads on the surface of the raw part. Then, reduce the heat, or move the meat away from the heat, for the heat to diffuse inside. Proceed in the same way for the other side.	Resistant to the touch. The blood will seep profusely on the surface of the sealed crust.
Well done (very slow cooking)	8 to 12 min in all The same procedure as for 'medium' cooking but leave to cook longer	Firm to the touch

Foods for stewing or casseroling

Food	What to choose	Cooking time	Weight per serving
Beef	Bottom round, brisket, chuck, heel of round, neck [clod], shank [shin]	2½ - 4 hours, depending on tenderness of cut	½ lb / 250 g
Veal	Scrag, shank [knuckle], veal for stew [pie veal]	1½ - 2 hours	½ lb / 250 g
Lamb	Neck, lamb for stew	1½ - 2 hours	½ lb / 250 g
Pork	Hand, hock [knuckle], spareribs [fresh belly]	2 hours	6 - 8 oz / 175 - 250 g
Variety meats [offal]	Brain, oxtail, tongue, etc.	See individual recipes	
Poultry and game	Stewing chicken [boiling fowl], rabbit, older game birds, less prime cuts of game animals	See individual recipes	
Vegetables	Potatoes, root vegetables	See individual recipes	
Fish and shellfish	Clams, crab, lobster, mussels, shrimp	See individual recipes	

Deep frying

Deep frying is plunging various foods, (fish, vegetables, eggs, raw or cooked foods), covered in batter or bread crumbs or combined with choux pastry, into a large amount of oil or fat raised to a high temperature.

Suitable foods for frying

Food	Type	Best parts for frying
Fish	Eel, brill, fresh cod, hake, sparling, gudgeon, sole, dabs, sand eels etc.	Slices, fillets, small fish, small pieces.
Vegetables	Eggplant [aubergines], mushrooms, zucchini [courgettes], potatoes, salsify etc.	See chapters on vegetables and potatoes.
Coated food	Fritters, croquettes etc.	Food coated in batter, bread crumbed, combined with choux pastry etc.

Attereaux
Attereaux consist of veal or lamb sweetbreads, brain, tongue, kidneys, ham, shellfish, fish, poultry, game, vegetables, fruit, whole or cut into squares or rectangles, threaded onto a wooden stick covered with sauce and bread crumbs.

Fruit fritters

Cooking

1. Do not fry until ready to serve.
2. Place the *attereaux* in a frying basket.
3. Plunge in small quantities into the fat (350°F / 180°C).
4. Fry gently for 4 to 5 mins.
5. Take out the *attereaux* and drain them on a serviette or kitchen paper.
Serve hot, arranged on a serviette-covered dish.

Fritters
There are three sorts of fritter: with batter, choux pastry or without batter or pastry.

With batter
1. When appropriate, put the food to soak 1 hour in advance.
2. Dip each piece in batter.
3. Put in a frying basket and plunge into the hot fat (350°F / 180°C).
4. Cook for 4 to 5 minutes.
5. Turn the fritters while they are cooking.
6. Take them out, drain on a serviette or kitchen paper.
7. Salt or sugar lightly.

With choux pastry
1. Combine the food to be fried with the choux pastry.
2. Put the pieces in hot fat (350°F / 180°C) with a spoon and leave to fry without touching them, until they become puffy and golden brown.
3. Take them out and drain on a serviette or kitchen paper.
4. To serve, arrange in the form of a pyramid on a serviette-covered dish.

Fruit fritters without batter or pastry
1. Core and peel the fruit, and cut into slices.
2. Spread them out on a plate, and sprinkle with superfine [caster] sugar. Sprinkle with calvados or cognac.
3. Leave to stand in a cool place.
4. When ready to serve, cook as for fritters in batter.
5. To serve, you can arrange the fritters in the form of a crown and sprinkle them with confectioners' [icing] sugar.

Cromeskies
These are of various foods: fish, poultry, mushrooms etc, cut into small pieces, bound together, rolled into a ball and then dipped in batter.

Cooking

1. Do not fry until you are ready to serve.
2. Place the cromeskies in a frying basket and lower them gently into the very hot fat (at least 350°F / 180°C), to give them a crusty golden brown jacket.
3. Leave to cook for 3 to 4 minutes without touching.
4. Take them out and drain on a serviette or kitchen paper.
5. To serve, you can arrange the cromeskies in the form of a pyramid on a serviette-covered plate.

Croquettes
Croquettes also consist of various foods: ham, fish, mushrooms, tongue etc, cut into small pieces and coated with bread crumbs.

Fritots

These are types of fritter consisting of pre-cooked food: poultry, poached fish fillets, mushrooms etc. marinated in advance and then coated in bread crumbs and fried.

Cooking

1. Marinate the food to be fried 1 hour in advance.
2. Follow any pre-cooking instructions in the individual recipe.
3. Dip the fritots one by one into the hot fat (350°F / 180°C).
4. Leave to fry for about 4 to 5 minutes.
5. Turn the fritots with a fork while they are cooking.
6. Take them out and drain on a serviette or kitchen paper and give a light sprinkling of salt.
To serve, you can arrange the fritots in the form of a pyramid on a serviette-covered plate. Serve with tomato sauce or tartare sauce.

Shallow frying or sautéing

There is little difference between frying and sautéing. The expression 'sauter' is often used for small food (potatoes, carrots, sliced onions), which are too small to be turned over individually and for frying meats that are cooked in hot fat and turned over half way through. The surface of the meat is sealed to form a crust which prevents the juices from escaping, but the success of this way of cooking depends largely on the flavor of the sauce and therefore on the way in which this sauce is made.

Before they are fried, certain foods (pork, veal) may be dipped in flour, or beaten egg and bread crumbs.

Panure à l'anglaise

Egg and Bread Crumb Coating

00:10   will vary according to the food

American	Ingredients	Metric/Imperial
1 cup	Flour	125 g / 4 oz
2	Eggs	2
1 tsp	Oil	1 tsp
	Salt and pepper	
2½ cups	Dry bread crumbs	150 g / 5 oz

1. Place the flour on a plate. Lightly beat the eggs with the oil and salt and pepper to taste in a shallow dish. Place the bread crumbs on another plate.
2. Coat the food to be breaded with flour. Shake off the excess, then dip in the beaten egg. Leave to drain, then place in the bread crumbs and press them on firmly on all sides to help them adhere.
3. Cook for the required cooking time.
4. The food may be coated with flour 20-30 minutes in advance, but must be dipped into the egg and bread crumbs immediately before cooking. Dry bread crumbs can also be used alone, without the flour and egg.

Foods for frying

Food	What to choose	Cooking time	Weight per serving
Beef	All prime steaks, ground [minced] beef	Will vary depending on taste	5 - 8 oz / 150 - 250 g
Veal	Chops, steaks or cutlets [escalopes], ground [minced] veal	4 - 8 min per side	5 oz / 150 g
Lamb	Chops, steaks, ground [minced] lamb	3 - 5 min per side	2 - 3 chops
Pork	Chops, cutlets [escalopes], ground [minced] pork, sausages	4 - 8 min per side	5 - 8 oz / 150 - 250 g
Poultry and game	Pieces of chicken, duck, rabbit, turkey, etc., small game birds (whole or cut up), venison steaks	See individual recipes	
Variety meats [offal]	Slices of liver, kidneys	5 - 20 min, depending on size	½ lb / 250 g
Fish and shellfish	Fish steaks and fillets, small whole fish, frogs' legs, scallops, shrimp	See individual recipes	

Poaching

When we speak of poaching, we normally think of food being cooked quickly in simmering water. However, the term also refers in general to the process of cooking food in a liquid. This method of cooking therefore applies to a great number of foods: fish cooked in a court-bouillon, crustaceans plunged quickly into boiling salted water, boiled beef in a pot-au-feu, steamed potatoes, veal sweetbreads poached in water, for example. These various methods of cooking in liquid are described in detail in each recipe.

Chief poaching foods

Foods	What to choose	Cooking time	Weight per serving
Beef	Bladebone, shoulder and stewing steak, clod, tail, thin ribs, brisket, knuckle, tenderloin	3½ hours (1¼ hours in pressure cooker)	5 - 8 oz / 150 - 250 g
Lamb	Leg, breast, neck, top cutlets, shoulders	15 min per lb 1½ hours (30 min in pressure cooker)	5 - 8 oz / 150 - 250 g
Veal	Shoulder, chump end, breast, flank, neck, top of rib, knuckle, round, shoulder	1¾ hours (35 min in pressure cooker)	5 - 8 oz / 150 - 250 g
Pork	Belly, knuckle, shoulder, spare ribs, top ribs, flank	1¾ hours (35 min in pressure cooker)	5 - 8 oz / 150 - 250 g

Sauerkraut (see page 403)

Braising

This is a method of cooking less tender cuts of meat and other foods to retain their succulence. There are two stages:

1. Pieces of food are first cooked quickly in hot fat to seal in the juices.
2. The food is then left to cook slowly in a tightly covered vessel over a very gentle heat so that the fibers break down and the juices are released.

Foods for braising or pot-roasting

Food	What to choose	Cooking time	Weight per serving
Beef	Aitchbone, blade, brisket, chuck, flank or skirt, rib, round, rump, short ribs, silverside, topside	45 min per 1 lb / 500 g (minimum 2 hours for pot-roasts)	½ lb / 250 g
Veal	Breast, chops, shank [knuckle], steaks	40 min per 1 lb / 500 g (minimum 1 ½ hours for pot-roasts)	½ lb / 250 g
Lamb	Breast, chump chops, neck, shank, shoulder	40 min per 1 lb / 500 g (minimum 1 ½ hours for pot-roasts)	½ lb / 250 g
Pork	Back ribs, chops, shoulder, spareribs, tenderloin or fillet	45 min per 1 lb / 500 g (minimum 2 hours for pot-roasts)	5 - 8 oz / 150 - 250 g
Poultry and game	Chicken (whole or in pieces), duck, goose, rabbit, turkey, game birds and animals (less prime cuts)	See individual recipes	
Fish and shellfish	Whole fish, or in steaks or fillets, scallops, squid, etc.	See individual recipes	
Vegetables	Celery, lettuce, etc.	See individual recipes	
Fruit	Peaches, pears, plums, apples, etc.	See individual recipes	

CHAPTER 8

Sauces

Sauces

This is not a definitive collection of recipes for sauces, but it includes those that are most often found in French cooking.

For ease of reference the sauces are divided into four broad categories.

1. Composite butters
2. Sauce stocks and thickenings
3. Cold sauces
4. Hot sauces

Some special sauces and stuffings will be explained in greater detail in individual recipes.

Composite butters

Beurre d'anchois
Anchovy Butter

00:20 plus soaking		00:00

American	Ingredients	Metric/Imperial
½ lb	Salted anchovies	250 g / 8 oz
1	Garlic clove	1
1 cup	Butter, at room temperature	250 g / 8 oz
	Pepper	

1. Put the anchovies into a mixing bowl, cover with water and leave to soak for 2 hours, changing the water several times. Drain.
2. Fillet the anchovies, discarding all skin and bones. Rinse and pat dry with paper towels.
3. Place the anchovies in a mortar. Peel the garlic and add to the mortar. Pound with the pestle to make a fine cream. Gradually add the butter and mix until very smooth. Season lightly with pepper.
4. This anchovy butter, which may be kept at least 3 weeks in the refrigerator, gains in flavour if you make it about 1 hour before using.
5. To serve anchovy butter warm, melt it in a bowl standing in a pan of hot water, whisking it as you do so. To make it finer, you may put it through a very fine strainer to remove fragments of anchovy.

Beurre d'escargot
Snail Butter

00:20 plus standing		00:00

American	Ingredients	Metric/Imperial
5	Shallots	5
4	Garlic cloves	4
1 cup	Butter, at room temperature	250 g / 8 oz
½	Lemon	½
	Ground fennel	
	Salt and pepper	
3 tbsp	Chopped fresh parsley	3 tbsp

1. Peel and finely chop the shallots. Peel and crush the garlic.
2. Mix together the butter, juice of the ½ lemon, a pinch of fennel, and salt and pepper to taste. Work the butter, adding the garlic, shallots and parsley gradually.
3. Leave to stand for 30 minutes before stuffing the snail shells (see page 192).
4. Will keep for 10 days in the refrigerator.

Beurre d'ail
Garlic Butter

00:10		00:00

American	Ingredients	Metric/Imperial
3	Garlic cloves	3
½ cup	Butter, at room temperature	125 g / 4 oz
	Salt and pepper	

1. Peel the garlic cloves. Crush them as finely as possible using a mortar and pestle.
2. Blend the garlic with the butter, working with the pestle to obtain an even paste. Add salt and pepper to taste.
3. Shape the garlic butter into a roll and wrap in foil. Chill until firm.
4. The butter will keep, in the refrigerator, for a few days. Cut it into equal slices to serve.

Cook's tip: if you don't like the aftertaste of garlic, chew some fresh parsley at the end of the meal.

Crush garlic to extract the maximum flavor

Beurre fondu

Drawn or Clarified Butter

⊿ 00:05   00:05 ⊖

American	Ingredients	Metric/Imperial
½ cup	Butter	125 g / 4 oz
½	Lemon (optional)	½
	Salt and pepper	

1. Warm the butter in a bowl placed over a saucepan of boiling water. As soon as the butter has melted, leave it to cool until it is lukewarm. After a moment or two, you will see a whitish deposit forming at the bottom of the bowl: this is the whey.
2. Pour the melted butter very gently into a container so that the whey is left behind. Add the juice of the ½ lemon, if liked, and season to taste.

Beurre maître d'hôtel

Parsley Butter

⊿ 00:15   00:00 ⊖

American	Ingredients	Metric/Imperial
⅔ cup	Butter, at room temperature	150 g / 5 oz
1 tbsp	Chopped fresh parsley	1 tbsp
½	Lemon	½
	Salt and pepper	

1. Put the butter on a plate. Mash it with a fork, then add the chopped parsley and juice of the ½ lemon. Add salt and pepper to taste. Work the mixture with the fork so as to make it very smooth.
2. Shape the butter into a roll and wrap in foil. Place in the refrigerator, where it will keep for a few days, and chill until firm.
3. When required, cut into equal slices and place on broiled [grilled] meat or fish.

Beurre de roquefort

Roquefort Butter

⊿ 00:10   00:00 ⊖

American	Ingredients	Metric/Imperial
½ cup	Butter, at room temperature	125 g / 4 oz
2 oz	Roquefort cheese	50 g / 2 oz
1 tsp	Cognac	1 tsp
1 tbsp	Prepared mustard	1 tbsp
	Pepper	

1. Mix the butter and roquefort with a fork, then add the cognac, mustard and pepper to taste. Continue to work the butter with the other ingredients to form a cream.
2. Shape into a roll, wrap in foil and chill until set.
3. You may serve roquefort butter, cut into thin slices, on canapés topped with tomatoes, gherkins or sausage.

Anchovy butter and snail butter

Beurre manié

Kneaded Butter

⊿ 00:02   00:00 ⊖

American	Ingredients	Metric/Imperial
1 tbsp	Butter, at room temperature	15 g / ½ oz
1 tbsp	Flour	1 tbsp

1. Mix the butter with the flour, using a fork, to make a paste.
2. Add the kneaded butter in one lump to a boiling sauce, and cook for a further 3-4 minutes, stirring constantly.
3. This quantity will thicken 2 cups [500 ml / ¾ pint].

Beurre noir

Black Butter

⊿ 00:00   00:05 ⊖
Black butter is the traditional accompaniment for skate.

American	Ingredients	Metric/Imperial
1 cup	Butter	250 g / 8 oz
5 tbsp	Vinegar	5 tbsp
3 tbsp	Capers	3 tbsp
	Salt and pepper	

1. Heat the butter in a frying pan over a brisk heat until it is a beautiful brown color. Remove from the heat.
2. Gently add the vinegar and capers. Add salt and pepper to taste. Stir to mix.

Sauce stocks and thickenings

Courts-bouillons and concentrates

Courts-bouillons and concentrates form the basis of a large number of fish soups and preparations for fish and shellfish. These are sometimes obtainable ready made, but their flavor does not compare at all with those you can make yourself. The recipe given here for a court-bouillon with vinegar, is extremely good for poaching fat fish (mackerel, tuna, salmon, etc), and that for a fish stock with white wine for lean white fish (sole, bream, etc).

Concentrate (fumet) is prepared from the bones and heads of fish, and is normally used for poaching. Courts-bouillons and concentrates may be kept in the freezer for several months.

Stocks

Stocks made from meat, poultry, fish or just vegetables form the basis for many soups, sauces and stews, and are also used for braising.

White stock, made from white meats (veal or poultry) and flavorings, is used for all dishes based on velouté sauce. Brown stock is made from beef, veal or poultry and flavorings first browned in butter. It is used for making soups, brown sauces, and for moistening stews and braises made with dark meats.

Stocks will keep perfectly for several months in the freezer.

Brown stock is used in the making of sauces as well as soups

Court-bouillon au vin blanc
Court-Bouillon with White Wine

▭▷ 00:15		00:40 ⌣
American	**Ingredients**	**Metric/Imperial**
4	Carrots	4
4	Large onions	4
2	Celery stalks	2
2 quarts	Dry white wine	2 l / 3½ pints
2 quarts	Water	2 l / 3½ pints
1	Fresh thyme sprig	1
1	Bunch of fresh parsley	1
4	Cloves	4
8	Black peppercorns	8
	Salt	

1. Peel the carrots and cut into slices. Peel and thinly slice the onions. Cut the celery into pieces about ¾ in / 2 cm long.
2. Pour the wine into a large saucepan and add the water, carrots, onions, celery, thyme, parsley, cloves, peppercorns and salt to taste. Bring to a boil and simmer for 40 minutes.
3. Leave to cool before straining.

Fonds brun
Brown Stock

This is made from beef, veal, poultry and vegetables, browned in butter before simmering in water with herbs and flavorings. It serves as a base for a large number of sauces.

▭▷ 00:15		05:00 ⌣
American	**Ingredients**	**Metric/Imperial**
3 tbsp	Butter or oil	3 tbsp
4	Carrots	4
4	Onions	4
1	Garlic clove	1
2 lb	Meaty bones (beef and veal), cut into pieces by the butcher	1 kg / 2 lb
1 lb	Beef for stew	500 g / 1 lb
2 quarts	Water	2 l / 3½ pints
1	Fresh thyme sprig	1
1	Bay leaf	1
2	Fresh parsley sprigs	2
	Salt and pepper	

1. Put the butter or oil into a large roasting pan.
2. Peel the carrots, onions and garlic and cut into large pieces. Place in the roasting pan with the bones and pieces of beef. Brown over a vigorous heat.
3. Add one-quarter of the water and scrape the bottom of the pan with a wooden spatula to detach the sediment.
4. Pour into a stewing pot and add the remaining water, the thyme, bay leaf, parsley, and salt and pepper to taste. Bring to a boil and simmer for 5 hours, skimming the scum from the surface occasionally.
5. Strain the stock through a dampened cloth placed over a large bowl. Twist the corners of the cloth to squeeze out all the liquid. Leave to cool.
6. Store the stock in the freezer if you are not going to use it during the following week.

Fonds blanc
White Stock

| | 00:30 | 04:00 |
| Makes about 3 quarts [3 l / 5 pints] | | |

American	Ingredients	Metric/Imperial
	Giblets from 3 chickens or 3 carcasses	
1½ lb	Shoulder of veal	750 g / 1½ lb
2 lb	Shin [knuckle] of veal	1 kg / 2 lb
4 quarts	Cold water	4 l / 7 pints
5	Carrots	5
4	Onions	4
2	Leeks	2
1	Celery stalk	1
1	Fresh thyme sprig	1
1	Bay leaf	1
2	Fresh parsley sprigs	2
	Salt and pepper	

1. Put the giblets into a cooking pot together with the shoulder of veal and the veal shin [knuckle]. Add the cold water. Place the pot over a medium heat and bring to a boil.
2. Meanwhile, peel and slice the carrots and onions. Slice the leeks and celery lengthwise. Skim the stock, then add the vegetables, thyme, bay leaf, parsley, and salt and pepper.
3. Simmer steadily for 3½ hours.
4. Leave the stock to cool until it is lukewarm, then remove any fat from the surface.
5. Strain the stock through a dampened cloth placed over a large bowl. Twist the corners of the cloth so as to squeeze out all the liquid. Cool completely.
6. Remove any remaining fat from the surface of the liquid.

Court-bouillon au vinaigre
Court-Bouillon with Vinegar

| | 00:15 | 00:40 |

American	Ingredients	Metric/Imperial
4	Carrots	4
4	Large onions	4
2	Celery stalks	2
2	Garlic cloves	2
1¼ - 2 cups	Wine vinegar	300 - 450 ml / ½ - ¾ pint
2 quarts	Water	2 l / 3½ pints
2	Fresh thyme sprigs	2
2	Bay leaves	2
6	Cloves	6
12	Black peppercorns	12
	Salt	

1. Peel and slice the carrots. Peel and thinly slice the onions. Cut the celery into pieces about ¾ in / 2 cm long. Peel and crush the garlic.
2. Pour the vinegar into a large saucepan and add the water, carrots, onions, celery, thyme, bay leaves, garlic and cloves. Bring to a boil, then add the peppercorns and salt to taste. Simmer for 40 minutes.
3. Leave to cool, then strain.

Fumet de poisson
Fish Stock

Fish stock forms the basis for a large number of sauces.

| | 00:15 | 01:00 |
| Makes 2 cups [500 ml / ¾ pint] | | |

American	Ingredients	Metric/Imperial
2	Large onions	2
2	Shallots	2
2	Large carrots	2
1½ lb	Fish trimmings (heads and bones)	750 g / 1½ lb
1	Bouquet garni	1
½	Lemon	½
1 cup	White wine	250 ml / 8 fl oz
1 quart	Water	1 l / 1¾ pints
	Salt and pepper	

1. Peel and finely chop the onions, shallots and carrots. Roughly crush the fish trimmings.
2. Place the vegetables and fish trimmings in a large saucepan and add the bouquet garni and the ½ lemon cut in two. Pour in the wine and water. Add salt and pepper to taste.
3. Bring to a boil, then reduce the heat and simmer for 1 hour.
4. Strain the stock. It will keep several months in the freezer.

Sauce espagnole (simplifiée)
Rich Brown Sauce
simplified

| | 00:20 | 04:00 |
| Makes 2 cups [500 ml / ¾ pint] | | |

American	Ingredients	Metric/Imperial
1 lb	Meaty veal bones, cut into pieces by the butcher	500 g / 1 lb
	Giblets from 2 chickens	
2	Carrots	2
2	Onions	2
1	Leek	1
3	Tomatoes	3
6 tbsp	Lard	75 g / 3 oz
1½ tbsp	Flour	1½ tbsp
1 tbsp	Tomato paste [purée]	1 tbsp
1 quart	Water	1 l / 1¾ pints
2 cups	White wine	500 ml / ¾ pint
	Salt and pepper	
1	Bouquet garni	1

1. Place the bones and giblets in a frying pan and brown.
2. Meanwhile, peel and chop the carrots and onions. Chop the leek. Peel the tomatoes (first plunging them in boiling water for 10 seconds) and cut into large pieces.
3. Melt the lard in a stewpan and add the onions, leek, carrots and tomatoes. Sprinkle with the flour. Mix well, then add the tomato paste diluted in the water, the wine, and salt and pepper to taste. Add the browned bones and giblets and bouquet garni. Bring to a boil. Leave to cook, uncovered, over a gentle heat for about 4 hours. Skim off the scum from the surface from time to time.
4. Strain the sauce. Leave it to cool, then remove any fat from the surface. Keep in the refrigerator until ready to use.

Aspic

This is a clear meat or fish stock which, once it has cooled, solidifies because of the gelatinous substances it contains. Aspics may be obtained naturally or by adding gelatin.

To color aspic
In order to obtain a beautiful amber tint, use caramel or food coloring which you add just before putting the aspic to cool. If you want to amuse your guests, tint it red, or why not green! Use the same colors as for confectionery or cocktails.

To flavor aspic
You may use different wines, spirits or liqueurs which you add, to taste, when the aspic has cooled but not set.

To chop aspic
Turn the firmly-set aspic onto a damp cloth, so that it does not stick, and chop it with a large knife.

To glaze food with aspic
Melt the set aspic without boiling. As soon as it is liquid, remove from the heat and leave to cool, stirring it with a wooden spoon in order to avoid air bubbles. As soon as the aspic begins to take on the consistency of a syrup, ladle it over the very cold food once or twice, putting the food in the refrigerator between the applications.

Gelée de viande

Aspic

This is a recipe for aspic made without gelatin, prepared from naturally gelatinous meat and bones.

�merican	Ingredients	Metric/Imperial
	00:35 — Makes 2½ quarts [2.5 l / 4½ pints]	05:00
American	**Ingredients**	**Metric/Imperial**
¼ cup	Butter	50 g / 2 oz
2 lb	Beef for stew (from the leg)	1 kg / 2 lb
1 lb	Shin [knuckle] of veal	500 g / 1 lb
1 lb	Crushed veal and beef bones	500 g / 1 lb
4	Carrots	4
2	Onions	2
1	Large leek	1
1	Celery stalk	1
4 quarts	Water	4 l / 7 pints
2	Boned calf's feet and the crushed bones	2
½ lb	Fresh bacon rind	250 g / 8 oz
1	Bouquet garni	1
	Salt and pepper	
½ lb	Chopped lean beef	250 g / 8 oz
3	Egg whites	3
1 tbsp	Chopped fresh tarragon	1 tbsp
1 tbsp	Chopped fresh chervil or parsley	1 tbsp

1. Heat the butter in a roasting pan and add the leg of beef, shin of veal, cut into pieces, and the crushed bones. Cook until well browned.
2. Meanwhile, peel and chop the carrots and onions. Chop the leek and celery.

3. Place the chopped vegetables in the bottom of a large stewpot together with the meat and place the bones on top. Pour on the water and add the sediment from the roasting pan. Bring to a boil, skimming off the scum that forms on the surface.
4. Add the calf's feet together with the crushed bones, the bacon rind and bouquet garni. Season with salt and pepper and simmer for about 4 hours.
5. Strain the stock. Leave to cool until lukewarm, then skim off the fat from the surface.
6. To clarify the stock, place it in a large saucepan with the chopped beef, egg whites, tarragon and chervil. Blend the whole thoroughly with a wooden spoon. Cook just at simmering point for 35 minutes.
7. Strain the stock through a dampened cloth, squeezing the cloth to extract all the liquid. Leave to cool, then place in the refrigerator to chill for 1-2 hours.
8. You may flavor the aspic before it has cooled using fortified wines such as port, sherry, madeira, etc, ⅔ cup [150 ml / ¼ pint] to each quart [1 l / 1¾ pints] aspic, or with dry white wine, 1¼ cups [300 ml / ½ pint] to each 1 quart [1 l / 1¾ pints] aspic.
9. The aspic will keep well in the freezer.

Gelée de poisson

Fish Aspic

This is a fish stock concentrate to which gelatin is added.

	00:30 — Makes 2 quarts [2 l / 3½ pints]	00:55
American	**Ingredients**	**Metric/Imperial**
2	Large carrots	2
2	Onions	2
2	Shallots	2
1 lb	Fish bones and trimmings	500 g / 1 lb
2	Fresh parsley sprigs	2
2	Fresh thyme sprigs	2
2	Bay leaves	2
⅔ cup	White wine	150 ml / ¼ pint
2 quarts	Water	2 l / 3½ pints
	Salt and pepper	
¾ lb	Whiting fillets	350 g / 12 oz
1	Bunch of fresh tarragon	1
2	Egg whites	2
2 envelopes	Unflavored gelatin	4 sachets

1. Peel and finely chop the carrots, onions and shallots. Crush the fish bones and trimmings. Place in a large saucepan and add the parsley, thyme, bay leaves, wine, water, and salt and pepper to taste. Cook for 30 minutes over a gentle heat, skimming off any froth that rises to the surface.
2. Meanwhile, chop the whiting fillets and tarragon. Place in a large bowl together with the egg whites and 1 cup [250 ml / 8 fl oz] water. Blend using a whisk.
3. Remove the fish stock from the heat and leave to cool. Strain the stock and add to the whiting mixture.
4. Pour the mixture back into the stewpot and bring to a boil over a gentle heat, stirring constantly with a wooden spoon. Simmer for 25 minutes.
5. Dissolve the gelatin in the remaining water. Stir into the fish stock.
6. Strain the fish stock through a dampened cloth, squeezing the cloth to extract all the liquid. Leave to cool, then place in the refrigerator to chill for 30 minutes before use.

Glace de viande
Meat Glaze

	00:30	07:00
	Makes about 1 quart [1 l / 2 pints]	

American	Ingredients	Metric/Imperial
9 lb	Veal bones, sawn into pieces	4 kg / 9 lb
4	Carrots	4
4	Onions	4
2	Garlic cloves	2
1	Celery stalk	1
2 lb	Tomatoes	1 kg / 2 lb
5 quarts	Cold water	5 l / 9 pints
	Bouquet garni	
1 tbsp	Tomato paste [purée]	1 tbsp
	Salt and pepper	

1. Preheat the oven to 500°F / 250°C / Gas Mark 9-10.
2. Place the bones in a roasting pan and bake until browned.
3. Meanwhile, peel and coarsely chop the carrots, onions and garlic. Put the garlic on one side. Chop the celery. Peel the tomatoes (first plunging them in boiling water for 10 seconds) and chop them.
4. Add the chopped carrots, onions and celery to the roasting pan and brown with the bones in the oven.
5. Transfer the browned vegetables and bones to a stewpot. Add the cold water and bring to a boil. Skim off any scum that rises to the surface.
6. Add the garlic, bouquet garni, tomatoes, tomato paste and salt and pepper to taste. Leave to cook for 7 hours over a low heat.
7. Strain the stock. Return it to the pan and boil, skimming frequently, until reduced to the consistency of a dark syrup. Strain again and leave to cool. Keep in the refrigerator.

Thickenings

To thicken a sauce or liquid preparation, flour, starch, cream, egg yolk, butter or blood is added.

Liaisons au beurre
Butter Thickenings

These can be difficult to make. To thicken a hot liquid, add cold butter cut into small pieces, whisking rapidly to emulsify it. (See also recipe for kneaded butter, page 112.)

Liaisons à la crème
Cream Thickenings

For it to become really silky, cream must lose half its initial volume through evaporation. Thus, if 1 cup [250 ml / 8 fl oz] crème fraîche is added to the same quantity of a sauce or other liquid, the thickening will occur when there is only ½ cup [125 ml / 4 fl oz] left.

To save time, boil the liquid to reduce it, then add the cream, stirring continuously, and leave to reduce once more, until the sauce is of the desired consistency.

Liaisons à la farine ou à la fécule
Flour Thickenings

Dissolve 1 tablespoon flour in 2 tablespoons cold liquid (water, milk, stock, court-bouillon, etc). Add the mixture to 2 cups [500 ml / ¾ pint] sauce to be thickened, stirring continuously until it just returns to a boil and leave to thicken.

Liaisons au jaune d'oeuf
Egg Yolk Thickenings

An egg yolk thickening makes a sauce silky and enriches it. To thicken 2 cups [500 ml / ¾ pint] of sauce, put 2 egg yolks into a bowl and beat them lightly. Add 1 tablespoon of the sauce, mixing continuously with a wooden spoon. Add half the sauce, continuing to stir. Return this mixture to the remainder of the sauce in the saucepan and warm over a gentle heat, stirring constantly, until thickened. Be very careful not to boil the sauce or it will curdle.

Liaisons au sang
Blood Thickenings

Add 2 tablespoons vinegar to animal blood to prevent it congealing. Away from the heat, trickle the blood into the sauce, beating vigorously. Be very careful not to boil.

Marinades
Foods such as meat, game, fish and poultry are often left to soak in a mixture of oil, wine or vinegar, herbs and spices before cooking. This liquid, or marinade, tenderizes and flavors the food.

Marinade-express pour grillade
Marinade for Broiled [Grilled] Meat

For small roasts, poultry, fish, etc.

	00:10	00:00

American	Ingredients	Metric/Imperial
	Pepper	
2	Large onions	2
1	Shallot	1
1	Bunch of fresh parsley	1
1	Garlic clove (optional)	1
1	Fresh thyme sprig	1
1	Bay leaf	1
2	Fresh tarragon sprigs	2
2 cups	Oil	500 ml / ¾ pint
1	Lemon	1

1. Place the meat to be marinated in a shallow dish. Sprinkle pepper over the meat. Do not salt: salt brings out the juices and prevents the meat from being sealed.
2. Peel and grate the onions and shallot. Chop the parsley. Peel and crush the garlic. Scatter the onions, shallot, parsley, garlic, thyme, bay leaf and tarragon over the meat.
3. Cover with the oil and the juice of the lemon. Leave to marinate for 2 hours, turning the meat frequently.

Marinade cuite, au vinaigre

Cooked Marinade with Vinegar

For meat or game.

▱ 00:15   00:30 🥘

American	Ingredients	Metric/Imperial
3	Medium-size carrots	3
2	Large onions	2
2	Shallots	2
1	Garlic clove	1
1	Celery stalk	1
1	Fresh parsley sprig	1
1 tbsp	Oil	1 tbsp
2	Fresh thyme sprigs	2
2	Bay leaves	2
8	Black peppercorns	8
1	Clove	1
1 quart	Dry white or red wine	1 l / 1¾ pints
1¼ cups	Vinegar	300 ml / ½ pint
	Salt and pepper	

1. Peel and slice the carrots, onions, shallots and garlic. Slice the celery. Chop the parsley.
2. Heat a little oil in a saucepan, add the carrots, onions, shallots, celery, garlic, parsley, thyme, bay leaves, peppercorns and clove. Cook over a gentle heat until the vegetables are golden and beginning to soften.
3. Add the wine and vinegar. Bring to a boil and cook over a low heat for 30 minutes. Leave to cool.
4. Place the meat or game in a mixing bowl. Add plenty of salt and pepper. Pour over the cooled marinade and leave to marinate for 24-48 hours in a cool place, but not in the refrigerator, turning the meat over two or three times.

Marinade crue à l'huile sans vinaigre

Uncooked Marinade without Vinegar

▱ 00:15   00:00 🥘

American	Ingredients	Metric/Imperial
3	Medium-size carrots	3
2	Large onions	2
2	Shallots	2
1	Garlic clove	1
	Celery stalk	
1	Fresh parsley sprig	1
2	Fresh thyme sprigs	2
2	Bay leaves	2
8	Black peppercorns	8
1	Clove	1
	Salt and pepper	
1 quart	Dry white wine	1 l / 1¾ pints
2 cups	Oil	450 ml / ¾ pint
6	Coriander seeds (optional)	6
6	Juniper berries (optional)	6

1. Peel and grate the carrots, onions, shallots and garlic. Grate the celery. Chop the parsley.
2. Put half the grated vegetables into the bottom of a mixing bowl. Add the parsley, thyme, bay leaves, peppercorns and clove.
3. Place the food to be marinated on top. Add salt and pepper to taste. Cover with the remainder of the vegetables. Add the wine and oil.
4. Leave to marinate in a cool place for 12-24 hours, turning the food frequently.

Cook's tip: if you are preparing this marinade for game, add the coriander seeds and crushed juniper berries.

Roux

A roux — a cooked mixture of butter and flour — is the basis of a large number of preparations and sauces such as white sauce, béchamel sauce, velouté sauce, burgundy sauce, madeira sauce, game sauce and so on.

There are three sorts of roux: white, golden and brown. The color will depend on how long the roux is cooked. It is particularly important, even in the case of white roux, which must not be allowed to color, to make sure that the roux is cooked for long enough to dispel the taste of the raw flour.

Roux blanc

White Roux

▱ 00:00   00:15 🥘

Take equal quantities of butter and flour. Melt the butter in a thick-bottomed saucepan. Add the flour all at once and stir vigorously over a very low heat. Continue to cook, stirring constantly, keeping the heat low to prevent the roux from coloring.

Roux blond

Golden Roux

▱ 00:00   00:15 🥘

Take equal quantities of butter and flour. Melt the butter in a thick-bottomed saucepan over a medium heat. Add the flour all at once and stir vigorously until the roux turns a golden color.

Roux brun

Brown Roux

▱ 00:00   00:15 🥘

Take equal quantities of butter and flour. Melt the butter in a thick-bottomed saucepan over a brisk heat. Add the flour all at once and stir vigorously over a brisk heat until the roux turns an even, light brown color. Take care not to burn the roux, otherwise it will be bitter. A brown roux is used for thickening brown sauces.

Cold sauces

Sauce tartare
Tartare Sauce

	00:25	00:00
	Makes 2 cups [500 ml / ¾ pint]	

American	Ingredients	Metric/Imperial
2 cups	Mayonnaise (see page 119)	500 ml / ¾ pint
2 tsp	Vinegar	2 tsp
8	Gherkins	8
1 tsp	Capers	1 tsp
2 tbsp	Chopped mixed fresh chives, tarragon and chervil	2 tbsp
	Salt and pepper	

1. If the mayonnaise is too thick, thin it with a little more vinegar, mixing vigorously.
2. Cut the gherkins into very small cubes. Chop the capers. Add to the mayonnaise with the herbs, and salt and pepper to taste. Mix well.
3. Keep in a cool place.

Aïoli
Garlic Mayonnaise

	00:15	00:00
	Makes 1 cup [250 ml / 8 fl oz]	

American	Ingredients	Metric/Imperial
7	Garlic cloves	7
1 cup	Olive oil	250 ml / 8 fl oz
1 - 2	Egg yolks, at room temperature	1 - 2
2 tbsp	Lemon juice	2 tbsp
	Salt and pepper	

1. Peel the garlic and crush in a mortar. Reduce to a cream by adding 1 or 2 tablespoons oil.
2. Add the egg yolks, then the remainder of the oil in a trickle, stirring the sauce continuously to thicken it like a mayonnaise. Add the lemon juice, and salt and pepper to taste.
3. Keep in a cool place.

Cook's tip: garlic mayonnaise is served as a dip with raw and cooked young vegetables, and with cold fish and boiled chicken.

Mayonnaise
Mayonnaise

	00:20	00:00
	Makes 2 cups [500 ml / ¾ pint]	

American	Ingredients	Metric/Imperial
2	Egg yolks, at room temperature	2
2 cups	Peanut [groundnut] oil	500 ml / ¾ pint
1 tbsp	Strong prepared mustard	1 tbsp
2 tbsp	Lemon juice or vinegar	2 tbsp
	Salt and pepper	

1. For the mayonnaise to be a success, the egg yolks and oil must be at the same temperature. Place the egg yolks and mustard in a large bowl. Add a very small quantity of oil and whisk it in with a balloon whisk or electric beater.
2. Add the remaining oil, very slowly at first. As soon as the sauce is thickening, the oil may be added more rapidly. While adding the oil, whisk or beat constantly. (The mayonnaise may also be made in a blender or food processor.)
3. Add the lemon juice or vinegar, a large pinch of salt, and pepper to taste. Mix well.

Cook's tip: if your mayonnaise separates or curdles, you can save it as follows: put 1 tablespoon of ice water in a clean bowl and gradually whisk or beat in the curdled mayonnaise.

Sauce au basilic (Pesto)
Basil Sauce

	00:15	00:00

American	Ingredients	Metric/Imperial
1	Large bunch of fresh basil	1
4	Garlic cloves	4
1 cup	Olive oil	250 ml / 8 fl oz
	Salt and pepper	

1. Crush the basil leaves and peeled garlic cloves in a mortar.
2. Transfer to a mixing bowl and add the oil, and salt and pepper to taste. Beat with an electric beater or whisk to obtain a green paste or use a blender or food processor.
3. Serve with roasted or broiled [grilled] veal or with pasta and rice and grated parmesan cheese.

Cook's tip: this sauce may be kept for several weeks in the refrigerator.

Garlic mayonnaise

Sauce vinaigrette
Vinaigrette Dressing

| | 00:07 | 00:00 |
| | Makes 4 tablespoons | |

American	Ingredients	Metric/Imperial
	Salt and pepper	
1 tbsp	Vinegar	1 tbsp
1 tsp	Prepared mustard	1 tsp
3 tbsp	Oil	3 tbsp
	Chopped mixed fresh herbs (parsley, tarragon, chervil chives) to taste	

1. Dissolve a pinch of salt in the vinegar. Mix in the mustard. Add pepper to taste.
2. Add the oil and chopped herbs. Mix thoroughly.

Sauce vinaigrette à la crème
Vinaigrette Dressing with Cream

| | 00:05 | 00:00 |
| | Makes 5 tablespoons | |

American	Ingredients	Metric/Imperial
½	Lemon	½
	Salt and pepper	
3 tbsp	Crème fraîche (see page 122)	3 tbsp
	Chopped mixed fresh herbs (parsley, tarragon, chervil chives) to taste	

1. Squeeze the ½ lemon and strain the juice. Dissolve a pinch of salt in the lemon juice.
2. Add the crème fraîche, chopped herbs and pepper to taste. Mix thoroughly.

Anchoyade
Anchovy and Garlic Purée

	00:05	00:00
	plus soaking	
	Makes about 1 ½ cups [350 ml / 12 fl oz]	

American	Ingredients	Metric/Imperial
16	Salted anchovies	16
1	Shallot	1
2 - 3	Garlic cloves	2 - 3
1 - 2 tbsp	Vinegar	1 - 2 tbsp
1 cup	Olive oil	250 ml / 8 fl oz
	Pepper	

1. Place the anchovies in a bowl and cover with cold water. Let them soak for 2 hours, changing the water several times.
2. Meanwhile, peel and chop the shallot. Peel and crush the garlic. Put the shallot and garlic into a blender or food processor.
3. Drain the anchovies. Fillet them, then rinse with cold water and pat dry on paper towels. Add to the blender.

4. Blend the anchovies, garlic and shallot to a smooth purée.
5. Add half the vinegar, then the oil in a trickle, blending continuously. Add pepper to taste (the sauce must be quite well seasoned) and the remainder of the vinegar.
6. Alternatively, the purée may be made in a mortar and pestle, or using a wooden spoon.
7. Serve the purée as a dip for raw vegetables or spread on warm toast. It also goes very well with broiled [grilled], fried or boiled fish.

Sauce aux noix et au roquefort
Walnut and Roquefort Sauce

| | 00:10 | 00:00 |

American	Ingredients	Metric/Imperial
3 oz	Roquefort cheese	75 g / 3 oz
⅓ cup	Walnuts	25 g / 1 oz
¼ cup	Olive oil	4 tbsp
1 tsp	Paprika	1 tsp
	Salt and pepper	

1. Crush the roquefort with a fork.
2. Place the walnuts in a blender, food processor or nut grinder. Reduce to a very fine powder.
3. Add the roquefort and then, gradually, the olive oil in a trickle. Continue blending the sauce until all the oil has been used.
4. Add the paprika, and salt and pepper to taste.

Rouille
Hot Pepper and Potato Mayonnaise

| | 00:15 | 00:00 |

American	Ingredients	Metric/Imperial
2	Garlic cloves	2
1	Small hot red pepper [chilli]	1
1	Slice of bread	1
1	Egg yolk	1
⅔ cup	Olive oil	150 ml / ¼ pint
2	Potatoes, boiled in fish soup or stew	2
	Salt and pepper	

1. Peel the garlic. Core the hot pepper and discard the seeds. Place the garlic and pepper in a mortar and crush with a pestle.
2. Soak the bread in a little water and squeeze dry. Add to the mortar and pound to a smooth paste.
3. Add the egg yolk and whisk the sauce, gradually incorporating the oil in a trickle. Mash the potatoes and blend into the sauce. Add salt and pepper to taste.
4. Alternatively, the sauce may be made in a blender or food processor.
5. This sauce is very strong and should be used in moderation. It is normally added to fish soups such as bouillabaisse (see page 145).

Sauce ravigote
Herb and Mustard Sauce

	00:10		00:00

American	Ingredients	Metric/Imperial
1	Hard-cooked egg	1
1 tbsp	Vinegar	1 tbsp
1 tbsp	Prepared mustard	1 tbsp
	Salt and pepper	
3 tbsp	Oil	3 tbsp
1	Garlic clove	1
	Chopped mixed fresh herbs (parsley, tarragon, chervil chives) to taste	

1. Place the egg in a mortar and crush with a pestle. Add the vinegar and mustard. Add salt and pepper to taste.
2. Work with the pestle so that the ingredients are well blended. Pour on the oil gradually, mixing continuously.
3. Peel and crush the garlic. Mix into the sauce. Add the herbs.

Egg and herb sauce

Sauce rémoulade
Rémoulade Sauce

	00:10		00:00

American	Ingredients	Metric/Imperial
3	Hard-cooked egg yolks	3
1	Egg yolk	1
1 tsp	Prepared mustard	1 tsp
1 cup	Oil	250 ml / 8 fl oz
1 tbsp	Vinegar or lemon juice	1 tbsp
	Salt and pepper	

1. Using a fork, mix the hard-cooked egg yolks with the raw egg yolk and mustard to make a very smooth paste.
2. Pour on the oil gradually, stirring with a wooden spoon until the mixture thickens and has the consistency of mayonnaise.
3. Alternatively, the sauce can be made quickly in a blender or food processor.

4. Add the vinegar or lemon juice, and salt and pepper to taste.

Sauce gribiche
Egg and Herb Sauce

	00:20		00:00

American	Ingredients	Metric/Imperial
4	Hard-cooked eggs	4
1 tbsp	Strong prepared mustard	1 tbsp
1 tbsp	Vinegar	1 tbsp
	Salt and pepper	
1 cup	Peanut [groundnut] oil	250 ml / 8 fl oz
1	Small bunch of fresh parsley	1
3	Fresh tarragon sprigs	3
6	Chive blades	6
1 tbsp	Capers	1 tbsp
1	Shallot	1
1	Small hot red pepper [chilli]	1

1. Shell the eggs and separate the yolks from the whites. Chop the whites. Put the yolks into a mixing bowl and mash them to a paste. Add the mustard, vinegar, and salt and pepper to taste.
2. Pour in the oil gradually in a trickle, beating vigorously with a whisk. Whisk the sauce like a mayonnaise until it is thick.
3. Chop the parsley, tarragon, chives and capers. Peel and chop the shallot. Mix into the sauce with the chopped egg whites. If you like very spicy sauces, add the hot pepper, crushed.

Sauce verte
Green Sauce

	00:35		00:05

American	Ingredients	Metric/Imperial
2	Egg yolks, at room temperature	2
1 tbsp	Strong prepared mustard	1 tbsp
2 cups	Peanut [groundnut] oil	500 ml / ¾ pint
2 tbsp	Wine vinegar	2 tbsp
	Salt and pepper	
2 oz	Watercress	50 g / 2 oz
2 oz	Spinach	50 g / 2 oz
1	Bunch of fresh chervil	1
1	Bunch of fresh parsley	1
1	Bunch of fresh tarragon	1

1. Put the egg yolks into a mixing bowl and add the mustard. Blend with a whisk, then add the oil gradually in a trickle, whisking continuously.
2. When the mayonnaise is thick, add the vinegar, and salt and pepper to taste.
3. Put the watercress, spinach and herbs into boiling salted water and cook for 5 minutes. Drain and cool under running water. Drain on paper towels.
4. Put the greens into a blender or food processor and blend to a smooth purée.
5. Add the purée to the mayonnaise and mix well.

Sauce raifort
Horseradish Sauce

	00:15		00:00

American	Ingredients	Metric/Imperial
2 - 3 tbsp	Grated horseradish	2 - 3 tbsp
2 tbsp	White wine vinegar	2 tbsp
2 tsp	Sugar	2 tsp
½ tsp	Mustard powder	½ tsp
½ tsp	Salt	½ tsp
½ tsp	White pepper	½ tsp
1 cup	Chilled crème fraîche (see page 122)	250 ml / 8 fl oz

1. Drain the horseradish, if necessary. Mix the horseradish with the vinegar, sugar, mustard powder, salt and white pepper.
2. Put the crème fraîche into another mixing bowl and whip until thick. Fold in the horseradish mixture. Taste and adjust the seasoning, if necessary.
3. Serve with red meats and broiled [grilled] and smoked fish, especially trout.

Crème fraîche
Crème Fraîche

	00:05		00:00
	plus maturing and chilling		

American	Ingredients	Metric/Imperial
1 cup	Heavy [double] cream	300 ml / ½ pint
1 cup	Sour cream	300 ml / ½ pint

1. Combine the creams in a mixing bowl and whisk lightly together.
2. Cover the bowl loosely with plastic wrap and leave in a warm place (at warm room temperature is sufficient) overnight for the culture to develop. (In cold weather, this may take up to 24 hours). At the end of the maturing time, the cream mixture will be thick and subtly tart.
3. Transfer the bowl to the refrigerator and chill for at least 4 hours.
4. Crème fraîche will keep in the refrigerator for 2-3 weeks, and will continue to develop its delicate tartness as it matures.

Cook's tip: crème fraîche can be purchased, or made at home if time permits. If you have no crème fraîche, heavy [double] cream may be used instead for cooked dishes, and sour cream for cold dishes.

Sauce vinaigrette au lard
Vinaigrette with Bacon

	00:00		00:05

American	Ingredients	Metric/Imperial
6 tbsp	Diced bacon	6 tbsp
2 tbsp	Vinegar	2 tbsp
	Salt and pepper	

1. Cook the diced bacon in a frying pan until crisp and brown and rendered of fat.
2. Pour the bacon and fat over a salad such as dandelion leaves, corn salad [lamb's lettuce] or red cabbage.
3. Pour the vinegar into the still-warm frying pan and stir to mix in the sediment on the bottom and sides of the pan. Pour over the salad. Add salt and pepper to taste and toss.

Artichokes can be served with melted clarified butter (see page 113) or hollandaise sauce (see page 126)

Hot sauces

Beurre blanc
White Butter Sauce

White butter sauce is a hot emulsified sauce which is often served with fish. It is rather tricky to make, because it is an unstable emulsion which tends to curdle. To make it successfully, add the cold butter cut into small pieces all at once to the boiling wine and shallots, whisking quickly to emulsify it.

	00:20		00:15	
American	**Ingredients**		**Metric/Imperial**	
12	Shallots		12	
⅔ cup	Dry white wine		150 ml / ¼ pint	
1 cup	Very cold butter		250 g / 8 oz	
1 tbsp	Crème fraîche (see page 122)		1 tbsp	
	Salt and pepper			

1. Peel and finely chop the shallots. Place in a saucepan with the wine. Bring to a boil and boil over a moderate heat until the mixture is reduced to one-third.
2. Meanwhile, cut the butter into pieces the size of a walnut.
3. Add the butter all at once to the shallots and cook over a gentle heat, whisking continuously to blend in the butter. Whisk in the crème fraîche.
4. As soon as the sauce has turned white (hence the name of the sauce), add salt and pepper to taste and pour it into a sauceboat.
5. If the sauce has curdled, put 1-2 tablespoons of cold water and 2 teaspoons very cold butter in a saucepan. Place over a gentle heat and gradually incorporate the curdled sauce, whisking vigorously.

Coulis de tomates
Thick Tomato Sauce

	00:20		00:45	
American	**Ingredients**		**Metric/Imperial**	
3 lb	Tomatoes		1.5 kg / 3 lb	
2	Garlic clove		2	
2	Small onions		2	
⅔ cup	Olive oil		150 ml / ¼ pint	
1	Bouquet garni		1	
5	Fresh basil leaves or		5	
1	Fresh tarragon sprig		1	
	Salt and pepper			
1 tbsp	Butter		1 tbsp	
1 tbsp	Flour		1 tbsp	

1. Peel the tomatoes (first plunging them into boiling water for 10 seconds), remove the seeds and chop into large pieces.
2. Peel and chop the garlic and onions. Place in a saucepan with the oil, bouquet garni, basil (or tarragon) and tomatoes. Add salt and pepper to taste. Cover and cook over a gentle heat for 25 minutes.
3. Uncover and cook for a further 10 minutes.
4. Remove the bouquet garni, squeezing it to extract the liquid. Strain the sauce into a clean saucepan. Return to the heat and bring back to a boil.

5. Mix the butter and flour to a smooth paste. Add this kneaded butter (beurre manié) to the boiling sauce and cook for 3-4 minutes, stirring continuously, until thickened.

Sauce aurore
Tomato Cream Sauce

	00:05		00:25	
American	**Ingredients**		**Metric/Imperial**	
1	Onion		1	
2 tbsp	Butter		25 g / 1 oz	
2 tbsp	Flour		2 tbsp	
2 cups	Milk		500 ml / ¾ pint	
1	Small bouquet garni		1	
2 tbsp	Tomato paste [purée]		2 tbsp	
2 tbsp	Crème fraîche (see page 122)		2 tbsp	
	Grated nutmeg			
	Salt and pepper			

1. Peel and coarsely chop the onion. Melt the butter in a saucepan, add the onion and cook for 5 minutes without browning. Add the flour and cook for 2 minutes, stirring continuously.
2. Remove from the heat and add the cold milk. Bring to a boil, stirring continuously. Add the bouquet garni and leave to simmer for 20 minutes.
3. Strain the sauce and return it to the saucepan. Add the tomato paste and crème fraîche. Add nutmeg, and salt and pepper to taste. Mix well.

Sauce barbecue
Barbecue Sauce

	00:10		00:25	
American	**Ingredients**		**Metric/Imperial**	
3	Onions		3	
5 tbsp	Olive oil		5 tbsp	
1 cup	Tomato paste [purée]		250 ml / 8 fl oz	
¼ cup	Vinegar (preferably cider vinegar)		4 tbsp	
⅔ cup	White wine or stock		150 ml / ¼ pint	
⅔ cup	Worcestershire sauce		150 ml / ¼ pint	
3	Fresh thyme sprigs		3	
1	Bay leaf		1	
2	Garlic cloves		2	
¼ cup	Honey		4 tbsp	
1 tsp	Prepared mustard		1 tsp	
	Salt and pepper			
	Tabasco sauce			

1. Peel and finely chop the onions. Heat the oil in a heavy saucepan, add the onions and soften over a moderate heat.
2. When the onions begin to brown, add the tomato paste mixed with the vinegar. Bring to a boil.
3. Add the wine, worcestershire sauce, thyme, bay leaf, peeled and crushed garlic, honey and mustard. Leave to simmer uncovered for 12 minutes.
4. Add salt and pepper and 2 or 3 drops of tabasco sauce.

Sauce béchamel
Béchamel Sauce

▬▭ 00:05   00:45 🍲

American	Ingredients	Metric/Imperial
5 tbsp	Butter	5 tbsp
5 tbsp	Flour	50 g / 2 oz
1 quart	Milk	1 l / 1¾ pints
	Grated nutmeg	
	Salt and pepper	
1	Medium-size onion (optional)	1
1	Clove	1
1	Small bouquet garni (optional)	1

1. Melt the butter in a heavy saucepan. Add the flour and stir vigorously with a wooden spoon until the butter completely absorbs the flour. Cook, stirring, for 2-3 minutes.
2. Remove from the heat and gradually pour in the milk, stirring continuously. Return the saucepan to the heat and bring slowly to a boil, stirring. Cook over a gentle heat for 10 minutes. Add nutmeg, salt and pepper to taste. The sauce is now ready to serve.
3. If liked, peel and halve the onion and stud with the clove. Add to the sauce with the bouquet garni and leave to simmer for a further 25-30 minutes, stirring frequently. Strain through a fine sieve.
4. This sauce keeps very well in the refrigerator. Cover it with a sheet of plastic wrap to prevent a skin forming.

Sauce chaud-froid
White Coating Sauce

This sauce is used to coat cooked poultry, fish or eggs.

▬▭ 01:00   03:30 🍲

American	Ingredients	Metric/Imperial
1½ lb	Shin [knuckle] of veal	750 g / 1½ lb
3	Carrots	3
3	Onions	3
3	Leeks	3
1	Celery stalk	1
3 quarts	Cold water	3 l / 5 pints
	Giblets from 3 chickens	
1	Bouquet garni	1
2 - 3	Cloves	2 - 3
	Salt and pepper	
16	Egg yolks	16
⅔ cup	Crème fraîche (see page 122)	150 ml / ¼ pint
1½ cups	Very fresh butter	350 g / 12 oz

1. Soak the veal in cold water for 3 hours.
2. Meanwhile, peel the carrots and onions and slice thinly. Slice the leeks and celery.
3. Drain the veal and put it in a large saucepan. Add the measured cold water, chicken giblets, sliced vegetables, bouquet garni, cloves, and salt and pepper to taste. Cook for 3 hours over a low heat, skimming off the scum from the surface from time to time.
4. Strain the stock through a dampened cloth placed over

another large saucepan. Twist the corners of the cloth to squeeze out all the liquid. Boil to reduce over a low heat until only 1 quart [1 l / 1¾ pints] remains.
5. Beat the egg yolks with the crème fraîche in a cold bowl. Gradually add the stock, whisking continuously. Finally add the butter, cut into small pieces, stirring well. Taste and adjust the seasoning.
6. Place the food to be coated on a rack over a tray. Spoon over the sauce several times. Leave to cool completely before serving.

Sauce bourguignonne
Burgundy Sauce

▬▭ 00:00   00:30 🍲

American	Ingredients	Metric/Imperial
¼ lb	Mushrooms	125 g / 4 oz
3 - 4	Shallots	3 - 4
¼ lb	Fresh pork sides [belly pork]	125 g / 4 oz
6 tbsp	Butter	75 g / 3 oz
1 quart	Red wine	1 l / 1¾ pints
1	Bouquet garni	1
	Salt and pepper	
2 tbsp	Flour	25 g / 1 oz

1. Chop the mushrooms. Peel and chop the shallots. Dice the pork very finely.
2. Melt 2 tablespoons [25 g / 1 oz] butter in a saucepan, add the mushrooms and pork and cook until lightly browned.
3. Add the red wine, shallots, bouquet garni, and salt and pepper to taste. Bring to a boil and reduce by half.
4. Remove the bouquet garni. Blend the flour and 2 tablespoons [25 g / 1 oz] butter to a paste (beurre-manié) and add to the sauce, stirring it with a whisk. Boil for 3-4 minutes until thickened, then add the remainder of the butter and whisk it in.

Burgundy sauce

Sauce bordelaise

Bordelaise Sauce

This sauce usually accompanies steak. The traditional recipe is a very complicated brown sauce enriched with poached beef marrow, but the one given here is a simplified version which is quicker and less expensive.

00:10   **00:15 to 00:20**

American	Ingredients	Metric/Imperial
5	Shallots	5
1¼ cups	Red wine	30 ml / ½ pint
1	Fresh thyme sprig	1
1	Bay leaf	1
	Salt and pepper	
¼ cup	Butter	50 g / 2 oz
1 tbsp	Flour	1 tbsp
1¼ cups	Beef stock	300 ml / ½ pint
2 oz	Beef marrow	50 g / 2 oz
2 - 3 tbsp	Meat juice	2 - 3 tbsp
1	Small bunch of fresh parsley	1

1. Peel and chop the shallots and place in a saucepan. Add the red wine, thyme, bay leaf and a pinch of salt. Bring to a boil and reduce by half.
2. Meanwhile, melt 1 tablespoon [15 g / ½ oz] butter in another saucepan. Add the flour and cook, stirring, until the roux has browned. Add the stock and salt and pepper to taste, stirring well. Cook over a low heat for 15 minutes, stirring frequently.
3. Dice the marrow. Poach for 5 minutes in boiling water, then drain.
4. Remove the thyme and bay leaf from the wine reduction. Add the wine to the other saucepan. Add the marrow cubes, adjust the seasoning and leave to simmer for 2-3 minutes.
5. Add the meat juice. Remove from the heat and add the remainder of the butter and the chopped parsley, stirring continuously.
6. If you do not use the sauce immediately, keep it warm in a bowl standing over a pan of hot water.

Sauce brune

Brown Sauce

00:15   **00:35**

American	Ingredients	Metric/Imperial
3	Onions	3
5 oz	Bacon	150 g / 5 oz
6 tbsp	Butter	75 g / 3 oz
6 tbsp	Flour	75 g / 3 oz
1 quart	Beef stock	1 l / 1¾ pints
	Salt and pepper	
1	Bouquet garni	1

1. Peel and thinly slice the onions. Cut the bacon into small cubes. Melt the butter in a saucepan, add the onions and bacon and cook over a very gentle heat until lightly browned.
2. Add the flour and stir to mix. Cook, stirring, until the mixture becomes light brown.
3. Add the stock and bring to a boil, stirring well. Add salt and pepper to taste. Add the bouquet garni. Cook for 20 minutes over a very gentle heat.

4. Taste and adjust the seasoning, then boil the sauce to reduce it for a further 10 minutes.
5. Before serving skim off any fat or scum from the surface and discard the bouquet garni.

Béchamel sauce

Sauce diable

Devil Sauce

00:15   **00:45**

American	Ingredients	Metric/Imperial
4	Shallots	4
2 cups	White wine	450 ml / ¾ pint
5 tbsp	Vinegar	5 tbsp
1	Fresh thyme sprig	1
1	Bay leaf	1
	Salt and pepper	
¼ cup	Butter	50 g / 2 oz
3 tbsp	Flour	25 g / 1 oz
2 cups	Beef stock	500 ml / ¾ pint
1	Bunch of fresh parsley	1

1. Peel and chop the shallots. Place them in a saucepan with the wine, vinegar, thyme sprig, bay leaf, and salt and pepper to taste. Boil until reduced to ½ cup [125 ml / 4 fl oz] liquid.
2. Meanwhile, melt 2 tablespoons [25 g / 1 oz] butter in a heavy saucepan over a medium heat. Add the flour and stir with a wooden spoon until the roux turns light brown in color. Add pepper to taste and pour on the stock, stirring constantly. Cook gently for 15 minutes, stirring from time to time.
3. Add the reduced wine mixture to the sauce and stir. Leave to cook over a low heat for about 5 minutes longer.
4. Chop the parsley. Remove the saucepan from the heat. Discard the thyme sprig and bay leaf. Swirl in the rest of the butter and the chopped parsley. Serve hot.

Sauce blanche
White Sauce

White sauce is prepared like béchamel (see page 124), but the milk is replaced by the same quantity of water or stock.

Sauce choron
Tomato Béarnaise Sauce

	00:20		00:30

American	Ingredients	Metric/Imperial
2 lb	Tomatoes	1 kg / 2 lb
1 quantity	Béarnaise sauce (see page 126)	1 quantity

1. Cut the tomatoes into large pieces and place in a heavy saucepan. Cook over a medium heat until thick and well reduced.
2. Strain through a food mill or conical strainer: you should obtain a very thick purée.
3. Mix the tomato purée with the béarnaise sauce.

Sauce béarnaise
Béarnaise Sauce

This sauce can be difficult to make. The secret of success is to stir it continuously during preparation. Also, the butter must be fresh and of excellent quality.

	00:10		00:20

American	Ingredients	Metric/Imperial
2	Shallots	2
2 - 3	Fresh tarragon sprigs	2 - 3
2	Fresh chervil or parsley sprigs	2
¾ cup	Butter	175 g / 6 oz
1 tbsp	Oil	1 tbsp
⅔ cup	Vinegar	150 ml / ¼ pint
	Salt and pepper	
3	Egg yolks, at room temperature	3
2 tbsp	Cold water	2 tbsp

1. Peel and finely chop the shallots. Chop the tarragon and chervil.
2. Heat 1 tablespoon [15 g / ½ oz] butter and the oil in a saucepan and add the shallots, half the chopped tarragon and chervil and the vinegar. Add pepper to taste. Place over a gentle heat and leave to reduce for 20 minutes until only 1 tablespoon of the vinegar remains.
3. Meanwhile, heat the remaining butter in a bowl standing over a pan of hot water. When the butter has melted, leave it to cool until it is lukewarm. After a moment or two, a whitish deposit will appear and fall to the bottom of the pan. Pour the melted butter into a bowl, leaving the sediment behind.
4. Place the egg yolks in a bowl over the pan of hot water, add the vinegar reduction and whisk well. Gradually incorporate the water, and salt and pepper to taste. Continue to whisk vigorously until the mixture becomes creamy. Remove from the

heat and, continuing to whisk, add the melted butter in a thin trickle. When all the butter has been incorporated, you will have a very smooth sauce.
5. Strain the sauce, if liked, then add the remaining tarragon and chervil.
6. If you do not use the sauce immediately, place the bowl over a pan of hot, but not boiling, water.

Cook's tip: Béarnaise sauce is taditionally served with all broiled [grilled] red meats, especially steak.

Sauce hollandaise
Hollandaise Sauce

	00:05		00:15

American	Ingredients	Metric/Imperial
1½ cups	Butter	350 g / 12 oz
4	Egg yolks, at room temperature	4
2 tsp	Cold water	2 tsp
½ tsp	Salt	½ tsp

1. Work the butter on a plate with a fork to soften it.
2. Place a saucepan half filled with water over the heat (choose a saucepan large enough for a large bowl to fit over it) and bring to a boil.
3. Put into a large bowl the egg yolks, cold water and salt. Place the bowl on the saucepan of boiling water and stir vigorously with a whisk.
4. As soon as the eggs begin to thicken, remove the bowl from the heat and add the softened butter in small pieces, whisking continuously (this is very important). You will then have a very smooth, pale yellow sauce. If you do not want to serve it immediately, place the bowl of hollandaise sauce back over the pan of hot but not boiling water, off the heat, to keep warm.

Cook's tip: when you incorporate the butter, if the sauce becomes too thick, immediately add a few more drops of cold water to thin it out.

Béarnaise sauce and Hollandaise sauce

Sauce Grand Veneur (simplifiée)

Grand Veneur Sauce
(simplified)

◢ 00:20   02:00 ⌷

American	Ingredients	Metric/Imperial
1	Garlic clove	1
2	Carrots	2
2	Onions	2
2	Shallots	2
¼ cup	Oil	4 tbsp
1¼ tbsp	Flour	1¼ tbsp
1 tbsp	Cognac	1 tbsp
⅔ cup	Vinegar	150 ml / ¼ pint
2 cups	Beef stock	500 ml / ¾ pint
2 cups	Red wine which was used for marinating game	500 ml / ¾ pint
	Salt and pepper	
6 tbsp	Red currant jelly	6 tbsp

1. Peel and crush the garlic. Peel the carrots, onions and shallots and cut into small cubes. Heat the oil in a frying pan, add the carrots, onions and shallots and cook over a very brisk heat, stirring, until lightly browned.
2. Sprinkle with the flour, stir well and leave to brown. Add the cognac, vinegar, beef stock, red wine which was used in the marinade and garlic. Bring to a boil, then season to taste with salt and pepper. Cook for 2 hours over a very gentle heat.
3. Place the red currant jelly in a saucepan and melt it over a very gentle heat. Cook until caramelized. Add to the sauce and cook for a further 5 minutes.
4. Strain the sauce into a clean saucepan, then boil to reduce it further until it has a silky consistency, skimming if necessary.

Sauce au kari

Curry Sauce

◢ 00:20   00:40 to 00:50 ⌷

American	Ingredients	Metric/Imperial
4	Medium-size onions	4
1 tbsp	Oil	1 tbsp
1 - 2 tbsp	Curry powder	1 - 2 tbsp
2 cups	Dry white wine	450 ml / ¾ pint
¼ cup	Water	4 tbsp
	Salt	
1 tbsp	Butter	1 tbsp
1 tbsp	Flour	1 tbsp
1 cup	Crème fraîche (see page 122)	250 ml / 8 fl oz

1. Peel and thinly slice the onions. Heat the oil in a saucepan, add the onions and cook gently until softened without browning (at least 25 minutes).
2. Sprinkle with 1 tablespoon curry powder and stir well. Pour on the wine and water. Add salt to taste but no pepper. Simmer for 20 minutes, stirring occasionally.
3. Purée the sauce in a blender or food processor, then return it to the saucepan. Add the second tablespoon of curry powder, if liked, and simmer for a further 5 minutes.

4. Meanwhile, mix the butter and flour to a paste (beurre manié) with a fork, then divide into small pieces. Add to the sauce and whisk to thicken.
5. Add the crème fraîche and heat through, stirring frequently. If the sauce is too thick, thin it out with a little boiling water.

Cook's tip: if this sauce is to be served with fish, substitute fish stock (see page 115) for the wine and water.

Sauce financière (simplifiée)

Madeira Mushroom Sauce (simplified)

◢ 00:30   00:30 ⌷

American	Ingredients	Metric/Imperial
14 oz	Small mushrooms	400 g / 14 oz
	Lemon juice	
6 tbsp	Butter	75 g / 3 oz
6 tbsp	Flour	75 g / 3 oz
1 quart	Chicken stock	1 l / 1¾ pints
	Salt and pepper	
1 - 2 tbsp	Truffle peelings	1 - 2 tbsp
1¼ cups	Madeira	300 ml / ½ pint

1. Clean the mushrooms and sprinkle with lemon juice to prevent them discoloring.
2. Melt the butter in a heavy saucepan over medium heat, add the flour and stir vigorously until the roux turns a golden color.
3. Add the chicken stock, stirring well. Add salt and pepper to taste. Add the whole mushrooms. Leave to cook over a low heat for 25 minutes.
4. About 5 minutes before serving, add the truffle peelings and madeira.

Sauce matelote

Sailor's Sauce

◢ 00:10   00:35 ⌷

American	Ingredients	Metric/Imperial
1	Garlic clove	1
1	Shallot	1
⅔ cup	Red wine	150 ml / ¼ pint
1¼ cups	Water	300 ml / ½ pint
1	Bouquet garni	1
	Salt and pepper	
6 tbsp	Butter	75 g / 3 oz
2 tbsp	Flour	25 g / 1 oz
2 tbsp	Cognac	2 tbsp

1. Peel and chop the garlic and shallot. Place in a saucepan with the wine, water, bouquet garni, and salt and pepper to taste. Boil to reduce to ⅔ cup [150 ml / ¼ pint] liquid.
2. Melt 2 tablespoons [25 g / 1 oz] butter in another saucepan over a very brisk heat. Add the flour and stir vigorously until the roux has browned. Add the reduced wine mixture and stir well to mix. Cook for a further 10 minutes.
3. Discard the bouquet garni. Add the cognac and remaining butter. Stir to mix and serve hot.

Sauce miroton

Brown Onion Sauce

	00:15		00:40

American	Ingredients	Metric/Imperial
4	Large onions	4
¼ cup	Lard	50 g / 2 oz
2 tbsp	Flour	25 g / 1 oz
2 tbsp	Tomato paste [purée]	2 tbsp
2½ cups	Beef stock	600 ml / 1 pint
	Salt and pepper	
2 tsp	Vinegar	2 tsp

1. Peel and finely chop the onions. Melt the lard in a saucepan, add the onions and brown slightly. Add the flour and stir vigorously until it browns.
2. Mix the tomato paste with the stock and add to the pan, stirring well. Add salt and pepper to taste. Leave to cook for a further 10 minutes, stirring frequently.
3. Stir in the vinegar and serve hot.

Sauce mornay

Cheese Sauce

	00:05		00:15

American	Ingredients	Metric/Imperial
6 tbsp	Butter	75 g / 3 oz
6 tbsp	Flour	75 g / 3 oz
1 quart	Milk	900 ml / 1½ pints
	Grated nutmeg	
	Salt and pepper	
1¼ cups	Grated gruyère cheese	150 g / 5 oz

1. Melt the butter in a heavy saucepan. Add the flour and cook, stirring with a wooden spoon, for 2-3 minutes. Remove from the heat and add the milk, stirring well. Return to the heat and cook, stirring, until the sauce has thickened. Leave to cook for about 10 minutes. Add nutmeg, salt and pepper to taste.
2. Add the cheese gradually, continuing to stir the sauce so that the cheese will melt evenly as it blends in.

Sauce mousseline

Whipped Cream Sauce

	00:00		00:10

American	Ingredients	Metric/Imperial
6 tbsp	Very fresh butter	75 g / 3 oz
½ cup	Crème fraîche (see page 122)	125 ml / 4 fl oz
⅔ cup	Vinegar	150 ml / ¼ pint
6	Black peppercorns	6
2	Egg yolks	2

1. Work the butter on a plate with a fork to soften it.
2. Pour the crème fraîche into an ice cold bowl. Whip until thick. Set aside.
3. Place the vinegar and peppercorns in a saucepan and cook over a low heat until only 1 tablespoon of liquid remains.

4. Remove from heat. Remove the peppercorns and beat in the egg yolks. As soon as the eggs begin to thicken, add the softened butter in small pieces, beating continuously.
5. Add the whipped cream and beat well. Serve the sauce with baked fish, or with lightly cooked young vegetables.

Sauce Nantua

Crayfish Sauce

	01:00		00:45

American	Ingredients	Metric/Imperial
2	Small onions	2
1	Shallot	1
10 tbsp	Butter	150 g / 5 oz
3 tbsp	Flour	3 tbsp
3 cups	Milk	750 ml / 1¼ pints
5	Fresh parsley sprigs	5
1	Fresh thyme sprig	1
	Grated nutmeg	
	Salt and pepper	
1	Small carrot	1
1	Small garlic clove	1
1	Small bouquet garni	1
8 - 10	Crayfish	8 - 10
1 tbsp	Vinegar	1 tbsp
1 cup	Crème fraîche (see page 122)	250 ml / 8 fl oz

1. Peel and finely chop one onion and the shallot. Melt 2 tablespoons [25 g / 1 oz] butter in a saucepan, add the onion and shallot and cook over a very moderate heat without browning. Sprinkle with the flour, stirring, and leave to cook for 2 minutes.
2. Pour on the milk, stirring well. Bring to a boil, stirring, then add the parsley, thyme and a pinch of nutmeg. Add salt and pepper to taste. Simmer over a very low heat until the sauce has reduced by about one-third.
3. Strain the sauce, pressing down on the solids to extract all liquid. Cover the surface with wax [greaseproof] paper to prevent a skin from forming and set aside.
4. Peel and thinly slice the remaining onion. Peel and grate the carrot. Peel and crush the garlic. Heat 2 tablespoons [25 g / 1 oz] butter in a frying pan, add the carrot, sliced onion, garlic and bouquet garni. Add pepper to taste and cook over a gentle heat until lightly browned.
5. Meanwhile, prepare the crayfish. Take them with one hand by the head, lowering the pincers forwards. With the other hand, grasp the central tail fin between the thumb and index finger. Twist and pull: a small black intestine will come out with the fin. Remove it. Pat the crayfish dry with paper towels.
6. Add the vinegar to the frying pan. Toss the crayfish into the pan and cook briskly until they turn red. Reduce the heat, cover and leave to cook for 8-10 minutes.
7. Remove from the heat. Leave to cool slightly, then peel the crayfish tails. Set aside. Crush the shells, heads and pincers in a mortar. Add the remainder of the butter and the vegetable mixture in the frying pan and knead it in with the pestle. Press the butter through a sieve with the pestle.
8. Uncover the white sauce and warm over a gentle heat. Add the crème fraîche and cook for 2-3 minutes, stirring.
9. Put the pan over another pan containing hot water. Incorporate the crayfish butter in small pieces. Add the crayfish tails.
10. Serve with eggs, fish and shellfish.

Crayfish sauce

Sauce madère (recette moderne)
Madeira Sauce
(modern recipe)

🚩 00:15   00:40 🍲

American	Ingredients	Metric/Imperial
½ lb	Beef for stew	250 g / 8 oz
3	Shallots	3
2	Small onions	2
½ cup	Butter	125 g / 4 oz
1	Fresh thyme sprig	1
1	Bay leaf	1
	Few fresh parsley sprigs	
3 tbsp	Cognac	3 tbsp
⅔ cup	Dry madeira	150 ml / ¼ pint
⅔ cup	Water	150 ml / ¼ pint
	Salt and pepper	
1 tbsp	Flour	1 tbsp
	Grated nutmeg	

1. Cut the meat into very small pieces. Peel and chop the shallots and onions.
2. Heat 1 tablespoon butter [15 g / ½ oz] in a saucepan, add the beef, shallots, onions, thyme, bay leaf and parsley and cook over a medium heat until the meat is browned. Sprinkle with the cognac, then pour on the madeira and water. Add salt and pepper to taste. Cover and simmer for 25-30 minutes.
3. Strain the sauce, pressing the solids to extract the liquid.
4. Melt 1 tablespoon [15 g / ½ oz] butter in the cleaned saucepan, add the flour and leave to brown, stirring continuously. Add the strained sauce, stirring, and bring to a boil. This sauce must be creamy but not thick so do not let it cook too long. Thin it out with a little boiling water if necessary.
5. Adjust the seasoning, and add a pinch of grated nutmeg. Remove from the heat and add the remaining butter in small pieces, whisking to blend it in.

Sauce moutarde
Mustard Sauce

🚩 00:10   00:10 to 00:12 🍲

American	Ingredients	Metric/Imperial
2	Shallots	2
¼ cup	Butter	50 g / 2 oz
2 tbsp	Flour	3 tbsp
1½ cups	Crème fraîche (see page 122)	350 ml / 12 fl oz
1 tbsp	Strong prepared mustard	1 tbsp
	Salt and pepper	
1	Egg yolk	1
	Lemon juice	

1. Peel and finely chop the shallots. Melt 2 tablespoons [25 g / 1 oz] butter in a saucepan, add the shallots and cook until soft but not brown.
2. Add the remainder of butter and, as soon as it has melted, add the flour. Cook for 2 minutes, stirring, then stir in the crème fraîche. Cook until the mixture thickens, stirring constantly.
3. Add the mustard. Add salt and pepper to taste. The sauce should be very spicy.

4. Lightly beat the egg yolk with a few drops of lemon juice and 1 tablespoon of the sauce. Add this mixture to the hot (but not boiling) sauce, stirring well. If the sauce seems too thick, thin it with a little boiling water added in small spoonfuls.
5. Serve with fish. The sauce may also be flavored with chopped herbs.

Sauce normande
Normande Sauce

🚩 00:15   00:15 🍲

American	Ingredients	Metric/Imperial
3 tbsp	Butter	40 g / 1½ oz
3 tbsp	Flour	40 g / 1½ oz
2 cups	Fish stock	500 ml / ¾ pint
	Salt and pepper	
1	Egg yolk	1
½ cup	Crème fraîche (see page 122)	125 ml / 4 fl oz

1. Melt the butter in a heavy saucepan. Sprinkle on the flour and cook, stirring, for 2-3 minutes.
2. Add the fish stock all at once, stirring continuously. Cook the sauce, stirring frequently, for 10 minutes.
3. Add salt and pepper to taste. Lightly beat the egg yolk with the crème fraîche. Add to the sauce and stir well. Do not allow the sauce to boil once you have added the egg yolk because it could curdle.

Sauce saupiquet
Spiced Wine Sauce

In the Middle Ages, saupiquet was simply a wine sauce thickened with toast which was served with roasted rabbit. Today it is served with chicken, veal and lamb.

🚩 00:10   00:35 🍲

American	Ingredients	Metric/Imperial
6	Shallots	6
8	Black peppercorns	8
⅔ cup	Wine vinegar	150 ml / ¼ pint
7	Juniper berries	7
¼ cup	Butter	50 g / 2 oz
1½ tbsp	Flour	1½ tbsp
1 cup	Beef stock	250 ml / 8 fl oz
1 cup	White wine	250 ml / 8 fl oz
⅔ cup	Crème fraîche (see page 122)	150 ml / ¼ pint
	Salt and pepper	

1. Peel and chop the shallots. Crush the peppercorns in a mortar. Place the shallots and peppercorns in a saucepan with the vinegar and juniper berries. Bring to a boil, then leave to reduce until the vinegar has completely evaporated.
2. Meanwhile, melt 2 tablespoons [25 g / 1 oz] butter in a heavy saucepan, add the flour and stir vigorously with a wooden spoon over a low heat. Add the stock and wine, stirring well. Leave to cook for 15 minutes, stirring frequently.
3. Add the shallot mixture to the sauce. Leave to cook for a further 15 minutes over a gentle heat, continuing to stir frequently. Strain the sauce.

4. Add the crème fraîche to the strained pepper sauce, and then the remainder of the butter. Add salt and pepper to taste. Serve very hot.

Sauce Périgueux

Madeira Truffle Sauce

Before making this sauce you will need to cook the madeira sauce and meat glaze.

American	Ingredients	Metric/Imperial
00:00		01:00
2 cups	White wine	500 ml / ¾ pint
1-2 tbsp	Truffle peelings	1-2 tbsp
2 cups	Madeira sauce (see page 130)	500 ml / ¾ pint
1 cup	Meat glaze (see page 117)	250 ml / 8 fl oz
1 tbsp	Cornstarch [cornflour]	1 tbsp
2 tbsp	Water	2 tbsp
6 tbsp	Butter	75 g / 3 oz

1. Place the wine, truffle peelings and madeira sauce in a heavy saucepan. Cover and simmer for 20 minutes.
2. Add the meat glaze and simmer for a further 20 minutes.
3. Dissolve the cornstarch in the water. Add to the sauce, stirring well, and cook for 5 minutes.
4. Add the butter gradually, stirring constantly. Cover the chosen food with the sauce just before serving.

Sauce poivrade

Game Sauce

This sauce is usually served with game.

American	Ingredients	Metric/Imperial
00:20		00:50
4	Carrots	4
4	Medium-size onions	4
3	Shallots	3
1	Leek, white part only	1
6 tbsp	Oil	6 tbsp
	Game trimmings (all the bits removed before cooking)	
1¼ lb	Flour	1¼ tbsp
2 cups	Wine from the game marinade or dry white wine	500 ml / ¾ pint
⅔ cup	Wine vinegar	150 ml / ¼ pint
	Salt and pepper	
1	Bouquet garni	1
6-7	Black peppercorns	6-7
1 tbsp	Red currant jelly	1 tbsp
¼ cup	Butter	50 g / 2 oz

1. Peel and chop the carrots, onions and shallots. Chop the leek. Heat the oil in a frying pan, add the chopped vegetables and game trimmings and cook until browned. Add the flour and stir well.

2. Add the wine and vinegar. Season to taste with salt and pepper. Add the bouquet garni, crushed peppercorns and red currant jelly. Cook for 5 minutes over a very low heat, stirring frequently.
3. Strain the sauce. Swirl in the butter.

Sauce poulette

Chicken Cream Sauce with Onions

American	Ingredients	Metric/Imperial
00:10		00:20
5 oz	Pearl [button] onions	150 g / 5 oz
½ cup	Butter	125 g / 4 oz
2 tbsp	Flour	2 tbsp
1¾ cups	Chicken stock	400 ml / 14 fl oz
	Salt and pepper	
½	Lemon	½
2	Egg yolks	2

1. Peel the onions. Set aside. Melt ¼ cup [50 g / 2 oz] butter in a heavy saucepan. Add the flour and stir well, then add the chicken stock. Stir over a gentle heat until boiling.
2. Place the onions in the saucepan. Add salt and pepper to taste. Simmer for 15 minutes over a very gentle heat.
3. About 5 minutes before cooking is completed, add the juice of the ½ lemon and bring back to a boil.
4. Mix the egg yolks with the remaining butter to obtain a cream. Add 1 tablespoon of the sauce, whisking continuously. Add the remaining sauce, continuing to stir. Serve hot.

Sauce suprême

Mushroom and Chicken Cream Sauce

American	Ingredients	Metric/Imperial
00:30		00:30
5 oz	Mushrooms	150 g / 5 oz
½	Lemon	½
¼ cup	Butter	50 g / 2 oz
¼ cup	Flour	50 g / 2 oz
5 cups	Chicken stock	1.2 l / 2 pints
½ cup	Crème fraîche (see page 122)	125 ml / 4 fl oz
2	Egg yolks	2
	Salt and pepper	

1. Cut the mushrooms into small cubes. Place them in a bowl of water to which the juice of ½ lemon has been added to prevent them from discoloring.
2. Melt the butter in a heavy saucepan. Add the flour and stir vigorously over a low heat. Stir in the chicken stock. Add the drained mushrooms. Leave to cook for 30 minutes over a low heat.
3. Add the crème fraîche and stir for a few minutes over a gentle heat.
4. Lightly beat the egg yolks in a mixing bowl. Add 2 tablespoons of the sauce and stir well. Gradually stir in the remaining sauce. Add salt and pepper to taste.

Sauce veloutée
Velouté Sauce

	00:15		00:03
	Makes 2 cups [500 ml / ¾ pint]		

American	Ingredients	Metric/Imperial
2 tbsp	Butter	25 g / 1 oz
1 tbsp	Flour	1 tbsp
⅔ cup	Cooking liquid from the dish to be accompanied	150 ml / ¼ pint
2	Egg yolks	2
½ cup	Crème fraîche (see page 122)	125 ml / 4 fl oz
	Lemon juice	
	Salt and pepper	

1. Melt the butter in a saucepan, add the flour and cook for 2 minutes, stirring.
2. Pour in the cooking liquid, stirring well. Bring to a boil and simmer for 1 minute over a gentle heat.
3. Leave to cool a little, then add the egg yolks mixed with the crème fraîche. Add a few drops of lemon juice, and salt and pepper to taste. Cook, stirring, until thick and smooth. Do not allow to boil.

Sauce riche
Rich Sauce

This is a variation of mushroom and chicken cream sauce (see page 131). To the diced mushrooms, add ⅔ cup [150 ml / ¼ pint] cognac, 1-2 tablespoons truffle peelings and, to be completely traditional, 1 tablespoon lobster butter.

Sauce zingara
Brown Julienne Sauce

This sauce is served with all roast meats.

	00:30		00:25 to 00:30

American	Ingredients	Metric/Imperial
3	Shallots	3
2	Carrots	2
1	Onion	1
1	Leek, white part only	1
7 tbsp	Butter	90 g / 3½ oz
2 cups	Beef stock	500 ml / ¾ pint
1	Bouquet garni	1
	Cayenne pepper	
¼ lb	Large mushrooms	125 g / 4 oz
½	Lemon	½
2 oz	Cooked tongue	50 g / 2 oz
2 oz	Cooked ham	50 g / 2 oz
¼ cup	Port wine	4 tbsp
1 - 2 tbsp	Truffle peelings	1 - 2 tbsp
	Salt and pepper	

1. Peel and chop the shallots, carrots and onions. Chop the leek. Melt 3 tablespoons [40 g / 1½ oz] butter in a saucepan and add the chopped vegetables, stock, bouquet garni and a pinch of cayenne pepper. Bring to a boil and leave to reduce for 15 minutes.

2. Meanwhile, dice the mushrooms. Place them in a bowl of water to which the juice of ½ lemon has been added to prevent them from discoloring. Cut the tongue and ham into small cubes. Place the drained mushrooms, tongue and ham in a heavy saucepan and add the port, 2 tablespoons [25 g / 1 oz] butter and the truffle peelings. Cook over a low heat until the port has reduced by half.
3. Strain the brown sauce into the saucepan containing the tongue, mushrooms and truffles and cook for 2-3 minutes, stirring well. Add salt and pepper to taste.
4. Swirl in the remainder of the butter.

Robert sauce

Sauce Robert
Robert Sauce

	00:05		00:25

American	Ingredients	Metric/Imperial
6	Onions	6
¼	Butter	50 g / 2 oz
3 tbsp	Flour	25 g / 1 oz
1 tbsp	Tomato paste [purée]	1 tbsp
⅔ cup	White wine	150 ml / ¼ pint
1 cup	Beef broth or stock	250 ml / 8 fl oz
	Salt and pepper	
2 tbsp	Prepared mustard	2 tbsp

1. Peel and thinly slice the onions. Heat the butter in a saucepan, add the onions and cook over a gentle heat, stirring frequently, until soft and golden. Add the flour and cook for a few minutes, continuing to stir.
2. Add the tomato paste. Stir in the white wine and broth. Add salt and pepper to taste. Leave to simmer for 20 minutes.
3. Add the mustard and mix thoroughly.

Sauce soubise

Onion Sauce

00:20   00:35

American	Ingredients	Metric/Imperial
10	Onions	10
1 cup	Stock or milk	250 ml / 8 fl oz
¼ cup	Butter	50 g / 2 oz
1¼ tbsp	Flour	1¼ tbsp
2 cups	Milk	500 ml / ¾ pint
	Grated nutmeg	
	Salt and pepper	

1. Peel and thinly slice the onions. Blanch them for 2 minutes in boiling water, then drain and rinse under cold running water. Drain again. Place them in a saucepan and cover with the stock or milk. Leave to cook gently for about 15 minutes.
2. Meanwhile, melt 2 tablespoons [25 g / 1 oz] butter in another saucepan. Add the flour and stir well. Cook gently, continuing to stir, for about 3 minutes. Add the milk, stirring vigorously. Bring to a boil and simmer for 10 minutes over a low heat.
3. When the onions have softened completely, increase the heat and boil off any liquid, stirring constantly. Purée the onions in a blender or food processor.
4. Add the onion purée to the sauce and heat, stirring.
5. Add a pinch of nutmeg, and salt and pepper to taste. Dot the remaining butter over the sauce to prevent a skin from forming and keep hot. Stir the sauce before serving.

Sauce tomate

Tomato Sauce

00:10   00:45

American	Ingredients	Metric/Imperial
3 lb	Tomatoes	1.5 kg / 3 lb
2	Small onions	2
2	Garlic cloves (optional)	2
⅔ cup	Olive oil	150 ml / ¼ pint
1	Bay leaf	1
1	Fresh thyme sprig	1
1	Bunch of fresh parsley	1
5	Fresh basil leaves or	5
1	Fresh tarragon sprig	1
	Salt and pepper	
1 - 2	Sugar cubes	1 - 2

1. Peel the tomatoes (first plunging them into boiling water for 10 seconds), remove the seeds and chop roughly. Peel and chop the onions and garlic.
2. Place the tomatoes, onions and garlic in a saucepan and add the oil, bay leaf, thyme, parsley and basil or tarragon. Add salt and pepper to taste. Cook over a high heat until excess liquid has completely evaporated. This will take about 40 minutes.
3. Taste and if you find the sauce too sharp, add the sugar cubes. Pass the sauce through a food mill or sieve.
4. You will obtain a more or less liquid sauce depending on the season and quality of the tomatoes. If after straining you find it rather thin, reduce it quickly over a brisk heat until it is of the desired consistency.
5. This sauce will keep for a week in the refrigerator.

Basil sauce (see page 119)

CHAPTER 9

Broths, Consommés and Soups

Guidelines

Vegetable stocks and broths
Soak dried legumes and pulses in water for several hours, then put them in fresh cold water to cook. Lentils are an exception to this rule, since they are not normally soaked.

Thicken soup when necessary with a spoonful of instant mashed potato flakes.

Beef or poultry stocks and broths
Try to make your stock the day before it is needed so the fat will have time to rise to the surface and solidify. You will be able to remove it in this form easily by drawing a skimming ladle or spoon over the surface.

Bouillon or stock cubes are often very salt, so keep this in mind when you are seasoning your soup.

Making a bouquet garni
Used to flavor soups and broths, a traditional bouquet garni consists of a fresh or dried bay leaf, several sprigs of fresh parsley or parsley stalks (with stems and roots) and a sprig of fresh or dried thyme, all tied together with kitchen thread. Try a selection of different herbs and flavorings for variety — tarragon, marjoram, basil, sage, fennel, oregano, rosemary or dried lemon and orange rind for example — or even a little celery or the green part of a leek.

Puréed vegetable soups
Wash the vegetables carefully to remove any dirt, but do not leave them to soak or they will lose most of their vitamins and mineral salts.

Raw vegetables will cook more quickly if you first mince them in a food processor. Remember that the flavor of garlic, shallots, onions and leeks is intensified by mincing so reduce the proportion of these foods accordingly. Process the vegetables once again after they have been cooked.

Croûtons
For best results, use stale rather than fresh bread. Toast croûtons instead of frying them for a healthy result. If you must fry croûtons, use only a little butter or oil and brown them over a gentle heat.

Leftovers
Save vegetable peelings (making sure you have scrubbed the vegetables first) and the water in which they have been cooked to make an economical basis for soups.

Bouillon de poule

Chicken Broth

	00:15		01:30

American	Ingredients	Metric/Imperial
	Giblets of 3 chickens	
2 quarts	Water	2 l / 3½ pints
1	Bouquet garni	1
3	Carrots	3
1	Turnip	1
1	Celery stalk	1
1	Large onion	1
2	Garlic cloves	2
3	Leeks	3
	Salt and pepper	

1. Place the giblets in a large saucepan and add the water and bouquet garni. Bring to a boil. Cover and simmer over a medium heat for 45 minutes.
2. Meanwhile, peel and dice the carrots and turnip. Chop the celery. Peel and quarter the onion. Peel the garlic and split the cloves in half. Trim the leeks, cut in half lengthwise and wash well in cold water, separating the leaves. Drain and chop coarsely.
3. Place all the vegetables in the pan. Add salt and pepper to taste. Return to a boil and simmer, covered, for a further 45 minutes.
4. Strain the broth into a warmed soup tureen. If liked, serve the giblets on a plate with a sauceboat of vinaigrette dressing (see page 120).

Soupe de poissons

Fish Soup

	00:20		00:40

American	Ingredients	Metric/Imperial
1	Porgy or scup [sea bream]	1
3	Small ocean perch [gurnards]	3
2	Whiting	2
6	Small red snappers or mullet	6
3	Slices of eel	3
6	Small sea bass	6
1	Onion	1
1	Leek, white part only	1
5 tbsp	Olive oil	5 tbsp
6	Garlic cloves	6
1	Fresh fennel sprig	1
1	Fresh thyme sprig	1
	Pared rind of 1 orange	
	Salt and pepper	
2 quarts	Water	2 l / 3½ pints
½ tsp	Saffron powder	½ tsp
1	Sliced french loaf	1
1 cup	Grated gruyère cheese	125 g / 4 oz

1. Ask your fish merchant to clean and scale all the fish. Cut the porgy, perch and whiting into slices. Peel and thinly slice the onion. Trim and thinly slice the leek.

2. Heat the olive oil in a large saucepan. Add the onion, leek, heads and tails from the larger fish, 4 garlic cloves (unpeeled but crushed), fennel, thyme and orange rind. Add salt and pepper to taste. Cook for 3-4 minutes, then cover with the water. Bring to a boil and leave to cook for 20 minutes.

3. Preheat the oven to 350°F / 180°C / Gas Mark 4.

4. Strain the soup. Return the strained soup to the pan and add the saffron, eel, perch and porgy. Bring to a boil over a brisk heat, then simmer for 5 minutes. Add the rest of the fish and leave to simmer for a further 5 minutes.

5. Meanwhile, rub the bread slices with the remaining garlic, peeled and halved. Discard the garlic. Sprinkle the bread with the cheese and arrange the slices on a baking sheet. Bake for 3-4 minutes or until the cheese has melted.

6. Arrange the fish on a warmed serving dish. Serve the fish with the soup and slices of french bread.

Fish soup

Bouillon gras

Beef Broth

	00:25		03:30

American	Ingredients	Metric/Imperial
2 lb	Beef for stew with bones	1 kg / 2 lb
2 tsp	Salt	2 tsp
6	Black peppercorns	6
3 quarts	Water	3 l / 5 pints
3	Carrots	3
3	Turnips	3
2	Leeks	2
1	Celery stalk	1
	Slices of bread for serving	

1. Put the beef and bones, salt and peppercorns into a large pan and cover with the cold water. Bring to a boil, skimming off the scum that rises to the surface.

2. Meanwhile, peel the carrots and turnips. Trim the leeks and celery.

3. Add the vegetables to the pan. Bring back to a boil, then lower the heat and leave to simmer for 3 hours.

4. A few minutes before serving, toast a few slices of bread and place them in a warmed soup tureen.

5. Skim off any fat from the surface of the broth and strain the broth into the tureen.

Cook's tip: if you leave the broth to cool, so much the better. The fat will set on the surface and can therefore be removed easily. For a more complete clarification refer to the recipe for consommé (page 138).

Crème aux champignons

Cream of Mushroom Soup

	00:15		00:35

American	Ingredients	Metric/Imperial
1½ lb	Mushrooms	750 g / 1½ lb
¼ cup	Lemon juice	4 tbsp
3	Shallots	3
6 tbsp	Butter	75 g / 3 oz
6 tbsp	Flour	75 g / 3 oz
1½ quarts	Chicken broth (see page 136)	1.5 l / 2½ pints
	Salt and pepper	
1¼ cups	Crème fraîche (see page 122)	300 ml / ½ pint

1. Set 6 mushrooms aside for the garnish and chop the remainder. Sprinkle with 3 tablespoons of lemon juice. Peel and chop the shallots.

2. Melt the butter in a saucepan, add the chopped shallots and mushrooms and cook until all the vegetable water has evaporated. Sprinkle with the flour and stir thoroughly.

3. Add the broth and bring to a boil, stirring continuously with a wooden spoon. Season with salt and pepper, if necessary. Leave to cook over a gentle heat for 15 minutes.

4. Put the soup into a food processor or blender and purée until smooth. Return to the saucepan and add the crème fraîche, beating with a whisk. Simmer over a medium heat for 10 minutes.

5. Meanwhile, chop the reserved mushrooms and sprinkle with the remaining lemon juice. Add to the soup and serve hot.

Consommé Belle-Hélène

Consommé with Eggs and Milk

	00:05		00:15

American	Ingredients	Metric/Imperial
3 cups	Cold broth (see left)	750 ml / 1¼ pints
1	Egg, separated	1
¼ cup	Ground rice	4 tbsp
3 cups	Milk	750 ml / 1¼ pints
1	Egg yolk	1
½ cup	Grated gruyère cheese	50 g / 2 oz

1. Remove the layer of fat from the broth using a skimming spoon. Heat the broth in a saucepan.

2. Beat the egg white in a bowl. Pour it in a trickle into the hot (but not boiling) broth. Stir gently until the egg white has solidified. Pour the whole through a strainer into a clean saucepan. You have now made what is referred to in culinary terms as a 'clarification.'

3. Return the consommé to the heat. Mix the ground rice with the cold milk, and when the consommé begins to boil, add the rice mixture, stirring thoroughly. When it boils for a second time, lower the heat and leave to simmer for 10 minutes.

4. Mix the egg yolks with 1 tablespoon cold milk in a soup tureen. Pour in the consommé, stirring continuously. Serve the consommé with the cheese.

Consommé

Consommé

This is a beef or chicken broth from which the impurities have been removed, thereby making it perfectly clear.

00:10 plus cooling   **01:40**

American	Ingredients	Metric/Imperial
2 quarts	Beef or chicken broth (see pages 136, 137)	2 l / 3½ pints
1	Carrot	1
1	Leek	1
1	Large celery stalk	1
2 - 3	Fresh chervil or parsley sprigs	2 - 3
1	Fresh tarragon sprig	1
4	Very ripe tomatoes	4
1 lb	Chopped meat	500 g / 1 lb
1	Egg white	1
	Pepper	

1. Cool the broth in the saucepan until the fat has set on the surface. Remove this fat using a skimming spoon.
2. Peel the carrot. Trim the leek and celery and slice them all finely. Chop the chervil, tarragon and tomatoes.
3. Mix together the vegetables, herbs, chopped meat and egg white. Add a little pepper and then a little water.
4. Pour the whole into the saucepan containing the broth and warm over a very gentle heat, scraping the bottom of the saucepan so that the egg white does not stick. Leave to cook gently for 1½ hours without stirring.
5. When the mixture froths and rises in the pan, skim off the fat and froth with a ladle, and leave to cook once again.
6. Strain the consommé through a fine sieve. All that now remains to be done is to season it in various ways.

Cook's tip: you can flavor your consommé by adding a liqueur glass of sherry when you are about to serve it.

Bilibi

Chilled Mussel Cream Soup

00:20 plus chilling   **00:35**

American	Ingredients	Metric/Imperial
1½ quarts	Cold water	1.5 l / 2½ pints
1 lb	Fish trimmings (bones and heads)	500 g / 1 lb
1	Bouquet garni	1
1	Celery stalk	1
	Salt and pepper	
6½ lb (5½ quarts)	Fresh mussels	3 kg / 6½ lb
2	Shallots	2
1 cup	White wine	250 ml / 8 fl oz
1 cup	Milk	250 ml / 8 fl oz
1 cup	Crème fraîche (see page 122)	250 ml / 8 fl oz
1 tbsp	Chopped fresh chives	1 tbsp

1. Pour the cold water into a large saucepan and add the fish trimmings, coarsely crushed, the bouquet garni, celery salt and pepper to taste. Bring to a boil and leave to simmer for 30 minutes.
2. Strain the fish stock and leave to cool.
3. Scrub the mussels thoroughly, changing the water at least 3 times. Peel and chop the shallots.
4. Place the mussels and shallots in a pan with the white wine and pepper to taste. Place over a brisk heat and cook until the mussels open, shaking the pan several times to turn the mussels over.
5. Remove the mussels from their shells and place on one side. Keep cool. Discard any mussels that remain closed. Strain the mussel cooking liquid through cheesecloth or muslin to remove any grit. Mix the liquid with the cooled fish stock. Whisk in the milk and crème fraîche.
6. Pour into a soup tureen and cover. Chill until ready to serve.
7. At the last moment, add the mussels and chopped chives. Taste and adjust the seasoning.

Bortsch

Beet Soup

01:00 plus cooling   **03:00 to 03:30**

American	Ingredients	Metric/Imperial
5 quarts	Cold water	5 l / 8¾ pints
2 lb	Brisket of beef	1 kg / 2 lb
3 - 4	Veal bones	3 - 4
2	Large onions	2
2	Garlic cloves	2
4	Tomatoes	4
¼	Head of celeriac	¼
3	Carrots	3
1	Medium-size raw beet [beetroot]	1
4	Medium-size leeks	4
1 lb	Kale	500 g / 1 lb
3 tbsp	Butter or lard	40 g / 1½ oz
1 tbsp	Oil	1 tbsp
2	Cloves	2
4	Fresh parsley sprigs	4
	Salt and pepper	
4	Potatoes	4
2 tbsp	Flour	2 tbsp
3	Fresh dill sprigs or	3
1 tbsp	Dried dill	1 tbsp
¾ cup	Sour or heavy [double] cream	175 ml / 6 fl oz

1. This dish is best prepared the day before. Put the cold water into a large saucepan and add the brisket of beef and veal bones. Bring to a boil, skimming thoroughly.
2. Meanwhile, peel and chop the onions and garlic. Peel the tomatoes (first plunging them in boiling water for 10 seconds), seed and chop. Peel the celeriac, carrots and beet. Cut the celeriac, carrots, beet and trimmed leeks into matchsticks. Shred the kale.
3. Melt 1 tablespoon butter or lard with the oil in a heavy saucepan and add the onions and garlic. Soften them without browning.
4. Add the tomatoes, leeks, kale, celeriac, beet and carrots. Stir, then cover and leave to cook for 10-15 minutes.
5. Add the vegetables to the saucepan containing the beef

and bones. Add the cloves, parsley and salt and pepper to taste. Leave to simmer, covered, for 3 hours.

6. Allow to cool, then remove any fat from the surface.

7. Bring the soup to a boil. Peel and dice the potatoes. Remove the beef and veal bones from the soup, and add the potatoes. Simmer until the potatoes are cooked, about 20 minutes. Meanwhile, dice the beef.

8. Melt the remaining butter in a saucepan and add the flour. Mix thoroughly and thin out with some of the soup.

9. Add the mixture to the remaining soup and simmer, stirring, until thickened. Stir in the diced beef and dill. Taste and adjust the seasoning.

10. Serve with the sour or heavy cream.

Bortsch

Crème du Barry
Cream of Cauliflower Soup

| | 00:25 | | 01:10 |

American	Ingredients	Metric/Imperial
4	Leeks, white part only	4
1	Cauliflower	1
6 tbsp	Butter	75 g / 3 oz
6 tbsp	Flour	75 g / 3 oz
1½ quarts	Chicken broth (see page 136)	1.5 l / 2½ pints
	Salt and pepper	
1¼ cups	Crème fraîche (see page 122)	300 ml / ½ pint
	Croûtons for garnish	

1. Clean the leeks, and chop finely. Break the cauliflower into small florets and rinse them under cold water. Drain well.

2. Heat the butter in a saucepan and add the leeks. Cover and cook gently, without browning, until softened, stirring occasionally. Sprinkle with the flour and mix thoroughly.

3. Gradually add the broth, stirring constantly. Bring to a boil. Add all but 6 of the cauliflower florets. Season to taste.

4. Simmer for about 50 minutes over a gentle heat.

5. Meanwhile, cook the reserved cauliflower florets in a saucepan of boiling water until tender. Drain and set aside.

6. Pour the soup into a blender or food processor and purée until smooth. Return to the saucepan and add the crème fraîche. Stir to mix. Taste and adjust the seasoning.

7. Reduce over a medium heat for 10 minutes, stirring frequently so that the soup does not stick to the bottom of the pan.

8. Break up the 6 cauliflower florets into small pieces and put them into a warmed soup tureen. Pour on the soup. Serve immediately, with croûtons.

Bisque de homard
Rich Lobster Cream Soup

| | 00:40 | | 01:00 |

American	Ingredients	Metric/Imperial
1 (2 lb)	Live lobster	1 (1 kg / 2 lb)
1	Onion	1
2	Shallots	2
1	Celery stalk	1
3	Carrots	3
¼ cup	Oil	4 tbsp
6 tbsp	Butter	75 g / 3 oz
⅔ cup	Cognac	150 ml / ¼ pint
2½ cups	Dry white wine	600 ml / 1 pint
1	Bouquet garni	1
3 tbsp	Tomato paste [purée]	3 tbsp
	Salt and pepper	
2 quarts	Fish stock (see page 115) or boiling water	2 l / 3½ pints
1¼ cups	Crème fraîche (see page 122)	300 ml / ½ pint
3	Egg yolks	3
1 tsp	Chopped fresh parsley	1 tsp

1. Holding the lobster firmly, kill it instantly by plunging the point of a sharp knife into the crack on top of the back bween the body and tail sections. This will sever the spinal cord. Cut the tail into 4 pieces and the body in half crosswise.

2. Peel and finely chop the onion. Peel and chop the shallots. Chop the celery. Peel and thinly slice the carrots.

3. Heat the oil and butter in a large saucepan over a brisk heat. Add the lobster pieces and onion and cook, stirring, for 5-7 minutes or until the lobster shells become red. Pour in the cognac. Leave to heat, then set alight.

4. When the flames have died down, remove the pieces of lobster with a slotted spoon and put them on one side.

5. Add the wine, shallots, celery, carrots, bouquet garni, tomato paste and salt and pepper to taste to the pan. Add the fish stock or water. Stir well and leave to simmer for 10 minutes.

6. Return the pieces of lobster to the pan and cook for a further 15 minutes.

7. Remove the pieces of lobster from the pan again and shell them. Set the lobster meat aside.

8. Put the shells, lobster head and any coral or roe into a food processor or blender and blend to a very fine purée. Add the purée to the saucepan and stir to mix. Strain through a fine sieve, pressing with a wooden spoon to extract the juices, and discard all the solids. Return the broth to the pan.

9. Dice the lobster meat. Add to the broth and reheat gently. Taste and adjust the seasoning.

10. Mix the crème fraîche with the egg yolks in a bowl, using a whisk. Pour into a pan, whisking vigorously. Remove from the heat as soon as the soup has thickened.

11. Pour into a warmed soup tureen. Sprinkle with chopped parsley and serve at once.

Consommé madrilène

Consommé with Tomatoes and Sherry

	00:10	00:45
American	**Ingredients**	**Metric/Imperial**
2 quarts	Cold chicken broth (see page 136)	2 l / 3½ pints
1	Egg white	1
6	Tomatoes	6
2 tbsp	Oil	2 tbsp
1	Fresh thyme sprig	1
½	Bay leaf	½
	Salt and pepper	
⅔ cup	Sherry	150 ml / ¼ pint

1. Remove the layer of fat from the broth.
2. Heat the broth in a saucepan. Beat the egg white in a bowl. Pour it in a trickle into the hot (but not boiling) broth. Stir gently until the egg white has solidified. Pour the whole through a strainer into a clean saucepan. You have now made what is referred to in culinary terms as a 'clarification.'
3. Return the consommé to the heat. Simmer uncovered to reduce by one-third (about 45 minutes).
4. Meanwhile, peel the tomatoes (first plunging them in boiling water for 10 seconds), then cut them into quarters and remove the seeds. Dice the flesh.
5. Heat the oil in a small frying pan. Add the tomatoes, thyme, bay leaf and salt and pepper to taste and leave to cook until the tomatoes have melted. Sieve the tomato mixture to make a purée, or blend it in a blender or food processor.
6. When the consommé is reduced, add the tomato purée together with the sherry. Mix and pour into cups.

Bisque de crevettes

Creamed Shrimp [Prawn] Soup

	00:25	00:30
American	**Ingredients**	**Metric/Imperial**
2 lb	Large raw shrimp [prawns]	1 kg / 2 lb
1	Large onion	1
2	Medium-size carrots	2
2 tbsp	Oil	2 tbsp
6 tbsp	Butter	75 g / 3 oz
2 tbsp	Cognac	2 tbsp
1	Bay leaf	1
1	Fresh thyme sprig	1
1	Fresh parsley sprig	1
	Salt and pepper	
	Cayenne pepper	
2 cups	Dry white wine	450 ml ¾ pint
2 tbsp	Tomato paste [purée]	2 tbsp
1 quart	Fish stock (see page 115)	1 l / 1¾ pints
3	Egg yolks	3
1¼ cups	Crème fraîche (see page 122)	300 ml / ½ pint

1. Rinse the shrimp and drain. Peel the onion and carrots and chop finely.
2. Heat the oil and butter in a wide saucepan over a brisk heat. Add the shrimp. As soon as the shells become red, pour on the heated cognac and set it alight immediately. Add the onion, carrots, bay leaf, thyme and parsley. Add salt and pepper to taste and a touch of cayenne pepper. Leave to cook for 5 minutes, stirring frequently.
3. Remove the shrimp and set aside. Add the wine to the pan, cover and cook over a gentle heat for 15 minutes.
4. Add the tomato paste and stir well. Cook for a further 10 minutes over a gentle heat.
5. Remove the thyme, bay leaf and parsley and discard. Add the fish stock to the pan and bring to a boil. Simmer for 5 minutes.
6. Meanwhile, peel the shrimp.
7. Purée the soup and shrimp in a blender or food processor until smooth. Taste and adjust the seasoning.
8. Place the egg yolks in a soup tureen with the crème fraîche and mix thoroughly with a sauce whisk. Gradually whisk in the puréed soup.
9. Serve immediately.

Bourride

Fish Stew with Garlic Mayonnaise

	00:30	00:40
American	**Ingredients**	**Metric/Imperial**
2	Onions	2
4	Garlic cloves	4
½ lb	Tomatoes	250 g / 8 oz
1	Orange	1
12	Fennel seeds	12
	Saffron powder	
1	Bouquet garni	1
⅔ cup	Olive oil	150 ml / ¼ pint
1¼ pints	Dry white wine	300 ml / ½ pint
2 quarts	Boiling water	2 l / 3½ pints
	Salt and pepper	
5 lb	Mixed fish (monkfish, red snapper or mullet, bream or porgy, gurnard or small ocean perch, John Dory, a piece of conger eel, etc.) cleaned and scaled if necessary	2.5 kg / 5 lb
1	Egg yolk	1
6	Slices of stale bread	6
	For the garlic mayonnaise:	
6 - 8	Garlic cloves	6 - 8
1 cup	Olive oil	250 ml / 8 fl oz
2	Egg yolks	2
2 tbsp	Lemon juice	2 tbsp
	Salt and pepper	

1. Peel and chop the onions and garlic. Peel the tomatoes (first plunging them in boiling water for 10 seconds) and chop them. Thinly pare ¼ of the rind from the orange.
2. Place the onions, garlic, tomatoes, orange rind, fennel seeds, a pinch of saffron and the bouquet garni in a large

saucepan. Pour on the oil and stir, then add the wine, boiling water and salt and pepper to taste. Bring to a boil and leave to simmer for 20 minutes.

3. Meanwhile, prepare the mayonnaise. Peel the garlic cloves and crush in a mortar, with a pestle, adding 1 or 2 tablespoons of the olive oil to obtain a paste. Add the egg yolks, then drizzle in the remaining oil in a trickle, blending with a whisk, as for mayonnaise. Add the lemon juice, and salt and pepper to taste.

4. Place all the fish in the pan and simmer for 15 minutes.

5. Drain the fish, place it on a warmed serving dish and keep hot. Put the vegetables into a blender or food processor with a little of the broth and blend to a purée. Pour this back into the remaining broth and reheat.

6. Mix the egg yolk with 2 tablespoons of the mayonnaise. Whisk in 1 ladle of the broth. Pour this mixture into the pan of broth, off the heat, and stir. Discard the bouquet garni.

7. Arrange the slices of bread on the bottom of a warmed soup tureen and pour over the thickened soup. Serve the fish with the soup and the remaining mayonnaise.

Crème d'asperges

Cream of Asparagus Soup

| | 00:45 | 00:30 to 00:40 | |

American	Ingredients	Metric/Imperial
1 quart	Milk	1 l / 1¾ pints
1	Medium-size onion	1
1	Clove	1
6	Black peppercorns	6
1	Bouquet garni	1
5 tbsp	Ground rice	5 tbsp
1 lb	Fresh asparagus	500 g / 1 lb
	Salt and pepper	
¼ cup	Butter	50 g / 2 oz
½ cup	Crème fraîche (see page 122)	125 ml / 4 fl oz

1. Put the milk into a saucepan, and add the peeled onion studded with the clove, the peppercorns and bouquet garni. Bring to a boil.

2. Dissolve the ground rice in a little cold water and pour this mixture into the boiling milk, stirring constantly. Lower the heat and leave to simmer for 20 minutes.

3. Meanwhile, trim the woody ends from the asparagus, and scrape the stalks if necessary.

4. Put just enough salted water into an asparagus steamer or tall saucepan to cover the stalks of the asparagus. Bring to a boil. Add the asparagus (the tips should be above the water), cover and steam until crisp-tender. This will take 8-20 minutes, depending on the age and size of the asparagus.

5. Remove the asparagus from the water, reserving the water, and drain on paper towels. Cut off the tips and keep them to garnish the soup. Chop the asparagus stalks.

6. Melt the butter in a saucepan. Add the chopped asparagus stalks and cook until very soft. Add to the flavored milk with 1 tablespoon of the reserved asparagus cooking water. Simmer until the asparagus breaks down.

7. Strain through a fine sieve, squeezing all liquid from the solids with the back of a spoon. Measure the strained milk, and add enough asparagus cooking water to make 1½ quarts [1.5 l / 2½ pints].

8. Add the crème fraîche and reserved asparagus tips. Taste and adjust the seasoning. Reheat gently and serve.

Cream of asparagus soup

Consommé Colbert

Consommé with Poached Eggs and Port Wine

| | 00:10 | 00:15 | |

American	Ingredients	Metric/Imperial
1½ quarts	Cold beef broth (see page 137)	1.5 l / 2½ pints
1	Egg white	1
1	Large carrot	1
1	Turnip	1
½ cup	Fresh shelled peas	50 g / 2 oz
6	Eggs	6
3 tbsp	Vinegar	3 tbsp
⅔ cup	Port wine	150 ml / ¼ pint

1. Remove the layer of fat from the broth using a skimming spoon.

2. Heat the broth in a saucepan. Beat the egg white in a bowl. Pour it in a trickle into the hot (but not boiling) broth. Stir gently until the egg white has solidified. Pour the whole through a conical strainer into a clean saucepan. You have now made what is referred to in culinary terms as a 'clarification.'

3. Return the consommé to the heat and bring back to a boil.

4. Meanwhile, peel the carrot and turnip and cut into small cubes.

5. Add the carrot to the boiling consommé and leave to cook for 5 minutes, then add the turnip and peas. Simmer for 7-10 minutes.

6. Meanwhile, poach the eggs: heat water in a wide saucepan or frying pan and add the vinegar. When the water is simmering, break one egg into a ladle. Slide the egg down the side of the pan and when it is in the water, quickly fold over the white around the yolk. Cook until the egg white has just set. Remove the egg with a slotted spoon and drain on paper towels. Poach the remaining eggs in the same way.

7. Trim the poached eggs to neaten the edges. Place an egg in each of 6 warmed soup plates.

8. Put the port into a soup tureen and strain the consommé into the tureen. Ladle the consommé over the poached eggs.

Bouillon de légumes

Vegetable Broth

00:10   **01:30**

American	Ingredients	Metric/Imperial
3	Carrots	3
3	Turnips	3
1	Celery stalk	1
1	Large onion	1
2	Garlic cloves	2
3	Leeks	3
1½ quarts	Water	1.5 l / 2½ pints
1	Bouquet garni	1
	Salt and pepper	
	Butter (optional)	

1. Peel the carrots and turnips and cut into very small cubes. Cut the celery into small cubes. Peel the onion and slice it thinly. Peel the garlic cloves and split each into quarters. Trim the leeks, cut in half lengthwise and wash well in cold water, separating the leaves. Drain and cut into small pieces.

2. Place all the vegetables in a large saucepan together with the water, bouquet garni and salt and pepper to taste. Bring to a boil over a brisk heat, then leave to simmer gently, uncovered, for 1½ hours.

3. Taste the broth and adjust the seasoning if necessary. Strain into a warmed soup tureen.

4. Serve very hot, adding a piece of butter to each serving, if you wish.

Cook's tip: if you make this broth in a pressure cooker, cook for no longer than 20 minutes. If you prefer a thicker soup, remove the bouquet garni, and purée the broth and vegetables in a blender or food processor, then reheat.

Garbure

Peasant Vegetable Stew

00:20
plus soaking
02:30

American	Ingredients	Metric/Imperial
1 cup	Dried [haricot] beans	175 g / 6 oz
1 lb	Lightly salted pork sides [belly pork]	500 g / 1 lb
1½ quarts	Water	1.5 l / 2½ pints
1	Leek	1
2	Turnips	2
3	Carrots	3
2	Onions	2
2	Garlic cloves	2
1	Bouquet garni	1
5	Black peppercorns	5
1	Small head of green cabbage	1
	Salt and pepper	
4	Potatoes	4
1	Can conserve of goose (confit d'oie)	1
1	Loaf of bread, sliced	1
½ cup	Grated gruyère cheese	50 g / 2 oz

1. Soak the beans in water to cover overnight. Drain.

2. Cut the pork into large pieces and place in a large pan. Cover with water. Bring to a boil, skimming thoroughly.

3. Meanwhile, cut the leek into small pieces. Peel and dice the turnips and carrots. Peel and chop the onions and garlic.

4. When there is no more scum rising in the pan, add all the prepared vegetables, the bouquet garni and peppercorns. Leave to cook for 1¼ hours.

5. Meanwhile, remove the damaged leaves and core from the cabbage. Separate the cabbage into leaves and rinse well. Toss into a saucepan of boiling salted water. When the water returns to a boil, cook for 3 minutes. Drain and cut into thin strips.

6. Peel the potatoes and slice thickly.

7. Add the cabbage and potatoes to the pan. Cover and leave to simmer for 45 minutes. Taste and adjust the seasoning.

8. Preheat the oven to 400°F / 200°C / Gas Mark 6.

9. Add the conserve of goose to the pan with a little fat and leave to cook for 10 minutes.

10. Using a strainer, remove the conserve with some of the vegetables and place in a shallow ovenproof dish. Top with slices of bread and sprinkle with the grated gruyère. Place in the oven and bake for 15 minutes.

11. Serve the meat and the rest of the vegetables at the same time or separately.

Peasant vegetable stew

Gratinée lyonnaise

Onion, Bread and Cheese Soup

00:15   **00:20**

American	Ingredients	Metric/Imperial
4	Large onions	4
¼ cup	Butter	50 g / 2 oz
⅔ cup	White wine	150 ml / ¼ pint
1 quart	Water	1 l / 1¾ pints
	Salt and pepper	
6	Slices of stale bread	6
2 cups	Grated gruyère cheese	250 g / 8 oz
1	Egg yolk	1
⅔ cup	Madeira wine	150 ml / ¼ pint

1. Peel and thinly slice the onions. Melt the butter in a saucepan. Add the onions and cook until light brown. Add the wine, then dilute gradually with the water. Add salt and pepper to taste and leave to simmer gently for 10-15 minutes.
2. Preheat the oven to 425°F / 220°C / Gas Mark 7.
3. Dice the bread. Half fill a deep round ovenproof dish with the diced bread and cover with a layer of grated cheese. Pour the onion soup over the bread. Scatter over the remainder of the cheese.
4. Place in the oven and bake for 15-20 minutes.
5. Beat the egg yolk and madeira together. Mix with a little of the soup and pour back into the remaining soup. Stir well and serve.

Gaspacho

Chilled Tomato and Pepper Soup

	01:00 plus chilling		00:05

American	Ingredients	Metric/Imperial
2	Medium-size cucumbers	2
3	Large tomatoes	3
1	Green pepper	1
1	Sweet red pepper	1
1	Large bermuda or spanish onion	1
1½ cups	Fresh bread crumbs	75 g / 3 oz
2 tbsp	Wine vinegar	2 tbsp
3	Garlic cloves	3
5 tbsp	Oil	5 tbsp
	Salt and pepper	
	Accompaniments:	
1	Cucumber	1
3	Shallots	3
4 - 6	Fresh chervil or parsley sprigs	4 - 6
1	Small bunch of fresh chives	1
3	Eggs	3
3 tbsp	Oil	3 tbsp
3	Slices of bread	3

1. Peel the cucumbers and cut into quarters lengthwise. Remove the seeds and cut the flesh into medium-size cubes. Peel the tomatoes (first plunging them in boiling water for 10 seconds), remove the seeds and dice the flesh. Cut the peppers in half, remove the seeds and the white parts and dice the flesh. Peel and coarsely chop the onion. Sprinkle the bread crumbs with the vinegar.
2. Place all the prepared ingredients in a blender or food processor and blend to a smooth purée.
3. Peel and crush the garlic. Put the garlic into a bowl and thicken it by gradually incorporating the oil, stirring continuously. Season to taste with salt and pepper. Add this to the puréed vegetable mixture. Stir thoroughly to mix and place in the refrigerator. Leave to chill.
4. To prepare the accompaniments, peel the cucumber, cut it into quarters lengthwise and remove the seeds. Cut the flesh into very small cubes. Peel the shallots and chop them. Rinse and drain the chervil and chives and cut finely with a pair of scissors. Put all these ingredients into small serving dishes.
5. Hard-cook the eggs for 10 minutes, then run them under cold water. Leave to cool and remove the shells. Cut the eggs in

half, and chop the yolks and whites separately into small cubes. Put into 2 serving dishes.
6. Heat the oil in a small frying pan. Cut the bread into small cubes and fry in the oil, until golden all over. Drain the croûtons on paper towels and put into a small serving dish.
7. Serve the gaspacho very cold with all the accompaniments.

Gratinée au porto

Onion Soup with Port Wine

	00:25		00:15

American	Ingredients	Metric/Imperial
1 lb	Onions	500 g / 1 lb
¼ cup	Butter	50 g / 2 oz
2 tbsp	Flour	2 tbsp
1½ quarts	Water	1.5 l / 2½ pints
	Grated nutmeg	
	Salt and pepper	
1	French loaf	1
2 cups	Grated gruyère cheese	250 g / 8 oz
6	Egg yolks	6
¾ cup	Port wine	175 ml / 6 fl oz

1. Preheat the oven to 400°F / 200°C / Gas Mark 6.
2. Peel the onions and slice them thinly. Melt the butter in a saucepan, add the onions and cook gently until softened.
3. Add the flour, mix well and cook for 2 minutes. Add the cold water all at once and bring to a boil, stirring vigorously. Add a pinch of nutmeg, and salt and pepper to taste and simmer for 10 minutes.
4. Cut the french loaf into slices and place under the broiler [grill] to dry out and brown lightly.
5. Pour the onion soup into 6 individual ovenproof bowls. Add the bread slices to the bowls, and sprinkle with the grated cheese.
6. Put into the oven and bake for 15 minutes.
7. Meanwhile, put each egg yolk into a small glass or cup. Pour a little port into each.
8. Each guest will lift the crust of his or her soup and pour in the contents of the glass, stirring gently with a fork to mix.

Panade

Bread and Milk Soup

	00:05		01:15

American	Ingredients	Metric/Imperial
½ lb	Stale bread	250 g / 8 oz
2 quarts	Cold water	2 l / 3½ pints
1 tbsp	Salt	1 tbsp
⅔ cup	Milk or crème fraîche (see page 122)	150 ml / ¼ pint

1. Roughly cut up the bread. Put it in a saucepan and add the water and salt. Bring to a boil and simmer for 1 hour.
2. Crush the bread with a fork, or put it through a blender or food processor to obtain a very smooth mixture.
3. Add the milk or crème fraîche. If the soup still seems to be too thick, add water or, for a richer soup, more crème fraîche.

Minestrone
Italian Vegetable Soup

	00:30 plus soaking		01:30

American	Ingredients	Metric/Imperial
¾ cup	Dried navy [haricot] beans	150 g / 5 oz
2 cups	Water	450 ml / ¾ pint
2	Carrots	2
3	Potatoes	3
2	Leeks	2
2	Zucchini [courgettes]	2
3	Tomatoes	3
¼	Head of celeriac	¼
2	Garlic cloves	2
¼ cup	Olive oil	4 tbsp
2 quarts	Beef stock	2 l / 3 ½ pints
4	Fresh basil sprigs	4
1	Fresh thyme sprig	1
3	Fresh parsley sprigs	3
	Salt and pepper	
1 tbsp	Noodles	1 tbsp
	Grated parmesan cheese	1 tbsp

1. Soak the beans in cold water overnight or for at least 4 hours.
2. Drain the beans and put them in a saucepan with the cold water. Bring to a boil and simmer, covered, for about 30 minutes.
3. Meanwhile, peel the carrots and potatoes and cut into small cubes. Clean the leeks, quarter lengthwise and wash under cold water, separating the leaves. Cut the leeks and zucchini into small cubes. Peel the tomatoes (first plunging them in boiling water for 10 seconds) and the celeriac, and dice them. Peel and crush the garlic.
4. Heat the olive oil in a large pan, add all the diced vegetables and cook gently, covered until softened, stirring from time to time.
5. Heat the beef stock, pour into the pan and add the garlic, the leaves from 2 basil sprigs, the thyme, parsley and beans with their cooking water. Season to taste with salt and pepper. Leave to simmer gently, covered, for 45 minutes.
6. Add the noodles and cook for a further 2-3 minutes.
7. Chop the rest of the basil leaves and add to the minestrone. Taste and adjust the seasoning. Remove and discard the thyme and parsley sprigs and serve immediately, accompanied if you wish by grated parmesan cheese.

Potage au cerfeuil
Chervil Soup

	00:10		00:20

American	Ingredients	Metric/Imperial
2 lb	Potatoes	1 kg / 2 lb
2 cups	Cold water	500 ml / ¾ pint
	Salt and pepper	
1	Large bunch of fresh chervil	1
½ cup	Crème fraîche (see page 122)	125 ml / 4 fl oz
¼ cup	Butter	50 g / 2 oz

1. Peel the potatoes and quarter them. Place in a saucepan and cover with the cold water. Add salt to taste. Bring to a boil and leave to cook for 20 minutes.
2. Meanwhile, rinse the chervil and shake well to drain. Cut it very finely with a pair of scissors.
3. Purée the potatoes and liquid in a blender or food processor until smooth. Return to the pan. Add the chervil, and salt and pepper to taste. Cover and infuse for 2 minutes off the heat.
4. Add the crème fraîche and butter and heat through without boiling, stirring with a whisk. Serve immediately.

Potage Crécy
Carrot Soup

	00:20		00:50

American	Ingredients	Metric/Imperial
4	Carrots	4
4	Medium-size potatoes	4
3	Turnips	3
2 quarts	Cold water	2 l / 3 ½ pints
	Salt and pepper	
5	Shallots	5
⅔ cup	White wine	150 ml / ¼ pint
½ cup	Butter	125 g / 4 oz
	Croûtons for serving	

1. Peel the carrots, potatoes and turnips and cut into small pieces. Put into a saucepan and add the cold water, and salt and pepper to taste. Bring to a boil and simmer gently for 30 minutes.
2. Meanwhile, peel the shallots and chop finely. Pour the wine into a small frying pan and add the shallots. Bring to a boil and reduce to one-third over a moderate heat.
3. Cut the cold butter into pieces the size of a walnut. Add them all at once to the shallots, beating with a whisk. Cook, stirring, over gentle heat until the mixture is pale and thickened.
4. Purée the soup in a blender or food processor until smooth. Return to the saucepan.
5. Gradually stir in the shallot-butter mixture and leave to cook for a further 20 minutes over a gentle heat. Season to taste.
6. Serve in a soup tureen accompanied by croûtons.

Potage velouté au cresson
Cream of Watercress Soup

	00:10		00:30

American	Ingredients	Metric/Imperial
1	Bunch of watercress	1
2 - 3	Potatoes	2 - 3
2 tbsp	Butter	25 g / 1 oz
2 quarts	Water	2 l / 3 ½ pints
	Salt	
½ cup	Crème fraîche (see page 122)	125 ml / 4 fl oz
2	Egg yolks	2
	Croûtons for serving	

1. Remove any damaged leaves from the watercress and rinse well, changing the water at least 3 times. Reserve a few nice leaves to decorate the soup. Drain the remaining cress in a salad basket.

2. Peel and slice the potatoes. Melt the butter in a large saucepan. Add the potatoes and cook for 5 minutes. Add the cress and cook until it is soft.

3. Cover with the water and add salt to taste. Bring to a boil and simmer for about 30 minutes.

4. Purée the soup in a blender or food processor until smooth. Return the soup to the saucepan and reheat.

5. Mix the crème fraîche with the egg yolks in a small bowl. Stir in some of the hot soup, then add this mixture to the remaining soup in the pan. Heat through, stirring, but do not boil.

6. Garnish with the reserved watercress leaves and serve the soup accompanied by croûtons.

Bouillabaisse

Provençal Fish Soup

	00:30		01:00

American	Ingredients	Metric/Imperial
4 lb	Mixed fish (gurnard or small ocean perch, John Dory, rascasse, whiting, monkfish, conger eel, etc.)	2 kg / 4 lb
2	Large onions	2
1	Leek, white part only	1
2	Large tomatoes	2
1	Garlic clove	1
2 quarts	Fish stock (see page 115)	2 l / 3½ pints
1	Fresh thyme sprig	1
1	Bay leaf	1
2 - 3	Parsley sprigs	2 - 3
⅔ cup	Olive oil	150 ml / ¼ pint
	Saffron powder	
	Salt and pepper	
12	Slices of bread	12

1. Clean the fish and scale if necessary. Cut large fish into pieces and leave small fish whole. Separate the firm-fleshed fish from the tender-fleshed fish.

2. Peel the onions. Chop them finely with the leek. Peel the tomatoes (first plunging them in boiling water for 10 seconds), remove the seeds and cut into pieces. Peel and crush the garlic.

3. Bring the fish stock to a boil.

4. Place the tomatoes, onions, leek, garlic, thyme sprig, bay leaf and parsley sprigs in a large saucepan. Pour on the olive oil and sprinkle with a little saffron. Stir to mix. Add the firm-fleshed fish, and pour on the hot stock so as to cover the fish. Add salt and pepper to taste. Leave to cook over a very brisk heat for about 8 minutes.

5. Add the tender-fleshed fish and simmer for a further 5 minutes.

6. Arrange the slices of bread around the edge of a shallow dish. Strain the cooking broth into a warmed soup tureen. Place the pieces of fish in the center of the shallow dish. Serve the fish and soup together.

Cook's tip: you can accompany this fish with hot pepper and potato mayonnaise (see page 120). The fish stock may be replaced by a simple court-bouillon (see page 114). The bread slices may also be lightly toasted in the oven.

Potage aux haricots blancs

White Bean Soup

	00:20 plus cooling		03:00

American	Ingredients	Metric/Imperial
1 cup	Dried navy [haricot] beans	250 g / 8 oz
1	Bouquet garni	1
1	Onion	1
1	Garlic clove	1
5	Celery stalks	5
2	Leeks, white part only	2
4	Large tomatoes	4
¼ cup	Butter	50 g / 2 oz
	Salt	
2	Egg yolks	2
	Garlic croûtons for serving	

1. Rinse the beans, place them in a large saucepan and cover with cold water. Cover the pan and bring very slowly to a boil (taking at least 45 minutes). Remove from the heat and allow to cool until lukewarm.

2. Drain the beans and put them back into the pan. Cover with plenty of fresh boiling water. Add the bouquet garni, peeled onion and peeled garlic clove. Return to a boil and leave to cook for about 1 hour or until the beans will crush easily.

3. Meanwhile, trim and chop the celery and leeks. Chop the tomatoes.

4. Melt half the butter in another saucepan. Add the leeks and celery and cook until softened. Stir in the tomatoes and leave to cook over a low heat for about 50 minutes.

5. When the beans are cooked, remove and discard the bouquet garni and onion. Purée the beans and liquid with the tomato mixture in a blender or food processor until smooth. Return to the saucepan.

6. Add salt to taste and bring to a boil, stirring well.

7. Mix the egg yolks with the remaining butter and 2 tablespoons of the soup. Add to the soup in the pan and heat through, stirring. Do not boil any further.

8. Serve with garlic croûtons.

White bean soup

Potage julienne
Vegetable Soup with Tapioca

⏱ 00:45   01:00 🍲

American	Ingredients	Metric/Imperial
¼	Head of white cabbage	¼
2	Carrots	2
2	Turnips	2
5 oz	Celeriac	150 g / 5 oz
½ lb	Potatoes	250 g / 8 oz
1	Leek	1
¼ lb	Green beans	125 g / 4 oz
2 quarts	Water	2 l / 3 ½ pints
	Salt and pepper	
1 cup	Peas	125 g / 4 oz
3	Fresh chervil sprigs	3
2 - 3	Lettuce leaves	2 - 3
⅓ cup	Tapioca	50 g / 2 oz
2 tbsp	Butter	25 g / 1 oz

1. Remove the damaged leaves and core from the cabbage. Peel the carrots, turnips, celeriac and potatoes. Trim the leek and beans. Rinse and drain the vegetables, then cut them into thin sticks [julienne].
2. Place the prepared vegetables in a large saucepan with the cold water and add salt and pepper to taste. Bring to a boil and leave to cook over a low heat for 30 minutes.
3. Add the peas. Chop the chervil and lettuce and add with the tapioca. Leave to cook for a further 30 minutes.
4. Cut the butter into small pieces.
5. Pour the soup into a warmed tureen. Add the butter and stir until melted. Serve immediately.

Potage liégeois
Sorrel, Potato and Tomato Soup

⏱ 00:20   00:45 🍲

American	Ingredients	Metric/Imperial
2	Leeks	2
5 oz	Sorrel (or spinach)	150 g / 5 oz
1	Celery stalk	1
6 tbsp	Butter	75 g / 3 oz
1 lb	Potatoes	500 g / 1 lb
2 quarts	Boiling water	2 l / 3 ½ pints
1	Bay leaf	1
2	Fresh chervil or parsley sprigs	2
	Salt and pepper	
½ lb	Tomatoes	250 g / 8 oz
2 tbsp	Crème fraîche (see page 122)	2 tbsp
	Croûtons for serving (optional)	

1. Trim the leeks and cut into pieces. Rinse the sorrel, removing the stalks. Trim and chop the celery.

2. Melt the butter in a large saucepan and add the prepared vegetables. Cook until softened, stirring occasionally.
3. Peel and slice the potatoes.
4. Add the boiling water, bay leaf, chervil, and salt and pepper to taste to the saucepan. Bring to a boil, then add the potatoes. Simmer for 45 minutes.
5. Peel the tomatoes (first plunging them in boiling water for 10 seconds) and purée them in a vegetable mill, blender or food processor.
6. Purée the soup until smooth. Mix in the tomato purée. Pour into a warmed soup tureen and add the crème fraîche, beating with a whisk. Serve with croûtons, if liked.

Potage paysanne
Country Vegetable Soup

⏱ 00:35   01:00 to 01:30 🍲

American	Ingredients	Metric/Imperial
	Giblets of 1 chicken	
6 - 8	Chicken feet or wing tips	6 - 8
2 quarts	Cold water	2 l / 3 ½ pints
	Salt and pepper	
3	Carrots	3
3	Turnips	3
3	Medium-size potatoes	3
3	Leeks, white part only	3
1	Celery stalk	1
½ cup	Butter	125 g / 4 oz

1. Place the giblets and chicken feet or wing tips in a large saucepan of boiling water and simmer for 3-4 minutes to clean them thoroughly. Drain. Carefully remove the skin and claws from the feet. Tie the feet together.
2. Put the cold water into a saucepan and add the giblets, feet or wing tips and salt and pepper to taste. Bring to a boil and simmer gently, covered, for about 45 minutes.
3. Peel the carrots, turnips and potatoes and cut into small cubes. Trim the leeks and celery and cut into small pieces.
4. Melt 1 tablespoon butter in a frying pan. Add the vegetables and cook until softened.
5. Add the vegetables to the saucepan and simmer gently, covered, for a further 30-40 minutes.
6. Remove the giblets and chicken feet or wing tips with a skimming spoon.
7. Cut the remaining butter into small pieces and stir into the soup. Taste and adjust the seasoning.

Potage velours
Tapioca Soup

⏱ 00:15   00:15 🍲

American	Ingredients	Metric/Imperial
2 quarts	Beef broth (see page 137)	2 l / 3 ½ pints
⅔ cup	Tapioca	125 g / 4 oz
2	Egg yolks	2
¼ cup	Butter	50 g / 2 oz

1. Pour the broth into a saucepan and bring to a boil. Add the tapioca, stirring to avoid lumps. Cook for 10 minutes, stirring continuously.

2. Mix the eggs yolks with a ladle of soup in a bowl and add the butter, cut in small pieces, stirring with a whisk.

3. Pour the remaining soup into a tureen. Add the egg yolk mixture, beating thoroughly. Taste and adjust the seasoning and serve very hot.

Cabbage soup

Soupe aux choux

Cabbage Soup

00:20   01:30

American	Ingredients	Metric/Imperial
1 (½ lb)	Piece of lightly salted bacon	1 (250 g / 8 oz)
2 quarts	Cold water	2 l / 3½ pints
1	Head of green cabbage	1
4	Medium-size carrots	4
4	Potatoes	4
2	Onions	2
2	Cloves	2
1	Celery stalk	1
1	Bouquet garni	1
	Salt and pepper	
1	Loaf of bread	1

1. Blanch the bacon in a large saucepan of boiling water for 5 minutes. Drain and return to the pan. Add the cold water. Bring to a boil and cook gently for 45 minutes.

2. Remove the core from the cabbage. Put the cabbage into a large saucepan of boiling water and blanch for 10 minutes. Drain and cut into 8 pieces.

3. Peel the carrots, potatoes and onions. Stud the onions with the cloves. Roughly chop the carrots and potatoes.

4. Add the cabbage, potatoes, carrots, onions studded with cloves, celery and bouquet garni to the bacon. Add salt and pepper to taste. Cover and leave to simmer for 40 minutes.

5. Remove and discard the bouquet garni. Remove the bacon and cut into thin slices. Add hot water to the soup if it is too thick, and taste and adjust the seasoning.

6. Serve the cabbage soup with the pieces of bacon and very thin slices of bread which can be put in each soup bowl before the soup is served.

Potage aux tomates

Tomato Soup

00:10   00:45

American	Ingredients	Metric/Imperial
1 lb	Tomatoes	500 g / 1 lb
3	Potatoes	3
1½ quarts	Beef broth (see page 137)	1.5 l / 2½ pints
	Salt and pepper	
	Chopped fresh chervil or parsley	

1. Peel the tomatoes (first plunging them in boiling water for 10 seconds) and potatoes. Chop the tomatoes and potatoes.

2. Place the tomatoes, potatoes and broth in a large saucepan and bring to a boil. Add salt and pepper to taste. Simmer for 45 minutes.

3. Purée the soup in a blender or food processor until smooth. Reheat if necessary.

4. Serve hot, sprinkled with chervil.

Soupe aux lentilles

Lentil Soup

00:15 plus soaking   02:00

American	Ingredients	Metric/Imperial
1¼ lb (2½ cups)	Lentils	625 g / 1¼ lb
1½ lb	Smoked pork shoulder [collar bacon]	750 g / 1½ lb
2	Carrots	2
2	Leeks	2
1	Onion	1
2	Cloves	2
6 tbsp	Butter	75 g / 3 oz
2 quarts	Water	2 l / 3½ pints
1	Bouquet garni	1
	Pepper	
2½ cups	Milk	600 ml / 1 pint
6	Slices of french bread	6

1. Soak the lentils in water to cover for 4 hours. If necessary, soak the pork in water to cover to remove excess salt.

2. Peel the carrots. Trim the leeks. Dice the carrots and leeks. Peel the onion and stud with the cloves.

3. Heat half the butter in a saucepan. Add the carrots and leeks, cover and cook gently until softened. Add the water, onion, bouquet garni, drained lentils and pork, and pepper to taste. Cook over a gentle heat, covered, for 1¾ hours.

4. Remove and discard the bouquet garni. Remove the shoulder of pork.

5. Purée the soup in a blender or food processor until smooth and pour back into the pan. Add the milk and heat, stirring. Taste and adjust the seasoning.

6. Toast the french bread slices. Put the remaining butter into a soup tureen, pour the soup on top and serve immediately, with the toasted bread.

Cook's tip: if you want to serve the pork with the soup, select a piece weighing at least 2¾ lb / 1.25 kg and extend the cooking time by 30 minutes.

Potage Saint-Germain
Cream of Split Pea Soup

| 00:10 | | 01:15 |

American	Ingredients	Metric/Imperial
5	Leeks	5
1	Celery stalk	1
3	Onions	3
¼ cup	Butter	50 g / 2 oz
2 cups	Split green peas	500 g / 1 lb
2 quarts	Water	2 l / 3½ pints
1 cup	Crème fraîche (see page 122)	250 ml / 8 fl oz
	Salt and pepper	
	Croûtons for serving	

1. Trim the leeks and celery. Peel the onions. Chop all the vegetables roughly. Melt the butter in a large saucepan and add the leeks, onions and celery. Cook over a low heat until golden brown.
2. Add the split peas and water. Bring to a boil and leave to cook for 1 hour.
3. Purée the soup in a blender or food processor until smooth. Return to the saucepan.
4. Add the crème fraîche. Bring to a boil and simmer for 15 minutes. Add salt and pepper to taste. Serve hot, sprinkled with croûtons.

Potage printanier
Spring Vegetable Soup

| 00:25 | | 01:00 |

American	Ingredients	Metric/Imperial
2	Turnips	2
1	Carrot	1
2	Potatoes	2
2	Leeks, white part only	2
1	Celery stalk	1
1 quart	Chicken broth (see page 136)	1 l / 1¾ pints
1	Cucumber	1
½ lb	Sorrel or spinach	250 g / 8 oz
3 tbsp	Butter	40 g / 1½ oz
	Salt and pepper	
1	Egg yolk	1
¼ cup	Crème fraîche (see page 122)	4 tbsp
	Chopped fresh parsley	

1. Peel and chop the turnips, carrot and potatoes. Trim and chop the leeks and celery.
2. Pour the chicken broth into a saucepan and bring to a boil, then add the prepared vegetables. Cook for 30 minutes.
3. Meanwhile, peel the cucumber, remove the seeds and cut into cubes. Set aside.
4. Clean and chop the sorrel. Melt the butter in a saucepan, add the sorrel and cook over a low heat until wilted.
5. Purée the soup in a blender or food processor until smooth and return to the pan. Place over a gentle heat and add the

sorrel and salt and pepper to taste. When the soup boils, stir in the cucumber and leave to cook over a low heat for 8 minutes.
6. Mix the egg yolk and crème fraîche with a ladle of soup in a small bowl. Add the mixture to the remainder of the soup in the pan and cook, stirring, until thickened. Do not boil.
7. Serve hot, sprinkled with chopped parsley.

Soupe à l'oignon
Onion Soup

| 00:20 | | 00:30 |

American	Ingredients	Metric/Imperial
¾ lb	Onions	350 g / 12 oz
¼ cup	Butter	50 g / 2 oz
1 tbsp	Flour	1 tbsp
1½ quarts	Beef broth (see page 137) or water	1.5 l / 2½ pints
	Salt and pepper	
¼ cup	Crème fraîche (see page 122)	4 tbsp
6	Slices of bread	6
1¼ cups	Grated emmental or gruyère cheese	150 g / 5 oz

1. Peel the onions and cut into fine strips. Heat the butter in a saucepan, add the onions and cook very gently until very soft and almost melted. Do not allow to burn.
2. When the onions are light brown, sprinkle with the flour and leave to cook for 2-3 minutes, stirring continuously, until the flour turns light brown.
3. Add the broth, stirring to avoid lumps. Add salt and pepper to taste and leave to cook for 30 minutes over a low heat.
4. Preheat the oven to 475°F / 240°C / Gas Mark 9.
5. Add the crème fraîche to the soup and pour into an ovenproof serving dish. Place the bread slices on the soup and sprinkle with the cheese.
6. Place in the oven and bake until the cheese has browned.

Soupe au cantal
Cheese and Potato Soup

| 00:10 | | 00:35 |

American	Ingredients	Metric/Imperial
8	Potatoes	8
	Salt and pepper	
2 quarts	Milk	2 l / 3½ pints
2	Garlic cloves	2
2 cups	Grated cantal	250 g / 8 oz
6 tbsp	Crème fraîche (see page 122)	6 tbsp

1. Peel the potatoes and cut into small cubes.
2. Add salt and pepper to the milk and bring to a boil in a large saucepan. Add the potato cubes and leave to cook over a very gentle heat for 25 minutes.
3. Rub a soup tureen with the halved garlic cloves and discard the garlic. Scatter the cheese on the bottom. Pour the soup into the tureen, add the crème fraîche and stir well to mix.

Soupe au pistou
Vegetable Soup with Basil Paste

⏱ 00:30   01:00 to 01:30 🍲

American	Ingredients	Metric/Imperial
1½ lb	Fresh broad beans	750 g / 1½ lb
3	Potatoes	3
2	Carrots	2
¾ lb	Green beans	350 g / 12 oz
¾ lb	Lightly salted lean bacon	350 g / 12 oz
3 quarts	Water	3 l / 5 pints
¼ lb	Noodles	125 g / 4 oz
2	Garlic cloves	2
15	Large fresh basil leaves	15
2	Tomatoes	2
1 cup	Grated gruyère cheese	125 g / 4 oz
5 tbsp	Olive oil	5 tbsp

1. Shell the broad beans. Peel the potatoes and carrots. Trim the green beans. Dice the potatoes, carrots and green beans.
2. Place the bacon in a saucepan with the water. Bring to a boil, then add the broad beans and carrots. Cover and leave to cook for 45 minutes.
3. Add the green beans and potatoes. Leave to cook for a further 30 minutes.
4. Add the noodles and leave to cook uncovered for 10 minutes.
5. Meanwhile, peel the garlic and place in a mortar with the basil. Crush to a paste with a pestle.
6. Peel the tomatoes (first plunging them in boiling water for 10 seconds) and remove the seeds. Add to the mortar and continue working with the pestle, adding the cheese and olive oil alternately, to make a paste.
7. Pour the paste into a soup tureen and gradually stir in the boiling soup. Leave to infuse for 5 minutes before serving.

Cook's tip: the basil paste can also be served as a delicious sauce for fresh pasta.

Soupe Parmentière
Thick Potato Soup

⏱ 00:10   00:15 🍲

American	Ingredients	Metric/Imperial
6	Potatoes	6
1½ quarts	Water	1.5 l / 2½ pints
	Salt and pepper	
1 cup	Crème fraîche (see page 122)	250 ml / 8 fl oz
2 cups	Grated gruyère cheese	250 g / 8 oz

1. Peel and grate the potatoes.
2. Pour the water into a saucepan, add a pinch of salt and bring to a boil. Add the grated potatoes and leave to cook over a gentle heat for 15 minutes.
3. In a soup tureen, mix together the crème fraîche and grated gruyère. Pour in the soup and stir well. Add pepper to taste.

Mussel soup

Soupe de moules
Mussel Soup

⏱ 00:25   00:45 🍲

American	Ingredients	Metric/Imperial
1	Fish head	1
	Few fish bones	
4	Onions	4
1	Bouquet garni	1
2 quarts	Water	2 l / 3½ pints
2	Carrots	2
2	Shallots	2
1 oz	Celeriac	25 g / 1 oz
2 tbsp	Olive oil	2 tbsp
3	Tomatoes	3
1¼ cups	Dry white wine	300 ml / ½ pint
	Saffron powder	
3 quarts	Fresh mussels	3 l / 5 pints
1 cup	Light [single] cream	250 ml / 8 fl oz
1½ cups	Grated edam cheese	175 g / 6 oz

1. Place the fish head, bones, 2 peeled onions and bouquet garni in a saucepan. Add the water and bring to a boil. Simmer for 20 minutes. Strain this stock.
2. Peel and dice the remaining onions, the carrots, shallots and celeriac. Heat the olive oil in a clean saucepan, add the vegetables and cook gently until softened.
3. Peel the tomatoes (first plunging them in boiling water for 10 seconds), then remove the seeds and chop the flesh. Add the tomatoes to the pan with half the wine, a pinch of saffron and the strained fish stock. Leave to cook for 20 minutes.
4. Scrub the mussels under running water. Place them in a saucepan with the remaining wine and cook until they open (discard any that remain closed). Remove the mussels from their shells and strain the liquor.
5. Add the strained cooking liquor, the mussels and cream to the soup and stir well.
6. Serve hot with the cheese.

Soupe de crabes
Crab Soup

00:20   01:00

American	Ingredients	Metric/Imperial
2	Carrots	2
2	Leeks	2
1	Celery stalk	1
3	Onions	3
4	Cloves	4
1	Garlic clove	1
3	Tomatoes	3
¼ cup	Olive oil	4 tbsp
2 lb	Small hard-shell crabs, cooked	1 kg / 2 lb
2 quarts	Water	2 l / 3½ pints
1	Fresh thyme sprig	1
1	Bay leaf	1
1	Fresh fennel sprig	1
2 - 3	Fresh parsley sprigs	2 - 3
	Saffron powder	
	Salt and pepper	
½ lb	Vermicelli	250 g / 8 oz

1. Peel and chop the carrots. Trim and chop the leeks and celery. Peel and thinly slice 2 onions. Stud the third peeled onion with the cloves. Peel and crush the garlic. Chop the tomatoes.
2. Heat the oil in a large saucepan. Add the carrots, leeks, celery, sliced onions and garlic. Cook until softened, then add the clove-studded onion, crabs, tomatoes, water, herbs, a pinch of saffron, and salt and pepper to taste. Simmer over a low heat for 45 minutes (the longer the soup cooks, the more accentuated will be its taste of crab).
3. Remove the crabs from the saucepan and set aside. Strain the soup and return it to the pan. Bring back to a boil, then add the vermicelli and simmer for 10 minutes or until just tender.
4. Meanwhile, crack open the crabs and remove the edible meaty parts.
5. Add the crabmeat to the soup. Taste and adjust the seasoning, and serve hot with croûtons and hot pepper and potato mayonnaise (see page 120), if liked.

Soupe aux poireaux
Leek Soup

00:10   01:00

American	Ingredients	Metric/Imperial
4	Large leeks	4
6	Potatoes	6
3 cups	Water	750 ml / 1¼ pints
1 quart	Milk	1 l / 1¾ pints
	Salt and pepper	
¼ cup	Butter	50 g / 2 oz

1. Clean the leeks, remove the roots and the green part of the leaves, and quarter the whites. Clean them under cold water, separating the leaves, then drain and cut into thin shreds crosswise. Peel the potatoes and cut into cubes.
2. Place the leeks and potatoes in a large saucepan together

with the water and milk. Add salt and pepper to taste and bring to a boil. Cover and simmer gently for 1 hour.
3. Purée the soup in a blender or food processor until smooth.
4. Put the butter in a soup tureen and pour the soup over it. Stir and serve very hot.

Chilled leek and potato soup

Soupe aux pois cassés
Split Pea Soup

00:05   01:10

American	Ingredients	Metric/Imperial
2 quarts	Water	2 l / 3½ pints
1 cup	Split peas	250 g / 8 oz
½	Pig's foot [trotter]	½
1	Celery stalk	1
1	Onion	1
1	Bouquet garni	1
	Salt and pepper	
¼ cup	Crème fraîche (see page 122)	4 tbsp
	Croûtons for serving	

1. Pour the cold water into a saucepan. Add the split peas, pig's foot, celery, peeled onion, bouquet garni and salt and pepper to taste. Bring to a boil and leave to cook for 1 hour 10 minutes.

2. Remove the pig's foot and put to one side. Remove and discard the onion and bouquet garni. Purée the soup in a blender or food processor until smooth and return it to the pan. If the soup is too thick, add a little water. Reheat the soup.

3. Cut the pig's foot into small pieces.

4. Add the crème fraîche to the soup and stir to mix. Serve hot with the pig's foot and croûtons.

Soupe au potiron
Pumpkin Soup

	00:10	00:50

American	Ingredients	Metric/Imperial
4 lb	Pumpkin	2 kg / 4 lb
⅔ cup	Water	150 ml / ¼ pint
1 quart	Milk	1 l / 1¾ pints
2 tbsp	Sugar	2 tbsp
	Salt	
2 tbsp	Butter	25 g / 1 oz
1 tbsp	Chopped fresh parsley	1 tbsp

1. Peel the pumpkin, remove the seeds and cut into cubes. Place in a saucepan, add the water and cook over a moderate heat for about 20 minutes. At the end of the cooking time, if there is too much liquid, evaporate it quickly over a brisk heat.

2. Purée the pumpkin in a blender or food processor until smooth.

3. Bring the milk to a boil in the saucepan. Add the pumpkin, sugar and a pinch of salt. Cook over a low heat for 25 minutes, stirring occasionally.

4. Stir in the butter and parsley and serve hot.

Vichyssoise
Chilled Leek and Potato Soup

	00:30 plus chilling	00:30

American	Ingredients	Metric/Imperial
4	Leeks, white part only	4
4	Onions	4
3 tbsp	Butter	40 g / 1½ oz
5	Potatoes	5
1½ quarts	Chicken stock (see page 136)	1.5 l / 2½ pints
⅔ cup	Crème fraîche (see page 122)	150 ml / ¼ pint
	Salt and pepper	

1. Clean the leeks and chop finely. Peel onions and cut into thin strips. Melt the butter in a saucepan, add the leeks and onions and cook for about 15 minutes over a gentle heat. Do not allow the vegetables to brown.

2. Peel and thinly slice the potatoes. Add to the pan and cook for 3-4 minutes, stirring continuously.

3. Bring the chicken stock to a boil. Add the vegetables and leave to cook for about 15 minutes or until the potatoes are tender.

4. Purée the soup in a blender or food processor until smooth,

then strain through a fine sieve. Leave to cool.

5. Add the crème fraîche and whisk vigorously, then add salt and pepper to taste. Chill until ready to serve.

Pumpkin soup

Velouté à la tomate
Tomato Cream Soup

	00:15	00:30

American	Ingredients	Metric/Imperial
2	Onions	2
2 tbsp	Butter	25 g / 1 oz
2 lb	Tomatoes	1 kg / 2 lb
1	Garlic clove	1
1	Fresh thyme sprig	1
1 quart	Water	1 l / 1¾ pints
3 tbsp	Cornstarch [cornflour]	3 tbsp
1 tsp	Sugar	1 tsp
¼ cup	Thick crème fraîche (see page 122)	4 tbsp
	Salt and pepper	
1	Egg yolk	1
2 tbsp	Chopped fresh parsley	2 tbsp
	Croûtons for serving	

1. Peel and thinly slice the onions. Melt half of the butter in a saucepan over a gentle heat and add the onions. Cook until softened.

2. Meanwhile, peel the tomatoes (first plunging them in boiling water for 10 seconds) and cut into small pieces. Add to the onions with the remaining butter and cook until the tomatoes are pulpy.

3. Add the peeled garlic clove, thyme and water. Bring to a boil and leave to cook for 25 minutes.

4. Remove and discard the thyme, then purée the soup in a blender until smooth. Return to the saucepan.

5. Mix the cornstarch with a little cold water and the sugar. Add to the soup and cook, stirring, until thickened. Remove from the heat and stir in the crème fraîche and salt and pepper to taste.

6. Mix the egg yolk and chopped parsley in a soup tureen. Gradually add the soup, stirring well. Serve with croûtons.

Tourin de Saint-Céré

Garlic Soup

00:20   00:40

American	Ingredients	Metric/Imperial
5	Onions	5
1 tbsp	Oil	1 tbsp
6	Tomatoes	6
6	Garlic cloves	6
2 quarts	Water	2 l / 3½ pints
1	Bouquet garni	1
	Salt and pepper	
1	Egg yolk	1
2 tbsp	Vinegar	2 tbsp
	Slices of toasted french bread	
1 cup	Grated gruyère cheese	125 g / 4 oz

1. Peel and thinly slice the onions. Heat the oil in a heavy saucepan, add the onions and cook until softened.
2. Meanwhile, peel the tomatoes (first plunging them in boiling water for 10 seconds) and quarter them. Peel the garlic. Place the tomatoes, garlic, water, bouquet garni and salt to taste in another saucepan and bring to a boil. Leave to cook for 10 minutes.
3. Pour the tomato mixture over the onions and stir well. Leave to cook over a brisk heat for 20 minutes.
4. Strain the soup, pressing down on the vegetables in the strainer to extract all their juices. Reheat the soup, if necessary.
5. Mix the egg yolk and vinegar in a soup tureen. Gradually stir in the soup. Add pepper to taste.
6. Serve hot, with the toasted bread and cheese.

Cook's tip: although garlic is very pungent when used raw, this soup does not have an overpowering flavor.

Velouté aux huîtres

Oyster Cream Soup

00:15   00:30

American	Ingredients	Metric/Imperial
½ lb	Whiting	250 g / 8 oz
½ lb	Sole or other white fish trimmings	250 g / 8 oz
1	Onion	1
1	Carrot	1
1	Fresh thyme sprig	1
½	Bay leaf	½
2 quarts	Water	2 l / 3½ pints
	Salt and pepper	
6 tbsp	Butter	75 g / 3 oz
2 tbsp	Flour	2 tbsp
5 oz	Mushrooms	150 g / 5 oz
2 - 3	Fresh parsley sprigs	2 - 3
18	Oysters	18
5 tbsp	White wine	5 tbsp
4	Egg yolks	4
⅔ cup	Crème fraîche (see page 122)	150 ml / ¼ pint
	Lemon juice	

1. Place the whiting, sole trimmings, peeled onion and carrot, thyme and bay leaf in a large saucepan. Add the water, and salt and pepper to taste. Bring to a boil and simmer for 30 minutes. Strain the stock and set aside.
2. Melt ¼ cup [50 g / 2 oz] butter in a saucepan and add the flour. Brown slightly over a gentle heat, stirring constantly. Add the strained fish stock, stirring well. Slice the mushrooms and add to the pan with the parsley sprigs. Leave to cook for 12-15 minutes, skimming the pan from time to time to remove any froth that may rise to the surface of the liquid.
3. Meanwhile, open the oysters and remove them from their shells. Reserve the oyster liquor.
4. Put the remaining butter and the white wine into a saucepan, bring to a boil and boil for 4 minutes. Add the oysters and their liquor and poach for 3 minutes.
5. Remove the oysters from the saucepan with a slotted spoon and set aside. Add the cooking juice to the fish broth.
6. Mix the egg yolks with the crème fraîche. Add to the soup, off the heat, stirring well. Return to the heat and cook gently, stirring, until thickened. Do not boil. Taste and adjust the seasoning, with lemon juice, salt and pepper.
7. Divide the oysters between individual soup bowls or plates and ladle in the soup.
8. Serve immediately, with french bread.

Velouté à l'oseille

Sorrel Cream Soup

00:10   00:30

American	Ingredients	Metric/Imperial
1	Large handful of sorrel	1
¼ cup	Butter	50 g / 2 oz
1 tbsp	Flour	1 tbsp
2 quarts	Water	2 l / 3½ pints
3	Potatoes	3
½ cup	Crème fraîche (see page 122)	125 ml / 4 fl oz
	Salt	
1	Bunch of fresh chervil or parsley	1
2	Egg yolks	2
	Croûtons for serving	

1. Put 4 or 5 of the sorrel leaves to one side. Remove the stalks from the remainder of the leaves. Rinse, drain and chop coarsely.
2. Melt the butter in a large saucepan and add the chopped sorrel. Cook, stirring frequently, until wilted. Sprinkle over the flour and stir well to mix, then add the water. Bring to a boil, stirring constantly to prevent sticking.
3. Peel and chop the potatoes. Add to the pan and simmer for about 15 minutes or until the potatoes are very tender.
4. Purée the soup in a blender or food processor until smooth. Return to the saucepan.
5. Cut the reserved sorrel leaves into thin strips. Add to the soup and heat. When the soup is almost at boiling point, remove from the heat and add the crème fraîche and salt to taste. Stir well.
6. Place the coarsely chopped chervil and egg yolks in a soup tureen and stir to mix. Pour the hot soup over this preparation and mix quickly. Serve with croûtons.

Cook's tip: Use fresh spinach to make this soup if sorrel is not available.

Onion soup

CHAPTER 10

First Courses

Cold hors d'oeuvres

Preparing raw vegetables

Asparagus
Hold the asparagus spear with its tip toward you. Using a swivel-bladed vegetable peeler and working towards the base of the spear, carefully peel away the outer skin.

Cabbage
With a large pointed knife, slice the cabbage in two and cut away the woody core of each half.

Endive [chicory] heart
Insert a small sharp knife at the base of the head to a depth of ¾ in / 2 cm, and cut out the cone formed by the center leaves.

Fennel and celery
Remove the leafy green part of the celery stalk or fennel bulb, then pull off any tough fibers or strings with a paring knife.

Garlic clove
Place the clove under the flat surface of a kitchen knife and press down firmly. This will flatten the garlic and burst the outer skin, which will then come away easily. Remove the outer skin and crush the garlic in a garlic press, or using a mortar and pestle.

Globe artichoke hearts
Cut off the stalk with a stainless steel knife. Pull the thick outside leaves away. Remove the choke with a grapefruit knife or a teaspoon and rub the cut surface of the heart with a slice of lemon to prevent discoloration.

Green beans
Make a cut across one end of the bean without severing it completely. Catching the string with the blade of your knife, pull it away along the bean's length. Repeat at the other end to remove the string from the other side.

Leeks
Remove any roots, cut off the damaged ends of the green leaves and slice the leek lengthwise into quarters. Holding the leaves open, wash each section thoroughly under cold running water.

Pumpkin
Cut the pumpkin into quarters and peel away its skin with a small sharp knife. Remove and discard the seeds and the coarse stringy material inside.

Shallots
Cut a thin slice from each end of the shallot, then remove and discard the papery skin and the first fleshy layer.

Spinach and sorrel leaves
Fold the leaf in two along the central stalk. Hold the folded leaf in one hand, and with the other tear the stalk away working from the base to the tip.

Sweet pepper [capsicum]
Cut the pepper in half lengthwise and remove the core, seeds and whitish membrane.

Tomatoes
Cut out the hard, green core around the stalk, then immerse the tomatoes in boiling water for 10 seconds if they are ripe, a little longer if they are not. The skins will then slip off easily. Cut in half to scoop or press out the seeds.

Asparagus with mousseline sauce

Asperges à la flamande

Asparagus, Flemish Style

00:30   00:30 to 00:45

American	Ingredients	Metric/Imperial
3 lb	Asparagus	1.5 kg / 3 lb
3	Eggs	3
2 tbsp	Chopped fresh chervil or parsley	2 tbsp
2 tbsp	Chopped fresh chives	2 tbsp
	Salt and pepper	
1 cup	Butter	250 g / 8 oz
1	Lemon	1

1. Trim the woody ends from the asparagus, then scrape the stalks. Tie the asparagus spears in 3 equal bunches. Set aside.
2. Hard-cook the eggs for 10 minutes in a saucepan of boiling water. Drain and cool, then shell the eggs. Chop them finely, or blend briefly in a blender or food processor. Add the chervil and chives and mix well.
3. Put salted water on to boil in a large saucepan. When the water is boiling, add the bunches of asparagus. As soon as the water returns to a boil, reduce the heat to keep the water simmering. Leave to cook for 5-20 minutes (depending on the age and size of the asparagus) or until tender.
4. Meanwhile, heat the butter in a heatproof glass bowl placed in a saucepan of simmering water (or use a double boiler). As soon as the butter has melted, remove the bowl from the pan and allow to cool. After a moment or two, a white sediment will form on the bottom of the bowl. Pour the clear melted butter very gently from the top into a serving bowl, leaving the sediment behind.
5. Add the juice of the lemon to the clarified butter. Add salt and pepper to taste. Stir in one-quarter of the egg and herb mixture.
6. Drain the asparagus and arrange on a warmed serving dish. Sprinkle with the remaining egg and herb mixture. Serve warm, accompanied by the butter sauce.

Asperges sauce mousseline
Asparagus with Mousseline Sauce

�▽ 00:20　　　　　00:35 🥘

American	Ingredients	Metric/Imperial
3 lb	Asparagus	1.5 kg / 3 lb
⅔ cup	Vinegar	150 ml / ¼ pint
6	Black peppercorns	6
	Salt	
2	Egg yolks	2
6 tbsp	Butter	75 g / 3 oz
⅔ cup	Heavy [double] cream	150 ml / ¼ pint

1. Trim the woody ends from the asparagus, then scrape the stalks. Tie the asparagus spears in 4 equal bunches, and set aside.
2. Place the vinegar and peppercorns in a small saucepan and bring to a boil. Boil until reduced to 1 tablespoon.
3. Meanwhile, put salted water on to boil in a large saucepan. When the water is boiling, add the bunches of asparagus. As soon as boiling resumes, reduce the heat to keep the water simmering. Leave to cook for 5-20 minutes (depending on the age and size of the asparagus) or until tender.
4. When the asparagus is cooked, remove it from the water and drain well. Arrange on a folded napkin on a warmed serving dish and keep hot.
5. Strain the peppercorns from the reduced vinegar. Remove the pan from the heat and add the egg yolks, whisking vigorously. Gradually incorporate the butter, cut into small pieces, continuing to whisk until thickened. Add salt to taste.
6. Whip the cream until thick and fold into the sauce.
7. Serve the mousseline sauce in a sauceboat with the asparagus.

Artichauts vinaigrette
Artichokes Vinaigrette

▮▽ 00:10　　00:25 to 00:30 🥘

American	Ingredients	Metric/Imperial
6	Globe artichokes	6
	Salt and pepper	
1 tbsp	Vinegar	1 tbsp
1 tbsp	Prepared mustard, preferably Dijon	1 tbsp
3 tbsp	Oil	3 tbsp
1	Fresh parsley sprig	1

1. Break off the stalks of the artichokes, pulling them to remove the strings also. Remove any damaged or discolored leaves.
2. Bring a large saucepan of salted water to a boil. Add the artichokes and leave to cook for about 30 minutes. To test if they are done, pull out one of the large leaves near the base. If it comes out easily, the artichokes are ready.
3. Remove the artichokes from the water, and drain upside-down in a colander.
4. For the dressing, dissolve a pinch of salt in the vinegar. Stir in the mustard. Season with pepper to taste. Add the oil and chopped parsley and mix thoroughly.
5. Serve the vinaigrette with the warm or cold artichokes.

Caviar d'aubergines
Eggplant [Aubergine] Caviar

▮▽ 00:20　　　　　00:35 🥘
plus chilling

American	Ingredients	Metric/Imperial
2	Eggplant [aubergines]	2
1	Large, very firm tomato	1
1	Shallot	1
1	Garlic clove (optional)	1
	Salt and pepper	
⅔ cup	Olive oil	150 ml / ¼ pint
1 tbsp	Chopped fresh dill or parsley	1 tbsp

1. Preheat the oven to 350°F / 180°C / Gas Mark 4.
2. Place the whole eggplant in the oven and bake until the skin becomes cracked and the eggplant are soft to the touch. Remove them from the oven and peel.
3. Peel the tomato (first plunging it in boiling water for 10 seconds), remove the seeds and cut into pieces.
4. Mince the eggplant and tomato purée in a blender or food processor until smooth.
5. Peel the shallot and garlic. Crush them in a mortar or blend to a purée.
6. Put all the puréed ingredients into a salad bowl and add salt and pepper to taste. Stir with a wooden spoon, gradually adding the olive oil in a trickle as for mayonnaise. You should obtain a thick paste. Chill lightly.
7. Add the chopped dill or parsley just before serving.

Cook's tip: choose firm glossy eggplant, as dull soft ones will be stale.

Aspics de foies de volaille
Chicken Livers in Aspic

▮▽ 00:20　　　　　00:08 🥘
plus chilling

American	Ingredients	Metric/Imperial
1	Shallot	1
3 tbsp	Butter	40 g / 1½ oz
1 lb	Chicken livers	500 g / 1 lb
	Salt and pepper	
	Dried thyme	
1 tbsp	Cognac	1 tbsp
1 quart	Liquid aspic (see page 116)	1 l / 1¾ pints
	Lettuce or other salad greens	
2 - 3	Tomatoes	2 - 3

1. Peel the shallot and chop finely. Melt the butter in a saucepan over a moderate heat, add the shallot and cook until softened.
2. Halve the livers and add to the pan. Cook over a brisk heat until they are firm and browned but still pink inside.
3. Add salt and pepper to taste. Add a pinch of thyme and the cognac. Remove from the heat and allow to cool completely.
4. Divide the livers between six individual molds and cover with warm aspic. Chill for at least 6 hours or until set.
5. Unmold the livers in aspic onto serving dishes garnished with salad greens and tomato quarters.

Assiette de crudités

Raw Vegetable Platter

	00:40 to 00:50 plus infusing	00:10

American	Ingredients	Metric/Imperial
2 tbsp	Cider vinegar	2 tbsp
½ cup	Oil	125 ml / 4 fl oz
2	Canned anchovy fillets	2
1 tbsp	Chopped fresh chives	1 tbsp
1 tbsp	Chopped fresh tarragon	1 tbsp
1	Small cauliflower	1
1	Head of red cabbage	1
6	Carrots	6
1	Head of celery	1
2	Cooked beets [beetroot]	2
1	Bunch of radishes	1
¾ lb	Mushrooms	350 g / 12 oz
1	Lemon	1
6	Eggs	6
	Salt and pepper	

1. About 2 hours before serving, prepare the vinaigrette. Mix the cider vinegar and oil in a bowl. Pound the anchovy fillets to a cream in a mortar with a pestle. Add to the oil and vinegar with the chives and tarragon. Leave to infuse for 2 hours, stirring occasionally. Do not add salt and pepper until you are ready to serve.

2. Break the cauliflower into florets. Core the red cabbage, and cut it into thin strips. Peel the carrots and grate them finely. Trim the celery and cut into small cubes. Peel the beets and dice them. Trim the radishes, leaving some of the leaves on them. Thinly slice the mushrooms, then sprinkle them with the juice of the lemon to keep them white.

3. Arrange all the vegetables on a large serving dish.

4. Hard-cook the eggs for 10 minutes in boiling water. Run them under cold water to cool, and remove the shells.

5. Cut the pointed tip off each egg. Remove the yolk from the cut-off pieces and crush it finely with a fork. Add the crushed yolk to the vinaigrette and season with salt and pepper. Decorate the serving dish with the rest of the eggs.

6. Serve the vegetables accompanied by the vinaigrette in a sauceboat.

Raw vegetable platter

Cervelle de canut

Herb-flavored Cream Cheese

	00:15 plus chilling	00:00

American	Ingredients	Metric/Imperial
2	Shallots	2
1 cup	Crème fraîche (see page 122)	250 ml / 8 fl oz
1 lb (2 cups)	Firm cream cheese	500 g / 1 lb
2 tsp	Chopped fresh parsley	2 tsp
1 tbsp	Chopped fresh chives	1 tbsp
3 tbsp	Chopped fresh chervil	3 tbsp
	Salt and pepper	
3 tbsp	Olive oil	3 tbsp
1 tsp	Vinegar	1 tsp

1. Peel and finely chop the shallots.

2. Whisk together the crème fraîche, cream cheese, chopped herbs and shallots. Add salt and pepper to taste. Continuing to stir, incorporate the olive oil and vinegar.

3. Line a round bowl with cheesecloth or muslin. Pour in the cheese mixture, heaping it up well. Fold-over the cheesecloth or muslin. Chill for 4 hours.

4. To serve, unwrap the cheese and unmold it onto a serving dish. Serve with raw vegetables or on its own before dessert. The French name for this cheese, which originated in Lyons, means 'silk weaver's brain.'

Citrons farcis au thon

Lemons Stuffed with Tuna

	00:30 plus chilling	00:00

American	Ingredients	Metric/Imperial
6	Large, thick-skinned lemons	6
1 (7 oz)	Can of tuna	1 (200 g / 7 oz)
1	Egg yolk	1
1 tsp	Prepared mustard	1 tsp
1 cup	Oil	250 ml / 8 fl oz
1 tbsp	Vinegar	1 tbsp
	Salt and pepper	
	Tabasco sauce (optional)	
6	Black olives	6

1. Cut off the pointed ends of the lemons and scrape out the pulp using a small spoon. Do not pierce the lemon skins. Set aside the lemon shells and cut-off ends.

2. Cut the lemon pulp into cubes and place these in a mixing bowl. Drain and flake the tuna and add to the diced lemon pulp.

3. Place the egg yolk in another bowl with the mustard and add the oil gradually in a trickle, blending with a whisk. When the mayonnaise is quite firm, incorporate the vinegar and season with salt, pepper and a few drops of tabasco sauce.

4. Add the mayonnaise to the tuna mixture and stir well. Stuff the lemon shells with the tuna mayonnaise. Garnish with olives and cover with the cut-off ends of the lemons. Chill until ready to serve.

Coeurs d'artichaut à la provençale

Artichoke Hearts Provençal Style

00:15   01:00

American	Ingredients	Metric/Imperial
36	Small purple globe artichokes	36
1	Lemon	1
4	Tomatoes	4
12	Pearl [button] onions	12
½ lb	Lightly salted bacon	250 g / 8 oz
6 tbsp	Olive oil	6 tbsp
1 tsp	Chopped fresh thyme	1 tsp
2	Bay leaves	2
	Salt and pepper	
1 tbsp	Chopped fresh basil	1 tbsp

1. Break off the artichoke stalks. Cut away the small outside leaves. Sprinkle the juice of half the lemon over the outside of the artichoke hearts so that they do not turn black. Continue cutting away all the side leaves, leaving only the center ones. Cut off the center leaves at their base. Completely remove the hairy choke, leaving the heart clean. Sprinkle with the remaining lemon juice.
2. Quarter and core the tomatoes. Peel the onions. Dice the bacon.
3. Place the bacon in a heavy saucepan and heat until it renders its fat. Drain the bacon on paper towels. Pour off the fat from the pan.
4. Heat the olive oil in a saucepan. Add the artichoke hearts, thyme and bay leaves cut into thin strips and cook until the artichoke hearts are lightly browned. Add the onions and brown lightly, turning them to cook evenly.
5. Return the bacon to the pan with the tomatoes, and salt and pepper to taste. Cover and leave to cook over a low heat for about 1 hour.
6. About 15 minutes before cooking is finished, add the basil. Serve hot or cold.

Concombres à la crème

Cucumbers in Cream

00:20   00:00
plus draining and chilling

American	Ingredients	Metric/Imperial
2	Cucumbers	2
	Salt and pepper	
10	Fresh tarragon sprigs	10
2	Lemons	2
1 cup	Crème fraîche (see page 122)	250 ml / 8 fl oz

1. Wipe the cucumbers and cut into thin slices. Place the slices in a colander and sprinkle with salt. Stir and leave to drain for 30 minutes.
2. Rinse the cucumber slices in cold water and drain again. Pat the slices dry with paper towels.
3. Chop the leaves from the tarragon sprigs and put in a salad bowl with the juice from the 2 lemons. Add pepper to taste. Gradually stir in the crème fraîche.
4. Add the cucumber slices and fold together gently. Chill well.
5. Serve very cold, garnished with a few leaves of tarragon.

Shrimp and rice vinaigrette

Coquilles aux crevettes

Shrimp [Prawns] and Rice Vinaigrette

00:20   00:18
plus marinating

American	Ingredients	Metric/Imperial
1½ cups	Water	350 ml / 12 fl oz
	Salt and pepper	
1 cup	Long grain rice	200 g / 7 oz
2	Red apples	2
2	Lemons	2
6	Celery stalks	6
1	Green pepper	1
2	Tomatoes	2
¾ cup	Peeled cooked shrimp [prawns]	150 g / 5 oz
1 tbsp	Vinegar	1 tbsp
1 tsp	Prepared mustard	1 tsp
3 tbsp	Oil	3 tbsp
1 tbsp	Chopped fresh parsley	1 tbsp
	Cooked shrimp [prawns] in shell for garnish	

1. Bring the water to a boil with salt to taste. Add the rice and simmer for 15-18 minutes or until tender. Drain in a colander and dry the rice by spreading it out on a cloth.
2. Dice the apples and sprinkle with the juice of the lemons so that they do not discolor.
3. Trim the celery. Core and seed the green pepper. Peel the tomatoes (first plunging them in boiling water for 10 seconds). Dice all these vegetables.
4. Put the rice, apples, celery, tomatoes and green pepper into a mixing bowl and add the shrimp.
5. Dissolve a pinch of salt in the vinegar. Stir in the mustard. Add the oil, parsley and pepper to taste.
6. Add this dressing to the shrimp mixture and fold together. Cover and leave to marinate for 30 minutes.
7. To serve, divide the mixture between 6 scallop shells or other individual dishes and garnish with a few shrimp in shell.

Feuilles de vigne farcies
Stuffed Grape Leaves

	01:00 plus cooling	01:00

American	Ingredients	Metric/Imperial
36	Grape or vine leaves	36
1¼ cups	Water	300 ml / ½ pint
	Salt and pepper	
¾ cup	Long-grain rice	150 g / 5 oz
6	Onions	6
1	Garlic clove	1
5 tbsp	Olive oil	5 tbsp
5	Fresh parsley sprigs	5
4 - 5	Fresh mint leaves	4 - 5
10	Coriander seeds	10
2	Bay leaves	2
1	Lemon	1

1. Plunge the grape leaves into boiling water, then drain and spread out on a cloth. Set aside.
2. Bring the water to a boil with salt to taste. Add the rice and simmer for 12 minutes: the rice should still be slightly crisp.
3. Meanwhile, peel and finely chop the onions and garlic. Heat 2 tablespoons of the oil in a saucepan, add the onions and garlic and cook over a very gentle heat until softened but not browned. Chop the parsley and mint leaves and add to the saucepan. Stir quickly over the heat.
4. Remove from the heat and add the rice. Season to taste with pepper and mix thoroughly.
5. Preheat the oven to 400°F / 200°C / Gas Mark 6.
6. Place a little pile of the rice mixture on each grape leaf. Fold over the sides, then roll up the leaf into a rather tight sausage.
7. Place the rolled leaves in an ovenproof dish. Cover with cold water and add the remaining olive oil, the coriander seeds and halved bay leaves. Put a plate on the rolled leaves to keep them submerged in the water.
8. Bake about 45 minutes or until the rice has absorbed most of the liquid, and you can pierce the rolls very easily with the point of a knife.
9. Remove the dish from the oven and leave to cool.
10. Drain the rolled grape leaves when cold. Squeeze the juice from half the lemon over the rolled leaves and garnish with the remaining lemon, thinly sliced.

Melons au jambon de Parme
Melon with Parma Ham

	00:05 plus chilling	00:00

American	Ingredients	Metric/Imperial
3	Ripe melons	3
12	Thin slices of parma ham or prosciutto	12
	Pepper	

1. Buy the melons the day before and choose well: they must be very heavy and sweet-smelling. Keep them in the refrigerator overnight.
2. About 30 minutes before serving, cut each melon into quarters and remove the seeds. Remove the peel. Return the melon quarters to the refrigerator to chill for 30 minutes.
3. Wrap each piece of melon in a slice of parma ham and arrange on a long dish. You may add pepper (pepper goes very well with melon).

Avocats garnis
Stuffed Avocado

	00:30	00:00

American	Ingredients	Metric/Imperial
3	Avocados	3
	Lemon juice	
	Salt and pepper	
1	Celery stalk	1
6	Lettuce leaves	6
1 cup	Black olives	150 g / 5 oz

1. Cut the avocados in half lengthwise and remove the seed. Brush the cut surfaces with lemon juice to prevent them from discoloring. Season the avocados with salt and pepper to taste.
2. Trim and dice the celery. Place each avocado half on a lettuce leaf, surrounded by a few olives and a little diced celery. Fill the hollows in the avocado halves with one of the following preparations:

Anchovy vinaigrette: prepare a vinaigrette dressing (see page 120) and season it to taste with anchovy paste or essence. Garnish the avocado with a few rolled anchovy fillets.

Shrimp: allow 1 tablespoon cooked peeled shrimp [prawns], a little diced celery and 1 tablespoon mayonnaise (see page 119) for each avocado half. Season with a few drops of tabasco sauce.

Crab: as for shrimp, using canned or freshly cooked crab meat, and decorate with a few black olives.

Tuna: allow 1 tablespoon flaked canned tuna and a little diced celery dressed with vinaigrette (see page 120) or mayonnaise (see page 119) for each half avocado.

Champignons à la grecque
Mushrooms, Greek Style

	00:30 plus cooling	00:40

American	Ingredients	Metric/Imperial
⅔ cup	Olive oil	150 ml / ¼ pint
3 cups	Water	750 ml / 1¼ pints
2	Lemons	2
1 tsp	Coriander seeds	1 tsp
1 tsp	Fennel seeds	1 tsp
1	Bouquet garni	1
2	Celery stalks	2
10	Black peppercorns	10
	Salt	
¾ lb	Small button mushrooms	350 g / 12 oz

1. Pour the olive oil and water into a heavy saucepan. Add the juice of the lemons, the coriander seeds, fennel seeds, bouquet garni, celery and peppercorns. Add salt to taste. Bring to the boil and leave to cook for 30 minutes.
2. Meanwhile, trim the mushrooms. If they are small, leave them whole. If they are large, quarter them.
3. Add the mushrooms to the saucepan and bring back to a boil. Simmer for 2 minutes, then immediately remove the saucepan from the heat. Leave the mushrooms to cool in the liquid.
4. Before serving, remove and discard the bouquet garni and celery.

Céleri rémoulade
Celeriac in Mayonnaise

	00:20	00:00
	plus marinating	

American	Ingredients	Metric/Imperial
1 (1 lb)	Head of celeriac	1 (500 g / 1 lb)
1	Lemon	1
	Salt and pepper	
1	Egg yolk	1
2 tbsp	Strong prepared mustard	2 tbsp
1 tbsp	Vinegar	1 tbsp
1 cup	Oil	250 ml / 8 fl oz
2 tbsp	Chopped fresh parsley	2 tbsp

1. Peel the celeriac and sprinkle it with the juice of half the lemon so that it does not discolor. Grate it coarsely.
2. Place the celeriac in a bowl and sprinkle with the remaining lemon juice in which you have dissolved ½ teaspoon of salt. Leave to blanch for 30 minutes to 1 hour, stirring occasionally.
3. Meanwhile, place the egg yolk in a bowl and add the mustard, vinegar, and salt and pepper to taste. Mix well. Gradually add the oil, whisking vigorously. The mayonnaise must be quite thick and adhere to the whisk. If it is too thick, add a little more vinegar.
4. Drain the celeriac, squeezing it in your hand, and place in a salad bowl. Add the mayonnaise gradually, stirring to combine the ingredients thoroughly.
5. Leave to stand for 30 minutes before serving, sprinkled with chopped parsley.

Chou rouge en salade
Red Cabbage Salad

	00:20	00:03
	plus soaking	

American	Ingredients	Metric/Imperial
1	Head of red cabbage	1
	Salt and pepper	
1¼ cups	Wine vinegar	300 ml / ½ pint
6	Eggs	6
1 cup	Crème fraîche (see page 122)	250 ml / 8 fl oz
1	Lemon	1
1 tbsp	Chopped fresh chervil or parsley	1 tbsp
1 tbsp	Chopped fresh chives	1 tbsp
1 tbsp	Chopped fresh fennel	1 tbsp

1. Remove the coarse and discolored outer leaves from the cabbage. Quarter the cabbage and remove the core. Cut the cabbage into thin strips (julienne).
2. Boil a large quantity of salted water in a saucepan. Add the cabbage. Return to a boil and continue boiling for 2 minutes. Drain the cabbage in a colander, run it under cold water and drain again. Put the cabbage into a mixing bowl and pour over the wine vinegar. Add salt and pepper to taste and leave to marinate for 1 hour, stirring frequently.
3. Hard-cook the eggs for 10 minutes in boiling water. Drain. Remove the shells and crush the eggs with a fork.
4. Mix the eggs with the crème fraîche, the juice of the lemon, the chervil, chives and fennel. Add salt and pepper to taste.
5. Drain the cabbage, discarding the marinade, and place in a salad bowl. Pour the cream sauce over and stir carefully.

Concombres à la menthe
Cucumbers with Yogurt and Mint

	00:15	00:00
	plus draining	

American	Ingredients	Metric/Imperial
3	Cucumbers	3
	Salt	
2 cups	Plain yogurt	450 ml / ¾ pint
3 tbsp	Olive oil	3 tbsp
1 tbsp	Chopped fresh fennel	1 tbsp
2 tbsp	Vinegar	2 tbsp
12	Fresh mint leaves	12

1. Peel the cucumbers, cut into quarters lengthwise and remove the seeds. Dice the cucumbers. Place in a colander, sprinkle with salt and leave to drain for 30 minutes.
2. Mix the yoghurt with the olive oil and fennel. Add the vinegar and mix very thoroughly.
3. Rinse the cucumbers under cold water, drain well and pat dry. Place in a salad bowl. Pour the yoghurt sauce over and sprinkle with the chopped mint leaves.
4. Just before serving, mix the cucumbers and sauce together.

Cook's tip: serve this as part of a summer hors d'oeuvre.

Cucumber with yogurt

Hors d'oeuvre d'hiver aux pois chiches

Mussel and Chick Pea Salad

00:10 plus soaking		01:30 to 02:00

American	Ingredients	Metric/Imperial
2 cups	Dried chick peas	500 g / 1 lb
1 quart	Mussels	750 g / 1½ lb
	Salt and pepper	
1 tbsp	Vinegar	1 tbsp
1 tbsp	Prepared mustard	1 tbsp
3 tbsp	Oil	3 tbsp
1 tbsp	Chopped fresh herbs (parsley, tarragon, chervil chives)	1 tbsp
3	Onions	3
1 cup	Black olives	125 g / 4 oz

1. Rinse the chick peas, place them in a bowl and cover with cold water. Leave to soak for 12 hours.
2. The next day, drain the chick peas, place them in a saucepan and cover with fresh cold water. Bring to a boil and cook for 1½-2 hours or until the chick peas are tender. Drain. Set aside to cool.
3. Thoroughly wash the mussels, changing the water at least 3 times. Place the mussels in a large saucepan over a brisk heat. As soon as they have opened, remove from the heat and take them out of their shells. (Discard any mussels that remain closed.) Allow to cool.
4. Dissolve a pinch of salt in the vinegar. Add the mustard and pepper to taste. Add the oil and herbs. Peel and finely chop 2 of the onions and add to the dressing. Mix well.
5. Combine the chick peas, mussels and dressing. Toss together gently.
6. Peel the remaining onion and slice thinly. Separate the slices into rings.
7. Garnish the salad with the onion rings and olives.

Hors d'oeuvre d'hiver aux endives

Winter Vegetable Salad

00:10		00:00

American	Ingredients	Metric/Imperial
3	Heads of Belgian endive [chicory]	3
1	Cooked beet [beetroot]	1
2	Apples	2
½	Lemon	½
1	Head of celery	1
1 cup	Walnuts	125 g / 4 oz
1	Egg yolk	1
1½ tsp	Strong prepared mustard	1½ tsp
	Salt and pepper	
1 cup	Oil	250 ml / 8 fl oz
1 tsp	Wine vinegar	1 tsp
1 tsp	Tomato paste [purée]	1 tsp

1. Remove the damaged leaves from the endives and slice crosswise. Peel and dice the beet. Peel and dice the apples, and sprinkle with lemon juice. Trim and dice the celery.

2. Combine the endive, beet, apples, celery and walnuts.
3. Put the egg yolk into a bowl and add the mustard, a pinch of salt and a pinch of pepper. Stir to mix, then add the oil gradually and in a thin trickle, stirring vigorously. Thin out the mayonnaise with the wine vinegar, and blend thoroughly. Add the tomato paste.
4. Add the mayonnaise to the salad ingredients and fold together gently.

Winter salad

Fonds d'artichaut vinaigrette

Artichoke Hearts Vinaigrette

00:20		00:30

American	Ingredients	Metric/Imperial
6	Large globe artichokes	6
	Salt and pepper	
3 tbsp	Chopped fresh chives	3 tbsp
	Lemon juice	
6	Eggs	6
2½ tbsp	Cider vinegar	2½ tbsp
1 tsp	Strong prepared mustard	1 tsp
⅔ cup	Oil	150 ml / ¼ pint
6	Tomatoes	6
1	Head of celery	1
1¼ cups	Black olives	400 g / 14 oz

1. Cook the artichokes in boiling salted water for 10 minutes. Drain upside-down.
2. Remove the artichoke leaves, keeping the hearts intact. Remove the hairy choke and set the hearts aside. Grate the flesh from the base of the leaves. Discard the leaves.
3. Mix the grated artichoke flesh with the chives and a few drops of lemon juice. Spread the mixture over the artichoke hearts.
4. Hard-cook the eggs in boiling water. Drain and remove the shells. Halve the eggs.
5. Dissolve a pinch of salt in the cider vinegar. Mix the mustard with the vinegar. Add the oil and pepper to taste, mixing thoroughly.
6. Serve each artichoke heart on a separate plate together with a quartered tomato, 2 egg halves, a few sticks of celery and olives. Serve the vinaigrette in a sauceboat.

Hors d'oeuvre d'hiver aux champignons de Paris

Raw Mushrooms in Cream

⏱ 00:10   🍲 00:00

American	Ingredients	Metric/Imperial
¾ lb	Mushrooms	350 g / 12 oz
1 tbsp	Lemon juice	1 tbsp
½ cup	Heavy [double] cream	125 ml / 4 fl oz
1 tsp	Strong prepared mustard	1 tsp
	Salt and pepper	
1 tbsp	Chopped fresh parsley	1 tbsp

1. Trim and wipe the mushrooms. Slice them and immediately sprinkle copiously with lemon juice to prevent them discoloring (you may use vinegar instead of lemon juice).
2. Mix the cream with the mustard. Add salt and pepper to taste. Put the mushrooms in a bowl and pour the cream over them. Fold together gently.
3. Sprinkle with the parsley.

Crudités aux poivrons

Raw Vegetables with Pimiento Paste

⏱ 00:45   🍲 00:10

American	Ingredients	Metric/Imperial
1	Cucumber	1
	Salt	
4	Potatoes	4
4	Eggs	4
4	Tomatoes	4
1	Head of celery	1
½	Can of pimientos	½
1½ tsp	Chopped fresh chervil or parsley	1½ tsp
1 cup	Mayonnaise (see page 119)	250 ml / 8 fl oz
	Toast for serving	

1. Wipe the cucumber and cut it into thin slices. Place in a colander, sprinkle with salt and leave to drain for 1 hour. Rinse under cold water, drain again and pat dry with paper towels.
2. Rinse the potatoes and put them unpeeled into a saucepan of cold salted water. Bring to a boil and leave to cook for about 20 minutes or until tender. Drain in a colander. When cool enough to handle, peel the potatoes and dice them.
3. Hard-cook the eggs in boiling water for 10 minutes. Drain and remove the shells.
4. Thinly slice the tomatoes. Trim and dice the celery. Drain the pimientos and pat dry with paper towels.
5. Purée the pimientos with the hard-cooked eggs in a blender or food processor until smooth . Add the chervil and mix it in, then add 1 tablespoon of the mayonnaise.
6. Put the pimiento paste into a cup in the middle of a serving dish, and surround with the raw vegetables. Serve with toast, which your guests will spread with pimiento paste instead of butter, and with the remaining mayonnaise — flavored, if liked, with chopped fresh herbs. You can replace the mayonnaise with a vinaigrette dressing (see page 120).

Pamplemousses froids

Chilled Grapefruit

⏱ 00:02   🍲 00:00
per fruit plus chilling

American	Ingredients	Metric/Imperial
3	Grapefruit	3
1 cup	Sugar	250 g / 8 oz

1. Cut the fruit in half crosswise. Using a very sharp pointed knife, remove the woolly center and the seeds.
2. Separate each section by cutting along the surrounding membrane as far as the peel. Using a serrated grapefruit knife, separate the flesh from the peel.
3. Serve chilled with the sugar.

Cracked wheat

Taboulé

Cracked Wheat or Tabbouleh

⏱ 00:30   🍲 00:00
plus soaking

American	Ingredients	Metric/Imperial
12	Small onions	12
1 lb	Ripe juicy tomatoes	500 g / 1 lb
5 - 10	Fresh parsley sprigs	5 - 10
1	Bunch of fresh mint	1
½ lb (1½ cups)	Couscous or cracked wheat	250 g / 8 oz
2	Lemons	2
6 tbsp	Oil	6 tbsp
	Salt and pepper	
4	Small firm tomatoes	4

1. Peel and thinly slice 8 of the onions. Peel and dice the ripe tomatoes. Chop the parsley and mint. Place all these ingredients in a mixing bowl and add the couscous, juice of the lemons, the oil and salt and pepper to taste.
2. Mix thoroughly and leave in a cool place for at least 2 hours, stirring from time to time. The couscous will swell in the juice.
3. Peel the remaining onions. Quarter the 4 small tomatoes.
4. Serve the salad in a bowl garnished with the onions, tomato quarters and a few mint sprigs.

Oignons à l'orientale
Sweet and Sour Onions

	00:20 plus cooling	00:40

American	Ingredients	Metric/Imperial
2 lb	Small onions of the same size	1 kg / 2 lb
¼ cup	Tomato paste [purée]	4 tbsp
10	White peppercorns	10
20	Coriander seeds	20
1	Bouquet garni	1
1 tbsp	Sugar or	1 tbsp
⅔ cup	Raisins	125 g / 4 oz
	Paprika	
1	Lemon	1
3 cups	Dry white wine	750 ml / 1 ¼ pints
¼ cup	Olive oil	4 tbsp
1 cup	Water	250 ml / 8 fl oz
	Salt	

1. Peel the onions and drop them into boiling water. Simmer for 5 minutes, then drain.
2. Place the onions in a saucepan and add the tomato paste, peppercorns, coriander seeds, bouquet garni, sugar or raisins and a pinch of paprika. Add the juice of the lemon, the wine, olive oil and water. Add salt to taste.
3. Bring to a boil and leave to simmer until the onions are tender (35-45 minutes, depending on size). When ready, the onions should be coated in the sauce which has reduced. If there is too much sauce, remove the onions and boil to reduce it still further over a brisk heat.
4. Allow to cool, and discard the bouquet garni before serving.

Cook's tip: mushrooms can be prepared in the same way, but add the juice of 2 lemons.

Hors d'oeuvre au tarama
Tarama Hors d'Oeuvre

	00:45 plus cooling Makes about 70	00:15

American	Ingredients	Metric/Imperial
14 oz	Smoked cod roe	400 g / 14 oz
14 tbsp	Butter	200 g / 7 oz
2	Lemons	2
½ cup	Milk	125 ml / 4 fl oz
	Salt	
½ cup	Flour	75 g / 3 oz
3	Eggs	3

1. Remove the skin from the cod roe and place the roe in a blender or food processor. Blend until smooth. Add 10 tbsp [150 g / 5 oz] of the butter and continue to blend, adding lemon juice until you have a paste which is fine, supple and easy to spread. Set aside in the refrigerator.
2. Preheat the oven to 430°F / 240°C / Gas Mark 8.
3. Place the milk, the remaining butter and a pinch of salt in a saucepan. Bring to a boil, stirring to melt the butter. Add the flour all at once and cook, stirring vigorously, until the paste comes away from the sides of the saucepan. Add 2½ of the eggs, one at a time, beating the paste vigorously after each addition. Put the paste into a pastry bag fitted with a small round nozzle.

4. Pipe small heaps of paste the size of a walnut onto lightly greased baking sheets. You should have approximately 70. Brush with the remaining egg, beaten.
5. Place in the oven, with the door half open, and bake for 15 minutes.
6. Leave the choux puffs to cool, then fill them with some of the cod roe paste. You can also serve the paste on small squares of toast. Garnish each square with a black olive.

Melons glacés au porto
Iced Melon with Port Wine

	00:05 plus chilling	00:00

American	Ingredients	Metric/Imperial
3	Ripe melons	3
¾ cup	Port wine	175 ml / 6 fl oz

1. Buy your melons the day before and choose well: they must smell sweet and above all they must be very heavy. Keep them in the refrigerator overnight.
2. About 30 minutes before serving, cut each melon in half and remove the seeds.
3. Pour 2 tablespoons of port wine into each melon half and return to the refrigerator to marinate for 30 minutes.

Tomates farcies
Stuffed Tomatoes

	00:20	00:30

American	Ingredients	Metric/Imperial
6	Ripe tomatoes	6
	Salt and pepper	
3	Fresh parsley sprigs	3
1	Fresh thyme sprig	1
1	Onion	1
1	Garlic clove	1
1½ cups	Ground [minced] cooked meat (beef, veal, etc)	350 g / 12 oz
1	Slice of bread	1
½ cup	Milk	125 ml / 4 fl oz
1	Egg	1
	Pinch of grated nutmeg	

1. Preheat the oven to 350°F / 180°C / Gas Mark 4.
2. Cut the tops off the tomatoes, and reserve them. Scoop the flesh and seeds out of the tomatoes using a small spoon. Season the insides of the tomatoes with salt and pepper, then leave them to drain, unside-down, on paper towels for 15 minutes.
3. Finely chop or mince the parsley, thyme, peeled onion and garlic. Place these ingredients in a mixing bowl and add the meat.
4. Soak the bread in the milk. Squeeze out excess milk, then add the bread to the bowl. Add the egg, nutmeg and salt and pepper to taste. Mix thoroughly.
5. Fill the tomatoes with the meat mixture and replace the tops. Arrange in a baking dish and bake for about 30 minutes. Serve hot or cold.

1. Using a very sharp stainless steel knife, peel the grapefruit without leaving any white pith. Separate the grapefruit into sections, discarding the membrane and seeds. Collect the juice by holding the grapefruit over a bowl as it is prepared.
2. Divide the grapefruit sections and juice between 6 small serving dishes and garnish each with a glacé cherry. Chill until ready to serve.
3. Serve with sugar.

Provençal sandwiches

Pan bagnat

Provençal Sandwiches

	00:10	00:10 to 00:15	
	plus peeling peppers		

American	Ingredients	Metric/Imperial
6	Small loaves of french bread or rolls	6
2 cups	Olive oil	500 ml / ¾ pint
3	Garlic cloves (optional)	3
3	Sweet red or green peppers	3
6	Small tomatoes	6
6	Medium-size onions	6
24	Black olives	24
1	Bunch of radishes	1
12 - 18	Canned anchovy fillets in oil	12 - 18

1. Preheat the oven to 450°F / 230°C / Gas Mark 8.
2. Cut the loaves or rolls in half and brush the cut surfaces generously with the olive oil. Peel and crush the garlic and sprinkle over the bread.
3. Place the peppers in the oven and bake until the skin blisters. Rub the peppers in a damp cloth and the skin will come off without any difficulty. Halve the peppers and remove the core and seeds. Cut the peppers into strips.
4. Slice the tomatoes. Peel the onions and cut into rings. Pit [stone] the olives, and trim and slice the radishes.
5. Top one half of each loaf or roll with tomato slices, onion rings, pepper strips, 2-3 drained anchovy fillets, 4 olives and radish slices. Cover with the other half of the loaf or roll and wrap tightly in foil. Set aside for a few minutes, even if you are to eat the sandwiches immediately.

Pamplemousses cocktail

Grapefruit Cocktail

	00:40	00:00	
	plus chilling		

American	Ingredients	Metric/Imperial
5 - 6	Grapefruit	5 - 6
6	Glacé or maraschino cherries	6
	Sugar	

Pamplemousses grillés

Broiled [Grilled] Grapefruit

	00:02	00:05 to 00:08	
	per fruit		

American	Ingredients	Metric/Imperial
3	Grapefruit	3
	Butter	
6 tbsp	Sugar	6 tbsp

1. Preheat the broiler [grill].
2. Prepare the fruit as in the previous recipe. Place a small pat of butter in the middle of each half and sprinkle with 1 tablespoon of sugar.
3. Arrange the grapefruit halves in a buttered ovenproof dish. Place under the broiler [grill] and cook slowly so that the fruit can be warmed through. Cook until browned on top.
4. Spoon the caramel in the dish over the grapefruit and serve hot, or chill for several hours.

Pommes fourrées au jambon

Apples Stuffed with Ham

	00:25	01:00	

American	Ingredients	Metric/Imperial
1	Onion	1
¼ cup	Butter	50 g / 2 oz
1	Small sweet red pepper	1
1	Small green pepper	1
5 oz	Cooked ham	150 g / 5 oz
6	Golden Delicious apples	6
2 tbsp	Chopped fresh chives	2 tbsp
6	Black olives	6

1. Preheat the oven to 350°F / 180°C / Gas Mark 4.
2. Peel and chop the onion. Melt the butter in a saucepan and add the chopped onion. Cook until softened without browning.
3. Core and seed the red and green peppers and cut into thin strips. Add to the saucepan and cook until softened. Dice the ham, add to the pan and cook for 5-8 minutes.
4. Cut the tops off the washed apples, and scoop out the insides without piercing the bottom, leaving a shell about ½ in / 1 cm thick.
5. Add the chives to the ham mixture, then use to fill the apples. Arrange in an ovenproof dish and bake for 30-40 minutes.
6. Serve hot, garnished with olives, or cold with salads.

Trois viandes en salade

Three Meats Salad

	00:20 plus chilling	00:00

American	Ingredients	Metric/Imperial
4	Boiled potatoes	4
4	Cooked carrots	4
1	Medium-size onion	1
1 cup	Diced cooked chicken meat	250 g / 8 oz
¾ cup	Diced cooked tongue	150 g / 5 oz
¾ cup	Diced garlic sausage	150 g / 5 oz
½ lb	Cooked green beans	250 g / 8 oz
3 cups	Cooked peas	350 g / 12 oz
1 cup	Mayonnaise (see page 119)	250 ml / 8 fl oz
1	Hard-cooked egg	1

1. Peel the potatoes and carrots and dice them. Peel the onion and cut into rings. Place these ingredients in a salad bowl and add the chicken, tongue, sausage, beans and peas.
2. Add the mayonnaise and incorporate into the salad. Garnish with slices of hard-cooked egg. Chill for 20 minutes before serving.

Tomatoes fourrées au thon

Tomatoes Stuffed with Tuna

	00:30 plus chilling	00:10

American	Ingredients	Metric/Imperial
6	Medium-size tomatoes	6
	Salt and pepper	
1 lb	Fresh peas in their shells	500 g / 1 lb
1 (3½ oz)	Can of tuna in brine	1 (75 g / 3 oz)
7	Garlic cloves	7
1 cup	Olive oil	250 ml / 8 fl oz
2	Egg yolks	2
2½ - 3 tbsp	Lemon juice	2½ - 3 tbsp
1 tbsp	Chopped fresh parsley	1 tbsp

1. Wipe the tomatoes. Cut off the tops and put to one side. Empty out the insides using a small spoon. Remove and discard the seeds from the flesh which you have taken out. Chop the flesh, add salt and pepper to taste and put to one side.
2. Shell the peas. Toss them into a saucepan of boiling salted water, bring back to a boil, and leave to cook for 2 minutes. Drain in a colander and run under cold water to chill.
3. Drain the tuna in a strainer and flake it.
4. Peel and crush the garlic in a mortar. Add 1-2 tablespoons of the olive oil and reduce to a paste. Add the egg yolks and mix well. Tip into a mixing bowl and add the rest of the oil in a trickle, whisking constantly until thickened to a mayonnaise. Add the lemon juice, salt and pepper to taste and mix well.
5. Mix the tuna, peas and tomato flesh. Fold in the garlic mayonnaise.
6. Fill the tomatoes with the tuna mixture and sprinkle each with chopped parsley. Replace the tops and serve the tomatoes lightly chilled.

Cook's tip: you can replace the tuna with flaked poached white fish.

Tapenade

Olive, Anchovy and Caper Spread

	00:25	00:00

American	Ingredients	Metric/Imperial
1½ cups	Large black olives	250 g / 8 oz
4 oz	Canned anchovy fillets	125 g / 4 oz
1½ tbsp	Capers	1½ tbsp
1¼ cups	Olive oil	300 ml / ½ pint
1	Lemon	1
	Salt and pepper	

1. Pit [stone] the olives, then put them into a food processor or blender with the anchovies and capers. Blend to a smooth cream.
2. Pour and scrape the mixture into a bowl. Gradually beat in the olive oil as if making mayonnaise, adding a few drops of lemon juice from time to time. Season with salt and pepper to taste.
3. Cover and keep in a cool place, in a tight-sealed container, until ready to serve.
4. Serve as a dip, or spread on small savory crackers [biscuits] or slices of french bread and sprinkle with a few more drops of lemon juice.

Poivrons grillés en salade

Broiled [Grilled] Pepper Salad

	00:30 plus marinating	00:15

American	Ingredients	Metric/Imperial
2 lb	Sweet red peppers	1 kg / 2 lb
1	Garlic clove	1
1¼ cups	Olive oil	300 ml / ½ pint
	Salt and pepper	

1. Preheat the broiler [grill].
2. Halve the peppers and place them cut sides down under the broiler. Cook until the skins are charred and blistered.
3. Wrap the peppers in paper and allow to cool for 10 minutes. Remove them from the paper and peel off the skins.
4. Remove the core and seeds from the peppers and cut them into strips. Peel and finely chop the garlic and sprinkle over the peppers. Cover with oil. Add salt and pepper to taste. Leave to marinate for at least 24 hours.
5. Serve as an hors d'oeuvre or condiment.

Vegetables make a colorful and appetizing hors d'oeuvre

Salads

The sauce or dressing which binds the ingredients of a salad usually has an oil and vinegar base. According to a Roman saying, four people are needed to make a good salad dressing: a miser to pour the vinegar, a squanderer to add the oil, a wise man for the salt and a madman to stir it.

Salade alsacienne

Cheese and Egg Salad

◁ 00:30   00:10 🍲

American	Ingredients	Metric/Imperial
¾ lb	Emmental cheese	350 g / 12 oz
5	Celery stalks	5
½ lb	Fribourg or other cheese	250 g / 8 oz
1 cup	Walnuts (optional)	125 g / 4 oz
2 tsp	Prepared mustard	2 tsp
2½ - 3 tbsp	Cider vinegar	2½ - 3 tbsp
⅔ cup	Crème fraîche (see page 122)	150 ml / ¼ pint
	Salt and pepper	
3	Eggs	3
1	Bunch of radishes	1

1. Cut the emmental and celery into thin sticks. Dice the fribourg. Put all these ingredients into a salad bowl and mix.
2. In a mixing bowl, mix the mustard with the cider vinegar. Add the crème fraîche gradually, stirring constantly for the ingredients to blend properly. Add salt and pepper to taste.
3. Hard-cook the eggs for 10 minutes in boiling water. Drain. Remove the shells and cut the eggs in half.
4. Trim and slice the radishes.
5. Put a few spoonfuls of the sauce into the salad bowl and toss well. Garnish with the egg halves and the radishes. Serve the remainder of the sauce separately.

Cheese and egg salad

Salade de boeuf

Beef Salad

◁ 00:10
plus marinating   00:10 🍲

American	Ingredients	Metric/Imperial
¾ lb	Cooked beef	350 g / 12 oz
2	Eggs	2
2	Shallots	2
	Salt and pepper	
1 tbsp	Vinegar	1 tbsp
1 tbsp	Strong prepared mustard	1 tbsp
3 tbsp	Oil	3 tbsp
1 tbsp	Chopped fresh parsley	1 tbsp

1. Remove the fat from the beef. Cut the meat into large cubes.
2. Hard-cook the eggs for 10 minutes in boiling water. Run them under cold water and remove the shells. Quarter the eggs and set aside.
3. Peel and chop the shallots.
4. Dissolve a pinch of salt in the vinegar. Mix with the mustard. Add the oil, shallots, parsley and pepper to taste. Mix together.
5. Pour the dressing over the meat and leave to marinate for 1 hour.
6. Stir and serve garnished with the egg quarters.

Salade camarguaise

Tuna, Anchovy and Rice Salad

◁ 00:45   00:20 🍲

American	Ingredients	Metric/Imperial
3 cups	Water	750 ml / 1¼ pints
	Salt and pepper	
2 cups	Long-grain rice	400 g / 14 oz
1	Cucumber	1
6	Very firm tomatoes	6
1	Green pepper	1
1	Onion	1
1	Garlic clove	1
1 (2 oz)	Can of anchovies in oil	1 (50 g / 2 oz)
3 tbsp	Capers	3 tbsp
¼ cup	Diced canned pimiento	4 tbsp
¾ cup	Black olives	125 g / 4 oz
2 tbsp	Vinegar	2 tbsp
2 tbsp	Prepared mustard	2 tbsp
1 cup + 3 tbsp	Oil	250 ml / 8 fl oz + 3 tbsp
2 tsp	Chopped fresh parsley	2 tsp
1	Egg yolk	1
	Lettuce leaves	
1 (7½ oz)	Can of tuna in oil	1 (200 g / 7 oz)

1. Place the water and salt to taste in a saucepan and bring to a boil. Add the rice and cover. Leave to cook for 15-20 minutes or until the rice is tender.
2. Drain the rice if necessary. Rinse in cold running water and drain again. Set aside to cool.
3. Wash the cucumber. Cut 10 very thin slices for the garnish,

and cut the rest into small cubes. Wash 4 of the tomatoes and cut into small cubes. Core and seed the green pepper, then dice it. Peel and finely chop the onion. Peel and crush the garlic. Finely chop the drained anchovies.

4. Mix the cucumber and tomato cubes, green pepper, onion, garlic, capers, pimiento, half the olives and anchovies with the rice.

5. Dissolve a pinch of salt in 1 tablespoon of the vinegar. Mix in 1 tablespoon mustard. Add 3 tablespoons of the oil, the chopped parsley and pepper to taste. Mix thoroughly. Pour this dressing over the rice salad, toss and leave to soak for 30 minutes.

6. Put the egg yolk into a bowl and add the remaining mustard, 1 teaspoon of the vinegar, and salt and pepper to taste. Stir vigorously with a whisk. Then add the remaining oil gradually in a thin trickle, stirring vigorously. When all the oil has been added, the mayonnaise should be thick. If it is too thick, thin it out with the remaining vinegar. Add the mayonnaise to the rice salad and toss well.

7. Put the salad into a serving dish lined with lettuce leaves. Garnish with the cucumber slices, the rest of the olives, and a few extra pieces of pimiento. Surround with the remaining tomatoes, cut into quarters, alternating with chunks of drained tuna.

Salade blanche

White Salad

	00:30		00:50	
	plus chilling			

American	Ingredients	Metric/Imperial
4	Potatoes	4
2	Apples	2
1	Head of celery	1
1	Fennel bulb	1
⅔ cup	Dry white wine	150 ml / ¼ pint
1 tbsp	Strong prepared mustard	1 tbsp
1½ tbsp	Vinegar	1½ tbsp
4½ tbsp	Oil	4½ tbsp
3 tbsp	Chopped fresh chives or parsley	3 tbsp
	Salt and pepper	
½ cup	Long-grain rice	90 g / 3½ oz
1 quart	Court-bouillon (see page 115)	1 l / 1¾ pints
¾ lb	Cod or other white fish fillet	350 g / 12 oz
1	Head of Romaine [cos] lettuce	1
1 cup	Mayonnaise (see page 119)	250 ml / 8 fl oz
½ cup	Walnuts	50 g / 2 oz
1 cup	Black olives	150 g / 5 oz

1. Place the potatoes in a saucepan and cover with cold water. Bring to a boil and cook for about 20 minutes or until tender. Drain and leave until cool enough to handle.

2. Meanwhile, peel, core and dice the apples. Trim and dice the celery. Cut the fennel into thin strips.

3. Peel and dice the potatoes. Place in a mixing bowl together with the apples, celery and fennel. Add the white wine.

4. Combine the mustard, vinegar, oil and chopped herbs. Season to taste with salt and pepper. Add this dressing to the potato mixture. Toss and chill for 1 hour.

5. Meanwhile, cook the rice in boiling salted water for about 15 minutes or until tender. Drain the rice and add to the potato.

6. Bring the court-bouillon to a simmer in a saucepan. Add the cod and poach for 5 minutes. Remove from the heat and allow the fish to cool in the liquid. Drain the fish and flake into small pieces. Add to the potato mixture.

7. Remove any damaged leaves from the lettuce. Wash in several changes of water and drain. Cut the leaves into strips and use them to line the bottom of a salad bowl.

8. Add half the mayonnaise to the fish salad and fold together gently. Pile on top of the lettuce. Garnish with the walnuts and olives. Serve accompanied by the remainder of the mayonnaise.

Salade de carottes

Carrot Salad

	00:20		00:00	

American	Ingredients	Metric/Imperial
1½ lb	Carrots	750 g / 1½ lb
	Salt and pepper	
1 tbsp	Vinegar	1 tbsp
1 tbsp	Prepared mustard	1 tbsp
3 tbsp	Oil	3 tbsp
1 tbsp	Chopped fresh chervil or chives	1 tbsp

1. Peel the carrots and grate them.

2. Dissolve a pinch of salt in the vinegar. Mix in the mustard. Add the oil and pepper to taste and mix well.

3. A few minutes before serving, sprinkle the carrots with the dressing and toss well. Sprinkle with the chervil or chives.

Cook's tip: you may replace the vinaigrette dressing with a mixture of crème fraîche (see page 122) and lemon juice.

Salade composée

Mixed Salad

	00:15		00:00	

American	Ingredients	Metric/Imperial
1	Head of chicory [curly endive]	1
2	Apples	2
	Lemon juice	
10	Radishes	10
3	Tomatoes	3
1	Head of celery	1
1 cup	Chopped walnuts	125 g / 4 oz
1 tbsp	Prepared mustard with green peppercorns	1 tbsp
¾ cup	Crème fraîche (see page 122)	175 ml / 6 fl oz
2 tbsp	Cider vinegar	2 tbsp
	Salt and pepper	

1. Rinse and drain the chicory. Cut into crosswise shreds with a pair of scissors. Peel and core the apples. Cut into thin slices, sprinkling them with lemon juice as you go to prevent them from discoloring. Trim and slice the radishes. Dice the tomatoes and celery. Place all these ingredients in a salad bowl and scatter over the walnuts.

2. In a mixing bowl, combine the mustard, crème fraîche, vinegar and salt and pepper to taste. Mix well. Serve with the salad.

Céleri en salade

Celery Salad with Roquefort

| ▶ 00:15 | 00:00 ◗ |

American	Ingredients	Metric/Imperial
2	Heads of celery	2
1 cup	Chopped walnuts	125 g / 4 oz
¼ lb	Roquefort or other blue cheese	125 g / 4 oz
1 tbsp	Cognac	1 tbsp
¼ cup	Walnut oil	4 tbsp
1 tbsp	Wine vinegar	1 tbsp
	Salt and pepper	

1. Trim the celery and remove tough strings, if necessary. Slice finely into a salad bowl. Add the walnuts.
2. Using a fork, crush the cheese and mash in the cognac. Add the oil, vinegar and salt and pepper to taste and mix well.
3. When ready to serve, pour the cheese dressing over the celery. Stir and serve immediately.

Salade capucine

Marinated Vegetable Salad

| ▶ 01:00 | 00:25 ◗ |
| plus marinating | |

American	Ingredients	Metric/Imperial
½ lb	Green beans	250 g / 8 oz
	Salt and pepper	
2 lb	Asparagus	1 kg / 2 lb
1	Cucumber	1
½	Cauliflower	½
1 tbsp	Vinegar	1 tbsp
1 tbsp	Prepared mustard	1 tbsp
3 tbsp	Oil	3 tbsp
1	Medium-size onion	1
1	Bunch of watercress	1
1	Bunch of fresh chervil or parsley	1
2	Fresh tarragon sprigs	2
1	Head of lettuce	1
½	Bunch of radishes	½
1 cup	Mayonnaise (see page 119)	250 ml / 8 fl oz

1. Cut the ends off the green beans and pull to remove any strings. Rinse the beans and cut into pieces. Cook in boiling salted water until crisp-tender. Drain and set aside.
2. Trim the hard ends from the asparagus spears, then scrape the stalks. Cut into pieces about 2 in / 5 cm long. Rinse the asparagus, then cook in boiling salted water for 5-15 minutes (depending on age and size of the spears) or until tender. Drain and set aside.
3. Cut the cucumber into very thin slices. Break the cauliflower into florets.
4. Dissolve a pinch of salt in the vinegar. Mix in the mustard. Add the oil and pepper to taste and mix thoroughly.
5. Peel the onion and chop very finely. Wash the cress leaves,

changing the water several times, then chop finely together with the chervil and tarragon. Add the herb mixture and onion to the dressing.
6. Rinse and drain the lettuce, then cut into thin strips. Trim the radishes and slice half of them. Cut the remaining radishes into 'roses'.
7. Put the beans, asparagus, cucumber, cauliflower and sliced radishes into a bowl and sprinkle with the dressing. Mix and leave to marinate for 20-30 minutes.
8. To serve, cover the bottom of a salad bowl with the shredded lettuce and pile the marinated salad on top. Scatter over the radish roses. Serve with the mayonnaise.

Marinated vegetable salad

Salade de langoustines

Shrimp [Prawn] Salad

| ▶ 00:20 | 00:10 ◗ |
| plus marinating | |

American	Ingredients	Metric/Imperial
2 tbsp	Golden raisins [sultanas]	2 tbsp
	Salt and pepper	
12	Raw jumbo shrimp [Dublin Bay prawns]	12
1	Head of celery	1
2	Apples	2
1 tbsp	Vinegar	1 tbsp
1 tbsp	Strong prepared mustard	1 tbsp
3 tbsp	Oil	3 tbsp
2 tbsp	Mayonnaise	2 tbsp

1. Put the raisins to soak in warm water.
2. Bring a large saucepan of salted water to a boil. Add the shrimp. When the water returns to a boil, cook for 6 minutes.
3. Drain the shrimp and cool in cold water. Peel and devein them and cut in half lengthwise.
4. Trim and dice the celery. Peel, core and dice the apples.
5. In a salad bowl, combine the shrimp, celery, apples and drained raisins.
6. Dissolve a pinch of salt in the vinegar. Mix in the mustard. Add the oil and pepper to taste. Stir in the mayonnaise.
7. Pour the dressing into the salad bowl and stir to mix. Leave to marinate for 10 minutes.

Salade Côte d'Ivoire
Ivory Coast Salad

01:00 plus chilling   00:20

American	Ingredients	Metric/Imperial
6	Large raw shrimp [prawns]	6
	Salt and pepper	
3	Whiting fillets	3
2	Grapefruit	2
1	Small ripe pineapple	1
3	Papayas	3
2	Avocados	2
	Lemon juice	
1	Egg yolk	1
1½ tsp	Strong prepared mustard	1½ tsp
	Tabasco sauce	
1 cup	Oil	250 ml / 8 fl oz
1 tsp	Wine vinegar	1 tsp

1. Cook the shrimp in boiling salted water until the shells turn pink. Remove with a slotted spoon and leave to cool.
2. Add the whiting fillets to the shrimp cooking water. As soon as the water returns to a boil, remove the saucepan from the heat and leave the fillets in the water for 5-7 minutes. Drain and carefully pat dry with paper towels. Cut the whiting fillets into pieces.
3. Peel the grapefruit. Divide into sections, removing all seeds and membrane. Catch the juice from the grapefruit in a bowl.
4. Peel the pineapple and cut into small pieces.
5. Cut the papayas in half lengthwise. Remove the seeds and a little of the surrounding flesh with a spoon, leaving shells about ½ in / 1 cm thick. Chop the removed flesh, and set the shells aside.
6. Peel the avocados and remove the seeds. Dice the flesh. Sprinkle immediately with lemon juice to prevent them from turning black.
7. Put the whiting, avocados, grapefruit sections, pineapple and chopped papaya flesh in a bowl and mix together. Divide between the papaya shells.
8. Put the egg yolk into a bowl and add the mustard and tabasco, salt and pepper to taste. Whisk to mix, then gradually add the oil in a thin trickle, whisking continuously. Thin out the mayonnaise with the vinegar. Lighten it with the reserved grapefruit juice.
9. Spoon some of the mayonnaise over the stuffed papaya halves and place the remainder in a sauceboat. Garnish each half with a peeled and deveined shrimp. Serve the salad lightly chilled.

Salade de moules
Mussel Salad

00:10 plus cooling   00:10

American	Ingredients	Metric/Imperial
2 quarts	Mussels	1.5 kg / 3 lb
1	Onion	1
	Salt and pepper	
1 tbsp	Vinegar	1 tbsp
1 tbsp	Strong prepared mustard	1 tbsp
3 tbsp	Oil	3 tbsp
1 tbsp	Chopped fresh parsley	1 tbsp

1. Scrub the mussels thoroughly and drain.
2. Put the mussels into a large stewpan over a brisk heat. As soon as they have opened, remove them from the heat and take them out of their shells. (Discard any mussels that remain closed.) Put them in a salad bowl and leave to cool.
3. Peel and finely chop the onion.
4. Dissolve a pinch of salt in the vinegar. Mix in the mustard. Add the oil, parsley, onion and pepper to taste. Mix well.
5. When ready to serve, cover the cold mussels with the vinaigrette dressing and mix.

Salade Françoise
Layered Beef Salad

01:00 plus cooling overnight   01:45

American	Ingredients	Metric/Imperial
1 (1 lb)	Piece of beef for pot roasting	1 (500 g / 1 lb)
5 oz	Tongue	150 g / 5 oz
	Salt and pepper	
1	Onion	1
1	Clove	1
1	Bouquet garni	1
6	Black peppercorns	6
2 cups	Peas	250 g / 8 oz
1	Sugar cube	1
1	Head of escarole	1
½	Head of celery	½
2	Shallots	2
3 tbsp	Chopped fresh parsley	3 tbsp
3 tbsp	Chopped fresh tarragon	3 tbsp
1 tbsp	Chopped fresh chervil	1 tbsp
3	Eggs	3
½ cup	Corn kernels	50 g / 2 oz
2	Canned pimientos	2
2 tbsp	Vinegar	2 tbsp
1 tbsp	Strong prepared mustard	1 tbsp
6 tbsp	Oil	6 tbsp

1. Cook the beef and tongue the day before: put them into a stewpot of salted water. Add the peeled onion studded with the clove, the bouquet garni and peppercorns. Bring to a boil and simmer for 1½ hours or until the beef is tender.
2. Drain the beef and tongue, leave to cool and keep in the refrigerator until needed.
3. The next day, remove any fat from the beef. Cut it and the tongue into ¾ in / 2 cm cubes.
4. Toss the peas into a large pan of boiling salted water. Add the sugar and cook for 10 minutes after boiling has resumed (less time if frozen peas are used). Drain the peas.
5. Remove any damaged leaves from the escarole, rinse and drain. Cut into strips. Dice the celery.
6. Peel and chop the shallots. Blend with the parsley, tarragon and chervil.
7. Hard-cook the eggs for 10 minutes in boiling water. Run them under cold water, shell and cut in half lengthwise.
8. Arrange the various salad ingredients in layers in a large salad bowl: beef and tongue, escarole, celery, corn, peas, pimientos cut into strips and eggs. Sprinkle each layer with the herb mixture.
9. Dissolve 2 pinches of salt in the vinegar. Mix in the mustard. Add the oil and pepper to taste and blend well.
10. Serve the dressing in a sauceboat with the salad.

Salade de crabes à la languedocienne

Languedoc Crab Salad

	00:20 plus chilling	01:10

American	Ingredients	Metric/Imperial
4	Carrots	4
2	Garlic cloves	2
4	Onions	4
1	Fresh thyme sprig	1
1	Bay leaf	1
2 quarts	Water	2 l / 3½ pints
1¼ cups + 3 tbsp	Vinegar	300 ml / ½ pint + 3 tbsp
	Salt and pepper	
2 (1 lb)	Crabs	2 (500 g / 1 lb)
2	Eggs	2
1 tsp	Prepared mustard	1 tsp
5 tbsp	Oil	5 tbsp

1. Peel and slice the carrots, garlic and onions. Place in a large saucepan together with the thyme, bay leaf, water, 1¼ cups [300 ml / ½ pint] vinegar, and salt and pepper to taste. Bring to a boil and simmer for 40 minutes.
2. Place the crabs in the simmering court-bouillon. Cook for 15 minutes.
3. Meanwhile, hard-cook the eggs for 10 minutes in boiling water. Drain and cool.
4. When the crabs are cooked, drain them. Detach the claws and legs, remove the flesh and cut into small pieces. Open the shell. Discard all inedible parts, then remove the creamy parts and the flesh and cut into small cubes.
5. Shell the eggs and cut in half. Cut the whites into thin strips and crush the yolks with a fork.
6. In a mixing bowl, mix the creamy parts of the crabs with the egg yolks until smooth. Add salt and pepper to taste, the mustard, the remaining vinegar and the oil, stirring well. Add the crabmeat to this dressing and toss to coat.
7. Place in a salad bowl. Scatter over the strips of egg white and chill for 1 hour before serving.

Salade Carmen

Chicken, Rice and Tarragon Salad

	00:20 plus cooling	00:40

American	Ingredients	Metric/Imperial
3 quarts	Water	3 l / 5 pints
	Salt and pepper	
1½ cups	Long-grain rice	300 g / 11 oz
2	Chicken wings	2
2	Sweet red peppers	2
2¾ cups	Peas	300 g / 11 oz
1	Sugar cube	1
1 tbsp	Vinegar	1 tbsp
1 tsp	Strong prepared mustard	1 tsp
3 tbsp	Oil	3 tbsp
2 tbsp	Chopped fresh tarragon	2 tbsp

1. Bring the water to a boil and add salt to taste. Add the rice and cook for approximately 15 minutes after boiling has

recommenced. Drain the rice, reserving the cooking water, and rinse in cold water. Leave to cool.
2. Skin the chicken wings, place them in a saucepan and cover with the rice water. Bring to a boil and simmer for about 30 minutes. Drain and leave to cool. Remove the meat from the bones and dice it. Set aside.
3. Preheat the oven to 450°F / 230°C / Gas Mark 8.
4. Place the peppers in the oven and bake until the skins blister. Take them out of the oven, wrap in a damp cloth and set aside for 5 minutes. The skin will then come off without any difficulty. When you have peeled the peppers, remove the core and seeds, and cut into cubes. Set aside.
5. Bring a saucepan of water to a boil and add the peas, sugar and salt to taste. Bring back to a boil and leave to cook for 10 minutes.
6. Meanwhile, dissolve a pinch of salt in the vinegar. Mix in the mustard. Add the oil, chopped tarragon and pepper to taste. Mix.
7. Drain the peas and put them in a salad bowl. Add the rice, chicken and diced peppers. Mix and add the vinaigrette dressing. Toss again. Serve cool.
8. If liked, garnish the salad with anchovy fillets and hard-cooked eggs.

Spinach salad

Salade d'épinards au lard

Spinach Salad with Bacon

	00:20	00:05

American	Ingredients	Metric/Imperial
½ lb	Smoked bacon	250 g / 8 oz
2	Eggs	2
1 tsp	Strong prepared mustard	1 tsp
1	Lemon	1
	Salt and pepper	
1¼ cups	Olive oil	300 ml / ½ pint
1 lb	Tender young spinach	500 g / 1 lb
1 tbsp	Vegetable oil	1 tbsp
2 tbsp	Wine vinegar	2 tbsp

1. Plunge the bacon into a pan of boiling water and leave to blanch for 5 minutes. Drain, cool and pat dry.
2. Remove any rind and cut the bacon into small pieces.
3. Hard-cook the eggs for 10 minutes in boiling water. Run

them under cold water and remove the shells. Separate the yolks from the whites and cut the whites into small cubes. Set the whites aside.

4. Crush the yolks with the mustard and the juice of the lemon until smooth. Add salt and pepper to taste. Incorporate the oil gradually, beating constantly with a wire whisk. Set this mayonnaise aside.

5. Remove the stalks from the spinach and rinse in several changes of water. Drain and pat or shake dry. Place in a salad bowl or on individual plates. Garnish the spinach with the diced egg white.

6. Heat the vegetable oil in a frying pan and add the bacon. Fry until brown and crisp. Drain the bacon on paper towels, then scatter over the spinach.

7. Pour away the oil from the frying pan. Add the vinegar to the pan and stir to mix with the sediment. Boil for a few seconds, then pour over the spinach.

8. Serve accompanied by the mayonnaise.

Mâche, Céleri, Betterave

Corn Salad with Beets and Celery

	00:10	00:00

American	Ingredients	Metric/Imperial
1	Head of celery	1
2	Cooked beets [beetroot]	2
¾ lb	Corn salad or lamb's lettuce	350 g / 12 oz
	Salt and pepper	
1 tbsp	Vinegar	1 tbsp
1 tbsp	Strong prepared mustard	1 tbsp
3 tbsp	Oil	3 tbsp

1. Cut the celery into small cubes. Peel the beets and cut into small pieces. Remove any damaged leaves from the corn salad. Rinse carefully and drain in a salad basket. Combine these vegetables in a salad bowl.

2. Dissolve a pinch of salt in the vinegar. Mix in the mustard. Add the oil and pepper to taste and blend.

3. Pour the dressing over the vegetables, toss and serve.

Chou en salade

Cabbage Salad

	00:20 plus marinating	00:00

American	Ingredients	Metric/Imperial
1	Head of white cabbage	1
2	Large lemons	2
5 tbsp	Olive oil	5 tbsp
	Salt and pepper	

1. Cut the cabbage into quarters and cut out the core. Cut the cabbage into very thin strips, removing the large ribs.

2. Place the cabbage in a salad bowl and add the juice of the lemons, the oil, and salt and pepper to taste.

3. Leave to marinate in a cool place for 1½-2 hours, stirring from time to time.

4. When you are about to serve, taste and adjust the seasoning if necessary. The salad should be quite well seasoned.

Salade au lard ardennaise

Bacon and Potato Salad

	00:10	00:35

American	Ingredients	Metric/Imperial
6	Large potatoes	6
	Salt and pepper	
¾ lb	Dandelion leaves	350 g / 12 oz
1	Shallot	1
1	Garlic clove	1
3 tbsp	Oil	3 tbsp
¾ lb	Bacon	350 g / 12 oz
¼ cup	Vinegar	4 tbsp

1. Peel the potatoes. Cook in boiling salted water for 30 minutes or until tender.

2. Meanwhile, rinse the dandelion leaves in cold water, removing any withered leaves. Drain. Peel and chop the shallot.

3. Rub the salad bowl with the cut sides of the halved garlic clove. Discard the garlic. Add the oil, chopped shallot, and salt and pepper to taste to the bowl. Cover with the dandelion leaves.

4. Drain the potatoes and cut into slices while they are still warm. Place in the salad bowl.

5. Dice the bacon and cook in a frying pan without fat until crisp. Pour the bacon and its fat over the salad. Pour the vinegar into the frying pan and boil for 4 minutes, stirring to mix in the sediment in the pan. Pour over the salad, toss and serve.

Chicorée frisée aux croûtons aillés

Chicory [Endive] with Garlic-Flavored Croûtons

	00:15	00:05

American	Ingredients	Metric/Imperial
1	Head of chicory [curly endive]	1
4	Slices of bread	4
7 tbsp	Oil	7 tbsp
2	Garlic cloves	2
	Salt and pepper	
1 tbsp	Vinegar	1 tbsp
1 tbsp	Strong prepared mustard	1 tbsp

1. Remove any damaged leaves from the chicory, rinse carefully and drain in a salad basket.

2. Remove the crust from the slices of bread and dice the bread. Heat 2 tablespoons of the oil in a frying pan and fry the bread dice until golden brown all over. Drain.

3. Peel the garlic, crush finely and mix with 1 tablespoon oil. Add the croutons to this mixture and stir so that they become saturated.

4. Mix a pinch of salt with the vinegar. Add the mustard and stir thoroughly. Add the remaining oil, pepper to taste and the garlic-flavoured croûtons. Blend. Pour over the chicory [endive] when you are about to serve.

Salade de flageolets

Bean Salad

	00:15	01:30

American	Ingredients	Metric/Imperial
2 cups (1 lb)	Dried or fresh flageolet beans	500 g / 1 lb
1	Onion	1
1	Clove	1
1	Garlic clove	1
1	Carrot	1
1	Bouquet garni	1
1	Knackwurst, saveloy or other large cooked pork sausage	1
	Salt and pepper	
1 tbsp	Wine vinegar	1 tbsp
1 tbsp	Prepared mustard	1 tbsp
3 tbsp	Oil	3 tbsp
	Chopped fresh herbs (parsley, chives, etc)	

1. Place the dried beans in a large saucepan containing at least 3 quarts [3 l / 5 pints] water and add the peeled onion studded with the clove, the peeled garlic, peeled carrot and bouquet garni. Bring slowly to a boil and leave to cook for at least 1½ hours. (Cook fresh beans briefly until just tender.)
2. Meanwhile, heat the sausage: toss it into a saucepan of boiling water, remove from the heat and allow the sausage to warm through for 10 minutes. Drain the sausage, skin it and cut into slices. Set aside.
3. Drain the beans and place in a mixing bowl.
4. Dissolve a pinch of salt in the vinegar. Mix in the mustard. Add the oil, pepper to taste and chopped herbs. Mix thoroughly.
5. Pour the dressing over the still warm beans and toss to coat. Spoon into a salad bowl, top with the sausage slices and serve.

Salade exotique

Exotic Salad

	00:15	00:00

American	Ingredients	Metric/Imperial
5	Tomatoes	5
1 (14 oz)	Can of palm hearts	1 (400 g / 14 oz)
2	Avocados	2
	Lemon juice	
1	Large grapefruit	1
1 cup	Black olives	125 g / 4 oz
	Salt and pepper	
⅓ cup	Cider vinegar	5½ tbsp
1 tbsp	Prepared mustard	1 tbsp
1 cup	Olive oil	250 ml / 8 fl oz

1. Slice the tomatoes and place around the edge of a serving dish. Drain the palm hearts and cut into rings. Arrange in the middle of the dish.
2. Peel the avocados. Halve them and remove the seeds. Sprinkle with lemon juice to prevent them from discoloring. Cut into lengthwise slices. Place around the slices of palm hearts.

3. Peel the grapefruit and separate the sections, discarding all seeds and membrane. Intersperse between the slices of avocado. Garnish with the olives.
4. Dissolve a pinch of salt in the vinegar. Mix in the mustard. Add the oil and pepper to taste and mix thoroughly. Serve this dressing with the salad.

Exotic salad

Salade au jambon

Ham Salad

	00:20	00:00

American	Ingredients	Metric/Imperial
3	Red apples	3
1	Bunch of radishes	1
¾ lb	Cooked ham	350 g / 12 oz
6	Celery stalks	6
2 tbsp	Chopped fresh herbs (chives, parsley)	2 tbsp
	Salt and pepper	
1 tbsp	Vinegar	1 tbsp
¼ cup	Oil	¼ cup
1 tbsp	Crème fraîche (see page 122)	1 tbsp
	Tabasco sauce	

1. Core the apples and cut them into thin slices. Trim the radishes and halve them. Cut the ham into thin sticks. Dice the celery. Combine these ingredients in a salad bowl. Add the chopped herbs and stir.
2. Mix a pinch of salt with the vinegar. Add the oil and stir. Add the crème fraîche and 3-4 drops of tabasco. Add pepper to taste.
3. Add the dressing to the salad and toss well. Leave to marinate for 10-15 minutes. Serve cool but not cold.

Laitue de Trévise
Radicchio Salad

American	Ingredients	Metric/Imperial
1 lb	Radicchio or red chicory	500 g / 1 lb
	Salt and pepper	
1 tbsp	Vinegar	1 tbsp
¼ cup	Oil	4 tbsp
2	Anchovy fillets	2
½	Garlic clove	½

1. Remove the damaged leaves from the radicchio, rinse carefully and drain thoroughly in a salad basket.
2. Mix a pinch of salt with the vinegar. Add the oil, crushed anchovy fillets, peeled and crushed garlic and pepper to taste. Stir and pour over the radicchio when you are about to serve.

Salade de harengs saurs
Smoked Herring Salad

American	Ingredients	Metric/Imperial
6	Smoked herring [kipper] fillets	6
1 cup	Milk	250 ml / 8 fl oz
6	Medium-size potatoes	6
2	Onions	2
1	Head of celery	1
3	Large dill pickles [gherkins]	3
5 tbsp	Cider vinegar	5 tbsp
3 tbsp	Oil	3 tbsp
	Salt and pepper	
1 - 2	Cooked beets [beetroot]	1 - 2
2	Eggs	2
1 cup	Crème fraîche (see page 122)	250 ml / 8 fl oz
2 tbsp	Chopped fresh herbs (parsley, chives and tarragon mixed)	2 tbsp
	Lemon juice	

1. Soak the fish fillets in the milk for 2 hours. Drain and cut into small pieces.
2. Scrub the potatoes and put them unpeeled into a saucepan. Cover with cold water. Bring to a boil and cook for 20 minutes. Drain and leave to cool until warm, then peel and dice.
3. Peel and chop the onions. Dice the celery and pickles.
4. Put the still-warm potatoes into a salad bowl together with the celery, pickles and onions. Sprinkle with the cider vinegar and oil. Add salt and pepper to taste, stir and leave to marinate.
5. Peel and dice the beets.
6. Hard-cook the eggs for 10 minutes in boiling water, then run them under cold water and remove the shells. Put the eggs in a food processor or blender and blend until coarse-fine.
7. Mix together the crème fraîche and herbs. Add salt and pepper to taste, and lighten with a little lemon juice.
8. When you are about to serve, arrange the herrings, beets and blended eggs over the marinated salad. Serve with the sauce.

Salade libanaise
Lebanese Salad

American	Ingredients	Metric/Imperial
1	Large bunch of fresh parsley	1
6	Small onions	6
2	Garlic cloves	2
5 tbsp	Olive oil	5 tbsp
1	Lemon	1
	Salt and pepper	
1	Cucumber	1
1	Green pepper	1
1	Sweet red pepper	1
5 oz	Corn salad or lamb's lettuce	150 g / 5 oz
3	Tomatoes	3

1. Preheat the oven to 450°F / 230°C / Gas Mark 8.
2. Wash the parsley and mince or finely chop the leaves. Peel and mince the onions. Peel and crush the garlic.
3. Put the olive oil into a bowl and add the juice of the lemon, the parsley, onion, garlic and salt and pepper to taste. Mix and set aside.
4. Peel the cucumber, quarter lengthwise, remove the seeds and dice the flesh.
5. Put the green and red peppers into the oven and bake for about 15 minutes or until the skins blister. Wrap them in a damp cloth and leave to cool for 5 minutes: the skin will then come off very easily. When you have peeled them, remove the seeds and core and dice them.
6. Remove any damaged leaves from the corn salad and rinse carefully in at least 3 changes of water. (If it is not the season for corn salad you can replace it with romaine [cos] lettuce or chicory [curly endive].)
7. Quarter the tomatoes.
8. Put the cucumber, peppers, corn salad and tomatoes into a salad bowl. Cover with the dressing but do not stir until you are about to serve.

Mesclun (Salade de Nice)
Mixed Young Salad Greens

American	Ingredients	Metric/Imperial
¾ lb	Mixed young salad greens (lettuce, corn salad or lamb's lettuce, dandelion leaves, watercress, endive, chicory, fennel, etc)	350 g / 12 oz
	Salt and pepper	
1 tbsp	Vinegar	1 tbsp
3 tbsp	Olive oil	3 tbsp

1. Wash the salad greens carefully after removing any damaged leaves. Drain in a salad basket.
2. Dissolve a pinch of salt in the vinegar. Add the olive oil and pepper to taste. Blend and pour over the salad greens when you are about to serve.

Salade napolitaine

Neapolitan Seafood Salad

	00:30 plus marinating		00:30

American	Ingredients	Metric/Imperial
1 lb	Squid	500 g / 1 lb
	Court-bouillon (see page 114)	
1 quart	Clams or cockles	750 g / 1½ lb
⅔ cup	Dry white wine	150 ml / ¼ pint
1 quart	Mussels	750 g / 1½ lb
1¼ cups	Olive oil	300 ml / ½ pint
½	Lemon	½
	Chopped fresh chives and parsley	
	Salt and pepper	
3	Tomatoes	3
	Salad greens	

1. Buy the squid already cleaned. Cut the triangular bodies into thin strips. Place these and the tentacles (if available) in a saucepan and cover with court-bouillon. Bring to a boil and simmer for 7-10 minutes. Do not overcook or the squid will be tough. Remove from the heat and leave to cool in the liquid. Drain.

2. Scrub the clams or cockles and place them in a large saucepan with the wine. Cook over a brisk heat, shaking the pan frequently, until they open. (Discard any that remain closed.) Take them out of their shells. Strain the cooking liquid through cheesecloth or muslin, or use a coffee filter. Set the liquid aside.

3. Scrub the mussels and place them in a stewpan over a brisk heat. Cook until they open, and remove them from their shells. (Discard any that remain closed.)

4. Combine two-thirds of the clam cooking liquid, the olive oil, lemon juice, herbs, and salt and pepper to taste. Mix well. Add the squid, clams or cockles and mussels and leave to marinate for 25-30 minutes, stirring occasionally.

5. Quarter the tomatoes.

6. Shred the salad greens and place over the bottom of a salad bowl. Pour in the seafood salad and garnish with the tomato quarters.

Fish, rice and vegetable salad

Endives, pommes, raisins de Smyrne

Endive [Chicory] with Apples

	00:15		00:00

American	Ingredients	Metric/Imperial
½ cup	Golden raisins [sultanas]	75 g / 3 oz
4	Heads of Belgian endive [chicory]	4
2	Apples	2
	Lemon juice	
	Salt and pepper	
1 tbsp	Vinegar	1 tbsp
1 tbsp	Strong prepared mustard	1 tbsp
3 tbsp	Oil	3 tbsp

1. Soak the raisins in warm water for 30 minutes.

2. Remove any damaged leaves from the endive. Cut into slices crosswise. Core and dice the unpeeled apples. Sprinkle with lemon juice to prevent them discoloring.

3. Dissolve a pinch of salt in the vinegar. Mix in the mustard. Add the oil and pepper to taste and blend.

4. Drain the raisins and combine with the endive and apples in a salad bowl. Pour over the dressing, mix and serve.

Salade orientale

Oriental Salad

	00:25 plus marinating		00:35

American	Ingredients	Metric/Imperial
1	Small chicken wing	1
	Salt and pepper	
2 - 3	Dried chinese mushrooms	2 - 3
3	Tomatoes	3
2	Thin slices of cooked ham	2
2	Eggs	2
1	Head of lettuce	1
¾ lb	Bean sprouts	350 g / 12 oz
3 tbsp	Oil	3 tbsp
3 tbsp	Nuoc-mâm (Oriental fish sauce)	3 tbsp
	Sugar	

1. Place the chicken wing in a saucepan of cold salted water. Bring to a boil and cook for 30 minutes. Drain. Remove the meat from the bones, discarding the skin, and cut into fine strips like matchsticks.

2. Put the mushrooms into warm water and leave to soak for 30 minutes.

3. Meanwhile, halve the tomatoes and remove the seeds, then dice. Remove any fat from the ham and cut into matchstick strips.

4. Hard-cook the eggs for 10 minutes in boiling water. Drain, remove the shells and cut the eggs into quarters.

5. Remove any damaged leaves from the lettuce. Rinse carefully and drain in a salad basket. Keep the nicest leaves to garnish the salad bowl and cut the remainder into fine strips. Rinse the bean sprouts and drain well.

6. Put the chicken, tomatoes, ham, shredded lettuce and bean sprouts into a mixing bowl. Add the oil, *nuoc-mâm* and a pinch of sugar. Add pepper to taste. Toss well and leave to marinate in a cool place for 15-20 minutes.

7. Pour the marinated mixture into a salad bowl lined with the reserved lettuce leaves. Garnish with the egg quarters. Put the drained mushrooms, more *nuoc-mâm* and soy sauce on the table so that guests can add seasoning to suit their taste.

Cook's tip: chinese mushrooms, nuoc-mâm, soy sauce, can be found in oriental grocery shops.

Salade montmartroise

Chicory [Endive], Bacon and Gruyère Salad

	00:15		00:05	

American	Ingredients	Metric/Imperial
½ lb	Smoked bacon	250 g / 8 oz
½	Loaf of french bread	½
3 - 4	Garlic cloves	3 - 4
5 oz	Gruyère cheese	150 g / 5 oz
1	Head of chicory [curly endive]	1
	Salt and pepper	
1 tbsp	Vinegar	1 tbsp
1 tsp	Prepared mustard	1 tsp
¼ cup	Oil	4 tbsp

1. Cut the bacon into chunks and blanch in boiling water for 5 minutes. Drain and allow to cool, then cook in a frying pan until browned and crisp. Drain and keep warm.

2. Cut the french loaf into thin slices. Toast them, then rub on both sides with the cut sides of the halved garlic cloves.

3. Cut the gruyère into ¾ in / 2 cm cubes.

4. Rinse the chicory, drain and tear into small pieces. Place in a salad bowl.

5. Dissolve a pinch of salt in the vinegar. Add the mustard and mix, then stir in the oil and pepper to taste.

6. Add the dressing to the chicory and toss. Scatter over the bacon and cheese cubes. Serve the toast separately.

Salade de morue

Salt Cod Salad

	01:00		02:00	

American	Ingredients	Metric/Imperial
14 oz	Soaked salt cod fillet	400 g / 14 oz
4	Globe artichokes	4
	Lemon juice	
	Salt and pepper	
2½ cups	Peas	300 g / 11 oz
4	Potatoes	4
4	Firm tomatoes	4
1	Head of celery	1
4	Eggs	4
6	Garlic cloves	6
1¼ cups	Oil	300 ml / ½ pint
1	Egg yolk	1

1. Put the cod into a saucepan of water. Bring to a boil, lower the heat immediately and leave to simmer for 5 minutes. Remove from the heat and leave the cod in the water for 20 minutes. Drain. Flake the cod, removing any skin and bones.

2. Remove the leaves and the hairy choke from the artichokes (see page 412). Only keep the hearts. Sprinkle them with lemon juice to prevent them discoloring. Cook in boiling salted water for 25-30 minutes until tender but still slightly firm. Drain and dry on paper towels. Cut each heart into 4-6 pieces.

3. Cook the peas in boiling salted water for 20 minutes or until tender (less time if frozen peas are used). Drain in a colander.

4. Put the unpeeled potatoes into a saucepan of cold water. Bring to a boil and cook for 20 minutes. Drain and when they are cold, peel and slice them.

5. Quarter the tomatoes. Dice the celery.

6. Hard-cook the eggs for 10 minutes in boiling water. Run them under cold water, remove the shells and slice them.

7. Peel and crush the garlic in a mortar and reduce them to a cream with 1-2 tablespoons of the oil. Add the egg yolk, then the remainder of the oil in a trickle, whisking the sauce to thicken it like a mayonnaise. Add salt and pepper to taste, and then add 2 tablespoons lemon juice. Mix well. Chill lightly.

8. Arrange all these ingredients in layers in a salad bowl: cod, artichokes, peas, potatoes, tomatoes and celery. Garnish with a few egg slices. (Serve the remainder of the eggs separately.)

9. Serve the salad with the garlic mayonnaise.

Salade aux noisettes

Hazelnut Salad

	00:40		00:00	

American	Ingredients	Metric/Imperial
1	Head of celeriac	1
	Lemon juice	
4	Carrots	4
1	Small head of celery	1
4	Tomatoes	4
1	Bunch of radishes	1
1	Head of escarole	1
2	Thick slices of cooked ham	2
½ cup	Hazelnuts	50 g / 2 oz
5 tbsp	Vegetable oil	5 tbsp
3 tbsp	Dry sherry wine	3 tbsp
1½ tsp	Wine vinegar	1½ tsp
1 tsp	Prepared mustard with herbs	1 tsp
	Salt and pepper	
12	Black olives	12

1. Peel the celeriac, grate it and sprinkle with a few drops of lemon juice to prevent it from discoloring.

2. Peel the carrots and grate them. Dice the celery. Quarter the tomatoes. Slice the radishes. Remove the damaged leaves from the escarole, rinse carefully and tear into small pieces. Cut the ham into thin strips. Crush the hazelnuts coarsely.

3. Put the celeriac, carrots, celery, tomatoes, radishes, escarole and ham into a salad bowl.

4. In a bowl mix together the oil, sherry, wine vinegar, mustard with herbs and the crushed hazelnuts. Add salt and pepper to taste and leave for a few minutes so the flavors can intermingle.

5. Pour the dressing over the salad. Add the olives, stir and serve.

Scarole, noix, truffe

Walnut and Truffle Salad

	00:15		00:00

American	Ingredients	Metric/Imperial
1	Head of escarole	1
1	Truffle	1
1 cup	Chopped walnuts	125 g / 4 oz
	Salt and pepper	
2 tbsp	Sherry vinegar	2 tbsp
¼ cup	Walnut or peanut oil	4 tbsp

1. Remove any damaged leaves from the escarole, rinse and drain in a salad basket. Peel the truffle and cut into thin sticks. Combine the escarole, truffle and walnuts in a salad bowl.
2. Dissolve a pinch of salt in the vinegar. Add the oil and pepper to taste. Blend and pour over the salad. Toss and serve immediately.

Salade niçoise

Tuna, Anchovy and Olive Salad

	00:45		01:30

American	Ingredients	Metric/Imperial
½ lb	Salted anchovies	250 g / 8 oz
	Olive oil	
4	Potatoes	4
½ lb	Green beans	250 g / 8 oz
	Salt and pepper	
1	Head of lettuce	1
1	Head of celery	1
4	Tomatoes	4
2	Sweet red or green peppers	2
2	Eggs	2
1 (7½ oz)	Can of tuna in oil	1 (200 g / 7 oz)
1 cup	Black olives	125 g / 4 oz
1 tbsp	Wine vinegar	1 tbsp
1 tbsp	Prepared mustard	1 tbsp
1 tsp	Chopped fresh parsley	1 tsp

1. Split open the anchovies in order to remove the backbone. Rinse well under cold running water. Drain and pat dry, then cover with olive oil. (If salted anchovies are not available, canned anchovy fillets may be used.)
2. Place the unpeeled potatoes in a saucepan of cold water. Bring to a boil and leave to cook for about 20 minutes. Drain in a colander, peel and cut into slices.
3. Trim the beans, removing any strings, and cook in boiling salted water for about 10 minutes or until tender but still firm. Drain and cut each bean into 2-3 pieces.
4. Rinse and drain the lettuce. Shred the leaves. Cut the celery into thin strips. Quarter the tomatoes. Core and seed the peppers and cut into thin rings.
5. Hard-cook the eggs for 10 minutes in boiling water. Drain, remove the shells and quarter the eggs.
6. Drain and flake the tuna.

7. Arrange in successive layers in a salad bowl the potatoes, the beans mixed with the lettuce, the celery, the tomatoes, the pepper rings, the drained anchovies and a few olives. Finally complete the garnishing of the salad with the tuna, eggs and the rest of the olives.
8. Dissolve a pinch of salt in the vinegar. Mix in the mustard. Add 3 tablespoons of olive oil, the parsley and pepper to taste. Mix thoroughly. Pour this dressing over the salad. Stir when you are about to serve.

Salade norvégienne

Norwegian Salad

	01:00 plus marinating		00:30

American	Ingredients	Metric/Imperial
½ lb	Cod fillets	250 g / 8 oz
6	Raw jumbo shrimp [Dublin Bay prawns] or	5
1 (7 oz)	Can of crabmeat	1 (200 g / 7 oz)
	Salt and pepper	
2 cups	Peas	200 g / 7 oz
½ lb	Potatoes	250 g / 8 oz
1	Apple	1
2	Large dill pickles [gherkins]	2
¼ lb	Celery	125 g / 4 oz
1	Onion	1
1	Orange	1
½	Lemon	½
1	Egg	1
1 cup	Mayonnaise (see page 119)	250 ml / 8 fl oz
1	Garlic clove	1
3 tbsp	Chopped fresh parsley	3 tbsp
3 tbsp	Chopped fresh chervil	3 tbsp
3 tbsp	Chopped fresh dill	3 tbsp
3 tbsp	Chopped watercress	3 tbsp
2 tbsp	Wine vinegar	2 tbsp
2 tbsp	Strong prepared mustard	2 tbsp
6 tbsp	Oil	6 tbsp
1	Head of lettuce	1

1. Plunge the cod fillets into a pan of cold salted water. Bring to a boil and leave to simmer for 5 minutes. Remove the saucepan from the heat and allow the fish to cool in the cooking water. Drain and flake, discarding any skin and bones.
2. If you are using shrimp, cook them in boiling salted water for 5 minutes. Drain. Peel and devein the shrimp and cut into pieces.
3. If you have chosen canned crab, drain, remove any cartilage and shell and break the meat into small pieces.
4. Cook the peas in a saucepan of boiling salted water for 20 minutes (less time if frozen peas are used). Drain.
5. Put the unpeeled potatoes into a saucepan of cold water. Bring to a boil and cook for 20 minutes. Drain and leave to cool, then peel and dice.
6. Peel and core the apple and dice it, together with the pickles and celery. Peel and chop the onion.
7. Put the cod, shrimp or crab, peas, potatoes, apple, pickles, celery and onion into a salad bowl. Mix without crushing, then sprinkle with the juice of the orange and the juice of the ½ lemon. Leave to marinate for 30 minutes to 1 hour in a cool place.

8. Hard-cook the egg for 10 minutes in boiling water. Drain, shell and put the egg into a blender or food processor. Blend until coarse-fine. Alternatively, press the egg through a sieve.
9. Divide the mayonnaise in half. Peel and crush the garlic and mix with one-half of the mayonnaise.
10. In a bowl, combine the parsley, chervil, dill and watercress.
11. Dissolve a pinch of salt in the vinegar. Mix in the mustard. Add the oil, 2 tablespoons of the chopped herb mixture, the sieved eggs, and pepper to taste.
12. Remove any damaged leaves from the lettuce, rinse carefully and drain well in a salad basket. Line the bottom of a salad bowl with the lettuce leaves.
13. Spoon the marinated salad onto the lettuce. Serve together with the egg and herb dressing, the plain mayonnaise, the garlic-flavored mayonnaise and the remaining herb mixture.

Norwegian salad

Salade de pissenlits au lard

Dandelion Salad with Bacon

| | 00:15 | 00:05 to 00:07 | |

American	Ingredients	Metric/Imperial
¾ lb	Lightly salted or smoked bacon	350 g / 12 oz
1½ lb	Dandelion leaves	750 g / 1½ lb
	Salt and pepper	
1 tbsp	Vinegar	1 tbsp
1 tsp	Prepared mustard	1 tsp
3 tbsp	Oil	3 tbsp

1. If the bacon is salty, put it into a saucepan of cold water, bring to a boil and blanch for 5 minutes. Drain, cool and pat dry.
2. Rinse the dandelion leaves in several changes of water and shake dry. Place in a salad bowl.
3. Dissolve a pinch of salt in the vinegar. Add the mustard, oil and pepper to taste. Pour over the drained dandelion leaves.
4. Cut the bacon into pieces as thick or as thin as you like. Cook in a frying pan, without fat, until crisp and well browned. Pour the bacon over the dandelion leaves together with the bacon fat in the pan. Take immediately to the table, toss and serve.

Tourteaux en salade

Crab Salad

| | 01:00 | 00:35 | |

American	Ingredients	Metric/Imperial
2	Small onions	2
	Salt and pepper	
1 tbsp	Vinegar	1 tbsp
5 tbsp	Oil	5 tbsp
2 (1½ lb)	Cooked crabs	2 (750 g / 1½ lb)
12	Cooked jumbo shrimp [Dublin Bay prawns]	12
2	Avocados	2
	Lemon juice	
2	Tomatoes	2
½ lb	Peeled cooked shrimp [prawns]	250 g / 8 oz
2 tbsp	Capers	2 tbsp
1 cup	Mayonnaise (see page 119)	250 ml / 8 fl oz
1	Head of lettuce	1

1. Peel and finely chop the onions.
2. Dissolve a pinch of salt in the vinegar. Add the oil and pepper to taste. Stir in the chopped onions.
3. Crack the crab claws and shell. Discard all inedible parts. Remove the creamy parts, mash with a fork and mix into the dressing. Set the crabmeat aside.
4. Peel and devein the jumbo shrimp.
5. Cut the avocados in half, remove the seeds and scoop out the flesh with a melon baller or teaspoon. Sprinkle the balls with lemon juice, as you shape them so that they do not turn black.
6. Cut the tomatoes into small cubes.
7. Place the crabmeat in a mixing bowl together with both kinds of shrimp, the avocado balls and tomatoes. Add the capers. Mix 3 tablespoons of the mayonnaise with the dressing. Add to the salad and toss together.
8. Remove any damaged leaves from the lettuce, rinse carefully and drain in a salad basket. Line 6 individual salad plates or bowls with lettuce leaves and fill with the crab salad. Serve the rest of the mayonnaise in a sauceboat.

Salade de tomates

Tomato Salad

| | 00:10 | 00:00 | |

American	Ingredients	Metric/Imperial
3	Scallions [spring onions]	3
8	Small, very firm tomatoes	8
1 cup	Small black olives	125 g / 4 oz
	Salt and pepper	
1 tbsp	Vinegar	1 tbsp
1 tsp	Prepared mustard	1 tsp
3 tbsp	Oil	3 tbsp

1. Trim and chop the scallions and place in a salad bowl. Cut each tomato into 4 slices and place on the scallions together with the olives.
2. Dissolve a pinch of salt in the vinegar. Mix in the mustard. Add the oil and pepper to taste and mix well.
3. Add the dressing to the tomatoes and serve.

Salade de poisson-maïs

Corn and Fish Salad

	00:40 plus marinating	00:30

American	Ingredients	Metric/Imperial
1 lb	Cod	500 g / 1 lb
2 quarts	Court-bouillon (see page 115)	2 l / 3½ pints
12	Raw jumbo shrimp [Dublin Bay prawns]	12
¼ lb	Peeled cooked shrimp [prawns]	125 g / 4 oz
3 cups	Peas	350 g / 12 oz
	Salt and pepper	
1	Grapefruit	1
3	Eggs	3
3	Tomatoes	3
4	Onions	4
1	Garlic clove	1
1 cup	Corn kernels	125 g / 4 oz
2 tbsp	Wine vinegar	2 tbsp
1¼ cups	Vegetable oil	300 ml / ½ pint
1	Head of lettuce	1
1	Egg yolk	1
1½ tsp	Strong prepared mustard	1½ tsp

1. Put the cod into the cold court-bouillon, bring slowly to a boil, and simmer for 5 minutes. Remove the fish with a slotted spoon. Dice the fish, discarding all skin and bones. Set aside.
2. Toss the jumbo shrimp into the court-bouillon and leave to cook for 5 minutes after boiling has resumed. Remove with a slotted spoon, and peel and devein the shrimp. Set aside.
3. Toss the cooked shrimp into the boiling court-bouillon and drain immediately in a colander. Set aside.
4. Cook the peas in a saucepan of boiling salted water for 15-20 minutes after boiling has resumed (less time if frozen peas are used). Drain.
5. Peel the grapefruit and divide into sections, discarding seeds and membrane. Keep half the sections whole and cut the other sections into 3 or 4 pieces each.
6. Hard-cook the eggs for 10 minutes in boiling water. Drain, run them under cold water and remove the shells. Slice 2 of the eggs. Place the third egg in a blender or food processor and blend until coarse-fine, or sieve the egg.
7. Slice 2 tomatoes and remove seeds. Chop the third.
8. Peel and chop the onions. Peel and crush the garlic.
9. Combine the diced fish, small shrimp, chopped grapefruit sections, onions, garlic, chopped tomato, sieved egg, peas and corn in a mixing bowl.
10. Dissolve a pinch of salt in 1 tablespoon of the vinegar. Add 4 tablespoons of the oil and pepper to taste and mix well. Pour the dressing over the fish mixture and leave to marinate in a cool place for 30 minutes.
11. Remove any damaged leaves from the lettuce, rinse carefully in several changes of water and drain in a salad basket. Cut into thin strips. Arrange the lettuce on the bottom of a salad bowl and sprinkle with salt.
12. Put the egg yolk into a bowl and add the mustard and salt and pepper to taste. Blend with a whisk. Pour in the remaining oil gradually, in a thin trickle, continuing to whisk vigorously. Thin out the mayonnaise with the remaining wine vinegar.
13. When ready to serve, add 3 tablespoons of the mayonnaise to the marinated mixture, stir and pour over the lettuce in the salad bowl. Top with the egg slices, tomato slices, whole grapefruit sections and the jumbo shrimp. Serve with the remainder of the mayonnaise.

Salade de poissons

Fish Salad

	00:15 plus chilling	00:20

American	Ingredients	Metric/Imperial
2 cups	Long-grain rice	300 g / 10 oz
	Salt and pepper	
½ tsp	Saffron powder	½ tsp
1 (7 oz)	Can of crabmeat	1 (200 g / 7 oz)
1½ lb	White fish fillets	750 g / 1½ lb
1	Head of lettuce	1
4	Tomatoes	4
1	Egg yolk	1
1½ tsp	Strong prepared mustard	1½ tsp
1 cup	Vegetable oil	250 ml / 8 fl oz
1 tbsp	Wine vinegar	1 tbsp

1. Cook the rice in boiling salted water, to which the saffron has been added, for about 20 minutes. Run it under cold water, drain in a colander and spread out on a cloth to dry thoroughly.
2. Drain the crab, discarding all cartilage and bits of shell.
3. Oil a ring mold 10 in / 25 cm in diameter and cover the bottom with the largest pieces of crab. Break the remainder of the crab into small pieces and mix it with the rice. Use to fill the mold, heaping it up with the back of a large spoon. Chill for 2 hours.
4. Plunge the fish fillets into cold salted water, bring to a boil and simmer for 5 minutes. Remove from the heat and leave the fish to cool in the water. Drain, remove any skin and bones and cut into 6-8 pieces.
5. Remove any damaged leaves from the lettuce and rinse carefully in several changes of water. Drain in a salad basket. Shred the large lettuce leaves. Slice the tomatoes.
6. Put the egg yolk into a bowl and add the mustard and salt and pepper to taste. Blend with a whisk. Pour in the oil gradually in a thin trickle, continuing to whisk vigorously. Thin out the mayonnaise with the wine vinegar. (Instead of mayonnaise you may use a tartare sauce — see page 119.)
7. Unmold the crab and rice salad onto a serving plate. Pile the shredded lettuce in the center and top with the pieces of fish and the tomato slices. Garnish with the small lettuce leaves. Serve with the mayonnaise.

Salade périgourdine

Perigord Salad

	00:40	00:25 to 00:30

American	Ingredients	Metric/Imperial
2	Globe artichoke hearts	2
	Lemon juice	
	Salt and pepper	
1 lb	Green beans	500 g / 1 lb
1 lb	Asparagus	500 g / 1 lb
1	Head of chicory [curly endive]	1
½ lb	Pâté de foie gras	250 g / 8 oz
6 tbsp	Oil	6 tbsp
2 tbsp	Sherry vinegar or dry sherry wine	2 tbsp

1. If the artichoke hearts are fresh, sprinkle them with lemon juice to prevent them from discoloring and cook in boiling salted water for about 25 minutes or until tender. Drain, run them under cold water and drain again. Cut each heart into 6.

2. Trim the beans and remove strings, if necessary. Cook in a large saucepan of boiling salted water for about 10 minutes or until tender but still crisp. Run them under cold water and drain.

3. Trim and scrape the asparagus. Cut all the spears to the same length, and tie them into 2 bunches. Cook in a large saucepan of boiling salted water for 5-20 minutes (depending upon age and size.) Run them under cold water and drain.

4. Remove any damaged leaves from the chicory and rinse carefully in several changes of water. Drain.

5. Divide the pieces of artichoke hearts, the beans, asparagus and chicory between 6 plates, and add 1-2 thin slices of pâté de foie gras to each plate.

6. In a bowl, combine the oil, sherry vinegar or dry sherry, and salt and pepper to taste and whisk to blend them thoroughly.

7. Sprinkle the dressing over the salads just before serving.

Perigord salad

Salade de poulet
Chicken Salad

◢▷ 00:45   00:30 ◣

American	Ingredients	Metric/Imperial
2 quarts	Court-bouillon with vinegar (see page 115)	2 l / 3½ pints
1 (2½ lb)	Chicken	1 (1.25 kg / 2½ lb)
1	Head of celery	1
1	Head of Romaine [cos] lettuce	1
2	Apples	2
5 oz	Gruyère cheese	150 g / 5 oz
2	Oranges	2
3	Tomatoes	3
⅔ cup	Raisins	125 g / 4 oz
	Salt and pepper	
2 tbsp	Vinegar	2 tbsp
2 tbsp	Prepared mustard	2 tbsp
1 cup + 3 tbsp	Vegetable oil	250 ml / 8 fl oz + 3 tbsp
1 tsp	Chopped fresh parsley	1 tsp
1	Garlic clove	1
1 cup	Chopped walnuts	125 g / 4 oz
1 cup	Black olives	150 g / 5 oz
1	Egg yolk	1

1. Bring the court-bouillon to a boil and add the chicken. Cook for 30 minutes, then leave to cool in the liquid.

2. Remove the chicken from the court-bouillon. Remove all the skin and take the meat from the carcass. Cut the meat into thin sticks.

3. Cut the celery into ½ in / 1 cm pieces. Rinse the lettuce and cut into thin strips. Peel and dice the apples. Cut the gruyère into cubes. Peel the oranges and cut into slices. Peel the tomatoes (first plunging them into boiling water for 10 seconds), remove the seeds and cut into pieces. Soak the raisins in warm water.

4. Dissolve a pinch of salt in 1 tablespoon of the vinegar. Mix in 1 tablespoon of the mustard. Add 3 tablespoons of the oil, the parsley, the peeled and crushed garlic, and pepper to taste. Mix well.

5. Blend the dressing thoroughly with the celery, lettuce, apples, gruyère, oranges, tomatoes, drained raisins, walnuts and olives. Keep in a cool place.

6. Meanwhile, put the egg yolk into a bowl and add the remaining mustard, 1 teaspoon vinegar and salt and pepper to taste. Whisk vigorously, then add the remaining oil in a very thin trickle, whisking constantly. If the mayonnaise is too thick, thin it with the remaining vinegar.

7. To serve, mix the mayonnaise with the salad.

Salade marisette
Fish and Rice Salad

◢▷ 00:30   00:15 to 00:18 ◣
plus soaking and marinating

American	Ingredients	Metric/Imperial
⅔ cup	Golden raisins [sultanas]	125 g / 4 oz
¾ lb	Cooked white fish	350 g / 12 oz
3	Tomatoes	3
1	Head of celery	1
1	Lemon	1
1 cup + 2 tbsp	Vegetable oil	250 ml / 8 fl oz + 2 tbsp
	Salt and pepper	
1 cup	Long-grain rice	200 g / 7 oz
1	Egg yolk	1
1½ tsp	Prepared mustard	1½ tsp
1 tsp	Wine vinegar	1 tsp

1. Soak the raisins in warm water for 1 hour. Drain and set aside.

2. Flake the fish, removing any skin and bones. Set aside.

3. Peel the tomatoes (first plunging them into boiling water for 10 seconds), remove the seeds and coarsely chop the pulp. Dice the celery.

4. Put the raisins, tomatoes and celery into a bowl and sprinkle with the juice of the lemon, 2 tablespoons of the oil and salt and pepper to taste. Stir and leave to marinate in a cool place.

5. Cook the rice in a large saucepan of boiling salted water for 15-18 minutes or until tender. Rinse in cold water, drain and spread out on a cloth to dry. Add the rice and fish to the ingredients which are marinating.

6. Put the egg yolk into a bowl and add the mustard and salt and pepper to taste. Whisk together. Gradually add the remaining oil in a thin trickle, continuing to whisk vigorously. Thin out the mayonnaise with the vinegar.

7. When you are about to serve, add the mayonnaise to the salad, and toss together. If liked, line the salad bowl with lettuce leaves and pile the rice salad on top.

Salade de riz à l'italienne

Italian Rice Salad

	00:20		00:30

American	Ingredients	Metric/Imperial
1½ cups	Water	350 ml / 12 fl oz
	Salt and pepper	
1 cup	Long-grain rice	250 g / 8 oz
1	Eggplant [aubergine]	1
2	Green peppers	2
6 tbsp	Oil	6 tbsp
½ lb	Tomatoes	250 g / 8 oz
1 tbsp	Prepared mustard	1 tbsp
1 tbsp	Vinegar	1 tbsp
1 tsp	Chopped fresh parsley	1 tsp

1. Pour the water into a saucepan, add a pinch of salt and bring to a boil. Rinse the rice and add to the boiling water. Cook for about 15 minutes or until tender and the water has been absorbed. Spread out the rice on a cloth to drain and dry.
2. Cut the eggplant into slices. Core and seed the green peppers and cut into thin strips. Heat 3 tablespoons of the oil in a large frying pan and cook the green pepper and eggplant until tender.
3. Add the rice and stir over a gentle heat so the rice is flavored by the vegetables. Add salt and pepper to taste. Leave to cool.
4. Peel the tomatoes (first plunging them into boiling water for 10 seconds) and dice them. Add to the rice mixture.
5. Mix a pinch of salt and the mustard with the vinegar. Add the remaining oil, chopped parsley and pepper to taste. Mix thoroughly.
6. Add the dressing to the rice and vegetable mixture just before serving and toss well.

Salade de pommes de terre

Potato Salad

	00:30		00:25 to 00:30

American	Ingredients	Metric/Imperial
3 lb	Potatoes	1.5 kg / 3 lb
	Salt and pepper	
1 cup	Dry white wine	250 ml / 8 fl oz
2 tbsp	Vinegar	2 tbsp
1 tsp	Prepared mustard	1 tsp
1¼ cups	Oil	300 ml / ½ pint
2	Shallots	2
2 tsp	Chopped fresh chervil or chives	2 tsp

1. Choose firm, waxy potatoes which will not fall to pieces when cooked. Cook the unpeeled potatoes in boiling salted water for 20 minutes. Drain and when cool enough to handle, peel and cut them into slices. Cover with the wine and toss so that they are thoroughly coated.
2. Mix a pinch of salt with the vinegar, then add the mustard and oil, stirring continuously. Add pepper to taste.
3. Peel and chop the shallots. Add to the dressing with the herbs and mix well.
4. When you are about to serve, sprinkle the potatoes with the dressing and stir carefully so as not to break them up. They are best served warm.

Salade verte

Green Salad

	00:40		00:20 to 00:30

American	Ingredients	Metric/Imperial
4	Globe artichokes	4
	Salt and pepper	
	Lemon juice	
1 lb	Asparagus	1 lb
2	Avocados	2
1	Bunch of chervil or parsley	1
1	Bunch of watercress	1
¼ lb	Mixed young salad greens or chicory [curly endive]	125 g / 4 oz
½	Cucumber	½
1	Lettuce heart	1
2 tbsp	Cider vinegar	2 tbsp
6 tbsp	Walnut oil	6 tbsp

1. Remove the leaves from the artichokes; leave the choke. Cook the hearts in boiling salted water, to which lemon juice has been added, for about 25 minutes or until tender. Drain, remove the hairy choke and cut the hearts into 6 or 8 pieces.
2. Scrape the asparagus stalks. Tie them together in 3 bunches and cook in boiling salted water for 5-20 minutes (depending on age and size). Drain in a colander.
3. Peel the avocados. Halve and remove the seeds. Slice and sprinkle with lemon juice so they will not turn black.
4. Rinse the sprigs of chervil and leave them whole. Remove the damaged leaves and stems from the watercress, rinse and drain in a salad basket.
5. Remove any damaged leaves from the salad greens or chicory, rinse and drain in a salad basket.
6. Peel the cucumber. Remove the seeds and dice the flesh. Sprinkle with salt and leave to drain for 20 minutes.
7. Rinse the lettuce heart.
8. Combine the artichoke hearts, asparagus, avocado slices, chervil sprigs, watercress leaves, salad greens or chicory, lettuce heart and diced cucumber in a salad bowl.
9. Dissolve a pinch of salt in the cider vinegar. Add the oil and pepper to taste. Stir.
10. Add the dressing to the salad, toss and serve.

Salade de salami

Salami Salad

	00:30		00:10

American	Ingredients	Metric/Imperial
2	Red apples	2
	Lemon juice	
12	Slices of salami	12
6	Eggs	6
1	Cooked beet [beetroot]	1
1	Head of lettuce	1
½	Bunch of radishes	½
1 cup	Mayonnaise (see page 119)	250 ml / 8 fl oz
1 tsp	Water	1 tsp
	Salt and pepper	

1. Core the apples. Cut into rather thick slices and then into thin sticks, dipping them in lemon juice so that they do not discolor.
2. Roll the apple sticks in the slices of salami and secure with wooden toothpicks.
3. Hard-cook the eggs for 10 minutes in boiling water. Drain, remove the shells and cut in half.
4. Peel the beet and dice. Remove any damaged leaves from the lettuce, rinse carefully in several changes of water and drain in a salad basket. Trim the radishes.
5. Line a salad bowl with the lettuce leaves and add the radishes, beet, egg halves and salami and apple rolls.
6. Lighten the mayonnaise with the water, and add salt and pepper to taste.
7. Serve the salad accompanied by the mayonnaise.

Salade russe
Russian Salad

	00:20 plus soaking	01:30

American	Ingredients	Metric/Imperial
½ cup	Small dried flageolet beans	125 g / 4 oz
½ lb	Carrots	250 g / 8 oz
½ lb	Turnips	250 g / 8 oz
½ lb	Green beans	250 g / 8 oz
1 lb	Peas	500 g / 1 lb
	Salt and pepper	
1	Cooked lobster tail or	1
12	Cooked jumbo shrimp [Dublin Bay prawns] or	12
1 (7 oz)	Can of crabmeat	1 (200 g / 7 oz)
4	Slices of cooked tongue	4
¼ lb	Lean cooked ham	125 g / 4 oz
½ lb	Button mushrooms	250 g / 8 oz
2 tbsp	Capers	2 tbsp
2 tbsp	Wine vinegar	2 tbsp
2 tbsp	Strong prepared mustard	2 tbsp
1 cup + 3 tbsp	Vegetable oil	250 ml / 8 fl oz + 3 tbsp
2 tsp	Chopped fresh parsley	2 tsp
4	Eggs	4
1	Egg yolk	1

1. Place the flageolet beans in cold water and soak for 2-3 hours. Drain and place in a large saucepan with fresh cold water to cover. Bring to a boil and simmer for 45 minutes.
2. Meanwhile, peel and dice the carrots and turnips. Trim the green beans and cut into ½ in / 1 cm pieces.
3. Add the carrots, turnips, beans, peas and salt and pepper to taste to the flageolet beans. Cook for a further 30 minutes.
4. Drain the vegetables in a colander and leave to cool.
5. Remove the lobster meat from the shell and dice it. Or peel, devein and chop the jumbo shrimp. Or drain the crab, removing any cartilage or bits of shell, and break the flesh into small pieces.
6. Dice the tongue and ham. Slice the mushrooms. Mix the tongue, ham and mushrooms in a large salad bowl with the cooked vegetables and lobster (or shrimp or crab). Add the capers.
7. Dissolve a pinch of salt in 1 tablespoon of the vinegar. Mix in 1 tablespoon of the mustard. Add 3 tablespoons of the oil, the parsley and pepper to taste. Blend this dressing with the ingredients in the salad bowl.

8. Hard-cook the eggs for 10 minutes in boiling water. Drain, remove the shells and cut in half.
9. Place the raw egg yolk in a bowl and add the remaining mustard, 1 teaspoon vinegar, and salt and pepper to taste. Whisk vigorously. Add the remaining oil in a very thin trickle, while continuing to whisk. If the mayonnaise is too thick, thin it out with the remaining vinegar.
10. When you are about to serve, add 3 tablespoons of the mayonnaise to the salad. Stir, then serve garnished with the remainder of the mayonnaise and the egg halves.

Russian salad

Salade scandinave
Scandinavian Salad

	00:20	00:10

American	Ingredients	Metric/Imperial
1	Head of lettuce	1
3	Eggs	3
3	Large dill pickles [gherkins]	3
3	Marinated herrings	3
½ lb	Saint Paulin or similar cheese	250 g / 8 oz
1	Bunch of fresh chervil or parsley	1
2 tsp	Chopped fresh chives	2 tsp
1 tsp	Prepared mustard with green peppercorns	1 tsp
3 tbsp	Oil	3 tbsp
½ cup	Crème fraîche (see page 122)	125 ml / 4 fl oz
1	Lemon	1
	Salt	

1. Rinse and dry the lettuce and separate the leaves.
2. Hard-cook the eggs for 10 minutes in boiling water. Drain, run under cold water, remove the shells and cut into slices.
3. Slice the pickles. Dice the herrings and cheese. Chop the chervil. Combine the eggs, pickles, herrings, cheese, chervil, chives and lettuce in a salad bowl. Keep in a cool place until ready to serve.
4. In a mixing bowl combine the mustard with the oil. Add the crème fraîche, the juice of the lemon and salt to taste.
5. Serve the salad with the dressing.

Salade Sylvie

Citrus, Ham and Cheese Salad

⏱ 00:30   00:00 🍲

American	Ingredients	Metric/Imperial
1	Lettuce heart	1
3	Oranges	3
2	Grapefruit	2
¼ lb	Gruyère cheese	125 g / 4 oz
1	Hard-cooked egg	1
5 oz	Cooked ham	150 g / 5 oz
¼ lb	Button mushrooms	125 g / 4 oz
1	Lemon	1
½ cup	Cream cheese	125 g / 4 oz
	Chopped fresh herbs (chives, tarragon, parsley, etc)	
	Salt and pepper	

1. Rinse and drain the lettuce. Tear into small pieces. Peel the oranges and grapefruit. Separate into sections, removing the seeds and membrane.
2. Cut the gruyère, egg, ham, mushrooms, oranges and grapefruit into small pieces.
3. Place all the prepared ingredients in a salad bowl.
4. Mix the juice of the lemon with the cream cheese. Add the chopped herbs, and salt and pepper to taste.
5. Pour the dressing over the salad, toss and serve.

Salade à la tapenade 👨‍🍳👨‍🍳

Piquant Olive Salad

⏱ 00:25   00:20 🍲

American	Ingredients	Metric/Imperial
1 lb	Small potatoes	500 g / 1 lb
1 lb	Small tomatoes	500 g / 1 lb
½ lb	Small onions	250 g / 8 oz
1	Garlic clove	1
2 tbsp	Olive, anchovy and caper spread (see page 166)	2 tbsp
6 tbsp	Olive oil	6 tbsp
1 tbsp	Vinegar	1 tbsp
2 tbsp	Chopped fresh parsley	2 tbsp
	Salt and pepper	
1 cup	Black olives	150 g / 5 oz

1. Put the unpeeled potatoes in a saucepan of cold water. Bring to a boil and cook for 20 minutes. Drain and leave to cool, then peel and quarter.
2. Quarter the tomatoes.
3. Peel and thinly slice the onions. Peel and crush the garlic.
4. Mix the olive, anchovy and caper spread in a bowl with the olive oil, garlic, vinegar and chopped parsley. Taste, then add salt and pepper.
5. Put the potatoes, tomatoes and onions in a salad bowl. Add the dressing and olives, toss and serve. You may also present this delicious salad with the dressing served separately in a sauceboat.

Saucisson en salade 👨‍🍳

Sausage Salad

⏱ 00:30   00:20 🍲

American	Ingredients	Metric/Imperial
1	Uncooked sausage with pistachios	1
½ lb	Smoked bacon	250 g / 8 oz
	Salt and pepper	
1 tbsp	Vinegar	1 tbsp
1 tbsp	Prepared mustard	1 tbsp
3 tbsp	Oil	3 tbsp
1	Head of chicory [curly endive]	1
	Toast for serving	

1. Prick the sausage. Place in a pan of boiling water and simmer for 20 minutes. Drain. Leave to cool, then slice.
2. Toss the bacon into a saucepan of boiling water and blanch for 5 minutes after boiling has resumed. Drain and pat dry, then cut into pieces. Brown the pieces in a frying pan without fat. Drain on paper towels, reserving the bacon fat in the pan.
3. Dissolve a pinch of salt in the vinegar. Mix in the mustard. Add the oil and bacon fat and blend.
4. Rinse the chicory, remove any damaged leaves and drain in a salad basket. Put the lettuce into a salad bowl together with the sausage and bacon. Sprinkle with the dressing and toss together.
5. Serve with slices of toast.

Corn salad

Hot hors d'oeuvres

Artichauts Barigoule

Stuffed Artichokes, Provençal Style

	01:00		00:40

American	Ingredients	Metric/Imperial
6	Globe artichokes or	6
12	Small purple artichokes	12
	Lemon juice	
	Salt and pepper	
½ lb	Button mushrooms	250 g / 8 oz
¼ lb	Unsmoked bacon	125 g / 4 oz
3	Shallots	3
2 tbsp	Olive oil	2 tbsp
1 tbsp	Chopped fresh parsley	1 tbsp
2	Onions	2
2	Carrots	2
6	Thin slices of smoked bacon	6
⅔ cup	White wine	150 ml / ¼ pint
1	Bouquet garni	1

1. Trim the stalks from the artichokes and remove all the leaves. Dip the peeled hearts immediately in lemon juice to prevent them from turning black.
2. Put some salted water and a little lemon juice into a saucepan, add the artichoke hearts and bring to a boil. Leave to cook for 15-30 minutes or until tender but still firm. Drain and remove the hairy chokes.
3. Preheat the oven to 425°F / 220°C / Gas Mark 7.
4. Finely chop the mushrooms. Chop the unsmoked bacon. Peel and chop the shallots.
5. Heat 1 tablespoon of the oil in a frying pan, add the bacon, mushrooms, shallots, parsley, and salt and pepper to taste and cook, stirring, until lightly browned. Drain off excess fat.
6. Peel and chop the onions and carrots and brown them in the remaining olive oil in another pan.
7. Wrap each artichoke heart in a slice of smoked bacon. Top with the mushroom mixture and then with the carrot mixture. Arrange the hearts in a casserole.
8. Add the wine and bouquet garni and cover the casserole. Put the casserole into the oven and braise for 30-40 minutes. Remove the lid 10 minutes before cooking finishes for the sauce to reduce.
9. Remove the bouquet garni and serve.

Bananes au bacon

Bananas with Bacon

	00:05		00:05

American	Ingredients	Metric/Imperial
6	Bananas	6
12	Small, thin slices of bacon	12
	Pepper	

1. Preheat the broiler [grill] to high.
2. Peel the bananas and cut in half crosswise. Wrap each banana half in a slice of bacon and push a wooden toothpick through the banana to hold the bacon securely in place.
3. Place the bananas in a flameproof baking dish. Add pepper to taste. (Do not add salt, because the bacon is already salty.)
4. Place the dish under the broiler and cook for about 5 minutes or until the bacon is crisp and browned. Turn the banana pieces to cook evenly. Serve hot.

Amuse-gueule saucisse

Sausage Cocktail Snacks

	00:20	00:10 to 00:15	
	plus thawing or making pastry	Makes 32	

American	Ingredients	Metric/Imperial
14 oz	Puff pastry (see page 458 or use frozen)	400 g / 14 oz
8	Cocktail sausages [chipolatas]	8
	Cayenne pepper	
1	Egg	1

1. If you are using frozen pastry, leave to thaw for 3 hours at room temperature.
2. Preheat the oven to 450°F / 230°C / Gas Mark 8.
3. Roll out the pastry ⅛ in / 3 mm thick, and cut out pieces which will *just* wrap around each sausage.
4. Lightly sprinkle the sausages with cayenne pepper and wrap each of them in a piece of pastry. Dampen the longest edge with water and press to seal. Coat the rolls with beaten egg. Cut each pastry-wrapped sausage into 4.
5. Arrange on a baking sheet and bake for 15 minutes. Pile them in a dish and pierce each of them with a toothpick. Serve hot.

Barquettes chaudes aux fines herbes

Hot Pastry Boats with Herbs

	00:10		00:06
	plus making pastry boats		

American	Ingredients	Metric/Imperial
6	Baked pastry boats (purchased or see page 89)	6
1	Small bunch of fresh herbs (tarragon, parsley, chives)	1
3	Eggs	3
¼ cup	Crème fraîche (see page 122)	4 tbsp
	Salt and pepper	

1. Preheat the oven to 325°F / 160°C / Gas Mark 3.
2. Arrange the pastry boats on a baking sheet and put them into the oven to heat through.
3. Meanwhile, finely chop the herbs. Break the eggs into a bowl and add the crème fraîche and salt and pepper to taste. Put this bowl into a saucepan half full of hot water and cook over a medium heat for about 5 minutes, stirring continuously. When the mixture is thick and very smooth, blend in the chopped herbs.
4. Fill the hot pastry boats with the herb mixture and serve immediately.

Aubergines farcies aux champignons de Paris

Eggplants [Aubergines] Stuffed with Mushrooms

	00:10	00:25

American	Ingredients	Metric/Imperial
6	Eggplants [aubergines]	6
3 tbsp	Olive oil	3 tbsp
1½ lb	Button mushrooms	750 g / 1½ lb
4	Onions	4
2	Garlic cloves	2
1	Small bunch of fresh parsley	1
¾ lb	Sausage meat	350 g / 12 oz
2	Egg yolks	2
	Salt and pepper	

1. Preheat the oven to 425°F / 220°C / Gas Mark 7.
2. Using a small pointed knife, remove the stalks from the eggplants. Split open the eggplants lengthwise. Using a sharp knife, score deep elongated diamond shapes in the pulp. Place the halves in an ovenproof dish. Sprinkle with a little of the olive oil, place in the oven and bake for 10 minutes.
3. Meanwhile, prepare the stuffing. Cut the mushrooms into small cubes. Cook gently for about 5 minutes in a little olive oil.
4. Peel and finely chop the onions and garlic. Chop the parsley.
5. Combine the mushrooms, onions, garlic and parsley in a mixing bowl. Add the sausage meat and egg yolks and mix well. Season with salt and pepper to taste.
6. Take the eggplants out of the oven. Using a grapefruit knife, cut all around the pulp ½ in / 1 cm from the skin, and without piercing the skin. Distribute the stuffing over the entire length of each half.
7. Put the dish back into the oven and bake for a further 15 minutes. Serve hot.

Beignets de jambon cru

Ham Fritters

	00:15	00:25

American	Ingredients	Metric/Imperial
1 cup	Water	250 ml / 8 fl oz
6 tbsp	Butter	75 g / 3 oz
	Salt	
1 cup	Flour	125 g / 4 oz
4	Eggs	4
1 (5 oz)	Thick slice of smoked ham	1 (150 g / 5 oz)
2 tbsp	Blanched almonds	2 tbsp
	Oil for deep frying	

1. Bring the water to a boil in a saucepan together with the butter and a pinch of salt. Add the flour all at once. Mix vigorously with a wooden spoon until the dough comes away from the sides of the pan. Remove the pan from the heat. Add one egg and mix thoroughly, then add another egg and mix. Continue adding eggs, incorporating each thoroughly before adding the next.
2. Cut the ham into small cubes and mix into the choux pastry, together with the almonds.

3. Heat oil for deep frying to 345°F / 175°C.
4. Take a teaspoon of the pastry and drop into the oil, using another spoon to loosen the pastry ball. Continue adding balls of pastry to the oil, cooking about 10-12 at a time. Cook the fritters for 6 minutes or until they are well browned.
5. Drain the fritters on a plate lined with paper towels, and serve hot.

Barquettes chaudes au cantal

Hot Pastry Boats with Cheese

	00:10 plus making pastry boats	00:10

American	Ingredients	Metric/Imperial
2 cups	Grated cantal or similar cheese	250 g / 8 oz
5 tbsp	Crème fraîche (see page 122)	5 tbsp
	Pepper	
1 tsp	Butter	1 tsp
⅓ cup	Chopped smoked lean bacon	60 g / 2½ oz
6	Baked pastry boats (purchased or see page 89)	6

1. Preheat the oven to 400°F / 200°C / Gas Mark 6.
2. Combine the cheese, crème fraîche and pepper to taste in a mixing bowl.
3. Melt the butter in a frying pan, add the bacon and fry until browned. Drain on paper towels.
4. Put the pieces of bacon into the pastry boats and cover with the cheese mixture. Bake for 5-7 minutes. Serve very hot.

Barquettes chaudes au saumon

Hot Salmon Pastry Boats

	00:10 plus making pastry boats	00:10

American	Ingredients	Metric/Imperial
1½ tbsp	Butter	20 g / ¾ oz
1½ tbsp	Flour	20 g / ¾ oz
⅔ cup	Milk	150 ml / ¼ pint
	Salt and pepper	
	Grated nutmeg	
1 (7 oz)	Can of pink salmon	1 (200 g / 7 oz)
¾ cup	Grated gruyère cheese	75 g / 3 oz
6	Baked pastry boats (purchased or see page 89)	6

1. Preheat the oven to 400°F / 200°C / Gas Mark 6.
2. Melt the butter in a saucepan, add the flour and mix thoroughly. Cook for 1 minute. Gradually stir in the milk and cook, stirring continuously with a wooden spoon, until smooth and thickened. Season with salt, pepper and a pinch of nutmeg.
3. Drain and flake the salmon. Add to the sauce together with

half the gruyère. Fill the pastry boats with the preparation and sprinkle with the remainder of the gruyère.

4. Place in the oven and bake until the gruyère on top is lightly browned. Serve immediately.

Beignets d'avocats
Avocado Fritters

	00:15 plus standing time	00:20

American	Ingredients	Metric/Imperial
2	Eggs	2
1 tsp	Salt	1 tsp
1¼ cups + 3 tbsp	Flour	150 g / 5 oz + 3 tbsp
	Pepper	
1 - 1½ cups	Beer	150 ml / ¼ pint
4	Avocados	4
	Oil for deep frying	
1	Egg white	1
	Lemon wedges	

1. Prepare the batter: whisk the whole eggs and salt in a mixing bowl and add 1¼ cups [150 g / 5 oz] of the flour and pepper to taste. Mix thoroughly. Gradually stir in the beer. Leave to stand for 2 hours.

2. Peel the avocados. Cut in half lengthwise, remove the seed and cut the flesh into ¾ in / 2 cm cubes. Coat in the remaining flour.

3. Heat oil for deep frying to 345°F / 175°C.

4. Beat the egg white into a firm snow and fold into the batter.

5. Dip the avocado cubes into the batter, then plunge into the oil. Cook until puffed and brown, then drain on paper towels. Serve hot, surrounded by lemon wedges.

Aubergines farcies
Stuffed Eggplants [Aubergines]

	00:20	00:50

American	Ingredients	Metric/Imperial
3	Eggplants [aubergines]	3
⅔ cup	Olive oil	150 ml / ¼ pint
8	Large tomatoes	8
3	Onions	3
1	Shallot	1
3	Garlic cloves	3
1	Small bunch of fresh parsley	1
	Salt and pepper	
¾ cup	Fresh bread crumbs	40 g / 1½ oz
1¼ cups	Grated gruyère cheese	150 g / 5 oz

1. Preheat the oven to 475°F / 240°C / Gas Mark 9.

2. With a small pointed knife, remove the stalks from the eggplants. Split open the eggplants lengthwise. Cut all around the pulp, ⅛ in / 3 mm from the skin, without piercing the skin. Score deep elongated diamond shapes in the pulp. Put the eggplant halves on a baking sheet, sprinkle with a little of the olive oil and bake until the pulp pulls away from the skin completely.

3. Meanwhile, peel the tomatoes (first plunging them for 10 seconds into boiling water). Remove the seeds and chop the pulp coarsely. Peel and chop the onions, shallot and garlic.

4. Using a spoon, carefully remove the pulp from the eggplant halves. Set the shells of skin aside. Heat the rest of the oil in a small frying pan and add the eggplant pulp, onions, garlic, shallot, chopped parsley and tomatoes. Add salt and pepper to taste. Leave to cook, stirring from time to time, until all of the liquid from the vegetables has evaporated.

5. Add about 1 teaspoon of the bread crumbs to the vegetable mixture and adjust the seasoning if necessary. Stuff the eggplant skins with this preparation and sprinkle with the gruyère mixed with the remaining crumbs.

6. Place in the oven and bake for 5-10 minutes or until the tops are golden brown. Serve piping hot.

Empanadas
Spicy Beef Turnovers

	00:30	00:15 to 00:18
	plus thawing or making pastry	

American	Ingredients	Metric/Imperial
¾ lb	Puff pastry (see page 458 or use frozen)	350 g / 12 oz
2	Eggs	2
⅓ cup	Raisins	50 g / 2 oz
¼ lb	Lightly salted bacon	125 g / 4 oz
2	Onions	2
1	Green pepper	1
1 lb	Ground [minced] beef	500 g / 1 lb
1 tbsp	Tomato paste [purée]	1 tbsp
2 tbsp	Chopped green olives	2 tbsp
	Sugar	
1 tsp	Dried thyme	1 tsp
	Tabasco sauce	
	Salt and pepper	

1. If using frozen pastry, set it aside to thaw. Hard-cook one of the eggs for 10 minutes in boiling water. Drain, run under cold water and remove the shell. Chop the egg.

2. Put the raisins to soak in warm water.

3. Grind [mince] the bacon together with the peeled onions. Put this mixture into a saucepan over a moderate heat and cook, stirring frequently, until the onions are soft and transparent.

4. Core, seed and dice the green pepper. Add to the saucepan and cook until the pepper is softened.

5. Add the beef, turn up the heat and cook quickly until the meat is browned and crumbly. Pour off excess fat.

6. Remove from the heat and add the tomato paste, the drained raisins, chopped green olives, chopped egg, a pinch of sugar, the thyme and 10 drops of tabasco. Add salt and pepper to taste and blend thoroughly.

7. Return to a medium heat and leave to simmer for 10 minutes, stirring frequently. Leave to cool.

8. Preheat the oven to 425°F / 220°C / Gas Mark 7.

9. Roll out the pastry to a thickness of ¼ in / 5 mm. Cut out 6 rounds using a saucer and a small pointed knife, and roll them out into oval shapes.

10. Cover half of each oval with one-sixth of the cooled stuffing. Dampen the edges of the pastry with water, and fold the pastry over the filling to form a turnover. Press with a fork to stick the two edges together. Glaze the pastry with the remaining egg, beaten.

11. Bake for 15-18 minutes. Serve hot, warm or cold.

Beignets de champignons
Mushroom Fritters

	00:25	00:03 to 00:04	
	plus standing time	for each batch of fritters	

American	Ingredients	Metric/Imperial
3	Eggs	3
1 cup + 2 tbsp	Oil	250 ml / 8 fl oz + 2 tbsp
1¾ cups	Flour	200 g / 7 oz
	Salt and pepper	
1 - 1½ cups	Beer	150 ml / ¼ pint
2	Garlic cloves	2
1 tsp	Prepared mustard	1 tsp
	Tabasco sauce	
1 tbsp	Vinegar or lemon juice	1 tbsp
2 tbsp	Lemon juice	2 tbsp
¾ lb	Button mushrooms	350 g / 12 oz
	Oil for deep frying	

1. Prepare the batter: whisk 2 of the eggs in a bowl. Add 2 tablespoons of the oil, 1¼ cups [150 g / 5 oz] of the flour and salt to taste. Blend thoroughly, then gradually beat in the beer. Leave to stand for 2 hours.

2. Separate the remaining egg. Peel and crush the garlic and place in a bowl with the egg yolk and mustard. Gradually add the remaining oil, whisking continuously, then add a dash of tabasco, the vinegar and salt and pepper to taste. Set aside.

3. Bring a large saucepan of water to a boil and add the lemon juice. Plunge the mushrooms into the boiling water, bring back to a boil and drain the mushrooms. Pat dry with paper towels. Coat the mushrooms with the remaining flour.

4. Heat the oil for deep frying to 345°F / 175°C.

5. Beat the egg white into a firm snow and fold into the batter. Dip the mushrooms in the batter, then plunge into the hot oil. Cook until puffed and brown. Drain on paper towels and serve hot, accompanied by the garlic mayonnaise.

Blinis
Russian Pancakes

	00:15	00:03	
	plus rising	for each pancake	

American	Ingredients	Metric/Imperial
1 package	Dry yeast	7 g / ¼ oz
½ tsp	Sugar	½ tsp
2 cups	Lukewarm milk	500 ml / ¾ pint
3 cups	Flour	350 g / 12 oz
3	Eggs, separated	3
½ tsp	Salt	½ tsp
¼ cup	Melted butter	50 g / 2 oz

1. Add the yeast and sugar to ½ cup [125 ml / 4 fl oz] of the milk and stir to dissolve.

2. Put ¾ cup [75 g / 3 oz] of the flour into a bowl. Add the yeast and milk mixture. Mix to a soft dough. Cover the bowl and leave to rise in a warm place for 2½ hours. The dough should double in size.

3. Place the remaining flour in a bowl and add the egg yolks, salt and the risen yeast dough. Mix in the rest of the warm milk gradually to obtain a smooth batter.

4. Cover the bowl with a cloth and leave to rise in a warm place for 30 minutes.

5. Stir the batter: it should be like a thick pancake batter. Beat the egg whites until stiff and fold into the batter.

6. Grease 2 small crêpe or frying pans with melted butter. Pour 2 tablespoons batter into each pan and cook over a gentle heat until the bottom of each pancake is set, but not browned. Turn them over and cook the other side (about 1½ minutes for each side). Cook 24 pancakes in this way.

7. Serve hot, accompanied by drawn or clarified butter with lemon (see page 113), cold crème fraîche (see page 122) or sour cream, lemon juice, salted or smoked fish or caviar.

Russian pancakes

Brioches chaudes fromage-chipolatas
Hot Cheese and Sausage Brioches

	00:20	00:20	

American	Ingredients	Metric/Imperial
6	Small individual brioches	6
3	Small pork link sausages [chipolatas]	3
2½ tbsp	Butter	30 g / 1¼ oz
2½ tbsp	Flour	30 g / 1¼ oz
1¾ cups	Milk	450 ml / ¾ pint
	Grated nutmeg	
	Salt and pepper	
1¼ cups	Grated gruyère cheese	150 g / 5 oz

1. Preheat the oven to 425°F / 220°C / Gas Mark 7.

2. Remove the tops of the brioches and scoop out the soft insides using a small spoon. Do not break the crust.

3. Pierce the sausages with a fork, place them in a frying pan without fat and brown them gently all over. Drain and cut into small cubes.

4. Melt the butter in a saucepan over a gentle heat, stir in the flour and cook for 1 minute. Gradually mix in the milk using a wire whisk. Cook, stirring, until the sauce is thick. Add a pinch of nutmeg, and salt and pepper to taste. Add the gruyère and sausage pieces and stir to mix.

5. Stuff the brioches with this preparation, put their tops back on and put them into an ovenproof dish. Heat for 5 minutes in the oven and serve immediately.

Corniottes
Cream Cheese Pastries

American	Ingredients	Metric/Imperial
1 quantity	Basic short pastry (see page 457)	1 quantity
4	Eggs	4
5 oz	Cream cheese	150 g / 5 oz
5 tbsp	Crème fraîche (see page 122)	5 tbsp
	Salt and pepper	

1. Preheat the oven to 450°F / 230°C / Gas Mark 8.
2. Roll out the pastry and cut out 4 in / 10 cm diameter rounds. Raise the edges of the rounds to form little tricorns, pinching them at the corners.
3. Break the eggs into a mixing bowl and beat to mix. Add the cream cheese, crème fraîche, and salt and pepper to taste, and work to obtain a smooth mixture.
4. Fill each tricorn with the cheese mixture. Place them on a baking sheet or in tartlet molds, if you think that the mixture will overflow.
5. Bake for 30 minutes.

Bouchées à la reine
Chicken Vol-au-Vents

American	Ingredients	Metric/Imperial
1 quart	Water	1 l / 1¾ pints
1	Onion	1
1	Carrot	1
1	Bouquet garni	1
	Salt and pepper	
2	Chicken wings	2
5 oz	Button mushrooms	150 g / 5 oz
	Lemon juice	
1	Small piece of veal sweetbread	1
½ cup	Butter	125 g / 4 oz
¼ cup	Flour	4 tbsp
	Grated nutmeg	
6	Baked patty shells (vol-au-vent cases)	6
3	Egg yolks	3
½ cup	Crème fraîche (see page 122)	125 ml / 4 fl oz
6	Small chicken dumplings	6

1. Put the water into a saucepan. Add the onion and carrot, both peeled, the bouquet garni and salt and pepper to taste. Bring to a boil and simmer until the carrot is tender.
2. Discard the bouquet garni. Add the chicken wings and leave to cook for 20 minutes.
3. Drain the chicken wings, reserving the cooking liquid. Discard the skin and bones and dice the meat. Strain the cooking liquid.
4. Preheat the oven to 400°F / 200°C / Gas Mark 6.
5. Slice the mushrooms and sprinkle with lemon juice to prevent them from discoloring.
6. Drop the veal sweetbread into a pan of boiling salted water

and blanch for 10 minutes. Drain. Remove all gristle and dice.
7. Melt the butter in a thick-bottomed saucepan and stir in the flour. Gradually add three-quarters of the reserved chicken cooking liquid. Bring to a boil, stirring until thickened. Add the diced chicken and veal sweetbread, the mushrooms and a pinch of nutmeg. Simmer over a gentle heat until well reduced and thickened.
8. Meanwhile, arrange the pastry cases on a baking sheet and heat through in the oven for 5 minutes.
9. Mix together the egg yolks and crème fraîche. Remove the saucepan from the heat and add the cream mixture. Stir thoroughly. Stir in the quenelles, sliced. Return the saucepan to a gentle heat and cook very gently, stirring, until piping hot. Do not allow to boil.
10. Fill the hot pastry cases with the chicken filling and serve.

Choux au fromage
Cheese Puffs

American	Ingredients	Metric/Imperial
1 cup	Water	250 ml / 8 fl oz
½ cup	Butter	125 g / 4 oz
1¼ cups	Flour	150 g / 5 oz
5	Eggs	5
¾ cup	Grated gruyère cheese	75 g / 3 oz
	Grated nutmeg	
	Salt and pepper	

1. Preheat the oven to 425°F / 220°C / Gas Mark 7.
2. Place the water and butter in a saucepan and bring to a boil. Add the flour all at once, and stir until the dough comes away from the sides of the pan. Remove from the heat. Add one egg and mix vigorously and thoroughly. Add another egg and mix. Continue adding the eggs, incorporating each thoroughly before adding the next. Beat in the gruyère, a pinch of nutmeg, and salt and pepper to taste.
3. Using a pastry bag fitted with a ½ in / 1 cm tube, pipe the pastry in balls on a greased baking sheet. Bake for 10-12 minutes.

Cheese puffs

Bouchées au roquefort
Roquefort Puffs

⊿ 00:40   00:15 to 00:18 🍲

American	Ingredients	Metric/Imperial
1 cup	Water	250 ml / 8 fl oz
¾ cup	Butter	175 g / 6 oz
	Salt	
1 cup	Flour	125 g / 4 oz
4	Eggs	4
½ lb	Roquefort cheese	250 g / 8 oz
1 tbsp	Crème fraîche (see page 122)	1 tbsp

1. Preheat the oven to 400°F / 200°C / Gas Mark 6.
2. Place the water, 5 tbsp [65 g / 2½ oz] of the butter and a pinch of salt in a saucepan. Bring to a boil. Add the flour all at once and stir until the dough comes away from the sides of the pan. Remove from the heat. Add one egg and mix thoroughly, then add another egg and mix. Continue adding the eggs, incorporating each thoroughly before adding the next.
3. Using a pastry bag fitted with a small tube, pipe the pastry onto a greased baking sheet. You should obtain 36 small heaps. Put into the oven and bake for 15-18 minutes or until risen and golden brown.
4. Turn off the oven and open the door. Leave the choux puffs inside for 2-3 minutes, then remove them.
5. Mix together the roquefort, remaining butter and crème fraîche, using a wooden spoon to obtain a very smooth mixture.
6. Split open the choux puffs with a knife and fill with the cheese mixture. Serve warm or cold.

Courgettes farcies
Stuffed Zucchini [Courgettes]

⊿ 00:20   00:30 🍲

American	Ingredients	Metric/Imperial
6	Zucchini [courgettes]	6
	Salt and pepper	
¾ lb	Cooked meat (pork, veal or beef)	350 g / 12 oz
4	Onions	4
2	Garlic cloves	2
1	Bunch of fresh parsley	1
2	Eggs	2
	Grated nutmeg	
½ cup	Grated gruyère cheese	50 g / 2 oz
¼ cup	Butter	50 g / 2 oz

1. Preheat the oven to 350°F / 180°C / Gas Mark 4.
2. Wipe the zucchini and cut them in half lengthwise. Remove most of the flesh with a small spoon and keep it in reserve.
3. Toss the zucchini shells into a saucepan of boiling salted water and cook for 2 minutes. Drain and run under cold water, then drain in a colander.
4. Grind [mince] together the cooked meat, peeled onions, peeled garlic cloves, parsley and the flesh from the zucchini. Add the eggs, a pinch of nutmeg, and salt and pepper to taste, mixing thoroughly with a fork.

5. Fill the zucchini shells with the stuffing and place them in a buttered baking dish. Sprinkle with the cheese and dot with small pieces of butter.
6. Place in the oven and bake for about 20 minutes. While they are cooking, baste the zucchini halves occasionally with the cooking juice.

Chavignols grillés
Baked Goat's Cheese Toasts

⊿ 00:15   00:12 to 00:13 🍲

American	Ingredients	Metric/Imperial
	Salt and pepper	
1 tbsp	Vinegar	1 tbsp
3 tbsp	Walnut oil	3 tbsp
15	Walnuts	15
1	Head of chicory [curly endive]	1
6	Crottin de Chavignol or similar small, soft goat's cheese	6
6	Slices of bread	6

1. Preheat the oven to 425°F / 220°C / Gas Mark 7.
2. Dissolve a pinch of salt in the vinegar. Add the oil, walnuts and pepper to taste. Place in the bottom of a salad bowl and set aside.
3. Rinse and drain the chicory. Separate the leaves. Add to the salad bowl but do not toss.
4. Cut a ½ in / 1 cm slice from the base of each cheese. Reserve these slices for another recipe. Cut the cheeses in half.
5. Trim the slices of bread so they are just slightly larger than the cheeses. Place a halved cheese on each slice of bread.
6. Arrange the toasts on a baking sheet and bake for 8 minutes. Then preheat the broiler [grill] and broil the cheese toasts for 4-5 minutes, watching them carefully.
7. Toss the chicory with the dressing. Serve with the hot cheese toasts.

Crêpes à la florentine
Spinach Crêpes

⊿ 00:20   00:30 🍲
plus standing time

American	Ingredients	Metric/Imperial
2	Eggs	2
1¼ cups	Flour	150 g / 5 oz
1¼ cups	Milk	250 ml / 8 fl oz
1 cup	Beer	150 ml / ¼ pint
	Salt and pepper	
6 tbsp	Butter	75 g / 3 oz
2 lb	Fresh spinach	1 kg / 2 lb
1¼ cups	Thick crème fraîche (see page 122)	300 ml / ½ pint
1 cup	Grated gruyère cheese	125 g / 4 oz

1. Prepare the crêpe batter: break the eggs into a mixing bowl, beat them together and add the flour. Stir with a wooden spoon to obtain a smooth batter and thin it out gradually with the milk. Blend thoroughly. Add the beer and a pinch of salt. Gently melt half of the butter in a saucepan. Incorporate it into the batter and leave to stand for 2 hours.

2. Preheat the oven to 450°F / 230°C / Gas Mark 8.

3. Carefully clean the spinach and remove the stalks. Add to a saucepan of boiling salted water and cook for 10 minutes. Drain, run under cold water and squeeze in your hands to extract all the water. Coarsely chop the spinach.

4. Put half the crème fraîche and half the gruyère into a small frying pan. Add the spinach and pepper to taste, and blend thoroughly. Leave to warm, with the lid on, over a gentle heat.

5. Melt a small piece of butter in a crêpe or frying pan. Add a ladleful of the batter and tilt the pan in all directions to spread the batter evenly over the bottom. Cook over a medium heat for 1½-2 minutes, then turn the crêpe over and cook the other side. Continue making crêpes in this way until all the batter has been used up.

6. Fill the crêpes with the spinach mixture and roll them up. Arrange in a buttered baking dish. Heat the remainder of the crème fraîche in a small saucepan and use to coat the crêpes. Sprinkle with the remainder of the grated cheese.

7. Place in the oven and bake until the top is golden brown and the crêpes are piping hot.

Spinach crêpes

Crêpes au roquefort

Roquefort Crêpes

	00:15 plus standing time	00:30

American	Ingredients	Metric/Imperial
2	Eggs	2
1¼ cups	Flour	150 g / 5 oz
1¼ cups	Milk	250 ml / 8 fl oz
1 cup	Beer	150 ml / ¼ pint
	Salt and pepper	
½ cup	Butter	125 g / 4 oz
2 oz	Roquefort cheese	50 g / 2 oz
	Melted butter for serving	

1. Prepare the crêpe batter: break the eggs into a mixing bowl, beat them together and add the flour. Stir with a wooden spoon to obtain a smooth batter and thin it out gradually with the milk. Blend thoroughly. Add the beer and a pinch of salt. Gently melt 3 tbsp [40 g / 1½ oz] of the butter in a saucepan. Incorporate it into the batter and leave to stand for 2 hours.

2. Finely crush the roquefort using a fork to obtain a smooth cream. Heat ¼ cup [50 g / 2 oz] of the butter and incorporate it into the roquefort cream. Add this mixture to the crêpe batter and whisk until very smooth. If the batter is too thick, add a little more beer.

3. Melt a small piece of butter in a crêpe or frying pan. Add a ladleful of the batter and tilt the pan in all directions to spread the batter evenly over the bottom. Cook over a medium heat for 1½-2 minutes, then turn the crêpe over and cook the other side. Continue making crêpes in this way until all the batter has been used up.

4. As each crêpe is cooked, coat it with a little melted butter before rolling it up. Keep warm between 2 plates placed over a saucepan of boiling water.

Crêpes aux champignons

Mushroom Crêpes

	00:30 plus standing time	00:45

American	Ingredients	Metric/Imperial
2	Eggs	2
1¼ cups + 3 tbsp	Flour	190 g / 6½ oz
3¼ cups	Milk	750 ml / 1¼ pints
1 cup	Beer	150 ml / ¼ pint
	Salt and pepper	
¾ cup	Butter	175 g / 6 oz
	Grated nutmeg	
14 oz	Button mushrooms	400 g / 14 oz
2	Shallots	2
1	Garlic clove	1
1 cup	Grated gruyère cheese	125 g / 4 oz

1. Prepare the crêpe batter: break the eggs into a mixing bowl, beat them together and add 1¼ cups [150 g / 5 oz] of the flour. Stir with a wooden spoon to obtain a smooth batter and thin it out gradually with 1¼ cups [250 ml / 8 fl oz] of the milk. Blend thoroughly. Add the beer and a pinch of salt. Gently melt 3 tablespoons [40 g / 1½ oz] of the butter in a saucepan. Incorporate it into the batter and leave to stand for 2 hours.

2. Meanwhile, melt 3 tablespoons [40 g / 1½ oz] of the butter in a saucepan, stir in the remaining flour and cook for 1 minute. Gradually stir in the remaining milk and then, continuing to stir, leave to thicken over a gentle heat for about 8-10 minutes. Season with salt, pepper and nutmeg to taste.

3. Finely chop the mushrooms. Peel and chop the shallots and garlic. Heat 3 tablespoons [40 g / 1½ oz] butter in a small frying pan, add the mushrooms, shallots and garlic and leave to cook over a gentle heat, stirring frequently, until all the liquid has evaporated. Add salt and pepper to taste.

4. Add half the sauce and mix thoroughly. Set aside.

5. Preheat the oven to 475°F / 240°C / Gas Mark 9.

6. Melt a small piece of butter in a crêpe or frying pan. Add a ladleful of batter and tilt the frying pan in all directions to spread the batter evenly over the bottom. Cook over a medium heat for 1½-2 minutes, then turn the crêpe over and cook the other side. Continue making crêpes in this way until all the batter has been used up.

7. Fill the crêpes with the mushroom mixture and roll them up. Arrange very tightly in a buttered baking dish. Cover them with the remainder of the sauce and dot with small pieces of butter. Sprinkle with gruyère.

8. Bake for 5-10 minutes and serve hot.

Croque-monsieur

Fried Ham and Cheese Sandwiches

	00:25		00:05 per sandwich
American	**Ingredients**		**Metric/Imperial**
3	Slices of cooked ham		3
12	Slices of bread		12
12	Thin slices of emmental cheese		12
¾ cup	Butter		175 g / 6 oz

1. Preheat the oven to 425°F / 220°C / Gas Mark 7.
2. Cut each slice of ham in half. On one slice of bread, place a slice of cheese, a piece of ham and another slice of cheese. Cover with a second slice of bread. Trim the edges of the ham and cheese so they don't hang out. Make 5 more sandwiches in the same way.
3. Melt half of the butter in a frying pan and add 3 of the sandwiches. Brown one side over a very moderate heat. Using a spatula and a fork, turn the sandwiches over and brown the other side, adding more butter, if necessary. (This first cooking must be done slowly so that the butter does not burn and so that the cheese will stick to the bread as it begins to melt.)
4. Transfer the sandwiches to a baking sheet and place them in the oven to keep hot while you cook the remaining sandwiches.
5. Serve the crusty, hot sandwiches as an entrée or a light lunch, accompanied by a green salad.

Endives au jambon

Endives [Chicory] with Ham

	00:10		01:10
American	**Ingredients**		**Metric/Imperial**
12	Medium-sized heads of endive [chicory]		12
½ cup	Butter		125 g / 4 oz
2 tsp	Sugar		2 tsp
	Salt and pepper		
1 tbsp	Flour		2 tbsp
⅔ cup	Milk		150 ml / ¼ pint
1 cup	Crème fraîche (see page 122)		250 ml / 8 fl oz
½ cup	Grated gruyère cheese		50 g / 2 oz
	Grated nutmeg		
12	Thin slices of cooked ham		12
12	Thin slices of gruyère cheese		12

1. Remove the damaged leaves from the endives [chicory]. Using a pointed knife, remove the hard part from the base of the leaves by hollowing out the center. Wash and drain.
2. Melt 2 tablespoons [25 g / 1 oz] butter in a thick-bottomed saucepan. When it froths, add the endives, sugar and salt and pepper to taste. Leave to cook over a gentle heat for approximately 40 minutes. The endives are done when they are slightly browned and the point of a knife can pass through them easily.

3. Meanwhile, melt 1 tablespoon butter in another thick-bottomed saucepan. Add the flour and cook, stirring, for 1 minute. Remove the saucepan from the heat and gradually add the milk, continuing to stir. Return to the heat and cook, stirring, until thickened. Add the crème fraîche, half of the grated gruyère, a pinch of nutmeg, and salt and pepper to taste. Leave to cook for 5 minutes over a gentle heat, stirring continuously.
4. Preheat the oven to 425°F / 220°C / Gas Mark 7.
5. On each slice of ham, place a slice of gruyère and then a braised endive. Roll up the ham which should go right around the endive. Arrange the rolls in a buttered ovenproof dish. Cover them with the sauce and sprinkle with the remaining grated gruyère.
6. Bake for about 30 minutes. Serve in the cooking dish.

Ficelles picardes

Ham and Mushroom Crêpes

	00:20 plus making crêpes		00:30
American	**Ingredients**		**Metric/Imperial**
1 lb	Button mushrooms		500 g / 1 lb
2 tbsp	Butter		25 g / 1 oz
1 cup	Crème fraîche (see page 122)		250 ml / 8 fl oz
1 cup	Grated gruyère cheese		125 g / 4 oz
	Salt and pepper		
6	Sliced of cooked ham		6
6	Crêpes (see page 458)		6

1. Preheat the oven to 400°F / 200°C / Gas Mark 6.
2. Chop the mushrooms. Heat the butter in a frying pan, add the mushrooms and cook until all their moisture has evaporated. Remove from the heat and add 1 tablespoon of the crème fraîche and 1-2 tablespoons of the gruyère. Add salt and pepper to taste.
3. Place a slice of ham on each crêpe. Cover with the mushroom mixture and roll up. Place the crêpes very close together in a buttered ovenproof dish. Pour over the remaining crème fraîche, which has been lightly seasoned with salt and pepper, and sprinkle with the remaining gruyère cheese. Place in the oven and bake for 30 minutes.

Escargots de Bourgogne

Snails with Garlic Butter

	01:00 plus standing time		00:30
American	**Ingredients**		**Metric/Imperial**
2 oz	Shallots		50 g / 2 oz
2	Garlic cloves		2
1 lb (2 cups)	Butter, at room temperature		500 g / 1 lb
2 tbsp	Chopped fresh parsley		2 tbsp
	Salt and pepper		
72	Canned snails with shells		72

1. Prepare the snail butter: peel and finely chop the shallots and garlic. Mix with the butter. Add the parsley and mash the mixture with a fork to blend thoroughly. Season to taste with salt and pepper.

2. Drain the snails. Drop them into a pan of simmering water and cook for 5 minutes. Drain, cool with cold water and drain again.

3. Put a pat of snail butter in each snail shell. Put the snails in the shells and fill with the rest of the snail butter.

4. Leave the snails in a cool place for 24 hours so that they absorb the flavor of the garlic butter.

5. Preheat the oven to 325°F / 160°C / Gas Mark 3.

6. Arrange the snails on snail dishes and put in the oven. Bake until the butter has melted and the snails are piping hot.

Crêpes farcies

Stuffed Crêpes

	00:25 plus standing time	00:20 to 00:25

American	Ingredients	Metric/Imperial
2	Eggs	2
1¼ cups	Flour	150 g / 5 oz
1¼ cups	Milk	250 ml / 8 fl oz
1 cup	Beer	150 ml / ¼ pint
	Salt and pepper	
10 tbsp	Butter	150 g / 5 oz
¼ lb	Cooked ham or	125 g / 4 oz
3	Eggs	3
1 lb	Spinach or beet tops	150 g / 5 oz
	Grated nutmeg	
1¼ cups	Grated gruyère cheese	150 g / 5 oz
½ cup	Crème fraîche (see page 122)	125 ml / 4 fl oz

1. Prepare the crêpe batter: break the 2 eggs into a mixing bowl, beat them together and add the flour. Stir with a wooden spoon to obtain a smooth batter and thin it out gradually with the milk. Blend thoroughly. Add the beer and a pinch of salt. Gently melt 3 tablespoons [40 g / 1½ oz] of the butter in a saucepan. Incorporate it into the batter and leave to stand for 2 hours.

2. Melt a small piece of butter in a crêpe or frying pan. Add a ladleful of batter and tilt the frying pan in all directions to spread the batter evenly over the bottom. Cook over medium heat for 1½-2 minutes, then turn the crêpe over and cook the other side. Continue making crêpes in this way until all the batter has been used up.

3. If preparing the crêpes the day before, wrap them in foil, interleaving each one with wax [greaseproof] paper and store in the refrigerator.

4. Preheat the oven to 400°F / 200°C / Gas Mark 6.

5. Chop the ham, or hard-cook the eggs in boiling water for 10 minutes. Drain, run under cold water and remove the shells. Chop the eggs.

6. Remove any damaged leaves and large ribs from the spinach or beet tops, rinse and toss into a saucepan of boiling salted water. Leave to cook for 5 minutes after boiling has resumed, then drain. Squeeze out excess moisture, then chop coarsely.

7. Melt 2 tablespoons [25 g / 1 oz] butter in a saucepan, add the spinach and leave to cook until all the vegetable water has evaporated. Add a pinch of nutmeg, ½ cup [50 g / 2 oz] of the gruyère, the chopped eggs or ham, and salt and pepper to taste. Mix thoroughly.

8. Fill the crêpes with the spinach mixture and roll them up. Arrange very tightly in a buttered ovenproof dish. Coat them with the crème fraîche, scatter over the remaining cheese and a few small pieces of butter. Bake for about 25 minutes.

Stuffed crêpes

Croûtes du skieur

Ham, Bread and Cheese Pudding

	01:00	00:15

American	Ingredients	Metric/Imperial
¼ cup	Butter	50 g / 2 oz
1 tbsp	Oil	1 tbsp
6	Slices of bread, ½ in / 1 cm thick	6
6 tbsp	Dry white wine	6 tbsp
6	Thin slices of cooked ham	6
1 tbsp	Vinegar	1 tbsp
7	Eggs	7
2 cups	Grated comté or similar cheese	250 g / 8 oz
2 tbsp	Crème fraîche (see page 122)	2 tbsp
	Grated nutmeg	
	Pepper	

1. Heat the butter with the oil in a frying pan. Add the bread slices and brown on both sides.

2. Place the bread in one layer in an ovenproof dish and moisten each with 1 tablespoon of the wine. Cover each with a slice of ham cut to the same size.

3. Heat 2 in / 5 cm of water in a saucepan and add the vinegar. Break 6 of the eggs, one at a time, into a ladle and plunge the ladle into the boiling water. When all the eggs are in the water, remove the saucepan from the heat, cover and leave to poach for 3 minutes. Remove the eggs and place them in a bowl of warm water. (Alternatively, use an egg poacher.)

4. Preheat the broiler [grill] to high.

5. Take the eggs out of the water and drain on a cloth. Cut off the excess white so as to give them a regular shape. Place an egg on each slice of ham.

6. Mix together the cheese, remaining egg and crème fraîche. Add a pinch of nutmeg and pepper to taste. Pour this mixture over the eggs in the dish.

7. Place under the broiler and cook for 5 minutes.

Escargots
du domaine d'Auriac

Fresh Snails Casseroled in Wine

	00:45 plus soaking	02:30 to 03:30

American	Ingredients	Metric/Imperial
240	Small fresh grey snails	240
2½ cups	Vinegar	600 ml / 1 pint
2 cups	Sea salt	500 g / 1 lb
	Flour	
3	Onions	3
5	Cloves	5
1	Bottle of white wine	1
1 tsp	Juniper berries	1 tsp
1	Bouquet garni	1
1	Bunch of fresh parsley	1
2	Garlic cloves	2
¼ cup	Butter, at room temperature	50 g / 2 oz
¾ lb	Cooked ham	350 g / 12 oz
3 tbsp	Olive oil	3 tbsp
1 cup	Tomato paste [purée]	200 g / 7 oz
	Salt and pepper	

1. Let the snails fast for two weeks. Tip them into a bowl and sprinkle with the vinegar, sea salt and a handful of flour. Leave them to soak for 2 hours.
2. Wash the snails under cold running water, rubbing them with your hands.
3. Drop the snails into a large pan of boiling water and blanch for 2 minutes. Drain well.
4. Peel one onion, stud with the cloves and put in a cooking pot. Add the white wine, juniper berries and bouquet garni. Put the snails in the pot and add enough water to cover. Bring to a boil and simmer for 2-3 hours.
5. Chop the parsley. Peel and crush the garlic. Mix into the butter with a fork. Set aside.
6. When the snails are cooked, drain them, reserving the cooking liquid. Remove them from their shells and remove the intestine. Set them aside. Strain the cooking liquid.
7. Peel and chop the remaining onions. Chop the ham. Heat the olive oil in a flameproof casserole. Add the chopped onions, ham and tomato paste. Cook until the mixture is lightly browned, then stir in the snail cooking liquid.
8. Add the snails, parsley butter, and salt and pepper to taste. Simmer for a further 30 minutes. Serve hot.

Feuilletés au roquefort

Roquefort Pastries

	00:25 plus thawing or making pastry	00:15

American	Ingredients	Metric/Imperial
¾ lb	Puff pastry (see page 458) or use frozen	350 g / 12 oz
½ lb	Roquefort cheese	250 g / 8 oz
1	Egg	1

1. If using frozen pastry, allow it to thaw. Preheat the oven to 450°F / 230°C / Gas Mark 8.
2. Roll out the pastry to a thickness of ⅛ in / 3 mm on a lightly floured surface. Cut into 16 rectangles measuring 3×4½ in / 7×11 cm.
3. Cut the roquefort cheese into 8 sticks the thickness of a finger. Place on 8 of the pastry rectangles.
4. Beat the egg. Brush the egg around the edges of the pastry rectangles on which the cheese has been placed.
5. Mark the remaining 8 pastry rectangles with a lattice pattern using the point of a knife. Lay these rectangles over the cheese and press with your fingers so that the pastry edges stick together. Brush the tops with beaten egg.
6. Place the rectangle on a lightly buttered baking sheet and bake for 10 minutes. Open the oven door and, leaving it ajar, continue baking for another 5 minutes.
7. Serve hot or warm.

Roquefort pastries

Friands à la viande

Meat Pastries

	00:20 plus making or thawing pastry	00:45

American	Ingredients	Metric/Imperial
14 oz	Puff pastry (see page 458) or use frozen	400 g / 14 oz
3	Shallots	3
5 oz	Button mushrooms	150 g / 5 oz
½ lb	Boneless breast of veal	250 g / 8 oz
½ lb	Smoked bacon	250 g / 8 oz
1	Bunch of fresh parsley	1
5 tbsp	Crème fraîche (see page 122)	5 tbsp
2 tbsp	Brandy	2 tbsp
	Salt and pepper	
2 tbsp	Butter	25 g / 1 oz
1	Egg	1

1. If using frozen pastry, allow it to thaw. Peel and chop the shallots. Chop the mushrooms. Grind [mince] the breast of veal, bacon and parsley. Mix the veal, bacon, parsley and mushrooms together. Add the crème fraîche, brandy and salt and pepper to taste.
2. Heat the butter in a frying pan, add the shallots and cook gently over a low heat, stirring frequently until softened. Add to the veal mixture.

3. Preheat the oven to 425°F / 220°C / Gas Mark 7.
4. Roll out the pastry to ⅛ in / 3 mm thick and cut into 6 squares. Divide the filling between the pastry squares and roll up to enclose the filling completely. Lightly moisten the edges to seal. Using a pointed knife, score the top of the pastries.
5. Break the egg into a bowl, beat it and brush the pastries with beaten egg. Arrange them on a baking sheet, and bake for 25-30 minutes. Serve very hot.

Flamiche aux poireaux
Leek Pie

American	Ingredients	Metric/Imperial
	01:15 plus making pastry	00:30
12	Leeks	12
¼ cup	Butter	50 g / 2 oz
	Salt and pepper	
1 quantity	Basic short pastry (see page 457)	1 quantity
2	Egg yolks	2
3 tbsp	Crème fraîche (see page 122)	3 tbsp

1. Trim the roots off the leeks, remove the damaged ends of the green leaves, and split the leeks into quarters. Clean under cold water, separating the layers. Cut into thin slices crosswise. Place in a saucepan with the butter and salt and pepper to taste and cook over a gentle heat for 1 hour, stirring occasionally.
2. Preheat the oven to 450°F / 230°C / Gas Mark 8.
3. Divide the pastry into 2 unequal portions. Roll out the larger portion, and use to line a deep pie pan.
4. Beat one of the egg yolks with the crème fraîche. Add to the cooked leeks and stir well. Pour into the pastry case.
5. Roll out the remaining pastry and lay it over the leeks. Moisten the pastry edges with a little egg white and press them together to seal. Brush the top with the beaten egg yolk.
6. Bake for 30 minutes. Serve warm.

Flammeküche
Bacon and Onion Bread

American	Ingredients	Metric/Imperial
	00:20	00:10
2	Onions	2
½ lb	Smoked bacon	250 g / 8 oz
¼ cup	Butter	50 g / 2 oz
14 oz	Risen bread dough (bought from a baker or homemade)	400 g / 14 oz
⅔ cup	Crème fraîche (see page 122)	150 ml / ¼ pint
	Salt	
	Cayenne pepper	
	Grated nutmeg	
1 tbsp	Oil	1 tbsp

1. Preheat the oven to 475°F / 240°C / Gas Mark 9.
2. Peel and slice the onions. Cut the bacon into dice. Heat the butter in a frying pan, add the bacon and cook gently until browned. Remove from the pan. Add the onions and leave to

cook gently for a few minutes until golden brown. Drain off excess fat.
3. Roll out the dough into a rectangle and place it on a baking sheet.
4. Mix together the bacon, onions and crème fraîche, and season to taste with salt, cayenne and nutmeg. Cover the top of the dough with this mixture. Pour the oil over it.
5. Place in the oven and bake for 15 minutes.

Fondue savoyarde
Savoy Fondue

American	Ingredients	Metric/Imperial
	00:20	00:20 to 00:25
1 lb	Emmental cheese	500 g / 1 lb
1 lb	Comté or similar cheese	500 g / 1 lb
1 lb	Beaufort or similar cheese	500 g / 1 lb
1	Garlic clove	1
1 quart	Dry white wine	1 l / 1¾ pints
	Pepper	
1 tbsp	Cornstarch [cornflour]	1 tbsp
⅔ cup	Kirsch	150 ml / ¼ pint
	French bread	

1. Remove any rind from the cheeses and cut them into thin slices.
2. Peel the garlic and rub the inside of a saucepan with it. Pour the wine into the saucepan, bring to a boil and add all the cheese. Stir until the cheese has completely melted. Add pepper to taste.
3. Dissolve the cornstarch in the kirsch. Pour into the saucepan and stir well until smooth and slightly thickened.
4. Cut the bread into cubes.
5. Put the saucepan on a spirit burner and serve immediately, with the bread cubes for dipping.

Galettes de blé noir
Buckwheat Crêpes

American	Ingredients	Metric/Imperial
	00:15 plus standing time	00:05 per crêpe
2¾ cups	Buckwheat flour	300 g / 11 oz
	Salt	
7	Eggs	7
3 cups	Water	750 ml / 1¼ pints
½ cup	Butter	125 g / 4 oz
6	Slices of cooked ham	6
1¼ cups	Grated gruyère cheese	150 g / 5 oz

1. Combine the flour and a pinch of salt in a mixing bowl. Add one of the eggs, then pour in the water in a trickle, beating to obtain a smooth batter. Leave to rest for 30 minutes.
2. Grease a crêpe or frying pan or griddle with a little butter. Pour on a spoonful of batter, spreading it out well. Cook the crêpe for 2 minutes, then turn it over with a spatula. Put a pat of butter on it, then break an egg on top and leave to cook for a few minutes. Season to taste with salt and pepper.
3. When the egg is cooked, put a slice of ham on the crêpe and sprinkle with grated gruyère cheese. Fold the crêpe into quarters and remove from the pan. Keep hot while you make 5 more crêpes in the same way.

Fonds d'artichaut farcis
Stuffed Artichoke Hearts

◤ 00:30   01:00 🍲

American	Ingredients	Metric/Imperial
6	Large globe artichokes	6
	Lemon juice	
	Salt and pepper	
½ lb	Cooked ham	250 g / 8 oz
½ lb	Button mushrooms	250 g / 8 oz
5 tbsp	Butter	65 g / 2½ oz
2 tbsp	Flour	2 tbsp
1⅓ cups	Milk	325 ml / 11 fl oz
	Grated nutmeg	
1 cup	Grated gruyère cheese	125 g / 4 oz
2 tbsp	Crème fraîche (see page 122)	2 tbsp

1. Remove the leaves and hairy choke (see page 412) from the artichokes. Peel the hearts with a knife, rubbing with lemon juice as you go along, so that they do not discolor. Cook the artichoke hearts in boiling salted water for 30-40 minutes or until the point of a knife will go through them easily.
2. Meanwhile, chop the ham. Chop the mushrooms and moisten with a few drops of lemon juice to keep them white. Heat 2 tablespoons [25 g / 1 oz] of the butter in a saucepan, add the mushrooms and cook until all the moisture has evaporated. Remove from the heat and mix the mushrooms with the chopped ham.
3. Preheat the oven to 400°F / 200°C / Gas Mark 6.
4. Melt the remaining butter in another saucepan over a gentle heat and add the flour. Stir well, then gradually stir in the milk and a pinch of grated nutmeg. Season to taste with salt and pepper, and leave to simmer for 10 minutes over a low heat, stirring occasionally.
5. Add 4 tablespoons of the white sauce and about one-third of the gruyère cheese to the ham and mushroom mixture, and mix well. Fill the drained artichoke hearts with the mixture, and arrange in an ovenproof dish.
6. Add the crème fraîche and remaining cheese to the rest of the white sauce. Mix and pour over the artichoke hearts.
7. Place in the oven and bake for 15-20 minutes.

Globe artichokes

Cromesquis
Ham Yeast Puffs

◤ 00:25   00:06 🍲
   plus rising

American	Ingredients	Metric/Imperial
2 cups + 1½ tbsp	Flour	270 g / 8¾ oz
1 tbsp	Oil	1 tbsp
1 package	Dry yeast	7 g / ¼ oz
¼ tsp	Sugar	¼ tsp
1 cup	Lukewarm water	250 ml / 8 fl oz
1½ tbsp	Butter	20 g / ¾ oz
1 cup	Milk	250 ml / 8 fl oz
	Salt and pepper	
2	Slices of cooked ham	2
1 cup	Bread crumbs	50 g / 2 oz
1	Egg white	1
	Oil for deep frying	

1. Put 2 cups [250 g / 8 oz] of the flour into a mixing bowl. Make a well in the center and pour in the oil, yeast and sugar. Mix with the warm water to make a smooth batter. Leave to rise for 2 hours.
2. Melt the butter in a saucepan over a gentle heat. Stir in the remaining flour and cook, stirring for 1 minute. Remove from the heat and gradually add the milk, stirring constantly. Return the saucepan to the heat, bring slowly to a boil and leave to cook for 10 minutes over a gentle heat, stirring continuously to prevent lumps from forming. Add salt and pepper to taste.
3. Chop the ham and mix with the sauce. Leave to cool.
4. Using a tablespoon, shape the sauce into small balls and coat them in the bread crumbs. Beat the egg white until stiff and fold into the batter.
5. Heat the oil for deep frying to 345°F / 175°C. Dip the small balls into the batter, then plunge them into the hot oil. Cook for 3-4 minutes or until puffed and brown. Remove carefully with a slotted spoon and drain on paper towels.
6. Pile the balls in a pyramid on a dish and serve hot, with a tomato sauce (see page 123) or mayonnaise (see page 119).

Gougère
Cheese Pastry Ring

◤ 00:20   00:40 🍲

American	Ingredients	Metric/Imperial
1½ oz	Gruyère cheese	40 g / 1½ oz
1 cup	Water	250 ml / 8 fl oz
	Salt and pepper	
5 tbsp	Butter	65 g / 2½ oz
1 cup	Flour	125 g / 4 oz
4	Eggs	4
1¼ cups	Grated gruyère cheese	150 g / 5 oz
1	Egg yolk	1

1. Preheat the oven to 350°F / 180°C / Gas Mark 4. Cut the piece of gruyère into thin slices.
2. Bring the water to a boil in a saucepan together with a pinch of salt and the butter. Add the flour all at once. Mix vigorously with a wooden spoon until the dough comes away from the sides of the pan. Remove the saucepan from the heat. Add one whole egg and mix thoroughly, then add another

whole egg and mix. Continue adding the remaining whole eggs, incorporating each thoroughly before adding the next. Add a pinch of pepper, ¾ cup [75 g / 3 oz] of the grated cheese and the slices of gruyère.

3. Butter and flour a baking sheet. Spoon the dough onto it in a ring. Brush with the beaten egg yolk and sprinkle with the rest of the grated gruyère.

4. Bake for about 40 minutes.

Cook's tip: do not open the oven door during the first 10 minutes of baking.

Pissaladière

Pizza Tart

00:30 plus thawing or making pastry		01:15

American	Ingredients	Metric/Imperial
½ lb	Puff pastry (see page 458) or use frozen	250 g / 8 oz
½ lb	Onions	250 g / 8 oz
1 tbsp	Olive oil	1 tbsp
	Salt and pepper	
2 lb	Tomatoes	1 kg / 2 lb
2 tbsp	Tomato paste [purée]	2 tbsp
1 (2 oz)	Can of anchovies in oil	1 (50 g / 2 oz)
	Dried marjoram	
15	Black olives, pitted [stoned]	15

1. Preheat the oven to 400°F / 200°C / Gas Mark 6. If using frozen pastry, allow it to thaw.

2. Peel the onions and cut into thin slices. Heat the oil in a saucepan, add the onions and fry gently until beginning to brown. Season lightly with pepper and a very little salt. Put to one side.

3. Slice the tomatoes.

4. Roll out the pastry to a thickness of ⅛ in / 3 mm, and use to line a buttered 10 in / 25 cm quiche or flan pan or dish.

5. Spread the tomato paste over the bottom of the pastry case, then put the onions, tomato slices and anchovy fillets on top (save the oil from the anchovies). Sprinkle with a little marjoram, pepper and the oil from the anchovies.

6. Bake for 20 minutes. Garnish with the olives.

Pizza tart

Grenouilles sautées

Sautéed Frogs' Legs

00:05 plus soaking		00:15 to 00:20

American	Ingredients	Metric/Imperial
24 - 36	Pairs of frogs' legs (according to size)	24 - 36
2 cups	Milk	500 ml / ¾ pint
	Salt and pepper	
6 tbsp	Flour	6 tbsp
¼ cup	Oil	4 tbsp
1 cup	Butter	250 g / 8 oz
1	Garlic clove	1
3 tbsp	Chopped fresh parsley	3 tbsp

1. Cut off the feet if necessary and place the frogs' legs in a mixing bowl. Pour over the cold milk, and add salt and pepper to taste. Soak for 30-45 minutes.

2. Drain the frogs' legs and coat them in the flour. Shake to remove excess flour.

3. Heat half the oil and 2 tablespoons [25 g / 1 oz] butter in a large frying pan. When it starts to smoke, put in about half of the frogs' legs — just enough to cover the bottom of the pan. They can be quite close together but not on top of each other. Cook until golden brown on both sides, turning carefully to keep them intact. Remove with a slotted spoon.

4. Add another 2 tablespoons [25 g / 1 oz] butter and the remaining oil to the pan. When hot, put in the remaining frogs' legs and brown as before. Drain.

5. Wipe out the frying pan. Melt the remaining butter in the pan over a low heat and add all the frogs' legs. Cook gently for 3-4 minutes.

6. Peel and finely chop the garlic. Sprinkle over the frogs' legs with the parsley and salt and pepper to taste. Toss briefly and serve hot.

Grenouilles à la provençale

Frogs' Legs Provençal

00:20		00:10

American	Ingredients	Metric/Imperial
24 - 36	Pairs of frogs' legs	24 - 36
	Salt and pepper	
6 tbsp	Flour	6 tbsp
6 tbsp	Oil	6 tbsp
5	Garlic cloves	5
1	Bunch of fresh parsley	1
2 cups	White bread crumbs	100 g / 4 oz
6 tbsp	Butter	75 g / 3 oz

1. Season the frogs' legs with salt and pepper. Roll them in flour and shake to remove the excess. Heat the oil in a large frying pan. Add the frogs' legs and cook on one side for about 5 minutes, then turn them and brown for a further 5 minutes on the other side.

2. Meanwhile, peel and chop the garlic. Wash and chop the parsley. Mix the bread crumbs with the garlic and parsley.

3. Arrange the frogs' legs on a serving dish and keep hot.

4. Pour off the oil from the frying pan. Melt the butter in the pan and when it froths, add the bread crumb mixture. Stir for several seconds, then sprinkle over the frogs' legs. Serve very hot.

Pirojki
Russian Meat Turnovers

| | 00:30 | 00:20 |
| | plus chilling Makes 12-15 | |

American	Ingredients	Metric/Imperial
1¾ cups	Flour	200 g / 7 oz
¾ cup + 2 tbsp	Butter	200 g / 7 oz
1 tsp	Confectioners' [icing] sugar	1 tsp
	Salt and pepper	
2	Egg yolks	2
6 tbsp	Water	3 tbsp
½ lb	Cooked beef	250 g / 8 oz
4	Eggs	4
1	Fresh dill sprig	1
1	Onion	1
1 tbsp	Vegetable oil	1 tbsp

1. Rub the flour, butter and sugar together with a pinch of salt until the mixture resembles fine crumbs. Add the egg yolks and enough water to mix to a smooth, fairly firm dough. Chill for 30-40 minutes.
2. Meanwhile, make the filling. Remove any fat from the meat, then chop it finely. Hard-cook 3 of the eggs in boiling water for 10 minutes. Drain, run under cold water and remove the shells. Chop the eggs. Mix with the meat and season to taste with salt and pepper. Chop the dill, and add to the mixture.
3. Peel and chop the onion. Heat the oil in a small pan, add the onion and fry until softened. Add the onion to the meat mixture and blend well.
4. Preheat the oven to 400°F / 200°C / Gas Mark 6.
5. Roll out the dough thinly and cut out 12-15 rounds with a diameter of 3 in / 7.5 cm.
6. Divide the meat filling between the dough rounds. Moisten the edges with the remaining egg, beaten, and fold over into a turnover shape. Press the edges with your fingers to seal. Glaze with beaten egg.
7. Bake for about 20 minutes. Serve hot or warm with beet soup, if liked (see page 138).

Quiche Lorraine
Egg and Bacon Quiche

| | 00:20 | 00:20 |
| | plus making pastry | |

American	Ingredients	Metric/Imperial
1 quantity	Basic short pastry (see page 457)	1 quantity
¼ lb	Smoked bacon	125 g / 4 oz
3	Eggs	3
½ cup	Crème fraîche (see page 122)	125 ml / 4 fl oz
1¼ cups	Grated gruyère cheese	150 g / 5 oz
	Salt and pepper	
	Grated nutmeg	

1. Preheat the oven to 450°F / 230°C / Gas Mark 8.
2. Roll out the pastry and use to line a buttered 10 in / 25 cm quiche or flan pan or dish. Prick the bottom with a fork.
3. Cut the bacon into dice and sprinkle over the bottom of the pastry case.
4. Break the eggs into a bowl and beat with the crème fraîche, grated gruyère cheese, a pinch of salt, a pinch of grated

nutmeg, and pepper to taste. Pour this mixture over the bacon in the pastry case.
5. Bake for 20 minutes and serve very hot.

Cook's tip: if you like the pastry very crisp, bake it 'blind' (unfilled) before adding the filling.

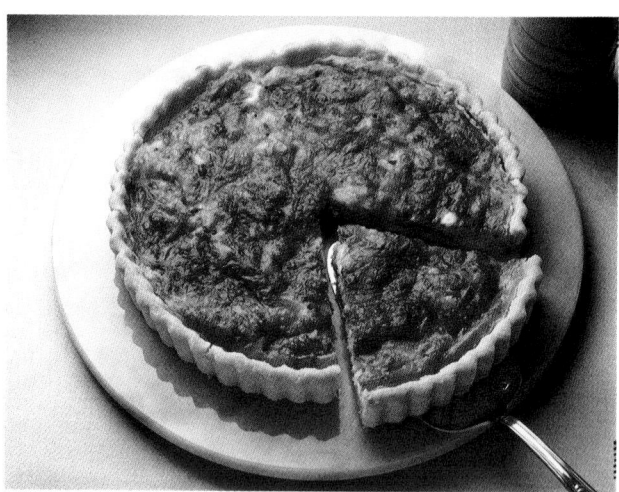

Egg and bacon quiche

Quiche aux petits pois
Pea and Bacon Quiche

| | 00:30 | 01:00 |
| | plus thawing or making pastry and chilling | |

American	Ingredients	Metric/Imperial
¾ lb	Puff pastry (see page 458) or use frozen	350 g / 12 oz
2 cups	Peas	250 g / 8 oz
	Salt and pepper	
5 oz	Smoked bacon	150 g / 5 oz
2	Cooked or canned artichoke hearts	2
1 cup	Crème fraîche (see page 122)	250 ml / 8 fl oz
2	Eggs	2
¼ cup	Grated gruyère cheese	25 g / 1 oz
2 tbsp	Butter	25 g / 1 oz

1. If using frozen pastry, allow it to thaw. Roll out the pastry to a thickness of ⅛ in / 3 mm and use to line a buttered 10 in / 25 cm quiche or flan pan or dish. Chill for 30 minutes.
2. Preheat the oven to 450°F / 230°C / Gas Mark 8.
3. Cook the peas in boiling salted water for 5 minutes, then drain. (If using frozen peas, just pour boiling water over them to thaw quickly and drain.)
4. Cut the bacon into very small dice. Drop into a saucepan of boiling water and blanch for 3 minutes. Drain. Brown the bacon dice lightly in a frying pan without any fat. Drain on paper towels.
5. Put the bacon dice in the pastry case, pressing them down so that they will not move. Arrange the artichokes and peas on top and press them lightly into the pastry.
6. Beat the crème fraîche and eggs in a bowl and add salt and pepper to taste. Pour this mixture into the pastry case. Sprinkle with the grated gruyère cheese, and dot with the butter cut into small pieces.
7. Bake for 15 minutes, then reduce the temperature to 350°F / 180°C / Gas Mark 4 and bake for a further 45 minutes.

Raclette

Melted Cheese with Potatoes

	00:08 to 00:10	00:30

American	Ingredients	Metric/Imperial
4 lb	Potatoes	2 kg / 4 lb
	Salt and pepper	
½ lb	Raclette or other melting cheese	250 g / 8 oz
	Pickled onions	
	Small dill pickles [gherkins]	

This dish was originally made by placing half the cheese by the fireplace. The cheese was scraped up as it melted, hence the name, which derives from the French for to scrape. Electrical appliances are now on the market for making raclette at the table, but a broiler [grill] can also be used.

1. Place the unpeeled potatoes in a saucepan of cold salted water and bring to a boil. Simmer for 25 minutes.
2. Meanwhile, preheat the broiler.
3. Cut the cheese into slices as long as a plate, and ⅛ in / 3 mm thick. Put each slice on an ovenproof plate.
4. Drain the potatoes and keep hot.
5. Put 2-3 plates under the broiler and cook until the cheese melts and turns a light golden brown. Take the plates to the table immediately, and put some more under the broiler.
6. Serve the cheese very hot, with plenty of pepper, the potatoes, pickled onions and pickles.

Rissoles

Savory Meat Turnovers

	00:30 plus chilling Makes 12	00:30

American	Ingredients	Metric/Imperial
½ cup + 2 tsp	Butter	125 g / 4 oz + 2 tsp
2 cups	Flour	250 g / 8 oz
1	Egg yolk	1
	Salt and pepper	
½ lb	Boneless veal shoulder	250 g / 8 oz
½ lb	Boneless pork shoulder	250 g / 8 oz
1	Shallot	1
1 tbsp	Chopped fresh parsley	1 tbsp
3 oz	Cooked ham	75 g / 3 oz
	Oil for deep frying	

1. Cut ½ cup [125 g / 4 oz] of the butter into small pieces and leave to soften at room temperature. Mix the flour with the egg yolk and a pinch of salt in a bowl. Add the pieces of butter, and mix rapidly to a dough. Roll the dough into a ball, and chill for about 1 hour.
2. Chop the veal and pork finely. Peel and chop the shallot. Melt the remaining butter in a frying pan and add the meat, shallot and parsley. Brown for about 15 minutes. Allow to cool. Dice the ham and stir into the meat mixture.
3. Heat the oil for deep frying to 345°F / 175°C.
4. Roll out the dough to a thickness of ⅛ in / 3 mm, and cut out 12 rounds with a diameter of 4 in / 10 cm.
5. Put 1 tablespoon of the meat filling on one side of each

pastry round. Moisten the edges of the pastry, and fold it over into a turnover, pressing the edges to seal.
6. Put the rissoles into the hot oil and fry them for about 15 minutes or until golden, turning them over occasionally. Drain on paper towels. Serve hot, with tomato sauce (see page 123) or ketchup.

Savory meat turnovers

Soufflé au jambon

Ham Soufflé

	00:30 to 00:35	00:30

American	Ingredients	Metric/Imperial
¼ lb	Cooked ham	125 g / 4 oz
¼ lb	Button mushrooms	125 g / 4 oz
5 tbsp	Butter	65 g / 2½ oz
2½ cups	Milk	600 ml / 1 pint
	Grated nutmeg	
	Salt and pepper	
¼ cup	Flour	50 g / 2 oz
5	Eggs, separated	5

1. Preheat the oven to 400°F / 200°C / Gas Mark 6.
2. Cut the fat off the cooked ham, and chop the ham very finely. Chop the mushrooms. Melt 1 tablespoon of the butter in a frying pan, add the mushrooms and cook, stirring occasionally, until all the moisture has evaporated. Mix the mushrooms with the chopped ham.
3. Season the milk with a pinch of nutmeg and salt and pepper to taste. Bring to a boil.
4. Melt the remaining butter in a heavy saucepan and add the flour. Stir well, then gradually add the boiling milk, stirring constantly. Cook for about 10 minutes, stirring.
5. Remove from the heat, and add the egg yolks, one by one, blending each in thoroughly before adding the next. Add the ham and mushrooms and mix well together.
6. Beat the egg whites until stiff and gently fold them into the ham mixture. Spoon into a well-buttered 8 in / 20 cm diameter soufflé dish. The dish should be two-thirds full.
7. Bake for 10 minutes, then raise the temperature to 425°F / 220°C / Gas Mark 7, and bake for 20 minutes longer. Serve immediately.

Royales à la tomate

Individual Tomato Custards

	00:40 plus chilling	00:45

American	Ingredients	Metric/Imperial
4	Large tomatoes	4
2	Garlic cloves	2
2	Shallots	2
2 tbsp	Olive oil	2 tbsp
1	Bouquet garni	1
1 tsp	Sugar	1 tsp
	Salt and pepper	
2 cups	Milk	500 ml / ¾ pint
3	Eggs	3
2	Egg yolks	2
1	Small bunch of fresh parsley	1
6	Black olives	6
6	Canned anchovy fillets	6

1. Peel the tomatoes (first plunging them into boiling water for 10 seconds). Remove the seeds and crush the flesh. Peel and crush the garlic. Peel and chop the shallots.
2. Heat the olive oil in a saucepan, add the shallots and cook gently until they begin to turn brown. Add the tomatoes, garlic, bouquet garni, sugar, and salt and pepper to taste. Stir well. Cover and leave to cook over a gentle heat for about 15 minutes.
3. Meanwhile, bring the milk to a boil. Beat the whole eggs and egg yolks together in a bowl, and add the boiling milk little by little. Chop the parsley and add to the custard.
4. If the tomato mixture is very liquid, boil it uncovered until excess moisture has evaporated. Discard the bouquet garni. Add the tomato mixture to the custard. Taste and adjust the seasoning.
5. Pour the mixture into 6 buttered ramekins and place them in a baking pan or wide shallow saucepan of simmering water. Cook for 45 minutes. Leave to cool for 2 hours.
6. To serve, unmold the tomato custards and garnish each with a black olive surrounded by an anchovy. Serve very cold.

Cook's tip: you can also cover the custards with tomato sauce (see page 123).

Tarte au Maroilles

Maroilles Cheese Tart

	00:30 plus making pastry and standing time	00:35

American	Ingredients	Metric/Imperial
1 quantity	Basic short pastry (see page 457)	1 quantity
½	Maroilles or similar cheese (not too fresh)	½
½ lb	Soft cream cheese	250 g / 8 oz
1 cup	Thick crème fraîche (see page 122)	250 ml / 8 fl oz
4	Eggs	4
	Pepper	

1. Roll out the pastry and use to line a buttered 10 in / 25 cm quiche or flan dish or pan. Set aside.

2. Remove the crust from the maroilles cheese. Crumble the cheese into a bowl, and add the cream cheese and crème fraîche. Mix to obtain a smooth consistency. Add the eggs one by one, and season to taste with pepper. Leave to rest for about 30 minutes in a cool place.
3. Preheat the oven to 425°F / 220°C / Gas Mark 7.
4. Fill the pastry case with the cheese mixture. Bake for about 35 minutes. Watch over the tart, and make sure that the top does not burn. If it is browning too much, cover it with foil. Serve hot.

Soufflé au bleu

Blue Cheese Soufflé

	00:25	00:30

American	Ingredients	Metric/Imperial
2 cups	Milk	500 ml / ¾ pint
	Salt and pepper	
¼ cup	Butter	50 g / 2 oz
¼ cup	Flour	50 g / 2 oz
½ lb	Auvergne or other blue cheese	250 g / 8 oz
6	Eggs, separated	6

1. Preheat the oven to 350°F / 180°C / Gas Mark 4.
2. Season the milk with salt and pepper to taste and bring to a boil. Melt the butter in a heavy saucepan and add the flour. Stir well, then gradually add the boiling milk, stirring constantly. Cook for about 10 minutes, stirring.
3. Remove from the heat, and add the crumbled blue cheese and the egg yolks, one at a time.
4. Beat the egg whites to stiff peaks, then fold them gently into the cheese mixture. Spoon into a buttered 8 in / 20 cm diameter soufflé dish. The dish should be two-thirds full.
5. Bake for 10 minutes, then raise the temperature to 425°F / 220°C / Gas Mark 7 and bake for 20 minutes longer. Serve immediately.

Cook's tip: do not open the oven door while the soufflé is cooking. If it comes into contact with cold air, it is liable to collapse.

Soufflé au fromage

Cheese Soufflé

	00:25	00:25 to 00:30

American	Ingredients	Metric/Imperial
2½ cups	Milk	600 ml / 1 pint
	Salt and pepper	
¼ cup	Butter	50 g / 2 oz
¼ cup	Flour	50 g / 2 oz
	Grated nutmeg	
5	Eggs, separated	5
¾ cup	Grated gruyère cheese	75 g / 3 oz

1. Preheat the oven to 350°F / 180°C / Gas Mark 4.
2. Season the milk with salt and pepper to taste and bring to a boil. Melt the butter in a heavy saucepan and add the flour. Stir well, then gradually add the boiling milk, stirring constantly. Cook for about 10 minutes, stirring. Add a pinch of grated nutmeg.

3. Remove from the heat and add the egg yolks one by one, blending each in thoroughly before adding the next. Stir in the grated gruyère cheese.

4. Beat the egg whites until stiff and gently fold into the cheese mixture. Spoon into a buttered 8 in / 20 cm diameter soufflé dish. The dish should be two-thirds full.

5. Bake for 10 minutes, then raise the temperature to 425°F / 220°C / Gas Mark 7 and bake for 20 minutes longer. Serve immediately.

Spinach tart

Tarte aux épinards

Spinach Tart

American	Ingredients	Metric/Imperial
¾ lb	Puff pastry (see page 458) or use frozen	350 g / 12 oz
1 lb	Spinach	500 g / 1 lb
	Salt and pepper	
	Grated nutmeg	
5 tbsp	Butter	65 g / 2½ oz
1 tbsp	Flour	2 tbsp
1 cup	Crème fraîche (see page 122)	250 ml / 8 fl oz
4	Eggs	4

00:20 plus thawing or making pastry — 00:50

1. Preheat the oven to 425°F / 220°C / Gas Mark 7. Thaw the pastry if using frozen.

2. Trim the stalks off the spinach. Wash, then cook in boiling salted water until tender. Drain and, when cool enough to handle, squeeze out excess moisture. Chop the spinach finely or process in a food processor until coarse-fine (not a purée). Season with a pinch of grated nutmeg, and salt and pepper to taste.

3. Melt the butter in a heavy saucepan and add the flour. Cook, stirring, for 1 minute, then add the crème fraîche. Allow to thicken, stirring constantly. Season to taste with salt and pepper. Remove from the heat and add the beaten eggs. Mix two-thirds of this sauce with the spinach, and taste and adjust the seasoning.

4. Roll out the pastry thinly and use to line a buttered and floured 10 in / 25 cm quiche or flan dish or pan. Prick the bottom with a fork. Pour in the spinach mixture, and cover with the rest of the egg sauce.

5. Bake for 15 minutes or until the filling is firm and set. Turn off the oven and leave the tart in the oven for about 5-10 minutes longer. Serve warm or cold.

Tourte de la Vallée de Munster

Munster Valley Pork Pie

American	Ingredients	Metric/Imperial
1 lb	Puff pastry (see page 458) or use frozen	500 g / 1 lb
1	Large onion	1
2 tbsp	Butter	25 g / 1 oz
1	Bread roll	1
⅔ cup	Milk	150 ml / ¼ pint
1	Garlic clove	1
1½ lb	Pork tenderloin [fillet] or boneless shoulder	750 g / 1½ lb
1	Egg	1
	Grated nutmeg	
	Salt and pepper	·
1	Egg yolk	1

00:40 plus thawing or making pastry — 00:40

1. If you use frozen pastry, thaw it. Preheat the oven to 425°F / 220°C / Gas Mark 7.

2. Peel and slice the onion. Heat the butter in a small saucepan, add the onion and fry gently until softened. Remove from the heat.

3. Crumble the bread roll in the milk. Peel the garlic. Cut the pork into large cubes. Put the onion, soaked bread, pork and garlic into a blender or food processor and blend until smooth. Add the whole egg and a pinch of grated nutmeg and mix well. Season to taste with salt and pepper.

4. Divide the pastry into 2 portions, one larger than the other. Roll out the larger piece and use to line a buttered 10 in / 25 cm deep pie or other ovenproof dish. Prick the bottom with a fork, then fill with the pork mixture.

5. Roll out the remaining pastry and lay over the filling. Pinch the edges to seal. Make a hole in the centre of the pie, and hold it open with a little piece of rolled-up cardboard (or use a pie funnel).

6. Brush the top of the pastry with the beaten egg yolk. Bake for 35 minutes. Serve hot.

Tarte à la moutarde

Mustard Cheese Tart

American	Ingredients	Metric/Imperial
¾ lb	Puff pastry (see page 458 or use frozen)	350 g / 12 oz
6	Tomatoes	6
5 tbsp	Dijon mustard	5 tbsp
5 oz	Gruyère cheese	150 g / 5 oz

00:25 — 00:40 to 00:50 plus thawing or making pastry

1. Preheat the oven to 450°F / 230°C / Gas Mark 8. Thaw the pastry if using frozen.

2. Peel the tomatoes (first plunging them into boiling water for 10 seconds), then cut into quarters and remove the seeds.

3. Roll out the pastry to a thickness of ⅛ in / 3 mm and use to line a buttered, lightly floured 10 in / 25 cm quiche or flan dish or pan. Spread the bottom with the mustard. Thinly slice the gruyère cheese and arrange over the mustard. Cover with the tomato quarters.

4. Bake for 40-50 minutes.

Tourte aux morilles
Morel Pie

	00:20 plus thawing or making pastry	00:40

American	Ingredients	Metric/Imperial
2 oz	Dried morels or other mushrooms	50 g / 2 oz
1¼ lb	Puff pastry (see page 458) or use frozen	625 g / 1¼ lb
1	Egg	1
1	Onion	1
¼ cup	Butter	50 g / 2 oz
1 cup	Crème fraîche (see page 122)	250 ml / 8 fl oz
	Salt and pepper	

1. Put the dried morels into warm water to soak for 2 hours.
2. Thaw the pastry if using frozen. Preheat the oven to 425°F / 220°C / Gas Mark 7.
3. Roll out half the pastry to about ⅛ in / 3 mm. Use to line a buttered 10 in / 25 cm quiche or flan dish or pan. Line the pastry with a sheet of wax [greaseproof] paper and fill the dish with dried beans. Roll out the rest of the pastry and lay over the beans, making a pastry lid. Moisten the edge, twist it up and make oblique cuts in it. Draw lozenges on the top with a pointed knife, and glaze with beaten egg.
4. Bake for 40 minutes.
5. Meanwhile, peel and chop the onion. Heat the butter in a saucepan, add the onion and cook gently until softened. Do not allow it to turn brown.
6. Drain the morels and cut into pieces if large. Add to the onion and cook until the moisture has completely evaporated.
7. Add the crème fraîche, and simmer until it thickens. Season to taste with salt and pepper.
8. To serve, carefully remove the hot pastry lid with a knife and take out the paper and beans. Pour in the morel mixture and replace the pastry lid. Serve hot.

Tourte au jambon
Ham Pie

	00:30 plus thawing or making pastry	01:00 to 01:15

American	Ingredients	Metric/Imperial
1¼ lb	Puff pastry (see page 458) or use frozen	625 g / 1¼ lb
6	Thin slices of cooked ham	6
14 oz	Emmental cheese	400 g / 14 oz
1	Egg	1

1. Preheat the oven to 450°F / 230°C / Gas Mark 8. Thaw the pastry if using frozen.
2. Roll out half the pastry to a thickness of about ⅛ in / 3 mm. Cut out a 10 in / 25 cm round and place it on a lightly oiled and floured baking sheet.
3. Arrange 3 slices of ham (with the fat cut off) on the pastry base. Cover with half of the emmental cheese, cut into thin slices, then place another 3 slices of ham on top of the cheese. Finally add a layer of the remaining cheese cut into thin slices. Leave a clear border of ½ in / 1 cm around the edge of the pastry round.
4. Roll out the other half of the pastry and cut out a round as before. Moisten the edge with beaten egg and place this round on top of the first one. Press down the edge to seal the pastry rounds together, and crimp or flute the edge.

5. Glaze the top with beaten egg. Prick in 3 or 4 places with a fork, and draw a pattern with the tip of a knife.
6. Bake for 30 minutes, then reduce the heat to 425°F / 220°C / Gas Mark 7, and bake for a further 30-45 minutes. Serve warm.

Ham pie

Vol-au-vent
Sweetbread Vol-au-Vent

	00:30	00:50

American	Ingredients	Metric/Imperial
1½ lb	Veal sweetbreads	750 g / 1½ lb
	Salt and pepper	
1	Calf's brain	1
1 tbsp	Vinegar	1 tbsp
14 oz	Button mushrooms	400 g / 14 oz
10 tbsp	Butter	150 g / 5 oz
1	Carrot	1
2	Shallots	2
3 tbsp	Flour	3 tbsp
1 tbsp	Tomato paste [purée]	1 tbsp
2 cups	Chicken stock	500 ml / ¾ pint
1¼ cups	Madeira wine	300 ml / ½ pint
2 tbsp	Oil	2 tbsp
5 tbsp	Brandy	5 tbsp
1	Large patty shell (vol-au-vent case)	1
1	Slice of cooked ham	1
1	Egg yolk	1
½ cup	Crème fraîche (see page 122)	125 ml / 4 fl oz

1. Put the sweetbreads in a saucepan of cold, salted water, bring to a boil, and simmer for 5 minutes. Drain and cool in cold water, then trim off any tough portions and outer membranes. Cut into large dice.
2. Wash the brain, and soak for 15 minutes in cold water to

which the vinegar has been added. Drain and remove all fiberlike membranes and surrounding threads. Rinse well and cut into dice.

3. Thinly slice the mushrooms. Melt 2 tablespoons [25 g / 1 oz] of the butter in a saucepan, add the mushrooms and cook until all the moisture has evaporated. Set aside.

4. Peel and dice the carrot. Peel and thinly slice the shallots. Melt 2 tablespoons [25 g / 1 oz] butter in another saucepan and add the carrot and shallots. Fry gently until softened, then sprinkle on 2 tablespoons of the flour and cook for a few moments, stirring.

5. Add the tomato paste, chicken stock and madeira. Season to taste with salt and pepper. Bring to a boil, then reduce the heat and leave to simmer gently for 20 minutes.

6. Leave the sauce to cool, then remove any fat which has risen to the surface. Strain the sauce.

7. Preheat the oven to 300°F / 150°C / Gas Mark 2.

8. Coat the diced sweetbreads with the remaining flour. Heat the oil and 2 tablespoons [25 g / 1 oz] butter in a frying pan, add the sweetbreads and brown on all sides for 10 minutes. Season with salt and pepper. Add the brandy and set it alight, then add the mushrooms and madeira sauce. Cover and leave to cook for 15 minutes over a gentle heat.

9. Meanwhile, heat the pastry case in the oven.

10. Melt the remaining butter in a frying pan, add the diced brain and cook until browned, for 5 minutes. Dice the ham. Add the brain and ham to the sweetbread mixture.

11. Mix the egg yolk in a bowl with the crème fraîche. Add to the sweetbread mixture, off the heat, then use to fill the hot pastry case. Serve immediately.

Tarte aux bettes

Swiss Chard Tart

00:45 plus thawing or making pastry		00:45
American	**Ingredients**	**Metric/Imperial**
¾ lb	Puff pastry (see page 458) or use frozen	350 g / 12 oz
2 lb	Swiss chard or beet tops [spinach beet]	1 kg / 2 lb
6 tbsp	Butter	75 g / 3 oz
	Grated nutmeg	
	Salt and pepper	
¾ lb	Onions	350 g / 12 oz
¾ lb	Tomatoes	350 g / 12 oz
2	Garlic cloves	2
1 tsp	Dried thyme	1 tsp
¾ cup	Grated gruyère cheese	75 g / 3 oz

1. Thaw the pastry if using frozen. Preheat the oven to 450°F / 230°C / Gas Mark 8.

2. Roll out the pastry and use to line a buttered and floured 10 in / 25 cm quiche or flan dish or pan. Prick the bottom with a fork and keep cool.

3. Remove the ribs from the chard, wash and cut them into thin strips. Melt 2 tablespoons [25 g / 1 oz] of the butter in a saucepan, add the chard and cook until all the moisture has evaporated. Add a pinch of grated nutmeg, and salt and pepper to taste.

4. Peel and slice the onions. Melt 2 tablespoons [25 g / 1 oz] of the butter in a frying pan, add the onions and cook until softened, without letting them turn brown.

5. Peel the tomatoes (first plunging them into boiling water for 10 seconds), then remove the seeds. Cut the flesh into pieces. Melt the remaining butter in a saucepan, add the tomatoes and cook until reduced to a pulp.

6. Peel and crush the garlic. Add to the tomatoes with the onions and thyme. Season to taste with salt and pepper.

7. Cover the bottom of the pastry case with half the tomato mixture. Sprinkle with half of the grated gruyère cheese and arrange the chard in an even layer on top. Cover with the remaining tomato mixture, and sprinkle with the rest of the cheese.

8. Bake for 20 minutes, then lower the heat to 350°F / 180°C / Gas Mark 4 and bake for 25 minutes longer. Serve warm or cold.

Tarte aux oignons

Onion Tart

00:45 plus chilling		00:50
American	**Ingredients**	**Metric/Imperial**
½ cup + 2 tbsp	Butter	150 g / 5 oz
	Salt and pepper	
2 cups + 2 tbsp	Flour	250 g / 8 oz + 2 tbsp
4	Egg yolks	4
1 lb	Onions	500 g / 1 lb
2 cups	Milk	500 ml / ¾ pint
	Grated nutmeg	

1. Cut ½ cup [125 g / 4 oz] of the butter into small pieces, and leave to soften at room temperature. Mix a pinch of salt, 2 cups [250 g / 8 oz] of the flour and 1 egg yolk in a bowl. Add the softened butter and mix to a dough. Roll the dough into a ball, and chill for 1 hour.

2. Preheat the oven to 425°F / 220°C / Gas Mark 7.

3. Roll out the dough thinly and use to line a buttered 10 in / 25 cm quiche or flan dish or pan. Prick the bottom with a fork.

4. Peel and slice the onions. Melt the remaining butter in a saucepan, add the onions and fry over a low heat, so that they will be softened before they start to brown.

5. Sprinkle the onions with the remaining flour and stir well to mix. Add three-quarters of the milk, and bring to a boil, stirring continuously. Add the rest of the milk. Remove from the heat and beat in the remaining egg yolks, one at a time. Season with salt and pepper to taste and a pinch of nutmeg.

6. Pour the onion mixture into the pastry case. Bake for 35-40 minutes. Serve warm.

Onion tart

Terrines, Pâtés and Galantines

Do you know the difference between a pâté and a terrine? The word pâté is used for all sorts of preparations based on meat or fish, covered with pastry and baked in the oven.

On the other hand, terrines are cooked in fireproof earthenware or china, stoneware, enameled iron, or glass containers. In everyday speech, terrines and pâtés are often confused. Many 'pâtés' are cooked in terrines.

Galantines, however, consist of chopped meat or fish rolled up in the animal's skin, then cooked in bouillon in a saucepan. The word 'galantine' is said to come from the words *geline* or *galine*, the Old French for 'chicken,' since this dish was at first made of poultry, and then later, at the end of the seventeenth century, of game and meat.

There are many varieties of pâté. Each region of France has its own recipe for pâtés, terrines and galantines. We have only selected a few simple ones for this chapter.

Guidelines

The ingredients

The ingredients used to make the filling can be many and varied: pork, mixtures of pork and veal, poultry and game (hare, duck, young wild boar, pheasant, quail, etc), foie gras, usually covered with a thin caul of pork and placed whole in the middle of the filling, panadas (a mixture of bread soaked in milk, flour, water, butter and egg, which is for binding light fillings such as fish or shellfish fillings), truffles, which give the filling their very characteristic flavor and note of refinement, and alcohols such as brandy, armagnac or calvados and white wine, madeira, port and sherry.

Lastly, the seasoning: only if none of the ingredients of the filling has been already salted, add salt.

Equipment

A meat grinder [mincer] or food processor is essential to grind the ingredients quickly and cleanly. It replaces our grandmothers' heavy mortar and pestle.

Cooking terrines and pâtés

The inside of a terrine must be lined with fat for the cooking process. The filling should also be covered with fat. A bay leaf and some sprigs of thyme are placed on top, and flavor the terrine by being concentrated under the lid during the cooking process. The terrine is next placed in a shallow baking pan, and surrounded by hot (but not boiling) water up to one-third of its height. Using a water bath or prevents the filling from drying out.

Checking the cooking process

You can usually expect the cooking to take about 1½ hours, but the time actually depends on the composition of the terrine or pâté. Check the fat surrounding the terrine. As soon as it becomes very clear, the terrine is cooked.

After cooking

The terrine must cool for 1 hour. The filling is then compressed by putting a board on it, on top of which is placed a weight, and the terrine is kept overnight in the refrigerator. It will keep for a week.

Cooking galantines

These are cooked slowly for about 1½ hours. The water or broth must be just barely simmering. The best way to check the temperature is to put a cooking thermometer in the liquid. To ensure that the galantine keeps its cylindrical shape during cooking, wrap it in cheesecloth or muslin.

Galantine

Galantine

	01:00 plus cooking and chilling	01:30 Serves 8
American	**Ingredients**	**Metric/Imperial**
1 (3½ lb)	Chicken	1 (1.5 kg / 3½ lb)
	Salt and pepper	
½ lb	Boneless pork shoulder	250 g / 8 oz
½ lb	Boneless veal shoulder	250 g / 8 oz
¼ lb	Veal kidney fat	125 g / 4 oz
¾ cup	Soft bread crumbs	40 g / 1½ oz
⅔ cup	Milk	150 ml / ¼ pint
3	Shallots	3
2	Onions	2
2 tbsp	Chopped fresh herbs (tarragon, parsley and chives)	2 tbsp
2	Eggs	2
2	Fresh thyme sprigs	2
	Grated nutmeg	
2	Chicken livers	2
2 quarts	Water	2 l / 3½ pints
1	Chicken bouillon [stock] cube	1
1 envelope	Unflavored gelatin	1 tbsp

1. Have the butcher or poulterer prepare the chicken if possible: remove the skin from the chicken, with the meat adhering to it, cut the wing and thigh joints, and remove and discard the carcass.
2. Spread out the skin. Cut away the area in front of the thighs, and sew up the tail opening with kitchen string. Season with salt and pepper to taste.
3. Finely grind [mince] all the chicken meat, including the breast fillets. Also grind the pork, veal and kidney fat. Mix these together in a bowl.
4. Moisten the breadcrumbs with the milk and squeeze out the excess. Peel and chop the shallots and onions. Add the breadcrumbs, shallots and onions to the meat mixture. Add the chopped herbs, eggs, crumbled thyme, a pinch of grated nutmeg and salt and pepper to taste. Mix the filling thoroughly.
5. Arrange half the filling on the chicken skin. Place the chicken livers on top, and cover with the rest of the filling. Fold over the edges of the skin and sew it up with kitchen string. Wrap the whole thing in cheesecloth or muslin and tie it up with string.
6. Bring the water to a boil in a saucepan and dissolve the bouillon cube in it. Put the galantine in the saucepan and bring back to a boil over a high heat. Reduce the heat and leave to simmer gently for 1½ hours. Leave to cool in the stock.
7. Take the galantine out of the stock, unwrap it, and leave to become completely cold. Boil the stock until reduced to 2 cups [500 ml / ¾ pint].
8. Dissolve the gelatin according to package directions, then add to the stock. Allow this aspic to cool until lukewarm.
9. Coat the galantine with the warm, jellying aspic and chill until set.

Pâté de foies de volaille
Chicken Liver Pâté

	00:30 plus chilling	00:35

American	Ingredients	Metric/Imperial
¾ lb	Onions	350 g / 12 oz
¼ cup	Goose fat or butter	4 tbsp
1¼ lb	Chicken livers	625 g / 1¼ lb
2 tsp	Dried thyme	2 tsp
	Salt and pepper	

1. Peel and chop the onions. Heat 2 tablespoons of the goose fat or butter in a frying pan, add the onions and cook until softened. Remove the onions with a slotted spoon and put to one side.

2. Put the rest of the goose fat or butter in the frying pan. Add the livers and cook for 5-7 minutes, stirring frequently. Add the thyme, mix together and allow to cool.

3. Put the livers and onions in a blender or food processor, or through a food mill, to obtain a very smooth purée. If necessary, put the mixture through twice. Season to taste with salt and pepper and mix thoroughly. Spoon the mixture into a 1½ quart [1.5 l / 2½ pint] terrine. Chill for several hours.

4. This pâté will keep perfectly for 8-10 days in the refrigerator. Ensure that the terrine is covered, so that it does not dry out.

Pâté de foie de porc
Pork Liver Pâté

	00:50 plus cooling	03:00

American	Ingredients	Metric/Imperial
3	Carrots	3
3	Turnips	3
4	Onions	4
3	Cloves	3
3	Leeks	3
2 lb	Pork bones	1 kg / 2 lb
1	Piece of bacon rind	1
1	Bouquet garni	1
	Salt and pepper	
3 quarts	Water	3 l / 5 pints
¼ lb	Fatty bacon	125 g / 4 oz
1 lb	Fresh pork sides [belly pork]	500 g / 1 lb
1	Bunch of fresh parsley	1
1	Large piece of pork caul	1
1 lb	Pork liver	500 g / 1 lb
2 tbsp	Brandy	2 tbsp
	Cayenne pepper	
	Grated nutmeg	
1	Bay leaf	1

1. Peel the carrots and turnips. Peel 1 onion and stud it with 2 of the cloves. Put these vegetables in a saucepan, together with the leeks, bones, bacon rind, bouquet garni, and salt and pepper to taste. Cover with the water, bring to a boil and simmer gently for 1½ hours.

2. Meanwhile, peel and chop the remaining onions. Grind the remaining clove to a powder. Finely grind [mince] the bacon and pork sides. Chop the parsley. Put the caul to soak in cold water.

3. Preheat the oven to 400°F / 200°C / Gas Mark 6.

4. After the stock has simmered for 1½ hours, add the pork liver and continue to simmer for 8-10 minutes. Drain the liver and leave it to cool, then grind it finely.

5. In a bowl, mix together the liver, bacon, pork, parsley and onions. Add the brandy, and season to taste with salt, pepper, cayenne and a pinch of grated nutmeg. Add the ground clove, and mix all these ingredients together thoroughly.

6. Carefully drain the caul and lay it out on a cloth. Pat it dry. Arrange it in a 1½ quart [1.5 l / 2½ pint] terrine, leaving it hanging over the sides. Put the bay leaf on the bottom, and fill the terrine with the liver mixture, heaping it up well. Fold the caul over the top.

7. Put the lid on the terrine and put it in a baking pan containing 2 in / 5 cm water. Put both in the oven and cook for 1¼ hours. The water must just simmer.

8. Remove the terrine from the oven. Take off the lid, put a board and then a weight on top of the pâté and leave to cool. Then place in the refrigerator and chill for several hours or overnight before serving.

Pâté chaud paysan
Hot Country Pâté

	00:20	01:00
	plus marinating, and thawing or making pastry	

American	Ingredients	Metric/Imperial
1 lb	Boneless pork shoulder	500 g / 1 lb
1 lb	Boneless veal shoulder	500 g / 1 lb
⅔ cup	Riesling or other white wine	150 ml / ¼ pint
1	Bay leaf	1
1	Fresh thyme sprig	1
1	Clove	1
	Chopped fresh parsley	
	Grated nutmeg	
	Salt and pepper	
2 tbsp	Oil	2 tbsp
¼ lb	Puff pastry (see page 458 or use frozen)	125 g / 4 oz
½ quantity	Basic short pastry (see page 457)	½ quantity
1	Egg yolk	1

1. Cut the pork and veal into thin slices. Put into a mixing bowl with the wine, crumbled bay leaf and thyme, crushed clove, chopped parsley, a pinch of grated nutmeg, and salt and pepper to taste. Add the oil and stir to mix. Leave to marinate in a cool place for 12 hours.

2. The next day, preheat to 425°F / 220°C / Gas Mark 7. Thaw the puff pastry if using frozen.

3. Roll out the basic short pastry on a lightly floured surface and cut into an 8×6 in / 20×15 cm strip. Use to line the bottom and sides of a terrine or loaf pan.

4. Pour the marinated meat mixture into the terrine.

5. Roll out the puff pastry and use to cover the meat filling. Press the edges of the pastries together to seal. Brush the surface with egg yolk. Make a small hole in the center and insert a piece of rolled-up cardboard as a 'chimney' or use a pie funnel.

6. Bake for 15 minutes, then reduce the temperature to 350°F / 180°C / Gas Mark 4 and bake for 45 minutes longer. Serve hot.

Lapin en gelée
Rabbit in Wine Aspic

	00:30 plus marinating	02:00

American	Ingredients	Metric/Imperial
1 (3½ - 4 lb)	Rabbit	1 (1.5 - 1.8 kg / 3½ - 4 lb)
6	White onions	6
2	Fresh thyme sprigs	2
1	Bunch of fresh parsley	1
6	Slices of smoked pork tenderloin [fillet]	6
	Salt and pepper	
2 cups	Dry white wine	500 ml / ¾ pint

1. Using a sharp knife, cut the rabbit into pieces.
2. Peel and chop the onions. Crumble the thyme. Chop the parsley. Mix all 3 ingredients together.
3. Line the bottom of a terrine with 4 slices of smoked pork. Cover with a layer of rabbit pieces, lightly season with salt and pepper, and sprinkle with the herb mixture. Add more rabbit pieces, salt, pepper and herbs. Finish with rabbit pieces, and cover with the last 2 slices of pork. Add half the dry white wine, and leave to marinate, without a lid, in a cool place for 5 hours.
4. Preheat the oven to 350°F / 180°C / Gas Mark 4.
5. Put the lid on the terrine, place it in the oven and cook for 30 minutes. Check to be sure the juice is not bubbling up over the sides. Leave to cook for a further 1½ hours, adding the rest of the white wine a little at a time.
6. Take the terrine out of the oven. Place a board on the meat, add a weight on top, and leave to cool completely before putting in the refrigerator. The terrine should keep for more than a week in the refrigerator.

Pâté de lapin
Rabbit Pâté

	01:00 plus marinating and chilling	01:30

American	Ingredients	Metric/Imperial
1 (3½ lb)	Rabbit	1 (1.5 kg / 3½ lb)
½ lb	Fatty bacon	250 g / 8 oz
½ lb	Sausage meat	250 g / 8 oz
1	Onion	1
⅔ cup	Cognac	150 ml / ¼ pint
1	Fresh thyme sprig	1
1	Dried bay leaf	1
1	Small bunch of fresh parsley	1
	Salt and pepper	
2 tbsp	Oil	2 tbsp
1	Piece of pork caul	1
1	Egg	1
1¼ cups	Crème fraîche (see page 122)	300 ml / ½ pint
1	Garlic clove	1

1. Cut the rabbit in half, separating the back from the breast. Bone the back and cut the meat into dice. Bone the breast and cut the meat into slices measuring about 1 in / 2.5 cm in length. Cut the bacon into thin slices. Crumble the sausage meat. Peel and chop the onion.
2. Put the ingredients in a mixing bowl with the cognac,

crumbled thyme and bay leaf, the chopped parsley, and salt and pepper to taste. Add the oil and stir to mix. Leave to marinate for 12 hours in a cool place.
3. Soak the caul in a bowl of cold water.
4. Preheat the oven to 400°F / 200°C / Gas Mark 6.
5. Remove the slices of rabbit from the marinade. Put the remaining marinated ingredients in a food processor or through a grinder [mixer] until coarse-fine. Mix with the egg, crème fraîche, peeled and chopped garlic, marinating liquid, and salt and pepper to taste. Work thoroughly together with a wooden spoon.
6. Drain the caul and pat dry. Line a terrine with it, making sure that it hangs over the sides. Fill with alternating layers of ground meat and rabbit slices, ending with ground meat. Fold the edges of the caul over the filling and put the lid on the terrine. Put the terrine in a baking pan containing 2 in / 5 cm of water and bring to a boil on top of the stove. Transfer to the oven and cook for about 1½ hours.
7. Remove the terrine from the oven. Take off the lid and replace it with a board with a weight on top. Leave to cool completely, then chill for 24 hours before serving.

Ballottine de dinde
Turkey Ballottine

	01:00 plus cooling and chilling	00:30 to each 2 lb / 1 kg

American	Ingredients	Metric/Imperial
1 (16 lb)	Turkey	1 (7 kg / 16 lb)
½ lb	Boneless lean veal	250 g / 8 oz
½ lb	Boneless lean pork	250 g / 8 oz
1 lb	Fatty bacon	500 g / 1 lb
5	Chicken livers	5
3	Eggs	3
5 tbsp	Brandy	5 tbsp
2 tbsp	Chopped truffles or truffle peelings	2 tbsp
1 tsp	Dried fennel	1 tsp
	Salt and pepper	
2	Carrots	2
1	Turnip	1
2	Onions	2
1	Calf's foot	1
2	Celery stalks	2
1	Bouquet garni	1
2 quarts	Water	2 l / 3½ pints
2 envelopes	Unflavored gelatin	15 g / ½ oz

1. Have the butcher or poulterer prepare the turkey if possible: take off the skin with the meat adhering to it, cut the joints of the wings and thighs, and finish by withdrawing the carcass. Remove the skin in front of the thighs and sew up the tail opening with kitchen string. Cut off the breast fillets remaining on the carcass and put aside. Reserve skin and carcass.
2. Finely grind [mince] the turkey meat (except for the breast fillets), veal, pork, bacon and chicken livers. Put it all into a bowl and mix together. Add the eggs, one by one, the brandy, truffles, fennel and salt and pepper to taste. Mix this filling thoroughly.
3. Spread out the turkey skin. In the center, place half the filling and cover it with the turkey breast fillets. Cover with the rest of the filling. Fold the skin to wrap up the filling, and sew it up. Wrap the ballottine in cheesecloth or muslin, and tie it up. Weigh the whole thing.

4. Peel the carrots, turnip and onions. Put these vegetables in a saucepan with the calf's foot, celery and bouquet garni. Add the turkey carcass and water. Bring to a boil, and leave to simmer for 45 minutes.

5. Put in the ballottine. Bring back to a boil, and simmer for 30 minutes to each 2 lb / 1 kg.

6. When the ballottine is cooked, allow it to cool in the stock, then drain and unwrap it. Rinse the cloth, and wrap the ballottine up again, tightly. Leave to cool for at least 6 hours.

7. Strain the cooking stock and return to the saucepan. Leave to cool, then remove the fat with a skimmer.

8. Preheat the oven to 450°F / 230°C / Gas Mark 8.

9. Boil the strained stock to reduce it to 1 quart (1 l / 1¾ pints). Dissolve the gelatin according to package directions, then add to the stock. Allow this aspic to cool until lukewarm.

10. Meanwhile, unwrap the ballottine, put it into an oven-proof dish, and brown it in the oven. Remove it from the oven and allow it to cool.

11. Coat the ballottine with the aspic and chill until set.

Terrine de lapin
Rabbit Terrine

American	Ingredients	Metric/Imperial
01:00 plus marinating and cooling		01:15
1 (3½ lb)	Rabbit	1 (1.5 kg / 3½ lb)
½ lb	Lightly salted fatty bacon	250 g / 8 oz
¾ lb	Boneless pork shoulder	350 g / 12 oz
2 tsp	Salt	2 tsp
1 tsp	Dried fennel	1 tsp
1 tsp	Crumbled dried thyme	1 tsp
⅔ cup	Dry white wine	150 ml / ¼ pint
3 tbsp	Oil	3 tbsp
3 tbsp	Brandy	3 tbsp
½ lb	Thin strips of pork fat back	250 g / 8 oz
3	Bay leaves	3
2 tbsp	Flour	2 tbsp
3 tbsp	Water	3 tbsp

1. Cut the rabbit into pieces, and remove the meat from the bones. Cut the bacon and pork into strips.

2. Put all the meat in a shallow dish and add the salt, fennel, thyme, white wine, oil and brandy. Stir, and marinate in a cool place (not the refrigerator) for 6-8 hours, stirring occasionally with a wooden spoon.

3. Drain the meat, reserving the marinade. Grind [mince] the meat until fine. Add to the marinade and mix well.

4. Preheat the oven to 400°F / 200°C / Gas Mark 6.

5. Flatten the strips of fat with a rolling pin. Line the bottom and sides of a 1½ quart (1.5 l / 2½ pint) terrine with about two-thirds of the strips of fat and then put in the filling, piling it up high. Cover with the remaining strips of fat. Put the bay leaves on the fat. Put the lid on. Mix the flour and water to make a very soft paste, and put this in a strip all around the lid to seal the terrine.

6. Put the terrine in a baking pan containing 2 in / 5 cm of water. Bring to a boil over a low heat, then put the whole thing in the oven, and leave to cook for 1¼ hours.

7. Turn off the oven, leave the door ajar, and allow the terrine to cool. When cold, take the terrine out of the oven, break the seal and open the terrine. Put a board on the meat and add a weight on top. Leave to cool completely. The terrine may be eaten 48 hours later.

Rabbit terrine

Terrine de foie gras
Foie Gras Terrine

American	Ingredients	Metric/Imperial
00:20 plus chilling		00:30
1 (1½ lb)	Goose liver	1 (750 g / 1½ lb)
2 tbsp	Coarse salt	2 tbsp
½ tsp	Dried fennel	½ tsp
	Pepper	
3 tbsp	Armagnac	3 tbsp
2 tsp	Unflavored gelatin	2 tsp
1½ cups	Port wine	350 ml / 12 fl oz
1	Piece of pork caul without holes	1

1. Remove the skin from the goose liver, then take out all the tubes. Sprinkle with coarse salt and chill for at least 24 hours in the refrigerator.

2. Rinse the liver in cold water to clean off the salt and pat dry. Put the liver in a bowl, season with the fennel and pepper to taste and rub in with your fingers. Add the armagnac. Dissolve the gelatin in 2 tablespoons of the port and add to the bowl. Chill for 48 hours.

3. Soak the caul in cold water.

4. Preheat the oven to 400°F / 200°C / Gas Mark 6.

5. Drain the caul and lay it out on a cloth. Pat dry. Wrap the liver in the caul and place in a small casserole. Add the remaining port, which should cover the liver. Cover the casserole.

6. Place in the oven. When the port starts to simmer, cook for a further 10 minutes.

7. Take the casserole out of the oven and allow to cool slightly, then drain the liver and put it into a small terrine. Reserve the liquid in the casserole. Cover the liver with a board, put a weight on top and leave to cool for 12 hours. Also allow the cooking liquid to cool.

8. Remove the fat from the cooled cooking liquid and pour it over the liver. Chill for at least 24 hours longer.

Gâteau de foies de volaille
Chicken Liver Cake

	00:20		00:30

American	Ingredients	Metric/Imperial
¼ lb	Pork fat	125 g / 4 oz
¾ lb	Chicken livers	350 g / 12 oz
4	Shallots	4
5 oz	Stale crustless bread	150 g / 5 oz
5 tbsp	Milk	5 tbsp
3 tbsp	Chopped fresh parsley	3 tbsp
2	Egg yolks	2
2½ tsp	Dried thyme	2½ tsp
	Salt and pepper	
	Grated nutmeg	
2 lb	Tomatoes	1 kg / 2 lb
2	Large garlic cloves	2
1	Large onion	1
2 tbsp	Olive oil	2 tbsp
	Cayenne pepper	

1. Preheat the oven to 425°F / 220°C / Gas Mark 7.
2. Cut the pork fat into dice, put in a frying pan over a medium heat and leave to soften and render some fat. Remove the cubes of fat with a slotted spoon and put to one side.
3. Add the chicken livers to the frying pan and stir for 1 minute over a high heat. Remove with the slotted spoon.
4. Peel and slice 2 of the shallots. Add to the frying pan and cook until translucent. Drain.
5. Put the stale bread into a bowl, moisten with the milk and, when soft, squeeze out excess milk with your hands.

Terrines and pâtés can be smooth- or coarse-textured

6. Combine the chicken livers, parsley, bread, pork fat cubes and cooked shallots in a blender or food processor and blend until smooth. Add the egg yolks and 2 teaspoons of the thyme. Season with salt and pepper and a pinch of grated nutmeg.
7. Put the mixture into a buttered 6 in / 15 cm soufflé dish and place it in a baking pan containing 2 in / 5 cm water. Bake for 30 minutes, keeping the water at a gentle simmer. Once the pâté pulls away from the side of the dish it is cooked.
8. Meanwhile, make the tomato sauce. Peel the tomatoes (first plunging them into boiling water for 10 seconds), cut them in half and remove the seeds. Cut the flesh into large dice. Peel and chop the garlic. Peel and chop the onion and remaining shallots. Heat the oil in a saucepan, add the onion and shallots and cook until softened. Add the tomatoes, remaining thyme, and salt, pepper and cayenne pepper to taste. Cook over a low heat for about 30 minutes or until all the moisture from the tomatoes has evaporated. Strain the sauce and keep hot.
9. Unmold the chicken liver cake onto a warmed serving dish. Coat with the tomato sauce, and serve immediately.

Terrine de faisan
Pheasant Terrine

	00:40		01:30

American	Ingredients	Metric/Imperial
1	Small pheasant, with giblets	1
½ lb	Boneless pork shoulder	250 g / 8 oz
½ lb	Boneless fatty veal shoulder	250 g / 8 oz
¾ lb	Lightly salted bacon	350 g / 12 oz
6	Dried sage leaves	6
1	Bay leaf	1
3	Fresh thyme sprigs	3
	Salt and pepper	
⅔ cup	Dry white wine	150 ml / ¼ pint
2 tbsp	Brandy	2 tbsp
2 - 4	Very thin strips of fatty bacon	2 - 4
1 tbsp	Flour	1 tbsp
2 tbsp	Water	2 tbsp

1. Preheat the oven to 400°F / 200°C / Gas Mark 6.
2. Bone the pheasant and remove the skin, trying not to tear it. Put the skin to one side. Also put aside the breast. Grind [mince] the rest of the pheasant meat, with the giblets, pork, veal, bacon, sage, bay leaf and thyme. Season with salt and a lot of pepper. Add the white wine, and carefully mix together all these ingredients.
3. Cut the pheasant breast into thin slices. Season to taste with salt and pepper. Line the bottom and sides of a terrine with the pheasant skin. Fill one third of the terrine with the ground meat, cover with half the pheasant breast slices, and repeat until the terrine is completely full, finishing with a layer of ground meat.
4. Prick here and there with a skewer, and pour over the brandy. Cover with the strips of bacon and put the lid on the terrine. Mix the flour and water to make a very soft paste and put this in a strip all around the lid to seal the terrine.
5. Place the terrine in a baking pan containing 2 in / 5 cm of water. Bake for 1½ hours.
6. Take the terrine out of the oven and let it cool slightly (10 minutes), then take off the lid. Put a board with a weight on top. Leave in a cool place for 12 hours before serving.

Preserves are a delicious accompaniment to pâtés, terrines and galantines

CHAPTER 11

Eggs

Guidelines

Are you sure you know how to boil an egg? Anyone can put an egg into a pan of boiling water, but the end result can easily go wrong unless you observe a few simple rules:

Take eggs out of the refrigerator at least 1 hour before cooking so they will not crack when placed in boiling water. Alternatively, take the chill off them by placing them in warm water for a few minutes.

Always cook eggs in simmering rather than rapidly boiling water. Plunge hard-cooked eggs into cold water immediately after boiling to stop the cooking process and cool the shell, which can then be easily removed.

Timing

The appearance and texture of your eggs will vary with the length of time they have been boiled. For accuracy, use a kitchen or egg timer.

3-5½ minutes
The white will be set, and the yolk still liquid in the center. This is a soft-cooked egg, which can be eaten plain or in a sauce.

6-7 minutes
The white will be thoroughly cooked, and the yolk set but still soft. This is an almost hard-cooked egg.

10 minutes
The white and the yolk will have the same firm consistency, but the yolk will be pale. This is the standard hard-cooked egg, which can be stuffed, chopped for use in all sorts of fillings, or added to a vinaigrette dressing.

Perfect scrambled eggs

More than 10 minutes
The white becomes rubbery, and the yolk dry with a greenish film around it. This egg is overcooked, indigestible and unappetizing.

To peel an egg

Tap the egg all over with the back of a spoon. The cracked shell and the membrane will then come away easily, but you should rinse the egg in case any small pieces of shell remain.

Storage

Eggs will stay at their freshest if you store them, pointed end down, in the special compartment of your refrigerator, or in their original carton on one of the shelves.

Freshness

Always check the date stamp when you are buying eggs, but if you are not sure how long they've been stored, you can test their freshness in two ways:

Water test
Place the egg in a bowl of salt water. If it sinks, it is fresh (because it contains only a small pocket of air). If it half sinks, with the wide end upwards, it is about a week old (since the air pocket has become larger and makes the egg lighter). If it floats, it is too old to be used.

Plate test
Break the egg onto a plate. If the yolk (which should be high and compact) is in the middle of a jellied white, the egg is fresh. If the white is very liquid and the yolk limp, the egg is stale.

Oeufs brouillés aux croûtons

Scrambled Eggs with Croûtons

⬜▭ 00:05   00:10 🍲

American	Ingredients	Metric/Imperial
6	Slices of stale bread	6
12	Eggs	12
	Salt and pepper	
4 - 6 tbsp	Butter	50 - 75 g / 2 - 3 oz
2 tbsp	Crème fraîche (see page 122)	2 tbsp
2 tbsp	Oil	2 tbsp

1. Cut the bread into small dice. Set aside. Gently mix the eggs without beating. Add salt and pepper to taste. Melt the butter in a saucepan in a larger saucepan of hot water. When the butter has melted, pour in the eggs and crème fraîche. Cook, stirring, for 10 minutes or until the eggs take on the consistency of thick cream. Turn off the heat.
3. Heat the oil in a frying pan. Add the diced bread and fry over a medium heat until the bread cubes are golden and have absorbed all the oil.
4. Serve the scrambled eggs garnished with the croûtons.

Cook's tip: the croûtons should be cooked in oil which is hot but not smoking. As soon as they have turned golden, remove them from the oil and drain on paper towels.

Oeufs au bacon
Bacon and Eggs

American	Ingredients	Metric/Imperial
24	Smoked bacon slices	24
6 tbsp	Butter	75 g / 3 oz
12	Eggs	12
	Salt and pepper	

00:00   00:10 per plate

1. Put the bacon slices in a frying pan without fat and cook to your taste (soft or crisp).
2. Put 1 tablespoon butter on each of 6 flameproof metal plates or gratin dishes, and place over a moderate heat. When the butter has melted, add 4 slices of cooked bacon to each plate and break 2 eggs onto it. Season with salt and pepper. Cook over a gentle heat for 8-10 minutes. If you like the edges of the egg white to be crispy, turn up the heat right at the end.

Oeufs Bénédictine
Eggs with Salt Cod in a Pie Crust

00:25   00:18

American	Ingredients	Metric/Imperial
6	Eggs	6
1	Small truffle	1
1½ cups	Salt cod cream (see page 266)	400 g / 14 oz
1 cup	Crème fraîche (see page 122)	250 ml / 8 fl oz
1 (8 in)	Baked pie crust with lid (bought from a baker or homemade)	1 (20 cm / 8 in)
2 tbsp	Butter	25 g / 1 oz
1 tbsp	Flour	1 tbsp
1 tbsp	Water	1 tbsp
	Grated nutmeg	
	Salt and pepper	

1. Preheat the oven to 300°F / 150°C / Gas Mark 2.
2. Place the eggs in a saucepan of boiling water. Bring the water back to a boil and cook exactly 6 minutes. Drain and put the eggs immediately in cold water. Peel them and leave in warm water to keep warm.
3. Peel the truffle. Slice part of it for the garnish and chop the remainder.
4. Heat the salt cod cream over a low heat, stirring frequently. Thin it, if necessary, with 1 tablespoon of the crème fraîche. Add the chopped truffle.
5. Place the pie crust and its lid into the oven to heat.
6. Melt the butter in a saucepan, add the flour, stir and leave to brown over a low heat. Add half the crème fraîche, the water, a pinch of grated nutmeg, and salt and pepper to taste and whisk together. Reduce to a thick paste, stirring over a low heat. Remove from the heat and add the remaining crème fraîche, whisking it in. Heat without boiling.
7. Fill the heated pie crust with the hot salt cod mixture. Put the hard-cooked eggs on top, standing up, and garnish with the truffle slices. Divide the pastry lid into portions and place on top of the pie. Serve the sauce in a sauceboat. Serve hot.

Oeufs brouillés à la portugaise
Scrambled Eggs Portuguese Style

00:20   00:35

American	Ingredients	Metric/Imperial
2	Sweet green and red peppers	2
2	Garlic cloves	2
1½ lb	Tomatoes	750 g / 1½ lb
1 tbsp	Olive oil	1 tbsp
1	Bouquet garni	1
12	Eggs	12
	Salt and pepper	
¼ cup	Butter	50 g / 2 oz

1. Cut the peppers in half, remove the core and seeds and cut the peppers into very thin strips. Peel and crush the garlic. Peel the tomatoes (first plunging them into boiling water for 10 seconds), then cut the flesh into small dice.
2. Heat the olive oil in a frying pan, add the pepper strips, tomatoes, garlic and bouquet garni and cook for 30 minutes over a low heat, stirring from time to time.
3. About 10 minutes before the end of the cooking time, break the eggs into a bowl and add salt and pepper to taste. Mix without beating. Melt the butter in a thick-bottomed saucepan, pour in the eggs and cook over a very low heat for about 5 minutes, stirring continuously.
4. Remove from the heat and pour in half the tomato mixture. Mix together and spoon into the center of a serving dish. Surround with the rest of the tomato mixture (discarding the bouquet garni) and serve immediately.

Bacon and eggs

Oeufs brouillés aux pointes d'asperges

Scrambled Eggs with Asparagus Tips

	00:50		00:13

American	Ingredients	Metric/Imperial
4 lb	Asparagus	2 kg / 4 lb
	Salt and pepper	
12	Eggs	12
6 tbsp	Butter	75 g / 3 oz
5 tbsp	Crème fraîche (see page 122)	5 tbsp

1. Break the tips off the asparagus spears, making the pieces about 2 in / 5 cm long. (Use the asparagus stalks for another recipe, such as soup.) Drop the tips into a saucepan of boiling salted water and cook for 4-5 minutes or until tender. Drain and keep warm.
2. Break the eggs into a bowl, add salt and pepper to taste and mix without beating. Melt ¼ cup [50 g / 2 oz] of the butter in a saucepan placed in a larger saucepan of hot water. Add the eggs and cook for 10 minutes, stirring, until they thicken.
3. Meanwhile, melt the remaining butter in a saucepan, add the asparagus tips and reheat gently.
4. Add the crème fraîche to the eggs and stir for a few more moments to heat through, then pour the scrambled eggs onto a hot plate. Garnish with the asparagus tips and serve.

Oeufs Bercy

Fried Eggs with Sausages and Tomato Sauce

	00:15		00:04 to 00:07

American	Ingredients	Metric/Imperial
1 cup	Tomato sauce (see page 133)	250 ml / 8 fl oz
	Cayenne pepper	
1 tsp	Oil	1 tsp
24	Small pork link sausages [chipolatas]	24
¾ cup	Butter	175 g / 6 oz
12	Eggs	12
	Salt and pepper	

1. Place the tomato sauce in a saucepan and reduce it over a low heat so that it becomes very thick. Season with a little cayenne pepper.
2. Meanwhile, heat the oil in a frying pan and add the sausages (pricked so that they do not burst). Brown them over a low heat.
3. Melt 2 tablespoons [25 g / 1 oz] butter on each of 6 flameproof plates. Break 2 eggs on each plate and arrange 2 sausages on the whites of each egg. Cook over a low heat for 4-7 minutes. Turn up the heat at the end of the cooking time to crisp the edges of the eggs.
4. Serve the eggs on the plates on which they were cooked, with the tomato sauce, salt and pepper, and hot toast.

Oeufs en darioles

Egg Molds

	00:10		00:20

American	Ingredients	Metric/Imperial
6 tbsp	Butter	75 g / 3 oz
¾ cup	Grated gruyère cheese	75 g / 3 oz
6	Eggs	6
5 tbsp	Crème fraîche (see page 122)	5 tbsp
	Salt and pepper	
1 tbsp	Oil	1 tbsp
6	Round slices of bread	6

1. Butter 6 ramekins and sprinkle the insides with a little of the grated gruyère cheese.
2. Beat the eggs in a bowl with the crème fraîche and remaining gruyère. Season to taste with salt and pepper. Pour this mixture into the ramekins, three-quarters filling them.
3. Heat about 1 in / 2.5 cm water in a pan large enough to hold the ramekins. When the water is almost simmering, put the ramekins in the pan. Cook gently for 20 minutes or until just firm to the touch. Make sure that the water continues to simmer and not boil, or the eggs will be spoiled.
4. Meanwhile, heat the oil in a frying pan, add the bread slices and fry until golden on both sides. Drain on paper towels.
5. Turn the molds onto the fried bread, and serve with a well-seasoned tomato sauce (see page 133).

Cook's tip: you can also serve these with a madeira mushroom sauce (see page 127).

Scrambled eggs with mushrooms

Oeufs brouillés au nid

Scrambled Egg Nests

	00:10		00:15

American	Ingredients	Metric/Imperial
6	Small brioches	6
2 tbsp	Crème fraîche (see page 122)	2 tbsp
6	Eggs	6
	Grated nutmeg	
	Salt and pepper	
3 tbsp	Butter	40 g / 1½ oz

1. Preheat the oven to 325°F / 160°C / Gas Mark 3.
2. Take the tops off the brioches and put to one side. Take out the soft center crumb and reserve it. Wrap the brioches and their tops in foil and put into the oven to heat through.
3. Meanwhile, put the soft center crumb from the brioches in a bowl and add 1 tablespoon of crème fraîche. Leave to soak, then mash finely with a fork.
4. Break the eggs into a bowl and add a pinch of nutmeg and salt and pepper to taste. Mix without beating. Melt the butter in a saucepan placed in a larger saucepan of hot water. Add the eggs and cook for 10 minutes, stirring, until they thicken. Add the remaining crème fraîche.
5. Add the soaked brioche crumbs and continue cooking until the eggs take on a good soft consistency. Taste and adjust the seasoning.
6. Fill the heated brioches with the scrambled eggs, put the tops back on and serve hot.

Cook's tip: any soft egg rolls can be used if brioches are not available.

Oeufs brouillés aux girolles

Scrambled Eggs with Chanterelle Mushrooms

	00:20		01:00

American	Ingredients	Metric/Imperial
½ lb	Chanterelles or other edible wild mushrooms	250 g / 8 oz
6 tbsp	Butter	75 g / 3 oz
	Salt and pepper	
¼	Garlic clove	¼
1 tbsp	Chopped fresh parsley	1 tbsp
9	Eggs	9
1 tbsp	Crème fraîche (see page 122)	1 tbsp

1. Rinse the chanterelles in several changes of water to remove all the sand. Drain in a colander, then put them on paper towels to absorb the rest of the moisture.
2. Melt 2 tablespoons [25 g / 1 oz] of the butter in a frying pan. Add the mushrooms and cook over a high heat until all the moisture has evaporated, stirring frequently. Season the mushrooms with salt and pepper, lower the heat and leave to cook gently, without letting them dry out, for about 15 minutes.
3. Peel and chop the garlic and mix with the parsley. Set aside.
4. Break the eggs into a bowl, add a pinch of salt and pepper

and stir without beating. Melt the remaining butter in a heavy saucepan over a very low heat, add the eggs and cook, stirring, for 10 minutes or until the eggs have the consistency of thick cream.
5. Add the crème fraîche and stir for a few moments.
6. Pour the scrambled eggs onto a warmed serving dish and put the mushrooms on top. Sprinkle with the parsley and garlic mixture. Serve immediately.

Oeufs à l'aurore

Eggs with Cheese Sauce

	00:15		00:25

American	Ingredients	Metric/Imperial
6	Eggs	6
2 tbsp	Butter	25 g / 1 oz
1 tbsp	Flour	1 tbsp
1 cup	Milk	250 ml / 8 fl oz
	Salt and pepper	
5 tbsp	Grated gruyère cheese	65 g / 2½ oz

1. Preheat the oven to 450°F / 230°C / Gas Mark 8.
2. Hard-cook the eggs for 10 minutes in boiling water. Drain, put them in cold water and remove the shells. Set aside.
3. Melt the butter in a saucepan, add the flour and stir well. Remove from the heat and gradually stir in the milk. Season to taste with salt and pepper. Bring to a boil, stirring continuously and cook for 10 minutes. Add the grated gruyère and mix well until the cheese has melted.
4. Cut the hard-cooked eggs in half lengthwise, and separate the whites from the yolks. Chop the whites and mix them with the white sauce. Crush the egg yolks.
5. Layer the yolks and white sauce in 6 buttered ramekins, finishing with a layer of egg yolk. Bake for 5 minutes and serve very hot.

Cook's tip: this is a quick and tasty dish for lunch when served with french bread and a green salad.

Fried eggs with sausages

Oeufs en brioche

Eggs in Brioche

00:30 **01:15**

American	Ingredients	Metric/Imperial
1	Onion	1
1	Carrot	1
¼ cup	Butter	50 g / 2 oz
	Dried thyme	
½	Bay leaf	½
¼ cup	Tomato paste [purée]	4 tbsp
⅔ cup	White wine	150 ml / ¼ pint
⅔ cup	Water	150 ml / ¼ pint
	Salt and pepper	
	Cayenne pepper or tabasco sauce	
6	Small brioches	6
6	Eggs	6
⅔ cup	Crème fraîche (see page 122)	150 ml / ¼ pint
1	Egg yolk	1

1. Peel and finely chop the onion. Peel and grate the carrot. Heat the butter in a saucepan, add the onion, carrot, a pinch of thyme and the bay leaf and cook until softened but not browned. Add the tomato paste, wine and water. Stir well. Cook over a low heat for 1 hour.
2. Preheat the oven to 400°F / 200°C / Gas Mark 6.
3. Strain the sauce and season with salt and pepper. Add a small pinch of cayenne pepper or a few drops of tabasco sauce. This sauce must be quite highly seasoned. Keep hot.
4. Take the tops off the brioches and hollow out the insides with a small pointed knife. Put the brioches in the oven, without their tops, for a few minutes to heat through.
5. Break an egg into each brioche. Season lightly with salt and pepper. Put back in the oven and bake for 12-15 minutes, just enough to cook the eggs. Heat the brioche tops as well.
6. Mix the crème fraîche with the egg yolk. Add to the sauce and heat through, stirring. Do not allow to boil. Serve the sauce with the eggs in brioche.

Oeufs en cocotte

Baked Eggs with Sorrel Cream

00:15 **00:06 to 00:08**

American	Ingredients	Metric/Imperial
1	Loaf of french bread	1
6 tbsp	Butter	75 g / 3 oz
	Chopped fresh chives	
	Chopped fresh parsley	
½ lb	Sorrel (or spinach)	250 g / 8 oz
	Salt and pepper	
1 cup	Crème fraîche (see page 122)	250 ml / 8 fl oz
12	Eggs	12

1. Preheat the oven to 400°F / 200°C / Gas Mark 6.
2. Cut the french loaf into 3 pieces, each 5 in / 12 cm long, and split each piece open. Butter the cut surfaces lightly.

Sprinkle with chopped chives and parsley. Cut each piece in half crosswise to make 6 pieces. Set aside.
3. Clean the sorrel, removing the stalks and keeping only the green part of the leaves. Rinse and drain. Put it in a saucepan with 2 tablespoons [25 g / 1 oz] of the butter, and salt and pepper to taste. Cover and cook for 1 minute, then remove the lid and continue cooking until the moisture has evaporated.
4. Bring the crème fraîche to a boil in a small saucepan. Season with salt and pepper, add the cooked sorrel and stir gently. Remove from the heat and keep hot.
5. Generously butter 6 ramekins. Sprinkle the bottoms with salt and pepper. Break 2 eggs into each ramekin without breaking the yolks. Place the ramekins in an ovenproof dish and add water to the dish to come halfway up the sides of the ramekins. Cover with foil and bake for 6-8 minutes, or until the whites become opaque and the yolks are still liquid. (This is a matter of taste: some people prefer both white and yolk well done.)
6. Take the ramekins out of the oven, cover with the sorrel sauce and serve very hot with the herbed bread.

Brioche

Oeufs aux fines herbes

Eggs with Herbs

00:05 **00:15**

American	Ingredients	Metric/Imperial
6 tbsp	Butter	75 g / 3 oz
6	Eggs	6
1½ cups	Crème fraîche. (see page 122)	350 ml / 12 fl oz
⅛ tsp	Cornstarch [cornflour]	⅛ tsp
1	Bunch of fresh chervil or parsley	1
1	Bunch of fresh chives	1
	Salt and pepper	

1. Melt the butter and divide between 6 small ramekins. Break an egg into each dish. Heat about 1 in / 2.5 cm water in a pan large enough to hold the ramekins. When the water is almost simmering put the ramekins in the pan. Cook gently until the eggs are just set.
2. Meanwhile, place the crème fraîche in a saucepan and boil to reduce by half. Add the cornstarch, dissolved in a tiny amount of water. The sauce should just coat the back of a spoon.
3. Add the chopped chervil and chives, and season with salt and pepper.
4. Pour the sauce onto the eggs and serve immediately.

Oeufs au gratin

Baked Eggs with Mushrooms

	00:10	00:25 to 00:30 including egg boiling	
American	**Ingredients**	**Metric/Imperial**	
8	Hard cooked eggs	8	
¼ lb	Mushrooms	100 g / 4 oz	
1	Shallot	1	
	Chopped fresh parsley		
⅓ cup	Tomato sauce (see page 133)	6 tbsp	
	Salt and pepper		
3 tbsp	Butter	40 g / 1½ oz	
2 tbsp	Dry bread crumbs	2 tbsp	

1. Preheat the oven to 400°F / 200°C / Gas Mark 6.
2. Peel the eggs and cut them in half lengthwise. Remove the yolks and mash them. Chop the mushrooms. Peel and chop the shallot. Add the mushrooms, shallot and parsley to the egg yolks and mix well.
3. Add the tomato sauce and season with salt and pepper. Melt 1 tablespoon [15 g / ½ oz] butter in a small heavy pan and cook the mixture for a few minutes.
4. Arrange the egg whites in a buttered gratin dish. Stuff the centers with the mixture. Sprinkle with the bread crumbs. Melt the remaining butter and pour over. Bake for 10-12 minutes or until the eggs are golden on top. Serve hot.

Oeufs en matelote

Eggs with Red Wine Sauce

	00:15	00:45	
American	**Ingredients**	**Metric/Imperial**	
1	Large onion	1	
2	Garlic cloves	2	
1	Bouquet garni	1	
2 cups	Water	500 ml / ¾ pint	
2 cups	Red wine	500 ml / ¾ pint	
	Salt and pepper		
6	Eggs	6	
¼ cup	Butter	50 g / 2 oz	
2 tbsp	Flour	2 tbsp	
6	Slices of toast	6	

1. Peel the onion and 1 clove of garlic and put in a saucepan with the bouquet garni. Add the water and red wine, then season to taste with salt and pepper. Bring to a boil and cook for 20 minutes.
2. Strain the liquid and return it to the pan. Put over a low heat. Break the eggs one by one into a ladle and put into the simmering liquid. Take the pan off the heat, cover and leave the eggs to poach for 3 minutes.
3. When the eggs are cooked, use a slotted spoon to transfer them to a bowl of warm water to keep hot. Strain the egg cooking liquid again.
4. Melt the butter in a saucepan, add the flour and cook, stirring, until the flour becomes golden. Add the strained liquid and stir until the sauce thickens.
5. Cut the remaining garlic clove in half and rub the cut surfaces over the toast. Discard the garlic.
6. Drain the eggs on paper towels and cut them into neat shapes, discarding any excess white.
7. Put one egg on each slice of toast and top with the hot sauce.

Oeufs en meurette

Eggs Poached in Wine

	00:00	01:00	
American	**Ingredients**	**Metric/Imperial**	
2	Onions	2	
2	Garlic cloves	2	
6 tbsp	Butter	75 g / 3 oz	
1	Bottle of red Burgundy wine	1	
	Salt and pepper		
1	Bouquet garni	1	
2	Cloves	2	
2 tbsp	Oil	2 tbsp	
6	Slices of bread	6	
1	Sugar cube (optional)	1	
6	Eggs	6	

1. Peel and chop the onions. Peel and crush 1 garlic clove. Heat ¼ cup [50 g / 2 oz] of the butter in a saucepan, add the onions and cook until golden brown. Add the wine, and season with salt and pepper. Add the bouquet garni, cloves and crushed garlic. Cover the saucepan and leave to cook for approximately 45 minutes.
2. Meanwhile, heat the oil in a frying pan, add the bread slices and fry until golden brown on both sides. Drain on paper towels. Halve the remaining garlic clove and rub the cut surfaces over the fried bread. Discard the garlic and keep the bread hot.
3. Taste the sauce: if you find it too acid, sweeten with the sugar.
4. Break the eggs one by one into a ladle, and put into the sauce. Take the saucepan off the heat, cover and leave the eggs to poach for 3 minutes. Take the eggs out of the sauce with a skimmer, and drain them on paper towels. Cut the eggs into neat shapes, discarding any excess white. Put the eggs on the fried bread and keep warm.
5. Strain the sauce and add the remaining butter. Leave to reduce and thicken over a low heat. Taste and adjust the seasoning.
6. Pour the hot sauce onto the eggs and serve immediately.

Oeufs aux crevettes

Eggs with Shrimp [Prawns]

00:20   00:20 to 00:25

American	Ingredients	Metric/Imperial
⅔ cup	Dry white wine	150 ml / ¼ pint
5 oz	Peeled cooked shrimp [prawns]	150 g / 5 oz
1 tbsp	Potato flour or cornstarch [cornflour]	1 tbsp
1 cup	Crème fraîche (see page 122)	250 ml / 8 fl oz
1 tbsp	Tomato paste [purée]	1 tbsp
	Salt and pepper	
½ cup	Butter	125 g / 4 oz
12	Medium eggs	12
12	Round slices of bread	12
2 tbsp	Oil	2 tbsp

1. Pour the wine into a saucepan and bring to a boil. Boil until reduced by half. Add the shrimp.
2. Mix the potato flour with a little cold water. Add this to the wine mixture, with the crème fraîche and tomato paste. Cook, stirring, until thickened and heated through. Season with salt and pepper to taste. Keep warm.
3. Generously butter 6 large ramekins. Break 2 eggs into each one.
4. Heat about 1 in / 2.5 cm water in a pan large enough to hold the ramekins. When the water begins to simmer, put the ramekins into the pan. Cover and cook for 6-7 minutes. The water must never boil. When cooked, the white of the egg should be firm, but the yolk still liquid.
5. Meanwhile, cut the crusts off the slices of bread. Heat the remaining butter with the oil in a frying pan, add the bread slices and fry until golden brown on both sides. Drain on paper.
6. Unmold the eggs onto the fried bread, cover with the shrimp sauce, and serve very hot.

Oeufs durs au fromage

Hard-cooked Eggs with Goat's Cheese

00:20   00:12
plus chilling

American	Ingredients	Metric/Imperial
6	Eggs	6
5 oz	Fresh goat's milk cheese	150 g / 5 oz
	Chopped fresh chives	
	Chopped fresh parsley	
	Chopped fresh chervil	
	Chopped fresh tarragon	
3	Shallots	3
12	Green peppercorns	12
	Salt and pepper	
2 tbsp	Olive oil	2 tbsp
	Lettuce leaves	

1. Hard-cook the eggs for 10 minutes in boiling water, then put them in cold water. Peel them, and leave to cool. Cut them in half lengthwise.

2. Put the goat's milk cheese in a blender or food processor. Add the herbs. Peel and chop the shallots. Add to the cheese mixture with the peppercorns.
3. Remove the yolks from the eggs with a small spoon, keeping the whites intact, and put into the blender with the cheese mixture. Season with salt and pepper to taste. Mix everything together, adding the olive oil a little at a time in order to make a smooth paste.
4. Fill the egg white halves with the cheese mixture and arrange them on a dish lined with lettuce leaves. If liked, sprinkle with a little more chopped parsley. Chill until ready to serve.

Oeufs en gelée

Eggs in Aspic

00:15   00:45
plus chilling

American	Ingredients	Metric/Imperial
1	Bunch of fresh tarragon	1
2 cups	Liquid aspic (see page 116)	500 ml / ¾ pint
2	Thin slices of cooked ham	2
1 tbsp	Vinegar, preferably white wine vinegar	1 tbsp
12	Eggs	12
2 tbsp	Coarsely chopped fresh chives	2 tbsp
	Lettuce leaves	

1. Arrange tarragon leaves on the bottoms of 12 small molds or ramekins. Carefully pour ½ in / 1 cm warm aspic into the bottom of each. Chill until set.
2. Cut the slices of ham into 12 diamond shapes.
3. Put 1 in / 2.5 cm of water and the vinegar in a large saucepan. Bring to a boil, then lower the heat to keep the water at a gentle simmer.
4. Break the eggs into the water one by one, using a ladle to put them into the liquid. Cover and poach for 3 minutes. Take the eggs out with a skimmer and drain on paper towels. Leave to cool, then trim the eggs into a neat shape, discarding any excess white.
5. Take the molds out of the refrigerator and put a poached egg into each. Add a few chives to each egg, and a diamond of ham, then cover with the remaining liquid aspic. Chill for 3-4 hours.
6. Unmold the eggs onto a dish lined with lettuce leaves.

Oeufs miroir

Baked Eggs with Cream

00:05   00:05

American	Ingredients	Metric/Imperial
6 tbsp	Butter	6 tbsp
12	Eggs	12
	Salt and pepper	
1 cup	Crème fraîche (see page 122)	250 ml / 8 fl oz

1. Preheat the oven to 350°F / 180°C / Gas Mark 4.
2. Put 1 tablespoon butter in each of 6 ramekins. Put into the oven to melt the butter.

3. Break 2 eggs into each dish. Season to taste with salt and pepper. Spoon over the crème fraîche.
4. Place in the oven and bake for 4-5 minutes or until the whites become opaque. Serve in the ramekins.

Cook's tip: before putting the eggs in the oven, you could sprinkle them with grated gruyère cheese.

Oeufs mimosa

Stuffed Eggs with Herbs and Tomatoes

◢▷ 00:30   00:12 🍲

American	Ingredients	Metric/Imperial
6	Eggs	6
2	Tomatoes	2
	Salt and pepper	
3 tbsp	Chopped fresh chives or parsley	3 tbsp
1 cup	Mayonnaise (see page 119)	250 ml / 8 fl oz
1	Lettuce heart	1

1. Hard-cook the eggs for 10 minutes in boiling water. Drain, put them in cold water and allow them to cool.
2. Cut the tomatoes into 3 slices each, and season with salt.
3. Peel and halve the hard-cooked eggs. Remove the yolks and put to one side. Reserve 6 egg white halves, and mash the other whites with a fork. Mix with the chopped herbs and add the mayonnaise spoonful by spoonful, to obtain an elastic but not soft consistency.
4. Fill the reserved egg white halves with the herb mixture and arrange each on a slice of tomato on top of a lettuce leaf. Sieve the egg yolks and sprinkle over the stuffed whites.

Oeufs mollets sauce verte

Soft-cooked Eggs in Green Sauce

◢▷ 00:30   00:05 to 00:06 🍲

American	Ingredients	Metric/Imperial
12	Eggs	12
¼	Bunch of watercress	¼
1	Bunch of fresh chervil	1
4	Fresh parsley sprigs	4
1 cup	Mayonnaise (see page 119)	250 ml / 8 fl oz
6 tbsp	Crème fraîche (see page 122)	6 tbsp
	Salt and pepper	

1. Cook the eggs in boiling water for 5-6 minutes. Drain and put them under cold water immediately. Peel and wipe them dry. Cut a small slice off the flat end so the eggs will stand upright. Arrange them in a serving dish and set aside.
2. Carefully wash the watercress and chop it very finely. Chop the chervil and parsley.
3. Mix the mayonnaise with the crème fraîche and chopped herbs. Taste and adjust the seasoning.
4. Cover the eggs with some of the herb sauce and serve the rest in a sauceboat.

Oeufs au parmesan

Eggs with Parmesan Cheese

◢▷ 00:10   00:05 🍲

American	Ingredients	Metric/Imperial
6	Eggs	6
1 cup	Grated parmesan cheese	125 g / 4 oz
5 tbsp	Butter	65 g / 2½ oz
⅔ cup	Crème fraîche (see page 122)	150 ml / ¼ pint
	Salt and pepper	

1. Preheat the oven to 350°F / 180°C / Gas Mark 4.
2. Separate the eggs, being careful not to break the yolks. Put the egg whites into a bowl and beat into stiff peaks. Spoon the egg white into 6 buttered ramekins.
3. Sprinkle the egg white with half the parmesan cheese, then gently rest a whole yolk on the white in each ramekin. Cover with the parmesan. Put a pat of butter on top of each.
4. Bake for 5 minutes.
5. Spoon over the crème fraîche, season to taste with salt and pepper and serve hot.

Oeufs pochés Bénédictine

Poached Eggs Benedict

◢▷ 00:10   00:20 🍲

American	Ingredients	Metric/Imperial
6	Slices of bread	6
2	Slices of cooked ham	2
1¾ cups	Butter	400 g / 14 oz
6	Egg yolks	6
6 tbsp	Crème fraîche (see page 122)	6 tbsp
	Salt and pepper	
½	Lemon	½
1 tbsp	White wine vinegar	1 tbsp
6	Eggs	6

1. Cut the crusts off the bread and toast lightly. Set aside.
2. Cut the slices of ham into 6 pieces the same size as the bread slices. Place the ham on the toast and set aside. Melt the butter and skim off the foam.
3. Half fill a large saucepan with water and bring to a boil. Lower the heat to keep the water at a simmer.
4. Put the egg yolks in a bowl and add the crème fraîche. Put the bowl over the pan of water and heat gently, beating with a whisk. When the mixture thickens, beat in the melted butter little by little. Season to taste with salt and pepper and add the juice of the ½ lemon. Leave the bowl standing in the pan of water to keep the sauce hot.
5. Put 2 in / 5 cm of water and the vinegar in a saucepan. Bring to a boil, then lower the heat to keep the liquid at a simmer. One by one, break the whole eggs into a ladle and slide them into the simmering liquid. Take the saucepan off the heat, cover and leave to poach for 3 minutes. Remove the eggs with a skimmer and drain on paper towels. Trim the eggs into neat shapes, discarding any excess white.
6. Arrange each egg on a piece of ham-topped toast. Cover with the hot sauce and serve.

Oeufs moulés
Egg Ramekins

	00:10		00:25

American	Ingredients	Metric/Imperial
12	Eggs	12
	Salt and pepper	
2 tbsp	Butter	25 g / 1 oz

1. Preheat the oven to 425°F / 220°C / Gas Mark 7.
2. Break 8 of the eggs into a bowl, season to taste with salt and pepper and stir to mix without beating. Heat the butter in a thick-bottomed saucepan, pour in the mixed eggs and cook over a low heat, stirring continuously, for about 6 minutes or until the mixture is thick and creamy. Remove from the heat.
3. Break the remaining eggs into a bowl and beat together, then add them to the cooked eggs. Adjust the seasoning.
4. Divide the egg mixture between 6 small metal molds or ramekins. Put the molds in a baking pan on top of the stove. Pour water into the pan to come halfway up the molds and bring to a boil.
5. Put the pan into the oven and bake for 18-20 minutes or until set.
6. Remove from the oven and leave to rest for 2 minutes, then turn the eggs out onto a warmed serving dish. Serve immediately with a sauce such as tomato sauce (see page 133) or Périgueux sauce (see page 131).

Oeufs pochés Nîmoise
Poached Eggs with Salt Cod Cream

	00:30		00:10

American	Ingredients	Metric/Imperial
6	Slices of bread, ¾ in / 2 cm thick	6
2 tbsp	Oil	2 tbsp
1 tbsp	Vinegar	1 tbsp
6	Eggs	6
1 cup	Salt cod cream (see page 266)	250 g / 8 oz
1 tbsp	Butter	15 g / ½ oz
1 tbsp	Flour	1 tbsp
1 cup	Crème fraîche (see page 122)	250 ml / 8 fl oz
	Salt and pepper	
1	Egg yolk	1
	Lemon juice	

1. Cut the crusts off the bread slices. Heat the oil in a frying pan, add the bread and fry until golden brown on both sides. Drain on paper towels and keep hot.
2. Put 2 in / 5 cm of water and the vinegar in a saucepan and bring to a boil, then lower the heat to simmer.
3. Break the whole eggs, one by one, into a ladle and put them in the simmering liquid. Take the saucepan off the heat, cover and leave the eggs to poach for 3 minutes.
4. Remove the eggs with a skimmer and put them in a bowl of warm water to keep hot.
5. Put the salt cod cream in a bowl in a saucepan of simmering water and leave to heat through.

6. Melt the butter in a saucepan, add the flour and stir well. Stir in the crème fraîche. Season to taste with salt and pepper. Simmer, stirring, until thickened. Remove from the heat. Add the egg yolk and a few drops of lemon juice and whisk well.
7. Make a small hole in the middle of each piece of fried bread. Fill with the hot cod mixture and put a drained poached egg on top. Cover with the hot cream sauce.

Oeufs pochés en salade
Poached Egg Salad

	00:30		00:03

American	Ingredients	Metric/Imperial
	Salt and pepper	
2 tbsp	Vinegar	2 tbsp
1 tsp	Prepared mustard	1 tsp
3 tbsp	Oil	3 tbsp
¼ lb	Mixed young salad greens	125 g / 4 oz
½	Head of chicory [endive]	½
6 oz	Thin slices of cooked ham	175 g / 6 oz
2 tbsp	Butter	25 g / 1 oz
6	Eggs	6

1. Dissolve a pinch of salt in 1 tablespoon of the vinegar. Season to taste with pepper. Mix in the mustard, then add the oil and mix thoroughly.
2. Remove any damaged leaves from the salad greens and chicory. Rinse and shake or spin dry.
3. Cut the ham into thin strips. Melt the butter in a frying pan, add the ham and cook for 3 minutes to heat through, stirring frequently. Remove from the heat and keep hot.
4. Put 2 in / 5 cm of water and the remaining vinegar in a saucepan. Bring to a boil, then lower the heat to keep the liquid simmering. One by one, break the eggs into a ladle and slip them into the simmering liquid. Take the saucepan off the heat, cover and leave the eggs to poach for 3 minutes.
5. Remove the eggs with a skimmer and drain them on paper towels. Trim the whites into a neat shape.
6. Mix the salad greens with the vinaigrette dressing and put into 6 small individual dishes. Add a poached egg and a little ham to each dish and serve.

Oeufs à la russe
Russian Style Eggs

	00:20		00:10

American	Ingredients	Metric/Imperial
6	Eggs	6
1 cup	Mayonnaise (see page 119)	250 ml / 8 fl oz
	Chopped fresh parsley or chives	

1. Hard-cook the eggs for 10 minutes in boiling water. Put under cold water and peel. Cut the base off each egg and carefully remove the yolk with a small spoon so as to keep the whites intact. Dice the egg white bases.
2. Put the yolks through a sieve or food mill. Put them in a serving dish and arrange the whites on top, with the opening upwards.
3. Fill each egg with the mayonnaise. Sprinkle with chopped herbs and the diced egg white.

Oeufs Toupinel
Eggs in Baked Potatoes

	00:30	01:30 to 02:00	

American	Ingredients	Metric/Imperial
6	Large potatoes	6
	Salt and pepper	
½ cup	Butter	125 g / 4 oz
6	Eggs	6
5	Slices of bacon	5
1 cup	Béchamel sauce (see page 124)	250 ml / 8 fl oz
1 cup	Coarsely chopped cooked ham	125 g / 4 oz
	Cayenne pepper	
½ cup	Grated gruyère cheese	50 g / 2 oz

1. Preheat the oven to 425°F / 220°C / Gas Mark 7.
2. Scrub the potatoes. With the point of a knife make an opening like a lid, cutting into the skin only. Leave the 'lid' in place. Bake for 1-1½ hours or until a small pointed knife will go through the potatoes easily.
3. Take off the lid. Hollow out the potato, leaving shells about 5 mm / ¼ in thick, and reserve the scooped-out potato. Season the inside of the potato shells lightly with salt and pepper. Put a pat of butter inside, and break an egg into each potato.
4. Coarsely chop the bacon and add to the béchamel sauce, together with the ham, scooped-out potato and a pat of butter. Add cayenne pepper and salt to taste.
5. Fill each potato shell with the bacon mixture and sprinkle with grated gruyère cheese.
6. Put the potatoes in the oven turned to the maximum setting and bake for 20 minutes.

Oeufs sur toasts
Eggs on Toast with Red Peppers

	00:20 plus marinating	00:20	

American	Ingredients	Metric/Imperial
2	Sweet red peppers	2
1	Garlic clove	1
	Olive oil	
3 tbsp	Oil	3 tbsp
6	Slices of bread	6
12	Slices of lean bacon	12
12	Medium eggs	12
½ cup	Butter	125 g / 4 oz

1. Cut the peppers in half, discard the core, seeds and white ribs and cut the peppers into thin strips.
2. Peel and crush the garlic. Put the strips of pepper in a bowl with the garlic and cover with olive oil. Leave to marinate for 12 hours. Drain.
3. Heat the 3 tablespoons of oil in a frying pan, add the bread slices and fry until golden brown on both sides. Drain on paper towels.
4. Cook the bacon in a frying pan without fat.
5. Put 2 slices of bacon on each slice of fried bread.
6. Fry the eggs, 4 at a time, in the butter until done to your taste.
7. Put 2 fried eggs on each piece of fried bread, and put 2 strips of red pepper on each yolk. Serve hot.

Omelette Brayaude
Ham and Potato Omelette

	00:30	00:10	

American	Ingredients	Metric/Imperial
½ lb	Slices of cooked country ham, ½ in / 1 cm thick	250 g / 8 oz
¾ lb	Potatoes	350 g / 12 oz
½ cup	Butter	125 g / 4 oz
6	Eggs	6
	Salt and pepper	

1. Cut the ham into dice and taste it. If salty, blanch for 5 minutes in boiling water. Drain.
2. Peel the potatoes and cut into dice. Heat half of the butter in a frying pan and add the potatoes. Cook until softened. Towards the end of the cooking time, add the ham. Continue cooking until the ham and potatoes are lightly browned.
3. Break the eggs into a bowl and season to taste with salt and pepper. Beat well with a fork for a few seconds. Pour the potatoes and ham into the eggs.
4. Heat the remaining butter in the frying pan, then add the egg mixture. Cook the omelette over a low heat, constantly pushing the cooked edges towards the center with a wooden spatula. Turn over with a plate to brown both sides.
5. In the Auvergne, this omelette is sometimes covered with 2-3 tablespoons of cream, or it can be sprinkled with grated gruyère cheese and then lightly browned under the broiler [grill].

Omelette danoise
Danish Omelette

	00:10	00:10	

American	Ingredients	Metric/Imperial
12	Eggs	12
2 tbsp	Milk	2 tbsp
	Salt and pepper	
6	Slices of smoked bacon, ½ in / 1 cm thick	6
¼ cup	Butter	50 g / 2 oz
1	Bunch of fresh chives	1

1. Break the eggs into a bowl and add the milk and salt and pepper to taste. Beat well with a fork for a few seconds.
2. Brown the bacon in a frying pan without fat. Drain on paper towels.
3. Melt the butter in a 9 in / 23 cm frying pan and pour in the beaten egg. Cook gently over a low heat, constantly pushing the cooked edges towards the center.
4. When the eggs have just set but the top is still soft, garnish with the bacon slices and sprinkle with chopped chives. Serve with a salad.

Omelette
Plain Omelette

	00:05	00:08

American	Ingredients	Metric/Imperial
12	Eggs	12
	Salt and pepper	
2 tbsp	Water, milk or crème fraîche (see page 122)	2 tbsp
¼ cup	Butter	50 g / 2 oz

1. Break the eggs into a bowl. Add salt and pepper to taste and the water, milk or crème fraîche, if desired. Beat well with a fork for a few seconds to obtain a uniform mixture.
2. Heat the butter in an 11 in / 28 cm frying pan. As soon as it foams (it must not be allowed to brown), pour in the beaten egg all at once. Cook over a low heat, constantly pushing the cooked part of the eggs at the edge towards the center with a wooden spatula. Shake the pan regularly to prevent the omelette from sticking.
3. Slide the omelette onto a dish and fold it over. Serve immediately.
4. You can also cook the omelette on both sides, in which case put a plate over the pan, turn it over quickly and tip out the omelette and slide the omelette back into the pan, cooked side upwards. This is a 'flat omelette'.

Omelette au fromage
Cheese Omelette

	00:06	00:05 to 00:08

American	Ingredients	Metric/Imperial
12	Eggs	12
2 tbsp	Milk	2 tbsp
1 cup	Grated gruyère cheese	125 g / 4 oz
	Salt and pepper	
¼ cup	Butter	50 g / 2 oz

1. Break the eggs into a bowl and add the milk, cheese and salt and pepper to taste. Beat well with a fork for a few seconds.
2. Melt the butter in a large frying pan, pour in the egg mixture and cook over a gentle heat, constantly pushing the cooked edges towards the center with a wooden spatula. When the omelette is cooked to your taste, slide it onto a warmed serving dish. Fold it over and serve immediately.

Omelette au four
Baked Omelette

	00:10 plus cooling	00:55

American	Ingredients	Metric/Imperial
1½ lb	Potatoes	750 g / 1½ lb
½ cup	Butter	125 g / 4 oz
1 tbsp	Oil	1 tbsp
1	Garlic clove	1
	Salt and pepper	
12	Eggs	12

1. Put the potatoes in a saucepan of cold water. Bring to a boil and cook for 20 minutes. Drain and allow to cool.
2. Preheat the oven to 475°F / 250°C / Gas Mark 9.
3. Peel the potatoes and cut them into slices. Heat 2 tablespoons [25 g / 1 oz] of the butter and the oil in a frying pan, add the potato slices and fry until golden. At the last minute, add the garlic clove, peeled and crushed.
4. Turn the potatoes into a buttered ovenproof dish and season to taste with salt and pepper.
5. Break the eggs into a bowl and season lightly with salt and pepper. Beat well with a fork for a few seconds, then pour the eggs onto the potatoes. Put the dish in the oven and bake for 15 minutes.
6. As soon as the top sets, dot it with the remaining butter and lower the oven heat to 350°F / 180°C / Gas Mark 4. Continue baking until the omelette comes away from the sides of the dish, about 15-20 minutes.
7. This omelette can be made with all the standard omelette fillings: mushrooms, bacon, herbs, etc. While it is difficult to make omelettes with more than 6 eggs in a frying pan, this omelette can have as many eggs as the dish can hold. It is an ideal recipe for improvised dinners.

Omelette au plat à la tomate
Baked Tomato Omelette

	00:10	00:15

American	Ingredients	Metric/Imperial
12	Eggs	12
	Salt and pepper	
½ cup	Grated gruyère cheese	50 g / 2 oz
1 tbsp	Chopped fresh chives or parsley	1 tbsp
3	Medium-size tomatoes	3
3 tbsp	Butter	40 g / 1½ oz

1. Preheat the oven to 425°F / 220°C / Gas Mark 7.
2. Break the eggs into a bowl and add salt and pepper to taste. Add the cheese and herbs. Beat well with a fork for a few seconds.
3. Peel the tomatoes (first plunging them into boiling water for 10 seconds) and slice them.
4. Heat the butter in an ovenproof dish. Arrange the tomato slices over the bottom of the dish and cover with the beaten eggs.
5. Bake for 15 minutes. Serve hot.

Omelette au haddock
Smoked Haddock Omelette

	00:10	00:25

American	Ingredients	Metric/Imperial
½ cup	Peas	50 g / 2 oz
½ lb	Smoked haddock fillets (finnan haddie)	250 g / 8 oz
6 tbsp	Butter	75 g / 3 oz
8	Eggs	8
	Salt and pepper	

1. Cook the peas in boiling water for 10 minutes (less time if using frozen peas), then drain them.
2. Put the haddock in a large saucepan of water, bring to a boil and simmer for 5 minutes. Take the saucepan off the heat and leave the fish to cool in the cooking water. Drain and cut into small pieces.
3. Heat 2 tablespoons [25 g / 1 oz] butter in a saucepan. Add the haddock and drained peas, cover and leave to cook over a very low heat.
4. Meanwhile, break the eggs into a bowl and add salt and pepper to taste. Beat well with a fork for a few seconds.
5. Melt the rest of the butter in a frying pan over a low heat and add the eggs. Cook the omelette, pushing the cooked edges towards the center, until done to your taste. Add the haddock and peas and fold the omelette over. Serve hot.

Omelette aux herbes
Herb Omelette

00:15   00:30

American	Ingredients	Metric/Imperial
3	Onions	3
1	Garlic clove	1
1	Bunch of fresh chives	1
2	Fresh basil sprigs	2
1	Handful of spinach	1
3 tbsp	Olive oil	3 tbsp
12	Eggs	12
	Salt and pepper	

1. Peel and slice the onions and garlic. Chop the chives and basil. Cut the stalks off the spinach. Rinse in plenty of water, drain and chop.
2. Heat 1 tablespoon oil in a frying pan and add the onions and garlic. Cook gently until translucent. Add the chives, spinach and basil. Cover and cook over a low heat until the mixture is reduced to a purée (about 15 minutes).
3. Break the eggs into a bowl and add salt and pepper to taste. Add the herb mixture. Beat well together with a fork for a few seconds.
4. Heat the remaining oil in a frying pan and add the egg mixture. Cook the omelette, constantly pushing the cooked edges towards the center until it is done to your taste. Slide onto a dish and fold over. Serve immediately.

Omelette paysanne
Peasant Omelette

00:10   00:06 to 00:08

American	Ingredients	Metric/Imperial
4	Scallions [spring onions]	4
1	Bunch of fresh parsley	1
	A handful of sorrel leaves	
12	Eggs	12
	Salt and pepper	
3-4 tbsp	Butter or bacon fat	40-60 g / 1½-2 oz

1. Chop the scallions, parsley and the sorrel leaves and mix together.

2. Break the eggs into a bowl, add salt and pepper and the vegetables and beat well together.
3. Melt the butter or bacon fat in a large omelette pan, pour in the mixture and cook over low heat. Keep moving the egg from the sides to the center as it cooks.
4. When the omelette is cooked to your liking slide it out onto a serving dish and fold it over. Serve at once.

Omelette aux oignons
Onion Omelette

00:10   00:35 to 00:40

American	Ingredients	Metric/Imperial
6	Medium-size onions	6
3 tbsp	Olive oil	3 tbsp
	Salt and pepper	
8	Eggs	8

1. Peel and slice the onions. Heat 2 tablespoons of the oil in a frying pan, add the onions and cook over a moderate heat until softened without browning. Season to taste with salt and pepper.
2. Break the eggs into a bowl and season lightly with pepper. Beat the eggs well for a few seconds.
3. Add the remaining oil to the onions, then pour over the eggs. Cook the omelette on both sides, using a plate to turn it over, until golden but still runny in the center.

Pipérade
Scrambled Eggs with Tomatoes and Peppers

00:20   00:30

American	Ingredients	Metric/Imperial
3	Onions	3
3	Garlic cloves	3
5 tbsp	Olive oil	5 tbsp
2 lb	Tomatoes	1 kg / 2 lb
2	Green peppers	2
6	Slices of bayonne ham or prosciutto	6
6	Eggs	6
	Salt and pepper	

1. Peel and chop the onions and garlic. Heat 2 tablespoons of the oil in a frying pan, add the onions and garlic and cook for about 10 minutes over a low heat.
2. Peel the tomatoes (first plunging them in boiling water for 10 seconds). Cut the peppers in half. Remove the core, seeds and white ribs, then cut the flesh into small pieces. Add the tomatoes and peppers to the frying pan and continue cooking for 30 minutes.
3. Heat the remaining oil in another frying pan, add the ham and cover. Brown over a low heat.
4. Break the eggs into a bowl. Season to taste with salt and pepper and beat well for a few moments. Add to the tomato mixture. Stir vigorously, then leave to cook over a low heat until the eggs are creamy.
5. Pour the pipérade into a serving dish, put the slices of ham on top and serve immediately.

Oeufs au vin blanc

Eggs with White Wine Sauce

	00:00		01:15

American	Ingredients	Metric/Imperial
1	Onion	1
1	Clove	1
2	Carrots	2
1	Garlic clove	1
1½ quarts	Dry white wine	1.5 l / 2½ pints
⅔ cup	Water	150 ml / ¼ pint
1	Celery leaf	1
	Chopped fresh parsley	
1	Fresh savory sprig	1
1	Bay leaf	1
1	Fresh tarragon sprig	1
2 tbsp	Oil	2 tbsp
12	Slices of bread	12
2 tbsp	Butter	25 g / 1 oz
1½ tbsp	Flour	25 g / 1 oz
1 tbsp	Vinegar	1 tbsp
12	Eggs	12

1. Peel the onion and stud it with the clove. Peel the carrots and garlic. Put the onion, garlic, carrots, wine, water, celery leaf, a handful of chopped parsley, the savory, bay leaf and tarragon in a saucepan. Cover and simmer for 1 hour. Strain and set aside.
2. Heat the oil in a frying pan and add the bread slices. Fry until crisp and golden brown on both sides. Drain on paper towels.
3. Heat the butter in a saucepan, add the flour and stir well. Gradually add the strained wine mixture, stirring to obtain a smooth consistency. Simmer, stirring, until thickened. Keep hot.
4. Put 2 in / 5 cm of water and the vinegar in a saucepan. Bring to a boil, then reduce the heat so the water is just simmering. Break the eggs, one by one, into a ladle and put into the simmering water. Take the saucepan off the heat, cover and leave the eggs to poach for 3 minutes.
5. Remove the eggs with a skimmer and drain on paper towels. Put them on the slices of fried bread. Cover with the sauce and serve.

Toasts aux oeufs au fromage

Fried Cheese Sandwiches with Egg

	00:15		00:05 per panful

American	Ingredients	Metric/Imperial
12	Thin slices of bread	12
¼ cup	Butter	50 g / 2 oz
¼ lb	Gruyère cheese	125 g / 4 oz
2	Eggs	2
2 tbsp	Milk	2 tbsp
	Salt and pepper	
6 tbsp	Oil	6 tbsp

1. Cut the crusts off the bread. Cut the slices in half and butter each side. Cut the gruyère cheese into 6 slices the same size as the bread, and sandwich each between two slices of bread.
2. Break the eggs into a bowl and add the milk, and salt and pepper to taste. Beat well together. Dip each sandwich into this mixture.
3. Heat the oil in a frying pan and fry the sandwiches on each side for 2 minutes. Serve hot.

Tortilla espagnole

Spanish Omelette

	00:10		00:15 to 00:17

American	Ingredients	Metric/Imperial
3	Large potatoes	3
3	Medium-size onions	3
½ cup	Oil	125 ml / 4 fl oz
12	Eggs	12
	Salt and pepper	

1. Peel the potatoes and cut them into small dice. Peel and chop the onions.
2. Heat 5 tablespoons of the oil in a frying pan, add the onions and potatoes and cook over a medium heat for 10 minutes, until the vegetables are golden brown.
3. Break the eggs into a bowl and beat them well to mix. Drain the potatoes and onions and add them to the bowl. Season to taste with salt and pepper.
4. Heat the remaining oil in a 7 in / 18 cm frying pan over a medium heat. Pour the contents of the bowl into the frying pan and cook until the edges of the omelette are set (a few minutes). When the bottom of the omelette is golden brown, turn it over with a plate and brown the other side for about 1 minute, ensuring that the inside is still runny. Serve hot or cold.

Oeufs en tomate

Eggs Baked in Tomatoes

	00:10		00:20

American	Ingredients	Metric/Imperial
6	Round tomatoes	6
6	Eggs	6
	Salt and pepper	
	Chopped fresh thyme and rosemary	
2 tbsp	Olive oil	2 tbsp
1	Garlic clove	1

1. Preheat the oven to 350°F / 180°C / Gas Mark 4.
2. Wash the tomatoes. Cut a large hole in the stalk end, and take out the seeds and part of the flesh.
3. Break an egg into each tomato, season with salt and pepper and sprinkle with herbs.
4. Oil an ovenproof dish with the olive oil. Peel and chop the garlic and sprinkle over the bottom of the dish. Arrange the tomatoes on top. Bake for 20 minutes. The egg whites should be set and the yolks firm, but not hard. Serve hot.

Cook's tip: serve with french bread and a green salad.

CHAPTER 12

Shellfish and Fish

Preparation

The term shellfish is used to describe both crustaceans (crab, lobster, shrimp etc.) and mollusks (oysters, scallops, mussels, squid etc.). Some of these creatures require special preparation, but you will find the small amount of extra work worthwhile.

To ensure freshness, choose crustaceans with a shiny carapace and bright, glossy eyes. Squid and octopus must be displayed on a bed of ice and their flesh should be firm and pearly with a pleasant smell.

Squid or cuttlefish
1. Rinse the squid in cold water. Hold the pouch containing the entrails and ink sac with one hand, and with the other take hold of the head just below the eyes. Pull to separate the two parts.
2. Remove the fine skin covering the white flesh and fins.
3. Cut the tentacles away from the head, leaving them connected to each other by a narrow ring of flesh.
4. Remove the bony beak from the head section and discard.

Scallops
1. To open the scallop shell, hold it with the flat side up, slide the point of a knife between the two halves at the 'corner' where the curve begins, and cut through the internal muscle.
2. Lift the top off the shell and detach the white muscle by slicing underneath it with a small sharp knife.
3. Reserve the muscle and coral (the orange, crescent-shaped part) and discard the black sac and the filaments. (If you are making fish stock for an accompanying sauce, the filaments can be added to this.)

Crab
1. With the cooked crab on its back, twist off the 8 legs and two claws as close to the body as possible.
2. Break the claws open with a nutcracker or a small hammer and carefully pick out the flesh without damaging it.
3. Remove the tail. Hold the upper shell in one hand and with the other grasp the body between the legs. Pull apart. Alternatively, slide the point of a knife between the upper half of the shell and the lower half (to which the legs are attached). Cut around the lower shell, using the knife as a lever to pry the two halves apart.
4. Spoon the meat from inside the upper shell, then remove and discard the abdominal sac and the long, soft 'fingers' around the lower shell. Cut this lower shell in half and remove the meat with a pointed implement such as a skewer. Pick out any meat in the holes left by the legs.

Preparing freshwater crayfish
To remove the digestive organs, grasp the 'fin' in the middle of the tail, twist half a turn, and pull to remove the blackish intestine that would give the dish a bitter taste.

Lobster or sea crayfish
1. With shell uppermost, cut right through the lobster with a sharp knife to divide in half.
2. Remove the khaki-colored liver and set aside. Female lobsters may have bright roe or coral. Remove this and reserve.
3. Remove the stomach (a hard sac near the head). Take out the flesh, discarding the intestinal vein beneath it.
4. Break off the claws and antennae by twisting them at the joint. Pull away and break in two.
5. Crack the shells of the claws with a nutcracker or hammer and remove the flesh in one piece.

A large tray of assorted shellfish

Preparing shellfish

Opening deep-shelled oysters
1. Insert the blade of a knife between the shells at the point where the muscle is located.

2. Push the blade in toward the center.

3. Pull the blade toward you, cutting through the muscle.

4. Lift the lid.

Opening flat oysters
1. Holding the oyster in the palm of your hand, place the blade of a knife against its tip.

2. Apply repeated pressure in a squeezing movement with your fingers until the blade has been forced into the oyster.

3. Pull the blade toward you, cutting through the muscle.

4. Lift the lid.

Cleaning mussels
1. Soak the mussels in fresh water.

2. Scrape them with a small, pointed knife.

3. Cut away the byssus (a fibrous attachment at the hinge of the valves).

4. Rinse the mussels quickly in a colander without leaving them to soak. (Although usually sold cleaned, mussels will need to be washed again before cooking.)

Oysters

Raw oysters should be opened by hand with the blade of a knife or special implement. Serve them with a drop of lemon juice and some buttered brown or rye bread. If you need oysters for a cooked dish choose large ones and place them in the oven or in a pan on top of the stove for a few seconds and the heat will open them.

Sea urchins

1. Using a glove or a cloth, hold the sea urchin upright, ie with the hole (mouth) at the top.

2. Pierce the mouth with a pair of scissors and cut a larger circular hole around the mouth. Remove this 'lid'.

3. Pour the liquid from inside the urchin into a bowl. Reserve the small orange masses that remain.

Guidelines

To make certain that a mollusk is safe to eat, first tap it lightly on the edge. It should remain firmly closed, so if it opens slightly, discard it. Once you have opened the shell, check that the inside smells fresh and pleasant. When you pinch the flesh at the edge (or fringe) or pour on a few drops of lemon juice, it should retract, and must be discarded if it does not.

Closed mollusks can be stored for 8-10 days if they are kept at a temperature between 32°F / 0°C and 41°F / 5°C — the vegetable compartment of your refrigerator is ideal. Once they are opened however, they must be eaten within 2 hours.

Mussels should be cooked without water until the shells are wide open. Allow about 2 quarts [4 lb / 2 kg] for 4 people.

Chipirons à l'encre

Cuttlefish in their Ink

	00:30	02:00

American	Ingredients	Metric/Imperial
4 lb	Cuttlefish, cleaned, with their ink	2 kg / 4 lb
2 tbsp	Oil	2 tbsp
3	Garlic cloves	3
2	Onions	2
1 ½ tbsp	Chopped fresh parsley	1 ½ tbsp
⅔ cup	White wine	150 ml / ¼ pint
	Vinegar	
	Salt and pepper	

1. Wash the cuttlefish thoroughly, and cut into round slices. Set the ink sacs aside.

2. Heat the oil in a wide saucepan, add the cuttlefish slices and cook over high heat until well browned.

3. Peel and very finely chop the garlic and onions. Add to the pan with the parsley, white wine, a dash of vinegar and the ink sacs. Season to taste with salt and pepper. Leave to cook for about 2 hours on a very low heat.

Follow the simple step-by-step instructions for preparing lobsters on page 247

Araignées de mer à la bretonne

Spider Crabs Breton Style

	00:45		00:15

American	Ingredients	Metric/Imperial
	Sea salt	
1	Bouquet garni	1
6	Medium-size spider crabs	6
5	Shallots	5
5	Gherkins	5
5	Hard-cooked eggs	5
1 tbsp	Prepared mustard	1 tbsp
1¼ cups	Oil	300 ml / ½ pint
	Salt and pepper	
1	Lemon	1

1. Bring a saucepan of water to a boil and add a handful of sea salt and the bouquet garni. Add the spider crabs and cook for 15 minutes at a simmer. Remove from the heat and leave the crabs to cool in the cooking water.
2. Peel and chop the shallots. Chop the gherkins. Cut 3 of the eggs in half and remove the yolks. (Discard the whites or keep them for another dish.) Mash the yolks in a bowl with the mustard and shallots. Add the oil in a thin stream, whisking vigorously as for mayonnaise. Add the chopped gherkins and season to taste with salt and pepper.
3. Drain the spider crabs. Break off the legs and remove the meat. Open the shells, and remove the creamy parts and the coral, as well as all the meat in the cells. Clean the shells thoroughly and put to one side.
4. Mash the coral and creamy parts and add the mayonnaise to them. Mix well. Stir in the meat and juice of the lemon. Fill the shells with this mixture.
5. Put the remaining 2 eggs through a food mill or sieve and sprinkle them over the filled shells. Serve cold.

Coquilles Saint-Jacques à l'ancienne

Old-Fashioned Style Scallops

	00:40		00:30

American	Ingredients	Metric/Imperial
2	Shallots	2
1 cup	Dry white wine	250 ml / 8 fl oz
	Salt and pepper	
12 - 18	Sea scallops	12 - 18
2 tbsp	Butter	25 g / 1 oz
1 tbsp	Flour	1 tbsp
1 cup	Crème fraîche (see page 122)	250 ml / 8 fl oz
½	Lemon	½
2	Egg yolks	2
	Bread crumbs	

1. Preheat the oven to 475°F / 240°C / Gas Mark 9. Peel the shallots and cut them into thin slices.
2. Pour the wine into a saucepan, season with salt and pepper and add the scallops. Bring to a boil and simmer for 2 minutes.

Remove from the heat and allow to cool, then remove the scallops with a slotted spoon. Set aside.
3. Add the shallots to the wine and boil until reduced to 3 tablespoons of liquid.
4. Melt the butter in a saucepan, sprinkle with the flour and brown lightly, stirring with a wooden spoon. Add the reduced wine and crème fraîche and bring to a boil, stirring. Remove from the heat. Add the juice of the ½ lemon and salt and pepper to taste. Add the egg yolks, one at a time, whisking vigorously.
5. Fill 6 scallop shells with the scallops and coat with the sauce. Sprinkle with bread crumbs and brown quickly in the hot oven.

Calmars sautés

Fried Squid

	00:30		00:30

American	Ingredients	Metric/Imperial
1½ lb	Cleaned squid	750 g / 1½ lb
2	Large onions	2
3	Garlic cloves	3
1¼ lb	Tomatoes	625 g / 1¼ lb
5 tbsp	Oil	5 tbsp
1	Bouquet garni	1
	Salt and pepper	

1. Cut the tentacles off the squid. Cut the bodies into strips and the tentacles into pieces.
2. Peel and chop the onions and garlic. Peel the tomatoes (first plunging them into boiling water for 10 seconds). Cut them into quarters, remove the seeds and coarsely chop the flesh.
3. Heat the oil in a frying pan, add the squid and cook for 3-4 minutes, stirring. Add the onions, tomatoes, garlic and bouquet garni. Season to taste with salt and pepper. Leave to cook for 30 minutes, stirring from time to time.
4. Discard the bouquet garni before serving.

Coques en salade

Cockle or Clam Salad

	00:20		00:10

American	Ingredients	Metric/Imperial
3 quarts	Cockles or small clams	3 l / 5½ pints
2 tbsp	Water	2 tbsp
1 cup	Mayonnaise (see page 119)	250 ml / 8 fl oz
1 tbsp	Chopped fresh chervil	1 tbsp
1 tbsp	Chopped fresh parsley	1 tbsp
3	Hard-cooked eggs	3

1. Put the cockles or clams into a saucepan with the water. Place over a high heat and cook, shaking the pan from time to time, until the shells open (discard any that remain closed).
2. Remove the cockles or clams from the shells, reserving any liquor. Rinse the cockles or clams to remove any sand.
3. Strain the liquor from the shells and the cooking liquid from the pan into a bowl. Add the cockles or clams and leave them in the liquid until ready to serve.
4. Drain the cockles or clams. Add the mayonnaise and stir. Sprinkle with the chervil and parsley. Quarter the eggs and arrange around the salad. Serve cold.

Araignées de mer farcies
Stuffed Spider Crabs

◣ 00:45   00:30 to 00:33 🥘

American	Ingredients	Metric/Imperial
	Sea salt	
1	Bouquet garni	1
6	Medium-size spider crabs	6
⅔ cup	Water	150 ml / ¼ pint
	Salt and pepper	
6 tbsp	Rice	6 tbsp
1 cup	Mayonnaise (see page 119)	250 ml / 8 fl oz
½ cup	Black olives, pitted [stoned]	50 g / 2 oz
2	Green peppers	2

1. Bring a saucepan of water to a boil and add a handful of sea salt and the bouquet garni. Add the crabs and cook for 15 minutes at a simmer. Remove from the heat and leave the crabs to cool in the cooking water.
2. Meanwhile, put the water into another saucepan. Add salt and bring to a boil. Pour in the rice and cook for 15-18 minutes or until tender. Drain the rice and spread out on a cloth to dry.
3. Carefully drain the crabs. Break the legs and remove the meat. Open up the shells and remove the creamy parts and the coral, as well as all the meat in the cells. Clean the shells thoroughly and put to one side.
4. Mash the coral and creamy parts. Add the mayonnaise and mix well, then add the crab meat and olives. Halve the green peppers, remove the core and seeds and dice the flesh. Add the diced peppers to the crab mixture with the rice.
5. Fill the crab shells with the crab meat mixture. Serve cold as an hors d'oeuvre on a bed of lettuce leaves.

Coquilles Saint-Jacques au beurre blanc
Scallops with White Butter Sauce

◣ 00:30   00:30 🥘

American	Ingredients	Metric/Imperial
18	Sea scallops	18
	Court-bouillon (see page 114)	
10	Shallots	10
⅔ cup	Cider vinegar	150 ml / ¼ pint
1 cup	Very cold butter	250 g / 8 oz
	Pepper	

1. Cut each scallop into 2-3 slices. Put them in a saucepan with their coral, if available, and just cover with court-bouillon. Bring slowly to a boil over a medium heat, then allow to simmer for 4-5 minutes.
2. Meanwhile, prepare the white butter sauce. Peel the shallots and chop them finely. Put them in a saucepan with the cider vinegar. Cook over a low heat until the shallots are soft and all the vinegar has evaporated. Cut the butter into small pieces and add little by little to the shallots, whisking vigorously. The mixture must not be allowed to boil. Season to taste with pepper.

3. Drain the scallops, arrange them on a serving dish and cover with the sauce. Serve immediately.

Cook's tip: if you prefer a smoother sauce, put it through a strainer before adding it to the scallops.

Coquilles Saint-Jacques à l'américaine
American Style Scallops

◣ 00:30   00:40 🥘

American	Ingredients	Metric/Imperial
1 lb	Small squid, cleaned	500 g / 1 lb
1	Garlic clove	1
6	Shallots	6
4	Tomatoes	4
1	Small carrot	1
2 tbsp	Olive oil	2 tbsp
½ cup	Butter	125 g / 4 oz
20	Sea scallops	20
1 tbsp	Tomato paste [purée]	1 tbsp
1¼ cups	Dry white wine	300 ml / ½ pint
	Cayenne pepper	
	Salt and pepper	
2 - 4 tbsp	Madeira wine or brandy	2 - 4 tbsp
1 tbsp	Chopped fresh parsley	1 tbsp

1. Cut the squid into strips. Peel and crush the garlic. Peel and chop the shallots. Peel the tomatoes (first plunging them into boiling water for 10 seconds) and coarsely chop the flesh. Peel and finely dice the carrot.
2. Heat the oil and 1 tablespoon of the butter in a saucepan. Add the scallops and cook over a high heat until lightly browned.
3. Remove the scallops with a slotted spoon. Put the squid in the saucepan and cook until all the liquid has evaporated. Add another tablespoon of butter, the shallots, carrot and garlic. Leave to soften over a medium heat, stirring frequently.
4. Add the tomato paste, white wine, a pinch of cayenne, and salt and pepper to taste. Cover and leave to cook over a low heat until the squid is tender and the sauce has thickened (about 40 minutes).
5. About 10 minutes before the end of the cooking time, add the madeira or brandy. Continue cooking uncovered. Add the scallops and heat through briefly.
6. Remove from the heat. Add the rest of the butter and stir thoroughly. Sprinkle with the chopped parsley and serve hot.

Coquilles Saint-Jacques aux feuilles d'oseille
Scallops with Sorrel

◣ 00:20   00:30 🥘

American	Ingredients	Metric/Imperial
2 lb	Sorrel leaves	1 kg / 2 lb
	Salt and pepper	
24	Sea scallops	24
¼ cup	Butter	50 g / 2 oz
1½ cups	Crème fraîche (see page 122)	350 ml / 12 fl oz

1. Trim the sorrel leaves and remove the stalks. Keep only the green part of the leaves. Wash in several changes of water, pat dry and put in a saucepan of cold salted water. Bring to a boil and cook for 20 minutes.
2. Meanwhile, cut each scallop in half. Melt the butter in a frying pan over a high heat, add the scallops and cook for 2 minutes on each side to seal them all over. Lower the heat and cook for a further 5 minutes.
3. Drain the sorrel leaves, pressing out excess moisture. Spread out on 6 heated plates. Remove the scallops from the frying pan with a slotted spoon and arrange on the sorrel.
4. Pour the crème fraîche into the frying pan. Season to taste with salt and pepper and boil to reduce for a few minutes until it thickens.
5. Pour the crème over the scallops and serve immediately.

Coquilles Saint-Jacques en brochettes

Scallop Skewers

00:30   00:05 to 00:08

American	Ingredients	Metric/Imperial
½ lb	Smoked ham	250 g / 8 oz
18	Sea scallops	18
18	Small button mushrooms	18
3 tbsp	Oil	3 tbsp

1. Preheat the oven to 425°F / 220°C / Gas Mark 7.
2. Thinly slice the ham and cut into 18 pieces. Wrap each scallop in a piece of ham. Trim the stalks from the mushrooms.
3. Thread the ham-covered scallops onto skewers, alternating with mushrooms. Brush the kebabs with oil and place in an ovenproof dish, balancing the skewers on the rim of the dish so that they can be easily turned during the cooking process.
4. Bake for 5-8 minutes, turning occasionally. Serve very hot, with barbecue sauce (see page 123).

Scallops with white butter sauce

Coquilles Saint-Jacques poêlées

Fried Scallops

00:15   00:10 to 00:15

American	Ingredients	Metric/Imperial
24	Sea scallops	24
	Flour	
⅔ cup	Olive oil	150 ml / ¼ pint
⅔ cup	Butter	150 g / 5 oz
	Salt and pepper	
2	Garlic cloves	2
1	Bunch of fresh parsley	1

1. Coat the scallops lightly in flour. Heat half of the oil in a frying pan, add the scallops and cook for about 4 minutes, stirring frequently. (Add a little more oil if necessary.)
2. Meanwhile, melt the butter in a saucepan over a low heat. Remove from the heat and cool slightly until the sediment from the butter sinks to the bottom of the pan. Carefully pour the clear part of the melted butter into another frying pan, leaving the sediment behind.
3. Remove the scallops from the oil with a slotted spoon and add them to the clarified butter. Season to taste with salt and pepper and leave to cook gently for 6-10 minutes.
4. Peel and chop the garlic. Chop the parsley. Mix the garlic with three-quarters of the parsley. About 5 minutes before the end of the cooking time, add the garlic-parsley mixture to the scallops. Stir well.
5. Serve hot, sprinkled with the rest of the chopped parsley.

Coquilles Saint-Jacques Newburg

Scallops Newburg

00:10   00:20 to 00:25

American	Ingredients	Metric/Imperial
24	Sea scallops	24
	Flour	
2 tbsp	Butter	25 g / 1 oz
2 tbsp	Brandy	2 tbsp
¾ cup	Madeira wine	175 ml / 6 fl oz
	Salt and pepper	
1	Small can of truffle peelings	1
1 cup	Crème fraîche (see page 122)	250 ml / 8 fl oz
3	Egg yolks	3

1. Cut each scallop into 2 or 3 slices, depending on their thickness. Coat the slices lightly in flour.
2. Melt the butter in a frying pan, add the scallops and cook until they are firm but not browned (about 2 minutes on each side). Add the brandy, madeira, and salt and pepper to taste. Boil briskly until the sauce is thick enough to coat the scallops.
3. Reserve some of the truffle for the garnish. Add the rest to the frying pan with the liquid in the can and 3 tablespoons of the crème fraîche. Cook over a low heat for 5-8 minutes, stirring from time to time.
4. Mix the egg yolks with the rest of the crème. Add this mixture to the pan and stir to thicken over a medium heat. Do not allow to boil.
5. Pour into a serving dish, sprinkle with the reserved truffle and serve immediately.

Scallops Newburg (see page 233)

Coquilles Saint-Jacques au safran
Scallops with Saffron

	00:20	00:30
	plus marinating	

American	Ingredients	Metric/Imperial
24	Sea scallops	24
3 tbsp	Brandy	3 tbsp
	Salt and pepper	
¼ cup	Butter	50 g / 2 oz
1 cup	Crème fraîche (see page 122)	250 ml / 8 fl oz
¼ tsp	Saffron powder	¼ tsp
	Cayenne pepper	
2	Egg yolks	2

1. Place the scallops in a mixing bowl, with their corals if available. Add the brandy, season to taste with salt and pepper and stir well. Leave to marinate for 30-40 minutes.
2. Put the 6 best corals to one side. Drain the others and mash them with a fork to make a purée. Put this purée through a food mill or sieve to make it smooth. Drain the scallops, reserving the marinade.
3. Melt the butter in a frying pan, add the scallops and cook until firm but not browned. Add the reserved marinade. Remove from the heat, cover the pan and leave to infuse for 5 minutes.
4. Remove the scallops with a slotted spoon and put to one side. Heat the butter-brandy mixture and add the crème fraîche, the puréed corals, saffron, and cayenne, salt and

pepper to taste. Bring to a boil, stirring frequently to obtain a velvety sauce. Add the scallops and the reserved whole corals.
5. Mix the egg yolks with 4 tablespoons of the sauce. Add this mixture to the remaining sauce and stir over a low heat, without boiling, until lightly thickened. Serve immediately.

Coquilles Saint-Jacques à la bretonne
Breton Style Scallops

	00:40	00:40

American	Ingredients	Metric/Imperial
6	Soft-shell crabs	6
1 tbsp	Oil	1 tbsp
1 tbsp	Butter	1 tbsp
3 tbsp	Brandy	3 tbsp
3	Shallots	3
1	Garlic clove	1
1	Fresh parsley sprig	1
1 lb	Cleaned squid	500 g / 1 lb
¼ cup	Tomato paste [purée]	4 tbsp
1¼ cups	Dry white wine	300 ml / ½ pint
	Salt and pepper	
6	Sea scallops	6

1. Rinse and drain the crabs. Heat the oil and butter in a saucepan, add the crabs and cook, stirring occasionally, until red (about 10 minutes). Add the brandy and set it alight. When the flames die down, remove the crabs with a slotted spoon.
2. Peel and chop the shallots and garlic. Chop the parsley. Add the shallots, garlic and parsley to the saucepan and cook until softened.
3. Cut the squid into small pieces and add to the saucepan. Mix the tomato paste with the wine. Add to the squid with salt and pepper to taste. Leave to cook gently for 20 minutes.
4. Add the scallops and crabs to the saucepan and continue cooking for 10 minutes. Serve hot.

Beignets de crevettes
Shrimp [Prawn] Fritters

	00:20	00:06 to 00:07
	plus resting time	

American	Ingredients	Metric/Imperial
1¼ cups	Flour	150 g / 5 oz
1 tbsp	Oil plus oil for deep frying	1 tbsp
½ cup	Water	4 tbsp
	Salt	
1	Egg white	1
1½ lb	Raw peeled shrimp [prawns]	750 g / 1½ lb

1. Sift the flour into a mixing bowl and make a well in the center. Add the tablespoon of oil, the water and a pinch of salt. Mix well. Leave to rest for 2 hours.
2. Beat the egg white into stiff peaks. Fold into the batter.
3. Heat oil for deep frying to 350°F / 180°C.
4. Dip the shrimp into the batter, then drop them into the oil. Cook for a few minutes until golden brown. Drain and serve hot, sprinkled with salt.

Coquilles Saint-Jacques à la crème

Scallops with Cream

⏲ 00:20　　　　00:20 🍲

American	Ingredients	Metric/Imperial
24	Sea scallops	24
3	Shallots	3
¼ cup	Butter	50 g / 2 oz
2 tsp	Flour	2 tsp
¼ cup	Dry white wine	4 tbsp
1 cup	Thick crème fraîche (see page 122)	250 ml / 8 fl oz
	Salt and pepper	
	Lemon juice	

1. Cut each scallop into 2 or 3 slices. Peel and finely chop the shallots.
2. Melt the butter in a saucepan, add the shallots and cook until they are soft and translucent. Add the scallops and cook, stirring, until all the moisture has evaporated. Sprinkle with the flour and stir well, then add the white wine and bring to a boil. Add the scallop coral, if available.
3. Add the crème fraîche, and salt and pepper to taste. Cover and cook over a low heat for 8-10 minutes.
4. Taste and adjust the seasoning if necessary, adding a few drops of lemon juice, and serve immediately.

Crabes farcies à l'antillaise

West Indian Style Stuffed Crabs

⏲ 00:50
plus chilling　　　　00:40 🍲

American	Ingredients	Metric/Imperial
2 quarts	Court-bouillon (see page 114)	2 l / 3½ pints
6 (1 lb)	Crabs	6 (500 g / 1 lb)
1	Small hot red pepper [chilli]	1
1	Clove	1
1	Shallot	1
2	Garlic cloves	2
¼ cup	Butter	50 g / 2 oz
¼ lb	Sausage meat	125 g / 4 oz
1 tbsp	Strong prepared mustard	1 tbsp
3 tbsp	Olive oil	3 tbsp
3 cups	Soft bread crumbs	175 g / 6 oz
3	Egg yolks	3
1 tbsp	Chopped fresh parsley	1 tbsp
	Salt and pepper	

1. Put the court-bouillon in a saucepan and bring to a boil. Add the crabs and bring back to a boil. Simmer for 15 minutes. Leave the crabs to cool in the stock.
2. Crush the hot pepper and clove. Peel and chop the shallot and garlic. Heat half of the butter in a frying pan, add the sausage meat and fry over a medium heat until lightly browned and crumbled. Drain.
3. When the crabs have cooled, drain them. Remove all the meat and the creamy part (see recipe for English style crabs). Put the shells to one side.

4. Flake the crab meat. Add the creamy part of the crab, the crushed hot pepper, clove, garlic, shallot, sausage meat, mustard, oil, two-thirds of the bread crumbs, the egg yolks, chopped parsley, and salt and pepper to taste. Mix well. Fill the crab shells with this mixture and chill for 12 hours.
5. When ready to cook, preheat the oven to 450°F / 240°C / Gas Mark 9. Sprinkle the crabs with the rest of the bread crumbs, dot with the remaining butter and bake for about 20 minutes. Serve very hot.

Coquilles Saint-Jacques aux herbes

Scallops with Herbs

⏲ 00:30　　　　00:10 to 00:15 🍲

American	Ingredients	Metric/Imperial
1 cup	Lightly salted butter	250 g / 8 oz
2 tbsp	Chopped mixed fresh herbs (tarragon, chives and parsley)	2 tbsp
	Pepper	
18 - 24	Sea scallops	18 - 24

1. Beat the butter with a wooden spoon to soften it into a paste. Add the herbs and pepper to taste. Keep cool.
2. Preheat the oven to 400°F / 200°C / Gas Mark 6.
3. Cut each scallop into 2 or 3 slices according to their thickness. Place the scallop slices in 6 scallop shells or other individual baking dishes and add a large teaspoon of herb butter to each. Arrange the filled shells on a baking sheet.
4. Bake for 10-15 minutes.

Crabes à l'anglaise

English Style Crabs

⏲ 00:15　　　　00:35 🍲

American	Ingredients	Metric/Imperial
	Salt and pepper	
6 (1 lb)	Crabs	6 (500 g / 1 lb)
6	Hard-cooked eggs	6
1 tbsp	Prepared mustard	1 tbsp
2 tbsp	Oil	2 tbsp
½ cup	Chopped fresh parsley	15 g / ½ oz
1 tsp	Vinegar	1 tsp
2 tbsp	Capers	2 tbsp

1. Bring a large saucepan of salted water to a boil. Add the crabs and bring the water back to a boil. Cook for 20 minutes.
2. Drain the crabs. Break the claws with a hammer and pick out the meat. Cut open the body shells, using a knife, along the 2 clearly drawn lines on the underside, near the legs. Separate the belly from the shell by pushing in your thumbs near the crab's mouth. Remove the creamy part from the shell and put it in a bowl. Discard all the inedible parts and add the meat to that from the claws. Dice the meat. Reserve the shells.
3. Shell the eggs. Mash 4 of them with a fork. Cut the remaining eggs into slices.
4. Mix the creamy meat from the crabs with the mashed egg, mustard and pepper to taste. Gradually add the oil, stirring constantly. Add the chopped parsley, vinegar, capers and diced crab meat. Mix thoroughly and adjust the seasoning.
5. Fill the 6 crab shells with the mixture and garnish with the egg slices. Keep cool until serving.

English style crabs (see page 235)

Crabes à l'indienne

Indian Style Crabs

	00:30		01:00

American	Ingredients	Metric/Imperial
2	Carrots	2
1	Celery stalk	1
1	Garlic clove	1
2	Large onions	2
1¼ cups	Wine vinegar	300 ml / ½ pint
1 quart	Water	1 l / 1¾ pints
1	Fresh thyme sprig	1
1	Bay leaf	1
3	Cloves	3
6	Black peppercorns	3
	Salt	
12	Medium-sized crabs	12
3 oz	Button mushrooms	75 g / 3 oz
7 tbsp	Butter	90 g / 3½ oz
6	Small tomatoes	6
1 tsp	Curry powder	1 tsp
¾ cup	Grated gruyère cheese	75 g / 3 oz

1. Peel and slice the carrots. Cut the celery into pieces about ¾ in / 2 cm in length. Peel and crush the garlic. Peel and coarsely chop the onions.

2. Pour the wine vinegar into a large saucepan. Add the water, carrots, onions, celery, sprig of thyme, bay leaf, garlic and cloves. Bring to a boil, then add the peppercorns and salt to taste. Simmer for 40 minutes.

3. Leave the stock to cool, then strain it. Add the crabs, bring to a boil and cook for 15 minutes.

4. Meanwhile, trim the mushroom stalks and slice the mushrooms thickly. Melt 3 tablespoons [40 g / 1½ oz] of the butter in a frying pan, add the mushrooms and cook over a very low heat for about 10 minutes.

5. Preheat the oven to 450°F / 240°C / Gas Mark 9.

6. Peel the tomatoes (first plunging them in boiling water for 10 seconds). Remove the seeds and purée the flesh in a food mill, blender or processor.

7. Drain the crabs. Remove all the meat and the creamy part (see English style crabs, page 235). Dice the meat, and set the shells aside.

8. Mix the creamy part of the crabs with the puréed tomatoes and curry powder. Add the mushrooms and crab meat. Mix well. Taste and adjust the seasoning.

9. Fill the crab shells with the crab mixture. Sprinkle with the cheese and dot with the remaining butter. Bake for 10 minutes. Serve hot.

Encornets farcis

Stuffed Squid

	00:30		00:40

American	Ingredients	Metric/Imperial
14	Small whole squid	14
10	Medium-sized onions	10
2	Garlic cloves	2
5 oz	Salted pork fat	150 g / 5 oz
½ cup	Olive oil	125 ml / 4 fl oz
2 tbsp	Chopped fresh parsley	2 tbsp
⅔ cup	Cooked long-grain rice	175 g / 6 oz
	Salt and pepper	
1	Strip of orange peel	1
⅓ cup	Brandy	5 tbsp
2 cups	White wine	450 ml / ¾ pint
1 tsp	Fresh thyme leaves	1 tsp
1	Bouquet garni	1
¼ cup	Tomato paste [purée]	4 tbsp
	Cayenne pepper	
1	Egg yolk	1

1. Buy whole squid, preferably all of the same size. Clean the squid, discarding the ink sac, eyes, head, bony mouth, visceral sac from the body or tail section and cartilage (or tail skeleton). Reserve the tentacles. Rinse the squid bodies under cold water without tearing them. Chop 2 of the squid bodies with the tentacles. Set the remaining 12 squid bodies aside, ready for stuffing.

2. Peel and chop 6 of the onions and 1 garlic clove. Chop the pork fat. Heat 1 tablespoon of the oil in a saucepan and add the chopped onions, garlic, pork fat, parsley and chopped squid. Cook, stirring occasionally for 5 minutes. Add the rice and season to taste with salt and pepper. Stir well. Fill each squid body with the rice mixture and close it up with a wooden toothpick.

3. Peel and chop the remaining onions. Heat 2 tablespoons of oil in a saucepan, add the onions and orange peel and leave to cook gently over a low heat until softened.

4. Meanwhile, heat 2 tablespoons oil in a frying pan, add the stuffed squid and brown quickly on all sides. As they are done, add them to the saucepan.

5. Add the brandy to the saucepan and set it alight. When the flames have died down, add the wine, remaining garlic, peeled and crushed, the thyme, bouquet garni, tomato paste, a pinch of cayenne pepper and a little salt. Leave to simmer for 40 minutes.

6. Put the egg yolk in a mixing bowl and gradually whisk in the remaining 3 tablespoons of oil. Mix with a few spoonfuls of the sauce, then stir into the remaining sauce. Discard the orange peel and bouquet garni before serving.

Crayfish in piquant wine sauce

Encornets sétoise
Squid in Chili Sauce

00:30   01:00 to 01:30

American	Ingredients	Metric/Imperial
2½ lb	Small squid	1.25 kg / 2½ lb
3	Tomatoes	3
2	Garlic cloves	2
2	Onions	2
⅔ cup	Olive oil	150 ml / ¼ pint
2 in	Piece of orange peel	5 cm / 2 in
2 tbsp	Brandy	2 tbsp
1 tbsp	Tomato paste [purée]	1 tbsp
1 cup	Dry white wine	250 ml / 8 fl oz
1	Bouquet garni	1
2	Hot red peppers [chillies]	2
	Salt and pepper	
1	Egg yolk	1

1. Clean the squid (see recipe for stuffed squid), discarding everything except the bodies. Rinse the bodies under cold running water. Pat dry with paper towels and cut into thin strips.

2. Peel the tomatoes (first plunging them in boiling water for 10 seconds) and chop the flesh coarsely. Peel and chop the garlic and onions.

3. Heat 2 tablespoons of olive oil in a frying pan. Add the strips of squid and cook over a high heat until all the moisture has evaporated. Add the onions, garlic and orange peel and stir for 3 minutes over a high heat. Add the brandy and mix well, then remove from heat and cover the frying pan. Leave to infuse for 5 minutes.

4. Put the frying pan back over the heat and add the tomatoes, tomato paste, wine, bouquet garni, hot peppers, crushed, and salt and pepper to taste. Leave to cool, covered, over a low heat for 1-1½ hours, adding a little water from time to time if necessary.

5. A few moments before serving, put the egg yolk in a mixing bowl and gradually whisk in the remaining olive oil. Add 4 tablespoons of the sauce and stir well. Take the frying pan off the heat, add the egg yolk mixture and stir well to bind the sauce. Discard the bouqet garni and serve immediately.

Crevettes grises
Boiled or Fried Shrimp

00:05   00:04 to 00:05

American	Ingredients	Metric/Imperial
2 quarts	Water	2 l / 3½ pints
6	Fresh thyme sprigs	6
4	Bay leaves	4
	Sea salt	
1 lb	Small raw shrimp	500 g / 1 lb
	Oil for deep frying	
	Bread	
	Lightly salted butter	

1. *Cooking in water:* Pour the water into a saucepan and add the thyme sprigs, bay leaves and a large handful of sea salt. Bring to a boil. Rinse the shrimp, put them into the stock and,

without waiting for it to come back to a boil, count 5 minutes cooking time. Remove from the heat and let cool for 2 minutes. Drain the shrimp and serve hot, warm or cold.

2. *Cooking in oil:* Rinse the shrimp in a strainer under cold running water and drain them on a cloth. Remove the shells. Heat oil for deep frying to 350°F / 180°C. Put in the shrimp and cook for 30 seconds. Remove the shrimp with a slotted spoon and arrange them on a dish lined with paper towels. Sprinkle with salt, and serve immediately with bread and butter.

Cooked crayfish

Écrevisses à la nage
Poached Crayfish

00:30   00:40 to 00:50

American	Ingredients	Metric/Imperial
1½ quarts	Water	1.5 l / 2½ pints
1	Bottle of dry white wine	1
12	Coriander seeds	12
1	Clove	1
1	Small bay leaf	1
½ tsp	Crushed black peppercorns	½ tsp
1	Hot red pepper [chilli]	1
12	Fennel seeds	12
	Pinch of dried savory	
1	Small fresh thyme sprig	1
	Salt	
2	Onions	2
2	Carrots	2
1	Celery stalk	1
1	Garlic clove	1
40 - 50	Crayfish	40 - 50

1. Pour the water into a large saucepan and add the wine, coriander seeds, clove, bay leaf, peppercorns, hot pepper, fennel seeds, savory, thyme sprig and salt to taste. Heat over a low heat.

2. Meanwhile, peel the onions and carrots and slice them. Chop the celery. Peel the garlic and cut it into quarters. Add these ingredients to the saucepan. Bring to a boil over a high heat, then simmer over a medium heat for 20 minutes.

3. Rinse the crayfish and clean them by pulling out the central fin of the tail, to remove the small black vein or bowel. Pat dry with paper towels.

4. Add the crayfish to the stock. Bring back to a boil and simmer for 15 minutes. Remove the crayfish with a slotted spoon. Set aside.

5. Strain the stock into another saucepan and boil to reduce it over a high heat until about 3 cups [750 ml / 1¼ pints] remain.

6. Serve the crayfish hot or cold in the reduced stock, or with the hot stock served separately in cups.

Crayfish in tomato wine sauce

Écrevisses cardinalisées

Crayfish in Piquant Wine Sauce

	00:15		01:40	

American	Ingredients	Metric/Imperial
1	Carrot	1
2	Onions	2
5	Shallots	5
2	Garlic cloves	2
1 oz	Fresh pork back fat	25 g / 1 oz
⅔ cup	Dry white wine	150 ml / ¼ pint
⅔ cup	White wine vinegar	150 ml / ¼ pint
⅓ cup	Meat gravy	5 tbsp
2½ tbsp	Brandy	2½ tbsp
2	Fresh thyme sprigs	2
½	Bay leaf	½
	Grated rind of ¼ orange	
1 tbsp	Sea salt	1 tbsp
1 tbsp	Black peppercorns	1 tbsp
	Ground white pepper	
	Cayenne pepper	
36	Crayfish	36

1. Peel the carrot, onions, shallots and garlic and chop them into dice. Cut the pork fat into small dice. Put the diced vegetables and pork fat into a stewpan and add the wine, wine vinegar, gravy, brandy, thyme sprigs, bay leaf, orange rind, sea salt, peppercorns, 2 pinches of ground white pepper and a pinch of cayenne pepper.

2. Bring to a boil and cook very gently until the sauce has reduced by half (about 1½ hours).

3. Meanwhile, rinse the crayfish and clean them by pulling out the central fin of the tail, to remove the small black vein or bowel. Pat dry with paper towels.

4. When the sauce has reduced, put in the crayfish and leave to cook for about 10 minutes.

5. Remove the crayfish with a slotted spoon and pile up in a serving dish. Strain the sauce and serve with the crayfish.

Écrevisses bordelaise

Crayfish in Tomato Wine Sauce

	00:20		00:40	

American	Ingredients	Metric/Imperial
2	Carrots	2
1	Onion	1
2	Shallots	2
1	Fresh thyme sprig	1
½ cup	Butter	125 g / 4 oz
2	Tomatoes	2
36	Crayfish	36
2 tbsp	Olive oil	2 tbsp
3 tbsp	Brandy	3 tbsp
1 tbsp	Chopped fresh parsley	1 tbsp
1 cup	Dry white wine	250 ml / 8 fl oz
	Cayenne pepper	
	Salt and pepper	

1. Peel the carrots and cut them into small dice. Peel and chop the onion and shallots. Take the leaves off the sprig of thyme. Heat 2 tablespoons [25 g / 1 oz] of the butter in a saucepan and add the carrots, onion, shallots and thyme leaves. Cover and cook over a low heat for 20 minutes.

2. Meanwhile, peel the tomatoes (plunge them in boiling water for 10 seconds first), remove the seeds and coarsely chop the flesh. Set aside. Rinse the crayfish and clean them by pulling out the central fin of the tail, to remove the small black vein or bowel. Pat dry with paper towels.

3. Heat the olive oil and 1 tablespoon of butter in a saucepan. Add the crayfish and cook, stirring, until they turn red. Add the brandy and set it alight.

4. Add the cooked vegetables, the tomatoes, half of the chopped parsley, the wine, a pinch of cayenne, and salt and pepper to taste. Bring to a boil over a high heat, then cover and cook over a low heat for 6-8 minutes, according to the size of the crayfish.

5. Remove the crayfish with a slotted spoon and keep hot. Leave the sauce to simmer, uncovered, for 10 minutes.

6. Remove the pan from the heat. Add the rest of the butter, cut into small pieces, then put the pan back over a very low heat. Stir in to bind the sauce. Taste and adjust the seasoning, adding more cayenne if liked.

7. Put the crayfish back in the sauce and reheat briefly. Pour into a warmed dish, sprinkle with the rest of the chopped parsley and serve immediately.

Homards à l'américaine
Lobsters in Rich Tomato Sauce

	00:40		00:25

American	Ingredients	Metric/Imperial
2	Carrots	2
3	Onions	3
2	Shallots	2
1	Garlic clove	1
3	Tomatoes	3
1 cup	Butter	250 g / 8 oz
1 tbsp	Oil	1 tbsp
3 (1 ½ lb)	Live lobsters	3 (750 g / 1 ½ lb)
⅓ cup	Brandy	5 tbsp
1 tbsp	Tomato paste [purée]	1 tbsp
2 cups	Dry white wine	500 ml / ¾ pint
1	Bouquet garni	1
	Cayenne pepper	
	Salt and pepper	
1 tbsp	Chopped fresh parsley	1 tbsp

1. Peel the carrots and grate them. Peel and chop the onions and shallots. Peel and crush the garlic. Peel the tomatoes (first plunging them in boiling water for 10 seconds) and chop the flesh roughly.

2. Heat 1 tablespoon of butter and the oil in a large saucepan. Add the carrots, onions and shallots. Cook over a low heat until all the ingredients have softened.

3. Meanwhile, cut up the lobsters. First sever the spinal cord by plunging a knife into the crack on top of the back between the body and tail sections. This will kill the lobster. Cut off the claws and cut the tail section from the body. Cut the tail into sections. Remove the greenish liver, or tomalley, and coral if any and put them in a mixing bowl.

4. Add the claws and tail sections to the saucepan and stir well until the shell turns red. Add the brandy and set it alight. Shake the pan gently until the flame goes out.

5. Mix the tomato paste with the wine and tomatoes. Add to the pan with the bouquet garni, garlic, a pinch of cayenne pepper, and salt and pepper to taste. Cover and cook over a medium heat for 20 minutes.

6. Remove the lobster pieces with a slotted spoon and put them on a dish. Add 2 tablespoons [25 g / 1 oz] of the butter to the lobster liver and mix well. Add this mixture to the sauce with the chopped parsley. Boil for 3 minutes over a high heat, stirring, then taste and adjust the seasoning.

7. Take the saucepan off the heat and add the rest of the butter, cut into small pieces. Whisk vigorously until the sauce is well bound. Discard the bouquet garni. Put the lobster pieces back into the sauce, reheat gently and serve immediately.

Homards grillés
Broiled [Grilled] Lobster

	00:05		00:15

American	Ingredients	Metric/Imperial
3 (1 ¼ lb)	Live lobsters	3 (625 g / 1 ¼ lb)
½ cup	Butter	125 g / 4 oz
	Lemon wedges	

1. Have the fish merchant kill the lobsters by severing the spinal cord, then split open the lobsters lengthwise.

2. Melt the butter in a bowl placed over a pan of hot water. Once the butter has melted, leave it to cool. After a moment you will see a whitish sediment form at the bottom of the bowl. Pour the melted butter very carefully into a container, leaving the sediment behind.

3. Preheat the broiler [grill].

4. Arrange the lobsters, cut sides up, in a shallow baking dish and brush them with the clarified butter. Broil for 15 minutes, brushing with more butter from time to time.

5. Serve with lemon wedges, and provide nutcrackers to break the claws.

Langoustines frites
Fried Breaded Scampi

	00:25 plus resting time	00:02 to 00:03	

American	Ingredients	Metric/Imperial
24	Scampi or Dublin Bay prawns	24
	Salt and pepper	
1	Egg	1
1 ½ tsp	Oil	1 ½ tsp
3 tbsp	Flour	3 tbsp
3 tbsp	Bread crumbs	3 tbsp
½ cup	Butter	125 g / 4 oz

1. If using frozen scampi, allow them to thaw completely. Remove the head and legs. Carefully shell the tails and take out the meat. Thread the scampi onto 6 skewers. Season with salt and pepper and leave to rest for 10 minutes.

2. Break the egg into a bowl and beat it lightly, then add the oil and mix thoroughly. Put the flour and bread crumbs into separate dishes.

3. Heat the butter in a large saucepan. (Alternatively, the scampi may be deep-fried in hot oil.)

4. Dip each skewer first into the flour, then into the beaten egg, and lastly into the bread crumbs. Fry in the butter for about 3 minutes, turning to brown evenly. Serve very hot with tartare sauce (see page 119) or mayonnaise (see page 119).

Huîtres chaudes au champagne
Hot Oysters with Champagne

	00:30		00:30

American	Ingredients	Metric/Imperial
36	Oysters	36
2	Shallots	2
1 tbsp	Butter	1 tbsp
¼ cup	Crème fraîche (see page 122)	4 tbsp
⅔ cup	Champagne	150 ml / ¼ pint
1 quantity	Hollandaise sauce (see page 126)	1 quantity

1. Open the oysters (see page 229), reserving the liquor, and set them aside on the half shell. Pour the liquor into a saucepan.

2. Peel and chop the shallots. Add them to the saucepan with the butter. Cook gently until the shallots become translucent. Add 2 tablespoons of the crème fraîche and the champagne. Leave to reduce over a low heat, stirring occasionally.
3. Meanwhile, whip the remaining crème until stiff.
4. Preheat the oven to 500°F / 250°C / Gas Mark 9.
5. Add the reduced champagne mixture to the hollandaise sauce, whisking vigorously. Fold in the whipped crème.
6. Coat each oyster with the sauce and put them on a baking sheet in the oven. Bake for a few minutes to brown. Serve hot.

Langoustines en beignets

Scampi Fritters

▬▷	00:30 plus resting time	00:20 ⊑

American	Ingredients	Metric/Imperial
1¾ cups	Flour	200 g / 7 oz
⅔ cup	Beer	5 tbsp
⅔ cup	Warm water	150 ml / ¼ pint
	Salt	
2 tbsp	Oil plus oil for deep frying	2 tbsp
	Sea salt	
24	Scampi or Dublin Bay prawns	24
2	Egg whites	2

1. Put 1¼ cups [150 g / 5 oz] of the flour in a mixing bowl. Add the beer and warm water and mix well, then add a pinch of salt and the 2 tablespoons of oil. Leave to rest for 2 hours.
2. If using raw scampi, pour 4 quarts [4 l / 7 pints] of water into a saucepan and add 2 handfuls of sea salt. Put in the scampi, bring to a boil and cook for 3-4 minutes over a high heat. Drain the scampi. (Allow frozen scampi to thaw completely.) Remove the head and legs. Carefully shell the tails, take out the meat and pat it dry on paper towels.

3. Heat oil for deep frying to 350°F / 180°C. Beat the egg whites until stiff and fold into the batter.
4. Coat the scampi lightly in the remaining flour, then dip them into the batter. Put them in the oil and fry for about 5 minutes or until golden. Remove them with a slotted spoon and arrange them on a dish lined with paper towels. Serve hot with a well-seasoned mayonnaise (see page 119) or with tartare sauce (see page 119).

Langoustes rôties

Baked Spiny Lobsters

▬▷	00:10	00:20 to 00:25 ⊑

American	Ingredients	Metric/Imperial
3 (1½ lb)	Live spiny or rock lobsters	3 (750 g / 1½ lb)
¼ cup	Olive oil	4 tbsp
1	Bunch of dried thyme	1
1 tbsp	Crumbled dried thyme	1 tbsp
3 tbsp	Pernod or Ricard	3 tbsp

1. Preheat the oven to 475°F / 240°C / Gas Mark 9.
2. Skewer each lobster under the tail and all the way along the body to keep it flat during cooking. Arrange the lobsters in an ovenproof dish and brush them with 2 tablespoons of the olive oil. Bake for 20-25 minutes.
3. Remove the skewers. Split the lobsters in half lengthwise and arrange them on a broiler [grill] rack, meat side upwards.
4. Put the leaves from the bunch of thyme in the broiler pan, add the rest of the oil and heat on top of the stove. Mix together the crumbled thyme and Pernod.
5. Put the rack holding the lobsters over the broiler pan and pour the Pernod mixture over them. Immediately set it alight, lifting up the lobsters so that everything is flamed. Serve as soon as the flames go out, together with some melted butter or lemon-flavored drawn or clarified butter (see page 113).

Shellfish

Homards hollandaise
Lobsters with Hollandaise Sauce

American	Ingredients	Metric/Imperial
3 (1 ½ lb)	Live lobsters	3 (750 g / 1 ½ lb)
4 quarts	Water	4 l / 7 pints
	Sea salt	
½ cup	Butter	125 g / 4 oz
1 tbsp	Fresh thyme leaves	1 tbsp
1 tbsp	Chopped fresh rosemary	1 tbsp
	Salt and pepper	
	Cayenne pepper	
1 tsp	Lemon juice	1 tsp
1 quantity	Hollandaise sauce (see page 126)	1 quantity

1. Have the fish merchant tie the lobster claws together. Put the water in a large saucepan with 2 large handfuls of sea salt. Put the lobsters into the water, bring to a boil and leave to simmer for 5 minutes. Take the pan off the heat and leave the lobsters in the cooking water for another 5 minutes. Drain and let cool a little.
2. Preheat the oven to 400°F / 200°C / Gas Mark 6.
3. Use scissors to detach the soft, transparent membrane under the lobster tail from both sides. Break the claws with a nutcracker or hammer, without detaching them from the body. Remove the greenish liver, or tomalley, and coral if any from the body and place them in a mixing bowl.
4. Put 2 tablespoons [25 g / 1 oz] of the butter, the thyme leaves and rosemary in a small frying pan. Melt over a low heat, without allowing the butter to foam. Season with salt, pepper and a pinch of cayenne pepper.
5. Lift the lobster tail meat and pour a little of this seasoned butter into the shells. Brush the meat with seasoned butter and put it back in the shells.
6. Add the rest of the butter to the liver and coral with the lemon juice. Heat over a very low heat, stirring, then pour this mixture into the lobster bodies.
7. Arrange the lobsters in a baking dish and bake for 12 minutes.
8. Coat with a little of the hollandaise sauce and brown quickly under the broiler [grill]. Serve immediately with the rest of the hollandaise sauce.

Langoustines nature
Scampi with Mayonnaise

American	Ingredients	Metric/Imperial
24 - 30	Scampi or Dublin Bay prawns	24 - 30
4 quarts	Water	4 l / 7 pints
	Sea salt	
1 cup	Mayonnaise (see page 119)	250 ml / 8 fl oz
	Tabasco sauce	

1. If using frozen scampi, allow them to thaw completely.
2. Put the water in a saucepan with a handful of sea salt. Put in the scampi, bring to a boil and cook for 2 minutes. Remove

the saucepan from the heat and leave the scampi in the water for 5 minutes.
3. Meanwhile, spice the mayonnaise with tabasco sauce to taste.
4. Drain the scampi in a strainer and cool them under cold running water. Serve cold with the mayonnaise.

Mussels in wine and cream

Mouclade
Mussels in Wine and Cream

American	Ingredients	Metric/Imperial
3 quarts	Fresh mussels	2 kg / 4 lb
2	Onions	2
1	Fresh thyme sprig	1
1	Bay leaf	1
1 ¼ cups	Dry white wine	300 ml / ½ pint
½	Lemon	½
	Curry powder	
	Salt and pepper	
2 tbsp	Crème fraîche (see page 122)	2 tbsp

1. Scrub the mussels thoroughly and rinse in cold water. Peel and chop the onions.
2. Place the mussels in a large pan with the onions, thyme sprig, bay leaf and wine. Cover and cook until all the mussels open. (Discard any that remain closed.)
3. Take the mussels out of the pan, discarding the empty half-shells. Keep the mussels on the half-shell hot in a dish.
4. Heat up the cooking juices and add the juice of the ½ lemon, a pinch of curry powder and salt and pepper to taste. At the last minute, stir in the crème fraîche. Pour the sauce over the mussels and serve immediately.

Macaronade de moules
Mussels in Tomato Sauce with Macaroni

00:40   00:30

American	Ingredients	Metric/Imperial
30	Large fresh mussels	30
3	Garlic cloves	3
3	Fresh parsley sprigs	3
2	Eggs	2
1½ lb	Pork sausage meat	750 g / 1½ lb
1 tbsp	Soft bread crumbs	1 tbsp
	Salt and pepper	
1 (5 oz)	Slice of salt pork [belly]	1 (150 g / 5 oz)
1	Onion	1
6 tbsp	Tomato paste [purée]	6 tbsp
3 cups	Water	750 ml / 1¼ pints
¾ lb	Macaroni	350 g / 12 oz
1 cup	Grated gruyère cheese	125 g / 4 oz

1. Scrub the mussels thoroughly and rinse with cold water. Place in a saucepan and heat until they open. (Discard any mussels that remain closed.) Drain upside-down.
2. Peel and chop the garlic. Chop the parsley. Mix together the eggs, sausage meat, garlic, parsley, bread crumbs and salt and pepper to taste in a bowl.
3. Put this filling into the mussel shells and close them up. Tie them with string so that they cannot open while cooking. Set aside.
4. Put the slice of salt pork into a pan of cold water. Bring to a boil and blanch for 3-4 minutes, then drain and rinse under cold water. Pat dry. Chop the salt pork. Peel and chop the onion.
5. Place the pork and onion in a saucepan and cook until lightly browned. Add the tomato paste and water and stir well. Add the mussels and cook for 30 minutes.
6. Meanwhile, cook the macaroni in boiling salted water for about 10 minutes or until tender but still firm.
7. Drain the macaroni and put it in a serving dish. Cover with the gruyère cheese and pour the mussels and sauce over the top. Serve immediately.

Moules Daniel
Mussels with Thyme

00:50   00:05

American	Ingredients	Metric/Imperial
50 - 60	Large fresh mussels	50 - 60
	Pepper	
3 tbsp	Crumbled thyme	3 tbsp
	Olive oil	

1. Scrub the mussels thoroughly and rinse with cold water. Open them with a knife and, as you do so, arrange them on their half-shells on a large flameproof dish.
2. Season the mussels with pepper and sprinkle with the thyme. Sprinkle a few drops of olive oil over each mussel.
3. Put the dish over a high heat and cook for about 5 minutes. When the mussels are cooked, sprinkle a little more olive oil over them and serve immediately.

Cook's tip: oil flavored with Provençal herbs is available in the shops and is ideal for this dish. It is also very useful for broiled [grilled], poached or baked fish.

Moules au fromage
Mussels with Cheese

00:30   00:20

American	Ingredients	Metric/Imperial
1½ quarts	Fresh mussels	1.5 kg / 3 lb
3	Celery stalks	3
1	Bay leaf	1
1	Fresh thyme sprig	1
1	Bunch of fresh parsley	1
⅔ cup	Water	150 ml / ¼ pint
	Salt and pepper	
½ lb	Tomatoes	250 g / 8 oz
1	Onion	1
1 cup	Grated cheddar cheese	125 g / 4 oz

1. Scrub the mussels thoroughly and rinse with cold water. Put them in a saucepan. Cut the celery into small dice. Add to the mussels with the bay leaf, thyme sprig, parsley, water and salt and pepper to taste.
2. Cover the pan and cook over a high heat for about 3 minutes, shaking the pan, until the mussels open. (Discard any mussels that remain closed.) Drain them and remove the empty half-shells. Arrange the mussels in an ovenproof dish.
3. Peel the tomatoes (first plunging them into boiling water for 10 seconds). Cut them into quarters, remove the seeds and finely chop the flesh. Peel and very finely chop the onion. Mix the cheese with the chopped tomatoes and onion. Season with salt and pepper to taste and cover each mussel with this mixture.
4. Preheat the broiler [grill]. Put the dish of mussels under the broiler and cook for about 15 minutes or until golden brown. Serve very hot.

Moules en brochettes
Mussel Kebabs

00:25   00:06

American	Ingredients	Metric/Imperial
1 quart	Fresh mussels	1 kg / 2 lb
	Salt and pepper	
5 oz	Thin smoked bacon slices	150 g / 5 oz
	Oil	

1. Scrub the mussels thoroughly and rinse with cold water. Put them in a saucepan, cover and cook over a high heat, shaking the pan from time to time, until the mussels open. (Discard any that remain closed.) Take the mussels out of their shells and season with salt and pepper.
2. Wrap the mussels, 2 at a time, in the slices of bacon and thread them onto 12 skewers.
3. Preheat the broiler [grill].
4. Baste the kebabs with oil, then arrange them under the broiler. Broil them for about 3 minutes, then turn them over and cook the other side.
5. Serve plain or with tartare sauce (see page 119).

Riz pilaf aux fruits de mer
Seafood Pilaf

	00:30		00:30

American	Ingredients	Metric/Imperial
2	Onions	2
¼ cup	Olive oil	4 tbsp
1¾ cups	Long-grain rice	350 g / 12 oz
2⅔ cups	Boiling water	600 ml / 1 pint
	Salt and pepper	
	Saffron powder	
1 pint	Clams or cockles	500 g / 1 lb
1 quart	Mussels	1 kg / 2 lb
12	Scampi or Dublin Bay prawns	12
6	Scallops	6
4	Small cleaned squid	4
3 tbsp	Flour	3 tbsp
3 tbsp	Butter	40 g / 1½ oz

1. Peel and chop the onions. Heat 2 tablespoons olive oil in a saucepan, add the chopped onions and cook until softened. Add the rice and stir for 3 minutes.
2. Remove from the heat and pour the boiling water carefully into the pan. Season to taste with salt and pepper and add a pinch of saffron. Cover the pan and leave the rice to cook for 15 minutes over a medium heat.
3. Meanwhile, scrub the clams or cockles and mussels thoroughly. Put them in a saucepan, cover and cook over a high heat, shaking the pan occasionally until they open. (Discard any that remain closed.) Drain them, take them out of their shells and rinse them under cold water to remove any sand.
4. Peel the scampi. Wipe the scallops. Cut the squid into rings.
5. Cook the squid for 15 minutes in boiling salted water. Drain and dry on paper towels.
6. Put the flour in a dish. Dip the mussels, clams or cockles, scampi, scallops and squid rings into the flour to coat on all sides. Shake to remove excess flour.
7. Heat the remaining olive oil and the butter in a frying pan. Fry all the floured ingredients in it one after the other until golden brown. When they have all been fried, put them together, season to taste with salt and pepper and add the rice. Mix well and serve immediately.

Pain aux moules
Mussel Loaf

	00:35		00:10

American	Ingredients	Metric/Imperial
1 (8 in)	Round loaf of bread	1 (20 cm / 8 in)
1	Large bunch of fresh parsley	1
3	Garlic cloves	3
4 quarts	Fresh mussels	2.5 kg / 5 lb
3 tbsp	Oil	3 tbsp
	Pepper	
1 cup	Crème fraîche (see page 122)	250 ml / 8 fl oz

1. Preheat the oven to 350°F / 180°C / Gas Mark 4.
2. With a pointed knife, cut a lid off the top of the loaf, then

scoop out the soft inside. Wrap the bread in foil and put it in the oven to heat.
3. Chop the scooped-out bread. Chop the parsley. Peel and chop the garlic.
4. Scrub the mussels thoroughly and rinse in cold water. Place the mussels in a pan, cover and cook over a high heat until they open. Remove the mussels from their shells. (Discard any mussels that remain closed.)
5. Heat the oil in a frying pan. Add the mussels, the chopped bread, parsley and garlic and stir to mix with a wooden spoon. Season lightly with pepper and cook for 2 minutes. Remove from the heat and stir in the crème fraîche.
6. Take the bread out of the oven and fill with the mussels and sauce. Put the lid back on and return to the oven to heat for 5 minutes longer.

Crêpes aux fruits de mer
Seafood Crêpes

	01:00		00:12 to 00:15

American	Ingredients	Metric/Imperial
1 quart	Fresh mussels	1 kg / 2 lb
1 quart	Clams or cockles	1 kg / 2 lb
12	Medium-sized scampi or Dublin Bay prawns	12
	Salt and pepper	
1	Shallot	1
½ cup	Butter	125 g / 4 oz
¼ lb	Cooked peeled shrimp [prawns]	125 g / 4 oz
6 tbsp	Madeira wine	6 tbsp
6 tbsp	Crème fraîche (see page 122)	6 tbsp
1	Egg yolk	1
12 (6 in)	Crêpes (see page 458)	12 (15 cm / 6 in)
1 tbsp	Flour	1 tbsp
½ cup	Grated gruyère cheese	50 g / 2 oz

1. Scrub the mussels and clams or cockles well and rinse in cold water. Put in 2 separate pans, cover and cook over a high heat until they open. (Discard any that remain closed.)
2. Strain the clam liquor (from the shells) and put to one side. Take the clams or cockles out of their shells and rinse quickly to remove any sand. Set aside. Take the mussels out of their shells and set aside.
3. Cook the scampi for 8 minutes in boiling salted water. Drain and leave to cool. Peel and cut them in half lengthwise.
4. Peel and finely chop the shallot. Heat 1 tablespoon butter in a saucepan, add the shallot and cook until softened. Add the shrimp [prawns] and 2 tablespoons of madeira. Remove from the heat, cover and leave to infuse for 10 minutes.
5. Return to the heat, uncovered, and add the clams or cockles, mussels, scampi and 1 tablespoon of crème fraîche. Season to taste with salt and pepper. Mix well. Taste and, if liked, add another tablespoon of madeira. Bring to a boil.
6. Remove from the heat. Add the egg yolk and mix carefully with a whisk. Leave to cool.
7. Preheat the oven to 475°F / 250°C / Gas Mark 9.
8. Fill each crêpe with the seafood mixture. Fold over into triangles and arrange them in an ovenproof dish.
9. Melt 2 tablespoons of butter in a heavy saucepan and add the flour. Stir in ½ cup [125 ml / 4 fl oz] of the clam liquor and the remaining madeira and crème fraîche. Season to taste with salt and pepper. Leave to cook for 10 minutes over a low heat, stirring frequently.

10. Cover the crêpes with the sauce and sprinkle them with the gruyère cheese. Place a pat of butter on each crêpe. Brown for 12-15 minutes in the oven.

Cassolettes aux fruits de mer

Seafood Ramekins

	00:30	00:30

American	Ingredients	Metric/Imperial
1 quart	Clams or cockles	1 kg / 2 lb
6	Scampi or Dublin Bay prawns	6
¾ lb	Cooked shrimp [prawns]	350 g / 12 oz
1 tbsp	Flour	1 tbsp
½ cup	Butter	125 g / 4 oz
5 tbsp	Crème fraîche (see page 122)	5 tbsp
	Salt and pepper	
10	Eggs	10

1. Wash the clams or cockles in cold water, then put them in a saucepan. Cover and cook over a high heat until the shells open. (Discard any that remain closed).
2. Remove the clams or cockles from their shells and rinse them to remove any sand. Set aside.
3. Peel the scampi and shrimp [prawns].
4. Put the flour in a dish and dip the scampi in it. Heat ¼ cup [50 g / 2 oz] of the butter in a frying pan. Add the scampi and cook until firm. Add the shrimp and stir for 3-4 minutes over a low heat. Add 2 tablespoons of the crème fraîche and salt and pepper to taste. Mix together, then add the clams or cockles. Cook, stirring, until the sauce is thick enough to coat the ingredients. Keep warm.
5. Break the eggs into a bowl, season with salt and pepper and mix the eggs without beating them. Heat the remaining butter in a thick-bottomed saucepan, pour in the eggs and stir over a very low heat until the mixture thickens. Add the remaining crème fraîche and continue to stir over a low heat until the mixture is amalgamated.
6. Add the seafood mixture to the scrambled eggs and fold together. Divide the mixture between 6 ramekins or other small dishes and serve immediately.

Moules marinière

Steamed Mussels in White Wine

	00:15 plus cooling	00:10

American	Ingredients	Metric/Imperial
2	Onions	2
½ cup	Butter	125 g / 4 oz
1 tbsp	Chopped fresh parsley	1 tbsp
2 cups	Dry white wine	500 ml / ¾ pint
3 quarts	Fresh mussels	2 kg / 4 lb
	Lemon juice	
	Salt and pepper	

1. Peel and chop the onions. Heat the butter in a saucepan, add the onions and cook over a low heat until softened but not browned. Add the chopped parsley and white wine. Bring to a boil. Remove from the heat, cover and leave to cool.
2. Meanwhile, scrub the mussels thoroughly and rinse in cold water. Add them to the saucepan. Add a few drops of lemon juice and salt and pepper to taste.
3. Place the covered pan over a high heat and cook, shaking the pan to cook the mussels evenly, until they open. (Discard any that remain closed.)
4. Serve very hot.

Cook's tip: accompany this dish with french or italian bread.

Timbale de fruits de mer

Seafood Mold

	00:30	00:40

American	Ingredients	Metric/Imperial
1	Lobster tail	1
12	Scampi or Dublin Bay prawns	12
½ lb	Sole fillets	250 g / 8 oz
2	Onions	2
1	Garlic clove	1
2	Tomatoes	2
¼ cup	Olive oil	4 tbsp
12	Scallops	12
2 cups	Dry white wine	500 ml / ¾ pint
1	Fresh thyme sprig	1
1	Bay leaf	1
5	Rosemary leaves	5
2	Lemon slices	2
⅔ cup	Water	150 ml / ¼ pint
1 tsp	Cornstarch [cornflour]	1 tsp
	Salt and pepper	
	Cayenne pepper	
1 tsp	Tomato paste [purée]	1 tsp

1. Remove the lobster meat from the shell and reserve the shell. Cut the meat into round slices. Pull the heads off the scampi and keep the heads. Peel the scampi and set aside. Chop the fillets of sole.
2. Peel the onions and cut them into thin slices. Peel and crush the garlic. Peel the tomatoes (plunge them into boiling water for 10 seconds first), then cut them in half, remove the seeds and coarsely chop the flesh.
3. Heat 3 tablespoons olive oil in a saucepan, add the scallops and the pieces of lobster meat and stir for 2 minutes over a high heat. Remove the scallops and lobster with a slotted spoon. Put the scampi in the saucepan and stir for 4 minutes over a high heat. Remove. Put the sole in the saucepan, stir until firm and remove.
4. Add the remaining oil to the saucepan and heat it, then add the scampi heads, lobster shell, onions and garlic. Stir for 3 minutes over a medium heat. Add the wine, chopped tomatoes, thyme sprig, bay leaf, rosemary leaves, lemon slices and water. Cover and simmer over a low heat for 20 minutes.
5. Mix the cornstarch with 1 tablespoon of water.
6. When the sauce is cooked, put it through a strainer over another saucepan. Press all the solids with a wooden spoon to extract as much liquid as possible. Season to taste with salt and pepper and a pinch of cayenne. Add the tomato paste and dissolved cornstarch. Stir over a low heat until the sauce is thickened and well mixed.
7. Add the scallops, lobster, scampi and sole to the sauce. Heat through gently, stirring, and serve hot.

Moules poulette
Mussels in Cream Sauce

	00:25	02:25

American	Ingredients	Metric/Imperial
1	Onion	1
6 tbsp	Butter	75 g / 3 oz
3 quarts	Fresh mussels	2 kg / 4 lb
⅔ cup	Dry white wine	150 ml / ¼ pint
10	Black peppercorns	10
1	Bouquet garni	1
1 tbsp	Flour	1 tbsp
1 cup	Crème fraîche (see page 122)	250 ml / 8 fl oz
2	Egg yolks	2
½	Lemon	½
	Salt and pepper	
1 tbsp	Chopped fresh parsley	1 tbsp

1. Peel and finely chop the onion. Melt 2 tablespoons [25 g / 1 oz] of the butter in a saucepan, add the chopped onion and cook over a low heat until it is soft.
2. In the meantime, scrub the mussels thoroughly and rinse in cold water.
3. When the onion is soft, add the white wine, peppercorns and bouquet garni. Boil for 1 minute. Add the mussels and cover the pan. Cook over a high heat, shaking the pan, until the mussels open. (Discard any mussels that remain closed.)
4. Remove all the empty shells and keep mussels on their half-shells hot. Strain the cooking liquid and reserve.
5. Melt the rest of the butter in a saucepan, sprinkle in the flour and stir over a low heat until the mixture is golden. Add the reserved cooking liquid and cook, stirring, over a low heat to thicken the sauce.
6. Mix the crème fraîche with the egg yolks and the juice of the ½ lemon. Add this mixture to the sauce and heat without allowing it to boil. Add salt and pepper to taste and the chopped parsley.
7. Put the mussels in the sauce, mix well and serve at once.

Soupe aux palourdes
Clam Soup

	00:15	00:30

American	Ingredients	Metric/Imperial
3	Leeks	3
3	Potatoes	3
3 tbsp	Butter	40 g / 1½ oz
1 quart	Water	1 l / 1¾ pints
1 quart	Clams	1 kg / 2 lb
	Salt and pepper	
⅔ cup	Crème fraîche (see page 122)	150 ml / ¼ pint
2	Egg yolks	2

1. Trim the roots off the leeks, remove the tops of the green leaves and split the leeks lengthwise into 4. Wash under running water and drain. Chop them finely. Peel the potatoes and cut into dice.
2. Heat the butter in a saucepan, add the leeks and potatoes and cook until softened without browning. Stir frequently. Add the water and simmer until the potatoes are very soft.

3. Meanwhile, scrub the clams thoroughly. Place them in a saucepan, cover and cook over a high heat, shaking the pan, until the shells open. (Discard any that remain closed.) Remove the clams from their shells and rinse off any sand. Strain the clam liquor (from the shells) and set aside.
4. Purée the leek and potato mixture in a blender or food processor, and return it to the saucepan. Season with a little salt and pepper. Add the clam liquor and enough water to make the liquid up to 2 quarts [2 l / 3½ pints]. Heat through until the mixture is piping hot.
5. Mix the crème fraîche with the egg yolks. Add the clams to the soup and heat for a few seconds, then add the egg and crème mixture. Stir for a few moments (do not allow to boil.) Serve in heated cups.

Soufflé aux fruits der mer
Seafood Soufflé

	00:40	00:35

American	Ingredients	Metric/Imperial
3	Scallops	3
5 oz	Sole fillets	150 g / 5 oz
2	Shallots	2
7 tsp + ¼ cup	Flour	7 tsp + 50 g / 2 oz
6	Small scampi or Dublin Bay prawns	6
5 tbsp	Butter	65 g / 2½ oz
⅔ cup	Dry white wine	150 ml / ¼ pint
	Salt and pepper	
1 tsp	Tomato paste [purée]	1 tsp
½ cup	Crème fraîche (see page 122)	125 ml / 4 fl oz
1 cup	Milk	250 ml / 8 fl oz
4	Eggs, separated	4

1. Cut the scallops into 2 or 3 slices. Cut the sole fillets into dice. Peel the shallots and cut into thin slices. Put 6 teaspoons of flour on a plate and dip the scallops and sole into it, then shake the pieces to remove excess flour and set aside.
2. Pull the heads off the scampi. Heat 2 tablespoons butter in a frying pan, add the scampi and stir for 3 minutes over a high heat. Remove the scampi, peel and put to one side.
3. Preheat the oven to 400°F / 200°C / Gas Mark 6.
4. Heat another teaspoon butter in the frying pan, add the shallots and soften over a low heat. Add the scallops and cook for 2-3 minutes or until they are just firm. Remove the scallops with a slotted spoon.
5. Add the sole dice and cook until just firm, then remove.
6. Add the wine to the frying pan. Bring to a boil and boil for 2 minutes. Add the scampi, scallops and sole. Season to taste with salt and pepper and mix well.
7. Put aside 3 tablespoons of the cooking juices. To the remainder add the tomato paste and the crème fraîche mixed with 1 teaspoon of flour. Stir for 5 minutes over a low heat.
8. Melt the remaining ¼ cup [50 g / 2 oz] butter in a saucepan. Add the remaining ¼ cup [50 g / 2 oz] flour and stir for 2 minutes. Add the milk and reserved 3 tablespoons of seafood cooking juice and mix with a whisk over a low heat until smooth. Remove from the heat and season to taste with salt and pepper. Add the yolks, one at a time, mixing them in thoroughly. Beat the egg whites into stiff peaks and fold them into the mixture.
9. Cover the bottom of a buttered 6½ in / 16 cm soufflé dish with the seafood mixture and spoon the soufflé mixture on top. Bake for 30 minutes. Serve immediately.

Preparing lobster

A simple to follow step-by-step guide to cooking a live lobster at home, then getting it ready for immediate eating, or for further cooking. If you haven't a special lobster pick or shell cracker, a spoon and hammer will do.

1. Before cooking a freshly caught lobster, sever the nerve cord with the point of a sharp knife where the head meets the body. Close the claws with rubber bands; with spiny lobsters, push antennae beneath body and tie round with string. Place in pan filled with cold water, cover firmly, and bring to a boil over moderate heat. Simmer for 15 minutes for first lb (450 g) and 10 minutes for each additional one.

2. Hold the cooked, drained and cooled lobster firmly with one hand and cut centrally through the shell – you need a sharp knife. Cut evenly through the shell and flesh.

5. Using a specially designed lobster pick or a spoon, remove the stomach (a hard sac near the head) and the intestinal vein. As this runs beneath the flesh, ease the flesh out of the shell with the pick or a curved grapefruit knife, then pull out the vein and discard it.

6. Use the pick or a knife to cut the flesh into bite-size pieces, then reassemble it back in the half shells – they can be rubbed with oil.

3. If you prefer you can divide the lobster in two starting at the tail end; then turn it, head towards you, and cut through the body. This is the best way of halving spiny lobster.

7. The claws and antennae are quite easily broken off by hand – just twist them at the joint, pull away and break in two to reveal flesh.

4. The bright roe or coral commonly found in female lobsters is a sort of inbuilt garnish to the flesh. The khaki-colored liver (tomalley) can be eaten or included in sauces.

8. Use kitchen scissors, a nutcracker or even a hammer to crack the shell so that the flesh in the claw can be removed in one piece.

9. The small part of the claw can be pulled away – lobster lovers even suck the gristly cartilage to savor all that the lobster has to offer.

Preparation

Buying fish

You can be sure that fish is fresh if it has:
- a pleasant, fresh smell with a hint of iodine
- bright, bulging eyes that fill their sockets
- pink or red gills, never gray
- shiny scales firmly adhered to the skin
- firm compact flesh that clings on to the backbone
- a rigid backbone. To test this, grasp the fish by the head and tail and pull. If it does not stretch, it is fresh, since softening of the backbone is one of the first signs of deterioration.

> ### Preparing salt cod
> Salt cod must be completely desalted before it is cooked. To do this, cut the fish into pieces and soak them in 3 or 4 changes of fresh water in a large container. The process will take 24 hours for a tail and 12 hours for fillets.

Storing fish

Fish keeps its freshness for a very short time indeed, so try to buy it on the day it is to be eaten. If you must keep it overnight, rinse it quickly under running water, wipe it carefully, wrap it in foil and put it in the refrigerator.

Frozen fish can be cooked without thawing if you double the cooking time.

Preparing fish

Scaling
Hold the fish by the tail and with the blade of a knife scrape off the scales, working towards the head.

Trimming
Using the scissors, cut off the back fin and the side, lower and tail fins.

Gutting the fish through the belly
With a sharp knife, make an incision through the belly of the fish. Grasp the end of the intestine nearest the head and pull it away along the length of the slit. Cut the intestine at the tail end.

Gutting the fish through the gills
Slip your index finger into the gills, bending it to make a hook, and gently pull out the intestine. Draw out the gills and the guts.

Skinning a flat fish
1. Cut off the fins on both sides. Lay the fish flat on a chopping board, brown side up, and score the skin with your fingernail or a sharp knife along the lines where the tail and fins meet the body.

2. Insert your thumb between the flesh and the skin at the tail end and use it to work the skin free. Hold the flesh steady with one hand and use the other to pull the brown skin. It will come off all at once. When you reach the head, remove the second (white) skin by detaching it under the jaw and sliding your thumb along underneath to lift it. Repeat on the white side.

Filleting a flat fish
1. Lay the fish flat on a chopping board. Mark out the fillets with a flexible knife, sliding the blade between the pinkish edges and the whiter flesh.

3. Lift the fillets by sliding the blade of the knife underneath them and cutting gently along the backbone. Turn the fish over and repeat.

2. Separate the 2 fillets by sliding the point of a knife along the backbone.

4. Gently flatten the fillets with a wooden spatula to stop them curling up during cooking.

Filleting a round fish
1. Place the cleaned fish on its right side. Holding the fish by its belly, insert the point of a knife in the back, close to the head. Cut all along the back fin.

3. To remove the lower fillet, turn the fish over and slide the blade of a knife along the backbone in the same way.

2. Make a deep cut just behind the head. Starting at the head, insert a knife between the flesh and the backbone and remove the fillet by sliding the knife gently toward the tail.

4. To skin the fillets, place them skin side downward on a cutting board and slide the blade of a knife, angled at a slant, between the skin and the flesh.

Boning a round fish
1. Gut and trim the fish. Use a small, pointed knife to extend the slit in the belly from the anal orifice to the tail.

2. Pull the two halves of the fish apart and remove the ribs (break them to detach them from the backbone). Then remove the backbone.

Skinning an eel
1. Make a cut right around the neck behind the head. Pull back the skin at this point (this is not easy; you may find it helps to hold the head in a pair of pliers). Hold the eel and skin with a cloth and pull the skin off backwards. It will come off all at once.

2. Slide the knife under the intestine and remove the guts.

Alose au beurre blanc

Shad with White Butter Sauce

⏱ 00:20　　　　00:40 🍲

American	Ingredients	Metric/Imperial
1 (3 lb)	Shad, scaled and cleaned	1 (1.5 kg / 3 lb)
2 tbsp	Marc or brandy	2 tbsp
3	Lemons	3
	Court-bouillon (see page 114)	
1¼ cups	Dry white wine	300 ml / ½ pint
1	Bouquet garni	1
9	Shallots	9
	Salt and pepper	
1 cup	Butter	250 g / 8 oz
1 tbsp	Crème fraîche (see page 122)	1 tbsp

1. Preheat the oven to 425°F / 220°C / Gas Mark 7.
2. Carefully rinse the shad in cold water, then wipe dry with paper towels. Pour the marc inside the fish. Thinly slice 1 lemon.
3. Place the fish in an ovenproof dish. Add enough court-bouillon to come halfway up the fish. Add half of the white wine and the bouquet garni, and put the lemon slices on the fish. Cover with foil and bake for about 40 minutes.
4. Meanwhile, make the sauce. Peel and chop the shallots. Put them in a saucepan with the remaining wine and salt and pepper to taste. Boil to reduce the liquid by two-thirds.
5. Cut the butter into small pieces. When the sauce has reduced, add the butter all at once, whisking vigorously, then add the crème fraîche, continuing to whisk. This will prevent the sauce from curdling. Pour the sauce into a warmed sauceboat.
6. Drain the fish and place on a warmed serving dish. Garnish with the remaining lemons, cut into quarters, and serve immediately with the white butter sauce.

Anguilles en matelote

Eels in Red Wine Stew

⏱ 00:40　　　　00:15 🍲

American	Ingredients	Metric/Imperial
2 lb	Fresh eels	1 kg / 2 lb
1	Medium-size onion	1
10 tbsp	Butter	150 g / 5 oz
1 tbsp	Oil	1 tbsp
1½ tsp	Flour	1½ tsp
1 quart	Red wine	1 l / 1¾ pints
2 tbsp	Brandy or marc	2 tbsp
2	Garlic cloves	2
1	Small ripe tomato	1
	Salt and pepper	
10	Pearl [button] onions	10
5 oz	Smoked bacon	150 g / 5 oz
½ lb	Mushrooms	250 g / 8 oz
	Lemon juice	

1. Clean and skin the eels, then cut them into segments.
2. Peel and chop the medium-size onion. Heat 2 tablespoons

[25 g / 1 oz] butter and the oil in a saucepan, add the chopped onion and cook until softened. Sprinkle in the flour and stir well. Add the pieces of eel and brown them all over.
3. Bring the wine to a boil in another saucepan. Heat the brandy or marc and pour over the eels. Set alight and shake the pan until the flames go out. Add the boiling red wine. Stir well.
4. Peel and chop the garlic. Peel the tomato (first plunging it into boiling water for 10 seconds), remove the seeds and crush the flesh. Add the garlic and tomato to the saucepan. Season to taste with salt and pepper and mix together. Cook for 15 minutes over a medium heat.
5. Peel the small onions. Heat ¼ cup [50 g / 2 oz] butter in a frying pan, add the onions and brown lightly on all sides. Add them to the saucepan.
6. Cut the bacon into dice and blanch for 5 minutes in boiling water. Drain and add to the saucepan.
7. Slice the mushrooms. Heat ¼ cup [50 g / 2 oz] butter in the frying pan, add the mushrooms and brown lightly. Add them to the saucepan.
8. Take the pieces of eel out of the saucepan and keep them hot in a serving dish.
9. Reduce the cooking liquid by half over a high heat. Remove from the heat and add the rest of the butter, whisking well. Add a few drops of lemon juice.
10. Coat the eel pieces with the sauce and serve.

Bar au cidre

Bass with Cider

⏱ 00:20　　　　00:50 🍲

American	Ingredients	Metric/Imperial
1 (4 lb)	Bass	1 (2 kg / 4 lb)
1	Carrot	1
2	Onions	2
1	Celery stalk	1
1	Bouquet garni	1
2 lb	White fish bones and trimmings	1 kg / 2 lb
	Salt and pepper	
2 quarts	Water	2 l / 3 pints
1 cup	Hard [dry] cider	250 ml / 8 fl oz
2 tsp	Butter	2 tsp
1 tsp	Cornstarch [cornflour]	1 tsp
⅔ cup	Crème fraîche (see page 122)	150 ml / ¼ pint
½	Lemon	½

1. Clean and scale the bass, reserving the head and trimmings. Cut the fish into 6 thick slices. Set aside.
2. Peel and thinly slice the carrot and onions. Thinly slice the celery. Put the vegetables in a large saucepan with the bouquet garni, fish bones and trimmings (including the bass head and trimmings) and ½ teaspoon salt. Add the water. Bring to a boil and cook over a high heat for 20-25 minutes. Strain the fish stock and leave to cool.
3. Preheat the oven to 400°F / 200°C / Gas Mark 6.
4. Arrange the 6 fish slices in a buttered ovenproof dish. Add the cider and 1 ladle of the stock. Season to taste with pepper.
5. Put the dish in the oven. When the liquid starts to simmer, cook for 15-20 minutes. Do not allow to boil.
6. Meanwhile, mash the butter and cornstarch to a paste.
7. Remove the fish pieces with a slotted spoon and arrange them on a hot serving dish. Keep warm. Strain the cooking juices into a saucepan and boil them to reduce.
8. Add the crème fraîche, whisk and add the juice of the

½ lemon. Taste and adjust the seasoning, adding a little more salt and pepper if necessary. Take the saucepan off the heat and add the butter and cornstarch mixture. Whisk well, then put back over the heat to thicken, still whisking. Coat the fish with the sauce and serve immediately.

Barbue farcie à l'oseille

Brill or Flounder with Sorrel Stuffing

00:30   00:40

American	Ingredients	Metric/Imperial
1 (4 lb)	Brill or flounder	1 (2 kg / 4 lb)
5	Shallots	5
1½ lb	Sorrel or spinach	750 g / 1½ lb
6 tbsp	Butter	75 g / 3 oz
2 cups	Dry white wine	500 ml / ¾ pint
	Salt and pepper	
1 tbsp	Flour	1 tbsp
1 cup	Crème fraîche (see page 122)	250 ml / 8 fl oz
2	Egg yolks	2

1. Preheat the oven to 350°F / 180°C / Gas Mark 4.
2. Have the fish filleted and keep the head and backbone.
3. Peel and chop the shallots. Rinse, drain and trim the sorrel. Heat 2 tablespoons [25 g / 1 oz] butter in a flameproof dish, add the chopped shallots and soften without browning. Add the fish backbone and head as well as the fillets (flattened with a spatula). Add the white wine and enough water so that the ingredients are just covered with liquid. Season to taste with salt and pepper. Bring to a boil over a low heat, then remove from the heat, cover the dish and poach the fillets for 10 minutes.
4. Meanwhile, heat the rest of the butter in a frying pan, add the sorrel leaves and soften them over a low heat, stirring. Sprinkle with the flour and mix together, then add 4 tablespoons of the crème fraîche and salt and pepper to taste. Cook, stirring, until thickened.
5. Remove the fillets with a slotted spoon and cut them into 12 pieces. Reserve the cooking liquid.
6. Put aside 2 tablespoons of the sorrel mixture, and spread the fish pieces with the rest. Arrange them in an ovenproof dish. Mix the rest of the crème fraîche with the egg yolks.
7. Strain the fish cooking liquid and return to the saucepan. Boil to reduce over a high heat until only about 1 cup [250 ml / 8 fl oz] remains. Add the reserved sorrel and crème and egg yolk mixture. Stir over a low heat, without allowing to boil, until thickened. Coat the fish with this sauce.
8. Bake for about 10 minutes until the top is lightly browned. Serve immediately.

Baked bass

Bar rôti
Baked Bass with Lemon

	00:10	00:30

American	Ingredients	Metric/Imperial
1 (3 lb)	Bass, cleaned and scaled	1 (1.5 kg / 3 lb)
	Salt and pepper	
6	Shallots	6
½ lb	Mushrooms	250 g / 8 oz
2	Lemons	2
1	Bouquet garni	1
2 cups	Dry white wine	500 ml / ¾ pint
¼ cup	Oil	4 tbsp

1. Preheat the oven to 450°F / 230°C / Gas Mark 8.
2. Wipe the bass. Make some slashes on the back of the fish and season with pepper. Place the fish in a buttered ovenproof dish.
3. Peel and chop the shallots. Thinly slice the mushrooms. Cut one lemon into slices. Surround the fish with the shallots and mushrooms and put the lemon slices on top. Add the bouquet garni. Pour over the wine, the juice of the second lemon and the oil.
4. Put the dish in the oven and cook for 30 minutes, basting the fish frequently with the juices and only adding salt after the first 15 minutes. Cover the fish with foil if it seems to be drying out too much.

Bar à la Dugléré
Bass with Tomato Sauce and Mushrooms

	00:30	00:30

American	Ingredients	Metric/Imperial
6	Medium-size tomatoes	6
2	Onions	2
2	Shallots	2
2	Garlic cloves	2
¾ lb	Mushrooms	350 g / 12 oz
1 (3 lb)	Bass	1 (1.5 kg / 3 lb)
3 tbsp	Chopped fresh parsley	3 tbsp
1	Bouquet garni	1
	Salt and pepper	
½ cup	Butter	125 g / 4 oz
2 cups	Dry white wine	500 ml / ¾ pint
2 tbsp	Oil	2 tbsp
1 tbsp	Flour	1 tbsp
	Cayenne pepper	

1. Preheat the oven to 400°F / 200°C / Gas Mark 6.
2. Peel the tomatoes (first plunging them in boiling water for 10 seconds) and chop them coarsely. Peel and chop the onions, shallots and garlic. Slice the mushrooms.
3. Clean and scale the bass and cut into 6 thick slices.
4. Generously butter an ovenproof dish and cover the bottom with half the tomatoes, onions and shallots. Add the garlic and parsley, and arrange the fish pieces over this layer. Cover with the rest of the tomatoes, onions and shallots. Add the bouquet garni and salt and pepper to taste. Dot ¼ cup [50 g / 2 oz]

butter, cut into pieces, over the top, then add the white wine. Put the dish in the oven and cook for 30 minutes.
5. Meanwhile, heat the oil in a frying pan and add the mushrooms. Stir thoroughly and season with salt and pepper, then leave to cook until all the moisture has evaporated. Keep hot. Mash 1 tablespoon of butter with the flour to make a paste. Set aside.
6. When the fish pieces are cooked, remove them with a slotted spoon and arrange them on a serving dish. Keep hot. Pour the cooking juices into a saucepan. Remove the bouquet garni and evaporate half the liquid by boiling over a high heat.
7. Whisk in the butter and flour mixture and adjust the seasoning, adding a pinch of cayenne pepper. Remove from the heat and add the rest of the butter, cut into small pieces, still whisking.
8. Coat the fish with the sauce. Surround with the mushrooms and serve immediately.

Fried anchovies

Anchois frits
Fried Anchovies

	00:40	00:05 to 00:06
		per batch

American	Ingredients	Metric/Imperial
2¾ lb	Fresh anchovies or other very small oily fish	1.25 kg / 2¾ lb
	Oil for deep frying	
	Flour	
	Salt and pepper	

1. Clean the anchovies by removing the heads. Rinse, then pat dry with paper towels.
2. Heat the oil to 345°F / 175°C.
3. Season some flour with salt and pepper. Coat the anchovies in it and shake them so that they retain only a thin film of flour. Arrange a batch of anchovies in a frying basket in one layer. (They must not stick together.)
4. Put into the oil and cook until the fish are just firm and golden brown, about 6 minutes. Drain on paper towels. Keep hot until all the anchovies have been fried.

5. Small fried fish soften quickly, so do not cook them too far in advance. Serve with bread, butter and lemon wedges.

Anguilles au vert
Eels in Green Sauce

◣▱ 00:30   00:20 to 00:30 ◥

American	Ingredients	Metric/Imperial
4 lb	Fresh medium-size eels	2 kg / 4 lb
½ lb	Sorrel or spinach	250 g / 8 oz
½ lb	Watercress	250 g / 8 oz
2	Onions	2
3	Celery stalks	3
¼ cup	Butter	50 g / 2 oz
1	Bottle of white wine	1
¾ cup	Chopped fresh parsley	25 g / 1 oz
¾ cup	Chopped fresh chervil	25 g / 1 oz
1 tsp	Chopped fresh sage	1 tsp
1 tsp	Chopped fresh mint	1 tsp
1 tsp	Chopped fresh savory	1 tsp
	Salt and pepper	
6	Egg yolks	6
1 cup	Crème fraîche (see page 122)	250 ml / 8 fl oz
	Lemon juice	

1. Clean and skin the eels (or have this done for you), then cut them into segments.
2. Trim the sorrel, removing the stalks and keeping only the green part of the leaves. Rinse it, drain well and cut it into thin strips. Remove the stalks from the watercress, rinse it and dry well.
3. Peel and finely chop the onions and celery. Heat the butter in a saucepan, add the onions and celery and soften over a medium heat.
4. Add the eel pieces and cook until they are just firm.
5. Add the wine, sorrel, watercress and herbs. Season to taste with salt and pepper. Cover and simmer for 15 minutes.
6. Remove from the heat. Add the egg yolks mixed with the crème fraîche, whisking vigorously. Add a few drops of lemon juice. Heat without boiling, stirring constantly, and serve hot or cold.

Bonite au four
Baked Bonito with Fennel

◣▱ 00:40   00:45 ◥

American	Ingredients	Metric/Imperial
1 (3 lb)	Bonito or tuna	1 (1.5 kg / 3 lb)
3	Garlic cloves	3
1	Small sweet red or green pepper	1
3	Fresh fennel sprigs	3
⅔ cup	Olive oil	150 ml / ¼ pint
	Salt and pepper	
1	Bunch of fresh thyme	1
1	Fresh rosemary sprig	1

1. Clean the fish, wipe it and put it in an ovenproof dish. Make 3 or 4 slashes on the top of the fish.
2. Peel and thinly slice one clove of garlic. Remove the core and seeds from the pepper and cut it into strips. Insert the garlic slices and pepper strips in the cuts in the fish. Stuff the fish with fennel sprigs.
3. Pour the olive oil into a bowl and season to taste with salt and pepper. Add the remaining garlic, peeled and crushed. Make a brush with the bunch of thyme and sprig of rosemary. Dip it into the flavored oil and brush the fish several times. Leave to marinate for at least 30 minutes.
4. Preheat the oven to 425°F / 220°C / Gas Mark 7.
5. Place the fish in the oven and bake for 45 minutes, basting it several times with the flavored oil.

Quenelles de brochet
Pike Dumplings

◣▱ 01:30   01:00 ◥

American	Ingredients	Metric/Imperial
1¼ cups	Water	300 ml / ½ pint
1¼ cups + 2 tbsp	Butter	300 g / 11 oz
	Salt and pepper	
1¼ cups	Flour	200 g / 8 oz
6	Eggs	6
1 (2 lb)	Pike, filleted	1 (1 kg / 2 lb)
	Cayenne pepper	
1 quart	Milk	1 l / 1¾ pints
	Grated nutmeg	
⅔ cup	Crème fraîche (see page 122)	150 ml / ¼ pint

1. Place the water and 2 tablespoons [25 g / 1 oz] of the butter in a saucepan. Add a pinch of salt. Bring to a boil, then remove from the heat and add ¾ cup [100 g / 4 oz] flour all at once, stirring vigorously. Stir over the heat to dry this paste. Remove from the heat again and add one egg, stirring quickly and carefully. Leave to cool completely, then place the panada in the refrigerator to chill.
2. Meanwhile, take the skin off the pike fillets. Put the flesh through a grinder [mincer] or food processor. Chill for 1 hour.
3. Put the bowl containing the puréed pike in a bowl of crushed ice. Season with salt, pepper and a pinch of cayenne and mix with a wooden spatula. Add the panada and stir over the ice until amalgamated. Add the remaining eggs, one at a time, stirring well.
4. Soften ¾ cup [175 g / 6 oz] butter with a wooden spatula and add it to the mixture. Work all the ingredients thoroughly together to obtain a fine homogeneous paste.
5. Flour your hands. Divide the paste into balls and roll them on a floured worktop to obtain cylinders 2½ in / 6 cm long and 1 in / 2.5 cm in diameter.
6. Heat a saucepan of water to 175°F / 90°C and poach the dumplings in it for 15 minutes, without allowing the water to boil. Remove the dumplings with a slotted spoon, put in cold water to cool and then drain.
7. Preheat the oven to 400°F / 200°C / Gas Mark 6.
8. Melt the remaining ½ cup [100 g / 4 oz] butter in a saucepan, add the remaining ½ cup [100 g / 4 oz] flour and mix well. Add the milk. Leave to thicken over a medium heat, stirring constantly, then season with salt, pepper and a pinch of grated nutmeg. Stir in the crème fraîche.
9. Butter a gratin dish and arrange the dumplings in it. Coat with the white sauce. Bake for 15 minutes. Serve at once.

Brochet au beurre blanc

Pike with White Butter Sauce

	00:20		01:25

American	Ingredients	Metric/Imperial
4	Carrots	4
3	Onions	3
3 quarts	Water	3 l / 5 pints
2 cups	Dry white wine	450 ml / ¾ pint
1	Bouquet garni	1
4	Cloves	4
8	Black peppercorns	8
	Salt and pepper	
1 (3 lb)	Pike, cleaned and scaled	1 (1.5 kg / 3 lb)
10	Shallots	10
1 cup	Very cold butter	250 g / 8 oz
1 tbsp	Crème fraîche (see page 122)	1 tbsp

1. Peel the carrots and onions and cut them into slices. Pour the water into a fish kettle or large saucepan and add 1¼ cups [300 ml / ½ pint] of the wine, the carrots, onions, bouquet garni, cloves, peppercorns and salt to taste. Bring to a boil and simmer for 30 minutes.
2. Add the pike and cook for 40 minutes over a medium heat.
3. Meanwhile, prepare the sauce. Peel the shallots and chop them finely. Put them in a saucepan with the remaining wine and boil over a moderate heat until the liquid has reduced by two-thirds (15 minutes).
4. Cut the butter into small pieces. When the sauce has reduced, add the butter all at once, whisking vigorously. Once the sauce has whitened, add the crème fraîche, then remove from the heat. Add salt and pepper to taste.
5. Drain the fish and put it on a serving platter. Cover with a little of the sauce and serve the rest separately.

Cabillaud au Chablis

Cod in White Wine

	00:20		00:40 to 00:50

American	Ingredients	Metric/Imperial
6	Shallots	6
4	Tomatoes	4
¼ cup	Butter	50 g / 2 oz
	Pinch of dried thyme	
½	Bay leaf	½
	Few fresh parsley stalks	
6 (6 oz)	Cod steaks	6 (175 g / 6 oz)
	Salt and pepper	
1	Bottle of dry white wine	1
2 tbsp	Crème fraîche (see page 122)	2 tbsp
	Lemon juice	
2 tbsp	Chopped fresh herbs (parsley, tarragon and chervil)	2 tbsp

1. Preheat the oven to 400°F / 200°C / Gas Mark 6.
2. Peel and thinly slice the shallots. Peel the tomatoes (first plunging them in boiling water for 10 seconds), remove the seeds and cut the flesh into dice.
3. Heat the butter in a frying pan, add the shallots and soften over a medium heat. When they are almost cooked, pour them and the butter into an ovenproof dish. Add the tomatoes, thyme, bay leaf and parsley stalks.
4. Arrange the cod steaks in the dish in one layer. Season with salt and pepper and pour over the wine.
5. Put the dish in the oven. When the wine starts to boil, turn off the oven and leave the dish inside for 5 minutes longer.
6. Remove the fish steaks with a spatula, arrange them on an ovenproof serving dish and keep hot.
7. Pour the cooking juices and vegetables into a saucepan. Boil to evaporate half the liquid over a high heat, then put it through the strainer into another saucepan, pressing the vegetables to extract all their juices. Add the crème fraîche and a few drops of lemon juice. Adjust the seasoning and reheat.
8. Coat the fish with the sauce. Heat in the oven until the sauce starts to simmer. Sprinkle with the chopped herbs and serve immediately.

Cabillaud portugaise

Portuguese Cod

	00:20		00:30 to 00:40

American	Ingredients	Metric/Imperial
3	Large cod steaks, 1 in / 2.5 cm thick	3
3 tbsp	Flour	3 tbsp
⅔ cup	Olive oil	150 ml / ¼ pint
12	Pearl [button] onions	12
2	Garlic cloves	2
4	Tomatoes	4
1	Sweet red pepper	1
1	Green pepper	1
1 tsp	Dried thyme	1 tsp
	Few fresh or dried rosemary leaves	
	Salt and pepper	
⅔ cup	Dry white wine	150 ml / ¼ pint

1. Preheat the oven to 475°F / 240°C / Gas Mark 9.
2. Season the cod steaks on both sides with salt and coat with the flour. Heat the oil in a frying pan over a medium heat, add the cod and brown on both sides. Remove the fish with a slotted spatula, drain and put in a flameproof casserole. Set aside.
3. Peel and chop the onions and garlic. Peel the tomatoes (first plunging them in boiling water for 10 seconds), remove the seeds and roughly chop the flesh.
4. Put the red and green peppers on an oven shelf in the oven and bake until blackened and blistered (about 15 minutes). Remove the peppers from the oven, wrap them in a damp cloth and let cool for 10 minutes. You will then be able to peel them easily. Remove the seeds and white pith and cut the flesh into strips.
5. Add the onions to the oil in the frying pan and brown lightly. Remove with a slotted spoon and add to the fish. Put the chopped tomatoes and garlic in the frying pan to soften. Add the tomatoes and strips of pepper to the fish. Season with the thyme, rosemary and salt and pepper to taste. Pour the wine over all the ingredients.
6. Cook over a medium heat, without stirring, for 20 minutes.

Lower the heat, cover the casserole and cook for a further 5 minutes.

Rôti de cabillaud
Roast Cod

| | 00:25 | | 00:40 |

American	Ingredients	Metric/Imperial
2 lb	Cod fillets	1 kg / 2 lb
	Salt and pepper	
3	Tomatoes	3
½ lb	Mushrooms	250 g / 8 oz
⅔ cup	Oil	150 ml / ¼ pint
⅔ cup	Dry white wine	150 ml / ¼ pint
1	Onion	1
2 tbsp	Chopped fresh parsley	2 tbsp
	Lemon wedges	

1. Preheat the oven to 400°F / 200°C / Gas Mark 6.
2. Pile the cod fillets on top of each other to make an evenly-shaped roast. Tie with string (not too tightly) so that it does not collapse during cooking. Season with salt and pepper and place in an ovenproof dish.
3. Halve the tomatoes. Quarter the mushrooms.
4. Surround the cod roast with the tomatoes and mushrooms and add the oil and white wine. Put in the oven and cook for about 40 minutes, basting from time to time with the liquid in the dish.
5. About 10 minutes before the end of the cooking time, sprinkle with the onion, peeled and chopped and the parsley. Remove the string.
6. Serve in the dish, garnished with lemon wedges.

Cabillaud au gratin
Cod in Mushroom Sauce

| | 00:30 | | 00:30 |

American	Ingredients	Metric/Imperial
6	Medium-sized potatoes	6
½ lb	Mushrooms	250 g / 8 oz
1 tbsp	Lemon juice	1 tbsp
1	Shallot	1
¼ cup	Butter	50 g / 2 oz
	Salt and pepper	
¼ cup	Flour	40 g / 1½ oz
2 cups	Milk	500 ml / ¾ pint
	Grated nutmeg	
¾ lb	Poached skinless boneless cod	350 g / 12 oz
½ cup	Grated gruyère cheese	50 g / 2 oz

1. Cook the potatoes in water to cover for about 20 minutes or until tender. Drain. Allow to cool, then peel and cut into slices. Divide between 6 individual ovenproof dishes.
2. Preheat the oven to 400°F / 200°C / Gas Mark 6.
3. Thinly slice the mushrooms and toss with the lemon juice. Peel and chop the shallot. Melt the butter in a frying pan, add the mushrooms and shallot and season with salt and pepper. Cook, stirring, until all the moisture has evaporated.
4. Sprinkle with the flour and stir for 1 minute, then add the milk and leave to thicken over a low heat, stirring constantly.

Season with a pinch of nutmeg.
5. Flake the fish with a fork. Add the fish to the mushroom sauce and fold the ingredients together. Spoon on top of the potatoes.
6. Sprinkle with the grated gruyère cheese and brown in the oven. Serve very hot.

Cook's tip: this dish can be made with any leftover cooked white fish or scallops.

Carrelet au cidre
Plaice or Flounder with Cider

| | 00:20 | | 00:30 |

American	Ingredients	Metric/Imperial
2 lb	Potatoes	1 kg / 2 lb
1 (2¾ lb)	Plaice or flounder, cleaned	1 (1.25 kg / 2¾ lb)
3	Onions	3
1 tbsp	Chopped fresh parsley	1 tbsp
½ tsp	Dried thyme	½ tsp
½	Bay leaf	½
2	Garlic cloves	2
	Salt and pepper	
	Hard [dry] cider	
6 tbsp	Butter	75 g / 3 oz

1. Peel the potatoes and cut them into thin slices. Arrange on the bottom of a saucepan. Place the fish on top of the potatoes.
2. Peel and slice the onions and cover the fish with them. Add the parsley, thyme, bay leaf, whole cloves of garlic, and salt and pepper to taste. Pour over enough cider to cover. Dot with the butter cut into pieces.
3. Simmer over a low heat for about 30 minutes.

Carrelets à la minute
Quickly Baked Plaice or Flounder

| | 00:15 | | 00:10 |

American	Ingredients	Metric/Imperial
6	Small plaice or flounder, cleaned	6
	Salt and pepper	
4	Shallots	4
1 cup	Dry white wine	250 ml / 8 fl oz
2 tbsp	Fresh bread crumbs	2 tbsp
2 tbsp	Chopped fresh parsley	2 tbsp
2 tbsp	Butter	25 g / 1 oz

1. Preheat the oven to 425°F / 220°C / Gas Mark 7.
2. Make a few slashes in the skin of the fish with the point of a knife. Arrange the fish in an ovenproof dish and season with salt and pepper.
3. Peel and chop the shallots. Sprinkle them over the fish, then add the wine. Sprinkle over the bread crumbs and parsley, and dot with the butter, cut into pieces.
4. Bake for 10 minutes.

Colin poché au court-bouillon

Poached Hake with Lemon Butter

	00:10		00:45

American	Ingredients	Metric/Imperial
2 quarts	Cold water	2 l / 3½ pints
⅓ cup	Vinegar	5 tbsp
2	Onions	2
2	Cloves	2
2	Carrots	2
1	Bouquet garni	1
	Salt and pepper	
1 (2 - 3 lb)	Hake, cleaned	1 (1-1.5 kg / 2-3 lb)
1 cup	Butter	250 g / 8 oz
1	Lemon	1

1. Put the water, vinegar, peeled onions studded with the cloves, peeled and sliced carrots, bouquet garni and salt and pepper to taste into a saucepan. Bring to a boil, then cover and leave to simmer gently for 30 minutes. Leave the stock to cool.
2. Add the hake to the stock, put back over a very low heat and simmer for about 15 minutes.
3. Meanwhile, melt the butter without allowing it to brown. Cool, then carefully pour the liquid, yellow butter into a bowl, without disturbing the white sediment at the bottom. Season with salt and pepper and add the juice of the lemon.
4. Drain the hake and serve with the lemon butter.

Cook's tip: you can replace the lemon butter with white butter sauce (see page 123) or hollandaise sauce (see page 126).

Carpe farcie au Sancerre

Stuffed Carp

	00:30		01:00

American	Ingredients	Metric/Imperial
2	Slices of bread	2
⅔ cup	Milk	150 ml / ¼ pint
3	Hard-cooked eggs	3
1	Onion	1
3	Garlic cloves	3
¾ lb	Pork sausage meat	350 g / 12 oz
1 (4 lb)	Carp, cleaned and scaled, with its roe (or other soft roe)	1 (2 kg / 4 lb)
	Salt and pepper	
2 tbsp	Butter	25 g / 1 oz
1 tbsp	Flour	1 tbsp
½	Bottle of dry white wine	½

1. Preheat the oven to 350°F / 180°C / Gas Mark 4.
2. Soak the bread in the milk. Chop the eggs. Peel and chop the onion and garlic. Mix together the eggs, onion, garlic, sausage meat, soaked bread and carp roe in a bowl. Season with salt and pepper.
3. Fill the fish with the stuffing and sew up with a trussing needle and fine string.
4. Melt the butter in a flameproof dish. Add the flour and

brown lightly, stirring. Stir in the wine. Put the fish in the dish.
5. Bake for about 1 hour, basting the fish with the liquid from time to time. Cut into fairly thick slices and serve hot with the sauce.

Cabillaud mornay

Cod in Cheese Sauce

	00:10		01:00

American	Ingredients	Metric/Imperial
1 (2¾ lb)	Cod, cleaned	1 (1.25 kg / 2¾ lb)
	Court-bouillon (see page 114)	
6	Fresh mussels	6
1 tbsp	Butter	1 tbsp
1 tbsp	Flour	1 tbsp
⅔ cup	Milk	150 ml / ¼ pint
⅔ cup	Crème fraîche (see page 122)	150 ml / ¼ pint
½ cup	Grated gruyère cheese	50 g / 2 oz
	Salt and pepper	

1. Put the cod into a large saucepan and cover with court-bouillon. Bring to a boil, then lower the heat and cook for 10 minutes. Turn off the heat, cover the saucepan and leave the fish to poach for a further 5 minutes. Drain the fish, reserving 1¼ cups [300 ml / ½ pint] of the cooking liquid. Remove all the skin and bones and break the flesh into pieces the size of an egg. Set aside.
2. Thoroughly scrub the mussels. Rinse and drain them.
3. Preheat the oven to 400°F / 200°C / Gas Mark 6.
4. Melt the butter in a saucepan, sprinkle with the flour and stir for 1 minute over a medium heat. Add the milk, reserved cooking liquid and crème fraîche. Leave to thicken over a low heat, stirring constantly. Add 2 tablespoons of the cheese and salt and pepper to taste.
5. Arrange the fish in an ovenproof dish with the mussels. Coat with the sauce. Sprinkle with the remaining cheese and dot with a little extra butter. Bake for 20 minutes.

Darnes de colin meunière

Sautéed Hake Steaks

	00:10		00:20 to 00:25

American	Ingredients	Metric/Imperial
⅔ cup	Milk	150 ml / ¼ pint
	Salt and pepper	
3 tbsp	Flour	3 tbsp
6	Hake steaks, 1 in / 2.5 cm thick	6
½ cup	Butter	125 g / 4 oz
⅓ cup	Oil	5 tbsp

1. Pour the milk into a dish and add ½ teaspoon salt. Put the flour in another dish. Dip the fish steaks first in the milk and then in the flour. Shake to remove the excess flour.
2. Preheat the oven to 425°F / 220°C / Gas Mark 7.
3. Heat the butter and oil in a large frying pan. Fry the fish steaks on one side until golden, then turn them over and fry the other side over a low heat.

4. Arrange the steaks on a serving dish, season lightly with salt and pepper and put the dish into the oven with the door open. Leave to crisp, about 3 minutes.

5. Serve with melted butter mixed with lemon juice.

Eglefins à la mode de Porto

Haddock with Tomato Rice

	00:15		00:45

American	Ingredients	Metric/Imperial
2 lb	Tomatoes	1 kg / 2 lb
3	Onions	3
2	Shallots	2
3	Garlic cloves	3
¼ cup	Oil	4 tbsp
1	Bouquet garni	1
	Salt and pepper	
1 cup	Long-grain rice	250 g / 8 oz
1½ quarts	Water	1.5 l / 2½ pints
6	Haddock steaks	6
1 quart	Dry white wine	1 l / 1¾ pints

1. Peel the tomatoes (first plunging them in boiling water for 10 seconds), remove the seeds and chop the flesh coarsely. Peel the onions, shallots and garlic and chop them.

2. Heat the oil in a saucepan, add the onions, garlic and shallots and brown them lightly. Add the tomatoes, bouquet garni, and salt and pepper to taste. Leave to cook over a low heat for 20 minutes, stirring occasionally.

3. Meanwhile, put the rice in a saucepan with the water. Bring to a boil and boil for 5-6 minutes.

4. Add the rice to the tomato sauce and stir to mix. Put the fish steaks on the top. Add the wine (which must cover the rice). Cover and cook over a low heat for 20 minutes. Serve very hot.

Porgy with white wine

Daurade au vin blanc

Porgy [Sea Bream] with White Wine

	00:10		00:30 to 00:40

American	Ingredients	Metric/Imperial
1 (3 lb)	Porgy [sea bream], cleaned and scaled	1 (1.5 kg / 3 lb)
	Salt and pepper	
2 tbsp	Olive oil	2 tbsp
1	Large onion	1
4	Medium-size tomatoes	4
1 cup	Dry white wine	250 ml / 8 fl oz
¼ cup	Butter	50 g / 2 oz
1 tbsp	Chopped fresh parsley	1 tbsp
1	Lemon	1

1. Preheat the oven to 425°F / 220°C / Gas Mark 7.

2. Season the inside of the fish with salt and pepper, and coat the outside with the olive oil. Put the fish in an ovenproof dish.

3. Peel and slice the onion. Break the slices into rings. Cut the tomatoes into quarters. Surround the fish with the tomatoes and cover it with the onion rings. Season with salt and pepper and add the wine.

4. Put the dish in the oven. When the liquid boils, cook for 30-40 minutes, basting with the juices from time to time.

5. Turn off the oven. Add the butter, cut into small pieces, to the dish with the parsley and the juice of the lemon. Leave in the oven for 5 minutes longer before serving.

Daurade au fenouil

Porgy [Sea Bream] with Fennel

	00:10		00:20 to 00:30

American	Ingredients	Metric/Imperial
2 (1½ lb)	Porgy [sea bream], cleaned and scaled	2 (750 g / 1½ lb)
	Salt and pepper	
2 tbsp	Fennel seeds	2 tbsp
⅔ cup	Olive oil	150 ml / ¼ pint
10	Fresh fennel sprigs	10
3	Lemons	3

1. Preheat the oven to 350°F / 180°C / Gas Mark 4.

2. Season the inside of the fish with salt and pepper, and put 1 teaspoon of fennel seeds in each fish. Season the outside with salt. Slash both fish twice and brush with a little olive oil.

3. Put the sprigs of fennel side by side in an ovenproof dish and place the fish on top. Cut one lemon into slices and arrange these over the fish. Put the dish in the oven and bake for 20-30 minutes without turning the fish over.

4. Meanwhile, put the remaining olive oil in a saucepan or bowl with the juice of a second lemon and the remaining fennel seeds. Season with salt and pepper to taste. Put the saucepan or bowl over another saucepan containing hot water and heat.

5. When the fish are cooked, arrange them on a serving dish and garnish with the remaining lemon, quartered. Serve with the lemon and fennel oil.

Harengs à la diable

Deviled Herrings

00:15   00:20 to 00:25

American	Ingredients	Metric/Imperial
6	Fresh herrings, cleaned, with roe	6
½ cup	Prepared mustard	125 g / 4 oz
	Cayenne pepper	
3 tbsp	Fresh white bread crumbs	3 tbsp
½ cup	Butter	125 g / 4 oz

1. Preheat the broiler [grill].
2. Make 2 or 3 slashes in each herring. In a bowl mix the mustard with a pinch of cayenne pepper. Coat the herring roe with a little of this mixture and put back inside the fish.
3. Brush the herrings generously with the mustard mixture, then coat with the bread crumbs. Arrange them on the rack in the broiler pan.
4. Melt the butter. Put the herrings under the heat and cook for about 10 minutes, brushing them from time to time with the melted butter. Turn the fish over carefully, brush with the rest of the melted butter and cook for 10-15 minutes longer. Serve very hot.

Harengs grillés à l'oseille

Broiled [Grilled] Herrings with Sorrel

00:25   00:30

American	Ingredients	Metric/Imperial
6	Fresh herrings, cleaned, with the roe	6
1 tbsp	Oil	1 tbsp
½ lb	Sorrel	250 g / 8 oz
1	Shallot	1
1 tbsp	Butter	1 tbsp
1 tbsp	Flour	1 tbsp
1 cup	Crème fraîche (see page 122)	250 ml / 8 fl oz
2 tbsp	Water	2 tbsp
½	Lemon	½
	Salt and pepper	
1	Egg yolk	1

1. Preheat the broiler [grill].
2. Make 2 or 3 slashes in each fish and brush them lightly with oil. Put the roe back inside. Arrange them on the rack, put them under the broiler and cook for about 10 minutes.
3. Meanwhile, cut the sorrel into thin strips. Peel and chop the shallot. Melt the butter in a frying pan, add the shallot and soften without browning. Sprinkle with the flour and stir well, then add crème fraîche, water and the juice of the ½ lemon. Add salt and pepper to taste and leave to cook over a very low heat.
4. Turn over the herrings and cook them for about 10 minutes on the other side.
5. Mix the egg yolk with a few spoonfuls of the sauce and whisk into the remaining sauce. Add the sorrel. Heat through gently, stirring, and pour into a sauceboat.
6. Arrange the herrings on a serving dish and serve at once with the sauce.

Harengs à la baltique

Baltic Herrings

00:25
plus marinating   00:15

American	Ingredients	Metric/Imperial
6	Medium-size fresh herrings, cleaned, with the roe	6
	Salt and pepper	
2 cups	Dry white wine	500 ml / ¾ pint
3 tbsp	Wine vinegar	3 tbsp
3	Crisp apples	3
½	Lemon	½
2	Large onions	2
1 cup	Crème fraîche (see page 122)	250 ml / 8 fl oz

1. Soak the herrings in cold water to cover for 1 hour. Drain, pat dry with paper towels and sprinkle them with salt. Set aside for 2 hours.
2. Remove the heads and tails from the fish. Split the fish in half and remove the backbones. Put the roe to one side.
3. Heat the wine in a saucepan with the vinegar and salt and pepper to taste. Add the roe and herrings. Bring to a boil and poach over a low heat for 10 minutes.
4. Leave to cool, then marinate for 2 days.
5. To serve, peel and core the apples, cut them into slices and sprinkle with the juice of the ½ lemon. Peel and slice the onions. Push the slices into rings. Mix the crème with salt and pepper to taste and 2 tablespoons of the marinade.
6. Arrange the herrings and roe in a serving dish. Cover with the apples and onion rings and spoon over the sauce. Chill.

Flétan à l'orange

Halibut with Orange Rice

00:20
plus marinating   00:30

American	Ingredients	Metric/Imperial
4	Juicy oranges	4
3 tbsp	Olive oil	3 tbsp
1	Garlic clove	1
	Salt and pepper	
6	Halibut or turbot steaks	6
2½ cups	Water	600 ml / 1 pint
1 cup	Long-grain rice	250 g / 8 oz
3 tbsp	Butter	40 g / 1½ oz

1. Using a vegetable peeler, thinly pare the rind from ½ an orange. Squeeze the juice from this orange and 2 others. Mix the juice with the oil. Peel and crush the garlic.
2. Put the oil and orange mixture in a shallow dish and add the garlic and salt and pepper to taste. Place the fish steaks in the dish and turn them over several times to coat them with the marinade. Leave to marinate for 30 minutes.
3. Put the water in a saucepan and bring to a boil. Add the orange rind, cut into small pieces, some salt and pepper and the rice. Cover and cook over a low heat for 15-18 minutes or until the rice is tender and the liquid has been absorbed.
4. Pour the rice into a serving dish. Dot with the butter, cut into small pieces, and keep hot.

5. Put the fish steaks in a frying pan, add the marinade and cook over a high heat for 4-5 minutes on both sides.
6. Cut the last orange into thin slices. Arrange the fish steaks on the rice, garnish with the orange slices and serve at once.

Congre à la mode de Caen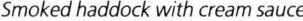
Caen Style Eel

	00:05	00:15

American	Ingredients	Metric/Imperial
2 lb	Fresh eels	1 kg / 2 lb
¼ cup	Oil	4 tbsp
2	Large onions	2
1 tbsp	Flour	2 tbsp
2 cups	Hard [dry] cider	500 ml / ¾ pint
	Salt and pepper	

1. Clean and skin the eels (or have this done for you), then cut them into segments.
2. Heat 1 tablespoon of oil in a frying pan. When the oil is hot, add the pieces of eel and cook for 5 minutes on each side. Remove the pieces, place in a serving dish and keep hot.
3. Peel and thinly slice the onions. Heat the remaining oil in the frying pan, add the onions and fry until golden. Sprinkle them with the flour, stir and add the cider. Season to taste with salt and pepper and leave to cook for 10 minutes.
4. Pour the cider sauce over the eel pieces and serve hot.

Haddock charentaise
Smoked Haddock with Cream Sauce

	00:10	00:20

American	Ingredients	Metric/Imperial
3-4	Small smoked haddock	3-4
2 cups	Milk	500 ml / ¾ pint
5 tbsp	Butter	65 g / 2½ oz
1 cup	Crème fraîche (see page 122)	250 ml / 8 fl oz
	Salt and pepper	
	Grated nutmeg	
	Lemon juice	

1. Put the fish in a saucepan, add the milk and enough water just to cover the fish and bring to a boil over a medium heat. Remove from the heat and leave to poach, covered, for 10-15 minutes. Drain and keep warm.
2. Meanwhile, put 6 tablespoons of the fish cooking liquid in a small bowl or saucepan and add the butter, cut into small pieces, and crème fraîche. Put the bowl or saucepan over another saucepan containing water and heat, whisking, until the mixture will coat the back of a spoon. Season to taste with salt, pepper and nutmeg and a few drops of lemon juice.
3. Arrange the fish on a serving dish and serve with the sauce.

Smoked haddock with cream sauce

Lotte au poivre vert

Monkfish with Green Peppercorns

00:10   00:30 to 00:40

American	Ingredients	Metric/Imperial
¼ cup	Butter	50 g / 2 oz
2¾ lb	Thin slices of monkfish (scaloppine or escalopes)	1.25 kg / 2¾ lb
	Salt	
2 tbsp	Bottled green peppercorns, drained	2 tbsp
1¼ cups	White wine	300 ml / ½ pint
1 cup	Crème fraîche (see page 122)	250 ml / 8 fl oz
2	Egg yolks	2

1. Heat the butter in a large frying pan, add the fish slices and cook until firm without browning (do not overlap them). Season with salt and cook gently for about 10 minutes. Remove the fish with a slotted spatula and keep hot.
2. Roughly crush the green peppercorns. Add them to the pan with the wine and boil over a medium heat to reduce to about half the quantity.
3. Return the fish to the pan. Add 6 tablespoons of the crème fraîche and bring to simmering point. Adjust the seasoning if necessary and leave to cook for a further 15-20 minutes.
4. Arrange the fish slices on a warmed serving dish and keep hot. Mix the egg yolks with remaining crème fraîche and 1 tablespoon of the sauce. Add this mixture to the rest of the sauce, whisking, then cook without boiling, stirring, until the mixture will coat the back of a spoon.
5. Pour the sauce over the fish and serve immediately.

Lotte en blanquette

Monkfish in White Sauce

00:20   00:45

American	Ingredients	Metric/Imperial
24	Pearl [button] onions	24
¾ cup	Butter	175 g / 6 oz
1 tbsp	Sugar	1 tbsp
	Salt and pepper	
2 lb	Monkfish fillet	1 kg / 2 lb
1½ cups	Dry white wine	350 ml / 12 fl oz
	Court-bouillon (see page 114)	
½ lb	Mushrooms	250 g / 8 oz
1	Lemon	1
2 tbsp	Flour	2 tbsp
1	Egg yolk	1
⅔ cup	Crème fraîche (see page 122)	150 ml / ¼ pint

1. Peel the onions. Put them in a saucepan with 3 tablespoons [40 g / 1½ oz] of the butter, the sugar, a pinch of salt and some pepper, and add just enough water to cover the onions. Cover and cook over a low heat until the onions are tender and the liquid has formed a clear caramel.

2. Meanwhile, cut the fish into large cubes. Melt 3 tablespoons [40 g / 1½ oz] butter in a saucepan, add the pieces of fish and cook until firm without browning. Add the wine and enough court-bouillon to cover the fish. Bring to a boil, then simmer for about 20 minutes.
3. While the fish is cooking, heat 3 tablespoons [40 g / 1½ oz] of the butter in a saucepan and add the mushrooms, the juice of the lemon, and salt and pepper to taste. Cover and cook for 10 minutes over a medium heat.
4. Melt the rest of the butter in a saucepan, add the flour and stir for 2 minutes over a low heat. Add the fish cooking liquid and cook, stirring, for 10 minutes over a medium heat until thickened. Add the mushrooms.
5. Mix the egg yolk in a bowl with crème fraîche. Add a few spoonfuls of the sauce, whisking vigorously, then stir this into the remaining sauce. Put the fish pieces in the sauce and heat without boiling.
6. Arrange the fish stew in a serving dish, surround with the onions and serve immediately.

Lotte en matelote

Monkfish Stew in Red Wine

00:30   01:00

American	Ingredients	Metric/Imperial
½ lb	Bacon, in a piece	250 g / 8 oz
½ lb	Pearl [button] onions	250 g / 8 oz
3 lb	Monkfish fillet	1.5 kg / 3 lb
¼ cup	Brandy	4 tbsp
2 cups	Red wine	500 ml / ¾ pint
1	Bouquet garni	1
	Salt and pepper	
5 tbsp	Butter	65 g / 2½ oz
½ lb	Mushrooms	250 g / 8 oz
2 tbsp	Flour	40 g / 1½ oz

1. Put the bacon in a saucepan of cold water, bring to a boil and blanch for 5 minutes. Drain and cut into dice. Peel the onions. Set aside.
2. Put the bacon dice in a sauce and brown over a low heat. Remove with a slotted spoon and put to one side.
3. Cut the fish into equal-size pieces. Add to the bacon fat in the pan and cook over a high heat, turning the pieces, until firm. Remove from the heat. Add the brandy and stir, then cover the saucepan and leave on one side for 10 minutes.
4. Put the saucepan back over the heat. Add the red wine and enough water to cover the fish. Add the bouquet garni and bacon. Season with salt and pepper. Cover and bring to a boil over a high heat, then leave to cook over a low heat for 20 minutes.
5. Meanwhile, melt 3 tablespoons [40 g / 1½ oz] butter in a saucepan, add the onions and fry them, with the lid on, over a medium heat until golden brown on all sides. Remove the onions with a slotted spoon and add to the fish. Put the mushrooms in the saucepan with the onion cooking butter, and cook until all their moisture has evaporated. Add to the fish and cook for a further 15-18 minutes.
6. Remove the bouquet garni. Mix the remaining butter with the flour to make a paste. Add to the fish stew, off the heat, stirring well. Put the pan back over the heat and boil for 2 minutes, stirring constantly, to thicken the sauce. Serve immediately.

Limandes à la provençale
Provençal Style Dabs

	00:15 plus soaking	00:40

American	Ingredients	Metric/Imperial
6	Dabs (portion-sized)	6
2	Lemons	2
1	Fennel bulb	1
4	Onions	4
1	Sweet red or green pepper	1
6	Tomatoes	6
3	Garlic cloves	3
5 tbsp	Oil	5 tbsp
1	Bouquet garni	1
	Salt and pepper	
1 cup	Rosé wine	250 ml / 8 fl oz
20	Olives	20

1. Cut all around the backbone of the dabs with scissors. Slash the flesh in 2 or 3 places with a sharp knife, and sprinkle the fish with the juice of the lemons. Leave to soak for 2 hours.
2. Trim and thinly slice the fennel. Peel and thinly slice the onions. Cut the pepper in half, remove the core and seeds and cut the flesh into strips. Peel the tomatoes (first plunging them in boiling water for 10 seconds) and coarsely chop the flesh. Peel and crush the garlic.
3. Heat the oil in a frying pan, add the fennel, onions and pepper strips and cook until softened. Add the tomatoes, garlic, bouquet garni and salt and pepper to taste. Leave to cook for about 15 minutes or until thickened, stirring occasionally.
4. Arrange the dabs on the tomato sauce. Add the wine. Cover and cook for 10 minutes over a medium heat.
5. Meanwhile, pit [stone] the olives. Add them to the frying pan and continue cooking for 10 minutes. Serve very hot.

Cook's tip: You can prepare sole or other flat fish in the same way as the dabs.

Lotte à l'américaine
Monkfish in Tomato Sauce

	00:15	00:25

American	Ingredients	Metric/Imperial
½ lb	Onions	250 g / 8 oz
2	Shallots	2
2	Garlic cloves	2
5	Tomatoes	5
3 lb	Monkfish fillet	1.5 kg / 3 lb
	Flour	
¼ cup	Olive oil	4 tbsp
2 tbsp	Brandy	2 tbsp
½	Bottle of dry white wine	½
1	Bouquet garni	1
2	Sugar cubes	2
1 tbsp	Tomato paste [purée]	1 tbsp
	Salt and pepper	
	Cayenne pepper	

1. Peel and chop the onions, shallots and garlic. Peel the tomatoes (first plunging them in boiling water for 10 seconds), remove the seeds and coarsely chop the flesh. Cut the fish into pieces and coat them in flour.
2. Heat 1 tablespoon of oil in a saucepan, add the onions, shallots and garlic and soften over a low heat, stirring frequently.
3. Heat the rest of the oil in a frying pan, add the pieces of fish and cook until the fish is golden brown on all sides.
4. Add the brandy to the fish and set it alight. When the flames die down, add the fish and its juices to the vegetables in the saucepan. Add the wine, bouquet garni, tomatoes, sugar and tomato paste. Season to taste with salt, pepper and cayenne.
5. Bring to a boil, then cover and cook over a low heat for 20-25 minutes. Serve hot.

Lamproie bordelaise
Bordeaux Lamprey

	00:25	02:40

American	Ingredients	Metric/Imperial
1 (3 lb)	Lamprey	1 (1.5 kg / 3 lb)
3	Leeks (white part only)	3
2	Celery stalks	2
1	Carrot	1
1	Large onion	1
½ lb	Mushrooms	250 g / 8 oz
6	Tomatoes	6
4	Shallots	4
4	Garlic cloves	4
¼ cup	Oil	4 tbsp
3 tbsp	Flour	3 tbsp
1	Bouquet garni	1
1 tbsp	Sugar	1 tbsp
1	Bottle of red wine	1
	Salt and pepper	
1 (5 oz)	Slice of cooked ham	1 (150 g / 5 oz)
6 tbsp	Butter	75 g / 3 oz
3 tbsp	Brandy	3 tbsp

1. Plunge the lamprey into a saucepan of boiling water. Bring back to a boil and simmer for 3 minutes. Drain the lamprey, skin it and cut it into 2 in / 5 cm pieces. Set aside.
2. Thinly slice the leeks and celery. Peel and thinly slice the carrot and onion. Remove the stems from the mushrooms and set aside. Dice the mushroom caps. Peel the tomatoes (first plunging them in boiling water for 10 seconds), remove the seeds and coarsely chop the flesh. Peel and chop the shallots and garlic.
3. Heat 3 tablespoons of oil in a saucepan, add the celery, leeks, carrot, shallots, onion, mushroom stems and cook over a low heat, stirring, until lightly browned. Sprinkle with the flour. Cook stirring, for 4 minutes. Add the bouquet garni, garlic, tomatoes, sugar, wine and salt and pepper to taste. Cover and simmer over a low heat for 2 hours.
4. In the meantime, cut the ham into dice. Heat the rest of the oil and the butter in a saucepan, add the ham and diced mushroom caps and cook until golden. Add the pieces of lamprey. Add the brandy and set alight.
5. Strain the wine sauce and add to the eel mixture. Cover and leave to cook over a low heat for 30 minutes.
6. Spoon the pieces of lamprey onto a serving dish and surround with the mushrooms and ham. Serve with the sauce.

Lotte à la bretonne
Breton Style Monkfish

00:15   **01:00**

American	Ingredients	Metric/Imperial
2 lb	Monkfish fillet	1 kg / 2 lb
	Court-bouillon (see page 114)	
¼ cup	Butter	50 g / 2 oz
2 tbsp	Flour	2 tbsp
1 cup	Crème fraîche (see page 122)	250 ml / 8 fl oz
	Salt and pepper	
2 tbsp	Grated gruyère cheese	2 tbsp

1. Preheat the oven to 450°F / 230°C / Gas Mark 8.
2. Cut the fish into equal-sized pieces. Put the pieces of fish in a large saucepan and add enough court-bouillon to cover. Bring to a boil over a high heat, then leave to simmer gently for 30 minutes.
3. Remove the fish pieces with a slotted spoon and put them in an ovenproof dish. Keep hot.
4. Strain the cooking liquid and return it to the saucepan. Boil to reduce by one-third over a high heat. Melt the butter in a saucepan, add the flour and stir for 3 minutes. Add ⅔ cup [150 ml / ¼ pint] of the reduced cooking liquid and the cream, and stir over a low heat until you obtain a light white sauce. Adjust the seasoning and add a little more cooking liquid.
5. Pour away the liquid in the ovenproof dish which has oozed out of the fish. Coat the fish with the sauce, sprinkle with the cheese and brown in the oven for 10 minutes. Serve very hot.

Lotte en gigot
Baked Monkfish with Mussels

00:10   **00:45**

American	Ingredients	Metric/Imperial
1 (2¾ lb)	Piece of monkfish, skinned	1 (1.25 kg / 2¾ lb)
2	Garlic cloves	2
	Salt	
2	Lemons	2
1 cup	Olive oil	250 ml / 8 fl oz
1 pint	Fresh mussels	500 g / 1 lb

1. Preheat the oven to 425°F / 220°C / Gas Mark 7.
2. Press down on the back of the fish to loosen the backbone. Peel the garlic and cut into slivers. With a sharp knife make slits all over the fish and insert the garlic slivers. Season with salt. Place in an ovenproof dish.
3. Cut one lemon into thin slices and squeeze the juice from the other lemon.
4. Arrange the slices of lemon on the fish. Add 5 tablespoons of the oil and put the dish in the oven. Bake until the fish releases its own moisture. Discard this liquid, then add the remaining oil and the lemon juice. Bake for 45 minutes, basting the fish from time to time with the cooking juices.
5. About 10 minutes before the end of the cooking time, thoroughly scrub the mussels. Rinse and drain them. Add the mussels to the dish and bake until they open (about 5 minutes). Discard any mussels that remain closed. Serve immediately.

Harengs marinés
Soused Herrings

00:30
plus marinating   **01:00**

American	Ingredients	Metric/Imperial
6	Medium-size fresh herrings, cleaned, with the roe	6
2 cups	Dry white wine	500 ml / ¾ pint
1 cup	Vinegar	250 ml / 8 fl oz
1	Carrot	1
3	Onions	3
3	Garlic cloves	3
3	Fresh thyme sprigs	3
1	Small bay leaf	1
1	Small bunch of fresh parsley	1
5	Fresh sage leaves	5
10	Black peppercorns	10
	Salt	

1. Put the roe back in the fish and arrange in a flameproof dish in one layer. Set aside.
2. Pour the wine and vinegar into a saucepan. Peel and slice the carrot and onions and add to the pan with whole cloves of peeled garlic, thyme, bay leaf, bunch of parsley, sage leaves, peppercorns and salt to taste. Bring to a boil and simmer for about 45 minutes.
3. Pour the boiling marinade over the herrings. Remove the parsley, thyme and garlic. Put over a low heat and poach, without boiling, for 10-13 minutes or until the fish is cooked.
4. Leave to cool, then cover and keep in a cool place. Serve very cold.

Loup poché
Poached Sea Bass

00:10   **00:12 to 00:25**

American	Ingredients	Metric/Imperial
1 (5½ lb)	Sea bass, cleaned and scaled	1 (2.5 kg / 5½ lb)
	Salt	
25	Black peppercorns	25
1	Bottle of white wine	1
	Court-bouillon (see page 114)	

1. Season the inside of the fish with salt and wrap it tightly in wet cheesecloth or muslin. Put it in a fish kettle or large saucepan. Add the peppercorns, some salt, the wine and enough court-bouillon to cover the fish with liquid.
2. Put the kettle over a high heat. As soon as scum forms on the surface, lower the heat and simmer the fish. Allow 25 minutes simmering if the fish is to be eaten hot, and 12 minutes if it is to be eaten cold.
3. To serve hot, remove the pan from the heat and leave the fish to poach for 5 minutes longer. Cover a serving dish with a folded napkin. Drain the fish, unwrap it and put it on the dish. Serve with a white butter sauce (see page 123), hollandaise sauce (see page 126), garlic mayonnaise (see page 119) or lemon-flavoured drawn or clarified butter (see page 113).
4. To serve cold, leave the fish to cool completely in its stock before draining it and removing the cheesecloth or muslin.

Serve with mayonnaise (see page 119), tartare sauce (see page 119), garlic mayonnaise (see page 119) or vinaigrette dressing with herbs (see page 120).

Cook's tip: If you have no fish kettle, cut the fish neatly into segments. If you try to curl the whole fish into a saucepan it is liable to break.

Loup flambé
Flamed Sea Bass

	00:10	01:05

American	Ingredients	Metric/Imperial
1 (4 lb)	Sea bass, cleaned and scaled	1 (2 kg / 4 lb)
	Olive oil	
	Salt and pepper	
2	Large bunches of dried thyme	2
2 tbsp	Pernod	2 tbsp
	Lemon halves	

1. Preheat the oven to 425°F / 220°C / Gas Mark 7.
2. Brush the fish with oil and sprinkle with salt and pepper. Put it on a rack in a roasting pan (line the latter with foil). Bake the fish for 20 minutes, then lower the heat to 350°F / 180°C / Gas Mark 4 and bake for about 45 minutes longer. To test if the fish is cooked, pierce it with the blade of a knife along the backbone. The knife should encounter no resistance.
3. Remove the foil from the roasting pan. Put the bunch of thyme in the pan, and add 2 tablespoons of oil. Put 1 tablespoon of thyme leaves in a bowl and add the Pernod. Put the fish, on the rack, back over the pan and coat the fish with the thyme-Pernod mixture. Set the thyme in the pan alight and raise the rack to flame the fish evenly.
4. Serve the flamed fish immediately, together with the oil flavored with Pernod and thyme and some lemon halves.

Merlans Colbert
Deep-Fried Whiting with Parsley Butter

	00:40	00:08 to 00:10
		per batch

American	Ingredients	Metric/Imperial
2	Eggs	2
3 tbsp	Flour	3 tbsp
2½ cups	Dry bread crumbs	200 g / 7 oz
6 (6 oz)	Whiting, cleaned and backbones removed	6 (175 g / 6 oz)
	Salt and pepper	
½ cup	Butter	125 g / 4 oz
1 tbsp	Chopped fresh parsley	1 tbsp
	Oil for deep frying	

1. Break the eggs into a shallow dish and beat them to mix. Put the flour and bread crumbs in 2 shallow dishes. Season the inside of the fish with salt and pepper.
2. Mash the butter with a fork to soften it, then add the parsley. Form the butter into a cylinder shape and wrap in foil. Put in the refrigerator to chill.

3. Heat the oil for deep frying. Open up the whiting. Dip them first in the flour, then in the beaten egg and then in the bread crumbs. Put them in the oil (which should be hot but not smoking) and fry for 8-10 minutes or until they are golden and rise to the surface of the oil. Drain on paper towels.
4. Arrange the fish on a warmed serving dish and season lightly with salt. Cut the parsley butter into 6 round slices and put them on the fish. Serve.

Filets de merlans frits
Fried Whiting Fillets

	00:20	00:10
		per batch

American	Ingredients	Metric/Imperial
6	Slices of crustless bread	6
2	Lemons	2
3 tbsp	Flour	3 tbsp
	Oil for deep frying	
6	Large whiting fillets	6
	Salt and pepper	

1. Cut the bread into dice. Peel the lemons, removing all the white pith, and cut the flesh into small pieces. Spread out the flour on a plate.
2. Heat the oil. Add the bread dice and fry until golden brown. Remove with a slotted spoon and drain on paper towels.
3. Dip the fish fillets in the flour and shake them to remove the excess. Put them in the oil, which should be hot but not smoking, and cook for 10 minutes or until golden. Drain on paper towels.
4. Season the fish with salt and pepper and put them on a warmed serving dish. Surround with the fried croûtons and small pieces of lemon.
5. The floured fillets can also be fried in hot butter. Turn them over with a spatula and do not allow the butter to brown. Add the pieces of lemon to the butter and pour it over the cooked fillets.

Poached sea bass

Maquereaux marinés

Marinated Mackerel

	00:45 plus marinating	00:35

American	Ingredients	Metric/Imperial
3	Onions	3
4	Shallots	4
2	Medium-size carrots	2
5 tbsp	Oil	5 tbsp
2 cups	Tarragon wine vinegar	500 ml / ¾ pint
1 quart	Water	1 l / 1¾ pints
1	Bunch of fresh parsley	1
10	Black peppercorns	10
2	Cloves	2
4	Bay leaves	4
	Salt	
6	Small mackerel, cleaned	6

1. Peel the onions, shallots and carrots and cut them into thin slices. Heat the oil in a saucepan, add the onions and shallots and soften without browning. Add the vinegar and water. Add the carrot slices, bunch of parsley, peppercorns, cloves, bay leaves and salt to taste. Cover and cook over a low heat for 30 minutes. Allow to cool. Remove the bunch of parsley.
2. Preheat the oven to 450°F / 230°C / Gas Mark 8.
3. Arrange the mackerel in an ovenproof dish, in one layer. Add the cold marinade and put the dish in the oven. When the liquid boils, open the oven door and with it ajar, simmer for 5 minutes.
4. Take the fish out of the oven and leave to cool completely. Cover and keep in the refrigerator for 4 days before serving. The mackerel will keep very well for about 2 weeks in the refrigerator, provided that they are always well covered with marinade.

Marinated mackerel

Maquereaux à la moutarde

Mackerel with Mustard

	00:05	00:25 to 00:30

American	Ingredients	Metric/Imperial
6 (6-8 oz)	Mackerel, cleaned	6 (175-250 g / 6-8 oz)
1 cup	Crème fraîche (see page 122)	250 ml / 8 fl oz
3 tbsp	Prepared mustard	3 tbsp
1	Lemon	1
2 tbsp	Chopped fresh parsley	2 tbsp
	Salt and pepper	
¼ cup	Butter	50 g / 2 oz

1. Preheat the oven to 400°F / 200°C / Gas Mark 6.
2. Arrange the fish in an ovenproof dish. Mix the cream with the mustard, the juice of the lemon, chopped parsley and salt and pepper to taste. Coat the fish with this sauce and dot with the butter.
3. Put the dish in the oven and bake for 25-30 minutes or until the sauce has slightly reduced and browned. Serve at once.

Morue en acras

Salt Cod Fritters

	00:30 plus soaking and resting	00:20

American	Ingredients	Metric/Imperial
¾ lb	Salt cod fillets	350 g / 12 oz
2	Eggs	2
	Salt and pepper	
2 tbsp	Oil plus oil for deep frying	2 tbsp
1¼ cups	Flour	150 g / 5 oz
1 cup	Beer	150 ml / ¼ pint
1	Garlic clove	1
1	Onion	1
1	Small sweet red pepper	1
1	Small bunch of fresh parsley	1
1	Small bunch of fresh chives	1
1	Egg white	1

1. Soak the cod fillets in cold water for at least 12 hours, changing the water from time to time.
2. Beat the whole eggs in a bowl. Add salt and pepper to taste and then the oil and flour. Stir well and gradually incorporate the beer. Leave to rest for 2 hours.
3. Peel the garlic and onion. Core and seed the red pepper.
4. Drain the fish and rinse it under cold running water. Put it in a heavy saucepan. Cover the fish with fresh cold water and bring to a boil over a low heat. Simmer for 2 minutes, then drain. Cut the fish into small pieces.
5. Put the fish in a blender or food processor with garlic, red pepper, onion, parsley, chives and pepper to taste. Stir the cod mixture into the batter. Beat the egg white into stiff peaks and fold into the cod batter.
6. Heat the oil for deep frying. Drop tablespoonfuls of the batter into the hot oil. Fry until the fritters are golden and puffed up. Drain on paper towels and serve hot with a salad, with raw vegetables as an hors d'oeuvre, or as canapés with cocktails.

Merlu koskera
Basque Style Hake

	00:45	00:45

American	Ingredients	Metric/Imperial
2	Garlic cloves	2
1 tbsp	Olive oil	1 tbsp
1 tbsp	Peanut or groundnut oil	1 tbsp
1 tbsp	Flour	1 tbsp
⅔ cup	Fish stock (see page 115)	150 ml / ¼ pint
6	Hake steaks	6
	Salt and pepper	
6	Scampi or Dublin Bay prawns	6
¾ lb	Clams or cockles	350 g / 12 oz
3	Hard-cooked eggs	3
6	Canned asparagus spears	6
1 (8 oz)	Can small green peas (petits pois), drained	1 (225 g / 8 oz)
2 tbsp	Chopped fresh parsley	2 tbsp

1. Peel and finely chop the garlic. Heat the olive and peanut oils in a saucepan, add the garlic and cook until golden brown. Add the flour and cook, stirring for 2-3 minutes. Add the fish stock.
2. Season the hake steaks with salt on both sides. Add to the pan and cook for 15 minutes over a low heat.
3. Meanwhile, cook the scampi in boiling salted water for 5 minutes. Drain and add to the saucepan.
4. Scrub the clams or cockles, then rinse and drain. Cut the eggs in half. Add the clams or cockles, eggs, asparagus, peas and parsley to the pan.
5. Cook for 3 minutes longer or until the clams open (discard any that remain closed). Serve hot.

Aïoli de morue
Salt Cod with Garlic Mayonnaise

	00:25	01:15
	plus soaking	

American	Ingredients	Metric/Imperial
1 (2¾ lb)	Tail piece of salt cod	1 (1.25 kg / 2¾ lb)
6	Tomatoes	6
6	Small purple artichokes	6
12	Small carrots	12
6	Potatoes	6
1 lb	Green beans	500 g / 1 lb
1 quart	Periwinkles [winkles]	1 l / 1¾ pints
	Salt	
6	Hard-cooked eggs	6
1 cup	Garlic mayonnaise (see page 119)	50 ml / 8 fl oz

1. Cut the cod into large pieces and soak for 24 hours in cold water, changing the water several times.
2. Rinse the tomatoes and artichokes. Do not cook them. Set aside.
3. Drain the fish. Put it in a saucepan, cover generously with fresh cold water and bring to a simmer over a low heat.

Remove from the heat, cover the saucepan and leave the cod to poach for about 5 minutes. Drain and keep hot.
4. Peel the carrots and potatoes. Trim the beans. Cook the vegetables separately in boiling water until crisp-tender. Drain.
5. Scrub the winkles, put them in a saucepan and cover them with cold water. Add a little salt. Bring to a boil and cook for 10 minutes. Drain.
6. Peel the eggs. Remove the skin and bones from the cod.
7. Place the fish on a serving dish and surround it with the winkles and eggs. Arrange the beans, carrots, potatoes, tomatoes and artichokes on another dish. Serve the fish with the vegetables and garlic mayonnaise.

Morue à la créole
Creole Style Salt Cod

	00:15	00:15
	plus soaking	

American	Ingredients	Metric/Imperial
1 (2¾ lb)	Piece of salt cod	1 (1.25 kg / 2¾ lb)
1	Large onion	1
1	Garlic clove	1
1 tbsp	Vinegar	1 tbsp
	Salt and pepper	
1 tsp	Prepared mustard	1 tsp
3 tbsp	Oil	3 tbsp
	Cayenne pepper	
1 tsp	Chopped fresh parsley	1 tsp

1. Soak the cod in cold water for 24 hours (change the water several times).
2. Drain the cod, put it in a saucepan and cover with fresh cold water. Bring to a boil over a low heat and simmer for 10 minutes.
3. Meanwhile, peel and chop the onion and garlic.
4. Mix the vinegar with a pinch of salt, then stir in the mustard and pepper to taste. Add the oil, onion, garlic, a pinch of cayenne pepper and the chopped parsley. Mix well.
5. Drain the cod. Remove the skin (which should come off easily) and bones and flake the fish into pieces. Put the fish on a serving dish and cover with the vinaigrette dressing. Serve immediately.

Mackerel with mustard

Brandade de morue

Salt Cod Cream

	00:30 plus soaking	00:15

American	Ingredients	Metric/Imperial
1 (2 lb)	Tail piece of salt cod	1 (1 kg / 2 lb)
1¼ cups	Olive oil	300 ml / ½ pint
1	Garlic clove	1
1¼ cups	Crème fraîche (see page 122)	300 ml / ½ pint
	Salt and pepper	
½	Lemon (optional)	½

1. Soak the cod for 24 hours in cold water (change the water several times).
2. Drain the cod, put it in a saucepan and cover with fresh cold water. Bring slowly to a boil. Simmer for 10 minutes.
3. Heat the olive oil. Peel and slice the garlic.
4. Drain the cod. Remove skin and bones and flake the flesh into small pieces. Place the fish in a heavy saucepan over a low heat and add garlic, crème fraîche and hot oil. Stir with a wooden spoon to obtain a smooth white purée. Add salt and pepper to taste, and the juice of the ½ lemon, if desired.

Morue aux haricots

Salt Cod with White Beans

	00:30 plus soaking	02:00

American	Ingredients	Metric/Imperial
1½ lb	Salt cod fillets	750 g / 1½ lb
2 cups	Dried navy [haricot] beans	500 g / 1 lb
2	Large carrots	2
3	Onions	3
1	Bouquet garni	1
2	Garlic cloves	2
2	Tomatoes	2
½ cup	Butter	125 g / 4 oz
⅔ cup	Crème fraîche (see page 122)	150 ml / ¼ pint
2 tbsp	Tomato paste [purée]	2 tbsp
	Salt and pepper	
	Grated nutmeg	
½ cup	Grated gruyère cheese	50 g / 2 oz

1. Soak the cod fillets in cold water for 24 hours (change the water several times).
2. Drain the fish, put it in a saucepan and cover with fresh cold water. Bring to a simmer over a low heat, then remove from the heat, cover and leave to poach for 10 minutes. Drain the fish and flake it, discarding skin and any bones. Set aside.
3. Put the beans in a large saucepan, add cold water to cover generously and bring to a boil over a low heat.
4. Meanwhile, peel the carrots and 2 of the onions. When the bean water begins to boil, drain the beans in a strainer and put them back in the saucepan. Add the carrots, onions, bouquet garni and fresh boiling water to cover generously. Simmer for about 1 hour or until the beans are soft.
5. Peel and chop the remaining onion and garlic. Slice the tomatoes.

6. Preheat the oven to 400°F / 200°C / Gas Mark 6.
7. When the beans are cooked, take a large cupful of them and purée in a blender, food processor or mill. Set aside.
8. Melt the butter in a saucepan, add the chopped garlic and onion and soften over a low heat without browning. Add a large cupful of the bean cooking liquid, crème fraîche and tomato paste, then little by little incorporate the bean purée to obtain a smooth sauce with the consistency of thin cream. Season to taste with salt and pepper and add a pinch of nutmeg.
9. Mix the cod with the remaining beans, drained, and pour into an ovenproof dish. Add the sauce and cover with the slices of tomato. Sprinkle with the cheese and brown in the oven for 10 minutes. Serve very hot.

Merlans en colère

'Angry' Whiting

	00:15	00:20

American	Ingredients	Metric/Imperial
6 (6-8 oz)	Whiting, cleaned	6 (175-250 g / 6-8 oz)
⅔ cup	Milk	150 ml / ¼ pint
	Salt and pepper	
1¼ cups	Flour	150 g / 5 oz
	Oil for deep frying	
	Lemon halves	

1. Put the tails of the whiting into their mouths, and carefully tie them with string to secure. Pour the milk into a bowl and season it with salt. Put the flour into another bowl.
2. Heat the oil for deep frying. Dip each whiting into the milk and then immediately into the flour, then put the fish in the oil and cook until golden. Drain on paper towels.
3. Arrange the fish on a serving dish and season with salt and pepper. Cut away the string with a knife. Garnish with lemon halves.

Morue à la crème

Salt Cod with Cream

	00:30	00:40

American	Ingredients	Metric/Imperial
1¼ lb	Salt cod fillet	625 g / 1¼ lb
1½ lb	Potatoes	750 g / 1½ lb
	Salt and pepper	
2	Medium-sized onions	2
1 tbsp	Butter	1 tbsp
1 tbsp	Flour	1 tbsp
1 cup	Heavy [double] cream	250 ml / 8 fl oz
2 tbsp	Chopped fresh parsley	2 tbsp

1. The day before making the dish, cut the salt cod into small pieces and soak for 24 hours in cold water, changing the water frequently.
2. Peel the potatoes and cook in boiling salted water.
3. Meanwhile, place the fish in a pan, cover with plenty of cold water and heat gently to boiling point. Turn off the heat, cover the pan and leave the fish to poach for 10-15 minutes.
4. Peel and chop the onions. Melt the butter in a frying pan, add the onions and soften without allowing them to brown. Sprinkle them with the flour and stir for 1 minute over a low heat. Add 4 tablespoons of the cooking liquid from the fish and

stir well. Stir in the cream. Season to taste with salt and pepper, remembering that the fish is already quite salty.

5. Drain the cod, and pat dry with paper towels. Flake the fish, discarding all skin and any bones, and add to the sauce. Heat gently without allowing the sauce to boil.

6. Drain the potatoes and cut into rounds. Arrange them on the bottom of a warmed serving dish and cover with the cod in cream sauce. Sprinkle with the chopped parsley and serve immediately.

Morue en Tourte

Salt Cod Pie

	00:45	01:35
	plus soaking and making or thawing pastry	

American	Ingredients	Metric/Imperial
1¼ lb	Salt cod	625 g / 1¼ lb
1 lb	Puff pastry (see page 457 or use frozen)	500 g / 1 lb
1½ lb	Potatoes	750 g / 1½ lb
1	Onion	1
2	Shallots	2
4	Fresh parsley sprigs	4
¼ cup	Butter	50 g / 2 oz
	Salt and pepper	
1	Egg	1
½ cup	Crème fraîche (see page 122)	125 ml / 4 fl oz

1. Remove the skin from the cod and cut the flesh into pieces. Soak for 24 hours in cold water to cover. Change the water frequently during this time.

2. If using frozen pastry, allow it to thaw.

3. Drain the cod and put in a flameproof casserole. Cover with fresh cold water and bring to a simmer. Remove the casserole from the heat and cover tightly with a lid or foil. Leave to poach for 10 minutes, without removing the cover.

4. Meanwhile, cook the potatoes, without peeling them, for 25 minutes in boiling water.

5. Drain the cod. Flake it, discarding all bones.

6. Drain the potatoes. Peel and slice them. Peel and chop the onion and shallots. Chop the parsley.

7. Preheat the oven to 425°F / 220°C / Gas Mark 7.

8. Roll out two-thirds of the puff pastry on a lightly floured board to a thickness of about ¼ in / 4 mm. Butter and lightly flour a deep 9 in / 24 cm pie dish and line with the pastry. Let the excess hang over the rim of the dish.

9. Make a layer of half the potatoes on the bottom of the pie dish. Add the flaked cod, onion and shallots and cover with the remaining potatoes. Sprinkle with the chopped parsley and dot with the butter cut into small pieces. Sprinkle with salt and pepper to taste.

10. Roll out the remaining pastry and use to cover the pie. With wet fingers, roll and twist the pastry edges together to seal. Make notches in the twisted edge with a pair of scissors. Prick the lid in 4 or 5 places with a skewer.

11. Lightly beat the egg with a fork. Brush the surface of the pie with beaten egg. Bake for 20 minutes, then reduce the oven temperature to 400°F / 200°C / Gas Mark 6. Bake for a further 40 minutes. If the pastry becomes too brown, cover with foil.

12. Remove the pie from the oven without turning off the heat. With a small, very sharp knife, carefully remove the lid at the twisted edge and add the crème fraîche. Put the lid back on the pie and return to the oven for a further 5 minutes baking. Serve immediately.

Portuguese salt cod

Morue portugaise

Portuguese Salt Cod

	00:30	01:00
	plus soaking	

American	Ingredients	Metric/Imperial
1 (2¾ lb)	Piece of salt cod	1 (1.25 kg / 2¾ lb)
6	Tomatoes	6
2	Large onions	2
2	Garlic cloves	2
4	Green or sweet red peppers	4
6 tbsp	Olive oil	6 tbsp
1	Bouquet garni	1
⅔ cup	Dry white wine	150 ml / ¼ pint
	Pepper	
	Cayenne pepper	
1 cup	Black olives	125 g / 4 oz

1. Soak the cod in cold water for 24 hours (change the water several times).

2. Drain the fish. Remove the skin and bones and cut the flesh into large pieces. Pat dry with paper towels. Set aside.

3. Halve the tomatoes and remove the seeds. Peel and finely chop the onions. Peel and crush the garlic. Cut the green or red peppers in half, remove the core and seeds and cut the flesh into strips. Heat half the oil in a frying pan, add the tomatoes, peppers and onions and cook until golden brown.

4. Meanwhile, heat the remaining oil in another frying pan, add the pieces of cod and brown lightly on all sides.

5. Put the cooked vegetables into a flameproof casserole. Add the garlic, bouquet garni, wine, and pepper and cayenne pepper to taste. Add the pieces of cod and mix together. Cover the casserole and cook over a low heat for 1 hour.

6. About 10 minutes before the end of the cooking time add the olives.

Morue parisienne

Parisian Salt Cod

	00:30	00:30
	plus soaking	

American	Ingredients	Metric/Imperial
2¾ lb	Salt cod	1.25 kg / 2¾ lb
2 lb	Potatoes	1 kg / 2 lb
2 tbsp	Peanut oil	2 tbsp
4	Garlic cloves	4
3 tbsp	Chopped fresh parsley	3 tbsp

1. Remove the skin and large bones from the cod. Cut the flesh into large pieces and soak for 24 hours in cold water to cover. Change the water frequently during this time.
2. Drain the cod. Put the pieces in a flameproof casserole and cover with fresh cold water. Bring to a simmer over a low heat. Remove from the heat, cover and leave to poach for 10 minutes.
3. Meanwhile, cook the potatoes, without peeling them, for 25 minutes in boiling water.
4. Drain the cod and pat dry on paper towels. Flake and set aside.
5. Drain the potatoes. Peel them and cut into large dice. Heat the oil in a frying pan, add the potatoes and brown on all sides.
6. Add the fish and cook until browned.
7. Peel and chop the garlic. Add to the frying pan with the chopped parsley. Stir for a further minute and serve.

Morue majorquine

Majorcan Salt Cod

	00:25	01:00
	plus soaking	

American	Ingredients	Metric/Imperial
2¾ lb	Salt cod	1.25 kg / 2¾ lb
2¾ lb	Potatoes	1.25 kg / 2¾ lb
1	Small bunch of fresh parsley	1
1	Fresh thyme sprig	1
1	Bay leaf	1
2	Garlic cloves	2
3	Medium-sized tomatoes	3
⅓ cup	Raisins	50 g / 2 oz
	Pepper	
1 tbsp	White bread crumbs	1 tbsp
⅔ cup	Olive oil	150 ml / ¼ pint

1. Soak the cod for 24 hours in cold water to cover. Change the water frequently during this time.
2. Put the cod in a flameproof casserole and cover with fresh cold water. Bring to a simmer over a low heat and cook gently for 10 minutes.
3. Drain the cod. Cut the thick end of the cod into 6 pieces, and flake the remainder. Set aside.
4. Cook the unpeeled potatoes for 25 minutes in boiling water.
5. Meanwhile, chop the parsley. Remove the leaves from the thyme sprig and crumble the bay leaf. Mix the herbs together.
6. Preheat the oven to 400°F / 200°C / Gas Mark 6.
7. Peel and crush the garlic. Slice the tomatoes.
8. Drain the potatoes. Peel and slice them.
9. Arrange half the potatoes over the bottom of a baking dish. Sprinkle with half of the garlic, half the mixed herbs and the

raisins. Cover with the flaked cod and add pepper to taste. Cover with the remaining potatoes and on top arrange the pieces of cod and the tomatoes. Sprinkle with the remaining garlic and herbs and the bread crumbs. Pour over the olive oil.
10. Bake for 25-30 minutes. Serve very hot.

Mulets flambés au fenouil

Flamed Mullet with Fennel

	00:10	00:15 to 00:25
	plus salting	

American	Ingredients	Metric/Imperial
6 (½ lb)	Striped [grey] mullet	6 (250 g / 8 oz)
	Salt	
1	Bunch of dried fennel leaves	1

1. Lightly salt the inside and outside of the fish.
2. Preheat the broiler [grill]. Dry the fish with paper towels, but do not scale them. Place them on the rack in the broiler pan. Cook under the broiler until tender.
3. Tie the fennel leaves with string to form a bundle. About 5 minutes before the end of the cooking time, put the bundle of fennel leaves in the broiler pan and set alight so that the aroma penetrates the fish.
4. When fish is cooked with the scales left on, the skin lifts off like a shell. Therefore, there is no need to worry if the skin turns dark. Serve the fish with hot pepper and potato mayonnaise (see page 120), garlic mayonnaise (see page 119), or a vinaigrette dressing with thyme (see page 120).

Raie au beurre noir

Skate with Brown Butter Sauce

	00:10	00:30

American	Ingredients	Metric/Imperial
2 ¾ lb	Skate	1.25 kg / 2¾ lb
	Court bouillon (see page 114)	
1 cup	Butter	250 g / 8 oz
⅓ cup	Vinegar	5 tbsp
5 tbsp	Capers	5 tbsp
¼ cup	Chopped fresh parsley	4 tbsp

1. Put the skate in a large stewpan and cover with court-bouillon. Bring to a simmer, then cook for 15-20 minutes, depending on the size of the fish.
2. Remove from the heat and leave to cool slightly, then drain the skate, reserving the cooking liquid.
3. Using scissors, trim off the edge of the fins. Remove and discard the black and the white skin. Divide the flesh into pieces, discarding the bones. Keep hot on a serving dish.
4. Melt the butter in a frying pan and cook until it is nut-brown in color. Strain 5 tablespoons of the reserved fish cooking liquid. Remove the butter from the heat and gradually add the vinegar and strained liquid, then the capers. Bring to the boil.
5. Sprinkle the skate with the chopped parsley and pour the caper butter over the top. Serve immediately.

Raie pochée sauce anchois

Poached Skate with Anchovy Sauce

	00:25		00:50

American	Ingredients	Metric/Imperial
2	Onions	2
2	Carrots	2
4	Cloves	4
1	Garlic clove	1
2 quarts	Water	2 l / 3½ pints
⅔ cup	Wine vinegar	150 ml / ¼ pint
1	Bouquet garni	1
	Salt and pepper	
	Black peppercorns	
3 lb	Skate wing	1.5 kg / 3 lb
3 tbsp	Butter	40 g / 1½ oz
½ cup	Flour	50 g / 2 oz
3 cups	Milk	750 ml / 1¼ pints
6 tbsp	Crème fraîche (see page 122)	6 tbsp
3 tbsp	Anchovy paste	3 tbsp
½	Lemon	½
1	Egg yolk	1

1. Peel the onions and carrots. Slice the carrots. Leave the onions whole and stick 2 cloves into each onion. Peel the garlic.
2. Pour the water and wine vinegar into a large stewpan and add the carrots, onions, garlic and bouquet garni. Season with salt and add a few peppercorns. Bring to a boil and simmer on a low heat for 30 minutes.
3. Cut the skate into sections if the wings are large. Add to the pan and simmer very gently for 10 minutes or until cooked.
4. Meanwhile, melt the butter in a heavy saucepan on a low heat. Add the flour and stir until the butter has absorbed the flour. Add the milk, season to taste with salt and pepper and cook, stirring, on a low heat until the sauce thickens (10 minutes).
5. Add crème fraîche, anchovy paste, the juice of the ½ lemon and the egg yolk and stir thoroughly.
6. To serve, drain the skate, remove the skin and bones and pour the anchovy sauce over the fish.

Rougets en papillotes

Red Mullet or Goatfish Baked in Paper

	00:30	00:15 to 00:18	

American	Ingredients	Metric/Imperial
3	Medium-sized onions	3
6	Red mullet or goatfish, cleaned	6
	Olive oil	
	Fennel seeds	
	Salt and pepper	

1. Preheat the oven to 350°F / 180°C / Gas Mark 4.
2. Using parchment [greaseproof] paper, cut out 6 heart shapes, each sufficiently large to wrap a fish. Peel and chop the onions.
3. Coat the fish with olive oil. Put a pinch of chopped onion, a few fennel seeds and a pinch of salt on one half of each paper heart. Put the fish on the paper hearts, season again with onions, fennel seeds, salt and pepper and fold over the other half of each heart. Roll the edges of the hearts, twisting the paper from the head down to the tail so that the fish is completely enclosed.
4. Arrange the wrapped fish on a rack in a roasting pan and bake for 15-18 minutes.
5. Serve the fish in the paper wrapping. When cooked in this way, they can be removed from the oven and kept hot for a few minutes without becoming dry.

Sardines grillées

Broiled [Grilled] Sardines

	00:05 plus salting	00:04 to 00:06	

American	Ingredients	Metric/Imperial
30	Fresh sardines or other small oily fish	30
2 tbsp	Sea salt	2 tbsp

1. Fresh sardines cooked in this way are not cleaned, scaled or washed. About 30-50 minutes before cooking, sprinkle the fish with the salt.
2. Preheat the broiler [grill].
3. Shake the sardines, holding them by the tail, so that the excess salt falls off. Arrange them on the broiler rack. Broil them for 2-3 minutes on each side, turning them over carefully. Do not overcook them as they will become dry. Cooked in this way, the skin comes off easily and the flesh underneath is moist and tender.
4. Serve with lemon wedges and garlic butter (see page 113).

Sardines à l'escabèche

Marinated Sardines

	00:15 plus marinating		00:15

American	Ingredients	Metric/Imperial
18	Medium-sized fresh sardines or other small oily fish, cleaned	18
3 tbsp	Flour	3 tbsp
⅔ cup	Olive oil	150 ml / ¼ pint
½	Garlic clove	½
4	Fresh mint leaves	4
	Salt and pepper	
1 tbsp	Vinegar	1 tbsp

1. Cut the heads off the fish. Coat the fish in flour.
2. Heat the olive oil in a frying pan, add the sardines and fry for about 1 minute on each side. The sardines are cooked when they are gold and firm. As soon as they are cooked, drain them and leave to cool. Reserve the oil.
3. Peel and crush the garlic. Chop the mint. Dissolve a pinch of salt in the vinegar. Season with pepper to taste. Add the reserved, cooled oil, garlic and chopped mint. Mix well.
4. Serve the sardines cold in the mint dressing.

Rouget au fenouil

Red Mullet or Goatfish with Fennel

00:20   00:45 to 01:00

American	Ingredients	Metric/Imperial
1 (3 lb)	Red mullet or goatfish, cleaned	1 (1.5 kg / 3 lb)
	Salt and pepper	
	Fresh fennel sprigs	
2	Garlic cloves	2
1	Onion	1
4	Tomatoes	4
2	Lemons	2
1¼ cups	Olive oil	300 ml / ½ pint
1 tsp	Fennel seeds	1 tsp

1. Preheat the oven to 400°F / 200°C / Gas Mark 6.
2. Season the inside of the fish with salt and pepper and add 2 sprigs of fennel. Peel and crush the garlic. Peel and slice the onion. Halve the tomatoes and remove the seeds. Slice one lemon.
3. Put the crushed garlic, onion slices and 2 or 3 sprigs of fennel in an ovenproof dish. Put the fish on top and cover with the slices of lemon and the tomato halves. Surround with a few more sprigs of fennel. Season with salt and pepper and sprinkle with 3 tablespoons of olive oil.
4. Put the dish in the oven. When the fish has browned (about 15 minutes), turn the oven down to 325°F / 160°C / Gas Mark 3. Continue cooking for 30-45 minutes, basting the fish frequently with the pan juices.
5. Meanwhile, pour the rest of the oil into a bowl or saucepan and add the fennel seeds and the juice of the remaining lemon. Season with salt and pepper. Place the bowl or saucepan over another saucepan half filled with water and heat until the sauce is very hot.
6. Serve the fish with the sauce in a sauceboat.

Rougets gratinés

Red Mullet or Goatfish au Gratin

00:30   00:25 to 00:30

American	Ingredients	Metric/Imperial
4	Tomatoes	4
¼ lb	Mushrooms	125 g / 4 oz
½	Lemon	½
3	Garlic cloves	3
5 - 6 tbsp	Oil	5 - 6 tbsp
	Salt and pepper	
1¼ cups	Red wine	300 ml / ½ pint
1 tbsp	Chopped fresh herbs (parsley, chervil, fennel)	1 tbsp
6	Red mullet or goatfish, cleaned	6
½ cup	Grated gruyère cheese	50 g / 2 oz

1. Preheat the broiler [grill].
2. Peel the tomatoes (first plunging them in boiling water for

10 seconds), cut them in half and remove the seeds. Roughly chop the flesh. Thinly slice the mushrooms. Squeeze the juice from the ½ lemon over them so that they do not blacken. Peel and crush the garlic.
3. Heat 2 tablespoons of oil in a frying pan, add the mushrooms and cook until all the liquid has evaporated. Remove the mushrooms with a slotted spoon and set aside. Put the tomatoes and crushed garlic in the pan and season with salt and pepper. Cook until reduced to a purée. Add the red wine and chopped herbs and stir for 2 minutes over a brisk heat. Remove from the heat and keep hot.
4. Brush the fish with the remaining oil. Broil [grill] for 10 minutes on one side, then turn them over and cook for 15 minutes on the other side.
5. Preheat the oven to 425°F / 220°C / Gas Mark 7.
6. Arrange the fish in an ovenproof dish. Pour the tomato sauce over the top, surround with the mushrooms and sprinkle with the grated cheese. Put the dish in the oven and bake for about 10 minutes.

Fried sardines

Sardines frites

Fried Sardines

00:30   00:05

American	Ingredients	Metric/Imperial
30 - 36	Fresh sardines or other small oily fish, cleaned	30 - 36
	Milk	
½ tsp	Grated nutmeg	½ tsp
2 tbsp	Chopped mixed fresh herbs (parsley, fennel, etc)	2 tbsp
½ cup	Flour	50 g / 2 oz
	Salt and pepper	
	Oil for deep frying	

1. Wipe the sardines to remove the scales. Place them in a shallow dish and cover with milk.
2. Mix together the nutmeg, herbs, flour and salt and pepper to taste.
3. Heat the oil for deep frying.
4. Remove the fish from the milk, one at a time, and shake off excess milk. Coat each fish in the flour mixture and drop it immediately into the oil, which should be hot but not smoking. Cook until firm and golden. Drain on paper towels and serve very hot.

Filets de sandre au riesling

Walleye [Pike-Perch] with Riesling

American	Ingredients	Metric/Imperial
	00:30	00:30
3	Shallots	3
6	Large white mushrooms	6
¼ cup	Butter	50 g / 2 oz
2 lb	Walleye [pike-perch] fillets	1 kg / 2 lb
	Salt and pepper	
2½ cups	Riesling or other white wine	600 ml / 1 pint
2 cups	Crème fraîche (see page 122)	450 ml / ¾ pint
1	Egg yolk	1

1. Peel and finely chop the shallots. Thinly slice the mushrooms. Melt the butter in a frying pan, add the shallots and mushrooms and cook, stirring occasionally, until all the liquid has evaporated.
2. Season both sides of the fish fillets with salt and pepper and put them in the frying pan. Add the wine. Cover and cook over a brisk heat for 4-5 minutes.
3. Remove the fillets with a slotted spatula and keep hot.
4. Reduce the sauce over a brisk heat until it has a syrupy consistency. Stir in crème fraîche. Adjust the seasoning. Add the egg yolk, beating with a whisk.
5. Pour the sauce over the fish and serve.

Cook's tip: for binding the sauce, the egg yolk can be replaced by kneaded butter (see page 112).

Roussette à la tomate

Dogfish with Tomatoes

American	Ingredients	Metric/Imperial
	00:30	00:20
2 lb	Tomatoes	1 kg / 2 lb
2	Garlic cloves	2
2¾ lb	Dogfish, huss or other shark fillet	1.25 kg / 2¾ lb
2 tbsp	Flour	2 tbsp
3 tbsp	Oil	3 tbsp
2 tbsp	Brandy	2 tbsp
2 tbsp	Chopped fresh parsley	2 tbsp
	Dried thyme	
1	Bay leaf	1
	Salt and pepper	

1. Peel the tomatoes (first plunging them in boiling water for 10 seconds), cut them in half, remove the seeds and dice the flesh. Peel and crush the garlic.
2. Cut the fish into 12 pieces. Coat the pieces of fish in the flour. Heat the oil in a stewpan, add the pieces of fish and brown on all sides. Remove the fish with a slotted spoon and put on a heatproof plate. Sprinkle with the brandy and set alight.
3. Add the garlic, parsley and tomatoes to the pan and cook gently until the tomatoes are pulped.
4. Add the fish and its liquid, a pinch of dried thyme and the bay leaf. Season with salt and pepper and cook for about 15 minutes on a low heat.

Saint-Pierre à l'oseille

John Dory With Sorrel

American	Ingredients	Metric/Imperial
	00:20	00:30
2 lb	Fresh spinach	1 kg / 2 lb
1 lb	Sorrel	500 g / 1 lb
3	Shallots	3
3	Medium-sized John Dory (or pompano or bream), skinned and filleted	3
1 cup	Butter	250 g / 8 oz
1 cup	Dry white wine	250 ml / 8 fl oz
	Salt and pepper	
1 tbsp	Flour	1 tbsp
2 tbsp	Crème fraîche (see page 122)	2 tbsp
6	Egg yolks	6
½	Lemon	½

1. Rinse the spinach and sorrel and remove all tough stalks. Peel and chop the shallots. Pound the fish fillets lightly with a wooden spatula to break down the fibers.
2. Preheat the oven to 350°F / 180°C / Gas Mark 4.
3. Melt 1 teaspoon of butter in a frying pan, add the shallots and fry until they are soft and translucent. Pour the white wine into the pan, season with salt and pepper and heat without allowing it to boil. Drop 4 fish fillets into this preparation and poach gently for 5 minutes, then remove them with a slotted spatula. Do the same with the remaining fillets. Keep the fish hot and reserve the cooking liquid.
4. While the fish is being cooked, drop the spinach into a pan of boiling water. Bring back to a boil and cook for 1 minute. Drain the spinach in a colander, then squeeze to remove excess moisture. Chop the spinach coarsely.
5. Heat 1 tablespoon of butter in a saucepan, add the sorrel and cook until it is soft and reduced to a purée. Add the spinach and stir. Sprinkle with the flour. Cook, stirring occasionally, until all moisture has evaporated. Add crème fraîche and season with salt and pepper. Remove from the heat and keep hot.
6. Boil the fish cooking liquid until reduced to ⅔ cup [150 ml / ¼ pint]. Pour it into a bowl or saucepan and place this over another pan half filled with hot water. Beating with a whisk, add the egg yolks, ½ cup [125 g / 4 oz] of butter cut into small pieces and the juice of the ½ lemon. Continue to beat until the mixture is frothy, then gradually add the remaining butter cut into small pieces, beating continuously.
7. Spread the spinach and sorrel mixture in an ovenproof dish. Arrange the fish fillets on top and pour over the sauce. Reheat in the oven without allowing the sauce to boil.

Roussette sauce moutarde

Dogfish with Mustard Sauce

	00:15	00:30

American	Ingredients	Metric/Imperial
2 ¾ lb	Dogfish or huss	1.25 kg / 2 ¾ lb
	Court-bouillon (see page 114)	
2	Shallots	2
1 tbsp	Butter	1 tbsp
2 tbsp	Flour	2 tbsp
1 cup	Crème fraîche (see page 122)	250 ml / 8 fl oz
	Salt and pepper	
1 tbsp	Strong prepared mustard	2 tbsp
2 tbsp	Chopped fresh parsley	2 tbsp

1. Cut the fish into 12 pieces. Arrange them in a single layer in a stewpan and cover with court-bouillon. Bring to a boil over a medium heat, then turn down the heat and simmer gently for 15 minutes. Meanwhile, peel and chop the shallots.
2. Drain the pieces of fish, reserving the cooking liquid. Strain the liquid and reserve 1 cup [250 ml / 8 fl oz].
3. Heat the butter in a saucepan, add the shallots and cook until they are soft and translucent. Sprinkle with the flour and stir for 2 minutes, then add the crème fraîche and bring to a boil, stirring continuously. Stir in the reserved cooking liquid to obtain a very thick sauce. Season with salt and pepper and add the mustard.
4. Arrange the pieces of fish in a flameproof serving dish. Pour the sauce over the top and heat very gently for 15 minutes. Sprinkle with chopped parsley before serving.

Saumon en koulibiac

Russian Salmon Pie

	01:00 Serves 8	01:30

American	Ingredients	Metric/Imperial
2 cups	Court-bouillon (see page 114)	500 ml / ¾ pint
2 cups	Dry white wine	500 ml / ¾ pint
1 (1 ¼ lb)	Piece of salmon, cleaned	1 (625 g / 1 ¼ lb)
¾ lb	Salmon and sole bones and trimmings	350 g / 12 oz
1 lb	Fresh spinach	500 g / 1 lb
4	Hard-cooked eggs	4
1 cup	Rice	250 g / 8 oz
3	Egg yolks	3
½ cup	Crème fraîche (see page 122)	125 ml / 4 fl oz
1	Lemon	1
1	Pork caul fat	1
2 quantities	Brioche dough (see page 457)	2 quantities
1	Egg white	1

1. Pour the court-bouillon and wine into a fish kettle or large saucepan. Add the salmon. Heat until the liquid simmers, then continue simmering for 15-20 minutes.

2. Drain the salmon, reserving the cooking liquid. Remove the skin from the salmon and separate the flesh into fillets, discarding the bones. Add the skin, with the salmon and sole bones and trimmings, to the fish cooking liquid. Simmer for 30 minutes.
3. Meanwhile, rinse the spinach and remove tough stalks. Cook for 10 minutes in boiling salted water, then drain in a colander. Press well to extract excess water. Chop coarsely. Slice the hard-cooked eggs.
4. Strain the fish stock and return it to the saucepan. Add the rice and cook for 20 minutes. Drain and cool, then add 2 of the egg yolks, the cream and the juice of the lemon. Mix well.
5. Preheat the oven to 400°F / 200°C / Gas Mark 6.
6. Soak the piece of caul in cold water. Drain. Spread it out carefully on a cloth, then line a cake pan with it, leaving it hanging over the sides. Put half the rice mixture on the bottom, cover with half the spinach and add the salmon fillets. Cover with the rest of the spinach, then with the rest of the rice mixture and put the slices of hard-cooked egg on top. Fold the caul over so that the contents are completely enclosed.
7. Roll out the brioche dough on a floured surface to a thickness of ½ in /1 cm. Carefully tip the caul-wrapped filling out of the pan and roll it up in the dough. Using a pastry brush dipped in the egg white, paint the edges of the dough and pinch them to seal the roll.
8. Put the stuffed brioche on a buttered baking sheet. Brush all over with the remaining egg yolk. Bake for 30 minutes.
9. Serve the pie as soon as it is taken out of the oven, accompanied by lemon-flavored drawn or clarified butter (see page 113).

Saumon froid

Cold Poached Salmon with Piquant Mayonnaise

	00:30 Serves 15–20	01:00

American	Ingredients	Metric/Imperial
1 (6 lb)	Salmon, cleaned	1 (3 kg / 6 lb)
1	Bottle of dry white wine	1
1	Court-bouillon (see page 114)	
3 cups	Mayonnaise (see page 119)	750 ml / 1 ¼ pints
1 tsp	Tabasco sauce	1 tsp
3 tbsp	Chopped fresh parsley	3 tbsp
2 tbsp	Chopped fresh tarragon	2 tbsp
3 tbsp	Chopped fresh chervil	3 tbsp
2	Gherkins	2
1 tbsp	Capers	1 tbsp
1	Garlic clove	1
1	Shallot	1
	Salt and pepper	

1. Put the salmon in a fish kettle. Pour in the wine and add enough court-bouillon to cover the fish completely. Heat rapidly until the liquid simmers, then continue simmering for 1 hour.
2. Take the fish kettle off the heat and leave the salmon to cool in the liquid. Keep in a cool place for 12 hours.
3. Drain the salmon and skin it carefully. Place it on a serving dish. Strain the cooking liquid and chill until it begins to set.
4. Meanwhile, combine the mayonnaise, tabasco sauce, parsley, tarragon and chervil. Finely chop the gherkins and capers. Peel and finely chop the garlic and shallot. Add to the mayonnaise. Taste and adjust the seasoning. Chill.

5. Paint several layers of the setting fish cooking liquid on the salmon with a pastry brush. Chill until set. Serve with the mayonnaise.

Cold poached salmon with piquant mayonnaise

Soles en gondoles

Sole in Baked Potatoes

00:45   01:15

American	Ingredients	Metric/Imperial
6	Large baking potatoes	6
2	Shallots	2
½ cup	Butter	125 g / 4 oz
1¼ cups	Dry white wine	300 ml / ½ pint
6	Sole fillets	6
½ lb	Peeled shrimp [prawns]	250 g / 8 oz
2 tbsp	Flour	50 g / 2 oz
½ cup	Crème fraîche (see page 122)	125 ml / 4 fl oz
	Salt and pepper	
½ cup	Grated gruyère cheese	50 g / 2 oz

1. Preheat the oven to 400°F / 200°C / Mark 6.
2. Scrub and prick the potatoes. Arrange them on a shelf in the oven and bake for 1 hour, turning them every 15 minutes.
3. Meanwhile, peel and chop the shallots. Heat 1 tablespoon of butter in a frying pan, add the shallots and fry until they are soft and translucent. Pour in the wine, stir and add the sole fillets. Simmer for 8-10 minutes. Remove the fish with a slotted spatula and set aside.
4. Add the shrimp to the frying pan. Stir, then cover, remove from the heat and leave to poach for 6-8 minutes. Drain the shrimp, reserving the liquid, and set aside.
5. Strain the liquid into a small saucepan and boil to reduce it to ⅔ cup [150 ml / ¼ pint].
6. Melt 1 tablespoon of butter in a saucepan, add the flour and stir for 1 minute over the heat. Add the reduced cooking

liquid and crème fraîche and cook over a low heat, stirring, until the sauce thickens. Season with salt and pepper. Mix half the sauce with the shrimp. Set aside.
7. Split open the potatoes and carefully scoop out some of the flesh with a small spoon, without damaging the skins. Mash 4 tablespoons of the scooped-out potato with 1 tablespoon sauce and salt to taste. Put this mixture back into the potato shells. Arrange the potatoes in an ovenproof dish.
8. Fill the potatoes with the shrimp mixture and put a sole fillet in each. Top with the remaining sauce. Sprinkle with the grated cheese and dot with the remaining butter. Brown in the oven for 10 minutes.

Filets de sole Marguerite

Sole in Cream Sauce

00:40   00:40

American	Ingredients	Metric/Imperial
1 quart	Dry white wine	1 l / 1¾ pint
1 quart	Water	1 l / 1¾ pint
1	Onion	1
1	Clove	1
1	Celery stalk	1
1	Bouquet garni	1
	Salt and pepper	
6	Sole fillets	6
1½ quarts	Fresh mussels	1.5 kg / 3 lb
¾ lb	Mushrooms	350 g / 12 oz
5 tbsp	Butter	65 g / 2½ oz
1½ tbsp	Flour	2 tbsp
⅔ cup	Crème fraîche (see page 122)	150 ml / ¼ pint
5 oz	Cooked peeled shrimp [prawns]	150 g / 5 oz
1 tbsp	Tomato paste [purée]	1 tbsp

1. Pour the white wine and water into a saucepan. Peel the onion and stud with the clove. Add to the pan with the celery and bouquet garni. Season with salt and pepper to taste. Bring to a boil.
2. Roll up the fillets of sole and tie with string. Put them in the boiling liquid, cover and simmer for 15 minutes.
3. Meanwhile, scrub the mussels thoroughly. Rinse and drain. Put them in a covered pan over a brisk heat and cook until they open, shaking the pan occasionally. (Discard any mussels that remain closed.) Remove the mussels from the shells and set aside. Reserve the liquid from the mussel shells.
4. Slice the mushrooms. Heat 1 tablespoon of butter in a frying pan, add the mushrooms and cook for 10 minutes or until all the liquid has evaporated.
5. Drain the sole fillets, reserving 2½ cups [600 ml / 1 pint] of the liquid in which they were cooked. Strain the liquid. Keep the sole hot.
6. Melt the remaining butter in a saucepan and add the flour. Stir until the flour has been absorbed, then add the strained liquid from the mussel shells and the reserved cooking liquid from the sole fillets. Bring to a boil, then add the crème fraîche, stirring continuously.
7. Add the shrimp to the sauce. Add the mushrooms, mussels and tomato paste. Stir to mix.
8. Preheat the broiler [grill]. Cut the string on the fillets of sole with scissors. Arrange the fillets in a flameproof serving dish. Pour the sauce over the top. Place under the broiler for a few minutes to brown the top.

Saumon au champagne
Salmon with Champagne

	00:30	01:15
	Serves 8–10	

American	Ingredients	Metric/Imperial
1 (4½-5 lb)	Salmon, cleaned	1 (2-2.4 kg / 4½-5 lb)
	Salt and pepper	
3	Shallots	3
¼ lb	Mushrooms	125 g / 4 oz
½ cup	Butter	125 g / 4 oz
½	Bottle of dry champagne or other sparkling white wine	½
½ cup	Crème fraîche (see page 122)	125 ml / 4 fl oz
2 - 3	Egg yolks	2 - 3

1. Preheat the oven to 400°F / 200°C / Gas Mark 6.
2. Season the inside of the salmon with salt and pepper. Wrap the head and tail in foil. Line the bottom of a roasting pan with foil so that you can remove the fish without breaking it.
3. Peel and finely chop the shallots. Finely chop the mushrooms. Spread the vegetables over the bottom of the roasting pan (on the foil). Put the fish on top and dot with pieces of butter. Season with salt and pepper and pour half the champagne over the top. Cover closely with foil and bake for about 1¼ hours. Baste frequently with the liquid in the pan, and gradually add the rest of the champagne, heated but not boiling. The liquid in the pan should not boil.
4. Check whether the salmon is done by cutting along the bone line with a knife: the flesh should separate from the bone. If not, continue cooking. Do not overcook or the fish will be dry.
5. Take the fish out with the aid of the foil. Skin it immediately on both sides, slide onto a serving dish and keep hot.
6. Pour the cooking liquid into a saucepan. Bring to a boil, remove from the heat and add the crème fraîche blended with the egg yolks, beating vigorously. Adjust the seasoning. Thicken without boiling, beating continuously with a whisk.
7. Pour some sauce over the fish and serve the rest in a sauceboat. In season, garnish the dish with cooked crayfish.

Saumon poché, sauce sabayon
Poached Salmon with Sabayon Sauce

	00:10	01:20
	plus cooling	

American	Ingredients	Metric/Imperial
3	Carrots	3
1	Onion	1
2	Cloves	2
1	Leek	1
1	Bouquet garni	1
2 cups	Dry white wine	500 ml / ¾ pint
2 cups	Water	500 ml / ¾ pint
1 (3 lb)	Piece of salmon, cleaned and scaled	1 (1.5 kg / 3 lb)
2½ cups	Crème fraîche (see page 122)	600 ml / 1 pint
4	Egg yolks	4
	Salt and pepper	

1. Peel and slice the carrots. Peel the onion and stud it with the cloves. Cut the leek in half. Put all the vegetables in a saucepan and add the bouquet garni, wine and water. Bring to a boil and simmer for 40 minutes.
2. Strain the stock and allow it to cool.
3. Put the salmon in a fish kettle (or a large saucepan) and add the stock. Poach for 40 minutes over a low heat.
4. About 10 minutes before the end of the cooking time, make the sauce. Put the cream in a bowl or saucepan and add the egg yolks, 4 tablespoons of the stock from the salmon, and salt and pepper to taste. Put the bowl or saucepan over another saucepan containing hot water and heat, stirring gently with a whisk. As soon as the mixture thickens, pour it into a sauceboat.
5. Drain the salmon and serve with the sauce.

Fried strips of sole

Soles en goujonnettes
Fried Strips of Sole

	00:20	00:06

American	Ingredients	Metric/Imperial
2 (1½ lb)	Soles, filleted	2 (750 g / 1½ lb)
4	Garlic cloves	4
1	Egg yolk	1
	Cayenne pepper	
	Paprika	
	Saffron powder	
	Salt and pepper	
1 cup	Olive oil plus oil for deep frying	250 ml / 8 fl oz
1¼ cups	Flour	150 g /5 oz
	Bread crumbs	
2	Eggs	2
2 tbsp	Water	2 tbsp

1. Cut the sole fillets into pieces ½ in / 1 cm wide and 3 in / 7.5 cm long. Set aside.
2. Peel the garlic, put it in a mortar and pound to a fine paste. Add the egg yolk, a pinch each of cayenne pepper, paprika and saffron, and salt and pepper to taste. Mix together. Add all but 2 tablespoons of the olive oil in a thin stream, beating with a whisk, as for mayonnaise. (If preferred, the spicy garlic mayonnaise may be made in a blender or food processor.) Set aside.

3. Spread out the flour and bread crumbs on 2 plates. Beat the eggs with the water and remaining oil in a shallow dish. Heat the oil for deep frying.

4. Dip the pieces of fish in flour, then in the beaten egg mixture and finally in the bread crumbs. Drop the pieces into the oil, which should be hot but not smoking, and fry for about 6 minutes or until golden.

5. Drain the pieces of fish on paper towels and serve immediately with the spicy garlic mayonnaise.

Filets de sole normande

Normandy Style Sole

00:20   00:40

American	Ingredients	Metric/Imperial
4 (¾ lb)	Soles, filleted (bones reserved)	4 (350 g / 12 oz)
	Court-bouillon (see page 114)	
	Hard [dry] cider	
⅔ cup	Water	150 ml / ¼ pint
1 pint	Fresh mussels	500 g / 1 lb
1 tbsp	Butter	1 tbsp
1 tbsp	Flour	1 tbsp
¼ cup	Crème fraîche (see page 122)	4 tbsp
	Grated nutmeg	
	Salt and pepper	

1. Roll up each sole fillet and secure with a wooden toothpick. Arrange all the fish rolls in a frying pan or flameproof casserole. Pour over half court-bouillon and half cider, enough liquid to cover the fish. Heat until the liquid simmers. Turn the fish rolls and cook for a further 5 minutes.

2. Remove the fish rolls with a slotted spatula and keep hot.

3. Add the fish bones to the pan with the water and simmer gently for 15 minutes.

4. Meanwhile, scrub the mussels thoroughly. Put them in a saucepan, cover and heat briskly, shaking the pan, until they open (discard any that remain closed). Remove the mussels from their shells, reserving all the liquid from the shells, and keep hot. Strain the liquid. Also strain the cider mixture.

5. Heat the butter in a saucepan, add the flour and stir for 2 minutes. Add crème fraîche and bring to a boil, stirring. Gradually blend in the strained mussel liquid and cider to obtain a thick cream sauce. Add a pinch of nutmeg and season to taste with salt and pepper. Stir in the mussels.

Sole with lemon butter

6. Remove the toothpicks from the fish rolls. Pour over the sauce and serve immediately.

Soles au Pouilly

Sole in White Wine Sauce

00:15   00:25

American	Ingredients	Metric/Imperial
12	Sole fillets	12
2	Shallots	2
¼ cup	Butter	50 g / 2 oz
½	Bottle of dry white wine	½
	Salt and pepper	
1 tbsp	Flour	1 tbsp
1 cup	Crème fraîche (see page 122)	250 ml / 8 fl oz
1 tsp	Tomato paste [purée]	1 tsp

1. Pound the sole fillets lightly with a wooden spatula so that they do not roll up during cooking. Peel and chop the shallots.

2. Heat 1 tablespoon of butter in a frying pan, add the shallots and cook until soft and translucent. Pour in the wine and season with salt and pepper. Bring to a simmer. Add 4 sole fillets and cook for 8 minutes. Remove the fish with a slotted spatula and keep hot. Cook the remaining 8 fillets in this way, remove and keep hot.

3. Reduce the cooking liquid by half, then strain it. Heat the rest of the butter in a saucepan, add the flour and stir for 1 minute. Add crème fraîche and bring to a boil, stirring. Add the reduced cooking liquid a little at a time and the tomato paste, just enough to color the sauce. Stir over a low heat to obtain a thick cream sauce. Adjust the seasoning if necessary.

4. Pour the sauce over the sole fillets and serve immediately.

Sole meunière

Sole with Lemon Butter

00:10   00:45

American	Ingredients	Metric/Imperial
3 tbsp	Flour	3 tbsp
	Salt and pepper	
6 (6 oz)	Soles, cleaned and skinned	6 (175 g / 6 oz)
1¼ cups	Oil	300 ml / ½ pint
1 cup	Butter	250 g / 8 oz
3	Lemons	3
2 tbsp	Chopped fresh parsley	2 tbsp

1. Season the flour with salt and pepper. Coat the soles with the flour.

2. Heat the oil in a frying pan and fry the soles, 2 or 3 at a time, for 8 minutes on each side. Drain the soles as they are cooked and keep hot on a serving dish.

3. When all the soles are cooked, pour the oil out of the frying pan and wipe the pan clean with paper towels. Cut the butter into small pieces and heat it in the frying pan until it bubbles. Add the juice of 1 lemon, stir well and pour over the soles. Sprinkle with the parsley.

4. Cut the remaining lemons into quarters or slices and arrange them around the fish. Serve immediately.

Thon grillé

Broiled [Grilled] Tuna

◣▱▱ 00:10   00:10 to 00:12 🍲

American	Ingredients	Metric/Imperial
¾ cup	Butter	175 g / 6 oz
2 tbsp	Chopped fresh parsley	2 tbsp
1	Lemon	1
	Salt and pepper	
6 (½ lb)	Tuna steaks	6 (250 g / 8 oz)
¼ cup	Oil	4 tbsp
	Parsley sprigs for garnish	
	Lemon wedges for serving	

1. Cream the butter with a wooden spoon. Add the chopped parsley and juice from the lemon. Blend well and season with salt and pepper. Put in the refrigerator to chill.
2. Preheat the broiler [grill].
3. Brush the tuna steaks with the oil. Put them on the broiler rack and broil for 10-12 minutes, turning them over halfway through the process.
4. When the tuna steaks are cooked, arrange them on a hot serving dish. Season with salt and pepper to taste and garnish with parsley sprigs and lemon wedges. Serve with the parsley butter.

Truites au bleu

Blue Trout

◣▱▱ 00:15   00:45 🍲

This recipe can only be made with freshly caught trout

American	Ingredients	Metric/Imperial
3	Carrots	3
2	Onions	2
3	Shallots	3
2 quarts	Water	2 l / 3½ pints
1	Bouquet garni	1
	Few fresh parsley sprigs	
	Salt and pepper	
6 (½ lb)	Trout, cleaned	6 (250 g / 8 oz)
3 cups	Wine vinegar	750 ml / 1¼ pints
	Chopped fresh parsley for garnish	
	Lemon wedges	

1. Peel the carrots, onions and shallots and cut them into thin strips. Put the vegetables into a saucepan with the water, bouquet garni, parsley sprigs, and salt and pepper to taste. Bring to a boil. Cover and simmer over a low heat for 30 minutes. Strain into a fish kettle or large pan and leave to cool.
2. Put the trout in a shallow dish. Boil the wine vinegar and pour it over the trout (this gives them their color). Leave to cool slightly, then plunge the fish into the stock in the fish kettle. Heat slowly until the liquid begins to simmer and simmer gently for 8-10 minutes.
3. Drain the trout carefully and arrange them on a serving dish. Sprinkle with chopped parsley and surround with lemon wedges. Serve with melted butter.

Truites à la parisienne

Parisian Style Trout

◣▱▱ 01:30   00:10 🍲

American	Ingredients	Metric/Imperial
1 envelope	Unflavored gelatin	1 sachet
1⅓ cups	Water	450 ml / ¾ pint
⅔ cup	Port wine	150 ml / ¼ pint
1 quart	Dry white wine	1 l / 1¾ pints
	Salt and pepper	
6 (½ lb)	Trout, cleaned	6 (250 g / 8 oz)
4	Tomatoes	4
4	Hard-cooked eggs	4
1 tbsp	Chopped fresh chives	1 tbsp

1. Dissolve the gelatin in the water, according to package directions, and stir in the port. Chill until this aspic is syrupy.
2. Meanwhile, bring the white wine to a boil. Season the inside and outside of the trout with salt and pepper and poach them in the wine for 10 minutes. Drain. Leave to cool, then remove the skin with a knife.
3. Put the trout on a grid placed over a dish. Pour a layer of the port aspic over them and put them in the refrigerator to set.
4. Meanwhile, peel the tomatoes (first plunging them for 10 seconds in boiling water), remove the seeds and slice them. Slice the eggs.
5. Garnish the trout with the tomato and egg slices and chopped chives. Pour a second layer of port aspic over the top. Chill until set.
6. Chill the rest of the port aspic until set. Before serving, dice it and arrange it around the trout.

Truite aux amandes

Trout with Almonds

◣▱▱ 00:20   00:15 🍲

American	Ingredients	Metric/Imperial
1¼ cups	Milk	300 ml / ½ pint
	Salt and pepper	
6 tbsp	Flour	6 tbsp
6 (6 oz)	Trout, cleaned	6 (175 g / 6 oz)
10 tbsp	Butter	150 g / 5 oz
3 tbsp	Oil	3 tbsp
1 cup	Flaked or sliced almonds	125 g / 4 oz
	Chopped fresh parsley for garnish	
	Lemon wedges for serving	

1. Pour the milk into a shallow dish and season with salt and pepper. Put the flour into another dish. Dip the trout in the milk, then roll them in the flour.
2. Heat ¼ cup [50 g / 2 oz] butter and oil in a large frying pan, add the trout and fry for 7 minutes on each side, turning them with a metal spatula.
3. Meanwhile, heat the remaining butter in a small saucepan. Add the almonds, stir well and brown lightly, shaking the pan from time to time.
4. When the trout are cooked, transfer them to a warmed serving dish. Pour over the almond butter mixture. Serve the trout sprinkled with the chopped parsley and surrounded with lemon wedges.

Trout with almonds

Truites aux pruneaux
Trout with Prunes

	00:15		00:15

American	Ingredients	Metric/Imperial
¼ cup	Potato starch or flour	50 g / 2 oz
6 (½ lb)	Trout, cleaned	6 (250 g / 8 oz)
6 tbsp	Butter	75 g / 3 oz
3 tbsp	Oil	3 tbsp
1 quart	Dry red wine	1 l / 1¾ pints
	Lemon juice	
	Salt and pepper	
1	Fresh thyme sprig	1
1	Bay leaf	1
	Grated nutmeg	
30	Prunes, soaked	30
2	Onions	2

1. Preheat the oven to 350°F / 180°C / Gas Mark 4.
2. Put the potato starch or flour on a plate and roll the trout in it one by one. Heat the butter and oil in a frying pan, add the trout and cook for 7 minutes on each side, turning them with a metal spatula.
3. Put the trout in an ovenproof dish. Pour in the red wine and add a few drops of lemon juice. Season with salt and pepper to taste. Add the thyme sprig, bay leaf, a pinch of grated nutmeg and the prunes. Peel and quarter the onions and add to the dish.
4. Bake for 15 minutes.

Truites en papillotes
Trout Baked in Foil

	00:20 plus marinating		00:20

American	Ingredients	Metric/Imperial
6 (6 oz)	Trout, cleaned	6 (175 g / 6 oz)
	Salt and pepper	
1 tbsp	Fennel seeds	1 tbsp
6	Coriander seeds	6
2	Fresh thyme sprigs	2
2	Bay leaves	2
¼ cup	Olive oil	4 tbsp
	Lemon wedges	

1. Season the inside and outside of the fish with salt and pepper. Put the fennel and coriander seeds in a mortar and grind them to a powder. Crumble the thyme and bay leaves. Arrange the trout in a deep dish. Sprinkle with thyme, bay, and the fennel and coriander mixture. Pour the oil over the top and leave to marinate for 1 hour in a cool place, but not in the refrigerator.
2. Preheat the oven to 425°F / 220°C / Gas Mark 7.
3. Cut out 6 large rectangles of foil. Without wiping the trout, place each one in the center of a foil rectangle. Fold the foil over so that each trout is completely enclosed and twist the edges to seal. Arrange on a baking sheet.
4. Bake for 20 minutes.
5. When the trout are cooked, set them on a serving dish without opening the foil, surround them with lemon wedges and serve immediately.

Thon basquaise
Basque Style Tuna

	00:40		01:00

American	Ingredients	Metric/Imperial
1	Garlic clove	1
1	Onion	1
	Oil	
1 lb	Tomatoes	500 g / 1 lb
1	Sweet red or green pepper	1
2 tbsp	Flour	2 tbsp
1 (3 lb)	Piece of tuna	1 (1.5 kg / 3 lb)
	Salt and pepper	
1¼ cups	Dry white wine	300 ml / ½ pint

1. Peel and finely chop the garlic and onion. Heat 1 tablespoon of oil in a frying pan, add the garlic and onion and fry until soft.
2. Peel the tomatoes (first plunging them in boiling water for 10 seconds), cut into quarters and remove the seeds. Remove the core and the seeds from the pepper and cut the flesh into thin strips. Put the tomatoes and pepper in the frying pan and cook over a low heat for 30 minutes, stirring occasionally.
3. Preheat the oven to 350°F / 180°C / Gas Mark 4.
4. Flour the piece of tuna lightly, season with the salt and pepper and put it in an ovenproof dish. Pour in the white wine. Add the tomato sauce. Bake for about 10 minutes. Serve hot.

Turbot à la normande
Normandy Style Turbot

	00:15		00:40

American	Ingredients	Metric/Imperial
1	Turbot, cleaned	1
½ lb	Onions	250 g / 8 oz
2	Carrots	2
1	Bouquet garni	1
	Salt and pepper	
2½ cups	Hard [dry] cider	600 ml / 1 pint
36	Fresh mussels	36
12	Scampi or Dublin Bay prawns	12
1 tbsp	Butter	1 tbsp
1 tbsp	Flour	1 tbsp
2	Egg yolks	2
½ cup	Crème fraîche (see page 122)	125 ml / 4 fl oz
½ lemon	Lemon	½

1. Cut the turbot into 6 pieces. Peel and slice the onions and carrots. Put the pieces of fish in a large pan with the onions and carrots. Add the bouquet garni and season with salt and pepper. Pour in the cider and add sufficient water to cover the pieces of fish. Bring to boil over a moderate heat, then turn down the heat and cook gently for 15-18 minutes.
2. Meanwhile, scrub the mussels thoroughly. Put them in a large saucepan and heat briskly, shaking the saucepan from time to time, until they open (discard any that remain closed). Remove the mussels from the shells and set aside. Reserve the liquid from the shells. Strain the liquid.
3. Cook the scampi in simmering water for 8 minutes. Drain and peel them.

4. Drain the pieces of fish, reserving the cooking liquid, and remove the skin. Arrange the fish on serving dish and keep hot. Strain the liquid into a saucepan and boil to reduce it by half. Add the liquid from the mussels.

5. Blend the butter with the flour to make a paste (beurre manié). Beat the egg yolks with the crème fraîche and the juice of ½ lemon. Add the beurre manié to the cooking liquid and simmer, stirring, until thickened. Remove from the heat. Add 1 tablespoon of this liquid to the egg yolk and crème fraîche mixture, mix well and pour back into the pan. Heat, whisking, and add salt and pepper to taste. Do not boil.

6. Surround the fish with the mussels and scampi and coat with the sauce. Serve immediately.

Turbot hollandaise
Turbot with Hollandaise Sauce

	00:30		00:32
American	**Ingredients**		**Metric/Imperial**
1	Turbot, cleaned and skinned		1
	Court-bouillon (see page 114)		
3	Egg yolks, at room temperature		3
2 tbsp	Cider vinegar		2 tbsp
	Pepper		
1 cup	Lightly salted butter		250 g / 8 oz
1	Lemon		1

1. Cut the turbot into 6 pieces and arrange in a large pan so that they do not overlap. Cover with court-bouillon. Bring to a boil, then cover and simmer for 15 minutes over a very low heat so that the liquid barely trembles. Remove from the heat, remove the lid and leave to cool slightly.

2. Meanwhile, put the egg yolks in a bowl or saucepan, add the vinegar and season with pepper. Stir and put the saucepan over another saucepan half filled with hot but not boiling water. Whisk until the mixture thickens, then gradually blend in the butter cut into small pieces. Continue to whisk until the sauce is smooth and thick. Gradually add the juice of the lemon and continue to whisk.

3. Drain the pieces of fish and place on a dish lined with a folded napkin. Serve the sauce separately.

Turbotin frit
Fried Turbot Steaks

	00:15	00:10 to 00:15	
American	**Ingredients**		**Metric/Imperial**
6	Turbot steaks, 1 in / 2.5 cm thick		6
	Salt and pepper		
1 cup	White bread crumbs		50 g / 2 oz
⅔ cup	Oil		150 ml / ¼ pint
1 cup	Butter		250 g / 8 oz
2	Lemons		2
	Tomato slices		
	Lemon slices		

1. Season the turbot steaks on both sides with salt and pepper. Coat with the bread crumbs, pressing them on well with a spatula so that they adhere firmly.

2. Heat the oil in a frying pan, add the fish and cook over a moderate heat for 10-15 minutes, turning them halfway through the process.

3. Meanwhile, melt the butter in a small bowl placed over a saucepan half filled with hot water. Season with salt, pepper and the juice of the lemons.

4. Arrange the fish steaks on a serving dish and garnish with the tomato and lemon slices. Serve the lemon butter separately in a sauceboat.

Thon braisé aux petits oignons
Braised Tuna with Onions

	00:30		01:20
American	**Ingredients**		**Metric/Imperial**
2	Carrots		2
2	Medium-size onions		2
1	Shallot		1
1	Garlic clove		1
¼ lb	Fresh pork sides [belly pork]		125 g / 4 oz
6 tbsp	Butter		75 g / 3 oz
1 (2¾ lb)	Piece of tuna		1 (1.25 kg / 2¾ lb)
1 tbsp	Flour		1 tbsp
⅔ cup	Fish stock (see page 115)		150 ml / ¼ pint
⅔ cup	Dry white wine		150 ml / ¼ pint
1	Bouquet garni		1
	Salt and pepper		
24	Tiny onions		24
1 tbsp	Sugar		1 tbsp
	Chopped fresh parsley		

1. Peel the carrots, onions, shallot and garlic. Chop the carrots, onions and shallot and crush the garlic. Remove any rind from the pork and cut the pork into strips.

2. Heat half of the butter in a flameproof casserole, add the strips of pork and brown slightly. Remove with a slotted spoon. Put the piece of tuna into the casserole. Brown it lightly on both sides and remove it. Put the carrots, chopped onion and shallot in the casserole, stir well and leave the vegetables to brown over a moderate heat.

3. Put the tuna and strips of pork back into the casserole. Sprinkle with the flour and brown, stirring constantly. Pour in the fish stock and white wine. Add the garlic and bouquet garni and season with salt and pepper. Cook, covered, for 1 hour over a low heat.

4. Meanwhile, peel the tiny onions. Put them in a heavy saucepan with the sugar and the remaining butter. Season to taste with salt and pepper. Cover with water and cook with the lid on over a low heat until the onions are tender and the sugar, butter and water have formed a caramel syrup. Roll the onions in the caramel so that they are coated all over and keep warm over a very low heat.

5. When the tuna is cooked, transfer it to a serving dish, using a slotted spatula. Strain the sauce onto the fish, sprinkle with chopped parsley and surround with the caramelized onions. Serve immediately.

Cook's tip: although tuna is more usually bought canned, it has an excellent flavor when used fresh.

Mixed Fish Dishes

Filets de poisson panés

Breaded Fried Fish Fillets

	00:15		00:04 per batch

American	Ingredients	Metric/Imperial
2 lb	Fish fillets	1 kg / 2 lb
2	Eggs	2
1 tsp	Oil	1 tsp
	Salt and pepper	
1 cup	Flour	125 g / 4 oz
1 cup	Dry white bread crumbs	50 g / 2 oz
	Oil for deep frying	
	Lemon wedges	

1. If the fish fillets are very large, cut them into equal-sized pieces. Break the eggs into a shallow dish, add the oil and salt and pepper to taste, and beat with a fork to mix. Put the flour on a plate and the bread crumbs on another plate. Dip the fillets in flour, then in beaten egg and lastly in bread crumbs.
2. Heat the oil for deep frying.
3. Fry the fish fillets in the hot but not smoking oil a few pieces at a time, to prevent the oil from cooling too much, for about 4 minutes or until they are golden. Lift them out with a slotted spatula and drain on paper towels.
4. Serve hot, garnished with lemon wedges. Alternatively, serve with tartare sauce (see page 119).

Friands de poisson

Fish Pies

	01:00 plus thawing or making pastry	00:20 to 00:25 Makes 12	

American	Ingredients	Metric/Imperial
1 lb	Puff pastry (see page 458 or use frozen)	500 g / 1 lb
1	Spiny lobster or crayfish tail	1
	Salt and pepper	
2	Shallots	2
2 (6 oz)	Soles, filleted	2 (175 g / 6 oz)
1 tsp	Potato starch or flour	1 tsp
½ cup	Crème fraîche (see page 122)	125 ml / 4 fl oz
¼ cup	Butter	50 g / 2 oz
⅔ cup	Armagnac	150 ml / ¼ pint
6 tbsp	Madeira wine	6 tbsp
2	Egg yolks	2
	Lemon juice	
1	Egg white	1

1. If using frozen pastry, allow it to thaw.
2. Drop the lobster or crayfish tail into a pan of boiling salted water. Bring back to a boil and cook for 10 minutes. Drain the lobster, remove the meat from the shell and chop roughly.
3. Peel and chop the shallots. Dice the sole fillets. Mix the potato starch with crème fraîche.
4. Melt the butter in a frying pan, add the shallots and cook until they are translucent. Add the diced sole and cook over a very low heat for 10-12 minutes or until firm but not browned. Remove the pan from the heat and mash the mixture with a fork. Add the chopped lobster meat, armagnac and madeira. Season with salt and pepper. Leave to marinate for 20 minutes.
5. Blend in the cream mixture. Return the pan to a brisk heat and stir with a wooden spoon until the mixture has the consistency of thick cream. Leave to cool, then blend in 1 egg yolk and a few drops of lemon juice. Taste and adjust the seasoning, if necessary.
6. Preheat the oven to 450°F / 250°C / Gas Mark 8.
7. Roll out the puff pastry dough to a thickness of ⅛ in / 3 mm and cut it into 4 in / 10 cm squares. Using a pastry brush, paint a ½ in / 1 cm border on each square with egg white.
8. Put a spoonful of filling on half of each square, fold over the other half and seal the edges, pinching them with the fingers. Draw a diamond shape on the top with the point of a knife. Brush with beaten egg yolk.
9. Place the pies on a dampened baking sheet and bake for 20-25 minutes. Serve piping hot.

Pain de poisson

Fish Loaf

	00:30		01:15

American	Ingredients	Metric/Imperial
1¼ lb	Whiting fillets	625 g / 1¼ lb
3 tbsp	Butter	40 g / 1½ oz
3 tbsp	Flour	3 tbsp
2 cups	Milk	500 ml / 16 fl oz
	Salt and pepper	
¼ lb	Peeled cooked shrimp [prawns]	125 g / 4 oz
2	Eggs	2
5	Egg yolks	5
	Grated nutmeg	
1 cup	Crème fraîche (see page 122)	250 ml / 8 fl oz
2 tsp	Tomato paste [purée]	2 tsp
	Lemon juice	

1. Preheat the oven to 400°F / 200°C / Gas Mark 6.
2. Put the whiting fillets through a food mill, or use a blender or food processor, to reduce them to a fine purée.
3. Melt the butter in a saucepan, add the flour and cook, stirring, for 2 minutes. Blend in the milk and thicken over a low heat, stirring continuously. Season with salt and pepper.
4. Put the whiting purée into a mixing bowl and add the shrimp, whole eggs and 3 egg yolks. Mix carefully. Add the remaining yolks to the sauce and add half of it to the fish mixture. Season to taste with salt, pepper and nutmeg.
5. Butter a 9 in / 24 cm charlotte mold. Fill it with the fish mixture and put the mold in an ovenproof dish. Pour 2 in / 5 cm of water into this dish and put it in the oven. Bake for 30 minutes, then reduce the temperature to 350°F / 180°C / Gas Mark 4. Bake for a further 1¼ hours without allowing the loaf to brown. Cover with foil if necessary.
6. Add crème fraîche, tomato paste and a few drops of lemon

juice to the rest of the white sauce. Heat very gently.

7. Turn the loaf out of the mold onto a serving dish, top with the sauce and serve.

Pauchouse

Burgundy Freshwater Fish Stew

	00:20		00:50
American	**Ingredients**	**Metric/Imperial**	
4 lb	Mixed freshwater fish, cleaned and scaled	2 kg / 4 lb	
1	Bottle of dry white wine	1	
1¼ cups	Water	300 ml / ½ pint	
3	Small garlic cloves	3	
1 tsp	Crumbled dried thyme	1 tsp	
	Salt and pepper		
	Cayenne pepper		
¼ cup	Butter	50 g / 2 oz	
3 tbsp	Flour	3 tbsp	
⅔ cup	Crème fraîche (see page 122)	150 ml / ¼ pint	

1. Remove the heads, fins and tails from the fish and place in a saucepan. Add 1¼ cups [300 ml / ½ pint] of the wine and the water. Bring to a boil, then simmer gently for 20 minutes.

2. Meanwhile, peel the garlic. Cut the fish into chunks. Put the pieces in a saucepan with the garlic, thyme, and salt, pepper and cayenne pepper to taste. Cover with the remaining white wine. Bring to a boil and cook for about 20 minutes.

3. Strain the fish stock. Drain the fish, reserving the cooking liquid. Keep hot.

4. Melt the butter in a heavy saucepan and add the flour. Gradually stir in the strained fish stock and then the cooking liquid from the fish. Cook for 10 minutes, stirring frequently. Strain the sauce and stir in the crème fraîche.

5. Serve the fish coated with the sauce.

Poisson au fenouil

Baked Fish with Fennel

	00:30	00:45 to 00:50	
American	**Ingredients**	**Metric/Imperial**	
12	Tiny onions	12	
1	Lemon	1	
½ cup	Butter	125 g / 4 oz	
1 tbsp	Flour	1 tbsp	
1 tbsp	Tomato paste [purée]	1 tbsp	
2 cups	Hard [dry] cider or white wine	450 ml / ¾ pint	
1 tsp	Fennel seeds	1 tsp	
	Salt and pepper		
1 cup	Crème fraîche (see page 122)	250 ml / 8 fl oz	
1 (3 lb)	Porgy, sea bream or mullet, cleaned and scaled	1 (1.5 kg / 3 lb)	
12	Small tomatoes	12	
	Fresh fennel sprigs		

1. Preheat the oven to 400°F / 200°C / Gas Mark 6.

2. Peel the onions. Pare the rind thinly from the lemon and cut it into strips. Squeeze the lemon to extract the juice.

3. Melt half of the butter in a frying pan, add the onions and fry until golden. Sprinkle with the flour and stir for 2 minutes over a medium heat. Add the tomato paste, cider or white wine and fennel seeds. Cook the mixture over a brisk heat, stirring continuously, until thickened. Season with salt and pepper. Stir in the crème fraîche, lemon rind and lemon juice and stir over a low heat without boiling.

4. Pour the sauce into a dish. Add the fish and dot with the remaining butter. Cover the dish with foil and put it in the oven. Bake for 25 minutes.

5. Put the tomatoes and fennel sprigs in the dish. Bake for a further 20-25 minutes, without the foil so that the fish browns. Serve hot.

Paella

Paella

	01:00	00:30 to 00:40	
American	**Ingredients**	**Metric/Imperial**	
1 (2¾ lb)	Chicken	1 (1.25 kg / 2¾ lb)	
¾ lb	Pork spareribs	350 g / 12 oz	
⅔ cup	Olive oil	150 ml / ¼ pint	
	Salt and pepper		
¾ lb	Squid, cleaned	350 g / 12 oz	
1	Sweet red or green pepper	1	
3	Onions	3	
2	Garlic cloves	2	
8	Spiny lobsters or crayfish, cooked	8	
4	Tomatoes	4	
2 cups	Unpolished long-grain rice	400 g / 14 oz	
2 lb	Fresh peas, shelled	1 kg / 2 lb	
	Cayenne pepper		
1 tsp	Saffron powder	1 tsp	
1 quart	Hot water	1 l / 1¾ pints	
12	Fresh mussels	12	

1. Cut the chicken into 12 pieces. Bone the pork and dice the the meat. Heat 3 tablespoons of the oil in a flameproof casserole, add the pieces of chicken and diced pork and cook over a low heat for 30 minutes without browning. Season with salt and pepper.

2. Meanwhile, cut the squid into strips. Cut the pepper in half, remove the seeds and cut the flesh into strips. Peel and chop the onions and garlic. Remove the lobster meat from the shells. Cut the tomatoes into quarters and remove the seeds.

3. Heat the rest of the oil in a paella pan or large frying pan and add the squid and pepper strips. Stir, then add the rice, onions and garlic. Cook, stirring, until the rice is translucent, then add the tomatoes. Cook until the tomatoes are soft.

4. Add the chicken and pork with their pan juices and the peas. Season to taste with salt, pepper and cayenne pepper. Dissolve the saffron in the hot water and add to the pan. Bring to a boil over a brisk heat, then cover and cook over a low heat for 15 minutes.

5. Add the lobster meat and cook for a further 5 minutes or until the rice has absorbed all the liquid.

6. Scrub the mussels thoroughly. Half bury them in the rice mixture and continue cooking until they open. Serve this colorful dish piping hot.

Poisson mayonnaise

Fish Salad

	00:30	00:10

American	Ingredients	Metric/Imperial
1¼ lb	Cooked white fish (cod or whiting)	625 g / 1¼ lb
2	Hard-cooked eggs	2
3	Tomatoes	3
	Tabasco sauce	
1 cup	Mayonnaise (see page 119)	250 ml / 8 fl oz
2 cups	Cooked navy [haricot] beans or green peas	250 g / 8 oz
6	Lettuce leaves	6
¾ cup	Black olives	125 g / 4 oz

1. Flake the fish, removing all skin and bones. Slice the eggs. Slice the tomatoes.
2. Add a few drops of tabasco to the mayonnaise. Mix the cooked beans or peas with 1 tablespoon of the mayonnaise.
3. Line 6 scallop shells or individual serving dishes with lettuce leaves. Cover with the beans or peas in mayonnaise and arrange the fish on top. Garnish with tomato and egg slices and coat with the mayonnaise. Decorate with the olives.
4. Keep in a cool place, but not in the refrigerator, until ready to serve.

Poisson lardé aux amandes

Larded Fish with Almonds and Cucumber

	00:30	00:30

American	Ingredients	Metric/Imperial
1	Onion	1
¼ lb	Bacon	125 g / 4 oz
1 (3 lb)	Carp or pike, cleaned and scaled	1 (1.5 kg / 3 lb)
1 tbsp	Chopped fresh parsley	1 tbsp
	Salt and pepper	
1 tbsp	Flour	1 tbsp
¼ cup	Lard	50 g / 2 oz
1 cup	Flaked or sliced almonds	125 g / 4 oz
½	Cucumber	½
¼ cup	Tomato paste [purée]	4 tbsp
1 tsp	Sugar	1 tsp
1 tsp	Paprika	1 tsp
	Ground cloves	
3 tbsp	Vinegar	3 tbsp

1. Preheat the oven to 400°F / 200°C / Gas Mark 6.
2. Peel and chop the onion. Cut the bacon into small narrow strips for larding. Stuff the inside of the fish with the chopped parsley and onion and season with salt and pepper. Lard the fish by inserting a small pointed knife right through the thick part and sliding the strips of bacon along the blade.
3. Sprinkle the fish with the flour and put it in an ovenproof dish. Pour half the lard, melted, over the top and bake for 20-25 minutes, turning the fish halfway through the process.
4. Meanwhile, put the almonds in a dry frying pan and toast

over a low heat, stirring continuously. Remove from the heat.
5. Slice the cucumber. Melt the remaining lard in the frying pan, add the cucumber slices and cook over a low heat until softened.
6. Put the tomato paste, sugar, paprika, a pinch of cloves, vinegar and almonds into a saucepan. Add a pinch of salt. Stir over a low heat until the sauce is hot and well blended.
7. Pour the sauce into a serving dish. Put the fish on top, sprinkle it with its pan juices and surround with the cucumber slices.

Fish salad

Poisson à la sicilienne

Sicilian Style Fish

	00:30	00:30

American	Ingredients	Metric/Imperial
1 (3 lb)	Mullet or sea bass, cleaned and scaled	1 (1.5 kg / 3 lb)
¼ cup	Olive oil	4 tbsp
	Salt and pepper	
1½ lb	Tomatoes	750 g / 1½ lb
¾ cup	Pine nuts	125 g / 4 oz
¼ lb	Mushrooms	125 g / 4 oz
2	Onions	2
2 tbsp	Dried mixed herbs (parsley, fennel, thyme, marjoram)	2 tbsp
2 cups	Dry white wine	450 ml / ¾ pint
12	Black olives	12

1. Preheat the oven to 450°F / 230°C / Gas Mark 8.
2. Put the fish in an ovenproof dish, brush it with 1 tablespoon of the olive oil and season the inside with salt and pepper to taste. Put the fish in the oven and bake for 10 minutes, then turn it over. Brush again with 1 tablespoon of the olive oil and bake for a further 10 minutes, basting frequently with the cooking liquid so that it does not dry out.
3. Meanwhile, peel the tomatoes (first plunging them for 10 seconds in boiling water), cut them in half and remove the

seeds. Roughly chop the flesh.

4. Put the pine nuts in a dry frying pan and toast them over a low heat, stirring occasionally.

5. Quarter the mushrooms if they are large. Peel and chop the onions. Add the tomatoes, onions and mushrooms to the frying pan with the remaining olive oil. Heat briskly, stirring continuously. When the mixture is soft, add the mixed herbs and white wine. Season with salt and pepper and cook over a low heat until thickened.

6. Pour the sauce around the fish and add the olives. Return to the oven and bake for 10 minutes longer. Serve very hot accompanied by rice.

Zarzuela

Zarzuela

	01:00	01:20

American	Ingredients	Metric/Imperial
2 lb	Scampi or Dublin Bay prawns	1 kg / 2 lb
1	Bouquet garni	1
2 quarts	Water	2 l / 3½ pints
4	Onions	4
2	Fish heads	2
	Salt and pepper	
1	Slice of bayonne ham, ½ in / 1 cm thick	1
1 lb	Monkfish fillet	500 g / 1 lb
1 lb	Squid, cleaned	500 g / 1 lb
4	Garlic cloves	4
2 lb	Tomatoes	1 kg / 2 lb
1	Green pepper	1
1	Sweet red pepper	1
3	Small spiny lobsters or crayfish	3
1¼ cups	Olive oil	300 ml / ½ pint
	Saffron powder	
⅔ cup	Brandy	150 ml / ¼ pint
1 quart	Fresh mussels	1 kg / 2lb

1. Pull off the heads and legs from the scampi. Put the heads and legs in a saucepan with the bouquet garni and water. Peel 1 onion and add it to the pan with the fish heads and salt to taste. Bring to a boil and simmer gently for 1 hour.

2. Meanwhile, dice the ham. Cut the monkfish into slices. Cut the squid into thin strips. Peel and thinly slice the rest of the onions. Peel and crush the garlic. Peel the tomatoes (first plunging them in boiling water for 10 seconds), cut them in half, remove the seeds and chop the flesh roughly. Halve the peppers, remove the seeds and cut the flesh into strips. Cut the lobsters in half.

3. Strain the fish stock and set aside.

4. Heat 5 tablespoons of olive oil in a large flameproof casserole, add the sliced onions and crushed garlic and cook until softened. Add the tomatoes and cook over a low heat until these vegetables are reduced to a purée. Remove the casserole from the heat.

5. Heat the rest of the olive oil in a frying pan. Add the lobster halves and brown lightly. Remove with a slotted spoon and add to the tomato sauce in the casserole. Brown the scampi, squid, monkfish, ham and strips of pepper in the same way. When all these ingredients are in the casserole, season with salt and pepper, add a pinch of saffron and pour in the brandy and strained fish stock. Bring to a boil and simmer gently for 20 minutes.

6. Scrub the mussels thoroughly. Put them in a saucepan, cover and heat briskly until they open (discard any that remain closed).

7. Add the mussels to the stew and serve with french bread and garlic mayonnaise (see page 119).

Waterzoï de poisson

Flemish Fish Stew

	00:15	00:40

American	Ingredients	Metric/Imperial
3	Carrots	3
2	Large onions	2
3	Leeks, white part only	3
2	Celery stalks	2
6 tbsp	Butter	75 g / 3 oz
2¾ lb	Mixed freshwater fish, cleaned	1.25 kg / 2¾ lb
⅔ cup	Beer	150 ml / ¼ pint
	Salt and pepper	
1	Bouquet garni	1
18	Slices of stale french bread	18
1 cup	Crème fraîche (see page 122)	250 ml / 8 fl oz

1. Peel the carrots and onions. Finely dice all the vegetables. Heat 2 tablespoons [25 g / 1 oz] of the butter in a frying pan, add the diced vegetables and cook for 10 minutes over a low heat, covered.

2. Meanwhile, cut the fish into chunks. Butter the bottom of a saucepan, add the pieces of fish and cover with the vegetables. Pour in the beer and sufficient water to cover the fish completely. Season with salt and pepper and add the bouquet garni. Cover the pan and cook for 30 minutes over a medium heat.

3. Meanwhile, heat the remaining butter in the frying pan and brown the slices of french bread on both sides.

4. When the fish stew is cooked, remove the bouquet garni. Put the pieces of fish in a deep serving dish. Add crème fraîche to the cooking liquid, mix well and pour over the fish. Serve very hot with the fried bread.

Flemish fish stew

Matelote de la Marne
Marne Fish Stew

	00:45	00:45

American	Ingredients	Metric/Imperial
1 (3 lb)	Pike, cleaned and scaled	1 (1.5 kg / 3 lb)
2	Medium-sized onions	2
1	Shallot	1
½ lb	Mushrooms	250 g / 8 oz
1	Garlic clove	1
1	Bottle of champagne or other sparkling white wine	1
	Salt and pepper	
1 cup	Butter	250 g / 8 oz
2 tbsp	Oil	2 tbsp
6	Slices of stale bread	6

1. Cut the pike into large chunks. Peel the onions and shallot and slice finely. Detach the mushroom stems from the caps and set aside. Thinly slice the caps. Peel and crush the garlic.
2. Pour the champagne into a large pan and bring to a boil. Add the onions, shallot, garlic and mushroom stems. Season with salt and pepper. Add the pieces of pike and poach for 10 minutes without boiling.
3. Meanwhile, melt 2 tablespoons [25 g / 1 oz] of the butter in a frying pan, add the sliced mushrooms and cook, stirring occasionally, until all the liquid has evaporated.
4. Heat the oil in another frying pan, add the bread slices and fry until golden brown on both sides. Drain on paper towels.
5. Remove the fish from the pan with a slotted spoon and keep it hot. Boil the liquid to reduce by three-quarters, then strain it into a clean pan. Add the remaining butter, cut into small pieces, whisking vigorously.
6. Line a serving dish with the fried bread and mushrooms and arrange the fish on top. Coat with the sauce and serve immediately.

Cod and potato balls

Croquettes de poisson
Fish Croquettes

	00:30	00:20

American	Ingredients	Metric/Imperial
2	Onions	2
1	Large shallot	1
5 oz	Mushrooms	150 g / 5 oz
1	Bunch of fresh parsley	1
2 tbsp	Oil plus oil for deep frying	2 tbsp
¼ cup	Flour	4 tbsp
1 cup	Boiling milk	250 ml / 8 fl oz
¾ lb	White fish fillets	350 g / 12 oz
	Salt and pepper	
4	Eggs	4
3 tbsp	Dry bread crumbs	3 tbsp

1. Peel the onions and shallot. Finely chop them with the mushrooms and parsley, or process in a food processor or blender until coarse-fine. Heat the 2 tablespoons of oil in a frying pan, add the vegetables and cook over a low heat until all the liquid has evaporated and the vegetables are soft. Sprinkle with 2 tablespoons of flour and stir well, then pour in the boiling milk, stirring continuously.
2. Grind [mince] the fish fillets. Add them to the pan and season with salt and pepper. Cook over a low heat for 10-12 minutes. Remove from the heat.
3. Break 1 egg into a shallow dish and beat it lightly. Put the bread crumbs and remaining flour on 2 plates.
4. Beat the remaining eggs together and gradually blend into the fish mixture in a thin stream. Leave to cool.
5. Heat the oil for deep frying. Shape the fish mixture into walnut-size balls and flatten them slightly. Dip them in the flour, then in the beaten egg and finally in the bread crumbs. Drop the croquettes, a few at a time, into the hot but not smoking oil and fry for about 10 minutes or until golden. Drain on paper towels. Serve piping hot.

Fish ball
Cod and Potato Balls

	00:30	01:10

American	Ingredients	Metric/Imperial
2 lb	Baking potatoes	1 kg / 2lb
¾ lb	Cooked salt cod fillet	350 g / 12 oz
¾ lb	Cooked fresh cod fillet	350 g / 12 oz
	Grated nutmeg	
3	Eggs	3
	Salt and pepper	
3 tbsp	Dry bread crumbs	3 tbsp
3 tbsp	Flour	3 tbsp
	Oil for deep frying	

1. Preheat the oven to 400°F / 200°C / Gas Mark 6.
2. Scrub and prick the potatoes. Put them on the shelf in the oven and bake for about 1 hour or until a knife sinks into them easily.
3. Meanwhile, flake the salt and fresh cod using 2 forks. Put it through a food mill, or use a blender or food processor, to obtain a very fine purée.

4. When the potatoes are cooked, cut them in half and scoop out the pulp. Finely mash the pulp with a fork, season with a little nutmeg and add to the fish purée.

5. Divide the mixture into large egg-size portions and shape into balls. Beat the eggs lightly in a flat dish and season with salt and pepper. Put the bread crumbs on a plate and the flour on another plate.

6. Heat the oil for deep frying.

7. Dip the fish balls in the flour, then in the beaten egg and finally in the bread crumbs. Drop them into the oil and fry for about 10 minutes or until they are golden. Drain them on paper towels and serve immediately with lemon wedges or a tomato sauce (see page 133).

Marmite dieppoise

Dieppe Hot-Pot

00:30		00:50
American	**Ingredients**	**Metric/Imperial**
1 (¾ lb)	Sole, cleaned and skinned	1 (350 g / 12 oz)
1 (¾ lb)	Gurnard or flounder, cleaned	1 (350 g / 12 oz)
3	Small red mullet or goatfish, cleaned	3
1 (½ lb)	Piece of turbot, skinned	1 (250 g / 8 oz)
¾ lb	Fish bones and trimmings	350 g / 12 oz
2½ quarts	Court-bouillon (see page 114)	2.5 l / 4½ pints
	Salt and pepper	
5 oz	Mushrooms	150 g / 5 oz
1	Leek, white part only	1
2	Shallots	2
2 tbsp	Butter	25 g / 1 oz
1½ tbsp	Flour	3 tbsp
1	Bouquet garni	1
1 quart	Fresh mussels	1 kg / 2 lb
3	Egg yolks	3
½ cup	Crème fraîche (see page 122)	125 ml / 4 oz
	Lemon juice	

1. Cut the heads off the fish. Cut the fish into chunks, reserving all skin and bones. Put the fish heads and all the fish bones and trimmings in a large pan and add the court-bouillon. Season with salt and pepper. Bring to a boil and cook for 15 minutes. Strain this stock, pressing the fish trimmings well, and set aside.

2. Chop the mushrooms. Chop the white part of the leek. Peel and chop the shallots. Melt the butter in a saucepan, add the mushrooms, leek and shallots and cook over a low heat for 7-8 minutes or until softened but not brown. Spinkle with the flour and mix well. Pour in 1 quart [1 l / 1¾ pints] of the strained fish stock and stir to mix. Add the bouquet garni and boil for 10 minutes. Strain into a large saucepan.

3. Scrub the mussels thoroughly. Put them in another pan, cover and cook briskly until the mussels open (discard any that remain closed). Discard the empty half of each mussel shell and put aside the halves containing the flesh. Strain the liquid from the shells and add it to the first pan.

4. Put the pieces of fish into this liquid. Bring to a boil and simmer gently for 20-30 minutes. Add the mussels.

5. Mix together the egg yolks, crème fraîche and a few drops of lemon juice. Add 1 ladle of the sauce from the saucepan, stirring well. Pour back into the pan, stir and serve.

Dieppe hot-pot

Coquilles de poisson

Fish in Shells

00:15		00:30
American	**Ingredients**	**Metric/Imperial**
1 lb	White fish fillet	500 g / 1 lb
	Court-bouillon (see page 114)	
½ lb	Mushrooms	250 g / 8 oz
½	Lemon	½
2	Shallots	2
½ cup	Butter	125 g / 4 oz
	Salt and pepper	
2 tbsp	Flour	2 tbsp
½ cup	Crème fraîche (see page 122)	125 ml / 4 fl oz
1 cup	Dry white wine	250 ml / 8 fl oz
	Grated nutmeg	
2	Egg yolks	2
2 tbsp	Bread crumbs	2 tbsp
2 tbsp	Grated gruyère cheese	2 tbsp

1. Cut the fish into large chunks. Place in a pan and cover with court-bouillon. Bring to a boil over a moderate heat. Reduce the heat and simmer gently for 10 minutes. Drain the fish, reserving the liquid. Flake the fish, discarding any skin and bones.

2. Thinly slice the mushrooms and sprinkle them with the juice of the ½ lemon. Peel and finely chop the shallots.

3. Melt half the butter in a saucepan, add the shallots and cook until translucent. Add the mushrooms, season with salt and pepper and cook over a medium heat until all the liquid has evaporated. Sprinkle with the flour and stir for 2 minutes, then add crème fraîche, wine, 1 cup [250 ml / 8 fl oz] of the reserved fish cooking liquid and a pinch of nutmeg. Cover and cook over a low heat for 15 minutes.

4. Preheat the oven to 400°F / 200°C / Gas Mark 6.

5. Remove the sauce from the heat. Blend in the egg yolks, beating with a whisk, then add the fish.

6. Fill 6 scallop shells or other small ovenproof dishes with the fish mixture. Cover with the bread crumbs mixed with the cheese and dot the top with remaining butter. Brown in the oven for 5 minutes. Serve piping hot.

Cotriade

Breton Fish Soup

	00:20	00:40

American	Ingredients	Metric/Imperial
1½ lb	Cod fillet	750 g / 1½ lb
2	Whitings, cleaned	2
2	Mackerel	2
2	Firm, white-fleshed saltwater fish, such as gurnard, cleaned	2
1	Piece of fresh eel, cleaned and skinned	1
3 - 4	Fresh sardines or other small oily fish	3 - 4
2 lb	Potatoes	1 kg / 2 lb
2	Shallots	2
6 tbsp	Lightly salted butter	75 g / 3 oz
1½ quarts	Cold water	1.5 l / 2½ pints
2	Fresh thyme sprigs	2
1	Bay leaf	1
2 tbsp	Chopped fresh parsley	2 tbsp
1	Fresh marjoram sprig	1
	Salt and pepper	
6	Slices of stale bread	6

1. Cut the fish into large chunks. Peel and slice the potatoes. Peel and thinly slice the shallots.
2. Heat the butter in a large pan, add the shallots and cook until they are translucent. Add the cold water, potatoes, thyme sprigs, bay leaf, chopped parsley and marjoram. Season with salt and pepper. Cook over a moderate heat for 15 minutes.
3. Add the chopped fish and cook for a further 15-20 minutes.
4. Serve the fish and potatoes accompanied by vinaigrette dressing (see page 120). The strained cooking liquid can be served as a soup ladled over slices of stale bread.

Brochettes de poisson au poivre vert

Fish Kebabs

	00:20	00:20

American	Ingredients	Metric/Imperial
1 tbsp	Green peppercorns	1 tbsp
2 tbsp	Cider vinegar	2 tbsp
¾ lb	White fish fillets (turbot, flounder, brill, pompano, John Dory, sole, etc.)	350 g / 12 oz
3	Smoked bacon slices	3
12	Scallops	12
	Salt and pepper	
	Flour	
2 tbsp	Oil	2 tbsp
4	Egg yolks	4
1 cup	Butter	250 g / 8 oz
1 tbsp	Hot water	1 tbsp

1. Roughly crush the green peppercorns and set aside to steep in the cider vinegar.
2. Cut the fish into pieces 2½ in / 6 cm long and 1 in /2.5 cm wide. Cut the bacon into large strips. Thread the scallops, pieces of fish folded in half and strips of bacon onto 6 skewers. Season with salt and pepper and coat lightly in flour.
3. Heat the oil in a large frying pan and fry the skewers over a low heat until well browned on all sides.
4. Meanwhile, drain the green peppercorns over a small bowl or saucepan to collect the vinegar. Season the vinegar with salt and pepper and add the egg yolks. Stir to mix. Put this bowl or saucepan over another saucepan half filled with hot but not boiling water. Heat and gradually add the butter, cut into small pieces, beating with a whisk until the sauce has the consistency of mayonnaise. Add the hot water and whisk until the mixture is light. Stir in the green peppercorns if wished.
5. Serve the sauce separately in a sauceboat.

Turbot

Canned smoked oysters and fresh oysters, ready for eating or cooking

CHAPTER 13

Meat

Poultry and Game

Poultry is usually sold 'dressed' or 'drawn,' that is without the internal organs. Sometimes the giblets (liver, gizzard and heart) are included. More often than not, the butcher will prepare and truss the bird, but if not there is a very simple method of trussing all types of poultry that requires only a piece of kitchen string. When the bird is cooked, you only need to remove the string before carving.

Choosing poultry
The bird should be neither too plump (it could be too old) nor too thin (it was probably underfed). The drumsticks should be plump (the feet shrink with age). The breastbone should be soft and pliable. The skin should be smooth and glossy. Soft flesh tinged with red should be avoided. Ask your supplier for advice and look at the sell-by date on pre-wrapped poultry.

To test whether a bird is cooked
Pierce the fleshy part of the leg with a trussing needle, skewer or a small pointed knife. If the juice that runs out is clear the bird is done. If it is pink, cook for another 10 minutes or so and test again. This does not apply to duck which is served underdone when roasted or broiled [grilled].

Keeping poultry
Cooked poultry will keep in the refrigerator for 3-4 days. In a sauce, it will not keep for more than two days. Uncooked poultry should be consumed quickly — within two days. After buying, remove the wrapping, cover the bird with wax [greaseproof] paper and store in the refrigerator. If you want to freeze it, refer to the general table for preserving food.

Preparing poultry

Trussing a bird
1. Fold the flap of neck skin securely over the opening so that the stuffing does not come out during cooking.

3. Pass one end of the string under the drumstick, bring it under the wing and tie a knot around the wing.

2. Pass the string under the rump. Cross it and tie it around the drumsticks. Pull to bring the drumsticks and rump together above the opening (so that you do not need to sew it).

4. With the same piece of string, make a loop around the other wing, pull tightly, then knot with the other end of the string and cut off any excess.

Cutting up an uncooked chicken
1. Lay the chicken on its back on a chopping board. Spread one leg and cut the skin.

3. Lift the wing and make a wide incision in the flesh with a knife. Spread the wing completely and the joint will appear. Cut it from below and remove the wing and the breast.

2. Pull the leg outwards, lifting so as to dislocate the bone. Cut the joint. Remove the other leg in the same way.

4. Detach the thigh from the drumstick by cutting the joint. Cut the carcass in half. The chicken is now cut into 8 pieces.

Carving a cooked chicken
1. Lay the chicken on its back on a chopping board. Insert a carving fork into the breast. Slide the blade of a sharp knife between the leg and the breast, spread and cut through the joint.

3. Slide the blade of the knife into the angle formed by the breast and the wing. Cut the joint, then detach the wing with a small amount of breast. Remove the other leg and wing in the same way.

2. Detach the thigh from the drumstick.

4. Remove the breast by detaching it from the carcass. If it is very thick, carve it in thin slices parallel with the breast bone.

Cutting up an uncooked rabbit
1. Lay the rabbit on its back on a chopping board. Cut right through the backbone above the legs. Repeat the operation just below the shoulders.

3. Chop the shoulders and legs in half.

2. Chop the back into three pieces.

4. The rabbit is now cut into 7 pieces.

Poulet à la broche aux huîtres

Spit-Roasted Chicken

00:30　　　　　　01:15

American	Ingredients	Metric/Imperial
1 (3 lb)	Chicken	1 (1.5 kg / 3 lb)
	Salt and pepper	
6 tbsp	Butter	75 g / 3 oz
24	Oysters	24
1	Onion	1
½ tbsp	Flour	½ tbsp
⅔ cup	Dry white wine	150 ml / ¼ pint
1	Fresh thyme sprig	1
1	Bay leaf	1
6	Slices of bread,	6
1 tbsp	Crème fraîche (see page 122)	1 tbsp

1. Season the inside and outside of the chicken with salt and pepper and truss the bird securely. Coat it with 3 tablespoons [40 g / 1½ oz] butter and push the rotisserie spit through the chicken. Fasten firmly at each end. Place the spit on the rotisserie and cook for about 50 minutes, basting frequently.
2. Meanwhile, open the oysters and remove them from their shells. Keep the oyster liquor from the shells and strain it.
3. Peel and thinly slice the onion. Heat 1 tablespoon [15 g / ½ oz] butter in a saucepan, add the onion and cook until golden. Sprinkle with the flour and cook, stirring, until browned. Stir in the wine and the oyster liquor. Add the thyme, bay leaf and a pinch of pepper, but not salt, as the liquor is salty enough. Cook over a low heat for 30 minutes.
4. Heat the remaining butter in a frying pan and fry the slices of bread until golden brown on both sides. Drain.
5. Skim the fat from the juices that have dripped from the chicken and pour into the sauce. Add the oysters and poach them gently for 5 minutes over a very low heat. Whisk in the crème fraîche, warm through and remove from the heat.
6. Remove the chicken from the spit. Carve it into portions and arrange on a warmed serving platter. Surround with the oysters and fried bread and pour the sauce over the top.

Cooking times for poultry

To cook	Cooking time	Average weight per portion
Capon, roasted	20 min per pound	12 oz / 350 g
Chicken, boiled	1 hr 30-3 hr	10 oz / 300 g
Chicken, casseroled	45-50 min	10 oz / 300 g
Chicken, roasted	25-30 min per pound	10 oz / 300 g
Cornish game hen [pullet or poussin], roasted	20-40 min	1 or 2 per person
Duck breast fillets (scaloppine), fried	10 min (7-8 min on the skin side) 2 min on the flesh side	5 oz / 150 g
Duck breast fillets (scaloppine), roasted	15 min	5 oz / 150 g
Duck (cut up), sautéed	45 min	12 oz / 350 g
Duck or duckling, roasted	50 min to 1 hr 50 min	12 oz / 350 g
Goose	15-25 min per pound (according to age)	10 oz / 300 g
Pigeon, casseroled	40-45 min	1 or 2 per person
Guinea fowl, casseroled	55 min to 1 hr	8 oz / 250g
Guinea fowl, roasted	about 45 min	8 oz / 250 g
Guinea fowl, salmis	1 hr 10 min to 1 hr 15 min	7 oz / 200 g
Quail (cut up), casseroled	25-30 min	2 per person
Quail, roasted	about 15 min	2 per person
Rabbit, casseroled	1 hr to 1 hr 15 min	8 oz / 250 g
Rooster, (3 lb / 1.5 kg), casseroled	1 hr 30-2 hr (according to weight)	10 oz / 300 g
Turkey (whole), roasted	20 min per pound (including stuffing)	8 oz / 250 g
Young pigeon (squab), casseroled	25-30 min	1 per person
Young rabbit, casseroled, roasted or sautéed	50-55 min	8 oz / 250 g

Cailles rôties sur canapés

Roast Quails on Canapés

⏱ 00:10   00:20 🍲

American	Ingredients	Metric/Imperial
12	Slices of bread, ½ in / 1 cm thick	12
⅔ cup	Butter	150 g / 5 oz
12	Small quails with livers	12
24	Juniper berries	24
	Salt and pepper	
12	Thin bacon slices	12

1. Preheat the oven to 450°F / 230°C / Gas Mark 8.
2. Cut the crust off the slices of bread. Butter the bread sparingly and arrange in a greased ovenproof dish.
3. Put 1 liver and 2 juniper berries inside each quail. Season with salt and pepper and wrap a slice of bacon around each bird. Tie with string.
4. Arrange the quails on the buttered bread and roast for 10 minutes.
5. Remove the bacon and roast for a further 5-10 minutes, according to taste.

Duck with orange sauce

Cailles aux raisins
Quails with Grapes

| | 00:20 | | 00:30 |
American	Ingredients	Metric/Imperial
12	Thin bacon slices	12
6 (5 oz) or 12 small	Quails	6 (150 g / 5 oz) or 12 small
2 tbsp	Butter	25 g / 1 oz
¼ cup	Brandy	4 tbsp
1 lb	White grapes	500 g / 1 lb
1 tsp	Potato starch or flour	1 tsp
	Grated nutmeg	
	Salt and pepper	
3 tbsp	Oil	3 tbsp
6	Slices of bread, ½ in / 1 cm thick	6

1. Wrap a slice of bacon around each quail and tie with string. Brown the quails rapidly in a large frying pan without any fat, then remove. Throw away any fat and wipe the pan with paper towels.
2. Put half the butter in the pan. Return the quails to the pan and heat until the butter sizzles without turning brown. Add the brandy, then remove from the heat, cover the pan and set aside to infuse for 5 minutes so that the alcohol flavors the quails.
3. Meanwhile, squeeze the juice from one-third of the grapes (use a juicer, or liquidize briefly or press and strain). Mix the juice with the potato starch. Add this mixture to the quails in the saucepan. Season with a pinch of nutmeg and salt and pepper to taste. Leave to simmer for 15-20 minutes over a very low heat.
4. Meanwhile, cut the remaining grapes in half and remove the seeds. Heat them in a saucepan with the rest of the butter until the skins start to wrinkle.
5. Heat the oil in another frying pan. Remove the crusts from the bread and fry until golden on both sides.
6. Serve the quails on the fried bread surrounded by the grapes and topped with the sauce.

Canard à l'orange
Duck with Orange Sauce

| | 00:45 | | 01:15 |
American	Ingredients	Metric/Imperial
1	Carrot	1
1	Onion	1
½ cup	Butter	125 g / 4 oz
1 (5 lb)	Duck, trussed	1 (2.5 kg / 5 lb)
1	Bouquet garni	1
3 tbsp	Boiling water	3 tbsp
	Salt and pepper	
6	Oranges	6
¼ cup	Orange liqueur	4 tbsp
2 tbsp	Brandy	2 tbsp
1 tbsp	Vinegar	1 tbsp
2 tsp	Potato starch or flour	2 tsp

1. Peel the carrot and onion and cut into thin strips.
2. Melt 6 tablespoons [75 g / 3 oz] of the butter in a flame-proof casserole, add the duck and brown on all sides over a moderate heat. Add the carrot, onion and bouquet garni. Moisten with 1 tablespoon of boiling water and season to taste with salt and pepper. Cover and simmer very gently for 1 hour.
3. Meanwhile, peel 2 of the oranges with a vegetable peeler and cut the rind into thin strips. Blanch the strips of rind in boiling water for 5 minutes. Drain and set aside.
4. Squeeze the juice from the 2 peeled oranges and one other orange. With a sharp knife, peel the remaining oranges without leaving any white pith. Separate into sections, discarding the membrane and seeds. Collect any further juice by holding the oranges over a bowl as they are prepared. Set the sections and juice aside.
5. Sprinkle the duck with the orange liqueur and brandy. Remove from the heat and leave to infuse for 10 minutes. Remove the duck from the casserole and wrap it in foil and keep hot.
6. Add the vinegar and orange juice to the casserole. Simmer over a very low heat, skimming off the fat until the sauce is clear. Strain the sauce into a saucepan. Leave to cool, then remove any more fat which has floated to the surface.
7. Return the sauce to the heat. Dissolve the potato starch in the remaining water and add to the sauce. Bring to a boil, stirring constantly. Adjust the seasoning, if necessary.
8. Melt the rest of the butter in another pan. Add the orange sections and strips of rind, then add the sauce. As soon as the sauce begins to boil, remove from the heat.
9. Carve the duck into portions. Arrange on a serving platter, surround with the orange sections and pour the sauce over the top of the duck.

Canard aux cerises
Duck with Cherries

| | 00:25 | | 00:50 |
American	Ingredients	Metric/Imperial
3 tbsp	Butter	40 g / 1½ oz
2 (2¾ lb)	Ducklings, trussed	2 (1.25 kg / 2¾ lb)
1	Orange	1
1¼ cups	Port wine	300 ml / ½ pint
5	Cloves	5
	Ground cinnamon	
	Salt and pepper	
1 cup	Red currant jelly	350 g / 12 oz
1 (12 oz)	Can of pitted [stoned] cherries in natural juice	1 (350 g / 12 oz)

1. Heat the butter in a flameproof casserole, add the ducks and brown on all sides. Cover and cook over a moderate heat for 40 minutes. The ducks should be underdone.
2. Drain the ducks over the casserole so that the meat juices run into it, then keep them hot.
3. Finely grate the rind from the orange, then squeeze out the juice. Put in a large saucepan with the port, crushed cloves, a pinch of cinnamon and salt and pepper to taste. Simmer over a low heat until the mixture reduces by one-third.
4. Add the red currant jelly. Remove from the heat and stir until the jelly melts. Strain the sauce and add the drained cherries, reserving a few for decoration.
5. Carve the ducks, collecting the juice, then return the duck portions and the juice to the casserole. Add the sauce and cook for a further 10-12 minutes over a very low heat.
6. Arrange the portions of duck on a warmed platter. Garnish with the reserved cherries and a little of the sauce and serve the rest of the sauce separately.

Roast duck with turnips

Canard rôti aux navets

Roast Duck with Turnips

	00:30	01:00

American	Ingredients	Metric/Imperial
¼ lb	Smoked bacon	125 g / 4 oz
2	Chicken livers	2
2 (2¾ lb)	Ducks, with their livers	2 (1.25 kg / 2¾ lb)
¼ lb	Button mushrooms	125 g / 4 oz
1 cup	Green olives	125 g / 4 oz
	Salt and pepper	
½ cup	Butter	125 g / 4 oz
⅔ cup	Water	150 ml / ¼ pint
3 lb	Small, young turnips	1.5 kg / 3 lb
3 tbsp	Sugar	3 tbsp

1. Preheat the oven to 450°F / 230°C / Gas Mark 8.
2. Cut the bacon into thin strips. Cook in a frying pan until lightly browned. Remove the bacon and set aside.
3. Cut the chicken and duck livers into quarters and add to the bacon fat in the pan. Cook over a medium heat until browned on all sides. Remove the livers and set aside.
4. Thinly slice the mushrooms. Add to the pan and cook, stirring occasionally, until the liquid has evaporated.
5. Meanwhile, remove the pits [stones] from the olives. Blanch the olives in boiling water for 2 minutes, drain and pat dry.

6. Put the bacon, mushrooms and liver through a grinder [mincer] or food processor to obtain a smooth mixture. Add the olives, and salt and pepper to taste.
7. Stuff each duck with half of the olive mixture. Truss and coat each bird with 2 tablespoons [25 g / 1 oz] of butter seasoned with salt and pepper.
8. Put the ducks on a rack in a roasting pan and roast for 40 minutes, turning the ducks 4 times so that they brown evenly on all sides. When the fat in the roasting pan starts to burn, add the water.
9. Meanwhile, peel the turnips. Cook in boiling salted water for 10 minutes and drain. Melt the remaining butter in a frying pan over a low heat, add the turnips and cook gently until they begin to brown. Sprinkle them with the sugar and continue to cook over a moderate heat for 10-15 minutes.
10. Carve the ducks into portions and serve with the stuffing and glazed turnips. Serve the roasting juices separately.

Canetons aux pêches

Ducklings with Peaches

	00:15	01:00

American	Ingredients	Metric/Imperial
2 (2 lb)	Ducklings, with the livers	2 (1 kg / 2 lb)
½ cup	Butter	125 g / 4 oz
2 tbsp	Flour	2 tbsp
	Salt and pepper	
2	Carrots	2
2	Onions	2
2	Celery stalks	2
1	Bouquet garni	1
1 (1 lb 12 oz)	Can of yellow peaches in syrup	1 (800 g / 1 lb 12 oz)
2 tbsp	Brandy	2 tbsp
1 tbsp	Potato starch or flour	1 tbsp
2 tbsp	Sugar	2 tbsp
1 tbsp	Vinegar	1 tbsp

1. Preheat the oven to 400°F / 200°C / Gas Mark 6.
2. Truss the ducklings.
3. Work 2 tablespoons [25 g / 1 oz] butter with the flour to a smooth paste. Season the ducklings with salt and pepper and coat them with this beurre manié.
4. Peel and slice the carrots and onions. Slice the celery. Put the vegetables in a roasting pan with the bouquet garni and duck liver and place the metal rack for the ducklings on top. Put the ducklings on the rack and roast for 45 minutes.
5. Remove the ducklings from the pan and keep hot.
6. Leave the vegetables and liver to cook for a further 10 minutes, then strain the liquid into a frying pan. Skim as much fat as possible from the surface of the liquid, then add the peaches and 6 tablespoons of the peach syrup. Cook for 5-6 minutes, turning the peaches halfway through.
7. Carve the ducklings into quarters and arrange on a warmed serving platter. Reserve the carving juices. Arrange the drained peaches around the duckling pieces. Keep hot.
8. Pour the carving juices into the frying pan. Mix the brandy with the potato starch and add to the pan. Bring to a boil, stirring, and adjust seasoning to taste.
9. Meanwhile, dissolve the sugar in the vinegar in a small heavy saucepan over a moderate heat. As soon as you obtain a brown caramel, beat it into the sauce. Finally, whisk in the remaining butter. Serve the sauce with the duck.

Aiguillettes de canard

Duck Scaloppine [Escalopes]

| | 00:10 | 00:15 |

American	Ingredients	Metric/Imperial
6 (5 oz)	Duck breast fillets	6 (150 g / 5 oz)
3 tbsp	Butter	40 g / 1½ oz
2 tbsp	Honey	2 tbsp
1½	Lemons	1½
⅔ cup	Raisins	125 g / 4 oz
	Salt and pepper	
3 tbsp	White rum	3 tbsp

1. Cut the breast fillets into thin scaloppine, each weighing about 50 g / 2 oz.
2. Heat the butter in a frying pan, add the duck slices and cook gently for 10-15 minutes, turning frequently until the duck is lightly colored or cooked according to taste. Remove from the pan, arrange on a platter and keep hot.
3. Return the pan to a medium heat and add the honey. When it bubbles, add the juice of the lemons and the raisins. Season to taste with salt and pepper and cook gently for 3-4 minutes. Finally, add the white rum and heat through.
4. Pour the hot sauce over the scaloppine and serve immediately.

Canard rôti aux pommes

Roast Duck with Apples

| | 00:20 plus soaking | 00:35 |

American	Ingredients	Metric/Imperial
12	Prunes	12
⅔ cup	Port wine	150 ml / ¼ pint
3	Apples	3
1	Large onion	1
1 (3 lb)	Duck	1 (1.5 kg / 3 lb)
	Salt and pepper	
6 tbsp	Butter	75 g / 3 oz
⅔ cup	Chicken stock	150 ml / ¼ pint

1. The day before, put the prunes in a bowl, cover with the port and leave to soak for 12 hours.
2. Preheat the oven to 450°F / 230°C / Gas Mark 8.
3. Drain the prunes, reserving any remaining port. Remove the pits [stones] from the prunes. Peel the apples, remove the core and seeds and cut into quarters. Peel and finely chop the onion. Mix together the prunes, apples and onion.
4. Sprinkle the duck with salt and pepper inside and out. Stuff with half of the prune mixture. Truss.
5. Coat the duck with 3 tablespoons [40 g / 1½ oz] butter and put it in a roasting pan. Roast for about 40 minutes, basting frequently with the melted butter so that the duck browns well.
6. Meanwhile, melt the rest of the butter in a small heavy saucepan. Add the remaining prune mixture and cook over a low heat for about 15 minutes.
7. As soon as the duck is cooked, drain and keep hot.
8. Skim the fat from the juices in the roasting pan, then add

any remaining port and the chicken stock. Heat briskly, stirring to loosen the solids at the bottom of the pan.
9. Pour the prune mixture into the sauce and simmer until the liquid reduces by half.
10. Carve the duck and arrange on a platter with the stuffing and prune mixture from the sauce. Serve the sauce separately.

Chapon au champagne

Capon with Champagne

| | 00:15 | 02:00 |

American	Ingredients	Metric/Imperial
7 tbsp	Butter	90 g / 3½ oz
1 (6 lb)	Capon, trussed	1 (3 kg / 6 lb)
1	Onion	1
3	Shallots	3
3 tbsp	Brandy	3 tbsp
	Salt and pepper	
½	Bottle of champagne or other sparkling white wine	½
12	Small blood sausages [black and white puddings]	12
1 tbsp	Cornstarch [cornflour]	1 tbsp
1 tbsp	Cold water	1 tbsp
1 tbsp	Sugar	1 tbsp
1 tbsp	White vinegar	1 tbsp

1. Heat 3 tbsp [40 g / 1½ oz] of the butter in a flameproof casserole, add the capon and brown on all sides for 25 minutes, without allowing the butter to burn. Meanwhile, peel the onion and shallots. Thinly slice the shallots.
2. Sprinkle the capon with the warmed brandy. Set it alight and shake the casserole gently, until the flames die out.
3. Season to taste with salt and pepper. Add the whole onion and 5 tablespoons of the champagne and cook gently for 1½ hours.
4. About 20 minutes before the capon has finished cooking, preheat the broiler [grill]. Prick the skins of the blood sausages with a fork so that the fat runs out when they are being cooked. Put them under the broiler and cook for 12-15 minutes, turning them several times. Keep hot.
5. Remove the capon from the casserole and keep it hot. Allow the cooking liquid to cool slightly, then skim off the fat which floats to the surface.
6. Heat 1 tablespoon [15 g / 1½ oz] butter in a saucepan, add the shallots and soften. Add the remaining champagne. Bring to a boil and add the skimmed cooking liquid from the capon.
7. Remove from the heat. Dissolve the cornstarch in the cold water. Add to the saucepan and thicken over a low heat, stirring continuously. Strain the sauce.
8. Put the sugar and vinegar in a small heavy saucepan and cook until you obtain a dark brown caramel. Thin it with a few drops of boiling water, then add the caramel to the strained sauce and heat for a few minutes. Taste, and adjust the seasoning if necessary.
9. Remove the saucepan from the heat and vigorously beat in the rest of the butter, a little at a time.
10. Carve the capon and arrange on a hot serving platter. Surround with the blood sausages and coat with a little of the sauce. Serve the rest of the sauce separately.

Cook's tip: this dish should not be reheated.

Canard aux olives

Duck with Olives

00:25   01:00

American	Ingredients	Metric/Imperial
2½ cups	Green olives	300 g / 10 oz
2 (2¾ lb)	Ducks, with livers	2 (1.25 kg / 2¾ lb)
¼ lb	Bayonne ham or prosciutto	125 g / 4 oz
6	Garlic cloves	6
3 tbsp	Olive oil	3 tbsp
5 oz	Button mushrooms	150 g / 5 oz
	Salt and pepper	
⅔ cup	Dry white wine	150 ml / ¼ pint
2	Tiny onions	2
3 tbsp	Butter	40 g / 1½ oz

1. Remove the pits [stones] from the olives. Blanch the olives in boiling water for 5 minutes. Drain and set aside.
2. Dice the duck livers. Cut the ham into thin strips. Peel the garlic cloves.
3. Heat 1 tablespoon of olive oil in a frying pan, add the ham and cook for 1 minute. Add the diced livers and cook for a further minute. Remove the meat, then add the garlic. Brown lightly and remove from the pan. Finally add the mushrooms and cook until they begin to brown. Remove.
4. Put all these ingredients in a bowl and mix well. Season to taste with salt and pepper and add half the olives.
5. Stuff each duck with half the olive mixture and truss. Heat the remaining oil in a flameproof casserole, add the ducks and brown on all sides. Remove them and wipe the inside of the casserole with paper towels.
6. Return the ducks to the casserole, season to taste with salt and pepper and add the wine and peeled onions. Cover and simmer for 30 minutes over a very low heat, turning the ducks halfway through the cooking time. Add the rest of the olives and cook for a further 15 minutes.
7. Remove the ducks from the casserole, carve them and arrange the pieces on a warmed serving platter with the stuffing. Keep hot.
8. Add the butter to the cooking liquid a little at a time, beating with a whisk until thick and creamy. Pour a little sauce over the duck and serve the rest separately.

Coq au cidre

Chicken with Cider

00:20   01:15

American	Ingredients	Metric/Imperial
2 (2¾ lb)	Chickens	2 (1.25 kg / 2¾ lb)
	Salt and pepper	
6	Apples	6
½ cup	Butter	125 g / 4 oz
6	Shallots	6
2½ cups	Dry cider	600 ml / 1 pint
1	Bouquet garni	1
1 cup	Crème fraîche (see page 122)	250 m / 8 fl oz

1. Preheat the oven to 450°F / 230°C / Gas Mark 8.
2. Season the insides of the chickens with salt and pepper. Peel the apples, cut them into quarters and remove the cores and seeds. Put the apple quarters inside the birds and sew up the

openings with kitchen string.
3. Put the birds in a large buttered flameproof casserole and coat them with 6 tablespoons [75 g / 3 oz] of the butter. Bake for about 20 minutes, turning the chickens several times so that they are brown on all sides.
4. Meanwhile, peel and chop the shallots. Heat the remaining butter in a small pan, add the shallots and cook until translucent. Heat the cider in a saucepan over a very low heat.
5. Remove the casserole from the oven. Reduce the oven temperature to 375°F / 190°C / Gas Mark 5.
6. Add the shallots, hot cider and bouquet garni to the casserole. Salt lightly and season generously with pepper. Cover and return to the oven. Cook for 45 minutes.
7. Remove the birds (return the apple quarters to the casserole) and keep them hot. Remove the bouquet garni from the casserole and add the crème fraîche. Reduce the sauce over a brisk heat, stirring constantly. When thickened, put the sauce through a strainer, pressing the ingredients with a spoon.
8. Carve the birds. Arrange the pieces on a serving platter and pour the sauce over the top.

Dinde roulée du pot

Boiled Rolled Turkey with Vegetables

00:25   01:15

American	Ingredients	Metric/Imperial
4	Leeks	4
1	Celery stalk	1
2	Onions	2
4	Cloves	4
6	Carrots	6
2	Turnips	2
2 lb	Brussels sprouts	1 kg / 2 lb
5 quarts	Water	5 l / 9 pints
	Salt and peper	
1	Bouquet garni	1
1 (2 lb)	Rolled boneless turkey roast	1 (1 kg / 2 lb)
6	Slices of marrow bone	6

1. Quarter the leeks and clean them, ruffling back the layers. Tie the celery with the leeks to form a bundle. Peel the onions and stud each one with 2 cloves. Peel the carrots and turnips. Remove the outer leaves of the brussels sprouts.
2. Pour the cold water into a large saucepan and add a pinch of salt. Put in the carrots and bring to a boil. Simmer for 20 minutes, then add the leeks and celery tied together, the onions studded with cloves, the turnips and the bouquet garni. Cook for about 20 minutes over a moderate heat.
3. Remove the vegetables and put them aside.
4. Pour half the vegetable stock into another saucepan. Add the turkey roast, bring to a boil and simmer for about 40 minutes.
5. Meanwhile, pour the other half of the stock into another pan and add the brussels sprouts. Cook for about 10-15 minutes or until tender. Drain.
6. About 5 minutes before the end of the cooking time, take a small panful of stock from the turkey, put in the pieces of marrow bone and cook for 5 minutes over a moderate heat.
7. Shortly before the end of the turkey's cooking time, add all the vegetables to reheat them. Season with salt and pepper.
8. Serve the turkey surrounded with the drained vegetables and marrow bones. The stock will make a delicious clear soup.

Escalopes de dinde normande

Normandy Style Turkey Scaloppine [Escalopes]

00:15 00:30

American	Ingredients	Metric/Imperial
5 oz	Button mushrooms	150 g / 5 oz
	Lemon juice	
3 tbsp	Butter	40 g / 1½ oz
6	Turkey scaloppine [escalopes]	6
⅔ cup	Dry white wine	150 ml / ¼ pint
2 tsp	Tarragon mustard	2 tsp
½ cup	Crème fraîche (see page 122)	125 ml / 4 fl oz
	Salt and pepper	
2	Egg yolks	2

1. Sprinkle the mushrooms with lemon juice.
2. Melt the butter in a large frying pan. As soon as it bubbles, add the turkey scaloppine and seal on both sides for a few seconds without allowing them to color. Remove them from the frying pan and set aside.
3. Pour the wine into the pan and bring to a boil, then add the tarragon mustard. Stir to mix. Return the scaloppine to the frying pan. Add the mushrooms and crème fraîche. Season to taste with salt and pepper and cook for about 15 minutes over a moderate heat.
4. Arrange the turkey on a hot serving dish and keep warm.
5. Take 2 tablespoons of sauce and blend in a bowl with the egg yolks. Remove the frying pan from the heat and add this mixture to the remaining sauce, stirring thoroughly. If necessary, reheat the sauce but do not allow it to boil. Pour it over the turkey and serve immediately.

Rôti de dindonneau aux pommes

Roast Turkey with Apples

00:25 01:15

American	Ingredients	Metric/Imperial
1 (3 lb)	Young turkey	1 (1.5 kg / 3 lb)
6 tbsp	Butter	75 g / 3 oz
	Salt and pepper	
6	Sweet apples	6
1	Lemon	1
	Ground cinnamon	

1. Preheat the oven to 450°F / 230°C / Gas Mark 8.
2. Lightly butter an ovenproof dish. Spread the turkey with butter, season with salt and pepper and put it in the dish. Roast for about 1¼ hours, turning it 4 times. Baste at regular intervals with the roasting juices and add 6 tablespoons of water during the last 30 minutes of the cooking time.
3. Meanwhile, peel the apples leaving them whole. Remove the cores with an apple corer and sprinkle them with the juice of the lemon so that they do not turn brown. About 15 minutes before the end of the roasting time, put the apples in the baking dish around the turkey. Put a pat of butter in the center of each apple and sprinkle with pepper to taste and a little cinnamon. Finish roasting.

4. Arrange the turkey on a platter surrounded by the apples and serve the roasting juices separately.

Coq au vin

Chicken in Red Wine

00:30 01:30

American	Ingredients	Metric/Imperial
1 (3 lb)	Chicken	1 (1.5 kg / 3 lb)
6 tbsp	Butter	75 g / 3 oz
	Salt and pepper	
5 oz	Lighty salted lean bacon	150 g / 5 oz
15	Tiny onions	15
2 tbsp	Brandy	2 tbsp
1	Bottle of full-bodied red wine	1
1	Garlic clove	1
1	Bouquet garni	1
1 tbsp	Flour	1 tbsp
	Chopped fresh parsley for garnish	

1. Cut the chicken into pieces.
2. Heat ¼ cup [50 g / 2 oz] of the butter in a flameproof casserole and add the chicken pieces. Season with salt and pepper and brown the chicken on all sides over a medium heat.
3. Meanwhile, finely dice the bacon and put it in a saucepan of cold water. Bring to a boil and blanch for 5 minutes. Drain. Peel the onions.
4. Remove the pieces of chicken and keep them hot. Put the onions and bacon in the casserole and fry for about 10 minutes, stirring frequently.
5. Return the chicken to the casserole and add the brandy. Heat and set alight, then, when the flames have died out, add the red wine so that all the chicken is well covered. Season to taste with salt and pepper. Add the peeled garlic and bouquet garni. Cover and simmer for 1 hour.
6. About 15 minutes before the end of the cooking time, work the rest of the butter with the flour to form a soft paste. Beat in 2 tablespoons of hot sauce, then return this mixture to the casserole and stir well.
7. Serve garnished with a little chopped parsley.

Roast quails on canapés (see page 292)

Dinde de Noël
Christmas Turkey

🏁 00:10   02:30 🍲

American	Ingredients	Metric/Imperial
1	Large pear	1
	Salt and pepper	
1 (7 lb)	Turkey, with giblets	1 (3.5 kg / 7 lb)
⅔ cup	Water	150 ml / ¼ pint
¼ cup	Butter	50 g / 2 oz

1. Preheat the oven to 400°F / 200°C / Gas Mark 6.
2. Wash the pear and cut it into quarters without peeling. Roll the quarters in a mixture of salt and pepper and put them inside the turkey. Truss it.
3. Season the turkey with salt and pepper and put it on a rack in a roasting pan. Roast for 2 hours and 20 minutes. Turn it frequently so that it browns on all sides. Halfway through the cooking, pour the water into the pan.
4. Remove the turkey from the oven, wrap it in foil and keep it hot.
5. Purée the turkey liver and heart in a blender or food processor. Heat 1 tablespoon butter in a frying pan, add the puréed mixture and brown over a moderate heat for 2 minutes. Season with salt and pepper.
6. Carve the turkey, keeping the carving juices. If the pear quarters have not dissolved, used them to garnish the platter of turkey.
7. Mix the browned liver and heart mixture with the pan juices, then add the carving juices. Reheat and whisk in the remaining butter. Serve this sauce with the turkey.

Compote de lapereau
Rabbit and Plum Brandy Terrine

🏁 00:40   02:00 🍲

American	Ingredients	Metric/Imperial
2 (4 lb)	Young rabbits, boned and bones reserved	2 (1.8 kg / 4 lb)
	Salt and pepper	
1	Piece of caul fat	1
¼ lb	Carrots	125 g / 4 oz
¼ lb	Onions	125 g / 4 oz
2 tsp	Crumbled dried thyme	2 tsp
2 tsp	Crushed bay leaves	2 tsp
1½ cups	Plum or other fruit brandy	350 ml / 12 fl oz
1	Bouquet garni	1
1 envelope	Unflavored gelatin	1 sachet

1. Preheat the oven to 350°F / 18;°C / Gas Mark 4.
2. Cut the rabbit meat into large cubes and season with salt and pepper. Soak the caul fat in cold water. Peel and slice the carrots and onions.
3. Drain the caul fat carefully. Spread it out on a cloth and pat it dry, then place it in a 1½-quart [1.5 l / 2½ pint] terrine so that it hangs well over the sides all around. Put in the rabbit cubes in layers, alternating with carrots, onions, crumbled thyme and crushed bay leaves. Pour in all but 2 teaspoons of the plum brandy; the rabbit cubes should be covered with

liquid. Press down well and fold over the caul.
4. Cover the terrine and place it in a pan containing water. Bake for 2 hours.
5. Meanwhile, put the rabbit bones in a large saucepan. Cover them with water, add the bouquet garni and season with salt and pepper. Bring to a boil and simmer for 1¼ hours.
6. Strain the stock and let it cool, then remove the fat which rises to the surface. Add the dissolved gelatin and the remaining plum brandy.
7. Remove the terrine from the oven and leave it to cool. Pour the lukewarm gelatin mixture over the top and chill for 48 hours.

Lapin à la cauchoise
Rabbit with Cream and Mustard Sauce

🏁 00:10   00:50 🍲

American	Ingredients	Metric/Imperial
1 (2¾ lb)	Rabbit	1 (1.25 kg / 2¾ lb)
¼ cup	Butter	50 g / 2 oz
5 tbsp	Crème fraîche (see page 122)	5 tbsp
	Salt and pepper	
3 tbsp	Strong prepared mustard	3 tbsp
1¼ cups	Dry white wine	300 ml / ½ pint
2	Shallots	2

1. Cut the rabbit into portions.
2. Melt the butter in a large flameproof casserole. When it is hot, add the pieces of rabbit and brown them on all sides. As soon as they are golden, remove them from the casserole and throw away the fat.
3. Put 2 tablespoons of the crème fraîche into the casserole. Return the pieces of rabbit and turn so that they are well coated. Season to taste with salt and pepper. Cook very gently for about 30 minutes. Add 1 tablespoon of crème fraîche every 10 minutes.
4. In a small bowl mix together the mustard and wine. Peel the shallots, chop finely and add to this mixture. Pour this over the rabbit at the same time as the last spoonful of crème. Cook for a further 15-20 minutes. Serve very hot.

Dinde farcie aux marrons
Turkey with Chestnut Stuffing

🏁 00:30   03:00 🍲
Serves 8–10

American	Ingredients	Metric/Imperial
1 cup	Raisins	150 g / 5 oz
2 lb	Canned whole chestnuts in natural juice	1 kg / 2 lb
1 (6 lb)	Turkey, with giblets	1 (3 kg / 6 lb)
½ cup	Butter	125 g / 4 oz
	Salt and pepper	
2	Fresh thyme sprigs	3

1. Preheat the oven to 450°F / 230°C / Gas Mark 8.

2. Soak the raisins in warm water. Drain the chestnuts. Finely chop the turkey liver.

3. Heat 1 tablespoon of butter in a frying pan, add the chopped liver and cook over a medium heat for 2 minutes, stirring constantly. Remove from the pan. Melt 2 tablespoons [25 g / 1 oz] of butter in the pan and add half the chestnuts. Season with salt and pepper and add a sprig of thyme. Stir for 5 minutes over a medium heat, then remove from the heat and leave to cool.

4. Mix the cooked chestnuts, drained raisins and liver together and put inside the turkey. Sew up the opening with kitchen string.

5. Put the turkey in a roasting pan. Coat with plenty of butter, season with salt and pepper and sprinkle with a few leaves of thyme. Add 3 tablespoons of hot water and the remaining turkey giblets and roast for 3 hours, basting the turkey frequently with the pan juices. Add 3 tablespoons of hot water from time to time while the turkey is cooking and cover it with foil if it browns excessively.

6. About 15 minutes before the end of the cooking time, put the rest of the chestnuts and butter in a saucepan. Add salt and pepper to taste and 1 teaspoon of thyme leaves. Heat through gently.

7. Set the turkey on a warmed serving platter and keep it hot. Put the roasting pan on top of the stove, remove the giblets and add 5 tablespoons of hot water to the juices. Boil, stirring with a wooden spoon, until the sauce reduces, then strain it into a sauceboat. Arrange the chestnuts around the turkey.

Turkey with chestnut stuffing

Lapin chasseur

Rabbit in Mushroom and Wine Sauce

	00:15	00:55

American	Ingredients	Metric/Imperial
1 (2¾ lb)	Rabbit	1 (1.25 kg / 2¾ lb)
¼ lb	Bacon	125 g / 4 oz
2	Onions	2
3	Shallots	3
1	Garlic clove	1
1¼ cups	Dry white wine	300 ml / ½ pint
⅔ cup	Water	150 ml / ¼ pint
1	Bouquet garni	1
	Grated nutmeg	
	Salt and pepper	
½ lb	Button mushrooms	250 g / 8 oz
1 tbsp	Butter	1 tbsp
1 tbsp	Flour	1 tbsp
	Chopped fresh parsley for garnish	

1. Cut the rabbit into portions.
2. Put the bacon in a saucepan. Cover it with water, bring to a boil and blanch for 5 minutes. Drain and cut it into strips. Peel and chop the onions, shallots and garlic.
3. Put the strips of bacon in a flameproof casserole over a moderate heat and cook to render the fat. Add the rabbit pieces and brown gently for about 10 minutes so that the fat does not burn.
4. Add the onions, shallots and garlic. As soon as they start to cook, add the wine and water. Add the bouquet garni, a pinch of nutmeg, and salt and pepper to taste. Bring to a boil, then reduce the heat, cover and simmer for 30 minutes.
5. Thinly slice the mushrooms. Add them to the casserole and cook for a further 15 minutes.
6. Remove the pieces of rabbit from the casserole, place them on a serving dish and keep hot.
7. Mix the butter with the flour to a smooth paste. Add 3 tablespoons of the cooking liquid. Stir well, then return this mixture to the casserole. Bring to a boil and cook, stirring, until the sauce is thick and creamy.
8. Pour the sauce over the rabbit and serve sprinkled with chopped parsley.

Lapin aux pruneaux

Rabbit with Prunes

	00:30	01:00

American	Ingredients	Metric/Imperial
20	Large prunes	20
1¼ cups	Madeira wine	300 ml / ½ pint
1 (2¾ lb)	Young rabbit	1 (1.25 kg / 2¾ lb)
1 tbsp	Oil	1 tbsp
¼ cup	Butter	50 g / 2 oz
1 (5 oz)	Slice of cooked ham	1 (150 g / 5 oz)
	Salt and pepper	

1. Remove the pits [stones] from the prunes with a small pointed knife. Soak the prunes in the madeira for 1 hour.

2. Cut the rabbit into pieces. Heat the oil and 2 tablespoons [25 g / 1 oz] butter in a flameproof casserole. As soon as the butter bubbles, add the pieces of rabbit and brown lightly over a moderate heat.
3. Cut the ham into strips, add to the casserole and fry for 5 minutes. Season to taste with salt and pepper. Add the madeira and prunes. Cover and cook over a very low heat for 45 minutes to 1 hour, until tender.
4. Put the pieces of rabbit in a warmed serving dish with the prunes and ham. Bring the sauce back to a boil, then remove from the heat and beat in the remaining butter, a little at a time. Adjust the seasoning and pour the sauce over the rabbit.

Rabbit with cream and brandy sauce

Lapin en civet

Jugged Rabbit

	00:15	02:00

American	Ingredients	Metric/Imperial
1 (3 lb)	Rabbit	1 (1.5 kg / 3 lb)
½ lb	Bacon	250 g / 8 oz
4	Carrots	4
4	Shallots	4
3 tbsp	Flour	3 tbsp
	Salt and pepper	
1	Bottle of red wine	1
1	Bouquet garni	1
20	Tiny onions	20
	Grated nutmeg	

1. Cut the rabbit into pieces.
2. Put the bacon in a saucepan, cover with cold water and bring to a boil. Blanch for 5 minutes. Drain and cut into small strips. Peel and finely chop the carrots and shallots.
3. Put the flour on a plate. Roll the pieces of rabbit in the flour to coat all over, then shake to remove excess flour.
4. Brown the strips of bacon in a flameproof casserole over a moderate heat without adding any fat. Remove them from the casserole and set aside.
5. Add the pieces of rabbit to the casserole. Season to taste with salt and pepper. Lightly brown the rabbit over a brisk heat. Add the carrots and shallots. When the vegetables are browned, pour in the red wine. Add a little water if necessary so that the pieces of rabbit are just covered with liquid. Add the strips of bacon and the bouquet garni. Cover the casserole and simmer gently for 1 hour.
6. Meanwhile, peel the onions.
7. Taste the cooking liquid and adjust the seasoning. Add a

pinch of nutmeg and the onions. Leave the casserole uncovered and simmer gently for another hour, stirring from time to time, until the rabbit is tender.

8. Discard the bouquet garni before serving.

Lapin sauce poulette

Rabbit with Rich Mushroom Sauce

		00:25	01:00	

American	Ingredients	Metric/Imperial
1 (2¾ lb)	Rabbit	1 (1.25 kg / 2¾ lb)
3	Onions	3
2	Carrots	2
6 tbsp	Butter	75 g / 3 oz
2 tbsp	Flour	2 tbsp
1 cup	Dry white wine	250 ml / 8 fl oz
	Salt and pepper	
1	Bouquet garni	1
5 oz	Button mushrooms	150 g / 5 oz
½	Lemon	½
2	Egg yolks	2
1 cup	Crème fraîche (see page 122)	250 ml / 8 fl oz

1. Cut the rabbit into pieces. Peel and slice the onions and carrots. Melt the butter in a flameproof casserole. As soon as it bubbles, add the rabbit pieces, onions and carrots and fry over a moderate heat until light brown.

2. Sprinkle with the flour. Stir so that all the pieces are coated, and lightly brown the flour. Pour in the wine and add enough water so that the liquid covers the rabbit and vegetables. Season to taste with salt and pepper and add the bouquet garni. Cover and simmer for 45 minutes to 1 hour or until the rabbit is tender.

3. Sprinkle the mushrooms with the juice of the ½ lemon. About 15 minutes before the end of the cooking time, remove the bouquet garni from the casserole and add the mushrooms.

4. Mix the egg yolks with the crème fraîche.

5. Just before serving, remove the casserole from the heat and add the egg mixture. Stir thoroughly and adjust the seasoning, if necessary.

Lapin à la fine

Rabbit with Cream and Brandy Sauce

		00:10	00:30 to 00:40	

American	Ingredients	Metric/Imperial
2 (1½ lb)	Rabbits	2 (750 g / 1½ lb)
¾ lb	Tiny onions	350 g / 12 oz
2 tbsp	Butter	25 g / 1 oz
1 tbsp	Oil	1 tbsp
	Salt and pepper	
½ cup	Cognac	125 ml / 4 fl oz
¼ cup	Crème fraîche (see page 122)	4 tbsp
1 tbsp	Flour	1 tbsp

1. Cut the rabbits into pieces. Peel the onions. Heat 1 tablespoon [15 g / ½ oz] butter with the oil in a flameproof casserole, add the pieces of rabbit and brown gently for about 7 minutes. Add the onions and cook for a further 10 minutes or until golden brown.

2. Season to taste with salt and pepper. Add the cognac, cover and cook over a very low heat for 30-40 minutes.

3. Remove the rabbit and onions from the casserole and keep hot. Skim the fat from the cooking liquid. Add the crème fraîche and boil for a few seconds. Remove from the heat.

4. Blend the rest of the butter with the flour to a smooth paste. Add a tablespoon of the cooking liquid and stir well, then add to the casserole, whisking. Return to the heat and bring to a boil. The sauce should be creamy without being thick. Taste and adjust the seasoning.

5. Serve the rabbit and onions coated with the hot sauce.

Cook's tip: this recipe is best if young rabbits are used.

Lapin farci

Stuffed Rabbit

		00:25	01:00 to 01:30	

American	Ingredients	Metric/Imperial
15	Green olives, pitted [stoned]	15
½ lb	Smoked bacon	250 g / 8 oz
1 (2¾ lb)	Young rabbit	1 (1.25 kg / 2¾ lb)
2	Chicken livers	2
2	Small pork link sausages [chipolatas]	2
6	Tiny onions	6
6	Garlic cloves	6
5 oz	Button mushrooms	150 g / 5 oz
	Thyme leaves	
1	Bay leaf	1
	Salt and pepper	
2 tbsp	Olive oil	2 tbsp
1	Bouquet garni	1
⅔ cup	Dry white wine	150 ml / ¼ pint
¼ cup	Butter	50 g / 2 oz

1. Blanch the olives in boiling water for 5 minutes, then drain. Cut the bacon into small strips, put them in a frying pan and cook over a moderate heat until brown. Remove them from the frying pan and set aside.

2. Cut the rabbit liver, chicken livers and sausages into dice and brown in the bacon fat. Remove from the frying pan.

3. Peel the onions and garlic. Add to the pan and cook for 10 minutes. Remove and set aside.

4. Cut the mushrooms into quarters and add to the frying pan. Cook until the liquid escapes from the mushrooms, then return the bacon, sausages, livers, onions and garlic to the pan. Add the olives, a pinch of thyme leaves and the bay leaf, crushed. Mix well, adding salt and pepper to taste.

5. Stuff the rabbit with the liver mixture and tie securely.

6. Heat the olive oil in a flameproof casserole. Add the rabbit, season with salt and pepper and brown on all sides. Add the bouquet garni and wine. Cover and cook over a low heat for about 1½ hours.

7. Carve the rabbit and arrange it on a serving dish surrounded by the stuffing. Remove the casserole from the heat and add the butter to the sauce a little at a time, beating well. Serve the sauce separately.

Lapin à la moutarde
Rabbit with Mustard

00:10   01:15

American	Ingredients	Metric/Imperial
1	Large piece of caul fat	1
1 (3 lb)	Rabbit	1 (1.5 kg / 3 lb)
5 tbsp	Strong prepared mustard	5 tbsp
	Salt and pepper	
1¼ cups	Crème fraîche (see page 122)	300 ml / ½ pint

1. Soak the caul fat in cold water. Preheat the oven to 450°F / 230°C / Gas Mark 8.
2. Coat the rabbit with the mustard and season lightly with salt and pepper. Drain the caul fat, spread it out on a cloth and pat it dry. Wrap the rabbit in it.
3. Put the rabbit in a buttered roasting pan. Roast for 50 minutes, turning and basting frequently. When the rabbit is cooked, remove it from the pan and keep it hot.
4. Pour the crème fraîche into the roasting pan and cook on top of the stove, scraping the bottom of the pan with a wooden spatula to dissolve the sediment. Simmer until the sauce thickens.
5. Cut the rabbit into portions (the caul will have dissolved) and serve very hot with the sauce.

Lapin au pineau
Rabbit with Pineau des Charentes

Pineau des Charentes is an aperitif made from fresh grape juice and cognac.

01:00
plus marinating   00:40

American	Ingredients	Metric/Imperial
2	Onions	2
2	Shallots	2
3	Carrots	3
1	Bouquet garni	1
½	Bottle of Pineau des Charentes or sherry	½
	Salt and pepper	
1 (6 lb)	Rabbit	1 (3 kg / 6 lb)
½ cup	Butter	125 g / 4 oz
⅔ cup	Beef stock or broth (see page 114)	150 ml / ¼ pint
1 tbsp	Flour	1 tbsp
½ lb	Prunes	250 g / 8 oz

1. The day before cooking, prepare the marinade. Peel and slice the onions, shallots and carrots. Put them in a bowl with the bouquet garni and pour in the Pineau des Charentes. Season with salt and pepper.
2. Cut the rabbit into pieces. Place in the bowl and marinate for 12 hours. Turn the pieces of rabbit 2 or 3 times.
3. Drain the pieces of rabbit, reserving the marinade. Melt ¼ cup [50 g / 2 oz] butter in a flameproof casserole, add the pieces of rabbit and cook until they are well browned.
4. Strain the marinade and add it to the casserole with the stock or broth. Simmer for about 40 minutes.
5. Remove the pieces of rabbit and keep them hot. Mix the

remaining butter and the flour to a paste. Add to the cooking liquid a little at a time, stirring well, and cook until thickened. Add the prunes to this sauce and heat through.
6. Arrange the pieces of rabbit on a serving platter. Surround with the prunes and serve the sauce separately.

Lapin coquibus
Rabbit Casseroled with Onions and Bacon

00:20   01:15

American	Ingredients	Metric/Imperial
1 (3 lb)	Rabbit	1 (1.5 kg / 3 lb)
¼ cup	Butter	50 g / 2 oz
3 tbsp	Olive oil	3 tbsp
½ lb	Smoked bacon	250 g / 8 oz
24	Tiny onions	24
1 tbsp	Flour	1 tbsp
2 cups	Chicken stock	500 ml / ¾ pint
1¼ cups	White wine	300 ml / ½ pint
	Salt and pepper	
1	Bouquet garni	1

1. Cut the rabbit into 9 pieces. Heat the butter and oil in a flameproof casserole, add the pieces of rabbit and brown on all sides over a medium heat.
2. Meanwhile, cut the bacon into strips. Peel the onions.
3. Remove the pieces of rabbit from the casserole and set aside. Add the strips of bacon and onions to the casserole and brown them lightly. Return the pieces of rabbit to the casserole. Sprinkle with the flour and cook, stirring, until browned.
4. Pour in the stock and wine. Season with salt and plenty of pepper and add the bouquet garni. Cover and cook over a low heat for about 50 minutes.
5. Discard the bouquet garni. Put the pieces of rabbit in a warmed serving dish and pour the sauce over the top. Serve.

Pigeons aux herbes
Pigeons with Herbs

00:20
plus standing time   00:25 to 00:35

American	Ingredients	Metric/Imperial
1 cup	Cream cheese	250 g / 8 oz
2 tbsp	Dried herbs of Provence	2 tbsp
1 tsp	Brandy	1 tsp
6 tbsp	Butter	75 g / 3 oz
	Salt and pepper	
3	Large pigeons	3
9	Bacon slices	9
⅔ cup	Boiling water	150 ml / ¼ pint
2 tbsp	Oil	2 tbsp
6	Slices of bread, ½ in / 1 cm thick	6

1. About 2 hours before cooking the pigeons, mix the cream cheese with the herbs, brandy and 2 tablespoons [25 g / 1 oz] of butter. Season with salt and pepper. Divide this mixture in 3 and stuff the pigeons with it. Wrap 3 slices of bacon around each bird. Leave them to stand in a roasting pan for 2 hours at room temperature.

2. Preheat the oven to 425°F / 220°C / Gas Mark 7.

3. Roast the pigeons for about 30 minutes without adding any liquid. Turn several times to brown evenly.

4. Remove the pigeons from the pan and keep warm. Put the pan over a low heat on top of the stove and add the boiling water. Heat, stirring to dissolve the solids in the bottom of the pan. Leave the sauce to reduce for 5 minutes.

5. Meanwhile, heat 1 tablespoon butter and the oil in a frying pan and fry the bread over a brisk heat until golden brown on both sides.

6. Beat the remaining butter into the sauce. Season to taste with salt and pepper and pour into a hot sauceboat. Cut each pigeon in half and place a half on each slice of fried bread. Serve immediately.

Pigeons with herbs

Pintade au chou

Guinea Fowl with Cabbage

| | 00:30 | | 01:30 to 02:00 | |

American	Ingredients	Metric/Imperial
1	Large head of white cabbage	1
¾ lb	Smoked bacon	350 g / 12 oz
	Salt and pepper	
1	Large guinea fowl	1
4	Bacon slices	4

1. Cut the cabbage into quarters and remove the core. Put the quarters in a saucepan of boiling salted water. Bring back to a boil and cook for 10 minutes. Drain well.

2. Preheat the oven to 450°F / 230°C / Gas Mark 8.

3. Cut the smoked bacon into large strips. Put them into a flameproof casserole and cook gently so that the fat is rendered without the bacon browning. Remove the bacon from the casserole with a slotted spoon and set aside.

4. Add the cabbage to the casserole and cook in the bacon fat until it softens. Return the strips of bacon to the casserole.

Season to taste with salt and pepper. Cover and cook over a low heat for 30 minutes.

5. Meanwhile, season the guinea fowl with salt and pepper and cover with the slices of bacon. Truss the bird and roast for about 30 minutes or until well browned.

6. Put the guinea fowl in the casserole with the cabbage and finish cooking gently until the cabbage is very soft (about 1 hour).

7. Just before serving, if there is too much liquid, reduce it rapidly over a brisk heat. Serve the guinea fowl carved into portions, on a bed of cabbage and bacon.

Cook's tip: this recipe can be made in large quantities as it is very good when reheated.

Pintades farcies

Stuffed Guinea Fowl

| | 00:30 | | 00:40 | |

American	Ingredients	Metric/Imperial
⅔ cup	Milk	150 ml / ¼ pint
2 cups	Fresh bread crumbs	125 g / 4 oz
5 oz	Lightly salted bacon	150 g / 5 oz
1	Shallot	1
2 (2 lb)	Guinea fowl, with livers	2 (1 kg / 2 lb)
½	Chicken livers	250 g / 8 oz
1	Egg	1
3½ oz	Pâté de foie gras	100 g / 3½ oz
1	Fresh thyme sprig	1
	Salt and pepper	
	Grated nutmeg	
	Oil	
⅔ cup	Boiling water	150 ml / ¼ pint
¼ cup	Butter	50 g / 2 oz

1. Pour the milk over the bread crumbs and set aside to soak. Cut the bacon into strips, put them in a saucepan of cold water and bring to a boil. Blanch for 5 minutes. Drain.

2. Peel and thinly slice the shallot. Put the shallot and bacon in a frying pan and fry over a medium heat until the shallot becomes translucent. Add the guinea fowl livers and the whole chicken livers. Fry them lightly so that they are not completely cooked.

3. Preheat the oven to 425°F / 220°C / Gas Mark 7.

4. Squeeze the liquid from the bread crumbs and put them in a bowl. Add the egg, foie gras, the ingredients in the frying pan and the thyme leaves. Work all these ingredients with a fork, mashing the livers. Season to taste with salt and pepper and add a pinch of nutmeg.

5. Divide this mixture in half and use to stuff the guinea fowl. Truss them and brush the skin with a little oil. Place on a metal rack in a roasting pan and roast for about 40 minutes. Turn them while roasting so that they brown on all sides, and pour half the boiling water into the dish halfway through the process. When the birds are cooked, turn off the oven and leave them inside for 5 minutes.

6. Carve the guinea fowl into portions, keeping the juices, and arrange the pieces on a serving dish. Garnish the dish with the stuffing and keep warm.

7. Pour the remaining boiling water into the roasting pan and heat briskly on top of the stove for a few minutes, scraping the bottom well to loosen all the solids. Beat in the carving juices and the butter. Taste and adjust the seasoning if necessary. Serve this sauce with the guinea fowl.

Pintadeaux rôtis sur canapés

Roast Guinea Fowl with Foie Gras

00:10　　　　　00:40

American	Ingredients	Metric/Imperial
3 (1 lb)	Young guinea fowl (with the livers)	3 (500 g / 1 lb)
	Salt and pepper	
3 tbsp	Butter	40 g / 1½ oz
6	Bacon slices	6
3 tbsp	Water	3 tbsp
2 tbsp	Oil	2 tbsp
6	Slices of bread	6
1	Small can of pâté de foie gras	1
¼ cup	Brandy	4 tbsp

1. Preheat the oven to 425°F / 220°C / Gas Mark 7.
2. Season the inside of each guinea fowl with salt and pepper and put 1 tablespoon of butter inside each. Cover the birds with bacon and tie it on with string. Place the birds on a rack in a roasting pan. Roast for 10-15 minutes.
3. Pour the juices from the guinea fowl into the roasting pan. Add the water. Continue roasting for 30 minutes.
4. Meanwhile, heat the oil and brown the slices of bread in a frying pan on both sides. Mash the livers of the guinea fowl in a bowl using a fork. Season to taste with salt and pepper and add the pâté de foie gras. Mix well.
5. When the guinea fowl are cooked, pour the juice which remains inside them into the roasting pan. Add the brandy and scrape well to loosen all the sediment at the bottom of the pan. Add the liver mixture and bring to a boil.
6. Cut the guinea fowl in half and serve each piece on a slice of fried bread topped with some of the sauce. Serve the rest of the sauce in a sauceboat.

Pintade en cocotte aux cerises fraîches

Casserole of Guinea Fowl with Fresh Cherries

00:40　　　　　01:15

American	Ingredients	Metric/Imperial
2	Young guinea fowl	2
¼ cup	Brandy	4 tbsp
	Salt and pepper	
4	Thin bacon slices	4
½ cup	Butter	125 g / 4 oz
5	Shallots	5
½ lb	Button mushrooms	250 g / 8 oz
½	Lemon	½
1	Small fresh thyme sprig	1
2 lb	Cherries	1 kg / 2 lb
⅔ cup	Water	150 ml / ¼ pint
6 tbsp	Sugar	6 tbsp
1¼ cups	Crème fraîche (see page 122)	300 ml / ½ pint

1. Preheat the oven to 450°F / 230°C / Gas Mark 8.
2. Rub the insides of the guinea fowl with a few drops of

brandy, then season them with salt and pepper. Cover the back and breast of the guinea fowl with the bacon and tie with kitchen string. Heat ¼ cup [50 g / 2 oz] of the butter in a flameproof casserole, add the guinea fowl and brown on all sides over a medium heat.
3. Meanwhile, peel and chop the shallots. Thinly slice the mushrooms and sprinkle with the juice of the ½ lemon. Melt the rest of the butter in a frying pan, add the shallots and cook until softened. Add the mushrooms and cook until all the liquid has evaporated.
4. Add the mushrooms and shallots to the casserole. Pour the remaining brandy over the birds and set alight, lifting the guinea fowl so that their whole surface absorbs the flavor. Add the thyme. Cover the casserole, put it in the oven and cook for 30 minutes.
5. While the guinea fowl are cooking, wash the cherries and remove the pits [stones]. Put them in a saucepan with the water and sugar. Cover and cook over a low heat for 15 minutes.
6. Remove the guinea fowl from the casserole and discard the bacon. Return them to the casserole and cook, uncovered, for 10 minutes longer. Add the cherries and cook for a further 10 minutes.
7. Drain the birds, carve them into portions and arrange them on a serving dish. Keep hot. Pour the crème fraîche into the casserole and boil briskly to thicken, stirring constantly. Adjust the seasoning, if necessary.
8. Pour the sauce into a sauceboat and serve, very hot, with the guinea fowl.

Salmis de pintade

Salmis of Guinea Fowl

00:20　　　　　01:15

American	Ingredients	Metric/Imperial
5 tbsp	Butter	65 g / 2½ oz
2 (2¾ lb)	Guinea fowl, with giblets	2 (1.25 kg / 2¾ lb)
	Salt and pepper	
2	Onions	2
2	Shallots	2
2	Carrots	2
1	Garlic clove	1
¼ lb	Lightly salted bacon	125 g / 4 oz
¼ cup	Brandy	4 tbsp
1	Bottle of dry red wine	1
	Grated nutmeg	
1	Bouquet garni	1
2 tbsp	Flour	2 tbsp
3	Slices of bread, ½ in / 1 cm thick	3
2 tbsp	Oil	2 tbsp

1. Heat ¼ cup [50 g / 2 oz] butter in a flameproof casserole, add the guinea fowl and brown lightly on all sides over a low heat. Do not let them get too dark. Season to taste with salt and pepper. Cover and cook over a low heat for 30 minutes.
2. Meanwhile, peel and dice the onions, shallots, carrots and garlic.
3. Cut up the guinea fowl for serving and put the pieces aside. Chop the giblets.
4. Chop the bacon and put the pieces in a saucepan of cold water. Bring to a boil and blanch for 5 minutes, then drain. Put the bacon in the casserole with the diced vegetables and cook until golden. Add the giblets and brown over a brisk heat.
5. Add the brandy and set alight, then pour over the red wine.

The liquid should cover the contents of the casserole, so add a little water if necessary. Season with pepper and a pinch of nutmeg and add the bouquet garni. Cover and simmer for 45 minutes.

6. Strain the contents of the casserole into a bowl, pressing with the back of a spoon to extract as much liquid as possible from the solids.

7. Wipe the casserole and put in the remaining butter. Heat it, then add the flour, mixing well. Brown this roux. Add the strained liquid, stirring, and cook until the sauce thickens.

8. Put the pieces of guinea fowl in the sauce and simmer for 10 minutes.

9. Meanwhile, remove the crusts from the slices of bread and cut diagonally into quarters. Heat the oil in a large frying pan and fry the bread until golden brown on both sides.

10. Put the pieces of guinea fowl in a serving dish together with the sauce and garnish with the croûtons.

Roast guinea fowl with foie gras

Poularde en chaud-froid

Cold Chicken in Aspic Cream

	01:00 plus cooling and chilling		03:00

American	Ingredients	Metric/Imperial
1 lb	Carrots	500 g / 1 lb
2	Turnips	2
3	Onions	3
1	Garlic clove	1
3	Cloves	3
4	Leeks	4
1	Celery stalk	1
1	Bouquet garni	1
	Salt and pepper	
3 quarts	Water	3 l / 5 pints
1 (4 lb)	Chicken	1 (2 kg / 4 lb)
2	Calf's feet, halved	2
2 cups	Crème fraîche (see page 122)	450 ml / ¾ pint
½ oz	Truffle slices	15 g / ½ oz

1. Peel the carrots, turnips, onions and garlic. Stud each onion with a clove. Put all these vegetables in a large pan, and add the leeks, celery and bouquet garni. Season to taste and cover with the water. Bring to a boil and simmer for 30 minutes.

2. Remove from the heat and add the chicken. Wait 5 minutes, then return the pan to a medium heat. Bring slowly back to a boil and simmer gently for 1 hour. Allow the chicken to cool in the stock.

3. Take the chicken out of the pan. Carve into equal pieces and remove all the skin. Set aside. Strain the stock and put 1 quart [1 l / 1¾ pints] aside.

4. Put the remaining stock back into the pan. Add the halved calf's feet and simmer for 45 minutes.

5. Reduce the reserved stock by one-third over a brisk heat, then add 3 cups [750 ml / 1¼ pints] of the stock from the calf's feet. Again boil to reduce by one-third. Gradually add ⅔ cup [150 ml / ¼ pint] crème fraîche, stirring constantly.

6. Pour the reduced sauce into a bowl and gradually stir in the rest of the crème. Beat vigorously until the sauce becomes silky.

7. Dip the pieces of chicken in the sauce to coat them. Arrange them on a sheet of foil and garnish them with thin slices of truffle. Using a pastry brush, coat them with the rest of the sauce which should be still slightly liquid but on the point of setting. Chill thoroughly in the refrigerator before serving.

Pigeons en compote

Braised Pigeons

	00:15		01:00

American	Ingredients	Metric/Imperial
5 oz	Bacon	150 g / 5 oz
3	Large pigeons	3
¼ cup	Butter	50 g / 2 oz
3	Onions	3
1	Garlic clove	1
1 tbsp	Flour	1 tbsp
1 tbsp	Tomato paste [purée]	1 tbsp
⅔ cup	Chicken stock	150 ml / ¼ pint
⅔ cup	Dry white wine	150 ml / ¼ pint
	Salt and pepper	
1	Bouquet garni	1
½ lb	Button mushrooms	250 g / 8 oz
½	Lemon	½
1¼ cups	Crème fraîche (see page 122)	300 ml / ½ pint

1. Cut the bacon into small strips, plunge them into boiling water and blanch for 5 minutes. Drain and set aside.

2. Cut the pigeons in half. Heat half the butter in a flameproof casserole, add the pigeons and brown on all sides. Meanwhile, peel and thinly slice the onions. Peel and crush the garlic.

3. Drain the pigeon halves and set aside. Put the onions and strips of bacon into the casserole to brown. Sprinkle with the flour and stir to brown well.

4. Return the pigeon halves to the casserole. Mix the tomato paste with the stock and white wine and pour this mixture over the pigeons. Season to taste with salt and pepper. Add the garlic and bouquet garni. Cover the casserole and cook over a low heat for 45 minutes.

5. Meanwhile, thinly slice the mushrooms and sprinkle with the juice of the lemon. Heat the rest of the butter in a frying pan, add the mushrooms and cook until all the liquid has evaporated. Add the mushrooms to the casserole 5 minutes before the end of the cooking time.

6. Discard the bouquet garni. Drain the pigeon halves, put them in a deep serving dish and keep hot.

7. Add the crème fraîche to the casserole and stir for a few minutes over a moderate heat until the sauce thickens. Pour it over the pigeon halves. Serve immediately.

Pigeons aux petits pois

Pigeons with Peas

	00:15	00:40

American	Ingredients	Metric/Imperial
1 lb	Baby carrots	500 g / 1 lb
10	Tiny onions	10
6 small or 3 large	Pigeons	6 small or 3 large
9	Bacon slices	9
3 tbsp	Oil	3 tbsp
1 lb	Fresh young peas	500 g / 1 lb
1	Bouquet garni	1
1¼ cups	Water	300 ml / ½ pint
2	Sugar cubes	2
	Salt and pepper	

1. Peel and thinly slice the carrots. Peel the onions. Cover the pigeons with the bacon and truss.
2. Heat the oil in a flameproof casserole, add the pigeons and brown gently on all sides for about 10 minutes. Remove the pigeons from the casserole and throw away the oil.
3. Return the pigeons to the casserole with the onions, peas, carrots, bouquet garni, water and sugar cubes. Season to taste with salt and pepper and cook for 30 minutes over a low heat.
4. Serve the pigeons on the vegetables in a deep dish.

Oie de Noël farcie

Stuffed Christmas Goose

	00:50	02:30 to 03:00
	plus soaking	Serves 10–12

American	Ingredients	Metric/Imperial
1 lb	Prunes	500 g / 1 lb
2 lb	Apples	1 kg / 2 lb
2 tbsp	Sugar	2 tbsp
	Salt and pepper	
1 (10 / 12 lb)	Goose	1 (4.5 / 5 kg / 10 / 12 lb)
1 tbsp	Oil	1 tbsp
1	Large head of red cabbage	1
1	Lemon	1
2 tbsp	Goose fat	2 tbsp
2 tsp	Caraway seeds	2 tsp

1. The day before cooking, put the prunes in a bowl, cover them with cold water and leave them to soak for 12 hours.
2. The following day, drain the prunes and remove the pits [stones] with a small pointed knife. Peel and core the apples and slice them. Mix the apples and prunes together, add 1 tablespoon of sugar and season to taste with salt and pepper.
3. Preheat the oven to 425°F / 220°C / Gas Mark 7.
4. Stuff the goose with the prune and apple mixture. Coat it lightly with oil and put in a roasting pan. Calculate the total cooking time for the goose (allow 15 minutes to each pound).
5. Put the goose in the hot oven and roast for about 45 minutes until it has browned on all sides. Lower the temperature to 350°F / 180°C / Gas Mark 4 and continue

roasting. Prick the skin of the goose with a fork while it is cooking so that the fat runs out.
6. Meanwhile, remove any damaged leaves from the cabbage, cut it into quarters and cut out the core. Cut the cabbage into strips. Put it in a saucepan and just cover it with water. Add salt to taste, the juice of the lemon, the remaining sugar, the goose fat and caraway seeds. Cook for about 1 hour, then boil briskly until all the excess liquid evaporates.
7. Carve the goose and arrange on a hot serving dish, garnished with the stuffing and the red cabbage.

Oie en civet

Rich Stew of Goose

	00:30	01:30 to 02:00
	Serves 8–10	

American	Ingredients	Metric/Imperial
1 (5 - 6 lb)	Young goose, with giblets	1 (2.5 - 3 kg / 5 - 6 lb)
3	Onions	3
4	Shallots	4
1	Garlic clove	1
3 tbsp	Flour	3 tbsp
1	Bottle of full-bodied red wine	1
1	Bouquet garni	1
	Salt and pepper	

1. Ask your butcher to cut up the goose and collect the blood. Brown the pieces of goose in a frying pan without any fat, starting with the fattest pieces. Drain them as soon as they are browned and put them in a flameproof casserole.
2. Peel and chop the onions, shallots and garlic. Sprinkle the flour over the pieces of goose in the casserole and brown it, then add the wine and sufficient water to cover the goose. Add the onions, garlic, shallots, goose gizzard and bouquet garni. Season with salt and pepper. Cover and simmer for about 1 hour.
3. About 10 minutes before the end of the cooking time, discard the bouquet garni and add the goose liver. Skim any fat from the cooking liquid, and taste and adjust the seasoning if necessary. Cook for 5 minutes longer.
4. Mix the goose blood with a few spoonfuls of the cooking liquid and add to the remaining liquid, off the heat, stirring well. Return the casserole to a low heat and cook for a further 5 minutes. The sauce should not boil.

Poulet basquaise

Basque Style Chicken

	00:30	01:15

American	Ingredients	Metric/Imperial
1 (3 lb)	Chicken	1 (1.5 kg / 3 lb)
¼ cup	Olive oil	4 tbsp
⅔ cup	Dry white wine	150 ml / ¼ pint
1	Bouquet garni	1
	Salt and pepper	
2	Large green peppers	2
2	Large sweet red peppers	2
4	Medium-sized tomatoes	4
6	Medium-sized onions	6

1. Cut the chicken into pieces.

2. Heat 2 tablespoons of olive oil in a frying pan, add the chicken and brown over a moderate heat.

3. Remove the pieces of chicken from the frying pan and put them in a flameproof casserole. Add the white wine and bouquet garni, and season to taste with salt and pepper. Cover and cook over a moderate heat for about 1¼ hours.

4. Meanwhile, cut the green and red peppers in half. Remove the core, seeds and stalks and put the peppers under a hot broiler [grill]. Cook for about 15 minutes or until the skins are charred and blistered. Remove the peppers, put them in a plastic bag and seal the bag so that it is airtight. Leave them to cool in the bag for 10 minutes.

5. Peel the tomatoes (first plunging them into boiling water for 10 seconds), remove the seeds and chop coarsely. Peel and thinly slice the onions. Take the peppers out of the bag and remove the skins, which should come off easily. Cut the flesh into strips.

6. Heat the rest of the olive oil in the frying pan, add the onions and cook until soft. Add the peppers and cook for 10 minutes, then add the tomatoes and season to taste with salt and pepper. Cook over a low heat until all the ingredients are soft.

7. About 20 minutes before the chicken has finished cooking, add the contents of the frying pan to the casserole. Continue to simmer gently until the end of the cooking time.

Basque style chicken

Stuffed chicken with rice

Poule au riz

Stuffed Chicken with Rice

	00:30	02:30

American	Ingredients	Metric/Imperial
6 tbsp	Butter	75 g / 3 oz
½ lb	Chicken livers	250 g / 8 oz
1 (½ lb)	Slice of cooked ham	1 (250 g / 8 oz)
1	Shallot	1
2	Garlic cloves	2
1	Bunch of fresh parsley	1
3	Slices of bread	3
1¼ cups	Milk	300 ml / ½ pint
1	Egg	1
1	Grated nutmeg	1
	Salt and pepper	
1 (4 lb)	Chicken	1 (2 kg / 4 lb)
	Chicken stock	
3 cups	Water	750 ml / 1¼ pints
2 cups	Long-grain rice	400 g / 14 oz
2 tbsp	Flour	25 g / 1 oz
3	Egg yolks	3
⅔ cup	Crème fraîche (see page 122)	150 ml / ¼ pint
1	Lemon	1

1. Heat 2 tablespoons [25 g / 1 oz] butter in a frying pan, add the chicken livers and brown for a few minutes. Purée the livers in a blender or food processor with the ham, peeled shallot and garlic, and parsley. Put into a mixing bowl.
2. Remove the crusts from the bread and soak the slices in the milk. When they are saturated, squeeze out the excess milk and add the bread to the bowl. Add the whole egg and a pinch of grated nutmeg. Season with pepper and mix well.
3. Stuff the chicken with the liver mixture. Put the chicken in a large cooking pot and cover with chicken stock. Bring to a boil

over a medium heat, then turn down the heat and simmer gently for about 2½ hours.
4. When the chicken is cooked, remove 1½ quarts [1.5 l / 2½ pints] of the stock. Allow it to stand for a few minutes so that the fat floats to the surface, then skim off the fat carefully. Pour the stock into a saucepan and boil it briskly until it is reduced by half.
5. Meanwhile, bring the water to a boil in a saucepan. Add salt to taste and the rice and cook for 15-18 minutes or until tender and the water has been absorbed. Remove from the heat and keep hot.
6. Melt the rest of the butter in another saucepan, add the flour and cook, stirring, for a few minutes. Remove from the heat and add the reduced stock, beating vigorously with a whisk. Return to the heat and cook for 5 minutes, stirring continuously, until thickened.
7. Mix together the egg yolks, crème fraîche and juice of the lemon in a bowl. Pour the mixture into the sauce and heat, stirring, without allowing it to boil.
8. Carve the chicken into portions. Put the stuffing in the center of a serving platter, arrange the pieces of chicken all around and serve the sauce in a sauceboat. Serve with rice.

Poulet au blanc

Chicken in White Sauce

	00:10	01:30

American	Ingredients	Metric/Imperial
1 (3 lb)	Chicken	1 (1.5 kg / 3 lb)
3	Lemons	3
10	Tiny onions	10
2	Carrots	2
2 tbsp	Butter	25 g / 1 oz
2 tbsp	Flour	2 tbsp
1¼ cups	Water	300 ml / ½ pint
	Grated nutmeg	
	Salt and pepper	
2 cups	Dry white wine	500 ml / ¾ pint
1	Bouquet garni	1
½ lb	Button mushrooms	250 g / 8 oz
2	Egg yolks	2
⅔ cup	Crème fraîche (see page 122)	150 ml / ¼ pint

1. Truss the chicken. Squeeze 2½ lemons to extract the juice and rub about half the juice all over the chicken. Peel and slice the onions and carrots.
2. Heat the butter in a flameproof casserole. Add the flour and cook, stirring, for 2 minutes. Add the cold water a little at a time. Bring to a boil, stirring, then add a pinch of nutmeg and season to taste with salt and pepper.
3. Put the chicken in the casserole and add sufficient wine just to cover the bird. Add the onions, carrots and bouquet garni. Simmer over a low heat for 1¼ hours.
4. Sprinkle the mushrooms with lemon juice. Add them to the casserole 30 minutes before the end of the cooking time.
5. Remove the chicken from the casserole and keep it hot. Remove the bouquet garni from the sauce and discard. Blend the egg yolks with the crème fraîche and the remaining lemon juice and stir into the sauce. Taste and adjust the seasoning, if necessary. Reheat the sauce over a low heat. Do not allow to boil.
6. Carve the chicken into portions, arrange on a platter and pour a little sauce over the top. Serve the rest of the sauce separately.

Poulet au citron
Lemon Chicken

00:20   **01:30**

American	Ingredients	Metric/Imperial
1 (4 lb)	Chicken	1 (1.8 kg / 4 lb)
2	Lemons	2
30	Tiny onions	30
20	Green olives	20
3 tbsp	Olive oil	3 tbsp
	Salt and pepper	
¾ lb	Button mushrooms	350 g / 12 oz

1. Cut the chicken into pieces. Halve 1 of the lemons and rub the chicken pieces with the juice.
2. Peel the onions. Remove the pits [stones] from the olives.
3. Heat the oil in a flameproof casserole over a brisk heat. Add the pieces of chicken and brown them on all sides for about 15 minutes. Season to taste with salt and pepper.
4. Add the juice of the remaining lemon, cover the casserole and cook over a very low heat for 45 minutes.
5. Add the olives, mushrooms and onions and cook for 30 minutes longer. Serve hot.

Poule en daube
Braised Chicken

00:25   **02:00**

American	Ingredients	Metric/Imperial
1	Calf's foot	1
¼ lb	Bacon	125 g / 4 oz
6	Carrots	6
2	Onions	2
2	Shallots	2
1 (4 lb)	Chicken	1 (2 kg / 4 lb)
1	Bouquet garni	1
2 cups	Dry white wine	450 ml / ¾ pint
⅔ cup	Water	150 ml / ¼ pint
	Salt and pepper	

1. Split the calf's foot in half lengthwise so that the gelatin will run out easily during cooking. Cut the bacon into 2 in / 5 cm squares. Put the calf's foot and bacon in a saucepan of water. Bring to boil and blanch for 5 minutes. Drain and cool with fresh water.
2. Peel and dice the carrots, onions and shallots.
3. Line the bottom of a casserole with a few pieces of bacon and the calf's foot. Cut the chicken into pieces and put into the casserole with the carrots, onions, shallots and pieces of bacon in successive layers. Finish with a layer of vegetables and bacon. Add the bouquet garni.
4. Pour over the wine and water. Add salt and pepper to taste. Bring to a boil and simmer gently for 2 hours over a very low heat.
5. Remove the pieces of chicken from the casserole, drain them and set them on a serving dish. Discard the bouquet garni. Pour the cooking juices over the chicken and serve surrounded by the vegetable mixture.

Cook's tip: the chicken can be served hot immediately after cooking or chilled overnight in the refrigerator. The cooking juices will set and can be served cold, with the chicken.

Poulet à la crème
Chicken with Cream and Mushroom Sauce

00:25   **00:45**

American	Ingredients	Metric/Imperial
1 (3 lb)	Chicken	1 (1.5 kg / 3 lb)
	Salt and pepper	
3 tbsp + 1 tsp	Butter	40g / 1½ oz + 1 tsp
3 tbsp	Oil	3 tbsp
1	Thin bacon slice	1
1 lb	Button mushrooms	500 g / 1 lb
½	Lemon	½
4	Shallots	4
1¼ cups	White wine	300 ml / ½ pint
1 tsp	Flour	1 tsp
1¼ cups	Crème fraîche (see page 122)	300 ml / ½ pint

1. Cut the chicken into 6 pieces and season with salt and pepper. Heat 3 tablespoons [40 g / 1½ oz] butter with 2 tablespoons of the oil in a flameproof casserole. Add the pieces of chicken and brown on all sides over a medium heat.
2. Meanwhile, cut the bacon into small strips. Dice the mushrooms and sprinkle them with the juice of the ½ lemon. Peel and chop the shallots. Gently fry the strips of bacon in a frying pan without any fat, then drain them and set aside.
3. Heat the remaining oil in the frying pan. Add the mushrooms and shallots and cook until all the liquid has evaporated. Season to taste with salt and pepper.
4. Add the bacon, mushrooms and shallots to the casserole. Pour in the white wine. Cover and cook over a medium heat for 40 minutes.
5. Blend the flour with a teaspoon of butter to a paste.
6. Drain the pieces of chicken and put them on a warm serving platter. Add the crème fraîche to the casserole, then add the butter and flour paste and thicken over a brisk heat, stirring. Adjust the seasoning.
7. Pour this sauce over the chicken and serve immediately.

Poulet Vallée d'Auge
Auge Valley Chicken

00:15   **01:15**

American	Ingredients	Metric/Imperial
1 (4 lb)	Chicken	1 (2 kg / 4 lb)
⅔ cup	Butter	150 g / 5 oz
	Salt and pepper	
¼ cup	Calvados or applejack	4 tbsp
1¼ cups	Thick crème fraîche (see page 122)	300 ml / ½ pint

1. Cut the chicken into pieces.
2. Heat the butter in a flameproof casserole, add the chicken and brown for about 10 minutes. Season with salt and pepper. Cover and cook over a very low heat for 1 hour.
3. Pour the calvados into the casserole, heat and set alight. When the flames have died out, remove the pieces of chicken, arrange them on a warmed serving platter and keep hot.
4. Add the crème fraîche to the liquid, stir and bring to a boil. Simmer for 5-6 minutes or until the sauce has thickened. Pour the sauce over the chicken and serve immediately.

Poularde en gelée
Chicken in Brandied Aspic

	01:00		01:15	
	plus chilling			

American	Ingredients	Metric/Imperial
1 (4 lb)	Chicken, with giblets	1 (2 kg / 4 lb)
	Salt and pepper	
¼ cup	Butter	50 g / 2 oz
⅔ cup	Dry white wine	150 ml / ¼ pint
½ lb	Cooked ham	250 g / 8 oz
1 / 2 tsp	Unflavored gelatin	1 / 2 tsp
2 tbsp	Brandy	2 tbsp

1. Season the inside of the chicken with salt and pepper and truss it. Melt the butter in a flameproof casserole, add the chicken and giblets and brown on all sides.
2. Add the white wine and ham cut into dice. Cover and cook for about 1¼ hours over a low heat. Add salt and pepper to taste halfway through the cooking. Remove from the heat and allow the bird to cool in the cooking liquid.
3. When the chicken has cooled, take it out of the casserole, remove the skin and carve it into portions. Lay the pieces side by side on a long dish.
4. Dissolve the gelatin in a little water (follow the instructions on the package). Strain the cooking liquid into a bowl and skim off any fat from the surface. Add the dissolved gelatin and brandy. Let cool until syrupy.
5. Paint the pieces of chicken with a coat of the brandy aspic, then add another coating after a few minutes (put the bird in the refrigerator between the 2 applications). Chill overnight.
6. Melt the remaining aspic and paint several coats on the pieces of chicken. Chill until set. If any aspic remains, chill it until it is very firm, then dice it and use it to garnish the chicken.

Poulet antillaise
West Indian Chicken

	00:30		01:15	

American	Ingredients	Metric/Imperial
1 (3 lb)	Chicken	1 (1.5 kg / 3 lb)
	Salt and pepper	
2 tbsp	Oil	2 tbsp
2	Large onions	2
2	Shallots	2
⅔ cup	Rum	150 ml / ¼ pint
2 tbsp	Pineapple juice	2 tbsp
3 tbsp	Lemon juice	3 tbsp
	Cayenne pepper	
6	Slices of pineapple	6

1. Season the inside and outside of the chicken with salt and pepper. Heat the oil in a flameproof casserole, add the chicken and brown on all sides.
2. Peel and chop the onions and shallots and add them to the casserole. Heat the rum in a small saucepan, pour it over the chicken and set alight.
3. When the flames die away, sprinkle the chicken with the pineapple juice and lemon juice. Season with salt and pepper and add a pinch of cayenne pepper. Cover and cook for 30 minutes over a low heat.

4. Dice the pineapple slices and add them to the casserole. Adjust the seasoning and cook for about 45 minutes longer. Serve very hot.

Poule au pot
Boiled Chicken with Vegetables

	00:25		01:30 to 02:00	

American	Ingredients	Metric/Imperial
2 lb	Veal bones without marrow	1 kg / 2 lb
1 (4 lb)	Chicken, with giblets	1 (2 kg / 4 lb)
2	Onions	2
2	Cloves	2
2	Turnips	2
6	Carrots	6
4	Small leeks	4
2	Heads of celery	2
1	Bouquet garni	1
	Salt and pepper	

1. Preheat the oven to 475°F / 240°C / Gas Mark 9.
2. Put the veal bones in a large cooking pot. Add the chicken and giblets, cover with plenty of cold water and bring to a boil, skimming off any scum that rises to the surface.
3. Meanwhile, peel the onions and put them in a roasting pan. Bake for about 7 minutes or until they brown. Stud each onion with a clove and add them to the cooking pot.
4. Peel the turnips and carrots. Remove the roots and green tips from the leeks and split them into quarters. Wash them thoroughly under the cold tap. Remove the stringy part of the celery sticks. Put all these vegetables whole into the cooking pot with the chicken. Add the bouquet garni and season to taste with salt and pepper. Bring back to a boil and simmer gently for about 1½ hours.
5. Serve the chicken surrounded by vegetables and accompanied by condiments — coarse salt, mustard, dill pickles [gherkins] and the cooking juices.

Poulet cocotte grand-mère
Grandmother's Chicken

	00:25		01:45	

American	Ingredients	Metric/Imperial
1 (4 lb)	Chicken	1 (1.8 kg / 4 lb)
2	Garlic cloves	2
3 tbsp	Butter	40 g / 1½ oz
	Salt and pepper	
½ lb	Bacon	250 g / 8 oz
10 oz	Tiny onions	300 g / 10 oz
6	Carrots	6
1 lb	Potatoes	500 g / 1 lb
1	Bouquet garni	1
½ cup	Water	125 ml / 4 fl oz

1. Truss the chicken.
2. Peel and crush the garlic. Mix it with 1 tablespoon

[15 g / ½ oz] of butter, a good pinch of salt and some pepper. Put this mixture inside the chicken.

3. Melt the rest of the butter in a flameproof casserole, add the chicken and brown on all sides for at least 20 minutes.

4. Meanwhile, cut the bacon into small strips. Put them in a saucepan of water, bring to a boil and blanch for 5 minutes. Drain. Brown the bacon in a frying pan until it is crisp. Remove from the pan and drain on paper towels.

5. Preheat the oven to 400°F / 200°C / Gas Mark 6.

6. Peel and dice the onions, carrots and potatoes. Add to the frying pan and brown in the bacon fat. Drain the vegetables and add to the chicken in the casserole. Also add the strips of bacon and the bouquet garni. Season to taste with salt and pepper and pour in the water.

7. Put the casserole in the oven and cook for 1 hour and 20 minutes. Turn the chicken over twice while it is cooking and stir the vegetables.

8. Carve the chicken into portions and set it on a serving platter surrounded by vegetables. Serve the sauce separately.

Poulet à l'estragon

Chicken with Tarragon

00:15   00:55

American	Ingredients	Metric/Imperial
1 (4 lb)	Chicken	1 (1.8 kg / 4 lb)
3 tbsp	Oil	3 tbsp
¼ cup	Butter	50 g / 2 oz
6	Shallots	6
1	Carrot	1
2 tbsp	Brandy	2 tbsp
1 cup	White wine	250 ml / 8 fl oz
	Salt and pepper	
4	Fresh tarragon sprigs	4
1 cup	Crème fraîche (see page 122)	250 ml / 8 fl oz
1	Egg yolk	1
1 tsp	Flour	1 tsp
1	Fresh chervil sprig	1

1. Cut the chicken into pieces.

2. Heat the oil and 3 tablespoons [40 g / 1½ oz] butter in a flameproof casserole. Add the pieces of chicken and cook over a low heat for about 20 minutes, until lightly browned. Turn frequently and do not allow the butter to burn.

3. Meanwhile, peel and thinly slice the shallots and carrot.

4. Remove the chicken from the casserole and keep hot.

5. Add the remaining butter to the casserole, then put in the shallots and carrot. Cook for 5 minutes, then put in the chicken. Sprinkle with the brandy and set alight.

6. When the flames have died out, add the white wine and a little water so that the liquid covers the pieces of chicken. Season to taste with salt and pepper and add 2 of the tarragon sprigs. Cover the casserole, bring to a boil and simmer over a low heat for 30 minutes.

7. Remove the pieces of chicken from the casserole and arrange them on a serving platter. Keep hot.

8. Beat the crème fraîche in a mixing bowl with the egg yolk and flour, pour this into the cooking juices and heat, stirring well. When the sauce has thickened, pour it over the chicken through a strainer.

9. Finely chop the rest of the tarragon and the chervil and sprinkle over the chicken.

Poulet Fontainebleau

Chicken Fontainebleau

00:20   01:15 to 01:30

American	Ingredients	Metric/Imperial
½ cup	Butter	125 g / 4 oz
1 (4 lb)	Chicken, trussed	1 (1.8 kg / 4 lb)
4	Onions	4
¼ cup	Brandy	4 tbsp
	Salt and pepper	
2 lb	Fresh garden peas	1 kg / 2 lb
2	Sugar cubes	2
½ lb	Button mushrooms	250 g / 8 oz
1 cup	Crème fraîche (see page 122)	250 ml / 8 fl oz
	Lemon juice	

1. Heat 2 tablespoons [25 g / 1 oz] of the butter in a flameproof casserole, add the chicken and brown it gently on all sides for about 10 minutes. Remove the chicken from the casserole and discard the butter.

2. Peel and chop the onions. Heat another 2 tablespoons [25 g / 1 oz] butter in the casserole and add the chicken and the onions. Add the brandy, heat and set alight. After the flames have died out, season with salt and pepper and cover the casserole. Cook over a low heat for about 1¼ hours.

3. Meanwhile, shell the peas. Cook them in boiling salted water with the sugar cubes for 10-15 minutes, or until just tender. Drain well and return to the pan. Add 2 tablespoons [25 g / 1 oz] butter and keep hot.

4. Thinly slice the mushrooms. Melt the remaining butter in a frying pan, add the mushrooms and cook, stirring occasionally, until all the liquid has evaporated. Season to taste with salt and pepper and add 1 tablespoon of crème fraîche. Keep the mushrooms hot.

5. Carve the chicken into portions, reserving the carving juices. Arrange the pieces of chicken on a platter and surround with the peas and mushrooms.

6. Skim the fat from the cooking liquid in the casserole. Add the carving juices to it, then beat in the rest of the crème and a few drops of lemon juice. Adjust the seasoning. Pour some sauce over the chicken and serve the rest in a sauceboat.

Chicken fontainebleau

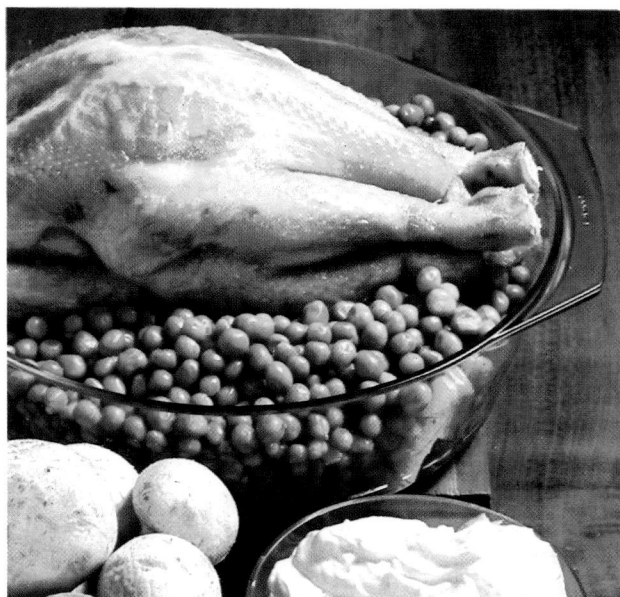

Poulet à la diable

Deviled Chicken

	00:10		00:45

American	Ingredients	Metric/Imperial
3 (1¼ lb)	Chickens	3 (625 g / 1¼ lb)
¼ cup	Olive oil	4 tbsp
	Salt and pepper	
⅔ cup	Dried white bread crumbs	50 g / 2 oz
2	Shallots	2
⅔ cup	Dry white wine	150 ml / ¼ pint
1¼ cups	Tomato ketchup	300 ml / ½ pint
1 tsp	Worcestershire sauce	1 tsp
	Tabasco sauce	

1. Preheat the oven to 375°F / 190°C / Gas Mark 5.
2. Cut the chickens into halves, flatten each half and coat with 3 tablespoons of olive oil. Season with salt and pepper and coat the skin with the bread crumbs, pressing to ensure that the crumbs adhere properly.
3. Put the chicken halves on a rack in a roasting pan. Bake, without basting, for 40 minutes. Turn off the oven and leave the chicken inside for 5 minutes longer.
4. Meanwhile, peel and finely chop the shallots. Heat the remaining olive oil in a saucepan, add the shallots and cook over a medium heat until golden. Add the white wine and boil to reduce by half. Add the ketchup, worcestershire sauce, 3 drops of tabasco and salt to taste. Bring to a boil. Pour the hot sauce into a sauceboat.
5. Remove the chicken from the oven and serve immediately with the hot deviled sauce.

Fricassée de poulet au vin rouge

Fricassee of Chicken with Red Wine

	00:30		01:00

American	Ingredients	Metric/Imperial
12	Tiny onions	12
7 tbsp	Butter	90 g / 3½ oz
1 tbsp	Sugar	1 tbsp
5 tbsp	Water	5 tbsp
½ lb	Button mushrooms	250 g / 8 oz
½	Lemon	½
	Salt and pepper	
1 (3 lb)	Chicken	1 (1.5 kg / 3 lb)
2 tbsp	Oil	2 tbsp
3	Shallots	3
2 cups	Red wine	500 ml / ¾ pint
2 tbsp	Brandy	2 tbsp
1	Bouquet garni	1
1 tbsp	Chopped fresh tarragon	1 tbsp
2 tbsp	Crème fraîche (see page 122)	2 tbsp

1. Peel and thinly slice the onions. Melt ¼ cup [50 g / 2 oz] butter in a small saucepan, add the onions and cook over a low heat until lightly browned. Sprinkle them with the sugar and add the water. Cover the saucepan and cook for 10 minutes.

2. Meanwhile, thinly slice the mushrooms. Heat 2 tablespoons [25 g / 1 oz] of butter in a frying pan, add the mushrooms and the juice of the ½ lemon and season with salt and pepper. Cook for 10 minutes.
3. Cut the chicken into 8 pieces and season with salt and pepper. Heat the oil and the rest of the butter in a flameproof casserole, add the pieces of chicken and cook for about 10 minutes or until browned on all sides.
4. Peel and chop the shallots. Add them to the chicken in the casserole. Pour in the red wine and the brandy. Add the bouquet garni and the cooking liquid from the mushrooms. Cover and cook for 30 minutes over a low heat.
5. Remove the chicken and arrange on a warmed platter. Add the tarragon, mushrooms and drained onions to the sauce. Discard the bouquet garni. Whisk in the creme fraîche.
6. Pour the sauce over the chicken and serve immediately.

Poulet à l'indienne

Indian Style Chicken

	00:20 plus marinating		01:30

American	Ingredients	Metric/Imperial
1¼ cups	Plain yogurt	300 ml / ½ pint
3 tbsp	Grated fresh ginger root or	40 g / 1½ oz
2 tbsp	Ground ginger	2 tbsp
2 tsp	Grated lemon rind	2 tsp
6	Fresh mint leaves or	6
1 tsp	Crushed dried mint	1 tsp
1 tbsp	Caraway seeds	1 tbsp
6	Cloves	6
	Ground cinnamon	
1 tbsp	Coriander seeds	1 tbsp
3	Very small hot peppers [chillies]	3
4	Garlic cloves	4
1 (3 lb)	Chicken	1 (1.5 kg / 3 lb)
2	Large onions	2
⅔ cup	Olive oil	150 ml / ¼ pint
	Saffron powder	
3 cups	Boiling water	750 ml / 1¼ pints
	Salt	
2 cups	Rice	400 g / 14 oz

1. Put the yogurt in a mixing bowl and add the fresh or ground ginger, grated lemon rind, fresh or dried mint, caraway seeds, cloves, a pinch of ground cinnamon, the coriander seeds, hot peppers and peeled and crushed garlic. Mix well.
2. Cut the chicken into pieces and add to the bowl. Turn to coat with the yogurt mixture, then leave to marinate for about 30 minutes.
3. Meanwhile, peel and finely chop the onions. Heat the olive oil in a flameproof casserole, add the onions and cook over a low heat, stirring frequently until they are translucent. Do not allow them to brown.
4. Add the chicken and the yogurt mixture. Bring to a boil slowly and simmer, covered, for 20-25 minutes.
5. Dissolve a pinch of saffron powder in the boiling water. Add salt to taste.
6. Add the rice to the casserole with the saffron water and bring to a boil over a brisk heat, stirring well. Reduce the heat, cover again and simmer over a low heat for 45 minutes or until the rice is tender and all the liquid absorbed. Serve hot.

Poulet Marengo

Chicken Marengo

▬▽ 00:25 01:00 🍲

American	Ingredients	Metric/Imperial
24	Green olives	24
1 (3 lb)	Chicken	1 (1.5 kg / 3 lb)
¼ cup	Olive oil	4 tbsp
	Salt and pepper	
3	Ripe tomatoes	3
1	Garlic clove	1
½ lb	Button mushrooms	250 g / 8 oz
1 cup	Dry white wine	250 ml / 8 fl oz
1 tbsp	Tomato paste [purée]	1 tbsp
1½ tsp	Butter	1½ tsp
1½ tsp	Flour	1½ tsp
1 tbsp	Chopped fresh parsley	1 tbsp

1. Remove the pits [stones] from the olives. Soak the olives for 1 hour in lukewarm water to remove excess salt.
2. Meanwhile, cut the chicken into pieces. Heat the oil in a frying pan, add the chicken and season with salt and pepper. Cook over a low heat for 40 minutes. Remove the chicken from the pan and keep hot. Pour the fat from the frying pan.
3. Peel the onions (first plunging them in boiling water for 10 seconds) and dice them finely. Peel and crush the garlic. Put the tomatoes and garlic in the frying pan and cook gently, stirring well.
4. Thinly slice the mushrooms or leave them whole if they are small. Add them to the frying pan with the wine and tomato paste. Season to taste with salt and pepper and simmer until the sauce has a creamy consistency.
5. If the sauce is too thin, add the butter blended with the flour (beurre manié) to thicken.
6. Return the chicken to the pan. Add the drained olives. Cover and cook, without boiling, for 10 minutes. Serve sprinkled with chopped parsley.

Poulet rôti

Roast Chicken

▬▽ 00:10 01:00 🍲

American	Ingredients	Metric/Imperial
1 (4 lb)	Chicken, with liver	1 (1.8 kg / 4 lb)
	Salt and pepper	
3	Bacon slices	3
7 tbsp	Butter, at room temperature	90 g / 3½ oz
⅔ cup	Water	150 ml / ¼ pint

1. Preheat the oven to 375°F / 190°C / Gas Mark 5.
2. Season the inside of the chicken with salt and pepper and put in the liver, the slices of bacon and 2 tablespoons [25 g / 1 oz] butter. Truss the chicken very securely. The bird will be juicier if the openings for evaporation are small.
3. Generously coat the skin of the chicken with ¼ cup [50 g / 2 oz] butter. Put the chicken on a rack in a roasting pan and roast for about 1 hour. While the bird is roasting, turn it twice so that it browns on all sides.
4. Drain the juices from the chicken into the pan. Carve it into portions and arrange on a serving platter and keep hot.

5. Pour the water into the roasting pan. Boil on top of the stove, scraping the bottom of the pan to dissolve the solids. Beat in the remaining butter. Serve the sauce in a sauceboat with the chicken.

Poulet Gaston-Gérard

Chicken Gaston-Gérard

▬▽ 00:05 01:30 🍲

American	Ingredients	Metric/Imperial
1 (3 lb)	Chicken	1 (1.5 kg / 3 lb)
1 tbsp	Oil	1 tbsp
1 tbsp	Butter	15 g / ½ oz
	Salt and pepper	
	Paprika	
2 cups	Grated gruyère cheese	250 g / 8 oz
1¼ cups	Dry white wine	300 ml / ½ pint
½ tbsp	Dijon mustard	½ tbsp
1¾ cups	Thick crème fraîche (see page 122)	400 ml / 14 fl oz
3 tbsp	Dried bread crumbs	3 tbsp

1. Cut the chicken into pieces.
2. Heat the oil and the butter in a flameproof casserole, add the pieces of chicken and brown on all sides. Season with salt, pepper and a pinch of paprika. Cover and cook gently for about 40 minutes.
3. Preheat the oven to 450°F / 230°C / Gas Mark 8.
4. Remove the chicken pieces from the casserole and arrange them in a baking dish. Set aside. Put three-quarters of the gruyère cheese in the casserole. Let the cheese melt, then add the white wine, mustard and crème fraîche. Heat until the sauce boils, stirring frequently.
5. Pour the cheese sauce over the chicken. Sprinkle with the bread crumbs and the rest of the gruyère cheese. Bake for about 10 minutes or until the topping is golden brown, and serve immediately.

Chicken marengo

Chicken with whiskey sauce

Poulet au whisky

Chicken with Whiskey Sauce

	00:15		00:50

American	Ingredients	Metric/Imperial
1 (4 lb)	Chicken	1 (1.8 kg / 4 lb)
6 tbsp	Butter	75 g / 3 oz
⅔ cup	Whiskey	150 ml / ¼ pint
5 oz	Button mushrooms	150 g / 5 oz
	Lemon juice	
1	Shallot	1
½ cup	Crème fraîche (see page 122)	125 ml / 4 fl oz
	Salt and pepper	
1 tsp	Cornstarch [cornflour]	1 tsp

1. Cut the chicken into quarters. Heat 2 tablespoons [25 g / 1 oz] butter in a flameproof casserole, add the chicken pieces and cook over a medium heat for about 10 minutes or until golden on all sides.
2. Pour the whiskey over the chicken. Remove from the heat, cover and leave to steep for 10 minutes.
3. Meanwhile, quarter the mushrooms and sprinkle with a few drops of lemon juice. Peel and chop the shallot. Melt the rest of the butter in a frying pan, add the mushrooms and cook, stirring occasionally, until all the liquid has evaporated. Add the chopped shallot and cook for a few minutes longer.
4. Put the mushrooms and shallot in the casserole with the chicken, add half the crème fraîche and season with salt and pepper. Cover and cook over a medium heat for about 30 minutes or until the chicken pieces are tender.
5. Arrange the pieces of chicken on a serving platter and keep hot. Return the casserole to the heat and bring back to a boil.

Mix together the remaining crème fraîche and cornstarch and add to the sauce, whisking well. Cook, stirring, until thickened. Add a few drops of lemon juice. Adjust the seasoning and pour the sauce over the pieces of chicken.

Aspic de volaille

Chicken in Aspic

	01:00 plus chilling		01:00

American	Ingredients	Metric/Imperial
3 quarts	Water	3 l / 5 pints
3	Carrots	3
3	Leeks	3
3	Onions	3
2	Cloves	2
2	Celery stalks	2
	Salt and pepper	
1	Bouquet garni	1
1 (3 lb)	Chicken	1 (1.5 kg / 3 lb)
2 envelopes	Unflavored gelatin	2 sachets
1 (½ lb)	Slice of cooked ham	1 (250 g / 8 oz)
1	Truffle (optional)	1
½ lb	Pâté de foie gras	250 g / 8 oz

1. Bring the water to a boil in a large pan. Meanwhile, peel the carrots. Cut the leeks into quarters. Peel the onions and stud one with 2 cloves. Add the carrots, leeks, onions and celery to the boiling water. Season with salt and pepper, add the bouquet garni and simmer gently for 30 minutes.
2. Add the chicken and cook for 1 hour.
3. Remove the chicken and set aside. Strain the cooking liquid through a strainer into a bowl, then through a fine strainer into a saucepan. Bring to a boil and simmmer until the liquid is reduced to 1 quart [1 l / 1¾ pints].
4. Dissolve the gelatin following the instructions on the package. Stir into the reduced cooking liquid and allow to cool until syrupy.
5. Pour a ½ in / 1 cm layer of the cooking liquid onto the bottom of an oiled 1½ quart [1.5 l / 2½ pint] charlotte mold. Chill until set.
6. Meanwhile, cut a ½ in / 1 cm wide strip from the slice of ham and dice it. Remove the chicken meat from the carcass, discarding all skin, and thinly slice the meat. Slice the truffle.
7. Arrange the truffle slices, diced ham and a few slices of chicken on the set aspic at the bottom of the mold. Cover with another layer of still liquid aspic and leave to set in the refrigerator.
8. Cut the rest of the ham into thin strips. Fold into the pâté. Remove the mold from the refrigerator and add a layer of the ham-pâté mixture. Cover with slices of chicken, then alternate the chicken and ham-pâté mixture until all the ingredients are used up.
9. Pour most of the remaining cold, but still liquid, aspic into the mold (warm the aspic again before pouring, if necessary), making sure that the aspic fills all the gaps between the mold and the filling.
10. Cover with a board, place a weight on top and chill for 6 hours.
11. To remove the chicken in aspic from the mold, carefully slide the blade of a knife between the aspic and the edge of the mold or plunge the mold into hot water for a few moments only. Put an inverted serving dish on top of the mold and turn them both over. Cut the rest of the aspic into small dice and arrange it around the chicken in aspic. Serve well chilled.

Poulet printanier

Chicken with Spring Vegetables

00:25   01:00

American	Ingredients	Metric/Imperial
¼ cup	Butter	50 g / 2 oz
1 (3 lb)	Chicken, trussed	1 (1.5 kg / 3 lb)
	Salt and pepper	
2 lb	Carrots	1 kg / 2 lb
1	Small lettuce heart	1
6	Small onions	6
3 lb	Garden peas	1.5 kg / 3 lb
2	Sugar cubes	2
1	Bouquet garni	1

1. Heat 1 tablespoon [15 g / ½ oz] butter in a flameproof casserole. Season the chicken inside and out with salt and pepper and add to the casserole. Brown it on all sides for about 10 minutes.

2. Peel and dice the carrots (or leave them whole if they are small). Rinse the lettuce heart and cut it in half. Peel the onions. Shell the peas. Add all these vegetables to the casserole with the sugar cubes and bouquet garni. Season to taste with salt and pepper. Add just enough cold water to cover the vegetables. Cover the casserole and bring to a boil, then reduce the heat and simmer for 1 hour. Do not stir during this time. At the end of the cooking time, take out and discard the bouquet garni.

3. To serve, remove the chicken from the casserole and carve it into portions. Remove the vegetables with a slotted spoon and arrange them on a serving platter with the pieces of chicken. Keep hot.

4. Reduce the cooking juices by half over a brisk heat. Add the rest of the butter a little at a time, beating with a whisk. Pour the hot sauce over the chicken.

Chicken with spring vegetables

Croquettes de volaille
Chicken Croquettes

	00:20 per batch	00:05

American	Ingredients	Metric/Imperial
1 (2 lb)	Cooked chicken	1 (1 kg / 2 lb)
5 oz	Button mushrooms	150 g / 5 oz
¼ cup	Butter	50 g / 2 oz
2 tbsp	Flour + flour for coating	25 g / 1 oz
1½ cups	Milk	350 ml / 12 fl oz
	Salt and pepper	
2	Egg yolks	2
	Oil for deep frying	
½ cup	Dried white bread crumbs	40 g / 1½ oz
1	Egg	1
2 tbsp	Olive oil	2 tbsp

1. Remove the chicken meat from the carcass, discarding all skin. Finely chop the chicken and the mushrooms.
2. Melt the butter in a heavy saucepan, add the flour and stir well, then gradually add the milk. Season to taste with salt and pepper. Add the chicken and mushrooms and cook until the mixture is very thick.
3. Remove from the heat. Add the egg yolks, mix well and leave to cool. When the mixture is cold, coat your hands with flour and shape the mixture into balls about 2 in / 5 cm in diameter. Flatten the balls into patties, if liked.
4. Heat the oil for deep frying to 340°F / 175°C.
5. Put the bread crumbs in a deep plate. Beat the whole egg with the olive oil in a shallow dish. Dip the croquettes first in the egg mixture, then in the bread crumbs to coat on all sides.
6. Plunge the croquettes, 4 or 5 at a time, into the hot oil. Cook until they are a dark golden color (about 5 minutes), then remove them and drain on paper towels. Serve hot.

Poulet aux fruits de mer
Chicken with Seafood

	01:00	01:00

American	Ingredients	Metric/Imperial
1 (3 lb)	Chicken	1 (1.5 kg / 3 lb)
3 tbsp	Butter	40 g / 1½ oz
4	Scallops	4
2	Shallots	2
⅔ cup	Dry white wine	150 ml / ¼ pint
1	Bouquet garni	1
	Salt and pepper	
4 - 5	Raw jumbo shrimp [Dublin Bay prawns]	4 - 5
1 quart	Clams or cockles	1 l / 2 pints
1 cup	Crème fraîche (see page 122)	250 ml / 8 fl oz
1 tbsp	Cornstarch [cornflour]	1 tbsp
2	Egg yolks	2
1 tsp	Lemon juice	1 tsp

1. Cut the chicken into pieces. Heat 2 tablespoons [25 g / 1 oz] of the butter in a flameproof casserole, add the chicken and cook gently for 10 minutes without letting it brown. Remove and keep hot.

2. Cut the scallops in half. Put them in the casserole and cook gently for 2-3 minutes, without allowing them to brown. Remove and keep hot.
3. Peel and thinly slice the shallots. Heat the rest of the butter in the casserole, add the shallots and cook until they are translucent.
4. Return the pieces of chicken to the casserole. Add the white wine and bouquet garni. Season to taste with salt and pepper and simmer for 1¼ hours over a very low heat.
5. Meanwhile, cook the shrimp in boiling salted water for 5 minutes, then drain. Peel and devein them. If they are large, halve them lengthwise.
6. Clean the clams or cockles and put them in a cooking pot over a brisk heat. Cook until they open and release their liquor. Remove them from the cooking pot with a slotted spoon and take them out of their shells (discarding any that have not opened). Set the clams and liquor aside.
7. Discard the bouquet garni from the casserole. Place the chicken on a platter and keep hot. Skim any fat from the sauce, then add the crème fraîche and 2 tablespoons of the clam liquor. Dissolve the cornstarch in 2 tablespoons of clam liquor and add to the sauce. Boil for a few minutes, stirring constantly. Taste and adjust the seasoning if necessary.
8. Add the shrimp, scallops and clams. Cook gently to heat through.
9. Quickly mix the egg yolks with the lemon juice and a few tablespoons of hot sauce. Stir the mixture into the remaining sauce away from the heat and pour the sauce over the chicken. Serve hot.

Gratin de volaille
Chicken Gratin

	00:30	00:40

American	Ingredients	Metric/Imperial
½ lb	Cooked chicken meat	250 g / 8 oz
2	Small onions	2
½ lb	Button mushrooms	250 g / 8 oz
	Lemon juice	
6 tbsp	Butter	75 g / 3 oz
⅔ cup	Crème fraîche (see page 122)	150 ml / ¼ pint
	Grated nutmeg	
	Salt and pepper	
¾ lb	Noodles	350 g / 12 oz
½ cup	Grated gruyère cheese	50 g / 2 oz

1. Preheat the oven to 400°F / 200°C / Gas Mark 6.
2. Cut the chicken into thin strips. Peel and chop the onions. Thinly slice the mushrooms and sprinkle them with the lemon juice.
3. Heat 2 tablespoons [25 g / 1 oz] butter in a saucepan, add the onions and mushrooms and cook, stirring occasionally, until all the liquid has evaporated. Add the chicken, crème fraîche and a pinch of nutmeg. Season to taste with salt and pepper and simmer for 5 minutes.
4. Meanwhile, cook the noodles in boiling salted water until just tender (5-10 minutes). Drain.
5. Put aside about 5 tablespoons of noodles and add the rest to the chicken and vegetable mixture, stirring well. Pour this mixture into a gratin dish. Cover with the remaining noodles, sprinkle with the grated gruyère cheese and dot with the rest of the butter, cut into small pieces.
6. Bake for 20 minutes or until the top is golden brown.

Game

Outside the hunting season (autumn and winter) you will only find farm-reared produce at the butcher's or poulterer's or at the supermarket. So it is very important to know what to look for when you are choosing game, so that you can be sure the meat will be tender.

- Young birds have pliable beaks, the feet are smooth, with elastic muscles, and the spurs short. In older birds the feet are rough and scaly. The feathers should be supple and soft to the touch.
- Venison (deer, moose, elk and so on) and small ground game (wild rabbit and hare) have soft, thin ears when the animal is young. If they are hard and stiff the animal is old. Another sign of freshness is the smell; be wary if the smell seems too strong.

When to cook
Should game be hung? It can be kept for a time to gain flavor and tenderize the flesh if it is too tough, but this is not a general rule.

Game bought at the butcher's or poulterer's has already been sufficiently hung; therefore, do not keep it too long.

If a hunter gives you game, it is worth knowing that small-game birds such as capercaillie, plover and teal are kept for three or four days unplucked (always in a cool place) and a woodcock is kept for no longer than a week.

Pheasant should be allowed to get high by hanging it by the feet, unplucked and undrawn, for at least three days in a cool, dry place or in the refrigerator wrapped in foil.

Wild duck and quail, however, should be cooked immediately, otherwise the flesh will have a bitter, acid taste.

Marinating
A marinade is a mixture of oil, vinegar and spices used for tenderizing and enhancing the flavor of large game. Marinating preserves the flesh for a few days and the marinade can be used for preparing the sauce in which the meat is subsequently cooked. Do not marinate young wild boar, but if you need to preserve it for 2 or 3 days before cooking, coat the meat with oil and put it in the refrigerator. Do the same with young deer. Marinating is suitable for older wild boar, which has firmer, tougher flesh.

Traditional accompaniments for game

Bécasses rôties

Roast Woodcock

	00:25	00:20 to 00:25	

American	Ingredients	Metric/Imperial
6	Woodcock	6
	Salt and pepper	
6	Bacon slices	6
¼ lb	Pâté de foie gras	125 g / 4 oz
	Cayenne pepper	
3 tbsp	Cognac or armagnac	3 tbsp
6	Slices of bread, ½ in / 1 cm thick	6
¼ cup	Butter, melted	50 g / 2 oz

1. Preheat the oven to 475°F / 240°C / Gas Mark 9.

2. Season the woodcock with salt and pepper. Cover them with bacon and tie it on with kitchen string.

3. Put the woodcock in a roasting pan and roast for 10-15 minutes. Remove the bacon and continue roasting for 5-10 minutes to brown the birds.

4. Remove the entrails from the woodcock and keep the birds hot. Pound the entrails with the pâté de foie gras, a pinch of cayenne pepper, the cognac or armagnac, and pepper to taste. Remove the crusts from the slices of bread and spread them with this mixture.

5. Brush a small baking sheet with the melted butter and arrange the bread on top in one layer. Bake for about 3 minutes.

6. Arrange the pâté canapés on a serving platter and put a woodcock on top of each. Serve immediately.

Côtes de chevreuil

Venison Chops with Game Sauce

	00:10	00:08	

American	Ingredients	Metric/Imperial
2 tbsp	Red currant jelly	2 tbsp
2 tbsp	Crème fraîche (see page 122)	2 tbsp
1 cup	Game sauce (see page 131)	250 ml / 8 fl oz
6	Slices of bread	6
3 tbsp	Butter	40 g / 1½ oz
3 tbsp	Olive oil	3 tbsp
6	Venison chops	6
	Salt and pepper	

1. Add the red currant jelly and crème fraîche to the game sauce and stir to mix. Keep hot in a bowl or pan placed in a saucepan containing hot water.

2. Cut the crusts from the bread. Heat 1 tablespoon [15 g / ½ oz] butter and oil in a frying pan and fry the bread slices until golden brown on both sides. Remove from the pan and keep hot.

3. Heat the remaining butter and oil in the frying pan. Add the venison chops and cook for about 4 minutes on each side, or until well browned and cooked to your taste. Season with salt and pepper.

4. Put the chops on the fried bread and serve immediately with the sauce.

Friands à la perdrix

Partridge Pies

	00:40		00:12 to 00:15

American	Ingredients	Metric/Imperial
1	Cooked partridge	1
¼ lb	Cooked, cold meat (pork, veal, poultry)	125 g / 4 oz
	Salt and pepper	
1 lb	Puff pastry (see page 458)	500 g / 1 lb
1	Egg, separated	1

1. Preheat the oven to 450°F / 230°C / Gas Mark 8.
2. Remove the meat from the partridge carcass, discarding all skin. Grind [mince] it finely or use a food processor. Grind the cold meat and mix the two meats together. Season with salt and pepper.
3. Roll out the puff pastry to a thickness of ⅛ in / 3 mm. Using a cutter or saucer with a diameter of about 3 in / 7.5 cm, cut the pastry into 24 rounds. Put 1 tablespoon of meat on 12 of the rounds, leaving ½ in / 1 cm edge all around.
4. Using a pastry brush dipped in egg white, moisten the edge of each filled round of dough. Cover them with the 12 remaining rounds and pinch the edges together to stick them firmly.
5. Brush the surfaces of the pies with beaten egg yolk. Make a pattern on the dough with the point of a knife and put the pies on a lightly oiled baking sheet.
6. Bake for 12-15 minutes, then turn off the oven and leave the pies inside with the door ajar for 5 minutes. Serve hot.

Faisans rôtis en cocotte

Casseroled Pheasant

	00:25		00:35

American	Ingredients	Metric/Imperial
2	Young pheasants, with the livers	2
4	Chicken livers	4
½ cup	Butter	125 g / 4 oz
2	Fresh thyme sprigs	2
3	Fresh sage leaves	3
	Salt and pepper	
5 tbsp	Brandy	5 tbsp
6	Slices of bread, ½ in / 1 cm thick	6

1. Chop the pheasant livers finely with the chicken livers. Add ¼ cup [50 g / 2 oz] of the butter, the leaves of one of the thyme sprigs and the sage leaves and season to taste with salt and pepper. Work the mixture together thoroughly. Stuff the pheasants with it. Truss them with kitchen string.
2. Heat 1 tablespoon [15 g / ½ oz] of butter in a flameproof casserole, add the pheasants and brown them on all sides over a moderate heat. Pour over the brandy, cover the casserole and remove from the heat. Leave to steep for 10 minutes.
3. Return the casserole to a low heat and cook, covered, for 35 minutes, turning the pheasants halfway through the cooking time.
4. Meanwhile, melt the remaining butter in a frying pan over a low heat and fry the slices of bread until golden brown on both sides. Drain and keep them hot.

5. Carve the pheasants into portions. Add their juices to the cooking liquid, and spread the slices of fried bread with the stuffing. Arrange the pieces of pheasant on the slices of fried bread and garnish with the rest of the fresh thyme. Serve immediately with the cooking liquid in a sauceboat.

Casseroled pheasant

Filet de chevreuil chasseur

Venison Steaks Braised in Red Wine

	00:45 plus marinating		01:00

American	Ingredients	Metric/Imperial
2 lb	Venison steaks	1 kg / 2 lb
3	Onions	3
2	Shallots	2
1	Garlic clove	1
4	Cloves	4
2	Bay leaves	2
	Salt and pepper	
2½ cups	Wine vinegar	600 ml / 1 pint
¼ cup	Oil	4 tbsp
3 oz	Bacon	75 g / 3 oz
1 cup	Red wine	250 ml / 8 fl oz
1 cup	Vegetable or beef stock	250 ml / 8 fl oz

1. If the meat is likely to be a little tough, marinate it before cooking. Put it in a dish or bowl in which it fits comfortably. Peel and slice the onions, shallots and garlic. Scatter these vegetables over the meat with the cloves, bay leaves and salt and pepper to taste. Pour the vinegar and oil over the top. Leave to marinate for 3-4 days, turning the meat over every day.
2. On the day of cooking, cut the bacon into strips. Cook them in a flameproof casserole until browned and rendered of fat.
3. Drain the venison, reserving the marinade, and add to the casserole. Brown it on all sides over a medium heat. Add the red wine, stock and 1 cup [250 ml / 8 fl oz] of the strained marinade.
4. Cover the casserole and simmer over a very low heat for 1 hour. Serve hot.

Perdreaux à la broche
Spit-Roasted Partridge

	01:00	00:30

American	Ingredients	Metric/Imperial
3	Partridges, with their livers	3
5 tbsp	Brandy	5 tbsp
	Salt and pepper	
9	Large grape or vine leaves	9
3	Bacon slices	3
3 tbsp	Goose fat or lard	3 tbsp
6	Chicken livers	6
6	Slices of bread, ½ in / 1 cm thick	6
6 tbsp	Butter	75 g / 3 oz

1. Brush the inside of each partridge with a few drops of brandy and season with salt and pepper. Wrap each bird in 3 grape leaves and cover with a piece of bacon. Tie on with kitchen string. Put the partridges on a rotisserie spit and cook them above a dripping pan for about 18 minutes, basting them frequently with the juices that drip from them.
2. Meanwhile, heat the goose fat or lard in a frying pan, add the partridge livers and chicken livers and cook over a brisk heat until browned all over. Season with salt and pepper. Purée the livers in a blender or food processor. Add the rest of the brandy and mix well.
3. Remove the crusts from the slices of bread. Heat the butter in a large frying pan and fry the bread until golden brown on both sides. Spread these canapés with the liver mixture.
4. Remove the bacon and grape leaves from the partridges and cook the birds for a few more minutes to brown. Put the canapés in the oven and heat them until the liver mixture begins to bubble.
5. Cut each partridge in half. Sprinkle the canapés with the juices, arrange them on the serving dish and put the halved partridges on top. Serve immediately.

Faisan au chou
Pheasant with Cabbage

	00:25	01:15

American	Ingredients	Metric/Imperial
1	Large pheasant	1
	Salt and pepper	
1	Large head of green cabbage	1
½ lb	Bacon	250 g / 8 oz
1	Garlic clove	1
2 tbsp	Butter	25 g / 1 oz
1	Bouquet garni	1
1	Clove	1

1. Season the inside and outside of the pheasant with salt and pepper.
2. Wash the cabbage, remove the damaged outer leaves and core and cut the rest into strips. Cook the cabbage in boiling salted water for 10 minutes, then drain it thoroughly.
3. Cut the bacon into small strips. Peel and crush the garlic. Heat the butter in a flameproof casserole, add the pheasant

and half the bacon and cook until the pheasant is well browned on all sides (about 10 minutes). Reduce the heat, cover and cook for a further 35 minutes.
4. Cook the rest of the bacon strips in another flameproof casserole until browned and rendered of fat. Add the cabbage, bouquet garni, garlic and clove, and season to taste. Cover and cook over a low heat for 30 minutes, stirring frequently.
5. Spoon the cabbage and bacon mixture onto a warmed serving dish and put the pheasant, carved into portions, on top. Serve the cooking juices separately in a sauceboat.

Roast haunch of venison

Gigue de chevreuil
Roast Haunch of Venison

	00:10 plus marinating	01:15 to 01:30 Serves 8–10

American	Ingredients	Metric/Imperial
½	Bay leaf	½
2 tbsp	Olive oil	2 tbsp
1 tsp	Fresh thyme leaves	1 tsp
	Grated nutmeg	
	Salt and pepper	
1 (5 lb)	Haunch of venison	1 (2.5 kg / 5 lb)
6 tbsp	Water	6 tbsp
3	Shallots	3
3	Celery stalks	3
6 tbsp	Butter	75 g / 3 oz
1	Bouquet garni	1
½ lb	Crushed venison bones	250 g / 8 oz
1	Bottle of red wine	1
1 tsp	Potato starch or flour	1 tsp
3 tbsp	Brandy	3 tbsp
2 tbsp	Red currant jelly	2 tbsp

1. Finely crush the bay leaf. Mix the olive oil with the crushed bay leaf, thyme, a pinch of nutmeg, and salt and pepper to taste in a bowl. Add the venison haunch and turn to coat with the oil. Leave to marinate for 2 hours.
2. Preheat the oven to 450°F / 230°C / Gas Mark 8.
3. Put the venison on a rack in a roasting pan and place it in the oven. Roast for 1¼ / 1½ hours. Turn the meat halfway

through the cooking process and add 5 tablespoons of the water to the pan. Do not baste the meat.

4. While the meat is roasting, peel and chop the shallots. Chop the celery. Melt 1 tablespoon [15 g / ½ oz] butter in a saucepan and add the shallots, celery, bouquet garni and crushed venison bones. Pour in the red wine. Cook over a low heat until the wine has reduced by half.

5. Strain this sauce into a clean saucepan, pressing all the solids well with a wooden spoon. Season with a pinch of nutmeg, and salt and pepper to taste. Return to the heat.

6. Dissolve the potato starch in the remaining water and add to the pan. Stir with a whisk over a very low heat until the sauce thickens. Add the brandy and red currant jelly, and continue stirring until the sauce is smooth. Remove from the heat. Add the remaining butter cut into small pieces, beating with a whisk. Pour the sauce into a sauceboat.

7. Serve the venison with the sauce.

Cook's tip: do not overcook the meat; usually venison is eaten underdone.

Sanglier sauce moscovite

Wild Boar with Muscovite Sauce

	00:40 plus marinating		03:15

American	Ingredients	Metric/Imperial
3	Carrots	3
3	Shallots	3
1	Onion	1
1	Garlic clove	1
1¼ cups	Oil	300 ml / ½ pint
2	Fresh thyme sprigs	2
1	Bay leaf	1
3	Cloves	3
2 cups	Vinegar	450 ml / ¾ pint
1½ quarts	White wine	1.5 l / 2½ pints
1 (5 lb)	Haunch of wild boar or peccary	1 (2.5 kg / 5 lb)
	Salt and pepper	
½ lb	Lightly salted bacon	250 g / 8 oz
⅓ cup	Currants	50 g / 2 oz
1½ tsp	Potato starch or flour	1½ tsp
2 tbsp	Water	2 tbsp
2 tbsp	Butter	25 g / 1 oz
⅔ cup	Madeira wine	150 ml / ¼ pint
½ cup	Toasted pine nuts	50 g / 2 oz

1. Peel and thinly slice the carrots, shallots, onion and garlic. Heat 3 tablespoons of oil in a frying pan, add the carrots, shallots, onion and garlic and cook until softened. Add the thyme, bay leaf, cloves, vinegar and wine. Cover the pan and cook gently for 30 minutes. Allow to cool, then add the rest of the oil to this marinade.

2. Run the haunch of wild boar with 1 tablespoon of salt. Put it in bowl and pour over the marinade. Marinate in a cool place for 4-5 days, turning the meat frequently.

3. Preheat the oven to 400°F / 200°C / Gas Mark 6.

4. Drain the haunch, reserving the marinade. Strain the marinade keeping all the flavorings. Cut the bacon into strips.

5. Brown the haunch in a flameproof casserole with the strips of bacon until it is well colored on all sides. Pour in enough

strained marinade to come halfway up the haunch. Place in the oven and braise for 2 hours, turning the meat frequently. Cover with foil halfway through the process.

6. When the haunch is cooked, pour the cooking juices into a saucepan and keep the meat hot. Add the rest of the strained marinade to the saucepan as well as the reserved flavorings and boil to reduce over a brisk heat until only half the liquid remains.

7. Meanwhile, soak the currants in warm water so that they swell. Mix the potato starch with the water. Cut the butter into small pieces. Warm the madeira.

8. When the marinade has reduced sufficiently, strain it into another saucepan, pressing all the flavorings well with a wooden spoon. Add the warm madeira, the drained currants, toasted pine nuts, dissolved potato starch and pepper to taste. Stir over a brisk heat until the sauce thickens, then remove from the heat and add the pieces of butter, beating rapidly. Serve immediately with the boar.

Wild boar with muscovite sauce

Faisans aux raisins

Pheasant with Grapes

	01:00		00:45

American	Ingredients	Metric/Imperial
4	Bacon slices	4
2	Young pheasants	2
4 lb	White grapes	2 kg / 4 lb
5 tbsp	Cognac or armagnac	5 tbsp
6 tbsp	Butter	75 g / 3 oz
	Salt and pepper	

1. Wrap the slices of bacon around the pheasants and truss them.

2. Extract the juice from one-third of the grapes (use a juice extractor, or liquidize briefly or press and strain). Peel the remaining grapes and leave to steep in the cognac.

3. Heat the butter in a large flameproof casserole, add the pheasants and brown on all sides over a medium heat. Sprinkle them with the grape juice and season to taste with salt and pepper. Cook, covered, over a medium heat for 30 minutes.

4. Remove the bacon from the pheasants, then add the peeled grapes to the casserole. Continue cooking for 15 minutes longer.

5. Carve the pheasants into portions and arrange the pieces on a warmed serving dish. Surround them with the grapes and pour the cooking liquid over the top. Serve very hot.

Faisans bohémienne

Bohemian Style Pheasant

	00:30 plus standing time	00:40

American	Ingredients	Metric/Imperial
½ lb	Fresh foie gras	250 g / 8 oz
	Paprika	
½ cup	Butter	125 g / 4 oz
	Salt and pepper	
2	Young pheasants	2
6	Slices of bread ½ in / 1 cm thick	6
¼ cup	Brandy	4 tbsp
½ cup	Crème fraîche (see page 122)	125 ml / 4 fl oz

1. Cut the foie gras into dice and roll it lightly in paprika. Leave for 1 hour to absorb the flavor.
2. Preheat the oven to 425°F / 220°C / Gas Mark 7.
3. Melt 1 teaspoon of butter in a frying pan, add the diced foie gras and brown lightly. Season with salt, then remove from the pan with a slotted spoon and allow to cool. Put aside the frying pan containing the butter.
4. Stuff the pheasants with the foie gras and sew up the openings with kitchen string. Put the pheasants in a roasting pan and roast for 40 minutes, turning them over carefully after 20 minutes.
5. Just before the pheasants have finished cooking, cut the crusts from the bread and cut each slice in half, diagonally. Heat the rest of the butter in the frying pan used earlier and fry the slices of bread until golden brown on both sides.
6. Heat the brandy in a saucepan. Pour it over the pheasants and set alight. When the flames have died away, remove the string from the pheasants and catch the juices which run out in the pan. Add the crème fraîche and a pinch of paprika to the juices. Heat, stirring to loosen all the sediment at the bottom.
7. Spread the pieces of fried bread with the melted foie gras. Put the pheasants on a serving platter, pour the sauce over them and surround with the garnished fried bread. Serve.

Lièvre à la crème

Hare with Cream Sauce

	00:15	01:30 to 02:00

American	Ingredients	Metric/Imperial
¼ cup	Butter	50 g / 2 oz
1 (4 lb)	Young hare	1 (2 kg / 4 lb)
4	Shallots	4
1 (½ lb)	Slice of cooked ham	1 (250 g / 8 oz)
⅓ cup	Vinegar	5 tbsp
⅔ cup	Dry white wine	150 ml / ¼ pint
	Salt and pepper	
1 cup	Crème fraîche (see page 122)	250 ml / 8 fl oz
1 tbsp	Cornstarch [cornflour]	1 tbsp

1. Melt the butter in a flameproof casserole, add the hare and brown on all sides.
2. Peel and finely chop the shallots. Add them to the casserole with the slice of ham. Cook for 2-3 minutes, then pour in the vinegar and one-third of the wine. Season to taste.

3. Cover and cook over a very low heat for 1 hour, adding the rest of the wine during this time.
4. Add the crème fraîche and cook for a further 30 minutes to 1 hour or until the hare is very tender.
5. Remove the ham, shallots and hare to a deep serving dish. Mix the cornstarch with 2 tablespoons of the cooking liquid and add to the casserole. Cook over a low heat until the sauce thickens. Pour over the hare and serve immediately.

Civet de lièvre

Jugged Hare

	00:30 plus marinating	02:30 to 03:00

American	Ingredients	Metric/Imperial
1 (4 lb)	Ready-to-cook hare, with the liver	1 (2 kg / 4 lb)
1 tbsp	Vinegar	1 tbsp
2	Onions	2
5 tbsp	Brandy	5 tbsp
2 tbsp	Olive oil	2 tbsp
	Salt and pepper	
1	Garlic clove	1
½ cup	Butter	125 g / 4 oz
2 tbsp	Flour	2 tbsp
1	Bottle of full-bodied red wine	1
1	Bouquet garni	1
½ lb	Slightly salted bacon	250 g / 8 oz
20	Tiny onions	20
1 tsp	Sugar	1 tsp
⅔ cup	Water	150 ml / ¼ pint
½ lb	Button mushrooms	250 g / 8 oz

1. Ask your butcher to skin the hare and collect the blood. Add to it the vinegar to prevent coagulation. Cut the hare into portions and put the liver aside.
2. Peel 1 onion and slice it thinly. Put the pieces of hare in a mixing bowl, add the onion slices, brandy and olive oil and season with salt and pepper. Stir and leave to marinate in a cool place for 6 hours.
3. Peel the remaining onion and the garlic clove and chop them finely. Melt 2 tablespoons [25 g / 1 oz] of butter in a flameproof casserole, add the flour and stir for 2 minutes over a medium heat. Add the pieces of hare. Stir, then pour in the marinade and red wine. Add the bouquet garni, garlic and onion and cook, covered, over a low heat for 2½-3 hours.
4. Meanwhile, cut the bacon into strips. Blanch the bacon in boiling water for 3 minutes and drain. Put the bacon in a frying pan and cook until browned and rendered of fat. Remove with a slotted spoon.
5. Peel the tiny onions. Drop into a pan of boiling water and boil for 2 minutes, then drain. Add 1 tablespoon [15 g / ½ oz] of butter to the frying pan containing the bacon fat, add the onions and sprinkle with sugar. Pour in the water and cook, uncovered, over a low heat until the water has evaporated.
6. Heat 1 tablespoon [15 g / ½ oz] of butter in another frying pan, add the mushrooms and cook until all the liquid has evaporated. Season with salt and pepper.
7. When the hare is tender, take the pieces from the casserole and carefully remove and discard all the bones. Set the meat aside. Mash the hare's liver with a fork and blend in the blood and vinegar mixture. Add this to the sauce together with the bacon, tiny onions and mushrooms.
8. Return all the meat to the casserole, mix well and heat through. Serve immediately.

Perdreaux aux morilles

Partridge with Morels

⏲ 00:40　　　　　00:30 🍲

American	Ingredients	Metric/Imperial
1 oz	Dried morels or other wild mushrooms	25 g / 1 oz
3	Partridges, with their livers	3
	Salt and pepper	
½ lb	Bacon slices	250 g / 8 oz
½ cup	Butter	125 g / 4 oz
4	Chicken livers	4
2	Fresh parsley sprigs	2
2	Fresh thyme sprigs	2
6 tbsp	Brandy	6 tbsp
	Grated nutmeg	
1 tbsp	Oil	1 tbsp
6	Slices of bread, ½ in / 1 cm thick	6

1. Carefully wash the dried morels in a colander under the cold tap, then put them in a bowl, cover them with lukewarm water and leave to soak for 2-3 hours. Drain them and dry well on paper towels.

2. Season the insides of the partridge with salt and pepper, then cover with some of the bacon and tie on with string.

3. Preheat the oven to 450°F / 230°C / Gas Mark 8.

4. Heat 2 tablespoons of butter in a frying pan, add the partridge livers and chicken livers and brown on all sides. Remove them from the pan with a slotted spoon and purée in a blender or food processor. Also purée the morels, the remaining bacon, the parsley and thyme. Combine all the puréed ingredients, add a few drops of brandy and season with salt, pepper and a pinch of nutmeg.

5. Stuff the inside of each partridge with a large piece of butter and the morel mixture. Put the partridges on a rack in a roasting pan and roast for 30 minutes. Turn the partridges twice during this time and, after 15 minutes, add a few tablespoons of cold water to the roasting pan.

6. Melt the oil and remaining butter in a frying pan and fry the slices of bread until golden brown on both sides. Drain.

7. Pour the rest of the brandy into the roasting pan and set it alight. When the flames die away, cut the partridges in half, and put each on a slice of fried bread. Serve with cooking liquid.

Jugged hare

Marcassin sauce poivrade

Young Wild Boar in Game Sauce

	00:15 plus marinating	02:00

American	Ingredients	Metric/Imperial
1	Onion	1
4	Garlic cloves	4
4	Shallots	4
1	Carrot	1
2	Fresh thyme sprigs	2
1	Bay leaf	1
3	Fresh parsley sprigs	3
6	Black peppercorns	6
⅔ cup	Wine vinegar	150 ml / ¼ pint
1	Bottle of red wine	1
1 (3 lb)	Young wild boar or peccary fillet	1 (1.5 kg / 3 lb)
	Salt and pepper	
4	Bacon slices	4
¼ cup	Butter	50 g / 2 oz
1 tbsp	Oil	1 tbsp
¼ cup	Tomato paste [purée]	4 tbsp

1. Peel and slice the onion, garlic, shallots and carrot. Put them in a mixing bowl with the herbs, peppercorns, wine vinegar and red wine. Add the boar fillet. Season with salt and pepper and leave to marinate for 12 hours.
2. Preheat the oven to 450°F / 230°C / Gas Mark 8.
3. Drain the boar fillet, reserving the marinade. Wrap it with bacon slices and tie on securely with string. Put it in a roasting pan with the butter and roast for 2 hours.
4. Meanwhile, strain the marinade and take out the garlic, onion, shallot and carrot. Chop them finely. Heat the oil in a saucepan, add the chopped vegetables and cook until they are golden. Add the tomato paste and pour in the strained marinade. Bring to a boil, stirring, and leave to reduce over a low heat to a smooth sauce.
5. Slice the boar and serve the sauce separately in a sauceboat.

Wild rabbit in mushroom and wine sauce (see page 300)

Bohemian style pheasants (see page 322)

Perdreaux aux choux

Partridge with Cabbage

	00:30	02:30

American	Ingredients	Metric/Imperial
2	Heads of savoy cabbage	2
½ lb	Bacon	250 g / 8 oz
2	Onions	2
2	Carrots	2
¼ cup	Goose fat or lard	4 tbsp
1	Old partridge	1
1	Bouquet garni	1
1 cup	Dry white wine	250 ml / 8 fl oz
6 tbsp	Brandy	6 tbsp
	Salt and pepper	
	Grated nutmeg	
3	Young partridges	3
1 tsp	Butter	1 tsp
½ lb	Fresh sausages	250 g / 8 oz

1. Cut the heads of cabbage into quarters, remove the cores and shred the leaves finely. Plunge them into a pan of boiling water and boil for 10 minutes. Drain well. Set aside.
2. Cut the bacon into strips. Peel and halve the onions. Peel the carrots and cut them into quarters lengthwise. Heat 1 tablespoon of goose fat or lard in a flameproof casserole, add the old partridge and the strips of bacon and brown well.
3. Add the cabbage to the casserole with the rest of the goose fat or lard, the carrots, onions, bouquet garni, white wine and brandy. Season with salt, pepper and a pinch of nutmeg. Cover the casserole and cook for 2 hours over a low heat.
4. Preheat the oven to 425°F / 220°C / Gas Mark 7.
5. About 40 minutes before the old partridge finishes cooking, season the young partridges with salt and pepper and put them in a roasting pan. Roast them for 30 minutes.
6. Melt the butter in a frying pan, add the sausages and brown on all sides. Add to the casserole for the final 15 minutes of cooking.
7. Remove and discard the bouquet garni. Remove the old partridge and either cut the meat into small pieces and mix into the cabbage, or set the meat aside for use at another time.
8. Transfer the cabbage mixture to a large, warmed serving dish. Cut each young partridge in half and arrange, with the sausages, on top of the cabbage.

Meat

How can you recognize high quality meat? What factors determine the suitability of the various cuts available for different cooking methods? Even though you can always ask your butcher for his recommendations, you should learn how to choose meat that is fresh, tasty and appropriate for the method of preparation you have in mind.

This chapter offers a useful guide to buying meat, plus a wide choice of recipes, each one giving the name of the cut needed to prepare it.

Grade and quality

Each country has a different system of grading meat, but most are concerned mainly with the part of the animal the cut comes from, and therefore with its tenderness. Because the hardest work is done by the muscular forequarters, the meat from this section will have a high proportion of bone, fat and connective tissue, making it tougher than the more expensive cuts from the hind quarters. Many grading systems also take into account the breed of the animal, its age and its diet.

Once you have established the appropriate grade for your purpose (bearing in mind that tougher cuts will need longer, slower cooking than the tender ones used for steak and chops), you should examine the meat on display to ascertain its quality.

Check that:
- the fibers are fine and closely textured.
- the color is bright red for beef, bright pink for lamb, and paler pink for pork. Veal should be pinkish. Avoid any meat that looks grayish or translucent.
- the fat is light cream-colored for beef (depending on the fattening method — the fat of animals fed on corn [maize] is fairly yellow, while on pasture-fed animals it is white), white for pork, veal and mutton.
- there are fine lines of fat in the grain of the meat as well. This characteristic (called marbling) is a sign of very high quality.
- the smell is pleasant and not too strong.
- the meat feels firm and elastic — supple to the touch, but not too soft.

Storing meat

Fresh raw meat should be wrapped in foil and kept in the refrigerator for not more than three days — two days if it is cooked. You should consume ground [minced] meat immediately since it is particularly vulnerable to contamination.

If your meat is sold pre-packed on polystyrene or cardboard trays, replace this packaging with foil as soon as possible to ensure adequate ventilation and prevent the meat from 'sweating'.

Make sure that any meat you buy for freezing is of the highest quality.

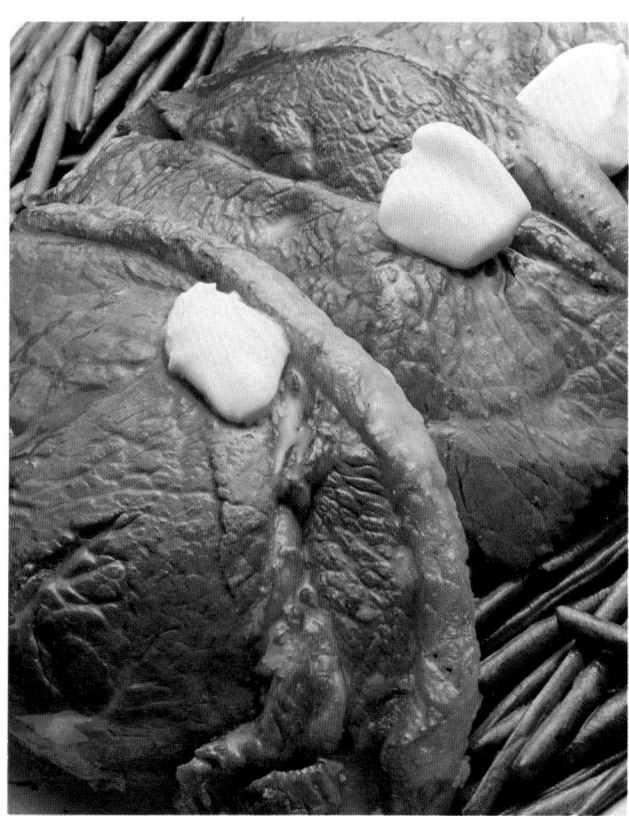

Buying and cooking beef

American cuts to choose	Cooking methods	British cuts to choose	
Rib, rib eye, tenderloin, rolled boneless rump (high quality), tip (high quality)	roast	aitchbone, fillet, rib (including fore, top and back or middle, and wing or prime), rump, sirloin, topside	roast
chuck steak (high quality), rib steak, rib eye steak, top loin steak, sirloin steak, porterhouse steak, tenderloin steak (filet mignon), flank steak (top quality), ground beef patties, cubes for kebabs	broil, fry	chateaubriand steak, entrecote steak, fillet steak or tournedos, porterhouse steak, rump steak, t-bone steak, minced beef patties, cubes for kebabs	grill, fry
boneless chuck eye roast, blade steak, blade roast, pot-roast, short ribs, flank or skirt steak, rump steak, boneless rump, tip roast, top round, bottom round, eye of round, round steak, brisket	braise, pot roast	aitchbone, top rump (or thick flank), leg, skirt, silverside and brisket, back and top rib, flank, topside, chuck, blade bone	braise, stew
shank, boneless chuck, neck, bottom round, heel of round, brisket and corned beef, oxtail	stew	clod (or sticking or neck), shin, stewing steak, oxtail	stew

Beef cuts

Beef: American cuts
1. Butt end or knuckle bone
2. Top round; round steak
3. Aitchbone
4. Bottom round
5. Rump roast
6. Sirloin tip
7. Sirloin steak (tail end of section); rib or club steak (head end of section)
8. Rib roast
9. Chuck roast; stewing beef
10. Shank
11. Knuckle
12. Brisket
13. Rattleran
14. Shortribs; plate (tail end of section)
15. Flank
16. Tenderloin & Porterhouse (T-bone)

Beef: English cuts
1. Shin
2. Round; round steak & topside; silverside and rump (tail end of section)
3. Aitchbone
4. Rump steak (tail end of section); sirloin steak (head end of section)
5. Baron (whole section both sides of back); this section is usually divided into either sirloin steak (head end of section)
6. Rib roast
7. Chuck
8. Neck
9. Shin
10. Knuckle
11. Brisket
12. Shoulder
13. Short or rolled ribs (head end of section); flank or skirt (tail end of section)
14. Fillet

Beef: French cuts
1. Crosse
2. Jarret or trumeau
3. Tende de tranche
4. Gite à la noix
5. Tranche grasse
6. Aiguillette & pointe de culotte
7. Entrecôte; contre filet; aloyau (in one piece)
8. Côte de boeuf (in one piece)
9. Paleron
10. Macreuse
11. Jarret or trumeau
12. Crosse
13., 15. & 17. Poitrine
14. Train de côtes (découvert)
15. Milieu de poitrine
16. Plat de côtes; entrecôte when boned
17. Milieu de tendron
18. Onglet
19. Flanchet
20. Filet; Chateaubriand

Alouettes sans têtes
Beef Birds

| | 00:30 | 02:15 to 02:30 | |

American	Ingredients	Metric/Imperial
12 (¼ lb)	Slices of flank steak, skirt steak or top round [top rump] steak	12 (125 g / 4 oz)
2	Medium-size onions	2
2 lb	Ripe tomatoes	1 kg / 2 lb
2	Garlic cloves	2
¼ lb	Slightly salted bacon	125 g / 4 oz
3 tbsp	Chopped fresh parsley	3 tbsp
	Salt and pepper	
3 tbsp	Oil	3 tbsp
1 cup	Dry white wine	250 ml / 8 fl oz
	Grated nutmeg	

1. Place the slices of beef between sheets of wax [greaseproof] paper and pound until thin. Do not make any holes in the meat.
2. Peel and finely chop the onions. Quarter the tomatoes, then push them through a food mill or sieve to make a purée. Peel and finely chop the garlic.
3. Place the bacon in a saucepan of water. Bring to a boil and blanch for 5 minutes. Drain the bacon and chop it finely.
4. Mix together the bacon, garlic and chopped parsley. Add pepper to taste.
5. Spread each slice of beef out flat on a board. Divide the bacon mixture beween the slices and roll them up. Tie the rolls with string.
6. Heat the oil in a flameproof casserole. Add the beef rolls and brown on all sides for about 5 minutes. Add the onions and cook for about 2 minutes. Gradually stir in the wine.
7. Lower the heat and cook until the wine has almost evaporated, turning the beef rolls occasionally. Add the puréed tomatoes, a pinch of nutmeg, and salt and pepper to taste. Cover the casserole and simmer for about 2 hours or until the meat is tender and the sauce thick.

Boeuf bourguignon
Beef in Burgundy

| | 00:20 | 01:30 to 02:00 | |

American	Ingredients	Metric/Imperial
½ lb	Slightly salted pork sides [belly pork]	250 g / 8 oz
20	Small onions	20
2¼ lb	Fresh beef brisket or chuck steak	1.25 kg / 2¼ lb
1 tbsp	Lard	15 g / ½ oz
2 tbsp	Flour	2 tbsp
1	Bottle of red Burgundy-type wine	1
1	Bouquet garni	1
	Salt and pepper	

1. Cut the pork into strips and blanch in boiling water for 3 minutes. Drain. Peel the onions. In a flameproof casserole, cook the pork strips over a low heat until they render their fat. Add the onions and brown with the pork. Remove the pork and onions with a slotted spoon and set aside.

2. Cut the beef into large cubes. Add the lard to the casserole and when melted, add the beef cubes. Brown on all sides. Sprinkle over the flour and allow this to color, stirring well.
3. Pour over the wine and add enough water just to cover the meat. Add the bouquet garni and season with a little salt and plenty of pepper. Bring to a boil over a high heat.
4. Add the pork strips. Reduce the heat, cover and cook for 1½-2 hours.
5. About 20 minutes before the end of the cooking time, add the onions.
6. Check the seasoning and discard the bouquet garni before serving. Serve with boiled potatoes.

Steak with shallots

Bavette aux échalotes
Steak with Shallots

| | 00:05 | 00:12 to 00:13 | |

American	Ingredients	Metric/Imperial
4	Shallots	4
¼ cup	Butter	50 g / 2 oz
6 (½ lb)	Sirloin [rump] steaks	6 (250 g / 8 oz)
2 tbsp	Oil	2 tbsp
	Salt and pepper	

1. Preheat the broiler [grill], unless you prefer to cook the steaks in a frying pan or on a steak grill.
2. Peel and finely chop the shallots. Heat the butter in a small saucepan, add the shallots and cook gently until translucent. Do not allow to brown.
3. Meanwhile, score the steaks with a sharp knife in a criss-cross pattern on both sides and brush all over with oil.
4. Place the steaks under the broiler or in the hot pan and reduce the heat slightly. Cook until well browned, then turn the steaks over using tongs or a spatula and continue cooking until done to your taste (7-8 minutes for rare meat). Place the steaks on a heated serving dish, season with salt and pepper and pour over the shallot butter. Serve immediately.

Cook's tip: see Basic Techniques for other cooking times.

Boeuf bourgeoise

Beef Pot Roast with Vegetables

◢▷	00:30		03:00 ⬱

American	Ingredients	Metric/Imperial
3 tbsp	Oil	3 tbsp
1 (3 lb)	Boneless chuck eye [blade or brisket] roast	1 (1.5 kg / 3 lb)
1	Calf's foot	1
2	Onions	2
1 tbsp	Butter	1 tbsp
1 quart	Red wine	1 l / 1¾ pint
1 cup	Tomato paste [purée]	250 g / 8 oz
2 cups	Water	500 ml / ¾ pint
1	Bouquet garni	1
	Salt and pepper	
14 oz	Carrots	400 g / 14 oz
14 oz	Turnips	400 g / 14 oz
14 oz	Potatoes	400 g / 14 oz
14 oz	Green beans	400 g / 14 oz

1. Preheat the oven to 425°F / 220°C / Gas Mark 7.
2. Heat the oil in a frying pan. Add the beef and calf's foot and brown on all sides over a high heat.
3. Peel and chop the onions. Melt the butter in a flameproof casserole, add the onions and cook until lightly browned.
4. Add the beef and calf's foot to the casserole. Moisten with the wine, tomato paste and water. Add the bouquet garni, and salt and pepper to taste. Bring to a boil, then cover the casserole and transfer to the oven. Cook for 2½-3 hours.
5. Meanwhile, peel the carrots, turnips and potatoes. Trim the green beans. Cut all the vegetables into thin strips. Cook them separately in boiling water until tender. Drain and keep hot.
6. Remove the meat to a warmed serving platter and keep hot. Bring the cooking liquid to a boil again and reduce to about half. Discard the bouquet garni.
7. Chop the calf's foot into small pieces and mix with the vegetables. Arrange around the meat. Serve sauce separately.

Boeuf en daube

Rich Beef Casserole

◢▷	00:10 plus marinating		04:00 ⬱

American	Ingredients	Metric/Imperial
2 lb	Boneless beef shank [shin] or chuck steak	1 kg / 2 lb
2	Carrots	2
2	Onions	2
4	Garlic cloves	4
4	Juniper berries	4
1	Bouquet garni	1
1	Clove	1
6	Black peppercorns	6
	Salt	
2 cups	Red wine	500 ml / ¾ pint
1	Calf's foot	1
1	Piece of orange rind	1

1. Carefully remove all fat from the beef, and cut it into 12 pieces. Place the meat in a casserole.
2. Peel and slice the carrots. Peel the onions. Peel and crush the garlic. Crush the juniper berries. Add all these ingredients to the casserole with the clove, peppercorns, and salt to taste. Cover with the wine and marinate for 12 hours in a cool place.
3. Preheat the oven to 400°F / 200°C / Gas Mark 6.
4. Add the calf's foot cut in half and the orange rind to the casserole. Cover and cook in the oven for 3¾ hours. Uncover and cook for a final 15 minutes to reduce the liquid.

Cook's tip: any vegetable in season can be served with this dish: Belgian endive [chicory], tomatoes, cauliflower, turnips, salsify or potatoes.

Aloyau aux cèpes

Sirloin of Beef with Cèpes

◢▷	00:15 plus marinating		01:20 ⬱

American	Ingredients	Metric/Imperial
2	Carrots	2
4	Shallots	4
1	Garlic clove	1
1 (3 lb)	Tenderloin [fillet] or boneless sirloin roast	1 (1.5 kg / 3 lb)
1	Bouquet garni	1
1 tbsp	Olive oil	1 tbsp
½	Bottle of good red wine	½
5 oz	Bayonne ham or prosciutto	150 g / 5 oz
½ lb	Fresh cèpes or other mushrooms	25. g / 8 oz
¼ cup	Butter	50 g / 2 oz
¼ cup	Brandy	4 tbsp
	Salt and pepper	
	Grated nutmeg	
¼ lb	Beef marrow	125 g / 4 oz
1 tbsp	Flour	1 tbsp

1. Peel and slice the carrots and shallots; peel and crush the garlic. Place the beef in an earthenware pot or deep glass dish. Add the shallots, carrots, garlic and bouquet garni and pour over the olive oil and wine. Leave to marinate for 24 hours, turning the meat often.
2. The next day, cut the ham into small dice. Clean the cèpes and cut off the end of the stems. Rinse the cèpes under running water and slice thinly.
3. Heat half of the butter in a flameproof casserole, add the ham and cook until golden brown. Remove the ham with a slotted spoon and reserve.
4. Remove the meat from the marinade and wipe dry with paper towels. Set aside. Pour the marinade into the casserole and bring to a boil. Simmer over a gentle heat for 20 minutes, then strain, pressing all the solids well. You should have 1 cup [250 ml / 8 fl oz] liquid.
5. Place the meat in a frying pan without any fat and brown on all sides. Put it in the casserole and add the cèpes, diced ham, brandy and reduced marinade. Season with salt, pepper and a pinch of nutmeg. Bring to a boil quickly, then cover and cook over a low heat for about 35 minutes. Turn the meat once during cooking.
6. Meanwhile, dice the marrow. Drop into a pan of boiling

salted water and cook for 3 minutes. Drain well and set aside.

7. Mix the flour with the rest of the butter to a paste. About 10 minutes before the meat has finished cooking, add the flour and butter paste and stir well to thicken the liquid. Add the marrow.

8. Serve very hot.

Boeuf miroton
Beef in Onion Sauce

	00:20		00:50	

American	Ingredients	Metric/Imperial
¾ lb	Onions	350 g / 12 oz
1½ lb	Cooked beef	750 g / 1½ lb
3 tbsp	Oil	3 tbsp
2 cups	Beef stock	450 ml / ¾ pint
⅔ cup	Vinegar	150 ml / ¼ pint
2 tbsp	Sliced dill pickles [gherkins]	2 tbsp
	Salt and pepper	

1. Peel and thinly slice the onions. Slice the cooked beef. Heat the oil in a flameproof casserole, add the onions and cook until they are translucent but not colored.

2. Add the beef stock and vinegar and bring to a boil. Boil for 15 minutes, stirring occasionally, until the mixture has taken on the consistency of cream.

3. Add the beef slices. Cover and cook gently, without letting it boil, for 10 minutes.

4. Add the gherkins, and salt and pepper to taste.

Boeuf au gratin
Potato-Topped Beef Casserole

	00:30		00:40 to 00:45	

American	Ingredients	Metric/Imperial
2 lb	Potatoes	1 kg / 2 lb
2 tbsp	Butter	25 g / 1 oz
1 cup	Milk	250 ml / 8 fl oz
	Salt and pepper	
	Grated nutmeg	
2	Medium-size onions	2
1	Small garlic clove	1
2 tbsp	Lard	25 g / 1 oz
1 lb	Ground [minced] beef	500 g / 1 lb
1¼ cups	Tomato sauce (see page 133)	300 ml / ½ pint
1 tbsp	Chopped fresh parsley	1 tbsp
	Dried thyme	
2 tbsp	Golden raisins [sultanas]	2 tbsp
¼ cup	Grated gruyère cheese	50 g / 2 oz
2 tbsp	White bread crumbs	2 tbsp

1. Peel and quarter the potatoes. Place them in a saucepan of cold water, bring to a boil and cook for 20 minutes.

2. Preheat the oven to 425°F / 220°C / Gas Mark 7.

3. Drain and mash the potatoes, or purée them in a food mill. Put the potatoes back in the saucepan over a medium heat, add the butter and milk and beat to a smooth consistency. Season with salt, pepper and a very little nutmeg. Set aside.

4. Peel and chop the onions and garlic. Heat the lard in a frying pan, add the onions and cook until golden brown. Add the beef and cook until browned and crumbly. Add the tomato sauce, parsley, thyme and garlic. Season with salt and pepper. Simmer over a low heat for 7-10 minutes, then add the raisins and mix well.

5. Pour the beef mixture into a shallow baking dish and cover with the potatoes. Sprinkle with the gruyère mixed with the bread crumbs.

6. Bake for 20-25 minutes or until piping hot and the top is browned.

Boeuf à la ficelle
Beef Tied with String

	00:30		03:00	

American	Ingredients	Metric/Imperial
8	Carrots	8
7	Turnips	7
2	Onions	2
4	Cloves	4
9	Leeks	9
1¼ lb	Beef shank [shin]	625 g / 1¼ lb
2 lb	Beef bones	1 kg / 2 lb
5 quarts	Water	5 l / 9 pints
	Salt	
5	Black peppercorns	5
6	Potatoes	6
1	Stick of celery	1
6	Small pieces of beef marrow	6
1 (2½ lb)	Piece of top round [top rump] steak	1 (1.25 kg / 2½ lb)

1. Peel and dice 2 of the carrots and 1 turnip. Peel the onions and stud each with 2 cloves. Dice 3 of the leeks. Put these vegetables into a stewpot with the beef shank, bones and water. Add a handful of sea salt and the peppercorns and bring to a boil. Simmer for 2 hours.

2. Meanwhile, prepare the accompanying vegetables. Peel the remaining carrots and turnips and the potatoes. Trim the celery and separate the stalks. Tie the leeks and celery stalks into bundles with string. Place the turnips in a large square of cheesecloth or muslin and tie the four corners together; do the same with the carrots and the pieces of marrow. Tie up the steak, leaving a good length of string at each end.

3. When the stock is ready, strain it and return to the stewpot. Bring back to a boil and add the carrots. Cook for 10 minutes, then add the celery and leeks. Cook for another 10 minutes.

4. Tie the two ends of spare string on the steak to the two handles of the stewpot so that the meat is immersed in the stock without touching the bottom of the pot. Add the marrow. Simmer for 20 minutes, then remove from the heat and leave the meat in the stock for 20 minutes.

5. Meanwhile, cook the potatoes in boiling salted water for about 20 minutes or until tender.

6. To serve, drain the meat and place on a warmed serving dish. Unwrap or untie all the vegetables and arrange around the meat with the marrow. Skim the fat from the stock and serve in soup cups with the meat.

Boeuf en gelée

Beef in Aspic

	00:20 plus chilling	02:00

American	Ingredients	Metric/Imperial
1 (4 lb)	Piece of top round [top rump] steak	1 (2 kg / 4 lb)
1 tbsp	Oil	1 tbsp
1 lb	Carrots	500 g / 1 lb
4	Onions	4
1	Garlic clove	1
1	Bouquet garni	1
	Salt and pepper	
	Grated nutmeg	
⅔ cup	Dry white wine	150 ml / ¼ pint
⅔ cup	Water	150 ml / ¼ pint
1 envelope	Unflavored gelatin	1 sachet
1	Sugar cube	1
¾ lb (3 cups)	Fresh shelled peas	350 g / 12 oz

1. Trim all the fat from the beef and prick it all over with a fork. Heat the oil in a flameproof casserole, add the beef and brown all over on a medium heat for 5 minutes.
2. Peel and slice the carrots, onions and garlic. Add them to the meat with the bouquet garni. Season with salt, pepper and a pinch of nutmeg. Cover and cook over a low heat for 30 minutes.
3. Moisten with the wine and water. Cover again and leave to simmer over a very low heat for 1½ hours.
4. Take the meat and vegetables out of the casserole and set aside. Strain the cooking liquid and skim off any fat. Dissolve the gelatin in this liquid. Set the aspic aside.
5. Bring a saucepan of water to a boil. Add salt and the sugar cube, then the peas. Cook for 15 minutes or until the peas are tender but still firm. Drain.
6. Line the bottom of a cake pan or earthenware dish with a layer of peas and carrot slices. Cover with a little of the aspic and chill for about 20 minutes.
7. Slice the meat thinly and put back together in its original shape. Place the meat on top of the vegetables in the pan. Cover with the rest of the aspic, and then add the remaining vegetables. Cover and chill for 12 hours.
8. Unmold the beef in aspic and serve with a green salad.

Boeuf braisé

Braised Beef

	00:20	01:30

American	Ingredients	Metric/Imperial
3 lb	Shank [shin]	1.5 kg / 3 lb
3	Onions	3
1	Garlic clove	1
2 tbsp	Lard	25 g / 1 oz
1 cup	Dry white wine or water	250 ml / 8 fl oz
1	Bouquet garni	1
	Salt and pepper	
½ lb	Bacon	250 g / 8 oz
3	Uncooked pork and beef sausages flavored with herbs	3

1. Ask your butcher to tie up the beef like a roast but without barding fat, and to give you a few bones. Peel and chop the onions and garlic.
2. Heat the lard in a flameproof casserole, add the beef and brown gently on all sides. Moisten with the wine or water and add the bones, onions, garlic, bouquet garni, and salt and pepper to taste.
3. Cover and simmer over a very gentle heat for 1½ hours, turning the meat from time to time.
4. Cut the bacon into slices, about ½ in / 1 cm thick, and blanch for 5 minutes in boiling water. Drain. Brown the bacon slices in their own fat in a frying pan.
5. Prick the sausages so that they do not burst, then cook in barely simmering water for 10 minutes. Let them cool slightly in the water, then drain and slice fairly thickly.
6. About 20 minutes before the meat is cooked, add the bacon and sausage slices to the casserole.
7. Discard the bouquet garni and serve the meat sliced with the bacon, sausages and gravy.

Boeuf aux carottes

Beef with Carrots

	00:45	04:00

American	Ingredients	Metric/Imperial
3 lb	Carrots	1.5 kg / 3 lb
5 oz	Fresh bacon rind	150 g / 5 oz
¼ cup	Oil	4 tbsp
1 (3 lb)	Boneless chuck eye roast, [topside], larded and tied	1 (1.5 kg / 3 lb)
2 tbsp	Brandy	2 tbsp
¼ cup	Butter	50 g / 2 oz
	Salt and pepper	
1	Fresh thyme sprig	1
2	Bay leaves	2

1. Preheat the oven to 350°F / 180°C / Gas Mark 4.
2. Peel and thinly slice the carrots. Cut the bacon rind into strips.
3. Heat 3 tablespoons of the oil in a flameproof casserole, add the beef and brown on all sides for about 5 minutes.
4. Take out the meat and discard the cooking oil. Replace the meat in the casserole, sprinkle with the brandy and set alight. Shake the casserole until the flame goes out. Remove the meat and set aside.
5. Scatter the bacon rind over the bottom of the casserole. Place the meat on top.
6. Heat the rest of the oil and butter in a frying pan, add the carrot slices and cook for about 8 minutes without letting them brown. Season with salt and pepper.
7. Add the carrots, thyme and bay leaves to the casserole. Cover the casserole with a sheet of oiled wax [greaseproof] paper, place the casserole lid on top and put in the oven. Cook for about 4 hours.
8. To serve, slice the meat and arrange on the serving dish. Surround it with the carrots. Discard the herbs from the cooking liquid and serve with the meat.

Cook's tip: you can also serve this dish cold in aspic. Add 1 tablespoon unflavored gelatin dissolved in 1 cup [250 ml / 8 fl oz] water to the cooking liquid. Pour a ¼ in / 5 mm layer of this over the bottom of an earthenware dish, add a layer of carrots and then a little more aspic. Place the meat on top, surround with the rest of the carrots and pour on the rest of the aspic. Chill for 12 hours or until set. To serve, unmold onto a serving dish.

Braised beef with carrots

Boeuf mode
Braised Beef with Carrots

	00:25		03:00

American	Ingredients	Metric/Imperial
2 lb	Carrots	1 kg / 2 lb
3	Onions	3
1	Leek	1
2	Tomatoes	2
½ lb	Button mushrooms	250 g / 8 oz
2	Pieces of beef bone	2
¼ cup	Butter	50 g / 2 oz
1 (2 lb)	Piece of braising beef, larded	1 (1 kg / 2 lb)
1	Large piece of fresh pork rind	1
1 tbsp	Flour	1 tbsp
1 tbsp	Tomato paste [purée]	1 tbsp
	Salt and pepper	
½	Calf's foot, boned	½
1	Bouquet garni including a celery stalk	1
2 cups	Beef stock	500 ml / ¾ pint

1. Preheat the oven to 450°F / 260°C / Gas Mark 9.
2. Peel and dice the carrots and onions. Dice the leek. Peel the tomatoes (first plunging them in boiling water for 10 seconds), scoop out the seeds and chop the flesh. Trim the stems of the mushrooms and slice thinly.
3. Place the beef bones in the oven and bake until they crack.
4. Meanwhile, heat the butter in a frying pan, add the beef and a piece of the pork rind and brown on all sides. Discard the rind and put the beef on one side.
5. Add the onions, leek and mushrooms to the pan and cook until softened. Add the flour and cook until golden brown. Add the tomatoes and tomato paste; season to taste.
6. Cover the bottom of a flameproof casserole with the rest of the pork rind. Spread the cooked vegetables on top, then place the beef on the vegetables. Add the bones, calf's foot and carrots. Season well and add the bouquet garni and beef stock, which should come halfway up the meat. Cover the casserole and bring to a boil.

7. Transfer the casserole to the oven, and reduce the heat to 350°F / 180°C / Gas Mark 4. Cook for 3 hours.
8. Remove the meat and place it on a carving board. Strain the sauce. Slice the meat and serve with the sauce.

Carpaccio
Marinated Raw Beef

	00:35		00:00
	plus marinating		

American	Ingredients	Metric/Imperial
2 lb	Beef tenderloin [fillet]	1 kg / 2 lb
4	Lemons	4
1 cup	Olive oil	250 ml / 8 fl oz
	Salt and pepper	
1	Head of lettuce	1
	Chopped fresh parsley	

1. Cut the meat into very thin slices (about the thickness of Parma ham slices). Put them in a deep dish. Squeeze the lemons and pour the juice over the slices of meat — its acidity will 'cook' the raw meat. Then pour over the olive oil and season with salt and pepper.
2. Marinate for 1 hour in the refrigerator.
3. Wash the lettuce, keeping the leaves whole.
4. Serve the beef with the lettuce, sprinkled with parsley.

Brochettes sauce piquante
Kebabs with Barbecue Sauce

	00:15	00:15 to 00:20	

American	Ingredients	Metric/Imperial
¾ lb	Smoked bacon	350 g / 12 oz
1½ lb	Boneless sirloin [rump steak]	750 g / 1½ lb
3	Onions	3
⅔ cup	Wine vinegar	150 ml / ¼ pint
1 tsp	Salt	1 tsp
½ tsp	Sugar	½ tsp
1 tsp	Black pepper	1 tsp
¼ cup	Tomato paste [purée]	4 tbsp
2 tbsp	Water	2 tbsp
½ tsp	Cayenne pepper	½ tsp
6 tbsp	Butter	75 g / 3 oz

1. Preheat the broiler [grill] or light the barbecue.
2. Cut the bacon and steak into large cubes. Peel and finely chop the onions.
3. Pour the vinegar into a small saucepan and add the onions, salt, sugar and pepper. Cook over a low heat until the vinegar has reduced to half the quantity, about 5 minutes.
4. Add the tomato paste, water and cayenne pepper. Simmer for 5 minutes over a very low heat.
5. Meanwhile, thread the beef and bacon alternately onto 6 skewers. Cook the kebabs for 5-6 minutes under the broiler or on the barbecue, turning frequently.
6. When the sauce is ready, cut the butter into small pieces and whisk into the sauce. Serve with the kebabs.

Boeuf aux olives

Beef with Olives

	00:20		03:00

American	Ingredients	Metric/Imperial
1 (¼ lb)	Piece of smoked bacon	1 (125 g / 4 oz)
2	Shallots	2
2	Carrots	2
10	Onions	10
1	Garlic clove	1
¼ lb	Button mushrooms	125 g / 4 oz
1 (2½ lb)	Chuck steak [brisket]	1 (1.25 kg / 2½ lb)
1	Bouquet garni	1
	Salt and pepper	
⅔ cup	Madeira or red wine	150 ml / ¼ pint
1½ cups	Green olives	250 g / 8 oz

1. Cut the bacon into strips. Peel and thinly slice the shallots, carrots and onions. Peel and crush the garlic. Quarter the mushrooms.
2. Cook the bacon strips in a flameproof casserole until they have rendered their fat, without browning. Remove the bacon with a slotted spoon. Add the piece of beef to the casserole with the onions and carrots and cook until the meat is browned on all sides. Add the bouquet garni and season with a little salt and plenty of pepper. Cook, covered, over a low heat for 20 minutes, turning the meat once.
3. Add the shallots, garlic, madeira or wine and bacon strips. Continue cooking, still covered, over a gentle heat for about 1½ hours.
4. Meanwhile, remove the pits [stones] from the olives. Blanch them in boiling water for 3 minutes, then drain.
5. Add the olives and mushrooms to the casserole. Continue cooking covered, over a gentle heat for 45 minutes longer.
6. Season and discard the bouquet garni before serving.

Boeuf en salade

Beef Salad

	00:20		00:25

American	Ingredients	Metric/Imperial
6	Potatoes	6
	Salt and pepper	
1¼ lb	Cooked beef	625 g / 1¼ lb
1	Large onion	1
4	Shallots	4
2	Garlic cloves	2
	Few fresh parsley sprigs	
1	Small bunch of fresh chives	1
1 tbsp	Prepared mustard	1 tbsp
2 tbsp	Vinegar	2 tbsp
¼ cup	Oil	4 tbsp
⅔ cup	White wine	150 ml / ¼ pint
6	Hard-cooked eggs	6

1. Scrub the potatoes and put them in a saucepan of cold water with a handful of sea salt. Bring to a boil and cook for about 20 minutes.

2. Meanwhile, cut the meat into small cubes. Peel and slice the onion and shallots and separate the slices into rings. Peel and chop the garlic. Chop parsley; snip chives into small pieces.
3. In a mixing bowl, combine the mustard with the vinegar, parsley, garlic, oil, onions and some pepper. Add the diced meat and mix well. Adjust the seasoning if necessary by adding a little salt, vinegar and pepper.
4. Drain the potatoes, then peel and slice them into a large salad bowl. Heat the wine in a small saucepan and when very hot, pour it over the hot potatoes. Sprinkle with the chives and shallots and season with salt and pepper. Fold together gently.
5. Put the meat mixture on top of the potatoes. Cut the eggs into quarters and arrange on top of the meat salad. Serve immediately.

Beef stroganoff

Boeuf strogonoff

Beef Stroganoff

	00:20		00:40

American	Ingredients	Metric/Imperial
1 tbsp	Mustard powder	1 tbsp
1½ tsp	Sugar	1½ tsp
	Salt and pepper	
8	Onions	8
1 lb	Button mushrooms	500 g / 1 lb
5 tbsp	Oil	5 tbsp
2½ lb	Beef tenderloin [fillet]	1.25 kg / 2½ lb
2 cups	Crème fraîche (see page 122)	500 ml / ¾ pint

1. Mix together the mustard, sugar and a pinch of salt. Add a little water to make a thick cream. Set aside.
2. Peel and thinly slice the onions. Thinly slice the mushrooms.
3. Heat 2 tablespoons of the oil in a frying pan, add the onions and mushrooms and season with salt and pepper. Cook, covered, over a gentle heat for about 20-30 minutes or until all the liquid has evaporated. Set aside.
4. Cut the beef into slices ¾ in / 1.5 cm thick and then cut these slices into strips ¼ in / 5 mm wide. Heat 2 tablespoons of the oil in another frying pan over a high heat, add one-third of the meat and cook, stirring, for about 2 minutes or until the meat strips are just brown. Remove these with a slotted spoon and place in the other pan on top of the onions and mushrooms. Brown the remaining beef strips, adding a little more oil if necessary, and add to the onions and mushrooms.

5. Heat all the ingredients over a gentle heat. Add the mustard mixture, stirring all the time. Cook, covered, over a very gentle heat for 2-3 minutes.
6. Stir in the crème fraîche and add seasoning to taste. Heat through gently and serve.

Côte de boeuf marchand de vin

Rib of Beef with Red Wine Sauce

	00:10	00:30

American	Ingredients	Metric/Imperial
3	Large onions	3
½ cup	Butter	125 g / 4 oz
1 tsp	Flour	1 tsp
1	Bouquet garni	1
2 cups	Full-bodied red wine	500 ml / ¾ pint
	Salt and pepper	
1 (3 lb)	Rib roast	1 (1.5 kg / 3 lb)

1. Preheat the broiler [grill].
2. Peel and thinly slice the onions. Heat half the butter in a saucepan, add the onions and cook until soft and translucent. Sprinkle with the flour and stir well, then add the bouquet garni and wine. Bring to a boil, stirring. Season to taste with salt and pepper. Cover and cook for 10-12 minutes.
3. Meanwhile, put the beef on the rack in the broiler pan and broil on one side for 10 minutes or until well browned. Turn and cook the other side for 15-20 minutes.
4. Strain the sauce into a clean saucepan. Add the rest of the butter, cut into small pieces, whisking well.
5. Carve the meat and serve with the sauce.

Côte de boeuf rôtie

Roast Rib of Beef

	00:03	00:45 to 01:00

American	Ingredients	Metric/Imperial
1 (3 lb)	Rib roast	1 (1.5 kg / 3 lb)
	Salt and pepper	
4 - 5 tbsp	Hot water	4 - 5 tbsp
2 tbsp	Butter	25 g / 1 oz

1. Remove the meat from the refrigerator 2 hours before cooking to bring it up to room temperature.
2. Preheat the oven to 450°F / 260°C / Gas Mark 9.
3. Place the meat on a rack in a roasting pan and sprinkle with salt and pepper. Roast for about 15 minutes or until the meat begins to brown, then reduce the temperature to 425°F / 220°C / Gas Mark 7. Add 3 tablespoons of hot water to the roasting pan and continue roasting for 30 minutes (for very rare meat), 35 minutes (for rare meat) or 45 minutes (for medium rare meat). Turn the meat 4 times while it is roasting and baste from time to time with the juices in the roasting pan.
4. Put the meat on a serving platter and keep hot in the oven with the door ajar. Add the remaining hot water to the roasting pan and boil to reduce over a brisk heat, scraping the bottom of the pan with a spatula. Add the butter and whisk in well.
5. Pour the sauce into a sauceboat and serve with the meat.

Boulettes au basilic et à la tomate

Basil and Tomato Meatballs

	00:35	00:45

American	Ingredients	Metric/Imperial
2 lb	Ripe but firm tomatoes	1 kg / 2 lb
2	Onions	2
1¼ cups	Cold water	300 ml / ½ pint
3 tbsp	Olive oil	3 tbsp
1	Garlic clove	1
1¼ lb	Lean ground [minced] beef	625 g / 1¼ lb
5 tbsp	Grated gruyère cheese	5 tbsp
2	Eggs	2
3 tbsp	Chopped fresh basil	3 tbsp
	Salt and pepper	
5 tbsp	Milk	5 tbsp
2 cups	Bread crumbs	125 g / 4 oz

1. Peel the tomatoes (first plunging them in boiling water for 10 seconds), remove the seeds and purée the flesh. Peel and finely chop the onions.
2. Put the onions in a saucepan with the water and olive oil. Cover and cook over a gentle heat for 15 minutes, then add the puréed tomatoes. Cook, uncovered, over a medium heat for 20 minutes.
3. Meanwhile, prepare the meatballs. Peel and chop the garlic. Put the beef in a mixing bowl and add the garlic, cheese, eggs, 2 tablespoons of the basil, and salt and pepper to taste. Mix all these ingredients together with your hands.
4. Heat the milk in a small saucepan. When it is hot, add the bread crumbs. Remove from the heat and stir with a fork until a thick paste is formed. Drain the excess milk from the bread crumbs and add them to the meat mixture. Mix well.
5. Shape into about 50 meatballs, wetting your hands frequently so the mixture does not stick.
6. Add the meatballs to the tomato sauce and cook for 10 minutes over a medium heat.
7. Sprinkle the meatballs with the remaining tablespoon of basil and serve very hot.

Côte de boeuf au gros sel

Rib of Beef in a Salt Crust

	00:05	00:30

American	Ingredients	Metric/Imperial
2 lb (5 cups)	Sea salt	1 kg / 2 lb
1 (2½ lb)	Rib roast	1 (1.25 kg / 2½ lb)

1. Preheat the oven to 450°F / 260°C / Gas Mark 9.
2. Cover the bottom of an ovenproof dish with two-thirds of the sea salt. Place the meat on top and cover it with the rest of the salt.
3. Put the meat in the oven and roast for 25 minutes. Turn the oven off and let the meat rest inside for 5 minutes. This will produce medium rare meat.
4. Crack the salty crust and remove it. Carve the meat and serve hot.

Chateaubriands au poivre et au madère
Pepper Steak in Madeira Sauce

◥　00:10　　　00:04 to 00:08 🍲

American	Ingredients	Metric/Imperial
3 tbsp	Crushed black peppercorns	3 tbsp
6 (½ lb)	Boneless sirloin [fillet] steak	6 (250 g / 8 oz)
⅔ cup	Butter	150 g / 5 oz
	Salt	
¼ cup	Brandy	4 tbsp
1 tsp	Potato starch or flour or cornstarch [cornflour]	1 tsp
1 cup	Madeira wine	250 ml / 8 fl oz

1. Sprinkle a chopping board or worktop with the crushed peppercorns and press both sides of each steak into them. Press with the palm of the hand to ensure the peppercorns stick to the meat well.

2. Heat ¼ cup [50 g / 2 oz] of the butter in a large frying pan. When it has turned golden brown, reduce the heat and add the steaks. Cook for 2-4 minutes on each side according to individual taste. Sprinkle with a little salt.

3. Pour the brandy over the steaks and set alight, lifting the steaks up so that the flames burn all over them. Remove the steaks with a slotted spoon, arrange on a serving dish and keep hot.

4. Dissolve the potato starch or cornstarch in 1 tablespoon of the madeira. Pour the rest of the madeira into the frying pan and bring to a boil, scraping the bottom of the pan with a wooden spatula. Remove the pan from the heat and add the dissolved potato starch. Return to a medium heat and stir until the sauce is slightly thickened. Remove from the heat again and gradually add the rest of the butter, cut into small pieces, whisking constantly.

5. Pour the sauce over the steaks and serve.

Chateaubriands béarnaise
Chateaubriand with Béarnaise Sauce

◥　00:20　　　00:25 🍲

American	Ingredients	Metric/Imperial
2	Shallots	2
2	Fresh tarragon sprigs	2
2	Fresh chervil sprigs	2
¾ cup + 1 tbsp	Butter	190 g / 6½ oz
1 tbsp	Oil	1 tbsp
⅔ cup	Vinegar	150 ml / ¼ pint
	Salt and pepper	
3	Egg yolks, at room temperature	3
2 tbsp	Water	2 tbsp
6 (½ lb)	Chateaubriand steaks (from thickest part of beef tenderloin or fillet)	6 (250 g / 8 oz)

1. Peel and finely chop the shallots. Chop the tarragon and chervil leaves.

2. Heat 1 tablespoon [15 g / ½ oz] of butter with the oil in a heavy saucepan. Add the shallots, half of the tarragon and chervil, the vinegar and pepper to taste. Reduce over a gentle heat for 20 minutes (put a heatproof mat under the pan to diffuse the heat) until only 1 tablespoon of vinegar remains.

3. Meanwhile, heat the rest of the butter in a bowl placed over a pan of hot water or in a double boiler. When the butter has melted you will see a whitish deposit at the bottom: this is the whey. Pour the melted butter very carefully into a bowl so as to leave the whey behind.

4. Preheat the broiler [grill].

5. Put the egg yolks into another bowl over the pan of hot water. Add the reduced vinegar mixture, beating with a whisk. Gradually whisk in the water, a pinch of salt and some pepper and whisk until the mixture becomes creamy. Remove from the heat and, still whisking, dribble in the melted butter. Strain the sauce, then stir in the rest of the tarragon and chervil. Keep warm over the pan of hot water.

6. Cook the steaks under the broiler for 3-5 minutes on each side, depending on whether you like them rare, medium or well done.

7. Serve the steaks accompanied by the hot béarnaise sauce.

Carbonade flamande
Flemish Beef Stew

◥　00:10　　　02:30 🍲

American	Ingredients	Metric/Imperial
2½ lb	Chuck steak	1.25 kg / 2½ lb
¼ cup	Lard	50 g / 2 oz
5	Onions	5
1½ tbsp	Flour	1½ tbsp
1 tbsp	Brown sugar	1 tbsp
1 tbsp	Vinegar	1 tbsp
1	Bouquet garni	1
2 cups	Beef stock	500 ml / ¾ pint
2 cups	Light beer [pale ale]	500 ml / ¾ pint
	Salt and pepper	
6	Potatoes	6

1. Cut the beef into large cubes. Heat the lard in a flameproof casserole, add the beef cubes and brown on all sides, stirring from time to time. Meanwhile, peel and thinly slice the onions.

2. When the meat is browned, take it out with a slotted spoon and set aside. Add the onions to the pan and brown lightly, stirring occasionally.

3. Replace the meat in the casserole. Sprinkle over the flour and stir until the flour has turned golden brown. Add the brown sugar, vinegar, bouquet garni, beef stock, beer, and salt and pepper to taste. Cover and cook over a gentle heat for about 2½ hours.

4. Meanwhile, peel and halve the potatoes. Cook in boiling salted water for 20 minutes or until tender. Drain.

5. Pour the stew into a heated serving dish, surround with the potatoes and serve very hot.

Cook's tip: you can also cook the potatoes in the steam from the meat. To do this, cut them in quarters and place in a steaming basket over the meat 40 minutes before the end of the cooking period. Make sure that the steamer has a very well-fitting lid.

Entrecôtes bercy
Rib Steaks in Bercy Sauce

	00:10		00:20

American	Ingredients	Metric/Imperial
6	Shallots	6
1 cup	Dry white wine	250 ml / 8 fl oz
	Salt and pepper	
6 (½ lb)	Boneless rib [sirloin or entrecôte] steaks	6 (250 g / 8 oz)
2 - 3 tbsp	Oil	2 - 3 tbsp
1	Bunch of fresh parsley	1
6 tbsp	Butter	75 g / 3 oz

1. Peel and finely chop the shallots. Put them in a small saucepan with the wine and salt and pepper. Cook over a medium heat until only 2-3 tablespoons of liquid remain.
2. Meanwhile, heat a steak or chop grill or griddle. Brush the steaks with the oil, lay them on the grill and cook for 3-4 minutes on each side. Season with salt and pepper.
3. Chop the parsley. When the shallot sauce has reduced, add the chopped parsley and the butter cut into small pieces, whisking well.
4. Serve the steaks coated with the sauce.

Cook's tip: add the salt to the steaks as each side is browned.

Émincé de boeuf
Beef Strips in Mustard Sauce

	00:15		00:20

American	Ingredients	Metric/Imperial
2 lb	Boneless sirloin [rump] steak	1 kg / 2 lb
4	Shallots	4
¼ cup	Butter	50 g / 2 oz
1 cup	Crème fraîche (see page 122)	250 ml / 8 fl oz
1 tsp	Strong prepared mustard	1 tsp
	Salt and pepper	

1. Trim any fat from the steak, then cut into slices ¼ in / 5 mm thick. Cut these slices into strips ¼ in / 5 mm wide. Peel and finely chop the shallots.
2. Heat half of the butter in a frying pan and add half of the meat strips. Cook over high heat, stirring, until browned all over. Remove with a slotted spoon. Brown the rest of the meat strips and remove.
3. Melt the rest of the butter in the frying pan over a medium heat, add the shallots and cook until soft and translucent. Add 4 tablespoons of the crème fraîche and stir, scraping the bottom of the pan with a wooden spatula. Cook until the mixture is a golden color, then add the rest of the crème and the mustard. Season with salt and a lot of pepper. Bring to a boil and cook, stirring, to thicken the sauce.
4. Add the meat strips and any juices from the frying pan and heat through quickly, stirring. Do not let the mixture boil again. Serve immediately.

Entrecôtes bordelaise
Rib Steaks in Bordelaise Sauce

	00:15		00:05 to 00:10

American	Ingredients	Metric/Imperial
1 tbsp	Oil	1 tbsp
⅔ cup	Butter	150 g / 5 oz
6 (½ lb)	Boneless rib [sirloin or entrecôte] steaks	6 (250 g / 8 oz)
6	Shallots	6
½	Bottle red wine (preferably Bordeaux)	½
1	Fresh thyme sprig	1
1	Bay leaf	1
	Salt and pepper	
1	Small bunch of fresh parsley	1
½	Lemon	½

1. Heat the oil with ¼ cup [50 g / 2 oz] of the butter in a frying pan. Add the steaks and cook over a high heat for 2-4 minutes on each side, according to taste. When they are cooked, arrange them on a warmed serving platter and keep hot.
2. Discard the fat left in the frying pan. Peel and finely chop the shallots. Put them in the frying pan with the wine, thyme, bay leaf, and salt and pepper to taste. Bring to a boil, scraping the bottom of the pan to loosen the sediment. Reduce by at least half over a high heat.
3. Chop the parsley. Squeeze the juice from the ½ lemon. Strain the sauce and add the lemon juice, parsley and the remaining butter, cut into small pieces. Whisk the sauce well.
4. Pour the sauce over the hot steaks and serve immediately.

Entrecôtes au roquefort
Rib Steaks with Roquefort Cheese

	00:15		00:06 to 00:10

American	Ingredients	Metric/Imperial
6 tbsp	Butter	75 g / 3 oz
¼ cup	Flour	50 g / 2 oz
1 quart	Hot milk	1 l / 1¾ pints
6 (½ lb)	Boneless rib [sirloin or entrecôte] steaks	6 (250 g / 8 oz)
1 cup	Crème fraîche (see page 122)	250 ml / 8 fl oz
½ lb	Roquefort cheese	250 g / 8 oz

1. Melt ¼ cup [50 g / 2 oz] of the butter in a saucepan over a gentle heat. As soon as it begins to foam, add the flour and stir until completely absorbed. Add the milk and cook, stirring well, over a gentle heat for about 10 minutes.
2. Meanwhile, heat the remaining butter in a frying pan, add the steaks and cook for 3-5 minutes on each side.
3. Stir the crème fraîche into the sauce. Add two-thirds of the cheese and mix carefully.
4. Pour the sauce over the steaks. Crumble the rest of the cheese over the steaks and serve very hot.

Estouffade de boeuf

Beef in Red Wine Sauce

00:20   03:30 to 04:00

American	Ingredients	Metric/Imperial
1 lb	Chuck steak	500 g / 1 lb
1½ lb	Flank steak	750 g / 1½ lb
½ lb	Lightly salted bacon	250 g / 8 oz
4	Onions	4
2	Garlic cloves	2
2 tbsp	Olive oil	2 tbsp
¼ cup	Flour	25 g / 1 oz
	Salt and pepper	
1	Bottle of red wine	1
1	Bouquet garni	1
½ lb	Button mushrooms	250 g / 8 oz
1 tbsp	Tomato paste [purée]	1 tbsp
⅔ cup	Black olives	125 g / 4 oz

1. Cut the meat into chunks. Cut the bacon into strips. Blanch the bacon in a pan of boiling water for 5 minutes, then drain and pat dry with paper towels. Peel and quarter the onions. Peel and crush the garlic.

2. Preheat the oven to 350°F / 180°C / Gas Mark 4.

3. Heat 1 tablespoon of oil in a flameproof casserole over a medium heat, add the bacon and cook until golden brown. Remove with a slotted spoon.

4. Coat the meat in the flour. Add to the casserole and brown on all sides. Season with salt and pepper and pour over the wine. Bring to a boil over a high heat and reduce the liquid to about half.

5. Add just enough water to cover the meat. Add the garlic and bouquet garni, then cover the casserole with a sheet of foil and put the lid on top. Transfer to the oven and cook for 3 hours.

6. Meanwhile, quarter the mushrooms. Heat the rest of the oil in a frying pan, add the mushrooms and cook until all their liquid has evaporated. Set aside.

7. Pour the meat mixture into a strainer placed over a large bowl. Return the meat to the casserole together with the bacon and mushrooms.

8. Skim the fat from the cooking liquid. Add the tomato paste and olives. Adjust the seasoning if necessary by adding a little salt and pepper, then pour the sauce over the meat in the casserole. Cover and cook over a gentle heat for 20-25 minutes longer. Serve with rice or noodles.

Entrecôtes grillées

Broiled [Grilled] Rib Steaks

00:05   00:05 to 00:10
according to taste

American	Ingredients	Metric/Imperial
2 (1¾ lb) or 1 (3 lb)	Boneless rib [sirloin or entrecôte] steaks	2 (900 g / 1¾ lb) or 1 (1.5 kg / 3 lb)
	Melted butter or oil	
	Salt and pepper	
½ cup	Butter	125 g / 4 oz
	Chopped fresh parsley or	
2	Shallots	2

1. Trim any fat and gristle from the steaks. About 30 minutes before cooking, brush the steaks very lightly with melted butter or oil, and shake or grind pepper over both sides of the meat. Season to taste with salt.

2. Heat a chop or steak grill or griddle.

3. Place the meat on the grill and cook on both sides according to taste. Cooking time will depend of the thickness of the meat, the exact temperature of the grill and on individual tastes. As a general rule, when the topmost side becomes shiny with moisture, the meat is cooked.

4. Dot the steak with shavings of butter mixed with chopped parsley or peeled and chopped shallots.

Cook's tip: the steak may be cooked on a barbecue over charcoal, if preferred.

Filet de boeuf en croûte

Beef Fillet in a Pastry Case

01:00   01:00 to 01:15
plus making dough

American	Ingredients	Metric/Imperial
1 (3 lb)	Tenderloin [fillet]	1 (1.5 kg / 3 lb)
	Salt and pepper	
2 quantities	Brioche dough (see page 457)	2 quantities
1	Egg	1

1. Heat a heavy-based frying pan, add the meat without any fat and brown on all sides. Remove the meat from the pan and immediately sprinkle all over with salt and pepper. Allow to become completely cold.

2. Preheat the oven to 400°F / 200°C / Gas Mark 6.

3. Roll out the brioche dough to ¼ in / 5 mm thick. Put the meat in the center of the dough and wrap and fold so that the meat is completely enclosed.

4. Lightly beat the egg and brush over the edges of the dough. Press them together to seal well. Brush the dough all over with beaten egg. Place on a buttered baking sheet, joins on top.

5. Bake until the pastry becomes golden, then cover with foil and continue cooking for 54-60 minutes.

6. When the meat is cooked, turn off the oven and leave the meat inside for another 10 minutes before serving. Serve with madeira sauce (see page 130).

Filet de boeuf au poivre

Roast Beef with Pepper

00:20   00:30 to 00:35

American	Ingredients	Metric/Imperial
1 (3 lb)	Beef tenderloin [fillet]	1 (1.5 kg / 3 lb)
1 tbsp	Oil	1 tbsp
	Salt	
2 tbsp	Crushed black peppercorns	2 tbsp
½ cup	Brandy	125 ml / 4 fl oz
¼ cup	Butter	50 g / 2 oz
1 tbsp	Strong prepared mustard	1 tbsp
1¼ cups	Crème fraîche (see page 122)	300 ml / ½ pint

1. Preheat the oven to 425°F / 220°C / Gas Mark 7.
2. Brush the meat with oil, sprinkle with salt and coat it all over with the peppercorns. Heat a frying pan, add the meat and brown it on all sides in its own fat over a high heat.
3. Transfer the meat to a roasting pan and continue cooking in the oven for 20-25 minutes.
4. Remove the meat from the pan and keep hot. Put the pan over a gentle heat and brown the meat residue in the bottom slightly without burning it. Add the brandy and heat, then scrape the meat residue from the bottom with a wooden spoon. Boil to reduce by half and keep warm.
5. Melt the butter in a saucepan and stir in the mustard and crème fraîche. Cook for 2-3 minutes, then mix this sauce into the cooking juices in the roasting pan.
6. Slice the meat and pour any meat juices into the sauce. Arrange meat on a warmed platter and serve with the sauce.

Langue braisée
Braised Tongue

| | 01:00 | 03:00 to 03:30 | |

American	Ingredients	Metric/Imperial
1 (4 lb)	Fresh beef [ox] tongue	1 (2 kg / 4 lb)
4	Onions	4
½ lb	Carrots	250 g / 8 oz
¼ lb	Fresh pork rind	125 g / 4 oz
1	Bouquet garni	1
	Salt and pepper	
⅔ cup	Dry white wine	150 ml / ¼ pint
1 quart	Beef stock	1 l / 1¾ pints
2 tbsp	Butter	25 g / 1 oz
1 tbsp	Flour	1 tbsp
	Capers	
	Chopped dill pickles [gherkins]	

1. Place the tongue in a stewpot, cover with plenty of water and bring to a boil. Simmer for 25 minutes, skimming off the scum. Peel the onions and slice them. Peel and dice the carrots.
2. Drain the tongue and immediately plunge it into cold water. Put it in a colander and run cold water over it until it is almost cold. Remove the white skin from the tongue.
3. Line the bottom of a large flameproof casserole with the pork rind, skin side down. Place the tongue on top with the onions and carrots. Add the bouquet garni, and salt and pepper to taste. Cook, covered, over a medium heat for about 20 minutes or until the pork rind begins to crisp.
4. Preheat the oven to 400°F / 200°C / Gas Mark 6.
5. Pour over the wine and bring to a boil, uncovered. Cook over a high heat until the wine has almost all evaporated. Add enough stock to reach two-thirds of the way up the tongue and bring to a boil.
6. Grease a sheet of wax [greaseproof] paper with half of the butter and lay it over the tongue. Cover with the lid. Place the casserole in the oven and cook the tongue for at least 3 hours, turning it over 4 times during the cooking period. Check that it is cooked by piercing with a skewer: it should go in easily.
7. Place the tongue on a warmed serving dish and keep hot. Strain the cooking liquid and reserve.
8. Melt the remaining butter in a saucepan, sprinkle with the flour and stir for 2 minutes over a medium heat. Add the reserved cooking liquid and cook, stirring, until thickened. Add capers and dill pickles to taste. Pour the sauce into a sauceboat and serve immediately with the tongue.

Grillade normande
Normandy Grill

| | 00:15 to 00:20 plus infusing | 00:45 to 01:00 | |

American	Ingredients	Metric/Imperial
1	Bunch of fresh parsley	1
¼ cup	Crème fraîche (see page 122)	4 tbsp
	Salt and pepper	
3 lb	Small new potatoes	1.5 kg / 3 lb
6 tbsp	Butter	75 g / 3 oz
3 tbsp	Oil	3 tbsp
2 (1 lb)	Boneless sirloin steaks	2 (500 g / 1 lb)

1. Chop the parsley finely. Mix it with the crème fraîche in a bowl and add salt and pepper to taste. Set aside to infuse in a cool place for 2 hours.
2. Scrape or peel the potatoes. Heat the butter and 2 tablespoons oil in a frying pan, add the potatoes and cook about 45 minutes or until they are golden and soft.
3. About 10 minutes before the potatoes are cooked, brush the steaks very lightly with the remaining oil. Cook in a frying pan for 7-10 minutes. Season with salt and pepper.
4. Heat the crème and parsley mixture gently.
5. Arrange the potatoes on a serving dish and put the meat on top. Pour over the crème and parsley mixture.

Ragoût de boeuf à l'hongroise
Goulash

| | 00:15 | 01:45 to 02:00 | |

American	Ingredients	Metric/Imperial
3 lb	Flank steak	1.5 kg / 3 lb
6	Onions	6
2 tbsp	Lard	25 g / 1 oz
1 tbsp	Flour	1 tbsp
1 tbsp	Mild (sweet) Hungarian paprika	1 tbsp
1 tsp	Strong (hot) Hungarian paprika	1 tsp
1 tsp	Cumin seeds or ground cumin	1 tsp
	Salt	
	Cayenne pepper	
4	Tomatoes	4
1	Bouquet garni	1

1. Preheat the oven to 425°F / 220°C / Gas Mark 7.
2. Cut the meat into large chunks. Peel and chop the onions. Heat the lard in a flameproof casserole, add the meat and onions and brown on all sides over a medium heat. Sprinkle with the flour, the mild and strong paprika and the cumin. Add salt and cayenne to taste and stir well. Cover the casserole and remove from the heat. Set aside.
3. Peel the tomatoes (first plunging them in boiling water for 10 seconds) and chop roughly. Add them to the casserole with the bouquet garni. Pour enough boiling water into the casserole so that the meat is almost covered. Stir well. Place the casserole in the oven, uncovered, and cook for 1¾-2 hours. The liquid in the casserole should be just bubbling.
4. Serve in the casserole with noodles, rice or boiled potatoes.

Faux-filet à la moelle
Sirloin Steaks with Beef Marrow

00:30   00:15 to 00:20

American	Ingredients	Metric/Imperial
2 (1 lb)	Boneless sirloin or rib steaks	2 (500 g / 1 lb)
2	Shallots	2
1	Small garlic clove	1
6	Slices of beef marrow	6
	Salt and pepper	
½ cup	Butter	125 g / 4 oz
½	Bottle of full-bodied red wine	½
6	Black peppercorns	6
	Dried thyme	
1	Small bunch of fresh parsley	1
½	Bay leaf	½
1 - 2 tbsp	Brandy	1 - 2 tbsp

1. Trim as much fat as possible from the steaks. Cut each into 3 equal pieces. Peel and chop the shallots. Peel and crush the garlic.
2. Poach the marrow for 2 minutes in boiling water, then remove from the heat.
3. Season the steaks with salt and pepper. Heat 1 tablespoon [15 g / ½ oz] of butter in a frying pan, add the steaks and cook about 3-5 minutes each side. Drain the slices of beef marrow.
4. Arrange the steaks on a warmed serving dish. Top with the drained slices of marrow and keep hot.
5. Add a little more butter to the frying pan, add the shallots and cook until soft and translucent. Add the wine, peppercorns, a pinch of thyme, the parsley and bay leaf. Bring to a boil and reduce the sauce by two-thirds. Add the brandy and garlic. Just before the sauce comes back to a boil, remove from the heat and add the rest of the butter, cut into small pieces, whisking well.
6. Strain the sauce, pressing the solids to remove all liquid, and spoon over the steaks.

Gras-double
Tripe

00:30   02:00

American	Ingredients	Metric/Imperial
4 lb	Fresh tripe	2 kg / 4 lb
1 tbsp	Butter	15 g / ½ oz
2	Onions	2
4	Shallots	4
4	Garlic cloves	4
	Dried thyme	
1	Bay leaf	1
1¼ cups	White wine	300 ml / ½ pint
1 lb	Carrots	500 g / 1 lb
	Saffron powder	
	Salt and pepper	

1. Cut the tripe into small pieces. Heat the butter in a flameproof casserole, add the tripe and cook to let it render its liquid.
2. Meanwhile, peel and finely chop the onions and shallots. Peel and crush the garlic. Add these ingredients to the casserole, together with some thyme and the bay leaf. Add the wine and cook for 1 hour.
3. Peel and slice the carrots. Add to the casserole, and season to taste with saffron, salt and pepper. Cook for another hour.

Tripe

Ragoût de boeuf à l'africaine
African Beef Stew

00:40   02:30

American	Ingredients	Metric/Imperial
2½ lb	Shank [shin]	1.25 kg / 2½ lb
3	Onions	3
3	Carrots	3
3	Garlic cloves	3
2 tbsp	Oil	2 tbsp
3 tbsp	Tomato paste [purée]	3 tbsp
5	Cloves	5
½ tsp	Ground ginger	½ tsp
	Cayenne pepper	
1 tbsp	Vinegar	1 tbsp
2 cups	Water	450 ml / ¾ pint
1	Bay leaf	1
	Salt and pepper	
½ cup	Peanut butter	125 g / 4 oz
2 tbsp	Flour	2 tbsp
2 tbsp	Honey	2 tbsp

1. Cut the beef into medium-sized cubes with a very sharp knife. Peel and thinly slice the onions and carrots. Peel and crush the garlic.
2. Heat the oil in a flameproof casserole, add the meat, carrots and onions and brown on all sides, stirring with a wooden spoon. Add the tomato paste, cloves, garlic, ginger, a pinch of cayenne pepper, the vinegar, water, bay leaf, and salt and pepper to taste. Stir in half of the peanut butter. Cover and cook over a gentle heat for 2½ hours.
3. Take 2 tablespoons of liquid from the casserole and put it in a bowl. Add the rest of the peanut butter, the flour and honey and mix together. Add to the casserole and stir until the sauce thickens.

Paupiettes de boeuf provençale

Provençal Beef Olives

00:50   01:30

American	Ingredients	Metric/Imperial
6	Thin slices of flank steak, skirt steak or top round [top rump] steak	6
½ lb	Smoked bacon	250 g / 8 oz
1	Garlic clove	1
1 tsp	Dried thyme	1
2 tbsp	Chopped fresh parsley	2 tbsp
	Ground allspice	
	Salt and pepper	
1	Carrot	1
1	Onion	1
1	Large piece of pork rind	1
1	Bay leaf	1
1	Fresh thyme sprig	1
⅔ cup	Dry white wine	150 ml / ¼ pint
⅔ cup	Beef stock	150 ml / ¼ pint
1 tbsp	Potato starch or flour	1 tbsp
1 tbsp	Water	1 tbsp

1. Place the slices of beef between sheets of wax [greaseproof] paper and pound until thin. Trim the slices of beef so that they measure about 3 in / 7 cm wide and 4 in / 10 cm long. Finely grind [mince] the pieces trimmed off, together with the bacon. Peel and chop the garlic.
2. Mix the ground [minced] meat trimmings and bacon with the garlic, dried thyme and parsley. Season with a pinch of allspice, a little salt and a lot of pepper.
3. Divide the stuffing into 6 equal portions and place on the slices of beef. Roll them up and tie with kitchen string.
4. Peel and grate the carrot. Peel and thinly slice the onion. Lay the pork rind in a flameproof casserole, skin side down, and add the carrot, onion, bay leaf and thyme sprig. Lay the beef rolls on top and cook, covered, over a medium heat for 30 minutes.
5. Pour over the wine. Bring to a boil over a high heat, then add the stock. Cook gently, covered, for 45 minutes.
6. Preheat the oven to 425°F / 220°C / Gas Mark 7.
7. Take the lid off the casserole and transfer the dish to the oven. Continue cooking for 15 minutes, basting the beef rolls with the cooking liquid often.
8. Arrange the beef rolls on a warmed serving dish and keep hot. Take the rind out of the casserole and skim the fat from the sauce. Dissolve the potato starch in the water, add to the casserole and stir over a gentle heat to thicken the sauce.
9. Pour the sauce over the beef rolls and serve.

Queue de boeuf aux carottes

Oxtail and Carrots

00:20   02:30

American	Ingredients	Metric/Imperial
2 lb	Oxtail	1 kg / 2 lb
5	Large onions	5
¼ cup	Oil	4 tbsp
10	Carrots	10
1	Fresh thyme sprig	1
1	Bay leaf	1
2	Fresh tarragon sprigs	2
	Salt and pepper	
1 cup	Dry white wine	250 ml / 8 fl oz

1. Have the butcher cut the oxtail into pieces about 3 in / 7 cm long.
2. Peel and thinly slice the onions.
3. Heat the oil in a flameproof casserole. Add the pieces of oxtail and onions and cook over a gentle heat for about 6-8 minutes or until golden brown.
4. Peel and thinly slice the carrots. Add them to the casserole with the thyme, bay leaf, tarragon, and salt and pepper to taste. Add the wine. Cover and simmer very gently for 2½ hours. Serve with rice or noodles.

Fondue bourguignonne

Beef Fondue

00:40   00:00
done at table

American	Ingredients	Metric/Imperial
1 quart	Mayonnaise (see page 119)	1 l / 1¾ pints
2	Garlic cloves	2
1 tbsp	Capers	1 tbsp
3	Fresh tarragon sprigs	3
1	Small bunch of fresh chives	1
2 tbsp	Tomato ketchup	2 tbsp
1 tsp	Curry powder	1 tsp
	Salt and pepper	
2½ lb	Steak tenderloin [fillet, sirloin, rump]	1.25 kg / 2½ lb
	Small pickled cocktail onions	
	Assorted dill pickles [gherkins]	
1 quart	Oil	1 l / 1¾ pints

1. Divide the mayonnaise equally into 5 portions. Peel and crush the garlic. Finely chop the capers, the tarragon leaves and the chives. Flavor the first portion of mayonnaise with the tomato ketchup, the second with the garlic, the third with the capers, chives and tarragon, and the fourth with the curry powder. Leave the fifth plain. Check the seasoning of each of the sauces and adjust if necessary with salt and pepper. Keep cool.
2. Cut the meat into large chunks. Put the onions and pickles in small serving dishes.
3. Heat the oil and pour into a metal fondue pot. Place over a burner in the center of the table. Each diner cooks his meat in the hot oil, and eats it with the sauce of his choice.

Langue de boeuf au gros sel
Tongue with Vegetables

	00:00	03:00
American	**Ingredients**	**Metric/Imperial**
1 (4 lb)	Fresh beef [ox] tongue	1 (2 kg / 4 lb)
2½ quarts	Water	2.5 l / 5 pints
1	Onion	1
1	Bouquet garni	1
1	Clove	1
	Sea salt	
6	Carrots	6
6	Leeks	6
6	Turnips	6
6	Potatoes	6
	Salt	

1. Place the tongue in a flameproof casserole, cover with plenty of cold water and bring to a boil over a medium heat. Turn down the heat and simmer very gently for 25 minutes, skimming off the scum from time to time.
2. Drain the tongue and immediately plunge it in cold water. Leave it there until it is almost completely cold.
3. Drain the tongue. Remove the white skin. Wash out the casserole and replace the tongue in it. Cover with the measured water and bring to a boil.
4. Peel the onion and add to the casserole, together with the bouquet garni, clove and 2 teaspoons sea salt. Half-cover and simmer gently for 1 hour.
5. Peel the carrots, leeks and turnips. Add them to the casserole and cook for 45 minutes longer.
6. Meanwhile, scrub the potatoes and cook them in boiling salted water for 20 minutes. Drain and peel. Keep warm.
7. Remove the tongue from the casserole and slice it thinly. Arrange the slices on a warmed serving dish and surround with the drained vegetables and potatoes. Pour some of the cooking liquid over everything. Serve the rest of the cooking liquid separately and have on the table dishes of sea salt, dill pickles [gherkins], mustard and pickled onions.

Queue de boeuf en hochepot
Oxtail Hot Pot

	00:30	03:30
American	**Ingredients**	**Metric/Imperial**
2 lb	Oxtail	1 kg / 2 lb
2	Fresh pig's feet	2
1	Pig's ear	1
	Sea salt	
1	Small head of cabbage	1
4	Onions	4
8	Carrots	8
6	Turnips	6
8	Potatoes	8

1. Have the butcher cut the oxtail into 3 in / 7 cm pieces. Quarter the pig's feet.
2. Place the pieces of oxtail, pig's feet and ear into a stewpot. Cover with plenty of water and add a handful of sea salt. Bring to a boil, skimming off the scum, then cover and simmer gently for 1½ hours.

3. Quarter the cabbage and cut out the core. Peel the onions, carrots and turnips.
4. Add the onions, carrots and turnips to the stewpot. Cook for 45 minutes longer, then add the cabbage. Continue cooking for 45-50 minutes, still simmering gently.
5. Cook the potatoes in boiling salted water and drain.
6. Remove the pig's ear with a slotted spoon and cut it into wide strips. Place these in the center of a warmed serving dish together with the pig's feet and the pieces of oxtail. Surround with the drained vegetables and serve very hot with sea salt, mustard, small pickled onions and dill pickles [gherkins].

Oxtail hotpot

Rosbif
Roast Beef

	00:05	00:45
American	**Ingredients**	**Metric/Imperial**
1 (3 lb)	Boneless sirloin roast, tied with string	1 (1.5 kg / 3 lb)
¼ cup	Butter	50 g / 2 oz
	Salt and pepper	
½ cup	Very hot water	125 ml / 4 fl oz

1. Take the meat out of the refrigerator 1 hour before cooking.
2. Preheat the oven to 450°F / 260°C / Gas Mark 9.
3. Put the meat in a roasting pan and roast for 15 minutes. Take the meat out of the oven and remove the covering of fat. Dot the meat with the butter cut into pieces, sprinkle with salt and return to the oven. Reduce the heat to 425°F / 220°C / Gas Mark 7 and continue roasting for 20-30 minutes, according to the thickness of the meat and how well done you want it to be.
4. Transfer the roast to a carving board, sprinkle with more salt and keep warm.
5. Pour the very hot water into the roasting pan and bring to a boil over a high heat on top of the stove, scraping the bottom of the pan with a wooden spatula. Pour this gravy into a sauceboat.
6. Slice the meat and pour any juice produced into the gravy.

Palets du Poitou à la moelle

Poitou Meatcakes with Beef Marrow

◤▷	00:20		00:15 ⊑

American	Ingredients	Metric/Imperial
1 cup	Milk	250 ml / 8 fl oz
2 cups	Bread crumbs	125 g / 4 oz
2	Medium-size onions	2
¼ cup	Butter	50 g / 2 oz
¾ lb	Beef marrow	350 g / 12 oz
1¼ lb	Lean ground [minced] beef	625 g / 1¼ lb
2	Eggs	2
	Grated nutmeg	
	Salt and pepper	
3 tbsp	Oil	3 tbsp
2 tbsp	White wine	2 tbsp
1	Lemon	1
1 tbsp	Chopped fresh parsley	1 tbsp

1. Heat the milk in a small saucepan and add the bread crumbs. Stir well to make a smooth, slightly sticky mixture. Remove from the heat and allow to cool.
2. Peel and chop the onions. Heat half the butter in a frying pan, add the onions and cook gently until slightly colored.
3. Mash the beef marrow in a bowl with a fork. Add the beef and mix well. Add the bread crumb mixture, onions, eggs, a pinch of nutmeg, and salt and pepper to taste. Mix all the ingredients thoroughly together with your hands.
4. Divide the mixture into 6 equal portions and shape into flat cakes or patties about ¾ in /1.5 cm thick.
5. Heat the oil with the rest of the butter in the frying pan. Add the patties and cook over a gentle heat for about 15 minutes or until golden brown on both sides. Arrange the patties on a warmed serving dish and keep hot.
6. Discard the fat from the pan. Add the wine to the pan and bring to a boil, scraping the bottom of the pan with a wooden spatula to detach the meat residue. Add the juice of the lemon and the parsley.
7. Pour the sauce over the meatcakes and serve immediately.

Steaks grillés

Pan-Broiled [Grilled] Steak

◤▷	00:00	00:04 to 00:08 ⊑

American	Ingredients	Metric/Imperial
6 (5 oz)	Steaks	6 (150 g / 5 oz)
3 tbsp	Oil	3 tbsp
	Salt and pepper	
¼ cup	Butter	50 g / 2 oz

1. Heat a steak or chop grill or griddle for 15 minutes before cooking.
2. Brush the steaks with the oil and place on the grill. Cook 2-4 minutes on each side, according to taste.
3. Transfer the steaks to a warmed serving platter and sprinkle with salt and pepper. Put a pat of butter on each steak and serve hot.

Grillade des bateliers du Rhône

Rhone Boatmen's Casserole

◤▷	00:30		02:00 ⊑
	plus marinating		

American	Ingredients	Metric/Imperial
1¾ lb	Chuck steak	900 g / 1¾ lb
1¼ lb	Onions	625 g / 1¼ lb
⅔ cup	White wine	150 ml / ¼ pint
	Salt and pepper	
¾ cup	Butter	175 g / 6 oz
2	Garlic cloves	2
1	Bouquet garni	1
3	Salted anchovies or	3
6	Canned [tinned] anchovy fillets	6
1 tbsp	Flour	1 tbsp

1. Cut the beef into 3 thick slices. Place in an earthenware pot or glass bowl. Peel and chop the onions and add to the bowl with the wine and salt and pepper. Marinate overnight.
2. The next day, drain the meat, reserving the marinade. Heat ¼ cup [50 g / 2 oz] butter in a frying pan, add to the meat slices and brown on all sides.
3. Strain the marinade into a cast iron casserole. Add the meat slices, peeled and crushed garlic and bouquet garni (which should not contain too much thyme or bay leaf). Simmer gently for 2-3 hours.
4. Meanwhile, bone the anchovies by lifting up the flesh from the tail end with a small pointed knife. Remove the skin and all the bones under running water (this will also make the fish less salty). If using canned fillets, drain from their oil, rinse under running water and dry on paper towels. Mash the fish in a bowl with the rest of the butter and the flour.
5. Add a little cooled sauce from the casserole to the anchovy butter, then mix into the sauce in the casserole. Serve hot.

Hamburger steak

Hamburgers

◤▷	00:15	00:04 to 00:05 ⊑

American	Ingredients	Metric/Imperial
2 lb	Ground [minced] steak	1 kg / 2 lb
¼ cup	Butter	50 g / 2 oz
	Salt and pepper	
	Chopped scallions [spring onions] or chives	
6	Eggs (optional)	6

1. Divide the steak into 6 equal portions and shape into patties.
2. Heat the butter in a large frying pan. Add the hamburgers and cook for 2-4 minutes on each side; they are medium-rare when small drops of blood collect on the surface.
3. Season with salt and pepper, and sprinkle with chopped scallions or chives.

Cook's tip: you can top each hamburger with a fried egg. Or you can spread the hamburgers generously with mustard, top with a thick slice of gruyère, comté or gouda cheese and brown in the oven or under the broiler [grill].

Pot-au-feu
Beef Stew

	00:30		03:00

American	Ingredients	Metric/Imperial
4 quarts	Water	4 l / 7 pints
2 lb	Flank steak	1 kg / 2 lb
1¼ lb	Shank [shin]	625 g / 1¼ lb
	Salt	
6	Leeks	6
1	Head of celery	1
1	Onion	1
4	Cloves	4
6	Carrots	6
6	Turnips	6
1	Bouquet garni	1
10	Black peppercorns	10
3	Beef marrow bones	3

1. Pour the water into a stewpot, add the meat and 1 tablespoon of salt and bring to a boil over a high heat. Skim off the froth as it appears. Cover and simmer gently for 1 hour.
2. Meanwhile, prepare all the vegetables. Trim and clean the leeks, then tie them together with kitchen string. Trim and clean the head of celery and tie the stalks together in a bundle with kitchen string. Peel the onion and stud with the cloves. Peel the carrots and turnips and leave them whole.
3. Add the carrots, onion and bouquet garni to the stewpot. About 30 minutes later, add the leeks, celery, turnips and peppercorns. Add a little more water if necessary. Continue cooking for 1½ hours, still covered and still simmering gently.
4. Wrap the marrow bones separately in small pieces of cheesecloth or muslin. A few moments before serving, add the marrow bones to the stewpot.
5. Discard the bouquet garni and onion. Arrange the pieces of meat on a warmed serving dish and surround them with the drained vegetables. Unwrap the marrow bones and put them in a serving bowl; pour some of the stock over them to keep them hot.
6. Serve immediately with sea salt, dill pickles [gherkins] and mustard.

Steaks hachés sur toasts
Hamburgers with Ham and Cheese

	00:15		00:10

American	Ingredients	Metric/Imperial
1	Large onion	1
2	Large tomatoes	2
5 tbsp	Butter	65 g / 2½ oz
2 lb	Ground [minced] steak	1 kg / 2 lb
1	Handful of chopped fresh parsley	1
	Salt and pepper	
6	Slices of white bread	6
3	Slices of cooked ham	3
6	Slices of emmental or gruyère cheese	6

1. Preheat the oven to 430°F / 230°C / Gas Mark 8.
2. Peel and finely chop the onion. Cut the tomatoes into slices about ½ in /1 cm thick.
3. Heat 1 tablespoon [15 g / ½ oz] of butter in a saucepan, add the onion and cook until softened. Put the onion in a large mixing bowl and add the steak and parsley. Season generously with salt and pepper; the mixture should be well-seasoned. Mix well with the hands, then divide into 6 equal portions and shape into patties.
4. Melt the rest of the butter in a frying pan. Add the patties and brown over high heat on both sides (2-4 minutes). Drain and keep hot.
5. Toast the bread. On each slice, place half a slice of ham, cut to fit, a slice of tomato and a hamburger. Top with a slice of cheese.
6. Place on a baking sheet and brown in the oven.

Pepper steak

Steaks au poivre à la crème
Pepper Steak with Cream

	00:07		00:04 to 00:08
	plus resting		

American	Ingredients	Metric/Imperial
6 (6 oz)	Filets mignons [fillet steaks]	6 (175 g / 6 oz)
	Salt	
	Crushed black peppercorns	
2 tbsp	Butter	25 g / 1 oz
3 tbsp	Brandy	3 tbsp
6 tbsp	Crème fraîche (see page 122)	6 tbsp

1. Sprinkle the steaks with salt and cover both sides with crushed peppercorns. Press with the palm of the hand to make the peppercorns stick on well. Set aside for 30 minutes.
2. Heat the butter in a frying pan, add the steaks and cook for 2-4 minutes on each side, according to taste. Heat the brandy in a small saucepan, pour it over the steaks and set alight, lifting the steaks up so that the flame burns all over the meat.

When the flame goes out, transfer the steaks to a warmed serving dish and keep hot.

3. Add the crème fraîche to the frying pan and heat through, scraping the bottom of the pan with a wooden spatula. Spoon this sauce over the steaks and serve.

Steak aux trois fromages

Hamburgers with Three Cheeses

	00:10	00:04 to 00:08

American	Ingredients	Metric/Imperial
6 tbsp	Cream cheese	6 tbsp
1½ lb	Ground [minced] steak	750 g / 1½ lb
3 - 4 tbsp	Grated parmesan cheese	3 - 4 tbsp
6 tbsp	Grated gruyère cheese	6 tbsp
3 tbsp	Chopped fresh parsley	3 tbsp
	Grated nutmeg	
	Salt and pepper	
¼ cup	Oil	4 tbsp

1. Put the cream cheese in a mixing bowl and add the steak. Mix together well, then add the parmesan, gruyère, parsley, a pinch of nutmeg, and salt and pepper to taste. Mix together with the hands.

2. Divide into 6 equal portions and shape into patties.

3. Heat the oil in a frying pan, add the patties and cook for about 2-4 minutes on each side, according to taste.

Steak tartare

Steak tartare

	00:10	00:00

American	Ingredients	Metric/Imperial
6	Egg yolks	6
3 tbsp	Prepared mustard	3 tbsp
	Worcestershire sauce	
2	Lemons	2
	Salt and pepper	
1 cup	Oil	250 ml / 8 fl oz
2 lb	Ground [minced] steak	1 kg / 2 lb
1 cup	Capers	125 g / 4 oz
1	Bunch of fresh chives or parsley	1
4	Onions	4

1. Put the egg yolks into a mixing bowl and add the mustard, a trickle of Worcestershire sauce, and the juice of the lemons, and salt and pepper to taste. Gradually add the oil, beating all the time with a wire whisk as if you were making mayonnaise.

2. Add the meat (which should be best quality lean steak) and mix well. Finely chop the capers and chives or parsley and add to the bowl. Peel and finely chop the onions and add. Mix well.

3. Divide the meat mixture into 6 equal portions and shape into patties. Serve immediately.

Cook's tip: you could also serve all the seasoning ingredients in small bowls and the meat on its own, with the egg yolks in their shells placed on top of each portion.

Rognons de boeuf au bordeaux

Kidneys with Red Wine Sauce

	00:30	00:30

American	Ingredients	Metric/Imperial
2	Large onions	2
4	Shallots	4
1	Garlic clove	1
2 tbsp	Lard	25 g / 1 oz
1¼ cups	Red wine (Bordeaux)	300 ml / ½ pint
⅔ cup	Water	150 ml / ¼ pint
2 tbsp	Butter	25 g / 1 oz
2 tbsp	Flour	2 tbsp
1	Fresh thyme sprig	1
½	Bay leaf	½
	Cayenne pepper	
	Salt and pepper	
2	Beef kidneys	2

1. Peel and finely chop the onions and shallots. Peel and crush the garlic. Heat half of the lard in a flameproof casserole, add the onions and shallots and cook over a gentle heat until very soft. Pour over the wine and water and cook, covered, at a gentle simmer for 20 minutes.

2. Mix 1 tablespoon [15 g / ½ oz] of butter with the flour to make a paste.

3. Remove the casserole from the heat. Add the butter/flour paste, the leaves from the thyme sprig, the garlic, bay leaf, a pinch of cayenne, and salt and pepper to taste. Stir over a gentle heat until the sauce begins to thicken, then remove from the heat and set aside.

4. Clean the kidneys, cutting out the core and white parts with a knife or pair of scissors. Cut the kidneys into large cubes.

5. Heat the rest of the lard and butter in a large frying pan, add the cubes of kidney and cook, stirring, until browned all over and a lot of juice has been rendered.

6. Pour the contents of the frying pan into the casserole and continue cooking for about 8 minutes, stirring the mixture occasionally.

7. Taste and adjust the seasoning and discard the bay leaf. Serve with fried potato cubes sprinkled with chopped chervil and chives.

Cook's tip: cooked this way, kidneys have an excellent flavor and are juicy and succulent.

Steaks à la poêle

Fried Steak

	00:05	00:02 to 00:04 each side

American	Ingredients	Metric/Imperial
3 tbsp	Oil	3 tbsp
6 (5 oz)	Steaks	6 (150 g / 5 oz)
	Salt and pepper	

1. Heat the oil in a frying pan. When it is hot, add the steaks and cook for 2-4 minutes on each side according to taste.

2. Place the hot steaks on a warmed serving dish and sprinkle with salt and pepper.

Tajine aux oeufs d'or

Spiced Beef with Golden Eggs

	00:30		04:00

American	Ingredients	Metric/Imperial
2 lb	Chuck steak	1 kg / 2 lb
1 lb	Shank [shin]	500 g / 1 lb
2	Garlic cloves	2
1 lb	Onions	500 g / 1 lb
¼ cup	Oil	4 tbsp
	Saffron powder	
2 tsp	Ground ginger	2 tsp
3 cups	Water	750 ml / 1 ¼ pints
	Salt	
1	Small bunch of fresh coriander	1
6	Hard-cooked eggs	6
1 tbsp	Butter	15 g / ½ oz
2 cups	Blanched almonds	250 g / 8 oz

1. Cut the beef into large chunks and set aside. Peel and chop the garlic. Peel and thinly slice the onions.
2. Heat the oil in a flameproof casserole. Remove from the heat and add the garlic, 2 pinches of saffron powder, the ginger and ⅔ cup [150 ml / ¼ pint] water. Sprinkle with salt and mix all these ingredients together.
3. Add the meat to the casserole, stirring so that it becomes well coated with the spices. Add the onion slices, remaining water and, finally, the bunch of coriander. Place the casserole on a medium heat and cover. When boiling point is reached, lower the heat and simmer the casserole for 4 hours over a very low heat.
4. Remove the meat with a slotted spoon and keep hot. Pour the cooking liquid into a small saucepan and reduce for about 10 minutes over a medium heat until thick.
5. Meanwhile, add 4 pinches of saffron powder to a pan of boiling water. Add the shelled eggs and stir until they have taken on a uniform golden color. Drain.
6. Heat the butter in a frying pan, add the almonds and cook until lightly browned.
7. Return the meat to the reduced sauce and reheat for a few minutes. Place in a deep serving dish and arrange the eggs on top. Sprinkle over the almonds.

Tournedos à la moelle

Steaks with Beef Marrow

	00:10		00:04 to 00:12

American	Ingredients	Metric/Imperial
6 (5 oz)	Filets mignons [fillet steaks]	6 (150 g / 5 oz)
1 tbsp	Oil	1 tbsp
	Salt and pepper	
5 oz	Beef marrow	150 g / 5 oz
¼ cup	Butter	50 g / 2 oz
3 tbsp	Chopped fresh parsley	3 tbsp

1. About 30 minutes before cooking, brush the steaks with oil and sprinkle with pepper.
2. Cut the marrow into 6 slices ½ in / 1 cm thick. Cook them gently in simmering salted water for 3-4 minutes.
3. Meanwhile, cook the steaks. Use a frying pan with no extra fat, (or a little butter, if preferred), or a very hot steak or chop grill [griddle] or the broiler [grill]. Allow 2 minutes on each side for very rare meat, 4 minutes for rare meat, and 6 minutes for medium rare.
4. Arrange the steaks on a warmed serving dish and put a pat of butter on top of each. Place a drained slice of marrow on each steak and sprinkle with the chopped parsley.

Cook's tip: this delicious dish reaches the heights of haute cuisine if served with a burgundy sauce (see page 124).

Tournedos maître d'hôtel

Steaks with Parsley Butter Sauce

	00:10		00:04 to 00:08

American	Ingredients	Metric/Imperial
½ cup	Butter	125 g / 4 oz
1 tsp	Lemon juice	1 tsp
1 tsp	Prepared mustard	1 tsp
2 tbsp	Chopped fresh parsley	2 tbsp
	Salt and pepper	
6 (5 oz)	Filets mignons [fillet steaks]	6

1. If you are using a steak or chop grill [griddle], preheat it until it is as hot as possible.
2. Melt the butter over a low heat and whisk until it takes on the consistency of cream. Remove from the heat and add the lemon juice and mustard, still whisking. Add the parsley and salt and pepper to taste and stir to mix.
3. Place the steaks on the very hot grill and cook for 2-4 minutes on each side, according to taste. Alternatively, cook the steaks in butter in a frying pan.
4. Arrange the steaks on a warmed serving dish, sprinkle with salt and serve the parsley butter sauce in a sauceboat.

Cook's tip: you can also serve the steaks with a béarnaise sauce (see page 126).

Saffron: an essential ingredient for spiced beef with golden eggs

Rôti à l'ail en chemise

Braised Beef with Garlic

⊳ 00:10   00:30 to 00:40 🍲

American	Ingredients	Metric/Imperial
1 (2½ lb)	Boneless rump [topside] or tip roast	1 (1.25 kg / 2½ lb)
5	Garlic cloves	5
3 tbsp	Oil	3 tbsp
	Salt and pepper	
3	Fresh rosemary sprigs	3
⅔ cup	Water	150 ml / ¼ pint

1. The piece of tied beef should be about 2½ in / 6 cm thick.
2. Remove all but the innermost layer of skin from the cloves of garlic. With a pointed knife, cut a groove the length of each clove.
3. Heat the oil in a flameproof casserole, add the meat, and cook for 3 minutes on each side over high heat, until it is well browned. Turn down the heat to the lowest possible setting. Season with salt and pepper, add the cloves of garlic and the rosemary and continue cooking for 25 minutes for rare meat, or 40 minutes for medium-rare meat. Turn the meat every 10 minutes using a spatula (do not prick it with a fork or the juices will run out).
4. Untie the meat and slice it thinly. Arrange the meat on a warmed serving dish and surround with the cloves of garlic. Keep hot.
5. Discard three-quarters of the cooking fat and pour the water into the casserole. Bring to a boil, scraping up the meat residue with a wooden spoon. Pour this gravy into a sauceboat and serve with the meat.

Chateaubriand – slices of beef fillet

Tournedos Rossini

Steaks with Truffle Sauce

⊳ 00:10   00:20 🍲

American	Ingredients	Metric/Imperial
3 oz	Bacon	75 g / 3 oz
2	Shallots	2
1 tbsp	Oil	1 tbsp
2 tbsp	Flour	2 tbsp
1 tbsp	Tomato paste [purée]	1 tbsp
2 tbsp	Chopped fresh parsley	2 tbsp
⅔ cup	Beef broth	150 ml / ¼ pint
	Salt and pepper	
1	Small can of truffle peelings	1
2 tbsp	Butter	25 g / 1 oz
6 (5 oz)	Filets mignons [fillet steaks]	6 (150 g / 5 oz)

1. Cut the bacon into matchstick strips. Peel and finely chop the shallots. Heat the oil in a small heavy-based saucepan, add the bacon and shallots and cook until the bacon is golden brown. Remove the bacon and set aside.
2. Add the flour to the pan and cook, stirring, until the flour is golden. Add the tomato paste, parsley and cooked bacon. Gradually stir in the stock. Add salt and pepper to taste and simmer for a few minutes.
3. Remove the bacon with a slotted spoon and discard it. Purée the sauce in a blender or food processor. Add the drained truffles and keep warm.
4. Melt the butter in a frying pan, add the steaks and cook for 2-4 minutes on each side, according to taste.
5. Serve the steaks coated with the sauce.

Buying and cooking veal

American cuts to choose	Cooking methods
leg, loin, rib (rack), boneless shoulder	roast
steaks or cutlets (scaloppine), chops, cubes for kebabs	broil, fry
breast, riblets, chops, steaks or cutlets, shank	braise
veal for stew	stew

British cuts to choose	Cooking methods
best end, breast, leg (including topside or cushion), loin, shoulder or oyster, fillet	roast
chump chops, best end neck cutlets, loin chops, escalopes, fillet steak, cubes for kebabs	grill, fry
breast, riblets, knuckle, middle neck cutlets	braise
shin, pie veal, scrag	stew

Veal in wine and mustard sauce (see page 352)

Veal cuts

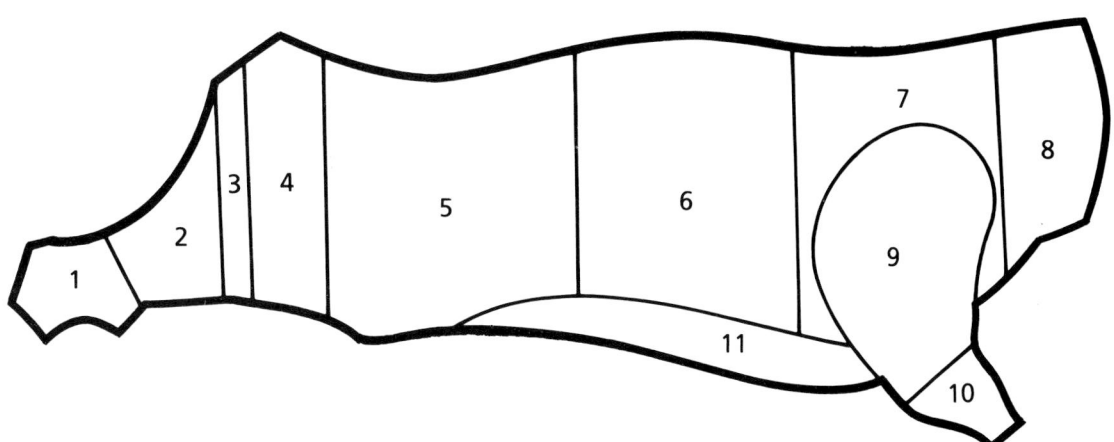

Veal: American cuts
1. Knuckle
2. Leg from which veal birds are made; if boned, round roast
3. Round steaks (scallops)
4. Rump roast
5. Loin roast: loin chops; loin steaks (nearest to tail end)
6. Center rib chops or roast
7. Shoulder chops
8. City chicken, when cut into cubes
9. Shoulder
10. Shank
11. Breast

Veal: English cuts
1. Knuckle or shin
2. Leg
3. Escallops or scallops
4. Fillet roast; escallops in slices
5. Rump end of loin
6. Saddle, if both sides of back are used; loin roast or loin cutlets
7. Best end of neck cutlets, or roast if boned
8. Middle neck cutlets, or roast if boned
9. Scrag end of neck
10. Shoulder
11. Knuckle and foot
12. Breast

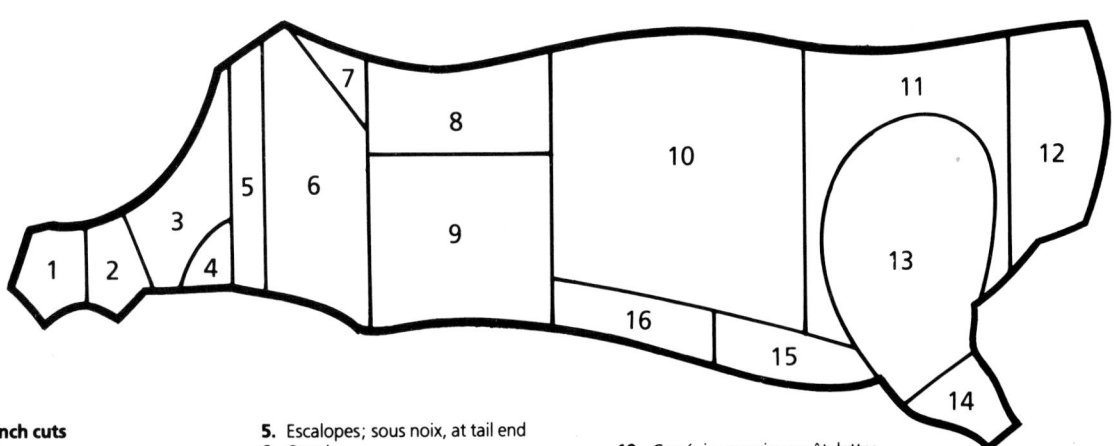

Veal: French cuts
1. Crosse
2. Jarret
3. Noix (cuiseau): grenadins; rouelles, nearest to tail
4. Fricandeau
5. Escalopes; sous noix, at tail end
6. Quasi
7. Noix patissière
8. Selle; if both sides of back are used: filet; longe
9. Longe, rognon, and rognonnade
10. Carré, in one piece; côtelettes premières
11. Côtelettes découvertes
12. Collet
13. Épaule
14. Jarret
15. Poitrine (flanchet)
16. Tendron

Côtes de veau normande
Normandy Veal Chops

◣▷ 00:30 — 00:30 ▭

American	Ingredients	Metric/Imperial
⅔ cup	Butter	150 g / 5 oz
6 (6 oz)	Veal loin chops	6 (175 g / 6 oz)
	Salt and pepper	
1 cup	Crème fraîche (see page 122)	250 ml / 8 fl oz
6 tbsp	Calvados or applejack	6 tbsp
2 lb	Golden Delicious apples	1 kg / 2 lb
1 tbsp	Sugar	1 tbsp

1. Preheat the oven to 350°F / 180°C / Gas Mark 4.
2. Heat ¼ cup [50 g / 2 oz] of the butter in a frying pan. Add the chops a few at a time and brown on both sides. As they are browned, transfer them to an ovenproof dish. Season the chops with salt and pepper and put to one side.
3. Add the crème fraîche to the frying pan and stir to scrape up the meat residue from the bottom of the pan. Reduce by one-third over a medium heat. Stir in the calvados.
4. Pour the crème sauce over the chops. Place in the oven and bake for 15-20 minutes.
5. Meanwhile, peel the apples and cut into quarters. Remove the seeds and core. Heat the rest of the butter in a frying pan, add the apple quarters and cook until golden. Halfway through this cooking period, sprinkle with the sugar.
6. To serve, arrange the chops on a warmed serving dish and surround with the apples. Adjust the seasoning of the sauce and pour over the chops.

Chaussons au jambon et au fromage
Veal, Ham and Cheese Turnovers

◣▷ 00:10 — 00:10 ▭

American	Ingredients	Metric/Imperial
6 (¼ lb)	Thin veal scaloppine [escalopes]	6 (125 g / 4 oz)
	Grated nutmeg	
12	Large fresh basil leaves	12
3	Thin slices of bayonne ham or cooked ham	3
¼ lb	Gruyère cheese	125 g / 4 oz
2 tbsp	Oil	2 tbsp
6 tbsp	Butter	75 g / 3 oz
	Salt and pepper	
5 tbsp	White wine	5 tbsp

1. Lay the slices of veal out flat and sprinkle with a little nutmeg. Lay 2 basil leaves on each one. Cut the ham slices in half and lay these on the veal. Cut the cheese into 6 thin slices and arrange these on top of the ham, making sure to leave a ½ in / 1 cm gap all around the edge of the meat.
2. Fold over each scaloppine in half and pin the edges together with a wooden toothpick.
3. Heat the oil in a frying pan and add the butter. As soon as the butter foams, add the veal turnovers and cook for 5 minutes on each side. Season with salt and pepper during cooking.

4. Transfer the veal to a warmed serving platter and keep hot.
5. Pour the wine into the frying pan and bring to a boil over a high heat, scraping up all the meat residue from the bottom of the pan. Reduce by about half, then spoon over the veal and serve hot.

Brochettes de veau
Veal Kebabs

◣▷ 00:10 plus marinating — 00:10 to 00:15 ▭

American	Ingredients	Metric/Imperial
2 lb	Boneless veal from the round [topside or cushion]	1 kg / 2 lb
2 tsp	Olive oil	2 tsp
	Paprika	
	Salt	
¼ lb	Smoked bacon slices	125 g / 4 oz

1. Cut the veal into 1½ in / 4 cm cubes. Put them in a mixing bowl and add the oil, a pinch of paprika and salt to taste. Marinate for 1 hour.
2. Preheat the broiler [grill] or heat a steak or chop grill.
3. Halve the bacon slices crosswise and roll them up loosely.
4. Thread the veal cubes and bacon rolls alternately onto 6 skewers. Cook the kebabs for 10-15 minutes. If cooking under the broiler, baste the kebabs with the marinating oil when you turn them.

Confit à la sauge
Veal Cooked in Goose Fat

◣▷ 00:10 plus macerating — 02:00 ▭

American	Ingredients	Metric/Imperial
3 tbsp	Sea salt	3 tbsp
2 tsp	Sugar	2 tsp
1 (2½ lb)	Piece of boneless veal round [topside or cushion], rolled, larded and tied	1 (1.25 kg / 2½ lb)
4	Garlic cloves	4
1 tsp	Pepper	1 tsp
4	Fresh sage leaves	4
3 lb (6 cups)	Goose fat	1.5 kg / 3 lb

1. Mix together the salt and sugar. Rub this mixture all over the veal so that it penetrates the meat. Leave to macerate for 12 hours.
2. The next day, rinse the veal under running water and pat dry with paper towels.
3. Peel the garlic cloves, cut each one in half and roll in the pepper. Cut the sage leaves in half. Make 8 deep incisions in the veal with a small pointed knife and insert in each one half a clove of garlic and half a sage leaf. If there is any pepper left over, sprinkle it over the meat.
4. Put the veal in a flameproof casserole and add the goose fat. Cover the casserole and cook over a gentle heat for 2 hours, never allowing the goose fat to boil — it should be just simmering.
5. Drain the veal and slice it. Serve hot, accompanied by noodles and a green vegetable.

Côtes de veau en papillotes

Veal Chops Baked in Foil

⏱ 00:10   00:40 🍲

American	Ingredients	Metric/Imperial
4	Onions	4
4	Shallots	4
1½ lb	Button mushrooms	750 g / 1½ lb
½ cup	Butter	125 g / 4 oz
	Salt and pepper	
6	Thin slices of bayonne ham or prosciutto	6
6 (6 oz)	Veal chops	6 (175 g / 6 oz)

1. Preheat the oven to 425°F / 220°C / Gas Mark 7.
2. Peel and finely chop the onions and shallots. Chop the mushrooms as finely as possible. Melt half of the butter in a frying pan, add the onions and shallots and cook for 5 minutes over a gentle heat until softened. Turn up the heat, add the chopped mushrooms and continue cooking for 10 minutes, stirring well, until no liquid remains. Remove from the heat, season with salt and pepper and set aside.
3. Cut the slices of ham in half. Set aside.
4. Melt the remaining butter in the frying pan, add the veal chops and cook for 4-8 minutes on each side to brown well. Remove from the pan and season with salt and pepper.
5. Cut 6 pieces of foil each large enough to wrap a chop. Butter each piece of foil. Place ½ slice of ham on each, then add a spoonful of the mushroom mixture. Put the chops on top. Add the remaining mushroom mixture and finally another ½ slice of ham to each. Seal the packages securely.
6. Place the packages on a rack in the oven and cook for 15 minutes. Serve very hot in the foil.

Blanquette de veau

Veal in a White Sauce

⏱ 00:10   02:00 🍲

American	Ingredients	Metric/Imperial
2½ lb	Boneless breast of veal	1.25 kg / 2½ lb
2	Carrots	2
1	Onion	1
1	Shallot	1
1	Bouquet garni	1
	Salt and pepper	
5 oz	Button mushrooms (optional)	150 g / 5 oz
2 tbsp	Butter	25 g / 1 oz
2 tbsp	Flour	2 tbsp
1	Egg yolk	1
½ cup	Crème fraîche (see page 122)	125 ml / 4 fl oz
½	Lemon	½

1. Cut the veal into 1 in / 2.5 cm wide strips. Put them into a flameproof casserole and just cover with cold water. Bring to a boil, skimming off the froth.
2. Meanwhile, peel and slice the carrots, onion and shallot. Add to the casserole with the bouquet garni. Season with salt and pepper and simmer very gently for 2 hours.

3. Halfway through the cooking period, add the mushrooms, if used.
4. With a fork, mix the butter and flour together to a paste. Take the casserole off the heat and add this paste. Bring to a boil, stirring, and cook for 5 minutes.
5. Just before serving, mix the egg yolk with the crème fraîche. Remove the casserole from the heat and add the egg yolk mixture, stirring all the time. Add the juice of the ½ lemon. Discard the bouquet garni and serve.

Veal in white sauce

Coeurs de veau braisés

Braised Calves' Hearts

⏱ 00:10   01:20 🍲

American	Ingredients	Metric/Imperial
2	Calves' hearts	2
2 lb	Carrots	1 kg / 2 lb
20	Small onions	20
6 tbsp	Butter	75 g / 3 oz
1 tbsp	Oil	1 tbsp
1	Bouquet garni	1
3	Garlic cloves	3
	Salt and pepper	
½	Bottle of dry white wine	½
⅔ cup	Chicken stock	150 ml / ¼ pint

1. Rinse the hearts to remove any blood clots and pat dry. Peel and thinly slice the carrots. Peel the onions.
2. Melt the butter with the oil in a large flameproof casserole. Add the hearts and brown all over. Add the onions and carrots and cook over a high heat for about 5 minutes or until golden brown.
3. Add the bouquet garni and peeled garlic. Season with salt and pepper and add the wine and stock. Cover and cook for at least 1 hour.
4. To serve, slice the hearts and surround with the vegetables. Reduce the cooking liquid by one-third over a fast heat, discard the bouquet garni and pour into a sauceboat.

Cervelles de veau panées

Breaded Calves' Brains

	00:15 plus soaking and marinating	00:10

American	Ingredients	Metric/Imperial
2	Pairs of calves' brains	2
2 tbsp	Vinegar	2 tbsp
2	Garlic cloves	2
6 tbsp	Oil	6 tbsp
2	Lemons	2
1 tsp	Dried thyme	1 tsp
	Ground bay leaf	
	Salt and pepper	
1 cup	Bread crumbs	50 g / 2 oz
4	Eggs	4
1 cup	Flour	125 g / 4 oz
	Oil for deep frying	
1	Bunch of fresh parsley	1

1. Put the brains in a deep bowl and cover with cold water. Leave them to soak for 30 minutes.
2. Drain the brains and remove all fiberlike membranes and threads. Put the vinegar in the bowl, add fresh cold water and rinse the brains. Drain again and pat dry with paper towels. Cut the brains into thick slices. Place in a deep bowl.
3. Peel and crush the garlic and put into a small bowl. Add 6 tablespoons oil, the juice of the lemons, thyme, a pinch of ground bay leaf, and salt and pepper to taste. Mix well and pour over the slices of brain. Marinate for 1 hour.
4. Put the bread crumbs in a shallow dish. Break the eggs into another dish and beat to mix, then add 2 tablespoons of the marinade. Mix well. Put the flour in another dish.
5. Heat the oil for deep frying.
6. Dip the slices of brain first in the flour, then in the beaten egg and finally in the bread crumbs. Deep fry until golden, about 10 minutes. Remove with a slotted spoon and drain on paper towels. Deep fry the bunch of parsley for a few seconds or until golden. Drain and crumble over the slices of brain. Serve immediately.

Fricadelles au beurre

Rich Veal Patties

	00:20	00:10

American	Ingredients	Metric/Imperial
2 cups	Bread crumbs	125 g / 4 oz
¼ cup	Crème fraîche (see page 122)	4 tbsp
1	Large onion	1
½ cup	Butter, at room temperature	125 g / 4 oz
2	Eggs	2
1 lb	Ground [minced] veal	500 g / 1 lb
	Salt and pepper	
	Grated nutmeg	
3 tbsp	Oil	3 tbsp

1. Put the bread crumbs in a small saucepan and add the crème fraîche. Heat gently, stirring, to make a sticky paste. Remove from the heat.

2. Peel and finely chop the onion. Melt 2 tablespoons [25 g / 1 oz] of the butter in a frying pan, add the onion and cook over a gentle heat, stirring, until it becomes translucent.
3. Break the eggs into a large mixing bowl. Add the veal, the rest of the butter, the bread crumb paste and the onion. Season with salt, pepper and a pinch of nutmeg. Mix well with the hands, then shape into 6 patties.
4. Heat the oil in a frying pan, add the patties and cook for 3 minutes on each side over a medium heat or until browned and cooked through. Serve hot.

Cervelles au court-bouillon

Brains Poached in Court-Bouillon

	00:10 plus soaking	00:10

American	Ingredients	Metric/Imperial
2	Pairs of calves' brains	2
2 tbsp	Vinegar	2 tbsp
1 quart	Court-bouillon with white wine (see page 114)	1 l / 1¾ pints
1	Lemon	1

1. Put the brains in a deep bowl and cover with cold water. Leave them to soak for 30 minutes.
2. Drain the brains and remove all fiberlike membranes and threads. Put the vinegar in the bowl, add fresh cold water and rinse the brains. Drain again.
3. Pour the court-bouillon into a large saucepan and add the juice of the lemon and the brains. Bring to a boil slowly and simmer gently for 5 minutes, then remove from the heat and allow the brains to cool in the court-bouillon.
4. Drain the brains and pat dry carefully with paper towels.

Côtes de veau braisées

Braised Veal Chops

	00:15	01:15

American	Ingredients	Metric/Imperial
5	Carrots	5
3	Onions	3
1	Celery stalk	1
3 tbsp	Butter	40 g / 1½ oz
1	Piece of fresh pork rind	1
6	Veal chops	6
2	Garlic cloves	2
1 tbsp	Tomato paste [purée]	1 tbsp
⅔ cup	Dry white wine	150 ml / ¼ pint
⅔ cup	Chicken stock	150 ml / ¼ pint
1	Bouquet garni	1
	Salt and pepper	

1. Preheat the oven to 400°F / 200°C / Gas Mark 6.
2. Peel and dice the carrots and onions. Dice the celery. Heat the butter in a flameproof casserole, add the pork rind and allow this to render its fat for 2 minutes, stirring. Add the diced vegetables. Cook, stirring well, until golden brown.
3. Add the veal chops. Cover the casserole and cook over a gentle heat for 15 minutes, turning the chops once.

4. Peel and crush the garlic. Mix together the tomato paste, wine and stock. Add the garlic, tomato paste mixture, bouquet garni, and salt and pepper to taste to the casserole.
5. Cover the casserole, transfer to the oven and cook for 50 minutes. The liquid should be just simmering. If it bubbles too much, turn down the heat to 350°F / 180°C / Gas Mark 4.
6. Arrange the chops on a warmed serving dish. Discard the rind from the casserole. Skim the fat off the sauce, then strain it over the chops. Serve immediately.

Côtes de veau viennoise

Wiener Schnitzel

	00:30	00:12 to 00:16

American	Ingredients	Metric/Imperial
6	Boned veal loin chops, ¾ in / 1.5 cm thick	6
	Salt and pepper	
¼ cup	Flour	4 tbsp
1	Egg	1
2 tbsp	Oil	2 tbsp
1½ cups	Dry bread crumbs	125 g / 4 oz
3 tbsp	Butter	40 g / 1½ oz
6	Lemon slices	6
6	Anchovy fillets	6

1. Season the chops on both sides with salt and pepper and leave to one side for 10 minutes.
2. Put the flour on a plate. Lightly beat the egg with 1 tablespoon of the oil in another plate. Put the bread crumbs on a third plate. Coat the chops first in flour, then dip in egg and finally coat with crumbs.
3. Heat 1 tablespoon [15 g / ½ oz] of the butter and the rest of the oil in a frying pan. Add the chops and cook gently until they are golden, but not brown (about 6-8 minutes each side).
4. Top each chop with a lemon slice, a pat of butter and a rolled-up anchovy.

Côtes de veau flambées

Flamed Veal Chops

	00:10	00:35

American	Ingredients	Metric/Imperial
2 tbsp	Oil	2 tbsp
6 (6 oz)	Veal loin chops	6 (175 g / 6 oz)
14 oz	Button mushrooms	400 g / 14 oz
	Lemon juice	
3 tbsp	Butter	40 g / 1½ oz
½ cup	Brandy	125 ml / 4 fl oz
1 cup	Crème fraîche (see page 122)	250 ml / 8 fl oz
	Salt and pepper	
½ tsp	Flour	½ tsp

1. Heat the oil in a frying pan, add the chops — 2 or 3 at a time if necessary — and cook until they are golden but not brown, about 6-8 minutes on each side.
2. Meanwhile, reserve 6 of the mushrooms for the garnish and thinly slice the remainder. Sprinkle the mushrooms with a little lemon juice to keep them white. Melt 2 tablespoons [25 g /

1 oz] of butter in a frying pan, add all the mushrooms and cook, stirring occasionally, until all the liquid rendered has evaporated.
3. Drain the chops. Wipe out the frying pan, then melt the remaining butter in it. Return the chops to the pan. Pour over the brandy, heat briefly and set alight. Shake the pan until the flames have gone out.
4. Add the sliced mushrooms and half of the crème fraîche and simmer until the crème has reduced and colored, stirring occasionally.
5. Season with salt and pepper. Add the rest of the crème mixed with the flour. Cook, stirring, for 5 minutes. Serve very hot garnished with the whole mushrooms.

Flamed veal chops

Croque-signor

Veal and Cheese Parcels

	00:15	00:15

American	Ingredients	Metric/Imperial
6 (5 oz)	Thick veal scaloppine [escalopes]	6 (150 g / 5 oz)
½ cup	Oil	125 ml / 4 fl oz
6	Very thin slices of gruyère cheese	6
2	Eggs	2
6 tbsp	Dry bread crumbs	6 tbsp
	Salt and pepper	

1. Cut each piece of veal through the thickness so that it can be opened up like a book. Do not cut all the way through. Brush the inside of each piece of veal with 1 tablespoon of oil. Slip in a slice of cheese and close the veal over. Cut off any cheese that sticks out.
2. Beat the eggs in a shallow dish. Coat the veal on both sides in beaten egg, then coat with the bread crumbs. Sprinkle with salt and pepper.
3. Heat the remaining oil in a frying pan and add the veal parcels. Cook over a medium heat for 4-6 minutes on each side until golden.

Estouffade à la moutarde

Veal in Wine and Mustard Sauce

	00:20		02:15

American	Ingredients	Metric/Imperial
2 lb	Boneless breast of veal	1 kg / 2 lb
1 lb	Boned veal blade steaks [middle neck cutlets]	500 g / 1 lb
¼ lb	Lightly salted lean bacon	125 g / 4 oz
¼ lb	Bacon rind	125 g / 4 oz
4	Shallots	4
½ lb	Button mushrooms	250 g / 8 oz
½	Lemon	½
3 tbsp	Oil	3 tbsp
2 tbsp	Butter	25 g / 1 oz
1 tbsp	Flour	1 tbsp
1 cup	Dry white wine	250 ml / 8 fl oz
1 tbsp	Prepared mustard	1 tbsp
1	Fresh thyme sprig	1
1	Bay leaf	1
1 cup	Thin crème fraîche (see page 122)	250 ml / 8 fl oz
	Salt and pepper	

1. Preheat the oven to 350°F / 180°C / Gas Mark 4.
2. Cut all the veal into large cubes. Cut the bacon and bacon rind into matchstick strips. Peel and finely chop the shallots. Thinly slice the mushrooms. Sprinkle them with the juice of the ½ lemon and put to one side.
3. Heat the oil in a frying pan, add the veal and bacon and cook over a high heat for 5 minutes or until browned on all sides. Remove with a slotted spoon and place in a flameproof casserole.
4. Add the butter and shallots to the pan and cook over a medium heat for 3 minutes. Add to the casserole.
5. Sprinkle the flour over the casserole and mix in well. Add the wine, mustard, thyme, bay leaf, crème fraîche, mushrooms and their lemon juice, the bacon rind, and salt and pepper to taste. The meat should be completely covered; if it is not, add a little water. Mix everything together well.
6. Bring to a boil on top of the stove, then transfer the casserole to the oven. Cook for 2 hours or until the veal is tender.

Escalopes au cidre

Scaloppine with Cider Cream

	00:10		00:20

American	Ingredients	Metric/Imperial
3	Onions	3
6 (5 oz)	Veal scaloppine [escalopes]	6 (150 g / 5 oz)
	Salt and pepper	
3 tbsp	Butter	40 g / 1½ oz
2½ cups	Dry hard cider	600 ml / 1 pint
1½ cups	Crème fraîche (see page 122)	350 ml / 12 fl oz

1. Peel and finely chop the onions. Sprinkle the slices of veal with salt and pepper on both sides. Melt the butter in a frying pan, add the veal and cook for 4-5 minutes on each side, until golden brown. Remove and keep hot.
2. Add the onions to the pan and cook for about 5 minutes over a medium heat, scraping up the meat residue from the bottom of the pan with a wooden spatula. Pour in the cider and reduce over a high heat until only about 3 tablespoons of liquid remain.
3. Reduce the heat and add the crème fraîche. Reduce by half, stirring constantly. Season with salt and pepper.
4. Return the veal to the pan and reheat briefly in the sauce.

Foie de veau au bacon

Calves' Liver with Bacon

	00:05		00:06

American	Ingredients	Metric/Imperial
½ cup	Butter	125 g / 4 oz
6 (5 oz)	Slices of calves' liver	6 (150 g / 5 oz)
	Salt and pepper	
12	Thin bacon slices	12
½	Lemon	½
	Lemon wedges for serving	

1. Melt half of the butter in a frying pan over a high heat, add the liver slices and cook until browned on both sides. Season with salt and pepper when you turn them over. When they are cooked (still pink inside), arrange them on a warmed serving platter and keep hot.
2. Cook the slices of bacon in the frying pan until the fat becomes translucent. Lay them on the serving platter around the slices of liver.
3. Heat the rest of the butter in the frying pan until it foams. Add the juice of the ½ lemon and pour this sauce over the liver. Serve with lemon wedges.

Escalopes aux cèpes

Scaloppine with Cèpes

	00:15 plus soaking		00:40

American	Ingredients	Metric/Imperial
9	Dried or canned medium-size cèpes	9
3	Ripe tomatoes	3
2	Medium-size onions	2
6 (5 oz)	Veal scaloppine [escalopes]	6 (150 g / 5 oz)
3 tbsp	Flour	3 tbsp
¼ cup	Oil	4 tbsp
1 cup	Red wine	250 ml / 8 fl oz
	Salt and pepper	
1	Lemon	1

1. If using dried cèpes, rinse them well and soak in warm water to cover for 30 minutes; drain. Drain canned cèpes. Slice the cèpes thinly.
2. Peel the tomatoes (first plunging them in boiling water for 10 seconds), quarter them and mash with a fork. Set aside. Peel and thinly slice the onions.

3. Coat the veal slices in the flour. Heat the oil in a frying pan, add the veal and cook for 4-5 minutes on each side over a medium heat. Remove from the pan and keep warm.
4. Add the onions to the pan and cook for 5 minutes over a moderate heat, scraping the bottom of the pan well. Add the wine, mashed tomatoes and cèpes. Add seasoning to taste. Wash the lemon, grate the lemon rind and add to the mixture. Cook for 15 minutes over a high heat, stirring well.
5. Return the veal to the pan and reheat briefly in the sauce before serving.

Foie de veau sauté aux raisins
Calves' Liver with Grapes

American	Ingredients	Metric/Imperial
36	Large green grapes	36
1	Bunch of fresh parsley	1
6 (5 oz)	Slices of calves' liver	6 (150 g / 5 oz)
	Salt and pepper	
½ cup	Flour	50 g / 2 oz
½ cup	Butter	125 g / 4 oz
1¼ cups	Dry white wine	300 ml / ½ pint

1. Peel the grapes. Chop the parsley. Season the liver slices with salt and pepper and coat in the flour.
2. Heat the butter in a large frying pan, add the liver slices and cook over a high heat for 3-4 minutes on each side. Arrange on a warmed serving platter and keep hot.
3. Add the parsley and grapes to the frying pan and allow to color slightly over a medium heat, stirring gently. Pour over the wine. Reduce by half over a high heat, stirring often.
4. Pour the grape sauce over the liver and serve immediately.

Escalopes berrichonne
Scaloppine with Morels in Cream

American	Ingredients	Metric/Imperial
7 tbsp	Butter	90 g / 3½ oz
6 (5 oz)	Veal scaloppine [escalopes]	6 (150 g / 5 oz]
	Salt and pepper	
¾ lb	Fresh morels or other mushrooms	350 g / 12 oz
5 oz	Bayonne ham or prosciutto	150 g / 5 oz
3	Shallots	3
1 cup	White wine	250 ml / 8 fl oz
1 cup	Crème fraîche (see page 122)	250 ml / 8 fl oz
1 cup	Grated gruyère cheese	125 g / 4oz

1. Preheat the oven to 425°F / 220°C / Gas Mark 7.
2. Heat 3 tablespoons [40 g / 1½ oz] of the butter in a frying pan, add the slices of veal and cook until golden brown on both sides, about 15 minutes. Season with salt and pepper and arrange in an ovenproof dish. Set aside.

3. Trim the morels and chop them if they are large. Cut the ham into thin strips. Peel and chop the shallots.
4. Heat the rest of the butter in the frying pan, add the mushrooms and shallots and cook until softened and the liquid produced by the mushrooms has evaporated. Add the ham and wine and stir well. Add the crème fraîche and salt and pepper to taste and reduce the sauce over a very gentle heat for about 10 minutes.
5. Cover the veal with the grated cheese, then pour over the sauce. Bake for 15 minutes.

Cook's tip: if fresh morels are not available, you can substitute 4 oz / 125 g dried morels or other wild mushrooms. Rinse these well, then soak in warm water to cover for 30 minutes. Drain and proceed as above. Drained canned morels may also be used.

Escalopes farcies
Stuffed Scaloppine in Madeira

American	Ingredients	Metric/Imperial
4	Slices of stale bread	4
⅔ cup	Milk	150 ml / ¼ pint
3	Garlic cloves	3
5 oz	Chicken livers	150 g / 5 oz
5 oz	Pork sausage meat	150 g / 5 oz
1¼ cups	Madeira wine	300 ml / ½ pint
⅓ cup	Brandy	5 tbsp
	Salt and pepper	
	Grated nutmeg	
1	Small bunch of fresh parsley	1
6 tbsp	Butter	75 g / 3 oz
6	Veal scaloppine [escalopes]	6
¼ cup	Flour	50 g / 2 oz
⅔ cup	Dry white wine	150 ml / ¼ pint
1¼ cups	Veal or chicken stock	300 ml / ½ pint
1¼ cups	Crème fraîche (see page 122)	300 ml / ½ pint

1. Preheat the oven to 475°F / 250°C / Gas Mark 9.
2. Soak the bread in the milk in a bowl. Peel and chop one of the cloves of garlic. Chop the chicken livers. Mix together the bread, chopped garlic, sausage meat, chicken livers, half of the madeira and the brandy. Season with salt and pepper and a pinch of nutmeg. Chop the parsley finely and add it to the rest of the ingredients and mix.
3. Heat 2 tablespoons [25 g / 1 oz] butter in a frying pan, add the slices of veal and cook for 3-4 minutes on each side, until golden brown. Do not cook through. Transfer to an ovenproof dish.
4. Melt the rest of the butter and stir in the flour. Peel and chop the rest of the garlic and add to the pan with the wine and stock, stirring all the time. Season with salt, pepper and nutmeg. Cook for a few minutes, stirring constantly. Add the rest of the madeira and the crème fraîche. Bring to a boil, stirring.
5. Pile the chicken liver stuffing on top of the veal and pour over the sauce. Bake for about 20 minutes or until the veal is cooked through and serve piping hot.

Escalopes Casimir
Scaloppine with Artichokes

	00:20	01:00

American	Ingredients	Metric/Imperial
1 lb	Carrots	500 g / 1 lb
½ cup	Butter	125 g / 4 oz
1	Small can of truffle peelings	1
	Salt and pepper	
6	Canned artichoke hearts	6
6	Veal scaloppine [escalopes]	6
1 tsp	Paprika	1 tsp
¼ cup	Oil	4 tbsp
⅔ cup	Crème fraîche (see page 122)	150 ml / ¼ pint
1	Lemon	1

1. Peel and coarsely grate the carrots. Heat 3 tablespoons [40 g / 1½ oz] of the butter in a saucepan, add the carrots and cook, covered, over a gentle heat for about 20 minutes or until very tender.
2. Drain the truffle peelings, reserving their juice. Chop finely and add to the carrots. Season with salt and pepper. Keep warm.
3. Drain the artichoke hearts. Heat another 3 tablespoons [40 g / 1½ oz] of the butter in another saucepan, add the artichoke hearts and heat through gently.
4. Meanwhile, season the slices of veal with salt and pepper and sprinkle with paprika. Heat the rest of the butter and the oil in a large frying pan and cook the veal over a low heat until golden brown (about 4-6 minutes each side). If it produces any liquid, let it evaporate completely.
5. Arrange the artichoke hearts on a warmed serving dish, cover them with the carrot mixture and lay the scaloppine on top. Keep hot.
6. Pour off the fat from the frying pan and pour in the crème fraîche, the truffle juice and juice of the lemon. Cook over a high heat, scraping the bottom of the pan with a wooden spatula. When the sauce is thick, pour it over the veal and serve immediately.

Foie à l'aigre-douce
Sweet and Sour Liver

	00:10	00:15

American	Ingredients	Metric/Imperial
1 tbsp	Oil	1 tbsp
⅔ cup	Butter	150 g / 5 oz
6 (5 oz)	Slices of calves' liver	6 (150 g / 5 oz)
	Salt and pepper	
2 tbsp	Sugar	2 tbsp
3 tbsp	Red wine vinegar	3 tbsp
1½	Lemons	1½

1. Heat the oil and ¼ cup [50 g / 2 oz] of the butter in a frying pan. Add the slices of liver and cook for 5 minutes on each side over a medium heat. Season with salt and pepper while they are cooking.
2. Arrange the liver slices on a warmed serving platter and

keep hot. Discard all the cooking fat, and put the sugar and vinegar in the frying pan. Bring to a boil, scraping up the meat residue from the bottom of the pan with a wooden spoon. Reduce the vinegar until a reddish-brown caramel remains.
3. Add the juice of the lemons and bring this mixture to a boil, stirring often. Cut the remaining butter into small pieces and add all at once to the boiling liquid. Beat vigorously with a whisk over a very low heat until the sauce is thick and very smooth.
4. Pour the sauce over the liver slices and serve immediately.

Foie à la vénitienne
Venetian Liver

	00:10	00:25

American	Ingredients	Metric/Imperial
6	Onions	6
¼ cup	Olive oil	4 tbsp
6 (5 oz)	Slices of calves' liver	6 (150 g / 5 oz)
2 tbsp	Chopped fresh parsley	2 tbsp
2 tbsp	Lemon juice	2 tbsp
	Salt and pepper	

1. Peel the onions and slice very thinly. Heat the oil in a frying pan, add the onions and cook, covered, over a gentle heat for 20 minutes. Stir from time to time with a wooden spoon.
2. Meanwhile, cut the liver slices into small pieces.
3. Uncover the onions, turn up the heat slightly and cook until the onions are golden brown. Add the liver and cook for 3 minutes, stirring well to mix. Add the parsley and continue cooking for about 1 minute, stirring all the time.
4. Remove from the heat and add the lemon juice and salt and pepper to taste. Serve hot.

Fricandeau
Braised Veal Roast

	00:10 Serves 7–8	02:30

American	Ingredients	Metric/Imperial
1 (3 lb)	Boneless veal roast for braising, rolled and tied	1 (1.5 kg / 3 lb)
1	Carrot	1
1	Onion	1
1 tbsp	Oil	1 tbsp
¼ cup	Butter	50 g / 2 oz
1¼ cups	Dry white wine	300 ml / ½ pint
2 cups	Chicken stock	500 ml / ¾ pint
	Salt and pepper	

1. Ask your butcher to lard the surface of the roast with pork fat.
2. Peel and thinly slice the carrot and onion. Set aside.
3. Heat the oil and half the butter in a flameproof casserole. Add the veal roast and seal on all sides for about 5 minutes. Do not brown the meat. Remove and set aside.
4. Discard all the cooking fat in the casserole. Add the rest of the butter and the carrot and onion and cook for a few minutes. Add half of the wine and ⅔ cup [150 ml / ¼ pint] of the stock. Replace the meat in the casserole and cook over a high heat until all the liquid has evaporated, turning the meat often.

5. Add the rest of the wine and stock and season with salt and pepper. Half-cover the casserole and cook over a gentle heat for 2 hours, turning the meat from time to time.

6. Place the meat on a warmed serving dish. Keep hot. Reduce the cooking liquid over a medium heat until it has the consistency of a thick syrup. Strain a little over the meat and the rest into a sauceboat.

Escalopes panées milanaise

Breaded Scaloppine with Noodles

American	Ingredients	Metric/Imperial
3	Eggs	3
2 tbsp	Oil	2 tbsp
	Dried thyme	
	Salt and pepper	
½ cup	Flour	50 g / 2 oz
1 cup	Dry bread crumbs	75 g / 3 oz
6	Veal scaloppine [escalopes]	6
½ cup	Butter	125 g / 4 oz
1¼ lb	Fresh egg noodles (see page 442)	625 g / 1¼ lb
6	Lemon slices	6
	Grated parmesan or gruyère cheese	

1. Break the eggs into a shallow dish. Add the oil, and thyme, salt and pepper to taste and mix together well. Put the flour on one plate and the bread crumbs on another. Coat the slices of veal first in the flour, then in the beaten egg, and finally in the bread crumbs.

2. Heat half of the butter in a frying pan, add the veal and cook for 5 minutes each side.

3. Meanwhile, cook the noodles in boiling salted water for 5-7 minutes or until just tender but still firm. Drain well. Pour the noodles into a deep warmed dish, add the rest of the butter and some pepper and mix well. Keep hot.

4. Arrange the scaloppine on warmed serving platter and place a lemon slice on each. Serve immediately with the noodles and grated cheese.

Foie de veau au curry

Curried Calves' Liver

00:10 plus marinating   00:20

American	Ingredients	Metric/Imperial
8 (¼ lb)	Thin slices of calves' liver	8 (125 g / 4 oz)
1¼ cups	Plain yogurt	300 ml / ½ pint
5	Ripe tomatoes	5
3	Onions	3
1	Garlic clove	1
6 tbsp	Butter	75 g / 3 oz
2 tbsp	Curry powder	2 tbsp
1 tsp	Ground ginger	1 tsp
⅛ tsp	Cayenne pepper	⅛ tsp
	Salt	

1. Cut the liver slices into thin strips and place them in a bowl. Add the yogurt and toss to coat. Marinate for 1 hour.

2. Peel the tomatoes (first plunging them in boiling water for 10 seconds) and mash with a fork. Set aside.

3. Peel and finely chop the onions and garlic. Melt half of the butter in a frying pan, add the garlic and onions and cook over a gentle heat for about 10 minutes. Sprinkle with the curry powder, ginger and cayenne. Mix well, then add the tomatoes and salt to taste. Cook over a gentle heat for 5 minutes, stirring occasionally.

4. Drain the liver, reserving the yogurt. Add the yogurt to the frying pan. Mix well and continue cooking gently for 5 minutes. Do not boil.

5. Meanwhile, melt the rest of the butter in another frying pan. Add the strips of liver and cook for 5 minutes over a medium heat, stirring well. Add the liver to the sauce and mix well.

Foie de veau cocotte

Casseroled Calves' Liver

00:45 Serves 10–12   01:00

American	Ingredients	Metric/Imperial
1 (4 lb)	Whole calf's liver	1 (2 kg / 4 lb)
3	Shallots	3
2	Onions	2
1	Carrot	1
6 tbsp	Butter	75 g / 3 oz
1	Bouquet garni	1
⅔ cup	Madeira wine	150 ml / ¼ pint
1¼ cups	White wine	300 ml / ½ pint
	Grated nutmeg	
1	Clove	1
1 tbsp	Potato starch or flour	1 tbsp
2 tbsp	Water	2 tbsp
	Salt and pepper	
1	Small can of truffle peelings	1

1. Ask the butcher to lard the liver with pork fat in 5 or 6 places along its length, to wrap it in a piece of caul fat and to tie it up in the shape of a long roast.

2. Peel and chop the shallots and onions. Peel and slice the carrot. Heat 1 tablespoon of butter in a heavy-based saucepan, add the shallots, onions, carrot and bouquet garni and cook over a low heat until the onions and shallots are translucent. Add the madeira, white wine, a pinch of nutmeg and the clove, and simmer gently for 30 minutes.

3. Preheat the oven to 425°F / 220°C / Gas Mark 7.

4. Strain the liquid and discard the vegetables and flavorings.

5. Place the liver in a flameproof casserole and add the liquid, which should come about halfway up the liver. Cover and place in the oven. Cook for 30 minutes, then turn the liver over and continue cooking for 30 minutes. The liquid should not boil.

6. Take out the liver. Untie it and take off the caul fat. Keep hot. Skim the fat from the cooking liquid. Dissolve the potato starch in the water and add to the liquid. Bring to a boil, stirring well. Season with salt and pepper to taste. Add the remaining butter, cut into small pieces, beating with a whisk. Add the drained truffle peelings.

7. Serve the liver sliced, with the sauce in a sauceboat.

Veal shanks with cheese

Jarret de veau gratiné

Veal Shanks [Knuckle] with Cheese

	00:30	01:30

American	Ingredients	Metric/Imperial
2	Carrots	2
2	Onions	2
2	Large pieces of pork rind	2
6	Veal shank cross cuts [slices of knuckle]	6
	Salt and pepper	
1	Bouquet garni	1
2 tbsp	Brandy	2 tbsp
1¼ cups	Dry white wine	300 ml / ½ pint
½ cup	Crème fraîche (see page 122)	125 ml / 4 fl oz
1	Egg yolk	1
5 tbsp	Grated gruyère cheese	5 tbsp

1. Peel and thinly slice the carrots and onions. Place one of the pieces of pork rind on the bottom of a flameproof casserole, fatty side down. Cover this with the carrots and onions and lay the slices of veal on top. Season with salt and pepper and push the bouquet garni into the middle of the meat. Add the brandy and wine. Lay the other piece of rind on top.
2. Cover the casserole and simmer over a gentle heat for 1 hour 20 minutes.
3. Preheat the oven to 450°F / 230°C / Gas Mark 8.
4. Remove the rind, and place the drained meat and carrots in a shallow ovenproof dish. Set aside.
5. Strain the cooking liquid into a mixing bowl. Skim off the fat. Mix the crème fraîche with the egg yolk and add to the bowl. Stir well. Adjust the seasoning, pour over the meat and sprinkle with the grated cheese.
6. Bake for 15 minutes to brown the top.

Foie de veau lyonnaise

Calves' Liver with Onions

	00:10	00:20

American	Ingredients	Metric/Imperial
6 (5 oz)	Slices of calves' liver	6 (150 g / 5 oz)
	Salt and pepper	
½ cup	Flour	50 g / 2 oz
6	Medium-size onions	6
3 tbsp	Butter	40 g / 1½ oz
1 tbsp	Wine vinegar	1 tbsp
2 tbsp	Chopped fresh parsley	2 tbsp

1. Season the liver slices with salt and pepper on both sides, and coat them in the flour. Peel and thinly slice the onions.
2. Melt 2 tablespoons [25 g / 1 oz] of the butter in a frying pan, add the slices of liver and cook for 3-4 minutes on each side over a high heat. Arrange on a warmed serving dish and keep hot.
3. Add the rest of the butter and the onions to the frying pan and cook over a gentle heat for 15 minutes. Add the vinegar and salt and pepper to taste. Stir well over a gentle heat for 1 minute without boiling, then pour this sauce over the liver slices.
4. Sprinkle with the parsley and serve immediately.

Grenadins au vermouth

Veal Steaks in Vermouth

	00:25	00:30 to 00:35

American	Ingredients	Metric/Imperial
6 (5 oz)	Slices of veal tenderloin [fillet], about 1 in / 2.5 cm thick, wrapped in pork fat	6 (150 g / 5 oz)
2 tbsp	Flour	2 tbsp
¼ cup	Butter	50 g / 2 oz
1 cup	Dry red vermouth	250 ml / 8 fl oz
1 tsp	Grated lemon rind	1 tsp
4	Tomatoes	4
8	Medium-size onions	8
1	Bouquet garni	1
	Salt and pepper	
2 tbsp	Crème fraîche (see page 122)	2 tbsp

1. Lightly coat the veal steaks in the flour. Heat the butter in a frying pan, add the steaks and cook gently until they are golden on all sides. Do not let the butter burn.
2. Remove from the heat and pour over the vermouth. Add the lemon rind. Cover and leave to infuse for 5 minutes.
3. Meanwhile, quarter the tomatoes and remove the seeds. Peel the onions.
4. Replace the pan on a high heat and bring to a boil. Turn the heat down and add the tomatoes, onions and bouquet garni. Season with salt and pepper. Cover and simmer over a low heat for 25-30 minutes.
5. Arrange the steaks on a warmed serving dish and garnish with the onions. Keep hot. Add the crème fraîche to the sauce

and heat through, stirring. Strain the sauce, pressing the solids to extract all the liquid. Pour the sauce over the steaks.

Cook's tip: there should not be a lot of sauce, so if necessary, reduce it by boiling before adding the crème fraîche. If you do not like cream, substitute ¼ cup [50 g / 2 oz] butter. This should be added away from the heat, little by little, beating all the time.

Médaillons au porto
Veal Steaks with Port

▬▷ 00:05   00:10 🍲

American	Ingredients	Metric/Imperial
6	Slices of veal tenderloin [fillet], about ½ in / 1 cm thick	6
6 tbsp	Flour	6 tbsp
¼ cup	Butter	50 g / 2 oz
6 tbsp	Port wine	6 tbsp
1 cup	Crème fraîche (see page 122)	250 ml / 8 fl oz
	Salt and pepper	
1	Lemon	1

1. Coat the veal steaks with the flour. Melt the butter in a frying pan, add the veal and cook over a medium heat for 3-4 minutes on each side, until golden. Remove and keep warm.
2. Add the port to the pan and bring to a boil. Stir in the crème fraîche and season with salt and pepper. Grate the lemon rind and add to the pan. Boil briskly for 2 minutes, then turn down the heat.
3. Replace the veal steaks in the pan and turn them over in the sauce so that they are coated with it. Reheat briefly.

Noix de veau rôtie
Roast Veal Round [Topside]

▬▷ 00:02   01:15 🍲

American	Ingredients	Metric/Imperial
1 (3 lb)	Veal round roast [topside or cushion], at room temperature	1 (1.5 kg / 3 lb)
	Salt and pepper	
1 tbsp	Boiling water	1 tbsp
2 tbsp	Butter	25 g / 1 oz

1. Preheat the oven to to 425°F / 220°C / Gas Mark 7.
2. Rub the veal all over with salt and pepper. Place it on a rack in a roasting pan.
3. Roast until the meat browns, then turn it over and continue roasting for 1 hour, basting frequently with the pan juices.
4. Turn off the oven and leave the meat inside for 5 minutes. (With an electric oven, open the door and leave it ajar.)
5. Remove the meat from the pan and keep hot. Put the roasting pan over a gentle heat on top of the stove and cook until the meat juices color slightly without burning. Add the boiling water and butter and stir until melted. Add salt and pepper to taste.
6. Slice the meat and serve with the gravy.

Fricassée de foie de veau et de rognons
Fricassee of Calves' Liver and Kidneys

▬▷ 00:30   00:30 🍲

American	Ingredients	Metric/Imperial
2	Calves' kidneys	2
3	Slices of calves' liver	3
2	Medium-size onions	2
¼ cup	Butter	50 g / 2 oz
3 tbsp	Vinegar	3 tbsp
1¼ cups	Red wine	300 ml / ½ pint
	Salt and pepper	

1. Quarter the kidneys. Remove the white parts and the fat in the center. Cut the kidneys into pieces. Cut the slices of liver into small pieces of the same size.
2. Peel and chop the onions. Heat 1 tablespoon of the butter in a frying pan, add the onions and cook until they begin to turn golden brown (after about 10 minutes). Add the vinegar and wine. Bring to a boil and reduce until the mixture is syrupy. Pour this sauce into a bowl.
3. Wipe out the frying pan out but do not wash. Melt the rest of the butter, add the pieces of liver and kidney and cook over a high heat for 3 minutes, stirring. Season with salt and pepper.
4. Pour over the sauce and reheat briefly.

Grenadins au poivre vert
Veal Steaks with Green Peppercorns

▬▷ 00:20   00:20 to 00:30 🍲

American	Ingredients	Metric/Imperial
6	Slices of veal tenderloin [fillet], about 1 in / 2.5 cm thick, wrapped in pork fat	6
2 tbsp	Flour	2 tbsp
2 tbsp	Butter	25 g / 1 oz
½ cup	Brandy	125 ml / 8 fl oz
1¼ cups	Dry white wine	300 ml / ½ pint
1 tbsp	Green peppercorns	1 tbsp
1 cup	Heavy [double] cream	250 ml / 8 fl oz
1 tsp	Tomato paste [purée]	1 tsp
	Salt	

1. Lightly coat the veal steaks all over in flour. Heat half of the butter in a frying pan, add the veal and cook gently, until they are golden on all sides. Do not let the butter brown.
2. Transfer the veal to another frying pan. Pour over the brandy, cover and leave to macerate.
3. Add the wine to the first frying pan and bring to a boil, scraping up the meat residue from the bottom of the pan. Add the green peppercorns, crushed with a mortar and pestle or put through a food mill. Reduce the liquid by half. Pour over the veal steaks.
4. Mix the cream with the tomato paste and add to the veal. Add salt to taste. Cook over a very low heat for 20 minutes, turning the veal steaks once halfway through and stirring the sauce occasionally.

Longe de veau

Roast Loin of Veal with Kidneys

	00:05 plus standing time		01:15

American	Ingredients	Metric/Imperial
1 (3 lb)	Boneless loin of veal	1 (1.5 kg / 3 lb)
1 - 2	Calves' kidneys	1 - 2
	Salt and pepper	
1¼ cups	Water	300 ml / ½ pint

1. Ask your butcher to tie the veal up around the kidneys. Rub the roast all over with salt and pepper and set aside, at room temperature, for 1 hour.
2. Preheat the oven to 400°F / 200°C / Gas Mark 6.
3. Put the veal on a rack in a roasting pan and roast until one side is golden brown. Turn the meat over and pour half of the water into the pan. Continue roasting for 1 hour, basting the meat with the juices in the pan towards the end of the cooking time.
4. Turn off the oven and leave the meat inside for 10 minutes. (With an electric oven, open the door and leave it ajar.)
5. Slice the meat and keep hot. Place the roasting pan over a gentle heat on top of the stove and cook until the meat juices color slightly without burning. Add the remaining water and scrape the bottom of the pan with a wood spoon to dissolve the caramelized juices. Reduce the liquid by half. Add salt and pepper to taste.
6. Serve the gravy in a sauceboat with the sliced meat.

Noix de veau aux cèpes et à la crème

Braised Veal with Cèpes and Cream

	00:05 plus soaking		01:30

American	Ingredients	Metric/Imperial
2 tbsp	Oil	2 tbsp
¼ cup	Butter	50 g / 2 oz
1 (3 lb)	Veal round roast [topside or cushion], barded and tied	1 (1.5 kg / 3 lb)
2	Medium-size onions	2
	Salt and pepper	
1¼ cups	Dry white wine	300 ml / ½ pint
¼ lb	Dried cèpes	125 g / 4 oz
1 tsp	Cornstarch [cornflour]	1 tsp
1 tbsp	Cold water	1 tbsp
⅔ cup	Crème fraîche (see page 122)	150 ml / ¼ pint

1. Heat the oil and butter in a flameproof casserole, add the veal roast and seal all over for 10 minutes over a moderate heat. Remove the meat and set aside.
2. Peel and chop the onions. Add to the casserole and cook for 5 minutes over a gentle heat, stirring well with a wooden spoon to detach the meat residue from the bottom of the casserole.
3. Replace the meat in the casserole. Season with the salt and pepper and add the wine. Cook for 45 minutes over a low heat, turning the meat occasionally and adding a few spoonfuls of water from time to time as necessary so that the meat does not dry out.
4. Meanwhile, rinse the cèpes well and soak in warm water to cover for 30 minutes. Drain and slice thinly.
5. Add the cèpes to the casserole and cook for another 45 minutes.
6. Remove the meat from the casserole and keep warm. Dissolve the cornstarch in the cold water and add to the casserole with the crème fraîche. Cook over a moderate heat for 2-3 minutes, stirring, until the sauce thickens. Remove from the heat.
7. Remove the string and barding fat from the meat and carve into slices about 1 in / ½ cm thick. Arrange the slices in a deep serving dish and pour over the hot sauce.

Langue de veau braisée

Braised Tongue

	00:20 plus soaking and parboiling		02:00

American	Ingredients	Metric/Imperial
1	Fresh or cured calf's tongue	1
6	Carrots	6
3	Onions	3
1	Celery stalk	1
2	Garlic cloves	2
1 tbsp	Tomato paste [purée]	1 tbsp
2 cups	Beef stock	500 ml / ¾ pint
¼ cup	Butter	50 g / 2 oz
½	Calf's foot	½
1¼ cups	White wine	300 ml / ½ pint
1	Bouquet garni	1
	Salt and pepper	
⅔ cup	Vinegar	150 ml / ¼ pint
1 tbsp	Sugar	1 tbsp
1 tbsp	Flour	1 tbsp

1. If using a cured tongue, soak it in cold water for 24 hours, changing the water frequently. Drain.
2. Place the tongue (cured or fresh) in a saucepan, cover with fresh cold water and bring to a boil. Simmer for 10-20 minutes, depending on size. Drain.
3. Preheat the oven to 425°F / 220°C / Gas Mark 7.
4. Peel and dice the carrots, onions and celery. Peel and crush the garlic. Mix the tomato paste with the stock.
5. Heat 3 tablespoons [40 g / 1½ oz] of the butter in a flameproof casserole, add the carrot, onion, celery and the half calf's foot and cook until golden brown. Pour over the wine and the stock mixed with the tomato paste. Add the garlic, bouquet garni and salt and pepper. Place the tongue in the casserole.
6. Bring to a boil over a high heat, then cover the casserole and transfer to the oven. Cook for about 2 hours or until the tongue is tender.
7. Meanwhile, boil the vinegar and sugar in a small saucepan to make a liquid caramel. Mix together the rest of the butter with the flour to a paste.
8. Remove the tongue and plunge it into cold water. Drain and peel off the skin. Trim off any bones and gristle. Slice the tongue and keep hot.
9. Strain the cooking liquid into a saucepan and add the butter/flour paste and vinegar caramel. Cook, stirring, for 5 minutes or until thickened. Add the slices of tongue and heat through for 2-3 minutes.

Braised tongue

Ragoût aux pois frais et à la menthe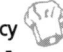

Veal with Peas and Mint

	00:15	01:35

American	Ingredients	Metric/Imperial
2½ lb	Boneless breast of veal	1.25 kg / 2½ lb
1 (2 oz)	Slice of Canadian [back] bacon	1 (50 g / 2 oz)
½ lb	Young carrots	250 g / 8 oz
2	Onions	2
1	Garlic clove	1
3 tbsp	Oil	3 tbsp
	Salt and pepper	
⅔ cup	Water	150 ml / ¼ pint
2 lb	Fresh peas	1 kg / 2 lb
1 lb	Fresh lima or broad beans	500 g / 1 lb
1 tbsp	Fresh mint cut into strips	1 tbsp

1. Cut the veal into large cubes. Cut the bacon into matchstick strips. Peel and slice the carrots and onions. Peel the garlic but do not crush it.
2. Heat the oil in a flameproof casserole, add the bacon and brown for 5 minutes over a medium heat. Add the veal cubes and brown all over for about 5 minutes.
3. Add the carrots, onions and garlic. Season with salt and pepper. Pour the water into the casserole and cook for 45 minutes over a medium heat.
4. Meanwhile, shell the peas. Shell the beans, removing the thin inner skin.
5. Add the beans to the casserole and continue cooking for 10 minutes. Add the peas and mix well. Cover the casserole and continue cooking for 30 minutes.
6. Add the mint. Cover again and cook for a further 10 minutes.

Rognons de veau bercy

Kidneys in Bercy Sauce

	00:15	00:15

American	Ingredients	Metric/Imperial
3	Calves' kidneys	3
1 cup	Butter	250 g / 8 oz
	Salt and pepper	
10	Shallots	10
1½ cups	Dry white wine	350 ml / 12 fl oz
1	Lemon	1
3 tbsp	Chopped fresh parsley	3 tbsp

1. Quarter the kidneys lengthwise. Cut out the tubes and the fatty core with a sharp pointed knife. Cut each piece of kidney into slices about ½ in / 1 cm thick.
2. Melt half the butter in a frying pan, add the kidneys and cook for 5 minutes over a high heat, stirring, to brown the kidney slices on both sides. Season with salt and pepper, then remove from the frying pan and put to one side.
3. Peel and chop the shallots. Add to the frying pan and cook for 3 minutes over a moderate heat, stirring. Add the wine and reduce it until only about 3 tablespoons are left. Add the juice of the lemon and return the kidneys. Cook for 2-3 minutes, stirring often. Remove from the heat.
4. Cut the rest of the butter into small pieces and gradually add to the sauce, beating well with a whisk. Taste and adjust the seasoning.
5. Serve hot, sprinkled with the parsley.

Noix de veau au lait

Veal Cooked in Milk

	00:10 plus macerating	03:15

American	Ingredients	Metric/Imperial
1 (3 lb)	Veal round roast [topside or cushion]	1 (1.5 kg / 3 lb)
1 quart	Milk	1 l / 1¾ pints
4	Garlic cloves	4
2 tbsp	Butter	25 g / 1 oz
½ tsp	Grated nutmeg	½ tsp
	Salt and pepper	
3 tbsp	Madeira wine	3 tbsp

1. Do not have the veal barded or tied. Place it in a large bowl and cover with the milk. Refrigerate for 12 hours. If the milk does not completely cover the meat, turn it occasionally.
2. Preheat the oven to 375°F / 190°C / Gas Mark 5.
3. Peel the garlic. Butter the inside of a flameproof casserole and place the meat, garlic and milk in it. Bake for 1½ hours.
4. Reduce the oven temperature to 350°F / 180°C / Gas Mark 4. Turn the meat over and season with the nutmeg and salt and pepper to taste. Continue cooking for 1½ hours.
5. Remove the meat from the casserole and place it on a warmed serving dish. Keep hot. Add the madeira to the casserole and cook over a high heat on top of the stove for about 5 minutes, beating until the milk, which will have curdled during cooking, takes on the consistency of cream. The sauce should be smooth and velvety.
6. Cut the meat into thin slices and serve the sauce separately in a sauceboat.

Tête de veau gribiche
Calf's Head with Sauce

⊳ 00:35   01:30 to 02:00 🍲

American	Ingredients	Metric/Imperial
2	Carrots	2
1	Onion	1
2	Leeks	2
1	Celery stalk	1
½	Calf's head, tied	½
1	Bouquet garni	1
2	Cloves	2
10	Black peppercorns	10
	Salt	
1 quantity	Egg and herb sauce (see page 121)	1 quantity

1. Peel and roughly chop the carrots and onion. Chop the leeks and celery.
2. Place the calf's head in a flameproof casserole and cover with plenty of water. Bring to a boil, skimming off the froth. As soon as it stops producing froth, add the carrots, leeks, onion, celery, bouquet garni, cloves, peppercorns, and salt to taste. Cover and simmer for 1½-2 hours, depending on size.
3. Drain the head and serve, sliced, with the egg sauce.

Osso bucco milanaise
Italian Braised Veal

⊳ 00:20   01:30 to 02:00 🍲

American	Ingredients	Metric/Imperial
½ lb	Carrots	250 g / 8 oz
½ lb	Onions	250 g / 8 oz
3 tbsp	Olive oil	3 tbsp
4	Tomatoes	4
1	Bouquet garni	1
1	Fresh basil sprig or	1
1 tsp	Dried basil	1 tsp
6	Fresh sage leaves	6
3 lb	Veal shank cross cuts [slices of knuckle]	1.5 kg / 3 lb
2 tbsp	Flour	2 tbsp
1 cup	Dry white wine	250 ml / 8 fl oz
1	Chicken bouillon [stock] cube	1
	Salt and pepper	
1	Garlic clove	1
1	Orange	1
1	Lemon	1
1 tbsp	Chopped fresh parsley	1 tbsp

1. Peel and grate the carrots and onions. Heat 1 tablespoon oil in a flameproof casserole and add the carrots and onions. Cook until golden brown.
2. Peel the tomatoes (first plunging them in boiling water for 10 seconds), remove the seeds and cut the flesh into pieces. Add the tomatoes to the casserole with the bouquet garni, basil and sage leaves. Cover and leave to simmer gently.
3. Meanwhile, coat the veal slices in the flour. Heat the rest of the oil in a frying pan, add the veal and brown all over. As the meat is browned, add the pieces to the casserole.

4. Pour the wine into the frying pan and bring to a boil, scraping up the meat residue from the bottom of the pan. Add this liquid to the casserole, and then just enough water to cover the meat. Finally add the bouillon cube and season with a little salt and pepper. Simmer over a gentle heat for about 1½ hours.
5. Peel and crush the garlic. Grate the rind from the orange and lemon. Mix together the rinds, garlic and parsley.
6. Add the parsley mixture to the casserole. Remove from the heat, stir and leave to infuse for 5 minutes before serving.

Poitrine de veau farcie
Stuffed Breast of Veal

⊳ 01:00   01:45 🍲
     plus soaking   Serves 6–8

American	Ingredients	Metric/Imperial
1	Calf's brain	1
2 tbsp	Vinegar	2 tbsp
2 lb	Fresh spinach	1 kg / 2 lb
8	Slices of stale bread without crusts	8
½ cup	Milk	125 ml / 4 fl oz
4	Onions	4
½ lb	Ground [minced] pork	250 g / 8 oz
1 tsp	Dried thyme	1 tsp
2 tsp	Dried marjoram	2 tsp
1	Egg	1
	Grated nutmeg	
	Salt and pepper	
1 (3 lb)	Boneless breast of veal	1 (1.5 kg / 3 lb)
3	Hard-cooked eggs	3
2	Garlic cloves	2
2	Carrots	2
¼ cup	Butter	50 g / 2 oz
1	Bouquet garni	1
½	Bottle of dry white wine	½

1. Place the brain in a deep bowl and cover with cold water. Leave to soak for 30 minutes.
2. Drain the brain and remove all fiberlike membranes and threads. Put the vinegar in the bowl, add fresh cold water and rinse the brain in the liquid. Drain again and grind [mince]. Set aside.
3. Remove the stalks from the spinach and cook the leaves in plenty of boiling water for 15 minutes.
4. Meanwhile, soak the bread in the milk, then squeeze out excess moisture. Peel and mince 2 of the onions.
5. Drain and mince the spinach. Put it in a mixing bowl and add the brain, pork, bread, onions, thyme, majoram, raw egg, a pinch of nutmeg, and salt and pepper to taste. Mix together with your hands.
6. Push half of this stuffing into the pocket in the breast of veal. Place the hard-cooked eggs in the middle and cover with the rest of the stuffing. Sew up the opening. Tie up the meat, giving it a regular shape.
7. Peel and thinly slice the garlic, carrots and remaining onions. Heat the butter in a flameproof casserole, add the garlic, carrots, onions and bouquet garni and cook until the vegetables are softened. Add the veal and brown it all over on a fast heat. Moisten with the wine and enough water to come three-quarters of the way up the meat. Season with salt and pepper. Reduce the heat and simmer for 1¾ hours, turning the meat over halfway through.
8. Serve cut into slices, accompanied by the strained gravy.

Paupiettes de veau

Veal Birds

	00:30		00:50

American	Ingredients	Metric/Imperial
8 (¼ lb)	Very thin veal scaloppine [escalopes]	8 (125 g / 4 oz)
½ lb	Cooked ham	250 g / 8 oz
1	Small bunch of fresh parsley	1
½ lb	Ground [minced] veal	250 g / 8 oz
1	Egg	1
⅔ cup	Crème fraîche (see page 122)	150 ml / ¼ pint
	Salt and pepper	
2 tbsp	Butter	25 g / 1 oz
4	Tomatoes	4
3	Shallots	3
2	Onions	2
⅔ cup	Port wine	150 ml / ¼ pint
1	Small bouquet garni	1

1. Trim the edges of the slices of veal to make regular rectangles. Set aside. Finely grind [mince] the meat trimmings with the ham and parsley. Place in a mixing bowl.
2. Add the ground veal, egg and a generous spoonful of crème fraîche to the bowl. Season to taste. Mix well.
3. Divide the stuffing between the slices of veal. Roll them up and tie with string. Melt the butter in a frying pan, add the veal rolls and cook gently for 20 minutes or until golden brown.
4. Peel the tomatoes (first plunging them in boiling water for 10 seconds) and halve. Peel and chop the shallots and onions.
5. Pour the port over the veal rolls and add the tomatoes, shallots, onions, bouquet garni, and salt and pepper to taste. Cover and simmer for 30 minutes.
6. Arrange the veal rolls on a warmed serving dish and keep hot. Add the rest of the crème fraîche to the sauce and heat through without boiling. Strain the sauce over the veal rolls.

Pain de veau

Veal Loaf

	00:20		00:45

American	Ingredients	Metric/Imperial
4	Onions	4
2	Garlic cloves	2
2	Celery stalks	2
2 tbsp	Olive oil	2 tbsp
1	Bay leaf	1
1 cup	Dry white wine	250 ml / 8 fl oz
½ cup	Bread crumbs	40 g / 1½ oz
1 tbsp	Butter	15 g / ½ oz
1½ lb	Ground [minced] veal	750 g / 1½ lb
½ lb	Ground [minced] pork	250 g / 8 oz
	Grated nutmeg	
3	Fresh thyme sprigs	3
2	Eggs	2
	Salt and pepper	
1	Piece of pork caul fat	1

1. Preheat the oven to 300°F / 150°F / Gas Mark 2.
2. Peel and mince the onions and garlic. Mince the celery. Heat the oil in a frying pan, add the onions, garlic, celery and bay leaf, crumbled, and cook until the vegetables are softened, do not let them brown.
3. Add ⅔ cup [150 ml / ¼ pint] of the wine. Bring to a boil and simmer for 5 minutes.
4. Remove from the heat. Add the bread crumbs and butter and mix well. Leave to rest for a few minutes, then pour into a mixing bowl.
5. Add the veal, pork, a pinch of nutmeg, the thyme, crumbled, the eggs, and salt and pepper to taste. Knead well with your hands. Shape into a neat sausage and wrap in the pork caul. Place in a baking dish.
6. Bake for 30 minutes, then turn the temperature up to 350°F / 180°C / Gas Mark 4. Pour the rest of the wine over the veal loaf and cook for 15 minutes longer.
7. Serve hot or cold.

Cook's tip: you could also cook this veal loaf in a flameproof casserole on top of the stove. In this case, first brown it lightly all over in 1 tablespoon of oil for about 25 minutes. Then moisten with the wine, cover and simmer for 45 minutes.

Jarret de veau
aux olives à la marocaine

Moroccan Veal Shanks [Knuckle]

	00:15		01:30

American	Ingredients	Metric/Imperial
4	Onions	4
3 tbsp	Oil	3 tbsp
1 tsp	Ground ginger	1 tsp
	Saffron powder	
	Salt	
2½ lb	Boneless veal shanks [knuckle]	1.25 kg / 2½ lb
24	Green olives, pitted [stoned]	24
2	Lemons	2
1 tsp	Mild paprika	1 tsp
1 tsp	Ground cumin	1 tsp
1 tbsp	Chopped fresh coriander	1 tbsp
1 tbsp	Chopped fresh parsley	1 tbsp

1. Peel and slice the onions. Put them in a flameproof casserole with the oil, ginger and a pinch of saffron. Add salt to taste and mix with a wooden spoon. Cut the veal into large cubes. Add to the casserole and stir to mix into the onion and spice mixture. Cover with cold water.
2. Place the casserole on a low heat, cover and cook for about 1 hour 20 minutes or until the meat is very tender.
3. Meanwhile, blanch the olives in boiling water for about 5 minutes, then drain. Thinly pare one of the lemons and chop the rind. Squeeze the juice from the lemon. Set aside.
4. Remove the meat from the casserole with a slotted spoon and set aside. Add the paprika, cumin and lemon juice to the casserole and reduce the sauce for 5 minutes or until it has thickened.
5. Add the olives, lemon rind, coriander and parsley. Mix well, then replace the meat in the casserole. Reheat gently for 5 minutes.
6. Slice the second lemon thinly and use to garnish the dish.

Pieds de veau rémoulade
Calves' Feet with Rémoulade Sauce

	00:30	01:30

American	Ingredients	Metric/Imperial
6	Calves' feet	6
1	Carrot	1
2	Onions	2
3	Shallots	3
2	Garlic cloves	2
2	Cloves	2
2 quarts	Water	2 l / 3½ pints
1	Bouquet garni	1
	Salt and pepper	
1	Egg yolk	1
3	Hard-cooked egg yolks	3
1 tbsp	Mustard	1 tbsp
1 cup	Oil	250 ml / 8 fl oz
2 - 3	Gherkins	2 - 3
¼ cup	Capers	50 g / 2 oz
2	Fresh parsley sprigs	2

1. Split the calves' feet in half. Plunge them into a saucepan of boiling water and blanch for 5 minutes. Drain and cool.
2. Peel the carrot, onions, shallots and garlic. Stud the onions with the cloves. Pour the water into a large stewpot and add all the vegetables, the bouquet garni and salt and pepper to taste. Bring to a boil. Add the calves' feet, cover and cook over a low heat for at least 1½ hours.
3. Put the egg yolk in a bowl with the 3 hard-cooked egg yolks, the mustard, and salt and pepper to taste. Mix together to make a smooth paste. Add the oil little by little in a trickle, beating constantly until the mixture thickens and takes on the consistency of mayonnaise (but rather less smooth). Chop the gherkins, capers and parsley and add to the mayonnaise.
4. Serve the calves' feet hot with the rémoulade sauce.

Ris de veau jardinière
Sweetbreads with Spring Vegetables

	00:45 plus soaking	00:55

American	Ingredients	Metric/Imperial
2 (1½ lb)	Calves' sweetbreads	2 (750 g / 1½ lb)
½ lb	Lightly salted bacon	250 g / 8 oz
¼ cup	Butter	50 g / 2 oz
2	Shallots	2
2	Onions	2
	Grated nutmeg	
1	Bouquet garni	1
	Salt and pepper	
1 cup	Madeira wine	250 ml / 8 fl oz
1 lb	Fresh peas	500 g / 1 lb
8	Young carrots	8
1	Sugar cube	1

1. Soak the sweetbreads in cold water to cover for 10 hours, changing the water 2 or 3 times.
2. Drain the sweetbreads and place in a saucepan of fresh cold water. Bring to a boil slowly and boil for 4 minutes, then drain and rinse under cold running water. Take off the skin and all gristly parts.
3. Place the bacon in a saucepan of water, bring to a boil and simmer for 5 minutes. Drain and cut into strips.
4. Cook the bacon strips in a flameproof casserole until they start to brown. Remove with a slotted spoon and set aside. Add the sweetbreads to the casserole and cook over a moderate heat until golden all over. Remove the sweetbreads. Discard the fat in the casserole and wipe it out.
5. Heat 2 tablespoons [25 g / 1 oz] of the butter in the casserole, and replace the bacon and sweetbreads. Peel the shallots and onions and add to the casserole with a pinch of nutmeg, the bouquet garni, and salt and pepper to taste. Cook gently for 10 minutes. Add the madeira, cover and simmer for 25 minutes.
6. Meanwhile, shell the peas and cook in boiling salted water for 15 minutes. Peel the carrots and cook in boiling salted water for 10-15 minutes or until just tender.
7. Drain the carrots and peas and add them to the casserole, together with the sugar cube. Simmer for 15 minutes longer.
8. Add the rest of the butter. Remove and discard the bouquet garni, onions and shallots, and serve the sweetbreads, sliced, on top of the remaining vegetables.

Poitrine de veau roulée à l'oseille
Breast of Veal with Sorrel

	00:45	01:45

American	Ingredients	Metric/Imperial
5 oz	Fresh sorrel or spinach	150 g / 5 oz
6 tbsp	Butter	75 g / 3 oz
4	Shallots	4
1½ lb	Button mushrooms	750 g / 1½ lb
⅓ cup	Crème fraîche (see page 122)	5 tbsp
1 (3 lb)	Boneless breast of veal	1 (1.5 kg / 3 lb)
3	Thick slices of Bayonne ham or prosciutto	3
2	Onions	2
1	Carrot	1
2	Fresh rosemary sprigs	2
2	Fresh thyme sprigs	2
1	Small bunch of fresh parsley	1
1	Garlic clove	1
2 tbsp	Oil	2 tbsp
1 cup	Dry white wine	250 ml / 8 fl oz
1 - 2	Veal bones	1 - 2
	Grated nutmeg	
	Salt and pepper	

1. Remove the stalks from the sorrel and cut it into strips. Melt 2 tablespoons [25 g / 1 oz] of the butter in a frying pan, add the sorrel and cook for a few minutes or until it has softened. Remove the sorrel from the pan and put to one side.
2. Peel and finely chop the shallots. Chop the mushrooms. Melt another 2 tablespoons [25 g / 1 oz] of the butter in the frying pan, add the shallots and mushrooms and cook over a

moderate heat until the liquid produced by the mushrooms has evaporated. Add the crème fraîche, then remove the pan from the heat and mix well with the sorrel.

3. Spread the breast of veal out flat and lay the slices of ham on top. Spread the sorrel mixture on top of the ham. Roll up the breast and tie it into shape.

4. Peel and slice the onions. Peel and thinly slice the carrot. Tie the rosemary sprigs, thyme and parsley together. Peel the garlic.

5. Heat the oil and the rest of the butter in a flameproof casserole. Add the veal and brown all over for 10 minutes over a fairly high heat. Remove the meat and set aside. Discard the cooking fat.

6. Add the carrot and onions to the casserole and cook for a few minutes, stirring well with a wooden spoon. Replace the meat and add the wine, garlic and bouquet garni of herbs. Add the veal bones: they will add flavor to the sauce during cooking. Season with a pinch of nutmeg and salt and pepper to taste. Cook over a low heat for 1 hour, basting the meat frequently.

7. Halfway through the cooking period, prick the meat with a fork in 2-3 places so that the juices from the stuffing can mix with the sauce and flavor it.

8. To serve, untie the meat and slice it thinly. Serve the strained gravy separately. Stuffed veal breast can also be served cold.

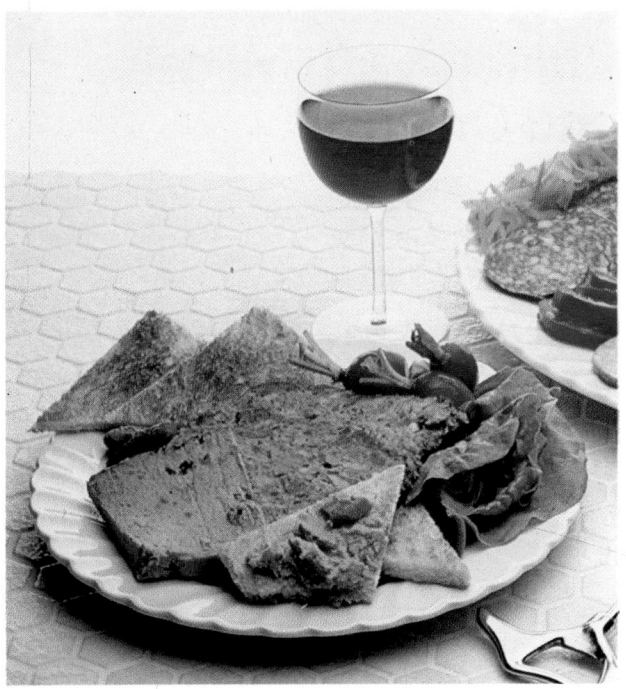

Ragoût de veau aux olives

Veal Ragoût with Olives

	00:30		01:30
American	**Ingredients**	**Metric/Imperial**	
2½ lb	Boneless breast of veal	1.25 kg / 2½ lb	
¼ lb	Slightly salted bacon	125 g / 4 oz	
50	Green olives, pitted [stoned]	50	
1 tbsp	Butter	15 g / ½ oz	
1 tbsp	Oil	1 tbsp	
3	Carrots	3	
1	Large onion	1	
1	Celery stalk	1	
½ lb	Shallots	250 g / 8 oz	
1 tbsp	Flour	1 tbsp	
1	Veal bone	1	
	Pepper		
1¼ cups	Veal or chicken stock	300 ml / ½ pint	
1¼ cups	White wine	300 ml / ½ pint	
¾ lb	Canned cèpes	350 g / 12 oz	

1. Cut the veal into 1 in / 2.5 cm wide strips. Set aside.

2. Place the bacon and olives in a large saucepan, cover with cold water and bring to a boil. Simmer gently for 5 minutes, then drain. Cut the bacon into small strips.

3. Heat the butter and oil in a large flameproof casserole, add the bacon strips and veal and brown lightly.

4. Peel and slice the carrots and onion. Slice the celery. Peel and chop the shallots. Add all these vegetables to the casserole and cook over a high heat for 2-3 minutes. Turn down the heat and sprinkle over the flour. Cook, stirring, until golden.

5. Add the olives, veal bone and a little pepper. Pour over the stock and wine, which should cover all the ingredients. Cook for about 1½ hours.

6. Drain the cèpes and add to the casserole. Heat through gently. Discard the bone before serving.

Rognons de veau aux champignons

Kidneys with Mushrooms

	00:10		00:35
American	**Ingredients**	**Metric/Imperial**	
6	Shallots	6	
14 oz	Button mushrooms	400 g / 14 oz	
6 tbsp	Butter	75 g / 3 oz	
3	Calves' kidneys	3	
¼ cup	Brandy	4 tbsp	
7 tbsp	Crème fraîche (see page 122)	7 tbsp	
	Salt and pepper		
2 tbsp	Dijon mustard	2 tbsp	

1. Peel and finely chop the shallots. Coarsely chop the mushrooms. Melt 2 tablespoons [25 g / 1 oz] of the butter in a frying pan, add the shallots and mushrooms and cook over a moderate heat, stirring often, until all the liquid produced by the mushrooms has evaporated. Remove the vegetables and set aside.

2. Add another 2 tablespoons [25 g / 1 oz] butter to the frying pan with the kidneys. Cook for 10 minutes over a moderate heat, turning the kidneys over halfway through to brown evenly.

3. Remove the kidneys from the frying pan. Quarter them lengthwise and cut out the tubes and fatty core with a small pointed knife. Cut each piece of kidney into slices about ¼ in / 5 mm thick. Set aside.

4. Add the brandy to the frying pan and reduce to about 1½ tablespoons. Return the shallots and mushrooms and add the crème fraîche and salt and pepper to taste. Reduce by half over a high heat, stirring often.

5. Remove from the heat and stir in the mustard. Put the kidneys back in the pan and add the remaining butter. Stir to coat the kidney slices with the sauce. Heat through gently without boiling.

Rognons de veau au madère et aux petits oignons

Kidneys with Madeira and Onions

	00:15	00:30

American	Ingredients	Metric/Imperial
1 lb	Very small onions	500 g / 1 lb
½ cup	Butter	125 g / 4 oz
1 tsp	Sugar	1 tsp
¼ cup	Water	4 tbsp
1 (½ lb)	Piece of bacon	1 (250 g / 8 oz)
3	Shallots	3
3	Large calves' kidneys	3
1 tsp	Cornstarch [cornflour]	1 tsp
1 cup	Madeira wine	250 ml / 8 fl oz
	Salt and pepper	
2 tbsp	Chopped fresh parsley	2 tbsp

1. Peel the onions. Place them in a frying pan with 3 tablespoons [40 g / 1½ oz] of the butter, the sugar and 3 tablespoons of the water. Cook for 20-25 minutes over a very gentle heat until the onions are tender. Shake the pan from time to time so that they cook evenly and become coated in a thin layer of golden caramel.
2. Meanwhile, cut the bacon into matchstick strips. Peel and finely chop the shallots. In another frying pan, melt 2 tablespoons [25 g / 1 oz] of the butter, add the shallots and bacon and cook for 10 minutes over a moderate heat, stirring with a spatula. Remove with a slotted spoon and set aside.
3. Add the kidneys to the pan and cook for 5 minutes over a moderate heat, turning to brown evenly. Remove the kidneys from the pan. Quarter them lengthwise and cut out the tubes and fatty core with a small pointed knife. Cut each piece of kidney into thin slices.
4. Pour off the fat from the frying pan and replace the kidneys, bacon and shallots. Add the rest of the butter. Reheat gently.
5. Dissolve the cornstarch in the remaining water and add to the kidney mixture. Cook, stirring, until thickened. Add the caramelized onions and madeira and continue to cook, stirring, for 1 minute. Add salt and pepper to taste. Sprinkle with the parsley and serve.

Saltimbocca

Veal with Sage and Ham

	00:05	00:10

American	Ingredients	Metric/Imperial
6 (¼ lb)	Veal cutlets [slices of fillet]	6 (125 g / 4 oz)
	Salt and pepper	
12	Fresh sage leaves	12
6	Slices of parma ham	6
5 tbsp	Butter	65 g / 2½ oz
6 tbsp	Dry white wine	6 tbsp

1. Ask your butcher to flatten the slices of veal to look like small, fairly thick scaloppine [escalopes]. Lay them flat on a working surface. Sprinkle with salt and pepper and place 2 sage leaves on each one. Cover with a slice of parma ham cut to the same size. Thread a wooden toothpick through to hold it all together.

2. Melt the butter in a frying pan, add the slices of veal and cook for 5 minutes on each side over a moderate heat, starting with the ham side. Remove the toothpicks and arrange the veal on a warmed serving dish. Keep hot.
3. Discard half of the cooking fat and add the wine to the pan. Reduce by half over a high heat for 3 minutes, scraping up the meat residue well from the bottom of the pan. Pour this gravy over the veal.

Cook's tip: this is a classical dish of Italian cuisine, particularly in Rome. The traditional wine to use is marsala, but the gravy will be equally delicious made with dry white wine.

Rôti de veau en cocotte

Pot Roast Veal

	00:10	01:15

American	Ingredients	Metric/Imperial
1 tsp	Lard	1 tsp
1 (3 lb)	Boneless veal round roast [topside or cushion]	1 (1.5 kg / 3 lb)
1 tsp	Butter	1 tsp
2 - 3	Veal bones	2 - 3
3	Onions	3
1	Bouquet garni	1
1 tbsp	Water	1 tbsp
	Salt and pepper	

1. Heat the lard in a flameproof casserole, add the veal and brown on all sides over a moderate heat, without letting the lard burn.
2. Discard the cooking fat. Add the butter, veal bones, peeled onions, the bouquet garni and water. Season with salt and pepper. Cover and cook for 1¼ hours.
3. To serve, carve the meat and pour over the strained sauce. Noodles make a fine accompaniment.

Pot roast veal

Rôti de veau à l'ananas

Roast Veal with Pineapple

 00:20   02:00

American	Ingredients	Metric/Imperial
1	Onion	1
1	Leek	1
1	Carrot	1
1 tbsp	Oil	1 tbsp
2 tbsp	Butter	25 g / 1 oz
1 (3 lb)	Boneless veal rump roast [topside or cushion], barded and tied	1 (1.5 kg / 3 lb)
1 cup	Chicken stock	250 ml / 8 fl oz
1	Apple	1
1	Firm banana	1
1 tsp	Curry powder	1 tsp
½ tsp	Ground ginger	½ tsp
	Salt	
1	Fresh pineapple	1
½ cup	Crème fraîche (see page 122)	125 ml / 4 fl oz

1. Peel and chop the onion. Thinly slice the leek. Peel and grate the carrot.

2. Heat the oil and butter in a flameproof casserole, add the veal and brown lightly all over for 10 minutes. Remove the meat and set aside.

3. Add the onion, carrot and leek to the casserole and cook for 5 minutes over a gentle heat, scraping the bottom of the casserole. Return the meat and add the stock. Bring to a boil over a gentle heat.

4. Peel and grate the apple and banana. Add to the casserole and stir well, then add the curry powder, ginger and salt to taste. Cover and cook over a gentle heat for 1½ hours, turning the piece of meat 2 or 3 times.

5. Meanwhile, cut off the ends of the pineapple and peel it. Remove the 'eyes' with the point of a peeler or knife. Cut into slices and remove the hard core from each slice.

6. Preheat the oven to 425°F / 220°C / Gas Mark 7.

7. Take the meat out of the casserole and cut into slices about ½ in / 1 cm thick. Arrange the slices in an ovenproof dish, alternating with the slices of pineapple. Set aside.

8. Purée all the remaining contents of the casserole in a blender or food processor. Pour the purée into a saucepan and add the crème fraîche. Bring to a boil and reduce the sauce until it is syrupy.

9. Pour the sauce over the meat and pineapple. Bake for 10 minutes. Serve hot.

Cook's tip: the slices of roast veal are best served from the ovenproof dish.

Roast veal with pineapple

Tripes à la mode de Caen

Normandy Tripe

00:15   **09:00**

American	Ingredients	Metric/Imperial
3 lb	Fresh tripe	1.5 kg / 3 lb
1	Calf's foot	1
1 lb	Onions	500 g / 1 lb
1 lb	Carrots	500 g / 1 lb
4	Garlic cloves	4
3	Leeks (white parts only)	3
14 oz	Fresh beef fat (preferably that surrounding the kidneys)	400 g / 14 oz
1	Bouquet garni	1
	Salt and pepper	
3 tbsp	Calvados or applejack	3 tbsp
1 quart	Dry hard cider	900 ml / 1 ½ pints
5 tbsp	Flour	5 tbsp

1. Preheat the oven to 325°F / 160°C / Gas Mark 3.
2. Put the tripe and halved calf's foot in a stewpot. Cover with plenty of water and bring to a boil. As soon as the water boils, drain the tripe and calf's foot and rinse under cold running water.
3. Peel and thinly slice the onions and carrots. Peel and crush the garlic. Tie the leeks into a bundle with string. Cut the tripe into 2 in / 5 cm squares. Cut the beef fat into thin slices.
4. Place the onions, carrots, tripe, calf's foot, garlic, bouquet garni and leeks into a large flameproof casserole. Season with salt and pepper. Add the slices of beef fat, the calvados and enough cider to cover all the ingredients.
5. Mix the flour with a little water to make a thick paste. Put the lid on the casserole and seal the join with the paste. Place the casserole in the oven and cook for about 8-9 hours.
6. When the tripe is cooked, break the paste seal. Take off the lid and discard the bouquet garni. Remove the bones from the calf's foot and cut the meat into pieces. Replace these in the casserole and serve very hot.

Tripes de granville

Tripe in Cider

00:30
plus cooling   **12:00**

American	Ingredients	Metric/Imperial
10	Small onions	10
2	Medium-size garlic cloves	2
4	Carrots	4
4	Leeks (white parts only)	4
¼ cup	Oil	4 tbsp
1	Calf's foot	1
3 lb	Fresh tripe	1.5 kg / 3 lb
1	Bouquet garni	1
1 tsp	Allspice berries	1 tsp
6	Cloves	6
	Salt and pepper	
2 cups	Dry hard cider	500 ml / ¾ pint
⅔ cup	Calvados or applejack	150 ml / ¼ pint
5 tbsp	Flour	5 tbsp

1. Preheat the oven to 325°F / 160°C / Gas Mark 3.
2. Peel the onions and garlic. Peel and slice the carrots. Chop the leeks. Heat the oil in a flameproof casserole, add the prepared vegetables and cook, without letting them color, until the onions are translucent. Cut the calf's foot into pieces and add to the casserole. Continue cooking for 3-4 minutes, stirring often.
3. Cut the tripe into 2 in / 5 cm squares. Add to the casserole and stir. Add the bouquet garni, allspice, cloves and salt and pepper to taste. Add the cider and calvados. Stir and bring slowly to a boil over a low heat. Simmer gently for 15 minutes.
4. Mix the flour with a little water to make a thick paste. Put the lid on the casserole and seal the join with the paste. Transfer the casserole to the oven and cook for 12 hours.
5. Allow to cool, then break the paste seal. Take off the lid and discard the bouquet garni. Skim the fat off the sauce with a spoon. Put the casserole over a low heat and heat through gently, stirring often. Serve very hot.

Veau Marengo

Veal Marengo

00:30   **01:45 to 02:00**

American	Ingredients	Metric/Imperial
24	Green olives (optional)	24
4	Tomatoes	4
3 lb	Boneless breast or shoulder of veal	1.5 kg / 3 lb
2 tbsp	Olive oil	2 tbsp
2	Onions	2
1	Garlic clove	1
½ lb	Button mushrooms	250 g / 8 oz
2 cups	Dry white wine	500 ml / ¾ pint
1 tbsp	Tomato paste [purée]	1 tbsp
1	Bouquet garni	1
1	Sugar cube	1
	Salt and pepper	
1 tbsp	Chopped fresh parsley	1 tbsp

Veal marengo

1. Pit [stone] the olives, if used. Plunge them into boiling water and blanch for 5 minutes. Drain and set aside. Peel the tomatoes (first plunging them in boiling water for 10 seconds), remove the seeds and chop. Set aside.
2. Cut the veal into chunks. Heat the oil in a flameproof casserole, add the veal and brown slowly on all sides. Remove from the casserole and put to one side.
3. Peel and chop the onions. Add to the casserole and cook until softened but not brown. Add the tomatoes. Peel and crush the garlic and add to the casserole. Cook over a gentle heat until well reduced to a mush, scraping up the meat residue from the bottom of the casserole with a wooden spatula. Do not let it burn.
4. Quarter the mushrooms. Add to the tomato sauce with the veal, wine, tomato paste, bouquet garni, sugar cube, and salt and pepper to taste. Cover and simmer very gently for 1¾-2 hours, stirring occasionally.
5. About 10 minutes before the end of the cooking period, add the olives. Serve sprinkled with the parsley.

Cook's tip: veal marengo is sometimes served garnished with small cooked sausages or bacon slices.

Tendrons de veau braisés

Braised Veal with Olives

	00:25		01:30	

American	Ingredients	Metric/Imperial
2½ lb	Boneless breast of veal	1.25 kg / 2½ lb
2 tbsp	Olive oil	2 tbsp
12	Small onions	12
½ lb	Button mushrooms	250 g / 8 oz
3 tbsp	Butter	40 g / 1½ oz
1 tbsp	Tomato paste [purée]	1 tbsp
⅔ cup	White wine	150 ml / ¼ pint
1	Bouquet garni	1
4	Garlic cloves	4
	Salt and pepper	
12	Green olives	12
12	Black olives	12

1. Cut the veal into 8 lengthwise strips. Heat the oil in a frying pan, add the pieces of veal and brown all over. Remove and place in a flameproof casserole.
2. Peel the onions. Add them to the frying pan and cook over a medium heat until golden on all sides, about 10 minutes. Place them in the casserole with the meat.
3. Quarter the mushrooms if they are large. Heat the butter in the frying pan, add the mushrooms and cook over a medium heat until all liquid produced by the mushrooms has evaporated. Add them to the casserole.
4. Mix the tomato paste with the wine and pour into the casserole. Add the bouquet garni. Peel and crush the garlic and add. Season with the salt and pepper. Cover and simmer for 1½ hours.
5. Plunge the green olives into boiling water and blanch for 5 minutes. Drain and remove the pits [stones]. Pit the black olives.
6. About 10 minutes before serving, add the black and green olives to the casserole.
7. To serve, put the meat on a warmed platter and pour the sauce round it.

Veau en gelée au sauvignon

Veal in Wine Aspic

	00:30 plus chilling		02:30	

American	Ingredients	Metric/Imperial
2 lb	Boneless breast of veal	1 kg / 2 lb
¼ lb	Fresh pork rind	125 g / 4 oz
1	Garlic clove	1
2	Small onions	2
2	Carrots	2
¼	Calf's foot, boned	¼
1	Bouquet garni	1
½ tsp	Black peppercorns	½ tsp
	Salt	
½	Bottle of dry white wine	½
1 tsp	Chopped fresh parsley	1 tsp
1 tbsp	Chopped fresh chervil	1 tbsp
1 tbsp	Chopped fresh tarragon	1 tbsp
1 tbsp	Chopped fresh chives	1 tbsp

1. Cut the breast of veal and the pork rind into large cubes. Peel and slice the garlic, onions and carrots.
2. Line the bottom of a cast iron or other flameproof casserole with the rind. Lay the onions and carrots on top. Add the pieces of veal, the calf's foot, bouquet garni, garlic and peppercorns. Add plenty of salt and pour the wine over. Cover the casserole and simmer over a low heat for 2½ hours.
3. Uncover the casserole and skim the fat off the surface. Discard the bouquet garni. Take out the calf's foot and cut it into thin slices.
4. Place the pieces of veal, rind, slices of calf's foot and vegetables, mixed together, into a terrine. Add the parsley, chervil, tarragon and chives to the cooking liquid, mix well and pour into the terrine. Cover and chill for at least 8 hours.

Braised veal with olives

Tendrons aux légumes nouveaux

Veal Breast with Spring Vegetables

00:20　　　　01:35

American	Ingredients	Metric/Imperial
2½ lb	Boneless breast of veal	1.25 kg / 2½ lb
1 lb	Young carrots	500 g / 1 lb
2 lb	Fresh peas	1 kg / 2 lb
12	Small onions	12
2 tbsp	Oil	2 tbsp
3 tbsp	Butter	40 g / 1½ oz
1	Bouquet garni	1
1 cup	Water	250 ml / 8 fl oz
	Salt and pepper	
½ lb	New potatoes	250 g / 8 oz

1. Cut the veal into 8 lengthwise strips. Peel and slice the carrots. Shell the peas. Peel the onions.
2. Heat the oil and butter in a flameproof casserole, add the pieces of veal and brown on all sides over a high heat for 5 minutes. Remove from the casserole and set aside.
3. Put the carrots and onions into the casserole and cook over a medium heat for 5-10 minutes or until the onions are just golden, turning to cook evenly.
4. Replace the pieces of meat in the casserole. Add the peas, bouquet garni and water. Season with salt and pepper. Cover and cook over a gentle heat for 50 minutes.
5. Peel (or just scrub) the potatoes and add them to the casserole. Continue cooking for 20-25 minutes, uncovered. If the vegetables and meat are not quite tender enough, cook for a little longer.
6. Discard the bouquet garni before serving.

Cook's tip: serve with noodles or buttered rice.

Veal and cheese parcels (see page 351)

Veal and juniper pâté

Rôti de rouelle

Roast Veal

00:10　　　　01:00

American	Ingredients	Metric/Imperial
4	Shallots	4
2	Garlic cloves	2
14 oz	Pork sausage meat	400 g / 14 oz
2 tbsp	Chopped fresh parsley	2 tbsp
	Salt and pepper	
3 tbsp	Olive oil	3 tbsp
1 (2 lb)	Veal round steak [slice of topside], 1½ in / 4 cm thick	1 (1 kg / 2 lb)
3 tbsp	Dry bread crumbs	3 tbsp
1 tbsp	Lemon juice	1 tbsp
1 tbsp	Water	1 tbsp

1. Preheat the oven to 425°F / 220°C / Gas Mark 7.
2. Peel and finely chop the shallots and garlic. Put the sausage meat, shallots and garlic into a mixing bowl and add the parsley. Mix well. Season with salt and pepper.
3. Grease a roasting pan with 1 tablespoon of the olive oil and place the meat in it. Spread the sausage meat mixture over the meat, pressing it on well. Sprinkle with the rest of the oil.
4. Roast for 15 minutes, then reduce the temperature to 400°F / 200°C / Gas Mark 6. Continue roasting for 30 minutes.
5. Sprinkle the meat with the bread crumbs and roast for a further 15 minutes.
6. Transfer the meat to a warmed serving platter and keep hot.
7. Pour the lemon juice and water into the roasting pan. Heat gently on top of the stove, scraping the meat residue from the pan. Pour the gravy into a sauceboat and serve with the meat.

Sauté de veau aux endives

Veal with Creamed Endive [Chicory]

◢ 00:10   01:35 🍲

American	Ingredients	Metric/Imperial
2 lb	Belgian endive [chicory]	1 kg / 2 lb
2½ lb	Boneless shoulder of veal	1.25 kg / 2½ lb
1 tbsp	Oil	1 tbsp
3 tbsp	Butter	40 g / 1½ oz
1 tbsp	Flour	1 tbsp
1¼ cups	Crème fraîche (see page 122)	300 ml / ½ pint
	Salt and pepper	

1. Trim the outside layer of leaves from the endive. Remove the hard core by hollowing it out from the bottom. Slice the endive thinly. Set aside.

2. Cut the veal into cubes. Heat the oil and butter in a flameproof casserole, add the veal cubes and brown all over for 5 minutes. Remove the meat with a slotted spoon.

3. Add the endive to the casserole and cook over a moderate heat for 7-8 minutes or until it is just golden. Sprinkle over the flour and mix well, then add the crème fraîche. Bring to a boil, stirring.

4. Return the meat and season with salt and pepper. Cover the casserole and cook over a gentle heat for 1 hour 20 minutes.

Terrine au genièvre

Veal and Juniper Pâté

◢ 00:15   01:30 🍲
plus macerating and chilling

American	Ingredients	Metric/Imperial
2 (5 oz)	Slices of calves' liver	2 (150 g / 5 oz)
3 tbsp	Gin	3 tbsp
1	Piece of pork fat	1
¾ lb	Ground [minced] veal	350 g / 12 oz
½ lb	Ground [minced] pork	250 g / 8 oz
	Salt and pepper	
12	Juniper berries	12

1. Cut the slices of liver into small cubes and pat dry with paper towels. Put them in a large bowl and sprinkle over 2 tablespoons of the gin. Refrigerate for 2 hours.

2. Preheat the oven to 350°F / 180°C / Gas Mark 4. Line the bottom and sides of a terrine with the pork fat, making sure that it hangs over the rim.

3. Put the veal and pork into a large mixing bowl. Season with salt and pepper and mix well together with your hands.

4. Put one-third of the pork and veal mixture on the bottom of the terrine and pack down well. Drain the liver and make a layer of half of the pieces of liver in the terrine. Scatter over 6 juniper berries. Add another one-third of the pork and veal mixture and press well down, then add the rest of the liver and juniper berries. Finish with the remaining pork and veal mixture and press down. Sprinkle over the remaining gin. Fold the pork fat over the top and cover with the lid.

5. Place the terrine in a roasting pan half full of hot water. Bake for 1½ hours.

6. When the pâté is cooked, take it out of the oven and let it cool, then chill for 12 hours before serving.

Veal orloff

Veau Orloff

Veal Orloff

◢ 00:30   01:00 🍲

American	Ingredients	Metric/Imperial
1 (2½ lb)	Veal rump or round roast [topside or cushion], larded and tied	1 (1.25 kg / 2½ lb)
¾ lb	Button mushrooms	350 g / 12 oz
	Lemon juice	
6 tbsp	Butter	75 g / 3 oz
¼ cup	Flour	50 g / 2 oz
1½ cups	Milk	300 ml / ½ pint
	Grated nutmeg	
	Salt and pepper	
2	Eggs, separated	2

1. Preheat the oven to 425°F / 220°C / Gas Mark 7.

2. Place the meat in a roasting pan and roast for 45 minutes.

3. Meanwhile, chop the mushrooms and sprinkle with lemon juice so that they do not discolor. Heat 2 tablespoons [25 g / 1 oz] of the butter in a saucepan, add the mushrooms and cook until any liquid they produce has evaporated. Set aside.

4. Melt the rest of the butter in a heavy-based saucepan over a gentle heat. As soon as it foams, add the flour and stir until the butter has absorbed the flour. Add the milk and stir until the sauce has thickened. Season with a pinch of nutmeg and salt and pepper to taste. Remove from the heat.

5. Add the mushrooms and egg yolks to the sauce and mix well. Keep warm.

6. When the meat is cooked, cut it into slices, retaining the juices produced. Spread each slice thinly with some of the sauce, then put the roast back together on an ovenproof serving dish. Stir the meat juices into the remaining sauce.

7. Beat the egg whites until very stiff and fold into the sauce. Pour over the meat. Bake for 10 minutes or until the sauce puffs up slightly and turns golden.

Buying and cooking lamb

American cuts to choose	Cooking methods	British cuts to choose	
leg, crown roast, rack or rib, shoulder	roast	best end of neck, breast, leg (including fillet and knuckle), loin, saddle, shoulder	roast
shoulder chops, rib chops, loin chops, sirloin chops, leg chops or steaks, cubes for kebabs, ground lamb patties	broil, fry	chump chops, cutlets, loin chops, lamb steaks from the leg, noisettes (boneless loin or best end steaks), cubes for kebabs, minced lamb patties	grill, fry
neck slices, shoulder chops, breast, riblets, shanks, lamb for stew	braise, stew	shoulder, middle neck cutlets, breast, chump chops, loin chops, leg	braise
		middle neck, scrag end of neck	stew

North African lamb casserole (see page 380)

Lamb cuts

Lamb & mutton: American cuts
1. Shank end of leg
2. Leg steaks

2. & 3. French leg or gigot
4. & 5. Saddle, only when cut takes in both sides of back; centerloin chops

6. Whole cut is called a 'rack'; if cut, rib chops; crown roast
7. Shoulder, if boned, rolled shoulder

8. Neck
9. Shank
10. Breast

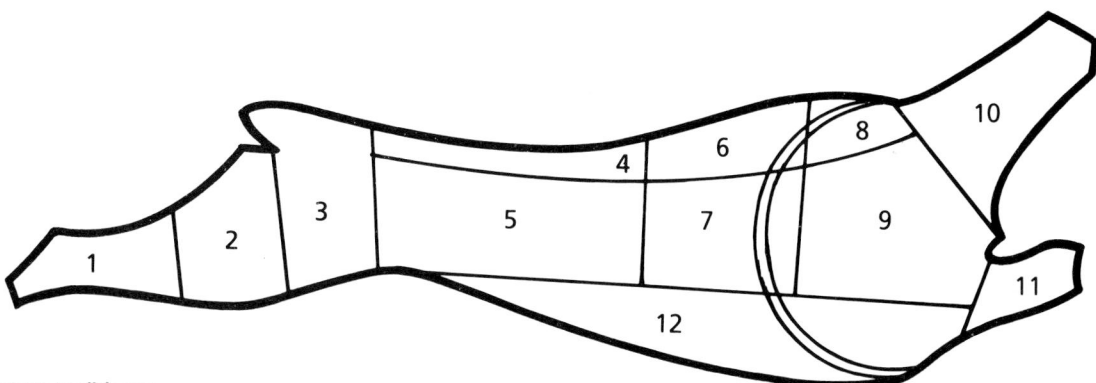

Lamb & mutton: English cuts
1. Shank end of leg
1. & 2. Leg (gigot in Scotland)
3. Fillet
4. & 5. Saddle, only when cut takes in both sides of back; loin or centerloin chops

6. Best end (fair end in Ireland) of neck roast; best end of neck chops if cut; crown roast
7. Cutlets

8. Middle neck chops or cutlets (gigot chops in Ireland)
8. & 9. Shoulder

10. Scrag end of neck
11. Shank
12. Breast

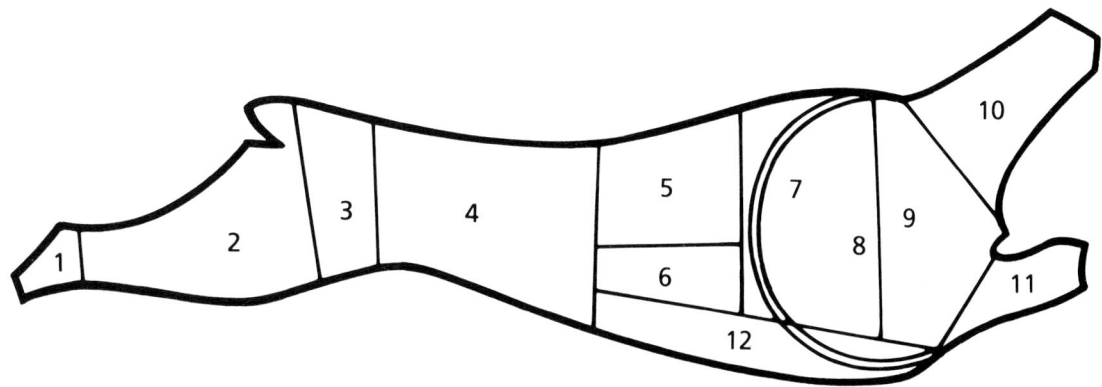

Lamb & mutton: French cuts
1. Pied
2. Gigot; baron d'agneau if cut takes in both leg parts

3. Selle d'agneau, when cut takes in both sides of back
4. Filet (top half); côte de filet (bottom half)

5. Côtes or côtelettes première
6. Haute de côtelette
7. Carré
8. Côtes or côtelettes découvertes

7., 8. & 9. Épaule
10. Collet
11. Pied
12. Poitrine

Agneau de lait poulette
Baby Lamb in Cream Sauce

	00:15	01:00
American	Ingredients	Metric/Imperial
3 lb	Boneless shoulder of baby lamb	1.5 kg / 3 lb
3	Small onions	3
1 tbsp	Butter	15 g / ½ oz
2 tbsp	Flour	2 tbsp
1¼ cups	Dry white wine	300 ml / ½ pint
1¼ cups	Water	300 ml / ½ pint
1	Bouquet garni	1
	Salt and pepper	
½ lb	Button mushrooms	250 g / 8 oz
2	Egg yolks	2
½ cup	Crème fraîche (see page 122)	125 ml / 4 fl oz
	Lemon juice	

1. Cut the lamb into chunks. Brown them in a frying pan without any fat. Remove and set aside.
2. Peel and chop the onions. Heat the butter in a flameproof casserole, add the onions and cook over a gentle heat until they are translucent.
3. Add the meat to the casserole and heat, stirring, then sprinkle with the flour. Shake the casserole so that the flour coats all the pieces of meat. Add the wine, water, bouquet garni, and salt and pepper to taste. Cover and simmer over a gentle heat for 30 minutes.
4. Add the mushrooms and simmer for 10-15 minutes longer. Remove from the heat. Discard the bouquet garni.
5. Mix the egg yolks in a bowl with the crème fraîche. Add a few drops of lemon juice and a little of the cooking liquid, then pour this mixture into the casserole. Reheat without boiling.

Baron d'agneau aux herbes de Provence
Baron of Lamb with Provençal Herbs

	00:10 Serves 12-16	01:40
American	Ingredients	Metric/Imperial
5	Large garlic cloves	5
1 (8 lb)	Lamb double loin roast [saddle] with 2 hind legs attached	1 (4 kg / 8 lb)
⅔ cup	Butter	150 g / 5 oz
¼ cup	Mixed dried Provençal herbs (thyme, oregano, bay leaf and savory)	4 tbsp
	Salt and pepper	
3 tbsp	Water	3 tbsp

1. Preheat the oven to 450°F / 230°C / Gas Mark 8.
2. Peel the garlic cloves and slice them thinly. With a small pointed knife, prick the meat all over and slide a piece of garlic into each incision along the knife blade. Melt the butter and stir in the herbs. Place the meat in a large roasting pan. Season with salt and plenty of pepper and pour over the herby butter. Add the water to the roasting pan.
3. Roast for 1 hour and 40 minutes, basting several times. If the surface of the meat starts to get too brown, cover with foil. To check whether the meat is cooked enough, insert a skewer: the juices that run out should be pink. (Cook longer if you prefer your meat more well done.)
4. The baron should be brought to the table and carved in front of your guests. Pour the cooking juices into a sauceboat and serve at the same time.

Blanquette d'agneau
Lamb in a White Sauce

	00:15	00:45
American	Ingredients	Metric/Imperial
2 lb	Boneless breast of lamb	1 kg / 2 lb
1	Onion	1
2 tbsp	Oil	2 tbsp
1	Carrot	1
1	Bouquet garni	1
1¼ cups	Water	300 ml / ½ pint
	Salt and pepper	
1 tbsp	Butter	15 g / ½ oz
1 tbsp	Flour	1 tbsp
1	Egg yolk	1
2 tbsp	Crème fraîche (see page 122)	2 tbsp

1. Cut the lamb into cubes. Peel and thinly slice the onion. Heat the oil in a flameproof casserole, add the onion and cook until golden. Add the lamb cubes and cook over a moderate heat for a few minutes, without letting them color.
2. Meanwhile, peel and slice the carrot. Add this to the casserole with the bouquet garni and water. Season with salt and pepper and stir well. Cook over a medium heat for 40 minutes.
3. Remove the meat with a slotted spoon and keep warm on a serving dish. Strain the cooking liquid and set aside.
4. Melt the butter in a small saucepan over a low heat, add the flour and stir well until the butter has absorbed the flour. Gradually add the strained cooking liquid, stirring well. Cook over a gentle heat for 5 minutes until thick, stirring constantly. Remove from the heat.
5. Mix the egg yolk in a bowl with the crème fraîche. Season with salt and pepper. Add this mixture to the sauce, stirring briskly.
6. Pour the sauce over the meat and serve hot.

Carré d'agneau printanier
Roast Spring Lamb

	00:05	00:25 to 00:30
American	Ingredients	Metric/Imperial
1	Rack of lamb [best end of neck], comprising 8 chops, chined	1
	Salt and pepper	

1. Preheat the oven to 475°F / 250°C / Gas Mark 9.
2. Place the meat on a rack in a roasting pan, fat side down.

Roast for 15 minutes, then turn the meat over. Season with salt and pepper and continue roasting for 15 minutes.
3. Turn the oven off and leave the lamb inside for 5-8 minutes. (With an electric oven, open the door and leave it ajar.)
4. To serve, cut the meat between the bones of the chops.

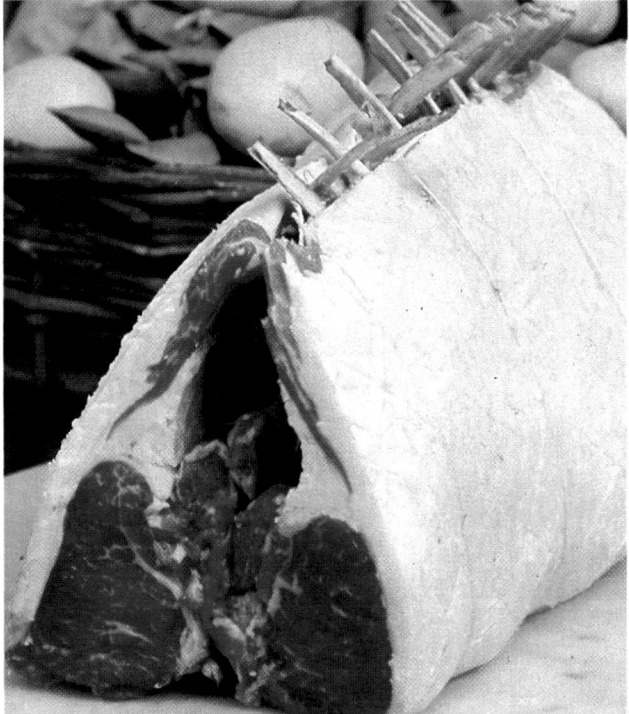

Roast spring lamb

Cervelles d'agneau grenobloise
Piquant Lambs' Brains

	00:20		00:15

American	Ingredients	Metric/Imperial
6	Lambs' brains	6
	Salt and pepper	
	Vinegar or lemon juice	
½ cup	Butter	125 g / 4 oz
2 tbsp	Oil	2 tbsp
12	Small cubes of bread	12
1	Lemon	1
¼ cup	Capers	50 g / 2 oz
	Chopped fresh parsley for garnish	

1. Soak the brains in cold water to cover for 6 hours, changing the water 3 or 4 times. Drain and remove the membrane.
2. Bring a large saucepan of water to a boil and add salt and a dash of vinegar or lemon juice. Add the brains and simmer for 5 minutes, then drain and pat dry.
3. Heat the butter in a frying pan until it is nut-brown color. Add the brains and cook until golden all over, about 10 minutes.
4. Meanwhile, heat the oil in another frying pan, add the cubes of bread and fry until browned on all sides. Drain on paper towels. Peel and dice the lemon.
5. Remove the brains to a warmed serving dish and keep hot. Add the lemon, croûtons and capers to the pan and stir to mix with the juices from the brains. Season with salt and pepper. Pour this mixture over the brains and sprinkle with parsley.

Carré d'agneau bonne femme
Country Style Lamb

	00:25		01:00

American	Ingredients	Metric/Imperial
5 oz	Slightly salted bacon	150 g / 5 oz
1½ lb	Potatoes	750 g / 1½ lb
½ cup	Butter	125 g / 4 oz
1	Rack of lamb [best end of neck], comprising 8 chops, chined	1
	Salt and pepper	
24	Tiny onions	24
1 tbsp	Sugar	1 tbsp

1. Preheat the oven to 450°F / 230°C / Gas Mark 8.
2. Cut the bacon into strips. Place them in a saucepan of cold water, bring to a boil and boil gently for 5 minutes. Drain and pat dry. Peel and cube the potatoes.
3. Grease an ovenproof dish with 2 tablespoons [25 g / 1 oz] of the butter. Place the lamb in it and add the bacon and potatoes. Sprinkle all over with salt and pepper. Melt half of the remaining butter and pour over the meat, bacon and potatoes. Place in the oven and cook for at least 30 minutes.
4. Meanwhile, peel the onions. Put them in a shallow pan, cover with water and add the rest of the butter. Bring to a boil. Add the sugar and salt to taste and stir. Cover the onions closely with a sheet of parchment [greaseproof] paper and simmer very gently until all the liquid has evaporated (about 30 minutes). Remove the paper and simmer a little longer, stirring gently, until the onions are golden.
5. When the meat is cooked, turn off the oven, cover the dish with a sheet of foil and leave inside for 15 minutes. (With an electric oven, open the door and leave it ajar.)
6. To serve, cut the meat between the bones of the chops, then put it back together again on a serving platter. Garnish with the potatoes, bacon and onions.

Chachlik
Lamb and Tomato Kebabs

	00:15	00:12 to 00:15	
	plus marinating		

American	Ingredients	Metric/Imperial
2 lb	Lean boneless lamb	1 kg / 2 lb
1 tsp	Ground cumin	1 tsp
	Salt and pepper	
⅓ cup	Olive oil	5 tbsp
36	Tiny onions or	36
6	Medium-size onions	6
10	Small, very firm tomatoes	10

1. Cut the meat into 1½ in / 4 cm cubes; there should be 24 cubes. Put them in a deep bowl and sprinkle with the cumin and salt and pepper to taste. Stir to season all the lamb cubes, then pour over the olive oil. Leave to marinate for 25 minutes.
2. Preheat the broiler [grill].
3. Peel the onions. Quarter them if using larger onions.
4. Thread the lamb cubes onto skewers, alternating with the onions and tomatoes. Cook for 12-15 minutes.

Côtelettes d'agneau provençale

Provençal Lamb Chops

	00:05	00:25
	plus marinating	

American	Ingredients	Metric/Imperial
⅔ cup	Olive oil	150 ml / ¼ pint
1 tbsp	Dried thyme	1 tbsp
12 (3 oz)	Lamb chops	12 (75 g / 3 oz)
3	Eggplant [aubergines]	3
	Salt	
6	Tomatoes	6
1	Garlic clove	1
3 tbsp	Chopped fresh parsley	3 tbsp

1. Mix the oil in a bowl with the thyme and leave to infuse for 1 hour.
2. Brush each chop with the herby oil and leave to marinate for 30 minutes.
3. Meanwhile, peel and thickly slice the eggplant. Lay them on paper towels, sprinkle with salt and leave to drain for 30 minutes. Rinse and pat dry, then dice.
4. Preheat the broiler [grill].
5. Heat 2 tablespoons of the herby oil in a frying pan, add the eggplant and cook over a low heat until golden, about 25 minutes. Stir occasionally.
6. Meanwhile, cut the tomatoes in half and remove the seeds. Sprinkle with a few drops of herby oil and set aside. Peel and chop the garlic.
7. Arrange the chops on the broiler rack and cook for 3-5 minutes on each side. Add the tomatoes when you turn the chops and cook until golden brown and softened.
8. Spoon the eggplant into the center of a warmed serving platter and sprinkle with the garlic and half of the parsley. Arrange the chops around the eggplant and garnish with the tomatoes. Sprinkle the tomatoes with the remaining parsley.

Épaule d'agneau farcie

Kidney-Stuffed Shoulder of Lamb

	00:20	00:40

American	Ingredients	Metric/Imperial
1	Shallot	1
¼ lb	Cooked ham	125 g / 4 oz
2	Fresh thyme sprigs	2
1	Small bunch of fresh parsley	1
2	Small lamb's kidneys	2
¼	Butter	50 g / 2 oz
	Salt and pepper	
6	Small firm tomatoes	6
1 (2 lb)	Boneless shoulder of lamb with shank (knuckle) attached	1 (1 kg / 2 lb)

1. Preheat the oven to 425°F / 220°C / Gas Mark 7.
2. Peel the shallot. Put it through a food mill or grinder [mincer] with the ham, thyme and parsley.
3. Halve the kidneys and cut out the cores. Melt 2 tablespoons [25 g / 1 oz] of the butter in a frying pan, add the kidneys and

cook for 3-4 minutes without letting them brown. Sprinkle with salt and pepper. Remove from the pan.
4. Add the shallot and ham mixture to the pan and cook until softened, scraping up the residue. Season with salt and pepper.
5. Spread the ham mixture in the cavity in the shoulder of lamb. Arrange the kidneys on top in a single layer. Roll up the meat in a long roll and tie. Place in an ovenproof dish.
6. Peel the tomatoes (first plunging them in boiling water for 10 seconds). Sprinkle with salt and pepper and arrange them around the meat.
7. Roast for about 40 minutes.
8. Turn off the oven. Add the remaining butter and a few drops of water. Leave the meat inside for 8-10 minutes. (With an electric oven, open the door and leave it ajar.)
9. Serve carved in slices with the tomatoes and pan juices.

Épaule de mouton berrichonne

Stuffed Shoulder of Lamb with Puréed Vegetables

	00:30	01:20

American	Ingredients	Metric/Imperial
2	Onions	2
1 tbsp	Oil	1 tbsp
1 cup	Fresh white bread crumbs	50 g / 2 oz
½ lb	Pork sausage meat	250 g / 8 oz
2 tbsp	Chopped fresh parsley	2 tbsp
1	Egg	1
1	Garlic clove	1
	Grated nutmeg	
	Salt and pepper	
1 (2 lb)	Boneless shoulder of lamb	1 (1 kg / 2 lb)
1	Celeriac	1
2	Turnips	2
3	Carrots	3
4	Leeks	4
1	Bouquet garni	1
3	Medium-size potatoes	3
1 tbsp	Butter	15 g / ½ oz

1. Peel and thinly slice one of the onions. Heat the oil in a frying pan, add the onion and cook until golden. Tip the onion into a mixing bowl. Set aside.
2. Soak the bread crumbs in hot water for 2-3 minutes. Drain the bread crumbs and squeeze with your fingers to remove excess water. Add the bread to the bowl.
3. Add the sausage meat, parsley and egg. Peel and chop the garlic and add it. Season with a pinch of nutmeg and salt and pepper to taste. Mix well together.
4. Lay the lamb out on a working surface. Spread with the stuffing and roll up the meat. Tie into shape with string. Place the meat in a flameproof casserole and cover with water. Bring to a boil.
5. Meanwhile, peel and dice the celeriac, turnips and carrots. Finely chop the leeks. Peel and thinly slice the remaining onion. When the water in the casserole has reached boiling point, add all the vegetables and the bouquet garni. Season with salt and pepper. Simmer gently over a low heat for 1 hour.
6. Peel and dice the potatoes. Add to the casserole and simmer for 20 minutes longer.

7. Remove the vegetables from the casserole with a slotted spoon and purée them in a blender or food processor until coarse-fine. Do not blend until smooth. Reheat this purée in a saucepan over a very gentle heat, adding the butter in small pieces.

8. Drain the lamb and cut it into medium thick slices. Remove the string. Arrange the meat on a warmed serving platter and surround with the vegetable purée.

Épaule d'agneau en gigot

Shoulder of Lamb 'Leg-of-Mutton' Style

▭▷ 00:10   00:40 🍲

American	Ingredients	Metric/Imperial
1	Garlic clove	1
1	Boneless shoulder of lamb with the shank [knuckle] attached	1
¼ cup	Butter	50 g / 2 oz
	Salt and pepper	
1 tbsp	Boiling water	1 tbsp

1. Preheat the oven to 475°F / 250°C / Gas Mark 9. Preheat the broiler [grill].

2. Peel the garlic and cut into slices. With a small pointed knife, prick the meat here and there, sliding in a piece of garlic along the knife blade at each incision. Spread 1 tablespoon [15 g / ½ oz] of the butter all over the meat and sprinkle with salt and pepper.

3. Place the meat on a rack in a roasting pan. Put it in the oven and roast for 15 minutes, then transfer to the broiler, placing the meat as far as possible from the heat. Cook for 25 minutes, turning occasionally to brown evenly.

4. Remove the meat from the heat and leave to rest for 8 minutes.

5. Carve the meat, and pour the juices produced back into the roasting pan. Add the boiling water and then the rest of the butter, beating well. Heat gently.

6. Serve the meat with the gravy.

Shoulder of lamb 'leg-of-mutton' style

Épaule d'agneau rôtie

Roast Shoulder of Lamb with Herbs

▭▷ 00:20   00:40 🍲
plus seasoning

American	Ingredients	Metric/Imperial
1 (2 lb)	Boneless shoulder of lamb, rolled and tied	1 (1 kg / 2 lb)
	Salt and pepper	
2	Bay leaves	2
3	Fresh thyme sprigs	3
3	Fresh rosemary sprigs	3
⅓ cup	Water	5 tbsp
¼ cup	Butter	50 g / 2 oz

1. Sprinkle the meat with salt and pepper. Slide the bay leaf and thyme and rosemary sprigs under the string tying the meat.

2. Preheat the oven to 425°F / 220°C / Gas Mark 7.

3. Place the lamb on a rack in a roasting pan. Roast about 20 minutes, then turn the meat over. Add the water to the roasting pan and continue cooking for 20 minutes.

4. Turn off the oven and leave the lamb inside for 5 minutes. (With an electric oven, open the door and leave it ajar.)

5. Carve the meat, and pour the juices produced back into the roasting pan. Add 1 tablespoon of hot water and bring to a boil on top of the stove, scraping up the caramelized meat residue from the bottom of the pan. Reduce by half, then add the butter, stirring with a whisk to incorporate well.

6. Serve the meat with the gravy.

Épaule de mouton aux olives

Shoulder of Lamb with Olives

▭▷ 00:15   01:00 🍲

American	Ingredients	Metric/Imperial
1	Boneless shoulder of lamb, barded and tied	1 (1 kg / 2 lb)
	Salt and pepper	
3	Onions	3
4	Carrots	4
3 tbsp	Oil	3 tbsp
1	Bay leaf	1
1	Fresh thyme sprig	1
2	Cloves	2
⅔ cup	Hot water	150 ml / ¼ pint
¾ cup	Green olives	125 g / 4 oz

1. Sprinkle the meat with salt and pepper. Peel and thinly slice the onions and carrots.

2. Heat the oil in a flameproof casserole, add the meat and brown for 5 minutes on each side. Add the carrots, onions, bay leaf, thyme, cloves, and salt and pepper to taste. Add the hot water and mix the vegetables together well. Cover and cook over a medium heat for 30 minutes.

3. Meanwhile, plunge the olives into boiling water, then drain.

4. Add the olives to the casserole and cook over a gentle heat for 30 minutes longer.

5. Carve the meat into slices and serve with the vegetables and gravy.

Gigot boulangère
Leg of Lamb with Potatoes and Onions

	00:25	02:50

American	Ingredients	Metric/Imperial
4 lb	Potatoes	2 kg / 4 lb
1	Onion	1
1 tsp	Dried crumbled bay leaf	1 tsp
1 tsp	Dried thyme	1 tsp
	Salt and pepper	
½ cup	Butter	125 g / 4 oz
2	Garlic cloves	2
1 (3 lb)	Leg of lamb, at room temperature	1 (1.5 kg / 3 lb)

1. Preheat the oven to 425°F / 220°C / Gas Mark 7.
2. Peel and thinly slice the potatoes. Peel and finely chop the onion. Mix the onion with the bay leaf and thyme. Season with salt and pepper.
3. Grease the bottom of an ovenproof dish with 2 tablespoons [25 g / 1 oz] of the butter and lay half the potatoes in a layer in it. Sprinkle with half the onion mixture. Add the remaining potatoes in an even layer and sprinkle with the rest of the onion mixture. Dot with ¼ cup [50 g / 2 oz] of the butter, cut in pieces, and moisten with warm water; the water should just cover the potatoes.
4. Place in the oven and bake for 1¾-2 hours or until there is hardly any water left in the bottom of the dish.
5. Mash the rest of the butter with salt and pepper to taste. Peel the garlic and cut into small slivers. With a small pointed knife, prick the meat here and there, sliding in a piece of garlic along the knife blade at each incision. Spread the seasoned butter over the meat.
6. Place the meat on top of the potatoes and roast for 45 minutes, turning it to brown evenly.
7. Turn off the oven and leave the meat inside for 5 minutes. (With an electric oven, open the door and leave it ajar.)
8. Carve the meat at the table and serve with the potatoes and pan juices.

Gigot farci
Kidney-Stuffed Leg of Lamb

	00:30	01:00

American	Ingredients	Metric/Imperial
¼ cup	Butter	50 g / 2 oz
3	Lambs' kidneys	3
2 tsp	Mixed dried Provençal herbs	2 tsp
	Salt and pepper	
1 (2½ lb)	Boned leg of lamb, bone reserved	1 (1.25 kg / 2½ lb)
1	Garlic clove	1
3 tbsp	Hot water	3 tbsp

1. Preheat the oven to 450°F / 230°C / Gas Mark 8.
2. Heat 2 tablespoons [25 g / 1 oz] of the butter in a frying pan, add the kidneys and cook over a high heat for about 3-4 minutes. Sprinkle with 1 teaspoon of the herbs, and salt and pepper to taste. Remove the kidneys with a slotted spoon. Add the remaining herbs to the fat in the pan and set aside.
3. Place the kidneys into the cavity in the lamb. Then put back the bone and tie to give the leg of lamb its original shape.
4. Peel the garlic and cut into small slivers. With a small pointed knife, prick the meat here and there and slide a piece of garlic along the blade of the knife into each incision. Brush the meat with the butter in which the kidneys were cooked and season with salt and pepper.
5. Place the meat on a rack in a roasting pan. Roast for 20 minutes, then turn the meat over and reduce the heat to 425°F / 220°C / Gas Mark 7. Roast for 40 minutes longer.
6. Turn off the oven, open the door and leave it ajar. Let the meat rest inside for 5 minutes.
7. Transfer the meat to a carving board and keep warm. Add the hot water to the roasting pan and scrape up the meat residue from the bottom. Bring to a boil. Remove from the heat and add the rest of the butter, beating well.
8. Carve the meat and add the carving juices to the gravy.

Cook's tip: you can buy dried Provençal herbs ready mixed (Herbes de Provence), or mix them yourself: 1 tsp dried thyme and ½ each dried basil, rosemary and savory.

Gigot grillé au beurre d'ail
Lamb Steaks with Garlic Butter

	00:10 plus chilling	00:08 to 00:12

American	Ingredients	Metric/Imperial
3	Garlic cloves	3
½ cup	Butter, at room temperature	125 g / 4 oz
	Salt and pepper	
6	Lamb leg steaks (slices cut from top of leg)	6
6 tbsp	Oil	6 tbsp

1. Peel the garlic and crush as finely as possible using a mortar and pestle or with the blade of a knife. Mix with the butter. Season with salt and pepper. Roll the garlic butter into a cylindrical shape. Wrap in foil and chill until firm.
2. Preheat the broiler [grill].
3. Brush the lamb steaks with the oil. Place the steaks on the rack of the broiler pan and cook for 4-6 minutes on each side, according to taste.
4. Cut the garlic butter into 6 or 12 slices and place 1 or 2 on each lamb steak. Serve hot.

Gigot rôti
Roast Leg of Lamb

	00:05 plus seasoning meat	01:20

American	Ingredients	Metric/Imperial
1 (4 lb)	Leg of lamb	1 (2 kg / 4 lb)
2	Garlic cloves	2
⅓ cup	Water	5 tbsp
¼ cup	Butter	50 g / 2 oz
	Salt and pepper	

1. If the meat has been stored in the refrigerator, take it out 4 hours before cooking. About 1 hour before cooking, peel the garlic and cut into small slivers. Prick the meat here and there with a small pointed knife and slide in a piece of garlic along the knife blade at each incision.

2. Preheat the oven to 475°F / 250°C / Gas Mark 9.

3. Place the meat on a rack in a roasting pan. Roast for 15 minutes, then lower the oven temperature to 400°F / 200°C / Gas Mark 6 and continue roasting for about 1 hour. Halfway through, add the water to the roasting pan. Baste the meat several times.

4. Check that the meat is cooked by inserting a skewer: the juice which runs out should be pink. Turn off the oven and leave the meat inside for 5 minutes.

5. Carve the meat, reserving the juices. Add the juices to the roasting pan with the butter, cut into pieces. Season with salt and pepper. Serve this gravy in a sauceboat.

Moussaka
Greek Lamb Casserole

	01:00		01:00
	plus draining		

American	Ingredients	Metric/Imperial
4 - 6	Eggplant (aubergines)	4 - 6
	Salt and pepper	
5 tbsp	Olive oil	5 tbsp
4	Onions	4
1	Garlic clove	1
1 tsp	Dried thyme	1 tsp
1	Bay leaf	1
1½ lb	Ground [minced] shoulder of lamb	750 g / 1½ lb
2	Eggs	2
1 tbsp	Chopped fresh coriander	1 tbsp

1. Peel the eggplant and cut them lengthwise into ½ in / 1 cm thick slices. Spread them out on a linen towel and sprinkle with salt. Leave to drain for 30 minutes.

2. Rinse the eggplant slices and pat dry. Heat 4 tablespoons oil in a frying pan, add the eggplant slices and brown quickly on both sides. Do not try to cook them through. Drain on paper towels.

3. Line a 6½ in / 16 cm charlotte mold with the best eggplant slices, starting at the bottom and overlapping the slices like flower petals. Then line the sides, allowing the slices to overhang the rim of the mold so that they can be folded over the filling. Set the remaining eggplant slices aside.

4. Peel and chop the onions and garlic. Heat the remaining oil in a heavy saucepan, add the onions and garlic and cook for a few minutes until soft. Add the thyme and bay leaf, broken into pieces. When the onions are translucent, add the lamb and brown, stirring frequently. Season with salt and pepper, cover and simmer gently for 15 minutes.

5. Preheat the oven to 350°F / 180°C / Gas Mark 4.

6. Remove the lamb mixture from the heat. Cool slightly, then mix in the eggs and coriander.

7. Put a layer of the meat mixture into the mold and cover with a layer of eggplant slices. Press down slightly. Continue layering the ingredients, finishing with a layer of eggplant, then fold over the overhanging eggplant slices used to line the mold.

8. Cover the mold and bake for 50 minutes to 1 hour.

9. Remove from the oven and cool for 5 minutes, then skim off any fat which has come to the surface. Unmold onto a serving dish and serve with tomato sauce (see page 133) seasoned with a large pinch of cayenne pepper.

Greek lamb casserole

Poitrine de mouton farcie
Stuffed Breast of Lamb

	00:45		01:30

American	Ingredients	Metric/Imperial
⅔ cup	Currants	125 g / 4 oz
2½ cups	Water	600 ml / 1 pint
	Salt and pepper	
1½ cups	Long-grain rice	350 g / 12 oz
½ cup	Butter	125 g / 4 oz
1 cup	Flaked almonds	125 g / 4 oz
2 tbsp	Honey	2 tbsp
½	Lemon	½
1	Clove	1
1 (3 lb)	Boneless breast of lamb, with a pocket in it for stuffing	1 (1.5 kg / 3 lb)

1. Preheat the oven to 450°F / 230°C / Gas Mark 8.

2. Soak the currants in warm water for 30 minutes.

3. Meanwhile, put the water in a saucepan and add salt to taste. Bring to a boil. Add the rice and cook for 15-18 minutes or until tender. Heat 1 tablespoon [15 g / ½ oz] butter in a frying pan, add the almonds and fry until golden. Mix the honey and the juice of the ½ lemon. Season with salt and pepper and add the clove, crushed.

4. Drain the currants. Drain the rice, if necessary and rinse under cold water to remove excess starch. Mix the flavored honey into the rice, then add the currants, almonds and 2 tablespoons [25 g / 1 oz] of the butter. Mix well.

5. Sprinkle the pocket in the lamb with salt and pepper. Fill with one-third of the rice mixture. Sew up the pocket with kitchen string and spread the rest of the butter over the meat. Place it in a roasting pan.

6. Roast for about 1 hour.

7. Add the rest of the rice mixture to the roasting pan and cook for 10 minutes longer.

Navarin de mouton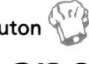

Lamb and Vegetable Stew

00:15   01:30 to 02:00

American	Ingredients	Metric/Imperial
3 lb	Boneless shoulder of lamb	1.5 kg / 3 lb
2 tbsp	Flour	2 tbsp
¼ lb	Small onions	125 g / 4 oz
2 tbsp	Lard or goose fat	2 tbsp
⅔ cup	Dry white wine	150 ml / ¼ pint
1	Bouquet garni	1
	Grated nutmeg	
	Salt and pepper	
¾ lb	Fresh peas	350 g / 12 oz
½ lb	Green beans	250 g / 8 oz
1 lb	Carrots	500 g / 1 lb

1. Cut the lamb into 1½ in / 2 cm cubes and coat with the flour. Peel the onions.

2. Melt the lard or goose fat in a flameproof casserole, add the lamb and brown all over without letting the fat burn. Pour in the wine, then add the onions, bouquet garni, a pinch of nutmeg, and salt and pepper to taste. Cover. When the liquid comes to a boil, turn down the heat and simmer very gently for about 45 minutes.

3. Shell the peas. Trim the beans and remove strings if necessary. Peel the carrots.

4. Add the vegetables to the casserole and cook, covered, for 30 minutes longer over a very low heat.

Gigot aux légumes nouveaux

Leg of Lamb with Spring Vegetables

01:00   01:00

American	Ingredients	Metric/Imperial
1	Garlic clove	1
1 (3 lb)	Leg of lamb	1 (1.5 kg / 3 lb)
2 tbsp	Oil	2 tbsp
	Salt and pepper	
1	Bouquet garni	1
1 lb	Small white turnips	500 g / 1 lb
2	Medium-size cucumbers	2
1 lb	Carrots	500 g / 1 lb
¾ lb	Small green beans	350 g / 12 oz
1	Small bunch of celery	1
1 lb	Fresh peas	500 g / 1 lb
1¼ lb	Potatoes	625 g / 1¼ lb
¾ lb	Onions	350 g / 12 oz
¼ cup	Butter	50 g / 2 oz

1. Peel the garlic and cut into small slivers. Prick the meat with a small pointed knife, sliding in a piece of garlic along the knife blade at each incision.

2. Heat 1 tablespoon of the oil in a flameproof casserole, add the lamb and brown all over. Sprinkle with salt and pepper and

add the bouquet garni. Cover and cook for 45-55 minutes.

3. Meanwhile, peel the turnips. Peel the cucumbers and carrots. Trim the beans and remove strings, if necessary. Cut all the vegetables, as well as the celery, into small dice. Shell the peas. Cook the vegetables separately in boiling salted water until tender but still firm: allow 10 minutes for the turnips, 10-15 minutes for the celery, 5 minutes for the cucumber, 10 minutes for the carrots, 20-25 minutes for the peas, and 5-10 minutes for the beans. Drain and set aside.

4. Peel and dice the potatoes. Peel and finely chop the onions. Heat 1 tablespoon [15 g / ½ oz] butter and the rest of the oil in a frying pan, add the potatoes and onions and cook gently for about 15 minutes.

5. Preheat the oven to 450°F / 230°C / Gas Mark 8.

6. Transfer the lamb to a roasting pan and roast for 10-12 minutes. Skim off and reserve the fat from the cooking liquid in the casserole. Use this fat to baste the lamb once or twice while it is roasting.

7. Put all the vegetables in the casserole with the cooking liquid from the meat. Add the rest of the butter and mix well. Cover and reheat quickly. Discard the bouquet garni, and season with salt and pepper.

8. Serve the meat sliced and surrounded by the vegetables.

Méchoui

Spit-Roasted Whole Lamb

00:45   05:00
plus lighting fire and marinating
Serves 15-20
according to the size of the lamb

American	Ingredients	Metric/Imperial
2	Garlic bulbs	2
1	Fat lamb (without head)	1
12	Dried hot peppers [chillies]	12
10	Black peppercorns	10
	Sea salt	
1	Large bunch of fresh mint	1
4	Lemons	4
1½ cups	Melted butter	350 g / 12 oz
1 cup	Olive oil	250 ml / 8 fl oz
6 tbsp	Dried oregano	6 tbsp
¼ cup	Harissa or other hot chili-based sauce	4 tbsp
2 tbsp	Black pepper	2 tbsp
3 tbsp	Dried mint	3 tbsp
2 tbsp	Salt	2 tbsp

1. Peel all the cloves of one bulb of garlic and place inside the lamb, together with the hot peppers, peppercorns, a handful of sea salt and the bunch of fresh mint.

2. Peel all the cloves of the other bulb of garlic and crush them. Grate the rind from the lemons and squeeze out the juice. In a large bowl, combine the melted butter with the oil, crushed garlic, lemon rind and juice, oregano, harissa, black pepper, dried mint and 2 tablespoons of salt. Mix very well.

3. Brush the lamb with the lemon mixture and leave to marinate for 2 hours.

4. Meanwhile, prepare the barbecue: dig a hole in the ground 3 ft / 1 m long, 20 in / 50 cm wide and 16 in / 40 cm deep. Fill the hole with wood, either on its own or mixed with charcoal, and light the fire. Leave to burn until reduced to embers.

5. Tie the lamb firmly to a rotisserie spit, with its fore and hind legs well stretched out. Place over the fire and cook the lamb, turning it constantly and basting with the lemon mixture. To check whether the lamb is cooked, insert a skewer — the juice which runs out should be clear, not pink.

6. Take the lamb off the spit and lay it on a large board. Carve it or let your guests help themselves.

Lamb-chop

Lamb Chops with Herb Butter

American	00:05	00:05 to 00:10

American	Ingredients	Metric/Imperial
½ cup	Butter, at room temperature	125 g / 4 oz
2 tbsp	Chopped fresh herbs (chives, parsley, tarragon)	2 tbsp
1	Garlic clove	1
6 (5 oz)	Thin lamb loin double chops	6 (150 g / 5 oz)
	Salt and pepper	

1. Mash all but 2 tablespoons (25 g / 1 oz) of the butter with the herbs and peeled and crushed garlic. Chill until firm.
2. Melt the remaining butter in a large frying pan. Add the chops to the pan — in one layer — and cook for 5-10 minutes according to taste, turning over halfway through. Keep a close eye on how the 'tails' of the chops are cooking; they should not be cooked as much as the thicker meat.
3. Arrange the chops on a warmed serving dish. Sprinkle with salt and pepper and top each chop with a spoonful of the seasoned butter. Serve hot.

Haricot de mouton

Lamb with White Beans

	00:15 plus soaking	02:30

American	Ingredients	Metric/Imperial
3 cups	Dried navy (haricot) beans	750 g / 1 ½ lb
2 ½ lb	Boneless shoulder of lamb	1.25 kg / 2 ½ lb
2	Carrots	2
2	Onions	2
2	Garlic cloves	2
¼ cup	Lard or goose fat	50 g / 2 oz
1	Bouquet garni	1
	Salt and pepper	

1. Soak the beans overnight in cold water to cover.
2. Drain the beans and place them in a saucepan. Cover with fresh cold water. Bring to a boil and simmer for about 2 hours or until the beans are tender.
3. Meanwhile cut the lamb into 1 in / 2.5 cm cubes. Peel and slice the carrots and onions. Peel the garlic.
4. Heat the lard in a flameproof casserole, add the lamb cubes and brown on all sides. Add the carrots, onions, garlic and bouquet garni. Cover and simmer over a very low heat for 1 hour.

5. Drain the beans, reserving their cooking liquid. Add them to the meat and moisten with a few spoonfuls of the reserved cooking liquid. Season with salt and pepper. Cover and simmer for 15 minutes longer. Serve very hot.

Mixed grill

Mixed Grill

	00:15	00:40

American	Ingredients	Metric/Imperial
½ cup	Butter	125 g / 4 oz
6	Small lamb rib chops	6
6 (3 - 4 oz)	Slices of calves' liver	6 (75 - 100 g / 3 - 4 oz)
6	Lambs' kidneys	6
6	Small sausages	6
3	Small tomatoes	3
6	Small button mushrooms	6
	Lemon juice	
	Salt and pepper	

1. Heat 3 tablespoons [40 g / 1½ oz] butter in each of two frying pans. Add the chops, slices of liver, kidneys, sausages and halved tomatoes and sauté quickly until browned but not cooked through. Remove from the heat.
2. Heat the rest of the butter in a saucepan, add the mushrooms and sprinkle with a few drops of lemon juice and salt and pepper to taste. Cook until all the liquid they produce has evaporated, stirring from time to time. Remove from the heat.
3. Preheat the broiler [grill].
4. To make serving easier, you could thread all the ingredients onto skewers in the following order: lamb chop, liver, kidney, sausage, mushroom. Sprinkle with salt and pepper.
5. Place the 'kebabs' under the broiler and cook for a few minutes. When one side starts to sizzle, turn them over. Heat through the tomato halves. Serve very hot.

Sauté d'agneau de lait

Sautéed Lamb with Parsley

	00:10	00:45

American	Ingredients	Metric/Imperial
2 ½ lb	Boneless shoulder of baby lamb	1.2 kg / 2 ½ lb
¼ cup	Butter	50 g / 2 oz
1	Small bunch of fresh parsley	1
2	Garlic cloves	2
	Salt and pepper	

1. Cut the lamb into pieces. Melt the butter in a heavy frying pan, add the pieces of lamb and brown, without burning the butter, for about 20 minutes.
2. Meanwhile, chop the parsley. Peel and chop the garlic.
3. Add the parsley and the garlic to the pan. Season with salt and pepper. Cover and cook over a very low heat for about 25 minutes, stirring from time to time.

Ragoût de mouton aux navets

Braised Lamb with Turnips

	00:30	02:00 to 02:30

American	Ingredients	Metric/Imperial
4 lb	Lamb riblets	2 kg / 4 lb
3 tbsp	Lard or	40 g / 1½ oz
¼ cup	Equal parts butter and oil	4 tbsp
2 tbsp	Flour	2 tbsp
4	Onions	4
1	Garlic clove	1
1	Bouquet garni	1
4 lb	Small white turnips	2 kg / 4 lb
	Salt and pepper	
8	Medium-size potatoes	8

1. Quickly seal the pieces of meat in a frying pan without any fat. When they are a nice golden color, remove with a slotted spoon and place in a flameproof casserole.
2. Add 1 tablespoon [15 g / ½ oz] lard (or 2 tablespoons of oil) and sprinkle with the flour. Shake the casserole to distribute the flour evenly. Cook for a few moments until it has turned golden.
3. Peel and thinly slice the onions and garlic. Add to the casserole with the bouquet garni. Cook very gently for 30 minutes, stirring occasionally.
4. Meanwhile, peel and quarter the turnips. Heat the rest of the lard (or the 2 tablespoons [25 g / 1 oz] butter) in a frying pan, add the turnips and cook gently until golden, about 25 minutes.
5. Drain the turnips and add to the casserole. Season with salt and pepper. Cook very gently for 1¼ hours longer. Add a little water to the casserole from time to time as necessary.
6. Peel the potatoes. Add them to the casserole and cook for a final 30 minutes.
7. Skim the fat off the cooking liquid and discard the bouquet garni before serving.

Tajine de mouton

North African Lamb Casserole

	00:30	01:30 to 02:00

American	Ingredients	Metric/Imperial
1 (4 lb)	Shoulder of lamb, shank [knuckle] piece	1 (2 kg / 4 lb)
1 tsp	Ground ginger	1 tsp
½ tsp	Saffron powder	½ tsp
	Salt and pepper	
1 cup	Olive oil	250 ml / 8 fl oz
2 lb	Green beans	1 kg / 2 lb
3	Tomatoes	3
1	Preserved lemon (see page 37)	1
1	Fresh lemon	1
1 tbsp	Flour	1 tbsp

1. Chop the lamb into 12 pieces of about the same size. Place them in a flameproof casserole, sprinkle with the ginger,

saffron and salt to taste and add the oil. Cover with water. Bring to a boil and simmer for about 10 minutes over a high heat.
2. Trim the beans and add them to the casserole. Cover and cook over a very low heat for 1½ hours, stirring from time to time and adding more water if necessary.
3. Quarter the tomatoes. Cut the preserved lemon into quarters. Scrape off the flesh and discard. Squeeze the juice from the fresh lemon. Dissolve the flour in 1 tablespoon of cold water.
4. Take the casserole off the heat and add these prepared ingredients. Stir well, then continue cooking for 5 minutes over a gentle heat.
5. If there is too much liquid, reduce over a fast heat at the end of the cooking period. Add pepper before serving.

Riz au curry

Lamb Curry with Saffron Rice

	00:20	01:30

American	Ingredients	Metric/Imperial
½ lb	Onions	250 g / 8 oz
2	Garlic cloves	2
4	Tomatoes	4
3 lb	Boneless shoulder of lamb	1.5 kg / 3 lb
¼ cup	Olive oil	4 tbsp
1	Fresh thyme sprig	1
1	Bay leaf	1
¼ cup	Curry powder	4 tbsp
	Cayenne pepper	
⅔ cup	Plain yogurt	150 ml / ¼ pint
5⅔ cups	Water	1.3 l / 2¼ pints
	Salt and pepper	
2½ cups	Long-grain rice	625 g / 1¼ lb
	Saffron powder	
1	Apple	1
2	Bananas	2

1. Peel and chop the onions and garlic. Peel the tomatoes (first plunging them in boiling water for 10 seconds), remove the seeds and chop the flesh. Cut the lamb into large pieces.
2. Heat half the olive oil in a large saucepan, add the onions and garlic and cook over a gentle heat for 5 minutes or until softened. Add the tomatoes, thyme, bay leaf, curry powder and a large pinch of cayenne pepper and leave to cook gently.
3. Heat the remaining oil in a frying pan and add the pieces of lamb. Brown on all sides over a high heat. Add the browned meat to the saucepan with the yogurt and ⅔ cup [150 ml / ¼ pint] of the water. Season with salt and pepper. Cover, and cook over a gentle heat for 1½ hours or until the lamb is tender.
4. Meanwhile, put the remaining water in another saucepan and bring to a boil. Add the rice, 1 teaspoon of salt and a pinch of saffron. Bring back to a boil, then cover and cook over a gentle heat for 18 minutes, without lifting the lid. Do not stir the rice. Taste it and let it cook for a few more minutes if you prefer it very tender. Keep hot.
5. Peel and dice the apple and bananas. When the lamb is cooked, add the fruit to the saucepan and stir. Cook for 5 minutes longer.
6. Serve the lamb curry and rice separately with both mild and hot chutneys as accompaniments.

Ragoût de mouton
Lamb Stew

| | 00:25 plus macerating | 01:30 to 02:00 | |

American	Ingredients	Metric/Imperial
3 lb	Boneless breast or shoulder of lamb	1.5 kg / 3 lb
	Salt and pepper	
1 tbsp	Lard (or butter)	15 g / ½ oz
2 tbsp	Flour	2 tbsp
1 quart	Water	1 l / 1¾ pints
¼ cup	Tomato paste [purée]	4 tbsp
1	Bouquet garni	1
20	Small onions	20
1 tbsp	Butter	15 g / ½ oz
1 tsp	Sugar	1 tsp
20	Small potatoes	20
1 tbsp	Chopped fresh parsley	1 tbsp

1. Cut the meat into 18 pieces of about the same size. Place them in a mixing bowl and sprinkle with salt and pepper. Stir and leave to macerate for about 10 minutes.

2. Heat the lard in a flameproof casserole, add the pieces of lamb and brown all over without letting the fat burn. Sprinkle with the flour and stir to distribute the flour evenly. Cook until the flour has turned golden brown.

3. Add the water and tomato paste. Stir to mix, scraping up the flour sticking to the bottom of the casserole. Add the bouquet garni. Cover and simmer for 1 hour.

4. Meanwhile, peel the onions. Heat the butter with the sugar in a frying pan, add the onions and cook over a low heat until golden on all sides. Peel the potatoes.

5. Remove the bouquet garni from the casserole. Add the onions and potatoes, but do not press them down into the sauce. Cover and cook for 30 minutes longer over a low heat.

6. Remove from the heat and cool slightly so that surplus fat can rise to the surface. Skim off this fat with a spoon.

7. Serve the meat sprinkled with the parsley, and surrounded by the onions, potatoes and sauce.

Selle d'agneau aux citrons verts
Saddle of Lamb with Lime

| | 00:20 | 01:00 | |

American	Ingredients	Metric/Imperial
¼ cup	Butter	50 g / 2 oz
1 (3 lb)	Lamb double loin roast [saddle]	1 (1.5 kg / 3 lb)
3	Limes	3
2	Carrots	2
2	Onions	2
1	Celery stalk	1
	Salt and pepper	
1	Bouquet garni	1
⅔ cup	Vinegar	150 ml / ¼ pint
1 tbsp	Sugar	1 tbsp
⅔ cup	Vermouth	150 ml / ¼ pint

1. Preheat the oven to 450°F / 230°C / Gas Mark 8.

2. Melt the butter in a flameproof casserole, add the lamb roast and brown on all sides. Meanwhile, pare the rind thinly from the limes. Set the rind aside. Squeeze the juice from the limes. Peel and finely dice the carrots and onions. Dice the celery.

3. Remove the meat from the casserole. Add the diced vegetables to the casserole and brown them, then replace the meat. Sprinkle with salt and pepper and pour over the lime juice. Add the bouquet garni. Cover the casserole and transfer it to the oven. Cook for about 30 minutes.

4. Meanwhile, cut the lime rind into fine shreds and blanch in boiling water for 1 minute. Drain. Heat the vinegar with the sugar in a small saucepan, add the shreds of rind and allow the liquid to evaporate over a medium heat.

5. When the meat is cooked, place it on a warmed serving platter and keep hot. Pour the vermouth into the casserole and boil, stirring, to reduce slightly. Pour into a sauceboat.

6. Garnish the meat with the lime rind and serve.

Spit-roast lamb

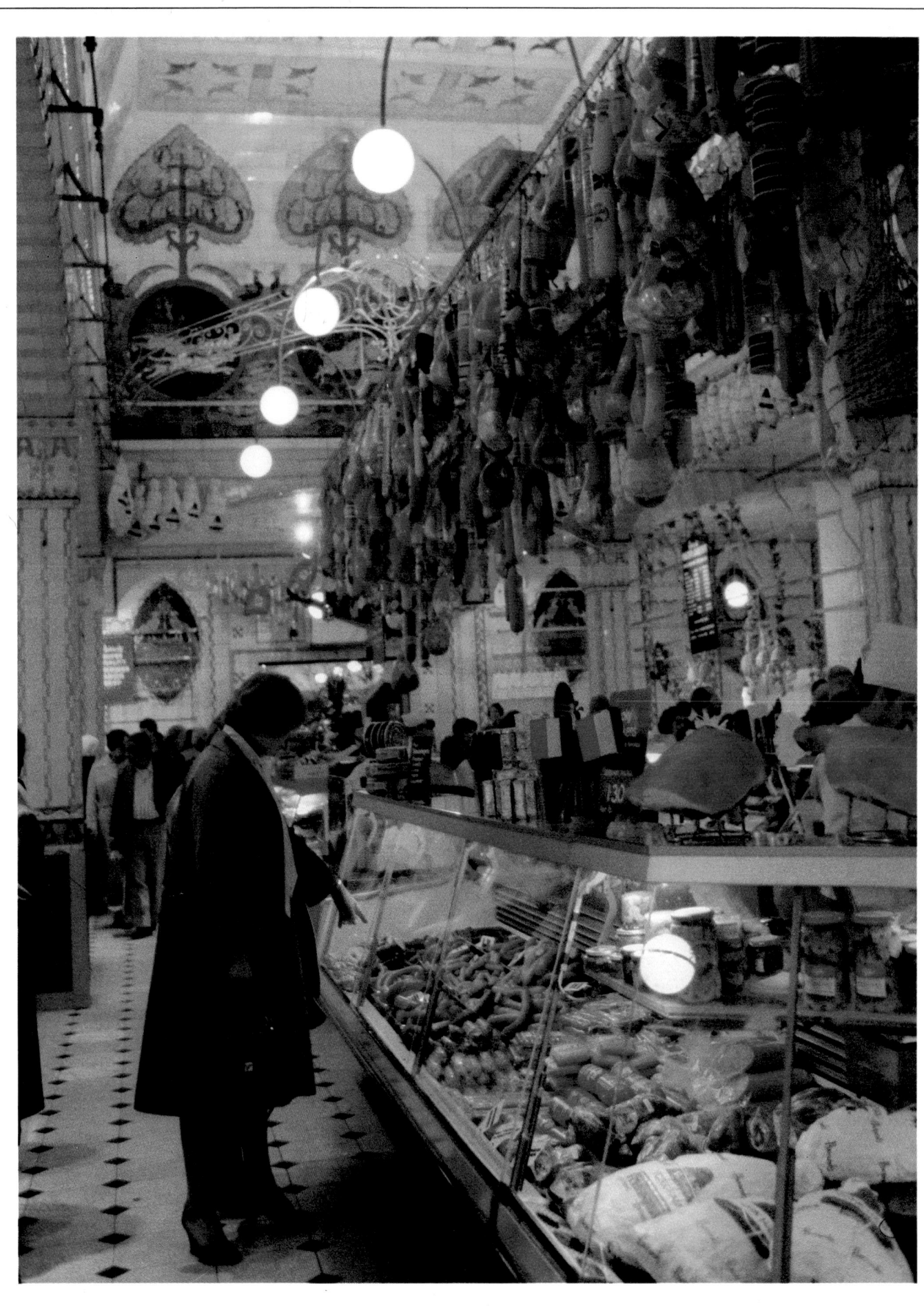

Buying and cooking pork

American cuts to choose	Cooking methods	British cuts to choose	
loin, crown, arm picnic shoulder, blade boston shoulder, tenderloin, back ribs, spareribs and country-style ribs	roast	fresh belly, leg, loin, neck end, spare rib, fillet, blade, hand, knuckle, spareribs	roast
rib chops, loin chops, shoulder steaks, cubes for kebabs, ground pork patties, sausages (fresh)	broil, fry	chump chops, loin chops, spare rib chops, escalopes, cubes for kebabs, minced pork patties, sausages (fresh)	grill, fry
chops, spareribs and country-style ribs, back ribs, tenderloin, shoulder steaks, cubes	braise	fillet, spare rib	braise
spareribs and country-style ribs, hocks	stew	fresh belly, knuckle	stew

Buying and cooking cured pork

American cuts to choose	Cooking methods	British cuts to choose	
ham, smoked pork loin, smoked arm picnic shoulder, smoked shoulder roll (butt), Canadian-style bacon	roast, bake	prime collar, middle back or through cut, corner gammon, middle gammon, bacon butt, ham	roast, bake (boil first if necessary)
ham slices, smoked pork loin chops, bacon, Canadian-style bacon, ground ham patties	broil, fry	gammon steaks, bacon rashers, short back and long back steaks	grill, fry
country-style ham, smoked arm picnic shoulder, smoked shoulder roll, smoked hocks	boil, braise, stew	end and middle bacon collar, gammon knuckle or hock, gammon slipper, bacon butt, bacon fore slipper, bacon small hock	boil, braise, stew

Stuffed whole suckling pig (see page 388)

Pork cuts

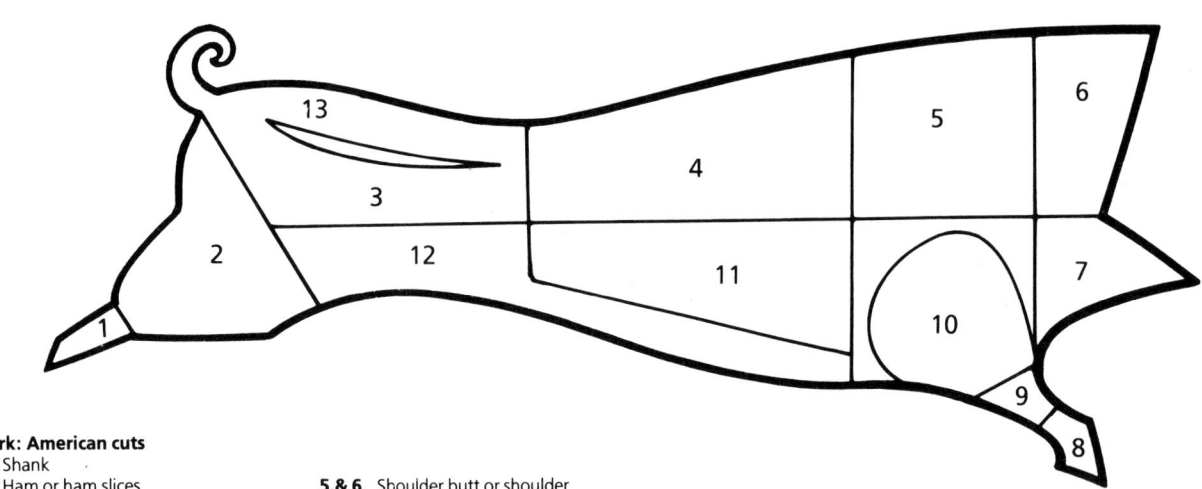

Pork: American cuts
1. Shank
2. Ham or ham slices
3. Loin roast; butterfly chops if both sides of back are used
4. Loin chops; loin roast (in one piece)
5.& 6. Shoulder butt or shoulder slices
7. Jowl butt
8. Foot
9. Hock
10. Picnic shoulder
11. Spareribs
12. Bacon piece
13. Tenderloin

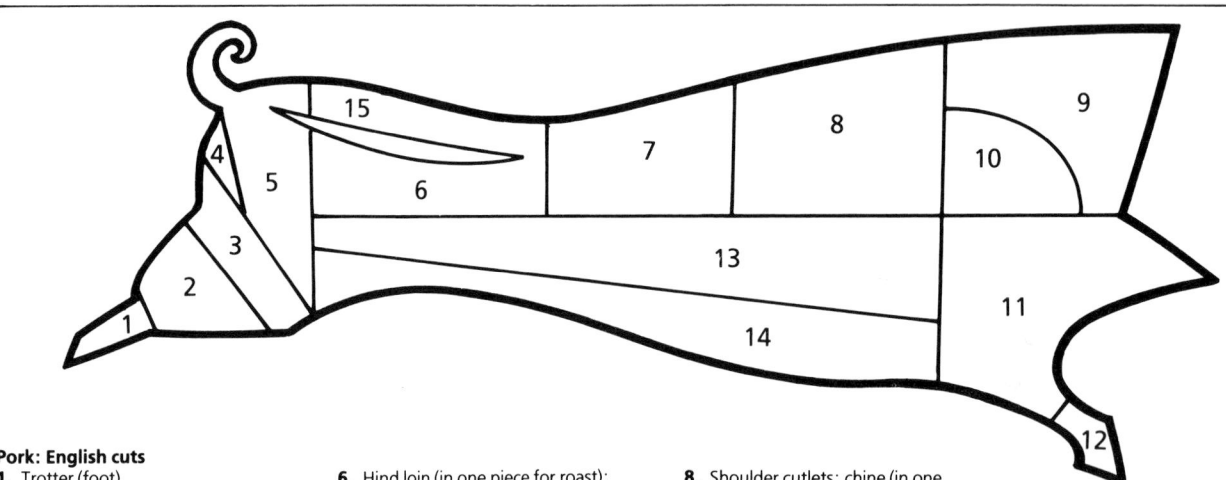

Pork: English cuts
1. Trotter (foot)
2. Knuckle or hock
3. Leg or gammon slices
4. Slipper
4.& 5. Gammon
6. Hind loin (in one piece for roast); chump chops (near tail end); loin chops also called centreloin chops
7. Fore loin (in one piece for roast); fore loin chops
8. Shoulder cutlets; chine (in one piece)
9. Spareribs
10. Bladebone
11. Hand
12. Trotter (foot)
13. Streaky bacon
14. Belly
15. Fillet (pork steak in Ireland)

Pork: French cuts
1. Pied
2. Jambonneau
3. Jambon
4. Pointe de filet; longe
5. Côtes (whole section); near head end, carré
6. Échine or palette
7. Gorge
8. Pied
9. Épaule or jambonneau
10. Plat de côtes
11. Poitrine
12. Filet

Aspic au jambon

Ham in Aspic

	00:40 plus setting		00:15

American	Ingredients	Metric/Imperial
¼ lb	Fresh peas	125 g / 4 oz
	Salt	
3	Hard-cooked eggs	3
2 cups	Aspic (see page 116)	500 ml / ¾ pint
½ lb	Prunes	250 g / 8 oz
12	Stuffed green olives	12
1 lb	Cooked ham	500 g / 1 lb

1. Shell the peas. Cook in boiling salted water for 15 minutes or until tender. Drain and set aside.
2. Shell the eggs. Dice the whites and mash the yolks.
3. Pour some of the liquid aspic into a decorative 1½ quart [1.5 l / 2½ pint] mold. Chill for 15 minutes or until set.
4. Meanwhile, remove the pits [stones] from the prunes with a small pointed knife. Quarter the prunes lengthwise.
5. Arrange 6 olives, 3 tablespoons of the peas and the diced white of one of the eggs on the layer of aspic in the mold. Cover with more aspic and chill for another 15 minutes.
6. Meanwhile, cut the ham into small dice.
7. As soon as the second layer of aspic has set well, layer the ham, remaining olives, remaining peas, the prunes, remaining egg whites and the mashed egg yolks in the mold. Cover with the rest of the aspic, and chill for 6 hours.
8. To serve, unmold onto a serving dish.

Andouillettes grillées sauce moutarde

Broiled [Grilled] Sausages with Mustard Sauce

	00:10		00:20

American	Ingredients	Metric/Imperial
6	Andouillettes or other small cooked pork sausages	6
3 tbsp	Oil	3 tbsp
2	Fresh tarragon sprigs	2
¾ cup	Butter	175 g / 6 oz
3 tbsp	Strong prepared mustard	3 tbsp
3 tbsp	Lemon juice or wine vinegar	3 tbsp
	Salt and pepper	

1. Preheat the broiler [grill].
2. Brush the sausages with the oil. Do not prick them, but lay them on the rack of the broiler pan and cook for 20 minutes, turning to brown evenly.
3. About 5 minutes before the end of cooking, remove the leaves from the tarragon sprigs and chop them. Cut the butter into small pieces. Mix the mustard and lemon juice or vinegar together in a small saucepan and heat gently, stirring. When the mixture boils, add the pieces of butter. Continue stirring over a low heat without boiling. Add the tarragon and salt and pepper to taste and mix well. Pour into a sauceboat.
4. Serve the sausages with the sauce.

Andouille à la purée

Sausage with Creamed Potatoes

	01:00		00:30

American	Ingredients	Metric/Imperial
½ lb	Andouille or other large cooked pork sausage	250 g / 8 oz
8	Medium-size potatoes	8
3 tbsp	Crème fraîche (see page 122)	3 tbsp
	Salt and pepper	
1	Small bunch of fresh parsley	1
2 tbsp	Dry bread crumbs	2 tbsp
2 tbsp	Butter	25 g / 1 oz

1. Cut the sausage into thin slices and remove the skin. Set aside.
2. Peel the potatoes and put them in a saucepan of cold water. Bring to a boil and cook for 20 minutes.
3. Preheat the oven to 425°F / 220°C / Gas Mark 7.
4. Drain the potatoes, then purée them using a potato ricer or food mill, or mash them. Add the crème fraîche and salt and pepper to taste. Chop the parsley. Add to the potato purée and mix in well.
5. Spread a layer of the potato purée on the bottom of a deep ovenproof dish. Cover with a layer of sausage slices, then add another layer of potato. Continue making layers until the ingredients are used up, finishing with a layer of potato.
6. Sprinkle with the bread crumbs and dot with the butter. Bake for 10 minutes or until the top is browned.

Boudin blanc aux pommes

White Sausage with Apples

	00:15		00:30

American	Ingredients	Metric/Imperial
6	Apples	6
6 tbsp	Butter	75 g / 3 oz
2 tbsp	Sugar	2 tbsp
6	Boudins blancs (white pork and poultry sausage or pudding)	6
	Salt and pepper	

1. Peel the apples. Cut each into 8 wedges and remove the core and seeds. Heat half of the butter in a frying pan, add the apples and cook for a few minutes over a moderate heat. Sprinkle with the sugar and cook over a gentle heat for a further 10 minutes or until golden. Keep warm.
2. Remove all the skin from the sausages. Melt the rest of the butter in a large frying pan over a gentle heat. Lay the puddings in the pan side by side and cook very gently until golden (without the skin, white sausages do not color so much). Turn very carefully using two spatulas, and cook the other side. Sprinkle with salt and pepper during cooking.
3. Serve the sausages with the apples.

Andouillettes à l'échalote

Sausages with Shallots

American	Ingredients	Metric/Imperial
2 tbsp	Lard or	25 g / 1 oz
2 tbsp	Oil	2 tbsp
6	Andouillettes or other small cooked pork sausages	6
3	Shallots	3
2	Lemons	2
	Salt and pepper	

1. Preheat the oven to 350°F / 180°C / Gas Mark 4.
2. Heat the lard or oil in a frying pan, add the andouillettes and brown all over on a medium heat, for 20 minutes. Drain and arrange on a warmed serving dish. Keep hot.
3. Peel and chop the shallots. Add to the frying pan and cook until soft and translucent. Add the juice of the lemons and salt and pepper to taste. Cook over a high heat, stirring well to scrape the sausage drippings from the bottom of the pan.
4. Pour this sauce over the sausages and serve immediately.

Carré de porc aux fruits

Loin of Pork with Fruit

American	Ingredients	Metric/Imperial
½ cup	Butter	125 g / 4 oz
1 (2½ lb)	Pork loin (center cut)	1 (1.25 kg / 2½ lb)
	Salt and pepper	
	Cayenne pepper	
4	Fresh sage leaves	4
6	Apples	6
	Ground cinnamon	
3	Bananas	3
3 tbsp	Rum	3 tbsp
6	Canned pineapple rings with syrup	6

1. Heat 2 tablespoons [25 g / 1 oz] of the butter in a flameproof casserole, add the pork and brown all over. Season with salt and pepper to taste and a pinch of cayenne pepper. Add the sage leaves and 1 tablespoon water and cook, covered, over a gentle heat for about 1½ hours, adding a little more water during cooking if necessary.
2. Meanwhile, peel the apples and cut into quarters. Remove the core and seeds. Heat 3 tablespoons [40 g / 1½ oz] of the butter in a frying pan, add the apples and cook, covered, over a gentle heat until golden. Sprinkle with a little cinnamon.
3. Peel the bananas and cut in half lengthwise. Heat the rest of the butter in another frying pan, add the banana halves and cook, covered, over a gentle heat until golden. Keep the bananas and apples warm.
4. When the meat is cooked, pour over the rum and set it alight. Lift up the meat so that the flame burns all over it. Transfer the meat to a warmed serving dish and surround with the apples, bananas and pineapple slices. Keep hot.

5. Pour ⅔ cup [150 ml / ¼ pint] pineapple syrup into the casserole and bring to a boil, scraping the bottom of the casserole with a wooden spatula. Reduce by half. Pour into a sauceboat and serve with the pork.

Cook's tip: in summer, you could use peaches instead of apples and bananas. Canned pineapple could be replaced by fresh pineapple cubes, sprinkled with sugar and fried in butter, or, if you want to be really original, cubes of fresh or canned mango.

Andouillettes au four

Baked Sausages

American	Ingredients	Metric/Imperial
3 tbsp	Butter	40 g / 1½ oz
6	Andouillettes or other small cooked pork sausages	6
3	Shallots	3
2 cups	Dry white wine	450 ml / ¾ pint
	Salt and pepper	

1. Preheat the oven to 425°F / 220°C / Gas Mark 7.
2. Heat half the butter in a frying pan, add the sausages and brown quickly on all sides.
3. Meanwhile, peel and chop the shallots. Heat the remaining butter in a saucepan, add the shallots and cook until softened. Do not let them burn.
4. Lay the sausages in an ovenproof dish and add their cooking liquid, the shallots and the wine. Season with salt and pepper. Bake for 20 minutes, turning them over once.
5. Remove the sausages to a warmed serving dish and keep hot. Pour the cooking liquid into a saucepan and boil to reduce by two-thirds. Pour this sauce over the sausages.

Loin of pork with fruit

Cervelas aux épinards
Cervelat [Saveloys] with Spinach

	00:20	00:15

American	Ingredients	Metric/Imperial
6	Medium-size cervelat [saveloys] or other smoked cooked pork sausage	6
1 tbsp	Oil	1 tbsp
2 lb	Fresh spinach or	1 kg / 2 lb
14 oz	Frozen spinach	400 g / 14 oz
	Salt and pepper	
¼ cup	Butter	50 g / 2 oz
6	Eggs	6

1. Split the sausages ¾ of the way through their thickness. Heat the oil in a frying pan, add the sausages and heat gently for 10 minutes.
2. Meanwhile, remove the stalks from fresh spinach and cook in boiling salted water for 10 minutes. Drain and squeeze to extract all excess water. Chop the spinach. (Cook frozen spinach according to the instructions on the package.)
3. Heat 2 tablespoons [25 g / 1 oz] of the butter in a saucepan, add the spinach and heat through over a very low heat.
4. Meanwhile, break the eggs into a mixing bowl and beat for a few seconds with a fork. Season with salt and pepper. Melt the rest of the butter in a saucepan, add the eggs and cook over a very gentle heat, stirring, until the eggs are lightly scrambled.
5. Spoon the spinach into the center of a warmed serving dish. Surround with the sausages and fill them with scrambled eggs where they have been split down the middle. Serve very hot.

Boudin mousseline
Blood Sausage [Black Puddings] with Creamed Potatoes

	00:05	00:25

American	Ingredients	Metric/Imperial
4 lb	Potatoes	2 kg / 4 lb
	Salt and pepper	
6	Boudins noirs (blood sausages or black puddings)	6
⅔ cup	Boiling milk	150 ml / ¼ pint
½ cup	Butter	125 g / 4 oz
	Grated nutmeg	
	Prepared mustard	

1. Preheat the oven to 425°F / 220°C / Gas Mark 7.
2. Scrub the potatoes and cook them in boiling salted water for 20 minutes.
3. Meanwhile, prick the sausages with the point of a knife and lay them on the rack of a roasting pan. Bake for 20 minutes.
4. Drain the potatoes, peel them and return to the saucepan. Mash with a potato masher. Gradually beat the boiling milk

into the potatoes over a gentle heat. Add the butter, a large pinch of nutmeg and salt and pepper to taste. Beat the purée over the heat until piping hot.
5. Put the potatoes in the center of a warmed serving dish and arrange the sausages all around. Serve with the mustard.

Andouillettes à la lyonnaise
Sausages in White Wine

	00:10	00:20 to 00:30

American	Ingredients	Metric/Imperial
6 tbsp	Butter	75 g / 3 oz
6	Andouillettes or other small cooked pork sausages	6
¾	Bottle of dry white wine	¾

1. Preheat the oven to 450°F / 230°C / Gas Mark 8.
2. Generously grease an ovenproof dish with 2 tablespoons [25 g / 1 oz] of the butter and arrange the sausages in it. Cut the rest of the butter into small pieces and scatter these over the sausages. Pour ¼ of the wine over the sausages.
3. Bake for 20-30 minutes, gradually adding the rest of the white wine.
4. Serve the sausages in the ovenproof dish.

Filet de porc charentaise
Pork Loin Charentaise

	00:10 plus marinating	02:30

American	Ingredients	Metric/Imperial
½	Sugar cube	½
1 tbsp	Sea salt	1 tbsp
1 tsp	Black peppercorns	1 tsp
	Ground allspice	
1	Fresh thyme sprig	1
1	Bay leaf	1
⅓ cup	Brandy	5 tbsp
1 (2½ lb)	Boneless loin of pork, bones reserved	1 (1.25 kg / 2½ lb)
1	Onion	1
1	Carrot	1
1 quart	Hot water	1 l / 1¾ pints
	Salt and pepper	

1. Put the sugar, sea salt and peppercorns in a mortar and crush with the pestle. Put these spices in a mixing bowl. Add a pinch of allspice, leaves from the thyme sprig, bay leaf, crumbled, and the brandy. Put the meat in a dish and rub all over with this mixture; leave it to marinate for 12 hours.
2. Preheat the broiler [grill].
3. Peel and chop the onion and carrot. Put them with the pork bones and brown for 10 minutes under the broiler.
4. Transfer the bones and vegetables to a flameproof casserole. Add the meat. Pour over the hot water and season with salt and pepper. Simmer for 1 hour.
5. Preheat the oven to 425°F / 220°C / Gas Mark 7.
6. Drain the meat, reserving the stock, and place on a rack in a roasting pan. Roast for about 1½ hours, basting frequently with the strained stock.

Carré de porc rôti
à la compote de pommes

Roast Loin of Pork with Apple Compote

00:15   01:15

American	Ingredients	Metric/Imperial
1 (3 lb)	Pork loin (center cut)	1 (1.5 kg / 3 lb)
1 tbsp	Oil	1 tbsp
	Salt and pepper	
1	Fresh sage sprig	1
4 lb	Apples	2 kg / 4 lb
⅔ cup	Sugar	150 g / 5 oz

1. Preheat the oven to 425°F /220°C / Gas Mark 7.
2. Place the meat in an ovenproof dish. Brush with the oil and sprinkle with salt and pepper. Remove the sage leaves from the stalks, chop them and add to the meat dish. Roast for 1¼ hours, adding 1 or 2 tablespoons of water from time to time. If the meat starts to get too brown, cover with foil.
3. Meanwhile, peel the apples and cut into quarters. Remove the core and seeds. Place in a frying pan with 2 tablespoons of water, the sugar and a pinch of salt. Cook, covered, over a gentle heat until the apples are very soft, then uncover and boil to evaporate the excess liquid. Mash the apples with a wooden spoon. Keep warm.
4. Carve the pork and serve with the hot apple compote.

Cochon de lait entier farci

Stuffed Whole Suckling Pig

01:00   02:30
Serves 8–10

American	Ingredients	Metric/Imperial
1 (8½ lb)	Suckling pig, liver reserved	1 (4 kg / 8½ lb)
¾ lb	Unsmoked bacon	350 g / 12 oz
⅔ cup	Oil	150 ml / ¼ pint
6 cups	Fresh white bread crumbs	350 g / 12 oz
1 cup	Milk	250 ml / 8 fl oz
2 lb	Pork sausage meat	1 kg / 2 lb
2	Eggs	2
¼ cup	Brandy	4 tbsp
1	Bay leaf	1
1	Bunch of fresh thyme	1
3 tbsp	Chopped fresh parsley	3 tbsp
	Salt and pepper	
3	Onions	3
4	Shallots	4
1	Carrot	1
1	Apple	1
½ cup	Hot water	125 ml / 4 fl oz
¼ cup	Butter	50 g / 2 oz

1. Preheat the oven to 450°F / 230°C / Gas Mark 8.
2. Cut the liver and bacon into cubes. Heat 1 tablespoon of the oil in a frying pan, add the liver and bacon and brown quickly. Transfer to a mixing bowl.

3. Soak the bread crumbs in the milk, then squeeze out excess liquid. Add the crumbs to the liver and bacon. Add the sausage meat, eggs, brandy, crumbled bay leaf, the leaves from the thyme and the chopped parsley. Season with salt and pepper. Mix this stuffing together thoroughly.
4. Sprinkle the inside of the pig with salt and pepper and fill with the stuffing. Sew up the opening firmly with string. Fold back the pig's feet and tie them in place. Hold the head in position with a wooden skewer. Sprinkle all over with salt and pepper and brush with the remaining oil. Wrap the ears in foil. Put a wooden plug in the mouth to keep it open.
5. Place the pig on the rack of a large roasting pan. Roast for 30 minutes, then reduce the heat to 400°F / 200°C / Gas Mark 6 and roast for a further 2 hours, basting from time to time with the cooking juices.
6. Peel and thinly slice the onions, shallots and carrot. Put them in the roasting pan under the rack halfway through the cooking period.
7. When the pig is cooked, transfer it to a large serving platter and keep hot. Remove the foil from the ears and replace the wooden plug with a small apple.
8. Place the roasting pan on top of the stove. Skim off the fat from the cooking liquid. Add the hot water and bring to a boil over a high heat, scraping up the meat residue from the bottom of the pan. Remove from the heat and add the butter little by little. Strain and pour into a sauceboat.
9. Once you have shown the cooked pig to your guests, take it back to the kitchen and carve it. Serve with the gravy.

Crépinettes au vin blanc

Sausage Patties with White Wine

00:15   00:15

American	Ingredients	Metric/Imperial
5	Shallots	5
⅔ cup	Butter	150 g / 5 oz
1¼ cups	Dry white wine	300 ml / ½ pint
1½ cups	Chicken stock	350 ml / 12 fl oz
¼ cup	Tomato paste [purée]	4 tbsp
	Salt and pepper	
3 tbsp	Oil	3 tbsp
12	Crépinettes (small fresh pork sausage patties)	12
12	Slices of white bread	12

1. Peel and finely chop the shallots. Melt 2 tablespoons [25 g / 1 oz] of the butter in a saucepan, add the shallots and cook gently until translucent. Add the wine, stock, tomato paste and salt and pepper to taste. Reduce by half over a moderate heat.
2. Meanwhile, heat 2 tablespoons [25 g / 1 oz] butter and one tablespoon oil in a frying pan, add the crépinettes and cook for 15 minutes over a moderate heat, turning to brown evenly.
3. Remove the crusts from the bread. Heat 3 tablespoons [40 g / 1½ oz] butter and the remaining oil in another frying pan, add the bread slices and fry until golden brown on both sides. Drain on paper towels.
4. Place the crépinettes on top of the fried bread and keep warm on a serving dish.
5. When the sauce has reduced by half, remove from the heat and add the rest of the butter, a little at a time. Taste and adjust the seasoning. Pour a little sauce over the sausages and serve the rest in a sauceboat.

Chipolatas au vin blanc

Sausages with Rich Wine Sauce

American	Ingredients	Metric/Imperial
1 tbsp	Butter	15 g / ½ oz
12	Thin pork sausages [chipolatas], 5 in / 12 cm long	12
2	Shallots	2
1½ cups	Dry white wine	350 ml / 12 fl oz
1 tbsp	Oil	1 tbsp
6	Slices of white bread	6
2	Egg yolks	2
1 tbsp	Crème fraîche (see page 122)	1 tbsp
	Salt and pepper	
1 tsp	Tomato paste [purée]	1 tsp
	Chopped fresh parsley for garnish	

1. Melt the butter in a small heavy-based frying pan, add the sausages, pricked with a fork so that they do not burst, and cook over a low heat for 10 minutes, turning to brown evenly. Remove and keep hot.
2. Peel and finely chop the shallots. Discard half the cooking fat from the frying pan, add the shallots and cook until translucent. Add the wine and boil to reduce by one-third over a moderate heat.
3. Meanwhile, heat the oil in another frying pan, add the slices of bread and fry until golden brown on both sides. Drain on paper towels.
4. Beat the egg yolks with the crème fraîche. Add to the sauce and allow to thicken over a low heat, stirring all the time. Do not boil. Season with salt and pepper. Stir in the tomato paste.
5. Arrange the sausages on the fried bread and sprinkle with chopped parsley. Serve with the sauce.

Sausages with rich wine sauce

Côtes de porc charcutière

Pork Chops with Charcutière Sauce

American	Ingredients	Metric/Imperial
6 (6 oz)	Pork chops	6 (175 g / 6 oz)
	Salt and pepper	
2	Onions	2
¼ cup	Lard or butter	50 g / 2 oz
1 tbsp	Flour	1 tbsp
1¼ cups	Dry white wine	300 ml / ½ pint
⅔ cup	Cold water	150 ml / ¼ pint
1 tsp	Prepared mustard	1 tsp
2 tbsp	Sliced gherkins	2 tbsp

1. Sprinkle the chops with salt and pepper. Set aside.
2. Peel and chop the onions. Heat 1 tablespoon [15 g / ½ oz] of the lard or butter in a saucepan, add the onions and cook until soft over a low heat. Stir in the flour and let it color, then add the wine. Bring to a boil, stirring. Add the water. Simmer over a very low heat, stirring frequently, for 30 minutes.
3. Melt the rest of the lard or butter in a frying pan, add the chops and brown on both sides over a high heat. Reduce the heat and cook for 12-15 minutes longer.
4. Transfer the chops to a warmed serving dish and keep hot. Discard the fat in the frying pan. Add 1 or 2 tablespoons of hot water to the pan and scrape up the meat residue which has caramelized on the bottom. Pour this juice into the sauce.
5. Add the mustard and sliced gherkins to the sauce. Season with salt and pepper. Mix together and heat through for a few minutes.
6. Serve the chops with the sauce.

Filet de porc à la catalane

Pork Tenderloin [Fillet] Cooked in Milk

American	Ingredients	Metric/Imperial
2 tbsp	Butter	25 g / 1 oz
1 (2½ lb)	Pork tenderloin [fillet]	1 (1.25 kg / 2½ lb)
1½ quarts	Boiling milk	1.5 l / 2½ pints
	Salt and pepper	
2	Fresh thyme sprigs	2
1	Bay leaf	1
	Grated nutmeg	
⅔ cup	Beef stock	150 ml / ¼ pint

1. Heat the butter in a flameproof casserole, add the meat and brown all over. Pour over the boiling milk. Season with salt and pepper and add the thyme, bay leaf and a pinch of nutmeg. Simmer gently, covered, for 2 hours. The cooking should be gentle, so that the milk does not boil over.
2. Remove the meat, slice it and arrange on a warmed serving platter. Keep hot.
3. Add the stock to the casserole (most of the milk will have evaporated) and boil for 3 minutes, scraping the residue from the bottom of the pot. Pour sauce over the meat and serve.

Haricots au lard
Bacon with White Beans

	00:20 plus soaking	02:30 to 03:00

American	Ingredients	Metric/Imperial
2 cups	Dried navy [haricot] beans	500 g / 1 lb
1 (1½ lb)	Piece of bacon	1 (750 g / 1½ lb)
2	Onions	2
2	Tomatoes	2
1 tbsp	Lard	15 g / ½ oz
1	Bouquet garni	1
1	Garlic clove	1
	Salt and pepper	

1. Soak the beans in cold water to cover for 1 hour. Drain and place in a saucepan. Cover with fresh cold water, bring to a boil and simmer for 45 minutes over a low heat.
2. Meanwhile, put the bacon in a saucepan, cover with cold water and bring to a boil. Simmer for 5 minutes, the drain and set aside.
3. Peel and thinly slice the onions. Peel the tomatoes (first plunging them in boiling water for 10 seconds), remove the seeds and chop.
4. Add the bacon and bouquet garni. Peel and crush the garlic and add. Cover with boiling water. Cook, covered, for 45 minutes over a low heat.
5. Drain the beans, reserving the cooking liquid, and add to the tomato sauce. Add enough of the cooking liquid from the beans just to cover them. Cover and simmer for 1 hour. Add a little more of the liquid from the beans from time to time, so that they are always covered. At the end of the cooking period, boil to reduce the liquid.
6. Remove the bacon and cut it into thin slices. Arrange on a warmed serving dish.
7. Season the beans with salt and pepper and pour over the bacon.

Roast pork loin

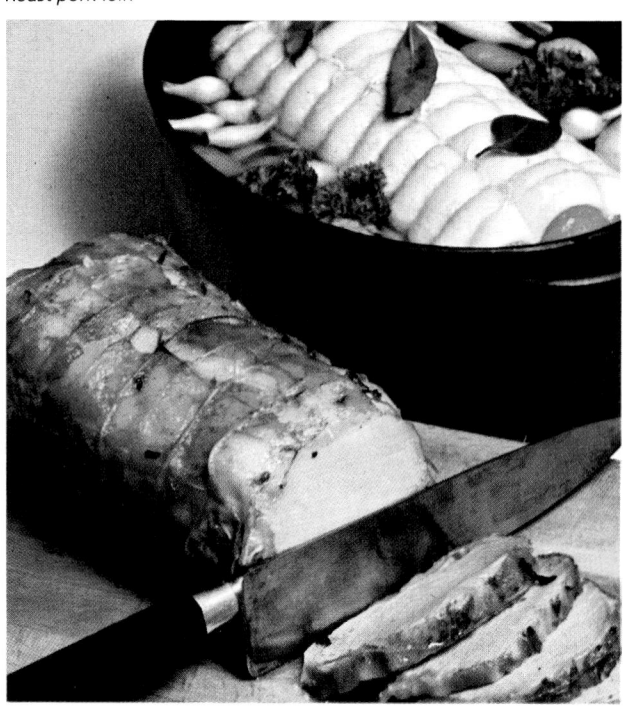

Filet de porc rôti
Roast Pork Loin

This roast is cooked by first simmering in flavored water, then roasting in the oven. With this method, only about 10% of the weight of the meat is lost (as opposed to about 20% at least if cooked only in the oven), and results in very tender, juicy meat.

	00:10	01:15

American	Ingredients	Metric/Imperial
2	Carrots	2
4	Shallots	4
4	Garlic cloves	4
2	Onions	2
1	Bouquet garni	1
3	Bay leaves	3
	Salt and pepper	
1 (2½ lb)	Boneless loin of pork	1 (1.25 kg / 2½ lb)
1 tbsp	Butter	15 g / ½ oz

1. Peel the carrots, shallots, garlic and onions. Slice the onions. Place the prepared vegetables in a casserole in which the meat will fit comfortably. Just cover these ingredients with water and add the bouquet garni, bay leaves, and salt and pepper to taste. Simmer for 10 minutes.
2. Add the meat and simmer for 45 minutes longer, turning the meat over halfway through.
3. Preheat the oven to 425°F / 220°C / Gas Mark 7.
4. Remove the casserole from the heat and cool for 5 minutes. Drain the meat and place it on a rack in a roasting pan. Roast for 20 minutes.
5. To serve, carve the meat, retaining all the juices. Add these juices to those in the roasting pan, together with the butter, to make a gravy.

Cook's tip: roast pork is just as delicious cold, so you could cook enough for two meals.

Jambon à la bourguignonne
Burgundy Ham

	00:15	00:25

American	Ingredients	Metric/Imperial
6	Slices of cooked ham	6
2	Shallots	2
¼ cup	Butter	50 g / 2 oz
⅔ cup	Dry white wine	150 ml / ¼ pint
2 tbsp	Vinegar	2 tbsp
1 cup	Crème fraîche (see page 122)	250 ml / 8 fl oz
1 tbsp	Tomato paste [purée]	1 tbsp
1	Egg yolk	1
	Grated nutmeg	
	Salt and pepper	

1. Lay the slices of ham on a gratin dish or other flameproof serving dish. Set aside.
2. Peel and finely chop the shallots. Melt the butter in a saucepan, add the shallots and cook until golden brown. Add the wine and vinegar. Boil to reduce until only 3 tablespoons of liquid remain.
3. Add the crème fraîche and tomato paste. Heat through,

then add the egg yolk, a pinch of nutmeg and salt and pepper to taste. Cook, stirring with a whisk, until you have a smooth sauce. Do not boil.

4. Strain this sauce over the ham. Heat gently for 20 minutes. Do not allow to boil. Serve in the cooking dish.

Côtes de porc à la moutarde

Pork Chops with Mustard

	00:05		00:30

American	Ingredients	Metric/Imperial
½ cup	Crème fraîche (see page 122)	125 ml / 4 fl oz
3 tbsp	Prepared mustard	3 tbsp
1 tbsp	Capers	1 tbsp
¼ cup	Butter	50 g / 2 oz
6 (6 oz)	Pork chops	6 (175 g / 6 oz)
	Salt and pepper	

1. Mix the crème fraîche with the mustard and capers. Set aside.
2. Melt the butter in a large frying pan, add the pork chops and cook for 7-8 minutes on each side. Sprinkle with salt and pepper.
3. Pour the mustard sauce over the chops. Reduce the heat, cover and cook over a low heat for 10-12 minutes. Serve hot.

Jambon à la crème

Ham with Rich Cream Sauce

	00:10		00:25

American	Ingredients	Metric/Imperial
⅔ cup	Dry white wine	150 ml / ¼ pint
⅔ cup	Chicken stock	150 ml / ¼ pint
6	Medium-thick slices of cooked ham	6
5 oz	Button mushrooms	150 g / 5 oz
¾ cup	Crème fraîche (see page 122)	175 ml / 6 fl oz
	Salt and pepper	
2	Egg yolks	2
½	Lemon	½

1. Heat the wine and stock together in a deep frying pan. Add the ham slices and heat through very gently for 15-20 minutes.
2. Meanwhile, thinly slice the mushrooms. Put the crème fraîche in a saucepan and bring to a boil. Add the mushroom slices and cook for 5 minutes. Season with salt and pepper. Add the cooking liquid from the ham and remove from the heat.
3. Beat the egg yolks in a large bowl. Pour 1 tablespoon of the hot sauce over the eggs, beating constantly with a whisk. Add half of the sauce, still stirring. Finally add this mixture to the rest of the sauce in the pan. Put on a low heat and stir until thick, but do not allow to boil. Add the juice of the ½ lemon.
4. Arrange the slices of ham on a warmed serving dish and pour over the hot sauce. Serve immediately.

Jambon au champagne

Ham with Champagne Sauce

	00:30 plus soaking		03:00 Serves 10-12

American	Ingredients	Metric/Imperial
1 (6½ lb)	Piece uncooked country ham	1 (3 kg / 6½ lb)
2	Shallots	2
2	Onions	2
2	Garlic cloves	2
2	Carrots	2
1	Bouquet garni	1
1	Bottle of brut champagne	1
	Confectioners' [icing] sugar	
1 tbsp	Potato starch or flour or cornstarch [cornflour]	1 tbsp
1 tsp	Tomato paste [purée]	1 tsp
	Salt and pepper	

1. Soak the ham for 18-24 hours in cold water to cover, to remove excess salt, changing the water 2 or 3 times. Drain.
2. Peel the shallots, onions, garlic cloves and carrots. Place them in a large flameproof casserole, add the ham and bouquet garni, and cover with cold water. Cover, bring to a boil over a moderate heat and simmer for 1½ hours.
3. Preheat the oven to 425°F / 220°C / Gas Mark 7.
4. Drain the ham, discarding the cooking liquid and vegetables. Remove the rind and excess fat from the ham. Put the ham back in the casserole and pour over the champagne. Place in the oven and cook for 1-1½ hours, basting frequently. The ham will be cooked when the small shank [knuckle] bone can be pulled out but offers a slight resistance.
5. Remove the ham from the casserole. Place it in a roasting pan and sprinkle it with confectioners' [icing] sugar. Increase the oven temperature to 450°F / 230°C / Gas Mark 8, return the ham to the oven and cook until it is golden.
6. Meanwhile, boil to reduce the champagne in the casserole. Add the potato starch or cornstarch, dissolved in 1 tablespoon cold water, and the tomato paste and stir well. Taste the sauce and adjust the seasoning.
7. Serve the ham carved into slices, with a little sauce poured over. Serve the rest of the sauce in a sauceboat.

Ham with champagne sauce

Grillades de porc
Grilled Pork Steaks

	00:05 plus seasoning		00:15

American	Ingredients	Metric/Imperial
6 (6 oz)	Boneless pork chops or steaks	6 (175 g / 6 oz)
2 tbsp	Oil	2 tbsp
	Salt and pepper	

1. Trim all the fat from the meat and score the surface. Brush each side with oil and sprinkle with salt and pepper. Set aside for 1 hour.
2. Heat a steak or chop grill [griddle] over a moderate heat.
3. Place the steaks on the hot grill and cook for 10-15 minutes, turning over halfway through.

Échine de porc bourbonnaise
Roast Pork with Cabbage and Chestnuts

	00:20		01:20

American	Ingredients	Metric/Imperial
1	Red cabbage	1
2	Garlic cloves	2
1 (3 lb)	Boneless pork blade Boston roast [spare rib]	1 (1.5 kg / 3 lb)
	Salt and pepper	
1 (½ lb)	Piece of lightly salted bacon	1 (250 g / 8 oz)
6 tbsp	Butter	75 g / 3 oz
1	Bouquet garni	1
1 cup	Red wine	250 ml / 8 fl oz
1	Can or bottle of unsweetened chestnuts	1
1	Fresh thyme sprig	1

1. Preheat the oven to 425°F / 220°C / Gas Mark 7.
2. Remove any damaged outer leaves from the cabbage. Cut it into quarters and remove the center core. Cut each quarter into thin slices. Set aside.
3. Peel the garlic and cut into small slivers. Pierce the meat here and there with a small pointed knife and slide a garlic sliver along the knife blade into each incision.
4. Place the pork in an ovenproof dish. Sprinkle with salt and pepper and add 3 tablespoons of water. Roast for 1 hour 20 minutes, basting often with its own juices. Add 1 or 2 tablespoons of hot water if necessary during cooking.
5. Meanwhile, put the shredded cabbage in a stewpot. Cover with plenty of cold salted water and bring to a boil. Simmer for 5 minutes, then drain and rinse well under cold running water. Drain again well.
6. Cut the bacon into strips. Blanch in boiling water for 5 minutes, then rinse under cold running water and drain.
7. Heat 2 tablespoons [25 g / 1 oz] of the butter in a flameproof casserole, add the bacon and cook until lightly browned. Add the cabbage, bouquet garni, and salt and pepper to taste. Pour over the wine and leave to cook, covered, over a low heat until the pork is ready.
8. Drain the chestnuts, reserving their juice. Put them in a frying pan with 3 tablespoons of their juice, the rest of the butter, the thyme, and salt and pepper to taste. Heat gently, covered.
9. When the pork is cooked, take the dish out of the oven and surround the meat with the chestnuts and the cabbage mixture. Serve immediately.

Côtes de porc au chou rouge
Pork Chops with Red Cabbage

	00:20		01:00

American	Ingredients	Metric/Imperial
3	Onions	3
1 tbsp	Butter	15 g / ½ oz
3	Bacon slices	3
6	Pork chops	6
1	Red cabbage	1
2	Small apples	2
6	Sugar cubes	6
3 cups	Red wine	750 ml / 1 ¼ pints

1. Peel and thinly slice the onions. Heat the butter in a flameproof casserole, add the bacon, pork chops and onions and cook for 15 minutes, turning the chops over half-way through.
2. Meanwhile, discard any damaged outer leaves from the cabbage. Cut it into quarters and remove the center core. Cut each quarter into thin slices. Peel the apples. Remove the core and seeds and cut the apples into matchstick strips.
3. Add the cabbage, apples, sugar cubes and wine to the casserole. Season with salt and pepper. Cover and simmer over a gentle heat for 1 hour, stirring occasionally.

Pork chops with cabbage

Daube de porc aux aubergines

Pork and Eggplant [Aubergine] Stew

	00:40		01:30

American	Ingredients	Metric/Imperial
2½ lb	Boneless pork shoulder or blade	1.25 kg / 2½ lb
2 tbsp	Flour	2 tbsp
2 tbsp	Oil	2 tbsp
4	Onions	4
2	Garlic cloves	2
	Salt and pepper	
2	Fresh thyme sprigs	2
2	Eggplant [aubergines]	2
1¼ cups	Hot water	300 ml / ½ pint

1. Cut the pork into 1½ in / 2 cm pieces. Coat with the flour. Heat the oil in a flameproof casserole, add the pork pieces and brown on all sides.
2. Peel and thinly slice the onions. Peel and crush the garlic. Add the onions and garlic to the casserole. Season with salt and pepper. Add the thyme. Cook over a low heat for 15 minutes, stirring often to brown the ingredients evenly.
3. Meanwhile, peel and slice the eggplant. Add to the casserole with the hot water. Simmer gently for 1¼ hours.

Filet de porc à l'ail

Loin of Pork with Garlic

	00:10		01:30
	plus seasoning		

American	Ingredients	Metric/Imperial
7	Garlic cloves	7
1 (2½ lb)	Boneless loin of pork, bones reserved	1 (1.25 kg / 2½ lb)
	Salt and pepper	
2	Onions	2
2	Fresh thyme sprigs	2
1	Bay leaf	1
⅔ cup	White wine	150 ml / ¼ pint
⅓ cup	Water	5 tbsp

1. Peel 2 of the garlic cloves and cut into slivers. Pierce the meat here and there with a small pointed knife and insert a sliver of garlic in each incision. Rub in some salt and pepper mixed together and leave for 1 hour.
2. Preheat the oven to 425°F / 220°C / Gas Mark 7.
3. Place the meat in a roasting pan with the bones. Roast for 10 minutes, turning the meat to brown it evenly.
4. Peel and quarter the onions. Add to the roasting pan with the rest of the garlic, unpeeled, the thyme and bay leaf. Pour over the wine and water. Lower the heat to 350°F / 180°C / Gas Mark 4 and continue cooking for 1¼ hours, basting and turning the meat twice.
5. Turn off the oven, leave the oven door ajar and leave the meat inside for 10 minutes. Transfer the pork to a warmed serving platter and keep hot.
6. Add 1 tablespoon of boiling water to the juices in the

roasting pan. Bring to a boil on top of the stove, scraping the meat residue from the bottom of the pan. Strain the gravy and serve with the pork.

Fromage de tête

Head Cheese [Brawn]

	00:15		02:30
	plus chilling		

American	Ingredients	Metric/Imperial
2	Carrots	2
2	Medium-size onions	2
3 quarts	Water	3 l / 5½ pints
	Salt and pepper	
½	Pig's head	½
1	Leek (white part only)	1
1	Bouquet garni	1
	Black peppercorns	
1	Garlic clove	1
2	Shallots	2
2	Small onions	2
1	Small bunch of fresh parsley	1

1. Peel the carrots and the 2 medium-size onions. Place the water in a large stewpot, add a little salt and bring to a boil. Add the ½ pig's head, peeled onions, carrots, leek, bouquet garni and a few peppercorns. Simmer very gently for 2½ hours.
2. Drain the pig's head. Strain the cooking liquid and reserve. Remove the bones from the head. Chop the meat and place in a deep round bowl or mold.
3. Peel the garlic, shallots and the 2 small onions. Mince these finely with the parsley.
4. Mix the minced vegetables with the meat. Season with salt and pepper and pour over 4 ladlefuls of the strained cooking liquid, or enough to cover. Chill for 12 hours.
5. To serve, unmold the head cheese by dipping the bowl or mold into hot water for a few seconds.

Côtes de porc poêlées

Fried Pork Chops

	00:00		00:14 to 00:18

American	Ingredients	Metric/Imperial
2 tbsp	Oil	2 tbsp
6 (6 oz)	Pork chops	6 (175 g / 6 oz)
	Salt and pepper	
	Lemon juice	

1. Heat the oil in a frying pan, add the chops and cook over a medium heat for 8-10 minutes, according to thickness.
2. Season with salt and pepper and turn the chops over. Cook on the other side for 6-8 minutes longer. Season again with salt and pepper 3 minutes before the end of the cooking period.
3. Sprinkle the chops with a few drops of lemon juice and serve.

Cook's tip: you can also cook pork chops on a steak or chop grill [griddle]. Brush them first with oil on each side and cook on the very hot grill. Serve sprinkled with any fresh herbs you like.

Paipet fier

Smoked Sausage with Potatoes

American	Ingredients	Metric/Imperial
2 lb	Potatoes	1 kg / 2 lb
2	Smoked Montbéliard sausages or other large smoked pork sausages	2
1	Onion	1
3	Garlic cloves	3
1	Small bunch of fresh parsley	1
¼ cup	Butter	50 g / 2 oz
¼ cup	Flour	50 g / 2 oz
	Dried thyme	
	Powdered bay leaf	
	Salt and pepper	
	Wine vinegar	

1. Put the potatoes in a saucepan of cold water, bring to a boil and cook for 20 minutes.
2. Meanwhile, cook the sausages in simmering water for 15 minutes. Drain, reserving the cooking water.
3. Drain the potatoes and cool slightly, then peel them and slice fairly thinly. Peel and thinly slice the onion. Peel and crush the garlic. Chop the parsley.
4. Melt the butter in a saucepan. Add the flour and stir. Add enough of the sausage cooking liquid to make a sauce. Add the onion, garlic, parsley, a pinch of thyme, a pinch of bay leaf, and salt and pepper to taste.
5. Cut the sausages into thin slices. Add them to the sauce with the potatoes and cook for about 15 minutes.
6. Just before serving, add a dash of wine vinegar.

Oreilles de cochon panées

Breaded Pigs' Ears

00:20 plus cooling   02:10

American	Ingredients	Metric/Imperial
1 quart	Water	1 l / 1¾ pints
1¼ cups	White wine	300 ml / ½ pint
1	Fresh thyme sprig	1
1	Fresh rosemary sprig	1
1	Bay leaf	1
1	Slice of lemon	1
2	Carrots	2
1	Onion	1
6	Pigs' ears	6
	Salt and pepper	
⅔ cup	Dry bread crumbs	50 g / 2 oz
6 tbsp	Butter	75 g / 3 oz

1. Pour the water and wine into a saucepan. Add the thyme, rosemary, bay leaf and lemon slice. Peel and thinly slice the carrots and onion, add to the pan with the pigs' ears. Season with salt and pepper. Simmer over a low heat for 2 hours.
2. Remove from the heat and allow to cool, then drain the ears.

3. Coat the ears all over with the bread crumbs. Melt 2 tablespoons [25 g / 1 oz] of the butter in a frying pan, add the ears and cook for 5 minutes on each side over a fairly high heat. Remove from the frying pan and keep warm.
4. Discard the cooking fat, and melt the rest of the butter in the pan. Pour this butter over the ears, sprinkle with salt and pepper and serve hot.

Pieds de porc grillés

Broiled [Grilled] Pigs' Feet

00:10   03:34 to 03:36 according to size

American	Ingredients	Metric/Imperial
6	Fresh pigs' feet [trotters]	6
2	Eggs	2
	Flour	
	Salt and pepper	
	Dry bread crumbs	

1. Place the pigs' feet in a large saucepan, cover with water and bring to a boil. Simmer for 3½ hours, adding more water to the pan from time to time as necessary.
2. Drain the pigs' feet and pat dry.
3. Preheat the broiler [grill].
4. Lightly beat the eggs in a shallow dish. Season the flour with salt and pepper. Coat the pigs' feet with flour, then dip them in the eggs and finally coat all over with bread crumbs. Pat on the crumbs lightly to help them adhere.
5. Broil the pigs' feet for 4-6 minutes, turning to brown evenly.

Palette de porc paysanne

Smoked Pork [Bacon] Peasant Style

00:20 plus soaking   02:30

American	Ingredients	Metric/Imperial
2 cups	Lentils	500 g / 1 lb
1 (3 lb)	Uncooked, smoked pork shoulder roll [bacon collar or fore slipper]	1 (1.5 kg / 3 lb)
3	Carrots	3
1	Large onion	1
2	Leeks	2
1 (½ lb)	Piece of bacon	1 (250 g / 8 oz)
2 tbsp	Lard or goose fat	25 g / 1 oz
3	Garlic cloves	3
	Salt and pepper	
2 cups	Red wine	500 ml / ¾ pint
1	Large uncooked pork sausage	1
1	Bouquet garni	1

1. Soak the lentils in cold water to cover for 2-3 hours. Soak the pork in cold water to remove excess salt, if necessary. Drain and pat dry.
2. Peel and dice the carrots and onion. Dice the leeks. Cut the bacon into strips. Heat the lard or goose fat in a large flameproof casserole, add the diced vegetables and bacon and cook until browned.

3. Peel the garlic and cut into small slivers. Prick the pork here and there with a small pointed knife and insert a piece of garlic along the knife blade at each incision. Sprinkle with salt and pepper. Put the pork in the casserole and pour over the wine. Cover and simmer for 1 hour.

4. Drain the lentils. Put them in a large saucepan, cover with fresh cold water and bring to a boil slowly over a low heat.

5. Add the boiling lentils to the casserole with the sausage and bouquet garni. Continue cooking, covered, for 1½ hours.

6. Discard the bouquet garni. Cut the sausage into slices and the pork into pieces. Place the meats in a deep dish and surround with the drained lentils. Serve very hot.

Parsleyed ham mold

Jambon persillé

Parsleyed Ham Mold

	01:00		03:00
	plus soaking and chilling		Serves 10-12

American	Ingredients	Metric/Imperial
1 (6½ lb)	Uncooked country ham	1 (3 kg / 6½ lb)
1	Onion	1
5	Garlic cloves	5
2	Carrots	2
3	Shallots	3
2	Calf's feet	2
1 tsp	Dried thyme	1 tsp
1	Bouquet garni	1
	Grated nutmeg	
	Pepper	
2 cups	Dry white wine	500 ml / ¾ pint
2 quarts	Water	2 l / 3½ pints
2	Bunches of fresh parsley	2
	Vinegar	

1. Soak the ham for 18-24 hours in cold water to cover, to remove excess salt, changing the water 2 or 3 times. Drain.

2. Peel the onion, 2 garlic cloves, the carrots and 1 shallot. Put

these vegetables in a large flameproof casserole and add the calf's feet, thyme, bouquet garni, a pinch of nutmeg, and pepper to taste. Place the ham in the casserole and pour over the wine and water.

3. Cover the casserole and bring to a boil. Simmer for about 3 hours, adding more water if necessary.

4. Meanwhile, peel the remaining garlic and shallots. Put them in a blender or food processor with the parsley and blend until fine. Set aside.

5. Drain the ham, reserving the cooking liquid. Remove the rind and excess fat from the ham, then cut the ham into large, equal-sized pieces. Chop the calf's feet, and mix with the parsley mixture. Strain the cooking liquid.

6. In a large bowl or mold, arrange a layer of pieces of ham, making sure that they all lie horizontally. Add a layer of the parsley mixture and a trickle of vinegar. Continue layering the ingredients in this way until they are used up. Pour over the cooking liquid, which should fill up all the gaps in the layers.

7. Cover the bowl with a plate of nearly the same diameter and put a weight on top to press the ham down well. Chill for at least 2 hours.

Jambon au madère

Ham with Madeira Sauce

	00:30		03:00
	plus soaking		Serves 10-12

American	Ingredients	Metric/Imperial
1 (6½ lb)	Uncooked country ham	1 (3 kg / 6½ lb)
	Court-bouillon (see page 114)	
3	Shallots	3
2	Onions	2
1	Carrot	1
2 cups	Madeira wine	500 ml / ¾ pint
1¼ cups	Water	300 ml / ½ pint
1	Bouquet garni	1
6	Black peppercorns	6
1 tbsp	Potato starch or flour	1 tbsp
	Salt and pepper	
2 tbsp	Butter	25 g / 1 oz

1. Soak the ham for 18-24 hours in cold water to cover, to remove excess salt, changing the water 2 or 3 times. Drain.

2. Place the ham in a large flameproof casserole. Cover with cold court-bouillon and bring to a boil. Cook for 1½ hours.

3. Let the ham cool in the stock, then drain it. Remove the rind and excess fat. Reserve the fat.

4. Preheat the oven to 450°F / 230°C / Gas Mark 8.

5. Peel the shallots, onions and carrot. Grate the carrot, and slice the shallots and onions thinly. Put a few bits of fat from the ham in the clean casserole and heat until melted. Add the vegetables and cook until soft.

6. Pour over the madeira and water. Add the bouquet garni and peppercorns. Return the ham to the casserole.

7. Place the casserole in the oven and cook for 1½ hours turning the ham often so that it browns all over. Cooking is finished when the shank [knuckle] bone can be pulled out but still offers slight resistance.

8. Remove the ham and keep warm. Strain the sauce into a saucepan and add the potato starch dissolved in 1 tablespoon of cold water. Taste and adjust the seasoning. Remove from the heat and add the butter, beating.

9. Serve the ham with the sauce.

Jambon Moivriot
Ham Slices in Red Wine

00:15   00:25

American	Ingredients	Metric/Imperial
6	Slices of dried country ham or cooked ham about ¼ in / 5 mm thick	6
3	Onions	3
1	Garlic clove	1
2 tbsp	Lard	25 g / 1 oz
1 tbsp	Flour	1 tbsp
2 cups	Full-bodied red wine	450 ml / ¾ pint
7 tbsp	Water	7 tbsp
1	Bouquet garni	1
	Salt and pepper	

1. Simmer the ham slices in water to cover for 10 minutes.
2. Meanwhile, peel and chop the onions. Peel and crush the garlic. Heat the lard in a frying pan, add the onions and cook, stirring, until they become pale golden (about 10 minutes). Sprinkle with the flour and stir well, then add the wine, water, bouquet garni, garlic, and salt and pepper to taste. Cover and cook over a gentle heat for 10 minutes. If the sauce evaporates too much, add a little more wine.
3. Drain the ham slices and add to the sauce. Simmer for a few minutes, then turn the slices over and cook for a few minutes longer.
4. Remove the bouquet garni before serving.

Poule verte
Pork-Stuffed Cabbage Roll

00:30   02:45

American	Ingredients	Metric/Imperial
1	Large green cabbage	1
2	Garlic cloves	2
2	Onions	2
1	Bunch of fresh parsley	1
¾ lb	Ground [minced] pork	350 g / 12 oz
1 cup	Fresh white bread crumbs	50 g / 2 oz
1	Egg	1
	Salt and pepper	
1 (¾ lb)	Piece of bacon	1 (350 g / 12 oz)
6	Carrots	6
2	Turnips	2
6	Black peppercorns	6
1 cup	Tomato sauce (see page 133)	250 ml / 8 fl oz

1. Remove any damaged outer leaves from the cabbage and put it whole into a large saucepan of cold water. Bring to a boil and simmer for 15 minutes. Remove the cabbage from the water, rinse under cold runnning water and drain.
2. Peel 1 clove of garlic and 1 onion. Mince the garlic and onion with the parsley. Place these ingredients in a mixing bowl and add the pork, bread crumbs, egg, and salt and pepper to taste. Mix together well.
3. Take off the large outer leaves of the cabbage. Remove the

thick central ribs and spread out the leaves flat in a line, overlapping them. Spread the pork stuffing on top. Roll up like a long loaf of bread, and tie like a roast of meat. Reserve the remaining cabbage.
4. Put the piece of bacon in a saucepan of cold water, bring to a boil and simmer for 10 minutes. Drain.
5. Peel the carrots, turnips and remaining onion and garlic. Place the vegetables in a stewpot with the cabbage roll, peppercorns and bacon. Cover with water. Bring to a boil, then cover and cook for 1¼ hours.
6. Remove the core and large ribs from the remaining cabbage and cut into strips. Add to the pot and cook for another hour.
7. Serve the cabbage roll and the bacon cut into slices, surrounded by the drained vegetables. Accompany with the tomato sauce.

Cook's tip: the stock, poured boiling hot over thick slices of stale bread, makes a delicious soup.

Pork-stuffed cabbage roll

Porc braisé au chou
Braised Pork with Cabbage

00:20   02:15

American	Ingredients	Metric/Imperial
1 (¼ lb)	Piece of bacon	1 (125 g / 4 oz)
3 tbsp	Oil	3 tbsp
1 (2 lb)	Boneless pork roast	1 (1 kg / 2 lb)
1	Small green cabbage	1
	Salt and pepper	
1	Small bunch of fresh parsley	1
1¼ lb	Potatoes	625 g / 1¼ lb

1. Cut the bacon into small dice. Heat the oil in a flameproof casserole, add the bacon and cook until browned. Add the pork and brown on all sides. Cover and reduce the heat. Leave to cook gently.

2. Meanwhile, remove any damaged outside leaves of the cabbage. Cut into quarters and remove the hard stalk at the base of the leaves. Drop the cabbage quarters into a saucepan of boiling salted water and cook for 10 minutes.

3. Drain the cabbage and rinse under cold water, then add to the casserole. Add the parsley. Cook, covered, over a gentle heat for 1 hour.

4. Peel the potatoes and add to the casserole. Season with salt and pepper. Cover again and cook gently for 45 minutes longer.

5. To serve, cut the meat into slices and arrange on top of the cabbage in a deep dish. Surround by the potatoes. Pour over the cooking liquid.

Ragoût de porc
Pork Stew

	00:20		02:00

American	Ingredients	Metric/Imperial
3 lb	Boneless shoulder of pork	1.5 kg / 3 lb
2 tbsp	Oil	2 tbsp
1 tbsp	Flour	1 tbsp
3	Onions	3
2	Tomatoes	2
1	Bouquet garni	1
	Salt and pepper	
8	Potatoes	8

1. Trim excess fat from the pork, then cut the meat into 1½ in / 2 cm pieces. Heat the oil in a frying pan, add the pork and brown the pieces on all sides. Drain the pork and place in a flameproof casserole.

2. Sprinkle the flour over the meat and stir to coat the meat evenly with the flour.

3. Peel the onions and add to the casserole with the tomatoes (whole) and bouquet garni. Add enough water so that the meat is just covered. Season with salt and pepper. Bring to a boil, then simmer very gently for 1½ hours.

4. Peel the potatoes and put them on top of the other ingredients in the casserole. Cook for 25-30 minutes longer or until they are tender.

5. Discard the bouquet garni before serving.

Rôti de porc boulangère
Roast Pork
with Potatoes

	00:20		01:45

American	Ingredients	Metric/Imperial
1 (3 lb)	Boneless loin of pork, bones reserved	1 (1.5 kg / 3 lb)
	Salt and pepper	
2	Garlic cloves	2
4 lb	Potatoes	2 kg / 4 lb
4	Fresh thyme sprigs	4
2	Bay leaves	2
	Grated nutmeg	
1 tbsp	Lard	15 g / ½ oz

1. Preheat the oven to 400°F / 200°C / Gas Mark 6.

2. Bring a large saucepan of water to a boil. Add the pork and bones and season with salt and pepper. Bring back to a boil and simmer, covered, for 20 minutes.

3. Meanwhile, peel 1 clove of garlic and rub the inside of an ovenproof dish. Discard the garlic. Peel and thinly slice the potatoes. Arrange them in the dish in 3 layers, seasoning each layer with the thyme, the bay leaves, crumbled, a large pinch of nutmeg, and the remaining garlic, peeled and crushed. Moisten with some of the liquid from the meat and add sufficient boiling water just to come up to the top of the potatoes. Dot with the lard.

4. Place in the oven and cook for 15 minutes.

5. Drain the pork, discard the bones and place on top of the potatoes. Continue cooking for 1½ hours, turning the pork occasionally so that it browns all over. This dish is cooked when the potatoes have absorbed nearly all the liquid.

Petit salé aux lentilles
Lentils with Salt
Pork and Sausage

	00:20 plus soaking	02:30 to 03:00	

American	Ingredients	Metric/Imperial
2½ cups	Small green lentils	625 g / 1¼ lb
1 (1 lb)	Piece of salt pork	1 (500 g / 1 lb)
1 (2 lb)	Uncooked smoked pork loin [lean bacon joint]	1 (1 kg / 2 lb)
1	Large carrot	1
2	Onions	2
1	Bouquet garni	1
6	Montbéliard sausages or other smoked pork sausages	6
	Salt and pepper	
2 tbsp	Butter (optional)	25 g / 1 oz

1. Soak the lentils in cold water to cover for 2-3 hours. Soak the salt pork and pork loin in cold water to remove excess salt, if necessary. Drain.

2. Place the salt pork and pork loin in a saucepan and cover with fresh cold water. Simmer gently for about 2 hours.

3. Meanwhile, drain the lentils and put into another saucepan. Peel the carrot and onions and add to the pan with the bouquet garni. Cover with water. Bring to a boil very slowly and simmer very gently for about 30-40 minutes. It is important not to let the lentils boil fast, or their skins will burst. Green lentils have a very thin skin, and cook quickly.

4. Add the sausages, pricked so that they do not burst, to the meats and simmer gently for a further 10 minutes.

5. Add a little salt to the lentils and then drain as soon as they are cooked. (Reserve the cooking liquid together with the vegetables as this will make an excellent soup.)

6. Drain the meats, reserving the cooking liquid. Cut the meats into pieces or slices and place them in a heavy-based saucepan. Cover with the lentils and moisten with a small ladleful of the meat cooking liquid, taken from the top so as to include a little fat (or else with the fat skimmed off and the liquid enriched instead with the butter). Add a little pepper and cover. Cook over a very low heat for 15-20 minutes.

7. To serve, arrange the meat on a warmed platter and spoon over the lentils and sauce.

Jambonneau en potée

Ham Hotpot

	00:30	03:15

American	Ingredients	Metric/Imperial
1 (2½ lb)	Uncooked boneless ham [gammon joint]	1 (1.25 kg / 2½ lb)
4 quarts	Water	4 l / 7 pints
	Salt and pepper	
1 (½ lb)	Piece of bacon	1 (250 g / 8 oz)
1	Veal shank [knuckle]	1
2	Pigs' tails (optional)	2
1	Onion	1
3	Cloves	3
½ lb	Young carrots	250 g / 8 oz
½ lb	Young turnips	250 g / 8 oz
½ lb	New potatoes	250 g / 8 oz
1	Spring cabbage	1
¼ lb	Fresh broad or lima beans	125 g / 4 oz

1. Soak the ham in cold water to cover to remove excess salt, if necessary. Drain.
2. Place the ham in a large cooking pot and cover with the water. Add a little pepper. Bring to a boil and cook for 40 minutes over a moderate heat.
3. Cut the bacon into large pieces. Add to the pot with the veal shank and pigs' tails. Peel the onion and stud with the cloves. Add to the pot. Simmer, covered, for 2 hours.
4. Meanwhile, peel the carrots, turnips and potatoes. Remove the hard inner core from the cabbage to leave only the leaves. Shell and peel the beans, if necessary.
5. Add the whole carrots and cabbage leaves to the pot and cook for 10 minutes, then add the turnips and beans. Cook for 10 minutes longer and add the potatoes. Cook for a final 15 minutes.

Saucisse aux pois cassés

Sausages with Split Peas

	00:05	00:40 to 00:50

American	Ingredients	Metric/Imperial
2 cups	Split peas	500 g / 1 lb
1	Onion	1
1	Bouquet garni	1
6	Thick fresh sausages, 6 in / 15 cm long	6
¼ cup	Butter	50 g / 2 oz
	Grated nutmeg	
	Salt and pepper	

1. Rinse the split peas, put them in a saucepan and cover with plenty of cold water (1 in / 2.5 cm above the peas).
2. Peel the onion and add to the peas with the bouquet garni. Bring to a boil over a moderate heat and simmer for 40-50 minutes or until tender. Add more boiling water whenever the peas come above the surface of the water.
3. Meanwhile, prick the sausages with a fork, so that they do not burst while cooking. If a long sausage is used, roll it into a coil. Place in a frying pan and cook over a moderate heat for 25 minutes on each side. Add a little fat to the pan if necessary.
4. Drain the peas. Remove the onion and bouquet garni. Purée

the peas in a food mill, blender or food processor. Beat in the butter. Add a pinch of nutmeg and season with salt and pepper. If the purée is too thick, thin it with a little milk or warm water.
5. Serve the purée with the well-drained sausages.

Sauté de porc provençale

Provençal Pork Sauté

	00:25	01:30

American	Ingredients	Metric/Imperial
2 lb	Boneless shoulder of pork	1 kg / 2 lb
2 tbsp	Olive oil	2 tbsp
	Salt and pepper	
2	Onions	2
2	Garlic cloves	2
3	Shallots	3
1	Bouquet garni	1
2 tbsp	Flour	2 tbsp
1 cup	Dry white wine	250 ml / 8 fl oz
15	Young carrots	15
2	Sweet red peppers	2
½ lb	Fresh peas	250 g / 8 oz
1 cup	Green and black olives	150 g / 5 oz

1. Cut the pork into large pieces. Heat the olive oil in a flameproof casserole. Add the pieces of pork and brown on all sides. Sprinkle with salt and pepper.
2. Peel and thinly slice the onions, garlic and shallots. Add them to the casserole with the bouquet garni. Cook until the vegetables are golden, then add the flour and mix well. Cook until the flour turns a light golden color. Add the wine, stirring all the time. Bring to a boil.
3. Meanwhile, peel the carrots. Core and seed the red peppers and cut into thin strips. Shell the peas.
4. Add the carrots, pepper strips, peas and olives to the casserole. Cover and simmer over a low heat for 1 hour. Serve very hot.

Saucisses en croûtes

Sausages in Pastry

	00:30	00:15 to 00:18
		plus making or thawing pastry

American	Ingredients	Metric/Imperial
½ lb	Puff pastry (see page 458 or use frozen)	250 g / 8 oz
3	Large fresh pork sausages	3
	Cayenne pepper	
1	Egg, beaten	1

1. If using frozen pastry, allow it to thaw.
2. Preheat the oven to 450°F / 230°C / Gas Mark 8.
3. Cut each sausage into 3 and sprinkle with a little cayenne.
4. Roll out the pastry to ⅛ in / 3 mm thick. Cut into 9 strips. Roll up each piece of sausage in a strip of pastry and seal the edges with egg. Score a few lines on the top of the pastry with the point of a knife, and brush the surface with egg.
5. Place on a baking sheet. Bake for 10-12 minutes, then turn down the heat to 400°F / 200°C / Gas Mark 6 and bake for 5 minutes longer. Serve hot.

Sausages are the basis of many French country dishes

Mixed Meat Dishes

Baeckeoffa

Alsatian Meat and Potato Stew

	00:40 plus marinating		02:00

American	Ingredients	Metric/Imperial
1 lb	Boneless loin or shoulder of pork	500 g / 1 lb
1 lb	Boneless shoulder of lamb	500 g / 1 lb
1 lb	Flank steak	500 g / 1 lb
½ lb	Onions	250 g / 8 oz
2	Garlic cloves	2
	Bouquet garni	
1 quart	Dry white wine	1 l / 1¾ pints
	Salt and pepper	
2 lb	Potatoes	1 kg / 2 lb

1. Cut all the meats into 1½ in / 2 cm cubes. Peel and slice 2 onions. Peel the garlic. Place these prepared ingredients in a large mixing bowl and add the bouquet garni, wine, and salt and pepper to taste. Cover and leave to marinate in a cool place for 12 hours.
2. Preheat the oven to 350°F / 180°C / Gas Mark 4.
3. Remove the meat from the marinade with a slotted spoon. Strain the marinade and set aside.
4. Peel and thinly slice the remaining onions and the potatoes.
5. Arrange half the potatoes on the bottom of an earthenware casserole and cover with the pieces of meat. Add a layer of half the onions, then the remaining potatoes, and top with the rest of the onions. Season to taste and pour over the strained marinade.
6. Cover the casserole, place in the oven and cook for at least 2 hours. Serve in the casserole.

Alsatian meat and potato stew

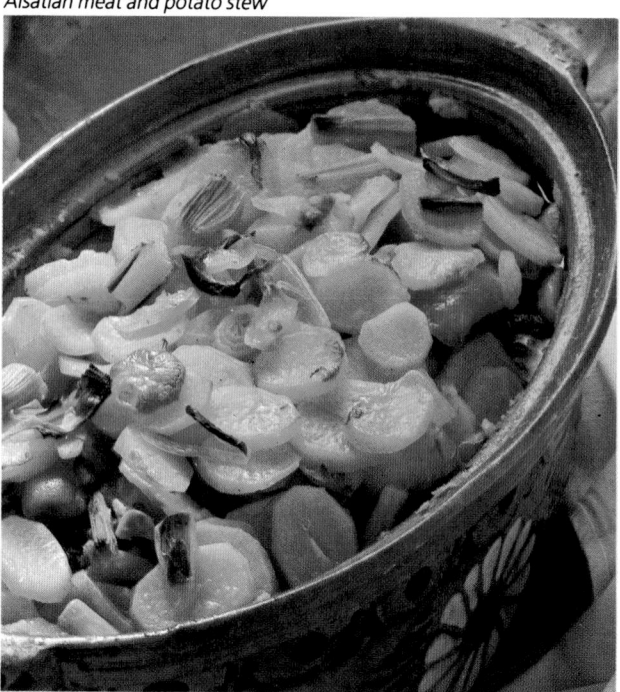

Cassoulet de Bonnac

White Bean Stew with Preserved Goose

	00:10 plus soaking		02:00 to 03:00

American	Ingredients	Metric/Imperial
4 cups	Dried navy [haricot] beans	1 kg / 2 lb
½ lb	Bacon rind	250 g / 8 oz
½ lb	Smoked ham	250 g / 8 oz
1	Garlic clove	1
	Salt and pepper	
1	Wing and leg of preserved goose (confit d'oie)	1

1. Soak the beans overnight in cold water to cover.
2. Rinse the beans and drain. Cut the bacon rind into pieces and place in the bottom of a large flameproof casserole. Add the beans, ham and peeled garlic and enough water to cover. Cover the pot, bring slowly to a boil and simmer for 3 hours. Do not stir. It may be necessary to add extra water occasionally if the beans seem to be drying out.
3. About 30 minutes before the end of the cooking time, season with salt and pepper and add the preserved goose.

Cassoulet de Castelnaudary

Bean Stew with Mixed Meats

	00:40 plus soaking		02:30

American	Ingredients	Metric/Imperial
4 cups	Dried navy [haricot] beans	1 kg / 2 lb
3	Carrots	3
2	Onions	2
3	Cloves	3
½ lb	Bacon rind	250 g / 8 oz
¾ lb	Piece of bacon	350 g / 12 oz
1	Bouquet garni	1
2 lb	Boneless goose breast	1 kg / 2 lb
2 lb	Boneless shoulder of lamb	1 kg / 2 lb
1 cup	Goose fat or lard	250 g / 8 oz
3	Garlic cloves	3
2 tbsp	Flour	2 tbsp
1 quart	White wine	1 l / 1¾ pints
	Salt and pepper	
5 oz	Garlic sausage	150 g / 5 oz
8	Small pork sausages [chipolatas]	8
1 cup	Tomato paste [purée]	250 g / 8 oz
2 cups	Bread crumbs	125 g / 4 oz

1. Soak the beans overnight in cold water to cover.
2. Rinse and drain the beans. Put them in a large cooking pot and cover with cold water.
3. Peel 2 carrots. Peel 1 onion and stud with the cloves. Tie together the bacon rind with string. Add all these ingredients to the pot. Add the bacon and bouquet garni. Bring to a boil and simmer for 2 hours.

4. Meanwhile, cut the goose and lamb into 1½ in / 2 cm pieces. Set aside 1 tablespoon of goose fat and heat the rest in a large saucepan. Add the pieces of goose and lamb and brown on all sides.

5. Peel and slice the remaining carrot and onion. Peel and crush the garlic. Add these to the meat and sprinkle with the flour. Cook until browned, stirring frequently. Add the wine and enough water to cover the meat. Season with salt and pepper. Cook for 2 hours over a low heat.

6. Remove the bacon rind from the beans and chop into pieces. Season the beans with salt to taste. Drain the beans and bacon.

7. Take the pieces of meat out of the saucepan and set aside. Add the chopped bacon rind and beans to the pan. Leave to simmer for 15 minutes.

8. Slice the bacon and the garlic sausage.

9. Heat the remaining goose fat in a frying pan; add the small sausages and the tomato paste and cook over a very low heat for 10 minutes.

10. Preheat the oven to 450°F / 230°C / Gas Mark 8.

11. Arrange a layer of beans in a large gratin dish. Add a layer of pieces of meat and then another layer of beans. On top of this make a layer of slices of bacon, the small sausages and the slices of garlic sausage. Add a final layer of beans and sprinkle with the bread crumbs.

12. Bake for 10 minutes. Serve very hot.

Couscous semoule

Couscous with Chick Peas

	01:00 plus soaking		03:30 Serves 8–10
American	**Ingredients**		**Metric/Imperial**
2 cups	Dried chick peas		500 g / 1 lb
2 cups	Golden raisins [sultanas]		350 g / 12 oz
4 lb (8 cups)	Couscous		2 kg / 4 lb
	Salt and white pepper		
⅔ cup	Butter		150 g / 5 oz
1 tbsp	Cayenne pepper		1 tbsp
1 tbsp	Caraway seeds		1 tbsp
1 tbsp	Quatre-épices or apple pie spice [mixed spice]		1 tbsp
¼ cup	Tomato paste [purée]		4 tbsp
½ cup	Chicken stock		125 ml / 4 fl oz

1. Soak the chick peas overnight in cold water to cover.

2. Drain the chick peas, place in a saucepan and cover with cold water. Bring to a boil and simmer gently for 3 hours.

3. Meanwhile, soak the raisins in lukewarm water. Place the couscous in a mixing bowl, cover with cold water and add 2 tablespoons of salt. Soak until all the water has been absorbed by the grain.

4. Pour the couscous into the top of a couscoussier or steamer. Steam over boiling water for 30 minutes without removing the lid.

5. Pour the couscous into the mixing bowl again and moisten with 1 cup [250 ml / 8 fl oz] of water. Return to the steamer and steam for a further 25-30 minutes.

6. Return the couscous to the bowl and work out any lumps. Add the butter a little at a time and mix well. Add the drained raisins. Drain the chick peas, add to the couscous and mix well. Return to the steamer and cook for a further 30 minutes.

7. Meanwhile, combine the cayenne pepper, caraway seeds, quatre-épices, ½ teaspoon pepper, the tomato paste and stock

in a saucepan. Heat for a few minutes.

8. To serve, separate the couscous grains using a fork, add more salt if necessary and pour into a deep serving dish. Serve with the sauce.

Couscous viandes

Couscous with Meat

	00:00 plus soaking	02:00 plus preparing couscous
American	**Ingredients**	**Metric/Imperial**
1 (3 lb)	Chicken with giblets	1 (1.5 kg / 3 lb)
1½ lb	Flank steak	750 g / 1½ lb
4 quarts	Water	4 l / 7 pints
6	Carrots	6
6	Onions	6
6	Turnips	6
6	Leeks	6
1	Bunch of celery	1
1	Bouquet garni	1
	Salt and pepper	
4	Zucchini [courgettes]	4
4	Tomatoes	4
1 lb	Ground [minced] beef	500 g / 1 lb
1 lb	Ground [minced] veal	500 g / 1 lb
	Cayenne pepper	
	Caraway seeds	
	Ground coriander	
2 tbsp	Oil	2 tbsp
8	Merguez or other spicy lamb sausages	8
8	Lamb chops	8
1 quantity	Couscous with chick peas (see previous recipe)	1 quantity
1 quantity	Spicy sauce (see previous recipe)	1 quantity

1. Place the chicken and its giblets and the flank steak in a large cooking pot. Cover with the cold water. Bring to a boil and simmer for 1 hour, skimming off the fat at regular intervals.

2. Peel the carrots, 4 onions and the turnips and add to the pot. Tie together the leeks and celery stalks in small bunches and add to the pot with the bouquet garni. Season with salt and pepper. Bring back to a boil. Thickly slice the zucchini and tomatoes and add to the pot. Simmer gently for a further 20 minutes.

3. Meanwhile, peel and finely chop the remaining onions. Mix with the ground beef and veal. Season with salt and pepper and add a pinch of cayenne pepper, a pinch of caraway seeds and 2 pinches of ground coriander. Mix together well. Shape into little balls using a tablespoon and set aside for 15 minutes.

4. Heat the oil in a frying pan, add the meatballs, spicy sausages and lamb chops. Cook until browned all over and cooked through.

5. To serve, untie the leeks and celery, discard the bouquet garni and pour the stock and vegetables into a soup tureen. Carve the chicken and arrange with the lamb chops on a platter. Serve the couscous in a deep serving dish, topped with the meatballs and the spicy sausages. Serve the spicy sauce separately.

Cook's tip: any seasonal vegetables that can be cooked in water can be added to this recipe.

Stuffed cabbage

6. Put the strips of pork fat in the form of a cross on the work surface. Place the cabbage in the center of the cross and spread out the leaves. Put one-quarter of the stuffing and 3 prunes in the center of the cabbage and fold in some of the leaves over the stuffing to keep it firmly in place. Cover with one-third of the remaining stuffing, add another 3 prunes and fold over another layer of leaves. Repeat twice more using the remaining stuffing and prunes.

7. Wrap the strips of fat around the cabbage and tie securely with string. Place the cabbage in a casserole and add the wine. It should come three-quarters of the way up the cabbage. Cover and bake for 2½ hours.

8. Before serving, untie the cabbage, remove the pork fat and cut the cabbage into thick slices using a sharp knife. Serve with the cooking juices.

Farci périgourdin

Ham-Stuffed White Cabbage

00:30　Serves 6–8　02:00

American	Ingredients	Metric/Imperial
1 lb	Piece of bacon	500 g / 1 lb
¾ lb	Potatoes	350 g / 12 oz
3	Carrots	3
2	Turnips	2
1	Onion	1
1	Clove	1
1	Veal shank [knuckle]	1
1	Leek	1
1	Bunch of celery	1
	Salt and pepper	
1	Bouquet garni	1
1 (½ lb)	Slice of smoked ham	1 (250 g / 8 oz)
2 (¼ lb)	Slices of cooked ham	2 (125 g / 4 oz)
4 cups	Diced white bread (crusts removed)	350 g / 12 oz
2	Shallots	2
3	Garlic cloves	3
1 cup	Chicken stock	250 ml / 8 fl oz
⅓ cup	Cognac	5 tbsp
6	Eggs	6
1	White cabbage	1

1. Place the bacon in a saucepan of cold water, bring to a boil and simmer gently for 5 minutes. Rinse in cold water and drain.

2. Peel the potatoes, carrots, turnips and onion. Stud the onion with the clove. Place all these vegetables in a large saucepan with the bacon, the veal shank, leek and celery. Season with salt and pepper and add the bouquet garni. Cover with water and bring to a boil. Simmer gently for about 40 minutes.

3. Meanwhile, dice all the ham and mix with the diced bread in a mixing bowl. Peel and chop the shallots and garlic and add to the bowl. Moisten with the stock and stir. Add the cognac and then the eggs, stirring well. Set aside.

4. Remove any damaged leaves from the cabbage. Cut out the core and separate the cabbage leaves. Cook in boiling water for 2 minutes. Drain, rinse under cold running water and drain again carefully.

5. Line a deep mixing bowl with cheesecloth or muslin, leaving the edges draped over the side. Place a cabbage leaf on the

Chou farci

Stuffed Cabbage

00:40　02:30

American	Ingredients	Metric/Imperial
1	Green cabbage	1
1	Bunch of fresh parsley	1
1 cup	Fresh bread crumbs	50 g / 2 oz
	Milk	
2	Garlic cloves	2
2	Onions	2
12	Prunes	12
1 lb	Ground [minced] pork	500 g / 1 lb
½ lb	Ground [minced] cooked ham	250 g / 8 oz
½ lb	Ground [minced] bacon	250 g / 8 oz
1	Egg	1
	Salt and pepper	
2	Thin strips of pork fat	2
2 cups	Dry white wine	500 ml / ¾ pint

1. Preheat the oven to 350°F / 180°C / Gas Mark 4.

2. Remove any bruised and withered outer leaves of the cabbage. Place the whole cabbage in a large saucepan, cover with plenty of cold water and bring to a boil. Simmer gently for 20 minutes.

3. Drain the cabbage. Cut out the core. Place the cabbage on a work surface, spread open the leaves and remove the heart (leaving a hollow about the size of a grapefruit).

4. Mince or finely chop the cabbage heart and parsley. Soak the bread crumbs in a bowl of milk. Peel and slice the garlic and onions. Remove the pits [stones] from the prunes using a small pointed knife.

5. Squeeze the bread to extract excess milk and place in a mixing bowl. Add the cabbage heart, parsley, garlic, onions, pork, ham, bacon and egg. Mix together well. Season with salt and pepper.

bottom of the bowl and arrange the others around the sides, allowing them to overlap the rim of the bowl. Reserve one leaf for the top.

6. Pour the ham mixture into the bowl. Fold the cabbage leaves over the stuffing and top with the reserved leaf. Wrap the cheesecloth securely around the stuffed cabbage and tie it at the top.

7. Take the stuffed cabbage in its wrapping out of the bowl and immerse in the boiling stock. Simmer for 1 hour.

8. Drain the cabbage, unwrap the cheesecloth and place on a serving dish. Cut the cabbage into slices. Serve the meat and vegetables in stock separately.

Choucroute

Sauerkraut with Pork and Sausages

American	Ingredients	Metric/Imperial
00:30 plus soaking		04:00 Serves 6–8
14 oz	Salt pork	400 g / 14 oz
4	Large onions	4
3	Carrots	3
4	Cloves	4
4 lb	Sauerkraut	2 kg / 4 lb
	Salt and pepper	
½ lb	Bacon rind	250 g / 8 oz
⅔ cup	Lard at room temperature	150 g / 5 oz
1	Bouquet garni	1
6	Juniper berries	6
1 (3 lb)	Uncooked smoked pork shoulder [bacon collar or fore slipper]	1 (1.5 kg / 3 lb)
6	Slices of cooked ham	6
2 cups	White wine	500 ml / ¾ pint
6	Strasbourg or Montbéliard sausages or other smoked pork sausages	6

1. Place the salt pork in a mixing bowl, cover with cold water and leave to soak for 1½ hours, changing the water once. Drain.

2. Peel the onions and carrots. Stud each onion with a clove. Drain the sauerkraut and squeeze out excess water. Separate the shreds using a fork, and season with salt and pepper.

3. Place three-quarters of the bacon rind in a flameproof casserole. Grease the sides of the casserole with the lard. Put half the sauerkraut into the pot and add the onions, carrots, bouquet garni, juniper berries, pork, cooked ham and salt pork. Cover with the remaining sauerkraut. Pour in the wine and add a little water if necessary to ensure that the sauerkraut is nearly covered. Top with the remaining bacon rind.

4. Bring to a boil over a moderate heat and simmer for 2½ hours.

5. Remove the salt pork. Continue simmering for 15 minutes, then remove the pork and ham. Keep the meats warm. Simmer the sauerkraut for a further 1 hour.

6. Add the sausages to the sauerkraut and simmer for a final 15 minutes.

7. To serve, slice the cuts of meat. Remove the vegetables and bouquet garni, and pile the sauerkraut in the center of a warmed serving dish. Arrange the slices of meat and ham around the sides, and top with the remaining ingredients.

Kig et far

Pork and Bacon on a Buckwheat Dumpling

American	Ingredients	Metric/Imperial
00:40		03:00
1 (1½ lb)	Piece of bacon	1 (750 g / 1½ lb)
2 cups	Buckwheat flour	250 g / 8 oz
1 cup	Milk	250 ml / 8 fl oz
3	Eggs	3
⅔ cup	Crème fraîche (see page 122)	150 ml / ¼ pint
½ cup	Melted butter	125 g / 4 oz
1 tbsp	Superfine [caster] sugar	1 tbsp
	Salt	
1 (2 lb)	Pork leg, shank portion [knuckle]	1 (1 kg / 2 lb)

1. Place the bacon in a saucepan of cold water. Bring to a boil and simmer for 10 minutes. Drain and set aside.

2. Sift the flour into a mixing bowl. Make a hollow in the center and add the milk, eggs, crème fraîche and melted butter. Add the sugar and a pinch of salt. Mix all the ingredients well together until a smooth thick batter is formed. Do not beat as this would incorporate too much air.

3. Put the batter in a clean linen towel, bring up the corners over the top and tie securely with string. Place in a large pan of boiling water. Add the pork and bacon and simmer for 3 hours.

4. Drain the meats and batter dumpling. Untie the string and flatten the dumpling in the linen towel. Slide it onto a deep warmed serving dish and place the sliced pork and bacon on top. Serve hot.

Cook's tip: serve this hearty winter dish with any colorful vegetable.

Sauerkraut with pork and sausages

Individual meat and vegetable stews

Petite marmite

Individual Meat and Vegetable Stews

	00:20		02:00

American	Ingredients	Metric/Imperial
1 (1½ lb)	Boneless beef chuck roast [top rib], bones reserved	1 (750 g / 1½ lb)
4 quarts	Water	4 l / 7 pints
2 lb	Carrots	1 kg / 2 lb
1 lb	Turnips	500 g / 1 lb
4	Leeks	4
1	Bunch of celery	1
1	Small cabbage	1
¼ lb	Beef bone marrow	125 g / 4 oz
	Grated nutmeg	
	Salt and pepper	
1 (2 lb)	Chicken	1 (1 kg / 2 lb)
1 lb	Ground [minced] beef	500 g / 1 lb
6	Slices of bread	6
½ cup	Grated gruyère cheese	50 g / 2 oz

1. Place the beef roast and bones in a large flameproof casserole. Cover with the water and bring to a boil, skimming off any fat. Peel the carrots and add them to the casserole. Simmer gently for 30 minutes over a low heat, skimming off any scum that may rise.
2. Peel the turnips. Cut the leeks in half. Separate the celery

into stalks, discarding the root. Add the turnips, leeks and celery stalks to the casserole.
3. Remove any withered outer leaves from the cabbage. Plunge whole into a pan of boiling water and simmer for 5 minutes. Drain. Remove 6 large leaves and put a piece of marrow in each leaf. Add a pinch of nutmeg and salt and pepper to taste. Form each leaf into a little parcel and tie up with string. Tie up the heart of the cabbage also. Add the parcels and cabbage heart to the casserole. Continue simmering for 10 minutes.
4. Add the chicken and cook for 20 minutes longer.
5. Remove the casserole from the heat and leave to cool. Remove the surface fat using a skimming ladle.
6. Preheat the oven to 425°F / 220°C / Gas Mark 7.
7. Remove the beef from the casserole and cut it into small pieces. Remove the chicken, take the meat from the carcass and cut it into small pieces, discarding the skin. Remove the whole vegetables and chop them. Remove the cabbage heart, untie it and chop. Remove the cabbage parcels. Divide all the ingredients, with the ground beef, between 6 small ovenproof dishes (or the special earthenware pots called *petites marmites*). Moisten with the strained broth.
8. Cover the dishes and bake for 30 minutes.
9. Meanwhile, toast the slices of bread and sprinkle with the grated cheese.
10. Serve the little stews very hot, with the cheese toasts.

Riz à la Valencienne

Spanish Style Rice Casserole

	00:30 Serves 6–8		00:30

American	Ingredients	Metric/Imperial
6	Small purple globe artichokes	6
	Lemon juice	
5	Medium-size tomatoes	5
½ lb	Fresh peas	250 g / 8 oz
3	Small sweet peppers	3
1 (2 lb)	Tender young rabbit	1 (1 kg / 2 lb)
1 lb	Boneless shoulder of pork [spare rib]	500 g / 1 lb
5 tbsp	Olive oil	5 tbsp
3	Medium-size onions	3
2	Garlic cloves	2
1	Bay leaf	1
3⅔ cups	Water	900 ml / 1½ pints
	Salt and pepper	
2 cups	Long-grain rice	400 g / 14 oz
	Saffron powder	
3	Hard-cooked eggs	3

1. To prepare the artichoke hearts, cut off the stalks and trim the points from the outer leaves. Rub the cut surfaces with lemon juice so that they do not discolor. Spread open the top leaves and pull out the inside leaves to reveal the hairy choke. Remove the choke using a teaspoon. Halve the artichokes lengthwise and sprinkle all over with the lemon juice. Set aside.
2. Quarter the tomatoes. Shell the peas. Core the peppers, remove the seeds, and cut into strips.
3. Cut the rabbit into 9 pieces. Cut the pork into cubes. Heat 3 tablespoons olive oil in a paella pan or a large frying pan, add the pork and rabbit pieces and brown them on all sides, over a moderate heat.

4. Peel and chop the onions and garlic. Add to the frying pan with the bay leaf, halved artichoke hearts, tomatoes, peas, the remaining olive oil, ⅔ cup [150 ml / ¼ pint] water, and salt and pepper to taste. Simmer the mixture over a gentle heat for about 20 minutes.

5. Add the rice, remaining water and add a pinch of saffron. Do not stir, but allow to simmer gently for 30 minutes longer or until the rice has absorbed all the water.

6. Remove from the heat and leave to cool for 5 minutes.

7. Garnish the dish with the shelled, hard-cooked eggs, cut into quarters, and serve immediately.

Fréginat

Carcassonne Pork Stew

⬦ 00:20 01:00 🥘

American	Ingredients	Metric/Imperial
3 lb	Boneless loin of pork or tenderloin [fillet]	1.5 kg / 3 lb
3 tbsp	Lard	40 g / 1½ oz
4	Garlic cloves	4
3	Onions	3
1 tsp	Crushed dried thyme	1 tsp
1	Bay leaf	1
	Salt and pepper	
3	Egg yolks	3
	Vinegar	

1. Cut the pork into small pieces. Melt the lard in a heavy saucepan, add the pork and seal the pieces quickly on all sides, until they are golden brown.

2. Peel and chop the garlic and onions and add these to the pan. Add water to half cover the meat. Add the thyme and crumbled bay leaf and season with salt and pepper. Simmer for 1 hour. By the end of the cooking time almost no liquid should be left.

3. Mix the egg yolks in a bowl with a few drops of vinegar. Remove the pan from the heat and mix in the egg yolks. Serve hot.

Marmite sarthoise 🧑‍🍳

Chicken and Rabbit Sauté with Cream

⬦ 01:30 00:50 🥘

American	Ingredients	Metric/Imperial
¾ lb	Boneless chicken breast	350 g / 12 oz
½ lb	Boneless rabbit	250 g / 8 oz
¼ lb	Fresh pork sides [belly of pork]	125 g / 4 oz
3 tbsp	Flour	3 tbsp
6 oz	Button mushrooms	175 g / 6 oz
¾ lb	White cabbage	350 g / 12 oz
¼ lb	Carrots	125 g / 4 oz
2 tbsp	Walnut oil	2 tbsp
1 cup	Dry white wine	350 ml / 12 fl oz
1 cup	White stock	350 ml / 12 fl oz
1 cup	Crème fraîche (see page 122)	150 ml / ¼ pint
	Salt and pepper	

1. Cut the chicken breast, rabbit and pork sides into strips. Coat the chicken and rabbit strips with the flour. Set aside.

2. Slice the mushrooms. Remove any withered outer leaves from the cabbage, core it and cut into strips. Peel the carrots and cut into strips lengthwise.

3. Steam the cabbage and carrots over boiling water for 20 minutes.

4. Meanwhile, heat the walnut oil in a frying pan, add the rabbit and chicken strips, mushrooms and pork strips and cook over a high heat for 5-10 minutes, stirring often to prevent them burning, until golden brown and cooked through.

5. Transfer the meat mixture to a warmed serving dish. Add the steamed vegetables and keep hot.

6. Add the white wine to the frying pan and bring to a boil, scraping the meat juices from the bottom of the pan. Reduce by one-quarter over a moderate heat. Add the stock and crème fraîche and blend well. Season to taste. Heat for 1 minute.

7. To serve, pour the sauce over the meat and vegetables.

Glazed carrots and green beans with garlic – colorful accompaniments to many meat dishes

Boiled smoked pork and sausages

Potée Lorraine

Boiled Smoked Pork and Sausages with Vegetables

	00:30	03:00
	plus soaking	Serves 6–8

American	Ingredients	Metric/Imperial
2 cups	Dried navy [haricot] beans	400 g / 14 oz
1 (2½ lb)	Boneless smoked shoulder of pork [bacon collar]	1 (1.25 kg / 2½ lb)
1 (1 lb)	Piece of smoked bacon	1 (500 g / 1 lb)
1	Morteau sausage or other large smoked pork liver sausage	1
4	Small smoked sausages	4
1	Bouquet garni	1
2 lb	Carrots	1 kg / 2 lb
3	Turnips	3
3	Onions	3
6	Leeks	6
1	Medium-size cabbage	1
8	Potatoes	8
	Salt	

1. Soak the beans overnight in cold water to cover. If necessary, soak the pork shoulder and smoked bacon in cold water to remove excess salt. Drain.
2. Place the pork, bacon, morteau sausage and small smoked sausages in a large flameproof casserole. Cover with 4 quarts [4 l / 7 pints] of water and bring to a boil. Simmer for 2 hours.
3. Meanwhile, place the beans in a saucepan with 3 quarts [3 l / 5 pints] of water and add the bouquet garni. Bring to a boil and cook for 1 hour.
4. Peel the carrots, turnips and onions. Add these vegetables to the casserole with the leeks and cook for a further 30 minutes.

5. Quarter the cabbage, remove the stalk and cut into strips. Cook the cabbage in boiling water for 5 minutes, then drain it and add to the casserole. Continue cooking for 30 minutes.
6. Meanwhile, peel the potatoes and cook in boiling salted water for 25 minutes or until tender. Drain.
7. Drain the pork, bacon and sausages, slice them and arrange on a warmed serving platter. Drain the vegetables and beans. Surround the meats with the vegetables, beans and potatoes.

Cook's tip: the cooking broth makes an excellent soup.

Potée Champenoise

Boiled Chicken and Sausages with Vegetables

	00:30	02:30
	plus soaking	Serves 8–10

American	Ingredients	Metric/Imperial
2 cups	Dried navy [haricot] beans	400 g / 14 oz
1	Small lightly salted uncooked ham [gammon]	1
1 (1¼ lb)	Piece of lightly salted bacon	1 (625 g / 1¼ lb)
6	Carrots	6
1	Onion	1
3	Turnips	3
1	Uncooked Lyons sausage with truffles	1
1	Small Morteau sausage or other smoked pork liver sausage	1
1	Bunch of celery	1
10	Black peppercorns	10
2	Cloves	2
5 quarts	Water	5 l / 9 pints
1 (4 lb)	Chicken	1 (2 kg / 4 lb)
1	Bouquet garni	1
12	Medium-sized potatoes	12
	Salt and pepper	

1. Soak the beans overnight in cold water to cover. Drain.
2. Place the ham and bacon in a saucepan of cold water. Bring to a boil and simmer for 10 minutes, then drain.
3. Peel the carrots, onion and turnips. Place these vegetables in a large flameproof casserole. Add the ham, bacon, sausage, celery stalks, peppercorns and cloves. Cover with the cold water. Bring to a boil and simmer gently for 20 minutes.
4. Add the beans to the casserole with the chicken and bouquet garni. Bring back to a boil and simmer gently for 1½ hours.
5. Peel the potatoes and add them to the casserole. Season with salt and pepper. Continue cooking for 25 minutes.
6. Drain the meats and vegetables. Slice the meats and place on a large warmed serving platter. Carve the chicken and add to the platter. Put the vegetables in another serving dish. Serve with mustard, gherkins, oil, vinegar and barbecue sauce.

Cook's tip: the stock can be used for cooking a cabbage, cut into thin strips, for 10 minutes. This cabbage would be served at another meal with very thin slices of farmhouse bread.

Boiled chicken and sausages

Hochepot des Flandres

Flanders Hotpot

	00:30	02:30 to 03:00	
	Serves 8–10		

American	Ingredients	Metric/Imperial
1	Oxtail	1
2 lb	Flank steak	1 kg / 2 lb
1 (3 lb)	Boneless shoulder of lamb, rolled and tied	1 (1.5 kg / 3 lb)
1 lb	Carrots	500 g / 1 lb
4	Leeks (white part only)	4
2	Large onions	2
4	Cloves	4
2	Garlic cloves	2
20	Juniper berries	20
12	Black peppercorns	12
	Salt and pepper	
1	Small green cabbage	1
4	Turnips	4
1	Bunch of celery	1
¾ lb	Green beans	350 g / 12 oz
1	Uncooked sausage	1
2	Pigs' ears	2
8	Potatoes	8
1 cup	Grated gruyère cheese	150 g / 5 oz
	Slices of toast	

1. Cut the oxtail into convenient-size pieces. Place them in a large flameproof casserole and add the flank steak and lamb shoulder. Cover with plenty of cold water. Bring to a boil, skimming off any fat, then lower the heat and simmer for 30 minutes.
2. Peel the carrots. Quarter the leeks. Peel the onions and stud each one with 2 cloves. Add these vegetables to the casserole with the unpeeled garlic, juniper berries, peppercorns and 2 pinches of salt. Simmer for 1 hour.
3. Remove any wilted outer leaves from the cabbage. Cut it into quarters and remove the tough stalks from the base of the leaves. Cook the leaves in boiling water for 5 minutes. Drain. Peel the turnips. Separate the celery into stalks, discarding the root. Add the cabbage, turnips and celery stalks to the casserole and cook for a further 30 minutes.

4. Trim the beans and remove any strings. Add them to the casserole with the sausage, pricked with a fork to prevent it bursting, and the pigs' ears. Continue to simmer for 30 minutes to 1 hour.
5. Meanwhile, cook the potatoes separately. Peel them and place in a saucepan of water. Add a pinch of salt and bring to a boil. Simmer for 25 minutes. Drain and keep hot.
6. Drain the meats and vegetables, reserving the broth. Slice the meats and arrange on a warmed serving platter. Put the vegetables in another warmed serving dish. Keep hot.
7. Skim fat from the broth. Strain into a tureen. Season and serve with the cheese and toast. Follow with the meat and vegetables.

Puchero

Stew of Mixed Meats and Vegetables

	01:00	03:00 to 03:30	
	plus soaking	Serves 6–8	

American	Ingredients	Metric/Imperial
1 cup	Dried chick peas	250 g / 8 oz
1 (3 lb)	Beef shank [shin]	1 (1.5 kg / 3 lb)
	Salt	
1	Celeriac	1
8	Carrots	8
4	Turnips	4
2	Onions	2
4	Cloves	4
6	Leeks	6
1	Bouquet garni	1
1	Fresh pork hock	1
1 (3 lb)	Chicken	1 (1.5 kg / 3 lb)
1	Large uncooked pork sausage	1
8	Very small ears of corn (husks and silk removed)	8
10	Black peppercorns	10
8	Potatoes	8
1	Strong chorizo sausage	1

1. Soak the chick peas overnight in cold water to cover.
2. Drain the chick peas, put them in a saucepan and cover with fresh cold water. Bring to a boil and simmer gently for 3 hours.
3. Meanwhile, place the beef in a large flameproof casserole, cover with cold water and add some salt. Bring to a boil, skimming off the scum until the water is clear. Lower the heat and simmer gently for 1 hour.
4. Peel and slice the celeriac. Peel the carrots, turnips and onions. Stud each onion with 2 cloves. Quarter the leeks and tie them into 2 bunches.
5. Add the carrots, the onions studded with cloves and the bouquet garni to the beef. Cook for a further hour, then add the celeriac, turnips, pork hock and chicken. Continue cooking for about 45 minutes.
6. Add the sausage, leeks, corn and peppercorns. Cook for about 30 minutes longer.
7. Meanwhile, peel the potatoes and cook in boiling salted water for 20 minutes. Heat the chorizo in simmering water for 5 - 7 minutes. Drain the potatoes and chorizo and keep hot.
8. Drain the meats and vegetables, reserving the broth. Slice the beef, pork and sausages and arrange on a warmed serving platter. Carve the chicken and add to the platter. Put all the vegetables in another serving dish. Skim all fat from the broth and strain it into a sauceboat. Serve with gherkins and mustard.

CHAPTER 14

Vegetables, Rice and Pasta

Cooking fresh vegetables

Guidelines

Boiling

When a lot of water is used, this method of cooking often entails a considerable loss of nutritive value as the nutrients are thrown away with the cooking water. For this reason many people prefer to cook vegetables in as little water as possible in a tightly covered pan. However, if little water is used, vegetables are more likely to alter in appearance and taste because they take longer to become tender. Green vegetables, such as green beans, that need to be cooked for only a short time, are best added to a large quantity of boiling water. This holds heat longer and quickly cooks the vegetables through. The lid should be left off the pan to prevent them discoloring. Root vegetables which are more dense than those grown above the ground cook more evenly when placed in cold water which is brought to a boil. Keep the water left after cooking vegetables as a basis for soups, sauces or gravies. Salt is added to water for taste reasons, but salt also raises the water's boiling point and makes food cook more quickly. This is why it is added to quickly cooked vegetables at the start of cooking and – since it also draws out the natural juices in food – at the end of cooking to recipes which are simmered slowly for a long period of time.

Certain vegetables (artichoke hearts, salsify, scorzonera, celeriac, jerusalem artichokes, cardoons) become discolored during cooking. To prevent this, cook them in a white stock. To 1 quart [1 l / 1¾ pints] water, add 1 tablespoon of flour and the juice of half a lemon; bring to a boil and add salt to taste. The vegetables are protected by the thin film of flour and the acidity of the lemon and retain their color during cooking.

Steaming

The great advantage of this method is that it retains nutrients and the color and texture of fresh and frozen vegetables. The vegetables are placed in a steamer over a pan of boiling water, or in a metal fold-up basket on legs, which stands in a pan containing only a small quantity of boiling water. In both methods the vegetables do not come into contact with the water and are cooked by the steam as it rises in the pan and circulates around the food. Though steam is hotter than boiling water, it does not cook more quickly and when steaming vegetables you should allow about 10 minutes more than boiling time. As a general rule, only young and tender vegetables should be steamed and the cooking time will vary according to the size of the vegetables. Both fresh and frozen vegetables are steamed for the same length of time. The amount of water you will need depends on the size and type of steamer, the usual amount is about 1 quart [1 l / 1¾ pints]. When steaming, add salt to the vegetables (not to the water) or season them at the table. It is a good idea to have a kettle of boiling water ready so that you can replenish the quantity of water in the steamer if necessary.

Most vegetables can be steamed, but those with a very pronounced flavor (particularly the cabbage family) are improved by first being blanched for a minute or two in boiling salted water. Both fresh and frozen vegetables are steamed for the same length of time.

Steaming is a very economical method of cooking if you use the pan to cook several things at the same time. For instance, if you are boiling potatoes, other even-sized vegetables can be wrapped in separate foil packages and placed on top of them.

The foil-wrapped vegetables will cook in the steam from the heat created by the boiling water. The steam needs to circulate so the packages should not be too close together. Chinese bamboo steamers which stack on top of each other over a saucepan, also allow a number of different ingredients to be cooked at the same time. The food that takes the longest time goes to the bottom section, close to the boiling water. The top basket must be covered with a closely fitting lid.

Pressure cooking

In a pressure cooker, the steam is sealed in and because it is increased in temperature by pressure, it makes food tender in one-third or less of the cooking time. Pressure cooking saves fuel and food retains more flavor and nutritive value. When cooking vegetables in a pressure cooker, the pan should be no more than two thirds full. Consult the manufacturer's instructions for more detailed information on cooking vegetables under pressure.

Dried legumes [pulses]

Dried peas and beans are generally cheaper than their fresh or canned equivalents, and are easy to cook and very nutritious. Most of them need to be soaked before they are cooked and they should be washed before soaking; any that float on the surface of the water should be removed.

Dried legumes are soaked before cooking to restore the moisture lost in drying and you can do this in two ways.
1. Place them in a bowl, cover them with 3 times their volume of cold water and leave them to soak for 4 to 12 hours, depending on the variety – smaller peas or beans need less soaking time than large ones.
2. A quicker method, is to place the peas or beans in a pan of cold water (do not add salt), bring to a boil and boil for about 5 minutes. Remove the pan from the heat and leave to soak for 1 hour.

In both cases, drain the peas or beans after soaking and rinse under running water. Lentils and split peas are better for soaking, but do not require it.

To cook the peas or beans, put them in a flameproof casserole and cover with water. Do not add salt until the end of the cooking time. Bring to a boil and add flavorings such as carrots, onions, celeriac or garlic. Continue cooking over a low heat for the required length of time. Beans, such as kidney beans, should be boiled fast for 10 minutes at the beginning of the cooking time to kill off harmful organisms.

If you are cooking dried legumes in a casserole with meat, they should be first soaked, with the exception of lentils or split peas. In this case, add extra water to the casserole during cooking as the meat juices will not provide sufficient liquid.

Cooking times for legumes [pulses]

Beans	– broad	1 hr 45 - 2 hr 15
	– flageolet	1 hr 15 - 1 hr 30
	– kidney	1 hr 15 - 1 hr 30
	– navy [haricot], small	1 hr 30 - 1 hr 45
	– pinto [borlotti]	1 hr 15 - 1 hr 30
Lentils	– brown/green	45-60 min
	– red	35-50 min
Peas	– chick	3 hr
	– dried	1 hr 45 - 2 hr 15
	– split	45-60 min

Vegetable cooking times

	Steaming	Pressure
Artichoke, jerusalem	25-30 min	20 min
Asparagus	15-20 min	10 min
Beet, sliced	10-15 min	8 min
Brussels sprouts	12-18 min	5 min
Cabbage, green	20-25 min	8 min
Carrots	15-20 min	12-15 min
Cauliflower	20-25 min	8 min
Chinese artichokes	10-15 min	10-12 min
Eggplant [aubergine], sliced	30-40 min	5 min
Endive [chicory]	25-35 min	12-15 min
Fennel	15-20 min	15 min
Green beans	10-15 min	6-7 min
Leeks	20-35 min	10 min
Peas	15-20 min	20 min
Potatoes (medium-sized)	18-20 min	12 min
Salsify	15-20 min	15 min
Spinach	12-15 min	5 min
Swiss chard ribs	10-15 min	8 min
Turnips	15-20 min	12-15 min

Six ways of cutting up vegetables

Brunoise
Peel the vegetables (carrots, potatoes, turnips) and cut into wide, thin slices. Pile up several slices and cut into thin, regular-sized sticks and then into small dice.

Jardinière
Peel the vegetables (carrots, potatoes, turnips). Cut them into sections and then into thick slices. Pile up several slices and cut into uniformly medium-sized sticks.

Julienne
Peel the vegetables (carrots, turnips, leeks). Cut them into thin slices and then into sticks. Cut the sticks into uniformly-sized thin sticks, about the size of matchsticks. To cut a leek into fine strips, clean it, remove the withered leaves and trim the dark green ends. Cut the leek into 2-3 in [7-8 cm] pieces, then cut these in half lengthwise. Place them, flat surface downwards on the work top and cut the pieces into long, very thin strips.

Macédoine
Peel the vegetables (carrots, turnips, but not potatoes). Cut them into slices, then into sticks. Cut the sticks into regular-shaped cubes, rather smaller than the dice used for brunoise. To prepare green beans, take a handful and cut into ½ in [1 cm] pieces.

Mirepoix
Used for flavoring: carrots, celery, thyme, bay leaves and parsley stalks. Wash all the ingredients and chop them coarsely.

Paysanne
Clean the vegetables (carrots, turnips, potatoes). Cut into thin slices and then chop coarsely into small pieces, without trying to achieve a uniform size.

Cook's tips
- You can use a colander to convert a saucepan into a steamer. It should fit inside the pan without its base touching the water. It must be metal and the top should be covered with foil so that the steam cannot escape.
- Vegetables such as asparagus and broccoli which have delicate tops and tough stalks can be steam boiled. To do this, choose a deep pan and prop up bundles of the vegetables with crumpled foil or stand them in an empty can which has holes punched in the bottom and sides. Add boiling water as necessary to the pan and cook the vegetables for the same length of time as when boiling.
- As water evaporates during steaming, add boiling water from a kettle to the required level. A metal jam jar lid or down-turned saucer placed in the water will have more space to rattle in as the water level sinks — good warning of time to replenish.
- If you have to devise a menu quickly, it is useful to have a small reserve of canned vegetables. Drain and rinse the vegetables before using them and follow the cooking directions on the can. It is generally sufficient simply to heat them through.
- Do not use or buy cans which have tops or bases that are not flat; any bulges mean that the vegetables have fermented and emitted a gas that has swollen the can.
- If you have to keep an opened can of vegetables for 2 or 3 days, transfer the contents to a glass or china bowl, cover and refrigerate.
- If you want to prepare vegetables in advance, cook them in an uncovered pan until they are tender but not soft, drain them and rinse in cold water to prevent further cooking. Just before serving, toss the vegetables in melted butter over a good heat.

Côtes de bettes gratinées

Swiss Chard in Cheese Sauce

	00:20	00:45

American	Ingredients	Metric/Imperial
1½ lb	Swiss chard	750 g / 1½ lb
1	Small celeriac	1
	Salt and pepper	
1	Lemon	1
2 cups	Cheese sauce (see page 128)	500 ml / ¾ pint
½ cup	Grated gruyère cheese	50 g / 2 oz
2 tbsp	Butter	25 g / 2 oz

1. Remove the green leaves from the chard as they are not used in this recipe. Scrape the white stems, wash well and cut into pieces 2½ in / 7 cm long. Slice into sticks a little thicker than matchsticks ('julienne' style, see page 411).
2. Peel, wash and cut the celeriac into sticks of the same size as the chard stems.
3. Bring some salted water to a boil in a saucepan. Add the juice of the lemon and the celeriac. Cook for 5-7 minutes and add the chard stems. Continue cooking until the chard is tender, but not soft.
4. Preheat the oven to 400°F / 200°C / Gas Mark 6.
5. Drain the vegetables well and arrange in a buttered gratin dish. Cover with the cheese sauce, sprinkle with the cheese and dot with the butter.
6. Bake for 20-30 minutes until the top is golden brown.

Brocolis au gratin

Broccoli in Cheese Sauce

	00:20	00:40 to 00:50

American	Ingredients	Metric/Imperial
	Salt and pepper	
2 lb	Broccoli	1 kg / 2 lb
¼ cup	Butter	50 g / 2 oz
2 tbsp	Flour	25 g / 1 oz
2 cups	Milk	500 ml / ¾ pint
⅔ cup	Crème fraîche (see page 122)	150 ml / ¼ pint
	Grated nutmeg	
1 cup	Grated gruyère cheese	125 g / 4 oz

1. Boil some salted water in a saucepan.
2. Thoroughly wash the broccoli and trim. Add to the pan and cook for about 10 minutes or until just tender.
3. Drain well and chop into large pieces. Preheat the oven to 400°F / 200°C / Gas Mark 6.
4. Melt 2 tablespoons [25 g / 1 oz] of the butter in a frying pan. Add the broccoli and cook gently to evaporate any remaining water. Season with salt and pepper. Remove the pan from the heat.
5. Melt the remaining butter in a heavy-bottomed saucepan over a low heat. Add the flour and mix together until the butter has absorbed all the flour. Gradually add the milk and continue

stirring over a low heat for about 10 minutes or until the sauce thickens. Finally, stir in the crème fraîche, a pinch of nutmeg and half the gruyère and season with salt and pepper.
6. Arrange the broccoli in a gratin dish, pour over the cheese sauce and sprinkle with the remaining cheese. Bake for 20-30 minutes or until golden brown. Serve hot.

Carottes aux raisins

Carrots with Raisins

	00:15 plus soaking	01:00

American	Ingredients	Metric/Imperial
1⅓ cups	Raisins	200 g / 7 oz
2 lb	Carrots	1 kg / 2 lb
½ cup	Butter	125 g / 4 oz
	Salt	
1 tsp	Sugar (optional)	1 tsp

1. Put the raisins in a bowl, cover with warm water and leave to soak.
2. Peel the carrots and cut them into thin slices. Melt the butter in a heavy-bottomed saucepan and add the carrots. Stir well then cover and cook over a very low heat for 40 minutes, taking care that they do not stick to the bottom of the pan.
3. Drain the raisins and mix with the carrots.
4. Cook for 10 minutes longer or until the carrots are tender. Add a little salt. If the carrots are not sweet enough, add the sugar. Serve very hot.

Broccoli in cheese sauce

Cèpes à la parisienne

Cèpes French Style

	00:20	00:30 to 00:40

American	Ingredients	Metric/Imperial
4 lb	Cèpes or other fresh mushrooms	2 kg / 4 lb
¼ cup	Oil	4 tbsp
1	Lemon	1
3	Shallots or	3
2	Garlic cloves	2
1⅓ cups	Coarse dry bread crumbs	125 g / 4 oz
1 tbsp	Chopped fresh parsley	1 tbsp

1. Separate the mushroom caps from the stems. Slice the stems into quarters lengthwise.
2. Heat 1 tablespoon of the oil in a flameproof casserole. Add the juice of the lemon and the mushroom caps and stems. Cook over a low heat for about 10 minutes or until all the liquid has evaporated. Remove from the pan and cut the caps into even-sized pieces. Set aside one-third of the stems.
3. Heat the remaining oil in the casserole. Return the mushroom caps and remaining stems to the pan, season with salt and pepper and cook for a further 15-25 minutes.
4. Finely chop the shallots (or garlic) together with the reserved mushroom stems.
5. A few minutes before serving, add this mixture with the bread crumbs to the cèpes and stir quickly. Turn onto a warmed serving dish and sprinkle with the parsley.

Cardons béchamel
Cardoons in Béchamel Sauce

◣ 00:10　　　00:40 to 00:50 🥘

American	Ingredients	Metric/Imperial
1	Lemon	1
3 lb	Cardoons (with a few leaves)	1.5 kg / 3 lb
¼ cup	Flour	25 g / 1 oz
2 quarts	Water	2 l / 3½ pints
1 tbsp	Salt	1 tbsp
1 tbsp	Beef drippings or oil	1 tbsp
3 cups	Béchamel sauce (see page 124)	750 ml / 1¼ pints

1. Squeeze the lemon. Cut away the outer stems and leaves and wash and dry the cardoons. Cut them into 4 in / 10 cm pieces and sprinkle with a little lemon juice.
2. Mix the flour with a little of the water then put in a large saucepan with the rest of the water. Add the salt, the remaining lemon juice and the drippings or oil. Bring to a boil and add the cardoons. Cover and cook for 30-40 minutes until just tender.
3. Drain and dry the cardoons and place them in a deep frying pan. Coat them with the béchamel sauce and heat through over a low heat for 10 minutes. Serve very hot.

Artichauts au naturel
Globe Artichokes

◣ 00:05　　　00:25 to 00:30 🥘

American	Ingredients	Metric/Imperial
	Salt	
½	Lemon	½
6	Globe artichokes	6

Cook by either of the methods given below.
In a saucepan:
1. Bring a large saucepan of salted water to a boil. Add the juice of the half lemon.
2. Break the stems of the artichokes, pulling them to remove the strings. Remove any damaged or discolored outer leaves.
3. Place the artichokes in the boiling water and cook for about 30 minutes, or until a leaf pulls out easily.

4. Drain upside-down and serve warm with melted clarified butter or hollandaise sauce (see page 126).

In a steamer:
1. Prepare the artichokes as above.
2. Fill the bottom of the steamer with water. Put the artichokes in the top of the steamer, above the water, cover, and steam for 25-30 minutes (depending on the size of the artichokes).

Cook's tip: after cooking, the leaves and hairy choke can be removed, and the hearts cooked gently in a frying pan with a little butter.

Swiss chard in cheese sauce

Carottes forestière
Carrots with Mushrooms in Cream

◣ 00:20　　　00:30 🥘

American	Ingredients	Metric/Imperial
2 lb	Young carrots	1 kg / 2 lb
2 cups	Chicken stock	500 ml / ¾ pint
1 tbsp	Sugar	1 tbsp
6 tbsp	Butter	75 g / 3 oz
	Salt and pepper	
	Grated nutmeg	
¾ lb	Button mushrooms	350 g / 12 oz
⅔ cup	Crème fraîche (see page 122)	150 ml / ¼ pint
	Chopped fresh chervil	

1. Peel the carrots, cut them into small strips and place in a saucepan with the stock, sugar, half the butter, salt, pepper and a pinch of nutmeg. Cover and cook over a moderate heat until the liquid has completely evaporated.
2. Meanwhile, clean the mushrooms and trim the stems. Cut into thin slices. Heat the remaining butter in a frying pan, add the mushrooms and season with salt and pepper. Cook until the liquid from the mushrooms has evaporated. Add the mushrooms and the crème fraîche to the carrots once they are cooked, mix together and sprinkle with the chervil.

Choux de Bruxelles au lard

Brussels Sprouts with Chestnuts

△ 00:45   01:00 🥘

American	Ingredients	Metric/Imperial
	Salt and pepper	
1 lb	Chestnuts	500 g / 1 lb
1 quart	Chicken stock	1 l / 1¾ pints
1½ lb	Brussels sprouts	750 g / 1½ lb
½ lb	Lightly salted bacon	250 g / 8 oz
1 tbsp	Lard	1 tbsp

1. Heat a saucepan of salted water. With the point of a knife, pierce the rounded part of the chestnuts. Add to the pan and bring back to a boil. Cook for 30 minutes.
2. Remove the saucepan from the heat and shell the chestnuts one at a time, leaving the rest to keep hot in the water.
3. Heat the stock in a saucepan. Add the shelled chestnuts and simmer gently for 10-15 minutes. Take care that the chestnuts do not disintegrate during cooking.
4. Meanwhile, cut the stems and outer leaves from the sprouts. Cook the sprouts in boiling salted water for 10-15 minutes. Be sure not to overcook them — they should remain firm.
5. Place the bacon in a saucepan and cover with water. Bring to a boil and simmer for 10 minutes. Drain and cut into strips.
6. Heat the lard in a saucepan and add the bacon. Cook gently until golden brown, then add the sprouts and drained chestnuts. Season with salt and pepper and stir gently. Cook for a further 5 minutes until well heated through.

Chou-fleur gratiné

Cauliflower in Cheese Sauce

△ 00:10   00:30 to 00:35 🥘

American	Ingredients	Metric/Imperial
1	Large cauliflower	1
¼ cup	Butter	60 g / 2 oz
6 tbsp	Flour	40 g / 1½ oz
1 cup	Crème fraîche (see page 122)	250 ml / 8 fl oz
1 cup	Grated gruyère cheese	150 g / 5 oz
	Grated nutmeg	
	Salt and pepper	

1. Preheat the oven to 375°F / 190°C / Gas Mark 5.
2. Remove the outer leaves from the cauliflower. Cut into the hard stem and separate the cauliflower into large florets.
3. In a saucepan bring some salted water to a boil. Add the cauliflower and bring back to a boil. Lower the heat and simmer gently, without a lid, for 10-15 minutes. Pierce the cauliflower with the blade of a knife. The florets should be cooked but still firm.
4. Meanwhile, melt 3 tablespoons [40 g / 1½ oz] of the butter in a saucepan, add the flour and stir until it is absorbed. Gradually stir in the crème fraîche and cook, stirring, until thickened. Flavor with two-thirds of the grated cheese, a pinch of nutmeg, and salt and pepper to taste.

5. Drain the cauliflower well, arrange in a gratin dish and cover with the sauce. Sprinkle with the remaining cheese and dot with the remaining butter.
6. Bake for about 20 minutes, or until the surface is golden brown.

Choux de Bruxelles à l'étouffée

Braised Brussels Sprouts

△ 00:20   00:40 🥘

American	Ingredients	Metric/Imperial
1½ lb	Brussels sprouts	750 g / 1½ lb
1	Medium-sized onion	1
½ lb	Bacon	250 g / 8 oz
2 tbsp	Lard or oil	2 tbsp
2 tsp	Flour	2 tsp
2 cups	Chicken stock	500 ml / ¾ pint
	Salt and pepper	

1. Trim and wash the sprouts. Peel the onion and cut into thin slices. Cut the bacon into small strips.
2. Heat the lard or oil in a saucepan and brown the onion for 2-3 minutes. Add the strips of bacon and brown for 3-4 minutes, stirring constantly. Sprinkle with the flour, mix well, and add the stock a little at a time. Slowly bring to a boil. Add the sprouts and season with salt and pepper. Cover and cook over a low heat for 30 minutes.

Chou rouge braisé

Braised Red Cabbage

△ 00:25   02:00 🥘

American	Ingredients	Metric/Imperial
1 (3 lb)	Head of red cabbage	1 (1.5 kg / 3 lb)
¼ cup	Lard (or oil)	4 tbsp
2 tbsp	Sugar	2 tbsp
2 tbsp	Vinegar	2 tbsp
⅔ cup	Water	150 ml / ¼ pint
	Salt and pepper	
2	Crisp eating apples	2
¼ cup	Red currant jelly	4 tbsp

1. Preheat the oven to 325°F / 160°C / Gas Mark 3.
2. Wash the cabbage, remove any damaged outer leaves and cut into thin slices.
3. Place the lard or oil in a large flameproof casserole with the sugar, vinegar, water, salt and pepper. Bring to a boil and add the cabbage. Stir and bring back to a boil.
4. Cover the casserole and place in the oven. Cook for 2 hours.
5. After 1 hour, stir the cabbage and add a little water if necessary.
6. About 20 minutes before the end of the cooking time add the apples, cored and chopped, and the red currant jelly.
7. If the cabbage has produced a lot of water, reduce over a high heat on top of the stove, stirring constantly, before serving.

Cook's tip: serve with pork or ham.

Chou-fleur en soufflé

Cauliflower Soufflé

	00:20	00:45

American	Ingredients	Metric/Imperial
1	Cauliflower	1
	Salt and pepper	
⅔ cup	Milk	150 ml / ¼ pint
1 cup	Bread crumbs	50 g / 2 oz
4	Eggs, separated	4
¾ cup	Grated gruyère cheese	75 g / 3 oz

1. Remove the leaves from the cauliflower. Cut into the hard stem and separate into large florets. Wash and drain.
2. Bring a pan of salted water to a boil and add the cauliflower. Bring back to a boil, lower the heat and simmer, without a lid, for 15-20 minutes.
3. Drain the cauliflower well and purée in a blender or food processor. Put the purée in a large bowl.
4. Preheat the oven to 350°F / 180°C / Gas Mark 4.
5. Heat the milk and pour it over the bread crumbs in a bowl. Leave to soak for a few minutes then squeeze out the bread and add to the cauliflower purée, along with the 4 egg yolks and the grated gruyère cheese. Season with salt and pepper and mix well.
6. Beat the egg whites until stiff and carefully fold them into the cauliflower mixture.
7. Butter a 6½ in / 16 cm soufflé dish. Fill it three-quarters full with the mixture. Bake for 10 minutes then increase the heat to 425°F / 220°C / Gas Mark 7. Bake for a further 15 minutes and serve immediately.

Chou-fleur

Cauliflower

	00:10	00:08 to 00:15

American	Ingredients	Metric/Imperial
2	Medium-sized cauliflowers (or 1 large)	2
	Salt and pepper	
1 tbsp	Flour	1 tbsp
½ cup	Butter	125 g / 4 oz
1 cup	Bread crumbs	50 g / 2 oz
2 tbsp	Vinegar	2 tbsp
1 tsp	Prepared mustard	1 tsp
¼ cup	Oil	4 tbsp

1. Remove the outer leaves from the cauliflower. Cut into the hard stem and separate the cauliflower into large florets.
2. Bring a saucepan of salted water to a boil and add the cauliflower and the flour mixed with a little cold water. Bring back to a boil, lower the heat and simmer gently, without a lid, for 10-15 minutes. Drain well.
3. If you prefer to use a steamer or pressure cooker, keep the cauliflower whole. Steam for 15 minutes, or for 4 minutes from the moment the steam begins to flow in a pressure cooker.
4. When the florets are cooked, but still firm, remove from the heat and drain well.
5. The cauliflower can be sprinkled with parsley and served with lemon clarified butter (see page 113). Or with bread crumbs (à la chapelure): heat the butter with the bread crumbs in a small saucepan over a low heat. Reshape the cauliflower in

a serving dish and coat with the butter and bread crumb sauce. Or with vinaigrette dressing (à la vinaigrette): dissolve a pinch of salt in the vinegar. Mix in the mustard and season with pepper. Add the oil and mix well. Pour the vinaigrette over the cauliflower and serve hot or cold.

Chou pommé à la crème

Creamed Cabbage

	00:15	01:00

American	Ingredients	Metric/Imperial
1 (3 lb)	Head of white cabbage	1 (1.5 kg / 3 lb)
	Salt and pepper	
1 tbsp	Lard (or oil)	1 tbsp
1	Garlic clove	1
1	Bouquet garni	1
⅔ cup	Chicken stock	150 ml / ¼ pint
3 tbsp	Crème fraîche (see page 122)	3 tbsp

1. Wash the cabbage and remove any damaged outer leaves. Cut into quarters and cut away the thick stem. Wash again, if necessary.
2. Bring a large saucepan of salted water to a boil. Add the cabbage and bring back to a boil. Cook for 10 minutes then drain.
3. Heat the lard or oil in a saucepan. Peel and chop the garlic clove and add to the pan. Stir, making sure that it does not brown.
4. Add the cabbage to the saucepan along with the bouquet garni. Moisten with the stock and season with salt and pepper. Cover and simmer for 45 minutes to 1 hour. Check from time to time that there is still some liquid in the bottom of the pan. Add a little more stock if necessary.
5. Remove the pan from the heat. Add the crème fraîche, stir well and serve immediately.

Chanterelles ou girolles au beurre

Buttered Chanterelles or Girolles

	00:10	00:30

American	Ingredients	Metric/Imperial
1 lb	Fresh chanterelles or girolles	500 g / 1 lb
½	Lemon	½
¼ cup	Butter	50 g / 2 oz
3	Shallots	3
6	Fresh parsley sprigs	6
1	Garlic clove	1
	Salt and pepper	

1. Trim the mushrooms and sprinkle with a little lemon juice. Melt the butter in a frying pan, add the mushrooms and brown for 10 minutes over a moderate heat, stirring frequently and carefully with a wooden spatula.
2. Meanwhile, peel and finely chop the shallots and parsley. Add them to the frying pan, along with the peeled, but whole, garlic clove. Season with salt and pepper, cover and cook for 20 minutes.

Cèpes bordelaise

Stuffed Cèpes Bordelaise

	00:30		00:20

American	Ingredients	Metric/Imperial
2 lb	Cèpes or other fresh mushrooms	900 g / 2 lb
3	Shallots	3
3 or 4	Garlic cloves	3 or 4
1	Lemon	1
⅓ cup	Olive oil	6 tbsp
2 tbsp	Chopped fresh parsley	2 tbsp
	Salt and pepper	

1. Trim the stems of the cèpes and then separate from the caps. Shred the stems using a blender, vegetable mill or food processor. Peel and chop the shallots. Peel and crush the garlic. Squeeze the juice from the lemon.
2. Heat half the olive oil in a frying pan, add the shredded stems, shallots and parsley and season with salt and pepper. Cook over a low heat for about 10 minutes, or until the liquid has completely evaporated.
3. Heat the remaining oil in a large frying pan and add the mushroom caps. Cook for about 5 minutes on each side over a low heat.
4. Arrange the mushroom caps, stem side upwards, on a serving dish and fill with the mixture of stems, shallots and parsley. Sprinkle with lemon juice and serve immediately.

Céleri-rave en purée

Creamed Celeriac

	00:20	00:30 to 00:40	
	Serves 8		

American	Ingredients	Metric/Imperial
2	Lemons	2
3	Celeriac	3
1 lb	Potatoes	500 g / 1 lb
2 tbsp	Flour	2 tbsp
1 cup	Milk	250 ml / 8 fl oz
½ cup	Crème fraîche (see page 122)	125 ml / 4 fl oz
	Grated nutmeg	
2 tbsp	Butter	25 g / 1 oz
	Salt and pepper	

1. Squeeze the lemons, reserving the juice of one half. Peel the celeriac and rub with lemon juice immediately so that it does not discolor. Cut into slices. Peel the potatoes.
2. Mix the flour with the remaining lemon juice and add to a saucepan of water. Bring to a boil then add the celeriac and potatoes. Cook for 20-30 minutes until the celeriac is tender.
3. Drain the vegetables and put through a blender, vegetable mill or food processor. Put the purée in a saucepan, reduce for a few minutes over a gentle heat then add the milk. Stir until the purée has a good, smooth consistency. Add the crème fraîche and a pinch of nutmeg. Mix well and add the butter. Season with salt and pepper and serve very hot.

Cook's tip: this dish can be served as a first course, or to accompany roasts.

Aubergines à la catalane

Eggplant [Aubergines] with Tomatoes

	00:30		00:45

American	Ingredients	Metric/Imperial
4	Long eggplant [aubergines]	4
	Salt and pepper	
	Oil for deep frying	
3	Tomatoes	3
1	Small bunch of fresh parsley	1
2	Garlic cloves	2
1 tbsp	Bread crumbs	1 tbsp
1 tbsp	Olive oil	1 tbsp

1. Cut the eggplant into slices, lengthwise. Sprinkle each slice with a little salt, place in a colander and drain for 30 minutes.
2. Heat a deep-fryer to 330°F / 175°C. Rinse and dry the eggplant and plunge them into the fryer one at a time, to brown them without completely cooking them. Drain well and place in an ovenproof dish.
3. Preheat the oven to 400°F / 200°C / Gas Mark 6.
4. Halve the tomatoes, remove the seeds and place in the dish on top of the eggplant. Season with salt and pepper.
5. Finely chop the parsley. Peel and finely chop the garlic. Mix together in a bowl with the bread crumbs. Cover the tomatoes with three-quarters of the mixture.
6. Sprinkle with olive oil and bake for 30 minutes until the top is golden brown. Before serving, sprinkle with the remaining bread crumb mixture.

Champignons farcis

Stuffed Mushrooms

	00:40		00:25

American	Ingredients	Metric/Imperial
12	Large cup [open] mushrooms	12
6	Medium-sized mushrooms	6
6 tbsp	Butter	75 g / 3 oz
2	Thin slices of cooked ham	2
3 tbsp	Flour	40 g / 1½ oz
2 cups	Milk	500 ml / ¾ pint
¾ cup	Crème fraîche (see page 122)	200 ml / ⅓ pint
2	Egg yolks	2
	Grated nutmeg	
	Salt and pepper	
¾ cup	Grated gruyère cheese	75 g / 3 oz

1. Preheat the oven to 425°F / 220°C / Gas Mark 7.
2. Clean the mushrooms and trim the stems. Melt 2 tablespoons [25 g / 1 oz] of the butter in a frying pan. Remove the stems of the large mushrooms and place the caps in the pan. Cook over a very gentle heat for about 10 minutes, taking care not to break them.
3. Chop the stems from the large mushrooms with the

remaining mushrooms. Place them in a saucepan with 2 tablespoons [25 g / 1 oz] of butter and cook over a moderate heat until the liquid from the mushrooms has evaporated.

4. Chop the slices of ham and add to the chopped mushrooms.

5. Melt the remaining butter in a heavy-bottomed pan, add the flour and mix well. Gradually add the milk and stir over a gentle heat until the sauce thickens. Remove from the heat. Pour in the crème fraîche, the egg yolks and a pinch of nutmeg. Season with salt and pepper and stir.

6. Add half the sauce and a quarter of the grated cheese to the chopped mushrooms and ham. Taste, and adjust the seasoning if necessary.

7. Fill the large mushrooms with the mixture. Place the rest of the mixture in a gratin dish, and top with the stuffed mushrooms.

8. Coat with the rest of the sauce mixed with the remaining cheese and a little milk.

9. Bake for 15 minutes until the top is golden brown and serve very hot.

Mushrooms baked in cream

Champignons en gratin
Mushrooms Baked in Cream

	00:30		00:30	

American	Ingredients	Metric/Imperial
2 lb	Button mushrooms	1 kg / 2 lb
1	Lemon	1
2	Shallots	2
¼ cup	Butter	50 g / 2 oz
1	Garlic clove	1
¾ cup	Crème fraîche (see page 122)	200 ml / ⅓ pint
⅔ cup	Milk	150 ml / ¼ pint
1	Egg yolk	1
1 tbsp	Cornstarch [cornflour] or potato starch or flour	1 tbsp
	Salt and pepper	

1. Preheat the oven to 400°F / 200°C / Gas Mark 6.

2. Clean the mushrooms, trim the stems and cut into thin slices. Sprinkle with a little lemon juice.

3. Peel the shallots and chop finely. Melt three-quarters of the butter in a frying pan and add the mushrooms and the chopped shallots. Cook until the liquid from the mushrooms has evaporated, stirring frequently. Do not allow to dry out completely.

4. Rub a gratin dish with the garlic clove and discard.

5. Mix the crème fraîche in a bowl with the milk, the egg yolk and the cornstarch or potato starch. Season with salt and pepper.

6. Put the mushrooms and shallots into the gratin dish and pour over the mixture of egg, flour and crème fraîche. Dot with the remaining butter.

7. Bake for about 30 minutes, without allowing the mixture to boil.

Carottes glacées
Glazed Carrots

	00:10		00:20 to 00:30	

American	Ingredients	Metric/Imperial
4 lb	Young carrots	2 kg / 4 lb
½ cup	Butter	125 g / 4 oz
2 tbsp	Sugar	2 tbsp
	Salt and pepper	

1. Peel, wash and chop the carrots into equal lengths. Trim into the shape of large olives, if liked.

2. Melt the butter in a heavy-bottomed saucepan and add the carrots, sugar, and salt and pepper to taste. Cover with water.

3. Cook, uncovered, over a gentle heat for 20-30 minutes, until the water has evaporated and the carrots are coated with the golden, syrupy liquid.

Cook's tip: this vegetable dish is a delicious accompaniment to Carcassonne Pork Stew (see page 405).

Champignons sautés
Sautéed Mushrooms

	00:10		00:15 to 00:20	

American	Ingredients	Metric/Imperial
2 lb	Button mushrooms	1 kg / 2 lb
1	Lemon	1
6 tbsp	Butter	75 g / 3 oz
	Salt and pepper	
3 tbsp	Chopped fresh parsley	3 tbsp
1	Garlic clove (optional)	1

1. Clean the mushrooms and trim the stems. Leave the mushrooms whole if they are small; if not, cut them into slices and sprinkle with lemon juice.

2. Heat half the butter in a frying pan and add the mushrooms and the juice of half a lemon. Cook over a moderate heat, stirring frequently, until all the liquid from the mushrooms has evaporated.

3. Add the remaining butter, season with salt and pepper and cook gently over a very low heat until the mushrooms are cooked. Do not allow the butter to brown.

4. To serve, sprinkle with chopped parsley or with a mixture of parsley and peeled and crushed garlic.

Endives aurore

Belgian Endive [Chicory] with Cheese Sauce

	00:10		00:20

American	Ingredients	Metric/Imperial
12	Heads of Belgian endive [chicory]	12
	Salt and pepper	
2 tbsp	Butter	25 g / 1 oz
2 tbsp	Flour	2 tbsp
2 cups	Milk	500 ml / ¾ pint
6 oz	Cooked ham	175 g / 6 oz
1¼ cups	Grated gruyère cheese	150 g / 5 oz
2 tbsp	Tomato paste [purée]	2 tbsp
3	Egg yolks	3

1. Remove any damaged leaves from the endive and cut out the hard core using a small pointed knife. Wash and drain. Boil some salted water in a saucepan. Add the endive and cook for 10 minutes.
2. Meanwhile, melt the butter in a saucepan, sprinkle with the flour, stir for 3 minutes over a low heat then gradually add the milk. Cook for about 10 minutes, stirring often. Remove from the heat.
3. Preheat the broiler [grill].
4. Dice the ham and add to the sauce together with the grated cheese, the tomato paste, salt and pepper. Return to a low heat, stir until the cheese has melted and then remove from the heat. Mix in the egg yolks, stirring vigorously.
5. Drain the endive well and place in a gratin dish. Cover with the sauce and brown under the broiler for 6-7 minutes.

Endives en gratin

Gratin of Belgian Endive [Chicory]

	00:10		00:40

American	Ingredients	Metric/Imperial
4 lb	Belgian endive [chicory]	2 kg / 4 lb
⅓ cup	Butter	75 g / 3 oz
½	Lemon	½
1 tbsp	Flour	1 tbsp
¾ cup	Crème fraîche (see page 122)	200 ml / 7 fl oz
1 cup	Grated comté or gruyère cheese	125 g / 4 oz
	Salt and pepper	

1. Preheat the oven to 400°F / 200°C / Gas Mark 6.
2. Remove any damaged outer leaves from the endive and cut out the hard core using a small pointed knife. Rinse quickly and wipe dry. Cut into pieces ¾-1 in / 1½-2 cm long and place in a frying pan over a low heat with ¼ cup [50 g / 2 oz] of the butter and the juice of half a lemon. Stir well.
3. Cook until the endive is soft and all the liquid has evaporated, then sprinkle with the flour. Stir, and cook over a low heat for a further 10 minutes.

4. Add the crème fraîche and three-quarters of the grated cheese. Season with salt and pepper.
5. Pour into a buttered ovenproof dish and sprinkle with the remaining cheese. Dot with the rest of the butter. Bake for 20 minutes until the gratin is piping hot and the top is golden brown.

Endives braisées

Braised Belgian Endive [Chicory]

	00:10		00:20

American	Ingredients	Metric/Imperial
12	Heads of Belgian endive [chicory]	12
3 tbsp	Butter	40 g / 1½ oz
⅔ cup	Water	150 ml / ¼ pint
2 tsp	Sugar	2 tsp
½	Lemon	½
	Salt and pepper	

1. Remove any damaged outer leaves from the Belgian endive and then cut out the hard core using a small pointed knife. Wash and wipe dry.
2. Melt the butter in a frying pan and add the endive, the water, the sugar and the juice of the half lemon. Season with salt and pepper. Cover and cook for about 20 minutes over a low heat.
3. Place the endive in a serving dish and serve immediately.

Cook's tip: if the endive produces a lot of liquid during cooking, reduce over a high heat before serving.

Coulemelles en fricassée

Braised Mushrooms

	00:20		00:20

American	Ingredients	Metric/Imperial
2 lb	Large mushrooms	1 kg / 2 lb
2	Onions	2
1	Carrot	1
¼ cup	Butter	50 g / 2 oz
2 tbsp	Flour	25 g / 1 oz
1	Fresh thyme sprig	1
1	Fresh rosemary sprig	1
1	Bay leaf	1
	Salt and pepper	
1¼ cups	Water	300 ml / ½ pint
2	Egg yolks	2
1	Lemon	1

1. Remove the stems from the mushrooms, clean the caps carefully and chop them.
2. Peel and thinly slice the onions and carrots. Heat the butter in a frying pan and brown the onions. Sprinkle the flour into the pan, and add the chopped mushrooms, carrot, the thyme, rosemary and the bay leaf. Season with salt and pepper and add the water. Cover and cook over a low heat for 20 minutes.
3. Place the egg yolks in a bowl. Remove all the ingredients

from the frying pan using a slotted spoon so that only the cooking liquid is left, and keep them warm.

4. Add a tablespoon of the liquid to the egg yolks and stir with a wooden spoon. Add half the remaining liquid, stir well and then return this mixture to the liquid in the pan. Place over a low heat and add all the vegetables. Stir to thicken the sauce, but do not allow it to boil or the egg yolk will curdle. Squeeze the juice from the lemon over the top and serve hot.

Beignets de courgettes
Zucchini [Courgette] Fritters

	00:25 plus standing time		00:05 per batch of fritters
American	**Ingredients**	**Metric/Imperial**	
2	Eggs	2	
	Salt		
1 cup	Flour	150 g / 5 oz	
2 tbsp	Oil	2 tbsp	
⅔ cup	Beer	150 ml / ¼ pint	
2 lb	Zucchini [courgettes]	1 kg / 2 lb	
	Oil for deep frying		
1	Egg white	1	

1. Beat the eggs in a bowl (or use a blender or food processor) and add a pinch of salt, the flour and 2 tablespoons of the oil. Beat together well and add the beer a little at a time. Leave to stand for 1 hour.

2. Peel the zucchini and cut them into thin slices or sticks. Spread out on a clean cloth and dry well.

3. Heat the oil in a deep pan to 340°F / 175°C.

4. Put some flour in a deep dish and coat the zucchini in it.

5. Beat the egg white until stiff and fold into the batter.

6. Dip the zucchini in the batter and plunge them in the oil, which should be hot, but not smoking. Cook for a few minutes until puffed and brown and then drain them on paper towels. Keep them warm while cooking the rest of the fritters. Serve hot with a garlic mayonnaise (see page 119).

Crosnes sautés
Sautéed Chinese Artichokes

	00:15 Serves 4		00:20
American	**Ingredients**	**Metric/Imperial**	
	Coarse salt		
2 lb	Chinese artichokes	1 kg / 2 lb	
	Salt and pepper		
¼ cup	Butter	50 g / 2 oz	
2 tbsp	Chopped fresh parsley	2 tbsp	
½	Garlic clove	½	

1. Sprinkle the coarse salt onto a cloth and place the artichokes on top. Rub them to remove the thin outer skin and then rinse them as quickly as possible.

2. Put the artichokes in a saucepan with just enough salted water to prevent them burning. Bring to a boil, cover and cook for about 10 minutes.

3. Melt the butter in a frying pan, add the artichokes, cover the pan and brown them over a low heat for a further 10 minutes. Season with pepper.

4. Serve sprinkled with a mixture of chopped parsley and finely chopped garlic. This dish is a good accompaniment to roasts.

Épinards béchamel
Spinach with Béchamel Sauce

	00:15		00:30
American	**Ingredients**	**Metric/Imperial**	
5 lb	Fresh spinach	2.5 kg / 5 lb	
	Salt and pepper		
3 cups	Béchamel sauce (see page 124)	750 ml / 1¼ pints	
	Grated nutmeg		

1. Preheat the oven to 425°F / 220°C / Gas Mark 7.

2. Remove the stems from the spinach and wash the leaves thoroughly. Put in a large saucepan with a large pinch of salt (no extra water should be needed) and cook over a medium heat for 8 minutes, stirring occasionally. Drain well.

3. Butter an ovenproof dish. Put half the spinach in the bottom of the dish and cover with half the sauce. Add another layer of spinach and top with the remaining sauce.

4. Bake for 10 minutes until golden brown. Serve very hot.

Cook's tip: add a soft-boiled or poached egg to each serving for a quick lunch or supper dish; or sprinkle with grated gruyère cheese for extra goodness.

Gratin de courgettes
Baked Zucchini [Courgettes]

	00:05		00:25
American	**Ingredients**	**Metric/Imperial**	
2 lb	Zucchini [courgettes]	1 kg / 2 lb	
	Salt and pepper		
3	Eggs	3	
1 cup	Crème fraîche (see page 122)	250 ml / 8 fl oz	
1 cup	Grated gruyère cheese	125 g / 4 oz	
	Grated nutmeg		

1. Preheat the oven to 425°F / 220°C / Gas Mark 7.

2. Wash the zucchini and cut into slices ½ in / 1 cm thick. Cook in a little boiling salted water for about 10 minutes then drain well.

3. Place the zucchini in a buttered ovenproof dish. Beat the eggs in a bowl with the crème fraîche, grated cheese, salt and pepper and a pinch of nutmeg. Pour over the zucchini. Brown in the oven for 15 minutes. Serve very hot.

Jardinière de légumes
Mixed Spring Vegetables

	00:45		00:30

American	Ingredients	Metric/Imperial
¾ lb	Turnips	350 g / 12 oz
¾ lb	Carrots	350 g / 12 oz
¾ lb	New potatoes	350 g / 12 oz
¾ lb	Fresh peas	350 g / 12 oz
¾ lb	Green beans	350 g / 12 oz
	Salt and pepper	
1 tsp	Sugar	1 tsp
3 tbsp	Chopped fresh mixed herbs	3 tbsp
1 cup	Butter at room temperature	250 g / 8 oz

1. Peel and dice the turnips, carrots and potatoes. Shell the peas. String the beans, if necessary, wash and cut them into pieces ½ in / 1 cm long.
2. Boil some salted water in 3 separate saucepans.
3. Put the diced carrot in one saucepan and cook for 5 minutes before adding the turnips. Cook for a further 5 minutes, and drain well.
4. Add the beans to another saucepan, cook for 5 minutes and then add the peas and the sugar. Cook for a further 5-10 minutes and drain well.
5. Add the potatoes to the third saucepan, bring to a boil and cook for 10-15 minutes over a gentle heat so that the potatoes do not disintegrate. Drain well.
6. While the vegetables are cooking, mix the fresh herbs with three-quarters of the butter. Season with salt and pepper. Roll into a sausage shape and wrap in foil. Place in the refrigerator to harden.
7. Place the drained vegetables in a serving dish with the remaining butter. If you are not serving them immediately, keep them warm over a saucepan of boiling water so that the butter melts without cooking.
8. Serve very hot with the herb butter.

Marrons bouillis
Boiled Chestnuts

	00:30		00:45

American	Ingredients	Metric/Imperial
3 lb	Chestnuts	1.5 kg / 3 lb
1 quart	Chicken stock	1 l / 1¾ pints
	Salt and pepper	
	Butter	

1. Using a small pointed knife, cut around the chestnuts, just piercing both skins. Place in a saucepan, cover with cold water and bring to a boil. Boil for 7 minutes and then remove from the heat.
2. Remove the chestnuts from the water one by one, peeling them as you go along. Put the chicken stock in a large saucepan, add the chestnuts, and a little water if necessary, so that the chestnuts are covered by the liquid. Bring to a boil and simmer gently for 25-35 minutes.
3. Drain the chestnuts and place in a warmed serving dish. Add salt, pepper and butter to taste.

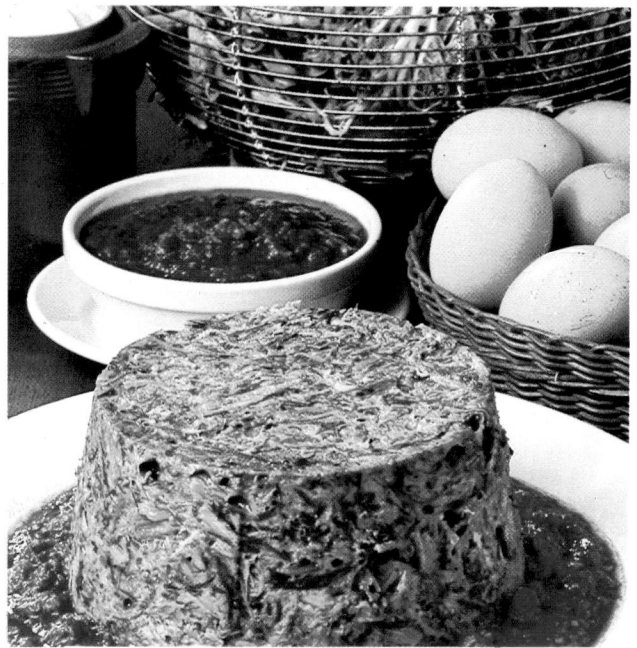
Chicory loaf

Pain de chicorée
Chicory [Curly Endive] Loaf

	00:30		01:00

American	Ingredients	Metric/Imperial
6	Heads of chicory [curly endive]	6
	Salt and pepper	
1 cup	Béchamel sauce (see page 124)	250 ml / 8 fl oz
4	Eggs	4
	Grated nutmeg	
1 (2 lb)	Can[s] tomato sauce	2 (400 g / 14 oz)
6 oz	Cooked ham	150 g / 6 oz

1. Preheat the oven to 350°F / 180°C / Gas Mark 4.
2. Remove the outer leaves from the chicory, wash thoroughly and drain.
3. Heat a large saucepan of salted water. Add the chicory, bring back to a boil and cook for 15 minutes. Drain well and chop coarsely.
4. Mix together the sauce and the chicory. Beat the eggs and add to the mixture together with a pinch of nutmeg. Taste and adjust the seasoning.
5. Grease a 1 quart [1 l / 2 pint] charlotte mold generously with butter and pour in the mixture. Place the mold in an ovenproof pan filled with water.
6. Bake for about 1 hour. The top of the loaf should hardly change color and the water in the pan should not boil. To check whether the loaf is cooked, pierce with a knife. If the blade comes out dry, then the loaf is ready.
7. Boil the tomato sauce to reduce it by one-third. Dice the ham and add to the sauce.
8. Remove the loaf from the oven and let cool 5 minutes before unmolding it onto a serving dish. Pour around the tomato sauce and serve.

Cook's tip: a Walnut and Roquefort Sauce (see page 120) could be served as an alternative accompaniment to this dish.

Pain d'épinard
Spinach Loaf

	00:40		01:00

American	Ingredients	Metric/Imperial
6 lb	Fresh spinach	3 kg / 6 lb
	Salt and pepper	
3 tbsp	Butter	40 g / 1½ oz
3 tbsp	Flour	40 g / 1½ oz
¾ cup	Crème fraîche (see page 122)	200 ml / ⅓ pint
4	Eggs	4
	Grated nutmeg	

1. Preheat the oven to 350°F / 180°C / Gas Mark 6.
2. Remove the stems from the spinach and wash thoroughly.
3. Put the spinach in a large pan with a pinch of salt and cook for 5-8 minutes. Drain well then chop coarsely.
4. Melt the butter in a saucepan, add the flour and stir until it is absorbed. Gradually stir in the crème fraîche and cook, stirring, until thickened. Add the beaten eggs, a pinch of grated nutmeg, salt and pepper and mix well.
5. Mix together the sauce and the spinach. Taste, and adjust the seasoning. Pour into a buttered 1 quart [1 l / 2 pint] charlotte mold and place the mold in an ovenproof pan filled with water.
6. Bake for 1 hour, without allowing the mixture to brown. To check whether it is cooked, pierce the loaf with a knife. If the blade comes out dry then it is ready.
7. Serve with a cheese sauce (see page 128).

Pain de laitue
Lettuce Loaf

	00:45		00:45

American	Ingredients	Metric/Imperial
	Salt and pepper	
3	Heads of soft-leaved lettuce	3
4	Eggs	4
2½ cups	Béchamel sauce (see page 124)	600 ml / 1 pint
	Grated nutmeg	
2	Slices of cooked ham	2

1. Preheat the oven to 350°F / 180°C / Gas Mark 4.
2. Bring a saucepan of salted water to a boil. Cut the heads of lettuce in half and plunge into the boiling water. Cook for 2 minutes. Drain well. Chop the lettuce finely.
3. Break the eggs into a bowl and beat well. Add the lettuce and half the sauce. Mix well.
4. Butter an 8 in / 20 cm savarin mold. Cut the slices of ham into triangles and arrange in the bottom of the mold. Pour the lettuce mixture into the mold and place in a large ovenproof dish. Fill the dish with water to halfway up the sides of the mold.
5. Bake for 45 minutes.
6. To serve, turn out of the mold and cover with the remaining béchamel sauce.

Oseille à la crème
Sorrel with Cream

	00:15		00:30

American	Ingredients	Metric/Imperial
2 lb	Sorrel	1 kg / 2 lb
	Salt and pepper	
⅓ cup	Butter	75 g / 3 oz
⅔ cup	Crème fraîche (see page 122)	150 ml / ¼ pint

1. Remove the stems from the sorrel and wash the leaves. Bring a saucepan of salted water to a boil. Add the sorrel and cook for 5 minutes. Drain well.
2. Melt the butter in a frying pan, add the sorrel and cook for 10-15 minutes, stirring constantly. Season with salt and pepper and add the crème fraîche. Stir over a moderate heat until the sauce thickens. Adjust the seasoning if necessary and serve immediately.

Petits pois surprise
Peas and Chicken in Aspic

	01:00		01:20

American	Ingredients	Metric/Imperial
2	Carrots	2
2	Onions	2
1	Leek	1
8 cups	Water	2 l / 3½ pints
2	Bouquets garnis	2
	Salt and pepper	
1 (2 lb)	Chicken	1 (1 kg / 2 lb)
1 envelope	Unflavored gelatin	20 g / 1 packet
4 lb	Fresh peas, shelled	2 kg / 4 lb
1 tbsp	Sugar	1 tbsp
3	Fresh mint sprigs	3

1. Peel the carrots and onions and place in a saucepan with the leek and water. Add one bouquet garni, salt and pepper, and bring to a boil. Cook for 20 minutes. Add the chicken and cook for 35-40 minutes.
2. Remove the chicken. Take the meat from the carcass and cut it into small pieces, discarding the skin. Leave to cool.
3. Strain the stock and reduce it to 3 cups [750 ml / 1¼ pints]. Sprinkle in the gelatin, stir well and set to one side to cool.
4. Place the peas in a saucepan with a little boiling water. Season with salt, pepper, the sugar, the remaining bouquet garni and the mint. Cook for 10-15 minutes. The peas should still be quite firm. Refresh under cold water and drain well.
5. Arrange ½ in / 1 cm of peas in the bottom of a 10 in / 26 cm savarin mold and add a little of the lukewarm aspic to cover. Leave in a cool place for 15 minutes.
6. Place the diced chicken on top of the peas and garnish the sides of the mold with peas as you go along.
7. Once the mold is full, moisten it with the remaining aspic until it reaches the top. Chill for 6 hours.
8. To remove from the mold, dip the mold in lukewarm water for a few seconds before turning out. Serve with mayonnaise (see page 119) or a vinaigrette dressing with herbs (see page 120).

Concombres au gratin

Cucumbers in Cheese Sauce

◣▱ 00:30   00:30 🍲

American	Ingredients	Metric/Imperial
3	Cucumbers	3
	Salt and pepper	
1	Onion	1
2 tbsp	Butter	25 g / 1 oz
2 tbsp	Flour	25 g / 1 oz
¾ cup	Crème fraîche (see page 122)	200 ml / 7 fl oz
½ cup	Grated gruyère cheese	50 g / 2 oz
	Grated nutmeg	

1. Preheat the oven to 425°F / 220°C / Gas Mark 7.
2. Peel the cucumbers and cut into quarters, lengthwise. Remove the seeds and dice the flesh.
3. Add the cubes of cucumber to a pan of boiling salted water and blanch for 10-12 minutes. Drain and place in a gratin dish.
4. Peel and finely chop the onion. Heat the butter in a saucepan, add the onion and cook over a low heat, without browning. Sprinkle in the flour, mix well and add the crème fraîche, stirring constantly until the mixture has thickened. Stir in the grated cheese, a small pinch of nutmeg and salt and pepper to taste.
5. Pour the sauce over the cucumber. Bake for 20 minutes until the top is golden brown.

Cook's tip: this is a delicious first course, but it also goes well with roasts.

Épinards en gâteau

Spinach Cake

◣▱ 00:15   00:30 🍲

American	Ingredients	Metric/Imperial
2 lb	Spinach	1 kg / 2 lb
2 cups	Flour	250 g / 8 oz
3	Medium-sized eggs	3
1 cup	Butter	250 g / 8 oz
⅓ cup	Crème fraîche (see page 122)	6 tbsp
1 cup	Ricotta or curd cheese	250 g / 8 oz
	Salt and pepper	
	Grated nutmeg	

1. Preheat the oven to 400°F / 200°C / Gas Mark 6.
2. Remove the stems from the spinach and wash the leaves thoroughly. Drain and dry in a clean cloth then place on a chopping board and chop coarsely.
3. Place the flour in a bowl, form a hollow and add to it the eggs, the butter, the crème fraîche, the cheese, salt, pepper and a pinch of nutmeg. Work the mixture together using your hands, as if making pastry.
4. Add the chopped spinach, mix together and place in a buttered ovenproof dish.
5. Bake for 30 minutes. Check whether the cake is cooked by inserting a knife — if it comes out dry the cake is ready.

Gratin de courgettes au riz

Zucchini [Courgettes] and Rice

◣▱ 00:25   00:40 🍲

American	Ingredients	Metric/Imperial
4 lb	Zucchini [courgettes]	2 kg / 4 lb
	Salt and pepper	
3 tbsp	Long-grain rice	3 tbsp
3	Eggs	3
1 cup	Crème fraîche (see page 122)	250 ml / 8 fl oz
1¾ cups	Grated cheese	200 g / 7 oz
	Grated nutmeg	

1. Preheat the oven to 350°F / 180°C / Gas Mark 4.
2. Cut the zucchini into thick slices. Cook for about 5 minutes in a little salted water and drain well.
3. Arrange in a gratin dish and sprinkle with the rice.
4. In a bowl beat the eggs with the crème fraîche and the grated cheese. Flavor with a pinch of nutmeg and season with salt and pepper.
5. Pour the sauce over the zucchini and mix well together.
6. Bake for 40 minutes or until the rice has absorbed the water from the zucchini and the top is lightly browned.

Épinards au gratin

Layered Spinach Casserole

◣▱ 00:40   00:30 🍲

American	Ingredients	Metric/Imperial
4 lb	Fresh spinach	2 kg / 4 lb
	Salt and pepper	
1½ lb	Button mushrooms	750 g / 1½ lb
1	Lemon	1
¼ cup	Butter	50 g / 2 oz
3 tbsp	Flour	40 g / 1½ oz
1¼ cups	Crème fraîche (see page 122)	300 ml / ½ pint
	Grated nutmeg	
½ cup	Grated gruyère cheese	50 g / 2 oz
3-4 tbsp	Milk	3-4 tbsp

1. Preheat the oven to 400°F / 200°C / Gas Mark 6.
2. Remove the stems from the spinach and wash the leaves thoroughly. Put in a large saucepan with a pinch of salt (no extra water should be needed) and cook over a medium heat for 8 minutes, stirring from time to time. Drain well.
3. Clean and slice the mushrooms and put them in a large saucepan with a little salted water, a few drops of lemon juice and a tablespoon [15 g / ½ oz] of butter. Cook until all the liquid has evaporated.
4. Melt the remaining butter in a saucepan, add the flour and stir until it is absorbed. Gradually stir in the crème fraîche and cook, stirring, until thickened. Season with salt and pepper and add a pinch of nutmeg. Pour 4 tablespoons of the sauce over the mushrooms, stir together and put through a blender, vegetable mill or food processor to make a purée.

5. Arrange 3 layers of spinach, alternating with 2 layers of mushroom purée in an ovenproof dish. Mix the remaining sauce with the grated cheese and, if necessary, dilute with a few tablespoons of milk. Pour over the spinach.

6. Bake for 30 minutes. The top should be brown but not burned.

Fèves au lard

Broad or Lima Beans with Bacon

	00:30		00:25

American	Ingredients	Metric/Imperial
4 lb	Fresh broad or lima beans	2 kg / 4 lb
½ lb	Bacon	250 g / 8 oz
2 tbsp	Butter	20 g / ¾ oz
	Salt and pepper	
5 tbsp	Crème fraîche (see page 122)	5 tbsp
2	Egg yolks	2

1. Shell the beans and cut the bacon into small strips. Heat the butter in a frying pan and brown the bacon for 3 or 4 minutes. Drain.

2. Place the beans in a saucepan with the bacon. Cover with a little water and season with pepper. Bring to a boil then lower the heat, cover, and cook for 10-15 minutes.

3. Meanwhile, place the crème fraîche in a bowl, add a pinch of salt and the egg yolks and mix well.

4. When the beans are cooked, remove the saucepan from the heat and add the egg and crème mixture. Return it to a very low heat and stir for 1 minute without letting it boil. Adjust the seasoning if necessary, and serve.

Fenouil meunière

Baked Buttered Fennel

	00:10		00:30 to 00:40

American	Ingredients	Metric/Imperial
1	Lemon	1
	Salt and pepper	
6-9	Heads of fennel	6-9
⅓ cup	Butter	75 g / 3 oz
2 tbsp	Chopped fresh parsley	2 tbsp

1. Preheat the oven to 300°F / 150°C / Gas Mark 2.

2. Squeeze the juice from the lemon and add to a saucepan of water. Season with salt and bring to a boil.

3. Trim the heads of fennel and cut them in half. Rinse and add them to the pan. Cook for 10-15 minutes until just tender. The point of a knife should penetrate fairly easily when they are done. Take care not to overcook as this results in a loss of flavor.

4. Drain the fennel well and cut each piece in half again. Arrange in an ovenproof dish and dot with pieces of the butter.

Grind a little pepper over the top and bake for 20-30 minutes. Do not allow them to brown, and moisten from time to time with a little water, if necessary.

5. Sprinkle with the chopped parsley and serve as an accompaniment to any meat.

Morilles à la crème

Morels with Cream

	00:10		00:20

American	Ingredients	Metric/Imperial
3 lb	Fresh morels or other mushrooms	1.5 kg / 3 lb
5	Shallots	5
½ cup	Butter	125 g / 4 oz
	Salt and pepper	
1¼ cups	Dry white wine	300 ml / ½ pint
1¼ cups	Crème fraîche (see page 122)	300 ml / ½ pint

1. Trim the stems of the mushrooms, wash quickly and wipe dry. Peel and finely chop the shallots. Melt the butter in a large saucepan, add the mushrooms and cook over a moderate heat for 10 minutes, until all the liquid has evaporated.

2. Add the shallots and season with salt and pepper. When the shallots are translucent, add the wine. Cook, uncovered, over a moderate heat for 10 minutes, or until the wine has completely evaporated.

3. Add the crème fraîche, stir to thicken over a high heat and serve immediately.

Haricots verts frais

Green Beans with Garlic

	00:20	00:10 to 00:15	

American	Ingredients	Metric/Imperial
2 lb	Green beans	1 kg / 2 lb
	Salt and pepper	
⅓ cup	Butter	75 g / 3 oz
1	Onion	1
1	Garlic clove	1
1 tbsp	Chopped fresh parsley	1 tbsp

1. Trim the beans, stringing them if necessary. Rinse them in cold water.

2. Bring some salted water to a boil in a saucepan. Add the beans and cook, partially covered, for about 8 minutes or until barely tender.

3. Meanwhile, melt half the butter in a small pan. Peel and finely chop the onion and garlic and add to the pan. Cook until the onion is translucent.

4. When the beans are cooked, rinse them under cold water and drain.

5. Return to the saucepan and reheat gently, without a lid, with the rest of the butter.

6. Stir in the onion and garlic mixture and season with salt and pepper. Finally, stir in the chopped parsley and serve immediately.

Haricots Périgourdine
White Beans in Tomato Sauce

| | 00:30 plus soaking | | 01:00 |

American	Ingredients	Metric/Imperial
2 cups	Dried navy [haricot] beans	500 g / 1 lb
3	Garlic cloves	3
½ lb	Bacon	250 g / 8 oz
1	Small bunch of fresh parsley	1
3	Tomatoes	3
1	Onion	1
2	Cloves	2
	Salt and pepper	

1. Soak the beans overnight in water to cover.
2. Drain the beans and place them in a saucepan. Cover with fresh water. Bring to a boil and simmer for 1 hour.
3. Peel the cloves of garlic and put them through a blender, vegetable mill or food processor with the bacon and parsley.
4. Peel the tomatoes (first plunging them into boiling water for 10 seconds), and remove the seeds. Peel the onion and stud with the cloves.
5. Add the tomatoes, onion and bacon mixture to the beans and stir well. Cook over a gentle heat for a further 30-45 minutes or until the beans are tender.
6. Discard the onion before serving. Serve as an accompaniment to spareribs with barbecue sauce (see page 123).

Pieds-de-mouton en fricassée
Mushroom Fricassée

| | 00:35 | | 01:00 |

American	Ingredients	Metric/Imperial
2 lb	Mushrooms	1 kg / 2 lb
6	Shallots	6
6 tbsp	Butter	75 g / 3 oz
⅔ cup	Chicken stock	150 ml / ¼ pint
1	Garlic clove	1
1	Onion	1
1	Bouquet garni	1
	Salt and pepper	
1	Egg yolk	1
6	Slices of bread ½ in / 1 cm thick	6

1. Clean the mushrooms and trim the stems. Peel and finely chop the shallots.
2. Heat three-quarters of the butter in a saucepan. Brown the mushrooms and sprinkle with the shallots.
3. Heat the stock and pour over the mushrooms. Peel the garlic clove and cut it in half. Peel the onion and cut it into quarters. Add the garlic and onion to the saucepan along with the bouquet garni. Season with salt and pepper and cook for 30-45 minutes over a moderate heat.
4. At the end of this time, remove the vegetables using a slotted spoon and keep warm. Strain the cooking liquid.
5. Place the egg yolk in a bowl, and mix with 1 tablespoon of the strained cooking liquid. Gradually add half the remaining liquid, stirring constantly, and then pour this mixture into the

rest of the liquid. Place over a low heat and stir to thicken, without allowing the sauce to boil.
6. Cut the crusts from the bread and cut into triangles. Fry in the remaining butter until golden brown on both sides.
7. Place the mushrooms in a serving dish and cover with the sauce. Garnish with the bread triangles and serve very hot.

Petits pois à la Parisienne
Braised Peas

| | 00:25 | | 00:30 |

American	Ingredients	Metric/Imperial
1	Head of romaine [cos] lettuce	1
4	Onions	4
1	Bunch of fresh parsley	1
2	Scallions [spring onions]	2
¼ cup	Butter	50 g / 2 oz
1 tbsp	Flour	1 tbsp
2 cups	Water	500 ml / ¾ pint
2 lb	Fresh peas	1 kg / 2 lb
	Salt and pepper	
3	Egg yolks	3

1. Wash the lettuce. Drain. Cut into thin strips. Peel the onions and cut into thin slices. Finely chop the parsley and scallions.
2. Melt the butter in a saucepan, add the flour and stir until the butter has absorbed all the flour. Stir in the water, a little at a time, and bring to a boil. Add the peas, onions, lettuce, scallions and parsley and season with salt and pepper. Cover and cook over a low heat for 20-30 minutes.
3. To serve, remove the saucepan from the heat and add the egg yolks, one by one, stirring vigorously. Adjust the seasoning, if necessary, and serve immediately.

Poireaux gratinés
Leeks in Cheese Sauce

| | 00:15 | | 00:55 |

American	Ingredients	Metric/Imperial
18	Leeks	18
	Salt and pepper	
6 tbsp	Butter	75 g / 3 oz
¼ cup	Flour	50 g / 2 oz
3 cups	Milk	750 ml / 1 ¼ pints
1 ¼ cups	Grated gruyère cheese	150 g / 5 oz
	Grated nutmeg	

1. Preheat the oven to 425°F / 220°C / Gas Mark 7.
2. Trim the leeks to leave the white part only and wash well. Boil some salted water in a saucepan and add the leeks. Simmer, without a lid, for about 20 minutes, or until the leeks are just cooked.
3. Meanwhile, melt three-quarters of the butter in a heavy-bottomed saucepan, sprinkle with the flour and stir for 2-3 minutes over a low heat until the butter has absorbed all the

flour. Add the milk a little at a time and stir over a gentle heat, until the sauce thickens. Add two-thirds of the grated cheese, and season with salt, pepper and a little freshly grated nutmeg. Remove from the heat.
4. Drain the leeks carefully and arrange in a buttered gratin dish. Cover with the cheese sauce, sprinkle with the remaining cheese and dot with the rest of the butter.
5. Bake for about 15 minutes until golden brown.

Petits pois bonne femme
Peas with Ham and Onions

	00:20	00:50

American	Ingredients	Metric/Imperial
12	Small onions	12
¼ cup	Butter	50 g / 2 oz
1	Bouquet garni	1
	Salt and pepper	
2 lb	Fresh peas, shelled	1 kg / 2 lb
½ lb	Cooked ham	250 g / 8 oz
	Grated nutmeg	
2 tsp	Sugar	2 tsp
2	Egg yolks	2
1 tbsp	Water	1 tbsp

1. Peel the onions and place in à heavy-bottomed saucepan. Add half the butter, the bouquet garni and a little water. Cook over a low heat until the liquid has evaporated and the onions have softened.
2. Meanwhile, heat ½ in / 1 cm of salted water in a large saucepan. Add the peas and cook, covered for 15 minutes.
3. Dice the ham and add to the onions. Cook until the ham begins to brown.
4. When the peas are cooked, drain and add to the onions and ham with the remaining butter, a little freshly grated nutmeg and the sugar. Season with salt and pepper, cover and heat for 5 minutes over a low heat, stirring to mix well.
5. Discard the bouquet garni. Remove the saucepan from the heat and add the egg yolks mixed with the water. Stir well and serve very hot.

Purée de carottes
Creamed Carrots

	00:20	00:30 to 00:40

American	Ingredients	Metric/Imperial
3 lb	Carrots	1.5 kg / 3 lb
	Salt	
1	Onion	1
6 tbsp	Butter	75 g / 3 oz
1 lb	Potatoes	500 g / 1 lb
½ cup	Crème fraîche (see page 122)	125 ml / 4 fl oz
1 tsp	Sugar (optional)	1 tsp
2	Egg yolks	2
	Grated nutmeg	

1. Peel the carrots and cut into thick slices. Heat a small amount of salted water in a saucepan. Add the carrots and cook for 10 minutes. Drain.
2. Peel and slice the onion. Heat half the butter in a saucepan and add the carrots and onion. Cover and cook over a low heat, without allowing either vegetable to brown, until the carrots are tender.
3. Meanwhile, peel the potatoes and cook in boiling salted water for 25 minutes or until soft. Drain.
4. Purée the vegetables using a blender, vegetable mill or a food processor, and place in a saucepan over a low heat. Stir in the crème fraîche a little at a time together with the sugar, if necessary. Finally, stir in the remaining butter and the egg yolks and season with a little freshly grated nutmeg. Serve very hot.

Cook's tip: a leek purée (see page 428) and cauliflower purée (see page 411) can be prepared and served at the same time.

Ratatouille (see page 429)

Poireaux braisés
Braised Leeks

	00:15	00:40

American	Ingredients	Metric/Imperial
18	Leeks	18
½ cup	Butter	125 g / 4 oz
	Salt and pepper	
½ lb	Bacon	250 g / 8 oz
1 tbsp	Oil	1 tbsp
¼ cup	Crème fraîche (see page 122)	4 tbsp

1. Trim the leeks, removing the roots and the very green leaves. Wash well under cold water and wipe dry.
2. Melt the butter in a saucepan, add the leeks, salt and pepper, cover and cook over a gentle heat for 30 minutes.
3. Meanwhile, cut the bacon into small strips. Heat the oil in a frying pan and brown the bacon over a moderate heat for 5 minutes, stirring constantly. Drain.
4. When the leeks are cooked, remove from the pan with a slotted spoon. Arrange in a serving dish and keep warm. Pour the crème fraîche into the saucepan together with the bacon and stir over a moderate heat for a few minutes until the sauce thickens. Cover the leeks with the sauce and serve immediately.

Gratin d'aubergines

Eggplant [Aubergine] Casserole

◣▷ 00:40   00:20

American	Ingredients	Metric/Imperial
4 lb	Eggplant [aubergines]	2 kg / 4 lb
	Salt and pepper	
1½ lb	Tomatoes	750 g / 1½ lb
2	Garlic cloves	2
5	Fresh basil leaves	5
3	Fresh parsley sprigs	3
1	Fresh thyme sprig	1
1 tbsp	Olive oil	1 tbsp
	Oil for deep frying	
1 cup	Grated gruyère cheese	125 g / 4 oz

1. Peel the eggplant and cut lengthwise into ½ in / 1 cm slices. Place in a colander and sprinkle each slice with cooking salt. Leave for 30 minutes to extract excess moisture which could make the dish watery.

2. Meanwhile, peel the tomatoes (first plunging them in boiling water for 10 seconds). Cut them in halves and remove the seeds. Place in a saucepan with the peeled garlic, basil, parsley, thyme leaves and olive oil. Cook over a high heat until the tomatoes become creamy. Purée in a blender or food processor. Season with salt and pepper.

3. Preheat the oven to 400°F / 200°C / Gas Mark 6.

4. Rinse the salt from the eggplant and dry on paper towels.

5. Heat the oil for deep frying to 340°F / 175°C. The oil should be hot but not smoking. Add some slices of eggplant to the pan. Leave to brown for a few minutes then remove and drain on paper towels. Continue until all the eggplant has been cooked.

6. Place a layer of the tomato purée in a large ovenproof dish and cover with a layer of eggplant. Sprinkle with a little grated cheese. Repeat until all the ingredients are used up, finishing with a layer of grated cheese.

7. Bake for about 20 minutes or until the casserole is hot right through and the top is golden brown.

Lentilles au lard

Lentils with Bacon

◣▷ 00:20 plus soaking   00:50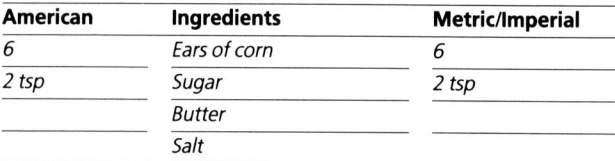

American	Ingredients	Metric/Imperial
2 cups	Dried lentils	500 g / 1 lb
1	Onion	1
5 oz	Bacon	150 g / 5 oz
2 tbsp	Lard (or oil)	2 tbsp
1 tbsp	Flour	1 tbsp
1½ quarts	Water	1.5 l / 2½ pints
2	Tomatoes	2
1	Bouquet garni	1
1	Garlic clove	1
	Salt and pepper	

1. Soak the lentils for at least 6 hours (preferably overnight) in water to cover.

2. Peel the onion and cut into thin slices. Dice the bacon and place in a saucepan of water. Bring to a boil. Simmer for 5 minutes and drain.

3. Heat the lard or oil in a large pan and brown the bacon and the onion. Sprinkle with the flour and stir well, then add the water.

4. Drain the lentils and add to the saucepan. Peel the tomatoes (first plunging them in boiling water for 10 seconds), remove the seeds and cut into pieces. Add to the pan together with the bouquet garni and the peeled garlic. Season with salt and pepper and cover. Slowly bring to a boil and simmer for about 35 minutes or until the lentils are cooked. If necessary, add a little boiling water during cooking.

Jets de houblon

Hop Shoots with a Cream Sauce

◣▷ 00:10   00:15

American	Ingredients	Metric/Imperial
1 lb	Hop shoots	500 g / 1 lb
	Salt and pepper	
1	Lemon	1
5 tbsp	Crème fraîche (see page 122)	5 tbsp
2	Egg yolks	2
3 tbsp	Butter	40 g / 1½ oz

1. Rinse the hop shoots quickly with plenty of cold water. Drop into a saucepan of boiling salted water and add the juice of the lemon. Simmer for 10-15 minutes.

2. Meanwhile, place the crème fraîche, the egg yolks, the butter, salt and pepper in a saucepan standing over a pan of hot water. Cook over a moderate heat for 10 minutes to thicken the mixture. Stir frequently.

3. Drain the hop shoots well and place in a warmed serving dish. Cover with the sauce and serve immediately.

Cook's tip: hop shoots are the edible tip of the male flower; the female cone is only used in brewing beer. They are cooked like asparagus in France.

Maïs en épis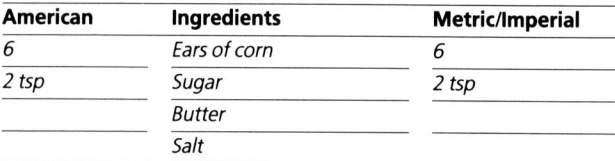

Corn on the Cob

◣▷ 00:10   00:05 to 00:10 (in water) 00:25 to 00:45 (in the oven)

American	Ingredients	Metric/Imperial
6	Ears of corn	6
2 tsp	Sugar	2 tsp
	Butter	
	Salt	

Select the freshest possible corn. The husk (outer leaves) should be green and not yellow; small kernels will be sweeter than larger ones. To cook, you can choose between boiling or roasting them in the oven.

1. Boiling. Strip the husks and silk from the ears. Place them in unsalted boiling water (salt prevents the corn from softening) and add the sugar. Simmer for 5-10 minutes (depending on the size and age of the ears). When cooked, drain well and serve with lightly-salted butter or butter and salt.

2. In the oven. Preheat the oven to 375°F / 190°C / Gas Mark 5. Carefully pull back the husk and remove the silk from the ears. Replace the husk. Lay the ears on a rack in a dish and bake for 25-45 minutes, turning frequently to ensure even cooking. Serve as above.

Laitues braisées
Braised Lettuce

	00:20		00:40
American	**Ingredients**		**Metric/Imperial**
24	Small white onions		24
½ cup	Butter		125 g / 4 oz
2 tbsp	Sugar		2 tbsp
	Salt and pepper		
6	Heads of romaine [cos] lettuce		6
1	Bouquet garni		1

1. Peel the onions. Melt 2 tbsp [25 g / 1 oz] of the butter in a heavy-bottomed pan. Add the onions and sprinkle them with half the sugar and a pinch of salt. Cook over a moderate heat until they turn a caramel color.

2. Meanwhile, cut the heads of lettuce in half, wash thoroughly and drain.

3. Place ¼ cup [50 g / 2 oz] of the butter in a large saucepan, add the lettuce, sprinkle with the rest of the sugar and simmer over a gentle heat for about 15 minutes.

4. Remove the halves of lettuce from the saucepan and roll up lengthwise. Place in a casserole with the onions, the remaining butter and the bouquet garni. Season with salt and pepper. Cover and cook over a gentle heat for 15-20 minutes, or until the lettuce is tender.

5. If the lettuce has produced a lot of liquid by the end of the cooking time, boil to reduce over a high heat.

6. To serve, arrange the lettuce around the sides of a serving dish and pile the onions in the center.

Macédoine d'hiver
Mixed Winter Vegetables

	00:40		00:45
American	**Ingredients**		**Metric/Imperial**
4	Globe artichokes		4
1	Lemon		1
	Salt and pepper		
¾ lb	Carrots		350 g / 12 oz
½ lb	Chinese or Jerusalem artichokes		250 g / 8 oz
½ lb	Button mushrooms		250 g / 8 oz
½ cup	Butter		125 g / 4 oz
¾ lb	Frozen peas		400 g / 14 oz
1	Fresh thyme sprig		1
3	Fresh parsley sprigs		3

1. Cut off the stems from the globe artichokes then the rows of large leaves. Pull away the center leaves then remove the choke from the hearts using a teaspoon. Rub the hearts with a little lemon juice. Bring some salted water to a boil and cook the artichoke hearts for 10-15 minutes. They should remain firm. Drain and dice them.

2. Peel the carrots and dice them. Cook in boiling salted water for 8-12 minutes. Drain.

3. Peel the chinese or jerusalem artichokes and rinse quickly. Cook in enough salted water to prevent them burning for 5-15 minutes. Take care not to overcook them. Drain.

4. Wash the mushrooms and cut them into thin slices. Sprinkle with a little lemon juice so that they do not discolor. Heat half the butter in a frying pan, add the mushrooms and cook for 10-15 minutes until all their liquid has evaporated.

5. Cook the frozen peas in boiling salted water for 5-10 minutes. Drain.

6. Place all the vegetables in a saucepan with the remaining butter, the thyme and salt and pepper to taste. Heat through over a very low heat, stirring frequently. Finely chop the parsley and sprinkle over the vegetables.

Navets glacés
Glazed Turnips

	00:10		00:30
American	**Ingredients**		**Metric/Imperial**
4 lb	Small, round turnips		2 kg / 4 lb
½ cup	Butter		125 g / 4 oz
	Salt and pepper		
2 tbsp	Sugar		2 tbsp

1. Do not peel the turnips unless they are old. Simply trim the tops and bottoms.

2. Melt the butter in a heavy-bottomed saucepan and add the turnips, salt and pepper, and the sugar. Add water until they are just covered.

3. Cook over a low heat, uncovered, for 20-30 minutes until all the water has evaporated and the turnips are coated with the sweet buttery glaze.

4. Serve very hot.

Cook's tip: turnips cooked in this way are usually served as an accompaniment to roasts. Sprinkle with the meat juices just before serving.

Oignons glacés
Glazed Onions

	00:20		00:30
American	**Ingredients**		**Metric/Imperial**
1 lb	Small white onions		500 g / 1 lb
⅓ cup	Butter		75 g / 3 oz
2 tbsp	Sugar		2 tbsp
	Salt		

1. Peel the onions. Place in a saucepan and just cover with water. Add the butter and bring to a boil.

2. Add the sugar and a pinch of salt. Stir and cook over a low heat for 20-30 minutes until the water has evaporated and the onions are thinly coated with the sweet buttery glaze. Serve as an accompaniment to any meat.

Potiron en gratin
Creamed Pumpkin

▭▷ 00:20   00:30 🥘

American	Ingredients	Metric/Imperial
4 lb	Pumpkin	2 kg / 4 lb
7 tbsp	Butter	90 g / 4½ oz
2 tbsp	Flour	2 tbsp
1 cup	Milk	250 ml / 8 fl oz
1 cup	Crème fraîche (see page 122)	250 ml / 8 fl oz
	Salt and pepper	
	Grated nutmeg	
4	Eggs	4

1. Peel the pumpkin, discard the seeds and take out the stringy center. Cut the flesh into pieces. Place in a saucepan with ¼ cup [50 g / 2 oz] of the butter and cook for about 20 minutes over a moderate heat, stirring frequently, until the pumpkin is tender.
2. Purée in a blender, vegetable mill or food processor. The pumpkin purée should be quite thick. If it is too liquid, reduce by stirring it over a high heat.
3. Preheat the oven to 400°F / 200°C / Gas Mark 6.
4. Heat 2 tbsp [25 g / 1 oz] of the butter in a saucepan, sprinkle with the flour and cook for 2 or 3 minutes. Gradually stir in the milk and then the crème fraîche and cook for a few minutes until the sauce thickens. Add the puréed pumpkin and season with salt and pepper and a little freshly grated nutmeg. Stir in the eggs and leave to cool for a few minutes.
5. Butter an ovenproof dish and pour in the purée. Dot with the remaining butter and bake for 10 minutes.

Purée de chicorée
Chicory [Curly Endive] Purée

▭▷ 00:20   00:25 🥘

American	Ingredients	Metric/Imperial
4 lb	Chicory [curly endive]	2 kg / 4 lb
	Salt and pepper	
2 tbsp	Butter	60 g / 2 oz
1½ cups	Béchamel sauce (see page 124)	350 ml / 12 fl oz
4	Slices of bread ½ in / 1 cm thick	4

1. Remove any damaged leaves from the chicory, cut into quarters and wash. Boil some salted water in a saucepan, add the chicory and simmer for 15 minutes.
2. Drain the chicory well and put it through a blender, vegetable mill or food processor. Add to the béchamel sauce. Taste and adjust the seasoning if necessary. Pour into a warmed serving dish and keep hot.
3. Melt the butter in a frying pan and fry the slices of bread until golden brown on both sides. Cut into small cubes and arrange on the chicory. Serve immediately.

Cook's tip: although this vegetable is more usually served raw in salads, it is equally good cooked. Try this delicious alternative as an accompaniment to crisp bacon.

Ratatouille Niçoise
Ratatouille

▭▷ 00:40   01:30 to 02:00 🥘

American	Ingredients	Metric/Imperial
6	Eggplant [aubergines]	6
	Salt and pepper	
2	Sweet green or red peppers	2
6	Tomatoes	6
4	Medium-size onions	4
2	Garlic cloves	2
4	Zucchini [courgettes]	4
¼ cup	Olive oil	4 tbsp
1-2 tsp	Sugar	1-2 tsp
1	Bouquet garni	1

1. Preheat the broiler [grill].
2. Peel the eggplant and cut them into slices. Place them in a colander, sprinkle with salt and leave for 30 minutes to drain off the liquid.
3. Meanwhile, skin the peppers by placing them under the hot broiler until the skins are charred. The skin should then peel off easily under cold running water. Remove the seeds and cut the flesh into thin strips.
4. Peel the tomatoes (first plunging them into boiling water for 10 seconds). Cut in half and remove the seeds. Peel the onions and cut into slices. Peel and crush the garlic. Slice the zucchini.
5. Heat the olive oil in a large flameproof casserole and add the onions and garlic. Cook until soft but not browned.
6. Rinse the eggplant and dry on paper towels. Add to the pan together with the peppers. Cover and cook for 15 minutes over a medium heat.
7. Put in the zucchini and tomatoes and stir well. Season with salt, pepper and a little sugar. Add the bouquet garni and simmer, uncovered, over a moderate heat for about 50 minutes or until the vegetables are cooked and most of the cooking liquid has evaporated.
8. Serve hot or cold.

Purée de chou-fleur
Cauliflower Purée

⏱ 00:15		00:30 🍲
American	**Ingredients**	**Metric/Imperial**
1	Large cauliflower	1
¼ cup	Butter	50 g / 2 oz
¼ cup	Crème fraîche (see page 122)	4 tbsp
1 tsp	Sugar	1 tsp
	Salt and pepper	

1. Remove the leaves from the cauliflower, cut off the stem and wash carefully.
2. Cook the cauliflower in a saucepan, steamer or pressure cooker until it is just tender.
3. Drain the cauliflower thoroughly and purée it in a blender, vegetable mill or food processor. Place the purée in a saucepan over a gentle heat so that any excess water evaporates.
4. Add the butter, crème fraîche and sugar, season with salt and pepper and stir well.

Cook's tip: serve as an accompaniment to all roasts.

Poivrons farcis braisés
Stuffed Peppers

⏱ 01:00		00:45 🍲
American	**Ingredients**	**Metric/Imperial**
2 lb	Tomatoes	1 kg / 2 lb
1	Large onion	1
2 tbsp	Olive oil	2 tbsp
1	Bouquet garni	1
1	Garlic clove	1
	Salt and pepper	
2	Medium-size onions	2
½ cup	Butter	125 g / 4 oz
½ cup	Long-grain rice	125 g / 4 oz
1¼ cups	Water	300 ml / ½ pint
1 lb	Ground [minced] lamb or beef	500 g / 1 lb
	Cayenne pepper	
6	Sweet green or red peppers	6

1. Peel the tomatoes (first plunging them in boiling water for 10 seconds). Cut into quarters and remove the seeds. Peel the large onion and cut into thin slices. Place the tomatoes and onion in a frying pan with the oil and add the bouquet garni and peeled and crushed garlic. Season with salt and pepper. Reduce, uncovered, over a gentle heat for 15 minutes. Remove the bouquet garni and purée in a blender or food processor.
2. Peel the medium-size onions and chop finely. Soften, without browning, in a saucepan with ¼ cup [60 g / 2 oz] of the butter.
3. Add the rice to the saucepan and stir well. Add the water together with a pinch of salt. Cover and cook, without stirring, until the rice has absorbed all the liquid.
4. Melt the remaining butter in a frying pan and brown the ground lamb over a moderate heat. Add the meat to the rice, along with 3 tablespoons of the tomato sauce and a pinch of cayenne pepper. Cook for a further 10 minutes.

5. Heat a saucepan of salted water, add the peppers and boil for 5 minutes. Drain and wipe them dry. Carefully cut out the stems of the peppers and remove the seeds. Stuff with the rice and meat mixture. Replace the pepper stems.
6. Place the peppers upright in a flameproof casserole and pour in the rest of the tomato sauce. Cover and simmer gently for about 45 minutes or until the peppers are tender.

Artichoke hearts with herbs

Poivrade en ragoût
Artichoke Hearts with Herbs

⏱ 00:20		00:30 🍲
American	**Ingredients**	**Metric/Imperial**
12	Small globe artichokes	12
	Lemon juice	
12	Small white onions	12
1½ lb	Small new potatoes	750 g / 1½ lb
2 tbsp	Olive oil	2 tbsp
1	Bay leaf	1
2 tsp	Dried thyme	2 tsp
2	Garlic cloves	2
	Dried savory	
	Dried basil	
	Salt and pepper	

1. Cut the stems and outer leaves from the artichokes and remove the remaining leaves and hairy choke with a small pointed knife until only the hearts remain. Rub these with a little lemon juice so that they do not turn black.
2. Peel the onions and press one into each artichoke heart.
3. Scrape or peel the potatoes, wash and drain them. Heat the olive oil in a heavy pan and add the artichoke hearts and the potatoes along with the bay leaf, thyme, peeled and crushed garlic, a pinch each of savory and basil, salt and pepper. Add water just to cover the ingredients and cook over a gentle heat for 25-30 minutes.

Tchaktchouka

Baked Eggs in Pepper Ragoût

	00:40		00:45

American	Ingredients	Metric/Imperial
4	Sweet peppers	4
2	Onions	2
2	Garlic cloves	2
3 tbsp	Olive oil	3 tbsp
2 lb	Tomatoes	1 kg / 2 lb
	Cayenne pepper	
1	Bay leaf	1
2	Fresh thyme sprigs	2
	Salt	
6	Eggs	6

1. Preheat the broiler [grill]. Place the peppers under the hot broiler and cook, turning constantly, until the skin is charred. Wrap them in a damp cloth and let them cool for 10 minutes. Peel and remove the seeds, then cut the flesh into thin strips. Peel and finely chop the onions and garlic.
2. Preheat the oven to 425°F / 220°C / Gas Mark 7.
3. Heat the oil in a frying pan, add the peppers and onions and cook until softened.
4. Peel the tomatoes (first plunging them into boiling water for 10 seconds), remove the seeds and cut into pieces. Add the tomatoes to the peppers, along with a pinch of cayenne pepper, the garlic, crushed bay leaf and the thyme leaves. Cook over a moderate heat until the mixture becomes thick. Add salt to taste.
5. Place the vegetable mixture in an ovenproof dish. Make 6 hollows using the back of a soup spoon and break an egg into each.
6. Place in the oven and bake until the egg whites are set but the yolks still soft. Serve immediately.

Cook's tip: the pepper ragoût can also be served without the eggs as an accompaniment to meat dishes.

Salsifis sautés

Sautéed Salsify

	00:40		00:30 to 00:40

American	Ingredients	Metric/Imperial
1	Lemon	1
3 lb	Salsify or scorzonera	1.5 kg / 3 lb
2 tbsp	Flour	2 tbsp
	Salt and pepper	
⅓ cup	Butter	75 g / 3 oz
½	Garlic clove	½
3 tbsp	Chopped fresh parsley	3 tbsp

1. Fill a bowl with water and add the juice of the lemon. Peel the salsify, cut into 1-1½ in / 3-4 cm pieces and add to the bowl.
2. Mix the flour with a little cold water. Heat some salted water in a pan and add the flour paste as it is about to boil. Stir until it boils and add the drained salsify. Cook over a moderate heat for 15-20 minutes or until just soft. Drain and refresh under cold running water.

3. Melt the butter in a frying pan and add the salsify. Cook gently, stirring frequently, for about 20 minutes. Season with salt and pepper.
4. Peel and chop the garlic and mix with the chopped parsley. Sprinkle over the salsify a few minutes before serving.

Tomates à la provençale

Baked Tomatoes with Herbs

	00:05		00:25

American	Ingredients	Metric/Imperial
3 lb	Tomatoes	1.5 kg / 3 lb
	Salt and pepper	
2 tsp	Dried thyme	2 tsp
1 tsp	Dried rosemary	1 tsp
3 tbsp	Olive oil	3 tbsp
4	Garlic cloves	4
1	Small bunch of fresh parsley	1
2 tbsp	Bread crumbs	2 tbsp

1. Preheat the oven to 400°F / 200°C / Gas Mark 6.
2. Wash the tomatoes and cut in half. Place them, flat side up, in a buttered ovenproof dish. Sprinkle each half with salt, pepper, thyme and rosemary. Pour the olive oil over them and bake for 15-20 minutes.
3. Peel and finely chop the garlic, and chop the parsley. Mix together with the bread crumbs.
4. Take the tomatoes out of the oven and increase the heat to 475°F / 240°C / Gas Mark 9. Sprinkle each tomato half with a heaped teaspoon of the garlic, parsley and bread crumb mixture. Return to the oven for 5 minutes or until the tops are brown.

Cook's tip: this dish is usually served hot, but is equally delicious cold.

Tomates farcies au riz

Tomatoes Stuffed with Rice

	00:30		00:50

American	Ingredients	Metric/Imperial
6	Large tomatoes	6
	Salt and pepper	
1 cup	Long-grain rice	180 g / 6 oz
½ cup	Butter	125 g / 4 oz
1	Small bunch of fresh parsley	1
6	Fresh chives	6
2	Hard-cooked eggs	2
1 cup	Grated gruyère cheese	125 g / 4 oz
2	Fresh chervil sprigs	2

1. Wash the tomatoes, slice off the tops and scoop out the insides with a small spoon, being careful not to puncture the shells. Sprinkle inside the tomato shells with a little salt and place them upside-down on a plate.

2. Boil a large pan of salted water and add the rice. Bring back to a boil and simmer for 6 minutes. Drain the rice and mix with the butter. Return it to the saucepan, cover and cook for 25 minutes over a gentle heat.
3. Preheat the oven to 400°F / 200°C / Gas Mark 6.
4. Place the rice in a mixing bowl. Chop the parsley and the chives and add to the rice. Shell the hard-cooked eggs, mash them and stir into the mixture.
5. Tip the liquid from each tomato and fill with the rice mixture. Arrange in a buttered ovenproof dish. Sprinkle with the grated cheese and chopped chervil and put in the oven. Bake for 25 minutes. Serve hot.

Cook's tip: these could also be served as a hot hors d'oeuvre.

Purée de marrons

Chestnut Purée

	00:40		00:30

American	Ingredients	Metric/Imperial
3 lb	Chestnuts	1.5 kg / 3 lb
¼	Celeriac	¼
	Salt and pepper	
1 cup	Milk	250 ml / 8 fl oz
¼ cup	Butter	60 g / 2 oz
2 tbsp	Crème fraîche (see page 122)	2 tbsp

1. Using a small pointed knife, cut around the chestnuts, piercing the 2 skins. Place in a saucepan, cover with cold water and bring to a boil. Boil for about 7 minutes and remove from the heat.
2. Remove the chestnuts one by one, and peel them. Peel the celeriac.
3. Place the chestnuts in a saucepan with the celeriac and cover with cold salted water. Bring to a boil and cook for about 30 minutes then drain well.
4. Purée in a blender, vegetable mill or food-processor and pour the purée into a saucepan. Place over a gentle heat and stir in the milk a little at a time. Add the butter and crème fraîche. Adjust the seasoning if necessary and serve very hot.

Cook's tip: serve with roast goose or turkey.

Topinambours sauce béchamel

Jerusalem Artichokes with Béchamel

	00:15		00:40

American	Ingredients	Metric/Imperial
2 lb	Jerusalem artichokes	1 kg / 2 lb
	Salt and pepper	
2 cups	Béchamel sauce (see page 124)	500 ml / ¾ pint
	Grated nutmeg	

1. Peel the artichokes and cook in a small amount of boiling, salted water for 15-20 minutes.
2. Drain the artichokes and add to the sauce. Simmer gently for 10 minutes and serve very hot.

Soufflé aux épinards

Spinach Soufflé

	00:20		01:00

American	Ingredients	Metric/Imperial
3 lb	Fresh spinach	1.5 kg / 3 lb
	Salt and pepper	
¼ cup	Butter	50 g / 2 oz
¼ cup	Flour	50 g / 2 oz
2½ cups	Milk	600 ml / 1 pint
	Grated nutmeg	
½ cup	Grated gruyère cheese	50 g / 2 oz
4	Eggs, separated	4

1. Wash the spinach thoroughly and remove the stems. Put in a large saucepan with a large pinch of salt and cook over a medium heat for 8 minutes. Drain well. Leave to cool a little then press the leaves between the palms of the hands to extract all the water. Chop the spinach finely and set aside.
2. Preheat the oven to 425°F / 220°C / Gas Mark 7.
3. Melt the butter in a saucepan, add the flour and stir until it has been absorbed. Gradually stir in the milk and cook, stirring, until thickened. Season with salt and pepper and add a little freshly grated nutmeg and the grated cheese.
4. Add 2 tablespoons of the sauce to the egg yolks and beat well. Stir in the rest of the sauce. Add the spinach.
5. Beat the egg whites until they are stiff and carefully fold into the spinach mixture.
6. Pour into a buttered 8 in / 21 cm soufflé dish to fill it three-quarters full. Bake for 30 minutes without opening the oven door, then increase the temperature of the oven to 450°F / 240°C / Gas Mark 8 and bake for a further 5 minutes. Serve immediately.

Cook's tip: make this soufflé with tender young spinach leaves and serve with glazed carrots (see page 417) and a bowl of hollandaise sauce (see page 126) for an appetizing spring lunch.

Purée de navets

Turnip Purée

	00:20		00:25

American	Ingredients	Metric/Imperial
3 lb	Turnips	1.5 kg / 3 lb
	Salt and pepper	
⅓ cup	Butter	75 g / 3 oz
1 tbsp	Sugar	1 tbsp
3 tbsp	Crème fraîche (see page 122)	3 tbsp

1. Peel the turnips. Bring some salted water to a boil in a saucepan and add the turnips. Simmer gently, uncovered for 15 minutes or until tender.
2. Drain the turnips and purée in a blender, vegetable mill or food processor. Cook the purée in a saucepan over a low heat for 5 minutes so that any liquid evaporates.
3. Add the butter, sugar and crème fraîche. Adjust the seasoning, if necessary. Stir for 5 minutes over a low heat and serve very hot.

Cook's tip: serve with ham and bacon dishes.

Rice

Rice is one of the world's most important foods and although most is grown and consumed in Asia, it is also grown in other temperate and tropical countries and is a very important crop in the USA, Brazil, Spain, Italy and Egypt. Natural unpolished rice (brown rice) is a prime source of nutrition since it provides vitamins, minerals, protein, fat and carbohydrate. Rice is a cheap and quick source of energy, for it is digested in about an hour instead of the two to four hours needed for most other foods.

Types of rice
There are basically two kinds of rice, long grain and short grain, and both kinds — while they are growing in the fields and before the grain is husked — are known as paddy rice.
Brown rice is the wholegrain that is left after the paddy rice is harvested and the inedible husk covering each grain is removed. It contains more nutrients and vitamins than other kinds of rice. It takes about 45 minutes to cook.
Parboiled rice, also known as non-stick, pre-fluffed or easy-to-cook, is processed before it is milled so more of the natural minerals and vitamins remain. It is not pre-cooked and it takes about 5 minutes longer to cook than ordinary white rice. It is prepared from rice that has been soaked in water, steamed and dried before hulling and milling.
Long grain rice is the kind that is most often eaten with savory dishes. The texture is light and fluffy and the grains remain separate when cooked.
White or polished rice is the most common form of long grain rice. It is less nutritious than brown rice because the bran and germ are removed during milling. It cooks in about 15 minutes.
Pre-cooked or instant long grain rice is completely cooked after milling. Depending on the brand, cooking time can be 1-10 minutes.
Medium grain rice is used for croquettes and puddings. It is not as translucent as long grain, has more starch and is stickier when cooked.
Short or round grain rice is most popular in Japan and parts of China. It is sticky when cooked and in the West is the traditional pudding rice as it softens well in milk. It is well suited to being eaten with chopsticks, and in Japan it is served plain and unsalted as an accompaniment to a savory dish.
Italian rice is another short grain variety with a hard core needing slow cooking without much liquid. It is used for making dishes such as risottos in which the sauce is cooked in with the rice.
Wild rice is not a true rice, it is an aquatic plant which grows in bogs and swamps in Canada, the USA, the Far East and northern Italy. Wild rice is very expensive, is usually eaten with game and has a delicate nutty flavor. It contains more protein and vitamins than regular rice and when cooked has a slightly purplish color.

Risotto à la milanaise
Milanaise Risotto

00:15   00:20

American	Ingredients	Metric/Imperial
2 lb	Tomatoes	1 kg / 2 lb
3	Onions	3
2	Garlic cloves	2
¼ cup	Olive oil	4 tbsp
1	Fresh thyme sprig	1
2 cups	Long grain rice	400 g / 14 oz
3 cups	Boiling water	750 ml / 1¼ pints
	Salt and pepper	
	Saffron	
	Grated parmesan or gruyère cheese	

1. Peel the tomatoes (first plunging them into boiling water for 10 seconds). Cut in half, remove the seeds and chop coarsely. Peel and finely chop the onions and the garlic.
2. Heat half the olive oil in a large saucepan and add the onions. Soften over a low heat, stirring constantly, for about 3 minutes. Add the tomatoes, thyme, and chopped garlic. Cook over a gentle heat for 10 minutes.
3. Heat the remaining oil in a frying pan, add the rice and stir for 3 minutes. Add the boiling water.
4. Pour the rice and water into the saucepan and season with salt, pepper and a pinch of saffron. Cover and simmer gently for 16-18 minutes, without removing the lid. The water should have been completely absorbed by the rice.
5. Serve hot, sprinkled with grated cheese.

Riz cantonais
Cantonese Rice

00:25   00:30 to 00:35
plus soaking time

American	Ingredients	Metric/Imperial
2 oz	Dried mushrooms	50 g / 2 oz
2 cups	Short grain rice	350 g / 12 oz
½ lb	Boneless chicken breast	250 g / 8 oz
	Salt and pepper	
5 oz	Canned bamboo shoots	150 g / 5 oz
4	Eggs	4
⅔ cup	Oil	150 ml / ¼ pint
½ lb	Cooked peeled shrimp [prawns]	250 g / 8 oz
½ lb	Fresh shelled peas	250 g / 8 oz
2 cups	Chicken stock	500 ml / ¾ pint
2 tbsp	Soy sauce	2 tbsp

1. Place the dried mushrooms in a bowl, cover with boiling water and leave to soak for 2 hours.
2. Rinse the rice under cold water, place it in a saucepan and cover with water. Cook for 20 minutes.
3. Meanwhile, cut the chicken into ½ in / 1 cm squares and season with salt and pepper. Cut the bamboo shoots into thin strips. Drain the mushrooms and chop them finely.
4. Beat the eggs in a bowl. Heat 1 tablespoon of the oil in a large frying pan, add the beaten eggs and cook for 2-3 minutes on one side. Turn the omelette over and cook on the other side until it is dry. Slide onto a chopping board, roll it and then cut into strips.

5. Heat 1 tablespoon of the oil in the frying pan and cook the diced chicken for 3 minutes. Repeat the process with the bamboo shoots, shrimp and peas, adding 1 tablespoon of oil each time.

6. Put all these ingredients into a saucepan and add the stock. Cover and cook over a moderate heat for 5-10 minutes. Add the soy sauce, then stir in the drained rice and the pieces of omelette. Mix together gently and heat for 3 minutes. Serve very hot in individual bowls.

Riz à l'ananas
Rice with Pineapple

	00:15		00:45

American	Ingredients	Metric/Imperial
8	Small onions	8
⅓ cup	Oil	6 tbsp
2 cups	Long grain rice	400 g / 14 oz
3 cups	Boiling water	750 ml / 1¼ pints
3	Sweet green or red peppers	3
1 lb	Lean boneless veal	500 g / 1 lb
1 tbsp	Curry powder	1 tbsp
1 tbsp	Flour	1 tbsp
⅔ cup	Cold water	150 ml / ¼ pint
	Salt and pepper	
1	Can of pineapple chunks	1
3 tbsp	Crème fraîche (see page 122)	3 tbsp

1. Peel the onions and cut them into slices. Heat half the oil in a frying pan and add half the onions. Soften, stirring frequently, for 3 minutes.

2. Add the rice and stir for three minutes, then gradually stir in the boiling water. Cook over a gentle heat for 20-25 minutes.

3. Meanwhile, heat the remaining oil in a frying pan and brown the rest of the onions.

4. Wash the peppers, remove the seeds and dice. Dice the veal. Add the veal and peppers to the frying pan with the onions. Add the curry powder, flour and cold water. Season with salt and pepper and leave to simmer over a gentle heat for 20 minutes. About 5 minutes before the end of the cooking time add the drained pineapple chunks.

5. To serve, place the rice in a deep serving dish and mix in the veal and pineapple mixture and the crème fraîche.

6. Serve hot.

Riz complet
Brown Rice

	00:05		00:30

American	Ingredients	Metric/Imperial
1 quart	Water	1 l / 1¾ pints
	Salt and pepper	
2 cups	Long grain brown rice	500 g / 1 lb
¼ cup	Butter	50 g / 2 oz

1. Put the water in a large pan. Season with salt and pepper and bring to a boil.

2. Rinse the rice under running water and then add it to the pan. Cook over a low heat for about 30 minutes until the grains of rice have absorbed the water and are tender.

3. Add the butter, toss and serve.

Cook's tip: this plain though nutritious rice dish may be enlivened by adding chopped fresh herbs such as thyme or basil, or lightly sautéed mushrooms, with the butter. It would also be good as an accompaniment to a robust country dish, such as Pork Chops with Charcutière Sauce (see page 389).

Rice can be served as an accompaniment to many dishes

Riz pilaf persan
Persian Rice

00:25   00:45

American	Ingredients	Metric/Imperial
12	Chicken livers	12
2	Onions	2
2	Garlic cloves	2
1 quart	Chicken stock	1 l / 1¾ pints
½ lb	Carrots	250 g / 8 oz
½ cup	Chicken fat or butter	125 g / 4 oz
1½ cups	Long grain rice	350 g / 12 oz
½ tsp	Saffron powder	½ tsp
	Cayenne pepper	
	Salt and pepper	
1 tbsp	Chopped fresh parsley	1 tbsp
2	Tomatoes	2

1. Cut the chicken livers into large pieces. Peel the onions and cut into thin strips. Peel and crush the garlic. Heat the chicken stock over a gentle heat. Peel and grate the carrots.
2. Heat the fat in a large saucepan and add the chicken livers. Stir over a high heat for 2 minutes or until just cooked. Remove from the pan with a slotted spoon and set aside.
3. Add the onion and the carrot to the saucepan and stir for 3-4 minutes. Add the rice. Stir for 5 minutes, then season with the saffron, a pinch of cayenne pepper and salt and pepper to taste. Add the crushed garlic and chopped parsley and stir together well. Finally, stir in the hot stock.
4. Leave to cook over a moderate heat for 30 minutes, without removing the lid.
5. Meanwhile, peel the tomatoes (first plunging them in boiling water for 10 seconds) and dice. Once the rice is cooked add the tomatoes and chicken livers. Stir gently and serve very hot.

Riz à la syrienne
Syrian Rice

00:20   00:40
plus soaking time

American	Ingredients	Metric/Imperial
2 cups	Long grain rice	400 g / 14 oz
2	Onions	2
¾ cup	Butter	175 g / 6 oz
¾ lb	Lean ground [minced] pork	350 g / 12 oz
	Grated nutmeg	
	Salt and pepper	
1 cup	Blanched almonds	125 g / 4 oz
1 quart	Water	1 l / 1¾ pints

1. Place the rice in a bowl and cover with warm water. Leave to soak for at least 4 hours.
2. Peel the onions and cut into slices. Melt the butter in a frying pan and add the onions along with the ground pork and a pinch of nutmeg. Season with salt and pepper and cook for 20 minutes over a medium heat. Remove the mixture from the pan with a slotted spoon and keep warm.
3. In the same frying pan, brown the almonds over a moderate heat. When they are a golden color, remove them and add to the pork mixture. Keep hot.

4. Put the water in the frying pan, bring to a boil and add the drained rice. Cook for 15-20 minutes, taking care not to let the rice stick to the bottom of the pan.
5. To serve, place the rice in a deep dish and mix in the meat and almond mixture.

Riz pilaf (à la turque)
Turkish Rice

00:15   00:18 to 00:20

American	Ingredients	Metric/Imperial
2	Onions	2
3 tbsp	Olive oil	3 tbsp
2 cups	Long grain rice	400 g / 14 oz
1 quart	Boiling water	1 l / 1¾ pints
	Salt and pepper	
	Saffron powder	

1. Peel and chop the onions. Heat the olive oil in a saucepan, add the onions and cook for 5 minutes over a moderate heat. Add the rice and cook, stirring well, for 3 minutes or until the rice becomes milky.
2. Add the boiling water, 1 teaspoon of salt, pepper and a pinch of saffron. Cover and cook over a moderate heat for 18-20 minutes, without removing the lid.
3. The rice is cooked once it has absorbed all the water and the surface is pitted with holes.

Cook's tip: this rice can be served as a main dish or as an accompaniment to fish, roasts or casseroles.

Riz à la vapeur
Steamed Rice

00:05   00:25 to 00:30

American	Ingredients	Metric/Imperial
2 cups	Long grain rice	400 g / 14 oz
	Salt	
3 tbsp	Butter	40 g / 1½ oz

1. Pour water into the bottom of a steamer. Bring to a boil.
2. Meanwhile, rinse and drain the rice. Line the upper section of the steamer with cheesecloth or muslin, pour the rice into it and steam for 25-30 minutes until it is tender.
3. To serve, season with salt, add the butter and toss.

Riz sauté
Sautéed Rice

00:00   00:25

American	Ingredients	Metric/Imperial
½ cup	Butter	125 g / 4 oz
2 cups	Long grain rice	400 g / 14 oz
3 cups	Chicken stock	750 ml / 1¼ pints
	Salt and pepper	

1. Melt the butter in a saucepan over a high heat. Add the rice and brown it for 5 minutes until it has absorbed all the butter.
2. Add the stock and season with salt and pepper. Bring to a boil and cook over a gentle heat for 20 minutes. Serve very hot.

Buttered wild rice

 Riz au safran

Saffron Rice

	00:10		00:25

American	Ingredients	Metric/Imperial
1	Onion	1
5 oz	Bacon	150 g / 5 oz
2 tbsp	Oil	2 tbsp
2 cups	Long grain rice	400 g / 14 oz
1 tsp	Saffron powder	1 tsp
	Salt and pepper	
3 cups	Boiling water	750 ml / 1¼ pints

1. Peel the onion and cut into thin slices. Dice the bacon. Heat the oil in a saucepan and cook the bacon and the onion until they are golden brown.
2. Put the rice in a large saucepan. Add the onion, bacon and saffron and season with salt and pepper. Add the boiling water, then cover and cook for 18-20 minutes, checking that the rice does not boil dry. Add a little extra water if necessary. Serve hot.

 Riz sauvage au beurre

Buttered Wild Rice

	01:00		00:45

American	Ingredients	Metric/Imperial
2 cups	Wild rice	400 g / 14 oz
1½ quarts	Cold water	1.5 l / 2½ pints
	Salt	
3 tbsp	Butter	40 g / 1½ oz

1. Place the rice in a bowl. Cover with warm water and leave to soak for 1 hour.
2. Drain the rice using a sieve. Pour the cold water into a large pan and add the rice and some salt.
3. Bring to a boil. Stir the rice, then lower the heat and cook for about 45 minutes or until the grains have absorbed all the water and are tender.
4. Add the butter and toss.

Cook's tip: serve wild rice with leg of lamb, poultry, or game.

Riz de Bayonne

Rice with Ham and Cheese

	00:05		00:20 to 00:25

American	Ingredients	Metric/Imperial
2	Onions	2
¼ cup	Oil	4 tbsp
2 cups	Long grain rice	400 g / 1 lb
3 cups	Boiling water	750 ml / 1¼ pints
	Salt and pepper	
2 (5 oz)	Slices of cooked ham or prosciutto	2 (150 g / 5 oz)
1 cup	Grated gruyère cheese	125 g / 4 oz

1. Peel the onions and cut into slices. Heat the oil in a frying pan and cook the onions for a few minutes.
2. Add the rice to the frying pan and stir for 3 minutes, then add the boiling water. Season with salt and pepper and cook for 20-25 minutes until the rice has absorbed all the water.
3. Meanwhile, dice the ham. When the rice is cooked add the grated cheese and the diced ham. Mix together and serve hot.

Riz Créole

Buttered Rice

	00:05		00:15 to 00:18

American	Ingredients	Metric/Imperial
1½ cups	Long grain rice	350 g / 12 oz
2¼ cups	Water	600 ml / 1 pint
	Salt	
⅓ cup	Butter	75 g / 3 oz

1. Rinse the rice in cold water until the water runs clear. Put the water in a saucepan, add salt and bring to a boil. Add the rice to the boiling water and cook for 15-18 minutes, according to taste.
2. Drain the rice in a sieve and rinse it under cold water. Drain thoroughly.
3. Preheat the oven to 400°F / 200°C / Gas Mark 6.
4. Cut the butter into small pieces and place in a gratin dish. Add the rice and bake for 5-8 minutes, stirring the rice from time to time with a fork. Once the rice is dry and the grains separate, remove from the oven and serve immediately.

Cook's tip: this rice may be served as an accompaniment to dishes with sauces, or it can be used cold or hot in salads.

Pasta

Pasta is one of the most versatile of foods; it comes in an incredible range of shapes and sizes and can be filled or unfilled, can be eaten in soup or boiled or baked. The best pastas are made with hard durum wheat — *semola di grano dúro.* Dry pasta, *pasta secca,* is made with flour and water; *pasta all'uovo* has the addition of eggs, green pasta is flavored with spinach. Pasta comes in cords, tubes, flat noodles (some of which come in nests), some pastas are smooth, others are wavy or ridged. The best known of the cord pastas are spaghetti and vermicelli, and macaroni of the tubular ones. Noodles range from the tiny tagliarini to the wide lasagne and there are tiny fancy shapes to eat in soup — stars, bow ties, letters of the alphabet, butterflies, thimbles and umbrellas. Some of the most versatile pastas for salad are elbow macaroni and shells. If you are going to use pasta in a cold salad, rinse it in cold water after it has been cooked and drained. This stops the cooking and chills the pasta ready for tossing with the dressing.

If you have the patience, you can make fresh pasta (the recipe for it appears on page 442) and there are electric machines which make pasta very quickly. Fresh pasta cooks in half the time of dried pasta.

In Italy, there are firm traditions about which sauces go with which pasta shape — shellfish are usually served with thin spaghetti, hollow shell shapes and tubes with meat sauces. However, outside the country of origin, the only limitation is that of the cook's imagination. Our recipes are simple and the choice of pasta to use is flexible. It is up to you, how you mix the different pastas and flavors. Purists will tell you that the only cheeses to serve with pasta are parmesan and pecorino romano (strong sheep's cheese). But gruyère, comté or emmental cheese go well with it, as do mozzarella, bel paese, port-salut, fontina, fontal or raclette.

To cook pasta

Allow 3-4 oz [75-125 g] of pasta per person. Fill a very large, deep saucepan with water, allowing about 1 quart [1 l/ 2 pints] of water for every 4 oz [125 g] of pasta. Heat the water and when it comes to a boil, add a good spoonful of salt and then the pasta little by little as the water comes back to a boil. To prevent the pasta sticking, add 1 tablespoon oil to the boiling water when you add the salt. Cooking time for spaghetti is about 10-12 minutes. When cooked, it should be *al dente,* that it, still quite firm when bitten into, so taste it before removing from the saucepan. As soon as the pasta is cooked, drain it and place immediately in a dish with the sauce. It should arrive at the table still steaming.

Cook's tip: these are the basic cooking times for different kinds of durum wheat pasta: vermicelli — 3 minutes; spaghetti, 10-12 minutes; shells, 10-12 minutes; macaroni, 15-20 minutes; cannelloni, 15-20 minutes. If you are cooking fresh pasta, it will take about half the time of dried pasta.

Opposite: a selection of pasta showing just some of the many shapes that are available. From left to right, starting at the top:
Small ridged macaroni, also called rigatoni;
Long macaroni and a fine kind of spaghetti called **vermicelli.** Other kinds of spaghetti, according to size are called capellini, fidelini, spaghettini, spaghettoni.
Penne macaroni, named after the sharp nib-like ends;
Trinette, with a wavy and straight edge and **fusilli,** long strands of spiraled spaghetti;
Marziani, or malloredus, looks like coiled springs;
Farfalle, butterflies, also called bow ties, cravattine;
Conchiglioni, sea shells;
Stornelli verdi, spinach colored, tiny curled ridged macaroni;
Tagliatelle, also known as fettucine, is shown in the basket in nests of various widths. One of the widest kinds is pappardelle.

Mezze maniche rigate (in the spoon), these pasta tubes are named after ribbed short sleeves;
Pasta alla chitarra, nests of square-cut spaghetti;
Capelli d'angelo, nests of very fine vermicelli;
Pastina or **semi di melone,** pasta shaped like melon seeds.

Above: a selection of filled pastas. From the top, left to right:
Cappelletti, which look like little hats;
Large tortellini, which look like folded table napkins;
Half-moon tortelloni, with fluted edges;
Agnolotti, which look like large postage stamps;
Small tortellini;
Ravioli or tortelloni, small half-moon shapes.

Gnocchi de semoule

Semolina Gnocchi

	00:30 plus cooling		00:40

American	Ingredients	Metric/Imperial
3 cups + 1 tbsp	Milk	750 ml / 1¼ pints + 1 tbsp
⅔ cup	Butter	150 g / 5 oz
	Salt and pepper	
	Grated nutmeg	
1⅓ cups	Semolina	250 g / 8 oz
1 cup	Grated parmesan cheese	125 g / 4 oz
3	Egg yolks	3

1. In a large saucepan, bring to a boil 3 cups [750 ml / 1¼ pints] of the milk, together with one third of the butter, some salt, a little freshly grated nutmeg and a pinch of pepper. Sprinkle in the semolina, stirring constantly to prevent lumps from forming. Cook over a low heat, stirring with a wooden spoon, for about 5 minutes or until the spoon will stand up in the mixture.

2. Remove the saucepan from the heat and add 2 tablespoons of the grated cheese. Mix the egg yolks with 1 tablespoon of milk and carefully stir into the mixture. Turn out onto a damp pastry board. Using a metal spatula dipped in water, spread out the paste to a thickness of ½ in / 1 cm. Leave to cool.

3. Preheat the oven to 400°F / 200°C / Gas Mark 6.

4. Using a pastry cutter or small wine glass, cut out little rounds of the paste. Melt the rest of the butter in a small saucepan. Fill a buttered ovenproof dish with 4 or 5 layers of gnocchi, adding melted butter and the rest of the grated cheese to each layer. Finish with a layer of cheese.

5. Bake for about 20 minutes, or until the gnocchi are hot and well browned. Serve immediately.

Lasagne bolognaise au four

Lasagne

	00:10		01:20

American	Ingredients	Metric/Imperial
1 lb	Tomatoes	500 g / 1 lb
3	Garlic cloves	3
1	Large onion	1
1	Bunch of fresh parsley	1
2 tbsp	Olive oil	2 tbsp
1 lb	Ground [minced] beef	500 g / 1 lb
	Salt and pepper	
½ lb	Lasagne	250 g / 8 oz
5 oz	Mozzarella cheese	150 g / 5 oz
¼ cup	Melted butter	50 g / 2 oz
1½ cups	Grated parmesan cheese	150 g / 6 oz

1. Peel the tomatoes (first plunging them into boiling water for 10 seconds) and chop coarsely. Peel and crush the garlic. Peel the onion and cut into thin slices. Chop the parsley.

2. Heat the olive oil in a saucepan and add the crushed garlic, the onion and the parsley. Stir over a moderate heat for 5 minutes then add the beef and mix together well. Cook for about 15 minutes over a low heat. Add the tomatoes and season with salt and pepper. Cover and cook for about 45 minutes over a gentle heat until the sauce is thick.

3. Meanwhile, bring a large cooking pot of salted water to a boil. Add the lasagne and cook for 5-10 minutes or until 'al dente' (see page 437). Remove the lasagne with a slotted spoon and leave to drain on a damp cloth.

4. Preheat the oven to 400°F / 200°C / Gas Mark 6.

5. Cut the mozzarella cheese into thin strips. Pour the melted butter into a gratin dish.

6. Arrange a layer of lasagne on the bottom of the dish. Spread this with a layer of meat sauce and some cheese. Repeat this until all the ingredients are used up, finishing with a layer of meat sauce, mozzarella and parmesan cheese.

7. Bake for 30-45 minutes until the top is golden brown. Serve very hot.

Gnocchi au fromage

Potato Gnocchi with Cheese

	00:45		00:45

American	Ingredients	Metric/Imperial
4 lb	Floury potatoes	2 kg / 4 lb
	Salt	
3½ cups	Flour	400 g / 14 oz
5 oz	Fontina or a similar cheese	150 g / 5 oz
½ cup	Butter	125 g / 4 oz
2 cups	Tomato sauce (see page 123)	500 ml / ¾ pint
1 cup	Grated parmesan cheese	125 g / 4 oz

1. Peel the potatoes and place them in a large saucepan of salted water. Bring to a boil and cook for about 25 minutes, or until the potatoes are soft. Drain well.

2. Mash the potatoes and add the flour. Mix together well to obtain a smooth purée. Separate the mixture into small balls and then shape them into 1 in / 2 cm diameter sausages. Cut each piece into smaller sausages 1½ in / 3 cm long and curve them by pinching them in the middle between thumb and index finger.

3. Sprinkle some flour onto a clean cloth and place the gnocchi on it as you make them.

4. Boil a large quantity of water in a cooking pot and add 1 teaspoon of salt. Add the gnocchi to the boiling water a few at a time. As soon as they rise to the surface they are ready. Remove them with a slotted spoon, place in a warmed serving dish and keep hot.

5. Cut the fontina into thin strips and sprinkle over the gnocchi. Heat the butter in a saucepan. Once it turns brown, pour it over the gnocchi. Serve immediately, accompanied by tomato sauce and grated parmesan cheese.

Pâtes fraîches vertes

Fresh Green Pasta

	00:45		00:03

American	Ingredients	Metric/Imperial
½ lb	Fresh spinach	250 g / 8 oz
4 cups	Flour	500 g / 1 lb
3	Eggs	3
	Salt	
1 tbsp	Oil	1 tbsp

1. Wash the spinach in several changes of water and cut off the stems. Place in a large saucepan and cook for 5 minutes, stirring several times. Drain the spinach using a colander, rinse under cold water and press to extract all the water. Chop the leaves finely, or put them through a blender, vegetable mill or food processor.

2. Place the flour on the work surface, make a hollow in the center and add to it the eggs, a large pinch of salt, the oil and spinach. Carefully blend together all the ingredients to obtain a uniformly green paste and then roll it into a ball and leave to rest for at least 1 hour.

3. Roll and cut the pasta using a pasta machine (as in the recipe for fresh egg pasta, see page 442) and prepare according to taste.

Spaghetti carbonara
Spaghetti with Eggs and Bacon

00:10   **00:20**

American	Ingredients	Metric/Imperial
6 oz	Bacon	175 g / 6 oz
1 tbsp	Oil	1 tbsp
	Salt and pepper	
1 lb	Spaghetti	500 g / 1 lb
6	Eggs	6
½ cup	Grated parmesan cheese	50 g / 2 oz
½ cup	Crème fraîche (see page 122)	125 ml / 4 fl oz
¼ cup	Butter	50 g / 2 oz

1. Cut the bacon into strips and brown in the oil for about 5 minutes. Remove from the pan with a slotted spoon.

2. Bring to a boil a large amount of salted water in a cooking pot. Add the spaghetti and cook for about 10 minutes or until 'al dente' (see page 437).

3. Meanwhile, break the eggs into a bowl, beat well and add the grated cheese, salt, pepper and crème fraîche.

4. Melt the butter in a saucepan and heat for about 4 minutes. Once it turns brown add the egg and cream mixture. Stir for 5 minutes to lightly cook the eggs. Add the well-drained spaghetti and bacon. Mix together over a gentle heat so that all the ingredients are hot. Add a generous amount of freshly ground black pepper to the dish and serve immediately.

Spaghetti amatriciana
Spaghetti with Bacon and Tomato Sauce

00:15   **00:40**

American	Ingredients	Metric/Imperial
6 oz	Bacon	175 g / 6 oz
1	Small onion	1
5	Tomatoes	5
2 tbsp	Oil	2 tbsp
	Salt and pepper	
1 lb	Spaghetti	500 g / 1 lb
¾ cup	Grated parmesan cheese	75 g / 3 oz

1. Cut the bacon into small strips. Peel and finely chop the onion. Peel the tomatoes (first plunging them into boiling water for 10 seconds). Cut in half, remove the seeds and chop coarsely.

2. Heat the oil in a frying pan and brown the bacon for about 5 minutes, stirring occasionally. Remove with a slotted spoon and set on one side. Add the chopped onion to the pan, stir for about 2 minutes and then add the tomatoes. Season with salt and pepper to taste. Stir well to mix and leave to cook over a moderate heat for 10 minutes.

3. Meanwhile, bring to a boil a large quantity of salted water in a cooking pot. Add the spaghetti and boil for about 10 minutes or until 'al dente' (see page 437).

4. Add the bacon to the tomato sauce and warm over a low heat.

5. Drain the pasta, and turn into a warmed serving dish. Add half the parmesan cheese and the bacon and tomato sauce. Mix gently together and serve the rest of the parmesan cheese separately in a small dish.

Pappardelle vertes au ragoût
Green Pappardelle with Meat Sauce

00:20   **01:30**

American	Ingredients	Metric/Imperial
1 lb	Tomatoes	500 g / 1 lb
3	Garlic cloves	3
1	Large onion	1
1	Bunch of fresh parsley	1
2 tbsp	Olive oil	2 tbsp
1 lb	Ground [minced] beef	500 g / 1 lb
	Salt and pepper	
¼ lb	Chicken livers	125 g / 4 oz
⅓ cup	Butter	75 g / 3 oz
1¼ lb	Green pappardelle	600 g / 1¼ lb
3 cups	Grated parmesan cheese	350 g / 12 oz
5 oz	Mozzarella cheese	150 g / 5 oz

1. Peel the tomatoes (first plunging them into boiling water for 10 seconds) and chop them coarsely. Peel and crush the garlic. Peel the onion and cut into thin slices. Chop the parsley.

2. Heat the olive oil in a saucepan and add the garlic, the onion and the parsley. Stir over a moderate heat for about 5 minutes. Add the beef, mix well and cook for about 15 minutes over a low heat. Add the tomatoes and season with salt and pepper. Cover and cook for about 45 minutes over a moderate heat until the sauce is thick.

3. Dice the chicken livers. Melt 1 tablespoon [15 g / ½ oz] of butter in a frying pan, brown the livers quickly and add to the sauce.

4. Preheat the oven to 400°F / 200°C / Gas Mark 6.

5. Boil a large quantity of salted water in a cooking pot. Add the pappardelle a few at a time and cook for 5-8 minutes if the pasta is fresh, 10-12 minutes if dried. Drain and leave to cool on a damp cloth.

6. Generously butter a gratin dish and fill with alternate layers of pasta, sauce and parmesan, ending up with a layer of parmesan. Melt the remaining butter in a small saucepan and pour over the pasta. Thinly slice the mozzarella and arrange over the top.

7. Bake for 20-25 minutes until the top is golden brown. Serve immediately.

Polenta
Polenta

| | 00:05 | 00:30 to 01:00 |

American	Ingredients	Metric/Imperial
1 quart	Water	1 l / 1¾ pints
2 tsp	Salt	2 tsp
8 oz	Coarse yellow corn meal [polenta]	225 g / 8 oz

1. Bring the water and the salt to a rapid boil. Sprinkle in the corn meal very slowly, stirring all the time with a wooden spoon.
2. When the mixture is thick and smooth, cover the pan and lower the heat. Cook for 30-40 minutes or until the corn meal is coming away from the sides of the saucepan.
3. Polenta can be served soft and very hot, like a purée, accompanied by various garnishes, or with butter and parmesan cheese. Or leave the prepared polenta to cool on a board and it can then be reheated in a variety of ways. Cut into squares, cover with tomato or other sauce and bake in a moderate oven; fry until golden in oil and butter; or try polenta fritters — coated in egg and bread crumbs and deep-fried.

Penne à la diable
Penne with Bacon and Mushroom Sauce

| | 00:30 | 00:45 |

American	Ingredients	Metric/Imperial
¾ lb	Button mushrooms	350 g / 12 oz
6 oz	Bacon	175 g / 6 oz
1 lb	Tomatoes	500 g / 1 lb
1	Fresh basil sprig	1
½	Sweet green or red pepper	½
2	Garlic cloves	2
6 tbsp	Butter	75 g / 3 oz
	Salt and pepper	
1 lb	Penne	500 g / 1 lb
¾ cup	Grated parmesan cheese	75 g / 3 oz

1. Clean the mushrooms and cut into thin slices. Cut the bacon into small strips. Peel the tomatoes (first plunging them into boiling water for 10 seconds) and cut in half. Remove the seeds and chop coarsely. Chop the basil leaves. Remove the seeds and white parts of the pepper and cut the flesh into very thin strips. Peel and crush the garlic.
2. Heat half the butter in a frying pan and brown the bacon for about 5 minutes. Remove with a slotted spoon and set aside.
3. Add the mushrooms to the same pan and cook for 10 minutes or until all the liquid has evaporated. Remove with a slotted spoon and place on one side.
4. Add the pepper and crushed garlic to the pan, cook for 2-3 minutes and then remove with a slotted spoon.
5. Place the tomatoes in the pan, season with salt and pepper and cook over a moderate heat for 20 minutes, stirring from time to time.
6. Return the bacon, mushrooms, pepper and garlic to the pan and add the chopped basil. Keep warm over a low heat.
7. Boil a large cooking pot of salted water and add the penne. Bring back to a boil and cook for about 10 minutes or until 'al

dente' (see page 437). Drain well and place in a warmed serving dish. Sprinkle with the parmesan cheese and dot with the remaining butter. Finally, pour over the sauce and toss just before serving.

Tagliatelle aux cèpes
Tagliatelle with Cèpes

| | 00:15 | 00:25 |

American	Ingredients	Metric/Imperial
1 lb	Fresh cèpes or other mushrooms	500 g / 1 lb
2	Garlic cloves	2
¼ cup	Olive oil	4 tbsp
	Salt and pepper	
1 tbsp	Chopped fresh parsley	1 tbsp
¼ cup	Crème fraîche (see page 122)	4 tbsp
1 lb	Tagliatelle	500 g / 1 lb
½ cup	Grated parmesan cheese	50 g / 2 oz

1. Clean and trim the mushrooms and cut into thin slices. Peel and chop the garlic cloves.
2. Heat the olive oil in a frying pan and cook the mushrooms over a low heat. Season with salt and pepper and add the garlic and the chopped parsley. Cook until all the liquid from the mushrooms has evaporated. Stir in the crème fraîche. Remove from the heat and keep hot.
3. Boil a large cooking pot of salted water. Add the tagliatelle and boil for 5-8 minutes if the pasta is fresh, 10-12 minutes if dried. Drain well and toss with the sauce over a gentle heat.
4. To serve, sprinkle with the grated parmesan cheese.

Macaroni au gratin
Macaroni Cheese

| | 00:20 | 00:20 to 00:25 |

American	Ingredients	Metric/Imperial
	Salt and pepper	
1 tbsp	Oil	1 tbsp
1 lb	Macaroni	500 g / 1 lb
⅔ cup	Crème fraîche (see page 122)	150 ml / ¼ pint
2 cups	Grated gruyère cheese	250 g / 8 oz
	Grated nutmeg	
¼ cup	Butter	50 g / 2 oz

1. Bring to a boil a large quantity of salted water in a cooking pot. Add the oil and the macaroni and cook for about 10 minutes or until 'al dente' (see page 437). Drain well.
2. Preheat the oven to 400°F / 200°C / Gas Mark 6.
3. Put the macaroni in a large saucepan, add the crème fraîche and cook for 6 minutes, stirring from time to time. Remove from the heat and add two-thirds of the grated cheese, salt, if necessary, pepper and a little freshly grated nutmeg. Mix together and place in a gratin dish. Sprinkle with the remaining grated cheese and dot with the butter.
4. Bake for 20-25 minutes until the top is golden brown.

Tagliatelle au basilic
Tagliatelle with Basil Sauce

	00:20	00:05 to 00:12

American	Ingredients	Metric/Imperial
1	Large bunch of fresh basil	1
3	Garlic cloves	3
¼ lb	Mozzarella cheese	125 g / 4 oz
1	Large fresh parsley sprig	1
⅔ cup	Olive oil	150 ml / ¼ pint
	Salt and pepper	
1 lb	Tagliatelle	500 g / 1 lb
¼ cup	Butter	50 g / 2 oz

1. Wash and remove the leaves from the basil. Peel the garlic. Cut the mozzarella into small pieces. Place the basil, parsley, garlic and mozzarella in a mortar or food processor. Crush with a pestle or process these ingredients, adding the olive oil a little at a time. Continue pounding until you have a smooth paste. Season with salt and pepper.
2. Bring a large cooking pot of salted water to a boil and add the tagliatelle. Boil for 5-7 minutes if the pasta is fresh, 10-12 minutes if dried, until 'al dente' (see page 437).
3. Drain, and turn into a deep dish. Add the butter, cut into small pieces, and cover with the basil sauce. Toss together and serve hot.

Spaghetti bolognaise
Spaghetti with Meat Sauce

	00:15	01:00

American	Ingredients	Metric/Imperial
1 lb	Tomatoes	500 g / 1 lb
3	Garlic cloves	3
1	Large onion	1
1	Bunch of fresh parsley	1
2 tbsp	Olive oil	2 tbsp
1 lb	Ground [minced] beef	500 g / 1 lb
	Salt and pepper	
1 lb	Spaghetti	500 g / 1 lb
¼ cup	Butter	50 g / 2 oz
1 ¼ cups	Grated parmesan cheese	150 g / 5 oz

1. Peel the tomatoes (first plunging them into boiling water for 10 seconds) and chop coarsely. Peel and crush the garlic. Peel and slice the onion. Chop the parsley.
2. Heat the olive oil in a saucepan and add the garlic, onion and parsley. Stir over a moderate heat for about 5 minutes. Add the beef and mix together. Cook for about 15 minutes over a low heat then add the tomatoes and season with salt and pepper. Cover and continue cooking over a low heat for 45 minutes until the sauce is thick.
3. About 15 minutes before the end of cooking time for the sauce, bring a large quantity of salted water to a boil in a cooking pot. Add the spaghetti and cook for about 10 minutes until 'al dente' (see page 437).
4. Drain the spaghetti in a colander and place in a large serving dish. Add the butter, cut into small pieces, sprinkle with the parmesan cheese and cover with the sauce. Mix together just before serving.

Raviolis niçoise
Spinach and Beef Ravioli

	00:40	03:00
	plus preparation of pasta	plus marinating

American	Ingredients	Metric/Imperial
1 lb	Lean beef	500 g / 1 lb
3 tbsp	Oil	3 tbsp
5 oz	Bacon	150 g / 5 oz
1 lb	Carrots	500 g / 1 lb
3	Large onions	3
3	Garlic cloves	3
2 lb	Tomatoes	1 kg / 2 lb
2 cups	Red wine	500 ml / ¾ pint
½ cup	Cognac	125 ml / 4 fl oz
	Salt and pepper	
1 lb	Spinach (fresh or frozen)	500 g / 1 lb
1	Egg	1
¾ cup	Grated parmesan cheese	75 g / 3 oz
½ lb	Fresh white pasta (see page 442)	250 g / 8 oz

1. Dice the beef and brown in a heavy saucepan with 1 tablespoon of the oil. Cut the bacon into small strips and add to the pan.
2. Peel the carrots and cut into thin slices. Peel the onions and the garlic and chop finely. Peel the tomatoes (first plunging them into boiling water for 10 seconds). Remove the seeds and cut into pieces. Add all these ingredients to the saucepan and pour in the red wine and the cognac. Season with salt and pepper and simmer gently for about 3 hours. Remove from the heat and leave the mixture to stand for at least 12 hours.
3. The next day, put the mixture through a blender, vegetable mill or food processor.
4. Cut the stems from the spinach and wash thoroughly. Put in a saucepan and cook for 5-8 minutes. Drain well and press to extract all the water. Put through a blender, vegetable mill or food processor. If using frozen spinach, put it straight into a saucepan and cook gently for 15-20 minutes. Add the spinach to the meat mixture along with the egg and the grated parmesan cheese. Mix the ingredients together and adjust the seasoning, if necessary.
5. Divide the pasta into two equal amounts. Roll out each half as thinly as possible using a rolling pin. Place small spoonfuls of the stuffing on one of the layers at regular intervals, about 2 in / 5 cm apart.
6. Cover with the other layer of pasta and press around the stuffing to seal. Cut out 2 in / 5 cm squares using a pastry cutter or small pointed knife to form the ravioli. Pinch the edges very firmly to seal them.
7. Bring a large cooking pot of salted water to a boil. Add the remaining oil to prevent the ravioli from sticking to each other during cooking. Add the ravioli a few at a time. Cook until tender, about 6-8 minutes. During this time the ravioli will rise to the surface. Remove carefully with a slotted spoon and put in a hot serving dish.
8. Serve simply, with butter and grated parmesan cheese, with a cream sauce (see page 128) or with a tomato sauce (see page 123).

Fresh pasta

Timbale de macaroni
Macaroni Casserole

◢	00:20		00:35 🍲

American	Ingredients	Metric/Imperial
½ lb	Cooked ham	250 g / 8 oz
½ lb	Button mushrooms	250 g / 8 oz
1	Garlic clove	1
1 cup	Green olives	125 g / 4 oz
6 tbsp	Butter	75 g / 3 oz
	Salt and pepper	
6	Small pork link sausages [chipolatas]	6
1 lb	Macaroni	500 g / 1 lb
1 cup	Crème fraîche (see page 122)	250 ml / 8 fl oz
1 cup	Grated parmesan cheese	125 g / 4 oz

1. Dice the ham. Clean the mushrooms and cut into thin slices. Peel and crush the garlic. Remove the pits [stones] from the olives and cut them into quarters.
2. Heat 2 tablespoons [25 g / 1 oz] of butter in a frying pan and add the mushrooms, garlic, salt and pepper. Cook for about 15 minutes, or until the liquid from the mushrooms has evaporated.
3. Meanwhile, heat 2 tablespoons [25 g / 1 oz] of butter in another frying pan and cook the sausages for about 10 minutes until brown.
4. Once the mushrooms are cooked, add the olives and diced ham to the pan and leave over a low heat to keep warm.
5. Boil a large cooking pot of salted water and add the macaroni. Boil for about 10 minutes or until the pasta is 'al

dente' (see page 437). Drain well and return to the pot.
6. Add the mushrooms, ham and olives, the crème fraîche, the parmesan cheese and the remaining butter. Mix all the ingredients gently together and adjust the seasoning, if necessary. The dish should have a robust flavor, without being too salty.
7. To serve, pour into a warmed serving dish and garnish with the sausages.

Pâtes fraîches blanches
Fresh Egg Pasta

◢	01:00		00:05 🍲

American	Ingredients	Metric/Imperial
4 cups	Flour	500 g / 1 lb
4	Eggs	4
1 tbsp	Oil	1 tbsp
	Salt	

1. Place the flour on the work surface, make a hollow in the center and add to it the eggs, oil and a pinch of salt. Fold and stir the flour in towards the center with the fingers. Roll into a ball and knead with the heel of your palm for 8-10 minutes. The dough should be smooth and elastic.
2. Process the pasta according to the instructions of your pasta machine. Place the pasta over a rolling pin as you make it and leave to dry for about 30 minutes.
3. To cook the pasta, boil 4 quarts [4 l / 7 pints] of salted water in a saucepan. Add the pasta and cook for about 5 minutes. Drain and prepare it according to taste.

Cook's tip: fresh pasta is delicious, and well worth the trouble of making at home.

Fusilli au basilic
Fusilli with Basil Sauce

◢	00:05		00:15 🍲

American	Ingredients	Metric/Imperial
	Salt and pepper	
1 lb	Fusilli	500 g / 1 lb
2	Garlic cloves	2
1	Bunch of fresh basil	1
3 tbsp	Olive oil	3 tbsp
	A few pine nuts	
½ cup	Grated parmesan cheese	50 g / 2 oz

1. Bring a large saucepan of salted water to a boil. Add the fusilli and bring back to a boil. Cook for 10-12 minutes or until the pasta is 'al dente'.
2. Meanwhile, peel and finely chop the garlic. Wash, dry and chop the fresh basil very finely.
3. Heat the olive oil in a saucepan. Add the garlic, the basil and a few pine nuts. Season with salt and pepper and stir over a low heat.
4. Drain the pasta thoroughly and add to the basil sauce. Stir well so that all the fusilli are covered in the sauce. Add the grated parmesan cheese, toss and serve immediately.

Cook's tip: fresh parsley can be used instead of fresh basil.

5. Preheat the oven to 400°F / 200°C / Gas Mark 6.
6. Spread the cheese and ham mixture onto the rectangles of pasta. Roll up the pasta and seal the sides by pressing together with wet fingers. Arrange the cannelloni in a buttered baking dish and cover with the tomato sauce. Sprinkle with half the parmesan cheese and dot with the remaining butter.
7. Bake for about 20 minutes until the top is golden brown. Serve very hot with the remaining parmesan cheese in a separate dish.

Cannelloni

Cannelloni à la napolitaine
Cannelloni

01:00   00:40

American	Ingredients	Metric/Imperial
4 cups	Flour	450 g / 1 lb
6	Eggs	6
½ tbsp	Oil	½ tbsp
	Salt and pepper	
1 lb	Tomatoes	500 g / 1 lb
2	Fresh basil sprigs	2
¼ cup	Butter	50 g / 2 oz
½ lb	Mozzarella cheese	250 g / 8 oz
2 oz	Smoked ham	50 g / 2 oz
1 cup	Grated parmesan cheese	125 g / 4 oz

1. Place the flour on the work surface. Make a hollow in the center and add 4 of the eggs, the oil and a pinch of salt. Fold the flour in toward the center and stir. Work to a smooth dough then knead until it is elastic and shiny. This will take about 10 minutes. Dip a cloth in warm water and wring it out until almost dry. Wrap the ball of dough in the cloth and leave to rest for 30 minutes.
2. Meanwhile, peel the tomatoes (first plunging them in boiling water for 10 seconds). Remove the seeds and chop roughly. Chop the basil leaves finely. Heat half of the butter in a frying pan and add the tomatoes, basil, salt and pepper. Cook over a gentle heat for 15 minutes, stirring from time to time.
3. Cut the mozzarella into thin slices, and the ham into very thin, short strips. Place in a bowl, season with salt and pepper, and add the remaining eggs. Work the ingredients together carefully until well blended.
4. Roll out the pasta dough with a rolling pin to a thickness of 1/16 in / 2 mm and cut it into 3×4 in / 8×10 cm rectangles. Boil a large quantity of water in a cooking pot. Add 1 tablespoon of salt and then the pasta. Bring back to a boil and cook for about 5 minutes. As soon as the pasta rises to the surface and floats, it is ready. Remove each piece of pasta with a slotted spoon and leave to drain on a damp cloth.

Cravattine au beurre et au fromage
Cravattine with Butter and Cheese

00:00   00:10 to 00:12

American	Ingredients	Metric/Imperial
	Salt and pepper	
1 lb	Cravattine	500 g / 1 lb
¼ cup	Butter	50 g / 2 oz
1 cup	Grated parmesan cheese	125 g / 4 oz

1. Boil a large quantity of salted water in a large cooking pot. Add the cravattine and bring back to a boil. Cook for 10-12 minutes or until the pasta is 'al dente' (see page 437).
2. Drain the cravattine in a colander. Pour into a warmed dish and add the butter and the grated cheese. Mix well, season with pepper and serve very hot. The cheese can also be served separately.

Cook's tip: all pasta can be cooked and served in this way.

Fettuccine vertes aux quatre fromages
Green Fettuccine with Mixed Cheese Sauce

00:10   00:20

American	Ingredients	Metric/Imperial
	Salt	
1 lb	Green fettuccine	500 g / 1 lb
½ lb	Mozzarella cheese	250 g / 8 oz
4 oz	Fontina cheese	125 g / 4 oz
4 oz	Bel Paese cheese	125 g / 4 oz
2 tbsp	Butter	25 g / 1 oz
½ cup	Grated parmesan cheese	50 g / 2 oz
⅔ cup	Crème fraîche (see page 122)	150 ml / ¼ pint

1. Boil a large quantity of salted water in a large cooking pot. Add the fettuccine and cook for 5-8 minutes if the pasta is fresh, 10-12 minutes if dried.
2. Meanwhile, dice the mozzarella, fontina and bel paese cheeses.
3. Drain the fettuccine in a colander. Melt the butter in a saucepan and add the pasta. Add all the cheeses, stir well and then mix in the crème fraîche. Cook over a gentle heat, stirring carefully, until the cheese has melted. Turn the pasta into a hot dish and serve immediately.

Potatoes

Potatoes are to the West what rice is to the East — the major accompaniment for a variety of other foods. The characteristics of the different types of potatoes are important, and you should choose them according to how they are to be cooked. Basically, potatoes can be divided into two groups, those with a waxy flesh and those with a floury texture. The waxy potatoes are good for all those dishes that need a firm texture — potato salads, dauphinoise potatoes (see page 446), boulangère potatoes (see page 448) or potatoes with onion (see page 450). The floury potatoes can be mashed, made into croquettes, baked and stuffed. If you are lucky enough to grow your own, then you can choose from a wide variety which offer different tastes and textures, whereas if you buy commercially grown potatoes, your choice will be very limited. During the last few years the potato fell out of nutritional favor, largely because it was believed to be responsible for weight gain and to have very little food value. Now it is generally recognized that the minerals and vitamins found in potatoes are an important contribution to our diet.

Cook's tips:
1. Ideally potatoes should be boiled in their skins and peeled after they are cooked, to conserve the minerals and Vitamin C which lie just below the skin. If this is not possible, peel them very thinly and reserve the water they are cooked in to use as a basis for soups.
2. Always place potatoes in cold salted water, bring to a boil and reduce the heat to a simmer — fast boiling causes the cells of the potatoes to break up, making them mushy.
3. Some varieties of potato break up very easily when they are boiled and the most successful way of cooking them is by steaming.
4. New potatoes only need wiping or washing before being boiled in their skins, then toss in butter and serve.
5. To make potato purée for savory croquettes, use freshly-cooked floury potatoes — not leftovers which don't have the same flavor and are more difficult to work. Mash the drained and peeled potatoes over a low heat or, for a finer purée, press through a potato rake or sieve, then return to the pan and heat gently to dry if necessary.
6. Cut down the cooking time for baked potatoes by spearing them on metal skewers, called baked potato prongs or spikes.
7. A well-made sauce can add to the flavor and appearance of bland vegetables like potatoes. As well as making them easier

and more enjoyable to eat, it can transform them into an interesting, unusual vegetable dish or a simple lunch or supper. Especially helpful in improving plain potatoes are fresh herbs, white wine, shellfish or cream, or more robust ingredients like garlic, cheese or tomato. The waxy varieties of potato are the best to use as they retain their shape and texture even when cooked in or coated with a sauce.
8. When sautéeing potatoes, the heat should be moderate and the potatoes turned frequently so they cook evenly without becoming over-browned. Never leave them to cook by themselves for they will stick to the pan.

Creamed potatoes with cheese

Aligot

Creamed Potatoes with Cheese

	00:20	00:45
American	**Ingredients**	**Metric/Imperial**
2½ lb	Potatoes	1.25 kg / 2½ lb
	Salt and pepper	
1	Garlic clove	1
1 lb	Soft cantal or gruyère cheese	500 g / 1 lb
⅓ cup	Butter	75 g / 3 oz
3 tbsp	Crème fraîche (see page 122)	3 tbsp

1. Peel and cut up the potatoes. Place in a saucepan, cover with cold, salted water and cook over a brisk heat for 30 minutes.
2. Drain and mash the potatoes. Peel and crush the garlic. Cut the cheese into fine strips.
3. Transfer the mashed potatoes to a thick-bottomed pan over a low heat and add the butter. Mix thoroughly with a wooden spatula. When the butter has melted remove the pan from the heat and add the garlic. Gradually work in the cheese, lifting up the mixture from the bottom of the pan with the spatula so as to draw out the mixture. During this process, which takes 10-15 minutes, return the pan to the heat from time to time.
4. Add the crème fraîche and pepper and continue working the mixture.
5. Serve the potatoes on a hot plate.

Pommes de terre nouvelles au basilic

New Potatoes with Basil

	00:15		01:00

American	Ingredients	Metric/Imperial
3 lb	Small new potatoes	1.5 kg / 3 lb
6	Medium-size onions	6
⅔ cup	Olive oil	150 ml / ¼ pint
3	Garlic cloves	3
3	Fresh basil sprigs	3
2 cups	Bread crumbs	125 g / 4 oz
	Salt and pepper	

1. Scrape or peel the potatoes. Peel and quarter the onions.
2. Heat half the olive oil in a frying pan, add the potatoes and cook gently over a low heat for 30 minutes. When they begin to brown add the onions and cook for a further 30 minutes.
3. Peel the garlic and crush with the basil leaves in a mortar or food processor. Gradually work in the remaining olive oil to produce a thick paste.
4. When the potatoes are golden brown, remove from the pan with a slotted spoon.
5. Tip the bread crumbs into the oil in the frying pan and cook for a few minutes until golden brown.
6. Return the potatoes to the frying pan and add the basil mixture. Stir over the heat for 1 minute. Season with salt and pepper and serve very hot.

Pommes surprises

Spinach Soufflé Potatoes

	00:15		01:50

American	Ingredients	Metric/Imperial
6	Very large potatoes	6
1 lb	Spinach, fresh or frozen	500 g / 1 lb
½ cup	Butter	125 g / 4 oz
	Salt and pepper	
½ cup	Crème fraîche (see page 122)	125 ml / 4 fl oz
	Grated nutmeg	
8	Eggs	8

1. Preheat the oven to 350°F / 180°C / Gas Mark 4.
2. Scrub the potatoes, prick all over and wrap each separately in foil. Bake for 1½ hours.
3. Meanwhile, wash the spinach thoroughly — if using fresh — and remove the stems. Put the leaves in a large pan and cook for about 8 minutes. If using frozen spinach allow 10 minutes extra cooking time to allow the spinach to thaw. Drain well.
4. Chop the spinach, return to the pan and place over a low heat. Add three-quarters of the butter and season with salt and pepper. Cook to evaporate any excess liquid, then remove from the heat.
5. When the potatoes are cooked, open the foil, cut the top off each potato and remove most of the flesh with a teaspoon, taking care not to break the skins. Put the flesh to one side.
6. Fill the bottom of each potato shell with 2 tablespoons of

spinach. Add 1 tablespoon of crème fraîche and a little freshly grated nutmeg to each potato. Season with salt and pepper. Break an egg into each potato and sprinkle with a little salt.
7. Separate the remaining eggs. Mash the potato flesh and mix in the remaining butter and the egg yolks. Beat the egg whites until stiff and fold into the mixture. Season with salt and pepper.
8. Cover each potato with this mixture and arrange in a buttered baking dish. Return to the oven and bake for 20 minutes until the tops are golden brown.

Potato puffs (see page 449)

Soufflé de pommes de terre

Potato Soufflé

	00:25		01:00

American	Ingredients	Metric/Imperial
3 lb	Potatoes	1.5 kg / 3 lb
	Salt and pepper	
2 cups	Milk	500 ml / ¾ pint
⅓ cup	Butter	75 g / 3 oz
1½ cups	Grated gruyère cheese	175 g / 6 oz
6	Eggs, separated	6

1. Peel and cut up the potatoes. Place in a pan, cover with cold salted water and cook over a brisk heat for 30 minutes.
2. Heat the milk. Drain the potatoes, mash and transfer to a mixing bowl. Add the butter and gradually beat in the hot milk, then add the grated cheese. Beat well until completely smooth.
3. Preheat the oven to 350°F / 180°C / Gas Mark 4.
4. Beat the egg yolks into the warm potato mixture, blend thoroughly, and season with pepper.
5. Beat the egg whites until stiff and fold gently into the potato purée with a wooden spoon.
6. Butter a 10 in / 24 cm soufflé dish and pour in the potato mixture. Bake for 15 minutes, then increase the heat of the oven to 425°F / 220°C / Gas Mark 7. Bake for a further 10 minutes and serve immediately.

Potato croquettes

Croquettes de pomme de terre

Potato Croquettes

00:45 plus chilling

00:30 plus 2 minutes frying time per batch

American	Ingredients	Metric/Imperial
2 lb	Potatoes	1 kg / 2 lb
	Salt and pepper	
6 tbsp	Butter	75 g / 3 oz
3	Egg yolks	3
	Grated nutmeg	
	Flour	
2 cups	White bread crumbs	125 g / 4 oz
1	Egg	1
	Oil for deep frying	

1. Peel and cut up the potatoes. Place in a saucepan, cover with cold, salted water and cook over a brisk heat for 30 minutes.
2. Drain and mash the potatoes. Transfer the mashed potato to a saucepan and stir for a few minutes over a moderate heat to evaporate excess moisture.
3. Remove the pan from the heat. Add the butter and 3 egg yolks to the hot mashed potato, working each egg in well before adding the next.
4. Season with salt and pepper and add a pinch of grated nutmeg. Spread the potato mixture on a flat dish and chill in the refrigerator for 1 hour. This will make it easier to handle.
5. Flour a pastry board and knead the potato until completely smooth. Take some of the potato and shape by hand into a sausage. Cut into shorter sausage shapes and repeat until all the potato has been used up.
6. Spread the bread crumbs on a plate. In a bowl beat the whole egg with a pinch of salt. Dip each croquette into the beaten egg and then roll in the bread crumbs. Leave to dry for 10 minutes.
7. Heat the oil to about 340°F / 175°C until it is hot but not smoking. Drop the croquettes into the oil and brown for about 2 minutes.
8. Remove the croquettes with a slotted spoon and place on paper towels. Repeat until you have fried all the croquettes. Keep hot until ready to serve.

Beignets au fromage

Cheese Fritters

00:20

00:35

American	Ingredients	Metric/Imperial
2 lb	Potatoes	1 kg / 2 lb
	Salt and pepper	
1 cup	Milk	250 ml / 8 fl oz
1¾ cups	Grated gruyère or comté cheese	200 g / 7 oz
⅔ cup	Butter	150 g / 5 oz
3	Eggs	3
	Grated nutmeg	
	Oil for deep frying	

1. Peel and cut up the potatoes. Place in a saucepan, cover with cold, salted water and cook over a brisk heat for 30 minutes.
2. Meanwhile gently heat the milk.
3. When the potatoes are cooked, drain and mash them. Transfer to a saucepan and place over a low heat. Add the hot milk, grated cheese and butter and mix well.
4. Stir in the eggs and a pinch of nutmeg and continue beating with a wooden spatula. Season to taste with salt and pepper.
5. Heat the oil to 340°F / 175°C. Take 1 tablespoon at a time of the potato mixture and drop into the oil. Fry for 2-3 minutes until light brown and then remove with a slotted spoon. Drain on paper towels and serve very hot.

Gratin dauphinois

Dauphinois Potatoes

00:25

01:00 to 01:30

American	Ingredients	Metric/Imperial
2 lb	Waxy potatoes	1 kg / 2 lb
1¼ cups	Milk	300 ml / ½ pint
1	Garlic clove	1
	Butter	
2	Eggs	2
⅔ cup	Crème fraîche (see page 122)	150 ml / ¼ pint
	Salt and pepper	
	Grated nutmeg	
1¼ cups	Grated gruyère cheese	150 g / 5 oz

1. Preheat the oven to 350°F / 180°C / Gas Mark 4.
2. Peel the potatoes and wipe dry, then cut into thin slices. Heat the milk.
3. Peel the garlic and rub around the inside of a shallow ovenproof dish. Generously butter the dish.
4. Beat together the eggs, crème fraîche and warm milk. Season with salt and pepper and a little freshly grated nutmeg.
5. Cover the bottom of the dish with a layer of potato, sprinkle with a little grated cheese and moisten with a little of the crème mixture. Repeat until you have used all the ingredients, ending with a layer of cheese.
6. Bake for 1-1½ hours until the potatoes are tender and the top is golden brown.

Cook's tip: an authentic Dauphinois Potatoes contains no gruyère cheese, but this does add extra flavour.

Nid d'oeufs
Egg Nests

	00:15		01:40

American	Ingredients	Metric/Imperial
3	Large potatoes	3
¼ cup	Butter	50 g / 2 oz
	Salt and pepper	
6	Eggs	6

1. Preheat the oven to 425°F / 220°C / Gas Mark 7.
2. Scrub the potatoes, prick all over and wrap each in foil. Bake for 1½ hours.
3. Melt the butter in a small pan over a low heat.
4. When the potatoes are cooked, remove from the oven and cut each potato in half lengthwise. With a small spoon hollow out each potato half to make a nest. Lightly salt the hollow. Break an egg into each nest, season with salt and pepper and sprinkle with the melted butter.
5. Place the nests in an ovenproof dish and return to the oven for a few minutes until the egg whites are firm. Serve immediately.

Pommes allumettes
Matchstick Potatoes

	00:25		00:05 per batch

American	Ingredients	Metric/Imperial
3 lb	Potatoes	1.5 kg / 3 lb
	Oil for deep frying	

1. Peel the potatoes, then cut into slices ⅛ in / 3 mm thick. Place the slices on top of each other a few at a time and cut into sticks about ⅛ in / 3 mm wide.
2. Soak in cold water for 10 minutes and then dry thoroughly on paper towels.
3. Heat the oil for deep frying until hot but not smoking (340°F / 175°C). Tip in some of the sticks of potato and cook for about 5 minutes until golden. Drain and season with salt immediately before serving as an accompaniment to roast game or other roast meats.

Pommes de terre à l'anglaise
Parsleyed Potatoes

	00:20		00:20 to 00:25

American	Ingredients	Metric/Imperial
2 lb	New potatoes	1 kg / 2 lb
	Salt	
½ cup	Butter	125 g / 4 oz
2 tbsp	Chopped fresh parsley	2 tbsp

1. Wash the potatoes but do not peel them. Place them in a saucepan, cover with cold salted water and cook over a brisk heat for 20-25 minutes.
2. Drain the potatoes and peel, if preferred. Place in a hot serving dish. Melt the butter in a small pan. Pour the melted butter over the potatoes and sprinkle with the chopped parsley. Serve immediately.

Hachis Parmentier
Cottage Pie

	00:30		01:00

American	Ingredients	Metric/Imperial
2½ lb	Potatoes	1.25 kg / 2½ lb
	Salt and pepper	
¾ lb	Cooked beef	350 g / 12 oz
5 oz	Cooked ham	150 g / 5 oz
3	Shallots	3
⅔ cup	Beef stock	150 ml / ¼ pint
2 cups	Milk	500 ml / ¾ pint
⅓ cup	Butter	75 g / 3 oz
	Grated nutmeg	
½ cup	Grated gruyère cheese	50 g / 2 oz

1. Preheat the oven to 425°F / 220°C / Gas Mark 7.
2. Peel and cut up the potatoes. Place in a saucepan, cover with cold salted water and cook over a brisk heat for 30 minutes or until the potatoes are soft.
3. Meanwhile, grind [mince] the beef and the ham without removing the fat. Peel and finely chop the shallots and add to the meat. Pour over the beef stock, season with salt and pepper and mix thoroughly.
4. Generously butter a shallow baking dish and spread the meat mixture evenly over the bottom of the dish.
5. Heat the milk. Drain and mash the potatoes. Gradually add the boiling milk, stirring continuously. Beat in the butter and add freshly grated nutmeg, and salt and pepper to taste. Stir thoroughly.
6. Cover the meat with the mashed potato and top with the grated cheese.
7. Bake for about 30 minutes until the pie is really hot and the top is golden brown.

Crique ardéchoise
Ardèche Potato Cakes

	00:20		00:10 per batch

American	Ingredients	Metric/Imperial
6	Large potatoes	6
2	Medium-size onions	2
1	Fresh parsley sprig	1
2 tbsp	Flour	2 tbsp
3	Eggs	3
	Salt and pepper	
	Oil for frying	
⅔ cup	Vinegar or lemon juice	150 ml / ¼ pint

1. Peel and grate the potatoes. Rinse in cold water and dry on paper towels.
2. Peel the onions and cut into thin rings. Chop the parsley.
3. Transfer the grated potato to a bowl and add the parsley, the onion rings, the flour and the eggs. Season with salt and pepper. Stir the mixture then shape into small potato cakes about ½ in / 1 cm thick.
4. Heat some oil in a frying pan until hot. Add several potato cakes and brown on one side, then turn and brown the other side. Drain the cakes on paper towels and keep hot. Repeat until all the potato cakes are cooked.
5. To serve, sprinkle with vinegar or lemon juice.

Galettes de pomme de terre

Creamed Potato Cakes

	00:20		00:35
American	**Ingredients**	**Metric/Imperial**	
1½ lb	Potatoes	750 g / 1½ lb	
	Salt and pepper		
1 cup	Milk	250 ml / 8 fl oz	
3 tbsp	Flour	3 tbsp	
6	Eggs	6	
5 tbsp	Crème fraîche (see page 122)	5 tbsp	
⅔ cup	Butter	150 g / 5 oz	

1. Peel and cut up the potatoes. Place in a saucepan, cover with cold salted water and cook over a brisk heat for 30 minutes. Drain.
2. Heat the milk in a saucepan. Mash the potatoes and add the hot milk. Season with salt and pepper to taste. Mix thoroughly with a wooden spatula and leave to cool.
3. When the potato is cold add the flour and mix well. Then work in the eggs one at a time together with the crème fraîche. Mix thoroughly. Take one tablespoon of the potato mixture at a time and shape into a flat cake.
4. Melt the butter in a frying pan. When the butter is very hot fry the potato cakes for 1 minute each side and serve immediately.

Cook's tip: use a floury variety of potato to make these cakes.

Pommes de terre boulangère

Boulangère Potatoes

	00:25		01:30
American	**Ingredients**	**Metric/Imperial**	
3 lb	Waxy potatoes	1.5 kg / 3 lb	
½	Garlic clove	½	
1	Bay leaf	1	
4	Fresh thyme sprigs	4	
4	Fresh parsley sprigs	4	
¼ cup	Goose fat, beef drippings or lard	50 g / 2 oz	
	Salt and pepper		

1. Peel the potatoes and cut into very thin slices using a sharp knife or mandoline. Rinse under cold water to remove starch and drain in a colander.
2. Peel and crush the garlic. Crumble the bay leaf and thyme and chop the parsley. Mix the garlic and herbs together. Grease the bottom and sides of a shallow flameproof dish with half the fat.
3. Cover the bottom of the dish with one-third of the potatoes. Season with salt and pepper and sprinkle with half the herb mixture.
4. Add another layer of potatoes and season with salt and pepper and the remaining herbs.
5. Cover with the remaining potatoes and season once more.
6. Dot the top with the remaining fat and add hot water to the level of the potatoes.
7. Bring to a boil over a medium heat. Lower the heat and simmer for 1 hour until all the water has evaporated.

8. Preheat the oven to 425°F / 220°C / Gas Mark 7.
9. Put the potatoes in the oven to complete the cooking and to color the top. When the potatoes are golden brown, reduce the heat to 325°F / 160°C / Gas Mark 3 and cook for a further 20 minutes.

Pommes darphin

Baked Potato Cake

	00:20 plus standing time		00:40
American	**Ingredients**	**Metric/Imperial**	
2 lb	Waxy potatoes	1 kg / 2 lb	
6 tbsp	Oil	6 tbsp	
½ cup	Butter	125 g / 4 oz	
	Salt and pepper		

1. Peel the potatoes and leave to stand in cold water for 1 hour. Drain, then cut into fine strips with a coarse grater or mandoline. Dry thoroughly.
2. Preheat the oven to 400°F / 200°C / Gas Mark 6.
3. In the oven heat half the oil in a shallow pan. In a frying pan melt half the butter and then add half the grated potatoes. Season with salt and pepper and stir over a high heat for 5 minutes. Transfer the potatoes to the shallow pan with a slotted spoon. Press down firmly into the pan. Heat the remaining butter in the frying pan and cook the rest of the potatoes in the same way. Add to the shallow pan and press down well.
4. Sprinkle the potatoes with the remaining oil and bake for 20-25 minutes or until golden brown. Turn onto a round dish to serve.

Cook's tip: serve with eggs and bacon for lunch or supper.

Pommes de terre farcies

Potatoes Stuffed with Pork

	00:25		01:00
American	**Ingredients**	**Metric/Imperial**	
2 lb	Medium-size potatoes	1 kg / 2 lb	
1	Garlic clove	1	
2	Shallots	2	
¼ lb	Cooked ham	125 g / 4 oz	
¼ lb	Pork sausage meat	125 g / 4 oz	
1 tsp	Chopped fresh parsley	1 tsp	
	Salt and pepper		
⅓ cup	Butter	75 g / 3 oz	
2 tbsp	Oil	2 tbsp	

1. Peel the potatoes and cut a lid off each.
2. With a small pointed knife carefully remove the inside of each potato, taking care not to cut through the outside. Reserve the inside flesh.
3. Peel the garlic and shallots. Grind [mince] these ingredients in a blender, vegetable mill or food processor with the ham and scooped-out potato.
4. In a mixing bowl work the sausage meat with a fork, then add the ham mixture and season with the chopped parsley and

salt and pepper. Stir well until the mixture is completely smooth.

5. Stuff the potatoes with this mixture. Heat the butter and oil in a flameproof casserole and brown the potatoes for a few minutes. Cover and continue cooking over a low heat for 1 hour. Serve very hot.

Pommes duchesse
Duchesse Potatoes

	00:25		00:40

American	Ingredients	Metric/Imperial
3 lb	Potatoes	1.5 kg / 3 lb
	Salt and pepper	
⅔ cup	Butter	150 g / 5 oz
7	Egg yolks	7
3	Egg whites	3

1. Peel the potatoes. Place in a pan, cover with cold salted water and cook over a brisk heat for 30 minutes.

2. Drain. Mash the potatoes and transfer to a mixing bowl. Add the butter in small pieces and season with salt and pepper to taste.

3. Add six of the egg yolks to the potato mixture. Beat the egg whites until stiff and fold into the mixture.

4. Preheat the oven to 425°F / 220°C / Gas Mark 7.

5. Form the potato mixture into a ball. Flour a pastry board and gently roll out the potato mixture to 2 in / 5 cm thick. Using a small, pointed knife, cut into squares or diamonds.

6. With a pastry brush coat each shape with the remaining egg yolk and transfer to a buttered baking sheet. Bake for 10 minutes and serve hot.

Pommes dauphine
Potato Puffs

	00:15 plus making of choux pastry		00:30 plus 5 minutes per batch

American	Ingredients	Metric/Imperial
2 lb	Potatoes	1 kg / 2 lb
	Salt and pepper	
1 quantity	Choux pastry (see page 457)	1 quantity
	Grated nutmeg	
	Oil for deep frying	

1. Peel and cut up the potatoes. Place in a pan, cover with cold salted water and cook over a brisk heat for 30 minutes. Drain and mash the potatoes.

2. Return the mashed potato to the pan and warm over a low heat for a few minutes to evaporate the excess moisture. Remove from the heat and leave to cool.

3. Mix the choux pastry into the potato, adding two parts pastry mixture to one part potato. Season with salt, pepper and freshly grated nutmeg to taste.

4. Heat the oil to 340°F / 175°C. The oil should be hot but not smoking. Form the potato mixture into balls with a teaspoon and add 5 or 6 balls at a time to the hot oil. The potato balls will double in size in seconds. Drain on paper towels. Repeat until all the potato mixture has been cooked. Serve immediately.

Cook's tip: grated gruyère cheese makes a tasty addition.

Pommes chips
Potato Chips [Crisps]

	00:30		00:08 to 00:12 per batch

American	Ingredients	Metric/Imperial
2 lb	Potatoes	1 kg / 2 lb
	Oil for deep frying	
	Salt	

1. Peel the potatoes and cut into very thin rounds.

2. Place the potato slices in a bowl of cold water to soak for 10 minutes and then drain and dry.

3. Heat the oil until it is hot but not smoking. Add the potato slices a handful at a time and cook until golden brown. Drain and season with salt immediately before serving.

Pommes frites
French Fried Potatoes

	00:25		00:12 to 00:15

American	Ingredients	Metric/Imperial
3 lb	Potatoes	1.5 kg / 3 lb
	Oil for deep frying	
	Salt	

1. Peel the potatoes and cut into slices ½ in / 1 cm thick. Cut each slice into ½ in / 1 cm sticks. Rinse and dry on paper towels.

2. Heat the oil in a deep pan or deep fryer until hot but not smoking. Place the potatoes in the oil and fry until they are cooked but still white.

3. Remove the potatoes from the oil with a slotted spoon and keep warm.

4. Just before serving, reheat the oil and fry the potatoes once more for 2-5 minutes until golden brown. Drain well and sprinkle with salt. Serve immediately.

Pommes sautées
Sauté Potatoes

	00:05		00:45

American	Ingredients	Metric/Imperial
3 lb	Potatoes	1.5 kg / 3 lb
⅔ cup	Oil	150 ml / ¼ pint
3 tbsp	Butter	40 g / 1½ oz
3 tbsp	Chopped fresh mixed herbs	3 tbsp
	Salt	

1. Peel the potatoes. Leave whole if they are very small, otherwise cut into medium-sized slices.

2. Heat the oil in a frying pan.

3. Add the potatoes and cook for about 25 minutes over a low heat until they begin to color. Stir occasionally with a wooden spoon.

4. When they are golden, pour off any excess oil and add the butter. Cover the pan and finish cooking over a very low heat.

5. Serve with the butter from the pan and sprinkle with the chopped fresh herbs (parsley, chives or basil) and salt to taste.

Pommes de terre au lard

Potatoes with Bacon

	00:25	01:00

American	Ingredients	Metric/Imperial
¾ lb	Bacon	350 g / 12 oz
3 lb	Small new potatoes	1.5 kg / 3 lb
2 tbsp	Drippings, lard or oil	25 g / 1 oz

1. Cut the bacon into thick strips. Scrape the new potatoes.
2. Heat the fat or oil in a frying pan and add the potatoes and bacon. Cook over a low heat for 1 hour until golden, but not brown.

Pommes lyonnaise

Potatoes with Onions

	00:20	00:50

American	Ingredients	Metric/Imperial
3 lb	Waxy potatoes	1.5 kg / 3 lb
	Salt and pepper	
½ cup	Butter	125 g / 4 oz
1 tbsp	Oil	1 tbsp
1 lb	Onions	500 g / 1 lb
1 tbsp	Chopped fresh parsley	1 tbsp

1. Wash, but do not peel, the potatoes. Place in a pan, cover with cold salted water and cook over a brisk heat for 30 minutes. Drain and peel the potatoes and slice thinly.
2. Heat half the butter and the oil in a frying pan, add the potatoes and cook gently for about 20 minutes until golden brown.
3. Meanwhile, peel and slice the onions. In another frying pan heat the remaining butter and gently cook the onions for about 15 minutes, without allowing them to brown.
4. When both the potatoes and onions are cooked, add the onions to the the potatoes. Season with salt and pepper and stir over the heat for 2 or 3 minutes.
5. Sprinkle with chopped parsley before serving.

Pommes de terre hongroise

Hungarian Potatoes

	00:15	01:30

American	Ingredients	Metric/Imperial
6	Large, regular-shaped potatoes	6
½ cup	Butter	125 g / 4 oz
1¼ cups	Grated cheddar or similar cheese	150 g / 5 oz
1 tsp	Hungarian paprika	1 tsp
	Salt and pepper	

1. Preheat the oven to 350°F / 180°C / Gas Mark 4.
2. Scrub but do not peel the potatoes. Prick all over. Wrap each potato in foil and bake for 1½ hours.
3. Take the potatoes from the oven and remove the foil. Cut

each potato in half and with a teaspoon remove the flesh without breaking the skin. Put the flesh to one side.
4. In a small pan melt the butter. Add the potato flesh, cheese and paprika and season with salt and pepper. Mix well with a wooden spoon over a low heat.
5. Fill the potato skins with the mixture and garnish each with a pinch of paprika. Place the potatoes on a baking sheet and return to the oven for 5 minutes. Serve at once.

Pommes de terre au four

Baked Potatoes

	00:15	01:00 to 01:30

American	Ingredients	Metric/Imperial
6	Large, regular-shaped potatoes	6
1 cup	Cream cheese (optional)	250 g / 8 oz
	Butter (optional)	
	Salt and pepper	
3 tbsp	Chopped fresh chives	3 tbsp

1. Preheat the oven to 350°F / 180°C / Gas Mark 4.
2. Scrub and dry the potatoes, prick all over and wrap each separately in foil.
3. Bake for 1-1½ hours in the oven (or on the hot coals of a campfire).
4. Remove the potatoes from the oven, unwrap the foil and cut open the potatoes.
5. Garnish with cream cheese or butter if desired, season with salt and pepper and sprinkle with the chopped chives. Serve very hot.

Baked potatoes

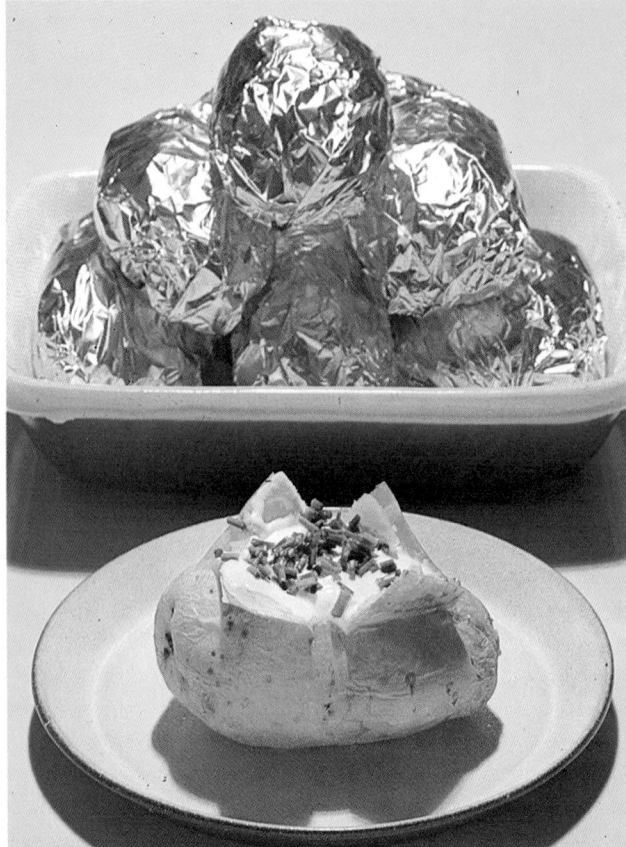

Purée de pommes de terre
Creamed Potatoes

	00:15		00:30

American	Ingredients	Metric/Imperial
3 lb	Potatoes	1.5 kg / 3 lb
	Salt and pepper	
1 cup	Milk	250 ml / 8 fl oz
⅓ cup	Butter	75 g / 3 oz
	Grated nutmeg	
2 tbsp	Crème fraîche (see page 122)	2 tbsp

1. Peel the potatoes and cut into quarters. Place in a pan, cover with cold salted water and cook over a brisk heat for 30 minutes.
2. A few minutes before the end of the cooking time bring the milk to a boil.
3. When the potatoes are cooked, drain and mash them. Add the butter and work in thoroughly, then gradually work in the boiling milk, stirring continuously. Season with salt and pepper and a pinch of nutmeg. Finally, add the crème fraîche and serve immediately.

Pommes vapeur
Steamed Potatoes

	00:20	00:18 to 00:20	

American	Ingredients	Metric/Imperial
3 lb	Potatoes	1.5 kg / 3 lb
	Salt	

1. Peel the potatoes. Leave whole if small, otherwise cut into quarters.
2. Bring some water to a boil in the bottom of a steamer over a high heat.
3. Place the potatoes in the top part of the steamer, cover and cook for about 20 minutes over a high heat.
4. When the potatoes are cooked (the point of a knife should pierce them easily) sprinkle with salt and serve hot, plain, or dotted with butter.

Cook's tip: if you prefer to use a pressure cooker, proceed in the same way, but cook for only 12 minutes from the time the steam begins to escape.

Truffade d'Auvergne
Pan-Fried Potatoes with Cheese

	00:15		00:35

American	Ingredients	Metric/Imperial
1½ lb	Waxy potatoes	750 g / 1½ lb
	Salt and pepper	
⅓ cup	Butter or goose fat	75 g / 3 oz
1½ lb	Tome de cantal or similar cheese	750 g / 1½ lb

1. Peel the potatoes and cut into thin slices. Place on a plate and season with salt and pepper.
2. Heat the fat in a frying pan. Add the potatoes and brown all over, turning with a wooden spatula. Lower the heat and cook for 20 minutes.
3. Cut the cheese into thin slivers, add to the potatoes and turn up the heat to melt the cheese. Stir with the spatula until the potatoes are coated in cheese. Cook for a further 5 minutes until brown and serve immediately.

Râpée stéphanoise
Potato and Egg Cake

	00:15		00:35

American	Ingredients	Metric/Imperial
1	Garlic clove	1
1	Shallot	1
1	Fresh parsley sprig	1
2 lb	Waxy potatoes	1 kg / 2 lb
2	Eggs	2
	Salt and pepper	
¼ cup	Butter	50 g / 2 oz

1. Peel and chop the garlic and shallot. Finely chop the parsley.
2. Peel the potatoes. Grate coarsely, and rinse and dry on paper towels.
3. Put the potato into a bowl. Add the eggs, parsley, garlic, shallots, salt and pepper and mix thoroughly.
4. Heat the butter in a frying pan.
5. Transfer the potato mixture to the frying pan and press down with a fork to form a cake. Cover the pan and cook over a low heat for 20 minutes. When the edges of the potato cake begin to brown, turn the cake over with the aid of a plate or saucepan lid. Cook for a further 15 minutes.

Tian de pommes de terre
Provençal Potatoes

	00:25		00:50

American	Ingredients	Metric/Imperial
2 lb	Potatoes	1 kg / 2 lb
	Salt and pepper	
¾ lb	Onions	350 g / 12 oz
1 lb	Tomatoes	500 g / 1 lb
1¼ cups	Grated gruyère cheese	150 g / 5 oz
1 tbsp	Fresh thyme leaves	1 tbsp
⅔ cup	Olive oil	150 ml / ¼ pint

1. Wash the potatoes, but do not peel. Place in a pan, cover with cold salted water and cook over a brisk heat for 30 minutes. Drain and leave to cool.
2. Peel the potatoes and cut into slices. Peel and chop the onions and slice the tomatoes.
3. Preheat the oven to 425°F / 220°C / Gas Mark 7.
4. In a shallow, ovenproof dish arrange alternate layers of potato, tomato, onion and cheese, sprinkling each layer with salt, pepper and thyme. Top with a layer of tomatoes sprinkled with cheese and thyme.
5. Moisten with the olive oil and bake for about 20 minutes until the top is golden brown.

CHAPTER 15

Desserts, Cakes and Pastries

Creams and basic pastries

Crème aux amandes
Almond Custard

	00:30	00:15 to 00:20

plus cooling and chilling
Makes about 1 quart 1 l / 1¾ pints

American	Ingredients	Metric/Imperial
1¼ cups	Milk	300 ml / ½ pint
¾ cup	Sugar	150 g / 5 oz
½ cup	Ground almonds	50 g / 2 oz
	Vanilla extract [essence]	
6	Egg yolks	6
1¼ cups	Butter	300 g / 10 oz

1. Put the milk and sugar in a saucepan and bring to a boil, stirring to dissolve the sugar. Add the ground almonds and a few drops of vanilla and warm over a very low heat for 2-3 minutes.
2. Place the egg yolks in a deep bowl and pour in the milk, stirring continuously.
3. Pour the mixture back into the pan and cook over a very low heat, stirring continuously. When the custard is thick enough to coat a spoon, remove the pan from the heat and leave to cool.
4. Whisk in the butter, a little at a time, and chill the custard until set.

Crème Chiboust
Alternative Filling for Saint-Honoré

	00:30	00:06

plus chilling
Makes enough to fill a Saint-Honoré cake
to serve 6-8 (see page 498)

American	Ingredients	Metric/Imperial
½	Vanilla bean [pod]	½
1 cup	Milk	250 ml / 8 fl oz
3	Eggs, separated	3
½ cup	Sugar	125 g / 4 oz
¼ cup	Cornstarch [cornflour]	25 g / 1 oz
2 tbsp	Water	2 tbsp
1	Egg white	1

1. Split the half vanilla bean. Put it in a saucepan with the milk and bring to a boil.
2. In a bowl mix egg yolks with 2 tablespoons [25 g / 1 oz] of the sugar and the cornstarch. Remove the vanilla bean from the milk and gradually pour the boiling milk onto the egg yolks, whisking vigorously. Return to the pan and stir over a low heat for 1 minute to thicken the custard. Remove from the heat and cover the pan to keep the custard warm.
3. Put the remaining sugar in a small pan with the water. Bring to a boil and boil for 5 minutes.
4. Beat the 4 egg whites until stiff. Pour the sugar syrup in a slow trickle onto the egg whites, beating vigorously. When all

the syrup has been incorporated, add the hot custard and mix quickly together with a wooden spoon. Continue stirring until completely cold.

Crème anglaise
Vanilla Custard Sauce

	00:05	00:15

plus cooling   Makes about 1 quart 1 l / 1¾ pints

American	Ingredients	Metric/Imperial
1 quart	Milk	1 l / 1¾ pints
1	Vanilla bean [pod] or	1
	Vanilla extract [essence]	
	Salt	
8 - 10	Egg yolks	8 - 10
¾ cup	Superfine [caster] sugar	150 g / 5 oz

1. Place the milk in a saucepan and add the vanilla bean, cut in half lengthwise, or a few drops of vanilla extract, and a pinch of salt. Bring to a boil, then remove from the heat and leave to infuse.
2. Beat together the egg yolks and sugar until the mixture becomes pale. Remove the vanilla bean from the milk and gradually whisk the milk into the eggs. Pour the mixture back into the pan and cook over a low heat for about 10 minutes, stirring constantly. On no account allow the custard to boil.
3. As soon as the custard is thick enough to coat a spoon, remove the pan from the heat and leave to cool, stirring from time to time to prevent a skin forming.

Cook's tip: if you are afraid of the custard separating, beat 1 teaspoon of flour or cornstarch [cornflour] with the egg yolks. This custard is the basis of many desserts and ice creams (see pages 463 and 511, 515).

Crème au caramel
Caramel Buttercream

	00:35	00:15

plus chilling

American	Ingredients	Metric/Imperial
1 cup	Sugar	250 g / 8 oz
¼ cup	Water	4 tbsp
1 cup	Heavy [double] cream	250 ml / 8 fl oz
1 cup	Butter	250 g / 8 oz

1. Put the sugar in a thick-based saucepan with the water. Heat, stirring to dissolve the sugar, then stop stirring. Cook over a moderate heat for 6-8 minutes until you have a golden syrup.
2. Pour the cream into a mixing bowl and slowly add the caramel, whisking continuously. Pour the mixture back into the pan and cook over a low heat for 10 minutes, stirring occasionally, until a little of the mixture dropped into cold water will form a small, fairly firm ball between the fingers.
3. In a mixing bowl, cream the butter with a wooden spoon until softened. Vigorously beat the caramel cream into the butter until smooth. Leave to cool, then chill until ready to serve.

Cook's tip: serve with a sponge cake (page 492), almond slices (page 500), meringues (page 494) or lady fingers [sponge fingers] (page 480).

Caramel

Caramel

	00:05	00:06 to 00:08

Makes enough to coat a 7 in / 18 cm mold

American	Ingredients	Metric/Imperial
½ cup	Sugar	125 g / 4 oz
¼ cup	Water	4 tbsp
1 tbsp	Wine vinegar	1 tbsp

1. Put the sugar into a small, thick-based pan and add the water. Bring to a boil, stirring to dissolve the sugar. Stop stirring and, watching carefully, cook until the syrup turns golden, or brown, depending on how you prefer it. On no account allow it to turn black or it will taste burnt and will be unusable.
2. Remove the pan from the heat and add the wine vinegar. This will stop any further cooking.
3. Tip the caramel into the mold and tilt the mold quickly until the bottom and sides are completely covered.

Cook's tip: for a more runny caramel which can be served as a sauce, dilute with a little hot water after adding the vinegar.

Crème au beurre

Buttercream

	00:15	00:06

plus chilling
Makes enough to cover a cake to serve 6

American	Ingredients	Metric/Imperial
4	Egg yolks	4
⅔ cup	Sugar	150 g / 5 oz
¼ cup	Water	4 tbsp
1 cup	Butter, at room temperature	250 g / 8 oz
	Vanilla extract [essence]	
¾ cup	Cocoa powder (optional)	75 g / 3 oz

1. Beat the egg yolks in a mixing bowl.
2. Put the sugar and water in a saucepan and heat, stirring to dissolve the sugar. Stop stirring and cook for about 6 minutes or until a drop of syrup forms a bead when dropped into cold water.
3. Pour the syrup in a fine stream into the egg yolks, beating vigorously. Continue beating until completely cold.
4. Add the butter a little at a time and continue to beat until the cream is smooth. Finally add vanilla to taste. Chill well.
5. If preferred, the cream can be flavored with cocoa. Dissolve the cocoa in a little hot water before adding to the cream.

Crème Chantilly

Chantilly Cream

	00:20	00:00

plus chilling

American	Ingredients	Metric/Imperial
2 cups	Thin crème fraîche (see page 122)	500 ml / ¾ pint
½ cup	Confectioners' [icing] sugar	50 g / 2 oz
	Vanilla extract [essence]	

1. The whole secret of this recipe's success lies in the correct temperature of the cream: place the crème fraîche in the bowl in which you intend to whip it, in the refrigerator 2 hours in advance.
2. Whip the cream gently until it doubles in volume and sticks to the blades of the beater. Do not whip too quickly or you risk turning the cream into butter.
3. With a wooden spoon slowly stir in the sugar, then a few drops of vanilla and mix well.
4. Chill until ready to serve.

Cook's tip: if you prefer to use thick crème fraîche, add some very cold milk (allowing 5 tablespoons milk to 1 cup [250 ml / 8 fl oz] crème fraîche).

Crème au kirsch

Kirsch Custard

	00:20	00:10

plus cooling

American	Ingredients	Metric/Imperial
1 quart	Milk	1 l / 1¾ pints
1	Vanilla bean [pod]	1
	Salt	
6	Egg yolks	6
1 cup	Flour	125 g / 4 oz
1 cup	Sugar	250 g / 8 oz
½ quantity	Chantilly cream (see page 455)	½ quantity
¼ cup	Kirsch	4 tbsp

1. Bring the milk to a boil with the halved vanilla bean and a pinch of salt. Remove from the heat and leave to infuse.
2. Meanwhile, beat the egg yolks with the flour and sugar. Remove the vanilla bean from the milk, and beat the milk into the egg yolk mixture. Return to the milk pan.
3. Return to a gentle heat and bring to a boil, stirring until the custard thickens.
4. Strain the custard into a bowl. Grease a piece of foil with butter and place on the surface of the custard to prevent a skin forming.
5. Just before serving fold in the chantilly cream and kirsch.

Crème au café

Baked Coffee Creams

	00:10	00:20

plus chilling

American	Ingredients	Metric/Imperial
3	Eggs	3
3	Egg yolks	3
⅔ cup	Superfine [caster] sugar	150 g / 5 oz
3 tbsp	Heavy [double] cream	500 ml / ¾ pint
5 tsp	Instant coffee powder	5 tsp
⅔ cup	Boiling water	150 ml / ¼ pint
2 cups	Milk	500 ml / ¾ pint

1. Preheat the oven to 325°F / 160°C / Gas Mark 3.
2. In a bowl beat together the eggs, yolks, sugar and cream.
3. Dissolve the coffee in the boiling water. Add the milk and slowly pour into the egg mixture, stirring continuously.
4. Pour into 6 ramekin dishes and place them in a shallow pan containing hot, but not boiling, water. Bake for about 20 minutes or until the cream has set.
5. Leave to cool, then chill for 1 hour before serving.

Crème pour choux au chocolat

Chocolate Custard for Choux Buns

	00:25		00:10

plus cooling
Makes enough to fill 12 large choux buns
(see choux pastry, page 457 and profiteroles, page 496)

American	Ingredients	Metric/Imperial
1 quart	Milk	1 l / 1¾ pints
4	Eggs, separated	4
2	Egg yolks	2
1 cup	Superfine [caster] sugar	250 g / 8 oz
¾ cup	Cornstarch [cornflour]	75 g / 3 oz
2 tsp	Unflavored gelatin	4 tsp
	Salt	
7 oz	Semisweet [plain] chocolate	200 g / 7 oz

1. Bring the milk to a boil.
2. Cream the 6 egg yolks with the sugar and cornstarch until the mixture is pale. Gradually add the boiling milk, whisking continuously.
3. Return the mixture to the milk pan. Return the pan to the heat and cook gently, stirring, for 2-3 minutes or until the custard begins to simmer. Remove the pan from the heat. Dissolve the gelatin in a little water. Stir into the custard until smooth.
4. Add a pinch of salt to the 4 egg whites and beat until very stiff. Fold gently into the custard.
5. Break the chocolate into small pieces. Place in a thick-bottomed pan with a tablespoon of milk or water and stir over a low heat until melted. Leave to cool, then stir into the custard.

Cook's tip: chocolate custard can also be served as a dessert. Chill in the refrigerator for several hours and top each serving with a spoonful of crème fraîche.

Crème moka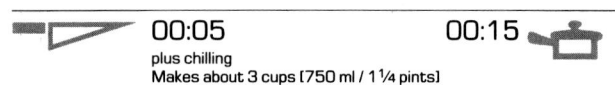

Chilled Mocha Creams

	00:20		00:10

plus cooling

American	Ingredients	Metric/Imperial
¼ cup	Cornstarch [cornflour]	25 g / 1 oz
1¼ cups	Cold milk	300 ml / ½ pint
1 cup	Very strong coffee	250 ml / 8 fl oz
¼ cup	Sugar	50 g / 2 oz
	Vanilla extract [essence]	
½ cup	Crème fraîche (see page 122)	125 ml / 4 fl oz
2 tbsp	Confectioners' [icing] sugar	2 tbsp
6	Sugar coffee beans	6

1. In a saucepan, whisk the cornstarch gently into the cold milk. Gradually whisk in the cold coffee and the sugar. Bring to a boil, stirring continuously. Add a few drops of vanilla and continue boiling for a few seconds. Allow to cool.
2. Meanwhile whip the very cold crème fraîche in a chilled bowl. Add the confectioners' sugar and continue whipping until it doubles in volume. Set aside in the refrigerator.
3. Divide the coffee cream between 6 individual glasses and chill until ready to serve.
4. Decorate with the whipped crème fraîche and the sugar coffee beans.

Crème pâtissière

Pastry Cream or Confectioner's Custard

	00:05		00:15

plus chilling
Makes about 3 cups (750 ml / 1¼ pints)

American	Ingredients	Metric/Imperial
2 cups	Milk	500 ml / ¾ pint
½ cup	Flour	50 g / 2 oz
3	Egg yolks	3
1	Egg	1
6 tbsp	Sugar	75 g / 3 oz
3 tbsp	Kirsch or rum or	3 tbsp
1 tsp	Vanilla extract [essence]	1 tsp

1. Set ⅔ cup [150 ml / ¼ pint] of the milk to one side and bring the rest to a boil.
2. Put the flour in a mixing bowl and beat in the egg yolks, whole egg and sugar. Gradually add the reserved milk, stirring.
3. When the mixture is smooth and creamy, stir in the boiled milk and return the mixture to the saucepan. Place over a low heat and cook, stirring continuously, until the cream is thick.
4. Add the kirsch (or rum or vanilla) and chill.

Cook's tip: pastry cream is used for a variety of desserts: cakes, tarts, fruit, pastries, etc.

Meringue italienne

Italian Meringue

	00:06		00:20

American	Ingredients	Metric/Imperial
⅔ cup	Superfine [caster] sugar	150 g / 5 oz
2 tbsp	Water	2 tbsp
	Vanilla extract [essence]	
3	Egg whites	3

1. Put the sugar in a small pan and add the water and a few drops of vanilla. Cook over a moderate heat for 5 minutes until you have a thick, but still fluid, syrup.
2. Beat the egg whites until stiff. Slowly trickle the boiling sugar syrup into the egg whites and continue beating until the mixture is almost cold.

Cook's tip: Italian meringue can be served with chantilly cream. It is also an important ingredient for iced soufflés.

Pâte d'amandes

Almond Paste

	00:10		00:00

American	Ingredients	Metric/Imperial
2 cups	Confectioners' [icing] sugar	250 g / 8 oz
1¾ cups	Ground almonds	200 g / 7 oz
1	Egg white	1

1. In a mixing bowl, stir together the sugar and ground almonds.

2. With a fork beat the egg white for 10 seconds, then add to the sugar and almonds and stir thoroughly with a wooden spoon until the paste is smooth.

Pâte brisée
Basic Short Pastry

	00:15		00:00
	plus chilling		
	Makes enough to line a 10 in / 25 cm pan		

American	Ingredients	Metric/Imperial
½ cup	Butter	125 g / 4 oz
2 cups	Flour	250 g / 8 oz
2 tbsp	Sugar	25 g / 1 oz
	Salt	
1	Egg yolk	1
½ cup	Water	5 tbsp

1. Cut the butter into small pieces and leave to soften. Sift the flour into a mixing bowl, make a well in the center and into the well put the sugar, a pinch of salt, the egg yolk and the cold water. Work quickly together. Incorporate the softened butter into the pastry without over-working it. Roll into a ball and leave to chill in the refrigerator for 1 hour.
2. When the pastry is ready for use, roll it out to ¼ in / 5 mm thick and fold in three. Repeat the rolling and folding process twice more as for puff pastry (see page 458). This will make the pastry smooth and supple.
3. If you are making pastry for a savory pie omit the sugar, use only 6 tbsp [75 g / 3 oz] butter and work the pastry with the palm of your hand until supple. Leave to stand. Pastry made like this is better for longer baking times.

Cook's tip: use as little flour as possible when rolling out.

Glaçage au fondant
Fondant Icing

	00:15		00:05
	Makes enough to ice a cake to serve 6		

American	Ingredients	Metric/Imperial
½ cup	Sugar	125 g / 4 oz
⅓ cup	Water	75 ml / 3 fl oz
¾ lb	Fondant	350 g / 12 oz
	Food coloring (red, green, yellow)	
	Cocoa powder	

1. Put the sugar and water in a pan and bring to a boil, then remove from the heat and leave to cool.
2. Place the fondant in a heatproof bowl and put over a pan half filled with water. Heat until the fondant melts, adding the sugar syrup very gradually until the fondant is warm and supple.
3. Stir in a few drops of food coloring. Add it a drop at a time to avoid giving the icing too deep a color.
4. Spread the icing over the cake with a metal spatula. (If you are icing small choux buns, dip them directly into the icing and smooth the surface with your finger.)
5. For chocolate icing, gradually add cocoa powder to the fondant along with the syrup. For coffee icing, dissolve 2 teaspoons of instant coffee in 2 teaspoons boiling water. Gradually add to the fondant with the syrup.

Pâte à brioche
Brioche Dough

	00:40		00:30
	plus rising		

American	Ingredients	Metric/Imperial
⅔ cup	Milk	5 tbsp
1 tbsp	Sugar	1 tbsp
1 package	Active dry yeast	½ sachet
⅔ cup	Butter	150 g / 5 oz
2¾ cups	Flour	300 g / 11 oz
5	Eggs	5
½ tsp	Salt	½ tsp

1. Warm the milk in a small saucepan and add ½ teaspoon of the sugar. Remove from the heat. Dissolve the yeast in the milk, and leave in a warm place for 15 minutes or until frothy.
2. Cream the butter with a wooden spoon until pale.
3. Sift the flour into a mixing bowl. Make a well in the center and pour in the milk and yeast mixture. Add the butter, 4 of the eggs, the remaining sugar and the salt. Work all the ingredients together thoroughly and shape the dough into a ball.
4. Knead the dough for about 20 minutes or until smooth and elastic. Leave in a warm place to rise for 6 hours or until doubled in bulk.
5. Punch down the dough to knock out the air, and knead again briefly.
6. Preheat the oven to 425°F / 220°C / Gas Mark 7.
7. To make a large brioche, take one-quarter of the dough and shape it into a ball with a 'tail'. Shape the remaining dough into a larger ball and place it in a buttered brioche mold. With your thumb, make a hole in the center of the dough in the mold, and place the smaller ball in it, tail downwards. Brush the surface with the remaining egg, beaten.
8. Bake for 30 minutes.

Cook's tip: the dough will keep well in the refrigerator, wrapped in foil. Allow the dough to come back to room temperature before using it.

Pâte à choux
Choux Pastry

	00:20		00:10
	Makes 15 choux buns or éclairs		

American	Ingredients	Metric/Imperial
1½ cups	Water	250 ml / 8 fl oz
1 tbsp	Superfine [caster] sugar (for sweet choux)	1 tbsp
	Salt	
5 tbsp	Butter	65 g / 2½ oz
1¼ cups	Flour	125 g / 5 oz
4	Eggs	4

1. Pour the water into a large saucepan and add the sugar (if using), a pinch of salt and the butter. Warm the liquid until the butter has melted, then raise the heat and bring the mixture to a boil. When the liquid rises in the pan remove immediately from the heat and tip in the flour all at once.
2. Beat with a wooden spoon until smooth, then return the pan to the heat and stir gently for ½-1 minute.
3. When the pastry comes away from the sides of the pan, remove from the heat once more. Thoroughly beat in the eggs one at a time. The dough should be shiny and should just fall from the spoon.

Crêpe batter

Pâte feuilletée quatre tours

Puff Pastry

	01:30 to 02:00	00:00
	including chilling Makes about 2 lb / 1 kg	

American	Ingredients	Metric/Imperial
4 cups	Flour	500 g / 1 lb
2 tsp	Salt	2 tsp
1½ cups	Water	250 ml / 8 fl oz
1¾ cups	Butter	400 g / 14 oz

1. The quantity of butter used for puff pastry can vary considerably, from equal quantities flour and butter to one-third the weight of flour. The more butter you use, the richer the pastry.
2. Sift the flour onto the worktop. Make a well in the center and into it tip the salt, the water and one eighth of the butter. Chill the remaining butter. Mix together into a smooth, firm pastry. Roll into a ball and chill for 30 minutes.
3. Roll out the pastry into a round about ¾ in / 2 cm thick. In the center place the remaining butter, cut into small pieces. Flatten the butter with the rolling pin, avoiding touching it with your hands, until it is spread thickly over the pastry.
4. Fold the pastry into three over the butter (stretching it a little if necessary) and seal the edges with the rolling pin.
5. Roll out again to ensure that the butter is evenly distributed. Fold into three and roll out into a rectangle. Fold the pastry into three once again. Turn the pastry a quarter turn to the right and again roll out into a rectangle. Fold in three again. You have now completed 2 turns, so make 2 finger marks in the pastry to remind yourself.

6. Return the pastry to the refrigerator and chill for 10-20 minutes, then remove it and repeat the rolling out, folding and turning as before. You have now completed 4 turns. (If you are not using the pastry immediately, it will keep for 6 days in the refrigerator or 2 months in the freezer, wrapped in foil or a plastic bag.)
7. Before using frozen pastry, thaw for 12 hours in the refrigerator in its wrapper, or for 3 hours at room temperature.
8. The more turns you give your puff pastry, the finer it will be. It may be as many as 6 (for very fine pastry), and is never less than 4, as for croissants.

Pâte à crêpes

Crêpe Batter

	00:10	00:03
	plus standing time Makes 15 crêpes	per crêpe

American	Ingredients	Metric/Imperial
3	Eggs	3
2 cups	Flour	250 g / 8 oz
2½ cups	Milk (or half milk and half beer)	500 ml / ¾ pint
2 tbsp	Oil	2 tbsp
	Salt	
3 tbsp	Rum, Grand Marnier or Cointreau	3 tbsp
3 tbsp	Warm water	3 tbsp
	Butter for frying	

1. Beat the eggs in a mixing bowl or in a blender or food processor. Add the flour. Beat until smooth then gradually beat in the milk (or milk and beer), the oil and a pinch of salt.
2. Leave the batter to stand for at least 2 hours, then add the rum or orange liqueur.
3. When you are ready to cook the crêpes, thin the batter with the warm water so that it is runny enough to cover the bottom of the pan immediately.
4. Put a pat of butter in a crêpe or frying pan and heat. Pour a ladle of batter into the pan and tip so that the batter is thinly spread. Cook for 2 minutes or until golden brown on the underside, then turn with a spatula and brown the other side. Slide the crêpe out of the pan and repeat with the remaining batter.

Cook's tip: crêpes can be cooked in advance. Wrapped in foil they will keep well in the refrigerator for 2-3 days. The batter itself will keep up to 24 hours in the refrigerator. Take care to store it in a container with a tight lid.

Praline aux amandes

Almond Praline

	00:05	00:25 to 00:30
	plus cooling	

American	Ingredients	Metric/Imperial
1 cup	Sugar	250 g / 8 oz
¼ cup	Water	4 tbsp
1¼ cup	Whole almonds	150 g / 5 oz

1. Place the sugar and water in a heavy-based saucepan and bring to a boil, stirring to dissolve the sugar. Stop stirring and boil over moderate heat until the syrup reaches 248°F / 120°C. This will take about 5 minutes.

2. Remove from the heat and add the nuts. Stir until the syrup starts to turn grainy. Return to the heat and cook, stirring, until the mixture becomes white and hardened. Continue cooking, stirring, until the crystallized syrup becomes liquid again. Cook for 10-15 minutes or until the syrup is a dark caramel color. Do not let the caramel burn or it will be bitter.

3. Remove the pan from the heat and pour the mixture onto an oiled marble or formica surface. Allow to cool completely, when the mixture will be totally hard.

4. Break up the praline and put it into a blender or food processor. Blend to a coarse powder, but not too fine. Store the praline in an airtight container.

Crème pour Paris-Brest

Praline Cream for Paris-Brest

	00:20		00:05
	Makes enough to fill a Paris-Brest (see page 492)		

American	Ingredients	Metric/Imperial
½ cup	Superfine [caster] sugar	125 g / 4 oz
3 tbsp	Water	3 tbsp
2	Egg whites	2
½ cup	Butter at room temperature	125 g / 4 oz
⅓ cup	Ground praline (see page 458)	65 g / 2 oz

1. Put the sugar in a pan and add the water. Bring to a boil, stirring to dissolve the sugar, and cook for 5 minutes until a drop of syrup forms a bead in cold water.

2. Beat the egg whites until very stiff. Trickle the boiling sugar syrup slowly onto the egg whites, beating vigorously. When all the syrup has been incorporated, continue beating until completely cold.

3. Cream the butter with the praline. Blend with the egg whites until completely smooth. Transfer the mixture to an icing bag and use to fill the Paris-Brest.

Pâte à beignets

Sweet Fritter Batter

	00:10		00:05
	plus standing time Makes 20 fritters (2 lb / 1 kg fruit)		per batch of fritters

American	Ingredients	Metric/Imperial
3 tbsp	Butter	40 g / 1 ½ oz
3	Eggs	3
	Salt	
2 cups	Flour	250 g / 8 oz
2 tbsp	Sugar	2 tbsp
	Vanilla extract [essence]	
1 ½ cups	Milk	250 ml / 8 fl oz
⅔ cup	Beer	150 ml / ¼ pint
3 tbsp	Rum or Grand Marnier (optional)	3 tbsp
2	Egg whites	2

1. Melt the butter. In a mixing bowl, beat together the whole eggs, a pinch of salt, the flour, melted butter, sugar and a few drops of vanilla.

2. Gradually add the milk and beer. The batter should be runny. Leave the batter to stand for 2 hours.

3. Just before use, add the rum or Grand Marnier if used. Beat the egg whites until stiff and fold into the batter.

Cook's tip: for a savory batter for meat or vegetables, omit the sugar, vanilla and rum.

Pâte à foncer

Rich Egg Pastry

	00:20		00:00
	plus standing time Makes enough to line a 10 in / 25 cm pan		

American	Ingredients	Metric/Imperial
2 cups	Flour	250 g / 8 oz
¼ cup	Superfine [caster] sugar	50 g / 2 oz
2	Eggs	2
½ tsp	Salt	½ tsp
7 tbsp	Butter	100 g / 3 ½ oz

1. Sift the flour onto the worktop and make a well in the center. Into the well put the sugar, beaten eggs, a pinch of salt and the butter, cut into small pieces. Work the ingredients together with your fingertips, gradually adding cold water until you obtain a smooth, supple pastry. The pastry is best if left to stand for 30 minutes at this stage, although it can be used immediately if necessary.

2. Roll out the pastry to about ¼ in / 5 mm thick. Use to line a buttered and floured pan, then chill for 30 minutes to prevent the pastry shrinking during cooking. Prick the bottom of the pastry case with a fork before filling.

Cook's tip: this pastry is suitable for 2 crust pies or flans. It can be used with fruits such as apples, plums, apricots.

Pâte à frire

Frying Batter

	00:10		00:05

	plus standing time	Makes 15 fritters	
American	**Ingredients**	**Metric/Imperial**	

American	Ingredients	Metric/Imperial
1 ¼ cups	Flour	150 g / 5 oz
1 tbsp	Oil	1 tbsp
	Salt	
½ cup	Water	4 tbsp
1	Egg white (from a large egg)	1
	Oil for deep frying	

1. Sift the flour into a mixing bowl and make a well in the center. Add the oil, a pinch of salt and the water. Beat thoroughly and leave to stand for 2 hours.

2. Beat the egg white until very stiff and gently fold into the batter.

3. Heat the oil for frying until hot but not smoking (340°F / 175°C). Add the fritters a few at a time and fry until golden.

Cook's tip: to check the temperature of the frying oil, drop in 1 teaspoon of batter. If it sticks to the bottom of the pan the oil is not hot enough. If it turns golden and rises to the top immediately the oil is too hot. If the batter takes 30 seconds to rise, the oil is the right temperature. All modern deep-fat fryers can be set at the required temperature.

Sabayon
Sabayon

00:05   **00:20 to 00:25**

American	Ingredients	Metric/Imperial
7	Egg yolks	7
1 cup	Superfine [caster] sugar	250 g / 8 oz
1 cup	Fortified wine such as port, marsala, madeira or sherry	200 ml / ⅓ pint

1. Place a saucepan or heatproof mixing bowl over a larger pan containing water. The water should be hot but not boiling. Place the egg yolks in the pan or bowl, add the sugar and beat until the egg becomes pale and the mixture runs off the beater in a continuous stream.
2. Remove the pan from the heat and continue to beat, gradually incorporating the wine, until the mixture becomes thick and frothy.
3. Turn the cream into individual glasses and serve immediately with madeleines (see page 491) or almond cookies [biscuits] (see page 500).

Pâte à fougasse
Yeast Dough

01:00
plus rising
Makes 2 lb / 1 kg dough   **00:10 to 00:12** (for rolls)

American	Ingredients	Metric/Imperial
1¼ cups	Milk	150 ml / ¼ pint
¼ cup	Sugar	50 g / 2 oz
2 packages	Active dry yeast	1 sachet
4 cups	Flour	500 g / 1 lb
1 tsp	Salt	1 tsp
3	Eggs	3
¾ cup	Butter	150 g / 5 oz

1. Warm half the milk in a small pan and add ½ teaspoon of sugar. Remove from the heat and dissolve the yeast in the liquid. Set aside in a warm place for 15 minutes or until frothy.
2. Sift one-quarter of the flour into a mixing bowl. Make a well in the center and pour in the yeast mixture. Mix together and form into a ball. Leave in a warm place to rise until the dough has doubled in bulk (about 20 minutes).
3. Sift the remaining flour onto a worktop and make a well in the center. Add the salt, remaining sugar and 2 of the eggs to the well. Work the ingredients together, moistening with the remaining milk, then add the yeast mixture. Knead the dough by lifting it, folding it back on itself and stretching it in the air, until it no longer sticks to your hands.
4. Soften the butter so it has the same consistency as the dough. Add it one-third at a time to the dough. Work each third in well before adding the next.
5. When the dough is smooth, roll it into a ball, place in a deep bowl and cover with a towel. Leave to rise in a warm place for 5-6 hours.
6. Punch down the dough to knock out the air. It is now ready.
7. To make small rolls, shape the dough into fingers, 3 in / 7 cm long and 1 in / 3 cm in diameter and arrange on a greased baking sheet, allowing space for them to spread. Leave in a warm place to rise for 1 hour or until the rolls have doubled in size. Brush with beaten egg, cut slits across the top and bake in a preheated 450°F / 230°C / Gas Mark 8 oven for 15 minutes.

Pâte sablée
Rich Flan Pastry

00:15
plus chilling
Makes enough to line a 10 in / 25 cm pan   **00:25**

American	Ingredients	Metric/Imperial
½ cup	Butter	125 g / 4 oz
6 tbsp	Superfine [caster] sugar	75 g / 3 oz
1	Egg yolk	1
	Salt	
	Vanilla extract [essence]	
2 cups	Flour	250 g / 8 oz

1. Cut the butter into small pieces and leave in a warm place to soften.
2. Place the sugar in a mixing bowl. Mix in the egg yolk, then add the softened butter, a pinch of salt and a drop of vanilla. Mix together, then add the flour. Quickly work all the ingredients together with your hands. Form into a ball and chill for 1 hour.
3. Roll out the dough and fold in three. Repeat the process twice more. This makes the pastry smooth and supple. Use the pastry to line a buttered and lightly floured pan. Prick the bottom with a fork and the pastry case is ready for use.

Cook's tip: this pastry can be used for any flan containing uncooked fruit such as strawberries or raspberries, or ready-cooked fruit, such as blackberries or pears. It is very fragile and will be difficult to remove from the pan unless you use one with a loose base. If you find the pastry difficult to roll, you can flatten it with the palm of your hand, place it in the pan and work it up the sides with your fingertips.

Pâte à génoise
Genoese Sponge Cake

00:30   **00:20 to 00:25**
Makes 2 lb / 1 kg batter or a 10 in / 25 cm cake

American	Ingredients	Metric/Imperial
7 tbsp	Butter	90 g / 3½ oz
8	Eggs	8
1 cup	Superfine [caster] sugar	250 g / 8 oz
	Salt	
2 cups	Flour	250 g / 8 oz

1. Preheat the oven to 300°-325°F / 140°-160°C / Gas Mark 2-3.
2. Melt the butter. Set aside.
3. Break the eggs into a large mixing bowl placed over a saucepan of hot water and add the sugar and a pinch of salt. Beat over heat until the mixture is thick and too hot to touch.
4. Remove from the heat and continue beating until the mixture has doubled in volume and runs off the beater in a continuous stream.
5. Fold in the flour in about 3 batches, alternating with the melted butter.
6. Pour the batter into a greased and lined 10 in / 25 cm cake pan. Bake for 35-40 minutes or until the cake is firm and golden brown and begins to shrink from the side of the pan. Take care not to open the oven door during the first 15 minutes of baking.
7. When baking is completed, leave the cake in the oven for a few minutes with the door open.

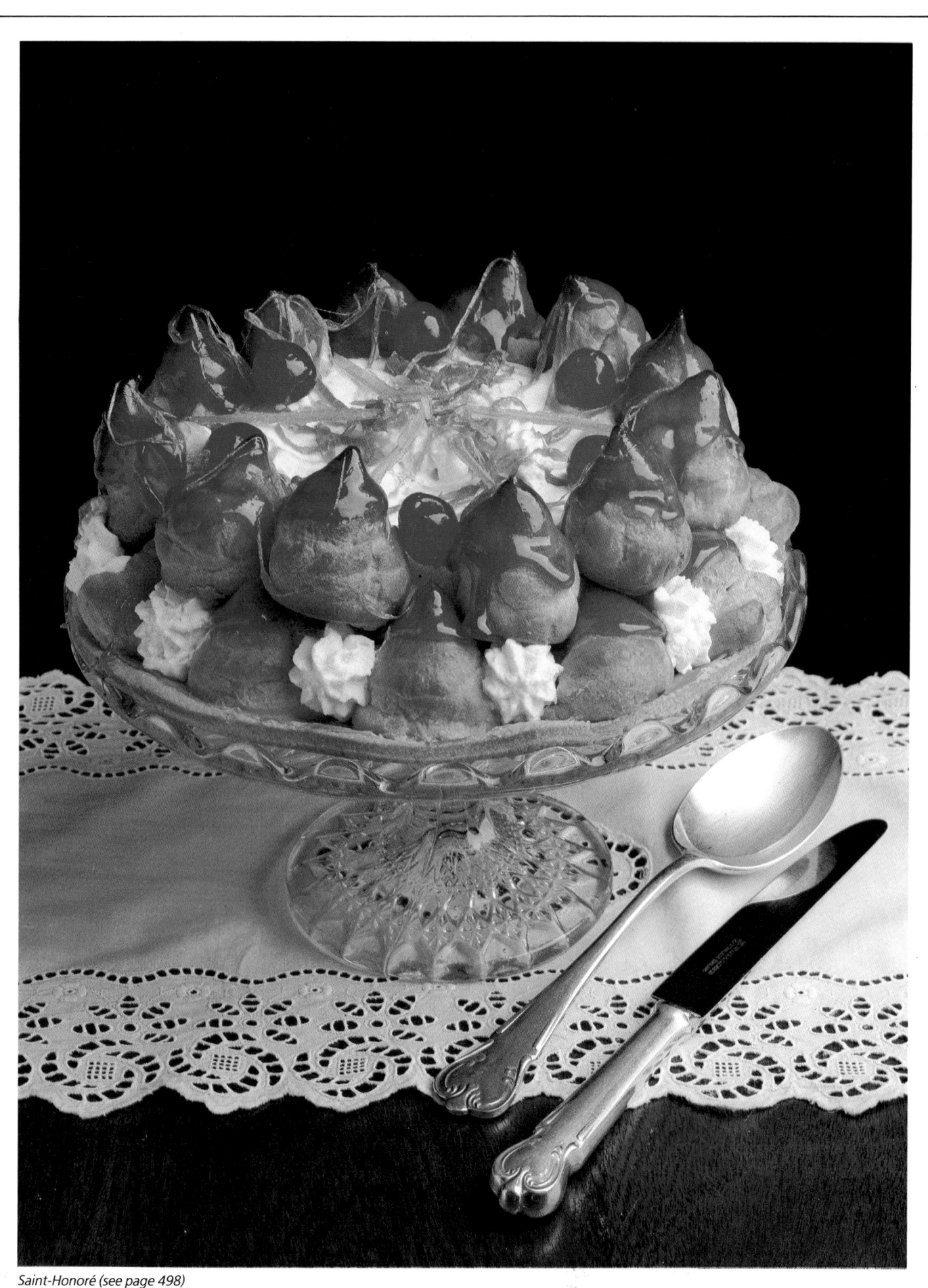

Saint-Honoré (see page 498)

Desserts

Blanc-manger
Almond Blancmange

	00:25 *plus chilling*	00:05

American	Ingredients	Metric/Imperial
	Oil	
3 cups	Blanched almonds	400 g / 14 oz
3 cups	Water	750 ml / 1 ¼ pints
2 envelopes	Unflavored gelatin	1 ½ sachets
1 ¾ cups	Sugar	350 g / 12 oz
3 tbsp	Rum	3 tbsp
12	Sugared almonds	12

1. Oil a bavarois or other deep mold and put into the freezer to chill.
2. Grind the almonds finely in a mortar and pestle, an electric grinder or food processor. Gradually add the cold water as you continue grinding, then strain the almond liquid into a large saucepan.
3. Dissolve the gelatin in a little water and add to the almond liquid with the sugar. Bring to a boil, stirring constantly. Remove from the heat and strain the mixture into a bowl. Leave to cool.
4. Stir in the rum and pour into the chilled mold. Chill in the refrigerator for at least 1 hour or until set.
5. Just before serving, unmold the blancmange on a plate and decorate with the sugared almonds.

Cook's tip: serve with a compote of fresh apricots or cherries.

Gâteau de semoule
Semolina Pudding

	00:10 *plus soaking*	00:20

American	Ingredients	Metric/Imperial
½ cup	Golden raisins [sultanas]	75 g / 3 oz
1 cup	Weak warm tea	250 ml / 8 fl oz
1 ¼ cups	Semolina	225 g / 8 oz
3 cups	Milk	750 ml / 1 ¼ pints
1	Vanilla bean [pod]	1
1 cup	Sugar	225 g / 8 oz
¾ cup + 2 tbsp	Butter	200 g / 7 oz
3	Egg yolks	3

1. Soak the raisins in the tea for 30 minutes. Drain.
2. Place the semolina in a fine strainer and rinse under warm water until the water runs clear.
3. Heat the milk with the vanilla bean, cut in half lengthwise and the sugar. Add the semolina and raisins. Cover the pan and cook for 10 minutes over a low heat, stirring from time to time.
4. Remove the vanilla bean. Add the butter and cook, covered, for a further 10 minutes over a low heat, stirring frequently. Leave to cool slightly, then beat in the egg yolks.
5. Pour the mixture into a buttered metal mold. Smooth the top and unmold onto a serving plate. Serve warm or cold.

Crème Mic-Mac
Chocolate and Vanilla Custard

	00:30 *plus chilling*	00:15

American	Ingredients	Metric/Imperial
1 quart	Milk	1 l / 1 ¾ pints
4 oz	Semisweet [plain] chocolate	125 g / 4 oz
¾ cup	Sugar	150 g / 5 oz
½ cup	Flour	50 g / 2 oz
3	Egg yolks	3
2	Eggs	2
¼ cup	Butter	50 g / 2 oz
	Vanilla extract [essence]	

1. Bring the milk to a boil in a large saucepan. Break the chocolate into a bowl, place in a pan of hot water and melt the chocolate.
2. Beat together the sugar, flour, egg yolks and whole eggs in a mixing bowl until smooth. Stir in the hot milk and pour the mixture back into the saucepan. Bring to a boil over a low heat, stirring constantly. Remove the pan from the heat and add the butter a little at a time.
3. Pour half the custard into a bowl and stir in a few drops of vanilla extract. Mix the melted chocolate thoroughly into the remaining custard.
4. Pour both custards simultaneously into a glass bowl. They will remain separate. Serve chilled but not frozen.

Crème au chocolat
Chocolate Cream

	00:20 *plus cooling*	00:10

American	Ingredients	Metric/Imperial
6	Egg yolks	6
1 cup	Superfine [caster] sugar	200 g / 7 oz
½ cup	Flour	75 g / 3 oz
8 oz	Semisweet [plain] chocolate	250 g / 8 oz
3 tbsp	Water	3 tbsp
1 quart	Milk	1 l / 1 ¾ pints
	Vanilla extract [essence]	
½ quantity	Chantilly cream (see page 455)	½ quantity

1. Beat the egg yolks with the sugar until pale. Add the flour a little at a time.
2. Break the chocolate into a heatproof bowl and add the water. Place the bowl in a pan of hot water and melt the chocolate. Bring the milk to a boil with a few drops of vanilla extract and stir in the melted chocolate. Gradually add this mixture to the beaten eggs, beating vigorously.
3. Return the mixture to the saucepan and cook over a low heat for 10 minutes, stirring constantly, until the custard coats the spoon. On no account allow the mixture to boil. Leave to cool, stirring from time to time to prevent a skin forming, then chill.
4. Just before serving fold in the chantilly cream.

Cook's tip: serve with savoy sponge cake (see page 478), ladyfingers [sponge fingers] (see page 480) or almond cookies [biscuits] (see page 500).

Île flottante
Floating Island

American	Ingredients	Metric/Imperial
1 cup	Praline (see page 458)	125 g / 4 oz
8	Egg whites	8
½ tsp	Salt	½ tsp
¼ cup	Superfine [caster] sugar	4 tbsp
½ cup	Granulated sugar	125 g / 4 oz
2 tbsp	Water	2 tbsp
1 quantity	Vanilla custard sauce (see page 454)	1 quantity

1. Coarsely crush the praline. Preheat the oven to 400°F / 200°C / Gas Mark 6.
2. Beat the egg whites with the salt. When they are frothy, gradually add the superfine sugar and continue beating until stiff. Fold in the crushed praline. Spoon the mixture into a buttered 1 quart [1 l / 1¾ pint] charlotte mold.
3. Bake for about 20 minutes or until a skewer inserted into the meringue comes out clean. Open the oven door and leave to set for a further 5 minutes. Unmold the meringue onto a serving dish and set aside.
4. Put the granulated sugar in a pan with the water. Melt over a medium heat, then cook until golden brown.
5. Drizzle the caramel syrup over the meringue 'island' and pour the custard sauce into the dish to surround the island. Serve chilled.

Crème renversée au chocolat
Upside-down Chocolate Custard

American	Ingredients	Metric/Imperial
8 oz	Semisweet [plain] chocolate	250 g / 8 oz
2 tbsp	Water	2 tbsp
1 quart	Milk	1 l / 1¾ pints
	Vanilla extract [essence]	
5	Eggs	5
5	Egg yolks	5
2 tbsp	Sugar	2 tbsp
1 quantity	Vanilla custard sauce (see page 454)	1 quantity

1. Preheat the oven to 325°F / 160°C / Gas Mark 3.
2. Break the chocolate into a bowl and add the water. Place over a pan of hot water to melt.
3. Meanwhile, bring the milk and a few drops of vanilla extract to a boil. In a mixing bowl, beat the whole eggs and egg yolks, then vigorously beat in the hot milk. Stir in the melted chocolate and add the sugar (this custard should not be too sweet).
4. Strain the custard into a 1 quart [1 l / 1¾ pint] charlotte mold. Place the mold in a shallow ovenproof dish and fill the dish to halfway up the mold with water.
5. Bake for 1 hour or until a skewer inserted into the center of the custard comes out clean.
6. Remove the mold from the dish in the oven and leave to cool. Chill for at least 6 hours.

7. When ready to serve, loosen the custard and unmold it onto a serving dish. Top with the cold vanilla custard sauce.

Candied fruit charlotte

Diplomate aux fruits confits
Candied Fruit Charlotte

American	Ingredients	Metric/Imperial
¼ lb (1 cup)	Assorted candied fruit	125 g / 4 oz
½ cup	Golden raisins [sultanas]	75 g / 3 oz
⅔ cup	Rum	150 ml / ¼ pint
1 (½ lb)	Stale brioche	1 (250 g / 8 oz)
¾ cup	Sugar	175 g / 6 oz
1 quart	Milk	1 l / 1¾ pints
	Vanilla extract [essence]	
6	Eggs	6
	Vanilla custard sauce (see page 454)	

1. Coarsely chop the candied fruit, keeping a few whole fruit in reserve for the decoration. Warm the rum and soak the chopped fruit and raisins in it for 30 minutes.
2. Preheat the oven to 325°F / 160°C / Gas Mark 3.
3. Slice the brioche and remove the crusts. Brown the sliced bread in the oven.
4. Butter a 1½ quart [1.5 l / 2½ pint] charlotte mold and sprinkle the inside with sugar. Cover the bottom of the mold with brioche and sprinkle this with a layer of the rum-flavored fruit. Fill the mold with alternate layers of brioche and fruit, finishing with a layer of brioche.
5. Heat the milk with a few drops of vanilla extract and the remaining sugar. Beat the eggs in a bowl and stir in the hot milk. Pour the mixture slowly into the mold until the milk is visible at the top.
6. Stand the mold in a shallow ovenproof dish and fill the dish to halfway up the mold with water. Bake for 1 hour without allowing the water to boil.
7. Leave to cool, then unmold and serve topped with vanilla custard sauce and decorated with the reserved whole candied fruits.

Crème caramel

Baked Caramel Custard

	00:20		01:00
	plus cooling		

American	Ingredients	Metric/Imperial
1¼ cups	Sugar	300 g / 10 oz
3 tbsp	Water	3 tbsp
1	Vanilla bean [pod]	1
1 quart	Milk	1 l / 1¾ pints
	Salt	
10	Eggs	10

1. Place ½ cup [125 g / 4 oz] of the sugar in a small pan with the water. Melt the sugar over a moderate heat and cook until the caramel is golden. Quickly remove from the heat and pour the caramel into a dry, hot 6 in / 15 cm diameter dish or mold. Tilt the dish or mold to coat all over and leave to cool.
2. Preheat the oven to 350°F / 180°C / Gas Mark 4.
3. Cut the vanilla bean in half lengthwise and put in a large saucepan with the milk and a pinch of salt. Bring to a boil, then stir in the remaining sugar.
4. Beat the eggs in a large mixing bowl. Gradually beat in the milk. Strain the mixture into the caramel mold and place in a shallow ovenproof dish. Fill the dish with water to halfway up the mold.
5. Bake for 1 hour. Test that the custard is ready by piercing with a knife. The blade should come out clean.
6. Remove the mold from the ovenproof dish and leave to cool. Just before serving, unmold the custard onto a serving plate.

Cook's tip: this dessert should be cooked at least 4 hours before it is required. Care should be taken not to overcook the custard.

Mont blanc

Chestnut Cream Cake

	01:30		00:30

American	Ingredients	Metric/Imperial
¾ cup + 2 tbsp	Butter	200 g / 7 oz
3	Eggs, separated	3
1	Egg yolk	1
6 tbsp	Superfine [caster] sugar	75 g / 3 oz
¾ cup	Flour	75 g / 3 oz
¼ cup	Rum	4 tbsp
1½ lb	Canned sweetened chestnut purée	750 g / 1½ lb
1 tbsp	Cocoa powder	1 tbsp
½ cup	Granulated sugar	125 g / 4 oz
⅓ cup	Water	5 tbsp
1 quantity	Chantilly cream (see page 455)	1 quantity

1. Preheat the oven to 450°F / 230°C / Gas Mark 8.
2. Melt 2 tablespoons [25 g / 1 oz] butter. Set aside. Beat the 4 egg yolks with half the superfine sugar. When pale, quickly work in the flour. Beat the 3 egg whites until very stiff and gradually beat in the remaining superfine sugar. Beat the egg whites and melted butter into the egg yolk mixture.
3. Pour the batter into a buttered 10 in / 25 cm cake pan. Bake for about 10 minutes or until a skewer inserted into the center

of the cake comes out clean. Remove the cake from the oven, unmold and leave to cool.
4. Mix half the rum with the chestnut purée in a warm bowl. Add the remaining butter and the cocoa. Beat well until smooth.
5. Put the chestnut paste into a pastry bag fitted with a plain ¼ in / 5 mm nozzle. Pipe over the sides of an oiled 10 in / 25 cm savarin mold in successive rings. Leave in the refrigerator to set.
6. Cut the cake into 2 layers.
7. Dissolve the granulated sugar in the water and remaining rum. Bring to a boil and boil for 2 minutes. Moisten the two cake layers with this syrup, and break one layer into pieces.
8. Place the whole cake layer on a flat serving plate. Slide the chestnut case out of the savarin mold and place the case on the cake layer. Fill the chestnut case with alternate layers of broken cake and chantilly cream. Place the rest of the chantilly cream in a pastry bag fitted with a plain ½ in / 1 cm nozzle and pipe the cream over the whole cake. Serve at once.

Chocolate mousse

Mousse au chocolat

Chocolate Mousse

	00:20		00:05
	plus chilling		

American	Ingredients	Metric/Imperial
3	Eggs, separated	3
½ cup	Superfine [caster] sugar	125 g / 4 oz
8 oz	Semisweet [plain] chocolate	250 g / 8 oz
2 tbsp	Water	2 tbsp
¼ cup	Butter	50 g / 2 oz
1	Egg white	1
	Salt	

1. Beat the egg yolks and sugar together until the mixture becomes pale.
2. Break the chocolate into another bowl and add the water. Place over a saucepan of hot water to melt. Remove the bowl from the heat and stir in the butter.
3. Add the chocolate to the egg yolk mixture. Beat the 4 egg whites with a pinch of salt until they form firm peaks, then gently fold into the chocolate mixture.
4. Spoon the mousse into a shallow dish or into 6 individual glasses and chill for at least 3 hours before serving.

Oeufs au lait

Baked Egg Custard

	00:10 plus cooling		01:00

American	Ingredients	Metric/Imperial
1	Vanilla bean [pod]	1
1 quart	Milk	1 l / 1¾ pints
8	Egg yolks	8
⅔ cup	Superfine [caster] sugar	150 g / 5 oz

1. Preheat the oven to 325°F / 160°C / Gas Mark 3.
2. Cut the vanilla bean in half lengthwise and put in a saucepan with the milk. Bring to a boil.
3. In a mixing bowl, whisk the egg yolks and sugar together until the mixture is pale. Remove the vanilla bean from the milk and gradually whisk the milk into the egg yolks.
4. Pour the custard into a porcelain baking dish. Place the dish in a roasting pan and fill the pan with water to halfway up the sides of the dish.
5. Bake for 1 hour, without allowing the water in the pan to boil, or until a skewer inserted into the center of the custard comes out clean.
6. Remove the dish from the roasting pan in the oven and leave to cool. Serve the custard from the porcelain dish.

Nègre en chemise

Cream-coated Chocolate Mousse

	00:30 plus chilling		00:10

American	Ingredients	Metric/Imperial
7 oz	Semisweet [plain] chocolate	200 g / 7 oz
1 tbsp	Milk	1 tbsp
1 cup	Butter	200 g / 7 oz
⅓ cup	Superfine [caster] sugar	75 g / 3 oz
4	Eggs, separated	4
2 cups	Crème fraîche (see page 122)	150 ml / ¾ pint
	Vanilla extract [essence]	
½ cup	Confectioners' [icing] sugar	50 g / 2 oz

1. Break the chocolate into a pan, add the milk and melt over a low heat. Cut the butter into small pieces and soften in a bowl with a wooden spoon. Beat in the superfine sugar and then the egg yolks one at a time. Finally beat in the melted chocolate.
2. Beat the egg whites until very stiff. Gently fold into the chocolate mixture with a wooden spoon. Spoon into a greased 1 quart [1 l / 2 pint] charlotte mold. Chill for 12 hours.

3. Chill the crème fraîche and just before serving, pour it into a chilled mixing bowl. Add a few drops of vanilla extract and the confectioners' sugar and whip until the cream has doubled in quantity.
4. Unmold the chocolate mousse onto a serving plate and cover it completely with the whipped cream.

Soufflé au citron

Lemon Soufflé

	00:30		00:15

American	Ingredients	Metric/Imperial
4	Eggs, separated	4
1	Egg yolk	1
¼ cup	Superfine [caster] sugar	4 tbsp
1 tbsp	Potato starch or flour	1 tbsp
1	Lemon	1

1. Preheat the oven to 400°F / 200°C / Gas Mark 6.
2. Whisk the 5 egg yolks with 2 tablespoons of the sugar until light and frothy. Add the potato starch and the finely grated rind of the lemon and whisk in lightly.
3. Beat the egg whites until very stiff, gradually incorporating the remaining sugar. Carefully fold the whites into the yolks.
4. Generously butter 6 4 in / 10 cm diameter ramekins and sprinkle inside with sugar. Fill each ramekin to the top with the soufflé mixture and bake for 15 minutes. Serve immediately.

Cook's tip: the ramekins can be filled before you start the meal and then put in the oven 15 minutes before they are to be served.

Soufflé au chocolat

Chocolate Soufflé

	00:30		00:30

American	Ingredients	Metric/Imperial
7 oz	Semisweet [plain] chocolate	200 g / 7 oz
1 tbsp	Water	1 tbsp
6	Eggs, separated	6
	Vanilla extract [essence]	
⅓ cup	Potato starch or flour	40 g / 1 ½ oz
½ cup	Superfine [caster] sugar	125 g / 4 oz
	Confectioners' [icing] sugar	

1. Preheat the oven to 425°F / 220°C / Gas Mark 7.
2. Break the chocolate into a bowl and place over a pan of hot water. Add the water and melt the chocolate over a low heat. Remove the bowl from the pan of water and beat in the egg yolks, 2 at a time, a few drops of vanilla extract and the potato starch mixed with three-quarters of the sugar.
3. Beat the egg whites until very stiff, then gradually beat in the remaining sugar. Fold the whites into the chocolate mixture.
4. Butter a 6 in / 15 cm soufflé dish and sprinkle with sugar. Fill the soufflé dish to the top with the chocolate mixture. Bake for 30 minutes. Serve sprinkled with confectioners' sugar.

Cook's tip: to make this soufflé at the last minute, prepare the chocolate mixture (step 2), then beat the whites and fold in just before you are ready to bake the soufflé.

Mousse aux marrons
Chestnut Mousse

	00:30 plus chilling	00:45

American	Ingredients	Metric/Imperial
2 lb	Chestnuts	1 kg / 2 lb
⅔ cup	Sugar	150 g / 5 oz
1	Vanilla bean [pod]	1
1 quart	Milk	1 l / 1¾ pints
	Salt	
1½ cups	Crème fraîche (see page 122)	350 ml / 12 fl oz
½ cup	Broken marrons glacés	150 g / 5 oz

1. With a pointed knife make an incision around each chestnut, cutting through both layers of skin, and place them in a saucepan. Cover with plenty of cold water. Bring to a boil and boil for about 5 minutes. Peel the chestnuts one at a time.

2. Place the peeled chestnuts in a pan with the sugar, the vanilla bean, cut in half lengthwise, the milk and a pinch of salt. Bring to a boil, then cover the pan and cook over a low heat for 40 minutes.

3. Remove the vanilla bean and purée the chestnut mixture in a vegetable mill, blender or food processor. Transfer the purée to a mixing bowl.

4. Pour the cold crème fraîche into a chilled mixing bowl and whip until it has doubled in quantity. Fold the whipped crème gently into the chestnut purée.

5. Spoon the chestnut mousse into a glass bowl. Decorate with pieces of marrons glacés and chill until ready to serve.

Riz à l'impératrice
Empress Rice Mold

	00:30 plus chilling	00:30

American	Ingredients	Metric/Imperial
	Salt	
1 cup	Round-grain rice	250 g / 8 oz
1 quart	Milk	1 l / 1¾ pints
1	Vanilla bean [pod]	25 g / 1 oz
2 tbsp	Butter	25 g / 1 oz
1 envelope	Unflavored gelatin	½ sachet
3 tbsp	Water	3 tbsp
¼ quantity	Vanilla custard sauce (see page 454)	¼ quantity
1 cup	Sugar	250 g / 8 oz
1¼ cups	Crème fraîche (see page 122)	300 ml / ½ pint
⅔ cup	Fruit jelly (apricot or gooseberry)	150 ml / ¼ pint
1 tbsp	Kirsch or rum	1 tbsp

1. Bring a large pan of lightly salted water to a boil. Add the rice; blanch for 2 minutes and drain.

2. Place the milk and vanilla bean, halved lengthwise, in a heavy saucepan and bring to a boil. Stir in the rice and butter. Cover the pan and simmer over a low heat for 25 minutes.

3. Meanwhile, dissolve the gelatin in the water. Stir into the custard sauce. Strain into a bowl and set aside.

4. When the rice is cooked, remove the vanilla bean. Stir in the sugar and leave to cool.

5. Whip the cold crème fraîche in a chilled bowl until it doubles in volume. Stir the rice into the custard, then fold in the whipped cream.

6. Transfer the mixture to a charlotte or savarin mold and chill for 3 hours or until set.

7. To serve, warm the fruit jelly with the kirsch until melted. Turn the rice mold onto a plate and spoon over the melted jelly.

Oeufs à la neige
Snow Eggs

	00:35 plus chilling	00:30

American	Ingredients	Metric/Imperial
	Salt	
8	Eggs, separated	8
1½ quarts	Milk	1.5 l / 2½ pints
1	Vanilla bean [pod]	1
⅔ cup	Superfine [caster] sugar	150 g / 5 oz
½ cup	Granulated sugar	125 g / 4 oz
2 tbsp	Water	2 tbsp

1. Add a pinch of salt to the egg whites and beat until firm. Set aside for 20 minutes, then beat again until very stiff.

2. Pour 5 cups [1.25 l / 2 pints] milk into a saucepan and add the vanilla bean, halved lengthwise, and half the superfine sugar. Bring to a boil, then lower the heat so that the milk is just simmering.

3. Take a large tablespoonful of egg white, float it on the surface of the milk and cook for 1 minute. Turn the poached meringue over and cook for a further minute. Remove the meringue with a slotted spoon and transfer to a cloth to drain. Repeat the process until all the egg white has been used.

4. Add enough milk to the pan to bring the quantity back to 1 quart [1 l / 1¾ pints]. Bring to a boil.

5. Add the remaining superfine sugar to the egg yolks and whisk until pale. Slowly add the boiling milk, whisking vigorously, then pour the mixture back into the pan. Stir over a low heat for about 10 minutes or until the custard is thick enough to coat the spoon. Pour the custard into a shallow dish and stir until just warm. Leave until completely cold.

6. When the custard is cold, carefully place the poached meringues on top.

7. Place the granulated sugar in a small pan with the water and melt over a moderate heat. Cook until the syrup turns to a golden brown caramel. Pour the caramel over the meringues and chill for 1 hour before serving.

Empress rice mold

Soufflé à l'orange
Orange Liqueur Soufflé

00:25 **00:40**

American	Ingredients	Metric/Imperial
2	Oranges	2
½ quantity	Vanilla custard sauce (see page 454)	½ quantity
1¼ cups	Mandarin or orange liqueur	300 ml / ½ pint
½ quantity	Pastry cream (see page 456)	½ quantity
4	Egg whites	4
12	Ladyfingers [sponge fingers]	12

1. Preheat the oven to 425°F / 220°C / Gas Mark 7.
2. Thinly pare the rind from 1 orange. Add to the custard sauce with 4 tablespoons of the liqueur. Set aside in the refrigerator.
3. Finely grate the rind from the remaining orange and squeeze out the juice. Stir the grated rind and juice into the pastry cream.
4. Beat the egg whites until stiff and fold carefully into the pastry cream.
5. Moisten the lady fingers with the remaining liqueur.
6. Butter a 6 in / 15 cm soufflé dish. Cover the bottom with a layer of ladyfingers, then add a layer of pastry cream. Continue the layers until you have used all the ingredients, finishing with a layer of the cream.
7. Bake for 25-30 minutes.
8. Remove the orange rind from the custard sauce and serve with the soufflé immediately it is removed from the oven.

Soufflé au Grand Marnier
Grand Marnier Soufflé

00:15 **00:30 to 00:35**

American	Ingredients	Metric/Imperial
1 cup	Milk	250 ml / 8 fl oz
¼ cup	Superfine [caster] sugar	50 g / 2 oz
¼ cup	Butter	50 g / 2 oz
2 tbsp	Flour	50 g / 2 oz
2 tbsp	Potato starch or flour	15 g / ½ oz
	Vanilla extract [essence]	
4	Eggs, separated	4
5 tbsp	Grand Marnier	5 tbsp
1	Ladyfinger [sponge finger]	1
	Confectioners' [icing] sugar	

1. Preheat the oven to 400°F / 200°C / Gas Mark 6.
2. Place the milk in a saucepan with the sugar and bring to a boil. Melt the butter in another saucepan and stir in the 2 tablespoons each of flour and potato starch or 4 tablespoons flour. Add the boiling milk and a few drops of vanilla extract. Cook, stirring, for about 3 minutes. Remove from the heat.
3. Carefully stir the egg yolks, one at a time, into the sauce, then add 4 tablespoons of the Grand Marnier.
4. Beat the egg whites until very stiff and fold gently into the mixture. Butter a 6 in / 15 cm soufflé dish and sprinkle with sugar. Half-fill the dish with the soufflé mixture.
5. Crumble the ladyfinger into a cup and moisten with the remaining Grand Marnier. Sprinkle over the soufflé mixture in

the dish, then fill the dish with the remaining soufflé mixture.
6. Bake for about 30 minutes (on no account open the oven door during this time) or until well risen. Serve immediately, sprinkled with a little confectioners' sugar.

Pudding de Bourgogne
Burgundy Pudding

00:25
plus cooling and chilling
01:00

American	Ingredients	Metric/Imperial
⅔ cup	Sugar	150 g / 5 oz
2½ tbsp	Water	2½ tbsp
1	Lemon	1
3 cups	Milk	750 ml / 1¼ pints
6 tbsp	Butter	75 g / 3 oz
6 tbsp	Flour	75 g / 3 oz
4	Eggs, separated	4

1. Put ¼ cup [50 g / 2 oz] of the sugar and 1½ tablespoons of the water into a deep cake pan. Cook over a moderate heat for 6-10 minutes or until the caramel is golden brown. Add the remaining water and stir to stop the caramel cooking further. Leave to cool.
2. Preheat the oven to 400°F / 200°C / Gas Mark 6.
3. Thinly pare the rind from the lemon and place in a saucepan with the milk and the rest of the sugar. Bring the milk slowly to a boil, then remove the pan from the heat. Cover the pan and leave to infuse for about 10 minutes.
4. Melt the butter in another saucepan, add the flour and stir for 3 minutes over a low heat. Remove the lemon rind from the milk and stir the milk, a little at a time, into the butter and flour roux. Bring to a boil, stirring, then remove the pan from the heat. Leave the sauce to cool for 5 minutes.
5. Stir the egg yolks into the sauce, one at a time. Beat the egg whites until very stiff and gently fold into the mixture.
6. Spoon into the cake pan and place in a shallow roasting pan containing about 1 in / 2.5 cm water. Bake for 1 hour.
7. Leave the pudding to cool until warm, then unmold onto a serving dish. Leave to cool completely, then chill before serving.

Grand Marnier soufflé

Tarts and flans

Pie aux pommes
Apple Pie

	00:30	00:30
	plus thawing or making pastry	

American	Ingredients	Metric/Imperial
14 oz	Puff pastry (see page 458 or use frozen)	400 g / 14 oz
3 large	Cooking apples	3 large
⅔ cup	Golden raisins [sultanas]	125 g / 4 oz
½ cup	Sugar	125 g / 4 oz
⅓ cup	Butter	75 g / 3 oz
1	Egg	1
1 cup	Crème fraîche (see page 122)	250 ml / 8 fl oz

1. If using frozen pastry, allow it to thaw.
2. Preheat the oven to 450°F / 230°C / Gas Mark 8.
3. Peel the apples and cut each into 8 segments. Cut out the cores and seeds. Arrange in layers in a deep pie dish with the raisins and sugar. Dot with the butter.
4. Roll out the pastry to ¼ in / 5 mm thick. Cut a strip the same width as the rim of the dish, roll out to ⅛ in / 3 mm thick and stick to the rim of the dish with beaten egg. Brush the pastry strip with beaten egg.
5. Cover the dish with the remaining pastry, pressing firmly around the rim, after brushing the rim once more with egg. Cut off any excess pastry. Press with the tines of a fork all around the rim. Make a hole in the center and insert a roll of card to keep it open. Brush the surface of the pie with beaten egg.
6. Bake for 30 minutes or until golden brown. Turn off the oven and wait a few minutes before removing the pie. Serve hot with crème fraîche.

Pie à la rhubarbe
Rhubarb Pie

	00:20	01:00
	plus making or thawing pastry	

American	Ingredients	Metric/Imperial
1 lb	Puff pastry (see page 458 or use frozen) or	500 g / 1 lb
1 quantity	Basic short pastry (see page 457)	1 quantity
1½ lb	Rhubarb	750 g / 1½ lb
3	Apples	3
2 cups	Sugar	500 g / 1 lb

1. If using frozen pastry, allow it to thaw.
2. Preheat the oven to 450°F / 230°C / Gas Mark 8.
3. Cut the sticks of rhubarb into ½ in / 1 cm lengths. Heat a little water in a saucepan and gently cook the rhubarb for 6-7 minutes. Drain.
4. Peel the apples. Cut each into 8 segments and cut out the core and seeds.
5. Arrange the fruit in a deep pie dish and stir in the sugar.
6. Roll out the pastry to ¼ in / 5 mm thick. Cut a strip the same width as the rim of the dish and stick it onto the rim with beaten egg.

7. Cut a few slits in the remaining pastry with the point of a knife and then cover the dish, sticking the lid to the pastry on the rim with beaten egg. Cut off any excess and press the edge down firmly with the tines of a fork. Brush the top of the pie with egg and brush again after a few minutes.
8. Bake for 45 minutes or until golden brown, pricking the pastry with the point of a knife when it rises.

Cook's tip: serve hot or cold with thick cream and sugar.

Pie aux fruits mélangés
Mixed Fruit Pie

	00:30	00:45
	plus making or thawing pastry	

American	Ingredients	Metric/Imperial
14 oz	Puff pastry (see page 458 or use frozen)	400 g / 14 oz
1½ lb	Fresh fruit (apricots, grapes, cherries, plums, etc)	750 g / 1½ lb
⅔ cup	Sugar	150 g / 5 oz
1	Egg	1
1 cup	Crème fraîche (see page 122)	250 ml / 8 fl oz

1. If using frozen pastry, allow it to thaw.
2. Preheat the oven to 450°F / 230°C / Gas Mark 8.
3. Remove the pits [stones] or seeds from the fresh fruit and arrange in a deep pie dish. Sprinkle with the sugar.
4. Roll out the pastry to ¼ in / 5 mm thick. Cut a strip of pastry the same width as the rim of the dish, roll it out to ⅛ in / 3 mm thick and stick to the rim of the dish with beaten egg. Brush the strip of pastry with beaten egg.
5. Cover the dish with the remaining pastry and press down firmly around the rim. Make a hole in the center and insert a piece of rolled card or a pie funnel to keep it open. Brush the surface of the pie with egg.
6. Bake for 10 minutes. When the pastry begins to rise, lower the heat to 350°F / 180°C / Gas Mark 4 and bake for a further 30 minutes.
7. Serve hot with crème fraîche.

Pie aux abricots
Apricot Pie

	00:35	00:45
	plus making or thawing pastry	

American	Ingredients	Metric/Imperial
14 oz	Puff pastry (see page 458 or use frozen)	400 g / 14 oz
1½ lb	Apricots	750 g / 1½ lb
⅔ cup	Sugar	150 g / 5 oz
1	Egg	1
1 cup	Crème fraîche (see page 122)	250 ml / 8 fl oz

1. If using frozen pastry, allow it to thaw.
2. Preheat the oven to 450°F / 230°C / Gas Mark 8.
3. Wash, drain and pit [stone] the apricots. Cut into quarters or sixths depending on size and arrange in a deep pie dish. Sprinkle with the sugar.
4. Roll out the pastry to ¼ in / 5 mm thick. Cut a strip the

same width as the rim of the pie dish and roll out to ⅛ in / 3 mm thick. Stick this strip to the rim of the dish with beaten egg, then brush the top of the strip with egg.

5. Cover the dish with the remaining pastry and press it down firmly around the rim. Make a hole in the center of the pastry lid and insert a piece of rolled card or a pie funnel to prevent it closing. Brush the top of the pie with beaten egg.

6. Bake for 15 minutes. When the pastry begins to rise, turn down the oven to 350°F / 180°C / Gas Mark 4 and bake for a further 30 minutes.

7. Serve hot with crème fraîche.

Apricot pie

Flan aux cerises
Cherry Flan

	00:25		01:00
	plus making or thawing pastry		

American	Ingredients	Metric/Imperial
14 oz	Puff pastry (see page 458 or use frozen)	400 g / 14 oz
2½ cups	Milk	500 ml / ¾ pint
4	Eggs	4
	Vanilla extract [essence]	
½ cup	Superfine [caster] sugar	125 g / 4 oz
½ cup	Flour	50 g / 2 oz
1 tbsp	Butter, at room temperature	15 g / ½ oz
½ lb	Pitted [stoned] cherries, fresh or bottled	250 g / 8 oz

1. If using frozen pastry, allow it to thaw.
2. Preheat the oven to 425°F / 220°C / Gas Mark 7.
3. Roll out the pastry and use to line a buttered 10 in / 25 cm tart or flan pan. Prick the bottom of the pastry case with a fork. Set aside.
4. Heat the milk. Put 2 whole eggs and 2 egg yolks into a bowl, add a few drops of vanilla extract and the sugar and beat until pale. Mix in the flour and butter, then stir in the hot milk.
5. Beat the 2 egg whites until stiff and fold into the mixture.
6. Arrange the cherries in the pastry case and pour on the mixture. Bake until the top is golden brown, then reduce the oven temperature to 400°F / 200°C / Gas Mark 6. Cover the

flan with foil and continue baking until the flan has cooked for a total of 1 hour.

Far aux pruneaux
Prune Pudding

	00:25		01:15
	plus soaking and cooling		

American	Ingredients	Metric/Imperial
1 cup	Prunes	125 g / 4 oz
3 cups	Milk	750 ml / 1 ¼ pints
½ cup	Sugar	125 g / 4 oz
1 cup	Flour	150 g / 5 oz
3	Eggs	3
3 tbsp	Rum	3 tbsp

1. Soak the prunes in water to cover for 12 hours.
2. Preheat the oven to 350°F / 180°C / Gas Mark 4.
3. Heat the milk. In a mixing bowl stir together the sugar and flour. Make a well in the center and add the eggs. Beat well, then gradually stir in the hot milk.
4. Drain the prunes and remove the pits [stones]. Add to the batter with the rum.
5. Pour the batter into a buttered 10 in / 25 cm cake pan or shallow ovenproof dish. Bake for about 1¼ hours. The pudding is cooked when the point of a knife inserted in the center comes out clean.
6. Leave to cool before removing from the pan.

Flan aux pruneaux
Prune Flan

	00:15		00:35
	plus making pastry and soaking prunes		

American	Ingredients	Metric/Imperial
3 cups	Pitted [stoned] prunes	400 g / 14 oz
2 cups	Weak tea	500 ml / ¾ pint
1 quantity	Basic short pastry (see page 457)	1 quantity
⅔ cup	Thick crème fraîche (see page 122)	150 ml / ¼ pint
2	Eggs	2
5 tbsp	Superfine [caster] sugar	65 g / 2½ oz
1 tbsp	Potato starch or flour	1 tbsp
⅔ cup	Milk	150 ml / ¼ pint
2 tbsp	Orange liqueur	2 tbsp
2 tbsp	Butter	25 g / 1 oz

1. Place the prunes in a bowl, cover with the weak tea and leave to soak for 4 hours.
2. Preheat the oven to 400°F / 200°C / Gas Mark 6.
3. Roll out the pastry to ¼ in / 5 mm thick and use to line a buttered 10 in / 25 cm tart or flan pan. Prick the bottom of the pastry case with a fork.
4. Drain the prunes and arrange in the pastry case.
5. Whip the crème fraîche with the eggs and sugar until thick. Dissolve the potato starch in the milk and orange liqueur and stir into the egg mixture. Pour over the prunes and dot the top with the butter.
6. Bake for 35 minutes. Remove from the pan and cool on a wire rack.

Tarte aux cerises

Cherry Tart

	00:30 plus making pastry	00:50

American	Ingredients	Metric/Imperial
1 quantity	Basic short pastry (see page 457)	1 quantity
1½ lb	Bottle pitted cherries (preferably morello)	625 g / 1½ lb
⅓ cup	Red currant jelly	100 g / 4 oz

1. Preheat the oven to 350°F / 180°C / Gas Mark 4.
2. Roll out the pastry and use to line a buttered 10 in / 25 cm tart pan. Prick with a fork.
3. Drain the cherries and arrange in the pastry case, starting from the outside edge and squeezing them closely together.
4. Bake for 30 minutes, then reduce the heat to 325°F / 160°C / Gas Mark 3 and bake for a further 20 minutes. The tart is cooked when the base is firm. Remove the tart from the pan and leave to cool.
5. Meanwhile, warm the red currant jelly over a low heat in a small pan until melted. Pour the jelly over the cherries and the sides of the tart.

Long pineapple tart

Tarte aux framboises

Raspberry Tart

	00:20 to 00:30 plus making pastry	00:20

American	Ingredients	Metric/Imperial
1 quantity	Basic short pastry (see page 457)	1 quantity
1 lb	Raspberries	500 g / 1 lb
⅓ cup	Red currant jelly	125 g / 4 oz
	Confectioners' [icing] sugar	

1. Preheat the oven to 400°F / 200°C / Gas Mark 6.
2. Roll out the pastry to ¼ in / 5 mm thick. Use to line a buttered 10 in / 25 cm tart pan. Prick the bottom of the pastry case with a fork. Bake 'blind' for 20 minutes.
3. Meanwhile, rinse and drain the raspberries and pat dry with paper towels. Remove any stalks.
4. Remove the pastry case from the pan and place it on a plate.
5. Melt the red currant jelly in a small pan over a low heat and

brush over the bottom of the tart case. Cover with the raspberries, then brush with the remaining jelly. Sprinkle with confectioners' sugar and serve chilled.

Clafoutis aux cerises

Baked Cherry Pudding

	00:15 plus standing time	00:35

American	Ingredients	Metric/Imperial
½ cup	Superfine [caster] sugar	125 g / 4 oz
	Salt	
6	Eggs	6
1¼ cups	Milk	250 ml / 8 fl oz
¾ cup	Flour	100 g / 3½ oz
1½ lb	Black cherries	750 g / 1½ lb

1. Place three quarters of the sugar and a pinch of salt in a mixing bowl. Beat in the eggs and then the milk. Add the flour and beat vigorously, then leave the batter to stand for 10 minutes.
2. Preheat the oven to 425°F / 220°C / Gas Mark 7.
3. Wash and dry the cherries and remove the stalks. Remove the pits [stones].
4. Spread out the cherries in a buttered 10 in / 25 cm cake pan or ovenproof dish and fill with the batter.
5. Bake for 35 minutes.
6. Leave to cool, then sprinkle with the remaining sugar.

Cook's tip: other soft fruit, such as apricots, can be used successfully in this dish.

Tarte longue à l'ananas

Long Pineapple Tart

	00:40 plus thawing or making pastry	00:40

American	Ingredients	Metric/Imperial
14 oz	Puff pastry (see page 458 or use frozen)	400 g / 14 oz
1	Egg	1
1	Fresh pineapple	1
1 quantity	Pastry cream (see page 456)	1 quantity
5 tbsp	Apricot jam	5 tbsp

1. If using frozen pastry, allow it to thaw.
2. Preheat the oven to 450°F / 230°C / Gas Mark 8.
3. Roll out the puff pastry into a rectangle about 6 in / 15 cm wide and about ¼ in / 5 mm thick. From each long side cut a strip of pastry about ¾ in / 2 cm wide.
4. Dampen a large baking sheet and place the rectangle of pastry on it. Brush the long edges with beaten egg and stick on the two narrow strips of pastry. Cut slits in the outside of this border with a knife at ¾ in / 2 cm intervals. Prick the pastry base with a fork. Bake for 12 minutes.
5. Meanwhile, cut off the two ends of the pineapple. Place the pineapple on a board and peel from top to bottom with a large knife. Cut out the eyes with a small pointed knife. Slice the pineapple crosswise and cut out the core. Cut each slice in half.
6. Remove the pastry case from the oven. Cover it with pastry cream, then arrange the pineapple slices on top. Reduce the heat of the oven to 400°F / 200°C / Gas Mark 6 and bake for a further 30 minutes.
7. Warm the apricot jam. Remove the tart from the oven and brush with hot apricot jam.

Cook's tip: if you prefer to make a round tart, proceed in exactly the same way, but cut the pastry using a large plate as a guide. Cut out a ¾ in / 2 cm border. Place the pastry base in a round tart pan and stick on the border with beaten egg. For the round tart cut the pineapple slices into quarters.

Tarte au fromage blanc

Cheese Tart

	00:30 plus making pastry	00:45 to 00:50

American	Ingredients	Metric/Imperial
1 quantity	Basic short pastry (see page 457)	1 quantity
2½ cups	Cream cheese	600 g / 1¼ lb
½ cup	Thick crème fraîche (see page 122)	125 ml / 4 fl oz
2	Eggs	2
2	Egg yolks	2
¾ cup	Superfine [caster] sugar	175 g / 6 oz
1 tbsp	Flour	1 tbsp
	Vanilla extract [essence] or	
1	Lemon	1
	Salt	
	Confectioners' [icing] sugar	

1. Preheat the oven to 425°F / 220°C / Gas Mark 7.
2. Roll out the pastry to ¼ in / 5 mm thick. Use to line a buttered and floured 10 in / 25 cm tart pan. Prick the bottom of the pastry case with a fork.
3. Beat the cream cheese until smooth, then beat in the crème fraîche. Add the whole eggs, one at a time, and then the egg yolks. Stir in the sugar mixed with the flour and a few drops of

vanilla extract or the finely grated rind of the lemon. Finally add a pinch of salt.
4. Pour the cheese mixture into the pastry case. Bake for 20 minutes, then lower the oven temperature to 350°F / 180°C / Gas Mark 4. If necessary, prick the filling with a fork to reduce bubbling and bake for a further 25 minutes. Serve hot or cold, sprinkled with confectioners' sugar.

Tarte aux poires

Pear Tart

	00:20 plus making pastry	00:20

American	Ingredients	Metric/Imperial
1 quantity	Basic short pastry (see page 457)	1 quantity
4	Large ripe pears	4
3	Eggs	3
1 cup	Crème fraîche (see page 122)	250 ml / 8 fl oz
1 tbsp	Cornstarch [cornflour]	1 tbsp
½ cup	Superfine [caster] sugar	125 g / 4 oz

1. Preheat the oven to 400°F / 200°C / Gas Mark 6.
2. Roll out the pastry to ¼ in / 5 mm thick and use to line a buttered 10 in / 25 cm tart pan.
3. Peel and quarter the pears. Remove the cores and cut into very thin slices.
4. Beat the eggs together and stir in the crème fraîche, cornstarch and sugar.
5. Arrange the sliced pears in the pastry case and cover with the egg mixture. Bake for about 20 minutes.
6. Remove the tart from the oven and allow to cool before removing from the pan.

Pear tart

Tarte à la rhubarbe

Rhubarb Tart

| | 00:30 | | 01:45 |
| | plus making pastry | | |

American	Ingredients	Metric/Imperial
1 quantity	Basic short pastry (see page 457)	1 quantity
1 cup	Hazelnuts	125 g / 4 oz
2 lb	Rhubarb	1 kg / 2 lb
½ cup	Granulated sugar	125 g / 4 oz
⅓ cup	Water	5 tbsp
5	Egg whites	5
1 cup	Superfine [caster] sugar	250 g / 8 oz

1. Preheat the oven to 350°F / 180°C / Gas Mark 4.
2. Roll out the pastry to ¼ in / 5 mm thick and use to line a buttered 10 in / 25 cm tart pan. Prick the bottom of the pastry case with a fork. Bake 'blind' for 20 minutes.
3. Grind the hazelnuts and toast without fat in a frying pan or in the oven.
4. Cut the rhubarb into short lengths and cook with the granulated sugar and water for about 15 minutes or until very soft. Purée in a vegetable mill, blender or food processor.
5. Remove the pastry case from the oven and reduce the temperature to 275°F / 120°C / Gas Mark 1. Fill the pastry case with the rhubarb purée.
6. Beat the egg whites until stiff, then gradually beat in the superfine sugar. Spread the meringue over the rhubarb purée.
7. Sprinkle the toasted hazelnuts over the meringue and bake for about 45 minutes. Serve warm.

Tarte à la vergeoise

Brown Sugar Tart

| | 00:30 | 00:15 to 00:18 |
| | plus rising time | |

American	Ingredients	Metric/Imperial
1½ cups	Milk	150 ml / ¼ pint
2 packages	Active dry yeast	1 sachet
2 tbsp	Granulated sugar	2 tbsp
4 cups	Flour	500 g / 1 lb
2	Eggs	2
	Salt	
½ cup	Melted butter	125 g / 4 oz
1⅓ cups	Light brown sugar	250 g / 8 oz

1. Heat the milk in a small pan over a low heat until lukewarm. Remove from the heat. Add the yeast and granulated sugar and stir well. Leave in a warm place for 15-20 minutes or until frothy.
2. Sift the flour onto a worktop and make a well in the center. Add the eggs and a pinch of salt. Work in with your fingertips. Moisten with the yeast mixture and add all but 2 tablespoons [25 g / 1 oz] of the melted butter. Knead the dough until it no longer sticks to your fingers or the worktop. Roll into a ball and leave to rise in a warm place for about 1 hour.
3. Preheat the oven to 400°F / 200°C / Gas Mark 6.
4. Roll out the dough into a round ½ in / 1 cm thick. Trim the edges, using a plate as a guide, to make the round neat. Place on a buttered and floured baking sheet.
5. Cover the top with the brown sugar, leaving a border ¾ in / 2 cm all the way around. Sprinkle with the remaining melted butter and bake for 15-18 minutes. Serve hot.

Redcurrant meringue tart

Tarte à la mirabelle

Plum Tart

| | 00:25 | 00:30 to 00:40 |
| | plus making pastry | |

American	Ingredients	Metric/Imperial
1 quantity	Basic short pastry (see page 457)	1 quantity
2 lb	Plums	1 kg / 2 lb
¼ cup	Sugar	50 g / 2 oz
⅓ cup	Apricot jam	125 g / 4 oz

1. Preheat the oven to 400°F / 200°C / Gas Mark 6.
2. Roll out the pastry to ¼ in / 5 mm thick and use to line a buttered 10 in / 25 cm tart pan. Prick the bottom of the pastry case with a fork. Bake 'blind' for 15 minutes.
3. Remove from the oven and increase the temperature to 425°F / 220°C / Gas Mark 7.
4. Remove the pits [stones] from the plums. Arrange in the tart case in a circular pattern and sprinkle with the sugar. Bake for 30 minutes. Remove from the oven and allow to cool.
5. When the tart is cold, warm the apricot jam in a small pan and pour over the plums.

Tarte meringuée aux groseilles

Red Currant Meringue Tart

| | 00:30 | | 01:30 |
| | plus making pastry | | |

American	Ingredients	Metric/Imperial
1 quantity	Basic short pastry (see page 457)	1 quantity
1 cup	Hazelnuts	125 g / 4 oz
¾ lb	Ripe red currants	250 g / 12 oz
6	Egg whites	6
1 cup	Superfine [caster] sugar	250 g / 8 oz
	Confectioners' [icing] sugar	

1. Preheat the oven to 400°F / 200°C / Gas Mark 6.
2. Roll out the pastry to ¼ in / 5 mm thick and use to line a 10 in / 25 cm tart pan. Prick the bottom of the pastry case with a fork. Bake 'blind' for about 20 minutes.
3. Remove the pastry case from the oven. Reduce the oven temperature to 275°F / 120°C / Gas Mark 1.
4. Grind the hazelnuts and toast them in a frying pan (or in the oven) without fat for a few minutes. Remove the stalks from the currants.
5. Beat the egg whites, gradually adding the sugar, until very stiff. Keep 4 or 5 tablespoons of egg white to one side, and fold the currants into the remaining whites.
6. Sprinkle the bottom of the pastry case with the hazelnuts. Cover with the currant meringue, then top with the plain meringue. Smooth over with a wooden spatula and sprinkle generously with confectioners' sugar.
7. Bake for 1 hour without allowing the meringue to brown. Serve hot or cold.

Tarte aux pommes

Apple Tart

	01:00 plus making pastry		00:35 to 00:40

American	Ingredients	Metric/Imperial
3 lb	Apples	1.5 kg / 3 lb
1	Lemon	1
3 tbsp	Sugar	3 tbsp
1 quantity	Rich flan pastry (see page 460)	1 quantity
¼ cup	Fruit jelly (currant, apricot, etc)	4 tbsp

1. Preheat the oven to 400°F / 200°C / Gas Mark 6.
2. Set aside 5 apples of similar size. Peel and core the remaining apples and purée them in a vegetable mill, blender or food processor. Add the juice of ½ lemon and 2 tablespoons sugar. Stir well.
3. Roll out the pastry and use to line a buttered 10 in / 25 cm tart pan. Prick the bottom of the pastry case with a fork and cover with the apple purée.
4. Peel the reserved apples. Cut into quarters, remove the cores and slice as thinly as possible. Arrange the apple slices in overlapping layers on the purée and sprinkle with the remaining sugar.
5. Bake for 35-40 minutes or until the pastry case is firm and golden.
6. Warm the fruit jelly and brush over the apple slices as soon as the tart is removed from the oven.

Tarte aux fraises

Strawberry Tart

	00:30 plus making pastry		00:25

American	Ingredients	Metric/Imperial
1 quantity	Rich flan pastry (see page 460)	1 quantity
⅔ cup	Red currant or raspberry jelly	250 g / 8 oz
¼ cup	Water	4 tbsp
1 lb	Strawberries	500 g / 1 lb
2 tbsp	Sugar	2 tbsp
½	Lemon	½

1. Preheat the oven to 350°F / 180°C / Gas Mark 4.
2. Roll out the pastry and use to line a buttered 10 in / 25 cm tart pan. Prick the bottom of the pastry case, then bake 'blind' for 20 minutes.
3. Meanwhile, combine the red currant or raspberry jelly and water in a small pan and cook for 10 minutes over a low heat to give a smooth syrup.
4. Rinse, drain and hull the strawberries.
5. Remove the pastry case from the pan and place it on a plate. Sprinkle with the sugar mixed with the grated rind of the ½ lemon and then fill with the strawberries. Just before serving glaze with the jelly syrup.

Brown sugar tart

Tarte au citron

Lemon Tart

	00:40 plus making pastry		00:30

American	Ingredients	Metric/Imperial
1 quantity	Basic short pastry (see page 457)	1 quantity
3	Lemons	3
2	Eggs	2
1 cup	Superfine [caster] sugar	250 g / 8 oz
1 cup	Ground almonds	125 g / 4 oz
1 cup	Water	250 ml / 8 fl oz
1	Vanilla bean [pod]	1
3	Glacé cherries	3

1. Preheat the oven to 350°F / 180°C / Gas Mark 4.
2. Roll out the pastry to ¼ in / 5 mm thick and use to line a buttered 10 in / 25 cm tart pan. Prick the bottom of the pastry case with a fork.
3. Finely grate the rind and squeeze the juice from 1 lemon. Beat the eggs with ¼ cup [50 g / 2 oz] of the sugar until pale, then stir in the ground almonds and lemon rind and juice.
4. Pour the mixture into the pastry case and bake for 30 minutes or until the filling is golden brown.
5. Meanwhile, thinly slice the remaining lemons. Dissolve the rest of the sugar in the water and add the vanilla bean, cut in half lengthwise. Boil for 10 minutes. Add the lemon slices and cook for 10 minutes longer. Drain, reserving the syrup.
6. Arrange the lemon slices in the tart case and garnish with halved glacé cherries. Pour over the syrup.

Cook's tip: if liked, cover the cooked tart with 2 egg whites stiffly beaten with ½ cup [125 g / 4 oz] superfine sugar and a pinch of salt. Brown in a cool oven.

Tarte Tatin

Upside-down Apple Tart

	00:25 plus making pastry	00:30

American	Ingredients	Metric/Imperial
1 lb	Firm apples	500 g / 1 lb
½ cup	Butter	125 g / 4 oz
¾ cup	Sugar	150 g / 5 oz
1 quantity	Basic short pastry (see page 457)	1 quantity
1 cup	Crème fraîche (see page 122)	250 ml / 8 fl oz

1. Preheat the oven to 350°F / 180°C / Gas Mark 4.
2. Peel, core and thickly slice the apples.
3. Butter a 9 in / 22 cm tart pan with 2 tablespoons [25 g / 1 oz] of the butter and sprinkle with half of the sugar. Arrange the apple slices in the pan and sprinkle with the remaining sugar. Cut the remaining butter into small pieces and dot over the apples.
4. Roll out the pastry to ¼ in / 5 mm thick and cut out an 11 in / 28 cm round. Place the pastry round over the apples and press the edges down well.
5. Put the pan over a high heat on top of the stove for 3 minutes to caramelize the sugar, then transfer to the oven and bake for 30 minutes.
6. To serve, turn the tart out of the pan onto a plate with the caramelized apples on top. Serve with crème fraîche.

Tarte aux myrtilles

Bilberry Tart

	00:40 plus making pastry	00:20

American	Ingredients	Metric/Imperial
1 quantity	Basic short pastry (see page 457)	1 quantity
¾ lb	Bilberries or blueberries	350 g / 12 oz
½ cup	Sugar	125 g / 4 oz
1 cup	Water	250 ml / 8 fl oz
2 tbsp	Apricot jam	2 tbsp

1. Preheat the oven to 400°F / 200°C / Gas Mark 6.
2. Roll out the pastry and use to line a 10 in / 25 cm tart pan. Prick the bottom of the pastry case with a fork. Bake 'blind' for 20 minutes.
3. Meanwhile, remove the stalks from the berries, and rinse and drain them.
4. Dissolve the sugar in the water and bring to a boil. Boil for 5 minutes over a moderate heat. Remove the pan from the heat and add the berries. Leave to infuse for 2 minutes, then return the pan to a low heat and cook the berries for 2 minutes or until they have absorbed the syrup.
5. Melt the apricot jam with 1 tablespoon of water over a low heat.
6. Pour the berries into the tart case and glaze with the jam. Leave to cool and then refrigerate for at least four hours before serving.

Cook's tip: bilberries are attractive mixed with other berries, such as raspberries, strawberries or red and black currants in an open tart.

Tarte rustique aux abricots

Country Style Apricot Tart

	00:30 plus making pastry	00:45 to 00:50

American	Ingredients	Metric/Imperial
1 quantity	Basic short pastry (see page 457)	1 quantity
2 tbsp	Superfine [caster] sugar	25 g / 1 oz
2 lb	Apricots	1 kg / 2 lb
	Confectioners' [icing] sugar	

1. Preheat the oven to 425°F / 220°C / Gas Mark 7.
2. Roll out the pastry to ¼ in / 5 mm thick and use to line a buttered 10 in / 25 cm tart pan. Prick the bottom of the pastry case with a fork and sprinkle with 1 tablespoon of sugar.
3. Cut the apricots in half and remove the pits [stones]. Arrange the apricots in the pastry case, cut side uppermost, and overlapping each other.
4. Bake for 20 minutes, then lower the temperature to 350°F / 180°C / Gas Mark 4. Sprinkle the apricots with the remaining sugar and bake for a further 20-25 minutes or until the pastry case is firm.
5. Serve hot or cold, sprinkled with confectioners' sugar.

Red, white and black currants are delicious in tarts and flans

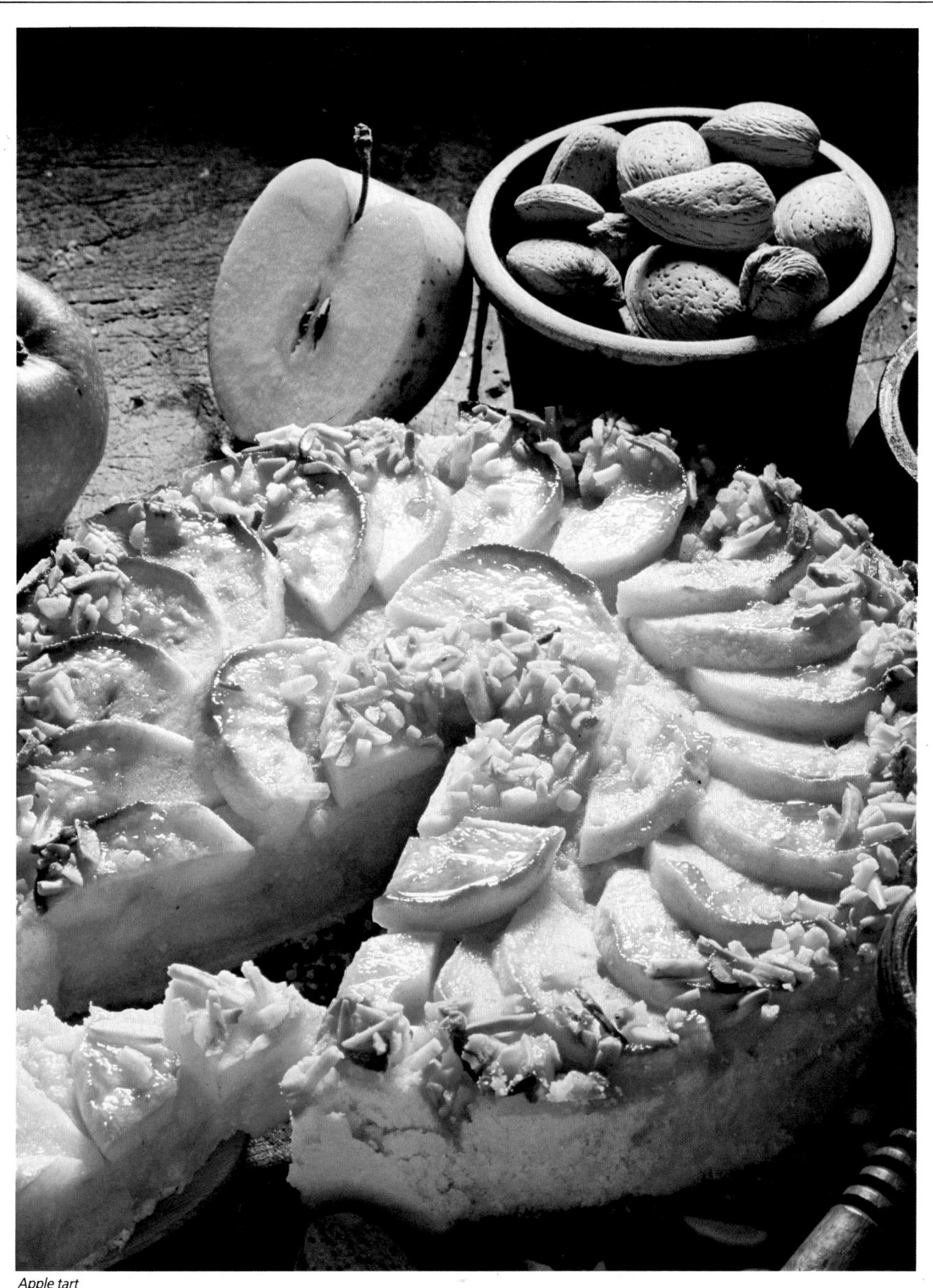

Apple tart

Cakes and pastries

Producing homemade cakes and pastries as good as those from the baker — and in many cases much better — is not only possible, it is also very easy. Even if you are not an experienced cook, the confections described in this chapter will present little difficulty once you have studied the general guidelines set out below. The most important thing to remember about these recipes is that they leave no room for improvisation; you must use only the ingredients listed, in exactly the quantities specified. All you need then is a reliable oven and a range of inexpensive equipment to guarantee success.

Choosing and using ingredients

The quality of the ingredients that go into your baked goods will be reflected in their taste and texture, so it's worth using the very best you can afford. Before you go shopping, familiarize yourself with the various types of sugar, flour etc. available, and the purposes for which each is intended.

Sugar
There are many different forms of sugar commonly used in baking — confectioners' or powdered [icing] sugar, superfine [caster] sugar, crystallized and cube or lump sugar among them — and the one you choose will affect the lightness and texture of your cakes and pastries.

Superfine [caster] sugar: the type most commonly used, this is a fine, quick-dissolving form of granulated sugar, and the best choice for cakes, as well as for fruit salads, creams and meringues. It is also excellent for dusting on crêpes and cooked fritters. The ordinary granulated sugar available in Europe is too coarse to be used for light, sponge-type cakes, but American granulated sugar is finer, and perfectly suitable for this purpose.

Cook's tip: when beating sugar with egg yolks, sprinkle it in slowly for best results. The mixture will turn pale in color and increase in volume as the sugar dissolves.

Vanilla sugar: fine sugar flavored with vanilla, this type is sold in sachets, but you can make your own by burying a vanilla bean [pod] in up to 4 cups [500 g / 1 lb] of sugar in an airtight jar. Use vanilla sugar instead of beans to enhance creams and ices as well as cakes.

Confectioners' or powdered [icing] sugar: a very fine form of sugar, this variety is extremely vulnerable to damp and must therefore be kept completely dry. Although mainly employed in icings, it is also useful on its own for cake decorating and in chantilly cream.

White sugar cubes or lumps: most often used crushed coarsely and sprinkled over cakes and sweet breads before baking. At one time, cube or lump (or loaf) sugar was the purest sugar, and therefore the first choice for many purposes, but now all forms of sugar are equally pure, so your choice should be made on grounds of flavor and texture alone.

Crystallized sugar: easily recognizable by the tiny, shiny crystals that give it its name, this type is used mostly for cake decoration, though it is sometimes sprinkled inside a greased cake pan before the batter [mixture] is poured in to prevent the cake from sticking.

Fondant: a thick white paste made by boiling sugar and water, and used to ice cakes or for making sweets. Fondant can be tinted with a few drops of food coloring or flavored with coffee, chocolate or any other suitable extract [essence].

Cook's tip: before using fondant, heat it in a bowl placed in a pan of water, but take care that the temperature does not exceed 104°F / 40°C. The paste is ready to use when it has reached spreading consistency and before it becomes runny, but you should work with it quickly, before it cools and hardens.

Flour
The nature and quality of the flour that is used for your baked goods will have more effect on the finished product than any other ingredient. There are several types of flour available, and these differ from country to country, but it is extremely important that you choose the right one for the purpose you have in mind. Whichever flour you are using, it must be sifted to get rid of any lumps. Although it is possible to buy pre-sifted flour, you should sift it again for best results.

Whole wheat flour: made from the entire wheat grain, this type of flour is good for you because it contains more nutrients than white flours and provides much of the fiber lacking in our modern diet. Cakes and pastries made with whole wheat flour, however, are not as light as those made from other kinds.

Once you have opened a bag of flour, store it in an airtight container in a dry place, where it will keep for several months.

Eggs
Eggs have a dual role in baking: the yolks bind mixtures, and the whites, when beaten until stiff, lighten them. Eggs are sold in a range of sizes, and the difference can be an important one (especially in delicate recipes such as choux pastry), so choose the medium size unless your instructions specify large or small.

Check to make sure the eggs are fresh (see page 212), then break each one into a saucer before you add it to the other ingredients to avoid spoiling the mixture if one egg is bad.

Egg whites will spoil at room temperature in 3-4 hours, so you should put them in the refrigerator immediately, where they will keep for up to 4 days — as will yolks, which should first be covered with a little water. Add leftover egg whites to omelettes or beat them with sugar to make a meringue topping. Yolks can be added to custards or quiches, or used to make mayonnaise.

Cook's tip: to separate eggs easily, break each one into a funnel with a small slot. When you tip the funnel slightly, only the white will pass through.

Fats and oils
Like eggs, fats perform several functions in cooking: they enhance flavor, act as emulsifying agents and allow especially baked foods to brown beautifully.

Butter: whether the butter you are using is salted, slightly salted or sweet (unsalted), its taste will strongly affect that of your cakes or pastries, so make sure it is completely fresh. Salted butter keeps longer than the unsalted variety, but it will go brown and burn at a lower temperature.

Cook's tips: if a recipe stipulates 'softened butter', take it out of the refrigerator 2 hours in advance. You will find it difficult to cream butter for making cakes and cookies [biscuits] when it is very cold and hard.

To cream butter, cut it into small pieces, place it in a warm bowl and beat it with a fork or wooden spoon.

Butter for melting should be measured into a heavy-based saucepan. Warm it over a very low heat, watching it carefully, and remove the pan before it begins to bubble.

Margarine: purists would never use anything but pure butter, but the best quality margarines, although they lack butter's distinctive taste, are sometimes easier to cream than butter, and always cheaper. Soft margarines are particularly suited to cake-making, while hard ones are best for pastry.

Oil: it is possible to use oil rather than butter or margarine for baking, but the finished product will have a very fine texture that is not to everyone's taste. You cannot substitute oil for butter directly in cake recipes, so look for those that have been specifically designed around liquid shortening. Do not use olive or walnut oil for this purpose since their flavors are too strong.

Similarly, use a neutral oil such as peanut [groundnut] or corn to fry fritters or doughnuts, and make sure the temperature is regulated correctly – the oil should not smoke.

Cornstarch [cornflour]

Cornstarch is a fine white powder milled from corn [maize] and used as a thickening agent. In France and other European countries, potato flour or starch is more commonly used, and this has a less pronounced flavor than that made from corn, which requires more careful mixing and cooking. To avoid a lumpy consistency and an unpleasant raw taste in your soups and sauces, dissolve the powder in a little cold water or milk, then add it to hot (but never boiling) liquid.

Yeast

A living organism that leavens by means of fermentation, yeast is sold in one of two forms:

Fresh or compressed yeast is sometimes difficult to find, but it is quick and easy to use. Check that it has an even, creamy color, a pronounced yeasty smell and a firm consistency without any tendency to crumble. Fresh yeast will keep for up to a week in the refrigerator, and up to a month in the freezer. Always dissolve fresh yeast in a little warm (not hot) water or milk before using.

Dried yeast comes in cans and packages and, if it is unopened, can be stored for up to a year. Once opened, however, it should be used within 2-3 months. Reconstitute dried yeast by sprinkling it onto warm milk or water in which a small amount of sugar has been dissolved. Remember that you will need only half the quantity of dried yeast as fresh.

Baking powder

A chemical raising agent, baking powder contains bicarbonate of soda, cream of tartar and a small amount of starch to keep the powder dry during storage. When this mixture is exposed to moisture and warmth, it gives off bubbles of carbon dioxide that expand and cause the dough or batter to rise.

Chocolate

The darker, less sweet types of chocolate have a stronger flavor and a firmer consistency than the lighter, milkier ones and are therefore the usual choice for cooking and baking. If you need to melt chocolate together with butter or liquid of some kind, the mixture can be put directly on to a very low heat in a heavy-based pan. To be melted by itself however, chocolate should be broken into small pieces and placed in a bowl over (but not touching) a pan of very hot, or just barely simmering, water. Be careful not to overheat it, since the taste of burnt chocolate will overpower all other ingredients.

Working with your oven

Even when you have prepared your recipe carefully and correctly, its success will not be guaranteed unless you can depend on your oven.

Precise cooking times are given in the recipes in this book, but every oven has its quirks, so you should get to know whether yours heats quickly or slowly, or if it tends to be slightly hotter or cooler than the temperature indicated.

Remember that cakes containing egg whites or yeast, i.e. mixtures that 'rise', must be at least 4 in / 10 cm below the roof of the oven. These need a moderate oven (350°F / 180°C / Gas Mark 4) since they will rise too quickly at a higher temperature, and then fall. All other types of mixture should be placed in the middle of the oven; if the top of your cake or pastry begins to brown too quickly, protect it by covering with a piece of foil.

Cherry sponge cake (see page 490)

Dame de pique

Queen of Spades

	01:00	00:30

American	Ingredients	Metric/Imperial
½ cup	Sugar	100 g / 4 oz
⅓ cup	Water	5 tbsp
⅓ cup	Golden raisins [sultanas]	50 g / 2 oz
⅔ cup	Rum	150 ml / ¼ pint
1 quantity	Genoese sponge cake batter (see page 460)	1 quantity
5 tbsp	Cocoa powder	5 tbsp
8 oz	Semisweet [plain] chocolate	250 g / 8 oz
1¼ cups	Chantilly cream (see page 455)	300 ml / ½ pint

1. Preheat the oven to 300°-325°F / 140°-160°C / Gas Mark 2-3.
2. Put the sugar into a small saucepan with the water and bring to a boil, stirring to dissolve the sugar. Boil for 5 minutes, then add the raisins. Remove from the heat and leave to steep in the syrup. When cool, add the rum.
3. Prepare the sponge cake batter, adding 4 tablespoons cocoa with the flour. Pour the batter into a buttered 7 in / 18 cm cake pan. Bake for 20-25 minutes.
4. When the sponge cake is cooked, remove it from the oven and turn it out onto a wire rack. Leave to cool.
5. Break 5 oz / 150 g of the chocolate into a small bowl and melt it over a pan of hot water. Allow to cool slightly.
6. Cut the cake into three layers with a serrated knife. Drain the raisins and brush the rum syrup over the cake layers.
7. Mix the melted chocolate with 1 heaping tablespoon of the chantilly cream, then gently stir in half the remaining chantilly cream. Keep the rest of the cream to decorate the cake.
8. Spread the cake layers with the chocolate cream and dot with the raisins. Place the layers one on top of the other, to reassemble the cake.
9. Cover the top of the cake with the remaining chantilly cream and sprinkle with the remaining chocolate, grated, and cocoa. Serve well chilled.
10. This cake will keep in the refrigerator for 24 hours.

Babas au rhum

Rum Babas

	00:45 plus rising	00:35 Makes 8

American	Ingredients	Metric/Imperial
¼ cup	Butter	50 g / 2 oz
1 package	Active dry yeast	½ sachet
2½ cups	Water	500 ml / ¾ pint
1 cup	Flour	125 g / 4 oz
	Salt	
1 tbsp	Superfine [caster] sugar	1 tbsp
2	Eggs	2
1 cup	Granulated sugar	250 g / 8 oz
1	Vanilla bean [pod]	1
⅔ cup	Rum	150 ml / ¼ pint

1. The dough used for rum babas is identical to that used for a savarin (see page 500). Melt the butter and leave to cool.

Dissolve the yeast in 1 tablespoon of the warm water. Sift the flour into a mixing bowl and add a pinch of salt, the superfine sugar and 1 egg. Mix well together. Add the dissolved yeast and stir well, then beat in the second egg. Beat for 5 minutes or until the dough is smooth and elastic. Add the melted butter and beat for a few more seconds.
2. Butter 8 baba molds and fill with the dough. Leave to rise in a warm place for 30 minutes.
3. Preheat the oven to 400°F / 200°C / Gas Mark 6.
4. Bake the babas for 15-20 minutes. Unmold them onto a wire rack and leave until cold.
5. Meanwhile, combine the granulated sugar, remaining water and vanilla bean, split in half lengthwise, in a heavy-bottomed pan. Bring to a boil and remove from the heat.
6. Dip the babas in the syrup until they stop bubbling, then transfer to a serving dish.
7. Pour all the excess syrup from the serving dish into a bowl and add the rum. Leave until cold, then pour over the babas. Chill until ready to serve.

Fruit fritters

Biscuit de Savoie

Savoy Sponge Cake

	00:20	00:30

American	Ingredients	Metric/Imperial
3 tbsp	Butter	40 g / 1½ oz
¾ cup	Superfine [caster] sugar	180 g / 6 oz
4	Eggs, separated	4
½ cup	Flour	60 g / 2 oz
½ cup	Potato starch or flour	60 g / 2 oz
	Vanilla extract [essence]	

1. Preheat the oven to 350°F / 180°C / Gas Mark 4.
2. Melt the butter in a small pan over a low heat.
3. Beat the sugar into the egg yolks until pale, then quickly work in the flour and potato starch.
4. Beat the egg whites until very stiff. Add the melted butter and few drops of vanilla extract to the egg yolk mixture, then fold in the whites.
5. Pour the mixture into a buttered and floured 10 in / 25 cm cake pan. Bake for 30 minutes.
6. Leave the sponge to cool in the pan.

Cake des débutants

Sponge Cake made with Oil

◢ 00:15		00:40 ◥
American	**Ingredients**	**Metric/Imperial**
4 cups	Flour	500 g / 1 lb
4 tsp	Baking powder	4 tsp
5	Eggs	5
1½ cups	Superfine [caster] sugar	300 g / 11 oz
1	Lemon	1
	Salt	
1¼ cups	Oil	300 ml / ½ pint
2 cups	Milk	450 ml / ¾ pint

1. Preheat the oven to 350°F / 180°C / Gas Mark 4.
2. Sift the flour into a mixing bowl with the baking powder and make a well in the center.
3. In another mixing bowl beat the eggs with the sugar, the finely grated rind of the lemon and a pinch of salt. When the mixture is frothy, stir in the oil and milk.
4. Slowly pour this mixture into the flour, beating well to prevent lumps.
5. Pour batter into a buttered and bottom-lined loaf pan.
6. Bake for 40 minutes, covering with foil if the top is browning too quickly. The cake is cooked when a skewer inserted in the center comes out clean.

Cook's tip: this cake will keep for over 10 days.

Cake aux fruits confits

Glacé Fruit Cake

◢ 00:25		01:50 ◥
American	**Ingredients**	**Metric/Imperial**
⅓ cup	Raisins	50 g / 2 oz
⅓ cup	Rum	5 tbsp
1 cup	Assorted glacé fruit (cherry, melon, pineapple, pear, apricot)	150 g / 5 oz
1	Lemon	1
⅔ cup	Butter	150 g / 5 oz
⅔ cup	Superfine [caster] sugar	150 g / 5 oz
4	Eggs	4
2 cups	Flour	225 g / 8 oz
2 tsp	Baking powder	2 tsp
1 cup	Blanched almonds	100 g / 4 oz

1. Preheat the oven to 400°F / 200°C / Gas Mark 6.
2. In a small pan, warm the raisins in the rum over a low heat, then set alight.
3. Dice the glacé fruit (apart from the cherries, which should be set aside). Finely grate the rind of the lemon, and add to the raisins together with the diced fruit. Leave to steep.
4. Cream the butter with the sugar until pale. Beat in the eggs one at a time, working each in well before adding the next. Stir in the steeped fruit mixture, flour and baking powder. The mixture must be quite thick or the fruit will sink.
5. Put half the cake batter into a buttered and lined 10 in / 25 cm long loaf pan. Dust the glacé cherries with a little

flour and arrange in the pan, then cover with the remaining batter. Arrange the almonds on top.
6. Bake for 20 minutes after which time the cake should have risen. Lower the oven temperature to 325°F / 160°C / Gas Mark 3 and bake for a further 1½ hours. Watch the color and cover with foil if it browns too quickly. The cake is cooked when a skewer inserted in the center comes out clean.
7. Turn the cake out of the pan onto a wire rack and leave to cool in the lining paper for 12 hours.

Cook's tip: this cake will keep for several days in an airtight tin in its lining paper.

Sponge cake made with oil

Beignets aux fruits

Fruit Fritters

◢ 00:30 plus making batter		00:05 per batch ◥
American	**Ingredients**	**Metric/Imperial**
2 lb	Fruit (apples, pineapple rings, bananas or oranges)	1 kg / 2 lb
¼ cup	Rum	4 tbsp
¼ cup	Superfine [caster] sugar	50 g / 2 oz
1 quantity	Sweet fritter batter (see page 459)	1 quantity
	Oil for deep frying	
	Confectioners' [icing] sugar	

1. Apple fritters: Peel and core the apples and cut into rounds ¼ in / 5 mm thick. Steep for 1 hour in the rum and sugar, mixed together. Dip the apple rings one at a time in the batter and drop into hot, but not smoking, oil. Fry until golden brown then lift out of the oil with a slotted spoon and drain on paper towels. Serve hot, sprinkled with confectioners' sugar.
2. Pineapple fritters: Cut large rings in half and steep and cook as for the apples. Take care to pat dry before coating in batter.
3. Banana fritters: Cut bananas in half and then in half lengthwise, and steep and cook as for the apples.
4. Orange fritters: Peel and slice, and steep and cook as for apples, but pat dry before coating in batter.

Bavarois à l'ananas
Pineapple Bavarois

�	01:00 plus chilling		00:00

American	Ingredients	Metric/Imperial
1 (1 lb)	Can of pineapple rings	1 (500 g / 1 lb)
2 envelopes	Unflavored gelatin	2 sachets
3 cups	Cold vanilla custard sauce (see page 454)	750 ml / 1 ¼ pint
⅔ cup	Kirsch	150 ml / ¼ pint
⅔ cup	Crème fraîche (see page 122)	150 ml / ¼ pint
1 tbsp	Confectioners' [icing] sugar	1 tbsp

1. Drain the pineapple, reserving the juice. Set aside several rings for decoration and chop the rest. Dissolve the gelatin in the pineapple juice.
2. Stir the chopped pineapple and gelatin mixture into the vanilla custard sauce and flavor with the kirsch.
3. Whip the chilled crème fraîche in a cold bowl until thick, gradually adding the confectioners' sugar. Set aside 2 tablespoons and gently fold the remaining crème into the pineapple custard.
4. Pour the mixture into an oiled 1½ quart [1.5 l / 2½ pint] bavarois mold. Chill for at least 3 hours or until set.
5. When ready to serve dip the base of the mold quickly in hot water. Place a plate over the mold and turn the bavarois onto the plate. Decorate with the reserved pineapple rings and the remaining cream.

Biscuits de Noël
Christmas Cookies [Biscuits]

�	00:40 Makes about 40	00:15 to 00:20

American	Ingredients	Metric/Imperial
1 cup	Superfine [caster] sugar	250 g / 8 oz
1 cup	Butter	250 g / 8 oz
2	Eggs	2
4 cups	Flour	500 g / 1 lb
	Salt	
	Cayenne pepper	
	Ground coriander	
	Ground aniseed	
1	Lemon	1
⅓ cup	Red jam	125 g / 4 oz
1½ cups	Confectioners' [icing] sugar	200 g / 7 oz
1 tsp	Rum	1 tsp
⅓ cup	Golden raisins [sultanas]	50 g / 2 oz

1. Preheat the oven to 350°F / 180°C / Gas Mark 4.
2. Cream the sugar with the butter until light and fluffy. Beat in the eggs one at a time. Sift in the flour and a pinch each of salt, cayenne pepper, coriander and aniseed.
3. Add the juice and finely grated rind of ½ lemon and knead until the dough is supple.
4. Roll out the dough to ¼ in / 5 mm thick. Cut into rounds or other shapes with a pastry cutter. Arrange the rounds on a buttered baking sheet.
5. Bake for 15-20 minutes. Cool on a wire rack.

6. Cut out the center of half the cookies. Spread the other half with jam and top with the cut cookies.
7. Mix the confectioners' sugar with the rum and 1 teaspoon of lemon juice. Ice the cookies and decorate each with a few raisins while the icing is still wet.

Biscuits à la cuillère
Ladyfingers [Sponge Fingers]

�	00:30 Makes about 50	00:12 to 00:15

American	Ingredients	Metric/Imperial
5	Eggs, separated	5
½ cup	Superfine [caster] sugar	125 g / 4 oz
1 cup	Flour	125 g / 4 oz
½	Lemon	½
1 cup	Confectioners' [icing] sugar	125 g / 4 oz

1. Preheat the oven to 350°F / 180°C / Gas Mark 4.
2. Beat the egg yolks with 6 tablespoons of the superfine sugar until pale in color. Add the flour and the grated rind of the half lemon.
3. Beat the egg whites until stiff. Gradually beat in the remaining superfine sugar.
4. Fold the egg whites carefully into the egg yolk.
5. Pipe the mixture onto a baking sheet, lined with parchment paper, in fingers about 4 in / 10 cm long. Sprinkle generously with confectioners' sugar and shake off any excess sugar.
6. Bake, with the oven door slightly open, for 12-15 minutes. Take great care not to open the door fully during the first 12 minutes or the fingers will fall.
7. Loosen the fingers using a metal spatula and cool on the baking sheet.

Cook's tip: these cookies will keep for at least 2 weeks in an airtight tin.

Biscuits au chocolat
Chocolate-coated Cookies [Biscuits]

▎readygraphic	00:30	00:30

American	Ingredients	Metric/Imperial
3 cups	Flour	350 g / 12 oz
¾ cup	Butter	175 g / 6 oz
1 tbsp	Baking powder	1 tbsp
	Salt	
¾ cup	Superfine [caster] sugar	175 g / 6 oz
2	Eggs	2
1 cup	Ground almonds	125 g / 4 oz
⅔ cup	Jam	250 g / 8 oz
¾ lb	Semisweet [plain] chocolate	350 g / 12 oz
2 tbsp	Milk	2 tbsp

1. Preheat the oven to 400°F / 200°C / Gas Mark 6.
2. Sift the flour into a mixing bowl and make a well in the center. Add the butter, cut into pieces, the baking powder, a

pinch of salt, the sugar and eggs. Beat until the mixture is well mixed, then add the ground almonds. Roll the dough into a ball. (Use a food processor, if preferred, to make this dough.)
3. Roll out the dough to ¼ in / 5 mm thick and cut into rounds with a cutter or small saucer.
4. Transfer the rounds to a buttered baking sheet. Bake for 15-20 minutes.
5. When the cookies are cooked, remove from the baking sheet using a metal spatula and leave to cool on a wire rack.
6. Spread half the cookies with jam and sandwich together with the remaining cookies.
7. Break the chocolate into a small bowl over a pan of hot water and add the milk. Melt over a low heat, stirring continuously.
8. Dip the sandwiched cookies one at a time in the chocolate using tongs. Place on a sheet of foil and leave to cool and set in the refrigerator.

Charlotte au pommes
Apple Charlotte

	00:30 plus chilling	00:15

American	Ingredients	Metric/Imperial
4 lb	Apples	2 kg / 4 lb
1½ cups	Sugar	300 g / 11 oz
1	Lemon	1
¼ tsp	Ground cinnamon	¼ tsp
⅔ cup	Butter	150 g / 5 oz
24	Ladyfingers [sponge fingers] (see page 480)	24
1½ cups	Thin crème fraîche (see page 122)	350 ml / 12 fl oz

1. Peel, quarter and core the apples. Place in a pan with the sugar, juice of the lemon, cinnamon and butter and cook for 15 minutes, stirring from time to time until the apples are soft and pulpy. Leave until completely cold.
2. Cover the bottom and sides of a charlotte mold with ladyfingers, curved side to the mold. Cut off the ends if they are taller than the mold.
3. Whip the chilled crème fraîche in a cold bowl until it has doubled in volume. Stir one-third of the whipped crème into the cooked apples and pour into the mold. Cover with the remaining ladyfingers.
4. Chill for at least 3 hours.
5. Just before serving, unmold the charlotte onto a plate. Decorate with the remaining whipped crème.

Cigarettes
Cigarettes

	00:20	00:05 per batch

American	Ingredients	Metric/Imperial
⅔ cup	Butter	150 g / 5 oz
1½ cups	Superfine [caster] sugar	300 g / 11 oz
	Vanilla extract [essence]	
6	Egg whites, at room temperature	6
1 tbsp	Thick crème fraîche (see page 122)	1 tbsp
1½ cups	Flour	175 g / 6 oz

1. Preheat the oven to 475°F / 240°C / Gas Mark 9.
2. Cream together the butter, sugar and a few drops of vanilla extract until fluffy. Beat in the egg whites two at a time, mixing well after each addition. Add the crème fraîche and sifted flour. Beat until very smooth and glossy.
3. Pipe small heaps of the mixture, about ¾ in / 2 cm in diameter, on to a buttered baking sheet. Take care that the heaps are widely spaced.
4. Bake for about 5 minutes or until the edges are brown. Quickly remove the cookies, one at a time, from the sheet with a sharp knife and wrap around a pencil or wooden spoon handle to give a cigarette shape. Cool on a wire rack.

Cook's tip: serve with sorbet, ice cream or mousse. These cookies will keep for at least a month in an airtight tin.

Sachertorte (see page 500)

Congolais
Chocolate Pyramids

	00:10	00:20

American	Ingredients	Metric/Imperial
1¾ cups	Cocoa powder	200 g / 7 oz
¾ cup	Sugar	150 g / 5 oz
	Vanilla extract [essence]	
2	Eggs	2
1	Egg yolk	1

1. Beat together the cocoa, sugar, a few drops of vanilla extract, the whole eggs and egg yolk until smooth. Leave to stand for 30 minutes.
2. Preheat the oven to 350°F / 180°C / Gas Mark 4.
3. Shape the mixture into egg-shaped balls and place on a lightly buttered baking sheet. Shape the balls into pyramids with your hands and a wet spatula, or flatten into cakes with a fork.
4. Bake for at least 20 minutes, without allowing them to brown.

Charlotte au chocolat
Chocolate Charlotte

	00:30 plus chilling	00:00 Serves 6–8

American	Ingredients	Metric/Imperial
1 cup	Sugar	250 g / 8 oz
1 cup	Water	250 ml / 8 fl oz
½ lb	Semisweet [plain] chocolate	250 g / 8 oz
½ cup	Butter at room temperature	125 g / 4 oz
5	Egg whites	5
½ lb	Ladyfingers [sponge fingers] (see page 480)	250 g / 8 oz
⅔ cup	Rum	150 ml / ¼ pint

1. In a saucepan, dissolve the sugar in 5 tablespoons of water, stirring with a wooden spoon. Cook over a low heat (without stirring) until you have a syrup that is thick but not colored. Remove from the heat and leave until warm.
2. Break the chocolate into a bowl and stand over a pan of hot water. Cook until the chocolate melts. Remove from the heat. Stir the butter into the chocolate until smooth.
3. Beat the egg whites until stiff. Beat in the sugar syrup. Stir in the chocolate mixture a little at a time to give a smooth cream.
4. Moisten the ladyfingers in the rum and remaining water mixed together. Use to line the bottom and sides of a lightly oiled 1 quart [1 l / 2 pint] charlotte mold. Cover the bottom of the mold with the chocolate cream, then add a layer of ladyfingers. Continue layering until the top layer of ladyfingers is slightly higher than the top of the mold (don't try to use all the cream).
5. Place a weighted board over the mold and chill in the refrigerator for 12 hours.
6. To serve, unmold onto a plate. Decorate the charlotte with chantilly cream (see page 455) or melted chocolate.

Chausson aux pommes
Apple Turnovers

	00:20 to 00:30 plus thawing or making pastry Makes 1 large or 10 small turnovers	00:45

American	Ingredients	Metric/Imperial
4	Apples	4
1 tbsp	Thick crème fraîche (see page 122)	1 tbsp
¾ cup	Sugar	150 g / 5 oz
1 lb	Puff pastry (see page 458)	500 g / 1 lb
1	Egg	1
2 tbsp	Butter	25 g / 1 oz

1. Preheat the oven to 450°F / 230°C / Gas Mark 8.
2. Peel, core and dice the apples. Roll in a mixture of the crème fraîche and sugar.
3. Roll out the pastry to ⅛ in / 3 mm thick. Cut into a round with the help of a large plate. Brush the outer 1 in / 2.5 cm with beaten egg.
4. Cover half the pastry with the apple mixture and dot with the butter. Fold over the other half of the pastry and pinch the edges together. Brush with beaten egg and when dry brush again. Make a design in the top with a pointed knife and prick with a fork. Place on a baking sheet.

5. Bake for 45 minutes, covering with foil if the turnover begins to get too brown.
6. To make small turnovers, cut the pastry into 4 in / 10 cm rounds and then roll into ovals. Divide the apple mixture evenly between them and stick the edges together with beaten egg. Decorate as for the large turnover and bake for 30 minutes.

Cheesecake
Cheesecake

	00:20	01:30

American	Ingredients	Metric/Imperial
4	Eggs, separated	4
2 cups	Cream cheese	500 g / 1 lb
½ cup	Flour	50 g / 2 oz
1 cup	Superfine [caster] sugar	200 g / 7 oz
⅓ cup	Cornstarch [cornflour]	40 g / 1½ oz
2 cups	Milk	500 ml / ¾ pint
1	Orange or lemon	1
5	Graham crackers [digestive biscuits]	5

1. Preheat the oven to 400°F / 200°C / Gas Mark 6.
2. Combine the egg yolks, cream cheese, sifted flour, half the sugar and the cornstarch. Beat well, then slowly add the milk, beating until smooth. Finely grate the rind of the orange or lemon and add to the mixture.
3. Beat the egg whites until very stiff, gradually adding the remaining sugar. Fold carefully into the cheese mixture.
4. Butter a 10 in / 25 cm cake pan and sprinkle lightly with sugar. Crumble the graham crackers and scatter over the bottom of the pan. Fill with the cheese mixture. Place the pan in a shallow ovenproof dish and add water to come halfway up the cake pan.
5. Bake for 30 minutes, then lower the oven temperature to 325°F / 160°C / Gas Mark 3 and bake for a further 1 hour.
6. Leave to cool until warm before removing the cake from the pan. Cool on a wire rack and chill until ready to serve.

Cook's tip: the cake will keep for a week in the refrigerator.

Honey crêpes

Cornes de gazelle
Almond Croissants

	00:30 Makes 15	00:15 to 00:20

American	Ingredients	Metric/Imperial
2¾ cups	Ground almonds	300 g / 11 oz
½ cup	Superfine [caster] sugar	125 g / 4 oz
¼ cup	Melted butter	50 g / 2 oz
1½ tbsp	Orange-flower water	1½ tbsp
1¼ cups	Flour	175 g / 6 oz
1 cup	Flaked almonds	125 g / 4 oz

1. Mix together the ground almonds and sugar. Add half the melted butter and ½ tablespoon of the orange-flower water, drop by drop, mixing well. Set the almond paste aside.
2. Combine the flour with the remaining melted butter and orange-flower water. Add a little water, if necessary, to give a supple dough.
3. Preheat the oven to 350°F / 180°C / Gas Mark 4.
4. Divide both mixtures into 15 equal portions. Roll out each portion of dough to form a small square. Roll the 15 portions of almond paste into sticks, slightly shorter than the diagonal of the 15 squares of pastry.
5. Tip the flaked almonds onto a plate. Place the squares of dough one at a time on the plate and place a stick of almond paste across them. Roll up and curve the points around to resemble a small croissant.
6. Arrange the croissants on a buttered baking sheet. Bake until golden brown (15-20 minutes).
7. Leave the croissants to dry out for a few minutes with the oven door open before serving.

Crêpes Suzette
Crêpes Suzette

	00:20 plus making batter	00:40

American	Ingredients	Metric/Imperial
1 quantity	Crêpe batter (see page 458)	1 quantity
1 cup	Orange liqueur	200 ml / ⅓ pint
	Butter for frying	
½ cup	Butter	125 g / 4 oz
1	Orange	1
½ cup	Sugar	125 g / 4 oz
⅔ cup	Brandy	150 ml / ¼ pint

1. Crêpes Suzette are finished just before serving, but the crêpes should be made in advance.
2. Prepare the crêpe batter, flavoring it with 4 tablespoons of orange liqueur.
3. Melt a little butter in a frying pan. Pour in a ladle of batter and tip the pan in all directions until the bottom is covered evenly with batter. Cook over a moderate heat until the underside of the crêpe is golden brown. Turn it over and cook the other side. Remove the crêpe. Repeat until you have used all the batter. Pile up the crêpes (interleaved with wax [greaseproof] paper) and set aside until ready to serve.
4. Cream the butter with the grated rind of the orange.
5. Just before serving, melt a little of the orange butter in a frying pan over a moderate heat (or in a chafing dish at the table). Add a crêpe and turn it immediately to coat both sides. Sprinkle with a little sugar. Fold in 4 and transfer the crêpe to a hot plate.

6. Repeat for all the crêpes, then return them all to the pan. Pour over the brandy and remaining orange liqueur and sprinkle with the rest of the sugar. Heat, then set alight and serve flaming.

Crêpes au miel
Honey Crêpes

	00:10 plus making crêpes	00:10 Makes 15

American	Ingredients	Metric/Imperial
⅔ cup	Liquid honey	250 g / 8 oz
¾ cup	Chopped nuts	75 g / 3 oz
½ cup	Ground almonds	50 g / 2 oz
15	Freshly made crêpes (see page 458)	15

1. Preheat the oven to 375°F / 190°C / Gas Mark 5.
2. Warm the honey with the nuts and ground almonds.
3. Brush a little of the honey mixture over each crêpe, roll up and arrange in a buttered ovenproof dish. Reheat in the oven for a few minutes and serve hot.

Diplomate au moka
Coffee Diplomat

	01:00 plus chilling	00:20

American	Ingredients	Metric/Imperial
2 cups	Milk	500 ml / ¾ pint
1	Vanilla bean [pod]	1
6	Egg yolks	6
¾ cup	Superfine [caster] sugar	150 g / 5 oz
2 tsp	Unflavored gelatin	2 tsp
1 tsp	Coffee flavoring	1 tsp
16	Ladyfingers [sponge fingers]	16
1 cup	Thin crème fraîche (see page 122)	250 ml / 8 fl oz
2 tbsp	Confectioners' [icing] sugar	2 tbsp
	Vanilla extract [essence]	

1. Bring the milk to a boil with the vanilla bean, split in half. Remove the pan from the heat, cover and leave to infuse for 10 minutes.
2. Meanwhile, beat the egg yolks with the sugar until pale. Remove the vanilla bean from the milk and beat the milk into the egg mixture. Pour the mixture back into the pan and cook over a low heat, stirring, until thickened. Do not allow the custard to boil. Remove from the heat.
3. Dissolve the gelatin in a little water, and stir into the custard. Add the coffee flavoring. Leave until cold and beginning to set.
4. Cover the bottom and sides of a buttered 1 quart [1 l / 2 pint] charlotte mold with the ladyfingers, curved side to the mold. Cut the tops to be level with the top of the mold.
5. Whip the crème fraîche in a chilled bowl with the confectioners' sugar and a few drops of vanilla extract. Fold the whipped crème into the coffee custard and pour into the mold. Chill for 2 hours or until set.
6. Unmold the coffee diplomat onto a serving dish. It will be easier to turn out if you dip the mold in hot water for a few moments as this melts the butter that sticks the ladyfingers to the mold.

Crêpes soufflées
Soufflé Crepes

00:25
plus making crêpes

00:15 to 00:20

American	Ingredients	Metric/Imperial
1 cup	Milk	250 ml / 8 fl oz
6	Eggs, separated	6
6 tbsp	Superfine [caster] sugar	75 g / 3 oz
¼ cup	Flour	25 g / 1 oz
	Vanilla extract [essence]	
2 tbsp	Orange liqueur	2 tbsp
15	Crêpes (see page 458)	15
2 tbsp	Melted butter	25 g / 1 oz
	Confectioners' [icing] sugar	

1. Preheat the oven to 400°F / 200°C / Gas Mark 6.
2. Heat the milk in a saucepan. Beat the egg yolks and sugar together until frothy. Beat in the flour, then stir in the hot milk.
3. Pour into the milk saucepan and heat, stirring, until thickened. Do not boil. Add a few drops of vanilla extract and the orange liqueur and leave to cool until warm.
4. Beat the egg whites until very stiff and fold gently into the mixture.
5. Cover half of each crêpe with 3 tablespoons of the mixture and fold over the other half. Arrange the crêpes in a buttered ovenproof dish. Brush with melted butter and bake until risen.
6. Remove from the oven, sprinkle with confectioners' sugar and serve at once.

Croissants
Croissants

00:30
plus rising and chilling

00:20
Makes 20

American	Ingredients	Metric/Imperial
4 cups	Flour	500 g / 1 lb
2 packages	Active dry yeast	1 sachet
⅓ cup	Warm water	5 tbsp
¼ cup	Superfine [caster] sugar	50 g / 2 oz
2 tsp	Salt	2 tsp
2½ cups	Milk	450 ml / ¾ pint
½ cup	Butter, chilled	125 g / 4 oz
1	Egg	1

1. Put 1 cup [125 g / 4 oz] flour in a bowl. Dissolve the yeast in the warm water and stir into the flour. Work to form a soft dough, adding more warm water, if necessary. Leave in a warm place for 20 minutes or until doubled in volume.
2. Mix the remaining flour with the sugar, salt and milk to make a dough. Add the yeast dough and mix well.
3. Cut the chilled butter into pieces. Roll out the dough thinly and dot with the pieces of butter. Fold the dough into 3, to enclose the butter. Roll out again, then fold into 3 and chill for 25 minutes. Make 2 further 'turns' (rolling out and folding).
4. Finally roll out the dough to ¼ in / 5 mm thick. Cut into strips 5 in / 12 cm wide and then into triangles 4 in / 10 cm along the base. Roll each into a tube from the base, stretching the top over slightly.
5. Place on an ungreased baking sheet and stretch the rolls slightly to shape into crescents.
6. Cover with a linen towel and leave to rise in a warm place until tripled in volume.

7. Preheat the oven to 475°F / 240°C / Gas Mark 9.
8. Brush the risen croissants with beaten egg and bake for 20 minutes.

Crêpes suzette

Éclairs
Chocolate and Coffee Éclairs

00:30
Makes 12 large or 36 small éclairs

00:30

American	Ingredients	Metric/Imperial
1 quantity	Choux pastry (see page 457)	1 quantity
1 quantity	Pastry cream (see page 456)	1 quantity
2 tbsp	Instant coffee powder	2 tbsp
2 tbsp	Cocoa powder	2 tbsp
1 lb	Fondant icing (see page 457)	500 g / 1 lb

1. Preheat the oven to 400°F / 200°C / Gas Mark 6.
2. Put the choux pastry into a pastry bag fitted with a ¾ in / 15 mm nozzle. Pipe the pastry in 3 in / 7 cm lengths onto a buttered baking sheet, leaving plenty of room for them to swell. Bake for 20 minutes, or until they have risen well.
3. Remove the éclairs from the oven and pierce each on the side to allow the steam to escape. Leave until cold.
4. Divide the pastry cream in half. Flavor one-half with 1 tablespoon of instant coffee powder and the rest with 1 tablespoon of cocoa.
5. Put the chocolate cream into a pastry bag fitted with a ½ in / 1 cm nozzle. Make a hole in the end of each éclair and fill half the éclairs with chocolate cream. Fill the remaining éclairs with coffee cream.
6. Warm the fondant over a low heat in a pan, stirring until smooth. Flavor half the fondant with the remaining coffee powder and the other half with the remaining cocoa.
7. Dip the top of each chocolate éclair into the chocolate fondant and place on a serving plate. Repeat with the coffee éclairs and coffee fondant.

Gâteau aux fruits secs
Currant and Almond Sponge Cake

00:30 Serves 8–10   **00:50 to 01:00**

American	Ingredients	Metric/Imperial
⅔ cup	Currants	100 g / 4 oz
2 oz	Petit-beurre or other plain sweet cookies [biscuits]	60 g / 2 oz
2 tbsp	Melted butter	30 g / 1 oz
5	Eggs, separated	5
1 cup	Superfine [caster] sugar	200 g / 8 oz
⅔ cup	Blanched almonds	100 g / 4 oz
2¼ cups	Flour	230 g / 9 oz
1 tsp	Baking powder	1 tsp

1. Soak the currants in warm water for 30 minutes.
2. Preheat the oven to 325°F / 160°C / Gas Mark 3.
3. Crush the cookies into fine crumbs. Brush the bottom and sides of a 10 in / 24 cm tart pan with the butter and sprinkle with the cookie crumbs. Press the crumbs into the butter and chill the pan.
4. Beat the egg yolks and sugar together until pale. Drain the currants and finely chop three-quarters of the almonds. Stir the currants and chopped almonds into the mixture. Add the flour and baking powder and mix well.
5. Beat the egg whites until stiff and fold in carefully with a wooden spoon.
6. Pour the batter into the tart pan and bake for 50-60 minutes. The cake is cooked when the blade of a knife inserted into the center comes out clean.
7. To serve, unmold and decorate with the remaining blanched almonds.

Galette des rois
Twelfth Night Tart

Whoever finds the bean in their piece of this tart is king — or queen — for the night.

00:15 plus making or thawing pastry   **00:45**

American	Ingredients	Metric/Imperial
1¼ lb	Puff pastry (see page 458 or use frozen)	625 g / 1¼ lb
1	Dried bean	1
1	Egg	1

1. If using frozen pastry, allow it to thaw.
2. Preheat the oven to 430°F / 240°C / Gas Mark 8.
3. Roll out the pastry into a round ¼ in / 5 mm thick. Make a border by pushing up all round with the point of a knife. Make a small cut in the pastry and place the bean in it. Turn the pastry round over and place it on a dampened baking sheet.
4. Decorate the top by cutting lightly with a pointed knife. Brush the top with beaten egg, taking care not to allow the egg to run down the sides. Bake for 20 minutes.
5. Remove the tart from the oven and brush with the remaining egg. Lower the oven temperature to 400°F / 200°C / Gas Mark 6 and bake for a further 25 minutes or until golden brown. Serve warm from the oven or reheat before serving.

Financières
Financiers

00:15 Makes 24   **00:18 to 00:20**

American	Ingredients	Metric/Imperial
1 cup	Flour	100 g / 4 oz
1 cup	Ground almonds	100 g / 4 oz
	Salt	
1½ cups	Superfine [caster] sugar	300 g / 12 oz
8	Egg whites	8
¾ cup	Butter	175 g / 6 oz
	Vanilla extract [essence]	

1. Preheat the oven to 400°F / 200°C / Gas Mark 6.
2. Sift the flour into a bowl and add the ground almonds, a pinch of salt and the sugar. Work in the egg whites thoroughly to give a smooth mixture.
3. Melt the butter over a low heat until golden brown, then pour the butter into the bowl. Add a few drops of vanilla extract and mix well.
4. Butter 24 barquette (boat-shaped) molds and fill them with the batter. Place on a baking sheet. Bake for 20 minutes or until golden brown. Cover the financiers with foil as soon as the edges begin to brown.
5. Remove the baking sheet from the oven and turn the financiers out of the molds. Leave to cool.

Gâteau glacé au chocolat
Iced Chocolate Cake

00:30 plus chilling   **01:00 to 01:15** Serves 8–10

American	Ingredients	Metric/Imperial
¾ lb	Semisweet [plain] chocolate	350 g / 12 oz
1 tbsp	Water	1 tbsp
¾ cup	Superfine [caster] sugar	150 g / 5 oz
¾ cup	Butter	170 g / 6 oz
6	Eggs, separated	6
1¼ cups	Flour	150 g / 5 oz
3 tbsp	Apricot jam	3 tbsp
¾ cup	Confectioners' [icing] sugar	90 g / 3 oz

1. Preheat the oven to 350°F / 180°C / Gas Mark 4.
2. Break half of the chocolate into a bowl, add the water and place the bowl over a pan of hot water. Heat until the chocolate melts.
3. Cream the superfine sugar and ⅔ cup [150 g / 5 oz] of the butter together until pale and fluffy. Beat in the egg yolks to give a creamy mixture. Stir in the melted chocolate.
4. Beat the egg whites until stiff. Fold alternative spoonfuls of egg white and flour into the chocolate mixture.
5. Pour the batter into a buttered and lined 8 in / 20 cm cake pan. Bake for 1 hour 10 minutes or until the blade of a knife inserted into the center of the cake comes out clean.
6. Unmold the cake onto a wire rack and leave until cold.
7. Melt the apricot jam and brush all over the cooled cake.
8. Break the remaining chocolate into a bowl, add the remaining butter and place over a pan of hot water. When the chocolate has melted, beat in the confectioners' sugar and a little hot water if necessary. Spread over the cake, using a spatula. Chill for 4 hours or until set.

Gâteau au café
Coffee Layer Cake

00:30   00:35 to 00:40
Serves 6–8

American	Ingredients	Metric/Imperial
1¼ cups	Butter	300 g / 10 oz
1 cup	Brown sugar	180 g / 6 oz
3	Eggs	3
2 tbsp	Coffee flavoring	2 tbsp
1 tsp	Baking powder	1 tsp
1½ cups	Flour	180 g / 6 oz
2 cups	Confectioners' [icing] sugar	260 g / 8 oz
1 cup	Shelled nuts	100 g / 4 oz

1. Preheat the oven to 400°F / 200°C / Gas Mark 6.
2. Cut ¾ cup [180 g / 6 oz] of the butter into small pieces and cream using a wooden spoon. Add the brown sugar, eggs, 1 tablespoon of coffee flavoring and the baking powder. Beat thoroughly, then stir in the flour.
3. Pour the batter into a buttered and bottom-lined 10 in / 25 cm cake pan. Bake for 20 minutes, then lower the oven temperature to 350°F / 180°C / Gas Mark 4. Bake for a further 15-20 minutes or until the blade of a knife inserted into the center of the cake comes out clean.
4. Unmold the cake onto a wire rack and leave until cold.
5. Using a large knife, cut the cake into 2 layers.
6. Cream the remaining butter, then work in the confectioners' sugar with the remaining coffee flavoring.
7. Keep 8 nuts to one side and grind the remainder. Stir the ground nuts into the coffee buttercream.
8. Sprinkle the top cake layer with a little extra confectioners' sugar. Spoon the buttercream into a pastry bag fitted with a fluted nozzle and pipe 8 whirls onto the confectioners' sugar. Top with the reserved 8 nuts. Spread the other cake layer with the remaining buttercream and cover with the decorated cake layer. Chill until ready to serve.

Gâteau au chocolat
Chocolate Almond Cake

00:15   00:25 to 00:30
plus chilling

American	Ingredients	Metric/Imperial
¾ lb	Semisweet [plain] chocolate	375 g / 12 oz
3 tbsp	Water	3 tbsp
6	Eggs, separated	6
1¼ cups	Superfine [caster] sugar	270 g / 10 oz
1 cup	Ground almonds	100 g / 4 oz
½ tsp	Baking powder	½ tsp
3 tbsp	Potato starch or flour	3 tbsp
1¼ cups	Butter at room temperature	250 g / 10 oz
	Salt	
1 cup	Confectioners' [icing] sugar	100 g / 4 oz

1. Preheat the oven to 400°F / 200°C / Gas Mark 6.
2. Break ½ lb / 250 g of the chocolate into a bowl, add 2 tablespoons of the water and place over a pan of hot water. Heat until the chocolate melts.

3. Beat the 6 egg yolks with all but 2 tablespoons of the superfine sugar until pale and creamy. Stir in the melted chocolate. Add the ground almonds, baking powder, potato starch and 1 cup [200 g / 8 oz] of the butter. Mix well.
4. Beat the egg whites with a pinch of salt until stiff and fold into the batter.
5. Butter a 10 in / 4 cm cake pan and sprinkle with the remaining superfine sugar. Pour in the cake batter. Bake for 25-30 minutes. (The cake must cook quickly so that the center remains moist.) Remove from the oven and leave to cool.
6. Melt the remaining chocolate with the remaining butter and water in a bowl over a pan of hot water. Stir in the confectioners' sugar a spoonful at a time to give a thick cream. Cover the cake with this icing and chill until set.

Forêt noire
Black Forest Gâteau

00:40   00:30
Serves 8–10

American	Ingredients	Metric/Imperial
24	Ripe black cherries (or bottled or canned)	24
3 tbsp	Brandy	3 tbsp
½ lb	Semisweet [plain] chocolate	250 g / 8 oz
6	Eggs	6
2 cups	Granulated sugar	425 g / 15 oz
	Vanilla extract [essence]	
½ cup	Cocoa powder	50 g / 2 oz
1 cup	Flour	100 g / 4 oz
⅔ cup	Melted butter	150 g / 6 oz
1½ cups	Water	350 ml / 12 fl oz
⅓ cup	Kirsch	6 tbsp
3 cups	Thick crème fraîche (see page 122)	750 ml / 1¼ pints
⅔ cup	Iced water	150 ml / ¼ pint
⅓ cup	Superfine [caster] sugar	75 g / 3 oz
12	Maraschino cherries	12

1. Preheat the oven to 400°F / 200°C / Gas Mark 6.
2. Remove the pits [stones] from the cherries and put them in a bowl with the brandy. Leave to steep.
3. Grate the chocolate and put in the refrigerator.
4. Beat the eggs with 1 cup [240 g / 8 oz] of the granulated sugar and a few drops of vanilla extract until the mixture is frothy. Stir in cocoa and flour. Stir in butter until smooth.
5. Divide the batter between three buttered and floured 9 in / 22 cm layer cake pans [sandwich tins]. Bake for 20 minutes. Unmold the cake layers onto a wire rack and leave until cold.
6. Pour the rest of the granulated sugar and the water in a pan and bring to a boil. Simmer for 10 minutes or until the mixture thickens without browning. Flavor with 3 tablespoons of the kirsch. Brush the kirsch syrup over the 3 cake layers.
7. Whip the crème fraîche with the iced water, the remaining kirsch and the superfine sugar until the crème has doubled in quantity. Drain the cherries.
8. Cover one of the cake layers with a layer of whipped cream ½ in / 1 cm thick and dot with 12 brandy-flavored cherries. Top with the second cake layer and cover this with a similar layer of whipped cream and cherries. Put the third cake layer in position and cover the top and sides of the cake with the remaining whipped cream.
9. Cover the sides of the cake with the chocolate and decorate the top with the maraschino cherries and the remaining chocolate. Chill until ready to serve.

Coffee layer cake

Gâteau lorrain
Lorraine Cake

00:10   00:20 to 00:25
plus making dough and pastry cream
Makes an 11 in / 28 cm cake

American	Ingredients	Metric/Imperial
1 quantity	Brioche dough (see page 457)	1 quantity
	Rum or kirsch	
½ quantity	Pastry cream (see page 456)	½ quantity
	Confectioners' [icing] sugar	

1. Shape the brioche dough into a ball and roll it out to a round, 11 in / 28 cm in diameter and ¼ in / 5 mm thick. Place on a buttered and lightly floured baking sheet. Leave to rise at room temperature for 1 hour.
2. Preheat the oven to 425°F / 220°C / Gas Mark 7.
3. Bake the dough for 20-25 minutes. Leave to cool.
4. Cut the cake into 2 equal layers and moisten each layer with a few drops of rum or kirsch.
5. Spread one of the cake layers with the pastry cream and cover with the other layer. Sprinkle the top generously with confectioners' sugar. Chill until ready to serve.

Gâteau lyonnais
Lyonnaise Cake

00:40   01:00 to 01:15

American	Ingredients	Metric/Imperial
1 cup	Butter	200 g / 8 oz
1 cup	Superfine [caster] sugar	200 g / 8 oz
4	Eggs	4
3 cups	Flour	300 g / 12 oz
1 tsp	Baking powder	1 tsp
	Vanilla extract [essence]	
2	Ripe pears	2
1 lb	Ripe apricots	500 g / 1 lb
½ cup	Praline (see page 458)	75 g / 3 oz
	Confectioners' [icing] sugar	
	Thick crème fraîche (see page 122)	

1. Preheat the oven to 350°F / 180°C / Gas Mark 4.
2. Cut the butter into small pieces and cream with a wooden spoon. Beat in the sugar, then the eggs, one at a time. When the mixture is smooth and light, work in the flour, baking powder and a few drops of vanilla extract.
3. Peel, quarter and core the pears, then thinly slice them. Halve the apricots and remove the pits [stones]. Coarsely grind the praline or crush with a rolling pin.
4. Pour a ¾ in / 1½ cm layer of cake batter into a buttered and floured 10 in / 24 cm cake pan. Cover with the sliced pears. Pour over a thin layer of cake batter and add the apricot halves, cut side down. Sprinkle with the crushed praline and cover with the remaining cake batter.
5. Bake for 10 minutes, then lower the oven temperature to 325°F / 160°C / Gas Mark 3. Bake for a further 15 minutes, then reduce the temperature to 300°F / 150°C / Gas Mark 2. Bake for 30 minutes longer. Turn off the oven and leave the cake inside for a final 10 minutes.
6. Unmold the cake and leave to cool before sprinkling with confectioners' sugar. Serve with a bowl of thick crème fraîche.

Gâteau de riz
Rice Cake

00:10   01:30
Serves 6-8

American	Ingredients	Metric/Imperial
1½ quarts	Milk	1.5 l / 2½ pints
1¾ cups	Sugar	400 g / 14 oz
1	Vanilla bean [pod]	1
1 cup	Short-grain (pudding) rice	170 g / 6 oz
5 tbsp	Water	5 tbsp
1 cup	Butter	200 g / 8 oz

1. Bring the milk to a boil with 1¼ cups [300 g / 10 oz] of the sugar and the vanilla bean, split lengthwise.
2. In another pan, bring some water to a boil and add the rice. Remove the pan from the heat and leave to soak for 3 minutes.
3. Drain the rice and stir into the boiling milk. Bring back to a boil and simmer for about 1½ hours or until the rice has absorbed all the milk.
4. Meanwhile, dissolve the remaining sugar in 4 tablespoons of the water and cook over a low heat until golden brown. Remove the pan from the heat and stir in the remaining water. Use the caramel to cover the bottom and sides of a 1½ quart [1.5 l / 3 pint] charlotte mold.
5. When the rice is cooked, add the butter a little at a time, stirring thoroughly with a wooden spoon. Pour the rice into the mold and chill for 12 hours.
6. To serve, unmold onto a serving plate.

Gâteau de potiron
Pumpkin Ring Cake

00:20   01:15

American	Ingredients	Metric/Imperial
1 lb	Pumpkin	500 g / 1 lb
	Salt	
4	Eggs	4
1¼ cups	Oil	300 ml / ½ pint
3 cups	Flour	350 g / 12 oz
1 tsp	Baking soda [bicarbonate of soda]	1 tsp
1 cup	Superfine [caster] sugar	250 g / 8 oz
1¾ cups	Chopped hazelnuts	200 g / 7 oz
1 tbsp	Ground cinnamon	1 tbsp
1	Lemon	1
1 cup	Confectioners' [icing] sugar	100 g / 4 oz

1. Preheat the oven to 325°F / 160°C / Gas Mark 3.
2. Peel the pumpkin and remove the seeds. Dice the pumpkin and cook in a little boiling salted water for 10 minutes. Drain very thoroughly, then purée in a vegetable mill, blender or food processor.
3. Beat the eggs with the oil and pumpkin purée. Add the flour, soda, sugar, chopped nuts, cinnamon and a pinch of salt. Mix well.
4. Pour the batter into a buttered and lightly floured ring mold. Bake for about 1¼ hours. The cake is cooked when the point of a knife inserted in the center comes out clean.
5. Unmold the cake onto a wire rack and leave to cool.
6. Mix the finely grated rind and juice of the lemon with the confectioners' sugar. Pour this icing over the cake.

Kugelhopf

Kougelhof

	00:20 plus soaking and rising	00:40

American	Ingredients	Metric/Imperial
½ cup	Currants	80 g / 3 oz
1 cup	Milk	150 ml / ¼ pint
1 ½ packages	Active dry yeast	1 sachet
2 tbsp	Sugar	25 g / 1 oz
2 cups	Flour	250 g / 8 oz
3	Eggs	3
1 tsp	Salt	1 tsp
½ cup	Butter at room temperature	130 g / 4 oz
	Confectioners' [icing] sugar	

1. Cover the currants with warm water and leave to soak for 1 hour.

2. Heat the milk until lukewarm and stir in the yeast with ½ teaspoon of sugar. Leave in a warm place for 15 minutes or until frothy.

3. Sift the flour into a mixing bowl and make a well in the center. Using your fingers work in the eggs, remaining sugar and salt. Add the liquid yeast and knead the dough for 15 minutes until supple.

4. Drain and dry the currants and work into the dough with the butter. Knead thoroughly, then leave the dough in a warm place to rise for about 45 minutes or until it has doubled in volume.

5. Preheat the oven to 400°F / 200°C / Gas Mark 6.

6. Fill a buttered kugelhopf or brioche mold with the dough and leave to rise for a further 15 minutes or until doubled in volume.

7. Bake for 40 minutes. Unmold the cake and sprinkle with confectioners' sugar.

Kugelhopf

Gâteau de Savoie aux cerises

Cherry Sponge Cake

00:20   00:50

American	Ingredients	Metric/Imperial
4	Eggs, separated	4
	Vanilla extract [essence]	
½ cup	Superfine [caster] sugar	125 g / 4 oz
1	Lemon	1
	Salt	
¾ cup	Flour	80 g / 3 oz
½ lb	Pitted [stoned] ripe cherries	250 g / 8 oz

1. Preheat the oven to 350°F / 180°C / Gas Mark 4.
2. Beat the egg yolks with a few drops of vanilla extract and half the sugar. Finely grate the rind from the lemon and squeeze the lemon to give 1 tablespoon of juice. Add the lemon rind and juice to the egg yolk mixture with a pinch of salt. Beat well, then mix in the flour.
3. Beat the egg whites until very stiff, adding the remaining sugar halfway through the process. Fold the egg whites into the lemon batter.
4. Pour the batter into a buttered 9 in / 22 cm cake pan. Top with the cherries and bake for 50 minutes. Remove the cake from the pan immediately it comes out of the oven and leave until cold.

Cook's tip: wrapped in foil, this cake will keep for several days in the refrigerator.

Gaufres

Waffles

00:30   00:03 to 00:05
plus rising   per batch

American	Ingredients	Metric/Imperial
3 cups	Milk	600 ml / 1 pint
2 packages	Active dry yeast	1 sachet
½ tsp	Sugar	½ tsp
4 cups	Flour	500 g / 1 lb
4	Eggs	4
⅔ cup	Melted butter	150 g / 5 oz
	Salt	
	Flavoring: vanilla, kirsch, orange-flower water, lemon rind, etc.	
	Confectioners' [icing] sugar or honey	

1. Heat the milk until lukewarm. Dissolve the yeast in a little of the milk with the sugar and set the rest of the milk aside to cool.
2. Sift the flour into a mixing bowl and make a well in the center. Add the eggs, melted butter, dissolved yeast, a pinch of salt, and the flavoring of your choice. Beat the mixture with a balloon whisk, gradually adding the remaining milk until it has the consistency of a heavy pancake batter.
3. Leave in a warm place for at least 1 hour or until the mixture has doubled in volume.
4. Cook the waffles following the instructions for your model of waffle-maker.
5. Serve the waffles dusted with confectioners' sugar or spread with honey.

Gâteau marbré

Marble Cake

00:30   00:45 to 00:50

American	Ingredients	Metric/Imperial
1½ cups	Butter	350 g / 12 oz
1½ cups	Superfine [caster] sugar	350 g / 12 oz
6 large (2 oz)	Eggs	6 standard (50 g / 2 oz)
3 cups	Flour	350 g / 12 oz
2 tsp	Baking powder	2 tsp
2 tbsp	Cocoa powder	2 tbsp
1	Lemon	1

1. Preheat the oven to 400°F / 200°C / Gas Mark 6.
2. Cut the butter into small pieces and cream until light and fluffy. Beat in the sugar and then the eggs, one at a time until smooth. Stir in the flour and baking powder until well blended.
3. Divide the cake batter in half and stir the cocoa into one portion. Finely grate the rind of the lemon and stir into the other portion.
4. Put half the lemon mixture into a buttered 10 in / 24 cm savarin mold. Add half the chocolate mixture, the remaining lemon mixture and finally the remaining chocolate mixture.
5. Bake for 50 minutes, making sure that the top of the cake does not brown too quickly. If necessary, cover with foil. The cake is cooked when a skewer inserted into the center comes out clean.
6. Remove the cake from the mold and cool on a wire rack.

Gâteau roulé

Sponge Roll

00:20   00:10
plus cooling

American	Ingredients	Metric/Imperial
5	Eggs, separated	5
½ cup	Superfine [caster] sugar	125 g / 4 oz
¾ cup	Cornstarch [cornflour]	75 g / 3 oz
¼ cup	Ground almonds	30 g / 1 oz
¼ cup	Flour	25 g / 1 oz
	Vanilla extract [essence]	
	Salt	
½ cup	Granulated sugar	100 g / 4 oz
⅓ cup	Water	5 tbsp
¼ cup	Rum	4 tbsp
	Filling: jam, chocolate cream (see page 462), buttercream (see page 455)	

1. Preheat the oven to 400°F / 200°C / Gas Mark 6.
2. Beat the egg yolks with the superfine sugar until pale. Stir in the cornstarch, ground almonds and flour. Add a few drops of vanilla extract.
3. Beat the egg whites with a pinch of salt until stiff. Carefully fold into the batter.
4. Cut a sheet of wax [greaseproof] paper the same size as your baking sheet. Place the paper on the baking sheet and butter it. Pour the batter over the paper and spread it out level with a spatula.
5. Bake for 10 minutes.
6. Remove from the oven, cover with a clean linen towel and leave until cold.

7. Put the granulated sugar and water in a small saucepan and bring to a boil. Simmer for 10 minutes, then add the rum. Allow to cool.

8. Sprinkle the sponge with some of the rum syrup then spread with the filling of your choice.

9. Loosen the cake from the paper and roll it up. Wrap tightly in paper to help the roll keep its shape. Leave to cool for 2 hours.

10. Lightly moisten the cake with the remaining rum syrup, then coat all over with extra superfine sugar.

Cook's tip: wrapped in its paper, this cake (unfilled) will keep for at least a week in a cool place.

Madeleines

Madeleines

⏲ 00:25 Makes 24		🍳 00:10
American	**Ingredients**	**Metric/Imperial**
2	Lemons	2
5	Eggs	5
1 cup	Superfine [caster] sugar	200 g / 8 oz
2 cups	Flour	200 g / 8 oz
2 tsp	Baking powder	2 tsp
	Salt	
1 cup	Melted butter	200 g / 8 oz

1. Finely grate the rind from the lemons. Beat the eggs with the sugar, then stir in the flour. Add the baking powder, a pinch of salt and the lemon rind and mix well. Add the butter and stir until well blended.

2. Preheat the oven to 450°F / 240°C / Gas Mark 9.

3. Butter 2 or 3 madeleine trays. Sprinkle with flour and shake out any excess. Fill each madeleine mold with the batter and leave to stand for 10 minutes.

4. Bake for 10 minutes. Remove the trays from the oven and unmold the madeleines immediately.

Manqué Praliné

Praline Cake

⏲ 00:20		🍳 01:00 to 01:15
American	**Ingredients**	**Metric/Imperial**
6	Eggs, separated	6
1 cup	Superfine [caster] sugar	200 g / 8 oz
	Vanilla extract [essence] or	
1	Lemon or	1
2 tbsp	Rum	2 tbsp
2 cups	Flour	200 g / 8 oz
1/4 cup	Melted butter	50 g / 2 oz
1/2 cup	Flaked almonds	50 g / 2 oz
1/4 cup	Granulated sugar	50 g / 2 oz
1	Small egg	1
	Confectioners' [icing] sugar	

1. Preheat the oven to 350°F / 180°C / Gas Mark 4.

2. Beat the egg yolks and 1 egg white with half the superfine sugar and a few drops of vanilla extract (or the grated rind of the lemon or the rum) until the mixture is pale and thick. Beat in the flour.

3. Beat the remaining 5 egg whites until beginning to stiffen. Add the remaining superfine sugar and continue beating until stiff. Carefully fold the whites and melted butter into the egg yolk mixture.

4. Pour the batter into a buttered and bottom-lined 10 in / 25 cm cake pan. Bake for 10 minutes, then reduce the oven temperature to 325°F / 160°C / Gas Mark 3. Bake for a further 1 hour or until the blade of a knife inserted into the center comes out clean.

5. Remove the cake from the oven and increase the temperature to 400°F / 200°C / Gas Mark 6.

6. Mix together the flaked almonds, granulated sugar and whole egg and brush this praline mixture over the top of the cake. Sprinkle with confectioners' sugar and return the cake to the oven. Bake for a few minutes to brown the praline.

7. Remove the cake from the pan and leave to cool.

Cook's tip: in a dry place this cake will stay fresh for several days.

Marquise au chocolat

Chocolate Marchioness

⏲ 00:30 plus chilling		🍳 00:00
American	**Ingredients**	**Metric/Imperial**
3/4 lb	Semisweet [plain] chocolate	350 g / 12 oz
1 tbsp	Water	1 tbsp
3/4 cup	Butter	175 g / 6 oz
1/2 cup	Superfine [caster] sugar	100 g / 4 oz
4	Eggs, separated	4
1/2 quantity	Chantilly cream (see page 455)	1/2 quantity

1. This cake should be made on the previous day and will keep for several days in the refrigerator.

2. Break the chocolate into a bowl and stand over a pan of hot water. Add the water and melt the chocolate.

3. Cream the butter with the sugar, then add the melted chocolate and mix well. Add the egg yolks, one at a time.

4. Beat the egg whites until very stiff and fold gently into the mixture with a wooden spatula.

5. Fill an oiled 1.5 quart [1.5 l / 3 pint] charlotte mold with the chocolate mixture. Press down well and chill for 12 hours.

6. Just before serving, unmold the cake onto a serving plate and decorate with chantilly cream.

Madeleines

Macarons
Macaroons

	00:30	00:12 to 00:15	
	Makes 36 single or 18 double macaroons		

American	Ingredients	Metric/Imperial
6	Egg whites	6
2 lb	Uncooked almond paste (see page 456 or use bought)	1 kg / 2 lb
3 cups	Confectioners' [icing] sugar	350 g / 12 oz
	Salt	
	Vanilla extract [essence]	

1. Preheat the oven to 350°F / 180°C / Gas Mark 4.
2. Mix 1 egg white into the almond paste until completely absorbed and the paste is firm and supple. Add a further egg white and work until well blended. Then add, all together, the sugar, a pinch of salt, a few drops of vanilla extract and the remaining egg whites. Work the ingredients together until smooth.
3. Cover a baking sheet with wax [greaseproof] paper. Put the mixture into a pastry bag fitted with a ½ in / 1 cm nozzle. Pipe 36 small blobs, about 1½ in / 4 cm in diameter, onto the paper.
4. Bake for 12-15 minutes or until golden. Remove the baking sheet from the oven and immediately remove the macaroons from the paper.

Mascotte
Buttercream Sponge Cake

	00:30	00:25 to 00:30	
	plus making cake and buttercream		

American	Ingredients	Metric/Imperial
½ cup	Ground praline (see page 458)	80 g / 3 oz
1 quantity	Buttercream (see page 455)	1 quantity
1 cup	Flaked almonds	100 g / 4 oz
½ cup	Sugar	100 g / 4 oz
2 tbsp	Water	2 tbsp
¼ cup	Rum	4 tbsp
1 (10 in)	Genoese sponge cake (see page 460)	1 (25 cm / 10 in)

1. Add the ground praline to the buttercream and mix well. Set aside.
2. Toast the flaked almonds under the broiler [grill] or in a frying pan, stirring continuously until light brown. Leave to cool.
3. Bring the sugar and water to a boil, stirring to dissolve the sugar. Remove from the heat and add the rum.
4. Cut the sponge cake into 3 equal layers and brush each with the rum syrup. Cover each layer with buttercream, spreading it with a spatula, then place them one on top of the other. Cover the sides of the cake with the remaining buttercream.
5. Sprinkle the toasted almonds over the cake. Cut several strips of paper ½ in / 1 cm wide and arrange them on the top of the cake at regular intervals. Sprinkle generously with confectioners' sugar, then slide the strips of paper carefully off the cake. Chill until ready to serve.

Millefeuille
Napoleons or Cream Slices

	00:30	00:35 to 00:40	
	plus making or thawing pastry		

American	Ingredients	Metric/Imperial
1 lb	Puff pastry (see page 458 or use frozen)	500 g / 1 lb
1 tbsp	Sugar	1 tbsp
½ quantity	Pastry cream (see page 456)	½ quantity
	Confectioners' [icing] sugar	

1. If using frozen pastry, allow it to thaw.
2. Preheat the oven to 400°F / 200°C / Gas Mark 6.
3. Roll out the pastry to ⅛ in / 3 mm thick and place on a buttered baking sheet. Leave to stand for 10 minutes.
4. Moisten the pastry slightly with water and sprinkle with sugar, then prick all over with a fork. Bake for 20-25 minutes or until dry and crisp. Leave to cool.
5. Cut the pastry sheet into 4 equal widths, each about 12×4 in / 30×10 cm. Spread 3 with pastry cream and place one on top of the other. Put the fourth piece of pastry on top. Sprinkle generously with confectioners' sugar and, if liked, decorate with criss-crossed lines.

Paris-Brest
Praline Filled Choux Ring

	00:15	00:30 to 00:45	
	plus making pastry		

American	Ingredients	Metric/Imperial
1 quantity	Choux pastry (see page 457)	1 quantity
2	Eggs	2
½ cup	Flaked almonds	50 g / 2 oz
1 cup	Milk	250 ml / 8 fl oz
1	Egg yolk	1
½ cup	Sugar	100 g / 4 oz
¼ cup	Cornstarch [cornflour]	30 g / 1 oz
⅔ cup	Butter	125 g / 5 oz
½ cup	Ground praline (see page 458)	75 g / 3 oz
	Confectioners' [icing] sugar	

1. Preheat the oven to 350°F / 180°C / Gas Mark 4.
2. Put the choux pastry into a pastry bag fitted with a plain ¾ in / 2 cm nozzle. Place an 8 in / 20 cm diameter plate upside-down on a baking sheet and pipe a ring of pastry ½ in / 1 cm from the rim of the plate. Remove the plate.
3. Beat 1 egg and brush the ring of pastry with beaten egg. Sprinkle with the flaked almonds and bake for 20-25 minutes. If the pastry begins to get too brown cover it with foil. When cooked remove the pastry ring from the oven, cut a slit in the side to allow the steam to escape and leave to cool.
4. Bring the milk to a boil in a saucepan. Beat the egg yolk with the remaining whole egg and add the sugar and cornstarch. Gradually whisk in the boiling milk, then pour the mixture into the pan. Cook, stirring, until the custard thickens. Remove from heat. Stir in half the butter, in small pieces, and leave until cold.

5. Cream the remaining butter and mix in the praline. Add this mixture to the cold custard and stir until smooth.

6. Cut across the ring of pastry to make two equal layers. Put the custard into a pastry bag fitted with a large fluted nozzle and pipe onto the bottom half of the ring. Replace the top half. Sprinkle with confectioners' sugar and chill until ready to serve.

Petits fours

Petits Fours

	01:00	00:00

American	Ingredients	Metric/Imperial
2 lb	Almond paste (see page 456 or use bought)	1 kg / 2 lb
	Food colorings: red, green and yellow	
	Rum or kirsch	
1	Egg white	1
1 cup	Whole hazelnuts	125 g / 4 oz
1 cup	Blanched almonds	125 g / 4 oz
1 cup	Shelled walnuts	125 g / 4 oz

Napoleons or cream slices

1. Divide the almond paste into 3 equal portions.

2. Hazelnut petits fours: place one portion of almond paste on a pastry board, make a hollow in the center and add 3 drops of red food coloring. Knead the paste using the palms of your hands until of uniform color. Add 1 teaspoon of rum or kirsch and knead once more. Roll the paste into a tube of ¾ in / 1.5 cm diameter and cut into ½ in / 1 cm slices. Stir, but do not beat, the egg white in a bowl and tip in the hazelnuts. Shape the slices of almond paste to resemble olives and decorate each with 3 hazelnuts.

3. Almond petits fours: color the second portion of almond paste with 3 drops of green food coloring and flavor with 1 teaspoon of rum or kirsch. Roll into a tube of ¾ in / 1.5 cm diameter and cut into 1½ in / 4 cm lengths. Dip the almonds in the egg white and decorate each piece of paste with 1 almond on top.

4. Walnut petits fours: color the remaining almond paste with 3 drops of yellow food coloring and flavor with 1 teaspoon of rum or kirsch. Roll the paste into a tube ¾ in / 1.5 cm in diameter and cut into slices. Shape each slice into a ball. Dip the walnuts in the egg white and place a walnut on opposite sides of each ball of paste.

Cook's tip: all these petits fours can be candied (see pages 30, 31). If you candy them, they should be eaten within 24 hours, otherwise they will keep for anytime up to 2 weeks in an airtight container.

Pain d'épice au miel
Honey Spice Bread

00:25 plus standing time   **00:45 to 01:00**

American	Ingredients	Metric/Imperial
½ cup	Honey	150 g / 6 oz
¼ cup	Butter	60 g / 2 oz
1 cup	Brown sugar	150 g / 6 oz
	Salt	
3 cups	Flour	300 g / 12 oz
1	Egg	1
1 tsp	Baking powder	1 tsp
1 tsp	Ground allspice	1 tsp
1 tsp	Ground ginger	1 tsp
1 tsp	Ground cinnamon	1 tsp
⅔ cup	Finely chopped candied peel (lemon and orange)	100 g / 4 oz
1 cup	Flaked almonds (optional)	100 g / 4 oz
3 tbsp	Milk	3 tbsp
½ cup	Sugar	100 g / 4 oz

1. Heat the honey, butter, brown sugar and a pinch of salt in a pan.
2. Sift the flour into a mixing bowl. Add the honey mixture and stir to give a thick paste. Cool until lukewarm, then add the egg, baking powder, allspice, ginger and cinnamon.
3. Add the candied fruit. Stir thoroughly, then leave to stand for 1 hour.
4. Preheat the oven to 350°F / 180°C / Gas Mark 4.
5. Line a 10×6 in / 25×15 cm loaf pan with buttered wax [greaseproof] paper and sprinkle with the flaked almonds, if liked. Pour the batter into the pan.
6. Bake for 45 minutes to 1 hour or until the spice bread is golden brown. The loaf is cooked when the point of a knife inserted in the center comes out clean. Reduce the oven temperature to 325°F / 160°C / Gas Mark 3.
7. Mix the milk with the sugar and brush over the loaf. Return to the oven for a few minutes to glaze.
8. Remove the bread from the pan immediately it comes out of the oven and leave to cool.

Meringues
Meringues

00:25 Makes about 44   **01:00**

American	Ingredients	Metric/Imperial
8	Egg whites	8
	Vanilla extract [essence]	
2 cups	Superfine [caster] sugar	500 g / 1 lb
½ cup	Flour	50 g / 2 oz
	Confectioners' [icing] sugar	

1. Beat the egg whites with a few drops of vanilla extract, gradually adding half the sugar and continuing to beat until very stiff. Gently fold in the remaining sugar mixed with the flour.
2. Preheat the oven to 275°F / 120°C / Gas Mark 1.
3. Pipe or spoon ovals of meringue onto a buttered and floured baking sheet. Sprinkle generously with confectioners' sugar (in the oven this will form small beads on the crust of the meringues).

4. Bake for 1 hour with the oven door slightly open. Watch the meringues carefully: they should not brown, but should be pale cream in color. Cover with a sheet of foil or wax [greaseproof] paper if the meringues are beginning to brown.
5. Loosen the meringues from the baking sheet and turn them over carefully. Leave them to dry out in the warm oven for 3-4 hours longer.

Honey spice bread

Puits d'amour
Cream Wishing Wells

00:40 plus making or thawing pastry Makes 6   **00:30**

American	Ingredients	Metric/Imperial
½ lb	Puff pastry (see page 458 or use frozen)	250 g / 8 oz
1	Egg	1
4	Egg yolks	4
½ cup	Superfine [caster] sugar	125 g / 4 oz
½ cup	Flour	60 g / 2 oz
2 cups	Milk	500 ml / ¾ pint
½ cup	Confectioners' [icing] sugar	60 g / 2 oz

1. Thaw the pastry if using frozen. Preheat the oven to 425°F / 220°C / Gas Mark 7.
2. Roll out the pastry to ¼ in / 5 mm thick. Cut into 12 rounds with a 3 in / 7 cm pastry cutter or use the rim of a glass. Place 6 rounds on a baking sheet. Cut the center out of the remaining 6 rounds with a 1¾ in / 4 cm pastry cutter or use a smaller glass.
3. Beat the whole egg and brush over the 6 rounds on the baking sheet. Place the 6 rings on top and press to secure to the bases, then brush all over with beaten egg. Bake for 18-20 minutes.
4. Meanwhile, beat the egg yolks with the superfine sugar until pale. Add the flour and mix well. Bring the milk to a boil in a pan. Beat into the egg yolk mixture, then pour back into the milk pan. Thicken over a low heat for about 5 minutes, stirring. Do not allow the custard to boil. Remove the pan from the heat and continue stirring the custard until cold.
5. Remove the pastry cases from the oven and leave until cold.
6. To serve, fill with the custard and sprinkle with confectioners' sugar. Caramelize for 1 minute under a hot broiler [grill] until golden brown.

Quatre-quarts
Lemon Sponge Cake

| | 00:20 | 00:35 to 00:40 |

American	Ingredients	Metric/Imperial
1	Lemon	1
1¼ cups	Butter	300 g / 10 oz
1¼ cups	Superfine [caster] sugar	300 g / 10 oz
	Salt	
5 large (2 oz)	Eggs, separated	5 standard (50 g / 2 oz)
2½ cups	Flour	300 g / 10 oz
1 tsp	Baking powder	1 tsp

1. Preheat the oven to 425°F / 220°C / Gas Mark 7.
2. Finely grate the rind of the lemon. Cream the butter, then beat in the sugar, a pinch of salt and the lemon rind. Beat in the egg yolks one at a time. Add the flour and baking powder and mix well.
3. Beat the egg whites with a pinch of salt until stiff. Stir one-quarter of the whites quickly into the mixture, then gently fold in the remaining whites.
4. Pour the batter into a buttered and floured 10 in / 26 cm cake pan. Bake for 15 minutes without opening the oven door. Then reduce the oven temperature to 400°F / 200°C / Gas Mark 6 and bake for a further 20 minutes. The cake is cooked when the blade of a knife inserted in the center comes out clean.

Cook's tip: prepared in this way the sponge mixture is quite soft. By not separating the eggs, and beating them in whole, you will produce a heavier textured cake.

Pain de Gênes
Genoa Bread

| | 00:20 | 01:00 |

American	Ingredients	Metric/Imperial
7	Eggs	7
2 cups	Ground almonds	250 g / 8 oz
1 cup	Sugar	250 g / 8 oz
2 tbsp	Pernod or Ricard (anise-flavored liqueur)	2 tbsp
2 tbsp	Rum	2 tbsp
¼ cup	Flour	25 g / 1 oz
¾ cup	Potato starch or flour	75 g / 3 oz
6 tbsp	Melted butter	75 g / 3 oz
2	Egg whites	2

1. Preheat the oven to 350°F / 180°C / Gas Mark 4. Separate 4 of the eggs.
2. Beat together the ground almonds, sugar, the 3 whole eggs and 4 egg yolks until the mixture is thick.
3. Add the liqueur, rum, flour and potato starch and mix well. Stir in the melted butter until well blended.
4. Beat the 6 egg whites until very stiff and fold gently into the mixture.
5. Pour the batter into a buttered and bottom-lined deep cake pan. Bake for about 1 hour or until the blade of a knife inserted into the center comes out clean. Turn out of the pan and leave until cold.

Moka
Coffee Sponge Cake

| | 01:00 plus making cake and chilling | 00:45 |

American	Ingredients	Metric/Imperial
1¾ cups	Sugar	350 g / 12 oz
½ cup	Water	120 ml / 4 fl oz
½	Vanilla bean [pod]	½
1 (10 in)	Genoese sponge cake (see page 460)	1 (25 cm / 10 in)
8	Egg yolks	8
1 cup	Butter at room temperature	250 g / 8 oz
1 tbsp	Coffee flavoring	1 tbsp
1 cup	Flaked almonds	100 g / 4 oz

1. Put ½ cup [100 g / 4 oz] of the sugar, half of the water, and the ½ vanilla bean split lengthwise, in a saucepan. Bring to a boil, then remove from the heat and leave until cold.
2. Cut the sponge cake into 3 equal layers. Place one on a serving plate and the other two on the worktop. Brush the 3 layers with the sugar syrup.
3. Put the remaining sugar and water in a pan and boil for about 10 minutes. Dip a spoon into the syrup, cool quickly and take a little between your thumb and index finger. It should form a thread between thumb and finger.
4. Beat the egg yolks and add the syrup in a slow stream, continuing to beat vigorously until cold. Work in the butter, cut into pieces, and beat to give a smooth cream. Finally, add the coffee flavoring.
5. Spread the flaked almonds on a baking sheet and toast under the broiler [grill], stirring from time to time.
6. Spoon a quarter of the coffee buttercream onto the center of the cake layer on the serving plate and spread it out evenly. Cover with the second layer, spread again with buttercream and then top with the third layer. Cover the whole cake with the remaining coffee buttercream and sprinkle the sides and top with toasted flaked almonds.
7. Chill for at least 3 hours or until the cake is firm.

Pains au chocolat
Chocolate Rolls

| | 01:00 plus making dough and rising time Makes 40 small chocolate rolls | 00:10 |

American	Ingredients	Metric/Imperial
2 quantities	Yeast dough (see page 460)	2 quantities
1	Egg	1
½ lb	Semisweet [plain] chocolate	250 g / 8 oz
1 tbsp	Water	1 tbsp

1. Divide the dough into small balls and roll into small sausage shapes. Arrange the rolls on 1 or 2 buttered and lightly floured baking sheets.
2. Leave to rise in a warm place for 1 hour.
3. Preheat the oven to 350°F / 180°C / Gas Mark 4.
4. Brush the rolls with beaten egg and bake for 10 minutes.
5. Meanwhile, melt the chocolate with the water in a bowl over a pan of hot water, stirring to a smooth paste.
6. Remove the rolls from the oven. Make a slit in each and fill with the chocolate. Serve very hot.

Oreillettes
Fried Cookies [Biscuits]

	00:30	00:03 to 00:04	
	plus standing time	per batch Makes 45-50	

American	Ingredients	Metric/Imperial
4 cups	Flour	1 kg / 2 lb
2 tsp	Baking powder	2 tsp
2	Eggs	2
	Vanilla extract [essence]	
½ tsp	Salt	½ tsp
2 cups	Milk	300 ml / ½ pint
½ cup	Butter	100 g / 4 oz
	Oil for frying	
	Confectioners' [icing] sugar	

1. Sift the flour and baking powder onto a worktop. Make a well in the center, and add the eggs, a few drops of vanilla extract and the salt. Work the ingredients together, gradually adding the cold milk. When all the ingredients are mixed, lightly flour the dough and knead until supple. Add the butter a little at a time and leave to stand for 2 hours.
2. Roll out the dough very thinly and cut into diamond shapes.
3. In a frying pan heat 1 in / 3 cm oil until hot but not smoking. Add a few diamonds at a time and fry until golden on both sides. Drain on paper towels.
4. Sprinkle with confectioners' sugar before serving.

Profiteroles
Profiteroles

	00:20	00:40	
	plus making pastry		

American	Ingredients	Metric/Imperial
1 quantity	Choux pastry (see page 457)	1 quantity
½ lb	Semisweet [plain] chocolate	250 g / 8 oz
⅓ cup	Milk	5 tbsp
2 tbsp	Butter	25 g / 1 oz
1¼ cups	Thick crème fraîche (see page 122)	300 ml / ½ pint
3 cups	Vanilla ice cream (see page 514 or use bought) or	750 ml / 1¼ pints
1 quantity	Chantilly cream (see page 455)	1 quantity

1. Preheat the oven to 400°F / 200°C / Gas Mark 6.
2. Put the pastry into a pastry bag fitted with a plain ¼ in / 5 mm nozzle. Pipe small balls of pastry onto a buttered baking sheet.
3. Bake for 20 minutes or until light golden brown and crisp. Make a small slit in each choux bun to allow steam to escape and cool on a wire rack.
4. Break the chocolate into a bowl and place over a pan of hot water. Add the milk and stir until the chocolate melts. Add the butter and stir until smooth, then mix in the crème fraîche. Keep warm over the pan of hot water.
5. Halve the choux buns and fill with vanilla ice cream or chantilly cream. Arrange in individual glasses.
6. Pour on the chocolate sauce and serve immediately.

Petits fours glacés
Candied Petits Fours

	01:00	00:20	
	plus drying	Makes 80	

American	Ingredients	Metric/Imperial
1½ cups	Prunes	250 g / 8 oz
1½ cups	Dates	250 g / 8 oz
⅔ cup	Glacé cherries	125 g / 4 oz
2 lb	Almond paste (see page 456)	1 kg / 2 lb
	Food coloring: red, green and yellow	
4 cups	Sugar	1 kg / 2 lb
⅔ cup	Water	150 ml / ¼ pint
2 tbsp	White vinegar	2 tbsp

1. Halve the prunes and dates and remove the pits [stones]. Halve the glacé cherries.
2. Divide the almond paste into 4 equal portions. Knead the first portion until very white and supple, then roll it into a tube ¾ in / 1.5 cm in diameter. Cut into ½ / 1 cm slices. Roll each slice into a ball and garnish each side with ½ glacé cherry.
3. Color the other 3 portions of almond paste (see recipe for petits fours page 493): the first with 3 drops of red food coloring, the second with 3 drops of green food coloring and the third with 3 drops of yellow food coloring. Roll each portion into a tube ¾ in / 1.5 cm in diameter and cut into ½ in / 1 cm slices. Shape to resemble olives. Use these 'olives' to stuff the prunes and dates and close up the fruit.
4. Leave for 24 hours to dry.
5. Dissolve the sugar in the water with the vinegar and cook over a moderate heat until the syrup begins to color.
6. Thread the fruit one at a time onto a skewer and dip in the caramel. Drain and place on a buttered baking sheet. Leave until quite dry.
7. Place each fruit in a paper case. Eat within 24 hours.

Pain perdu
French Toast

	00:10	00:04	
		per batch	

American	Ingredients	Metric/Imperial
1 cup	Milk	250 ml / 8 fl oz
½ cup	Sugar	100 g / 4 oz
	Vanilla extract [essence]	
5	Eggs	5
1 cup	Butter	250 g / 8 oz
12	Slices brioche (fresh or stale)	12

1. Warm the milk. Add the sugar and a few drops of vanilla extract and stir until dissolved.
2. Beat the eggs in a shallow dish.
3. Melt the butter in a bowl over a pan of hot water and leave to cool. A whitish deposit will form in the bottom of the bowl. Carefully pour the butter into a dish, leaving the deposit behind.
4. Dip the slices of brioche in the sweetened milk, then in the beaten eggs. Pour 1 tablespoon of the clarified butter into a frying pan and, when hot, add a batch of brioche. Fry until golden on both sides. Fry the remaining brioche, adding more clarified butter to the pan as necessary.
5. Serve hot with sugar and apricot jam.

Profiteroles

Négrillons aux noix
Chocolate and Nut Cakes

◣ 00:30
Makes 20   00:15 ⌁

American	Ingredients	Metric/Imperial
1 cup	Shelled walnuts	120 g / 4 oz
¼ cup	Butter	60 g / 2 oz
½ cup	Superfine [caster] sugar	120 g / 4 oz
3 oz	Semisweet [plain] chocolate	90 g / 3 oz
3	Egg whites	3
½ cup	Blanched almonds	50 g / 2 oz
⅓ cup	Glacé cherries	50 g / 2 oz

1. Preheat the oven to 350°F / 180°C / Gas Mark 4.
2. Finely grind the walnuts. Set aside.
3. Cream the butter and sugar together until pale and fluffy.
4. Break the chocolate into a bowl and place over a pan of hot water. Melt the chocolate and cool until just warm, then gradually stir it into the butter and sugar mixture. Add the ground walnuts.
5. Beat the egg whites until stiff and fold into the mixture.
6. Half fill 20 buttered tartlet pans with the mixture. Decorate the top of each with an almond and a few pieces of glacé cherry.
7. Bake for 15 minutes.
8. Remove from the pans immediately as this mixture tends to stick when cool.

Petits gâteaux à l'anis
Small Aniseed Cakes

◣ 00:25
plus cooling   00:25 to 00:30 ⌁
Makes about 20

American	Ingredients	Metric/Imperial
1 cup	Butter	250 g / 8 oz
2½ cups	Confectioners' [icing] sugar	280 g / 10 oz
2	Eggs yolks	2
	Rosewater	
3½ cups	Flour	400 g / 14 oz
½ tsp	Baking powder	½ tsp
1 tbsp	Ouzo or Pernod	1 tbsp
½ cup	Ground almonds	60 g / 2 oz
20	Cloves	20

1. Preheat the oven to 300°F / 150°C / Gas Mark 2.
2. Cream the butter in a mixing bowl, then beat in two-thirds of the sugar, the egg yolks, one at a time, and 6 drops of rosewater. Beat the mixture well, then add the flour, baking powder and ouzo or Pernod.
3. Toast the almonds in a dry pan for about 5 minutes, stirring continuously until golden. Add to the mixture and stir until smooth.
4. Using a teaspoon make 20 small heaps of the mixture on a baking sheet. Stick a clove in each. Bake for about 30 minutes without allowing the cakes to brown.
5. Roll each cake in the remaining confectioners' sugar while still hot and leave on a wire rack to cool. When cold roll once more in the sugar.

Pudding à l'orange
Orange Pudding

	00:30	01:00
	plus cooling and chilling	

American	Ingredients	Metric/Imperial
1 quart	Milk	1 l / 1¾ pints
3	Oranges	3
6 tbsp	Butter	80 g / 3 oz
1 cup	Flour	100 g / 4 oz
	Vanilla extract [essence]	
¾ cup	Sugar	150 g / 6 oz
	Salt	
6	Eggs, separated	6

1. Bring the milk to a boil and leave until lukewarm.
2. With a sharp knife, cut 2 oranges into very thin slices and use to cover the bottom of a 1½ quart [1.5 l / 3 pint] charlotte mold. Finely grate the rind of the remaining orange and set to one side.
3. Melt the butter in a pan over a low heat, add the flour and cook for a few minutes, stirring. Stir in the milk, a little at a time, then add a few drops of vanilla extract, the sugar, orange rind and a pinch of salt. Bring to a boil, stirring. Leave to cool.
4. Preheat the oven to 350°F / 180°C / Gas Mark 4.
5. Beat the egg yolks into the mixture.
6. Beat the egg whites until stiff and fold gently into the mixture. Spoon into the mold.
7. Stand the mold in a shallow ovenproof dish of water. Bake for 1 hour or until the blade of a knife inserted into the center of the pudding comes out clean.
8. Leave to cool, then chill. To serve, unmold the pudding onto a plate.

Quatre-quarts aux pommes
Apple Sponge Cake

	00:25	01:30

American	Ingredients	Metric/Imperial
1¼ cups	Butter	300 g / 10 oz
1¼ cups	Superfine [caster] sugar	300 g / 10 oz
	Salt	
5 large (2 oz)	Eggs	5 standard (50 g / 2 oz)
	Vanilla extract [essence] or	
2 tbsp	Rum	2 tbsp
2½ cups	Flour	300 g / 10 oz
4	Apples	4

1. Preheat the oven to 425°F / 220°C / Gas Mark 7.
2. Cream the butter, then beat in the sugar, a pinch of salt and the eggs, one at a time. Continue beating until creamy. Add a few drops of vanilla extract or the rum. Finally, fold in the flour until the mixture is smooth and well blended.
3. Pour the batter into a buttered and floured 10 in / 26 cm cake pan, half filling it.
4. Peel and core the apples. Cut each into 8 segments and arrange on the batter in the pan.
5. Bake for 15 minutes, then reduce the oven temperature to 400°F / 200°C / Gas Mark 6. Bake for 15 minutes longer. Finally reduce the temperature to 350°F / 180°C / Gas Mark 4 and bake for a final 50 minutes or until the blade of a knife inserted into the center of the cake comes out clean.

6. Remove the cake from the oven and leave it to cool for 5 minutes, then remove it from the pan and leave until cold.

Pancakes écossais
Pancakes or Drop Scones

	00:15	00:04 to 00:05
	Makes 12-16	per batch

American	Ingredients	Metric/Imperial
1 cup	Flour	125 g / 4 oz
1 tbsp	Baking powder	1 tbsp
1	Egg	1
1¼ cups	Milk	250 ml / 8 fl oz
2 tbsp	Sugar	30 g / 1 oz
2 tbsp	Melted butter	30 g / 1 oz
1 tbsp	Oil	1 tbsp

1. Sift the flour and baking powder into a bowl and beat in the egg, milk and sugar. Add the melted butter and mix well.
2. Heat a little oil in a griddle or heavy-based frying pan. Drop batter onto the griddle or pan, a spoonful at a time, leaving room for the batter to run. Cook until golden brown on the underside, then turn and cook on the other side.
3. Keep the pancakes hot until all are cooked.
4. Serve with butter and jam, apple purée or maple syrup.

Saint-Honoré
Saint-Honoré

	00:45	00:30
	plus making pastries and chilling	Serves 10

American	Ingredients	Metric/Imperial
1 quantity	Basic short pastry (see page 457)	1 quantity
7	Eggs	7
1 quantity	Choux pastry (see page 457)	1 quantity
2 cups	Superfine [caster] sugar	500 g / 1 lb
⅔ cup	Water	150 ml / ¼ pint
1 quart	Milk	1 l / 1¾ pints
1	Vanilla bean [pod]	1
¾ cup	Cornstarch [cornflour]	75 g / 3 oz
1 envelope	Unflavored gelatin	1 sachet

1. Preheat the oven to 400°F / 200°C / Gas Mark 6.
2. Roll out the short pastry to ⅛ in / 3 mm thick. Using an overturned plate as a guide, cut out a round, 8 in / 20 cm in diameter (there will be leftover pastry). Place on a buttered and floured baking sheet and prick the pastry round with a fork. Beat 1 egg in a bowl and brush over the edge of the pastry round.
3. Put the choux pastry into a pastry bag fitted with a plain ½ in / 1 cm nozzle and pipe a ring of choux pastry around the edge of the short pastry round, ⅛ in / 3 mm from the edge. Brush the choux pastry with beaten egg. Bake for 20 minutes.
4. Pipe the remaining choux pastry onto another buttered and floured baking sheet in 20 small balls, about ¾ in / 2 cm in diameter. Bake for 15 minutes.
5. Remove the baking sheets from the oven. Pierce the choux balls and the ring to allow the steam to escape and leave to cool.

6. Put half of the sugar and the water into a pan and bring to a boil, stirring to dissolve the sugar. When the syrup begins to caramelize, remove the pan from the heat. Dip the small choux buns one at a time in the caramel syrup and stick them onto the ring of choux pastry, placing them as close together as possible.

7. Bring the milk to a boil with the vanilla bean, split in half lengthwise. Separate the remaining 6 eggs. Beat the egg yolks with the remaining sugar and the cornstarch. When the mixture is pale in color, gradually whisk in the boiling milk (remove the vanilla bean). Pour back into the milk pan and cook over a low heat, stirring, until thickened. Remove from the heat.

8. Dissolve the gelatin in a little water. Stir into the custard and leave to cool.

9. Beat the egg whites until stiff and fold into the custard. Put the custard into a pastry bag fitted with a fluted nozzle and fill the center of the Saint-Honoré. Chill until ready to serve.

Rochers
Coconut Rocks

American	Ingredients	Metric/Imperial
3	Egg whites	3
¾ cup	Superfine [caster] sugar	180 g / 6 oz
	Vanilla extract [essence]	
	Salt	
2⅓ cups	Dried shredded [desiccated] coconut	200 g / 7 oz

1. Place the egg whites, sugar, a few drops of vanilla extract and a pinch of salt in a heavy-bottomed pan. Whisk over a low heat until frothy and hot, but not boiling. Remove the pan from the heat and continue whisking until cold.

2. Stir in the coconut.

3. Preheat the oven to 300°F / 150°C / Gas Mark 2.

4. Using a tablespoon, place small mounds of the coconut mixture on a buttered baking sheet.

5. Bake for 35 minutes without allowing the cakes to brown. Leave to cool on a wire rack.

Tuiles aux amandes
Almond Tiles

00:15   00:05

American	Ingredients	Metric/Imperial
¾ cup	Superfine [caster] sugar	170 g / 6 oz
1 cup	Flaked almonds	100 g / 4 oz
	Salt	
1 cup	Flour	100 g / 4 oz
2	Eggs	2
	Vanilla extract [essence]	
6 tbsp	Melted butter	70 g / 3 oz

1. Preheat the oven to 475°F / 240°C / Gas Mark 9.

2. Stir together the sugar, flaked almonds, a pinch of salt and the flour. Beat the eggs with a few drops of vanilla extract and stir into the dry ingredients with the melted butter until well blended.

3. Place teaspoons of the mixture on a buttered baking sheet,

leaving plenty of space between them, then flatten them with a fork dipped in cold water.

4. Bake for 4-5 minutes or until golden at the edges.

5. Remove the tiles from the baking sheet immediately they come out of the oven and roll them around a rolling pin to curve them. Leave to cool, and store in an airtight container where they will keep for up to 1 month.

Tôt-fait
Rich Lemon Sponge Cake

00:20   00:45 to 01:00

American	Ingredients	Metric/Imperial
2 cups	Flour	200 g / 8 oz
1 cup	Superfine [caster] sugar	200 g / 8 oz
	Salt	
6	Eggs	6
1 cup	Milk	150 ml / ¼ pint
1	Lemon	1
4	Egg whites	4
¾ cup	Melted butter	160 g / 6 oz

1. Preheat the oven to 425°F / 220°C / Gas Mark 7.

2. Beat together the flour, sugar, a pinch of salt, the whole eggs, milk and finely grated rind of the lemon, until smooth.

3. Beat the egg whites until stiff and fold gently into the mixture. Finally, fold in the melted butter.

4. Pour the batter into a buttered and floured 10 in / 24 cm cake pan. Bake for 45-60 minutes or until the blade of a knife inserted into the center of the cake comes out clean.

5. Leave the cake in the oven for a few minutes with the door open so that the cold air outside does not make the cake fall. Unmold the cake onto a wire rack and leave to cool before serving.

Truffes au chocolat
Chocolate Truffles

00:20   00:10
plus chilling
Makes 2 lb / 1 kg truffles

American	Ingredients	Metric/Imperial
1 lb	Semisweet [plain] chocolate	500 g / 1 lb
5	Egg yolks	5
2 cups	Confectioners' [icing] sugar	250 g / 8 oz
1 cup	Butter at room temperature	250 g / 8 oz
5 tbsp	Crème fraîche (see page 122)	5 tbsp
5 tbsp	Brandy	5 tbsp
1 cup	Cocoa powder	125 g / 4 oz

1. Break the chocolate into a bowl and place over a pan of hot water. Heat until melted.

2. Beat the egg yolks with the sugar until thick and creamy. Mix in the butter, then the melted chocolate, crème fraîche and brandy and stir until smooth.

3. Shape into small balls with your hands. Roll in cocoa. Chill for 12 hours before serving.

Reine de Saba
Queen of Sheba

	00:30	01:00

American	Ingredients	Metric/Imperial
½ lb	Semisweet [plain] chocolate	250 g / 8 oz
⅔ cups	Thin honey	250 g / 8 oz
1 cup	Butter at room temperature	250 g / 8 oz
6	Egg yolks	6
1 cup	Flour	100 g / 4 oz
2 tsp	Baking powder	2 tsp
1 cup	Chopped, toasted hazelnuts	125 g / 4 oz

1. Preheat the oven to 400°F / 200°C / Gas Mark 6.
2. Place the chocolate in a bowl over a pan of hot water and heat until melted. Warm the honey in a small saucepan.
3. Remove the bowl of chocolate from the pan of hot water. Add the honey and stir until smooth. Add the butter and egg yolks. When the mixture is well blended, add the flour and baking powder, and finally the chopped hazelnuts. Mix well.
4. Pour the batter into a buttered and floured 10 in / 26 cm cake pan. Bake for 1 hour or until the blade of a knife inserted into the center of the cake comes out clean.
5. Unmold the cake onto a wire rack and leave to cool.

Cook's tip: this cake will keep in a cool place for at least 1 week.

Sachertorte
Sachertorte

	00:30 plus cooling	00:35 Serves 8-10

American	Ingredients	Metric/Imperial
¾ lb	Semisweet [plain] chocolate	350 g / 12 oz
9	Eggs, separated	9
½ cup	Melted butter	125 g / 4 oz
	Vanilla extract [essence]	
1	Egg white	1
½ cup	Superfine [caster] sugar	125 g / 4 oz
1 cup	Flour	125 g / 4 oz
¼ cup	Apricot jam	100 g / 3½ oz
⅔ cup	Orange liqueur	150 ml / ¼ pint
1¼ cups	Confectioners' [icing] sugar	150 g / 5 oz
1 cup	Crème fraîche (see page 122)	250 ml / 8 fl oz

1. Preheat the oven to 350°F / 180°C / Gas Mark 4.
2. Break ½ lb / 250 g of the chocolate into a bowl and place over a pan of hot water. Heat until melted.
3. Beat 8 of the egg yolks in a mixing bowl, and work in the melted butter and chocolate and a few drops of vanilla extract.
4. Beat the 10 egg whites until stiff with 1 tablespoon of the superfine sugar. Gradually add the remaining superfine sugar and continue beating until very stiff. Gently fold ⅓ of the egg whites with the flour into the chocolate mixture. Then fold in

the remaining whites, lifting the mixture from the bottom of the bowl to avoid breaking up the whites.
5. Divide the batter between 2 buttered and lined 9 in / 22 cm layer cake pans [sandwich tins]. Bake for 30 minutes.
6. Unmold the cake layers onto a wire rack and leave until cold.
7. Warm the apricot jam with the orange liqueur until smooth. Spread thinly all over the 2 cake layers. Place one on top of the other.
8. Put the remaining chocolate in a heavy saucepan and add the confectioners' sugar, crème fraîche and a few drops of vanilla extract. Bring slowly to the boil, stirring, and simmer for 5 minutes.
9. Beat the remaining egg yolk in a bowl. Remove the chocolate mixture from the heat and stir in the egg a little at a time. Return the pan to the heat for a few seconds, stirring continuously to give a thick mixture. Do not boil. Leave until just warm.
10. Place the cake on a plate (or wire rack). Pour the chocolate icing onto the top and spread evenly over the top and sides with a spatula.
11. Keep the cake in the refrigerator, and bring it out 1 hour before serving.

Cook's tip: prepare, bake and assemble the cake 48 hours in advance, but do not make the icing until the day of serving.

Savarin aux fraises
Strawberry Savarin

	00:45 plus making dough, rising and chilling Serves 6-8	00:20 to 00:25

American	Ingredients	Metric/Imperial
1 quantity	Yeast dough (see recipe for rum babas, page 478)	1 quantity
1 cup	Sugar	250 g / 8 oz
1	Vanilla bean [pod]	1
2 cups	Water	500 ml / ¾ pint
1¼ cups	Rum	300 ml / ½ pint
⅔ cup	Apricot jam	200 g / 8 oz
1 cup	Assorted glacé fruit	100 g / 4 oz
1 pint	Strawberries	500 g / 1 lb
1 cup	Wild [alpine] strawberries	100 g / 4 oz

1. Put the dough into a buttered 9 in / 22 cm savarin mold. Leave to rise in a warm place for 30 minutes.
2. Preheat the oven to 400°F / 200°C / Gas Mark 6.
3. Bake the savarin for 20-25 minutes. Unmold it onto a wire rack and leave to cool, flat base down.
4. Put the sugar into a pan with the vanilla bean, split in half lengthwise, and the water. Bring to a boil, stirring to dissolve the sugar, and remove immediately from the heat. Place the savarin in a shallow dish and gradually brush on some of the syrup. Leave to cool, then sprinkle with three-quarters of the rum.
5. Warm the apricot jam in a small pan over a low heat until melted and brush over the savarin. Decorate with the glacé fruit.
6. Rinse and hull the strawberries and wild strawberries. Pat dry. Place in a dish and sprinkle with the remaining sugar syrup and rum. Leave to steep for 1 hour in the refrigerator.
7. Just before serving, tip the strawberries into the center of the savarin.

Black Forest gâteau

Fruit desserts

Fresh fruit in season must surely be one of the most healthy and mouth-watering of desserts. For a special occasion, select the more unusual fruits such as fresh figs, mangoes and fresh dates, tropical exotics, such as kiwis and passion fruits, and pile them decoratively on to a large platter. Add a bunch or two of white or black grapes, some nectarines, ripe pears and dessert apples, and garnish the platter with vine leaves and fresh flowers. Accompany with a selection of soft french cheeses (see pages 66-79) and a dessert wine – a Sauternes, or Muscat de Beaumes de Venise, or even one of the rare sweet champagnes. More simply, fresh fruit can also be used as the basis for easy-to-prepare desserts such as fruit salads, and for ice creams and sorbets.

To prepare pineapple shells:
Whole:
1. Cut off the leafy top to use as a lid.
2. Using a grapefruit knife, cut the flesh from the pineapple, taking care not to cut through the rind. Remove the center core and cut up the flesh.
3. Fill the pineapple shell with fruit salad and place on top the crown of leaves.

Halved:
1. Cut the pineapple in half lengthwise, cutting through the decorative crown of leaves.
2. Cut out the flesh of each half with a grapefruit knife and remove the core. Dice the flesh to use in the fruit salad.
3. Fill the pineapple halves with the salad and arrange the halves head to tail on a long dish.

To make pineapple rings:
1. Cut off each end of the pineapple. Place the pineapple on a board then, working from top to bottom, cut off the rind in downward strips.
2. Cut out the eyes with the point of a small knife.
3. Cut the pineapple into slices and remove the center core with a small pastry cutter or apple corer.

Fraises au citron ou à l'orange

Orange and Lemon Strawberries

American	00:15 plus steeping	00:00
American	**Ingredients**	**Metric/Imperial**
2 lb	Strawberries	1 kg / 2 lb
½	Lemon	½
½	Orange	½
½ cup	Granulated [caster] sugar	125 g / 4 oz

1. Rinse and hull the strawberries. Place in a large bowl. Sprinkle with the juice of the ½ lemon and ½ orange and the finely grated rind of ¼ orange or ¼ lemon.
2. Sprinkle with the sugar and leave to steep in the refrigerator for 2 hours.

Fraises à la crème

Strawberries and Cream

American	00:10 plus making Chantilly cream	00:00
American	**Ingredients**	**Metric/Imperial**
2 lb	Strawberries	1 kg / 2 lb
1 cup	Thick crème fraîche (see page 122) or chantilly cream (see page 455)	250 ml / 8 fl oz
	Superfine [caster] sugar	

1. Rinse and hull the strawberries.
2. Serve accompanied by crème fraîche or chantilly cream and sugar.

Fraises au vin

Strawberries in Wine

American	00:10 plus steeping	00:00
American	**Ingredients**	**Metric/Imperial**
2 lb	Strawberries	1 kg / 2 lb
½ cup	Superfine [caster] sugar	125 g / 4 oz
⅔ cup	White wine	150 ml / ¼ pint

1. Rinse and hull the strawberries. Sprinkle with the sugar and leave to stand for 1 hour.
2. Just before serving, pour on the wine.

Cream hearts with strawberries

Coulis de fraises ou de framboises
Strawberry or Raspberry Sauce

	00:05	00:00

American	Ingredients	Metric/Imperial
2 lb	Strawberries or raspberries	1 kg / 2 lb
1	Lemon	1
3 tbsp	Superfine [caster] sugar	3 tbsp

1. Rinse, drain and hull the fruit.
2. Reduce the fruit to a purée in a blender or food processor and then strain through a sieve to remove seeds.
3. Squeeze the juice from the lemon. Add to the purée together with the sugar and stir well. Chill in the refrigerator.
4. Serve this sauce with sorbet, ice cream or a fruit charlotte.

Coupe de fruits secs
Dried Apricot Compote

	00:05 plus soaking and chilling	00:15

American	Ingredients	Metric/Imperial
2½ cups	Dried apricots	400 g / 14 oz
3 cups	Water	750 ml / 1¼ pints
¾ cup	Sugar	150 g / 5 oz
	Vanilla extract [essence]	
18	Blanched almonds	18

1. The day before, rinse and dry the apricots and place in a shallow dish. Heat the water without allowing it to boil, pour over the apricots and leave to soak for 12 hours.
2. The next day, drain the apricot juice into a pan and add the sugar and a few drops of vanilla extract. Bring to a boil and cook for 1 minute over a high heat.
3. Add the apricots to the boiling syrup. Simmer gently for 10 minutes. Add the almonds and stir for 1 minute.
4. Pour the apricot mixture into a shallow dish. Allow to cool, then chill until serving.

Ananas de fête
Festive Pineapple

	00:30	00:05

American	Ingredients	Metric/Imperial
1	Large pineapple	1
4	Oranges	4
3	Bananas	3
1 cup	Sugar	200 g / 8 oz
12	Dates	12
⅔ cup	Glacé cherries	100 g / 4 oz
12	Glacé apricots	12

1. Cut off the top and base of the pineapple, then, using a wide, pointed knife cut around the inside of the skin. Remove the pineapple flesh and collect the juice. Reserve the tube of skin. Cut 8 slices from the pineapple and remove the core. Dice the remaining pineapple.

2. Thinly slice 2 oranges without peeling them. Peel the remaining oranges and cut into cubes. Reserve the juice. Peel and slice the bananas.
3. Place the pineapple skin in the center of the serving dish and fill with the cubed orange, bananas and diced pineapple. Sprinkle with 2 tablespoons of sugar.
4. Surround the pineapple with the slices of orange and pineapple, and decorate with the dates, cherries and apricots.
5. Prepare a syrup with the fruit juices by boiling with the remaining sugar for 5 minutes.
6. Serve the pineapple accompanied by the syrup.

Bananes flambées
Flambé Bananas

	00:05	00:20 to 00:30

American	Ingredients	Metric/Imperial
6	Bananas	6
	Flour	
¼ cup	Butter	60 g / 2 oz
¼ cup	Sugar	60 g / 2 oz
1 tbsp	Water	1 tbsp
¼ cup	Rum	4 tbsp

1. Preheat the oven to 300°F / 150°C / Gas Mark 2.
2. Peel the bananas and cut in half crosswise. Roll the bananas lightly in flour. Heat the butter in a shallow flameproof casserole, add the banana pieces and brown over a gentle heat.
3. Sprinkle with the sugar and moisten with the water.
4. Transfer the casserole to the oven and bake for 12-15 minutes or until the bananas are tender.
5. Remove from the oven a few minutes before serving. Leave to cool slightly, then sprinkle with hot rum. Set alight and shake the dish to loosen the caramelized sugar. Serve immediately.

Crémets aux fraises
Cream Hearts with Strawberries

	00:30	00:00

American	Ingredients	Metric/Imperial
2 cups	Thin crème fraîche (see page 122)	500 ml / ¾ pint
2	Egg whites	2
2 lb	Strawberries	1 kg / 2 lb
	Superfine [caster] sugar	

1. Whip the cream until doubled in volume.
2. Beat the egg whites until stiff. Gently fold into the whipped cream.
3. Cut some cheesecloth or muslin into 6 squares. Dampen them and wring out the excess moisture. Use them to line 6 perforated, heart-shaped cheese molds (coeur à la crème molds). Fill the molds with the cream mixture. Fold over the cheesecloth or muslin and leave to drain in a pan in the refrigerator for 4 hours.
4. To serve, unwrap the cheese hearts and arrange on a serving dish. Rinse, dry and hull the strawberries and arrange around the hearts. Serve a bowl of sugar separately.

Melon cups

Oranges meringuées
Meringue Oranges

	00:50	00:20 to 00:25	
	plus chilling		

American	Ingredients	Metric/Imperial
6	Oranges	6
1 cup	Raspberries (or pitted [stoned] cherries)	100 g / 4 oz
2	Bananas	2
2	Apples	2
1	Pear	1
½ cup	Granulated sugar	100 g / 4 oz
3	Egg whites	3
⅔ cup	Superfine [caster] sugar	150 g / 5 oz
1 cup	Crème fraîche (see page 122) or chantilly cream (see page 455)	250 ml / 8 fl oz

1. Cut a lid off each orange and remove the flesh without breaking the skins. Dice the flesh. Place the skins in an ovenproof dish and set aside.
2. Rinse, drain and hull the raspberries (or cherries). Peel and slice the bananas. Peel, core and slice the apples and pear. Place all the fruit in a bowl and sprinkle with the granulated sugar. Leave to steep in the refrigerator for 2 hours.
3. Preheat the oven to 275°F / 120°C / Gas Mark 1.
4. Pile the fruit salad into the orange skins.
5. Beat the egg whites, gradually adding the superfine sugar, until stiff. Transfer the meringue to a pastry bag and pipe onto the tops of the oranges. Take care that the fruit is completely covered.
6. Bake for about 25 minutes, without allowing the meringue to brown. Serve at once with crème fraîche or chantilly cream.

Cook's tip: if you would prefer to serve the oranges cold, use ¾ cup [180 g / 6 oz] sugar to make the meringue and bake for 1 hour. Allow to cool before serving.

Melon d'espagne fourré
Melon Cups

	00:30	00:00	
	plus chilling		

American	Ingredients	Metric/Imperial
1	Large cantaloupe melon	1
2 lb	Mixed fresh fruit: grapes, pears, strawberries, oranges	1 kg / 2 lb
½ cup	Sugar	100 g / 4 oz
¼ cup	Kirsch or maraschino liqueur	4 tbsp
1 cup	Thick crème fraîche (see page 122) or chantilly cream (see page 455)	250 ml / 8 fl oz

1. Cut a lid off the melon and scoop out the fruit in balls using a ball-cutter or a teaspoon. Discard the seeds.
2. Wash the fresh fruit and peel, dice and remove seeds where necessary. Place the fruit in a bowl with the melon balls and sprinkle with the sugar and liqueur. Leave to steep in the refrigerator for 1 hour.
3. Just before serving, fill the melon shell with the fruit salad. Serve well chilled with the crème fraîche or chantilly cream.

Coupe aux pommes et aux mûres
Blackberry and Apple Cup

	00:15	00:10 to 00:15	
	plus chilling		

American	Ingredients	Metric/Imperial
¾ lb	Blackberries (or raspberries)	350 g / 12 oz
3 tbsp	Water	3 tbsp
1 cup	Sugar	250 g / 8 oz
1½ lb	Apples	750 g / 1½ lb
1 cup	Thin crème fraîche (see page 122)	250 ml / 8 fl oz
½ cup	Confectioners' [icing] sugar	50 g / 2 oz

1. Rinse the blackberries (or raspberries) and place in a pan with the water and ½ cup [125 g / 4 oz] sugar. Cook without boiling for 10-15 minutes.
2. Set aside the blackberries (or raspberries) which are still whole after cooking (about half). Purée the remainder with the juice in a blender or food processor and then strain to remove the seeds.
3. Peel and core the apples. Cut into quarters and place in a pan. Just cover with water and add the remaining sugar. Cook without boiling for 10-15 minutes and leave to cool in the juice.
4. Divide the blackberry purée between 6 individual glasses and garnish with apple segments and whole blackberries. Chill.
5. Whip the crème fraîche in a chilled bowl, gradually adding the confectioners' sugar until it has doubled in volume.
6. Remove the glasses from the refrigerator and pipe a whirl of cream onto each.

Melon aux framboises

Melon with Raspberries

▬▬◣	00:20 plus chilling	00:00 ▭

American	Ingredients	Metric/Imperial
1 large or 2 medium	Cantaloupe melon(s)	1 large or 2 medium
½ lb	Raspberries	250 g / 8 oz
½ cup	Sugar	100 g / 4 oz
¼ cup	Kirsch	4 tbsp
1 pint	Raspberry ice cream (see page 516)	500 ml / 1 pint

1. Cut a zig-zag around the top of the melon and remove the lid. Remove the seeds and scoop out the flesh in balls using a ball-cutter or a teaspoon.
2. Rinse and hull the raspberries.
3. Mix the melon balls and raspberries. Sprinkle with the sugar and kirsch and leave to steep for 1 hour in the refrigerator, so that the flavors can mingle.
4. To serve, half fill melon with ice cream and top with fruit.

Fondue de pommes

Stewed Apples

▬▬◣	00:15 plus cooling	00:20 ▭

American	Ingredients	Metric/Imperial
1	Lemon	1
3 lb	Apples	1.25 kg / 3 lb
1 cup	Sugar	200 g / 8 oz
1	Vanilla bean [pod]	1
	Ground cinnamon	
⅔ cup	Water	150 ml / ¼ pint

1. Squeeze the juice from the lemon into a large bowl. Peel, core and thinly slice the apples. Add to the bowl and stir to coat with the lemon juice.
2. Transfer the apples and lemon juice to a pan and add the sugar, the vanilla bean split lengthwise, a good pinch of cinnamon and the water. Cover the pan and cook over a low heat for 15 minutes without stirring, then remove the lid and allow the water to evaporate (still over a low heat) for 5 minutes. Remove the vanilla bean.
3. Pour the stewed apples into a serving dish and leave to cool. Serve well chilled.

Pears Belle-Hélène

Poires Belle-Hélène

Pears Belle-Hélène

	00:30 plus chilling	00:20

American	Ingredients	Metric/Imperial
1 cup	Sugar	200 g / 8 oz
1 cup	Water	250 ml / 8 fl oz
6 medium or 3 large	Ripe pears	6 medium or 3 large
	Lemon juice	
½ lb	Semisweet [plain] chocolate	250 g / 8 oz
3 cups	Vanilla ice cream (see page 514 or use bought)	750 ml / 1¼ pints

1. In a thick-bottomed pan dissolve the sugar in ¾ cup [175 ml / 6 fl oz] of the water. Bring to a boil over a high heat and boil for 5 minutes.
2. Peel and halve the pears lengthwise, then remove the cores. Immerse the pears in the boiling syrup, without overlapping them if possible. Add a few drops of lemon juice. When the syrup returns to a boil, remove the pan from the heat. Leave the pears to cool in the syrup until just warm, then drain and chill them.
3. Break the chocolate into a bowl and add the rest of the water. Place the bowl over a pan of hot water and melt the chocolate to a thick cream. Keep hot.
4. Place a portion of vanilla ice cream in each of 6 chilled serving glasses and cover with 1 or 2 pear halves. Pour the hot chocolate sauce over the pears at the table.

Croûtes aux pêches

Peach Toasts

	00:25 plus chilling	00:25

American	Ingredients	Metric/Imperial
6	Large yellow peaches	6
1¼ cups	Sugar	300 g / 10 oz
2 cups	Water	500 ml / ¾ pint
¼ cup	Butter	60 g / 2 oz
6	Thick slices brioche	6
	Raspberry jelly	
	Few pieces candied angelica	

1. Blanch the peaches in boiling water for 30 seconds, then drain and peel them.
2. Put 1 cup [250 g / 8 oz] of the sugar and water in a saucepan and bring to a boil, stirring to dissolve the sugar. Add the peaches and simmer for 5 minutes. Remove the pan from the heat and leave the peaches to cool in the syrup.
3. Preheat the oven to 400°F / 200°C / Gas Mark 6.
4. Butter the slices of brioche. Sprinkle with the remaining sugar and arrange in an ovenproof dish. Brown the bread in the oven for about 10 minutes. Spread each slice with raspberry jelly and arrange on a serving dish.
5. Remove the peaches from their syrup using a slotted spoon. Add 2 tablespoons of raspberry jelly to the syrup and thicken over a low heat. Put the peaches back in the syrup and cook for 1 minute, turning them gently, then place the peaches on the brioche slices. Pour on the syrup. Decorate with angelica and leave until cold. Chill until ready to serve.

Poires Bourdaloue

Pears in Almond Custard

	00:15 plus chilling	00:20 to 00:25

American	Ingredients	Metric/Imperial
6	Pears	6
1	Lemon	1
2 cups	Milk	500 ml / ¾ pint
1 cup	Sugar	250 g / 8 oz
	Vanilla extract [essence]	
¼ cup	Cornstarch [cornflour]	25 g / 1 oz
½ cup	Ground almonds	50 g / 2 oz
5	Egg yolks	5
1 tbsp	Kirsch	1 tbsp
2 tbsp	Water	2 tbsp

1. Carefully peel the pears without removing the stalks, and sprinkle with the juice of the lemon.
2. Place the pears in a flameproof casserole, cover with cold water and top with wax [greaseproof] paper to prevent the pears going brown. Simmer gently for 12-15 minutes. Remove from the heat and leave to cool. When cold, drain the pears and arrange upright in a serving dish.
3. Bring the milk to a boil with ¾ cup [150 g / 6 oz] of the sugar and a few drops of vanilla extract.
4. Thoroughly beat the cornstarch and ground almonds with the egg yolks. Beat until the mixture has increased in volume. Add the boiling milk and pour back into the pan. Cook gently, stirring, for about 10 minutes or until the custard coats the spoon. Do not boil. Leave to cool, then flavor with the kirsch. Pour the custard around the pears.
5. Place the remaining sugar in a pan with the water and dissolve over a moderate heat. Cook until the syrup is golden brown. Cover the top of each pear with this caramel and chill until ready to serve.

Mousse aux marrons

Chestnut Cream

	00:20 Serves 8–10	00:00

American	Ingredients	Metric/Imperial
1 cup	Butter	200 g / 8 oz
¾ cup	Superfine [caster] sugar	150 g / 6 oz
¼ cup	Rum	4 tbsp
2 lb	Canned sweetened chestnut purée	1 kg / 2 lb
1¼ cups	Thin crème fraîche (see page 122)	300 ml / ½ pint
1½ cups	Broken marrons glacés	200 g / 8 oz
6	Marrons glacés (candied chestnuts)	6

1. Cream the butter until softened, then beat in the sugar and rum. Add the chestnut purée, a little at a time, and beat until well blended.
2. Whip the crème fraîche until thick and fold carefully into the chestnut mixture. Gently stir into the mixture the broken marrons glacés.
3. Divide the mousse between 8-10 individual glasses. Decorate with the whole marrons glacés and chill.

Salade d'oranges
Orange Salad

	00:20		00:05
	plus chilling		

American	Ingredients	Metric/Imperial
8	Oranges	8
½ lb	Purple [black] grapes	250 g / 8 oz
1 cup	Sugar	250 g / 8 oz
⅔ cup	Water	150 ml / ¼ pint

1. Peel 6 of the oranges and divide into segments, removing the membrane between the segments and all seeds. Collect the juice. Cut the remaining oranges into very thin slices without peeling.
2. Remove the seeds from the grapes.
3. Arrange some orange slices around the edge of a serving dish and pile the grapes and orange segments in the center. Cover with the remaining orange slices and sprinkle with the orange juice.
4. Dissolve the sugar in the water and bring to a boil. Boil for 5 minutes.
5. Pour the sugar syrup over the oranges and grapes. Cool, then chill well before serving.

Pêches au vin
Peaches in Wine

	00:20		00:10
	plus cooling and chilling		

American	Ingredients	Metric/Imperial
6	Large ripe peaches	6
1 cup	Sugar	250 g / 8 oz
1	Bottle of red wine	1
⅔ cup	Raspberry jelly	250 g / 8 oz

1. Blanch the peaches in boiling water for 30 seconds, then drain and peel off the skins.
2. Arrange the peaches side by side in a pan. Sprinkle with two-thirds of the sugar and just cover with wine. Bring to a boil.
3. Cover the pan and simmer until the peaches are just soft. Remove from the heat and leave to cool until just warm.
3. Remove the peaches from the pan with a slotted spoon and transfer to a serving dish. Reheat the syrup and stir in the raspberry jelly, any remaining wine and the rest of the sugar, if necessary.
4. Pour the syrup over the peaches and serve chilled.

Rabottes de pommes
Apple Dumplings

	00:30	00:30 to 00:35	
	plus making or thawing pastry		

American	Ingredients	Metric/Imperial
6	Apples	6
⅓ cup	Butter	80 g / 3 oz
½ cup	Sugar	125 g / 4 oz
½ lb	Puff pastry (see page 458 or use frozen)	250 g / 8 oz
1	Egg	1

1. Preheat the oven to 400°F / 200°C / Gas Mark 6.
2. Peel and core the apples, and keep the cores.
3. Cream the butter and sugar together and use to fill the center of each apple. Replace the cores.
4. Roll out the puff pastry to ⅛ in / 3 mm thick and cut into 6 squares, each large enough to wrap around an apple. Also cut out 6 1¾ in / 4 cm rounds with a pastry cutter.
5. Wrap each apple in a pastry square, bringing the corners up without overlapping them. Thread a pastry round over each apple stalk and stick to the pastry square with a little water. Decorate the pastry with the point of a knife.
6. Beat the egg and brush over the pastry. Place the apples on a baking sheet. Bake for 30-35 minutes. Check that they are cooked by piercing the apples through the pastry with a skewer. It should slide in easily.
7. Serve hot, warm or cold, with cream.

Pruneaux au vin
Prunes in Wine and Rum

	00:10		00:05
	plus maturing		

American	Ingredients	Metric/Imperial
5 cups	Full-bodied red wine	1.25 l / 2 pints
1 cup	Sugar	200 g / 8 oz
2	Vanilla beans [pods]	2
1¼ cups	Rum	300 ml / ½ pint
1 lb	Prunes	600 g / 1 lb

1. Pour the wine into a saucepan and add the sugar and vanilla beans, split lengthwise. Heat gently until the wine is covered in a white froth.
2. Remove the pan from the heat and add the rum. Remove the vanilla beans.
3. Pierce each prune with a skewer and place in preserving jars. Cover with the warm wine mixture and leave to cool.
4. Seal the jars and leave the prunes to mature for 3-4 weeks before serving.

Fruit salad with liqueur (see page 510)

Poires au sirop
Spiced Pears in Syrup

	00:10 plus chilling		00:20

American	Ingredients	Metric/Imperial
2 cups	Sugar	500 g / 1 lb
1 quart	Water	1 l / 1¾ pints
2	Fresh thyme sprigs	2
2	Bay leaves	2
3	Cloves	3
	Pepper	
¼ cup	Thin honey	4 tbsp
6	Ripe pears	6

1. Dissolve the sugar in the water in a large saucepan. Add the thyme, bay leaves, cloves, a pinch of pepper and the honey.
2. Peel the pears. Immerse them in the syrup and cook over a low heat for 20 minutes.
3. Transfer the pears to 6 individual glasses and cover generously with the syrup. Chill for 2 hours before serving.

Cook's tip: this unusual dessert with its flavor of thyme, bay leaves and cloves can be served with a Savoy sponge cake (see page 478) or, more originally, with a goat's milk cheese.

Pêches pochées au sirop
Poached Peaches

	00:05 plus cooling		00:25

American	Ingredients	Metric/Imperial
12	Yellow peaches	12
1½ cups	Sugar	350 g / 12 oz
3 cups	Water	750 ml / 1¼ pints
⅓ cup	Fruit liqueur (optional)	5 tbsp

1. Blanch the peaches in boiling water for 30 seconds, then drain and remove the skins.
2. Put the sugar and water in a saucepan and bring to a boil. Immerse the peaches in the boiling syrup and simmer for 15 minutes. Remove from the heat and leave the peaches to cool in the syrup.
3. Alternatively, drain the peaches with a slotted spoon and transfer to a shallow ovenproof dish. Sprinkle with a fruit liqueur of your choice and set alight. Pour on the syrup and chill until ready to serve.

Pommes rôties à l'orange
Baked Apples with Orange

	00:10		00:45

American	Ingredients	Metric/Imperial
3	Oranges	3
6	Apples	6
3 tbsp	Sugar	3 tbsp

1. Preheat the oven to 350°F / 180°C / Gas Mark 4.
2. Wash the oranges and cut 6 large slices from the middle of the fruit. Arrange on the bottom of an ovenproof dish or in 6 individual dishes.
3. Wash the apples and remove the core. Using a sharp knife cut the skin all the way around about two-thirds of the way up each apple. Place on the orange slices.
4. Bake for about 20 minutes.
5. Meanwhile, squeeze the juice from the remaining orange. Dissolve the sugar in the juice.
6. When the slits in the apples begin to separate, sprinkle the apples with the sweetened orange juice and bake for a further 20 minutes or until soft. Serve hot with extra sugar, if liked.

Pommes au four ou à la poêle
Baked or Fried Apples

	00:10 frying time: 00:15		00:30

American	Ingredients	Metric/Imperial
6	Apples	6
2 - 3 tbsp	Sugar	2 - 3 tbsp
¼ cup	Butter	60 g / 2 oz

1. Whichever method of cooking you choose, peel and core the apples.
2. To bake: preheat the oven to 375°F / 190°C / Gas Mark 5. Transfer to an ovenproof dish and fill the center of each apple with butter. Bake, sprinkling the apples with water 2 or 3 times, for about 30 minutes. When a knife will go into them easily they are cooked. Serve hot.
3. To fry: cut the apples into 8 segments. Melt the butter in a frying pan and add the apples. Sprinkle with 1 tablespoon of sugar and toss the apples to coat them well. Brown quickly over a high heat, then cook over a very low heat until tender. Shake the pan from time to time rather than stirring the apples.

Baked apples with orange

Mousse à l'orange
Orange Mousse

	00:10 *plus chilling*		00:10

American	Ingredients	Metric/Imperial
3 tbsp	Flour	25 g / 1 oz
3	Eggs, separated	3
½ cup	Superfine [caster] sugar	100 g / 4 oz
4	Oranges	4

1. In a saucepan stir together the flour, egg yolks, three quarters of the sugar and the finely grated rind of 1 orange. Place the pan on a low heat.
2. Squeeze the juice from all the oranges and add to the pan. Cook, stirring, for about 10 minutes or until the custard is thick enough to coat the spoon. Do not boil. Remove the pan from the heat and leave to cool, stirring from time to time to prevent a skin forming.
3. Beat the egg whites with the remaining sugar until stiff. Carefully fold the whites into the orange custard.
4. Pour the mousse into a large bowl and chill for at least 1 hour.

Cook's tip: this mousse is excellent to follow a filling main course. It can be served with petits fours (see page 493).

Mousse au citron
Lemon Cheese Mousse

	00:10 *plus soaking and chilling*		00:00

American	Ingredients	Metric/Imperial
1 cup	Currants	150 g / 6 oz
6	Petit suisse cheeses	6
¾ cup	Sugar	150 g / 6 oz
3	Lemons	3
⅔ cup	Thin crème fraîche (see page 122)	150 ml / ¼ pint
¼ cup	Confectioners' [icing] sugar	30 g / 1 oz

1. Put the currants in a bowl of warm water and leave to soak for 1 hour.
2. Put the cheeses, sugar, flesh of 2 lemons (without seeds) and the juice of the third lemon into a blender or food processor and blend to give a thick cream.
3. Whip the crème fraîche in a chilled bowl, gradually adding the confectioners' sugar, until stiff and doubled in volume.
4. Gently fold the cream and drained currants into the lemon cream.
5. Divide between 6 individual glasses and chill for 1 hour.

Mousse au citron vert
Lime Mousse

	00:20 *plus cooling and chilling*		00:10

American	Ingredients	Metric/Imperial
6	Eggs, separated	6
1 cup	Superfine [caster] sugar	200 g / 8 oz
3	Limes	3

1. Beat the egg yolks with the sugar until frothy, then add the juice of the limes.
2. Place the bowl over a pan of hot water and heat gently, stirring constantly, for 10 minutes or until the mixture will coat a spoon. Remove the bowl and leave until cold.
3. Beat the egg whites until very stiff and gently fold into the lime mixture.
4. Divide the mousse between 6 individual glasses and chill for 1 hour.

Cook's tip: the cooking over the pan of hot water is necessary for the success of this recipe.

Fruits rafraîchis
Fruit Salad with Liqueur

	00:20 *plus chilling*		00:10

American	Ingredients	Metric/Imperial
2	Oranges	2
2	Pears	2
2	Apples	2
½ lb	Pineapple (canned or fresh)	250 g / 8 oz
1 cup	Sugar	250 g / 8 oz
1¼ cups	Water	300 ml / ½ pint
½ lb	Strawberries	250 g / 8 oz
	Kirsch or maraschino liqueur	

1. Peel the oranges and cut into slices. Peel, core and slice the pears and apples. Cut the pineapple into chunks. Transfer all this fruit to a serving bowl.
2. Boil the sugar and water over a moderate heat for 10 minutes. Pour the syrup over the fruit and chill.
3. Just before serving, decorate the salad with strawberries or other seasonal fruit (raspberries, grapes, etc) and add a dash of kirsch or maraschino liqueur.

Pruneaux au Vouvray
Prunes in White Wine

	01:00 *plus soaking and chilling*		00:10

American	Ingredients	Metric/Imperial
1 lb	Semi-dried prunes	500 g / 1 lb
3	Lemons	3
1	Bottle of white wine	1
½ cup	Sugar	100 g / 4 oz
1	Vanilla bean [pod]	1
	Grated nutmeg	

1. Soak the prunes in a bowl of warm water for 1 hour.
2. Meanwhile, thinly pare the rind from the lemons. Pour the wine into a pan and add the sugar, vanilla bean split lengthwise, a pinch of nutmeg and the lemon rind. Bring to a boil and simmer for 10 minutes. Cool.
3. Drain the prunes and transfer to a serving bowl. Cover with the spiced wine and chill for at least 3 hours (or, better still, for 2-3 days).

Cook's tip: add a pinch of ground cinnamon to the wine and serve with chantilly cream (see page 455).

Ices

Of all the frozen desserts, ice creams and sorbets are the most spectacular and the simplest to make. They can provide a special dinner or an impromptu snack with an element of surprise and freshness which your guests will remember with pleasure. There are no hard and fast rules about serving either ice cream or sorbet; it depends entirely on your powers of imagination and the type of menu you are serving. Ice cream is made with cream or milk and eggs, a sorbet consists mainly of a sugar syrup and fruit purées or fruit juice. (Fruit with seeds or skins should be sieved − using a nylon strainer − to make a really smooth purée.)

An electric ice cream maker which is filled with the mixture and placed in the freezer or ice compartment of a refrigerator, or a more expensive model which sits on a worktop, is a very useful piece of equipment if you make ice cream or sorbets regularly. In it, the mixture is automatically beaten steadily until it is frozen and this gives a very smooth texture and more bulk than when the mixture is hand beaten. Without this appliance, you can still make good ice creams or sorbets. Set your freezer or refrigerator to the 'fast freeze' or coldest setting an hour before putting in the mixture and chill all your equipment before using it. To prevent the formation of large ice crystals, freeze the ice mixture in quantities of 1 quart [1 l / 1¾ pints] rather than larger amounts, using containers in which the mixture can be beaten. Beat the mixture once or twice during freezing to break down ice crystals and incorporate air.

After the second beating, or when the mixture in an ice cream maker is beginning to freeze, transfer the mixture to a mold and freeze for at least 4 hours. Molds come in a variety of shapes and sizes from 1 quart [1 l / 2 pints] down to individual plastic molds in the form of brightly colored fruit which children love. Ice creams and sorbets will keep for about 2 months in a freezer.

Iced strawberry soufflé (see page 518)

Café liégeois
Coffee Liégeois

	00:15 *plus freezing*	00:15

American	Ingredients	Metric/Imperial
1 quantity	Vanilla custard sauce (see page 454)	1 quantity
1 tsp	Coffee flavoring	1 tsp
¼ cup	Instant coffee powder	4 tbsp
1 cup	Water	250 ml / 8 fl oz
1 tbsp	Sugar	1 tbsp
2 cups	Thin crème fraîche (see page 122)	500 ml / ¾ pint
½ cup	Confectioners' [icing] sugar	50 g / 2 oz
6	Sugar coffee beans	6

1. Flavor the custard sauce with the coffee flavoring. Transfer the mixture to an ice cream maker and freeze, following the manufacturer's instructions.
2. Dissolve the instant coffee in the water and leave to cool. Add the sugar and place in the refrigerator.
3. Whip the crème fraîche, until it has doubled in volume, gradually adding the confectioners' sugar.
4. Pour a little cold sweetened coffee into 6 stemmed glasses and cover with coffee ice cream. With a pastry bag and fluted nozzle, pipe a whirl of whipped crème fraîche into each glass. Top with the sugar coffee beans and serve immediately.

Chocolat liégeois
Chocolate Liégeois

Replace the coffee flavoring with ¼ cup [50 g / 2 oz] cocoa powder. Place the chocolate custard sauce in an ice cream maker and freeze. When ready, scoop the chocolate ice cream into 6 large stemmed glasses, top with chantilly cream (see page 455) and sprinkle lightly with cocoa powder.

Café viennois
Viennese Coffee

	00:15 *plus cooling and chilling*	00:10

American	Ingredients	Metric/Imperial
6 tbsp	Instant coffee powder	6 tbsp
1 quart	Hot water	1 l / 1¾ pints
3 cups	Crème fraîche (see page 122)	750 ml / 1¼ pints
⅓ cup	Sugar	80 g / 3 oz
¼ cup	Confectioners' [icing] sugar	50 g / 2 oz

1. Dissolve the instant coffee in the water.
2. Heat 1 cup [250 ml / 8 fl oz] of the crème fraîche with the sugar. When the mixture begins to boil, stir it into the hot coffee. Cool, then chill for 1 hour.
3. Meanwhile, whip the remaining crème fraîche in a chilled bowl, gradually adding the confectioners' sugar. Continue whipping until the crème fraîche is stiff.
4. When the coffee is cold, whizz it in a blender until frothy and pour into 6 stemmed glasses. With a pastry bag and fluted nozzle, pipe a whirl of whipped crème fraîche on top.

Café granito
Coffee Granita

	00:15 plus freezing	00:03

American	Ingredients	Metric/Imperial
½ cup	Sugar	125 g / 4 oz
⅔ cup	Cold water	150 ml / ¼ pint
¼ cup	Instant coffee powder	4 tbsp
2 cups	Hot water	500 ml / ¾ pint
1 cup	Crème fraîche (see page 122)	250 ml / 8 fl oz
⅓ cup	Confectioners' [icing] sugar	40 g / 1½ oz
6	Sugar coffee beans	6

1. Dissolve the sugar in the cold water over a moderate heat without stirring. Remove the pan from the heat and leave the syrup to cool.
2. Dissolve the instant coffee in the hot water. Stir into the cold syrup.
3. Pour into an ice cube tray and freeze. Every 20-30 minutes, take the coffee mixture out of the freezer and stir with a fork to avoid ice crystals forming.
4. Meanwhile, whip the crème fraîche in a chilled bowl, gradually adding the confectioners' sugar, until the crème is thick.
5. To serve, divide the coffee ice between 6 frosted glasses. Using a pastry bag with fluted nozzle, pipe the whipped cream on top. Decorate with sugar coffee beans.

Cook's tip: this water ice should be slightly gritty in texture.

Cassata
Cassata

	00:30 plus freezing	00:15

American	Ingredients	Metric/Imperial
½ quantity	Vanilla custard sauce (see page 454)	½ quantity
½	Vanilla bean [pod]	½
½	Lemon	½
½ cup	Flaked almonds	60 g / 2 oz
⅓ cup	Crystallized fruit	60 g / 2 oz
3 tbsp	Kirsch	3 tbsp
1 cup	Thick crème fraîche (see page 122)	250 ml / 8 fl oz
⅔ cup	Chilled milk	150 ml / ¼ pint
½ cup	Confectioners' [icing] sugar	50 g / 2 oz

1. Prepare the vanilla custard sauce, adding the thinly pared rind of the ½ lemon with the vanilla bean. Transfer the custard to a mixing bowl and leave until completely cold, stirring from time to time.
2. Pour the custard into an ice cream maker and freeze, following the manufacturer's instructions.
3. Spread the ice cream over the bottom and sides of a chilled 1 quart [1 l / 2 pint] charlotte mold. Place a small bowl or jar in the center to keep the ice cream in place.
4. Meanwhile, spread the flaked almonds on a baking sheet and toast under a hot broiler [grill] for 3-4 minutes, stirring occasionally and taking care not to let them become too brown. Leave to cool.
5. Dice the crystallized fruit and mix with the kirsch in a small bowl.

6. Whip the crème fraîche and milk in a chilled bowl until frothy. Gradually add the confectioners' sugar and continue whipping until stiff. Fold in the flaked almonds and the drained crystallized fruit.
7. Remove the mold from the freezer. Take out the small bowl or jar and fill the center hollow with the almond mixture. Freeze for at least 4 hours.
8. To serve, dip the mold in warm water for a few seconds and turn out the cassata onto a serving plate.

Coupes glacées aux pruneaux
Iced Prune Creams

	00:15 plus soaking and freezing	00:20

American	Ingredients	Metric/Imperial
½ lb (1½ cups)	Prunes	250 g / 8 oz
½ cup	Superfine [caster] sugar	100 g / 4 oz
1 cup	Cream cheese	250 g / 8 oz
⅔ cup	Thin crème fraîche (see page 122)	150 ml / ¼ pint
	Vanilla extract [essence]	
6	Prunes in armagnac	6

1. Cover the prunes with water and leave to soak for 12 hours.
2. The next day, cook the prunes in the soaking water over a low heat for 15-20 minutes. Drain the prunes, remove the pits [stones] using a small pointed knife and purée in a blender or food processor. Add the sugar and cream cheese and blend well.
3. Whip the crème fraîche with a few drops of vanilla extract until thick. Carefully fold the whipped crème fraîche into the prune mixture.
4. Using a pastry bag and ¼ in / 5 mm nozzle, pipe the prune cream into 6 glasses. Freeze for 1 hour.
5. Serve topped with the prunes in armagnac.

Parfait au café
Coffee Parfait

	00:30 plus freezing	00:05

American	Ingredients	Metric/Imperial
1 cup	Sugar	200 g / 8 oz
⅓ cup	Water	5 tbsp
8	Egg yolks	8
⅔ cup	Very strong coffee	150 ml / ¼ pint
1 cup	Thin crème fraîche (see page 122)	250 ml / 8 fl oz

1. Dissolve the sugar in the water and cook over a low heat, without stirring, until it forms a thick syrup. Remove from the heat before the syrup begins to brown.
2. In a bowl gradually beat the syrup into the egg yolks. When thick, stir in the strong coffee.
3. Whip the crème fraîche and fold into the coffee mixture a little at a time.
4. Transfer the mixture to a 1½ quart [1.5 l / 2½ pint] freezer-proof mold and freeze for 6 hours.
5. To serve, dip the mold in warm water for a few seconds and turn out the parfait onto a plate.

Cook's tip: although this dessert is usually coffee-flavored it can also be made with chocolate, praline or vanilla.

Cassata

Glace au thé
Tea Ice Cream

	00:20	00:15
	plus freezing	

American	Ingredients	Metric/Imperial
1 quart	Milk	1 l / 1¾ pints
10 tsp	Orange pekoe tea leaves	10 tsp
½ cup	Thick crème fraîche (see page 122)	125 ml / 4 fl oz
8 - 10	Egg yolks	8 - 10
¾ cup	Superfine [caster] sugar	150 g / 6 oz
2 tbsp	Rum	2 tbsp
½ quantity	Chantilly cream (see page 455)	½ quantity

1. Bring the milk to a boil. Remove the pan from the heat and add the tea. Cover the pan and leave to infuse for 4 minutes. Strain the milk and stir in the crème fraîche.
2. Beat the egg yolks with the sugar until pale. Gradually beat in the cream mixture.
3. Return the mixture to the saucepan and stir over a low heat for 10 minutes until the custard will coat the spoon. Take care not to allow the custard to boil.
4. Leave the custard until cold, then add the rum. Pour into an ice cream maker and freeze according to the manufacturer's instructions.
5. Serve in individual glasses, topped with a whirl of chantilly cream, if liked.

Assorted iced soufflés

Glace à la vanille
Vanilla Ice Cream

	00:20	00:15
	plus freezing	

American	Ingredients	Metric/Imperial
⅔ cup	Thin crème fraîche (see page 122)	150 ml / ¼ pint
1 quantity	Vanilla custard sauce (see page 454)	1 quantity

1. Whip the crème fraîche until thick. Fold the whipped cream into the vanilla custard sauce.
2. Pour into an ice cream maker and freeze according to the manufacturer's instructions.
3. Transfer the ice cream to the refrigerator about 20 minutes before serving.

Cook's tip: if you do not have an ice cream maker pour the mixture into suitable freezer trays and freeze until half frozen (sides are frozen, center is still soft). Beat thoroughly to break down ice crystals. Return to freezer and freeze again. This process can be repeated to give a creamier consistency.

Glace aux marrons
Chestnut Rum Ice Cream

	00:15	00:10
	plus freezing	Serves 6-8

American	Ingredients	Metric/Imperial
1 quart	Milk	1 l / 2 pints
1	Vanilla bean [pod]	1
½ cup	Sugar	125 g / 4 oz
6	Egg yolks	6
1 lb	Canned sweetened chestnut purée	400 g / 14 oz
⅔ cup	Rum	150 ml / ¼ pint
1 cup	Broken marrons glacés (candied chestnuts)	150 g / 5 oz
6 or 8	Chestnuts in syrup	6 or 8

1. Put the milk in a saucepan with the vanilla bean, halved lengthwise, and the sugar. Bring to a boil.
2. Beat the egg yolks until frothy, then gradually add the boiling milk (discard the vanilla bean). Pour the mixture back into the pan and stir over a low heat for 10 minutes until the custard will coat the spoon. Do not boil.
3. Remove from the heat and stir in the chestnut purée. Leave until cold.
4. Stir in the rum, pour the mixture into an ice cream maker and freeze, following the manufacturer's instructions.
5. Fold in the broken marrons glacés. Freeze for a further 2 hours.
6. Half an hour before serving transfer the ice cream to the refrigerator and frost 6 or 8 glasses in the freezer.
7. To serve, scoop out the ice cream in balls, arrange in the individual glasses and decorate with the chestnuts in syrup.

Glace au chocolat
Chocolate Ice Cream

	00:30	00:10
	plus freezing	

American	Ingredients	Metric/Imperial
1 quart	Milk	1 l / 1¾ pints
¾ cup	Cocoa powder	70 g / 3 oz
8	Egg yolks	8
1 cup	Superfine [caster] sugar	200 g / 8 oz

1. Mix the milk and cocoa powder together and bring to a boil in a saucepan.
2. Beat the egg yolks with the sugar until pale. Gradually beat in the boiling milk.

3. Pour the mixture back into the pan and stir for 10 minutes over a low heat until the custard is thick enough to coat the spoon.
4. Pour the custard into a bowl and leave to cool, stirring occasionally to prevent a skin forming.
5. When cold, pour the custard into an ice cream maker and freeze according to the manufacturer's instructions.
6. Transfer the ice cream to the refrigerator about 20 minutes before serving.

Glace au café

Coffee Ice Cream

	00:30 plus freezing		00:10

American	Ingredients	Metric/Imperial
1 quart	Milk	1 l / 1¾ pints
1¼ cups	Superfine [caster] sugar	300 g / 10 oz
8	Egg yolks	8
¾ cup	Very strong coffee	175 ml / 6 fl oz
1 cup	Thin crème fraîche (see page 122)	250 ml / 8 fl oz
¼ cup	Confectioners' [icing] sugar	30 g / 1 oz

1. Bring the milk to a boil with half the sugar.
2. Beat the egg yolks with the remaining sugar until pale. Gradually beat in the boiling milk. Pour the mixture back into the pan and stir over a low heat for 10 minutes or until the custard is thick enough to coat the spoon. Do not boil.
3. Remove the pan from the heat and pour the custard into a bowl. Stir in the coffee and leave to cool.
4. When cold, pour the custard into an ice cream maker and freeze according to the manufacturer's instructions.
5. When ready to serve, whip the crème fraîche, gradually adding the confectioners' sugar.
6. Using an ice cream scoop, remove balls of coffee ice cream and arrange in individual glasses. Pipe the crème fraîche on top.

Glace Plombières

Ice Cream Plombières

	01:00 plus freezing		00:15

American	Ingredients	Metric/Imperial
½ quantity	Vanilla custard sauce (see page 454)	½ quantity
⅔ cup	Mixed candied fruit	125 g / 4 oz
2 tbsp	Kirsch	2 tbsp
2 tbsp	Thick crème fraîche (see page 122)	2 tbsp
½ quantity	Chantilly cream (see page 455)	½ quantity

1. Pour the custard sauce into an ice cream maker and freeze according to the manufacturer's instructions.
2. Meanwhile, finely chop the candied fruit. Sprinkle it with the kirsch and stir in the crème fraîche. Place in the freezer to chill the mixture to the same temperature as the ice cream.
3. When the ice cream is of a good consistency, fold in the fruit mixture. Transfer to a deep freezeproof mold and freeze for at least 6 hours.
4. To serve, dip the mold in warm water for a few seconds and turn out the ice cream. Decorate with chantilly cream and more candied fruit.

Glace au citron

Lemon Ice Cream

	00:10 plus freezing		00:00

American	Ingredients	Metric/Imperial
5	Lemons	5
1 quart	Water	1 l / 1¾ pints
1½ cups	Sugar	350 g / 12 oz
¼ cup	Thick crème fraîche (see page 122)	4 tbsp

1. Finely grate the rind of 1 lemon into a bowl. Squeeze the juice of the 5 lemons and strain into the bowl. Add the water, sugar and crème fraîche. Mix thoroughly.
2. Pour the mixture into an ice cream maker and freeze according to the manufacturer's instructions.
3. Transfer the ice cream to the refrigerator about 20 minutes before serving.
4. Serve the ice cream on its own with raspberry sauce (see page 504) or a syrup.

Sorbet à l'orange

Orange Sorbet

	00:15 plus freezing		00:00

American	Ingredients	Metric/Imperial
10	Oranges	10
	Sugar	

1. Squeeze the juice from the oranges and strain it. Measure the juice. For every 1 cup [250 ml / 8 fl oz], add 6 tablespoons of sugar. Stir well to dissolve the sugar.
2. Pour into an ice cream maker and freeze according to the manufacturer's instructions.
3. Transfer the sorbet to the refrigerator about 20 minutes before serving.
4. Serve in individual frosted glasses.

Glace aux raisins et au rhum

Rum and Raisin Ice Cream

	00:30 plus soaking and freezing		00:15

American	Ingredients	Metric/Imperial
⅓ cup	Raisins	50 g / 2 oz
1 cup	Thin crème fraîche (see page 122)	250 ml / 8 fl oz
1 quantity	Vanilla custard sauce (see page 454)	1 quantity
1 tbsp	Rum	1 tbsp

1. Soak the raisins in warm water for 1 hour.
2. Whip the crème fraîche until thick. Fold into the custard sauce with the rum and drained raisins.
3. Transfer the mixture to an ice cream maker and freeze according to the manufacturer's instructions.
4. Transfer the ice cream to the refrigerator about 20 minutes before serving.

Glace aux fraises ou aux framboises

Strawberry or Raspberry Ice Cream

	00:15 plus freezing		00:00
American	**Ingredients**	**Metric/Imperial**
2 lb	Strawberries or raspberries	1 kg / 2 lb
	Sugar	
2	Lemons	2
¼ cup	Crème fraîche (see page 122)	4 tbsp

1. Rinse and hull the strawberries or raspberries. Reduce the fruit to a purée in a blender or food processor and measure the quantity of purée. Add an equal amount of water.
2. For each 1 cup [250 ml / 8 fl oz] purée, add ¾ cup [150 g / 6 oz] sugar. Squeeze the juice from the lemons and add to the purée with the crème fraîche. Mix well.
3. Pour the mixture into an ice cream maker and freeze according to the manufacturer's instructions.
4. Transfer the ice cream to the refrigerator about 20 minutes before serving.
5. Serve the ice cream on its own or with vanilla ice cream (see page 514) strawberries, or raspberries and raspberry sauce (see page 504).

Cook's tip: peach, apricot or melon ice cream can be made by this same method.

Coupes glacées aux fruits

Fruit and Ice Cream Cups

	00:25		00:05
American	**Ingredients**	**Metric/Imperial**
3	Seasonal fruits (pears or peaches)	3
¾ cup	Sugar	180 g / 6 oz
⅓ cup	Water	5 tbsp
1	Lemon	1
6 tbsp	Apricot jam	6 tbsp
½ lb	Gingersnaps	200 g / 8 oz
1 pint	Vanilla ice cream (see page 514)	500 ml / 1 pint
6 tbsp	Chocolate sprinkles [chocolate vermicelli]	6 tbsp

1. Peel and quarter the fruit and remove the cores or pits [stones].
2. Dissolve the sugar in the water and bring to a boil. Add the juice of the lemon and cook over a moderate heat for 5 minutes.
3. Add the fruit to the syrup and cook gently for 5 minutes. Drain the fruit with a slotted spoon.
4. In a separate pan warm the apricot jam with 2 or 3 tablespoons of water. Dip the fruit into the jam so that each piece is coated.
5. Crush the gingersnaps. Put 2 tablespoons of crumbs in each of 6 individual glasses. Add a scoop of vanilla ice cream and then the fruit. Sprinkle with the remaining crumbs. Top with more vanilla ice cream and chocolate sprinkles.

Sorbet à la pomme verte

Green Apple Sorbet

	00:30 plus freezing		00:05
American	**Ingredients**	**Metric/Imperial**
1 cup	Sugar	200 g / 8 oz
⅔ cup	Water	150 ml / ¼ pint
5	Under-ripe green apples	5
	Lemon juice	
⅓ cup	Calvados or applejack	6 tbsp

1. Dissolve the sugar in the water and bring to a boil over a high heat. Boil for about 5 minutes or until a thick syrup is formed. Remove from the heat and leave the syrup to cool.
2. Wash the apples but do not peel them. Quarter and core them and rub each quarter with lemon juice. Grate the apples with the peel. Place the grated apple in a mixing bowl and sprinkle with the juice of 1 lemon. Stir in the cold syrup.
3. Pour the mixture into an ice cream maker and freeze according to the manufacturer's instructions.
4. Transfer the sorbet to the refrigerator about 20 minutes before serving.
5. To serve, scoop the sorbet into balls with an ice cream scoop and arrange in individual glasses. Sprinkle each serving with 1 tablespoon of calvados.

Ice cream plombières

Citrons glacés

Lemon Ices

	01:30 plus freezing		00:05
American	**Ingredients**	**Metric/Imperial**
2½ cups	Sugar	600 g / 1¼ lb
3 cups	Water	750 ml / 1¼ pints
12	Large lemons	12

1. Dissolve the sugar in the water and boil for 5 minutes.
2. Wash and dry 6 lemons. Thinly pare off the rind. Add the rind to the syrup, remove from the heat, cover the pan and leave to infuse.

3. Cut the tops off the remaining lemons and scoop out the flesh using a small spoon, taking care not to pierce the skins. Chill the skins and lids in the refrigerator. Purée the lemon pulp in a blender or food processor.

4. Stir the purée into the syrup. Pour it into an ice cream maker and freeze according to the manufacturer's instructions.

5. When the sorbet is of a good consistency, spoon it into the lemon skins and top with the lids. Freeze for a further 3 hours before serving.

Oranges givrées

Frosted Oranges

	01:00 plus freezing	00:00

American	Ingredients	Metric/Imperial
1	Lemon	1
6	Large oranges	6
	Sugar	
1	Egg white	1
¼ cup	Confectioners' [icing] sugar	30 g / 1 oz

1. Squeeze the juice from the lemon.

2. Cut a lid from each orange and scoop out the inside with a spoon, taking care not to pierce the skin. Frost the skins and lids in the freezer.

3. Purée the orange pulp in a blender or food processor and strain. Add the orange juice to the lemon juice and measure the liquid. For each 1 cup [250 ml / 8 fl oz] of juice, add 6 tablespoons of sugar. Stir well to dissolve the sugar.

4. Pour into an ice cream maker and freeze according to the manufacturer's instructions.

5. Beat the egg white with the confectioners' sugar until stiff. When the sorbet is set, fold in the egg white. Return to the freezer and continue freezing until set.

6. To serve, fill the frosted orange skins with sorbet and replace the lids. If you are not serving immediately, return them to the freezer.

Sorbet abricot

Apricot Sorbet

	00:20 plus freezing	00:15 to 00:20

American	Ingredients	Metric/Imperial
1 (1 lb)	Can of apricots in syrup	1 (500 g / 1 lb)
1	Lemon	1
1 cup	Sugar	200 g / 8 oz
1 cup	Water	250 ml / 8 fl oz
1	Egg white	1

1. Drain the apricots, reserving the syrup. Purée the apricots in a blender or food processor and add the juice of the lemon.

2. Dissolve the sugar in the water and bring to a boil. Boil for about 15 minutes, then stir into the puréed apricots. Cool.

3. When completely cold, pour the mixture into an ice cream maker and freeze, following the manufacturer's instructions.

4. Beat the egg white until stiff. When the sorbet has set, soften it in the blender or with an electric beater. Gently fold in the egg white. Return to the freezer and freeze for a further 2 hours.

5. To serve, make balls of sorbet with an ice cream scoop and place in individual glasses. Pour on the chilled apricot syrup.

Sorbet aux poires

Pear Sorbet

	01:00 plus freezing	00:20

American	Ingredients	Metric/Imperial
2 lb	Pears	1 kg / 2 lb
2 tbsp	Lemon juice	2 tbsp
2 cups	Sugar	450 g / 1 lb
6 tbsp	Water	6 tbsp
2 tbsp	Poire William (pear liqueur)	2 tbsp

1. Set aside 3 of the pears. Peel, quarter and core the rest. Purée in a blender or food processor with the lemon juice. Add sufficient water to make 1 quart [1 l / 2¾ pints] liquid and strain into a bowl.

2. Stir in 1¼ cups [300 g / 10 oz] of the sugar. Pour into an ice cream maker and freeze, following the manufacturer's instructions.

3. Meanwhile, peel the reserved pears. Cut into 4 or 6 wedges and remove the cores. Dissolve the remaining sugar in the water and boil for about 5 minutes. When the syrup begins to thicken, add the pears. Bring back to a boil, then remove from the heat. Leave until cold.

4. Arrange the drained pears in individual glasses. Boil to reduce the syrup to about 1¼ cups [300 ml / ½ pint] and pour over the pears. Chill.

5. When ready to serve, sprinkle each serving with 1 teaspoon of pear liqueur and cover with scoops of sorbet.

Sorbet aux pêches

Peach Sorbet

	01:00 plus freezing	00:20

American	Ingredients	Metric/Imperial
2 lb	Peaches	1 kg / 2 lb
2	Very ripe apricots	2
2 tbsp	Lemon juice	2 tbsp
2 cups	Sugar	450 g / 1 lb
6 tbsp	Water	6 tbsp
6 tbsp	Maraschino liqueur	6 tbsp

1. Set aside 3 peaches. Quarter the remaining peaches and the apricots and remove the pits [stones]. Purée the fruit in a blender or food processor. Add sufficient water to the purée to give 1 quart [1 l / 1¾ pints] of liquid.

2. Stir the lemon juice into the purée and strain. Add 1¼ cups [300 g / 10 oz] of the sugar.

3. Pour the mixture into an ice cream maker and freeze according to the manufacturer's instructions.

4. Meanwhile, blanch the reserved peaches in boiling water for 1 minute, then drain and remove the skins. Quarter the peaches and remove the pits.

5. Dissolve the remaining sugar in the water and boil over a high heat for 5 minutes or until the syrup thickens. Add the peach quarters. Bring the syrup back to a boil, then remove the pan from the heat. Leave to cool.

6. When the peaches are cold, arrange in 6 individual glasses and pour a little syrup over the top. Chill for an hour or two until ready to serve.

7. To serve, add 1 tablespoon of maraschino liqueur to each glass and cover the peaches with balls of sorbet cut with an ice cream scoop.

Soufflé glacé aux fraises

Iced Strawberry Soufflé

	00:35		00:10
	plus freezing		

American	Ingredients	Metric/Imperial
1¼ cups	Sugar	300 g / 10 oz
⅔ cup	Water	150 ml / ¼ pint
4	Egg whites	4
1 lb	Strawberries	400 g / 1 lb
3 cups	Thin crème fraîche (see page 122)	750 ml / 1¼ pints

1. Dissolve the sugar in the water and bring to a boil. Boil until a little syrup forms small beads when dropped in cold water.
2. Beat the egg whites until stiff. Gradually add the boiling syrup and continue beating vigorously until completely cold. Place in the refrigerator.
3. Rinse and hull the strawberries. Blend in a food processor or blender to a thick purée and place in the refrigerator to chill.
4. In a chilled bowl whip the crème fraîche until thick.
5. Add the strawberry purée and whipped crème fraîche to the egg white mixture and fold gently together until well blended.
6. Cut a strip of wax [greaseproof] paper 6 in / 16 cm wide and 2½ in / 6 cm longer than the circumference of an 8 in / 20 cm soufflé dish. Fold the paper strip in half lengthwise to give a double strip 3 in / 8 cm wide. Wrap the paper around the outer rim of the dish, to stand 2½ in / 6 cm above the rim, and secure in position with kitchen string or a large rubber band.
7. Pour the strawberry mixture into the dish to level with the top of the paper collar and freeze for at least 6 hours.
8. To serve, remove the paper collar.

Strawberry sorbet

Sorbet aux fraises ou aux framboises

Strawberry or Raspberry Sorbet

	00:10		00:10
	plus freezing		

American	Ingredients	Metric/Imperial
2 cups	Sugar	400 g / 14 oz
1¼ cups	Water	300 ml / ½ pint
3 lb	Strawberries (or raspberries)	1.5 kg / 3 lb

1. Dissolve the sugar in the water, then cook without stirring for about 10 minutes over a low heat until a thick, colorless syrup is formed. Leave to cool.
2. Rinse and hull the strawberries or raspberries. Reduce to a thick purée in a blender or food processor.
3. Stir the purée into the cold syrup and pour the mixture into a shallow pan. Freeze for at least 4 hours.
4. To serve, use an ice cream scoop or a spoon to make balls of sorbet. Place in individual frosted glasses and serve on its own or decorated with chantilly cream (see page 455).

Cook's tip: these sorbets keep for a long time in the freezer. Before serving leave them in the refrigerator for 1 hour to give them the right consistency.

Omelette norvégienne

Norwegian Omelette

	00:30		00:10
	plus chilling		

American	Ingredients	Metric/Imperial
1 (10 in)	Genoese sponge cake (see page 460)	1 (24 cm / 10 in)
⅔ cup	Grand Marnier	150 ml / ¼ pint
4	Eggs, separated	4
4	Egg whites	4
2 cups	Superfine [caster] sugar	400 g / 14 oz
1 pint	Ice cream: vanilla (see page 514), coffee (see page 515) or chocolate (see page 514) or use bought	500 ml / 1 pint
1 cup	Confectioners' [icing] sugar	100 g / 4 oz

1. Cut the sponge cake into a rectangle 8 in / 20 cm long and 4 in / 10 cm wide and place in the center of an ovenproof dish. In the cake cut out a second rectangle 2½ in / 6 cm wide, 7 in / 18 cm long and 1 in / 2 cm deep. Remove this rectangle and keep to one side to serve as a lid.
2. Moisten the cake with two-thirds of the Grand Marnier. Replace the lid and chill for 1 hour.
3. Preheat the oven to 475°F / 240°C / Gas Mark 9.
4. Beat the 4 egg yolks with the remaining Grand Marnier. Beat the 8 egg whites until very stiff, gradually adding the superfine sugar. Carefully fold the yolks into the whites.
5. Remove the cake from the refrigerator and take out the lid. Place the ice cream in the hole in the center and cover with the lid.
6. Fill a pastry bag with some of the egg mixture and completely cover the cake with the remaining egg. Level it with a metal spatula, then pipe the rest of the egg mixture over the top. Sprinkle generously with confectioners' sugar.
7. Bake for about 10 minutes or until the top of the omelette is golden brown. Serve immediately.

Pêche Melba
Peach Melba

	00:10 plus chilling		00:00

American	Ingredients	Metric/Imperial
¾ lb	Strawberries	300 g / 12 oz
¾ lb	Raspberries	300 g / 12 oz
2½ cups	Sugar	600 g / 1¼ lb
1 quart	Vanilla ice cream (see page 514 or use bought)	1 l / 2 pints
6	Peach halves in syrup (canned or freshly made)	6
½ cup	Flaked almonds	50 g / 2 oz
½ quantity	Chantilly cream (see page 455)	½ quantity

1. Rinse and hull the strawberries and raspberries. Purée in a blender or food processor. Stir in the sugar until completely dissolved. Strain to remove seeds. Chill for 12 hours.
2. To serve, place 1 tablespoon of fruit purée in each of 6 glasses and add a scoop of vanilla ice cream. Arrange half a peach on the ice cream. Sprinkle with flaked almonds, surround with chantilly cream and top with a little more fruit purée.

Cook's tip: Peach Melba can be made entirely with strawberries or raspberries, wild strawberries or even red currants, but always with equal quantities of fruit and sugar.

Peach Melba

Sorbet au Cointreau
Cointreau Sorbet

	00:15 plus freezing		00:05

American	Ingredients	Metric/Imperial
1 cup	Sugar	200 g / 8 oz
2 cups	Water	500 ml / ¾ pint
1	Vanilla bean [pod]	1
2	Oranges	2
5	Cloves	5
2 tbsp	Cointreau	2 tbsp

1. Dissolve the sugar in the water and bring to a boil. Add the vanilla bean, split lengthwise, and boil for 5 minutes. Remove from the heat.
2. Thinly pare the rind from 1 orange and add to the syrup together with the cloves. Leave the syrup until completely cold.
3. Strain the syrup and stir in the juice of the 2 oranges and the Cointreau.
4. Pour into an ice cream maker and freeze, following the manufacturer's instructions.
5. Transfer the sorbet to the refrigerator about 20 minutes before serving.
6. Serve the sorbet sprinkled with additional Cointreau.

Soufflés glacés à la framboise
Iced Raspberry Soufflés

	01:00 plus freezing		00:10

American	Ingredients	Metric/Imperial
2 cups	Sugar	450 g / 1 lb
½ cup	Water	125 ml / 4 fl oz
10	Egg yolks	10
1½ cups	Raspberries	150 ml / 5 oz
1 quart	Thin crème fraîche (see page 122)	1 l / 1¾ pints

1. Cut 6 strips of wax [greaseproof] paper 3 in / 8 cm wide and 1 in / 3 cm longer than the circumference of 6 ramekins or individual soufflé dishes. Oil the dishes and sprinkle with a little sugar. Wrap a strip of paper around the outer rim of each dish, taking it 1½ in / 4 cm higher than the rim. Secure in place.
2. Place the remaining sugar and the water in a saucepan and boil until a little syrup forms small beads when dropped in cold water.
3. Meanwhile, put the egg yolks into a bowl and beat until pale. Beat in the boiling syrup in a thin trickle. Place the bowl over a pan of hot water and continue to beat until the mixture is thick enough to stick to the blades of the beater. Leave until quite cold.
4. Rinse and hull the raspberries and purée them in a blender or food processor.
5. Whip the crème fraîche until thick. Fold the crème fraîche into the egg yolk mixture, then stir in the raspberry purée.
6. Fill the ramekins to the top of the paper collars with the mixture and freeze for 6 hours.
7. To serve, remove the paper collars.

Cook's tip: the same mixture can be used to fill a 7 in / 18 cm soufflé dish, in which case use a 3 in / 8 cm strip of paper and bring it 2½ in / 6 cm above the rim of the dish. Secure the paper with a large rubber band or kitchen string.

Sorbet citron
Lemon Sorbet

	00:30		00:05
	plus freezing		

American	Ingredients	Metric/Imperial
6	Lemons	6
6	Sugar lumps	6
2 cups	Sugar	500 g / 1 lb
2 cups	Water	500 ml / ¾ pint
1	Egg white	1
	Vodka (optional)	

1. Wash and dry 2 lemons. Rub the skins with the sugar lumps until the sugar is yellow (having absorbed the lemon zest or oil). Place the lumps in a pan with the sugar and water. Bring to a boil, stirring to dissolve the sugar, and cook for 20 minutes or until the syrup thickens.
2. Squeeze the juice from the 6 lemons. Add the syrup. Stir thoroughly, then leave to cool.
3. Pour into an ice cream maker and freeze, following the manufacturer's instructions.
4. Remove the sorbet from the freezer and soften in a blender or with an electric beater. Beat the egg white until stiff and fold gently into the sorbet. Return the sorbet to the freezer and freeze for at least 2 hours longer.
5. Transfer the sorbet to the refrigerator about 20 minutes before serving.
6. Serve the sorbet on its own or sprinkled with vodka. It could also be served with a strawberry sauce (see page 504).

Soufflé glacé à l'ananas
Iced Pineapple Soufflé

	00:25	00:03 to 00:04	
	plus steeping and freezing		

American	Ingredients	Metric/Imperial
1	Large can of pineapple slices	1
2	Lemons	2
3	Eggs, separated	3
½ cup	Superfine [caster] sugar	100 g / 4 oz
1 envelope	Unflavored gelatin	1 tbsp
⅔ cup	Thin crème fraîche (see page 122)	150 ml / ¼ pint
1 piece	Candied angelica	1 piece

1. Drain the pineapple slices, reserving the juice. Set aside 4 pineapple slices and finely chop the rest. Finely grate the rind from the lemons.
2. Combine egg yolks, lemon rind and half the sugar. Place bowl over a pan of hot, but not boiling, water and beat until the mixture is pale in color and has doubled in volume. Remove from the heat.
3. Dissolve the gelatin in 4 tablespoons of the pineapple juice. Stir the gelatin into the egg yolk mixture with the chopped pineapple.
4. Chill for 1-1½ hours or until the mixture begins to set.
5. Keep 4 tablespoons of the crème fraîche to one side and whip the rest until thick. Fold gently into the pineapple mixture.
6. Beat the egg whites until very stiff, gradually adding the remaining sugar. Fold the whites into the soufflé mixture.
7. Cut a strip of wax [greaseproof] paper 6 in / 16 cm wide and 2½ in / 6 cm longer than the circumference of an 8 in / 20 cm soufflé dish. Fold the paper strip in half lengthwise to

give a double strip 3 in / 8 cm wide. Wrap the paper around the outside rim of the dish to stand 2½ in / 6 cm above the rim. Secure in position with kitchen string or a large rubber band.
8. Pour the soufflé mixture into the dish to the level of the top of the paper collar and freeze for at least 6 hours.
9. To serve, whip the remaining crème fraîche until stiff, and cut the angelica into small diamonds. Remove the paper collar from the soufflé and decorate with piped crème fraîche, the 4 slices of pineapple and the angelica.

Cook's tip: canned pineapple is specified since the enzymes in the fresh fruit may prevent the gelatin from setting. But if you prefer, use a very ripe pineapple. Cut the pineapple into ½ in / 1 cm slices and cut off the peel and the core. Sprinkle the pineapple with 2 tablespoons of sugar and leave to steep for 2 hours.

Iced pineapple soufflé

Soufflé glacé au chocolat
Iced Chocolate Soufflé

	00:25		00:05
	plus freezing		Serves 8–10

American	Ingredients	Metric/Imperial
⅓ cup	Cocoa powder	40 g / 1½ oz
1 cup	Water	250 ml / 8 fl oz
2 cups	Thin crème fraîche (see page 122)	500 ml / ¾ cup
¾ cup	Sugar	150 g / 6 oz
8	Egg yolks	8
	Confectioners' [icing] sugar	

1. Dissolve the cocoa in ⅔ cup [150 ml / ¼ pint] of the water to give a smooth paste. In a chilled bowl whip the crème fraîche until thick. Stir in the cocoa.
2. Dissolve the sugar in the remaining water and cook over a low heat for 5 minutes. Beat the boiling syrup into the egg yolks and continue beating until completely cold.
3. Fold the cocoa mixture carefully into the egg yolk mixture.
4. Cut a strip of wax [greaseproof] paper 6 in / 16 cm wide and 2½ in / 6 cm longer than the circumference of an 8 in /

20 cm soufflé dish. Fold the paper strip in half lengthwise to give a double strip 3 in / 8 cm wide. Wrap the paper around the outer rim of the dish to stand 2½ in / 6 cm above the rim. Secure in position with kitchen string or a large rubber band.

5. Pour the chocolate mixture into the dish to level with the top of the paper collar and freeze for 12 hours.

6. To serve, remove the paper collar and sprinkle with confectioners' sugar.

Sorbet au Grand Marnier

Grand Marnier Sorbet

	00:20		00:05
	plus steeping and freezing		
American	**Ingredients**	**Metric/Imperial**	
1¼ cups	Sugar	300 g / 10 oz	
2 cups	Water	500 ml / ¾ pint	
¼	Lemon	¼	
6	Apples	6	
2 tbsp	Grand Marnier	2 tbsp	
1 tbsp	Thick crème fraîche (see page 122)	1 tbsp	

1. Dissolve the sugar in the water and bring to a boil. Boil for 5 minutes, then remove the pan from the heat.

2. Grate the rind from the lemon. Peel the apples. Add the lemon rind and apple peel to the syrup. Leave to steep for 3 hours.

3. Strain the syrup and stir in the Grand Marnier and crème fraîche.

4. Pour the mixture into an ice cream maker and freeze, following the manufacturer's instructions.

5. Transfer the sorbet to the refrigerator about 20 minutes before serving.

6. Serve the sorbet on its own, sprinkled with more Grand Marnier, or topped with melted chocolate.

Vacherin glacé aux framboises

Iced Raspberry Vacherin

	00:30		01:15
	plus freezing		Serves 8–10
American	**Ingredients**	**Metric/Imperial**	
9	Egg whites	9	
3 cups	Superfine [caster] sugar	700 g / 1½ lb	
2 lb	Raspberries	900 g / 2 lb	
2 cups	Thin crème fraîche (see page 122)	450 ml / ¾ pint	
¼ cup	Iced milk	4 tbsp	
¼ cup	Confectioners' [icing] sugar	25 g / 1 oz	
	Vanilla extract [essence]		

1. Preheat the oven to 300°F / 150°C / Gas Mark 2.

2. Butter a large baking sheet and sprinkle with flour. With your index finger outline 3 circles 8 in / 20 cm in diameter.

3. Beat 5 of the egg whites until firm, gradually adding 1 cup [250 g / 8 oz] sugar. Separately, beat the remaining egg whites with ⅞ cup [200 g / 7 oz] of sugar.

4. Spoon the whites into a pastry bag fitted with a ½ in / 1 cm nozzle. Working from the center outwards, fill the 3 circles on the baking sheet with flat spirals of meringue. Bake for 1¼ hours.

5. Meanwhile, rinse and hull the raspberries. Purée them in a blender or food processor. Strain out the seeds, if liked. Stir the remaining sugar into the purée. Pour the mixture into an ice cream maker and freeze, following the manufacturer's instructions.

6. Place a round of meringue on a serving plate and cover with a 1 in / 3 cm layer of ice cream. Top with a second round of meringue and a similar layer of ice cream. Top with the remaining round of meringue, then cover the top and sides of the vacherin with the remaining ice cream, spreading it with a metal spatula. Freeze for at least 3 hours.

7. A few minutes before serving, whip the crème fraîche with the milk. Add the confectioners' sugar and a few drops of vanilla extract and whip until thick. Put the cream into a pastry bag fitted with a fluted nozzle and use to decorate the vacherin. Serve immediately.

Fragrant fresh pineapple

Glossary

French cookery terms

A

Abats

Variety meats [offal]. Those parts of the animal which are not included in the main carcass. They are called red if they can be cooked directly (liver, kidney, tongue) and white if they must be blanched or boiled before the main cooking (foot, head, brain, sweetbreads, tripe, etc.).

Abattis

Giblets and other parts of a bird which are not included in the main carcass (neck, head, feet, liver, gizzard, heart).

Aiguille à brider

Trussing needle. Large steel needle through which kitchen string is threaded for the purpose of trussing poultry or game and for closing holes made (when stuffing, for example) in meat or fish.

Aiguillette

Originally a very thin slice of flesh cut from the breast of a bird. Now also applied to other meats.

Al dente

Borrowed from the Italian, meaning literally 'to the teeth'. Used to describe the texture of pasta or rice – firm to the bite, not too cooked.

Andouilles

Chitterlings. Various types of pork sausage, served hot or cold. Smaller varieties are known as *andouillettes*.

Aspic

Term used also in English. Clear savory jelly made from fish- or meat-stock, used as a garnish or to set cold dishes in molds.

Assiette anglaise

Dish of assorted sliced cold meats.

Attereau

Small skewer of savory foods that is deep fried.

B

Bain-marie

Water-bath used for keeping food hot or for cooking it gently. The food is placed in a saucepan or dish that is then placed over another saucepan or pan containing water kept at simmering point or just below. This gentle method of cooking is especially good for custards and creams and can be carried out in the oven as well as on top of the stove.

Ballottine

Similar to a **galantine** but whereas a galantine is always served cold, a ballottine may be eaten hot or cold.

Barder

To bard. To cover the breasts of poultry or game, or roasts of lean meat, with thin slices of pork fat to prevent them from drying out during cooking. The fat is usually removed a short time before the end of the cooking to allow the meat to brown.

Beurre manié

Kneaded butter. Equal quantities of butter and flour, mixed together to a paste and used to thicken sauces in the final stages of cooking.

Bisque

Thick creamy soup made from lobster (*bisque de homard*) and other crustaceans.

Blanchir

To blanch:
1. To boil meat or vegetables in water before the main cooking so as to remove excess bitterness or saltiness, clean and tenderize, or prepare for freezing.
2. To immerse food in boiling water so as to help remove the skin (tomatoes, almonds, peaches, etc.).

Bocal

Wide-mouthed glass jar, with a patent lid, used for storing preserved foods.

Bouchées

see **Vol-au-vents**

Bouillir

To boil. To bring a liquid to a boil before the addition of foods to be cooked.

Bouillon

Meat or vegetable stock from which soups and sauces are made. *See also* **Court-bouillon.**

Bouquet garni

Bunch or sachet of fresh or dried herbs, usually parsley, thyme and bay leaf, used for flavoring soups, sauces, meat dishes, etc.

Braiser

To braise:
1. To cook meat or poultry in a covered pot, with fat and very little liquid. An effective method of cooking for the cheaper cuts.
2. To cook vegetables (e.g. lettuce, spinach) in butter only, in a covered pan.

Brochette

Large skewer on which similarly-sized pieces of meat, fish or vegetables are threaded before broiling [grilling].

Brunoise

see **Macédoine**

C

Cèpe

see **Champignon**

Champignon

General term for mushroom. Some of the edible fungi enjoyed in France are:
champignon de Paris or **champignon de couche:** the cultivated mushroom.
Wild varieties of edible fungus include:
barigoule: a fungus that grows in southern France and is used for stuffing globe artichokes.
cèpe: the boletus, of great gastronomic importance in France.
chanterelle: yellow, cup-shaped fungus that is sometimes known as **girolle.**
coulemelle: parasol mushroom, also called *à la bague* (literally 'with the ring').
morille: morel. Highly-prized fungus that appears in the springtime in France and is used in cooking in a similar way to the cèpe.
russule: the bluet. A European autumn mushroom highly regarded in France.

Chanterelle

see **Champignon**

Chapelure

Bread crumbs made from bread that has been dried in the oven and then crushed with a rolling pin, etc. The process of coating food with bread crumbs before cooking, is known as **Panage.**

Charcuterie

1. French pork-butcher's shop.
2. The cooked meats sold by a *charcutier.*
There is no exact equivalent in English-speaking countries and charcuterie is not limited to pork-based products. The *charcutier* and his wares are extremely important in French cooking.

Chateaubriand

Thick steak cut from the middle of a fillet of beef.

Chiffonade

1. Strips of lettuce, etc., cooked in butter. The filling for a sorrel omelette is made in this way, sometimes mixed with a cream sauce.
2. Type of salad dressing. Recipes vary, but they include hard-cooked egg, vinaigrette, herbs and flavorings.

Chinois

Conical strainer with a fine mesh.

Clarifier

To clarify:
1. To clear stock for consommé or aspic by heating it and adding chopped beef or the white of an egg.
2. To heat butter to remove the salt and sediment. The butter is heated gently and then left for the sediment to settle. The clear fat is poured off, ready for use.

Cocotte

1. Small vessels, made of various materials, used for the cooking and serving of eggs (*oeufs en cocotte*).
2. Deep two-handled cooking pot with a tight cover. It may be round or oval.

Concasser

1. To chop roughly (e.g. tomatoes).
2. To pound in a mortar.

Condiments

Aromatic vegetable substances added to foods to give them more flavor (e.g. gherkins, mustard, chutney).

Confit

1. Preserve of pork or poultry meat that has been salted and cooked in its own fat.
Confits are an important item in the regional cooking of southwest France.
2. Fruit or vegetables preserved in alcohol, etc.

Coulis

1. Juices occurring naturally in meat.
2. Soups or sauces made from purées (e.g. tomato sauce, raspberry sauce).

Court-bouillon

Aromatic liquid used for cooking meat, fish, shellfish, poultry or vegetables. Water, or a mixture of water and wine, is flavored with vegetables and seasonings, and cooked for about 20 minutes before use.

Crème fraîche

Made from fresh heavy [double] cream that has been heated with sour cream and left to mature, giving it a slightly tart flavor. Widely used in traditional French cooking, it is not always easy to buy outside France, but it is simple to make (see page 122). For many of the recipes in this book, heavy cream can be substituted, but it will not give the same flavor as genuine crème fraîche. Sour cream may be used in recipes where it will not be boiled.

Crêpe

Type of thin pancake. Crêpes may be folded to enclose a variety of savory fillings, but crêpe suzette, the most famous kind, is sweet.

Crépine

Caul. Fatty membrane from the intestine of a pig or calf, used to wrap around food to give it flavor and moisture while cooking. The pig's caul is also used as the casing for a type of sausage known as *crépinettes*.

Croûte

Slice of fried or toasted bread on which food is served.

Croûtons

Small cubes of fried bread used to garnish soups, salads, etc.

Crudités

Mixture of chopped raw vegetables, sometimes with a vinaigrette dressing, served as an hors d'oeuvre at the beginning of a meal.

D

Dariole

Small cylindrical metal mold, used for entrées or cakes, which are given the same name.

Darne

Thick steak, cut from salmon or other fish.

Daube

Country method of cooking meat, game and poultry. Similar to **Braiser**. The ingredients are cooked slowly in a pot known as a *daubière*, in stock with added wine.

Déglacer

To make a sauce by dissolving the various sediments, left at the bottom of a pan after cooking meat, poultry and game dishes. A liquid is added (wine, cream, etc.) and brought to a boil, stirring well.

Dégorger

To prepare food for cooking by:
1. Removing impurities in meat or other food by soaking in cold water and draining.
2. Allowing blood to drain out of certain foods (e.g. brains and sweetbreads).
3. Sprinkling some kinds of vegetable (e.g. eggplant [aubergines]) with salt, to release the juices.

Dégraisser

To remove the fat from the surface of cooking liquid or bouillon with a skimmer or spoon.

Doubler

To double:
1. To fold meat, pastry, etc. over into two.
2. To cover pastry dishes in the oven with foil or other materials to prevent them from burning.

Douilles

Metal tubes or nozzles used with a pastry bag. Obtainable in various sizes and shapes, they are used for decorating pâtisserie, filling choux pastry, etc.

Duxelles

Mixture of onions, shallots and mushrooms, chopped finely and cooked slowly in butter. Stored dry and used in stuffings, etc.

E

Écumer

To remove, with a slotted spoon or ladle, the scum that forms on the surface when cooking bouillon, soups, *casseroles*, etc.

Émulsion

Emulsion. Dispersion of one liquid (in the form of tiny globules) into another liquid. Mayonnaise is an example of the process when cold, white butter sauce (*beurre blanc*) when hot.

Entremets

Dessert or sweet course served after the cheese course in France. The term does include pastry-based sweets.

Escalope

Thin boneless pieces of meat (usually veal), fried in butter or oil, sometimes enriched with cream and other ingredients. An escalope is usually beaten flat and thin before cooking.

Étuver

To stew. To cook food in a tightly covered vessel in a very cool oven.

F

Faitout

Literally translated as 'does everything'. Cast-iron stewpot with an enameled finish, also called a **rondin**.

Farce

Stuffing or forcemeat. Mixture of chopped or ground [minced] food used to fill boned meat, poultry, game, fish and vegetables and in terrines.

Fariner

To flour:
1. To coat food in flour before frying, sautéing, or covering in bread crumbs.
2. To sprinkle flour lightly over a work surface or mold to prevent pastry or other food from sticking.

Flamber

To flame:
1. To pour a spirit, such as brandy or rum, over food and set it alight. The alcohol burns off, leaving an aromatic flavor.
2. To pass a bird over a flame, so as to remove any feathers remaining after plucking.

Fleurons

Crescent-shaped pieces of puff pastry, fried or baked and used as a garnish.

Fonds

The stocks which require very lengthy cooking. Used a great deal in traditional French cooking. *Fonds blanc* (white stock) is the basis of veloutés and other creamy preparations. *Fonds brun* (brown stock) is the basis of *sauce espagnole* and numerous other sauces that accompany game.

Fontaine

A well. A hollow made in the center of a heap of flour to receive other ingredients that are to be mixed with it.

Fouetter

To whisk or whip.

Frapper

To ice, chill, or serve on ice.

Frémissement

To keep a liquid on a very low heat so that it barely moves.

Fricasser

To cook poultry in butter and then thicken the sauce with cream and yolk of egg.

Frire

To deep fry. To cook food in deep fat or oil.

Fritots

Fritters made from different foods, sweet or savory. The pieces are dipped in batter and deep fried.

Fumet

Concentrated stock, usually made from fish.

G

Galantine

Stuffed and boned poultry, game, meat or fish, cooked in stock and pressed under weights, then served cold with a surround of the jellied stock. *See also* **Ballottine**.

Garniture

Garnish. There are a huge number of garnishes in French cooking, some of them simple, some elaborate. Many of the famous classical garnishes have names that indicate their main ingredient. A *parmentier* must contain potatoes, and a *chasseur* will always include mushrooms, for example.

Gibier

Game:
1. *Gibier à poil* Game animals, or furred game.
2. *Gibier à plume* Game birds, or feathered game.

Gigue

Haunch of venison or wild boar.

Girolle

see **Champignon**

Glacer

To glaze:
1. To coat meat thinly in its own juice after cooking, and place briefly in a very hot oven or under the broiler [grill] to give it a shiny glaze.
2. To apply icing to some kinds of cakes and buns (e.g. chocolate éclairs)
3. To cook food (turnips, carrots, etc.) with sugar, water and butter until the water has evaporated and the food is lightly coated with caramel.

Gratiner

To brown a dish that is covered in grated cheese or bread crumbs in an oven or under a hot broiler [grill].

Grenadin

Thick, larded slice of veal tenderloin [fillet].

Griller

To broil [grill]. To cook food by exposing it directly to a radiant heat source. Used for red or white meat, poultry, kebabs, fish or vegetables.

H

Hacher

To grind [mince]. To reduce food to very small pieces with a sharp knife, or with a meat grinder or food processor.

J

Jardinière

Mixed cooked vegetables, cut into regular shapes and served as a garnish to meat dishes.

Julienne

Matchstick-like strips of vegetables, fruit, ham, etc.

Jus de viande

Juices that run out of meat during certain cooking processes. If allowed to cool and solidify, they are known as *jus en gelée*.

L

Larder

To lard. To insert strips of pork fat or bacon fat (*lardons*) through meat, using a larding needle (*lardoire*). Used to moisten lean meat during cooking.

Lèchefrite

Dripping pan. Dish in the oven or under a spit, designed to collect the cooking juices from roasts or broiled [grilled] meats.

Liaison

Addition of flour, starch, butter, egg yolk or blood to a sauce, soup or cream, to thicken or bind it.

M

Macédoine

Mixture of diced fruit or vegetables. A *brunoise* is made of smaller pieces than a macédoine and is used to garnish soups and sauces.

Macérer

To macerate. To flavor food (usually fruit) by soaking it in liqueur or wine. The liquid is served with the fruit.

Malaxer

To knead. To work butter, pastry or dough to soften it.

Mandoline

Type of metal grater for slicing vegetables very finely.

Manier

see **Beurre manié**

Mariner

To marinate. To soak meat, game, fish or poultry in an aromatic liquid before cooking so as to preserve and/or tenderize it. The liquid (*marinade*) may be made of wine, vinegar or lemon juice, often mixed with oil and flavorings, and may be either used in the cooking or discarded, according to the recipe.

Marmite

High-sided stewpot made of metal or earthenware.

Mie-de-pain

Bread crumbs made from fresh bread and used for coating meat or fish before cooking.

Mijoter

To simmer. To cook over a gentle heat.

Mirepoix

Mixture of chopped vegetables, used to add flavor to gravies, sauces or soups.

Morille

see **Champignon**

Mousseline

'Muslin'. Applied to a number of recipes, such as the classic *sauce mousseline*, that feature whipped cream. They may be served hot or cold.

P

Paillettes

'Little straws':
1. Vegetables cut into small sticks.
2. Sticks made from cheese-flavored pastry, served with consommé.

Panage

see **Chapelure**

Panne

Fat that covers pigs' kidneys. Melted down, it produces lard.

Panure

Similar to panage (*see* **Chapelure**) but the food is coated with egg or melted butter first to make the bread crumbs stick.

Papillotes

Pieces of foil or greased paper in which food, such as fish or veal cutlets, is wrapped before cooking. The method of cooking *en papillote* preserves all the juices and aromas, and the food is brought to the table still wrapped in the paper cases.

Pâte

Pastry. Used in various forms in an enormous number of sweet and savory French recipes. Some of the most important kinds are:
Pâte à brioche (a yeast dough); *pâte à choux* (choux pastry, essential for éclairs, etc.); *pâte a pâté*; *pâte brisée* (a short pastry from which open tarts are usually made); *pâte feuilletée* (puff or flaky pastry used for *vol-au-vents,* etc.); *pâte moulée* (often used for making pies); *pâte sablée* (crumbly pastry); *pâte sucrée* (sweet short pastry).
The term *pâte* may also refer to a batter (*pâte à frire*) or to pasta (*pâtes*).

Paupiette

Thin slice of meat or fish rolled around a stuffing and tied with string before cooking.

Pincée

A pinch. Small quantity taken between thumb and index finger. Equals about ⅙ oz / 5 g.

Pocher

To poach. To cook food gently in a simmering liquid.

Poêler

To pan fry or shallow fry. To cook food in fat in a frying pan.

Praline

Clear brown toffee with almonds, crushed and used for flavoring and decoration in pâtisserie.

Q

Quenelle

Very finely-textured dumpling made of pounded and sieved meat, fish or potatoes. Quenelles are poached gently and are usually served with a sauce.

Quiche

Open pastry tart with an egg-based filling. Various savory ingredients may be used but the classic *quiche lorraine* includes bacon.

R

Rafraîchir

To refresh:
1. To rinse food that has been cooked in boiling water quickly under cold water to prevent further cooking.
2. To 'set' the color (of vegetables).
3. To wash away any scum (e.g. brains, sweetbreads).

Raidir

To sear. To cook a food quickly in hot fat to seal in the juices, without allowing it to color.

Rassir

To hang. To leave meat and game for several days to tenderize it and to improve its flavor.

Réduire

To reduce. To evaporate a sauce or liquid over a high heat so as to concentrate its flavor and thicken it.

Relever

To season. To bring out the flavor of a dish with a condiment or spice.

Revenir, faire

To give food a brief preliminary cooking in very hot fat until it has colored slightly. Usually precedes braising, soup-making, etc.

Rondin

see **Faitout**

Rôtir

To roast. To cook meat, poultry, game, etc. by direct heat in the oven or on a spit.

Roulade

A roll:
1. Some kinds of **galantine** are referred to as roulades.
2. Stuffed rolled meat, fish or omelettes.

Roux

Mixture of hot butter and flour that forms the basis for many sauces.

Ruban, faire le

To beat to a ribbon. A mixture is said to form ribbons when it detaches itself from the blades of a wooden spoon or whisk and forms a ribbon that folds over itself.

Russule

see **Champignon**

S

Saignant

Meat served very rare is described as saignant ('bloody').

Saucisse

Pork sausage. Many kinds of saucisse are available in France. They vary in shape and are eaten hot or cold. The larger kinds, sliced and eaten raw, and known as **saucissons,** may contain other meats.

Saucisse de Montbéliard is flavored with caraway; *saucisse à la boudine* from Poitou is made from pork with sorrel or chard; *saucisse de Strasbourg* is a smoked beef and pork sausage; *saucisson d'Arles* is a dried pork and beef sausage; *saucisson à l'ail* is soft garlic sausage that is cooked before eating.

Saumure

Brine. Solution of sea salt, flavored or unflavored, in which food is cured.

Sauter

To cook small pieces of food in hot fat in a shallow heavy frying pan. The pan is shaken from time to time to prevent the food from sticking. (*sauter* = to jump)

Suer, faire

To make food 'sweat'. To reduce the water content of vegetables by frying. It usually precedes braising.

T

Terrine

Dish of fish, poultry, meat, and sometimes vegetables cooked in an earthenware, porcelain, cast iron or ovenproof glass container, called a *terrine*.

Timbale

1. Round mold with sloping sides, sometimes fluted.

2. Food made in such a mold (e.g. *timbale de riz*).
3. A variation on the theme, made of ovenproof materials and used for the cooking of soufflés, is known as a *timbale à soufflé*.

Tourte

Covered pie with a pastry crust and a savory filling. (Quiches are sometimes known as tourtes.)

Trousser

To truss. To tie or skewer the legs and wings of poultry or game into a neat shape before cooking.

V

Vol-au-vent

Patty shell. Puff pastry case with a lid, containing a savory filling and served hot or cold. The small individual versions are more correctly known as **bouchées**.

Z

Zeste

Outer, colored layer of the skin of citrus fruits.

Zester

To zest. To remove the skin of a citrus fruit with a sharp knife or zester.

French Index

English Index

Your Recipe Notes

The publishers would like to thank the following individuals and organizations for their kind permission to reproduce the pictures in this book:

APRIFEL; AOC; BRITISH CHICKEN INFORMATION SERVICE; FOOD & WINE FROM FRANCE; IGDA; IMAGE BANK; KENWOOD; MOULINEX; ORBIS, Bird, Brock, Elliott, Kay, Leale, Myers, O'Leary, Tuff, Williams; PHILLIPS; Martin Rigdale; SCOOP, Berdoy, Bouillard, Boys, Connors, Decros, Dirand, Ferrand, Fouili Elia, Gain, Hamot, Hispard, Holsnyder, Jannes, Jozefson, Korniloff, Leger, Lemaire, Leroy, Maltaverne, Pascal, Pedersen, Traeger; SEB; SOPEXA; TEFAL; VEDETTE.